THE NEW ROLLING STONE
RECORD GUIDE

THE NEW
Rolling Stone®
RECORD
GUIDE

**Revised, updated and more
complete than ever, this indispensable book
reviews and rates over 12,000 rock,
pop, soul, country, blues,
folk and gospel albums**

**Edited by Dave Marsh
and John Swenson**

Rolling Stone.

A Random House/Rolling Stone Press Book/New York

Library of Congress Cataloging in Publication Data

Marsh, Dave.
The new Rolling stone record guide.

Rev. ed. of: The Rolling stone record guide.
1. Music, Popular (Songs, etc.)—Discography.
2. Sound recordings—Reviews. I. Swenson, John.
II. Rolling stone. III. Title.
ML156.4.P6M37   1983   789.9'13645   82-40116
ISBN 0-394-72107-1

Manufactured in the United States of America
Typography and binding design by J. K. Lambert
9 8 7 6 5 4 3 2
First Edition

Acknowledgments

Before the beginning, there were Sarah Lazin and Rob Cowley, who had the faith that an updated, revised *Record Guide* would be a worthwhile project, and worked to gain us the resources with which to complete it. And once we got rolling, there was the equally indispensable Debbie Geller, who got things straight in the beginning and kept them that way to the bitter end. To each of these, our deepest, if disorganized, appreciation.

Randall Grass stepped in with an exhaustive knowledge of reggae and the ability and confidence to commit it to paper, thereby not only immeasurably improving the text but also teaching us a great deal about some especially intriguing sounds.

Patty Romanowski and her staff at Rolling Stone Press (Janis Bultman, Barry Jacobs, Jim Farber, Kenn Lowy, Jill Schoenstein, Steve Futterman, Michael Silberman) did yeoman work in checking facts, smoothing out grammar and syntax and generally picking up the pieces. Jim Nettleton, who compiled much of the dating, and Wayne King, whose mania for musical minutae was valuable in too many ways to count, are also owed much gratitude.

The record company publicists who continued to answer a seemingly endless series of telephone messages are once again praised and blessed by one and all. They too were an indispensable part of the book's creation, and if only they were not so numerous as to require a separate volume would deserve to be singled out, each and every one. We hope that this blanket acknowledgment, together with the sighs of relief on our end of the phone, tells them how much their assistance contributed.

But if anyone took the first edition of the *Record Guide* to heart, it was the record retailers of America. Their encouragement, at the unlikeliest times and in the strangest places, gave us a powerful sense that we'd done worthwhile work. We hope that this book lives up to expectations and would like to thank specifically the following: Greenworld Records, the House of Oldies and Robin Cohn of City Hall Records, all in New York City; John McCord and Frank Scott of Down Home Music (a store that is to record lovers what the local bar is to the town drunk). We also would like to thank Jeff Tamarkin of *Goldmine,* for sharing back issues and wisdom.

Contents

Introduction
to the Second Edition

The second edition of *The Rolling Stone Record Guide* is virtually a new book altogether. It's the product not only of four years' retrospective analysis but also of a virtual revolution in the way that popular records are marketed and distributed in America.

When our first manuscript was completed, in 1978, the record industry was dominated by five major multinational conglomerates. Only a few others, themselves typically quite large and well-financed, made any significant impact on the marketplace. Since then, while the majors have continued to produce the bulk of the top sellers, their actual influence and power have shrunk. If there's talk of a decline in record sales and profitability, for once it's the big guys who are hurting. Independents are flourishing as they have not done since the middle Sixties.

It's easy enough to see why. Inherent in the setup of the conglomerates is a level of bureaucracy that can't make the production of records that cater to minority tastes cost-effective. Independent labels have become a significant force once again by staking out turf in relatively remote but artistically important corners, where the audience is small but sizable enough to ensure some profit. Reggae, rap, traditional rock & roll or rhythm & blues, punk, art rock in both its European and American guises, and a fair share of post-disco dance music are all more likely to be on one of the independent labels than on CBS or Warner Bros. At least until one or more of these genres becomes powerful enough to enter the mainstream, that's likely to continue to be the case.

In addition, something similar has occurred in record distribution. Beyond the obvious fact that all of the independent sales represent sales outside the web of conglomerate distribution, the record buyer is now offered a number of alternatives. As the price of domestic albums has risen,

European and Japanese imports have become more widely available. And as the independents have had to cope with so much geographical territory and financial insecurity, more and more have turned to some kind of mail-order setup. Imports and mail order may now be the only guaranteed way to keep up with the increasing flow of new and *reissued* material.

The latter is especially important in our view, since it offers access to the American musical heritage in a way that the conglomerates have never considered. Since it is the first premise of the *Record Guide* that this heritage is worth preserving, this is a most welcome trend. And it is ultimately abetted even by the conglomerates, with their repackagings of historic music, from the Carter Family to Fats Domino to more current figures, at budget prices.

In other words, despite the dire warnings of catastrophe, the actual availability of rock & roll-era music has expanded many times in the past few years. In preparing this edition of the *Record Guide,* we were quite happily forced to discard many of the limitations we imposed on the first. There was no point in restricting ourselves only to domestic releases, for instance, since imports are now fairly easily available. This second edition includes reviews of thousands of small-label and imported albums, so many that we can no longer claim to be certain to have omitted nothing that's available. (You'd be surprised how elusive some records can be, even for the most tenacious researchers, all of whom, incidentally, worked on this book.)

In order to retain a complete picture, we've avoided deleting records which were reviewed in the first edition and have subsequently been cut out of catalogues— with the exception that artists whose entire work has gone missing are now eliminated, for reasons of space. (We made exceptions even there for artists of major importance, however.) We've kept so much deleted material because many of these records aren't truly off the shelves—they've only moved to the bargain bins or used-record stores. Additionally, the major labels, who've done most of the deletions, do have those budget-line reissue programs, which often recycle records to the active file with surprising rapidity.

We didn't, of course, try to cover records released and then deleted between the time when we completed the first edition (roughly, December 1978) and began work on the second (the spring of 1981). Anything that disappeared from the market that quickly has probably reviewed itself. The reviews are current through about mid-1982. Again, the purpose of the *Guide* is historical. *Rolling Stone* itself is still there for keeping up to the minute.

Unfortunately, when we assembled all of our new and revised material, we were left with enough for two volumes—far more than could be bound into one. Essentially, we had doubled the contents of the *Record Guide* itself. Faced with either creating an unwieldy, not especially useful book or omitting some reviews, we decided to have it both ways: we have eliminated the Jazz section, and this material will be included in a future *Rolling Stone Jazz Record Guide.* (We have retained what are to our mind the essential jazz-related figures in this edition, of course.) This has at least enabled us to combine all entries in a single alphabetical listing.

There have been two significant changes in our listings themselves. First, we have omitted record label catalogue numbers. We are confident that any serious record dealer can order albums for you with the label name only, and we've found that catalogue numbers, especially at the major labels, change with utterly chaotic frequency in any event.

More important, the individual album listings are now organized chronologically, rather than alphabetically. The date of the album is the date on which it was first released in that configuration, an important distinction, since, for example, MCA's *Twenty Golden Greats,* a Buddy Holly compilation first issued in 1978, is included here as a 1978 album, even though all of the music in it was recorded two decades earlier, when Holly was still alive. In general, the dates of all reissued material are deceptive in this sense. Reading the review text should dispel seeming discrepancies. (Albums we

have not been able to date with certainty are listed as "NA" for "not available." Anyone with additional information or corrections on this or other matters is welcome to write us at Rolling Stone Press, 745 Fifth Avenue, New York, N.Y. 10151.)

In addition to *Phonolog* and *Schwann,* we found the following major mail-order or importer catalogues as basic references. We have included addresses in this listing because these are also among the best places to obtain material in this book that isn't available at your corner record shop:

Down Home Music, Inc., 10341 San Pablo Avenue, El Cerrito, CA 94530. Indispensable for blues, R&B, vintage rock & roll, jazz, country, Cajun and folk.

JEM Records, 3619 Kennedy Road, South Plainfield, NJ 07080. European rock, much independent-label post-punk material and many post–British Invasion albums are available in this importer/distributor's impressive catalogue.

Shanachie Records, 1 Hollywood Avenue, Dalebrook Park, Ho-Ho-Kus, NJ 07423. The best reggae catalogue in the nation.

Rounder/Roundup Records, 1 Camp Street, Cambridge, MA 02140. In addition to the splendid music offered on the Rounder label, Roundup also serves as a clearinghouse for folk and acoustic music, some ethnic and blues recordings, and selected blues and jazz imports.

Each of the above has inexpensive catalogues that can be ordered by mail.

One of the greatest advantages of being an editor of a book like this is that one has the opportunity to revise and correct reviews that were inadequate or inaccurate in the earlier edition. We have changed judgments of the first edition with a free hand, either by rewriting ourselves or reassigning the material in question to another reviewer. In some cases, this has resulted in upgrading our assessment of a performer's work—the Clash, for instance. In others, it has resulted in downgrading it—Linda Ronstadt, for one. In both instances, and all the others we might mention, we feel that the new version more accurately describes what a listener will experience.

In the end, we are certain that this second edition of the *Record Guide* is both more useful and better organized than the first one. And we are pleased to note that our final comment in the last edition's introduction has been verified. It *will* stand, and it does.

Dave Marsh
November 4, 1982

Introduction
to the First Edition

In rock's twenty-five-year existence, hundreds of books have attempted to define or at least circumscribe the music or some part of the expereince of hearing it. But until now rock has lacked a basic reference work keyed to the central unit of consumption: the LP. The oldies guides list singles, and their ratings tend to reflect market value (that is, price) rather than aesthetics, scarcity rather than intrinsic worth. But whether it's on a blue Chess label or a more recent orange one, Chuck Berry's "Maybellene" has a worth that transcends its cost. In that sense, the best creations of rock artists are genuinely priceless, and the worst genuinely worthless. This book tries to sort them out, ignoring neither the guilty nor the innocent but standing them side by side, as they coexist on record shelves everywhere.

We haven't tried to codify rock. For one thing, the form is too new and, in the strictest sense, undefined to allow that. On the other hand, a good deal of what we have had to say is merely a repetition of what's conventionally understood: we aren't the people to tell you the Beatles were uncreative. We hope we can say that we have uncovered a certain number of unsuspected gems, and we have certainly been compelled to deflate the (critical or public) reputations of certain previously overestimated performers. In the main, we've probably been overgenerous, which is not necessarily a fault. This book is, after all, designed at least as much for the general reader as for the rock cultist. (For those who get too lost, though, there is a glossary to guide you through our reviews, and a bibliography to direct you to some of the better volumes on the subject.)

The Rolling Stone Record Guide is unprecedented for a reason. Compiling a comprehensive critical guide to such a volatile area is virtually impossible. When we first began to compile this book, in late 1976, the task seemed straightforward enough. By the time the job is finished, though, about one-third of the entries will represent artistic entities who did not exist when we began. Rock groups break up, reform and spin off solo performers more quickly than the somewhat ponderous processes of print can digest them. Those interested in up-to-the-minute evaluations are better off in the pages of *Rolling Stone* itself, which reviews about 500 records yearly—something like 15 percent of the U.S. record industry's annual output. The *Record Guide* is intended for those who would rather probe the music's past, those who don't stop in the front of the record store, where the new releases are kept, but keep on going to the back, where American musical history is stored.

In order to make the *Record Guide* workable, certain guidelines were necessarily established. We focused on records released in the United States, and more specifically, upon those that are in print—that is, records that could conceivably be ordered by your local record merchant, however unlikely it may be that the store would automatically have them in stock. We chose to do LPs rather than singles because LPs have a longer shelf life, and because most people orient their buying to albums (and tapes).

We've also limited ourselves to music that is rock, is associated with rock, has influenced rock or has been influenced by rock. That is quite enough, of course, since it inevitably impinges upon other areas: blues, jazz, gospel, mainstream pop itself. But we haven't attempted to create a survey that's as comprehensive in terms of jazz recordings, for instance, as for modern rock and pop. This is a task for someone else, and it needs to be done, if only so the uninformed can have a guide to what to hear. It is shocking that there is not a book like this for the jazz listener, or the blues newcomer.

Naturally, we violated every one of our rules when it served our purpose to do so. The most difficult problem was what's in print. Records are deleted from company catalogues almost as quickly as they're conceived—often too hastily in both cases. At most large companies, if an album doesn't sell a certain minimum number of copies—say, 5,000—in a calendar year, it is dropped. This means that the early work of Aretha Franklin or Smokey Robinson is available only in anthologies or bowdlerized budget editions, a situation less than ideal from a critical viewpoint. One of the things that creating the *Record Guide* constantly brought home to us was how cavalierly corporations treat music. With the increasing concentration of record-industry power in the hands of corporate conglomerates, with all their cost efficiency and bureaucracy, little hope can be extended for a change in such policies. Sad to say, rhythm & blues fans may someday be forced to pirate or bootleg Wilson Pickett's vintage work, just as jazz and classical fans now do with rare works of the past.

A related problem is what happens when a record company itself enters an area of uncertain ownership. At this writing, the Chess Records catalogue is in severe disrepair because it has changed ownership several times in the Seventies. The catalogue's current owner, All Platinum, began a promising reissue program in 1977 (when the material was first acquired), but that program has now fallen by the wayside. Similarly, Fantasy has done little with the vast collection of Stax treasures it now controls; it would be delightful to see reissues of the quality of Fantasy's Prestige and Milestone jazz and folk sets created for the Stax R&B material.

Our basic reference guide for determining what was available was *Phonolog,* that massive yellow ring-bound volume with which habitues of record stores are probably already familiar. *Phonolog* lists thousands of records, cross-referenced by artist, song title and LP title, updated thrice weekly (thus the ring binder). It is weak on small, less commercially oriented labels, and we supplemented its information with the monthly *Schwann Records & Tape Guide,* and where possible with the label catalogues themselves. Still, it is often some time between the deletion of an album and its official demise in any of these sources; the

result was that a number of entries were written concerning artists whose entire body of work (usually no more than two or three LPs) was cut out. Those reviews appear in this volume, both as a guide to what is likely to be turning up in bargain bins in the near future, and with an eye to the future. When a revised edition of the *Record Guide* is published, it will list all cutouts. At the very least, the phrase "now deleted" at the bottom of a review here indicates what might be turning up for $1.98 at Woolworth's.

Where only a portion of an artist's work is deleted, we have not listed that portion (although reference may be made to the cutouts in the text). This is an odd circumstance—it may mean that the work of a minor or a genuinely awful performer is more fully catalogued here than the work of a master. But given the editors' hope that the *Record Guide* will be of some value as a shopping aid, it seems the best compromise.

Imported records are listed only where essential—i.e., where the body of a major artist's work is ill represented in the U.S. issues, as is the case with Buddy Holly's. Once again, future editions of the *Record Guide* ought to supply more complete import editions, particularly as the upward spiral of American record prices makes import LPs more competitive.

We chose to organize the book by artist, since that is the best way in which to see work in its perspective; the alternative suggestion was to order it chronologically, but that is confusing (what year does one date an anthology?). The listings are similarly in alphabetical order, and undated, since the text provides enough temporal reference points to give the sense of an album's era. Immediacy is central to rock, but the *Record Guide* is concerned with how and why the best of it lasts.

Establishing criteria for including performers was as perplexing as any other problem we faced. Obviously it would be fatuous to ignore the Bee Gees, sectarian not to include Billy Joel, even though these are not "rock" performers in the critical sense of the term. We took it as our job to survey most Seventies pop, all rhythm & blues, a good deal of black pop and a limited amount of country music. The reason why we chose less country than black pop is simple: when C&W strays from its roots, it is more likely to drift toward MOR, while the interchange between rock and black popular forms is constant—Funkadelic owes a great deal to Sixties progressive rock, while modern rock borrows heavily (still) from innovations in black pop recording techniques (including disco). We also attempted to incorporate most pop artists who reflected a specific rock influence—not Ferrante and Teicher's Beatle interpretations but surely Barbra Streisand's recordings with rock-based rhythm sections. Also, we wanted mainstream pop performers who had some sort of influence on rock and R&B performers: Frank Sinatra as the teen idol most nearly antedating Elvis Presley, Nat "King" Cole for his influence upon Ray Charles and other R&B singers.

There are also supplemental sections on jazz, R&B and gospel, as well as a section of reviews of anthologies and soundtracks. It is worthwhile to emphasize once more that these do not attempt to be as comprehensive as the pop/rock listings; any reasonably well informed jazz buff could recite a truckload of omissions. Jazz performers, like blues and gospel ones, were chosen for their influence upon rock and R&B, or because they showed that influence, in the case of some more recent artists. A few—King Oliver, Jelly Roll Morton, Louis Armstrong, Duke Ellington and Count Basie, among others— were included because their influence upon *all* American music makes it impossible to ignore them in any survey. Again, there is a need for a comprehensive jazz survey, and it is the editors' hope that the limitations of the *Record Guide* supplement will spur someone qualified to do the job.

Given these restrictions, the present volume is comprehensive in terms of artists listed through about mid-1978, with the addition of a few significant debuts released a bit later than that (e.g., the Cars). The records within each artist listing are comprehensive through late 1978; we have been able to add a few of the more important early 1979 releases as well. We, too, wish that a more up-to-date volume was possible, but there's *Rolling Stone* itself for that. We had to stop somewhere or be trapped like Sisyphus. But since *The Rolling Stone Record Guide* is intended as a permanent reference work, the editors are already contemplating the arduous task of compiling future editions. Toward that end, we'd appreciate interested readers sending us their complaints, comments, notifications of omission and any additional relevant oddments to Rolling Stone Press, 745 Fifth Avenue, New York, N.Y. 10022. We'll attempt to incorporate as many of them as possible next time.

To the extent that the *Record Guide* has precedents, they are Robert Christgau's monthly "Consumer Guide" column in the *Village Voice,* which lists twenty albums by letter grade (A to F), and Leonard Maltin's *TV Movies,* which uses a star ranking system similar to our own to evaluate several thousand films that are likely to turn up on the airwaves. From Maltin, we took the notion of a comprehensive guidebook; from Christgau, the concept of the consumer guide as the most pungent, pithy (and acerbic) form of criticism.

But what we learned while putting the *Record Guide* together was of even greater value. Writing about performers as diverse as Roscoe Holcomb, Elvis Presley and the Sex Pistols ought to be confusing, but for us, it was extraordinarily enlightening, not only because there were connections we'd previously missed, great moments that lay dormant in our minds and new music to discover and evaluate, but also because, as we progressed, the whole of popular music began to seem a seamless web. There is a certain strength in hearing Ronnie Lane sing rock as modern as today in accents as old as the British Isles, or listening to Ry Cooder merge all sorts of North American music into an individual style; piecing together the disparate elements that comprise the *Record Guide,* we got to know a fragment of the joy that such men must feel in their creations. In his monumental *Mystery Train: Images of America in Rock 'n' Roll Music,* Greil Marcus has done an extensive study of such linkages—for example, between Sly Stone's "Thank You for Talkin' to Me Africa" and "Staggolee," a story as old as the folk blues.

We experienced such shocks of recognition over and over again, whether in finding Al Green quoting country blues in a disco number or simply by discovering that General Johnson, a contemporary black writer/performer, was the man who wrote and sang the Showmen's great anthem "It Will Stand." In the end, after all the months of winnowing and verifying, it is Johnson's words that stick with us, and we hope, with you:

Don't nickname it
You might as well claim it . . .
It'll be here forever and ever
Ain't gonna fade, never no never.
Dave Marsh
February 26, 1979

Ratings

★ ★ ★ ★ ★
Indispensable: a record that must be included in
any comprehensive collection.

★ ★ ★ ★
Excellent: a record of substantial merit, though flawed
in some essential way.

★ ★ ★
Good: a record of average worth, but one that might possess considerable
appeal for fans of a particular style.

★ ★
Mediocre: records that are artistically insubstantial,
though not truly wretched.

★
Poor: records in which even technical competence is at question,
or which are remarkably ill-conceived.

■
Worthless: records that need never (or should never) have been created.
Reserved for the most bathetic bathwater.

¶
Record that is out of print.

Reviewers

EDITORS

Dave Marsh (D.M.) is the author of the best-selling *Born to Run: The Bruce Springsteen Story*, *The Book of Rock Lists*, *Elvis*, and a biography of the Who, *Before I Get Old*. A founding editor of *Creem* and former *Rolling Stone* editor, Marsh has contributed essays, articles and reviews to a number of newspapers and magazines.

John Swenson (J.S.) grew up a Who fanatic in Brooklyn and began writing about his mania while in college. He contributed to the *Village Voice* in the early Seventies, before working as a record review editor at *Crawdaddy, Circus* and *High Times*, while writing books about the Who, the Beatles, Kiss, the Eagles, Bill Haley, Stevie Wonder and Simon and Garfunkel. Swenson has also written frequently for *Rolling Stone*.

CONTRIBUTORS

Billy Altman (B.A.) founded the first magazine called *Punk* in 1973. He is currently records review editor of *Creem* and a contributor to *Esquire* and the *Village Voice*.

George Arthur (G.A.) covered rock and pop for the *Seattle Post Intelligencer* for five years. He has also written for *Billboard, Circus, Crawdaddy, Rock, Helix, Performance*, the *Seattle Flag* and the *Everett Herald*.

Bob Blumenthal (B.B.) is a Massachusetts attorney who writes about jazz for *Rolling Stone, Downbeat, Musician* and the *Boston Phoenix*. He was one of six commissioners named by the Record Industry Association of America to select the Reagan White House record library.

Jean Charles Costa (J.C.C.) is a guitarist who was editor of the defunct music publication *Gig*.

Brian Cullman (B.C.), a contributing editor of *Musician*, is the former leader of the band Scattered Light. He is currently finishing his first solo album, *Everything That Rises*.

Dan Doyle (D.D.) is a former contributor to *Pop Top* magazine. He's also produced records for Johnny Copeland, Arthur Blythe, Steve Lacy and the Holy Modal Rounders.

Jim Farber (J.F.) is a music and film critic whose work has appeared in the *New York Times*, the *Village Voice, Rolling Stone* and many other publications.

Laura Fissinger (L.F.) has contributed to *Rolling Stone, Creem, Musician*, the *Boston Phoenix* and several midwestern newspapers and music publications.

Chet Flippo (C.F.), a senior writer at *People*, was formerly an editor at *Rolling Stone* and has a master's degree in journalism: he received at the University of Texas for writing a thesis on the rock press. He is also the author of *Your Cheatin' Heart: A Biography of Hank Williams*, and is writing a book about John Wayne.

David Fricke (D.F.) is an associate editor at *Musician* and the New York correspondent for the English pop music weekly *Melody Maker*. He has also been a frequent contributor to *Rolling Stone, People, New York Rocker, Trouser Press* and other music publications.

Aaron Fuchs (A.F.) has been an editor at *Cash Box* and a columnist at the *Soho News* and has contributed to *Rolling Stone*, the *Village Voice*, the *Daily News* and *Crawdaddy*. He now runs an R&B reissue label, Night Train Records.

Steve Futterman (S.F.) has written for *Rolling Stone, Musician* and the *Record*, and has contributed to the *Rolling Stone Encyclopedia of Rock & Roll* and the *Rolling Stone Rock Almanac*.

Debbie Geller (D.G.) has written for the *Record, Kicks* and *Stereo* and contributed to the *Book of Rock Lists*.

Russell Gersten (R.G.) works in educational research in the Pacific Northwest and has been writing about soul music for more than a decade.

Mikal Gilmore (M.G.) is a contributing editor at *Rolling Stone* and music editor at the *L.A. Weekly*.

Alan E. Goodman (A.E.G.) is a former disc jockey and reviewer for *Crawdaddy* who now works for Columbia Records.

Malu Halasa (Ml.H.), author of *The Beat: Twist and Crawl*, contributed to *The Book of Rock Lists* and has written for *Rolling Stone* and various American and English publications.

Peter Herbst (P.H.), a senior editor at *New York*, was formerly senior editor at *Rolling Stone* and music editor at the *Boston Phoenix*.

Stephen Holden (S.H.) is a pop critic for the *New York Times*, a frequent contributor to *Rolling Stone* and the author of a novel about the music business, *Triple Platinum*.

Martha Hume (M.H.) writes a weekly music column for the *New York Daily News*, is a former editor of *Country Music* and is the author of *You're So Cold I'm Turning Blue*, a book about country music.

Scott Isler (S.I.), editor of *Trouser Press*, has written for *Rolling Stone*, *Crawdaddy* and other publications.

Gary Kenton (G.K.) is a former editor of *Fusion* and *Creem*, and a contributor to *Musician*, *Country Rhythms* and other publications.

Wayne King (W.K.), a dedicated Who archivist, is assistant editor at the *Record*. He has also written for *Trouser Press* and contributed to the *Rolling Stone Rock Almanac*.

Kenn Lowy (K.L.), an electronic guitarist and e-bowist and a member of wrinklemuzik, has written for *Trouser Press* and contributed to *The Book of Rock Lists*.

Bruce Malamut (B.M.) has written about music extensively for *Rolling Stone*, *Crawdaddy*, *Circus* and the *Village Voice*. He is currently reviews editor for *Guitar World*.

Greil Marcus (G.M.), a former *Rolling Stone* editor and the author of *Mystery Train: Images of America in Rock 'n' Roll Music*, covers books and rock & roll for *California*.

Ira Mayer (I.M.) is pop music critic of the *New York Post* and American editor of the London-based *Music & Video Week*.

Joe McEwen (J.Mc.) was once known to Boston radio listeners as the disc jockey

Mr. C. He has written under both names for the *Boston Phoenix*, *Real Paper*, the *Village Voice* and *Rolling Stone*. McEwen is currently an A&R man at Columbia Records.

David McGee (D.Mc.), formerly assistant managing editor at *Record World*, has written for *Rolling Stone* and NBC radio. He is currently managing editor of the *Record*.

John Milward (J.B.M.) writes for many national magazines, including *Rolling Stone*, the *Village Voice* and *Penthouse*. He is the former music critic for the late *Chicago Daily News* and the *Chicago Reader*.

Teri Morris (T.M.) has contributed to *ZigZag*, *Bomp*, *Rolling Stone* and *BAM*.

John Morthland (J.Mo.) is a former editor of *Rolling Stone*, *Real Paper*, *Country Music* and *Creem*. He is also the author of *The Best of Country Music*.

Paul Nelson (P.N.) founded the *Little Sandy Review*, edited *Circus* and currently is a *Rolling Stone* contributing editor.

Alan Niester (A.N.) is a Toronto high school teacher who writes for a variety of American and Canadian magazines.

Rob Patterson (R.P.) writes syndicated music and entertainment features for United Features Syndicate and contributes to *Musician*, *Music Sound Output*, *Creem*, *Goldmine*, *Progressive Media*, *Modern Recording and Music*, *Audio Times* and other publications.

Kit Rachlis (K.R.) is music editor of the *Boston Phoenix* and and has written for *Rolling Stone*, the *Village Voice*, *Seventeen* and *Mother Jones*.

Ira Robbins (I.R.) is publisher and editorial director of *Trouser Press*. He's also contributed to *Crawdaddy*, *New Musical Express*, *Zoo World*, *Creem*, *Circus*, *Phonograph Record* and other publications.

Wayne Robbins (W.R.) is a former editor of *Creem* and a pop music critic at *Newsday*.

Frank Rose (F.R.), a contributing editor at *Esquire*, has written for *Rolling Stone* and the *Village Voice*. He is currently at work on a book about artificial intelligence.

Michael Rozek (M.R.) has written for *Rolling Stone*, *Texas Monthly*, *Omni*, *Cosmopolitan* and other publications. He currently lives in Moscow, Idaho, where he is working on two books.

Fred Schruers (F.S.) is a contributing editor at *Rolling Stone*. He's also contributed to the *New York Daily News*, the *Washington Post*, *Musician* and a number of other publications.

Dave Schulps (D.S.) is a co-founder and

former editor of *Trouser Press*. His writing has also appeared in *Crawdaddy, Gig, Cash Box, Sounds* and *Musician*. He is currently production coordinator for *Rock Quiz*, a syndicated radio program.

Tom Smucker (T.S.) works for the New York Telephone Company.

Ariel Swartley (A.S.) is a contributor to the *Boston Phoenix, Rolling Stone,* the *Village Voice* and other publications.

Bart Testa (B.T.) teaches film studies at Innis College, University of Toronto. He is the jazz critic for *McLean's* magazine and contributes to the *Globe and Mail, Canadian Forum* and *Toronto Life*.

Ken Tucker (K.T.), former rock music critic at the *Los Angeles Herald Examiner*, is now rock music critic for the *Philadelphia Inquirer*.

Charley Walters (C.W.) manages a record store on Nantucket Island, where he lives year-round.

Record Label Abbreviations

Abraham (**Abra.**)
Accent (**Ac.**)
Accent/GNP (**Ac./GNP**)
Accord (**Acc.**)
Adelphi (**Adel.**)
Advance (**Adv.**)
Advent Corporation
   (**Advent Corp.**)
Aerospace (**Aero.**)
Aircheck (**Air.**)
Airway (**Airw.**)
Albatross (**Alb.**)
All Ears (**All E.**)
All Platinum (**All Pl.**)
Alligator (**Alli.**)
Alshire (**Alsh.**)
Alston (**Als.**)
Althia (**Alt.**)
Ambient (**Amb.**)
American International
   (**Amer. Int.**)
Amherst (**Amh.**)
Andrew's Music (**Andr.**)
Anthem (**Anth.**)
Antilles (**Ant.**)
Archive of Piano Music
   (**Arc. Piano**)
Archives (**Arc.**)
Archives of Folk and Jazz
   (**Arc. Folk**)
Arhoolie (**Arhoo.**)
Ariola (**Ario.**)
Ariola-America (**Ario.-
   Amer.**)
Arista (**Ari.**)
Arista/Freedom (**Ari./
   Free.**)
Arista/GRP (**Ari./GRP**)
Arista/Novus (**Ari./No.**)
Aristocrat (**Arist.**)
Artists House (**Artists H.**)
Ashbourne (**Ashb.**)
Ashtree (**Ash.**)
Asylum (**Asy.**)

Atlantic (**Atl.**)
Audio Fidelity (**Audio Fi.**)
Audio Masterworks (**Audio
   M.**)
Audiophile (**Audiop.**)
Aural Explorer (**Aural**)
Avant-Garde (**Av.**)

Backbeat (**Back.**)
Backstreet (**Backs.**)
Bainbridge (**Bain.**)
Barclay (**Bar.**)
Bareback (**Bare.**)
Barking Pumpkin (**Bark.**)
Barnaby (**Barn.**)
Bearsville (**Bears.**)
Becket (**Beck.**)
Bee Hive (**Bee**)
Beserkley (**Beserk.**)
Bethlehem (**Beth.**)
Big Tree (**Big**)
Biograph (**Bio.**)
Billingsgate (**Bill.**)
Birthright (**Birthr.**)
Biscuit City (**Bisc.**)
Bizarre (**Biz.**)
Blackbird (**Black.**)
Black Lion (**Black L.**)
Black Saint (**Black S.**)
Blarney Castle (**Blar.**)
Blind Pig (**Blind**)
Blue Angel (**Blue A.**)
Bluebird (**Blueb.**)
Blue Canyon (**Blue C.**)
Blue Goose (**Blue G.**)
Blue Note (**Blue N.**)
Blues Beacon (**Blues Bea.**)
Blues Boy (**Blues B.**)
Blues Classics (**Blues C.**)
Blue Sky (**Blue S.**)
Bluesway (**Blues.**)
Blue Street (**Blue St.**)
Blues Spectrum (**Blues Sp.**)
Blue Thumb (**Blue Th.**)

Boardwalk (**Bdwalk**)
Boston Brass (**Boston B.**)
Boulevard (**Boul.**)
Brunswick (**Bruns.**)
Buckboard (**Buck.**)
Buddah (**Bud.**)
Bulldog (**Bulld.**)
Bullfrog (**Bull.**)
Butterfly (**Butter.**)

Cachalot (**Cach.**)
Cadence (**Cad.**)
Cadet Concept (**Cadet C.**)
Caedmon (**Caed.**)
Calliope (**Calli.**)
Cambridge (**Cam.**)
Camden (**Camd.**)
Candide (**Can.**)
Canto Libre (**Canto L.**)
Capitol (**Cap.**)
Capitol/Pickwick (**Cap./
   Pick.**)
Capitol/Sovereign (**Cap./
   Sov.**)
Capricorn (**Capri.**)
Caribou (**Cari.**)
Caroline (**Caro.**)
Carrerre (**Carr.**)
Casablanca (**Casa.**)
Casino (**Ca.**)
Cassandra (**Cass.**)
Catalyst (**Cata.**)
Caytronics (**Cay.**)
Chalfont (**Chal.**)
Chaloff (**Cha.**)
Charisma (**Char.**)
Checker (**Check.**)
Chelsea (**Chel.**)
Chiaroscuro (**Chi.**)
Chimneyville (**Chim.**)
Chiswick (**Chis.**)
Chi-Sound (**Chi-S.**)
Chi-Town (**Chi-T.**)
Chocolate City (**Choc.**)

Chrysalis (**Chrys.**)
Chrysalis/Warner Bros.
  (**Chrys./War.**)
Circuit (**Cir.**)
Citadel (**Cit.**)
Clappers (**Clap.**)
Claridge (**Clar.**)
Classic Jazz (**Class.**)
Clocktower (**Clock.**)
CMS/Summit (**CMS/Sum.**)
Collector's Classics (**Col.
  Clas.**)
Colonial (**Colo.**)
Columbia (**Col.**)
Columbia Special Products
  (**CSP**)
Commodore (**Comm.**)
Communications Archives
  (**Comm. Arc.**)
Concert-Disc (**Con.-Disc**)
Concord Jazz (**Conc. J.**)
Contemporary (**Contem.**)
Coral (**Cor.**)
Coronet (**Coro.**)
Cotillion (**Coti.**)
Counterpoint/Esoteric
  (**Count.**)
County (**Coun.**)
Cracker Barrel (**Crack.**)
Crazy Cajun (**Crazy C.**)
Creative Sound (**Cre.**)
Creative World (**Cre. W.**)
Crescendo (**Cres.**)
Crossover (**Cross.**)
Crown Prince (**Crown P.**)
Crystal (**Crys.**)
Curtom (**Cur.**)

Dark Horse (**Dark**)
Day Spring (**Day**)
Delmark (**Del.**)
Deptford Fun City (**Dept.**)
Different Drummer (**Dif.**)
Dimension (**Dimen.**)
Discreet (**Discr.**)
Dixieland Jubilee (**DJ**)
Douglas International
  (**Douglas**)
Dreamland (**Dreaml.**)
Dunhill (**Dun.**)
Dynamite (**Dyna.**)

ECM/Polydor (**ECM/
  Poly.**)
ECM/Warner Bros.
  (**ECM/War.**)
Editions EG (**Ed. EG**)
Electrola (**Elect.**)
Elektra (**Elek.**)
EmArcy (**Em.**)

Embassy (**Emba.**)
Embryo (**Emb.**)
Emergency (**Emer.**)
EMI America (**EMI**)
Ensign (**Ens.**)
Enterprise (**Enterp.**)
Entr'acte (**Entr.**)
Epiphany (**Epip.**)
ESP Disk (**ESP**)
Eubie Blake Music (**EBM**)
Euphoria (**Euph.**)
Everest (**Ev.**)
Evergreen (**Ever.**)
Excello (**Ex.**)
Exodus (**Exo.**)
Expériences Anonymes
  (**EA**)

Fabulous (**Fab.**)
Famous Charisma (**Fam.
  Char.**)
Famous Door (**Fam. D.**)
Fantasy (**Fan.**)
Fantasy/WMOT (**Fan./
  WMOT**)
Festival (**Fest.**)
Finnader (**Finn.**)
First Amendment (**First
  Amen.**)
First American (**First
  Amer.**)
First Artists (**First Ar.**)
Flashlight (**Flash.**)
Flying Crow (**Fly. C.**)
Flying Dutchman (**Fly. D.**)
Flying Fish (**Fly. Fish**)
Flyright (**Flyr.**)
Folk-Legacy (**Folk-Leg.**)
Folkways (**Folk.**)
Fontana (**Fon.**)
Fortune (**For.**)
Fredonia (**Fredo.**)
Free Spirit (**Free**)
Fretless (**Fret.**)

Galaxy (**Gal.**)
Gamble (**Gam.**)
Gateway (**Gate.**)
Geffen (**Gef.**)
Gemini Hall (**Gem. H.**)
Generation (**Gener.**)
Genesis (**Gen.**)
Joe Gibbs (**J. Gibbs**)
Glendale (**Glen.**)
GNP Crescendo (**GNP**)
Gold Mind (**Gold M.**)
Good News (**Good N.**)
Good Time Jazz (**GTJ**)
Gordy (**Gor.**)
Graduate (**Grad.**)

Granite (**Gran.**)
Grapevine (**Grape.**)
Grass Mountain (**Grass**)
Grateful Dead (**Grate.**)
Great Northwest (**Great
  N.**)
Grecophon (**Grec.**)
Green Linnet (**Green L.**)
Greensleeves (**Greens.**)
Grenadilla (**Grena.**)
Groove Merchant (**G.M.**)
Gryphon (**Gry.**)
Guitar Player Records
  (**Guitar**)
Guitar World (**Guit.**)

Halcyon (**Hal.**)
Hall of Fame (**Hall**)
Handshake (**Hands.**)
Hannibal (**Hann.**)
Harlequin (**Harl.**)
Harmony Music (**Har. M.**)
Harvest (**Harv.**)
Heartbeat (**Heartb.**)
Heartwarming (**Heartw.**)
Herwin (**Her.**)
Hickory (**Hick.**)
High Note (**High N.**)
Historical (**Hist.**)
Hitsville (**Hits.**)
Home Cooking (**Home C.**)
Horizon (**Hori.**)

Imperial (**Imper.**)
Impulse (**Imp.**)
Increase (**Inc.**)
India Navigation (**In. Nav.**)
Indian House (**In. H.**)
In-Fidelity (**In-Fi.**)
Infinity (**Inf.**)
Inner City (**Inner**)
Interzone (**Inter.**)
Invictus (**Inv.**)
Iron Horse (**Iron H.**)
Island (**Is.**)
Island/Ze (**Is./Ze**)
Ivory World (**Ivory W.**)

Jay Jay (**Jay**)
Jazz Classics (**Jazz Cl.**)
Jazzology (**Jazzo.**)
Jazz Trip (**Jazz T.**)
Jefferson (**Jeff.**)

Kaleidoscope (**Kal.**)
Kama Sutra (**Kam. S.**)
Kanawha (**Kan.**)
Karate (**Kar.**)
Kayvette (**Kayv.**)
Kenwood (**Kenw.**)

Kicking Mule (**Kick.**)
King Bluegrass (**King B.**)
Kirshner (**Kir.**)
Klavier (**Kla.**)

Lamb and Lion (**Lamb**)
Land o' Jazz (**Land**)
Laurel/Protone (**Laurel/
  Pro.**)
Laurie (**Laur.**)
Lava Mountain (**Lava M.**)
Legacy (**Leg.**)
Legrand (**Legr.**)
LeJoint (**LeJ.**)
Leviathan (**Lev.**)
Liberty (**Lib.**)
Lifesong (**Lifes.**)
Limelight (**Lime.**)
Lionsgate (**Lion.**)
Little David (**Lit. Dav.**)
Little Star (**Lit. Star**)
London (**Lon.**)
London/Decca (**Lon./Dec.**)
Lone Star (**Lone**)
Los Angeles (**L.A.**)
Louisianne (**L'anne**)
Louisville (**Lou.**)
Lyricord (**Lyr.**)

Magpie (**Mag.**)
Maiden America (**Maid.**)
Mainstream (**Main.**)
Malaco (**Mal.**)
Mamlish (**Maml.**)
Manhattan (**Manh.**)
Manticore (**Mant.**)
Mark/Creative (**Mark/
  Cre.**)
Marlin (**Mar.**)
Master Jazz (**Mas. J.**)
Matchbox (**Match.**)
Melodeon (**Mel.**)
Melodisc (**Melo.**)
Melodyland (**Melod.**)
Memphis (**Memp.**)
Mercury (**Mer.**)
Message (**Mess.**)
Midland (**Mid.**)
Midsong International
  (**Mid. Int.**)
Milestone (**Mile.**)
Mill City (**Mill**)
Millenium (**Millen.**)
Missing Link (**Miss. L.**)
Modern (**Mod.**)
Monitor (**Mon.**)
Monmouth-Evergreen
  (**Mon.-Ev.**)
Monterey (**Monte.**)
Monument (**Monu.**)

Morrhythm (**Morr.**)
Mother-in-Law (**Mother**)
Motown (**Mo.**)
Mountain Railroad
  (**Mount.**)
Movie Star (**Movie**)
Mowest (**Mow.**)
Mushroom (**Mush.**)
Music Is Medicine (**Music
  Is**)
Musicor (**Musi.**)

Nashboro (**Nashb.**)
Natural Resources (**Nat.**)
Nemperor (**Nemp.**)
Neutron Records (**Neut.
  Rec.**)
New Song (**New S.**)
New World (**New W.**)
New York International
  (**N.Y. Int.**)
Nighthawk (**Nighth.**)
No Holds Barred (**No H.**)
Nonesuch (**None.**)

Odyssey (**Odys.**)
Oldie Blues (**Oldie B.**)
Old Timey (**Old Ti.**)
Old Town (**Old T.**)
Olympic (University of
  Washington) (**Olym.**)
Omnisound (**Omni.**)
Opus One (**Op. One**)
Original Sound (**Orig.
  Sound**)
Ornament (**Orna.**)
Osmosis (**Osm.**)
Outrageous (**Outra.**)
Outstanding (**Out.**)
Ovation (**Ova.**)
Oyster (**Oy.**)
Ozark (**Oz.**)

Pablo Live (**Pablo L.**)
Pacific (**Pacif.**)
Pacific Arts (**Pac. A.**)
Pacific Fine Arts (**Pac.
  F.A.**)
Pacific Jazz (**Pac. J.**)
Painted Smiles (**Paint.**)
Paltram (**Pal.**)
Pandora (**Pand.**)
Parachute (**Parach.**)
Paradise (**Parad.**)
Paragon (**Parag.**)
Paramount (**Para.**)
Parlophone (**Parlo.**)
Parrot (**Par.**)
Passport (**Pass.**)
Pathways of Sound

(**Pathways**)
Pavillion (**Pav.**)
PBR International (**PBR**)
Peacock (**Pea.**)
Pelican (**Pel.**)
People (**Peo.**)
Peters International
  (**Peters**)
Pfeiffer (**Pfeif.**)
Philadelphia International
  (**Phil.**)
Philips (**Phi.**)
Phil.-L.A. of Soul (**Phil.-
  L.A.**)
Philly Groove (**Philly**)
Phonogram (**Phono.**)
Piccadilly (**Picca.**)
Pickwick (**Pick.**)
Piedmont (**Pied.**)
Pine Tree (**Pine**)
Plantation (**Plant.**)
Plastic Record (**Pl. Rec.**)
Playboy (**Play.**)
Pleiades (**Plei.**)
Polydor (**Poly.**)
Polydor Deluxe (**Poly.
  Del.**)
Polygram (**Polyg.**)
Portrait (**Por.**)
Poseidon (**Pos.**)
Potato (**Pot.**)
Powderworks (**Powd.**)
Power Pak (**Power**)
Precision (**Prec.**)
Prelude (**Prel.**)
President (**Pres.**)
Prestige (**Prest.**)
Prince Buster (**Prince B.**)
Private Stock (**Priv.**)
Prodigal (**Prod.**)
Progressive (**Prog.**)
Project 3 (**Proj.**)
Protone (**Prot.**)
Puritan (**Puri.**)
Pyramid (**Pyr.**)

Quality (**Qual.**)
Queen Disc (**Queen**)
Quintessence (**Quin.**)

Radio Archives (**Radio A.**)
Rampant (**Ramp.**)
Random Radar (**Ran. Rad.**)
Ranwood (**Ran.**)
Rare Earth (**Rare**)
Ravenna (**Rav.**)
Realgood (**Realg.**)
Recommended (**Rec.**)
Red Lightnin' (**Red L.**)
Red Star (**Red S.**)

Reformation (**Reform.**)
Regular (**Reg.**)
Renaissance (**Ren.**)
Reprise (**Rep.**)
Revelation (**Rev.**)
Richmond (**Rich.**)
Ridge Runner (**Ridge**)
Riverboat (**River.**)
Riverside (**Riv.**)
Roadshow (**Road.**)
Rockburg (**Rockb.**)
Rocket (**R.**)
Rockhouse (**Rockh.**)
Rocking Horse (**Rocking**)
Rockstar (**Rocks.**)
Roller Coaster (**Roller C.**)
Rolling Rock (**Roll. R.**)
Rolling Stone (**Rol.**)
Rooster (**Roos.**)
Rough Trade (**Rough T.**)
Roulette (**Rou.**)
Rounder (**Roun.**)
Roxbury (**Rox.**)

Sackville (**Sack.**)
Salsoul (**Sals.**)
Salvation (**Salv.**)
Sanskrit (**Sans.**)
Scotti Brothers (**Scotti**)
SeaBreeze (**Sea.**)
Serenus (**Ser.**)
Shadybrook (**Shady.**)
Shanachie (**Shan.**)
Shelter (**Shel.**)
Silk Purse (**Silk**)
Sine Qua Non (**Sine**)
Skyline (**Skyl.**)
Slash Records (**Slash**)
Solid Rock (**Solid R.**)
Solid Smoke (**Solid S.**)
Solid State (**Solid St.**)
Song Bird (**Song**)
Soul City (**Soul C.**)
Soul Note (**Soul N.**)
Soul Parade (**Soul Pa.**)
Soul Power (**Soul P.**)
Soul Train (**Soul T.**)
Sound Bird (**Sound B.**)

Sound State Seven (**Sound S.**)
Sountrak (**Sountr.**)
Southland (**So.**)
Southwind (**Southw.**)
Specialty (**Spec.**)
Spindizzy (**Spin.**)
Spoken Arts (**Sp. Arts**)
Spoken Word (**Sp. Word**)
Spotlite (**Spot.**)
Springboard (**Sp.**)
Standard (**Stan.**)
Stanyan (**Sta.**)
Starday (**Star.**)
Starflight (**Starf.**)
State Line (**State L.**)
Steeplechase (**Steep.**)
Stinson (**Stin.**)
Stony Plain (**Stony**)
Storyville (**Story.**)
Strawberry (**Straw.**)
Sugarhill (**Sugar.**)
Sunbeam (**Sunb.**)
Sunnyvale (**Sunny.**)
Sunset (**Suns.**)
Sunshine Sound (**Sunshine**)
Surfside (**Surf.**)
Swaggie (**Swag.**)
Swan Song (**Swan**)
Sweet Jane (**Sweet J.**)
Swing House (**Swing H.**)
Symposium (**Symp.**)

Tablight (**Tabli.**)
Takoma (**Tak.**)
Talisman (**Tal.**)
Tamla (**Tam.**)
Tangent (**Tan.**)
Taz-Jaz (**Taz.**)
Testament (**Test.**)
Tetragrammatron (**Tetra.**)
Texas Re-Cord Company (**Tex.**)
Threshold (**Thresh.**)
Tifton (**Tif.**)
Timeless (**Timel.**)
Tom 'n' Jerry (**Tom**)
Tomato (**Toma.**)
Top Ranking (**Top R.**)

Tortoise International (**Tort.**)
Tradition (**Trad.**)
Transatlantic (**Trans.**)
Triangle (**Tri.**)
Trojan (**Troj.**)
True North (**True**)
Twentieth Century-Fox (**20th Cent.**)
Twin Tone (**Twin T.**)

Unicorn (**Uni.**)
Union Pacific (**Un. Pac.**)
United Artists (**U.A.**)
Unlimited Gold (**Unli.**)
Up Front (**Up Fr.**)
Utopia (**Ut.**)

Vanguard (**Van.**)
Vanguard Twofers (**Van. T.**)
Vee Jay (**VJ**)
Vertigo (**Vert.**)
Vibration (**Vibr.**)
Virgin Front Line (**V.F.L.**)
Virgin International (**Virgin Int'l**)
Vocalion (**Voc.**)
Voyager (**Voya.**)

Wackies (**Wac.**)
Warner Bros. (**War.**)
Waterhouse (**Waterh.**)
Westbound (**Westb.**)
Western Hemisphere (**Western**)
Whitfield (**Whit.**)
Who's Who in Jazz (**Who's**)
Windsong (**Wind.**)
Wing and a Prayer (**Wing**)
Wizard (**Wiz.**)
Wonderland (**Won.**)
Wooden Nickel (**Wood.**)
World Jazz (**World**)
World Library of Sacred Music (**WLSM**)

Xanadu (**Xan.**)

ROCK, SOUL, BLUES, COUNTRY, GOSPEL AND POP

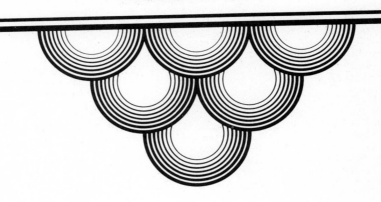

ABBA
★ ★ Waterloo / Atl. (1974)
★ ★ Abba / Atl. (1975)
★ ★ ★ Greatest Hits / Alt. (1976)
★ ★ Arrival / Atl. (1976)
★ ★ The Album / Atl. (1977)
★ ★ Voulez-Vous / Atl. (1979)
★ ★ ★ Greatest Hits, Vol. 2 / Atl. (1979)
★ ★ Super Trouper / Atl. (1980)
★ ★ The Visitors / Atl. (1981)

This Swedish quartet (two women, two men) is an international phenomenon; their sound—a compendium of white American pop hooks welded to mesmerizing synthesizers and the permanently anxious lead singing of the women—is pleasant and forgettable. In their conscious conquest of Everywhere, they are determined not to offend: a fixed cheeriness pervades, and thus Abba is best taken in small doses—i.e., their singles. Given this every-song-a-smiley-smash approach, the *Greatest Hits* volumes are of the highest quality, even if they are prone to induce both sleep and cavities.
— K.T.

ABC
★ ★ ★ Tears Are Not Enough / Neut. Rec. (1981), Br. imp.

Well-crafted funk from the industrial wilds of Sheffield in England's extreme north. ABC's only problem is that it surfaced at a time when everybody else was playing the same stuff. Not yet a nightclub narcotic, but their next album will be.
— ML.H.

ACCEPT
★ ★ Accept / Pass. (1980)
★ ★ Breaker / Pass. (1981) ¶

Journeyman heavy metal/hard rock; unexceptional stylists, unimaginative material. For genre fanatics only. — D.M.

AC/DC
★ ★ High Voltage / Atco (1976)
★ ★ Let There Be Rock / Atco (1977)
★ ★ Powerage / Atl. (1978)
★ ★ ★ If You Want Blood You've Got It / Atl. (1978)
★ ★ ★ Highway to Hell / Atl. (1979)
★ ★ ★ Back in Black / Atl. (1980)
★ ★ Dirty Deeds Done Dirt Cheap / Atl. (1981)
★ ★ ★ ★ For Those About to Rock, We Salute You / Atl. (1981)

Scathing, often libelous reviews have been a way of life for this Australian molten boogie band ever since they debuted in this country with *High Voltage* (a compilation of two earlier Aussie LPs). But what the critics don't know, the heavy-metal kids understand. Led by the tenacious axe-wielding Scots-born Young brothers Angus and Malcolm, AC/DC are nothing more or less than rock & roll party thunder, 110-decibel escapism fired up by panzer division riffs 'n' rhythms, Angus' mad-dog stage romps in a sweaty schoolboy uniform, and the lecherous growl of original singer Bon Scott.

The first three albums, produced by former Easybeats and hit Australian producers Harry Vanda and George Young (Angus and Malcolm's older brother), have their moments, and *If You Want Blood You've Got It* captures their live show with a white-noise vengeance. But both *Highway to Hell* and *Back in Black*—which features the lion's roar of Brian Johnson, who became the band's singer after Scott died in 1980—struck platinum on the strength of tighter songs and the meaty production of Robert John Lange. Ironically, their next best-seller, *Dirty Deeds Done Dirt Cheap,* was a collection of old tracks featuring Scott, which had been previously unissued in the States.
— D.F.

JOHNNY ACE
★ ★ ★ ★ **Johnny Ace Memorial Album /
Duke (NA)**
★ ★ ★ **Memorial Album for Johnny Ace /
Chis. (1982), imp.**
Johnny Ace achieved legendary status as
much for the way he died—losing a game of
Russian roulette on Christmas Eve 1954—as
for the series of plaintive (slightly off-key)
soul ballads he recorded in 1952–54, includ-
ing "Pledging My Love" and "Never Let Me
Go." These are the core of Duke's endearing
and historically important collection. The
Chiswick set, with its nearly identical cover
and title, features unreleased songs and alternate takes.   — R.G.

ACE
★ ★ **Five-a-Side / Anchor (1974)** ¶
★ **Time for Another / Anchor (1975)** ¶
★ **No Strings/Anchor (1977)** ¶
This five-man English band led by Paul Car-
rack competently reprised basic American
rock, including soul. *Five-a-Side* contains
their only hit, "How Long."   — S.H.

BARBARA ACKLIN
★ ★ ★ **Love Makes a Woman / Bruns.
(1968)**
★ ★ ★ **Seven Days of Night / Bruns. (1969)**
★ ★ ★ **Someone Else's Arms / Bruns. (1970)**
★ ★ ★ **I Did It / Bruns. (1970)**
★ ★ ★ **I Call It Trouble / Bruns. (1971)**
★ ★ ★ **Great Soul Hits of Barbara Acklin /
Bruns. (NA)**
Acklin has been a journeyman soul singer
since the late Sixties, and although her only
Top Twenty pop success came in 1968 (with
"Love Makes a Woman," which made No.
15), she turns in fine, light R&B perform-
ances on each of these records, in a groove
established (and probably handled better, if
not more pleasantly) by some of the lighter
Motown singers—Martha Reeves, for exam-
ple.   — D.M.

THE ACT
★ ★ ★ ★ **Too Late at Twenty / Hann. (1981)**
The Act's Nick Laird-Clowes plows turf
similar to Squeeze's Difford and Tilbrook
and shows himself nearly their equal in taking well-worn ideas and turning them into
something fresh. Like Squeeze, the Act uses
Lennon and McCartney circa 1966 as a
jumping-off point for its more individual excursions, but its sound already has a self-
assurance it took Squeeze three albums to
achieve. Though the Act lacks Squeeze's
cleverness, its music is tougher and more focused. A most impressive debut.   — D.S.

THE ACTION
★ ★ ★ **The Ultimate Action / Demon
(1980), Br. imp.**
The Action rank just below the Who and
the Small Faces in importance among London Mod bands of the early Sixties. Produced by George Martin, the singles collected in this album (which was compiled by
the Jam's Paul Weller) are in fact more typical of the mods' tastes in soul and R&B
than most early Who and Faces material.
The outstanding track is their version of
"The Harlem Shuffle," though throughout,
the singing leaves a good deal to be desired.
Those who enjoy blue-eyed soul will want to
pick up on this.   — D.M.

ROY ACUFF
★ ★ **Best of Roy Acuff / Cap. (1963)** ¶
★ ★ **Roy Acuff Sings Hank Williams /
Hick. (1966)**
★ ★ ★ ★ **Greatest Hits / Col. (1970)**
★ ★ **Roy Acuff's Greatest Hits, Vol. 1 /
Elek. (1978)**
★ ★ ★ **Roy Acuff's Greatest Hits, Vol. 2 /
Elek. (1979)**
Though he never had as many hits as his
reputation might suggest, Acuff is a crucial
figure in country music. He came to prominence as the star of the Grand Ole Opry in
the late Thirties and early Forties, when the
Western influence was beginning to permeate
country music. Acuff remained strictly traditional: his Smoky Mountain Boys were a
classic mountain string band, and his rough
singing style conveyed an unmistakable debt
to the church. The Columbia album contains
the songs that made his career ("Night Train
to Memphis," "The Great Speckled Bird,"
"Fire Ball Mail," "Wabash Cannonball" and
the scarifying "Were You There When They
Crucified My Lord." It is absolutely essential
to any country album collection. Later, more
modern versions of many of these songs appear on the Capitol and Elektra albums,
which are no substitute for the real thing.
— J.MO.

ADAM AND THE ANTS
★ ★ ★ **Dirk Wears White Sox / Do-It
(1979), Br. imp.**
★ ★ ★ **Kings of the Wild Frontier / Col.
(1980)**
★ ★ **Prince Charming / Col. (1981)**
Having struggled in the hinterland of the
1976 punk explosion, Adam finally found a
formula for success when he teamed up with
former Sex Pistols Svengali Malcolm
McLaren. Sounding like the drummers of
Burundi with heavy metal overtones, Adam

made his fortune in a fashion for pirate suits and Indian gear coupled with a passion for tribalism. Pure pap for nonpeople. — ML.H.

BRYAN ADAMS
★ ★ ★ **Bryan Adams / A&M (1980)**
★ ★ ★ ★ **You Want It, You Got It / A&M (1981)**
Canadian pop/R&B blue-eyed soul vocalist, multi-instrumentalist and writer impressed with a strong but uneven debut that featured Jeff "Skunk" Baxter in a session cameo. The second record, produced by Bob Clearmountain, is a very good Byrds-to-hard-rock medium for Adams' vocal and guitar skills. — J.S.

FAYE ADAMS
★ ★ ★ **Faye Adams / Savoy (1980)**
Adams' biggest hits—"Shake a Hand," "I'll Be True," "Hurts Me to My Heart"—were recorded for Herald Records in 1953. She had earlier recorded for Atlantic, where she also did good work. These sides, from the late Fifties and early Sixties, aren't so exceptional but they are strong, blues-oriented with gospel overtones. — D.M.

GAYLE ADAMS
★ ★ **Love Fever / Prel. (1981)**
Latter-day disco singer; something to yawn about. — D.M.

JOHNNY ADAMS
★ **After All the Good Is Gone / Ario. (NA)**
★ ★ ★ **Heart and Soul / SSS (1970)**
★ ★ **Stand by Me / Chel. (NA) ¶**
Heart and Soul is an interesting album of varied Sixties soul with heavy country and blues influences. Though Adams is from New Orleans, the record bears none of that city's distinctive musical flourishes. Notable songs include "Reconsider Me," "Losing Battle" and "I Won't Cry." Succeeding records unsuccessfully attempt to update the style. — J.MC.

ADC BAND
★ ★ **Renaissance / Coti. (1980)**
★ **Brother Luck / Coti. (1981)**
Sappy, inconsequential funk. — J.D.C.

ADDRISI BROTHERS
★ **Addrisi Brothers / Bud. (1977)**
Slick, processed disco sung by this songwriting duo and produced and recorded in Nashville by country session master Norbert Putnam. Will 1977 be remembered as the year of cracker disco? Probably not. — J.S.

ADVERTISING
★ ★ ★ **Jingles / EMI (1978), Br. imp.**
One of the first and best of England's 1978 post-punk power pop brigade released a couple of cute, bright and clever Merseybeat-tinged singles, "Lipstick" and "Stolen Love"—both included here—before being washed away in the ensuing critical backlash against just this kind of thing. Simon Boswell and Tot Taylor, the group's talented vocal/guitar/songwriting duo, are now with Live Wire and recording solo, respectively. — D.S.

THE ADVERTS
★ ★ ★ ★ **Crossing the Red Sea with the Adverts / Bright (1978), Br. imp.**
★ **Cast of Thousands / RCA (1979), Br. imp.**
After four singles that indicated real primal punk promise in 1977, the Adverts made two albums before splitting. *Crossing the Red Sea,* with some of those 45 sides, is an important document of punk energy. *Cast of Thousands* is a disaster; buried in miserable production, it suffers also from pretentiousness and a general lack of direction. — I.R.

AEROSMITH
★ ★ **Aerosmith (Featuring "Dream On") / Col. (1973)**
★ ★ **Get Your Wings / Col. (1974)**
★ ★ ★ **Toys in the Attic / Col. (1976)**
★ ★ **Rocks / Col. (1976)**
★ ★ ★ **Draw the Line / Col. (1977)**
★ ★ **Live Bootleg / Col. (1978)**
★ ★ **Night in the Ruts / Col. (1979)**
★ ★ ★ ★ **Aerosmith's Greatest Hits / Col. (1980)**
Each generation of rock fans needs its own heroes, and those who came of age in the mid-Seventies chose Aerosmith, a selection that at first seemed based more on looks than sound. Lead vocalist Steven Tyler, with his puffy, pouty lips and salacious eyes, had the manner of his lookalike, Mick Jagger, but none of Jagger's command of song or movement. And lead guitarist Joe Perry's role seemed initially a game but limited version of Keith Richards'. But by its third album, *Toys in the Attic,* Aerosmith had defined its own hard-rock style, and *Rocks* perfected it.

Unfortunately, the band remains erratic in its composing. One doesn't get even half an album of hard-rock gems like "Sweet Emotion" or "Back in the Saddle." *Live Bootleg* is marred by uninspired performances. *Aerosmith's Greatest Hits* is as solid a selection of mid-Seventies hard rock as anyone could hope for. — W.R.

JANE AIRE AND THE BELVEDERES
★ ★ ★ **Jane Aire and the Belvederes /
Virgin (1979), Br. imp.**
Akron, Ohio's other female export to the
U.K., Jane Aire is more of a rocker and less
of a wily ham than Rachel Sweet (who appears on this LP in a backup vocal role).
Aire's strong, Midwestern vocals have real
character and Liam Sternberg's excellent
production (and songwriting) gives it full
play. — I.R.

AIRPLAY
★ **Airplay / RCA (1980)**
L.A. studio *menschen* David Foster and Jay
Graydon go for the big bucks, Toto-style,
and fall flat on their asses. The most calculated and soulless pseudo-group of its kind,
which is saying something. — D.M.

AIR RAID
★ **Air Raid / 20th. Cent. (1981)**
Mediocre Southern rock band with expan-
sionist pretensions (i.e., pop to pomp). Not
worthy even as AOR radio fodder. — D.M.

AIR SUPPLY
■ **Lost in Love / Ari. (1980)**
■ **The One That You Love / Ari. (1981)**
Quintessential saccharin: ersatz, sickly sweet
and probably carcinogenic. — S.M.

AIRWAVES
★ ★ ★ **New Day / A&M (1978)**
★ ★ ★ **Next Stop / A&M (1979)**
Earnest, well-crafted pop-rock sound by a
band assembled at the famous Rockfield Studios in Wales, where Dave Edmunds spent
time as a producer. House producer/engineer
Pat Moran and studio guitarist Ray Marti-
nez, ex–Love Sculpture bassist John David
and ex–Help Yourself drummer Dave
Charles meshed well to produce a tight,
commercial sound rich in musical nuance.
— J.S.

FRANKLIN AJAYE
★ **Don't Smoke Dope, Fry Your Hair / Li.
Dav. (NA)** ¶
★ **Comedian / A&M (1973)**
★ **I'm a Comedian, Seriously / A&M (1974)**
Mix two parts Jimmy Walker and one part
David Brenner. Add stale material (ingredi-
ents: high school, being black, getting
stoned). Simmer for three albums. Yields:
Zilch. — K.T.

JAN AKKERMAN
★ ★ ★ ★ **Profile / Sire (1972)**
★ ★ ★ **Tabernakel / Atco (1974)**

★ ★ ★ **Jan Akkerman / Atl. (1978)** ¶
★ ★ ★ **Live / Atl. (1979)**
Akkerman is best known as the guitarist of
Focus, the Dutch rock group. His hard, aggressively agile and imaginative guitar paced
Profile's first side through muscular, often
frenetic jazz-rock jams, usually with only
bass and drums backing. Side two included
capable, unaccompanied classical guitar and
lute pieces, among more straightforward
electric rock playing. *Tabernakel* featured
medieval and original classically oriented
works, most with Akkerman alone on lute,
the others with a rock rhythm section and a
well-integrated and arranged orchestra.
— C.W.

ALABAMA
★ **My Home's in Alabama / RCA (1980)**
★ **Feels So Right / RCA (1981)**
★ **Mountain Music / RCA (1982)**
Flaccid country-rock band cranks out hit
singles—"Tennessee River" and "Why Lady
Why" from *My Home's*, "Old Flame" from
Feels and "Take Me Down" and the title
track from *Mountain Music*. For the modern
dentist. — J.S.

ALBERTOS Y LOS TRIOS PARANOIAS
★ ★ **Alberto y Los Trios Paranoias / Trans.
(1976)**
★ ★ **Italians from Outer Space / Trans.
(1977)**
★ ★ **Death of Rock and Roll / El Mambo
(1980)**
Wild music cum comedy group with an
early production assist from Nick Lowe.
Creators of the "snuff music" fad in England. — J.S.

ALDA RESERVE
★ ★ **Love Goes On / Sire (1979)**
If you concentrated on the bad imagist poetry and tinkly electric piano that makes up
the bulk of their sound, you might be able to
hammer together an argument making Alda
Reserve the Doors of the New York punk
scene. Then again, if bad imagist poetry and
tinkly electric piano were all there was to
the Doors in the first place, they'd have disappeared as quickly as Alda Reserve has.
— J.D.C.

ALESSI
★ **Alessi / A&M (1976)**
★ **All for a Reason / A&M (1977)**
★ **Driftin' / A&M (1978)**
★ **Words and Music / A&M (1979)**
Long Island twin brothers Billy and Bobby

Alessi stumble over the same problem that defeated their Beatle-esque aspiration in their previous group, Barnaby Bye: Lennon and McCartney weren't just masters of harmony, but also masters of rhythm and melody. And without something as gritty as "Long Tall Sally" to offset the vocalizing, all this fey power pop adds up to nothing more than the Lettermen without cardigans. — D.M.

KAREN ALEXANDER
★ **Isn't It Always Love** / **Asy. (1975)**
★ **Voyager** / **Asy. (1978)**
Singer/songwriter who sang on Wendy Waldman and Maria Muldaur LPs conceived of these rubbery songbooks while living in Iran. Perhaps that's why Ayatollah Khomeini banned Western music in that country. — J.S.

WILLIE ALEXANDER AND THE BOOM BOOM BAND
★ **Willie Alexander and the Boom Boom Band** / **MCA (1978)** ¶
★ **Meanwhile . . . Back in the States** / **MCA (1978)**
Barely competent funk from an old-timer on the Boston R&B scene; Alexander was associated with the city's late-Seventies new wave resurgence, but by the time he got to the recording studio, he was already over the hill. Hold out for Mink DeVille instead. — D.M.

ALIAS
★ **Alias** / **Mer. (1978)** ¶
★ **Contraband** / **Mer. (1979)**
Jacksonville, Florida, trio plies a fairly limp version of Southern rock. Woman vocalist Jo Jo Billingsly did stints with both Lynyrd Skynyrd and the Atlanta Rhythm Section. — J.S.

ALIBI
★ **Friends** / **Poly. (1980)**
Produced by Chris Rea, this band nevertheless sounds less like a white R&B outfit than retread Bee Gees. — J.S.

DR. ALIMANTADO
★ ★ ★ ★ **Best Dressed Chicken in Town** / **Greens. (1980)**
★ ★ ★ **Sons of Thunder** / **Greens. (1981)**
Equal doses of wackiness and profundity served up with some of the heaviest bass explosions on record made *Best Dressed Chicken* a punk cult classic (the cover alone would have assured its immortality). Alimantado has been one of the more interesting topical DJs, but as *Sons of Thunder*

shows, he's less convincing as a singer. Hard roots music nevertheless. — R.F.G.

JOHNNIE ALLAN
★ ★ ★ ★ **Good Timin' Man** / **Flyr. (1980), Br. imp.**
Allan's a Cajun rock 'n' roller, well-known in Louisiana though still obscure outside the bayous. He had a hit in England with Chuck Berry's "Promised Land," not included here, which brought him the opportunity to make this album. His broad range and C&W tremolo give him a latter-day Conway Twitty feel, particularly on slower numbers. But Allan cuts up best on "I Knew the Bride," "JuJu Man" and "Victim of Life's Circumstances," which cut the versions by Dave Edmunds, Nick Lowe's Brinsley Schwarz and Delbert McClinton, respectively. Fans of any of those performers are directed here posthaste. — D.M.

LAURA ALLAN
★ ★ ★ **Laura Allan** / **Elek. (1978)**
Pleasant, fairly lightweight California singer/writer; not Joni Mitchell, though she might like to be. But Allan sings funkier, a big plus. — D.M.

DEBORAH ALLEN
★ ★ ★ **Trouble in Paradise** / **Cap. (1980)**
A Nashville songstress with a voice eerily reminiscent of Stevie Nicks. The way Allen applies that voice—full of loping raspiness but able to phrase like the flight of a bird—is what makes her so promising. Her equally intriguing songwriting capabilities (especially when working with Rafe Van-Hoy) assure her future. — R.P.

PETER ALLEN
★ ★ ★ **Continental American** / **A&M (1974)**
★ ★ ★ **Taught by Experts** / **A&M (1976)**
★ ★ **It Is Time for Peter Allen** / **A&M (1977)**
★ ★ **I Could Have Been a Sailor** / **A&M (1979)**
★ ★ ★ **Bi-Coastal** / **A&M (1980)**
An Australian-born singer, Allen combines the blithe grace of Fred Astaire with the campy flash of Liberace. He came to prominence on New York's cabaret circuit, singing touching autobiographical songs like "Tenterfield Saddler," the title of one of two out-of-print Metromedia albums. Signed by A&M in 1974, he made two moody genre classics, *Continental American* and *Taught by Experts*, with art-pop producers Joel Dorn and Brooks Arthur; the latter introduced his Carmen Miranda–style signature

song, "I Go to Rio." After an uneven live album *(It Is Time)* and his weakest studio effort *(Sailor),* Allen collaborated with whiz L.A. producer David Foster on *Bi-Coastal,* a pop-funk tour de force that placed him squarely in the pop-rock mainstream, closer for once to Boz Scaggs than to Fred Astaire. — S.H.

PHYLICIA ALLEN
★ **Josephine Superstar / Casa. (1981)**
Disco concept set, dedicated to Josephine Baker. Pretentious even as the cabaret tripe it aspires to be, and absolutely useless as dance music, since the arrangements are hackneyed and not especially lively, and Allen isn't much of a singer. She enunciates like hell though. For those who believe that singing has more to do with enunciation than emotion. Produced by Village People auteur Jacques Morali. — D.M.

THE RANCE ALLEN GROUP
★ ★ ★ **The Rance Allen Group / Stax (1971)**
★ ★ ★ **Brothers / Stax (1973)**
★ ★ **Say My Friend / Cap. (1977)** ¶
★ ★ ★ **Straight from the Heart / Stax (1978)**
★ ★ ★ **I Feel Like Going On / Stax (1979)**
★ ★ ★ **Smile / Stax (1979)**
★ ★ ★ **Our Best to You / Stax (1981)**
★ ★ ★ **Truth Is Where It's At / Stax (NA)**
★ ★ ★ **Ain't No Need of Crying / Stax (NA)**
Although they've never clicked in a big way even on the soul charts, this trio of brothers perhaps purveys the most effectively modernized gospel-soul of the late Seventies and Eighties. With occasional production assistance from Motown vet Hank Cosby, the Allens (Rance sings lead and plays keyboards) have carved out a distinctive style with heart at a time when few stylists display even a glimmer of soul. A lack of outstanding material keeps the Rance Allen Group from the first-rank of pop-soul groups, but someday, when they shake that curse off, this group could develop into something genuinely moving and outstanding. For now, Allen's biting gospel leads are a pleasant antidote to both Pendergrass-level crooning and Clinton-esque funk snarls. — D.M.

WOODY ALLEN
★ ★ ★ **The Night Club Years 1964–1968 / U.A. (1972)**
In the mid-Sixties, Allen's stand-up style—a nervous but traditional barrage of one-liners—was counterrevolutionary: his comedic mentors were Bob Hope and Groucho Marx, not Lenny Bruce and Nichols and

May, the improvisationary deities of the period. However, Allen's subject matter and point of view was anarchic: he approached the world as if everyone were in analysis for having failed to score with the ideal woman (a stacked philosophy major). *The Night Club Years* catches him at his most tensely self-assured. — K.T.

LUTHER ALLISON
★ ★ ★ **Love Me Mama / Del. (1969)**
★ ★ ★ **Luther's Blues / Gor. (NA)**
★ **Night Life / Gor. (1975)**
Youngish Chicago blues guitarist who has never been able to consolidate his raw talent into a truly workable recording style. Motown's Gordy subsidiary is an odd place to find Allison, and the label's pop orientation proves disastrous on *Night Life,* where he's asked to truck with soul music. The others are better, but their preponderance of hot guitar licks lacks focus. — D.M.

DUANE ALLMAN
★ ★ ★ ★ **An Anthology / Capri. (1972)**
★ ★ ★ ★ **Anthology, Vol. 2 / Capri. (1974)**
★ ★ ★ ★ **Best of Duane Allman / Poly. (1981)**
These discs prove conclusively that Allman's vision extended far beyond his groundbreaking feats with the Allman Brothers Band. In his Hourglass recordings (as well as in some tracks cut in 1969 with an unnamed band that included the Allman Brothers' bassist, Berry Oakley), one hears the tentative beginnings of the Allman Brothers' distinctive style. Allman's genius asserted itself at other times too. Here some of his finest moments as a sessionman are catalogued, including "Layla," Wilson Pickett's powerhouse rendition of "Hey Jude" and King Curtis' "The Weight." These anthologies are of more than historical interest: they are enjoyable and instructive as well. — D.MC.

GREGG ALLMAN
★ ★ ★ ★ **Laid Back / Capri. (1973)**
★ ★ **The Gregg Allman Tour / Capri. (1974)** ¶
★ ★ **Playin' Up a Storm / Capri. (1977)**
Laid Back effectively recaptures much of the glory of the early Allman Brothers albums, although that group's exuberance is replaced here by a captivating sort of moroseness. At any rate, Allman turns in one superb vocal after another in his world-weary style ("Midnight Rider" and "These Days" are evocative in the extreme) and is aided by no-nonsense musicianship and some nifty arrangements.

If only the tour album were worthy of such praise. But after a fast start it disintegrates musically. An inappropriate twenty-four-piece orchestra and two spineless performances by Cowboy don't help matters. *Playin'* is also slack. — D.MC.

ALLMAN BROTHERS BAND

★ ★ ★ **Idlewild South / Capri. (1969)**
★ ★ ★ **The Allman Brothers Band / Capri. (1970)**
★ ★ ★ ★ ★ **Allman Brothers Band at Fillmore East / Capri. (1971)**
★ ★ ★ ★ **Eat a Peach / Capri. (1972)**
★ ★ **Brothers and Sisters / Capri. (1973)**
★ ★ ★ **Beginnings / Capri. (1973)** ¶
★ **Win, Lose or Draw / Capri. (1975)**
★ ★ ★ **The Road Goes On Forever / Capri. (1975)**
■ **Wipe the Window, Check the Oil, Dollar Gas / Capri. (1976)**
★ ★ ★ **Enlightened Rogues / Capri. (1979)**
★ **Reach for the Sky / Ari. (1980)**
★ **Brothers of the Road / Ari. (1981)**
★ ★ ★ **The Best of the Allman Brothers Band / Poly. (1981)**

Listening to the Allman Brothers Band's first two flawed but engaging albums (repackaged as *Beginnings* and also available separately), one senses a relentless search for grandeur within a singular style of blues-rock fusion that also encompassed elements of classical and country music. Fired by Duane Allman's stinging, inventive lead and slide guitar work and by a rhythm section that pumped ferociously, the Allmans snapped up the grail on a superb live set, *At Fillmore East.* Remarkably, with three of seven cuts clocking in at 19:06, 12:46 and 22:40, there are no wasted notes, no pointless jams, no half-realized vocals—everything counts, from Duane's forceful opening slide guitar statement on "Statesboro Blues" through the fading first notes of "Mountain Jam" on side four.

More than half of the band's next album, *Eat a Peach,* is culled from the Fillmore East date, including the two-sided "Mountain Jam," which abounds in breathtaking musical interplay, particularly between Dickey Betts and Duane Allman. Three songs recorded after Duane's death find the band still riding a creative peak. "Little Martha," a guitar-dobro duet by Betts and Allman, closes the album and can be considered a symbolic passing of the mantle that marks the beginning of the end for the band. Betts, with a lyrical but softer touch than Duane, was ill-suited to front a band. *Brothers and Sisters,* although it contains Betts'

"Ramblin' Man" (a hit single), is flabby. The songs lack punch, even with Gregg Allman's penetrating vocals, and there is no dynamic musicianship to pull the material out of the realm of the ordinary. *Win, Lose or Draw* is but further proof of the band's decline. Again, Gregg shines—on the title cut and on an update of Muddy Waters' "Can't Lose What You Never Had"—but his are the only notable performances. *The Road Goes On Forever* is a two-record set billed as "their greatest performances." *Comme çi, comme ça. Wipe the Windows, Check the Oil, Dollar Gas* is an album of live material culled from the band's appearances after Duane's death.

A reunion that worked, *Enlightened Rogues* was the best the brothers had been since *Eat a Peach.* Dickey Betts' guitar lines soared and wailed in the old style, and Gregg Allman's fervent vocals proved he hadn't forgotten how to get to the heart of a song. A duet between Betts and Bonnie Bramlett on "Crazy Love" is an especially riveting moment.

Brothers of the Road on the other hand, has an excellent song—"Straight from the Heart"—to recommend it, but not much of anything else. In fact the record finds the Allmans moving in a pop direction. No Southern band has ever sounded so sickly sweet. For diehards only. — D.MC.

GREG ALPER BAND

★ ★ ★ **Fat Doggie / Adel. (NA)**
Fairly good jazz-rock effort featuring Alper's funky saxophone playing. — J.S.

ALL-SPORTS BAND

■ **All-Sports Band / Radio (1981)**
The most offensive "uniform band" since the Village People. In the Sixties the all-American sports ethic was uncool to many rock fans, but with the more conservative and athletic ambiance of Seventies and Eighties arena-rock, the All-Sports Band must have seemed like a smart cash-in. No one bought it. Anyway, for such an allegedly butch project the music itself was incredibly wimpy, with dull, Foreigner-style corporate guitar riffs and air-pumped AM harmonies. — J.F.

ALPHA BAND

★ ★ **The Alpha Band / Ari. (1976)** ¶
★ ★ ★ **Spark in the Dark / Ari. (1977)** ¶
★ ★ **Statue Makers of Hollywood / Ari. (1978)** ¶
J. Henry Burnett, David Mansfield and Steven Soles formed the Alpha Band during

their stint as sidemen with Bob Dylan's Rolling Thunder Revue tour, and *The Alpha Band* and *Spark in the Dark* show a decided Dylan/Roger McGuinn influence, especially in Burnett's oblique lyrics and his singing. *Spark,* more slickly produced and featuring a serviceable session cameo from Ringo Starr, gets a slight edge in a close fit. *Statue Makers* might have been even better, except for its religious pretensions. — J.S.

ALTERNATIVE TV
★ ★ ★ **Action Time Vision / Dept. (1978)**
★ ★ ★ **What You See Is What You Are / Dept. (1978)**
★ ★ ★ **Vibing Up the Senile Man / Dept. (1979)**
★ ★ ★ **Strange Kicks / IRS (1981)**
Weird British band, led by conceptualizers Mark Perry and Dennis Burns, dabbles in surrealism, modern composition and electronic music, tongue-in-cheek profundity and a penchant for late-Sixties psychedelia. Strongly influenced by Zappa, whose "Why Don't You Do Me Right?" is included on the first record, *The Image Has Cracked* (listed here as *Action Time Vision.*) The band comes closest to living up to its name on the psycho-soap opera "The Radio Story" from the third LP, *Vibing.* — J.S.

AMANT
★ **Amant / Mar. (1981)**
One of the TK Records stable's less necessary products. — D.M.

AMAZING RHYTHM ACES
★ ★ ★ **Stacked Deck / ABC (1975)** ¶
★ ★ ★ **Too Stuffed to Jump / ABC (1976)** ¶
★ ★ ★ **Toucan Do It, Too / ABC (1976)** ¶
★ ★ **Burning the Ballroom Down / ABC (1978)** ¶
★ ★ **Amazing Rhythm Aces / Col. (1979)**
★ ★ **How the Hell Do You Spell Rhythm / War. (1980)**
Old-timey, bluegrass, Nashville steel, swing and R&B come together in the Aces' music, appropriately enough, since they're a Memphis band. If their eclecticism is sometimes disconcerting, their spirit is usually sufficient to carry listeners along. Traditionalists will be pleased with *Stacked Deck,* which renders such classics as "Life's Railway to Heaven" with stylish authenticity and presents original tunes that remain faithful to the conventions of blues and country music. *Too Stuffed to Jump* has a more contemporary sound (and cleaner production), but the Aces' passionate respect for their sources is no longer in evidence and the result is rather flat. Subsequent albums remain so. — A.S.

AMBOY DUKES
★ ★ **Survival of the Fittest / Poly. (1971)**
★ ★ ★ **Call of the Wild / Discr. (1974)**
★ ★ **Journeys/Migrations / Main. (1975)** ¶
★ ★ **Tooth, Fang and Claw / Discr. (1975)**
More than any other band of the late Sixties (save perhaps the Electric Prunes), the Amboy Dukes provided posterity with a working definition of the term "acid rock." Their albums, psychedelicized from covers (the original *Journey to the Center of the Mind* proudly displayed roughly fifty pot-smoking apparati) to song titles ("Why Is a Carrot More Orange Than an Orange," "The Inexhaustible Quest for the Cosmic Cabbage") to music ("Cabbage" is a two-part, ten-minute opus featuring an excerpt from Bartók's second string quartet interspersed with strains of atonal jazz and a one-minute Beach Boy parody), stand as testament to either just how far some people will go to make a buck or just how crazed rock music became during the more frenzied moments of the last decade. Like a Veg-a-Matic, the Amboy Dukes diced and sliced every kind of imaginable music genre until the group succumbed. The various early Amboy Duke aggregations were anchored by guitarist Ted Nugent, from whose warped brain most of this music stemmed.

The early Seventies found the Amboy Dukes changing their approach—Nugent bringing his man-of-the-loincloth philosophy more to the forefront and the Dukes sounding more like a heavy-metal hard-rock band than a gang of potential burnouts. *Call of the Wild* is the best of the later LPs, filled with ferocious instrumentals that bring to mind sweet images of rhinoceroses stampeding on a rainy, windswept day. — B.A.

AMBROSIA
★ ★ ★ **Ambrosia / War. (1975)**
★ ★ **Somewhere I've Never Travelled / War. (1976)**
★ ★ **Life Beyond L.A. / War. (1978)**
★ ★ **One Eighty / War. (1980)**
This band's debut album featured two outstanding songs, a Kurt Vonnegut takeoff called "Nice, Nice, Very Nice" and "Holdin' On to Yesterday," a catchy ballad that eventually became a minor hit. Otherwise, though, Ambrosia gets bogged down in a tedious rehash of art-rock ideas apparently inspired by bands like Yes. — J.S.

AMERICA
★ **America / War. (1972)**
★ **Homecoming / War. (1972)**
★ **Hat Trick / War. (1973)**

★ Holiday / War. (1974)
■ Hearts / War. (1975) ¶
★ ★ History: America's Greatest Hits / War. (1975)
★ Hideaway / War. (1976) ¶
★ Harbor / War. (1976) ¶
■ America Live / War. (1977)
★ Silent Letter / Cap. (1979)
★ Alibi / Cap. (1980)

America is a triple play of mellow California folkies noted for the hit singles "Horse with No Name," "Tin Man," "Sister Golden Hair" and "Ventura Highway." They represent the senescence of the once-vibrant West Coast folk scene. *History* is a greatest-hits set. — J.S.

AMERICAN NOISE
★ ★ American Noise / Planet (1980)

Suburban Cleveland bar band makes good; never to be heard of again, of course. The truest fulfillment of the fable. No reason for you to participate. — D.M.

AMERICAN STANDARD BAND
★ ★ American Standard Band / Is. (1979)

Instrumentally competent, lyrically clichéd, vocally dismal late-Seventies FM radio product—and proud of it, I guess. On the West Coast, bands like this sometimes grow up to become the Doobie Brothers; back east, they simply drift back to the bars. It's hard to say which is preferable, but we now know which fate befell these guys. — D.M.

ALBERT AMMONS
★ ★ ★ ★ ★ King of Blues and Boogie Woogie / Oldie Bl. (NA)

Chicago-born boogie-woogie pianist learned from Pinetop Smith and Meade Lux Lewis before coming to New York to establish his name at Café Society, where he worked as a team with pianist Pete Johnson. Ammons was one of the best practitioners of the genre. — J.S.

ERIC ANDERSEN
★ ★ Today Is the Highway / Van. (1965)
★ ★ ★ 'Bout Changes and Things / Van. (1966)
★ ★ ★ 'Bout Changes and Things, Take 2 / Van. (1968)
★ ★ More Hits from Tin Can Alley / Van. (1968)
★ A Country Dream / Van. (1968)
★ ★ ★ The Best of Eric Andersen / Van (1970)
★ ★ ★ ★ Blue River / Col. (1972)
★ ★ Be True to You / Ari. (1975) ¶

★ ★ Sweet Surprise / Ari. (1976) ¶
★ ★ The Best Songs / Ari. (1977) ¶

Eric Andersen was the first "new Dylan." The most self-consciously sexual of the Greenwich Village folksingers, he conveyed in his early work a romanticism that owed much to the Everly Brothers' innocence and effervescence. His career, however, was always undermined by bad luck and poor judgment. His response to Dylan's going electric was to re-record his best and most popular early album (*'Bout Changes and Things*) with a three-piece band (*'Bout Changes and Things, Take 2*) and to coat his next with florid production (*More Hits from Tin Can Alley*). Following the collapse of the folk scene, he pursued one fad after another: C&W (*A Country Dream*) and *Sgt. Pepper* orchestration (his out-of-print Warners albums). In 1971 he switched labels for the second time and produced his best work (*Blue River*), which balanced pop and traditional modes and faith and fatalism. After a two-year absence, caused in part by the loss of the masters for his follow-up album, Andersen moved to Arista, where he has produced two albums (*Be True to You* and *Sweet Surprise*). Despite the occasional brilliance of his writing—Andersen finally seems to recognize the limits of his romanticism—both are crippled by Tom Sellers' horrific production. Of the two best-of collections, the Vanguard contains the earlier material and is therefore preferable, but the Arista included several cuts from *Blue River,* arguably one of the most underrated albums by a singer/songwriter in the Seventies. — K.R.

AL ANDERSON
★ ★ ★ Al Anderson / Van. (1973)

This solo album was made by Anderson right after he joined NRBQ from the Wildweeds, and features NRBQ drummer Tom Staley, piano player Terry Adams and trombonist Donn Adams. Anderson sings and plays guitar on a variety of light-spirited country-blues tunes and down-tempo R&B numbers. — J.S.

JOHN ANDERSON
★ ★ ★ ★ John Anderson / War. (1980)
★ ★ ★ ★ John Anderson 2 / War. (1981)
★ ★ ★ ★ I Just Came Home to Count the Memories / War. (1981)

Anderson is a country traditionalist, not in the hard-core sense of Joe Ely, but working within the genre's more restrictive conventions. That means he's liable to include some real weeper trash among his raw-edged

honky-tonk gems, but you'll forgive it: Anderson's sonorous baritone voice and a pretty decent eye for material (just enough of it composed by himself) make him less likely than most to go the Eddie Rabbitt route.
— D.M.

JON ANDERSON
★ ★ **Olias of Sunhillow** / Atl. (1976)
★ **Song of Seven** / Atl. (1980) ¶
Ex-Yes lead vocalist applies his lumpy mythologizing and lightweight vocalizing to boring solo material. — A.N.

ANGEL
■ **Angel** / Casa. (1976)
■ **Helluva Band** / Casa. (1976)
■ **On Earth As It Is in Heaven** / Casa. (1977)
■ **White Hot** / Casa. (1978)
■ **Bad Publicity** / Casa. (1979)
■ **Live without a Net** / Casa. (1979)
■ **Sinful** / Casa. (1979)
Kiss stablemates tried to ride the Seventies heavy-metal glitter train behind the blown-dry pouting of guitarist Punky Meadows. They tried as hard as they could to get people to believe they were a mirror image of Kiss, even to the point of championing their lameness on *Bad Publicity.* They did rate a pop-history footnote by inspiring Frank Zappa to write the hilarious parody "Punky's Whips." — J.S.

ANGEL CITY
★ ★ ★ ★ **Face to Face** / Epic (1980)
★ ★ ★ **Dark Room** / Epic (1980)
★ ★ ★ **Night Attack** / Epic (1982)
Australia's top band in 1978 and 1979, Angel City (known as the Angels at home) aspires to make rock music of epic proportions not so much through lavish orchestration—the band's sound is basic, taut and spare—but in the intensity of the performance. Often enough the group succeeds.

Singer Doc Neeson might lack technical virtuosity, but he does spit, snarl, sneer and recite convincingly, and his onstage incarnation of the characters in the songs, combining mime and dance with the strutting arrogance of rock & roll, can be electrifying.

If you can sometimes hear traces of David Bowie and Lou Reed in Neeson's vocal style, the tense precision of the basic rock rhythms is peculiarly Angel City's own, anchored by bassist Chris Bailey and drummer Graham "Buzz" Bidstrup (replaced by Brent Eccles on 1982's *Night Attack*). The momentum of the songs owes a lot to the tightly complementary playing of the two guitarists, brothers John and Rick Brewster; the latter's

solos, while not astonishingly innovative, have a sharp simplicity and rightness.

The U.S. issue of *Face to Face* is a compilation of Angel City's first two Australian successes, and shows the band at its best. It's the implication of an explosive, almost hysterical energy being barely contained by the firm rhythms and elemental forms of the songs that give the band its moments of transcendence. The lurking dangers of Angel City's approach are pretentiousness and excess, and they're a little closer to the surface on 1981's *Dark Room,* with its gloomier tones and more portentous lyrics. 1982's *Night Attack* returns to the stripped-down simplicity of the first album, and the constraints of the song structures serve to recreate a sense of urgency that had been lost on *Dark Room.* The songs are just a little too similar, however, for the record to constitute as considerable an achievement as the first U.S. release, which remains the band's best recording. — S.M.

ANGLO-SAXON BROWN
★ **Songs for Evolution** / Atl. (1976)
Bad disco music meets mediocre cabaret jazz singing. — D.M.

THE ANIMALS
★ ★ **Best of Eric Burdon and the Animals, Vol. 2** / MGM (1967) ¶
★ **The Greatest Hits of Eric Burdon and the Animals** / MGM (1969)
★ ★ ★ ★ **Best of the Animals** / Abkco (1973)
★ ★ **Best of the Animals** / Sp. (1973) ¶
★ ★ ★ **Before We Were So Rudely Interrupted** / Jet (1977) ¶
★ ★ **Night Time Is the Right Time** / Sp. (NA)
The Animals were the only English act to approach soul and blues with the single-minded devotion of the Rolling Stones, at least in the early years (circa 1965). Led by singer Burdon, keyboard player Allan Price and bassist Chas Chandler (later, Jimi Hendrix and Slade's manager), the group was as resourceful and imaginative as any English Invasion band, and wittier than most—check "Story of Bo Diddley" on the Abkco set; a brief, amazing history of rock & roll.

The group's catalogue is in unfortunate disrepair; the originals were all on MGM and are well worth seeking out. Nevertheless, most of the hits are contained on the Abkco album, including the classics "House of the Rising Sun," "I'm Crying," "We've Gotta Get Out of This Place," an anthem, and "It's My Life," a statement of purpose.

The blues influence of John Lee Hooker and Bo Diddley's R&B are predominant. The LP also contains two of the key songs on the MGM *Best of:* "When I Was Young" and "A Girl Named Sandoz." But the MGM sets present a far different band—a more or less psychedelic one, which had hits with "San Franciscan Nights," "Monterey" and "Sky Pilot," at the height of the Haight-Ashbury fad. The latter are included on the MGM *Greatest Hits.* While they are, in a way, great fun as memorabilia, they are surely no more than that.

The Springboard sets contain material recorded before the group hooked up with an American label. *Night Time* has them backing Sonny Boy Williamson. The principal item of importance on *Best of* is a powerhouse version of Chuck Berry's "Almost Grown," one of the group's few guitar-dominated rockers. Both are to be preferred over the MGM collections.

Before is a surprisingly successful 1977 reunion one-shot, with the original group, again dominated by Price and Burdon, turning in fine, hard-nosed blues performances. — D.M.

PAUL ANKA

★ **Anka / U.A. (1974)** ¶
★ ★ **Paul Anka Gold / Sire (1974)**
■ **Feelings / U.A. (1975)** ¶
■ **My Way / Camd. (1975)**
★ **Remember Diana / RCA (1975)**
★ **She's a Lady / RCA (1975)** ¶
■ **Times of Your Life / U.A. (1975)**
■ **The Painter / U.A. (1976)** ¶
★ **Paul Anka Sings His Favorites / RCA (1976)**
★ **Essential Paul Anka / Bud. (1976)** ¶
■ **Songs I Wish I'd Written / RCA (1977)** ¶
■ **The Music Man / U.A. (1977)** ¶
★ **Vintage Years 1957–1961 / Sire (1977)** ¶
■ **Live / Barn. (NA)** ¶
★ **This Is Paul Anka / Bud. (NA)** ¶
■ **Paul Anka—His Best / U.A. (1980)**
Unctuous Fifties pop singer/writer, scored in Sixties by writing "My Way" for Sinatra, in the Seventies with "Having My Baby." Useless to the end; get Neil Sedaka instead. — D.M.

ANY TROUBLE

★ ★ **Where Are All the Nice Girls / Stiff (1980)** ¶
★ ★ ★ **Wheels in Motion / Stiff (1981)**
Manchester, England–based quartet bears down hard and owes more of a debt to Elvis Costello than is good for them. *Nice Girls* covers Springsteen's "Growing Up," *Wheels* features a better overall sound. — J.S.

APHRODITE'S CHILD

★ **666 / Vert. (1972)**
Pompous and pointless Greek rock concept album masterminded by keyboardist Vangelis. Not an omen. — J.S.

CARMINE APPICE

★ ★ **Carmine Appice / Pasha (1982)**
Solo debut from drummer whose career includes membership in Vanilla Fudge, Cactus and KGB and stints behind Jeff Beck and Rod Stewart. Adequate if not altogether inspired, this LP is less bombastic than might be expected from percussionist of "You Keep Me Hanging On" fame. Appice's original tunes are for the most part contentless, although the selection of "Paint It Black" (done as an instrumental) and "Be My Baby" is at least eccentric. — G.A.

APRIL WINE

★ ★ **The Whole World's Going Crazy / Lon. (1976)**
★ ★ **April Wine Live at the El Macambo / Lon. (1977)** ¶
★ ★ **First Glance / Cap. (1978)**
★ ★ **Harder . . . Faster / Cap. (1980)**
★ ★ **Castle Donnington / Poly. (1981)**
★ ★ **Nature of the Beast / Cap. (1981)**
April Wine is a Montreal-based band that has issued numerous albums in Canada. Those albums portray the group as a delightful high-school punk outfit dealing in crass, hard-driving two- and three-minute singles. Their work is characterized by a few good ballads repeated too many times and an unnecessary dependence on guitarist/vocalist Myles Goodwyn. — A.N.

AQUARIAN DREAM

★ ★ **Norman Connors Presents Aquarian Dream / Bud. (1976)**
★ ★ **Chance to Dance / Elek. (NA)**
★ ★ **Fantasy / Elek. (1978)**
Norman Connors produced the original Aquarian Dream album for Buddah in 1976, around the time of his biggest commerical successes. The Elektra albums came later. The Buddah record is somewhat more elastic in its manipulation of disco ready-mades than the records under Connors' own name, but he was never able to take his artificial dance group scheme anywhere, even on the successor LPs. — D.M.

ARGENT

★ ★ ★ **Argent / Epic (1970)** ¶
★ ★ ★ **Ring of Hands / Epic (1971)** ¶
★ ★ ★ **All Together Now / Epic (1972)**
★ ★ **In Deep / Epic (1973)** ¶

★ Nexus / Epic (1974) ¶
★ Encore / Epic (1974) ¶
★ Circus / Epic (1975) ¶
★ ★ Counterpoint / U.A. (1975) ¶
★ ★ ★ Anthology / Epic (1976)
Formed in 1970 by ex-Zombies lead singer/
keyboardist Rod Argent, this band leaned
heavily on its leader's talents. The first few
albums show Argent in good form, especially
on "Liar," "Schoolgirl" and "Dance in the
Smoke" from the first album. Guitarist Russ
Ballard provided the behind-the-scenes direction, writing much of the band's material, including two of its hits, "God Gave Rock
and Roll to You" and "It's Only Money."
Rod Argent wrote the band's biggest hit,
"Hold Your Head Up." But Argent never
really developed a strong identity. Ballard
left the band in 1974, and the group broke
up two years later — J.S.

ARMAGEDDON

★ ★ ★ Armageddon / A&M (1975)
The late Keith Relf never sang better, not
even with the Yardbirds, but the real show
here is guitarist Martin Pugh: sharp chords,
manic solos and refreshing acoustic textures—reminiscent of, alas, the Yardbirds.
Solid drumming from Bobby Caldwell. Raw
and powerful, though occasionally long-
winded. — C.W.

JOAN ARMATRADING

★ ★ Whatever's for Us / A&M (1973)
★ ★ Back to the Night / A&M (1975)
★ ★ ★ ★ Joan Armatrading / A&M (1976)
★ ★ ★ Show Some Emotion / A&M
(1977)
★ ★ To the Limit / A&M (1978)
★ ★ Steppin' Out / A&M (1979)
★ ★ Me, Myself, I / A&M (1980)
★ ★ Walk under Ladders / A&M (1981)
Joan Armatrading sets confessional lyrics
that are neither fuddled nor sappy (surprise)
to near-danceable acoustic funk, and the result is an album that's at once intimate and
stylish. Armatrading's songs are personal
without being self-indulgently revealing.
They are built around dialogue and incident,
and the observations on male-female relationships they contain are those of a survivor
rather than a victim. Actually, it may be her
voice, deep and flexible, that makes even ab-
ject statements sound self-respecting. Glyn
John's guitar-based production is refreshingly
simple, but Armatrading could have benefited from fuller arrangements. Of the earlier
albums, *Whatever's for Us* is the most appealing. Warm, enthusiastic, amateurish, it
features Armatrading on piano as well as

guitar. Perhaps as an attempt to capture a
wider audience, Armatrading got a new producer and backup bands for *Me, Myself, I*
and *Steppin' Out,* with mixed results; her
powerful voice is lost in the pop/new wave
and she sounds uncertain and uncomfortable.
— A.S.

BILLY BOY ARNOLD

★ ★ ★ More Blues on the Southside / Prest.
(1964)
★ ★ ★ Blow the Back Off It / Red L.
(1975), Br. imp.
★ ★ ★ Sinner's Prayer / Red L. (1976), Br.
imp.
★ ★ ★ Checkin' It Out / Red L. (1979), Br.
imp.
★ ★ ★ ★ Crying and Pleading / Charly
(1980), Br. imp.
Harpist/vocalist Arnold enjoyed his first success backing Bo Diddley on "Bo Diddley"/
"I'm a Man," his first hit. Arnold's music is
a refinement and extension of that record,
and some of the most exciting and energetic
music to come from the Southside in recent
years.
  Arnold's best-known song, "I Wish You
Would," is a classic Diddley-beat R&B
number, often covered (notably by the Yardbirds) but never surpassed. His best records,
made for Vee Jay in the Fifties, are on both
Crying and Pleading and *Blow the Back Off
It,* but the Charly LP has been mastered
from the original tapes. *Sinner's Prayer* is a
1970 set recorded in Chicago; the Prestige
album is a Sixties set recorded in the Windy
City. Both feature a number of notable local
blues players (Louis Myers, Sammy La-
whorn, Mighty Joe Young, Lafayette Leake).
Checkin' It Out is a surprisingly effective set
recorded with a British band led by guitarist
T. S. McPhee. All of the records are annotated, and all are well worth hearing.
— D.M.

KOKOMO ARNOLD

★ ★ ★ Kokomo Arnold/Peetie Wheatstraw /
Blues C. (1965)
★ ★ ★ ★ Kokomo Arnold / Casey Bill
Weldon: Bottleneck Trendsetters / Yazoo
(1971)
★ ★ ★ Kokomo Arnold / Col. Class. (1976),
Br. imp.
★ ★ ★ ★ Set Down Gal / Mag. (1976), Br.
imp.
A really fine slide guitarist and an affecting,
if rough-voiced singer, Arnold was one of
the most influential Thirties delta bluesmen.
His bottleneck style—held in his lap and
played with very fast fingerpicking—is Ar-

nold's stylistic signature. Arnold popularized the best-known version of "Milkcow Blues," which Elvis Presley later smashed to smithereens.

Though the Blues Classics is only half an album, it and the Collector's Classics LPs are the best representations of his material. (Wheatstraw and Arnold frequently played and traveled together, in any event.) All the material is of Thirties vintage. — D.M.

ARPEGGIO
★ ★ **Let the Music Play . . . /** Poly. **(1979)**
★ **Break Out /** Poly. **(1980)**
Failed funk. "Love and Desire (Part 1)" from *Let the Music Play . . .* started to climb the R&B charts but stalled—for reason, one imagines, of predictability. — D.M.

ART BEARS
★ ★ ★ **Hopes and Fears /** Rec. **(1978), Br. imp.**
★ ★ ★ **Winter Songs /** Ralph **(1979)**
★ ★ ★ **The World As It Is Today /** Rec. **(1981)**
Dense, demanding, but—if you have the stamina—intensely rewarding new music inventions by an offshoot of the maverick British band Henry Cow. The neo-operatic whoop of female singer Dagmar, drummer Chris Cutler's artful clatter, and Fred Frith's exploratory guitar voicings (along with a little violin here, the odd harmonium there) coalesce into a dramatic inventive whole topped by imagistic free-verse lyrics that deal with a kind of socialist politics of the heart. There are elements of good old rock & roll here as well as alien jazz fusion, but the total effect is more like Brecht in space. — D.F.

ARTFUL DODGER
★ ★ ★ **Artful Dodger /** Col. **(1975) ¶**
★ ★ ★ **Honor among Thieves /** Col. **(1976) ¶**
★ ★ **Babes on Broadway /** Col. **(1977) ¶**
★ ★ ★ **Rave On /** Ario. **(1980)**
Debut album offers hard-driving music—the buoyant lyricism of Sixties pop meets the instrumental punch of Seventies hard rock—mated with fervently delivered straightforward lyrics reflecting the confusion, the exultation and the naiveté of youth. "Wayside," "Think Think," "Follow Me" and "Silver and Gold" are superior songs. *Honor among Thieves* is a tentative but important step toward a tough, lean contemporary sound. Original songs—particularly "Scream," "Dandelion" and "Keep Me Happy"—show increasing sophistication of writers Billy Paliselli, Gary Herrewig and Gary Cox.

Only major error is a static remake of "Keep A-Knockin'." *Babes,* however, belied the band's early energy; desperate for an audience, Dodger resorted to formula.

After the disastrous *Babes on Broadway,* Artful Dodger came back with a record that recalled the pop glory of its first two LPs. Gary Herrewig and Billy Paliselli reasserted themselves as two of the finest songwriters in rock, and the band played with such ferocity and authority as to lay to rest any doubts that they might have gone soft. — D.MC.

ARTISTICS
★ ★ ★ ★ **I'm Gonna Miss You /** Bruns. **(1967)**
★ ★ ★ **Articulate Artistics /** Bruns. **(1968)**
★ ★ ★ **What Happened /** Bruns. **(1969)**
★ ★ ★ **I Want You to Make My Life Over /** Bruns. **(1969)**
★ ★ ★ **Look Out /** Bruns. **(1973)**
The Artistics, on the R&B charts fairly frequently from 1965 into the early Seventies, were specialists in Motown-era soul, with one lead singer who sounded a bit like David Ruffin, another who resembled Smokey Robinson. Their only two singles to make the pop charts, "I'm Gonna Miss You" and "Girl I Need You," from '66 and '67, are both included on *I'm Gonna Miss You.* — D.M.

THE A'S
★ ★ ★ ★ **The A's /** Ari. **(1979)**
★ ★ **A Woman's Got the Power /** Ari. **(1981)**
As power-poppers, the A's are smart enough to pump their songs full of sass and then step on the gas. Consequently, their self-titled debut was bright and snappy, getting by on sheer guts when inspiration ran thin (e.g., interpolating the Beatles' "Twist and Shout" into their own, otherwise predictable "Grounded"). Sadly, the second album is a botch, the A's attempt to go for a mass audience without really being sure what that mass audience is. — J.D.C.

ASHFORD AND SIMPSON
★ ★ **Gimme Something Real /** War. **(1973)**
★ **I Wanna Be Selfish /** War. **(1974)**
★ ★ ★ **Come As You Are /** War. **(1976)**
★ ★ **So So Satisfied /** War. **(1977)**
★ ★ **Send It /** War. **(1977)**
★ ★ **Keep It Comin' /** Tam. **(1977) ¶**
★ ★ ★ **Is It Still Good to Ya? /** War. **(1978)**
★ ★ ★ **Stay Free /** War. **(1979)**
★ ★ ★ **Musical Affair /** War. **(1980)**
Nick Ashford and Valerie Simpson wrote or

produced most of the famous Marvin Gaye-Tammi Terrell hits of the late Sixties, such as "Ain't No Mountain High Enough" and "You're All I Need to Get By." In 1973 they decided to start singing duets themselves.

So far their career has hardly equaled Marvin and Tammi's. Ashford and Simpson's albums are as irritating as they are interesting. Each has one or two excellent moments, but none has the power of their Motown work.

It's tempting to blame Ashford, whose voice is horrible and whose lyrics are oversentimental. Yet their decision to make ridiculously ultraromantic albums has been their saving grace; they've resisted current trends in soul and disco, never descending to formulas. At their best—"I Had a Love," "Somebody Told a Lie," "Anywhere"—lyrics, music and voices blend together, and one does have a sense of two people struggling to express their feelings through music. — R.G.

ASLEEP AT THE WHEEL
★ ★ ★ **Comin' Right at Ya** / U.A. (1973)
★ ★ ★ **Asleep at the Wheel** / Epic (1974) ¶
★ ★ ★ **Fathers and Sons** / Epic (NA)
★ ★ ★ **Texas Gold** / Cap. (1975)
★ ★ ★ **Wheelin' and Dealin'** / Cap. (1976)
★ ★ ★ ★ **The Wheel** / Cap. (1977)
★ ★ ★ **Collision Course** / Cap. (1978)
★ ★ ★ **Served Live** / Cap. (1979)
★ ★ ★ **Framed** / MCA (1980)
★ ★ ★ **American Band 3** / Cap. (1981)
Asleep at the Wheel was possibly the greatest of the Seventies country rockers, because they leaned so intelligently toward the most interesting elements of country, especially Western swing, as developed by Bob Wills. The group is a large one, and features horns as well as the usual country rhythm section complete with pedal steel. Their rather checkered career, which has seen some country audience acceptance but total apathy on the part of rock fans, began with the United Artists album, moved through a brief sojourn at Epic, and finally found a more or less substantial home at Capitol, which is also where they've made their best records. *Texas Gold* and *The Wheel* score highest because principal vocalists Chris O'Connell and Ernest Tubb-soundalike Ray Benson have better material to work with. Western Swing is hillbilly music's answer to jazz (Charlie Parker allegedly admired Wills) and in songs like "Let Me Go Home Whiskey" (*Gold*), "Miles and Miles of Texas" (*Wheelin'*) and "My Baby Thinks She's a Train" (*The Wheel*), Asleep lives up to all elements of the tradition. — D.M.

THE ASSOCIATES
★ ★ **The Affectionate Punch** / Fiction (1980), Br. imp.
Unusual British duo—Billy MacKenzie sings and writes the lyrics, Alan Rankine plays all the instruments except drums—overdubs its way into sub-Bowie (music) and sub-Joy Division (lyrics) territory. While they occasionally show promise—"Paper House" anticipated the sound of U2 by about half a year—most of what's here has been done better by others. — D.S.

ASWAD
★ ★ **Aswad** / Mango (1976)
★ ★ **Hulet** / Tuff Gong (1979)
★ ★ ★ ★ **Showcase** / Aswad (1980)
Some say Aswad is the hardest, most interesting live U.K. reggae band. On record (they've made only four LPs in six years) they often come off as bland Marley-derivatives due to their tendency to leaven elements of funk, rock, and jazz with Lettermen-style harmonies and marshmallow production. *Showcase,* by compiling several outstanding singles, shows their potential. — R.F.G.

THE ASSOCIATION
★ ★ **The Association's Greatest Hits** / War. (1968)
The pleasing ephemerality of songs like "Windy" and "Cherish" is made banal when you have to put it on the turntable rather than allow it to hit you on the radio. The Association was a prime Sixties AM radio group—leave them there in bliss. — K.T.

ASYLUM CHOIR
★ ★ **Look Inside the Asylum Choir** / Smash (1968)
★ ★ ★ **Asylum Choir II** / Shel. (1971)
Asylum Choir combined the talents of two L.A. session types—Leon Russell and Marc Benno—who were trying to find a niche for their individual talents in the late-Sixties rock boom. Their first album, complete with a toilet-roll cover, falls victim to the psychedelic excesses of the time. By contrast, the second shows them moving toward their eventual solo careers—Benno working in an attractive if ultimately lightweight blues vein, and Russell developing the tumbling piano-based style that would seem so novel on his debut solo album. — J.B.M.

ATHLETICO SPIZZ 80
★ Do a Runner / A&M (1980)
Post-Bowie, post-punk pseudo-artiste self-proclaimed minimalist quintet helps explain why British punk/new wave never did so well in the States. — J.S.

CHET ATKINS
★ ★ Best of / RCA (1964)
★ Chet Atkins Picks on the Beatles / RCA (1966)
★ Chet Atkins Picks the Best / RCA (1967)
★ Chet Atkins Picks on the Pops / RCA (1969)
★ This Is Chet Atkins / RCA (1970)
★ Me and Jerry / RCA (1970)
★ For the Good Times / RCA (1971)
★ Me and Chet / RCA (1972)
★ ★ Now and Then / RCA (1972)
★ Chet Atkins Picks the Hits / RCA (1972)
★ Alone / RCA (1973)
★ Christmas with Chet Atkins / RCA (NA)
★ Chester, Floyd, and Boots / Camd. (1975)
★ ★ The Atkins-Travis Traveling Show / RCA (1975) ¶
★ ★ ★ The Night Atlanta Burned (The Atkins String Company) / RCA (1975) ¶
★ Chet Atkins Goes to the Movies / RCA (1975)
★ ★ Best of Chet Atkins and Friends / RCA (1976)
★ ★ ★ Chester and Lester / RCA (1976)
★ ★ ★ A Legendary Performer / RCA (1977)
★ Chester, Floyd, and Danny / RCA (1977) ¶
★ Me and My Guitar / RCA (1977) ¶
★ American Salute / RCA (NA)
★ ★ Chet Atkins in Concert / Camd. (NA)
★ Country Pickin' / Camd. (NA)
★ Finger Pickin' Good / Camd. (NA)
★ ★ First Nashville Guitar Quartet / RCA (1979)
★ ★ Best/On the Road / RCA (1980)
★ Reflections / RCA (1980)
★ Country—After All These Years / RCA (1981)

Despite the fact that Chet Atkins is one of the most influential guitarists of the past thirty years, he has issued more dross than anyone in Nashville. A good general rule for the record buyer is to avoid any record with a title like "Chet Atkins Picks the Hits/Beatles/Rolling Stones/Minnie Pearl." Similarly, avoid titles like "Chet Atkins Goes to the Movies/Paris/Memphis/Cuba." Only fanatical guitar students and Chet Atkins' best friends will be interested in such records. All of these records consist of Chet Atkins, his guitar and long orchestral dubs in renditions of standard songs from the year or Hollywood or the Beatles and so forth.

That said, there are three Chet Atkins albums that show the man for the virtuoso musician that he is.

The Night Atlanta Burned, by the Atkins String Company, is a beautiful recording. The idea for the album comes indirectly from John D. Loudermilk, who ran across a fragmentary composition for a mandolin orchestra that had survived the destruction of Atlanta during the Civil War. Atkins and Loudermilk came up with the idea of putting together a country chamber ensemble. Lisa Silver plays violin and viola, Atkins plays guitar, Johnny Gimble adds mandolin and Paul Yandell plays acoustic rhythm guitar.

The Night Atlanta Burned is a successful musical experiment that should be repeated. Atkins' guitar, usually a diffident instrument, is inspired. The addition of violin, mandolin and viola give the music a texture that is lacking on any of Atkins' other albums. This record should be as well received by classical music fans as it has been by country music adherents.

Chester and Lester, a collaboration between Atkins and Les Paul, is not as experimental as it is improvisational and spontaneous. Paul's uninhibited nature provides a nice foil for the imperturbable Atkins both musically and in the brief conversations inserted between the songs. There is a sense of fun in this album, which is as close to jazz as Chet Atkins ever will come.

The Atkins-Travis Traveling Show pairs Atkins with Merle Travis, his mentor. It would be interesting to know why this album does not succeed as well as *Chester and Lester.* Both guitars are great, but I suspect that, even though they are a little different, Atkins' and Travis' styles are just too close to allow for the musical serendipity that happened with Les Paul. The between-songs patter is not as good, and the songs themselves are mostly country standards. While *The Night Atlanta Burned* and *Chester and Lester* are records that surpass the country label, *The Atkins-Travis Traveling Show* will be of interest only to country music scholars.

An overview of Chet Atkins' work suggests that Atkins works best only when challenged, and that the challenges must come from outside the field of country music. Ironically, rock musicians who learned the Atkins style seem to have seen the possibilities of his music before Atkins himself did. — M.H.

ATLANTA RHYTHM SECTION
★ ★ ★ **Atlanta Rhythm Section / MCA (1972)**
★ ★ ★ ★ **Third Annual Pipe Dream / Poly. (1974)**
★ ★ ★ **Dog Days / Poly. (1975)**
★ ★ ★ ★ **Red Tape / Poly. (1976)**
★ ★ ★ ★ ★ **A Rock and Roll Alternative / Poly. (1977)**
★ ★ ★ ★ **Champagne Jam / Pol. (1978)**
■ **Are You Ready / Poly. (1979)**
★ ★ **Underdog / Poly. (1979)**
★ ★ **Boys from Doraville / Poly. (1980)**
★ ★ ★ **Quinella / Col. (1981)**

The Atlanta Rhythm Section was formed in 1970 as a songwriter's cooperative. The group pooled the talents of two late-Sixties Atlanta bands, the Classics IV (producer Buddy Buie and guitarist J. R. Cobb) and the Candymen (drummer Robert Nix and keyboardist Dean Daugherty), with two young session players, guitarist Barry Bailey and bassist Paul Goddard.

The band put together a studio, used itself as the house band and slowly recorded two records in between bread-and-butter sessions backing up singers and recording television soundtracks. The two albums, *Atlanta Rhythm Section* and *Back Up Against the Wall*, are now reissued as a double set on MCA. *Atlanta Rhythm Section* used Rodney Justo as lead singer and was fairly inconsequential except for the fine "Another Man's Woman." On *Back Up Against the Wall* Ronnie Hammond replaced Justo as lead singer, and several tracks—the title song, "Cold Turkey Tennessee," Joe South's "Redneck" and Randall Bramblett's "Superman"—demonstrated tremendous potential.

Eventually the band's songwriting talent began to pay off. *Third Annual Pipe Dream,* the most representative early session, produced two excellent regional hits, "Doraville" and "Angel." Producer Buie had kept the ARS in tight check until that album, but after the hits, the band became more oriented to live performances and its sound changed.

Dog Days suffered from the transition as Buie's production sweetening worked against the live feel of the basic tracks. Buie changed his production strategy, and the next album, *Red Tape,* was much closer to the band's live sound, especially on the longer remake of "Another Man's Woman," highlighted by Goddard's remarkable bass solo. *A Rock and Roll Alternative* finally defined the band's recording on hard-rock tracks like "Sky High" and ballads like "So in to You." "So in to You" became a substantial nationwide hit

in 1977 and finally put the group over the top after years of struggling to make ends meet.

Charter drummer Robert Nix left around the time of *Are You Ready,* a double live album that shows off little of the group's in-concert power. *Boys from Doraville* and *Underdog* sound somewhat indifferent despite the addition of crack session drummer Roy Yeager. But *Quinella* signaled a strong comeback for the group via hot tracks like "Homesick," "Alien" and "Higher."
— J.S.

THE ATLANTICS
★ **Big City Rock / MCA (1979) ¶**
Hapless power pop. — D.M.

ATLANTIC STARR
★ **Atlantic Starr / A&M (1978)**
★ **Straight to the Point / A&M (1979)**
★ **Radiant / A&M (1980)**
Tedious nine-piece black pop ensemble proves that three strikes ought to be out in any league. — D.M.

ATOMIC ROOSTER
★ **Death Walks behind You / Elek. (1970)**
★ **Atomic Rooster IV / Elek. (1973) ¶**
Faceless early-Seventies English hard-rock act churned out pedestrian pseudo-rock with an occasional pause for *la grande ballade.* The best track here is keyboardist Vincent Crane's solo instrumental, "Moods" (on *IV*), which brings to mind Vince Guaraldi on an off day. — B.A.

AUDIENCE
★ ★ **The House on the Hill / Elek. (1971)**
■ **Lunch / Elek. (1972)**
Gus Dudgeon's echoey production of Audience's debut, *The House on the Hill,* bolstered the British group's weak instrumental palette. So they shake some complacent lunacy out of the title cut, "I Put a Spell on You," and "Jackdaw." Under careful handling, Howard Werth's voice pairs well with Keith Gemmell's ubiquitous, gruff sax. Much of their overall strategy was later to find success in some Roxy Music and David Bowie.

However, as a rock band Audience never rose above thin gruel, and its degeneration came quickly, on *Lunch,* where Werth trades his gothic atmospherics for a dabble in Americana. Flat-footed meandering results. — B.T.

BRIAN AUGER
★ ★ ★ **Befour / RCA (1970)**
★ ★ **Oblivion Express / RCA (1971)**

★ ★ ★ A Better Land / RCA (1971)
★ ★ Second Wind / RCA (1972)
★ ★ Closer to It / RCA (1973)
★ ★ ★ Straight Ahead / RCA (1974)
★ ★ Live Oblivion, Vol. 1 / RCA (1974)
★ ★ ★ Reinforcements / RCA (1975)
★ ★ Live Oblivion, Vol. 2 / RCA (1976)
★ ★ Happiness Heartaches / War. (1977)
★ ★ The Best of Brian Auger / RCA (1977)
★ ★ Encore / War. (1978)

This veteran keyboard player whose heart belongs to Jimmy Smith has used rock to gain a fair amount of popularity twice— once as backup to Julie Driscoll's vocals, later with Oblivion Express. Much of his work has been reissued on budget labels, and as a result, his recording history can be confusing. The Driscoll material is by now deleted; *Befour* appeared immediately after her departure. *Oblivion Express, Land* and *Wind* mark the inauguration of Oblivion Express, including a future Average White Band member, the late Robbie McIntosh, on drums. Here the sound is closer to English progressive rock in structure—both before and after the sound is jazzier, with *Befour* including some good cops from Traffic and Herbie Hancock. *Closer* and *Straight* have some Wes Montgomery and Marvin Gaye and had fair luck on the charts (jazz and R&B as well as pop). Auger's riffing organ dominates every facet. Both the *Live* LPs are redundant, while *Reinforcements* is a standout because he again deserts jazz for pop, this time in the Average White Band/Stevie Wonder mold. — A.N.

MIKE AULDRIDGE
★ ★ ★ Dobro/Tak. / Devi (1972)
★ ★ Blues and Bluegrass / Tak. (1974)
★ ★ Mike Auldridge / Fly. Fish (1976)
★ ★ Mike Aulridge and Old Dog / Fly. Fish (1977)
★ ★ Critic's Choice / Tak. (1979)
★ ★ Slidin' Smoke / Fly. Fish (1979)

Auldridge is a sophisticated dobro player who has recorded and performed with the Country Gentlemen and Seldom Scene bluegrass groups. He is surrounded on each of these discs with stellar lineups ranging from Linda Ronstadt to David Bromberg, Vassar Clements to Lowell George. The effect can be numbing when all fingers are flying at once, but on the debut *Dobro* in particular, the hot-licks effects are kept to a minimum and taste abounds. — I.M.

AU PAIRS
★ ★ ★ Playing with a Different Sex / Human (1981), Br. imp.

Since their inception in 1978, the two-girl, two-boy Au Pairs have honed down their original primal thrash into an earnest drive of funk and rhythm. Eminently danceable, the songs are politically inspired, centering around the gender dynamics of female anatomy and consciousness as demonstrated by the fertility-temperature-chart liner notes. A promising debut. — ML.H.

AURA
★ Aura / Mer. (1971)

Blood, Sweat and Tears–era jazz-rock, right down to the corny Vegas lounge horn charts and the gruesome David Clayton-Thomas vocal inflections. — D.M.

AURACLE
★ Glider / Chrys. (1978)
★ City Slickers / Chrys. (1979)

Despite production by Miles Davis maestro Teo Macero, this sextet seems to think that the essence of jazz-rock is appropriating the most banal clichés of both genres. The result is clinically tedious. — D.M.

PATTI AUSTIN
★ ★ End of a Rainbow / CTI (1976)
★ ★ ★ Havana Candy / CTI (1977)
★ ★ Live at the Bottom Line / CTI (1979)
★ ★ Body Language / CTI (1980)
★ ★ ★ Every Home Should Have One / Qwest (1981)

A polished session singer, Austin is an elegant, somewhat pop, jazz-fusion stylist. Her version of the Kurt Weill/Maxwell Anderson standard, "Lost in the Stars," on *Havana Candy* is the high point of a recording career that began under the aegis of fusion maestro Creed Taylor. A featured vocalist on Quincy Jones' all-star *Sounds . . . And Stuff Like That,* Austin was signed to Jones' label, Qwest, in 1981 and recorded a high-gloss pop-soul album, *Every Home Should Have One,* of considerable charm. — S.H.

AUTOMATIC MAN
★ ★ ★ Visitors / Is. (1976)
★ ★ ★ Automatic Man / Is. (1976)

Imaginative heavy metal paced by Bayeté's vocals and effortless keyboards, and ex-Santana member Michael Shrieve's deft drumming (on the first album only). The debut's successful combination of Hendrix, synthesizers, R&B and hard rock gives way to jazz rock and mainstream soul on *Visitors.*
— C.W.

JOHNNY AVERAGE BAND
★ ★ **Some People / Bearsv. (1980)**
Is that as in "some of the people all the
time," etc.? Or is this simply heartland-style
rock too muddled to know its own mind? At
any rate the self-deprecation doesn't work,
probably because there's so much to be self-
deprecating about.   — D.M.

AVERAGE WHITE BAND
★ ★ ★ **Show Your Hand / MCA (1973)**
★ ★ ★ ★ ★ **AWB / Atl. (1974)**
★ ★ **Cut the Cake / Atl. (1975)**
★ ★ ★ **Put It Where You Want It / MCA
(1975)**
★ **Person to Person / Atl. (1976)** ¶
★ ★ **Soul Searching / Atl. (1976)** ¶
★ ★ **Benny and Us / Atl. (1977)** ¶
★ ★ **Warmer Communications / Atl. (1978)**
★ **Feel No Fret / Atl. (1979)**
★ **Volume VIII / Atl. (1980)**
★ **Shine / Ario. (1980)**
At first the Average White Band seemed lit-
tle more than a gimmick with an ironic
moniker. They played black music so con-
vincingly that even blacks bought it. But the
debut LP, *Show Your Hand,* also suggested
considerable songwriting facility, and AWB's
energy, especially the rhythmic drive of
bassist Alan Gorrie and drummer Robbie
McIntosh, was far more propulsive than
what slavish imitators could hope to generate.

The Average White Band, you see, had a
leg up on white American bands who
wanted to play black—as Scots they were
British colonials, so they understood
cultural oppression. For AWB, black music
spoke a language to be internalized, not
aped.

The third album, *AWB,* proved to be the
one classic the band had in them. Nine of
the ten tunes were memorably melodic and
bristled with hooks. The singing of Alan
Gorrie and Hamish Stuart, gracefully mixed
to the fore by producer Arif Mardin,
brimmed over with an authoritative enthusiasm.

Unfortunately, this glorious success was
not to be repeated. *Cut the Cake* and *Soul
Searching,* both given to disco and modal
monotony, suggested that with Robbie
McIntosh's accidental-overdose death in September 1974, something in the group died as
well.   — P.H.

AVIARY
★ ★ **Aviary / Epic (1979)**
Seattle-based glam-rock throwback failed to
revive the glitter era.   — J.S.

AXE
■ **Axe / MCA (1979)**
■ **Living on the Edge / MCA (1980)**
Dreadful Southern heavy-metal band out of
Gainesville, Florida. Give it to 'em.   — J.S.

HOYT AXTON
★ ★ **Less Than the Song / A&M (1973)**
★ ★ ★ **Life Machine / A&M (1974)**
★ **My Griffin Is Gone / Col. (1974)**
★ ★ ★ **Southbound / A&M (1975)**
★ ★ ★ **Fearless / A&M (1976)**
★ ★ ★ **Snowblind Friend / MCA (1977)**
★ ★ ★ **Road Songs / A&M (1977)**
★ ★ **Free Sailin' / MCA (1978)**
★ **Rusty Old Halo / A&M (1979)**
★ **Where Did the Money Go? / A&M
(1980)**
Hoyt ("The Pusher") Axton is an anomaly:
a starry-eyed cynic, a hayseed wearing city
shoes. Despite his backwoods sensibility (and
he comes on as shaggy and sly as a honey
bear), Axton is a shrewd songwriter who's
been writing other people's hits for years
("Greenback Dollar" for the Kingston Trio,
"Joy to the World" for Three Dog Night).
Nevertheless, there are startling gaps in
Axton's sophistication. Like a square who
never recovered from the summer of love, he
can be positively hokey (cf. "Pet Parade" on
Life Machine). But if he sometimes out-
Nashville's Nashville with his brand of barefoot slick, he's learned country music's most
important lesson: simplicity. Based on precise observation and compact melodies, the
best of Axton's songs ("The Devil" on *Fearless;* "Lion in the Winter" and "Pride of
Man" on *Southbound;* "Boney Fingers" and
"When the Morning Comes" on *Life Machine*) achieve the timeless resonance of an
Appalachian hymn.

There is no definitive Axton album; the
good songs are sandwiched among the flops
and filler. *Life Machine* is probably his most
consistent effort; *My Griffin Is Gone,* a psychedelic relic, the most dispensable. But even
the failures are listenable, and the harmonies
that blend his deep, sweet, lazy voice with
those of country-accented sopranos like
Linda Ronstadt's are perfect.   — A.S.

KEVIN AYERS
★ ★ ★ ★ **Joy of a Toy/Shooting at the
Moon / Harv. (1970–1971),
Br. imp.**
★ ★ ★ **Whatevershebringswesing / Harv.
(1972), Br. imp.**
★ ★ ★ **Bananamour / Sire (1972)** ¶
★ ★ **The Confessions of Dr. Dream and
Other Stories / Is. (1974)** ¶

★ ★ ★ **Yes, We Have No Mañanas (So Get Your Mañanas Today) / ABC (1977) ¶**
A charter member of England's Canterbury art-rock mob and the original bassist with Soft Machine, Kevin Ayers is a charmingly idiosyncratic songwriter with a casual basso profundo singing style, a cracked sense of humor, and good taste in supporting musicians (Mike Oldfield, Ollie Halsall, David Bedford and Lol Coxhill have passed through his bands). Early records like *Joy of a Toy/ Shooting at the Moon* (a compilation of his first two LPs) and *Whatevershebringswesing* vividly capture Ayers' talent in dramatic offbeat instrumental colors. *Bananamour* and *Mañanas* are slightly more mainstream in tone but hardly compromised, although some of his more recent U.K. issues lack the old spark. *The Confessions of Dr. Dream* is undone by an overlong concept piece sprawled across side two. Unfortunately, none of Ayers' albums are in print in the United States, and most were never released here. — D.F.

AZTEC TWO-STEP
★ ★ ★ **Aztec Two-Step / Elek. (1972)**
★ ★ **Second Step / RCA (1975)**
★ ★ **Two's Company / RCA (1976) ¶**
★ ★ **Adjoining Suites / RCA (1977) ¶**
★ **Times of Our Lives / Waterh. (1979)**
Rex Fowler and Neal Shulman have pleasant, callow voices and harmonize relentlessly, if not imaginatively. Their debut LP, primarily acoustic folk rock, is still their best— "The Persecution and Restoration of Dean Moriarty (On the Road)," despite its melodic banality, was a sort of underground hit in the early Seventies. On the RCA albums, they attempt a more eclectic approach, with mixed effect. Generally, their voices are too pallid to compete with instrumental energy, and their ensemble sound is listenable but trite. — P.H.

BABE RUTH
★ ★ First Base / Harv. (1972)
★ ★ Stealin' Home / Harv. (1975)
★ Kid's Stuff / Harv. (1976) ¶
Babe Ruth featured Jenny Haan, a powerful vocalist in the Julie Driscoll–Lydia Pense mold, and multi-instrumentalist Alan Shacklock. Within their records can be found everything from Italian Western movie themes to rehashed soul and Frank Zappa, not to mention disco and all-out rock. Shacklock left after *Babe Ruth,* the group's third and best (but deleted) album, because of commercial strikeout; Haan followed after the fourth, *Stealin' Home.* Supporting cast carried on with hokey baseball clichés. Their best music came from giving Haan free rein—"Dancer" from *Babe Ruth* sounds like the result of a hot jam between Steve Marriott and Driscoll.   — A.N.

THE BABYS
★ ★ The Babys / Chrys. (1976)
★ ★ Broken Heart / Chrys. (1977)
★ Head First / Chrys. (1979)
★ Union Jacks / Chrys. (1980)
★ On the Edge / Chrys. (1980)
★ ★ Anthology / Chrys. (1981)
A minor paradigm of commercial rock's mistakes during the mid-Seventies, the Babys were an Anglo-American unit whose four-year, five-LP career was a comedy of marketing and trend-mongering errors. Presented as junior Rod Stewarts (or grown-up Bay City Rollers) in a massive prerelease publicity blitz, the Babys were unveiled just as punk became headline news—making the band seem like yesterday's stale commodity, the last train from Bloatsville. The band never recovered from that initial miscalculation. Despite some radio exposure and singles success ("Isn't It Time," "Every Time I Think of You," "Back on My Feet Again") the Babys' appeal was never up to the massive hype it came wrapped in. For all but diehard fans, *Anthology* presents the highlights of the abortive rise and terminal decline of the band, despite inclusion of a truly lame and previously unreleased version of "Money."   — G.A.

BURT BACHARACH
■ Reach Out / A&M (1967)
■ Make It Easy on Yourself / A&M (1969)
■ Burt Bacharach / A&M (1971)
■ Living Together / A&M (1973)
■ Burt Bacharach's Greatest Hits / A&M (1974)
■ Futures / A&M (1977)
■ Woman / A&M (1979)
Although he was, with Hal David, perhaps the best Tin Pan Alley–style writer of the Sixties, Bacharach is no performer—his voice is more affecting on TV commercials. The proof of his talent is in the recordings of Dionne Warwick and Gene Pitney, not here.   — D.M.

BACHMAN-TURNER OVERDRIVE
★ ★ Bachman-Turner Overdrive / Mer. (1973) ¶
★ ★ ★ Bachman-Turner Overdrive 2 / Mer. (1973)
★ ★ Not Fragile / Mer. (1974)
★ ★ ★ Best of Bachman-Turner Overdrive / Mer. (1976)
★ ★ Freeways / Mer. (1977) ¶
★ Street Action / Mer. (1978)
★ Rock 'n' Roll Nights / Mer. (1978)
Bachman-Turner Overdrive, organized by the former lead guitarist of the Guess Who, Randy Bachman, enjoyed a brief heyday from 1973 to 1976 as a pop alternative to heavy metal. Tougher and raunchier than the Guess Who's singles, their two biggest hits came in 1974. "Takin' Care of Business" was a brawny rocker without much subtlety, but "You Ain't Seen Nothin' Yet," which

made No. 1 in the fall of '74, was a direct steal from the Who, and an imaginative one. But that seemed to exhaust Bachman's imagination—everything before and since is simply sluggish.

Best of contains both of the above hits, plus the group's only other Top Twenty hit, "Roll On Down the Highway," the followup to "You Ain't Seen." *Bachman-Turner Overdrive 2* contains "Takin' Care of Business," but the group's best album is probably *Not Fragile,* which has the other songs mentioned above. Both *Street Action* and *Rock 'n' Roll Nights* were released after Randy Bachman's departure for a solo career. — D.M.

THE BACKWOODS BAND
★ ★ ★ **Jes' Fine / Roun. (1980)**
Rough-edged and engaging bluegrass quintet from Ithaca, New York. — J.S.

BAD BOY
★ ★ **Back to Back / U.A. (1978)** ¶
★ ★ **The Band That Made Milwaukee Famous / U.A. (NA)** ¶
Heartland heavy: not a thought to mar its musclebound features, either. Still, if you like it *pounded* out, this might work. — D.M.

BAD COMPANY
★ ★ ★ ★ **Bad Company / Swan (1974)**
★ ★ ★ **Straight Shooter / Swan (1975)**
★ ★ ★ **Run with the Pack / Swan (1976)**
★ ★ **Burnin' Sky / Swan (1977)**
★ ★ ★ **Desolation Angels / Swan (1979)**
This state-of-the-art mid-Seventies hard-rock band began as an apotheosis of supergroups, combining lead singer Paul Rodgers and drummer Simon Kirke from Free, guitarist Mick Ralphs from Mott the Hoople, and bassist Boz Burrell from King Crimson. On the strength of the solid first album, a modest hit in "Can't Get Enough," and the instant celebrity of Paul Rodgers' smooth but powerful vocal punch, the band has carved out a solid niche for itself on the arena concert circuit. The workmanlike but unflashy stolidness of the group's playing, which is virtually interchangeable on all the records, makes it at once effective and uninteresting, and while Bad Company has lived up to its commercial promise, the band must be viewed as an aesthetic failure for its inability to do anything more than exploit the hard-rock form. Rodgers' voice provides the transcendence, but the rest of the band just never leaves the ground. — J.S.

BADFINGER
★ ★ **Airwaves / Elek. (1979)**
★ ★ **Say No More / Radio (1981)**
All that these records have in common with the original (late Sixties/early Seventies) incarnation of Badfinger is the name, guitarist Joey Molland and bass player Tom Evans. The first Badfinger had some lovely melodic Beatle-style songs and on occasion came up with some convincing rock & roll. This time around, though, all they can muster is pedestrian MOR tripe. — D.G.

BAD MANNERS
★ ★ **Ska 'n' B / Magnet (1980), Br. imp.**
★ ★ **Loonee Tunes / Magnet (1980), Br. imp.**
★ ★ **Bad Manners / Magnet (1981), Br. imp.**
★ ★ **Gosh It's . . . / Magnet (1981), Br. imp.**
Adopting the style but not the content of the Eighties ska explosion in Britain, Bad Manners have become perhaps the most commercially popular band of the genre. Demonstrating that the lowest common denominator sells to the highest number of people, the only real "weight" in their repertoire is provided by lead personality, the stout and ever-jolly Buster Bloodvessel. — ML.H.

BAD NEWS TRAVELS FAST
★ **Look Out / Casa. (1979)**
★ **Ordinary Man / Casa. (1979)**
Not fast enough. — W.K.

JOAN BAEZ
★ ★ ★ ★ **Joan Baez / Van. (1960)**
★ ★ ★ ★ **In Concert, Part One / Van. (1962)**
★ ★ ★ ★ **Joan Baez / Van. (1963)**
★ ★ ★ ★ **In Concert, Part Two / Van. (1963)**
★ ★ ★ **Joan Baez / Van. (1964)** ¶
★ ★ ★ **Farewell, Angelina / Van. (1965)**
★ ★ ★ **Noel / Van. (1966)**
★ **Joan / Van. (1967)**
■ **Baptism / Van. (1968)**
★ ★ **Any Day Now / Van. (1969)**
★ ★ **David's Album / Van. (1969)**
★ ★ ★ **First Ten Years / Van. (1970)**
★ ★ **One Day at a Time / Van. (1970)**
★ ★ **Blessed Are / Van. (1971)**
★ ★ ★ **Ballad Book / Van. (1972)**
■ **Carry It On / Van. (1972)**
■ **Come from the Shadows / A&M (1972)**
★ ★ **Hits/Greatest & Others / Van. (1973)**
★ **Where Are You Now, My Son / A&M (1973)** ¶
★ ★ **Contemporary Ballad Book / Van. (1974)**
★ **Gracias a la Vida (Here's to Life) / A&M (1974)**

■ **Diamonds and Rust / A&M (1975)**
★ ★ ★ **Lovesong Album / Van. (1976)**
★ **From Every Stage / A&M (1976)**
★ **Gulf Winds / A&M (1976)** ¶
★ **Best of / A&M (1977)**
★ **Blowin' Away / Por. (1977)**
★ **Honest Lullaby / Por. (1979)**
Joan Baez was one of the two most influential performers of the early-Sixties folk movement; the other was the group Peter, Paul and Mary, and like them, Baez was essentially a popularizer. She played the pacifist radical—committed to civil rights, peace marches and traditional ballad singing—perfectly, partly because she so much looked the part. And when the young Bob Dylan emerged from Minnesota in 1961, it was only natural that they hooked up together. The most highly rated albums above—the first two records called *Joan Baez,* the *Ballad Book,* and both volumes of *In Concert*—all feature her on traditional material, since they were recorded before the contemporary, topical songwriters emerged in Dylan's wake.

When Dylan, Eric Andersen, Richard Fariña, Phil Ochs and others made their appearance, Baez was useful for the exposure she gave their songs; her soprano was far too perfect and emotionally remote to interpret them successfully, however. In consequence, the albums where she attempted to mix contemporary and traditional material are more successful than later records where she tried to do exclusively contemporary songs. *Any Day Now,* a two-record collection of Dylan material, highlights her problem: she makes the songs of the Sixties' greatest writer seem as humorless and stodgy as the poem she reads on *Baptism.*

Perhaps Baez's most salutary quality was her political commitment; for years, she refused to pay taxes because of the Vietnam War, and she consistently supported leftist causes, often at considerable personal and professional expense. But her approach to political music is so sanctimonious it's nearly unbearable, and her few attempts at wholly political album-making have been her most disastrous recordings: *Carry It On,* featuring her ex-husband David Harris, who did time as a war resister, and *Gracias a la Vida,* a smug attempt to educate the masses politically, are the most obnoxious.

In the Seventies, Baez's career has been more unfocused than ever. The folk boom long over, unable to communicate effectively whatever she may feel about the currently fashionable singer/songwriter material left for her to sing, she has retreated on two recent albums, *Diamonds and Rust* and *Gulf Winds,* to writing her own songs. *Come from the Shadows* included the egregious "To Bobby," a panting attempt to exhume interest in her long-lapsed affair with Dylan (which may or may not have helped her become part of the 1976 Rolling Thunder Revue), while "Time Rag" on *Blowin' Away,* took a slap at the popular press, always the last refuge of the artistically benighted.
— D.M.

THE BAILEY BROTHERS
★ ★ ★ **Take Me Back to Happy Valley / Roun. (1975)**
★ ★ **Just As the Sun Went Down / Roun. (1980)**
Slow-paced bluegrass instrumentals and mostly gospel-based vocal harmonies by this Forties-era brother act and their backup, the Happy Valley Boys. — J.S.

LAVERN BAKER
★ ★ **Let Me Belong to You / Bruns. (1970)**
★ ★ ★ **LaVern Baker Sings Bessie Smith / Atl. (NA), Br. imp.**
★ ★ ★ ★ **LaVern Baker / Atl. (NA), Br. imp.**
Baker was already a fine, mature rhythm & blues stylist when producer Jerry Wexler prodded her into singing rock & roll. The fact that she never liked her work in the field—which included the hits "I Cried a Tear," "Jim Dandy" and "Tweedlee Dee" as well as the surrealistic brag classic, "Jim Dandy Got Married"—did not prevent her from becoming one of the first superb women rock singers.

Proof of all her various talents is on the Atlantic imports listed above. The *Bessie Smith* LP is a tribute to one of Baker's mentors, with a fine band led by Buck Clayton. *LaVern Baker* has the cover packaging of her first Atlantic LP, right down to the track listings, but the music inside is a better-chosen selection of all her work for the label, including all four of the songs listed above. The band alone is worth the price of admission—the uncredited (but probably King Curtis) sax solo on "I Cried a Tear" is a definitive moment. Soaring over it all is Baker's throbbing voice, handling ballads with ease and the rockers with undeniable (if possibly patronizing) wit. Unfortunately, the Brunswick LP, from 1970, attempts to contemporize Baker's style in all the wrong ways. — D.M.

MICKEY BAKER
★ ★ **Take a Look inside Me/ Big Bear (1975), imp.**

★ ★ ★ **The Blues in Me / Black and Blue (1975), imp.**
★ ★ ★ **Blues and Jazz Guitar of Mickey Baker / Kick. (1978), imp.**
★ ★ **Up on the Hill / Roots (NA), imp.**
Mickey Baker is the greatest guitar player of the New York rock 'n' roll scene of the Fifties, the axeman on virtually all the important Atlantic and doo-wop hits of the day. He earned his nickname with an influential and incisive style, making "Guitar" Baker a name to conjure with. His fame spread after he wrote *Jazz Guitar,* his brilliant instruction book, a painstakingly developed explanation of this master craftsman's methodology, reduced to terms so lucid it remains *the* primer for aspiring guitarists.

In the early Sixties, Baker moved to Europe. Operating from his outpost in Paris, he has made these albums, but unfortunately, most of the material is acoustic, and most of the bands are filled out with starstruck European kids. The instruction-oriented Kicking Mule disc is perhaps his best, which is a shame. There must be someone out there willing to work with Baker's talent as effectively as Springsteen has with Gary Bonds or Tom Petty with Del Shannon.   — D.M.

BALANCE
★ ★ **Balance / Por. (1981)**
Balance isn't a bad band and their debut isn't a bad record, but they are a fine testament to the artistic folly of being an FM trend follower. Pepi Castro even has the supreme psychedelic-pop credentials of having led the seminal Blues Magoos. But the albeit well-played music here is even more formulated than the commercials Castro cuts in his spare time. Talent wasted in trying to make it, rather than trying to make something.   — R.P.

BALCONES FAULT
★ ★ **It's All Balcones Fault / Cream (1977)**
This wacky Texas Dixieland jazz cum lounge band runs through its weird assortment of Big Band comedy routines, rock & roll, Afro-Cuban jazz and Tex-Mex ranchero music with engaging if unsettling aplomb. The slickness that enables them to handle this odd assortment of arrangements deftly is also what ultimately keeps them from being believable.   — J.S.

THE BALFA BROTHERS
★ ★ ★ **J'ai Vu Le Loup, Le Renard et La Belette / Roun. (1977)**
Wonderful record of lilting Cajun music by this quartet of Louisiana brothers. Dewey and Will's violin playing set the tone for the waltzes that comprise most of the album.   — J.S.

MARTY BALIN
★ ★ **Balin / EMI (1981)**
Lack of professional production in combination with mediocre outside material makes the long-overdue solo debut of Jefferson Starship's leading man a major disappointment. Still, *Balin* yielded two hits—the Top Ten "Hearts" and "Atlanta Lady."   — S.H.

E.C. BALL
★ ★ ★ **E.C. Ball with Orna Ball and the Friendly Gospel Singers / Roun. (1973)**
Interesting record of fingerpicking guitar techniques by a well-regarded guitarist who previously chose not to secularize his predominantly spiritual approach by recording. This record includes crude but expressive vocal harmonies by Ball and his wife Orna.   — J.S.

HANK BALLARD AND THE MIDNIGHTERS
★ ★ ★ **Finger Poppin' Time / Power (NA)**
★ ★ ★ **20 Original Greatest Hits / King (NA)**
Ballard is best known for originating "The Twist," which Chubby Checker popularized in a version indistinguishable from Hank's. But Ballard made some of the raciest and most important early R&B hits of the Fifties, including the epochal "Work with Me Annie," and the "Annie" cycle of replies and sequels kept him going for the bulk of that decade. He also scored with the ballad "Teardrops on Your Letter," and a "Twist" sequel, "Finger Poppin' Time," among others. The beat is direct and seductive, the singing sweet and sensual.   — D.M.

RUSS BALLARD
★ ★ ★ **Winning / Epic (1976) ¶**
★ ★ **At the Third Stroke / Epic (1978)**
★ ★ **Russ Ballard and the Barnet Dogs / Epic (1980)**
★ ★ **Into the Fire / Epic (1980)**
Former Argent lead singer remains an interesting progressive pop singer even without the excellent material he had to work with in his former band. Unfortunately, singers without good material and arrangements aren't much fun to hear.   — D.M.

BALLIN' JACK
★ **Ballin' Jack / Col. (1971)**
Flaccid jazz-rock played by competent in-

strumentalists who sound like a musicians' union pickup group. — J.S.

THE BAND

★ ★ ★ ★ ★ **Music from Big Pink** / Cap. (1968)
★ ★ ★ ★ ★ **The Band** / Cap. (1969)
★ ★ ★ **Stage Fright** / Cap. (1970)
★ ★ **Cahoots** / Cap. (1971)
★ ★ ★ ★ ★ **Rock of Ages** / Cap. (1972)
★ ★ ★ **Moondog Matinee** / Cap. (1973)
★ ★ ★ **Northern Lights—Southern Cross** / Cap. (1975)
★ ★ ★ **The Best of the Band** / Cap. (1976)
★ ★ ★ ★ **Islands** / Cap. (1977)
★ ★ ★ **Anthology** / Cap. (1978) ¶
★ **Rock of Ages, Vol. 1** / Cap. (1982)
★ ★ **Rock of Ages, Vol. 2** / Cap. (1982)

The Band is a curious group that has never quite lived up to its reputation as *the* classic American rock band of the early Seventies, a reputation mostly acquired as backing band for the electric Bob Dylan during the late Sixties.

Music from Big Pink, their debut album, sported a cover painting by Bob Dylan and had a profound musical impact on its release. The two-keyboard approach was quickly picked up by a number of bands, but what was really unmatchable was the intensity of the group's performances, its incredible vocalizing, which involved key changes in voice that seemed to operate on the members' instincts as much as on writing or arranging, and the remarkable depth of the songwriting. Lead guitarist Robbie Robertson was not then the exclusive writer; Richard Manuel's contributions to the writing, including his collaborations with Bob Dylan, were nearly as important. Robertson's "The Weight" was the best song, trailed closely by "Chest Fever," "Long Black Veil," "Lonesome Suzie" and "I Shall Be Released."

The Band had been performing together—originally as the backup for Ronnie Hawkins (whose sole remaining Roulette album features Robertson's incredible playing on "Who Do You Love") in their native Canada, later in Arkansas as Levon (Helm, the drummer and only American) and the Hawks and finally with Dylan. On *The Band,* one of the greatest and most profound rock & roll albums ever made, this experience—of coming to America, of being Canadian, of the deep and sometimes exhilaratingly frightening experiences they'd shared—all came home. Songs like "Across the Great Divide," "The Night They Drove Old Dixie Down," "Jemima Surrender," "Look Out Cleveland" and many more define the late

Sixties and early Seventies for thousands of listeners. *The Band* is as close to a perfect statement of purpose as any rock group has ever come.

The Band, however, did not produce a hit single, and somehow has never quite lived up to its incredible implications. *Stage Fright,* which followed, had fine moments, most notably on the title song, "Time to Kill," and "The Shape I'm In." But it retrenched into a kind of conservatism inherent in the perfectionism of the first two albums, and transcended there by a feeling of release and freedom at finally standing on their own. More problematically, Robertson, who began to write all of the group's original material with the second LP (a practice that continued until *Northern Lights*), simply didn't turn out enough good material for a classic album. But if *Stage Fright* was a disappointment, *Cahoots* was a catastrophe. With the exception of "Life Is a Carnival" and Dylan's "When I Paint My Masterpiece," there simply isn't a good song on the record. The Band may have been rock masters, but they had to have some kind of material to work with.

What followed was retrenchment and confusion. *Rock of Ages,* the live album, managed to capture most of the group's best material, and incorporated some delightful horn arrangements (by Allen Toussaint), but contained nothing new—even the three new songs, "Get Up Jake," "I Don't Want to Hang Up My Rock and Roll Shoes" and Marvin Gaye's "Don't Do It"—had been part of the group's repertory for years. *Moondog Matinee* was a misguided oldies album, with obvious and trite selections, redeemed mostly by pianist/vocalist Richard Manuel's singing on "The Great Pretender."

Northern Lights—Southern Cross turned a corner, but it was a strange one. By now, the group's records, except for the first, were beginning to seem interchangeable. *Northern Lights* added another element—the kind of bizarre organ and synthesizer fills Garth Hudson had been experimenting with onstage for several years. While it contained no truly outstanding songs, it at least made some interesting instrumental innovations. *Islands* repeated the process, with Hudson taking an even larger role, though the material still left much to be desired. Surprisingly, however, at this crucial juncture, the group decided it had had enough and decided to disband. *The Best of the Band* followed at Christmastime in 1976; the only other project the members were expected to engage in collectively was a live LP from their final concert held at Thanksgiving of '76 in San Francisco. (A film, *The Last Waltz,* was also made of that show by director Martin Scorsese, and the soundtrack is available on Warner Bros.).

Singer/bassist Rick Danko and drummer Levon Helm moved immediately into outside projects, Danko on his own, Helm with the RCO All-Stars. Robertson, Manuel, and Hudson kept to themselves, announcing no plans, though Robertson continued to insist the Band would continue to record together. All that's known is that this group had provided some of the highlights of rock & roll for nearly a decade; what kept it from completely realizing its potential or continuing as an active musical force will undoubtedly remain a mystery. Capitol's two-disc repackaging of *Rock of Ages* is both aesthetically stupid and uneconomic. — D.M.

BANDERA
★ **Knights / MCA (1981)**
Bandera combines Austin-style Texas rock with Gainesville-style Southern boogie without capturing the fire of the former or the gritty swing of the latter. Misses the point completely. — J.D.C.

MOE BANDY
★ ★ **Hank Williams, You Wrote My Life / Col. (1976)** ¶
★ ★ **Here I Am Drunk Again / Col. (1976)**
★ ★ ★ **I'm Sorry for You, My Friend / Col. (1976)** ¶
★ ★ ★ ★ **Best of Moe Bandy / Col. (1977)**
★ ★ ★ **Cowboys Ain't Supposed to Cry / Col. (1977)**
★ ★ **Soft Lights and Hard Country Music / Col. (1978)**
★ ★ **Love Is What Life's All About / Col. (1978)**
★ ★ **It's a Cheating Situation / Col. (1979)**
★ ★ **One of a Kind / Col. (1980)**
Bandy was a country-music anachronism when he surfaced in 1974. He sang pure Texas honky-tonk, previously believed to be an extinct form. Honky-tonk is gutbucket C&W—drinking and cheating songs utilizing a fiddle instead of a violin section, a high harmony voice instead of vocal choirs, and a more prominent rhythm. Bandy made a few bows toward modern Nashville, but his albums are mostly models of light production that his sharp, stinging voice cuts through dramatically. *I Just Started Hatin' Cheatin' Songs Today* and *Bandy the Rodeo Clown,* his two best albums, have been available only in the bargain bins since GRC folded. However, the hit singles from his three GRC albums are included on Columbia's great *Best of* package.

His weakest effort is the first Columbia album *(Hank Williams),* which despite the title song contains his one foray into schmaltz. *Drunk Again* is only a slight improvement, but *Sorry* is much more in the old GRC groove. Since honky-tonk is, after all, a limited form, his albums tend to sound samey to the uninitiated; in that case, *Best of* is most wholeheartedly recommended. — J.MO.

MOE BANDY AND JOE STAMPLEY
★ ★ ★ **Just Good Ol' Boys / Col. (1979)**
★ ★ **Hey Joe, Hey Moe / Col. (1981)**
Journeyman honky-tonkers puttin' on airs together. More conventional than Bandy's best. — D.M.

TONY BANKS
★ ★ **A Curious Feeling / Char. (1979)**
Likably bland solo album by the Genesis keyboardist. — J.D.C.

BANKS AND HAMPTON
★ ★ **Passport to Ecstasy / War. (1977)** ¶
Carl Hampton and Homer Banks wrote such soul hits as "(If Loving You Is Wrong) I Don't Want to Be Right," "Who's Making Love," "If You're Ready (Come Go with Me)" and "Be What You Are." But you'd be hard pressed to discover that fact—or the talent—from what's included here. Recorded at the height of discomania, this set is a classic example of why craftsmen don't always make good performers, and of why talented soulmen were often ruined by the rigorous conventions of modern dance styles. I mean, the descent from "Who's Making Love" to "Get On Up, Shake Some Butt" may not seem like much to you, but to someone who cares about these things, it's murderously disappointing. — D.M.

THE BARBARIANS
★ ★ ★ **The Barbarians / Rhino (1979)**
Boston garage-punk from the mid-Sixties. This group is best known as the band with the drummer whose left hand was a hook (as featured in *The T.A.M.I. Show*); his story is told in "Moulty," included here, along with the band's two better-known songs, "Are You a Boy or Are You a Girl," a middle-finger salute of major proportions in '65, and "What the New Breed Say," a failed anthem but an interesting one. Not as much can be said for the rest, but devotees of Sixties punk will find this worth investigating for posture as much as sound. — D.M.

BARDE

★ ★ ★ ★ Images / Fly. Fish (1980)
Although this Canadian sextet shares some musical ground with DeDanaan and the Boys of the Lough, what sets them apart is the way they've worked British and French folk stylings into their Irish revivalist format. Strict traditionalists may be put off at first by the group's eclectic approach, but only if accuracy is valued over listening pleasure. — J.D.C.

BOBBY BARE

★ ★ ★ 500 Miles Away from Home / Camd. (1964)
★ ★ ★ This Is Bobby Bare / RCA (1973)
★ ★ ★ Bobby Bare Sings "Lullabies, Legends and Lies" / RCA (1973)
★ ★ Singin' in the Kitchen / RCA (1974) ¶
★ ★ Cowboys and Daddys / RCA (1975) ¶
★ ★ Paper Roses / Camd. (1975) ¶
★ ★ I'm a Long Way from Home / Camd. (1975)
★ Memphis, Tennessee / Camd. (1975)
★ ★ Country Boy and Country Girl / RCA (1976) ¶
★ ★ ★ ★ The Winner and Other Losers / RCA (1976) ¶
★ ★ ★ Me and McDill / RCA (1977) ¶
★ ★ ★ Bare / Col. (1978)
★ ★ ★ Sleeper Wherever I Fall / Col. (1978)
★ ★ ★ Sunday Mornin' Comin' Down / RCA (1979) ¶
★ ★ ★ Down and Dirty / Col. (1980)
★ ★ Drunk and Crazy / Col. (1980)
★ ★ My Country America / RCA (1980)
★ ★ As Is / Col. (1981)
Bare's career began as "Bill Parsons," who had the No. 2 hit in the country in 1958 with "All-American Boy," a takeoff on Elvis going into the army. As Bobby Bare he was, through out the Sixties, a staple minor-league country attraction, although he did not dent the pop charts again until 1974 with "Daddy What If."

When Bare is at his best, on the albums rated with three stars above, he sticks to a basically Western, macho stance and some of the most hard-edged music in country. On stuff like "Paper Roses," he's just silly. *Me and McDill* and *The Winner and Other Losers,* released in the mid-Seventies, attempted to redefine his image in terms of the outlaw cult developing around Waylon Jennings, Willie Nelson and Tompall Glaser. The move was not entirely successful, but it did play into Bare's strengths: a stronger rhythmic and dynamic sense than most country artists and an ability to project an adequately but not overbearingly tough male image. — D.M.

BAREFOOT JERRY

★ ★ ★ Watchin' TV / Monu. (1974)
★ ★ ★ You Can't Get Off with Your Shoes On / Monu. (1975)
★ ★ ★ Keys to the Country / Monu. (1976)
★ ★ ★ Barefoot Jerry's Grocery / Monu. (1976)
★ ★ ★ Barefootin' / Monu. (1977)
Marginal country rockers cut a choogling groove but never were able to do anything with it. — J.S.

RUSS BARENBERG

★ ★ ★ ★ Cowboy Calypso / Roun. (1979)
Tremendous folk-acoustic set covering an extraordinarily wide range of styles led by Country Cooking's Barenberg. John Miller, Tony Trischka and Andy Statman, among others, chip in instrumental accompaniment. Barenberg's guitar playing here is awesome. — J.S.

JESSE BARISH

★ Mercury Shoes / RCA (1980) ¶
Soulish white singer from San Francisco, a protégé of this album's producer, Marty Balin, sometimes of Jefferson Airship. No "Miracles" here, unfortunately. — D.M.

BAR-KAYS

★ ★ Gotta Groove / Stax (1969)
★ ★ Too Hot to Stop / Mer. (1976)
★ ★ Flying High on Your Love / Mer. (1977)
★ ★ Light of Life / Mer. (1978)
★ ★ Money Talks / Stax (1978)
★ ★ In Joy / Mer. (1979)
★ ★ As One / Mer. (1980)
Since their rebirth (all but two of the original Bar-Kays died in the same 1967 plane crash that killed Otis Redding), the Bar-Kays have been a band in search of an identity. *Too Hot,* their first album in years, is unashamedly derivative Ohio Players funk, and the others continued the process. The real thing isn't so great either. — J.M.

BARNSTORM

★ ★ ★ ★ Barnstorm / MCA (1973)
Guitarist Joe Walsh reportedly quit the James Gang because he was less interested in carrying a power trio with his soloing than in adding keyboards to the band and experimenting with a more layered sound. *Barnstorm,* Walsh's blueprint for an ideal band, involves piano, organ and guitar interlacing through a spectacular, languorous progression without sacrificing rock intensity, and may well turn out to be his only representative album. — J.S.

ELIZABETH BARRACLOUGH
★ ★ ★ **Hi / Bearsv. (1979)**
Competent blues-rock singer, in the Bonnie
Raitt vein. Never got the follow-up opportu-
nity that could have demonstrated whether
this album's potential was more than begin-
ner's luck. Produced by Hi impresario Willie
Mitchell. — D.M.

SYD BARRETT
★ ★ ★ **The Madcap Laughs/Barrett / Harv.
(1974)**
This double album brings together the two
disturbed solo LPs by this original Pink
Floyd singer/guitarist and elusive acid casu-
alty. By the time these records were first released in England in 1970, Barrett's psycho-
psychedelic vision as documented on Floyd's
manic debut *The Piper at the Gates of Dawn*
had mutated into the acoustic musings of a
child-poet, which is exactly how coproducers
David Gilmour and Roger Waters of Pink
Floyd captured him on *The Madcap Laughs.*
Barrett, produced by Gilmour and Floyd
keysman Richard Wright, is closer to the
quiet offbeat meditations on *Piper,* with soft
liquid keyboards and strains of Barrett's eccentric electric guitar. A fascinating if disconcerting case study of someone who went
the chemical distance and never returned.
— D.F.

ROBBIE BASHO
★ ★ **Voice of the Eagle / Van. (1972)**
★ ★ **Zarthus / Van. (1974)**
Basho's approach adapted John Fahey's
acoustic guitar wizardry to play even further
with Eastern modal concepts, but never quite
got off the ground as the psychedelic/
mystical folk music it was meant to be.
— D.M.

BATDORF AND RODNEY
★ **Off the Shelf / Atl. (1971)**
★ **Batdorf and Rodney / Asy. (1972)**
★ **Life Is You / Ari. (1975)** ¶
This duo's three albums blend the styles of
Seals and Crofts and Crosby, Stills and Nash
into slick television music. After they split
up, Batdorf put together the group Silver.
— S.H.

BAY CITY ROLLERS
★ **Bay City Rollers / Ari. (1975)**
★ **Rock 'n' Roll Love Letter / Ari. (1976)**
★ **Dedication / Ari. (1976)** ¶
★ **It's a Game / Ari. (1977)**
★ **Greatest Hits / Ari. (1977)**
★ **Strangers in the Wind / Ari. (1978)**
Trivial, sugary, preteenage pop product—

some watered-down oldies, but mainly original material. *Bay City Rollers* emphasized
the group's clean, passionless vocal harmonies, and toned down their simplistic, anonymous, almost incidental instrumentation.
Rock 'n' Roll Love Letter showed a slight
maturing but otherwise stuck to their proven
formula; *Dedication,* produced by the ordinarily estimable Jimmy Ienner, was a mere
continuation. *It's a Game,* Harry Maslin
producing, featured dull studio professionalism and orchestration, and made more of a
relaxed MOR pitch—it still lacked originality, energy and conviction. *Greatest Hits* assembled their numerous commercial successes, most notably "Saturday Night." — C.W.

B.C.G. (BOB CREWE GENERATION)
★ **Street Talk / Elek. (1976)**
★ ★ **Motivation / Elek. (1977)**
Crewe is one of rock's stranger figures: he
first emerged as a member of the Rays (their
hit was "Silhouettes") and became most successful in the early Sixties as a producer of
classic records by Mitch Ryder and the Detroit Wheels and Frankie Valli and the Four
Seasons. Those productions were all frankly
evocative of Phil Spector.
    Later he turned to disco, scoring a success
with Disco Tex and the Sex-o-lettes, a breakthrough for the notorious talk-show rocker
Monte Rock III. *Street Talk* continues the
disco groove, but *Motivation* is a different
matter, a vocal album produced by Jerry
Wexler and Barry Beckett. Wexler is perhaps
the greatest of the rock vocal producers, and
Crewe's voice isn't bad, but nothing can
completely redeem the self-penned material.
— D.M.

THE BEACH BOYS
★ ★ ★ **Surfin' U.S.A. / Cap. (1963)**
★ ★ ★ **Surfer Girl / Cap. (1963)**
★ ★ ★ **Little Deuce Coupe / Cap. (1963)**
★ ★ ★ ★ ★ **All Summer Long/California
Girls / Cap. (1964)**
★ ★ **Beach Boys' Christmas Album / Cap.
(1964)**
★ ★ **Beach Boys' Concert / Cap. (1964)**
★ ★ ★ **Best of the Beach Boys / Cap. (1966)**
★ ★ ★ **Best of the Beach Boys, Vol. 2 /
Cap. (1967)**
★ ★ ★ **Dance Dance Dance/Fun Fun Fun
/ Cap. (1971)**
★ ★ ★ ★ **Endless Summer / Cap. (1974)**
★ ★ ★ ★ **Spirit of America / Cap. (1975)**
★ ★ ★ **Stack O' Tracks / Cap. (1976)**
★ ★ **The Beach Boys / Sp. (NA)**
The Beach Boys burst out of Southern Cali-
fornia in 1962–63 with a teen-oriented sound

that predicted much of what would come later with the invasion of the British rock acts following the Beatles. Led by composer/singer/bassist Brian Wilson (with his two brothers—Dennis and Carl—and a cousin, Mike Love), the basic sound, as expressed in such songs as "Surfin' U.S.A.," "Little Deuce Coupe," "Fun, Fun, Fun" and "Surfin' Safari," was built around Chuck Berry's guitar sound, Eddie Cochran's antiphonal rockabilly and group vocal harmonies. The lyric themes were perfect encapsulations of middle-class suburban lifestyles, in the best sense: surfing, driving and just fooling around amounted to miniaturized acts of self-assertion, building an identity completely separate from that of adults. This inkling of rebellion was never more than implicit, though, one of the major differences between this group and the British acts that followed.

Brian Wilson's ballad style could be breathtaking. "Don't Worry Baby" used a drag race as a sexual metaphor; "Surfer Girl" was pure maudlin ode; "In My Room" a definition of wonderful rich-kid self-pity. These are great songs, and "Don't Worry Baby" alone would make Wilson and the Beach Boys major figures in rock history. While their harmony arrangements were never as soulful as those of the best R&B groups at Atlantic and Motown, nor as inventive as the Beatles', the Beach Boys helped shape a generation of pop taste—their influence can be heard in groups as diverse as America and the Who.

Toward the middle of the Sixties, Brian Wilson became fascinated with the production style of Phil Spector. *All Summer Long* was a concept album in the Spector spirit, a celebration of liberty from school and work—it contains "I Get Around," the group's best fast song, and "Wendy," a classic ballad. *California Girls* was most explicit in its emulation of Spector and the coterie of producers associated with him in New York and L.A. (notably Shadow Morton)—it includes a pretty takeoff on the Crystals' "Then He Kissed Me" and the Ad-Libs' "Boy from New York City," both rewritten for gender purposes.

Capitol's repackaging efforts on this music have been rather formless. *Surfer Girl, Surfin' U.S.A.* and *Little Deuce Coupe* are available cheaply and separately, with a couple of minor songs deleted. *All Summer Long* and *California Girls* make a great double package (at the price of one record), but the deletions hurt worse: there was little fluff on the originals. Similarly, *Dance Dance Dance/Fun Fun Fun* (originally titled *Beach Boys Today!* for

the former, *Shut Down, Volume 2,* for the latter). The anthologies are uneven: the Springboard is nearly worthless, a jumble of hits; the late-Sixties *Greatest Hits* is adequate, but the selection is both skimpy and obvious. *Endless Summer,* released in 1974 and an immediate hit that spurred a long-lasting revival, covers all of the group's best and best-known songs; as a result, *Spirit of America,* the 1975 followup, is a bit thin, though still more than worthwhile. *Stack O' Tracks* is an oddity: instrumental tracks only from a variety of the group's best-known songs—perfect for aspiring vocalists.

The Beach Boys were essentially a studio group, as all of their concert recordings confirm. *Concert* may very well be the best of these, but that says little. The *Christmas Album* is notable only for the hit single, "Little Saint Nick," and some of the most nasal carols ever put on wax.

★ ★ ★ ★ **20/20/Wild Honey / Rep. (1967)**
★ ★ **Beach Boys '69 / Cap. (1969)**
★ ★ ★ **Surf's Up / Rep. (1971)**
★ ★ ★ ★ **Pet Sounds / Rep. (1966, rerelease 1972) ¶**
★ ★ ★ **Friends/Smiley Smile / Rep. (rerelease, 1974)**

As the Sixties waned and mass freak-out advanced not only in California but throughout the world, Brian Wilson lost touch with the poetry of everyday joys and sorrows that was his true métier. As the mystical gobbledygook of the decade began to affect him, the Beach Boys were never much more than a front for his personality.

Pet Sounds was the band's first commercial failure, not surprisingly since it was also their most ambitious LP, a song cycle that attempted to create the sort of pastiche the Beatles later crafted on *Sgt. Pepper's*. *Pet Sounds* is arch, and its best songs ("Caroline No," "Wouldn't It Be Nice," "God Only Knows") are its simplest, but its principal flaw may have been attempting too much experimentation for the Beach Boys market. The album is powerful, but spotty: it's unlikely that the other Beach Boys ever really understood Brian's ambitions. *Wild Honey* is hardly less confused: the title track is an R&B-flavored smash, just the kind of music one would have bet that the Beach Boys couldn't do well. But the rest is either cute or strained. *20/20* and *Friends* are basically singles packaged pretentiously; some of these ("Do It Again" is the best) were moderate hits, but most weren't. They were released because Wilson had bigger game in mind, a total production, a conceptual masterpiece tentatively called *Smile*.

For a variety of reasons (best chronicled in *The Rolling Stone Illustrated History of Rock & Roll*), *Smile* was never released, although important fragments appeared on various LPs by the group from the late Sixties through the middle Seventies, by then its innovations seemed rather tepid and its focus misdirected. But Wilson's mystique, particularly among critics, grew larger as the group's audience diminished: *Smile* would have been a great album, we were assured each time the Beach Boys released a mediocre one. This myth remains forceful even though the title track of *Surf's Up*, which was meant to be the centerpiece of *Smile*, was far less forceful and arguably less innovative than Wilson's surf-era hits. The *Smile* legend is an exercise in myth-mongering almost unparalleled in show business: Brian Wilson became a Major Artist by making music that no one outside of his own coterie ever heard. That his public product in this period is so trivial is a bit amusing and a bit revolting.

★ ★ Sunflower / Rep. (1970) ¶
★ Carl and the Passions—So Tough/Pet Sounds / Rep. (1972) ¶
★ ★ Holland / Rep. (1973)
★ ★ The Beach Boys in Concert / Rep. (1973)
★ ★ ★ Good Vibrations—Best of the Beach Boys / Rep. (1975)
★ ★ 15 Big Ones / Rep. (1976)
★ ★ ★ The Beach Boys Love You / Rep. (1977) ¶
★ M.I.U. / Rep. (1978) ¶
★ L.A. (Light Album) / Cari. (1979)
★ Keepin' the Summer Alive / Cari. (1980)

The Beach Boys re-formed Brother Records in 1970; they also repurchased the rights to some of their early Capitol material. These are the albums listed as appearing on Reprise. But by now most of their best work was behind them. Mike Love became the band's exclusive lead singer, and with age, his nasality lost its charm. Brian Wilson was wiped out—he barely makes his presence felt on *Sunflower, Holland* or *Carl and the Passions*, though each of the latter two contains a class effort: "Sail On Sailor" and "Marcella," respectively. More often, Brian was hauled out as a totemic presence to justify the band's deterioration into an oldies act: thus, his appearances in concert around the 1976 fifteenth anniversary of the group, and his pathetic contributions to *15 Big Ones*. That record is strained and lifeless—so cruel it amounts to a documentary look at a worm on a hook, which bothered the band's cult not at all.

Since then the band has become primarily a live oldies act providing a large audience with painless nostalgia. On record, it has become a vehicle for the numbing platitudes of Mike Love's involvement with Maharishi Mahesh Yogi and transcendental meditation. From *M.I.U.* to *L.A.*, the result is a musical mush. — D.M.

THE BEAT

★ ★ ★ The Beat / Col. (1979)
This is power pop, L.A.-style: all revved up and no place to go. The band knows how to play hard and fast, and Paul Collins—who was in the Nerves, a band that also produced Jack ("Hanging On the Telephone") Lee—has a knack for strong hooks and vivid pop imagery. Despite their enthusiasm, all the Beat have to say is that they like rock & roll. And for that they need a whole record? (Not to be confused with the Coventry-based ska band, the Beat, marketed in the United States as the English Beat.) — J.D.C.

THE BEATLES

★ ★ ★ ★ ★ Meet the Beatles / Cap. (1964)
★ ★ ★ ★ ★ The Beatles' Second Album / Cap. (1964)
★ ★ ★ ★ Something New / Cap. (1964)
★ ★ ★ ★ ★ A Hard Day's Night / U.A. (1964)
★ ★ The Beatles' Story / Cap. (1964)
★ ★ ★ ★ ★ Beatles '65 / Cap. (1964)
★ ★ ★ ★ ★ The Early Beatles / Cap. (1965)
★ ★ ★ ★ Beatles VI / Cap. (1965)
★ ★ ★ ★ Help! / Cap. (1965)
★ ★ ★ ★ ★ Rubber Soul / Cap. (1965)
★ ★ ★ ★ Yesterday . . . And Today / Cap. (1966)
★ ★ ★ ★ ★ Revolver / Cap. (1966)
★ ★ ★ ★ ★ Sgt. Pepper's Lonely Hearts Club Band / Cap. (1967)
★ ★ ★ ★ Magical Mystery Tour / Cap. (1967)
★ ★ ★ ★ ★ The Beatles / Cap. (1968)
★ ★ Yellow Submarine / Cap. (1969)
★ ★ ★ ★ ★ Abbey Road / Cap. (1969)
★ ★ ★ ★ Hey Jude / Cap. (1970)
★ ★ ★ ★ ★ Let It Be / Apple (1970)
★ ★ ★ ★ ★ The Beatles/1962–1966 / Cap. (1973)
★ ★ ★ ★ ★ The Beatles 1967–1970 / Cap. (1973)
★ ★ ★ ★ ★ Rock 'n' Roll Music / Cap. (1976)
★ ★ ★ ★ Love Songs / Cap. (1977)
★ ★ ★ ★ Live at the Hollywood Bowl / Cap. (1977)
★ ★ ★ ★ Live! at the Star-Club in Hamburg, Germany; 1962 / Ling. (1977)

★ ★ **The Decca Tapes / Cir. (1979)**
★ ★ ★ **Rarities / Cap. (1980)**
★ ★ ★ ★ **Rock 'n' Roll Music, Vol. II /**
   Cap. (1980)

The Beatles took an existing rock & roll nomenclature, redefined it in such a new and exciting way that they created the line between Fifties and Sixties rock, then proceeded to push that music to its absolute limits before breaking up. In retrospect, the group's much-lamented decision to call it quits as the Seventies began was entirely appropriate; the collected work does not leave you with the impression that there were unfinished statements. There is a perfectly resolute and logical progression of ideas from *Meet the Beatles* to *Abbey Road*. They did it all, they did it right, and then they went their separate ways.

The records are not chronologically listed here because later releases covered material from the earliest days. The Beatles of the poorly recorded but fascinating *Star-Club* set from 1962 played with a speedy, manic frenzy. As the intensity of "Roll Over Beethoven," "Hippy Hippy Shake" and "Long Tall Sally" shows, they were raw but extremely powerful. They were already doing much of the material that would be recorded over the next couple of years and alternated rockers with ballads like "Red Sails in the Sunset" and "Bésame Mucho." The live energy is not in evidence on *The Decca Tapes*, on which the group sounds very much under wraps, singing ballads blandly and playing the rockers stiffly.

Of course, *The Decca Tapes* are demos so bad they never would have been released if the Beatles hadn't followed up with the mind-boggling sound that charged their 1963 British hits "Please Please Me," "She Loves You" and "I Want to Hold Your Hand." These sides, which featured the hard kick of new drummer Ringo Starr, were clearly intended to trade off the band's reputation as Liverpool's hottest live act.

The Beatles didn't crack the U.S. charts until 1964 when "I Want to Hold Your Hand" began the chain of hits that would soon make them the most popular recording artists in history. Because of the time lag between British and U.S. success, though, the early Beatles LPs released in the United States do not correspond to the records released in England. (The early British albums —*Please Please Me, With the Beatles* and *Beatles for Sale*—are all of five-star quality and readily available on import.) *Meet the Beatles,* the first U.S. release, doesn't include a number of songs from their first LP—not even the apocalyptic version of "Twist and Shout" and Ringo's driving rendition of "Boys." Those songs and other early tunes like "Please Please Me" are on the great *The Early Beatles,* while the ground-shaking "She Loves You" hooked *The Beatles' Second Album.*

By the time of the fourth U.S. release, *Something New,* the patchwork assemblage of U.S. albums took its toll: the record was obvious filler, some tracks reproduced on the *Hard Day's Night* soundtrack with a few oddities like "Komm, Gib Mir Deine Hand" thrown in. Still, "Things We Said Today" and "Anytime at All" were good original songs, and the spirited covers of "Slow Down" and "Matchbox" are tremendous. Capitol managed to squeeze one more LP into the Beatles-hungry market of 1964 with *The Beatles' Story,* a two-disc documentary souvenir set.

The Beatles finally came into phase on both sides of the Atlantic with the first of their classic "concept" albums, *Beatles '65.* The album worked as a musical whole, not merely the latest bunch of songs that could be assembled into a record in any order. "No Reply" and "I'm a Loser" showed the first signs of the maturation in Lennon/McCartney's songwriting, a reflection of Bob Dylan's influence. At first the band veered sharply between uptempo rockers and ballads, but as they went on, the group easily made the transition from mellow, folk-music-inspired slow songs to the hardest rock.

George Harrison's technique as what amounted to a session lead guitarist was always in the best taste. Harrison fit well into the sophistication of George Martin's arrangements and managed to play innovative guitar parts in short, often understated lines. The use of feedback as a sonic bridge in the transition between "She's a Woman" and "I Feel Fine" is a brilliant maneuver that uses fairly primitive recording equipment to produce an effect that would later become standard.

Beatles VI and the *Help!* soundtrack established a holding pattern until *Rubber Soul,* the breakthrough record which followed up the strategic ideas of *Beatles '65.* This was such an adept folk-rock album that it marked the beginning of McCartney's string of great ballads with "Michelle." Every song on the record is beautifully simple and rings with some unforgettable melodic phrase. "Norwegian Wood" features George on sitar. "I've Just Seen a Face," "The Word," "Wait" and "Run for Your Life" became Beatles classics.

"Yesterday," the 1965 hit, headlined *Yesterday . . . And Today.* This LP had the legendary "butcher" cover (which was pulled off the market) and included such tremendous songs as "Dr. Robert," "Day Tripper," "Nowhere Man" and "Drive My Car." Once again a McCartney ballad, "Eleanor Rigby," hooked the record, but it was the other three who would make people anticipate *Sgt. Pepper.* Harrison made his strongest contributions to date with "Taxman," "I Want to Tell You" and "Love You Too," which featured more sitar. Ringo once again managed a one-shot stroke with the zany "Yellow Submarine," and Lennon provoked and confused with his first experimental track, the Eastern/psychedelic "Tomorrow Never Knows."

Sgt. Pepper's Lonely Hearts Club Band was a landmark recording in its innovative use of technology. The dramatic use of effects—multilayered sounds and montage, especially—by Martin and the Beatles gave the album its unprecedented scope. Released in early 1967, *Sgt. Pepper* became a symbol of the "summer of love." The title track, "She's Leaving Home," "Lucy in the Sky with Diamonds," "When I'm Sixty-four" and "A Day in the Life" were the best-known tracks.

The era of psychedelic experimentation ushered in by *Sgt. Pepper* produced a lot of bad records, and the subsequent backlash was often justified. When the Beatles' self-produced film *Magical Mystery Tour* was a commercial disaster, people were quick to write off the soundtrack, but the songs are tremendous, a lush extension of *Pepper*'s production concepts: the title track, "The Fool on the Hill," "I Am the Walrus," "Hello Goodbye," "Strawberry Fields Forever," "Penny Lane," "Baby You're a Rich Man" and "All You Need Is Love."

The 1967–68 period was a bad time for the Beatles. Their attempts to radically change their music and lifestyles met with resistance, and they were plagued by poor management. The *Magical Mystery Tour* film failure was only a prelude to the full-fledged disaster that the Apple Corporation, the Beatles' experimental multimedia company, would become; and Lennon and McCartney were involved in a complex court proceeding over ownership of their song publishing. The seeds of the breakup had already been planted, and the next album, *The Beatles,* which is commonly referred to as the White Album, reflected the growing isolation of the group's members.

McCartney's vocal contributions to *The Beatles* were the most lighthearted songs on the set: "Back in the U.S.S.R.," "Rocky Raccoon," "Ob-La-Di, Ob-La-Da," "Mother Nature's Sun" and "Blackbird." Lennon wore his pain on his sleeve in the tortured rock of "Everybody's Got Something to Hide Except Me and My Monkey" and "Yer Blues" and on the pensive "Julia." Harrison's "Piggies" and "While My Guitar Gently Weeps" showed how the sadness affected his formerly optimistic world view, while Ringo's somber album closer, "Good Night," sounded a little too final.

Yellow Submarine, the soundtrack to the animated film, offered only four new songs (Harrison's "It's All Too Much" and "It's Only a Northern Song," and Lennon/McCartney's "All Together Now" and "Hey Bulldog"), and is burdened by one side of George Martin instrumentals.

Abbey Road, the group's swan song, reflected the growing rift between Lennon and McCartney. McCartney and George Martin wanted to make a grand statement out of the dozens of song ideas that were floating around, a pop symphony with no distinction between the individual songs. Lennon was convinced that rock had been conceptualized too far for its own good and wanted a stripped-down record of straight-ahead rock. The compromise gave Lennon control of side one, with McCartney and Martin free to try their experiment on the flip side.

"Come Together" started things off with a stark, gritty rock progression that clearly bore Lennon's signature, as did the heavy blues riff repeated over and over, "I Want You (She's So Heavy)" that finished the side. It's fortunate that McCartney got his wish because side two of *Abbey Road* is the best recorded music the band ever produced, an exquisite realization of the ideas the band had been putting forth crudely but boldly since *Beatles '65* and especially since *Sgt. Pepper.* By now the technology had advanced to the point where the dense, lush sounds the Beatles had sought in the studio were easily reached. The approach to recorded rock sound on *Abbey Road* became the standard of Seventies rock, a new system of sound moves and arrangement strategies still being employed to this day.

"Sun King" begins a beautiful suite that climaxes the album, breaking into "Mean Mr. Mustard," then the surging "Polythene Pam," followed by the crashing "She Came In Through the Bathroom Window" and the resolution of "Golden Slumbers," which sets up the incredible finale, "Carry That Weight," with its brilliant summation of the band's career, Harrison and Lennon trading short bursts of solos that defined a whole tradition of Seventies rock guitar sounds. The Beatles came in blaring and with "Carry That Weight" went out the same way.

Let It Be was put together and released before *Abbey Road* but in fact documents the group's breakup. The film makes it very clear that Lennon and McCartney had little use for each other at that point, while the soundtrack documents the Beatles' last public performance. They set up on the roof of Apple studios in London and played until the police came and made them stop. The last set: "Get Back," "Don't Let Me Down," "I Got a Feeling," "One After 909," "I Dig a Pony," then one final crack at "Get Back" before the plug was pulled. "Thank you very much," signs off John Lennon as the Beatles neatly cap an era. "I hope we passed the audition." — J.S.

BE-BOP DELUXE
★ ★ Axe Victim / Harv. (1974) ¶
★ ★ Futurama / Harv. (1975) ¶
★ ★ ★ Sunburst Finish / Harv. (1976) ¶
★ ★ ★ ★ Modern Music / Harv. (1976) ¶
★ ★ ★ ★ Live in the Air Age / Harv.
   (1977) ¶
★ ★ ★ Drastic Plastic / Harv. (1978) ¶
★ ★ ★ ★ The Best of . . . and the Rest of
   Be-Bop Deluxe / Harv. (1979) ¶
Be-Bop Deluxe's first two albums suffer from a misguided emphasis on Bill Nelson's flamboyant guitar style (Hendrix-derived glissandi with simmering sustains), with the often beautiful melodies and lyric fantasies taking a back seat to cluttered tempo changes and pointless gimmickry. *Sunburst Finish,* Be-Bop's first American success (albeit a modest one), works better, although Nelson's split role continues to diffuse the band's impact. With *Modern Music* he concentrated on coalescing his melodic strengths with the band's instrumental personality. The upshot, musically, is their most balanced and durable LP, and lyrically, an intriguing merger of Nelson's previous fantasy obsessions with a jarring quest for secular redemption (or at least escape). *Live in the Air Age* is everything you'd expect from this band in concert, while *Best of* is just that. Be-Bop fans should also seek out Nelson's solo effort, *Northern Dream* (JEM). — M.G.

JEFF BECK
★ ★ ★ ★ Truth / Epic (1968)
★ ★ Beck-Ola / Epic (1969)
★ ★ ★ ★ Jeff Beck Group/Rough and Ready
   / Epic (1971)
★ Jeff Beck Group / Epic (1972)
★ ★ ★ Beck, Bogert and Appice / Epic
   (1973)
★ ★ ★ ★ Blow by Blow / Epic (1975)
★ ★ ★ ★ Truth/Beck-Ola / Epic (1975) ¶
★ ★ ★ Wired / Epic (1976)
■ Live / Epic (1977)
★ ★ ★ There & Back / Epic (1980)

Although universally acknowledged as one of rock's premier and most influential guitarists, Jeff Beck has had problems as a solo artist and group leader. He is adept at conceiving and outfitting bands to use as vehicles for his immense talents, but apparently gets impatient, bored and/or angry with other musicians quickly—no single Jeff Beck Group has lasted for more than two albums. *Truth* and *Beck-Ola,* recorded in the late Sixties with Rod Stewart, Ron Wood (on bass) and Nicky Hopkins, both show flashes of brilliance ("I Ain't Superstitious," "You Shook Me" on the former, "Plynth," "Rice Pudding" on the latter), but Beck dominates so much he leaves the band in the dust. Stewart suffers the most; his style, not yet fully developed, is simply no match for Beck's frenetic lashings.

The next Jeff Beck Group (featuring Bob Tench, vocals; Max Middleton, keyboards; and Cozy Powell, drums) fares well at first. With a fairly anonymous band posing no threats to the infamous Beck ego, he relaxes a bit and plays (rather than toys) with the other musicians. Middleton brings some jazz texturing to the music, and Beck, picking up the cue, records some beautiful tracks, especially the long and introspective "Raynes Park Blues," on *Jeff Beck Group.* And "Situation" reveals that he has lost none of his ferocity. The promise doesn't last long, though; *Jeff Beck Group,* produced all too calmly by Steve Cropper, is easily the laziest, dullest LP in Beck's catalogue.

Apparently Beck was already planning a new band with Vanilla Fudge/Cactus veterans Tim Bogert and Carmine Appice. *Beck, Bogert and Appice* returns Beck to the field of hard rock with a vengeance. A power trio to end all power trios, *B, B and A* wears its excesses proudly. They fracture Stevie Wonder's "Superstitition," coyly croon Curtis Mayfield's "I'm So Proud" and beat Grand Funk at their own game with "Why Should I Care" and "Livin' Alone."

After the stormy demise of B, B and A, Beck changed course once again, and under George Martin's production recorded *Blow by Blow,* an all-instrumental album (no more vocalists to worry about) that shows off

Beck's consummate abilities as a guitarist as never before. All styles served here, from rock to funk to jazz, and its success has led Beck into jazz-rock circles. *Wired,* with Jan Hammer on keyboards, is Beck meeting the jazz-rock fusion forces. His playing is as terse and intelligent as on *Blow by Blow,* and Hammer's accompaniment shows unusual restraint. The live Beck/Hammer album, however, marks the nadir of this talented artist's career, as excess meets excess. Fortunately, Beck righted his fusion path with the hard-driving *There & Back,* which finally allowed him to present himself as the pure instrumentalist he always saw himself as.   — B.A.

FREDDIE BECKMEIER
★ ★ **Freddie Beckmeier / Casa. (NA)**
Ex-Etta James sideman's claim to fame is having played at the Monterey Pop Festival. — J.S.

BECKMEIER BROTHERS
★ ★ **Beckmeier Brothers / Casa. (NA)**
Hard funk-rock band whose members sessioned with Etta James, Billy Preston, Greg Allman and Frank Zappa before making this fairly anonymous record.   — J.S.

CAPTAIN BEEFHEART AND HIS MAGIC BAND
★ ★ ★ ★ ★ **Trout Mask Replica / Rep. (1970)**
★ ★ ★ ★ **The Spotlight Kid / Rep. (1971)**
★ ★ ★ ★ **Clear Spot / Rep. (1972)**
★ ★ ★ **Shiny Beast (Bat Chain Puller) / War. (1978)**
★ ★ ★ ★ **Doc at the Radar Station / Virgin (1980)**
Trout Mask Replica is a staggering double album about three steps beyond some combination of Delta blues and free jazz. Astonishingly advanced rhythmically, it also sports superb guitar work and some of the most spontaneous sax blowing (by Beefheart) ever recorded. His voice (range: four and a half octaves) sounds like a wild animal. His lyrics are often humorous, rambling discourses on the relationship between man and nature. The whole album has a wonderful childlike feeling about it.

In *Spotlight Kid* and *Clear Spot,* Beefheart attempted to hone this basic style down to something closer to the mainstream—but not much closer. *Spotlight Kid*'s guitar solos, especially, are more conventional and prominent. The lyrics aren't quite as personal, and Beefheart's blues leanings are more explicit. *Clear Spot* is quite similar; it even has one

delightful soul song ("Too Much Time") that sounds as though it could have been a hit single. *Shiny Beast* was an encouraging return that anticipated the brilliant *Doc at the Radar Station,* one of his best and most accessible albums.   — J.M.

THE BEE GEES
★ **Odessa / RSO (1969)**
★ ★ ★ ★ **Main Course / RSO (1975)**
★ ★ **Children of the World / RSO (1976)**
★ ★ ★ ★ **Bee Gees Gold, Vol. 1 / RSO (1976)**
★ ★ **Here at Last / RSO (1977)**
★ ★ ★ **Spirits Having Flown / RSO (1979)**
★ ★ **Bee Gees Greatest / RSO (1979)**
★ ★ **Livin' Eyes / RSO (1981)**
Except for a one-disc condensation of the two-disc *Odessa,* all of the Bee Gees' Sixties albums—made when they were an Australian version of the lightest aspects of the Beatles—are out of print. *Gold,* however, does a fine job of condensing the group's hits, from "New York Mining Disaster 1941" to really mushy stuff like "How Can You Mend a Broken Heart."

In the middle Seventies, just as their vogue seemed played out, the Bee Gees began to incorporate R&B into their lavish pop repertoire, and the result has made them a major, if not dominant, factor in the marketplace. *Main Course,* containing the hits "Jive Talkin'," "Nights on Broadway" and "Fanny," established a pop disco sound much indebted to Arif Mardin's towering productions, and the others followed suit. But the group's biggest hits came with the release of the soundtrack from *Saturday Night Fever* in 1978; the Bee Gees are now a household word, epitomizing the elaborate craftsmanship of late-Seventies pop, the cultural transference between black and white music that has occurred in the past few years, and the emotional vapidity dominating popular taste of late. *Spirits* was more pop than disco, ducking the issue, but containing what may be the best nondisco hit the Bee Gees have made, "Tragedy." With *Livin' Eyes,* the Bee Gees inexplicably reverted to their saccharine predisco style, completely abandoning R&B rhythms. The result is a commercial as well as aesthetic disaster. — S.H./D.M.

BEGINNING OF THE END
★ ★ ★ **Beginning of the End / Atco (1971)**
One-hit pop R&B wonders whose one hit— "Funky Nassau"—was worth the wait. — J.S.

ARCHIE BELL AND THE DRELLS
★ ★ ★ **Dance Your Troubles Away** / Phil.
(1975)
★ ★ **Where Will You Go, When the Party's
Over** / Phil. (1976) ¶
★ ★ ★ **Hard Not to Like It** / Phil. (1977)
★ ★ ★ **Strategy** / Phil. (1979)
★ ★ ★ **I Never Had It So Good** / Beck.
(1981)
The Drells' first Philly soul efforts (for Atlantic in the late Sixties) were quintessential Kenneth Gamble and Leon Huff productions: trashy, slick and raunchy, epitomized by "Tighten Up." By the mid-Seventies, however, disco had changed the prerequisites for dance songs, and most of these songs weigh in at four minutes plus, often too much for comfort. Still, Bunny Sigler's "I Could Dance All Night," from *Dance Your Troubles Away,* harks back to the old sound, and "Let's Groove" is rocking nouveau boogie. The other albums echo the previous successes more and more faintly, unfortunately.
— J.MC./D.M.

CAREY BELL
★ ★ ★ **Blues Harp** / Del. (1969)
★ ★ ★ ★ **Last Night** / Blues. (1973)
This expressive blues harpist and singer has gigged around Chicago since the Fifties as well as playing with Muddy Waters' and Willie Dixon's groups. *Last Night* is particularly good. — J.S.

MAGGIE BELL
★ ★ ★ **Suicide Sal** / Swan (1975)
Bell can really drive a song, but she relies more on grit than inspiration. On *Suicide Sal,* she's backed by Led Zeppelin's Jimmy Page, among others. A good time is had by all, and Bell's soul mannerisms are convincing in this rock setting. — A.S.

BELL & JAMES
★ ★ ★ **Bell & James** / A&M (1978)
★ ★ ★ **Only Make Believe** / A&M (1979)
★ ★ ★ **In Black and White** / A&M (1980)
Talent in the service of formula. LeRoy Bell, nephew of Philadelphia soul producer/songwriter Thom Bell, and Casey James are Pacific Northwest musicians who have had greater success as writers of others' hits— "Three Way Love Affair," "This Time Baby," "Mama Can't Buy You Love," etc.— than as a recording act. Soft-focus makeout music with a high-gloss finish, an LP's worth of such tracks is likely to strike the listener as bland and weightless in the extreme; not without charm, but utterly lacking in character. Bell and James achieved chart success in

spring and summer of 1979 with "Livin' It Up (Friday Night)." Thom Bell served as executive producer and the duo's guide in the ways of the music business. — G.A.

THE BELLAMY BROTHERS
★ **The Bellamy Brothers Featuring "Let
Your Love Flow"** / War. (1976)
■ **Plain and Fancy** / War. (1977) ¶
■ **Beautiful Friends** / War. (1978)
■ **Two and Only** / War. (1979)
■ **Sons of the Sun** / War. (1980)
■ **You Can Get Crazy** / War. (1980)
The guileless exuberance of "Let Your Love Flow," a 1976 hit, is belied by the rest of these LPs, which exemplify some of the worst tendencies of contemporary pop rock: slick, gauzy harmonies overlaid on a bed of chewing-gum rhythm. Pop without the snap and crackle, in other words. — D.M.

JORGE BEN
★ ★ ★ **Samba Nova** / Is. (1977)
★ ★ **Tropical** / Is. (1977)
Brazilian Jorge Ben's *Samba Nova* is much closer to the street music of *Black Orpheus* than to the more familiar superclub whisperings of bossa nova. Ben, a seductive acoustic guitarist and sweet-voiced singer (but with a nice rough edge), leads a mostly percussion band through a fine set of songs aided by a touch of orchestration and several crisp, sirenic backup singers. *Nova* presents Ben very well to the North American audience.

Tropical, however, is a disappointing foray into a disco/soul revisionism of Ben's samba for which his voice and writing are totally ill suited. The album features heavy electric versions of such Ben standards as "Mas Que Nada" and several ballads so poorly arranged that Ben sometimes sounds like Cat Stevens singing in Portuguese. Only "Taj Mahal" and "My Lady" retain Ben's typical rude rhythmic energy. — B.T.

PAT BENATAR
★ ★ **In the Heat of the Night** / Chrys.
(1979)
★ ★ **Crimes of Passion** / Chrys. (1980)
★ ★ **Precious Time** / Chrys. (1981)
When Pat Benatar came out of New York cabarets to record as a rock & roll singer, she was inaccurately referred to as part of the new wave. What Benatar actually does is what Peter Frampton used to: put touches of heavier music into a lightweight pop format, disguising the dirtier elements enough to guarantee airplay while still coming on tough. *In the Heat of the Night* is a tentative

first step toward developing her own Ronstadt-type formula, a balance between soft and loud numbers. Two Blondie soundalikes ("We Live for Love" and "Rated X"), along with too many slow showcases for her multioctave vocal range, make for a dispirited effort.

Crimes of Passion began to get things down pat, emphasizing her ability to belt out tunes aggressively. But as Benatar's sensitive yet tough pose became more pronounced, the deceit behind her image became apparent. The conflict between assertiveness and vulnerability in the Pretenders' Chrissie Hynde is never fully resolved; it is the dynamic caused by this internal struggle that makes Hynde's art so successful. Not having the direction come from her own intuition or sensibility leads Benatar to some ludicrous moments; *Crimes'* "Hit Me with Your Best Shot," believed by some to be an ode to sadomasochism, is followed by the anti-child abuse "Hell Is for Children."

Precious Time, despite atrocious cover versions of the Raiders' "Just Like Me" and the Beatles' "Helter Skelter" (there being no discernible purpose in the latter redoing this in its post-Manson context), made Benatar a superstar. Since the only way to judge such emotionally fraudulent music is, paradoxically, by its commercial acclaim (because turning a buck is really its prime motivation, the "art" of this stuff is shown precisely by the jingle of the cash register), *Time* is Pat Benatar's best record. That anybody actually cares about it or her is irrelevant; does anybody care about Peter Frampton any more?
— W.K.

MARC BENNO
★ ★ **Marc Benno / A&M (1970)**
★ ★ **Minnows / A&M (1971)**
★ ★ **Ambush / A&M (1972)**
★ **Lost in Austin / A&M (1979)**
Benno's records are early examples of what was to become the L.A. style—polished studio expertise. Various musicians set the tone for each of the albums: Booker T. Jones' chunky piano and Ry Cooder's bottleneck guitar help to create the easy-rocking intimacy of the debut. The full slate of studio musicians and the fuller production of David Anderle gave *Minnows* a slightly pop feel. *Ambush,* which utilized a pruned-down band with few additions, put Benno in a tougher setting that worked to his advantage.

While these albums demonstrate Benno's lightweight talents (pleasant voice, smooth guitar style), they create a paradox—while there is nothing to detract from his work,

there's also precious little to recommend it.
— J.B.M.

PIERRE BENSUSAN
★ ★ ★ ★ **Pres de Paris / Roun. (1978)**
★ ★ ★ ★ **Pierre Bensusan 2 / Roun. (1980)**
★ ★ ★ ★ **Musiques / Roun. (1980)**
Beautiful records by acoustic guitar virtuoso Bensusan, whose interests range from jazz and blues to various ethnic musics including Celtic, Breton, traditional English, and Spanish. Bensusan's deep emotional spirit and staggering technique combines elements of Bert Jansch, John Renbourne, Stefan Grossman, Ry Cooder and Lenny Breau. — J.S.

BROOK BENTON
★ ★ ★ **The Two of Us (with Dinah Washington) / Mer. (1960)**
★ ★ ★ ★ **Golden Hits / Mer. (1961)**
★ ★ ★ **Brook Benton Today / Coti. (1970)** ¶
★ **Brook Benton Sings a Love Story / RCA (1975)** ¶
★ ★ **This Is Brook Benton / All Pl. (1976)**
Nothing brings back the late Fifties like the sound of a blues riff delivered by 1001 strings. It was Benton's own idea to combine gospel intensity with lush pop arrangements, and the Mercury sides from the Fifties have more to offer than nostalgia. His singing is both smooth and smoky, and he's never lost the crisp delivery he learned in his early days with the Golden Gate Quartet. On *The Two of Us,* the duets themselves are fine, but the solo tunes are neither artist's best work. *Golden Hits,* on the other hand, is a classic. From rock to ballads to blues, Benton never drops his easy elegance, yet the pretty, swirling strings don't obscure his emotional intensity.

The RCA album is a remastered hash of outtakes; the Cotillion is from the period that produced Benton's last big hit, "Rainy Night in Georgia"; the All Platinum set is mid-Seventies Benton, not at the height of his powers but still good enough to make a disco version of "My Funny Valentine" credible. — A.S.

BUSTER BENTON
★ ★ **Spider in My Stew / Ronn (1979)**
★ ★ **Buster Benton in the Feeling / Ronn (1981)**
★ ★ **Blues Buster / Red L. (NA), Br. imp.**
Mediocre Chicago singer/guitarist. The Red Lightnin' LP has good notes, by Jim O'Neal of *Living Blues;* "Spider in My Stew," Benton's best moment, is available on the Red Lightnin', but the original's on Ronn.
— D.M.

CHUCK BERRY
★ ★ ★ ★ More Chuck Berry / Chess
(1960) ¶
★ ★ On Stage / Chess (1963)
★ ★ ★ ★ Chuck Berry's Greatest Hits /
Chess (1964) ¶
★ ★ ★ ★ Chuck Berry's Golden Decade /
Chess (1967) ¶
★ Chuck Berry's Golden Hits / Mer. (1967)
★ ★ The London Chuck Berry Sessions /
Chess (1972) ¶
★ ★ ★ ★ Chuck Berry's Golden Decade,
Vol. 2 / Chess (1973) ¶
★ ★ ★ Chuck Berry's Golden Decade, Vol. 3
/ Chess (1974) ¶
★ ★ Chuck Berry / Chess (1974) ¶
★ ★ ★ ★ Rockit / Atco (1979)
★ ★ Chuck Berry (Greatest Hits) / Arc.
Folk (NA)
★ ★ ★ ★ ★ Rockin' at the Hops / Chess
(NA), Fr. imp.
★ ★ ★ ★ Chuck Berry Is on Top / Chess
(NA), Fr. imp.

Chuck Berry is to rock what Louis Armstrong was to jazz. He established *the* basic mode of expression on the genre's key instrument, the guitar—an approach that shaped almost everything that was played after his rise. As a writer, his influence was hardly less great. The sagas of teenage hard luck and romance, the devoted pursuit of a half-comic, half-demonic American dream which he set down in "Maybellene," "Johnny B. Goode," "Back in the U.S.A." and a dozen others paint an America as big, brilliant and personal as anyone's.

The most striking characteristic of Berry's style when it first appeared, with "Maybellene" in 1955, was the fast, ringing tone of his electric guitar. Although he recorded in Chicago, in close proximity to such masters of urban blues as Howlin' Wolf and Muddy Waters, he effected a drastic change in their 12-bar style, speeding it up, simplifying it by merging it with the basic 32-bar pop-song format. Berry himself listed Louis Jordan and country & western as important sources. This basic guitar sound was simple enough to move any number of teenagers to copy it—everyone from Lonnie Mack to the Beach Boys, and in England, the Rolling Stones, the Beatles, the Animals and others—but was in fact almost endlessly adaptable, as anyone who has ever heard "Brown Sugar" can attest.

Chuck Berry's Golden Decade, at least the first two volumes, tells most of the story: "Nadine," "Brown Eyed Handsome Man," "Memphis," "Almost Grown," "Reelin' and Rockin'," "Sweet Little Sixteen," "Promised Land," "Let It Rock," "Carol," "You Never Can Tell" and a half-dozen others are at the heart of the rock repertoire. Most of these were not hits when first released—only four of Berry's records made the Top Ten from 1956 to 1960—but they have become familiar to almost every rock listener because so many bands use them to supplement their performances. This alone would make them essential to an understanding of the music. But Berry was as frequently inspired as any rock performer of his generation, ranking with Elvis Presley and perhaps Little Richard at the very pinnacle of the genre. The emotions are more often bright and lively than dark and brooding, something else that set him off from the bluesmen, but this can conceal the deadly ironic eye of songs like "School Day" or "Roll Over Beethoven" or the deeply moving saga of Little Marie in "Memphis" and its sequel, "Little Marie."

Greatest Hits and *More* (a mid-Sixties singles collection—its original title was *Twist*—which has somehow survived the Chess cutout policy) merely reiterate volumes 1 and 2 of *Golden Decade.* Volume 3 is without any hits, and in fact is filled out with much of Berry's always mediocre blues playing. It is still worth hearing, even in the abysmal fake stereo that robs all this material of much of its punch—if possible, listen in mono. (Unfortunately, none of these records are available in that format.) The French imports on Chess are reissues, in sterling mono, of original fifties Berry LPs. Expensive but worth every *sou.*

The Mercury and Archive of Folk and Jazz collections are from a brief, disastrous fling at the former label during the mid-Sixties. The song titles are the same, but that's about all. *On Stage* is only a mediocre live set—unfortunate, because Berry was a great, duckwalking showman in concert—and does *not* contain "Surfin' U.S.A.," no matter what the liner says.

London Sessions gave Berry his last hit (and first No. 1) in 1972 with the bathroom-risqué "My Ding-a-Ling," apart from which it is exceptional only for its sloppiness. The Chess *Chuck Berry* seems designed mostly to showcase the singing of his daughter, Ingrid Berry Gibson. One song, "Deuce," comes close to the inspired ribaldry of the early ones, and "Hi Heel Sneakers" is the only one of the classic covers that is up to snuff. *Rockit,* recorded at Berry Park, Chuck's Missouri home, is surprisingly potent, with a tough "Havana Moon" and a surreal paean to "California," where he'd just done time on a tax rap. Not the old days but nice stuff.

Apart from that you would be better off searching out such deleted albums as *Back Home* (containing the memorable "Tulane") or the magnificent *St. Louis to Liverpool,* one of the greatest rock & roll records ever made. — D.M.

BETHNAL

★ ★ **Dangerous Times** / Vert. (1978), Br. imp.

★ ★ **Crash Landing** / Vert. (1978), Br. imp.

Bethnal issued two LPs in 1978 and completely destroyed the new-wave credibility that the British press had created for them. Despite an uncommon lineup (lead singer doubling on violin) and the inspiration of Pete Townshend, both records expose a general lack of discernible talent. An audacious cover version of the Who's "Baba O'Riley" on *Dangerous Times* was the closest Bethnal ever came to being noteworthy.
— I.R.

DICKEY BETTS

★ ★ **Highway Call** / Capri. (1974) ¶

★ ★ **Dickey Betts and Great Southern** / Ari. (1977)

★ ★ **Atlanta's Burning Down** / Ari. (1978)

Launch the sucker and see if she floats. What could have been promise renewed turns out to be promises, promises. Rather than break new ground, Betts exhumes some of his moldiest clichés and struggles in vain to sound like he's interested in them. For the diehard. — D.M.

BEVERLY AND DUANE

★ ★ **Beverly and Duane** / Ario.-Amer. (1979)

Dispensable pop-disco duo. — D.M.

THE B-52'S

★ ★ ★ **The B-52's** / War. (1979)

★ ★ **Wild Planet** / War. (1980)

The conceit here is that the pop ready-mades of the pre-Beatle Sixties and the dance rhythms of the late Seventies are ripe for synthesis by a band of Georgia bohemians. Well, maybe. On the debut album, thanks to a hip dance novelty, "Rock Lobster," the blend works fine, but the group's cutesiness overwhelms its artfulness and eliminates all semblance of real emotion. Which means that without an equally strong blockbuster tune on album two, the B-52's simply supply more dance fodder. And pandering to club jocks is no better than pandering to FM or AM radio jocks. Besides, nobody here can sing as well as Darlene Love . . . or Donna Summer, for that matter. — D.M.

BIG BROTHER AND THE HOLDING COMPANY

★ ★ ★ ★ **Cheap Thrills** / Col. (1968)

The definitive late-Sixties acid-rock album, notable for sloppy, overlong cuts, inspired amateurish playing, thoroughly distorted electric lead guitar playing from James Gurley and the galvanic vocals of the era's most beloved and charismatic performer, Janis Joplin. You had to be there, but if you weren't, listening to this is about as close as you can come. — J.S.

BIG MACEO

★ ★ ★ ★ **Chicago Breakdown** / Blueb. (1975)

This double album spotlights the moving vocals and strong left-handed playing of a blues pianist perhaps second only to Otis Spann. — J.MO.

BIG MAYBELLE

★ ★ ★ **The Gospel Soul of Big Maybelle** / Bruns. (1968)

★ ★ ★ **The Great Soul Hits of Big Maybelle** / Bruns. (1969)

★ ★ **The Amazing Big Maybelle** / Up Fr. (NA) ¶

★ ★ **Last of Big Maybelle** / Para. (NA)

A strong-voiced belter in the Bessie Smith tradition, on record Big Maybelle never really showed what she was capable of. Her live performances were legendary, and you do get a sense of her power on the Brunswick records, but the Up Front and Paramount sides simply don't capture her. It's worth checking up on her pop sides recorded for Savoy in 1956, which are anthologized on *The Roots of Rock 'n' Roll.* "Candy," a hit for that label, is the best she sounded on record. — J.S.

BIG TWIST AND THE MELLOW FELLOWS

★ ★ ★ ★ **Big Twist and the Mellow Fellows** / Fly. Fish (1980)

The material is sub-Southside Johnny, the vocals are more gravelly Gravenites than true Blue Bland, but this is soulful and direct, and the horns and voices are perfectly integrated. For a hipster soul band that is, pretty damn good, even if it's not a substitute for the real thing. — D.M.

BIG YOUTH

★ ★ ★ ★ **Screaming Target** / Troj. (1973)

★ ★ **Hit the Road Jack** / Troj. (1976)

★ ★ ★ **Natty Cultural Dread** / Troj. (1976)

★ ★ **Isaiah, 1st Prophet of Old** / V.F.L. (1978)

★ ★ ★ ★ **Everyday Skank** / Troj. (NA)

★ ★ ★ **Some Great Big Youth / Heartb. (NA)**
After the initial breakthroughs of U. Roy, Dennis Alcapone and I. Roy, who together defined reggae's rapping style in the early Seventies, jewel-toothed Big Youth took toasting to another level with his acute social commentary and dread sensibility. Tunes such as "S-90 Skank" and "Cool Breeze," and *Screaming Target* used everyday ghetto life as a springboard for his transcendent spirit. His increasing (and unfortunate) tendency to sing has marred recent LPs. *Everyday Skank* is the essential compilation, while *Some Great Big Youth* compiles the better moments from his last three LPs, including the excellent *Progress* LP. — R.F.G.

BARNSLEY BILL
★ ★ **The Freewheeling Barnsley Bill / Mother (1981), Br. imp.**
The "new prime minister of super-heavy drinking," Bill savages the conventions of New York rap unmercifully. Okay as a taste of British working-class preoccupations, but unsuitable for the serious student of "party hearty." — ML.H.

BILLY & THE BEATERS
★ ★ ★ **Billy & the Beaters / Alfa (1981)**
Billy is Billy Vera, a tough-minded singer/songwriter who sounds like Billy Joel with soul. (He recorded with some success in the Sixties, as Atlantic's answer to Mitch Ryder.) Which is to say that although Vera has Joel's weakness for schlock, he also manages to transcend his clichés through sheer depth of feeling. Not on every song, unfortunately. Recorded live for extra grit; features guitarist Jeff Baxter. — J.D.C.

BIONIC BOOGIE
★ ★ **Bionic Boogie / Poly. (1977) ¶**
Relentless dance-floor thump from "conceptual group" organized (produced, written and instrumentally led) by Gregg Diamond. Makes competent if uninspired use of the era's disco clichés, which means that it probably sounded pretty decent once upon a time, but now is outdated. That is, they don't make 'em like this any more for a reason. — D.M.

EDWIN BIRDSONG
★ **What It Is / Poly. (1971) ¶**
★ **Edwin Birdsong / Phil. (NA)**
Unintentionally hilarious comments on earthy street experience (actual song title: "It Ain't No Fun Being a Welfare Recipient"

from *What It Is*) with born-again leanings. The best thing to get saved with these is the money you might have wasted. Nice piano playing, though. — D.M.

THE BIRTHDAY PARTY
★ ★ ★ **Door Door / Mush. (1979), Aust. imp.**
★ ★ ★ **The Birthday Party / Miss. L. (1980)**
★ ★ ★ **Prayers on Fire / Miss. L. (1981)**
The Birthday Party emerged from the new-wave scene that flourished in Melbourne, Australia, in 1976–77, paralleling the punk chic that evolved into new romanticism in Britain. Their first incarnation was as a band of stylishly nihilistic schoolboys known as the Boys Next Door. They released an album in 1979 titled *Door Door,* a competent and sometimes interesting statement of the ethos of world-weary desperation fashionable at the time. After developing a strong cult following in Melbourne's inner suburbs, they left for England, where they underwent a name change and a broadening of musical interests, principally in the direction of New Music electronics. Their angst-filled concerns gained an original, experimental flavor that has brought them considerable success on England's independent charts. — S.M.

ELVIN BISHOP
★ ★ **Rock My Soul / Epic (1972)**
★ ★ ★ **The Best of Elvin Bishop: Crabshaw Rising / Epic (1972) ¶**
★ ★ ★ **Let It Flow / Capri. (1974) ¶**
★ ★ ★ **Juke Joint Jump / Capri. (1977)**
★ ★ ★ ★ **Struttin' My Stuff / Capri. (1975)**
★ ★ ★ **Hometown Boy Makes Good / Capri. (1976) ¶**
★ ★ ★ ★ **Raisin' Hell / Capri. (1977)**
★ ★ ★ **Hog Heaven / Capri. (1978)**
Elvin Bishop was one of the guitarists in the original Paul Butterfield Blues Band—at first paired with Michael Bloomfield and later on his own. Bishop quickly developed the humorous, countrified persona Pigboy Crabshaw, who was equal parts the hick Tulsa kid Bishop might have been when he joined the Butterfield band, and the laconic, blues-playing sharpie that he certainly was by the time he left.
In 1970, Bishop left Butterfield for a solo recording deal with Bill Graham's Fillmore label (the material that now appears on the Epic albums). The three albums he cut for Graham were loose, funky R&B, ranging from covers of Fifties R&B tunes like "Feel It" and "So Fine" to jams with Santana's percussionists. There was also a self-effacing C&W stream of humor in the music—

typified by such songs as "Hogbottom," "Stealin' Watermelons," and "Party Till the Cows Come Home." Somehow it never quite jelled. The Epic *Best of* is a representative anthology of the period; *Rock My Soul* is the third and weakest album of the series.

Bishop moved to Capricorn Records in 1974, with a new band that played similarly funky material, in a bit more relaxed (and confident) fashion. The first couple of albums, the deleted *Let It Flow* and *Juke Joint Jump,* faltered mostly because of the weakness of Bishop's lead vocals; *Struttin' My Stuff,* which added singer Mickey Thomas, produced one of the best hit singles of 1976, "Fooled Around and Fell in Love." While the focus of the group's sound remained Bishop's blues-based guitar in interplay with Phil Aaberg's keyboards and Johnny Vernazza's second guitar, the emergence of Thomas gave Bishop a flexibility he had previously lacked—the version of "My Girl" here, while it can hardly be said to be in the same league as the original, was at least more ambitious than the boogie purveyed by other groups with similar roots.

The quality of the sequel, *Hometown Boy Makes Good,* suffered partly because the quality of the material fell off, partly because it was hard to determine whether Thomas or Bishop was in charge. But *Raisin' Hell,* a live album, reasserted Bishop's control. What might have been a simple boogie blues set, no less numbing than an evening with Charlie Daniels, was redeemed by Bishop's self-effacing humor (which reemerged now that his marketability had been demonstrated) and the simple, fine playing of the group. *Raisin' Hell* is fun in a way that very little white blues of the Seventies was, a kind of joyous celebration of collective spirit. Subsequent releases repeat the style, not the spirit, of Bishop's successes, which is to say that even such a loose and funky approach can become a formula.   — D.M.

STEPHEN BISHOP
★ ★ ★ **Careless / ABC (1976)**
★ ★ ★ **Bish / ABC (1978)**
★ ★ ★ **Red Cab to Manhattan / War. (1980)**
In 1977, when his debut LP was released, Bishop seemed no more than a whining but listenable post-James Taylor songwriter with a particularly (face it) unpleasant mug. But a year later, when *Bish* appeared, it was clear—on the basis of appearances on "Saturday Night Live" and in *Animal House*— that a good deal of what seemed too precious about Bishop was actually satire of a very subtle order. That doesn't make singles

like "On and On" and "Save It for a Rainy Day" much more pleasant as radio hits—the approximation of the typical singer/songwriter's maudlin self-pity is too close to comfort. But at least it makes you smile while you push the buttons.   — D.M.

THE BIZARROS
★ **The Bizarros / Mer. (1979)**
In Superman comics, the Bizarro world was a backwards parallel universe to Earth in which all things good and sensible were rendered corrupt and insane. These Bizarros came from Akron, along with Devo, to spearhead the first wave of post-punk American art rock, for which they may be forgiven in some universe, but not in this somewhat harmonious one.   — D.M.

BILL BLACK COMBO
★ **Award Winners / Hi (NA)**
★ **Memphis, Tennessee / Hi (NA)**
★ **Saxy Jazz / Hi (1960)** ¶
★ **Solid and Raunchy / Hi (1960)** ¶
★ **Untouchable Sound / Hi (1963)** ¶
★ ★ **Greatest Hits / Hi (1963)** ¶
★ **Bill Black Combo Plays the Blues / Hi (1964)** ¶
★ **Bill Black Combo Plays Tunes by Chuck Berry / Hi (1964)** ¶
★ **Bill Black Combo Goes Big Band / Hi (1964)** ¶
★ ★ **Greatest Hits, Vol. 2 / Hi (NA)** ¶
★ **More Solid and Raunchy / Hi (1969)** ¶
★ **Solid and Country / Hi (1975)** ¶
★ **World's Greatest Honky-Tonk Band / Hi (1975)** ¶
★ **It's Honky-Tonk Time / Hi (1977)** ¶
★ **Bill Black Combo / Zodiac (NA)** ¶
"Redneck MOR" was a good description of the Bill Black Combo. Black was the bass player in the first Elvis Presley band at Sun Records, and his combo turned out raunchy saxophone-dominated instrumentals for twenty years, even after he died. It's all interchangeable, characteristically hard-edged (after all, they're a Memphis band) and ultimately forgettable.   — J.S.

BLACKBYRDS
★ ★ ★ ★ **The Blackbyrds / Fan. (1974)**
★ ★ ★ ★ **Flying Start / Fan. (1974)**
★ ★ **City Life / Fan. (1975)**
★ **Unfinished Business / Fan. (1976)**
★ **Action / Fan. (1977)**
★ ★ **Night Grooves / Fan. (1978)**
★ ★ **Better Days / Fan. (1980)**
Originally Donald Byrd's backing band, the Blackbyrds stepped out into the light in the early Seventies as a jazz-funk fusion group

with something of their own to say. At least at first, the rhythmic bottom was solid and danceable, the vocals were appropriately spare, and the instrumentation—particularly the horn charts—was melodically adventurous and fulfilling. *The Blackbyrds* was their debut, and *Flying Start* represents a creative, if not a commercial, peak. But after the success of *Flying Start,* the Blackbyrds began to see themselves as a disco attraction rather than as a progressive R&B act, and *City Life* exhibited a dispiriting reliance on recycled riff-hooks and an embarrassing bent for hollow social and psycho-cybernetic commentary. The other albums simply continue the decline into self-parody.
— M.G.

BLACK FLAG
★ ★ ★ **Damaged** / SST (1981)
Black Flag is one of the leaders of contemporary L.A. punk—a small, sometimes violent cultural movement that transplanted 1977-style British hard-core punk anger to the Californian promised land. To many, this nihilistic approach seemed anachronistic and irrelevant coming from well-tanned L.A., but in fact only such a combination could accurately represent the glittering city. Black Flag's punk chords on its exciting, witty debut express anger amidst the Hollywood void. Obviously Black Flag lacks the firm purpose and eloquence of British punk's politics, but it does represent a credible suburban rebellion against boredom. Sort of like heavy metal if that ritualized form had the element of unfocused threat it always boasts about. — J.F.

J. D. BLACKFOOT
★ ★ ★ **Song of the Crazy Horse** / Fan. (1975)
★ ★ ★ **Southbound and Gone** / Fan. (1975) ¶
The American-born, New Zealand-based Blackfoot built his debut LP, *Song,* around its over-eighteen-minute-long title track, inspired by *Bury My Heart at Wounded Knee,* then followed it up with a better-than-average Southern rock record. — J.S.

BLACKFOOT
★ ★ ★ **No Reservations** / Is. (1975) ¶
★ ★ ★ **Flyin' High** / Epic (1976) ¶
★ ★ ★ ★ **Strikes** / Atco (1979)
★ ★ ★ **Tomcattin'** / Atco (1980)
★ ★ ★ ★ **Marauder** / Atco (1981)
High-energy Southern hard rock produced by Jimmy Johnson in Muscle Shoals and led by guitarist Rickey Medlock, grandson of

bluegrass musician and songwriter Shorty Medlock. Two members of Blackfoot played in the band that would later become Lynyrd Skynyrd. — J.S.

BLACK IVORY
★ ★ **Feel It** / Bud. (1975)
★ **Black Ivory** / Bud. (1977) ¶
★ **Hangin' Heavy** / Bud. (NA) ¶
Pedestrian soul group had a variety of R&B chartmakers in the early Seventies for the minor Today and Kwanza labels, but since signing with Buddah, only "Will We Ever Come Together" *(Feel It)* has clicked.
— D.M.

BLACKJACK
★ **Worlds Apart** / Poly. (NA) ¶
★ **Blackjack** / Poly. (1979)
Italian-American heavy-metal group led by vocalist Michael Bolotin. Guest appearance by David Sancious (on Blackjack) and a Vanilla Fudge–like cover of the Supremes' "My World Is Empty without You" are the only noteworthy moments. — J.S.

BLACKMORE'S RAINBOW
★ ★ **Ritchie Blackmore's Rainbow** / Poly. (1975)
★ **Rainbow Rising** / Oy. (1976)
★ **On Stage** / Poly. (1977)
★ **Long Live Rock 'n' Roll** / Poly. (1978)
★ **Down to Earth** / Poly. (1979)
★ **Difficult to Cure** / Poly. (1981)
Looking back over half a decade's plodding sludge, one finds it tempting to see former Deep Purple guitarist Blackmore's early work with his own band as promising, but that's an illusion abetted only by the disgraceful slothfulness and thorough lack of imagination displayed in everything from the live album onward. Blackmore is a proficient player when he chooses to be, but he seems trapped between bucks and boredom here, and even the addition of former Purple crony Roger Glover on bass beginning with *Long Live* does little to provoke him to anything but formula recitations of basic headbanger moves. The two most recent albums lack even the occasionally interesting drummer Cozy Powell. — D.M.

BLACK OAK ARKANSAS
★ **Black Oak Arkansas** / Atco (1971)
★ **Raunch 'n' Roll** / Atco (1973)
★ **X-Rated** / MCA (1975)
★ **Live, Mutha** / Atco (1976) ¶
★ **Balls of Fire** / MCA (1976) ¶
★ **Ten-Year Overnight Success** / MCA (1976) ¶

★ **Best of Black Oak Arkansas / Atco (1977)**
★ **Race with the Devil / Capri. (1977)** ¶
★ **I'd Rather Be Sailing / Capri. (1978)** ¶
Mindless gutbucket boogie hooked around the mealy-voiced antics of lead singer Jim Dandy Mangrum. Black Oak's distinguishing characteristic is that the band has three guitarists who collectively don't even add up to one good one. The pits of hard-rock senescence. — J.S.

BLACK SABBATH
★ **Black Sabbath / War. (1970)**
★ **Master of Reality / War. (1971)**
★ **Paranoid / War. (1971)**
★ **Black Sabbath, Vol. 4 / War. (1972)**
★ **Sabbath, Bloody Sabbath / War. (1973)**
★ **Sabotage / War. (1975)**
★ **We Sold Our Soul for Rock 'n' Roll / War. (1976)**
★ **Technical Ecstasy / War. (1976)**
★ **Never Say Die / War. (1978)**
★ **Heaven and Hell / War. (1980)**
★ **Mob Rules / War. (1981)**
These would-be English Kings of Heavy Metal are eternally foiled by their stupidity and intractability. In the early Seventies their murky drone was all the more appealing for its cynicism—the philosophy that everything is shit, and a flirtation with pre-*Exorcist* demonic possession. Time has passed them by; their recent stuff is a quaint bore. Their high point was *Paranoid,* a better example of their goofy malevolence than the *We Sold Our Souls* anthology, and cheaper. — K.T.

BLACK SATIN
★ ★ **Black Satin / Bud. (1976)**
This group is actually Fred Parris and the Five Satins in a contemporary guise. They had minor 1975 R&B hit with "Everybody Stand and Clap Your Hands (for the Entertainer)"; also recut "In the Still of the Night" and a Barry White song, which about covers it. — D.M.

BLACK SLATE
★ ★ ★ **Amigo / Alli. (1980)**
★ ★ ★ **Rasta Festival / Alli. (1981)**
British reggae (that made by West Indians in the U.K.) reflects the British West Indian experience and cannot be judged by Jamaican standards. Black Slate's reggae integrates soul and rock less self-consciously than most, producing at least one punky reggae standard in "Sticks Man" on *Amigo. Amigo's* propulsive pop-reggae gets the nod over the less convincing roots reggae of *Festival.*
— R.F.G.

BLACKSMOKE
★ ★ **Blacksmoke / Choc. (1977)**
Eight-piece disco band had minor '76 chartmaker, "Your Love Has Got Me Screamin'."
— D.M.

BLACK UHURU
★ ★ ★ ★ ★ **Showcase / Black Rose/D Roy (1979)**
★ ★ ★ ★ **Sensimillia / Mango (1980)**
★ ★ ★ ★ **Black Sounds of Freedom / Greens. (1981)**
★ ★ ★ ★ ★ **Red / Mango (1981)**
★ ★ ★ ★ ★ **Vital Selection / Virgin Int'l (1981)**
The two-man, one-woman vocal blend of Black Uhuru in combination with the production genius and instrumental wizardry of Sly and Robbie (reggae's greatest rhythm section) made Black Uhuru the first important reggae group of the Eighties. Lead singer and composer Michael Rose's keening, modal Afro-Arab vocal style and nitty-gritty lyric detail set them apart. So far, a sameness of melody has not diluted some of the most powerful, hypnotic reggae ever made. *Black Sounds* is a reissue of *Love Crisis,* a first LP by a different lineup that only hinted at the innovations to come. *Sensimillia's* electronic Africanisms are a bit dense, but *Red* and *Showcase* (*Vital Selection* duplicates *Showcase*) are awesome masterpieces.
— R.F.G.

OTIS BLACKWELL
★ ★ ★ **These Are My Songs / Inner (1978)**
Author of several important Fifties tunes, including "Don't Be Cruel" and "All Shook Up" for Elvis, Blackwell bears a remarkable vocal resemblance to Presley. The cover and liner notes would like to have you believe that this means Blackwell is the greater artist, which is silly. On the other hand, he is an interesting eccentric; although the band lets him down on occasion, this is worth hearing. — D.M.

NORMAN BLAKE
★ ★ **Home in Sulphur Springs / Roun. (1972)**
★ **Fields of November / Fly. Fish (1974)**
★ ★ ★ **Whiskey before Breakfast / Roun. (1976)**
★ **Live at McCabe's / Tak. (1976)**
★ ★ **Blackberry Blossom / Fly. Fish (NA)**
★ ★ **Norman Blake / Fly. Fish (NA)**
★ ★ **Directions / Tak. (NA)**
★ ★ **Old and New / Fly. Fish (NA)**
Blake is a superb guitarist capable of the flashiest, fastest picking this side of Doc

Watson. A Nashville staple, his duets with close friend/dobroist Tut Taylor and guitarist Charlie Collins can be awe-inspiring. (*Home* and *Whiskey* are both duo albums, the former with Taylor, the latter with Collins.) Blake's backup work with, and influence on, John Hartford, Kris Kristofferson and Joan Baez, however, is also estimable.

Unfortunately, when Blake is recording as leader (and on Taylor's Rounder LP), he takes on the additional role of vocalist, a "talent" of his that is considerably less than adequate.

The natural sound quality on the two Rounder sets, though, makes them particularly appealing. *Fields of November* is a generally uninspired performance, and the live disc doesn't justify itself in ambiance or technical levels. — I.M.

NORMAN BLAKE AND THE RISING FAWN STRING ENSEMBLE
★ ★ ★ ★ The Rising Fawn String Ensemble / Roun. (1979)
★ ★ ★ ★ Full Moon on the Farm / Roun. (1981)
Guitarist Blake's mostly instrumental LPs with the Rising Fawn String Ensemble are beautiful evocations of a multiplicity of styles from bluegrass to Cajun music. On the '79 set Blake's guitar is joined by Nancy Blake's cello and mandolin and James Bryan's fiddle. For *Full Moon . . .* Nancy also plays fiddle and vocals, while Charles Collins is added on fiddle and second guitar. — J.S.

RONEE BLAKLEY
★ Welcome / War. (1975)
This album represents an early foray by Los Angeles into mainstream country music. Although the attempt later succeeded in the form of L.A. takeovers of performers like Dolly Parton and Crystal Gayle, it fails here.

Blakley is a singer/songwriter in the California folk tradition. This album represents an attempt to capitalize on her starring role in Robert Altman's film *Nashville,* but the production, while tasteful, lacks heart; the compositions (all Blakley originals) lack authenticity. — M.H.

BOBBY "BLUE" BLAND
★ ★ ★ ★ ★ Two Steps from the Blues / Duke (NA)
★ ★ ★ ★ Call On Me / Duke (1963)
★ ★ ★ ★ Ain't Nothin' You Can Do / Duke (1964)
★ ★ ★ The Soul of the Man / Duke (NA)
★ ★ ★ ★ ★ The Best of Bobby Bland / Duke (1973)
★ ★ ★ ★ ★ The Best of Bobby Bland, Vol. 2 / Duke (NA)
★ ★ ★ Touch of the Blues / Duke (1968)
★ ★ ★ Spotlighting the Man / Duke (NA)
★ ★ ★ Introspective of the Early Years / Duke (NA)
★ ★ ★ His California Album / ABC (1973) ¶
★ ★ Dreamer / ABC (1974) ¶
★ B.B. King and Bobby Bland / Together for the First Time . . . Live / Imp. (1974)
★ ★ Get On Down with Bobby Bland / ABC (1975) ¶
★ ★ Bobby Bland and B.B. King/Together Again . . . Live / ABC (1976)
★ ★ Reflections in Blue / ABC (1977)
★ ★ Come Fly with Me / ABC (1978)
★ ★ I Feel Good, I Feel Fine / MCA (1979)
★ ★ Sweet Vibrations / MCA (1980)

The black Sinatra? Assuredly the smoothest of the hard R&B singers. Listening to Bland, one might also think that the evolution of rhythm & blues had been arrested when Ray Charles left Atlantic. The difference between them is that what Bland learned from gospel was purely technical, rather than the emotiveness Charles acquired. Bland's art, unique among bluesmen, is one of containment. His style is uncluttered, usually relying only on simple rhythm tracks with a touch of sax and brass backing, although some of his guitarists, notably Mel Brown, have been amazing.

Bland has recorded since the late Fifties, and thankfully, almost everything he has done is in print. Nearly every one of the Duke albums is a treasure, with exquisite moments: the power of Bland's voice, the delicacy of his phrasing, the sweep of what he does with songs as superficially ordinary as "Call On Me" or "It's My Life, Baby." Indeed, several of his hits are standards—"I Pity the Fool" and "Farther up the Road," particularly—although they usually seem overwrought in other hands.

The *Best of* collections provide an excellent overview of his chart hits (mostly the black charts, of course), while *Introspective* sticks closer to 12-bar, and generally more obscure, blues, to achieve a more limited end. *Two Steps* includes, in addition to the classic title track, one of the most heartrending soul ballads ever recorded, "Lead Me On," perhaps the definitive recording of blues crooning. *Call On Me* and *Ain't Nothin' You Can Do* are the kind of records Ray Charles might have made if pop hadn't dominated his career.

Like Charles, Bland began brilliantly when

he went to ABC (not by choice—Duke was sold). *California Album* and *Dreamer* have some of his most sophisticated music. But on the latter, a kind of erosion begins to set in. *Get On Down* attempts to repeat Charles' success with country songs in a blues context and mostly fails. It is charitable to describe the sessions with B.B. King as mistakes— Bland retains most of his energy and skill, King does not. The results are embarrassing for both, particularly since Bland was once B.B.'s valet.

There *are* treasures here. Given record company cutout policies, it might be wise to invest immediately. No telling how long this stuff will remain available. Bland's stature among collectors is already high—how he has missed attracting the young white audience King did is mysterious—and should these recordings be deleted, copies will become very valuable.   — D.M.

THE BLASTERS
★ ★ ★ ★ **The Blasters / Slash (1981)**
Fine raveup anchored in the band's appreciation of what one tune calls "American Music": R&B, rockabilly, Western swing, etc. The group triumphantly unifies elements around a driving backbeat and Phil Alvin's satisfying vocal delivery. LP includes Blasters' "Marie, Marie," a hit of sorts in the U.K. for Shakin' Stevens; "Never No More Blues," a Bob Wills tune convincingly updated; "Hollywood Bed," with its echo of the Joe Turner song of the same name and its well-executed New Orleans second-line rhythms, and finely detailed originals like "No Other Girl" and "Border Radio." Overall, the album has a spirit and verve uniquely its own. Lee Allen, New Orleans saxophonist of Ace Records/Cosimo's Studio glory days, is used to excellent effect. Second sax, Steve Berlin, is no slouch either. The best—if most traditional—band to emerge from L.A.'s new wave.   — G.A.

THE BLEND
■ **The Blend / MCA (1978)**
■ **Anytime Delight / MCA (1979)**
Miserable post-fusion band failed in its attempt to be a funky Steely Dan.   — J.S.

BLIND FAITH
★ ★ ★ **Blind Faith / RSO (1969)**
This forcibly created supergroup was meant to be the rage of 1969, because it included Eric Clapton and Ginger Baker from Cream, Steve Winwood from Traffic and the then-unknown Rick Grech from Family. Two problems intervened: first, businessmen had

engineered the situation from the outside, trying to cash in on reputations, and without regard to musical compatability. Second, the volatility of the performers ensured a one-album life span. It was a disappointment then, of course, but it looks a bit better now, highlighted by Clapton and Winwood's work on "Presence of the Lord" and a nice, gentle version of Buddy Holly's "Well All Right." In its day, the relatively racy cover caused rack jobbers to ban it. Today no one flinches, but then no one manufactures supergroups any more, either.   — D.M.

BLISS BAND
★ ★ ★ **Dinner with Raoul / Col. (1978)** ¶
★ ★ ★ **Neon Smiles / Col. (1979)**
Glib, smart rockers reproduced the Steely Dan formula deftly but missed its commercial content.   — J.S.

RORY BLOCK
★ ★ ★ **Intoxication / Chrys. (1977)** ¶
★ ★ ★ **You're the One / Chrys. (1978)**
Interesting, though rarely inspired, white blues singer. Block knows what to do with her material conceptually but she hasn't quite the heart to make her a major talent. Still, one of the worthier alternatives to the dread Ronstadt-clone syndrome.   — D.M.

BLODWYN PIG
★ ★ ★ ★ **Ahead Rings Out / A&M (1969)**
An early offshoot of the original Jethro Tull, this LP centers on guitarist Mick Abrahams and demon saxist Jack Lancaster. A spinoff of Tull's original hard-rock style, this sophisticated bruiser wears its age well. It was followed by a derivative effort, *Getting to This* (deleted), before the group disbanded.
  — A.N.

BLONDIE
★ ★ ★ **Blondie / Pri. (1977)**
★ ★ ★ **Plastic Letters / Chrys. (1978)**
★ ★ ★ ★ **Parallel Lines / Chrys. (1978)**
★ ★ ★ **Eat to the Beat / Chrys. (1979)**
★ **Autoamerican / Chrys. (1980)**
★ ★ ★ ★ **The Best of Blondie / Chrys. (1981)**
Although they emerged from the same fertile lower Manhattan scene that spawned the Ramones, Talking Heads and Television, Blondie was far more pop-oriented than any of those bands. The band's first efforts were a rough pastiche of girl-group arrangements, surf music, British beat, and just about every other type of pre-psychedelic Sixties sound. It was obvious, though, that like most of the new-wave groups that followed them, Blon-

die's music was as much a product of the distance between the group and its influences as an attempt to create a new synthesis. Unlike David Bowie and Bruce Springsteen, the Seventies rock artists with the greatest reach, Blondie was unable ever to demonstrate enough command or desire to turn its eclecticism into an arresting form of its own.

With *Parallel Lines,* the group did come close to achieving a balance of all its implicit directions. Producer Mike Chapman, formerly half of the Chinn/Chapman songwriting team that wrote many of the British glam-rock hits of the early Seventies, tightened up the sound; the heart of the mix was now Clem Burke's Keith Moon–inspired drumming. But it wasn't the most powerful rock number on the record ("Hangin' on the Telephone") that made Blondie's name; it was the first single to cross over into disco territory from the new-wave side, "Heart of Glass." Its No. 1 success became both boon and bane. The acclaim accorded "Glass" drew Blondie away from what seemed to be its most natural style, and added some musical dissension to an outfit already mildly schizophrenic because of the contradictions raised by Debby Harry's increasing popularity as a face for the Eighties and the "Blondie is a group" angle that the ads (and other band members) initially proclaimed.

Eat to the Beat was a muddled affair, as the band struggled with its new fame by hopping around stylistically. There were moments; "Dreaming" was the zenith of Blondie's rock & roll phase, and the lameness of a disco-beat track like "Atomic" suggested that their hearts were not yet into unabashed commercial pandering. All it meant, it turned out, was that to guarantee another shot at No. 1 with their peculiar fusion of dance styles they would have to turn to the source, in this case Eurodisco conceptualizer and Donna Summer mastermind Giorgio Moroder. He turned the trick with "Call Me," the theme to the film *American Gigolo*; unfortunately his propulsive production was only a vehicle for Harry's voice and revealed no sign of a working band. The dabbling in various forms that had always threatened to disrupt Blondie's tenuous vision became depressingly apparent on *Autoamerican,* where the only artistic gesture seemingly left was parody and camp ("Rapture" and "Faces," respectively). By this time, it apparently no longer mattered; now totally a studio entity, the group had become the darlings of those who champion style over substance (proof positive: the "special remixes" on *Best of,* a

necessity for keeping up with all the latest trends). With solo albums by Harry (a surprising sales dud) and keyboard man Jimmy Destri out, the band's status remained doubtful. But the idea that "Blondie is a group" was dispelled long ago, anyway. — W.K.

BLOODROCK
- **Bloodrock 2 / Cap. (1970)**
- **U.S.A. / Cap. (1971)**
- **Bloodrock 3 / Cap. (1971)**
- **Live / Cap. (1972)** ¶
- **Bloodrock 'n' Roll / Cap. (1975)**

Capitol's stablemate to Grand Funk Railroad, Bloodrock codified the nadir of early-Seventies heavy metal, added horns and became even worse. The absolute bottom of the barrel. — J.S.

BLOOD, SWEAT AND TEARS
★ ★ ★ ★ ★ **Child Is Father to the Man /** Col. (1968)
★ ★ ★ **Blood, Sweat and Tears / Col. (1969)**
★ ★ ★ **Greatest Hits / Col. (1972)**
★ ★ **New Blood / Col. (1972)** ¶
★ **No Sweat / Col. (1973)**
★ ★ **New City / Col. (1973)** ¶
★ **Mirror Image / Col. (1974)** ¶
★ ★ **More Than Ever / Col. (1976)** ¶
★ **Brand New Day / ABC (1977)** ¶
■ **Nuclear Blues / LAX (1980)**

It's easy to forget that Blood, Sweat and Tears began as an Al Kooper project in 1968, as part of a move toward bigger, not necessarily jazzier, rock sounds. *Child,* the only album made under Kooper's direction, is important not only because its jazz and art-song aspects expanded the scope of rock for both audience and musicians but also because it was one of the most perfectly listenable pop albums of its era. The performances are impeccable, and the song selection (numbers by Tim Buckley, Harry Nilsson, Randy Newman, Gerry Goffin and Carole King are included) is nearly perfect.

Blood, Sweat and Tears represents the pinnacle of the group's commercial success: Kooper out, vocalist David Clayton-Thomas (an acquired taste at best) in, and the group took over AM, FM and MOR playlists simultaneously by sticking to rockified Big Band jazz. But Clayton-Thomas left soon after and successive replacements were a constant headache; the band sounds more listless with each new album. Clayton-Thomas, his solo career a bust, returned for *New City, More Than Ever, Brand New Day* and *Nuclear Blues*; it helped, but not much. — A.N.

KEN BLOOM

★ ★ ★ **Ken Bloom** / **Fly. Fish (1978)**
Bloom is an honest-to-god musician's musician whose one album is a nominally folk affair of extremely wide appeal, primarily because he avoids the pitfalls of both "folk" and "virtuosity." He's also shed the burden of growing up in L.A., playing with names like Tom Scott, Tim Weisberg and Jim Gordon while still in high school, joining Michael Murphey's Lewis and Clark Expedition, playing sessions for the Monkees, and backing Linda Ronstadt with the then-fledgling Eagles. That's probably why this album feels like it was a liberating experience for him. Bloom fashions a stylistic sampler with some great twists, like slide concert zither on the blues gem "Sittin' on Top of the World," or the balalaika epic, "Nicholai." Bloom ranges across genres and plays almost anything with reeds (clarinet to Northumbrian small-pipes) or strings (bandura to some fine guitar). Guests include Steve Goodman, singer Claudia Schmidt and Toronto's Original Sloth Band. This could have been a staid lesson in music and cultures, but Bloom mixes styles and instruments with such cheeky aplomb that his LP becomes a dizzying world tour of the most inspired sort. — R.P.

MICHAEL BLOOMFIELD

★ ★ ★ **Triumvirate** / **Col. (1973)** ¶
★ ★ ★ **Analine** / **Tak. (1977)**
★ ★ ★ **If You Love These Blues, Play 'Em As You Please** / **Guitar (1977)** ¶
★ ★ ★ **Mike Bloomfield** / **Tak. (1978)**
★ ★ ★ **Between a Hard Place and the Ground** / **Tak. (1980)**
★ ★ ★ **Living in the Fast Lane** / **Waterh. (1981)**
★ ★ ★ ★ **Cruisin' for a Bruisin'** / **Tak. (1981)**
Following his memorable stints with the Butterfield Blues Band and the Electric Flag, Mike Bloomfield embarked on a solo career plagued by erratic follow-through. *Triumvirate* utilizes the funky blues voice of John Paul Hammond and Dr. John's keyboards to good effect, putting Bloomfield's guitar in the kind of group context where it works best. The result is a good solid blues album from a talented trio of journeymen. *If You Love These Blues* is meant as a blues guitar primer, with Bloomfield effectively evoking the styles of the form's masters. If his scholarly presentation seems silly—the last track features him saying thanks to enough guitarists to choke a horse—his fluid interpretations of various blues styles stand up to repeated listening. Ironically, Bloomfield had begun a full-scale comeback with the excellent *Cruisin'* . . . just before his death in 1981. — J.B.M.

KURTIS BLOW

★ ★ ★ **Kurtis Blow** / **Mer. (1980)**
★ ★ **Deuce** / **Mer. (1981)**
Blow's "The Breaks" was one of the earliest and best of the post-disco rap hits; his debut album also proved him a surprisingly gifted ballad singer. On *Deuce*, unfortunately, most of his promise went to waste on a poor selection of material and some fairly uninspired raps. This is one case of a gold 12-inch single where you might do well to seek out the LP it's on. — D.M.

DAVID BLUE

★ **Stories** / **Asy. (1971)**
★ **Com'n Back for More** / **Asy. (1975)**
★ **Cupid's Arrow** / **Asy. (1976)**
Of all the Dylan imitators of the folk-rock Sixties, David Blue was distinctly the most outrageous, because his emulation was most complete. Fortunately or not, all of those albums (for Elektra) have been deleted. Unfortunately, for sure, in the Seventies series of discs he made for Asylum, Blue's obsession with Dylan had dwindled, and until his death in 1983 he was just another scraggly-voiced singer/songwriter. — D.M.

LITTLE JOE BLUE

★ ★ **Don't Tax Me In** / **Flyr. (NA), Br. imp.**
B.B. King clone. Typical late-Seventies blues. — D.M.

BLUE ANGEL

★ ★ ★ ★ **Blue Angel** / **Poly. (1980)**
Rare delight from the New York new wave: a group steeped in girl-group drama and the Spector aesthetic, with the talent to put it across. The pleasures here are lightweight, but that's appropriate to the genre. If you can imagine the Crystals with punk hair and Fender guitars, you've got the picture. — D.M.

BLUE ASH

★ ★ **Front Page News** / **Play. (1977)** ¶
Blue Ash made a fresh, innocent Beatles-influenced album in the early Seventies, which garnered the Youngstown quartet critical acclaim and no sales. By the time this followup was released, the innocence was gone and the boys just seemed to be grinding it out. — D.M.

BLUE CHEER
★ ★ **Vincebus Eruptum** / Phi. (1968)
From one of the original heavy groups, this remnant of a bygone era is interesting only for their rudely rendered cover of Eddie Cochran's "Summertime Blues," the Top Twenty success of which preempted the release of a potential hit version by the then-struggling Who. — W.K.

THE BLUEGRASS CARDINALS
★ ★ ★ **The Bluegrass Cardinals** / Briar (1977)
Good traditional-style bluegrass quintet features exceptional vocal harmonies. — J.S.

BLUE JUG BAND
★ ★ **Blue Jug** / Ario.-Amer. (NA) ¶
Seattle-based country-rock outfit plays well but owes a little too much to the Band for comfort. — J.S.

BLUE MAGIC
★ ★ ★ **Blue Magic** / Atco (1974) ¶
★ ★ ★ **Magic of the Blue** / Atco (1974) ¶
★ ★ ★ **Thirteen Blue Magic Lane** / Atco (1975) ¶
★ ★ ★ **Mystic Dragons** / Atco (1976) ¶
★ ★ ★ **Message from the Magic** / Atco (1978) ¶
★ ★ **Welcome Back** / Cap. (1981)
★ ★ **Summer Snow** / WMOT (NA)
One of the more successful groups from the Philadelphia sophisticated soul axis, Blue Magic crossed over after strong disco response and the popularity of its 1974 single "Sideshow." The band follows the Philly formula perfectly—Norman Harris produces, MFSB is the backup band. — J.S.

BLUE OYSTER CULT
★ ★ ★ ★ **Blue Oyster Cult** / Col. (1972)
★ ★ ★ **Tyranny and Mutation** / Col. (1973)
★ ★ ★ **Secret Treaties** / Col. (1974)
★ ★ **On Your Feet or on Your Knees** / Col. (1975)
★ ★ ★ ★ **Agents of Fortune** / Col. (1976)
★ ★ ★ ★ **Spectres** / Col. (1977)
★ ★ **Some Enchanted Evening** / Col. (1978)
★ ★ ★ **Mirrors** / Col. (1979)
★ ★ ★ **Cultosaurus Erectus** / Col. (1980)
★ ★ ★ **Fire of Unknown Origin** / Col. (1981)
When BOC made its LP debut critics raved about its arcane and sinister lyrics, but Eric Bloom's vocals were barely audible, much less intelligible. What really made it magnetic was the hook-laden music with its parade of Buck Dharma's multilayered guitars and the Cult's reputation as a neo-fascist, vampirish New York band that would sooner suck your blood than take your money. The first three albums occasionally go off the deep end trying to preserve the claims to maniacal metalism, but when they stick, their sensation is nothing short of sexual.

On Your Feet or on Your Knees fails as an attempt to transfer the Cult's wondrously assaultive stage antics to vinyl, but not without a necksnapping riff or two. Better to wait for a video disc. *Agents of Fortune* represents BOC's most diversified offering, from Allen Lanier's doo-wop tango, "True Confessions," to the classic Cult relic, "(Don't Fear) The Reaper," a Top Ten single. Patti Smith co-wrote two songs, "Debbie Denise" and "Revenge of Vera Gemini," and has a watery, Ronnie Spector–like guest vocal on the latter. A new direction for the Cult, explored further on *Spectres*, featuring the bone-chilling anthems "I Love the Night" and "Death Valley Nights." But *Some Enchanted Evening* was a premature live set that indicated BOC might be running out of ideas, a notion which *Mirrors, Cultosaurus Erectus* and *Fire of Unknown Origin* went a long way toward confirming. — M.G.

BLUE RIDDIM BAND
★ ★ ★ **Restless Spirit** / Fly. Fish (1981)
Blue Riddim's synthesis of reggae rhythms and Sixties soul horn charts and vocal styles makes perfect sense when you consider that many reggae greats cut their teeth on American soul music. The record's sometimes flaccid composing and occasionally stiff studio performances can't keep me from hearing them as an ace party band. Respectable American reggae. — R.F.G.

THE BLUE RIDGE RANGERS
★ ★ ★ **The Blue Ridge Rangers** / Fan. (1973)
When *The Blue Ridge Rangers* was released, it seemed like a parenthesis in John Fogerty's career—a clearing of the air after the collapse of Creedence Clearwater Revival, a taking stock of past debts (in this case, to C&W and gospel) and future prospects (a rich and prolific solo career, one presumed). That parenthesis, however, has lasted more than eight years (including his second solo LP, *John Fogerty*) and what originally seemed like an aside has become the topic sentence in Fogerty's post-Creedence career. Fogerty is the Blue Ridge Rangers—its drummer, bass player, fiddler, backup chorus, horn section and more. It's a solo album with a vengeance—a one-man virtuoso act, a slap across rock's collective will, the product

of obsessive perfectionism. Too much of the album sounds mechanical (particularly the drumming), too much of it is plodding (Fogerty's song choices are imaginatively obscure, but often dull), but when it catches fire ("I Ain't Never," "Hearts of Stone," "She Thinks I Still Care"), *Blue Ridge Rangers* no longer seems like a retreat from rock & roll, but a reinvestment in its mythic past. For that it's worth it. — K.R.

THE BLUES BAND
★ ★ ★ **Ready! / Ari. (1980), Br. imp.**
★ ★ ★ **Official Blues Band Bootleg Album / Ari. (1980), Br. imp.**
Former Manfred Mann vocalist Paul Jones fronts a competent combo of long-standing blues academics for the "pleasure of playing." While not always inspired, their treatment of such old classics as "Diddy Wah Diddy," "Boom Boom Out Goes the Lights" and "Hallelujah I Love Her So," plus a handful of originals, at least has a certain charm and integrity. — ML.H.

THE BLUES BROTHERS
★ ★ ★ **Briefcase Full of Blues / Atl. (1978)**
★ **Made in America / Atl. (1980)**
★ ★ **The Blues Brothers—Original Soundtrack / Atl. (1980)**
★ ★ **Best of the Blues Brothers / Atl. (1981)**
When *Saturday Night Live* stars John Belushi and Dan Aykroyd first began performing their inspired shtick on television as Jake and Elwood Blues, white blues singers with a checkered past, who could have guessed that they would carry it as far as three records and a $30 million movie? Not anyone who was actually listening to the rather pale renditions of soul music on these albums. The Top Ten *Briefcase Full of Blues,* recorded live (as is *Made in America*), seems fairly sincere in its love for the form and features a tight band with former MGs Steve Cropper and Duck Dunn and James Cotton Band guitarist Matt Murphy. Not even those fine players can save *Made in America,* though, nor do passable performances from Aretha Franklin, Ray Charles and James Brown on the soundtrack prevent the feeling that tribute was turning into rip-off. — W.K.

BLUE SKY BOYS
★ ★ ★ **The Blue Sky Boys / Blueb. (1976) ¶**
★ ★ ★ **Blue Sky Boys / Roun. (1976)**
★ ★ ★ **Bluegrass Mountain Music / Camd. (NA)**
★ ★ ★ **Sunny Side of Life / Roun. (1973)**
★ ★ ★ **Together Again / Star. (NA)**

From 1936 (when they made their first recordings) until 1951, some of the most authentic American music around came from two North Carolina brothers. Bill Bolick, who played mandolin, and his guitarist brother Earl produced some of the finest country harmony singing ever heard. Much of their material was traditional British and American ballads, often very religious ones.

By the time they retired in 1951, after making 124 recordings, country music's audience had changed and there was no longer a great demand for the mournful mountain ballads. Now Bill works as a postal inspector in North Carolina and Earl is an employee of Lockheed Aircraft in Georgia. — C.F.

BLUE STEEL
★ ★ ★ **No More Lonely Nights / Inf. (1979) ¶**
★ ★ ★ **Nothing But Time / Asy. (1981)**
★ ★ ★ **Slip Away / Asy. (1981)**
While thin-sounding outfits like the Iron City Houserockers get the bar-band raves, this much more full-throated group is ignored, probably because nobody has done anything much with this offshoot of Southern hard rock since Skynyrd's plane went down. On *Nothing But Time,* they turn in a fine if excessively literal cover of Roy Orbison's "Oh Pretty Woman," and while the rest of the writing certainly isn't up to that standard (or Skynyrd's) it's good enough to justify the allusions. — D.M.

BLURT
★ **In Berlin / Ruby (1981)**
Live debut LP features Ted Milton's furious sax and angry, tuneless vocals running rampant over an almost-tape-loop-repetitive guitar-plus-drums rhythm section. At its best, Blurt manages to convey the feeling of Them's "Gloria" taken to its farthest imaginable extreme; at its worst, it's only grating noise. For anarchists only. — D.S.

BOATZ
★ ★ ★ **Boatz / Capri. (1979)**
An offshoot of the LeBlanc & Carr Band, Boatz are a curious pop duo, considering their ties to the Southern scene. This is intelligent and smooth FM radio pop, a tad low-key perhaps, but far more luscious and smart than your average stab at AOR radio acceptance. — R.P.

BOB B. SOXX AND THE BLUE JEANS
★ ★ ★ **Bob B. Soxx and the Blue Jeans / Spector (NA), Br. imp.**
Phil Spector's production was at its most

keenly driven rhythm & blues pitch on Bob B. Soxx's hits, "Zip a Dee Doo Dah" and "Why Do Lovers Break Each Other's Hearts"—that is, it was hardly bombastic at all, just light, pre-Motown teenage soul. The group isn't really outstanding enough to earn its own LP, but acquits itself handsomely on the stronger material at hand, thanks in no small part to anonomyous member *extraordinaire* Darlene Love. — D.M.

ANGELA BOFILL

★ ★ **Angie** / Ari./GRP **(1978)**
★ ★ ★ **Angel of the Night** / Ari./GRP **(1979)**
★ ★ **Something About You** / Ari. **(1981)**
Angela Bofill has an exceptional voice, one that combines the accuracy and open tone of classical singing with the emotional inflection of R&B. But for some reason, she seems to confine this wonderfully expressive instrument to tiresome psuedo-funk and platitudinous ballads. *Angel of the Night* is the only album that consistently features her strengths, and even then only 60 percent of the time. What a waste. — J.D.C.

DOCK BOGGS

★ ★ ★ **Dock Boggs, Vol. 2** / Folk. **(1965)**
★ ★ ★ **Dock Boggs Interviews** / Folk. **(1965)**
★ ★ ★ **Dock Boggs, Vol. 3** / Folk. **(1970)**
Traditional Virginia mountain musician— banjo and voice—who recorded in 1927 and 1928, then returned to work in the mines until rediscovered by Mike Seeger in 1963. These recordings (oddly, *Volume 1* is no longer available) chronicle his knowledge of the area's music and social lore—the interviews conducted by Seeger are fascinating, displaying some evidence of what mountain music must have been like before it was popularized by Jimmie Rodgers and the Carter Family and broadcast out of the area. Because Boggs is a rough-edged, unsophisticated singer and the instrumentation is minimal, he may be hard for rock-oriented listeners to listen to, but anyone with an interest in American music would do well to hear him. — D.M.

HAMILTON BOHANNON

★ ★ ★ **Stop and Go** / Dakar **(1973)**
★ ★ ★ **Keep on Dancin'** / Dakar **(1974)**
★ ★ ★ **Insides Out** / Dakar **(1975)**
★ ★ ★ **Mighty Bohannon** / Dakar **(1975)** ¶
★ ★ ★ **Dance Your Ass Off** / Dakar **(1976)**
★ ★ **Phase II** / Mer. **(1977)**
★ ★ ★ **On My Way** / Mer. **(1978)**
★ ★ ★ **Summertime Groove** / Mer. **(1978)**
★ ★ **Cut Loose** / Mer. **(1979)**

★ ★ **Music in the Air** / Mer. **(1980)**
★ ★ **One Step Ahead** / Phantom **(NA)**
★ ★ **Too Hot to Hold** / Mer. **(NA)**
Former Motown drummer Bohannon was one of the first to perceive the tremendous possibilities of disco for percussionists. He did it to death, stomping out a whole series of big-foot beat, highlighted by the 1975 hit, "Foot-Stompin' Music," and an array of similar black Sandy Nelson titles—"Disco Stomp," "Bohannon's Beat (Pts. 1 & 2)," etc. — D.M.

GORDON BOK

★ ★ **Peter Kagan and the Wind** / Folk-Leg. **(1972)**
★ ★ ★ **Bay of Fundy** / Folk-Leg. **(1976)**
A Maine fisherman, sailor and folklorist, the majority of Bok's traditional and original songs and tales are concerned with the sea. "Peter Kagan," a magnificent fable, is based on tales of the seal-folk. "Bay of Fundy" is probably his best-known composition. Bok's association with the Hudson River Restoration sloop, *Clearwater,* brought him to new audiences via such shipmates as Pete Seeger and Don McLean. *Bay of Fundy,* with Ann Mayo Muir singing harmonies, is a more appropriate introduction, though the fifteen-minute story of "Peter Kagan" will no doubt enter traditional sea lore. — I.M.

MICHAEL BOLOTIN

★ ★ **Michael Bolotin** / RCA **(1975)**
★ **Every Day of My Life** / RCA **(1976)**
Sounding like Joe Cocker on the first of these, Bolotin can be powerful but just as forced. His songwriting, however, is soulful, as is his backup: Wayne Perkins, Wilbur Bascomb and Dave Sanborn. *Every Day of My Life* gets away from Cocker, but doesn't do much else. Save Billy Elworthy's raw guitar, the playing is very ordinary. Both records suffer from the singer's poor cover versions. — C.W.

THE BOMBERS

★ ★ **Bombers** / West End **(1978)**
★ **Bombers 2** / West End **(1979)**
This funk act came close to having a dance-rock hit in 1979 with "(Everybody) Get Dancin'." Nothing came of it. — D.M.

JOHNNY BOND

★ ★ ★ **The Best of Johnny Bond** / Star. **(NA)**
Journeyman country singer has had long career, beginning as a Gene Autry sidekick in the Forties. Starday material is from the Six-

ties, and includes his biggest hits, "10 Little Bottles" and "Three Sheets in the Wind." Among rock & rollers, however, Bond is best known for "Hot Rod Lincoln," a 1952 proto-rockabilly hit revived in the early Seventies by Commander Cody and His Lost Planet Airmen. Bond's original, worth finding, isn't here. — D.M.

GARY U.S. BONDS
★ ★ ★ **Dedication / EMI (1981)**
★ ★ ★ ★ ★ **U.S. Bonds' Greatest Hits / Legr. (1963/1981)**
Whether recorded on a spaceship, in a remote cotton field in the dead of night, or simply in Frank Guida's Norfolk, Virginia, studio, "Quarter to Three," "School Is Out," "New Orleans," "Dear Lady Twist" and "Not Me" are some of the wildest, most raucous hits of the post-plane crash, pre-Beatles rock & roll interstice. That is, these songs, big gobs of sound somewhere on the fringe of rhythm & blues, are even more mythic than most oldies, because they are rock 'n' roll from the period when there was supposed to be no rock 'n' roll, and because they sounded ancient and weird even when hot off the presses. Despite producer Guida's sometimes obtuse and invariably self-promoting packaging, the Legrand LP is a must.

Dedication is one of the most successful comeback albums in rock & roll history, which has a great deal to do with producers Bruce Springsteen and Miami Steve, upon whom Bonds was a major influence. Springsteen contributed three original songs, including the hit, "This Little Girl," and added a duet with Bonds on a pumped-up "Jolé Blon." Van Zandt wrote only one song, "Daddy's Come Home," but it's the centerpiece of an album that sets out to prove that Bonds is not merely capable of repeating past formulas but can also stand as a modern interpreter (which he does on the best of the other material, particularly Jackson Browne's "The Pretender" and Bob Dylan's "From a Buick Six"). Not quite so glorious as the old days, *Dedication* comes close enough to be worth the attention of anyone who still remembers. — D.M.

JUKE BOY BONNER
★ ★ ★ **I'm Going Back to the Country / Arhoo. (1968) ¶**
★ **The Adventures of Juke Boy Bonner / Home C. (NA)**
★ ★ ★ **Legacy of the Blues / Sonet (NA)**
★ ★ **The One Man Trio / Fly. Fish (1979)**
★ ★ ★ **The Struggle / Arhoo. (NA)**

Texas/California bluesman of the Forties; relatively formless songs, effectively performed in the Lightnin' Hopkins mold, but with a tinge of black social consciousness. — D.M.

KARLA BONOFF
★ ★ ★ **Karla Bonoff / Col. (1977) ¶**
★ ★ ★ **Restless Nights / Col. (1979)**
Karla Bonoff came to prominence when her friend Linda Ronstadt chose three of her best songs ("If He's Ever Near," "Someone to Lay Down beside Me" and "Lose Again") for inclusion on *Hasten Down the Wind.* And on her debut LP, Bonoff pleasantly surprised almost everyone by doing warm, even versions of her own songs. Those three songs, plus a rendition of "Home" that stood on its own, proved Bonoff's self-sufficiency. Her admixture of country lamentation with urban neurosis was apt for the times, and she was quickly established as a mass-audience heartthrob with both intelligence and accessibility. — F.S.

THE BONZO DOG BAND
★ ★ ★ **Gorilla / Imper. (1967) ¶**
★ ★ **Keynsham / Imper. (1969) ¶**
★ ★ ★ ★ **Beast of the Bonzos / U.A. (1971)**
★ ★ ★ ★ ★ **The History of the Bonzos / U.A. (1974)**
When the Bonzo Dog Band first appeared in 1967, it was immediately taken to heart by the handful of critics, humorists and cultists who remain its only fans. Who had time for an absurdist horn band that sang about Mickey and Minnie Mouse's offspring or did a gurgling version of "I Left My Heart in San Francisco"? *Gorilla* was a spotty but innovative beginning—the group hit its peak on the now-deleted *Urban Spaceman* and *Tadpoles,* then adopted a more straightforward rock approach for *Keynsham,* which was problematic: the comedy suffered, and the music was pretty forgettable.

After *Keynsham,* the group split—Neil Innes and Viv Stanshall attempted to reform with the (deleted) *Let's Make Up and Be Friendly,* but without success—leaving us with the two anthologies as a legacy. *Beast* is a fine sampler, but *History* is indispensable for anyone who wants to understand such later comedic developments as "Monty Python's Flying Circus" and "Saturday Night Live." — M.G.

BOOKER T. AND THE MGs
★ ★ ★ ★ **The Best of Booker T. and the MGs / Atl. (1968) ¶**
★ ★ ★ ★ **Green Onions / Atl. (1968), Br. imp.**

★ ★ ★ **Booker T. and the MGs Greatest Hits / Stax (1974)**
★ **Universal Language / Asy. (1977)** ¶
★ ★ ★ **Free Rider / Stax (NA)**
A quartet consisting of organist Booker T. Jones, guitarist Steve Cropper, bassist Duck Dunn and drummer Al Jackson, the MGs set the style for soul backup and instrumental groups of the Sixties. As accompanists on a multitude of Stax hits, they were impeccable in their taste and restraint, remarkable for their simplicity. As a solo unit, their instrumentals (the best known of which is "Green Onions") stuck closely to simple melodic statement, incorporating a tightly structured rhythm approach, Cropper's thick, fuzzy chording, and Jones' organ embellishments.

The group went its separate ways in 1972—Dunn and Jackson continued as Memphis session players, most notably for Al Green; Jones dueted with Priscilla Coolidge, his wife and sister of Rita Coolidge; Cropper went into production—but reunited for an abortive LP on Asylum, shortly after Jackson's unfortunate murder. — J.MC.

BOOKER T. AND PRISCILLA
★ **Chronicles / A&M (1973)**
★ **Evergreen / Epic (1977)**
After the MGs broke up in 1972, Booker T. Jones, their organist, moved to California, where he recorded tepid country-flavored duets with his wife, Priscilla Coolidge, and a solo LP of no discernible direction. — J.MC.

BOOMTOWN RATS
★ ★ ★ **The Boomtown Rats / Mer. (1977)**
★ ★ ★ **A Tonic for the Troops / Col. (1979)**
★ ★ ★ **The Fine Art of Surfacing / Col. (1979)**
★ ★ ★ **Mondo Bongo / Col. (1980)**
Bob Geldof looked like a burgeoning rock & roll hero on his first couple of albums, released in the later part of the punk explosion, but was really closer to the bar/pub-band syndrome of Graham Parker and Bruce Springsteen. "Joey's on the Street Again," included on both *The Boomtown Rats* and the patched-together *A Tonic for the Troops,* is fine neo-Spectorian drama.

But even on that second album Geldof had already begun to decay into one of rock's most obnoxious posers, a nasty, cynical cross between Mick Jagger and Alice Cooper, with all the principles of the former and all the compassion of the latter. With the exception of one great song, "I Don't

Like Mondays," and one listenable one, "Elephant's Graveyard," *Surfacing* is all too self-descriptive and *Mondo Bongo* as jive as its name. "Pretentious and exploitative" isn't anybody's idea of a recommendation—I hope. — D.M.

DEBBY BOONE
★ **You Light up My Life / War. (1977)**
■ **Midstream / War. (1978)** ¶
■ **Debby Boone / War. (1979)**
■ **Love Has No Reason / War. (1980)**
■ **Savin' It Up / War. (1981)**
"You Light Up My Life," the best-selling single in Warner Bros. history, paces a hastily assembled debut from Pat Boone's daughter. Outtakes from the Boone sisters are used as filler. But even this second-generation schlock-and-roll is better than the drivel that makes up the rest of Boone's catalogue. — F.S.

PAT BOONE
★ ★ ★ **Sixteen Great Performances / ABC (NA)**
★ ★ **Texas Woman / Hits. (NA)** ¶
★ **The Lord's Prayer and Other Great Hymns / Dot (NA)** ¶
★ **Just the Way I Am / LLN (1981)**
Pat Boone is probably among the top five of soulless performers. But for those who were white, middle class, American, 'twixt twelve and twenty during the Fifties and *not* rebellious, the man has a certain archetypal heaviness that can't be denied. For what it is, his collection of golden oldies is pretty damn good. It's docked one star, however, for containing a couple of ringers that weren't hits and one, "Speedy Gonzales," that was racist even if it was a hit. Make that Thirteen Great Performances. The religious album on Dot is best ignored; Boone and his family have done much better work on the small gospel labels.

Texas Woman succeeds with its stew of right-wing politics, personalized Christian music and countryish L.A. middle-of-the-road. Whether anyone wants such a stew remains to be seen, but fans of American paradoxes should note that Mr. White Bucks also recorded on Motown's country label. — T.S.

BOOTSY'S RUBBER BAND
★ ★ ★ **Stretchin' Out in Bootsy's Rubber Band / War. (1976)** ¶
★ ★ ★ ★ **Ahh . . . the Name is Bootsy, Baby! / War. (1977)** ¶
★ ★ ★ ★ **Bootsy: Player of the Year / War. (1978)**

★ ★ ★ **This Boot Is Made for Funk In /
War. (1979)**
★ ★ ★ **Ultra Wave / War. (1980)**
It's like living inside some Ralph Bakshi cartoon—an intergalactic street world inhabited
by everything from pimps to Martians. And
it sounds like Hawkwind cloned with Sly all
transmuted through *Bitches Brew.*

Ask William Collins, a.k.a. Bootsy, why
he split Parliament/Funkadelic to form his
own brand of New Age Funk and he'll tell
you—the kids made him do it. The little
ones who turn on without drugs—they're
called "geepies," wee folk who defected from
the P/Funk camp to enroll in Bootsy's psy-
choticbumpschool. Actually, when Collins'
Hendrix-like charisma and amazingly elastic
space bass started garnering too much attention in P/Funk, George Clinton decided to
add another act to the P/Funk roster to be
led by Bootsy Collins. Pre-Funkadelic,
Bootsy was James Brown's bassist in the incomparable JB's, along with the formidable
hornmen Maceo Parker and Fred Wesley.
When Collins announced his solo move, they
signed aboard. Wesley's Rubber Band charts
are some of the most imaginative and subtle
funk you'll ever behold—his and Parker's
oblique maneuvers weaving in and around
the rhythm section's eternal pump are no
less than hypnotic.

And Bootsy's into Stars, so his specially
equipped bass—a Lamborghini amongst Che-
vettes—was custom-built into the shape of
Winky Dink. He's also into nursery rhymes,
so on the second album his hound-dog rock
comes packaged in the form of tunes like
"The Pinocchio Theory." The track swings
so hard *it hurts.* "Rubber Duckie" introduces Collins' vision of a Robin Hood who
"steals from the rich and gives to poor little
ole me!" It's all sorta zany, you can dance
to it and . . . I'm sure you get the point.
Without it, you just ain't with it.
— B.M.

THE BOPPERS
★ **The Boppers / Fan. (1978)**
Ten-piece funk unit with enough ideas to
keep, at most, two of them busy (the idea
they lifted from the Commodores, who got it
from Sly, and the one they overheard Miles
Davis suggesting on *Bitches Brew*). — D.M.

EARL BOSTIC
★ ★ ★ **Earl Bostic Plays / Star. (NA)**
★ ★ ★ **Earl Bostic: 14 Original Greatest
Hits / King (NA)**
Swinging alto saxophonist best known for his

1951 hit, "Flamingo." Bostic's biting style is
well worth hearing for genre fans, or for
those who believe Clarence Clemons sprang
from the head of a muse. — D.M.

BOSTON
★ ★ ★ **Boston / Epic (1976)**
★ ★ ★ **Don't Look Back / Epic (1978)**
Described as a cross between Led Zeppelin
and Yes, Boston's not nearly that gruesome.
Most of its harmonic sense comes from L.A.,
which balances out all the heaviness, and
guitarist/writer Tom Scholz uses his special-
effects guitar tastefully. *Boston* could use
more consistent songwriting, though that
didn't stop the debut from selling 6 million
copies. It did, however, prevent the lackluster *Don't Look Back,* from qualifying as anything but a failure. Boston has a terrific formula, which it executes competently, but
without inspiration, it may never amount to
much. — J.MO.

THE BOTHY BAND
★ ★ ★ ★ **Tommy Peoples and Paul Brady—
The High Part of the Road/Shan. (1976)**
★ ★ ★ ★ ★ **Best of the Bothy Band/Green
L. (1981)**
Best of is the first American release of the
top Irish traditional band, featuring Donal
Lunney on guitar and bouzouki and Tommy
Peoples on fiddle. The Bothy Band chal-
lenged the Chieftains as the prime represen-
tatives of traditional Irish music. The Peo-
ples/Brady offshoot album is a virtuoso's
tour de force. — D.D.

BOULDER
★ ★ **Boulder / Elek. (NA)**
The great thing about bands who use place
names for their moniker is you know exactly
where to tell them to go back to. — R.P.

DENNIS BOVELL (BLACKBEARD)
★ ★ ★ **I Wah Dub / RDC (1980)**
★ ★ ★ **Brain Damage / Phono. (1981)**
Someday people may call Dennis Bovell a
genius. Certainly his ability would have been
recognized by now if he had been creating in
a medium other than reggae. As leader of
Matumbi and one of the U.K.'s best producers, he continually stretches reggae toward
soca, rock, jazz, and funk. *Brain Damage*
moves easily from one musical style to another to produce many inspiring moments
limited by uneven material. — R.F.G.

BRIAN BOWER
★ ★ ★ **The View from Home / Fly. Fish
(1978)**

★ ★ ★ **Home on the Road / Fly. Fish (1980)**
Performances from Pacific Northwest auto-
harpist that avoid folkie lethargy by means
of innovation and openness to contemporary
sources. Bower, an occasional session player,
calls on a host of others for aid on his LPs,
including Steve Goodman and Jim Post.
— G.A.

DAVID BOWIE
★ ★ **Space Oddity / RCA (1972)**
★ ★ ★ **The Man Who Sold the World /
RCA (1972)** ¶
★ **Images 1966–1967 / Lon. (1973)** ¶
★ ★ **Don't Be Fooled by the Name / PRT
(1981), Br. imp.**
For a while it seemed as if David Bowie
would be to the Seventies what Elvis Presley
was to the Fifties, or the Beatles to the Sixties: a charismatic figure who would single-
handedly make over the entire pop music
scene in his image. Bowie did (and still does)
have charisma aplenty, but looking back on
his recorded output it's sometimes difficult to
understand what all the screaming was
about.

Judging from interviews, Bowie himself
hasn't always understood what he was doing.
His music reflects indecision; no other pop
idol has embraced and abandoned such a variety of styles. The nervous shedding of one
persona after another, however, has kept
Bowie the most fascinating and unpredictable rock performer from the Seventies to
the present.

Don't Be Fooled by the Name is a 10-inch
LP of Bowie's six sides cut for Pye in 1966.
The cover shot, which isn't as honest as
the album title, depicts Bowie during his
1978 tour, but the music is insipid Sixties
mod pop with hardly anything going for it
except historical post facto appeal. Strictly a
curio.

Images 1966–1967, dredged up in the first
flush of Bowiemania, is an embarrassing reissue of the artiste's first solo album padded
out to two LPs with a few rancid outtakes.
The songs are horrible little vignettes of people and places brimming over with wordly
philosophy and insights of which only a precious twenty-year-old is capable. Bowie's
vocal resemblance to Anthony Newley is
painfully obvious here; more importantly,
the schlocky music throughout most of
the album indicates Bowie's lack of
commitment to rock, if not downright
contempt for the "scene" (stated bluntly on
"Join the Gang"). In that respect, the *Images* songs mark the beginning of Bowie's

ongoing odyssey toward self-knowledge—and
little else.

Space Oddity and *The Man Who Sold the
World* are also reissues—they were originally
released on Mercury in 1969 and 1970, respectively—but their continued availability is
more justifiable than *Images.* Despite the
melodic hit single that leads off *Space Oddity,* the album marks a return to rock from
cabaret country. Tough music supports
tough lyrics on "Unwashed and Somewhat
Slightly Dazed" and "The Cygnet Committee" (probably influenced by William S. Bur-
roughs). An occasional imagistic misfire
points up Bowie's post-hippie sensibility, as
do the meandering, overlong songs. Still, an
improvement on "The Laughing Gnome"—
and his first U.S. hit album, in 1973.

The Man Who Sold the World continues
in the *Space Oddity* vein with even harder
music, thanks to producer Tony Visconti's
domineering bass and Mick Ronson's razzle-
dazzle lead guitar. For the first time Bowie
comes across as his own man, not a derivative hanger-on. His literate compositions—
still overwhelmingly narrative—clash nicely against amelodic "tunes"; there's even
an aharmonic jam on "She Shook Me
Cold." Heavy metal with an art-school
education.

★ ★ ★ **Hunky Dory / RCA (1972)**
★ ★ ★ **The Rise and Fall of Ziggy Stardust
and the Spiders from Mars / RCA (1972)**
★ ★ ★ **Aladdin Sane / RCA (1973)**
★ ★ **Pin-Ups / RCA (1973)**
★ ★ **Diamond Dogs / RCA (1974)**
★ **David Live / RCA (1974)**
Superficially, what was most surprising about
Hunky Dory following *The Man Who Sold
the World* was its rejection of sludge-rock
rock for sparse musical textures (Ronson is
here, but almost inaudible behind Rick
Wakeman's piano) and a return to hum-
mable melodies.

Hunky Dory presents a blatant roll call of
influences: "Andy Warhol," "Song for Bob
Dylan," the warmed-over Lou Reed of
"Queen Bitch." Bowie's acknowledgment of
his heroes is refreshing, but the songs remain
wordy and flaccid. As a slight consolation,
the introspective lyrics mesh (for a change)
with the delicate music. The effect is of an
artist who's shucked one identity without
finding another. (Was Bowie's version of Biff
Rose's drippy "Fill Your Heart" on the
level? What about his own love song to his
son, "Kooks"?) Only obsessive references to
"Homo Superior" ("Oh! You Pretty
Things") and supermen ("Quicksand") point
the way to the future.

Bowie's infamous concept/persona emerged full-blown on *Ziggy Stardust.* The album's insinuating tunes are plastered with potent outer-space/homosexual imagery ("Lady Stardust," "Ziggy Stardust," "Moonage Daydream," "Suffragette City"), with a little apocalypse thrown in for good measure ("Five Years," "Rock 'n' Roll Suicide"). Unfortunately, the vocals, more confident than ever before, are done in by thin production. The melodramatic "Rock 'n' Roll Suicide" can be seen as an extension of Bowie's Anthony Newley shtick. *A plus ça change . . .*

Aladdin Sane, in tandem with the "Space Oddity" single, finally established Bowie in the American marketplace. This time it all came together: Bowie buried his voice in the mix, and the band played hard rock that *sounded* like hard rock. The Bowie/Ziggy persona chattered Dylanesque fuzz for lyrics (and he still hadn't risen above an occasional gaffe: cf. "Lady Grinning Soul's cool canasta"), but it fit well with the music. Mike Garson's cocktail piano betrayed Bowie's lack of faith in rock, but not many people worried about it.

Aladdin Sane included a camped-up version of the Rolling Stone's "Let's Spend the Night Together," and an original, "Jean Genie" (Genet, geddit?), that sounded like the Yardbirds performing "I'm a Man." Bowie proudly displayed his Sixties London roots on *Pin-Ups,* which consisted entirely of songs of the era transmogrified into Ziggy-music via wooden, passionless vocals over chaotic playing. Its hollow-rock is successful inasmuch as Bowie's forte has always been interpretation, refining others' ideas. His stilted, tortuous delivery and super-charged arrangements of Who/Pretty Things/Kinks/etc. classics form an affectionate take-off—a tribute that sidesteps nostalgia.

Bowie's next "serious" album, *Diamond Dogs,* suffers from an Orwellian doomsday concept and the departure of Ronson, leaving Bowie as sole guitarist. The resulting de-emphasis on guitar makes for restrained music—the spotlight shifts to Garson's elegant keyboards—while Bowie flounders around in Burroughs-influenced bombast ("We Are the Dead," "Future Legend"). The cuts that have aged the best—"Rebel Rebel" and the title track—are Rolling Stones songs by any other name. *Diamond Dogs* was one Ziggy album too many, and Bowie knew it.

A change was apparent on the two-record *David Live,* with Pablo Rosario's congas and David Sanborn's sax adding Latin/R&B elements. Otherwise, this souvenir of the 1974 *Diamond Dogs* tour finds Bowie in strained voice on material drawn almost entirely from that LP, *Aladdin Sane* and *Ziggy Stardust.* For all the liner-note boasts about "no studio overdubs," the album just doesn't pack much excitement. Two previously unrecorded (by Bowie) songs forced collectors to shell out for this one: an affected "All the Young Dudes," his contribution to Mott the Hoople, and Eddie Floyd's "Knock on Wood"—another portent of things to come.

★ ★ ★ **Young Americans / RCA (1975)**
★ ★ ★ **Station to Station / RCA (1976)**
★ ★ **Changesonebowie / RCA (1976)**
Young Americans came as a shock to tarted-up Bowie fans who had yet to learn that their hero changes musical tactics the way a guitarist changes strings. Except for "Fame" and "Across the Universe," the album was recorded at Philadelphia's house of funk, Sigma Sound, with session musicians (notably bassist Willy Weeks and drummer Andy Newmark) who know their groove thang. As always with Bowie, lyrics are subordinate to overall feel; the running commentary in front of the bubbling music mainly allows Bowie to emote, a trait that began to appear on *Diamond Dogs.* The smooth approach often turns merely slippery (like the marble-featured portrait of the artist as disco idol on the cover), but "Fame" gave Bowie his only No. 1 single in the U.S. and provided a depressing epitaph for cocomposer/vocalist John Lennon.

For his next trick, Bowie integrated rock and soul. There's plenty of loud guitar (Earl Slick's) on *Station to Station,* yet the sensibility behind "Golden Years" (another hit single) and "TVC15" soars over petty musical boundaries. The thin white duke develops engine trouble only when buffeted by Nina Simone's "Wild Is the Wind."

Changesonebowie is an instant-product assemblage of singles sides from a decidedly nonsingles artist. All the selections but one—"John, I'm Only Dancing," a pleasant ditty from Bowie's "I think I'm gay" period—are on LPs where they make more sense, but *Changesone* is a good showcase for Bowie the pop craftsman. It was also a last hurrah for such music.

★ ★ ★ **Low / RCA (1977)**
★ ★ ★ **"Heroes" / RCA (1977)**
★ ★ **Stage / RCA (1978)** ¶
Low marked the beginning of a collaborative period with Brian Eno. The album is more than half instrumental, mostly quiet elec-

tronic drones reflecting Eno-esque theory. Regardless of who influenced whom, this was quite a bold move. The vocal tracks are jagged scraps of meaning set to disruptive musical phrases. *Low* is literally the sound of psychosis—disturbingly effective.

"Heroes" refined *Low's* outlook. There are more ethereal instrumentals (almost a side's worth) contrasted with disjunctive lyrics. The most coherent of these, the title tune, found popular favor; elsewhere Bowie is just too obscure to connect on any but the most rarefied levels.

Stage, another double-live set, might seem redundant, but it triumphs over the earlier *David Live.* Bowie is in much better voice than before, and the album (which lists no recording date or location) is organized sensibly: one side *Ziggy Stardust* tunes, one side from the *Young Americans/Station to Station* transition, and two sides of *Low/"Heroes"* material. This time the band sounds hot, and even the thorny newer compositions come off well. Intentionally or not, *Stage* conveniently seals off another era of Bowie.

★ ★ ★ ★ **Lodger / RCA (1979)** ¶
★ ★ ★ ★ **Scary Monsters / RCA (1980)**
★ ★ **Changestwobowie / RCA (1981)**
With these three albums Bowie seems (from this cramped perspective) to have reached full artistic maturity. *Lodger* dazzles with baroque arrangements, flawless pacing and—for once—lyrics that don't fall apart on the inner sleeve. Still obsessed with psychological dysfunction, Bowie widens his scope to project alienation on a global level ("African Night Flight," "Move On," "Yassassin") as well as through intriguing vignettes ("D.J.," "Look Back in Anger," "Boys Keep Swinging," "Repetition"). The best realized of his concept albums (even *Ziggy Stardust* was half-baked in that respect), *Lodger's* words and music work with, not against (or in spite of), each other.

Scary Monsters continued Bowie's winning streak. The same song ("It's No Game") in Japanese and English opens and closes the album in an obvious frame, but in between, the dense music veers blithely from metric singsong ("Up the Hill Backwards") to "Fame" stomp ("Fashion") to *Lodger*-style intricacy ("Teenage Wildlife"). For subject matter Bowie turns his sights on twisted individuals (the title track, "Because You're Young"), society ("Fashion"), and even himself ("Ashes to Ashes," a "sequel" to "Space Oddity"). Bowie's newfound lyrical confidence is again in evidence, drawing the listener into his fear-world instead of shutting her/him out.

Changestwobowie, another greed-inspired potpourri, is a schizoid jumble of old album tracks ("Oh! You Pretty Things," "1984") and recent singles-from-album-tracks ("D.J.," "Fashion," "Ashes to Ashes"). No "Heroes," surprisingly, but there is the obligatory "rare" cut: "John I'm Only Dancing (Again) 1975," a *Young Americans*-period revamping previously unreleased on LP. The single is cheaper.
— S.I.

BOW WOW WOW
★ **See Jungle! See Jungle! Go Join Your Gang, Yeah! City All Over, Go Ape Crazy / RCA (1981)**
One of Malcolm McLaren's stranger projects, Bow Wow Wow, led by the teenaged lovely Annabella, seemed fine as a one- or two-shot novelty act: the cassette-only single, "C-30, C-60, C-90, Go!" was a nice spoof on record-industry paranoia about the proliferation of homemade cassettes, while "Work," the group's other early British hit, threatened to articulate McLaren's politics and aesthetics. But extended to an album, especially an album that's almost all rhythm track and chanting, Bow Wow Wow is a headachy bore, a joke that doesn't know the limits of its own pretensions. And while McLaren, like all savvy entrepreneurial hustlers, may contend that it's that way on purpose, it's hard to buy his rationale this time—Bow Wow Wow stands as the genuinely talentless one-shot group he thought he had in the Sex Pistols (and maybe did until the singer turned out to have other thoughts on the matter). No such luck this time.
— D.M.

BILL BOYD AND HIS COWBOY RAMBLERS
★ ★ **Bill Boyd's Cowboy Ramblers / Blueb. (1975)** ¶
A fine example of the journeyman pro in Western swing. Boyd's groups were always small (string instruments and sometimes piano, never horns), and performed creditably, though seldom spectacularly. For Western swing diehards only. — J.MO.

EDDIE BOYD
★ ★ ★ **Legacy of the Blues, Vol. 10 / Sonet (1974), Br. imp.**
★ ★ ★ **Vacation from the Blues / Jeff. (1976)**
★ ★ **Eddie Boyd and Ulli's Blues Band / Blue A. (NA), Br. imp.**
★ ★ ★ **Five Long Years / L+R (NA), Br. imp.**

★ ★ ★ **Ratting and Running Around /
Crown P. (NA)**
★ ★ ★ **A Sad Day / Paris Album (NA), Br.
imp.**
Boyd, a Chicago singer and pianist, is most
important as a writer, and his best composition, "Five Long Years," has been widely
covered. His best material was done in the
Fifties, and it's best represented on *Ratting
and Running Around,* although some vintage
sides are also issued on *Vacation,* and the
Sonet set. *Five Long Years* is the product of
a 1965 session with Buddy Guy, and it's
quite nice. The Paris Album and Blue Angel
sets are recent, with European bands, and
competent at best. — D.M.

TERENCE BOYLAN
★ **Terence Boylan / Asy. (1977)**
★ **Suzy / Asy. (1980)**
The kind of singer you're *sure* is gonna turn
out to be an actor with a hobby. Questionable highlight of second LP is "Shake Your
Fiorucci," with direct quotes of the guitar
riffs from "Layla" and "Jumpin' Jack
Flash." The rest you'll forget as quickly as
did the high-priced L.A. session pros who
made it. — D.M.

THE BOYS
★ ★ ★ ★ **The Boys / NEMS (1977), Br. imp.**
★ ★ ★ **Alternative Chartbusters / NEMS
(1978), Br. imp.**
★ ★ **To Hell with the Boys / Safari (1978),
Br. imp.**
★ ★ **Boys Only / Safari (1980), Br. imp.**
The Boys began as part of punk's ambitious
hard core, a group for more than thunder 'n'
thrills, and their first two LPs are among the
most delightful holdovers from the period.
But they slid too easily into a power-pop
mode that renders the more recent albums
dispensable. — D.M.

THE BOYS OF THE LOUGH
★ ★ **The Boys of the Lough / Philo (1974)**
★ ★ ★ **The Piper's Broken Finger / Philo
(1976)**
Like the Chieftains, the Boys of the Lough
are purveyors of Scottish and Irish traditional music, though some would argue that
the Boys' style is a bit less formal (or polished) than the Chieftains'. The reels, jigs
and ballads, however, led by fiddler extraordinaire Aly Bain, are really a live music whose
bright textures are difficult to capture on record.
The Boys of the Lough was recorded live,
and the sound is muted and distant throughout. *The Piper's Broken Finger,* a studio ef-

fort, is more successful, and probably the
best paced of the group's LPs. — I.M.

BOYZZ
★ **Too Wild to Tame / Epic (1978)**
Too numskull to bother, more likely.
— D.M.

BOBBY BRADDOCK
★ **Between the Lines / Elek. (1979)**
★ **Love Bomb / Elek. (1980)**
High-school-assembly melodies and rather
too obvious social-awareness lyrics sort of
make Braddock the C&W Harry Chapin.
Unfortunately, Braddock also writes love
songs. — D.M.

PROFESSOR ALEX BRADFORD
★ ★ **Obey His Will / Check. (1967)**
★ ★ ★ ★ **Best of Alex Bradford / Spec.
(NA)**
★ ★ ★ **He Lifted Me / Spec. (NA)**
Combine Archie Brownlee with Alex Brad-
ford, add a horn section (and maybe some
strings), and you have a close approximation
of the Atlantic-era Ray Charles. Bradford,
who began his career in vaudeville, often expressed a desire to sing pop à la Dionne and
DeeDee Warwick (whom he discovered) and
LaVern Baker (for whom he wrote Top
Forty hits). His idols include Petie
Wheatstraw, Gatemouth Moore and Eddie
"Cleanhead" Vinson, and a blues feel perme-
ates all of Bradford's best material. This is
particularly true of his imagery—check out
his best-known song, "Too Close to Heav-
en." Bradford had an amazingly versatile
voice that went effortlessly from a deep
moan to a high shriek. *Best of* is essential to
any basic gospel collection, but the other
Specialty LP is surprisingly strong. *Obey,*
from late in his career, is a fascinating, off-
the-wall set of pop gospel, but it isn't always
effective, and Bradford's gravelly voice has
become weak and mannered. — J.MO.

THE BRAINS
★ ★ ★ **The Brains / Merc. (1980)**
★ ★ ★ **Electronic Eden / Merc. (1981)**
Excellent hard-edged new-wave combo from
Atlanta reached its pinnacle (so far anyhow)
on its debut LP with the anthemic "Money
Changes Everything," in which the real push
'n' pull of sexual warfare (the other kind,
too, one imagines) is identified, scorned and
mourned. The band doesn't come close to
anything so transcendent on all the rest of
these, but their playing is invariably solid
and the writing often intriguing, and always
committed. — D.M.

BRAINSTORM
★ **Stormin' / Tabu (1977)** ¶
★ **Journey to the Night / Tabu (1978)** ¶
★ **Funky Entertainment / Tabu (1979)** ¶
Truly mediocre nine-piece soul/funk unit;
clichés gathered from everywhere and
sprawled over nearly two hours' worth of
vinyl so far. There comes a time when even
the ability to set up a reasonable backbeat
doesn't count for much. Three albums of
aural wallpaper is that time. — D.M.

RANDALL BRAMBLETT
★ ★ ★ ★ **That Other Mile / Poly. (1975)** ¶
★ ★ ★ **Light of the Night / Poly. (1976)** ¶
Bramblett is a singer/songwriter/
instrumentalist of no small promise, one of
the most sought-after Southern session players (he's featured in Gregg Allman's touring
band) and probably the most urbane Southern songwriter this side of Randy Newman.
Both albums are classics of the Seventies
Southern rock renaissance. Bramblett later
joined Sea Level. — J.S.

DELANEY BRAMLETT
★ **Delaney Bramlett and Friends—Class
Reunion / Prod. (1977)**
The former leader of Delaney and Bonnie
and Friends found himself in such straits in
1977 that he wound up making this pathetic
and soul-shriven album for Motown's "rock"
label. At least Bonnie, his ex-wife, got sympathetic production at Capricorn. — D.M.

OSCAR BRAND
★ ★ **Bawdy Songs and Backroom Ballads /
Audio Fi. (1958)**
★ ★ **Bawdy Sea Shanties / Audio Fi. (1958)**
★ ★ **Concert at Town Hall / Folk. (1959)**
★ ★ **Bawdy Western Songs / Audio Fi.
(1960)**
★ ★ **Bawdy Songs Goes to College / Audio
Fi. (1961)**
★ ★ **Rollicking Sea Shanties / Audio Fi.
(1962)**
★ ★ **Sing Along Bawdy Songs / Audio Fi.
(1962)**
★ ★ **Bawdy Hootenanny / Audio Fi. (1963)**
★ **Brand X / Rou. (1971)**
★ ★ **Singing Holidays / Caed. (1976)**
★ ★ **Laughing America / Trad. (NA)**
★ ★ ★ **Pie in the Sky / Trad. (NA)**
★ ★ ★ **Best of Oscar Brand / Trad. (NA)**
★ ★ ★ **Oscar Brand and Jean Ritchie / Arc.
Folk (NA)**
★ **Wild Blue Yonder / Elek. (NA)**
Oscar Brand came out of the same Forties
radical left folk scene that produced Pete
Seeger and Woody Guthrie, and made Lead-

belly and the Weavers famous. Because his
politics were closer to the mainstream, however, he was able to survive the blacklists of
the McCarthy Fifties much more successfully. Like Seeger, his nearest leftist counterpart, Brand was obsessed with the folk tradition. But ideology never interfered with what
he wanted to do musically. This is not altogether salutary—in fact, it trivializes much
of what later made the early folkies important to the post-Dylan generation—but it can
often be more listenable and almost always is
less preachy.
Brand's real reputation was made with the
series of *Bawdy Songs* LPs he made for
Audio Fidelity in the late Fifties and early
Sixties. These were not the sorts of songs
that could find their way into schoolbooks,
and the always puritanical American left
never boasted much about this part of the
American working-class heritage either.
Today, though, after twenty years of increasingly explicit sexual reference in mainstream
pop music, Brand's bawdy songs seem dated
and fairly tame. How you gonna keep 'em
down on the farm after they've heard "Foxy
Lady"?
And Brand's other albums of traditional
music simply reveal his limits as a vocalist.
Far better interpretations of almost all the
nonbawdy material are available from a variety of sources, particularly singers like
Woody Guthrie and Ramblin' Jack Elliott.
To hear Brand best, pick up the Tradition
Best of or the album he made for that label
with the neglected Appalachian ballad singer
Jean Ritchie. — D.M.

BRAND X
★ ★ ★ **Live Stock / Pass. (1977)**
★ ★ ★ **Masques / Pass. (1977)**
★ ★ ★ **Product / Pass. (1979)**
Progressive English band, masterminded by
Genesis drummer Phil Collins (he seems
more interested here), toys also with jazz fu-
sion. Obtuse but effective. — D.M.

BRASS CONSTRUCTION
★ ★ ★ ★ **Brass Construction / U.A. (1975)**
★ ★ **II / U.A. (1976)** ¶
★ ★ **III / U.A. (1977)**
★ ★ **IV / U.A. (1978)**
★ ★ **V / U.A. (1979)**
★ ★ **VI / U.A. (1980)**
Their first album includes the hit "Movin"
and five other one-word titles of disco length
and style. Their music is accented by mis-
construed images of urban origin. *II* is
something of a departure; the vocals are
more upfront, standardized in the jive/Ohio

Players fashion. *III, IV, V* and *VI* continue in this vein. Numbering all your LPs instead of giving them titles doesn't make you Chicago. And even if it did . . .   — G.C.

BREAD
★ **Bread / Elek. (1969)**
★ **On the Water / Elek. (1970)**
★ ★ ★ **Manna / Elek. (1971)**
★ ★ ★ ★ **Baby I'm-a Want You / Elek. (1972)**
★ ★ ★ ★ **Guitar Man / Elek. (1972)**
★ ★ ★ ★ **The Best of Bread / Elek. (1973)**
★ ★ ★ ★ **The Best of Bread, Vol. 2 / Elek. (1974)**
★ ★ **Lost without Your Love / Elek. (1976)**
Especially in its later days, Bread was downright inspirational. Sparkling lyricism, lush melodicism, immaculate production dynamism, foolproof vocal harmonies (with soul, no less) and a nearly unchallenged hit-single-writing capacity. The two *Best of* collections contain twenty-four mellifluously rocking jewels. *Volume 2* recaptures the glory of three classic albums cut in Bread's 1969–1973 heyday, *Baby I'm-a Want You, Manna* and *Guitar Man.* It's pop, but transcendent pop. David Gates and James Griffin went on to solo fame before reuniting in 1976 to cut *Lost . . . Love,* but it was a depressingly slouch offering, especially considering the brilliance of Gates' recent solos.
— B.M.

BREAKFAST SPECIAL
★ ★ ★ ★ **Breakfast Special / Roun. (1977)**
One of the true supergroups of young bluegrass players, Breakfast Special featured Kenny Kosek on fiddle, Roger Mason on bass, Stacy Phillips on dobro, Andy Statman on mandolin, Jim Tolles on guitar and lead vocals, and Tony Trischka on banjo and pedal steel guitar.   — J.S.

BREAKWATER
★ ★ **Breakwater / Ari. (1979)**
★ ★ **Splashdown Time / Ari. (1980)**
Moderately popular, thoroughly formulized black pop.   — D.M.

BREATHLESS
★ ★ ★ **Breathless / EMI (1979)**
★ ★ **Nobody Leaves This Song Alive / EMI (1980)**
A spinoff of Cleveland's ever more successful Michael Stanley Band (Breathless' Jonah Koslen was MSB's original lead-guitarist), this band shares other traits with Stanley's outfit. Solid, workmanlike and likable, the group nonetheless never truly developed a

style, and could also use a little more energy.
— R.P.

BRENDA AND THE TABULATIONS
★ **I Keep Coming Back for More / Choc. (1977)**
Ex-girl group gone disco. Bad idea gone wrong.   — D.M.

BRICK
★ ★ **Good High / Bang (1976)**
★ ★ **Brick / Bang (1978)**
★ ★ **Stoneheart / Bang (1979)** ¶
★ ★ **Waiting on You / Bang (1980)**
★ ★ **Summer Heat / Bang (1981)**
Inoffensive "soulful disco jazz" (self-description from debut album notes)—a little Jr. Walker, a little Ramsey Lewis, a little Larry Graham bass, a little Family Stone chanting harmony. Not enough of anything, but nothing to get annoyed about, which is some kind of blessing, figuring your mind is on vacation and you just wanna relax to the Muzak.   — D.M.

THE BRIDES OF FUNKENSTEIN
★ ★ ★ **Funk or Walk / Atl. (1978)** ¶
★ ★ ★ **Never Buy Texas from a Cowboy / Atl. (1980)**
George Clinton's master plan seems to be to make one album for every record company there is. The result is this hybrid (girl group/funk band) and its two albums. The results are sort of like the Three Degrees meet Bootsy's Rubber Band in Giorgio Moroder's version of heaven: synthesizers, soprano harmonies, grunting bass, splashy percussion, aimless songs. "Disco to Go" from *Funk or Walk* was the Brides' one and only significant chartmaker; what's next, if anything, only Uncle Jam knows for sure. Not exactly a strikeout but also (and not unlike a great many Clinton projects) more interesting as an idea than as a reality.   — D.M.

ALICIA BRIDGES
★ **Alicia Bridges / Poly. (1978)**
★ **Play It As It Lays / Poly. (1979)**
Pop-disco chanteuse whose debut album was produced by Steve Buckingham at the Studio One in Georgia. Her one hit, "I Love the Night Life," was taken from that record.
— J.S.

DEE DEE BRIDGEWATER
★ ★ **Dee Dee Bridgewater / Atl. (1976)**
★ ★ **Just Family / Elek. (1978)**
★ ★ **Bad for Me / Elek. (1979)**
Dee Dee Bridgewater combines silky, precise articulation with a stirring dynamic range

(comparable to Streisand's but with a greater flair for jazz phrasing). She measures every vibrato, every blue note, every scream to full effect. Her sassy swagger on the rockers is commensurate with her near operatic control over the ballads. — M.G.

BRIGATI
★ **Lost in the Wilderness / Elek. (1976)**
If you were a fan of Eddie Brigati's steamy, ripping Rascals vocals, this is a maddening record. Eddie and David Brigati enlist some impressive New York sessionmen for such questionable fare as a hep disco version of "Groovin' " and a Philly-soul-Muzak-disco version of "You Send Me." A song called "Lost in the Wilderness (How 'Bout a Harlem in Your Life)" is the lyrical ploy to match their musical pandering to a black audience the Rascals once *earned.* — F.S.

BRIAN BRIGGS
★ ★ ★ **Brian Damage / Bearsv. (1980)**
Genuine pop eccentric. Under his real name, John Hillbrooks, Briggs has worked as an engineer, producer (of Bearsville stablemate Randy Van Warmer) and synthesizer sideman. On his own, he makes his music from straight pop, synthesizer art-rock, Clint Eastwood soundtracks, flutes, possibly some Jamaican rhythm here and there. None of it really adds up to more than high-tech easy listening, but it's *intelligent* high-tech easy listening. As far as I can tell. — D.M.

MARTIN BRILEY
★ **Fear of the Unknown / Mer. (1981)**
Veteran of Ian Hunter's band plays as if the title referred to musical innovation. Nasty hackwork. — D.M.

BRINSLEY SCHWARZ
★ ★ ★ ★ **Please Don't Ever Change / U.A. (1973), Br. imp.**
★ ★ ★ ★ **The New Favourites of Brinsley Schwarz / U.A. (1974), Br. imp.**
★ ★ ★ ★ **Brinsley Schwarz / Cap. (1978) ¶**
★ ★ ★ ★ **Fifteen Thoughts of Brinsley Schwarz / U.A. (1978), Br. imp.**
Brinsley Schwarz was the best of the British pub-rock bands, and a seminal influence on what later became the British new wave: lead guitarist Schwarz now backs up Graham Parker as part of the Rumour, while writer/bassist Nick Lowe, who has produced Parker and Elvis Costello, is a sidekick of Dave Edmunds, who produced the fine *New Favourites.*

The two-record set *Brinsley Schwarz* is a compilation of the first two of the group's albums. The debut LP is listless funk, without the verve of the followup (originally titled *Despite It All*), which is perhaps the best country-influenced rock LP ever made. "Country Girl" has the charm and fake innocence that make Lowe's solo albums so appealing, the recording is bright and the singing is grand. On its own, *Despite It All* would be worth five stars; together, these two records are surely worth five bucks. The two U.K. import anthologies, both of them astutely compiled, are pricier but still worth a listen. — D.M.

JOHNNY BRISTOL
★ **Bristol's Creme / Atl. (1976)**
★ **Strangers / Atl. (1978)**
Bristol is a former Motown producer who did some of Gladys Knight's best records there. On his own, he has had a couple of hits, most notably "Hang On in There Baby," a 1974 disco smash for MGM. But his specialty is a kind of post-feminism seduction, encouraging women to improve themselves flat on their backs. To which one can only respond: "Get funked." — D.M.

BRITISH LIONS
★ **British Lions / RSO (1978) ¶**
Useful primarily as the answer to the following trivia questions: What happened to the rest of Mott the Hoople after Ian Hunter and Mick Ronson left the band? (Buffin, Overend Watts and Morgan Fisher found a couple of new partners, John Fiddler and Ray Major, and carried on with this.) What is the worst version of Garland Jeffreys' "Wild in the Streets" ever recorded? (Side one, track two.) What is the only album in world history to contain a credit for slide glockenspiel? Now that you have this information, you surely don't need the record, no matter how much "All the Young Dudes" changed your life. — D.M.

BROADWAY
★ **Magic Man / Hilltak (1979) ¶**
As every New Yorker knows, Broadway is a dying institution. And this conceptual "group" (only lead vocalist Patti Williams and producer Willie Henderson are identified) is further proof that some clichés are correct—but that most are boring. — D.M.

JAIME BROCKETT
★ **Remember the Wind and the Rain / Cap. (1971)**
★ **North Mountain Velvet / Adel. (1977)**
These albums move as fast as a snail on the nod. Recommended for people who really

like contemporary talking blues, meaningful pauses and dulcimer solos. — A.S.

BROKEN HOME
★ Broken Home / Atl. (1980)
Pseudo-Foreigner produced by Robert John "Mutt" Lange. — J.S.

DAVID BROMBERG
■ David Bromberg / Col. (1972)
★ Demon in Disguise / Col. (1972)
★ ★ Wanted/Dead or Alive / Col. (1974)
★ Midnight on the Water / Col. (1975)
★ ★ How Late'll Ya Play 'Til? / Fan. (1976)
★ Reckless Abandon / Fan. (1977)
★ ★ Best: Out of the Blues / Col. (1977)
★ Hillbilly Jazz / Fly. Fish (1977)
★ Bandit in a Bathing Suit / Fan. (1978)
★ My Own House / Fan. (1978)
★ You Should See the Rest of the Band / Fan. (1980)
David Bromberg has the reputation of being an amusing performer, but most of his albums feature live recordings, which only shows that humorous asides and good-time jams seldom survive on vinyl. Bromberg's singing is terrible. When he tries to sound tough, his voice squeaks like an adolescent in the church choir; otherwise it simply grates. But his later efforts (on Fantasy) prove that singing wasn't his only problem.

In fact, though the fast-pickin' folkie-with-a-croak earned his reputation as a session guitarist, his solo albums demonstrate that when he loses his speed, little else remains. Bromberg delivers seven-minute cuts based on one lick, gets the notes right but seldom the spirit, and has no style of his own. Perhaps his worst sin is that he makes blues and bluegrass sound alike. — A.S.

HERMAN BROOD
★ Herman Brood & His Wild Romance / Ario.–Amer. (1979)
★ Go Nutz / Ario.–Amer. (1980)
Holland's answer to Ted Nugent. Your move. — J.S.

GARY BROOKER
★ ★ No More Fear of Flying / Chrys. (1980)
Former Procol Harum keyboardist/singer turns in solo album nearly as pompous as that band's later work. Brooker was an influential English art-pop singer, but you'd never guess it from this. Check out *A Salty Dog* instead. — D.M.

BROOKLYN DREAMS
★ ★ Brooklyn Dreams / Millen. (1977)
★ ★ Sleepless Nights / Casa. (1979)

★ ★ Joy Ride / Casa. (NA)
★ ★ Won't Let Go / Casa. (NA)
Led by Donna Summer's husband, Bruce Sudano, Brooklyn Dreams is expertly produced and manages a pretty commercial sound, but doesn't know whether to purvey disco or do Lou Reed imitations. They're better off rocking, lacking the precision to compete with Summer-style Eurodisco. — J.S.

ELKIE BROOKS
★ ★ Rich Man's Woman / A&M (1975)
★ ★ Two Days Away / A&M (1977)
★ ★ Shooting Star / A&M (1978)
★ ★ Live and Learn / A&M (1979)
The smoky, seductive singer from Vinegar Joe composes well and picks some good covers, but too often is lost in mediocre material and backup. Her bluesy wailing doesn't always mix well with pop-directed rock. — C.W.

LONNIE BROOKS
★ ★ ★ ★ Bayou Lightning / Alli. (1979)
★ ★ ★ ★ Turn On the Night / Alli. (1981)
Brooks has recorded on and off (under his own name and as Guitar Junior) since the mid-Fifties, both in his native Louisiana and, more often, in Chicago. His style is an amalgam of New Orleans rhythm & blues and Chicago blues, a style he carries off more adeptly than most because he is both a fine singer and a fine guitarist. *Bayou Lightning* is a simply electrifying set, and *Turn On the Night* isn't far behind it. — D.M.

PATTIE BROOKS
★ ★ ★ Love Shook / Casa. (1977)
★ ★ ★ Our Ms. Brooks / Casa. (1978)
★ ★ ★ Agatha / Casa. (NA)
★ ★ ★ Pattie Brooks / Casa. (NA)
★ ★ ★ Party Girl / Casa. (NA)
Vocally, Brooks is a ringer for Donna Summer, and her material isn't bad. But this demonstrates that Summer became Queen of Disco not on the strength of pipes alone, but with a combination of singing, good material and genuinely exciting production, which is the principal ingredient lacking here. If Brooks ever hooks up with an imaginative composer or producer, she could yet become something special, instead of just a better-than-average dance-oriented chanteuse. — D.M.

BIG BILL BROONZY
★ ★ Big Bill / Folk. (1957) ¶
★ ★ ★ Blues / Folk. (1959)
★ ★ ★ Big Bill Broonzy Sings Folk Songs / Folk. (1962)

★ ★ ★ ★ ★ Young / Yazoo (1968) ¶
★ ★ ★ ★ ★ Do That Guitar Rag / Yazoo
(1972) ¶
★ ★ Feelin' Low Down / Cres. (1973)
★ ★ ★ 1932–42 / Bio. (1973) ¶
★ ★ ★ Lonesome Road Blues / Cres. (1975)
★ ★ ★ Big Bill Broonzy / Ev. (NA)
★ ★ ★ ★ Big Bill Broonzy / RCA (NA)
★ ★ ★ Big Bill Broonzy / Story. (NA)
★ ★ ★ ★ Big Bill Broonzy / Queen (NA)
★ Big Bill Broonzy Sings Country Blues /
Folk. (NA)
★ ★ ★ ★ Big Bill's Blues / CBS (NA)
★ ★ ★ An Evening with Big Bill / Story.
(NA)
A strong singer who doubled on guitar and
fiddle, Broonzy was widely recognized as one
of the greatest folk bluesmen before his
death in 1958. His style is languid yet
charged with emotion, with plenty of space
left between notes to develop tension. He
traveled the classic country-blues route from
Mississippi to Arkansas and finally to Chicago, playing while holding down odd jobs and
occasionally recording. Broonzy is the key
transitional figure between the delta style of
Robert Johnson and the modern, electric
Chicago blues of Muddy Waters. The Everest, Biograph, Yazoo, RCA, Queen Disc,
CBS and Crescendo sides assemble some of
the pertinent material he did during the
Thirties and Forties, but nowhere near encompass the range of his repertoire, which is
considered to include over 350 original compositions. The Folkways material, recorded
shortly before his death and released posthumously, shows that Broonzy was still a
powerful singer despite his failing health
and a throat operation. *Blues* is with
Sonny Terry and Brownie McGhee. — J.S.

THE BROTHERS JOHNSON
★ ★ Right on Time / A&M (1972)
★ ★ Look Out for #1 / A&M (1976)
★ ★ Blam!! / A&M (1978)
★ ★ Light Up the Night / A&M (1980)
★ ★ Love Me by Name / A&M (1981)
Mediocre pop-funk, Seventies family style;
lots of hit singles in 1978–79, but nothing to
write home about yet. — D.M.

BROTHER TO BROTHER
★ ★ ★ Let Your Mind Be Free / Turbo
(1976)
★ ★ Shades in Creation / Turbo (1976)
Soul group had a mid-Seventies hit with Gil
Scott-Heron's "The Bottle" (not included on
these albums), but they haven't made very
much noise since then. — A.E.G.

CHARLES BROWN
★ ★ ★ Merry Christmas Baby / Big Town
(1976)
★ ★ Music Maestro Please / Big Town
(1976)
★ ★ Great R&B Oldies / Blues Sp. (1976)
★ ★ ★ ★ Sunny Road / Route 66 (1977), Br.
imp.
★ ★ I'm Gonna Push On / Stockholm
(1980), Br. imp.
★ ★ ★ ★ Race Track Blues / Route 66
(1981), Br. imp.
★ ★ ★ Driftin' Blues / Main (NA)
★ ★ Blues 'n' Brown / Jewel (NA)
Brown was an important figure in late For-
ties/early Fifties R&B singing, during the
transition to rock 'n' roll styles; although his
style was smoother and blander than Roy
Brown's, it was nonetheless influential.
Charles Brown's best record, "Merry Christmas Baby," is found in its original version
(along with many of his other vintage tracks)
on *Sunny Road,* as well as on *Merry Christmas Baby,* which is an all-Christmas-song
LP. *Race Track Blues* is also vintage material. The other albums consist of more recent
crooning and are highly dispensable.
— D.M.

CLARENCE "GATEMOUTH" BROWN
★ ★ ★ ★ ★ San Antonio Ballbuster / Red L.
(1975)
★ ★ Gate's on the Heat / Blue St. (1975)
★ ★ Bogalusa Boogie Man / Bar. (1976)
★ ★ ★ Blackjack / Music Is Medicine
(1978)
Brown's blasting voice and hard-edged, innovative guitar playing made him one of the
best practitioners of pre-rock rhythm &
blues. He was a huge star in Texas during
the late Forties and Fifties, his absolutely essential recordings for Peacock during that
time are anthologized on *San Antonio Ballbuster,* a great album that is all the Gatemouth you'll ever need. — J.S.

DENNIS BROWN
★ ★ ★ ★ ★ Visions / J. Gibbs (1978)
★ ★ ★ ★ Words of Wisdom / J. Gibbs
(1979)
★ ★ Live at Montreux / J. Gibbs (1979)
★ ★ ★ Joseph's Coat / J. Gibbs (1980)
★ ★ ★ ★ Money in My Pocket / Troj.
(1981)
★ ★ Foul Play / A&M (1981)
Dennis Brown first hit in Jamaica at age
fourteen in 1970 with "No Man Is an Is-
land" (score the like-titled Studio One LP if
you can find it). Since then, his smooth, full-
bodied baritone has made him the most pop-

ular singer of love songs in Jamaica—a virile purveyor of muscular, joyous romances. Yet he has written enough strong message material to give him credibility among roots audiences. *Money in My Pocket* is an excellent compilation of his early- and mid-Seventies work. *Visions* and *Words of Wisdom* present top-flight musicianship, uncluttered production, intelligent lyrics and powerful singing. *Live* offers lousy sound and tepid performances, while *Foul Play* is a patchy attempt at crossover. — R.F.G.

JAMES BROWN
★ ★ ★ **Revolution of the Mind / Poly. (1971)**
★ **Hot / Poly. (1971)** ¶
★ ★ ★ **Hot Pants / Poly. (1971)** ¶
★ ★ ★ ★ **Soul Classics, Vol. 1 / Poly. (1972)** ¶
★ ★ ★ **There It Is / Poly. (1972)** ¶
★ ★ **Payback / Poly. (1973)** ¶
★ ★ ★ **Hell / Poly. (1974)** ¶
★ **Sex Machine Today / Poly. (1975)** ¶
★ ★ **Everybody's Doin' the Hustle / Poly. (1975)** ¶
★ ★ **Get Up Offa That Thing / Poly. (1976)** ¶
★ ★ **Mutha's Nature / Poly. (1977)** ¶
★ ★ **Jam/1980s / Poly. (1978)**
★ ★ ★ **Take a Look at Those Cakes / Poly. (1978)**
★ ★ ★ **Original Disco Man / Poly. (1979)**
★ ★ ★ **People / Poly. (1980)**
★ ★ ★ ★ **Live and Lowdown at the Apollo, Vol. 1 / Solid S. (1980)**
★ ★ ★ **Live/Hot on the One / Poly. (1980)**

James Brown has never been the subject of a well-documented greatest-hits collection, and with the disappearance of King Records (and every James Brown album through 1970), *Soul Classics* is just about all that remains of his greatest period. For a guy whose prime stretched over fifteen years, the selection on *Soul Classics* is haphazard to say the least. The packaging is utterly devoid of dates, notes or enticing photos from the old days, and aesthetically it's hard to acknowledge "Super Bad" or "Make It Funky Pt. 3" as quintessential JB. Still, how can you argue with "Papa's Got a Brand New Bag," "It's a Man's, Man's, Man's World" and "Cold Sweat"?

Sadly, Brown's remaining work traces the decline of both his voice and his creative powers. By the time James Brown reached Polydor, he had virtually done away with any sense of lyric coherence in his songs;

words became secondary to sound. For a while it worked. His early hits on the label were a combination of verbal, stream-of-consciousness cacophony, and sizzling instrumental riffs. Gradually Brown's efforts became caught up in their own hypnotizing monotony. He finally ran out of rhythmic ideas, and by the time the disco phenomenon exploded, James Brown was reduced to recycling past hits under new names. Sometimes he didn't even bother to change that much ("Sex Machine Today"). The bottom was reached when he recorded a song on the *Sex Machine Today* album complaining that others were ripping him off and then a few months later released "Hot," a photocopy of David Bowie's "Fame." The Solid Smoke set is Brown's legendary Apollo performance. — J.MC.

OSCAR BROWN JR.
★ **Between Heaven and Hell / Col. (1962)**
★ **Movin' On / Atl. (1972)**
★ **Fresh / Atl. (1974)**
Jive, histrionic funk-jazz singer with pretension to "social relevance." — D.M.

PETER BROWN
★ ★ ★ **Fantasy Love Affair / Drive (1978)**
★ ★ **Stargazer / Drive (NA)**
Brown's "Fantasy Love Affair" was one of the more intriguing disco smashes of 1978: built on a dance rhythm structure, the song incorporated elements of post–rock & roll soft pop (Beatles, CSN&Y) into its evocation of love's chimerical pleasures, but insisted on viewing the dance floor as the essence of reality. The result is fascinating, if imperturbably smug (in the same way, it must be said, that those who view everything through the narrow lens of rock & roll are often smug). Unfortunately, *Stargazer* does not recapitulate such delights. — D.M.

RANDY BROWN
★ ★ ★ **Welcome to My Room / Parach. (1978)**
★ ★ ★ **Intimately / Parach. (1979)**
★ ★ ★ **Check It Out / Stax (1981)**
★ ★ ★ **Midnight Desire / Choc. (NA)**
★ ★ ★ **Randy / Choc. (NA)**
Brown has a terrific soul-shouter's voice, like a slightly less heavyweight version of Teddy Pendergrass. Unfortunately, he is given to stud philosophizing even more narcissistic than Teddy's. What else can you say about someone who has the temerity to suggest the confines of his bedroom as a vantage point for looking out at the universe? — D.M.

ROY BROWN

★ ★ ★ ★ ★ **Hard Luck Blues / King (NA)**

★ ★ ★ ★ **Laughing But Crying / Route 66 (1978), Br. imp.**

★ ★ ★ ★ **Good Rockin' Tonight / Route 66 (1978), Br. imp.**

New Orleans music historian John Broven called Brown "the first singer of soul," and if that's an arguable claim, it's also a defensible one. Brown's best records—perfectly represented on all of the above records—are models of pre–rock & roll blues-ballad singing. If it's true that Brown's best composition, "Good Rockin' Tonight," was done better by both Wynonie Harris and Elvis Presley, it is also true that Presley's ballad singing is inconceivable without Brown's influence. And much the same could be said of Little Junior Parker, Little Milton, Jackie Wilson and half a dozen others. Brown's deep crooning and powerhouse shouting has an unmatched subtlety; his best vocals seem to emerge from a well of emotion unfathomably deep. — D.M.

RUTH BROWN

★ ★ ★ ★ **Sweet Baby of Mine / Route 66 (1981), Br. imp.**

★ ★ ★ ★ **Ramblin' / RB (NA), Br. imp.**

Both of these records reissue some of Brown's fine Fifties sides. Recorded for Atlantic, they are interesting and significant rock 'n' roll transition period records— though Brown never loosened up as much as LaVern Baker, her prime label competitor. "Mama He Treats Your Daughter Mean" is the classic. Atlantic itself has no Brown albums in print. — D.M.

SHIRLEY BROWN

★ ★ ★ **Shirley Brown / Ari. (1977) ¶**

★ ★ ★ ★ **Woman to Woman / Stax (1974, 1979)**

★ ★ ★ **For the Real Feeling / Stax (1979)**

On her Arista album, Shirley Brown's magnificent voice overcomes unskilled and unsympathetic production. "A Mighty Good Feeling" and "Givin' Up" (and the single "Blessed Is the Woman") are the stand-outs here. Her Stax material is better, particularly *Woman to Woman,* which shows what the right production (by the late Al Jackson) can do for her on an Aretha Franklin–inspired set. — J.S.

STANKY BROWN GROUP

★ **Stanky Brown Group / Sire (1978)**

Pre-new wave Seventies New York City area rock band, more notable for its ability to get a recording contract than for its ability to do anything with it. — D.M.

TONI BROWN AND TERRY GARTHWAITE

★ ★ ★ ★ **Cross-Country / Cap. (1972) ¶**

This remarkable little one-shot stands as a kind of high point for this singer/songwriter team. Recorded in 1972 in between sessions with their regular group, Joy of Cooking, the album is a country-rock session produced by Wayne Moss and featuring Vassar Clements (fiddle), Charlie McCoy (harmonica), Dennis Linde (bass), Bill Aikins (piano), Kenny Malone (drums), Russ Hicks (steel guitar) and Jim Colvard (guitar). Brown and Garthwaite wrote some of their best material for this date, particularly "I Want to Be the One," "As I Watch the Wind" and "I Don't Want to Live Here." — J.S.

DUNCAN BROWNE

★ ★ **Streets of Fire / Sire (1979)**

★ **Wild Places / Sire (1978)**

Synthesizer pop that hardly lives up to the promise of the album titles. Fire and wildness, not to mention human passion, is just what this mechanical marvel lacks. — D.M.

JACKSON BROWNE

★ ★ ★ ★ **Jackson Browne / Asy. (1972)**

★ ★ ★ ★ **For Everyman / Asy. (1973)**

★ ★ ★ ★ **Late for the Sky / Asy. (1974)**

★ ★ ★ ★ ★ **The Pretender / Asy. (1976)**

★ ★ ★ ★ ★ **Running on Empty / Asy. (1978)**

★ ★ ★ ★ **Hold Out / Asy. (1980)**

Jackson Browne is the most accomplished lyricist of the Seventies. His miniaturist landscapes of life in the nether end of the century, as seen from the emotional and geographic climate of Southern California, provide rock's surest touchstone with the mood of the recent era; they have been instrumental in creating the Eagles–Linda Ronstadt axis of California singer/songwriter rock.

Browne's first three albums are highlighted by a preponderance of excellent songwriting. One thinks particularly of the *Jackson Browne*'s "Song for Adam," "Rock Me on the Water" and "Doctor My Eyes," his only hit single; of *For Everyman*'s momentous title track, "Ready or Not" and "These Days"; and of *Late for the Sky*'s brilliant philosophical depiction of death, "For a Dancer," as well as that album's "Fountain of Sorrow," "The Road and the Sky" and "Before the Deluge."

The themes—family, fate, death, honor, despair, with romance and the road providing the natural backdrop for all of it—are continuous and overlapping, from album to album and song to song. Browne's perspective has been described as apocalyptic, but it's really something else: a sweet-tempered survey of the doom around him, in which society at large and every smaller unit within it is finally dwarfed by the individual—sometimes an outlaw, sometimes a more common person—who stands, in the end, alone and if not triumphant, at least alive. There is great balance in his world view (if swinging from extreme to extreme can eventually constitute balance), and certainly more than the expected share of hope and humility.

If anything mars this first trio of LPs, it is Browne's occasional lapses as a performer. His singing is erratic, sometimes moving, sometimes almost callow; the arrangements range from tightly focused, almost traditional folk purity (in the melodies, and in David Lindley's guitar and violin accompaniment) to simply messy. But in *The Pretender* Browne found a perfect forum for all of his concerns, and the music came to its full flower at last. The melodies were brilliant, the songs deeply moving and perfectly constructed—"Here Come Those Tears Again" and "The Fuse" were the first successful out-and-out rock & roll he'd ever recorded—and the record's concept held together from start to finish. Indeed, moving from the opening song, "The Fuse," to the closing one, "The Pretender," led one nowhere except on the great circuitous route of life itself.

Running On Empty, released in late 1977, was the most ambitious live album project ever attempted. The performances came from everywhere—onstage, from the group's touring bus and its motel rooms, even from backstage—and the songs did the same: Browne rerecorded none of his previous repertoire and contributed only a couple of originals, supplementing them with songs written by members of his backup band like Danny Kortchmar, a tune written by his road manager, and the old Maurice Williams and the Zodiacs' hit, "Stay," which closed the set perfectly. (Both "Stay" and the rocking title song were hit singles.) It was a departure, but a fitting one. This was one outlaw who had found a society that could accept him.

Hold Out is lyrically the weakest set of songs Browne had ever assembled; it repeats old themes without opening up much new ground, sentimentalizes much of the best of his early work, and wallows in the ersatz streetlife of "Boulevard." On the other hand, the record contains Browne's most interesting music. Together with coproducer Greg

Ladanyi and keyboard player Craig Doerge, Browne creates a dense aural montage which effectively buoys his voice and adds a seductive element of rock & roll to his songs. In this regard, *Hold Out* is a good deal less than the obvious catastrophe it was on the surface. More likely, it represents the conclusion of one phase of Browne's lyric writing, though what comes next (given the tortoise pace at which he works) isn't even subject to guesswork. — D.M.

ED BRUCE
★ ★ **Ed Bruce** / MCA (1976)
★ ★ **One to One** / MCA (1981)
Bruce's most notable achievement is cowriting the Waylon Jennings' hit, "Mama Don't Let Your Babies Grow Up to Be Cowboys." Although that song appears on *Ed Bruce,* Bruce is such a lugubriously mellow singer that it doesn't have half the impact Jennings gives it. — D.M.

JACK BRUCE BAND
★ ★ ★ **How's Tricks** / RSO (1977)
★ ★ ★ **I've Always Wanted to Do This** / Epic (1980)
The powerful, melodic patterns woven by this ex-Cream bassist lie at the very heart of jazz-rock fusion. Bruce's conceptions are erratic (find his great out-of-print LPs *Things We Like* and *Songs for a Tailor*), but his playing is always interesting. On *Tricks* drummer Simon Phillips excels, while *This* features fusion superstar Billy Cobham on drums. — J.S.

LENNY BRUCE
★ **Berkeley Concert** / Rep. (1969)
★ ★ **Live at the Curran Theatre** / Fan. (1971)
★ **"Thank You Masked Man"** / Fan. (1972)
★ ★ ★ **The Real Lenny Bruce** / Fan. (1975)
★ **What I Was Arrested For** / Casa. (1977)
★ ★ ★ **The Best of Lenny Bruce** / Fan. (NA)
★ **Interviews of Our Times** / Fan. (NA)
★ **Lenny Bruce—American** / Fan. (NA)
★ **The Sick Humor of Lenny Bruce** / Fan. (NA)
★ **"Togetherness"** / Fan. (NA)
Bruce was always a fascinating talker, but if you're looking for laughs, the Presence of Modern Comedy is not the man to seek out. *The Best of Lenny Bruce* contains his finest early material, and is sporadically hilarious; *Live at the Curran* is a mesmerizing monologue about his arrests, but as a three-record set may strike you as a lot to shell out for interesting rambling. *The Real Lenny Bruce,*

a two-record set, contains his best, funniest routine, "Comic at the Palladium," a twenty-minute dissection of seedy show biz in both America and England, and compared with the rest of his recorded work, it seems to come out of nowhere: as acidly hysterical as his myth claims, and totally without embarrassing self-pity and intellectual pretensions. In general, Bruce tried to break down the structure of a stand-up monologue, allowing for new thoughts, new emphases, new accidents with every performance, but just wasn't imaginative or intelligent enough to feed his gabby gift with new premises from which to wing it. So often he just babbles until he provokes an inadvertent giggle. Simplistic moralism and lame dialect humor sinks half of this album list. And while Bruce may have made the frankness of, say, Richard Pryor possible, greater artists like Richard Pryor have made Bruce's recorded work seem tame, churlish, and even sentimental. — K.T.

BILL BRUFORD

★ ★ ★ ★ Feels Good to Me / Poly. (1978)
★ ★ ★ One of a Kind / Poly. (1979)
★ ★ The Bruford Tapes / Ed. EG (1980)
★ ★ ★ Gradually Going Tornado / Poly. (1980)

Feels Good to Me, the celebrated Yes/King Crimson drummer's first solo album, is a remarkably cohesive and inviting demonstration not just of Bruford's chops but of his compositional ability and excellent taste in musicians as well. Joined by art-rock and progressive jazz cult heroes Dave Stewart, Allan Holdsworth and Annette Peacock (among others), Bruford ran the gamut from frantic fusion races like "Beelzebub" to a combination of spatial funk and liquid jazz balladry in "Seems Like a Lifetime Ago." And Bruford wisely leaves all the solos to his sidemen.

One of a Kind and *Gradually Going Tornado,* recorded with the core band of the first album (John Clark later replaced Holdsworth on guitar), are for the most part impressive technically but are not as melodic and lack diversity in arrangements. Ditto *The Bruford Tapes,* a live reprise of the first two records. — D.F.

BRUSH ARBOR

★ Page One / Monu. (1976)
★ Straight / Monu. (1977)

Essentially nondescript country-rock band covering a range of bad material like Buzz Cason's "Emmylou" and the original composition "God Is Good, God Is Love." — J.S.

PEABO BRYSON

★ ★ ★ Peabo / Bullet (1976)
★ ★ ★ Reaching for the Sky / Cap. (1978)
★ ★ ★ Crosswinds / Cap. (1978)
★ ★ ★ We're the Best of Friends (with Natalie Cole) / Cap. (1979)
★ ★ ★ Paradise / Cap. (1980)
★ ★ ★ I Am Love / Cap. (1981)
★ ★ ★ Turn the Hands of Time / Cap. (1981)

A competent if uninspired soul singer who might amount to something someday if he could ever find a way to focus his mind on something more intriguing than the most conventional odes to heartbreak and lust. — D.M.

B.T. EXPRESS

★ ★ Non-Stop / Road. (1975) ¶
★ ★ Energy to Burn / Col. (1976)
★ ★ Function at the Junction / Col. (1977) ¶
★ ★ Shout / Col. (1978) ¶
★ ★ 1980 / Col. (1980)

As formulaic as the most assembly-line vocal group production, the music of B.T. Express is the prototype for a slew of faceless bar bands who have assumed disco and funk prominence. The songs are mindlessly simple and differ little from album to album. Their first hit, "Do It ('Til You're Satisfied)" (on their now-deleted Scepter album), provides the model: a repetitive vocal chant, lots of mid-range hand clapping to punctuate the beat (the bottom is all but removed from the mix), and a simple horn riff to give the barest hint of melody. If you've heard one, you've heard them all. — J.MC.

ROY BUCHANAN

★ Roy Buchanan / Poly. (1972)
★ Second Album / Poly. (1973)
★ That's What I'm Here For / Poly. (1974) ¶
★ In the Beginning / Poly. (1974)
★ ★ Live Stock / Poly. (1975)
★ ★ A Street Called Straight / Atl. (1976)
★ ★ Loading Zone / Atl. (1977)
★ ★ You're Not Alone / Atl. (1978)
★ ★ ★ My Babe / Waterh. (1980)

Roy Buchanan's career attests to the power both of suggestion and of the guitar in rock. He is, in a sense, the perfect example of why the best players aren't necessarily the best artists. As a technician, he has long been a legend, burning out electric solos with a trebly tone and high-volume sustain that produced distortion effects not unlike Beck's or Hendrix's. Lauded by other guitar players for his technique, in 1972 he suddenly found himself with a national audience. But Buchanan lacks the imaginative presence to do anything with either his technique or his base of listeners.

Part of this is due to the bands with which he has usually worked: decent veterans of the Maryland bars where Buchanan made his reputation, they moved *too* easily from country to rock to blues. Because they lacked a proper vocalist—Buchanan sings in a talking monotone that deserves never to have been recorded—the guitar had to carry the whole load. And while Buchanan's howling leads could elicit nods of appreciation from guitar aficionados, they couldn't supply a sufficient musical context.

The Atlantic albums, in which Buchanan is working with better-equipped professionals—Arif Mardin among others—give him a better showcase. Although a good deal of what's on them is still self-indulgent, the smoother backgrounds at least put it in relatively tasteful relief. *My Babe* is a strong return to his roots in Fifties rock, featuring great versions of the Little Walter title track and the ballad "Secret Love." — J.B.M.

BUCKEYE
★ **Buckeye / Poly. (1979)**
Exactly the kind of nowhere soft rock that record companies like to think is catchy . . . catch*ing* is more like it. The only thing worse than obscurity for records like this is success. — D.M.

LINDSEY BUCKINGHAM
★ ★ ★ **Law and Order / Asy. (1981)**
Solo LP from Fleetwood Mac guitarist that spawned successful single ("Trouble") upon release. *Law and Order* is most like Buckingham's contributions to Mac's *Tusk*. His active musical intelligence and curiosity and the precision of his execution nearly camouflage the slightness of Buckingham's underlying notions. The vocals suggest a Fifties teen balladeer lurking beneath the shimmering rock star glorified by the jacket's portrait. — G.A.

BUCKINGHAM NICKS
★ ★ **Buckingham Nicks / Poly. (1973)**
Pleasant, albeit middleweight Los Angeles folk rock. Stevie Nicks and Lindsey Buckingham present narcotic voice and guitar respectively, although only "Crystal" gives a hint of what would galvanize when they joined Fleetwood Mac. — J.B.M.

THE BUCKINGHAMS
★ ★ ★ **Greatest Hits / Col. (1969)**

★ ★ **Made in Chicago / Col. (1975) ¶**
The Buckinghams, Chicago's answer to the British Invasion and producer James William Guercio's first hit machine, encapsulated a number of influences (straight pop, R&B and progressive rock). *Made in Chicago* is a bloated two-record set that includes all their Columbia hits, while *Greatest Hits* is a more concise collection that has the distinct advantage of boasting their original organ-powered smash, "Kind of a Drag." In their heavily arranged approach, the Buckinghams predated the brass-pop sound of Chicago (also produced by Guercio) with a lighter pop consciousness that could produce indulgent dreck ("Foreign Policy") as well as sublime pop fluff—"Don't You Care," "Hey Baby (They're Playing Our Song)."
— J.B.M.

TIM BUCKLEY
★ ★ ★ **Goodbye and Hello / Elek. (1967)**
This is the late Tim Buckley's masterpiece, and in fact his only commercially successful album in the United States. His second record, it epitomizes the dense songwriting and elaborate production accorded the first wave of singer/songwriters in that period. The album's theme, also typical, is announced in the very long and very Dylan-influenced title song as the conflict between the "death and war" generation and the "life and love" generation that Buckley celebrates with a solipsist's abandon. Blood, Sweat and Tears was only one of several groups who covered songs from *Goodbye and Hello,* and it was promptly predicted that Buckley would soon become our new major songwriter.

That never happened, because in the many deleted albums after *Goodbye and Hello,* Buckley futilely sought a jazz-folk fusion, and in the process virtually abandoned regular songwriting completely. His writing became progressively sparser and his vocals increasingly eccentric in expression. From *Happy/Sad* through *Starsailor* made with the horn section of the original Mothers of Invention, Buckley was almost totally forgotten in the world of Cat Stevens and James Taylor.

Late in his failed career, however, Buckley made one burning, madly erotic rock album, *Greetings from L.A.* (Warner Bros.). Curiously, this is the Buckley album his fans outside the United States have kept in print, while outside the United States *Goodbye and Hello* is out of print along with all the others. *Greetings* is probably the best album Buckley recorded, and it is certainly the best album to remember him by, for it was made by a beaten man still capable of desperate ecstasies. — B.T.

THOMAS BUCKNASTY
■ Blast-O-Funk / RCA (NA)
Rot-o-record. — J.S.

BUCKS FIZZ
★ Bucks Fizz / RCA (1981), Br. imp.
With the Abba-esque "Making Your Mind Up," Bucks Fizz won the 1981 Eurovision Song Contest, an annual competition to identify and celebrate the blandest musical entertainers in Europe. The problem with the record is that you can't see the girls whip their skirts off. — ML.H.

BUDGIE
★ In for the Kill / MCA (1974) ¶
★ If I Were Brittania I'd Waive the Rules / A&M (1976)
★ Bandolier / A&M (1976)
★ Impeckable / A&M (1978)
Working in the now-traditional power trio format, this band suffers from a startling paucity of original ideas, riffs or songs. Their sound is thin, their music hackneyed and repetitive. — A.N.

NORTON BUFFALO
★ ★ ★ Lovin' in the Valley of the Moon / Cap. (1977)
★ ★ ★ Desert Horizon / Cap. (1978)
Steve Miller's harmonica player turns out to be a surprisingly capable performer on his own, with a mixture of blues and country rock and occasional dabblings with electronic effects. — D.M.

BUFFALO SPRINGFIELD
★ ★ ★ Buffalo Springfield / Atco (1966)
★ ★ ★ ★ ★ Buffalo Springfield Again / Atco (1967)
★ ★ ★ Last Time Around / Atco (1968)
★ ★ ★ Retrospective / Atco (1969)
★ ★ ★ ★ ★ Buffalo Springfield / Atco (1976)
Along with the Byrds, the Buffalo Springfield defined an eclectic country-rock style during the mid-Sixties that remains current and has been widely influential. Formed by a couple of itinerant folkies, Stephen Stills and Richie Furay, led by the macabre singer/songwriter/lead guitarist Neil Young, and anchored by ex-Dillards drummer Dewey Martin (bassists Bruce Palmer, then later Jim Messina rounded out the group), the Springfield made two brilliantly eccentric records before tearing themselves apart. The first, *Buffalo Springfield,* showcased Stills'

and Young's tremendous songwriting talent (Stills' "For What It's Worth" became the band's only major hit single) and Furay's distinctively countryish lead singing.

Their second, *Buffalo Springfield Again,* is the definitive album, with both Young and Stills at the top of their songwriting game, some weird and brilliant production assistance from Jack Nitzsche, and the meanest playing they got on record. The frenetic, eerily prophetic self-analysis in Young's "Mr. Soul" and "Broken Arrow" characterized his mystical songwriting, while Stills' "Rock & Roll Woman" and "Bluebird" are the finest songs he's ever written.

For all practical purposes the group no longer existed by *Last Time Around.* Except for Young's kiss-off, "On the Way Home," Stills' pretty "Uno Mundo" and Richie Furay's breathtaking country song "Kind Woman," the material doesn't match the band's prime output. They went their separate ways, Stills to Crosby, Stills and Nash; Young to a solo career with Crazy Horse, then later as part of Crosby, Stills, Nash and Young; Furay and Messina to Poco; and then Messina on to form Loggins and Messina.

For a group with such a short life span, the Springfield's influence becomes even more astounding. Their music has filtered relentlessly down into the work of the Eagles, Jackson Browne and countless others, a distinctly American rock style that has become the West Coast standard. Though *Again* is the definitive recording, the two-record anthology (*Buffalo Springfield,* 1976) is the best collection, highlighting pertinent material from all three records with the emphasis on the second album, including the original nine-minute version of "Bluebird," complete with the extended jam that had been edited out of the song as it appeared on *Again.* — J.S.

JIMMY BUFFETT
★ ★ ★ A White Sport Coat and a Pink Crustacean / Dun. (1973)
★ ★ Living and Dying in 3/4 Time / Dun. (1974)
★ ★ ★ A-1-A / Dun. (1974)
★ Havana Daydreamin' / ABC (1976)
★ ★ ★ Changes in Latitudes, Changes in Attitudes / ABC (1977)
★ ★ Son of a Son of a Sailor / ABC (1978)
★ ★ Live / ABC (1978) ¶
★ ★ You Had to Be There / MCA (1978)
★ ★ Volcano / MCA (1979)
★ ★ Somewhere over China / MCA (1981)
Buffett is a protean figure—part comic, part

drunkard, an inconsistent but occasionally great songwriter, leader of an ersatz country-rock group called the Coral Reefer Band. His songwriting is his strong suit. *Crustacean* featured a couple of crazed hippie anthems, "The Great Filling Station Holdup" and "Peanut Butter Conspiracy," and the pensive ode "Death of an Unpopular Poet." On the ensuing records, Buffett has a bad habit of indulging in overly camp material and too many woozy booze tunes, but there are bright moments on each album. High points are "This Hotel Room," "Kick It in Second Wind," and the title track from *Havana Daydreamin',* "Door #3," "Stories We Could Tell" and "Pirate Looks at Forty" from *A-1-A,* and the hit single off *Changes* that turned him from a cult figure to a pop star, "Margaritaville." — J.S.

BUGGLES
★ ★ **The Age of Plastic / Is. (1980)**
Aside from the wonderful "Video Killed the Radio Star"—perhaps the most successful recent example of a single where the production was catchier than the material—this is high-tech dreck. The idea here isn't selling pop songs, but impressing the listener with the all-around cleverness of Buggles Trevor Horn and Geoffrey Downes. Sadly, Horn and Downes shattered any such illusions by joining Yes shortly after the release of *The Age of Plastic.* — J.D.C.

BUGS TOMORROW
■ **Bugs Tomorrow / Casa. (1980)**
Someone must have thought they knew how to make a surefire hit record. Take all the rock clichés of the late Seventies and early Eighties, mix and match 'em, and everyone makes a million dollars. So half this bunch of L.A. no-talents is dressed in Devo costumes, the other half in punk regalia. Some of their songs are Springsteen-inspired "emotional" epics about the streets, cars and a girl, some of them Gary Numan futuristic, and the others power pop. Fortunately, no one bought this hideous product of marketing manipulation and Bugs Tomorrow has gone the way of most stupid ideas. — D.G.

SANDY BULL
★ ★ **Fantasias for Guitar and Banjo / Van. (1965)**
★ ★ **Inventions / Van. (1965)**
★ ★ **E Pluribus Unum / Van. (1970)**
★ ★ ★ **Demolition Derby / Van. (1972)**
★ ★ ★ **Essential / Van. (1974)** ¶
From the pristine string fantasias of his first album through the time when his drug habit

interrupted his progress in 1972, Sandy Bull made spellbinding music. A near prodigy on guitar and banjo at seventeen, he became a student of jazz as well as Indian and Arabic music. This eclectic streak resulted in "Blend," a twenty-two-minute side on *Fantasias for Guitar and Banjo.* On his second album, *Inventions,* he cut "Blend II," again working with veteran jazz drummer Billy Higgins.

He also played electric and acoustic takes of Gavotte No. 2 from Bach's Suite No. 5, and an instrumental version of Chuck Berry's "Memphis, Tennessee." Influenced by Pop Staples' gospel guitar work, he split his six-string Fender electric's signal between four kinds of amplification on *E Pluribus Unum:* "Electric Blend" and "No Deposit, No Return Blues" are a smack freak's workouts for 1970 acid eaters. His last recording, *Demolition Derby,* is a scary mix of Latin juking ("Gotta Be Juicy") and country warbling ("Tennessee Waltz" and Floyd Cramer's "Last Date"). *The Essential Sandy Bull* compilation covers the terrain, but *Demolition Derby* is a haunting promise from a career that may yet be revived. — F.S.

BULLDOG
★ **Smasher / Bud. (1974)** ¶
Ex-Rascals Gene Cornish (guitar) and Dino Danelli (drums) couldn't rescue this now-defunct foursome's anonymous hard rock. Nothing really wrong, but precious little on target. — C.W.

CINDY BULLENS
★ ★ **Desire Wire / U.A. (1978)**
★ ★ **Steal the Night / U.A. (1978)**
Bullens would like to come on as an authentic female hard rocker. Maybe she is, but her pair of solo albums are forced hard rock, and in that light, her most revealing credential may not be her work with occasional Real Thing Elton John but her appearance in the ultimate Anti-Rock Epic, *Grease.*
— D.M.

BULLSEYE
■ **On Target / Col. (1979)** ¶
Among its other nifty "original" songs, Bullseye has come up with one called "Seventh Heaven." For pathetic rockers like these, the operative image ought to be Ninth Circle.
— D.M.

VERNON BURCH
★ ★ ★ **When I Get Back Home / Col. (1977)** ¶
★ ★ ★ **Get Up / Choc. (NA)**
★ ★ ★ **Love-a-Thon / Choc. (NA)**

★ ★ ★ **Steppin' Out / Choc. (NA)**
On his deleted 1975 debut album (United Artists), Vernon Burch astounded people with his vocal similarity to Stevie Wonder. Burch mastered Wonder's touch, phrasing and general mood on songs like "Ain't Gonna Tell Nobody." He also played lead guitar, which had been his main bread-and-butter gig with the re-formed Bar-Kays, and his guitar work was as derivative (in the Stax/Volt psychedelic mode made popular by Isaac Hayes circa *Hot Buttered Soul*) as his singing. The subsequent albums move him closer to a disco style and add an Al Green touch to the Wonder influence.
— J.S.

ERIC BURDON AND WAR
★ ★ **Love Is All Around / ABC (1976)** ¶
War helped make Burdon's last great single, "Spill the Wine," but MGM has deleted their first LP—*Eric Burdon Declares War*—which is one of his best. *Love* is funky fooling around from the same era (1969–70, mostly) and ranks with Burdon's silliest—"A Day in the Life" as a blues song is foolish indeed. War has gone on to become one of the Seventies' most interesting and influential black bands. — D.M.

ERIC BURDON BAND
■ **Ring of Fire / Cap. (1974)** ¶
■ **Stop / Cap. (1975)** ¶
It wasn't uncommon for the early Burdon to cross the border from emotional involvement to hysteria. Generally he was saved by the excellence of his bands, War and the Animals. By 1974, when he made these records, he couldn't have cleared customs—even when recycling some of his old hits, the band is so clumsy, Burdon so overextended, that nothing works. — D.M.

SONNY BURGESS
★ ★ **Legendary Sun Performer / Charly (NA), Br. imp.**
Sun performer, yes. Burgess did rockabilly for Sam Phillips in the Fifties just like all the greats. Legendary, however . . . sorry, but Burgess managed to get through the experience without ever recording a single really exceptional track. Even his one putatively famous number, "We Wanna Boogie," is best known for a line Burgess simply throws away, not for any excellence of performance. Fanatics only. — D.M.

KENI BURKE
★ **You're the Best / RCA (1981)**
Former member of the Five Stairsteps, later a prominent session bassist, Burke originally recorded for George Harrison's Dark Horse label. This set is utterly pedestrian soul-funk, and explores what seems to be every cliché of contemporary black pop before stumbling to its conclusion. — D.M.

SOLOMON BURKE
★ ★ ★ ★ ★ **The Best of Solomon Burke / Atl. (1965)** ¶
★ **Music to Make Love By / Chess (1975)** ¶
★ **Back to My Roots / Chess (1977)** ¶
★ ★ ★ **Sidewalks, Fences and Walls / Inf. (1979)**
★ ★ ★ **From the Heart / Charly (1980), Br. imp.**
Unlike other soul stars of the Sixties, who sang their music with unflagging intensity—often to the point of hysteria—Solomon Burke was the master of control. The music on *The Best of Solomon Burke* is majestic and dignified, yet as powerful as the most volatile recorded performances of Wilson Pickett. But Burke's restraint was only part of his genius. He was also a most convincing storyteller, as well as a shameless eclectic, capable of absorbing a range of idioms and influences in his singing and songwriting. When Solomon said in the intro to "Everybody Needs Somebody to Love," "There's a song I sing, and I believe if everybody was to sing this song it would save the whole world," I believed him. So, it seems did Mick Jagger: Burke has proven to be one of Jagger's biggest influences as a vocalist.
  Solomon Burke needed a producer's touch in the studio. His self-productions have often been embarrassing. A Barry White imitation on *Music to Make Love By* provided a temporary commercial respite, but the hopefully titled *Back to My Roots* proved to be the nadir of his career. — J.MC.

BILLY BURNETTE
★ ★ **Billy Burnette / Poly. (1979)**
★ ★ **Between Friends / Poly. (1979)**
★ ★ ★ **Billy Burnette / Col. (1980)**
★ ★ **Gimme You / Col. (1981)**
Son of Dorsey, nephew of Johnny, lives up to his rockabilly lineage only on eponymous Columbia debut LP, where he even essays a passable version of Pop's "Honey Hush." *Gimme You* is a nonresonant rehash of that one, while the Polydor albums, cut before rockabilly again became voguish in the U.S., are bland pop-rock. — D.M.

BILLY JOE BURNETTE
■ **Welcome Home, Elvis / Gusto (1977)** ¶

Quickie release after The King's death. This one takes our hero all the way to heaven's gate itself, with recitatives and hymns, many of them done in pure Elvis-imitator style. This is the kind of music that deserves to be sold across the street from Graceland . . . and absolutely nowhere else. — D.M.

DORSEY BURNETTE
★ **Things I Treasure / Calli. (NA) ¶**
★ **Dorsey Burnette / Zirkon (NA)**
Brother of late Johnny Burnette, Dorsey was never quite as fine a rocker in the first place, and by the time of these Seventies LPs, had gone the way of all ex-rockabillies: to bland C&W. — D.M.

JOHNNY BURNETTE AND THE ROCK AND ROLL TRIO
★ ★ ★ ★ **Tear It Up / Solid S. (1976)**
★ ★ ★ **Johnny and Dorsey Burnette Together Again / Solid S. (1978)**
Excellent sampler of the late rockabilly artist's 1956 and 1957 recordings, with excellent liner notes and pristine monaural sound. Includes his seminal "Train Kept A-Rollin'," plus the remarkable "Rock Therapy," but not his pop hits, even "You're Sixteen." *Together Again* is raw takes, very marginal stuff. — D.M.

ROCKY BURNETTE
★ ★ ★ **Son of Rock & Roll / EMI (1980)**
Son of Johnny, nephew of Dorsey, has come closer than cousin Billy to living up to his genes, thanks to a perfect rockabilly update, "Tired of Toein' the Line," which became a Top Ten smash in 1980. Oddly, Burnette has yet to sustain as much energy as Billy on LP—*Son of Rock & Roll* contains constant reminders that Pop wound up a bathetic ballad singer after his Rock & Roll Trio beginnings. — D.M.

T-BONE BURNETTE
★ ★ ★ **Truth Decay / Tak. (1980)**
Burnette was one of the leaders of the Alpha Band and a key member of Bob Dylan's Rolling Thunder Revue, in which he played guitar. Here he has come up with an album of what can only be called mystic Christian blues, played fast, raw and loose. Burnette's not much of a singer, or this would rate higher. — D.M.

BURNING SPEAR
★ ★ ★ ★ ★ **Marcus Garvey / Is. (1976)**
★ ★ ★ ★ **Garvey's Ghost / Is. (1976)**
★ ★ ★ ★ **Man in the Hills / Is. (1976)**
★ ★ ★ **Dry and Heavy / Mango (1977)**
★ ★ ★ **Live / Is. (1978)**
★ ★ ★ ★ ★ **Harder Than the Rest / Mango (1979)**
★ ★ ★ ★ **Social Living / Is./UK/Burning Spear (1980)**
★ ★ ★ **Hail H.I.M. / Burning Spear (1980)**
Reggae is political music by definition, and Burning Spear is the genre's most stridently political group—their first album and its best-selling title track are named for the back-to-Africa leader of the Twenties who gave Rastafarianism its cultural impetus.

Garvey is a great reggae album, and *Garvey's Ghost*'s title track is one of the landmarks of the reggae offshoot called "dub," which involves releasing instrumental tracks, and heightening them for even more intensity. But despite the group's great sense of groove and the sporadic brilliance of vocalist Winston Rodney, after *Man in the Hills,* the music has grown colder, less approachable. Even the live album, which might have been as formidable as Rodney's stage presence, peters out in playing that is virtually directionless. Rodney has never compromised his relentless, hypnotic groove and has never made a bad record (his hard-to-get Studio One LPs are essential). *Social Living* offers a spacier dimension than usual—the title masterpiece and "Civilised Reggae" seem intergalactic in scope. *Hail H.I.M.* has dense textures and heavy rhythms and rocks monolithically. *Harder,* a compilation of Mango cuts, is one of the great reggae LPs. — D.M./R.F.G.

MARY BURNS
★ **Mary Burns / MCA (1980)**
What a great voice. What a lousy record. — R.P.

HAROLD BURRAGE
★ ★ ★ **She Knocks Me Out / Fly. (1981), Br. imp.**
Mid-Fifties Cobra label sides recorded by solid if derivative Chicago R&B shouter. Mostly, Burrage is in the Big Joe Turner mold (if not in Big Joe's league), although he occasionally rocks out à la Little Richard or comes close to Roy Brown's crooning. None of this adds up to a distinctive style, but all of it is sufficiently engaging for genre fans. — D.M.

J.C. BURRIS
★ ★ ★ **On the Road / Folk. (1959)**
Burris, the nephew of famed blues harpist Sonny Terry, follows in Terry's footsteps as

a singer and harp player. He has the energy
Sonny surely once had, but not yet the ri-
pening of talent that Terry's maturity has
brought him. — R.P.

PAT BURTON
★ ★ ★ **We've Been Waiting for This** / **Fly.
Fish (1974)**
★ ★ ★ **Slumberin' on the Cumberland** / **Fly.
Fish (1979)**
An associate of John Hartford, bluegrass
guitarist Pat Burton displays an equal facility
with instrument, voice and song. — R.P.

BUS BOYS
★ ★ ★ ★ **Minimum Wage Rock & Roll** /
Ari. (1980)
The Bus Boys make no bones about being a novelty act. Not only are they a rock & roll group
consisting of five blacks and a Chicano, but they
sing songs like "KKK" and "There Goes the
Neighborhood." You have heard songs like
these before—if you've heard Chuck Berry—
but not recently. What makes the Bus Boys
work on a level beyond novelty is that, lyrics to
the contrary, their rock & roll is not a shtick but
a genuine musical commitment. Few bands can
make basic bar-band licks sound this fresh.
— J.D.C.

KATE BUSH
★ ★ **The Kick Inside** / **Harv. (1978)**
English thrush who created a storm in cer-
tain critical quarters in late 1978. Not
exactly new wave, not exactly art-rock. Sort
of like the consequences of mating Patti
Smith with a Hoover vacuum cleaner.
— D.M.

DAVID BUSKIN
★ **David Buskin** / **Epic (1972)** ¶
East Coast acoustic singer/songwriter. Lightweight reflective songs crooned in pleasant
voice. — S.H.

CARL AND PEARL BUTLER
★ ★ ★ **Honky-Tonkitis** / **CMH (NA)**
Vocalists from the Grand Ole Opry reprise
their Sixties repertoire with a contemporary
backing of Nashville sessioneers. — J.S.

JERRY BUTLER
★ ★ ★ **All-Time Jerry Butler Hits** / **Trip
(NA)** ¶
★ ★ ★ **Sixteen Greatest Hits** / **Trip (NA)** ¶
★ ★ ★ **Just Beautiful** / **Kent (NA)** ¶
★ ★ **Starring Betty Everett** / **Trad. (NA)**
★ ★ ★ ★ ★ **The Best of Jerry Butler** / **Mer.
(1970)**
★ ★ **Love's on the Menu** / **Mo. (1976)**

★ **Suite for the Single Girl** / **Mo. (1977)** ¶
★ ★ **It All Comes Out in My Song** / **Mo.
(1977)** ¶
★ ★ ★ **Nothing Says I Love You** / **Phil.
(1978)**
★ ★ **Thelma and Jerry** / **Mo. (1977)** ¶
★ ★ ★ **The Best Love I Ever Had** / **Phil.
(1980)**
Butler began his singing career in a church
choir in Chicago that also included Curtis
Mayfield and Sam Gooder; together they
were the original Impressions, although after
Butler's "For Your Precious Love," a beauti-
ful, big-voiced soul ballad, became a national
hit in 1958, he left the group to go solo with
Vee-Jay Records, while Mayfield took the
Impressions in other directions. The Trip,
Kent and Tradition LPs feature his Vee-Jay
work, which also included "He Will Break
Your Heart," with Betty Everett; "Giving
Up on Love"; and an unfortunate amount of
straight pop material like "Moon River."
But Butler's most brilliant music was
made when he teamed with Philadelphia
producers Kenneth Gamble and Leon Huff
for a series of late-Sixties singles. The hits
"Only the Strong Survive," "Never Give
You Up," "Lost," "What's the Use of
Breaking Up," "Moody Woman" and "Hey
Western Union Man" resulted, and they are
an apex of the era's record-making, with an
appeal that stretches across pop and soul
boundaries. Butler's voice was the first vehicle Gamble and Huff found for their orchestral funk ideas, and it remains the most expressive. It is reserved but emotional—the
two excellent but depleted albums he made
with Gamble and Huff for Mercury were
called *Ice on Ice* and *The Iceman Cometh*—
with a nice trick of moving from verse to
verse in guttural drags. (The lyrics, particularly "Only the Strong Survive," were far
ahead of their time, and easily the best Gamble and Huff have written.)
Unfortunately, Butler has not been able to
keep pace with the changes in black pop
taste; the series of albums he's made for Motown are strained, unable to find a satisfactory compromise between his crooning naturalness and the rhythm attack of modern
disco production. The duet album with
Thelma Houston, which attempts to recapture the spirit of his duets with Everett, is
perhaps the best of them, but all are disappointing. — D.M.

JOAN CAROL BUTLER
★ ★ ★ **Joan Carol Butler** / **Cap. (1976)** ¶
A competent purveyor of down-home love

songs, Joan Butler can be good when she's not cloying. The backing by the Muscle Shoals rhythm section emphasizes Butler's similarity to Fleetwood Mac's Christine McVie. — J.S.

PAUL BUTTERFIELD

★ ★ ★ **The Paul Butterfield Blues Band /**
  Elek. (1965)
★ ★ ★ ★ **East-West / Elek. (1966)**
★ ★ ★ **The Resurrection of Pigboy**
  Crabshaw / Elek. (1968)
★ ★ ★ **In My Own Dream / Elek. (1968)** ¶
★ ★ **The Butterfield Blues Band/Live /**
  Elek. (1971)
★ ★ ★ **Golden Butter/The Best of the Paul**
  Butterfield Blues Band / Elek. (1972)
★ ★ ★ **It All Comes Back / Bears. (1973)** ¶
★ ★ ★ **Paul Butterfield/Better Days / Bears.**
  (1973) ¶
★ **Put It in Your Ear / Bears. (1976)** ¶
★ **North South / Bears. (1981)**
It would be easy to see Paul Butterfield purely in historical terms—he was, after all, the American musician most responsible for introducing urban blues to rock audiences— but that would overlook the music, which holds up surprisingly well. Perhaps none of it equals the bluesmen he emulated, but little of it is shoddy, either. Butterfield was a popularizer, but an authentic one, who gave credit where credit was due (Little Walter, Muddy Waters, Howlin' Wolf) and rejected imitation as strongly as he did bastardization. His first album, *The Paul Butterfield Blues Band,* seemed more imprisoned by blues than freed by it, but on the second, *East-West,* he cut traditional ties without losing track of them, shifting sources from Allen Toussaint's R&B to Cannonball Adderley's jazz. The album's centerpiece, however, was its title song, a thirteen-minute instrumental track whose lengthy and brilliant guitar passages (by Mike Bloomfield and Elvin Bishop) did as much as anything to establish the mystique and heroism of modern rock guitarists.

As his band continued to change personnel (Bloomfield left to form Electric Flag after *East-West*), Butterfield expanded into R&B (*The Resurrection of Pigboy Crabshaw* and *In My Own Dream*) and began to use a full horn section. If most of Butterfield's albums now seem a bit secondhand, it is in part because he was too humble a performer to conquer his sources. Unlike Van Morrison, for instance, Butterfield always conceived of blues as a tradition, not as a sensibility. Even after he disbanded the Blues Band and formed Better Days (a crack rock

& roll unit that included such players as Amos Garrett and Geoff Muldaur), he never projected himself, never conveyed a sense of who he was or what he wanted to say. While both the albums recorded with his early-Seventies group, Better Days (the debut album *Butterfield/Better Days* and *It All Comes Back*), boast a formal imagination, they lack a personal one. His last record, a collaboration with former King Records' producer Henry Glover, collapses altogether. An experiment in modern R&B, *Put It in Your Ear* buries Butterfield in a mountain of effects and he seems completely lost—a final metaphor for a rich but narrow career.
  — K.R.

THE BUZZARDS

★ ★ ★ **Jellied Eels to Record Deals / Chrys.**
  (1979), Br. imp.
An extensive (seventeen-track) career retrospective consisting of singles and unreleased studio sessions from a largely unknown but surprisingly clever London punk quartet. The (Leyton) Buzzards' self-effacing good humor, ragged instrumental clumsiness and substantial lyrical cleverness suggest latent intelligence and charm. — I.R.

BUZZCOCKS

★ ★ ★ ★ **Singles Going Steady / IRS (1979)**
★ ★ ★ **A Different Kind of Tension / IRS**
  (1980)
Hailing from Manchester, England, the Buzzcocks were at the forefront of the British punk upheaval. Original singer Howard Devoto booked one of the Sex Pistols' first major concerts outside London, and his group's 1977 debut EP, *Spiral Scratch,* remains a seminal document of British new-wave angst.

When Devoto left that same year to form Magazine, guitarist Pete Shelley took the helm as singer and main songwriter, and it was his troubled romanticism in combination with his pop savvy and the band's relentless drill-press sound that distinguished the Buzzcocks from the rest of the safety-pin bawlers. They recorded three albums before Shelley went solo early in 1981, but it was on singles that Shelley and the band expressed themselves best. *Singles Going Steady* compiles their first eight British singles, complete with B sides, and it is at once an exhilarating and harrowing experience, Shelley's powerful emotional outbursts ("Orgasm Addict," "What Do I Get?" "Ever Fallen in Love (With Someone You Shouldn't Have Fallen in Love With)?") caught up in the frantic rush of the band and his own riveting song hooks. *A Different Kind of Tension,* the Buzzcocks' only other U.S. release, couldn't help but pale in comparison. — D.F.

JOSEPH BYRD
★ ★ ★ **The American Metaphysical Circus /** Col. (1969)
★ **A Christmas Yet to Come** / Tak. (1975)
★ **Yankee Transcendoodle** / Tak. (1976)

Byrd is rock's original electronic experimentalist. After dropping out of UCLA and the experimental music scene to become a summer-of-lovester, he made *The American Metaphysical Circus,* a kind of pre-Glass, post-Riley rock-influenced electronic-noise concept album (by "Joe Byrd and the Field Hippies") and produced voguish "happenings." The results are sufficiently innocent to be appealing.

By the mid-Seventies, Byrd had tempered his ambitions, and the Takoma albums are merely synthesizer reworkings of standard tunes—carols and the like on *A Christmas Yet to Come,* patriotic airs and folk songs on *Transcendoodle.* These come a lot closer to Muzak than is allowable in these parts. — D.M.

THE BYRDS
★ ★ ★ ★ ★ **Mr. Tambourine Man** / Col. (1965)
★ ★ ★ ★ ★ **Turn! Turn! Turn!** / Col. (1966)
(Jim McGuinn, guitar; Gene Clark, tambourine; David Crosby, guitar; Chris Hillman, bass; Michael Clarke, drums)

The unmistakable sound of the Byrds—trebly electric twelve-string guitar, rock bottom bass and soaring vocal harmonies—marked the rise to prominence of West Coast folk rock. Intelligence, sensitivity and self-consciousness are reflected in the first two Byrds albums, which neatly blend traditional folk ("He Was a Friend of Mine," "Satisfied Mind," "Turn! Turn! Turn!"), new folk (a myriad of Dylan tunes) and thoughtful, original pop (Clark's "I'll Feel a Whole Lot Better," "The World Turns All Around Her"). They even have a sense of humor—*Tambourine Man* closes with that big hit from *Dr. Strangelove,* "We'll Meet Again," and *Turn!* drags Stephen Foster's "Oh! Susannah!" out of the cellar, tongue firmly in cheek.

★ ★ ★ ★ **Fifth Dimension** / Col. (1966)
★ ★ ★ ★ ★ **Younger Than Yesterday** / Col. (1967)
★ ★ ★ ★ ★ **Byrds' Greatest Hits** / Col. (1967)
★ ★ ★ ★ **The Notorious Byrd Brothers /** Col. (1968)

★ ★ ★ ★ **The Byrds Play Dylan** / Col. (1980)

Gene Clark's departure before the recording of *Fifth Dimension* tosses chief songwriting burdens on McGuinn and Crosby, and they fare more than adequately under the pressure. The group begins to experiment both lyrically and instrumentally, using the mysteries of space as exploratory grounds. "Eight Miles High," with its atonal, chaotic lead guitar (influenced by both John Coltrane and Indian ragas), ushers in psychedelia a year ahead of schedule. Roots are still revered, though, through lovely readings of traditional songs "John Riley" and "Wild Mountain Thyme." *Younger Than Yesterday,* with the last two Byrds hits, the ironic "So You Want to Be a Rock 'n' Roll Star" and the bittersweet cover of Dylan's "My Back Pages," again breaks new ground, as Hillman, a former bluegrass mandolinist, writes and sings lead on four songs, two of which ("Girl with No Name," "Time Between") are bona-fide country tunes. A *Greatest Hits* package was then released; Columbia correctly sensed that the era of Byrd hit singles was ending. Crosby drops out in the middle of recording sessions for *Notorious Byrd Brothers,* yet the band (McGuinn changes his first name to Roger at this time), using the production breakthrough that *Sgt. Pepper* made possible, keeps right on going. And they remain the Byrds, as exemplified by their transformation of Carole King's "Goin' Back," with its simple but emotional twelve-string solo.

★ ★ ★ ★ ★ **Sweetheart of the Rodeo** / Col. (1968)
(Roger McGuinn, guitar and banjo; Gram Parsons, guitar; Chris Hillman, bass and mandolin; Kevin Kelley, drums)

With a revamped lineup, the Byrds plunge into country music, achieving a delicate balance similar to their first two albums. Parsons, who dominates the record, pens the two originals ("Hickory Wind," "One Hundred Years from Now"), both gems. Songs by Dylan, Woody Guthrie, the Louvin Brothers and Merle Travis are all treated masterfully. Guest musicians include John Hartford and Clarence White, flatpicker extraordinaire.

★ ★ ★ **Dr. Byrds & Mr. Hyde** / Col. (1969)
★ ★ ★ **Untitled** / Col. (1970)
★ ★ ★ **The Ballad of Easy Rider** / Col. (1970) ¶
(Roger McGuinn, guitar; Clarence White, guitar; Gene Parsons, drums; John York, bass [*Dr. Byrds*]; Skip Battin, bass)

McGuinn's ambivalence about turning the group into a country band leads to Parsons' and Hillman's departure to form the Flying Burrito Brothers. The new Byrds do some country, but they also can rock out. White brings a new dimension to Byrds guitar, most evident on "King Apathy III" and Dylan's "This Wheel's on Fire." The new band is promising, and their next effort, *Easy Rider,* is a masterpiece. Battin replaces York for *Untitled,* a double set with one studio and one live LP. The live set works, with updated versions of Byrds oldies, but the studio side, save McGuinn's "Chestnut Mare" and White's rendition of Little Feat's "Truck Stop Girl," is mostly filler. Battin simply cannot write Byrd songs.
★ ★ **Best of the Byrds/Greatest Hits, Vol. 2 / Col. (1972)**
★ ★ ★ ★ **Preflyte / Col. (1973)**
The second *Greatest Hits* package, released just prior to the Byrds' final breakup in '72, is a hodgepodge of songs from the band's entire career with little to recommend it. *Preflyte* is a posthumous release of the original group's demo tape and illuminates the beauty of the initial conception. Nine of the eleven tracks hadn't been previously released, and most of them, especially "You Showed Me" and "You Won't Have to Cry" are first-rate. (The original band did re-form for one record, *Byrds* [Asylum, available as a cutout], in '73, but time had finally taken its toll, and it's an embarrassing disappointment.) — B.A.

ROBERT BYRNE
★ **Blame It on the Night / Mer. (1979)**
How about blaming it on Robert Byrne?
— D.M.

DAVID BYRON
■ **Take No Prisoners / Mer. (1976)** ¶
Histrionic ex-Uriah Heep singer may be the most irritating front man of Seventies rock, and his solo debut does nothing to alter that judgment. Definitely *not* a Byronic hero.
— J.S.

D. L. BYRON
★ ★ ★ **This Day and Age / Ari. (1980)**
Everyone was so busy shrugging "Springsteen clone" (justified) that they ignored this record (unjustified). Byron has a gorgeous rock & roll baritone, a mercilessly tight band and a measurable helping of that arcane magic that makes his resemblance to Springsteen (almost) beside the point. — L.F.

THE CADETS
★ ★ ★ **Rock 'n' Roll Hits of the Fifties /**
  United (NA)

Also known as the Jacks, the Cadets' claim
to fame was "Stranded in the Jungle," one
of the most bizarre examples of rhythm &
blues tomfoolery in history. There's nothing
else here to match that one transcendent moment, but the other tracks here are typical
group harmony from the period. Still,
"Stranded" is better heard as a single or,
more likely, on an anthology where it is surrounded by other vintage items—a kind of
vinyl radio experience, as it was meant to be.
  — D.M.

SHIRLEY CAESAR
★ ★ **First Lady / Road. (1977)**
★ ★ ★ ★ **Shirley Caesar / Up Fr. (NA)**
★ ★ ★ ★ **The Best of Shirley Caesar with**
  the Caravans / Savoy (NA)

Though young, Caesar reached her fame as a
note-bending preacher of gospel's old school;
she can also be the most mesmerizingly intense of modern singers. The Savoy sides are
crude and bluesy, her voice displaying astonishing power and range. (Though the Caravans—also including Inez Andrews and Al-
bertina Walker—were one of the most
popular gospel groups, it's mainly the sides
with Caesar that are of interest to rock fans.)

On her own, Caesar sang in a more old-
fashioned style; yet as a preacher, she also
rapped advice à la Millie Jackson and
showed abundant humor. These are her Hob
sides, some of which comprise the Up Front
compilation. *First Lady* is secular songs with
spiritual themes and proof that the transition
from gospel to soul isn't entirely natural:
constricted by the style's conventions, she is
an undistinguished soul singer. — J.MO.

CAFE JACQUES
★ ★ ★ ★ **Round the Back / Col. (1978)** ¶
★ ★ ★ **International / Col. (1978)**

Excellent British studio band whose dense
rhythmic mix and melodic keyboard textures
recall Traffic's lyricism and Little Feat's syncopation. — J.S.

JOHN CAGE
★ ★ ★ ★ ★ **Indeterminacy / Folk. (1959)**
★ ★ ★ ★ **Variations IV / Ev. (1965)**
★ ★ ★ ★ **Variations II / Col. (1967)**
★ ★ ★ **Electronics and Percussion / Col.**
  (1968)
★ ★ ★ **HPSCHD / None. (NA)**

Modern classical minimalist John Cage influenced Frank Zappa, Todd Rundgren, Brian
Eno and the other tape nuts of rock, but his
importance is also felt by dancers, film-
makers and artists all over the world. His
concept of Zenlike total harmony—not just
in the music, when it exists, but in the roles
of composition, performance, arena and participants—shifted the moment of creation,
demystified it and brought it into the concert
hall. His pieces can seem heavily manufactured, yet primordial. And with the freedom
he gives to his musicians (they do not impro-
vise, as jazz musicians do, but follow his
scores at will), he always makes sure some
certain somethings happen. Each performance is caught in time, impossible to pre-
dict, for the audience or for Cage.

Indeterminacy is ninety stories read by
Cage, each told within the space of a minute, and none having anything to do with
the next. They are inadvertently punctuated
by tape, piano and radio provided by David
Tudor, and become points of reference on a
map of magic and invention.

Variations IV, a live recording, mixes
tapes, sound effects, recorded stories, audience noise, records and live mikes. All were
controlled by Cage and Tudor (except, of
course, the audience) from two separate
rooms.

Tudor was at the amplified piano for *Variations II,* which uses a score of superim-

posed geometric drawings to create measurable "values" translated in the performance. *Electronics and Percussion,* five realizations by Max Neuhaus, includes one piece by Cage, "Fontana Mix." The Neuhaus version mixes feedback from contact mikes resting on percussion instruments in front of loudspeakers. Years before Hendrix, this was revolutionary, but maybe not so interesting.

You join the fun on *HPSCHD,* by Cage and Lejaren Hiller, a piece for harpsichords and computer-generated sound tapes. Each copy comes with its own computer-printout "score" for modulating volume, treble, bass and channels. "Good luck," Cage says in his notes to the work.   — A.E.G.

JONATHAN CAIN BAND
★ ★ **Windy City Breakdown / Bearsv.
(1977)** ¶
Cain has made a couple of charming folk-rock "message" singles: "Whispering Thunder," the story of Jonathan Jackson, and a great baseball meditation, "Home Run Willie." But neither of those are here, and the music that is present is bland and platitudinous post-hippie easy listening. This is not the guy from Journey   — D.M.

CALDERA
★ ★ ★ **Caldera / Cap. (1976)**
★ ★ ★ **Sky Islands / Cap. (1977)**
★ ★ ★ **Time and Chance / Cap.
(1978)**
★ ★ ★ **Dreamer / Cap. (1979)**
Caldera's music reflect the varied national backgrounds of the band's members—Brazil, Argentina, Cuba, Costa Rica and the United States. They meld their native sounds with a funky jazz-fusion style that is similar to acts like the Crusaders (whose Wayne Henderson produced *Caldera*) and Earth, Wind and Fire (whose Larry Dunn coproduced *Sky Islands*). Their imaginatively conceived instrumental sound bristles with potential, but never truly explodes into distinctive music.
  — R.P.

BOBBY CALDWELL
■ **Bobby Caldwell / Clouds (1978)**
■ **Cat in the Hat / Clouds (NA)**
Pompous disco balladeer. Must have stumbled into the studio on his way home from a George Benson soundalike wet T-shirt contest.   — D.M.

J. J. CALE
★ ★ ★ **Really, J. J. Cale / Shel. (1972)**
★ ★ ★ **Naturally . . . J. J. Cale / Shel.
(1972)**

★ ★ **Okie / Shel. (1974)**
★ ★ **Troubadour / Shel. (1976)**
★ ★ **5 / Shel. (1979)**
★ ★ **Shades / MCA (1981)**
J. J. Cale's music is like a softly repeated blues mantra; its appeal lies in his attractively smoky voice and rolling guitar style, its weakness his compositional repetition. The songs rarely strike out with a melody of their own, but rather become instrumental and vocal meditations around a few basic chords. For this reason, *Naturally* remains his best album, since it put this style in a fresh setting. *Really* incorporates a bit of country into the mix—Vassar Clements and Josh Graves participate—and the Muscle Shoals studio band is effectively featured on "Lies." Country and bits of harder guitar rock cropped up on Cale's last two albums, but the effect is still that of a simple song taken at a loping pace. While it can be attractive as such, it rarely pushes either Cale's voice or his guitar to levels that truly involve the listener.   — J.B.M.

JOHN CALE
★ ★ ★ **Vintage Violence / Col. (1970)**
★ ★ **Church of Anthrax [with Terry Riley] /
Col. (1971)**
★ ★ ★ ★ **Paris 1919 / Rep. (1973)**
★ ★ ★ **Fear / Is. (1974)** ¶
★ ★ ★ **Slow Dazzle / Is. (1975)** ¶
★ ★ **Helen of Troy / Is. (1975)**
★ ★ ★ **Guts / Is. (1977)**
★ ★ ★ **Honi Soit / A&M (1981)**
John Cale, a founding member of the Velvet Underground, is a classically trained musician who studied in Europe with classical avant-gardist La Monte Young. Arriving in New York in the early Sixties, he saw rock as the ripest and most amenable form open to the avant-garde.

Vintage Violence was Cale's first solo album (he left the Velvets after the 1968 *White Light/White Heat* LP), and melodically it's a comparatively light collection, the songs loosely constructed around a central cast of losers, lovers and ghosts. The playfulness of the music belies the often morose lyrical content and offsets Cale's flat-affect vocal style.

Church of Anthrax is a collaborative effort with avant-garde classical composer Terry Riley, and is closer to jazz than anything else. Riley (on keyboards and sax) and Cale (on guitar, viola and keyboards) spiraled off into lengthy, feverish modal exercises, harbinger of experiments Brian Eno, among others, would pursue in the mid-Seventies. (A later classical attempt, *The Academy in Peril,* is completely out of print.)

John Cale didn't make a record again until 1973, this time for Reprise with Richie Hayward and Lowell George of Little Feat in supportive roles. The result, *Paris 1919,* was his towering achievement, a gentle, introspective collection, similar in tenor to *Vintage Violence.* The following year found Cale on a new label, Island. *Fear* sported a tougher, more deranged rock sound than anything since his work with the Velvets. "Fear Is a Man's Best Friend" and "Gun" are wild, frightening insights about brutality, far more cathartic than Lou Reed's similar recordings. Cale filled his quota of lovely, folk-based melodies as well.

Slow Dazzle soon followed, and included a paean to Brian Wilson, a perverse remake of "Heartbreak Hotel" and the by now familiar amalgam of jagged, dissonant rockers and soothing, deceptive "ballads." Some critics dubbed Cale the new Jim Morrison, but those who'd been listening all along knew better.

In late 1975, Cale released his third album in less than a year, *Helen of Troy,* an assembly of grim obituaries for the living, bitter recollections, and predatory rock. It included "I Keep a Close Watch," a spitting version of "Pablo Picasso" (a track Cale had originally produced for the Modern Lovers in 1970), and a surprisingly subdued rendition of Jimmy Reed's "Baby What You Want Me to Do?" *Helen* was Cale's equivalent of Neil Young's scarifying *Tonight's the Night.* Island never even bothered to release it in the United States and promptly deleted *Slow Dazzle* and *Fear.* But they have released an excellent anthology of his work for the label, *Guts.*

In addition to his solo career, Cale has produced and/or worked extensively with the following artists: the Velvet Underground, Lou Reed, Iggy Pop and the Stooges, Nico, Terry Riley, Eno, Phil Manzanera, Kevin Ayers, Jonathan Richman and the Modern Lovers and Patti Smith.
— M.G.

CALICO

★ ★ ★ **Calico / U.A. (1975)** ¶
★ ★ **Calico, Vol. 2 / U.A. (1976)** ¶
Pleasant if uneventful country rock produced in Nashville. The first album gets a slight edge on the strength of the songwriting.
— J.S.

RANDY CALIFORNIA

★ **Kapt. Kopter and His (Fabulous) Twirly Birds / Epic (1972)**
Postpsychedelic dysfunction (circa 1977)

from a talented guitarist who is continually becoming lost in the sauce of his own peculiar indulgences. A variety of generes—from metallic soul ("I Don't Want Nobody") to Hendrix-influenced riff frenzy ("Downer")—are mangled here, and the covers are preposterous: the Beatles' "Rain" is transformed into a vengeful monsoon, for instance. Even the reunions of Spirit, California's original group, were less outrageous than this.
— B.A.

TERRY CALLIER

★ ★ ★ **Fire on Ice / Elek. (1978)**
★ ★ ★ **Turn You to Love / Elek. (1979)**
★ ★ ★ **Occasional Rain / Cadet (NA)**
★ ★ ★ ★ **What Color Is Love / Cadet (NA)**
★ ★ ★ ★ **I Just Can't Help Myself / Cadet (NA)**
Terry Callier came to minor prominence in Jerry Butler's Chicago songwriters' workshop as a songwriter for Butler, the Dells and other Chicago soul acts. But as a solo artist singing his own songs, Callier does not sing in a traditional soul form. Though a gospel chorus, an occasional saxophone, and strings are often featured on his records, Callier's music combines folk and blues elements. He strums an acoustic guitar while he sings and at times he's reminiscent of Richie Havens, though Callier's a superior vocalist and writer. The violins may tip his music into MOR territory but, as on both *What Color Is Love* and *I Just Can't Help Myself,* Terry Callier is capable of imaginative presentations. Charles Stepney produced all three. The Elektra sets continue Callier's style in more relaxed settings. — J.MC.

THELMA CAMACHO

★ ★ **Thelma Camacho / Casa. (1980)**
Singer/songwriter formerly with the Christy Minstrels and Kenny Rogers and the First Edition uses a pop/R&B context for her solo album. — J.S.

CAMEO

★ ★ **Cardiac Arrest / Choc. City (1977)**
★ ★ **Ugly Ego / Choc. City (1978)**
★ ★ **We All Know Who We Are / Choc. City (1978)**
★ ★ **Secret Omen / Choc. City (1979)**
★ ★ **Cameosis / Choc. City (1980)**
★ ★ **Feel Me / Choc. City (1980)**
★ ★ **Knights of the Sound Table / Choc. City (1981)**
Any group that has had this many albums—and a steadily growing series of soul hits—in only four years must have something going for it. But any eight-piece funk group that

never seems loud can't be worth much, either. So far, a career that amounts to rubberized Kool and the Gang. — D.M.

GLEN CAMPBELL
★ Gentle on My Mind / Cap. (1967)
★ ★ By the Time I Get to Phoenix / Cap. (1967)
★ ★ Wichita Lineman / Cap. (1968)
★ That Christmas Feeling / Cap. (1968)
★ ★ Galveston / Cap. (1969) ¶
★ "Live" / Cap. (1969) ¶
★ ★ Try a Little Kindness / Cap. (1970)
★ ★ ★ Glen Campbell's Greatest Hits / Cap. (1971)
★ ★ The Last Time I Saw Her / Cap. (1971)
★ ★ I Knew Jesus (Before He Was a Star) / Cap. (1973) ¶
★ ★ Arkansas / Cap. (1975) ¶
★ ★ Rhinestone Cowboy / Cap. (1975)
★ ★ ★ The Best of Glen Campbell / Cap. (1976)
★ ★ Bloodline / Cap. (1976)
★ ★ Southern Nights / Cap. (1977)
★ Live at the Royal Festival Hall / Cap. (1977)
★ ★ Basic / Cap. (1978)
★ Highwayman / Cap. (1979)
★ Somethin' 'Bout You Baby I Like / Cap. (1980)
★ ★ It's the World Gone Crazy / Cap. (1981)
In album after album, Campbell's true grit triumphs over schlock production and the necessity to cover a broad country-pop base. Campbell has long shown astute song selection, his association with Jimmy Webb ("By the Time I Get to Phoenix," "Wichita Lineman," "Galveston") having been particularly fruitful. For all but the devoted, any of the anthologies should suffice, *The Best of* being preferable because it contains the classic country boy's dream of making it in the city, "Rhinestone Cowboy," in addition to the Webb songs and "Gentle on My Mind."
— S.H.

RAY CAMPI
★ Gone Gone Gone / Roun. (1980)
Rockabilly artist more noteworthy for the persistence of his obsession than for his ability to reenact the exploits of the heroes (Gene Vincent, Elvis, et al.) he imitates.
— D.M.

CAN
★ ★ ★ ★ Monster Movie / U.A. (1969), Br. imp.
★ ★ ★ ★ Tago Mago / U.A. (1971), Br. imp.

★ ★ ★ Ege Bamyasi / U.A. (1973) ¶
★ ★ ★ ★ Future Days / U.A. (1974) ¶
★ ★ ★ ★ Soon over Babaluma / U.A. (1975) ¶
★ ★ Out of Reach / Peters (1978), Br. imp.
Mistakenly lumped in with such Teutonic cosmic technicians as Tangerine Dream, Amon Duul II and those transistorized pranksters Kraftwerk, Can were one of Germany's most revolutionary, consistently challenging, and undeniably exciting bands and the true impact of their influence is just now being felt in the English post-punk fallout of Public Image Ltd.
 Where most other German bands of the late Sixties and Seventies were out exploring musical space, Can were more concerned with alien sounds on earth. Their classic first two albums, *Monster Movie* and the two-record *Tago Mago* (neither issued in the U.S.) are a disturbing extension of the Velvet Underground's white-noise symphony, an application of keyboard player Irmin Schmidt and bassist Holger Czukay's studies under Stockhausen to the improvisational extremes of modern jazz and the primal beat of rock. The manic vocal ravings of black American Malcolm Mooney on *Monster Movie* and the ominous mumblings of former Japanese street singer Damo on later Can LPs also increased the physical intensity and sense of horror-show dread in their sound.
 Ege Bamyasi was a brief experiment with song forms (however raw) that actually yielded a German hit single in "Spoon." But *Future Days* and *Soon over Babaluma* are stunning impressionistic works, hypnotic soundscapes of heartbeat rhythms, guitar and violin explorations, and dramatic electronic color. *Out of Reach* and a number of later U.K. releases on Virgin found the band grappling with commercial demons (commercial by comparison, that is) and not succeeding. But there is no arguing that where Can first dared to go, others are now starting to follow. The above releases are out of print, but should be available as German imports.
— D.F.

CANDIDO
★ Drum Fever / Poly. (1973) ¶
★ Candi's Funk / SSL (NA) ¶
Some of the least intense Latin jazz ever recorded. — D.M.

CANNED HEAT
★ ★ Boogie with Hooker and Heat / Sp. (NA) ¶
★ Canned Heat / Sp. (NA) ¶
★ ★ Boogie with Canned Heat / U.A. (1968)

This group of blues aficionados (leader Bob "The Bear" Hite had a legendarily deep record collection) backed into a recording career in 1966, defined a certain wine-slugging festival spirit, then did a fast fade by the turn of the decade. Masterful guitarist and bumblebee-voiced singer Al Wilson died in 1970—the last stroke for the group.

The weak *Canned Heat* contains four warmed-over boogie numbers; each of these, except for "Bullfrog Blues," is found in John Lee Hooker's superior versions on *Boogie with Hooker and Heat.* But Hooker doesn't really seethe in their reverent company, so the two-record set is only pleasant. A dandy United Artists cutout (*The Very Best of Canned Heat*) is worth a search; it contains their epochal '68 hits "On the Road Again" and "Going Up the Country," plus stompers like "Let's Work Together." Bob Hite died in 1981. — F.S.

FREDDY CANNON
★ ★ **The Explosive Freddy Cannon / Sonic (1976), Br. imp.**
The difference between the nasality of Cannon and the nasality of say, Frankie Avalon has something to do with pitch, a bit more to do with the wildness of Cannon's material and arrangements (especially "Palisades Park" and "Tallahassee Lassie") but ultimately is not the kind of distinction that makes him a particularly worthwhile period memory. — D.M.

GUS CANNON
★ ★ ★ ★ ★ **Cannon's Jug Stompers/Gus Cannon as Banjo Joe 1927–1930 / Her. (NA)**
This record, extremely important in the history of twentieth-century music, collects all of Gus Cannon's recordings made in the period when he codified a jug-band tradition that thirty-five years later would have extensive repercussions on rock & roll. Cannon played banjo like a woodchopper, hitting the strings with a fierce rhythmic intensity that matched the ribald enthusiasm of his singing, whistling, jug blowing and kazoo playing. Cannon exuded an energy and love of playing on these sides that is incredibly infectious. His 1927 duets (as Banjo Joe) with guitarist Blind Blake include such classics as "Poor Boy, Long Ways from Home," the great story-song "Madison Street Rag" and the hilarious "My Money Never Runs Out."

The Stompers were a trio with Cannon, the brilliant harmonica player Noah Lewis, and Ashley Thompson on guitar. This group recorded "Minglewood Blues" and "Big

Railroad Blues," and if there's a Grateful Dead fan in the world who won't go out and get this album on that information alone, s/he's missing something. Later Thompson was replaced by Elijah Avery, who doubled on banjo, and this trio recorded another tune that Grateful Dead fans might recognize, "Viola Lee Blues." In 1929, banjo player Hosea Woods replaced Avery, and this unit recorded "Walk Right In," which would later become a huge hit for the Rooftop Singers in the early Sixties. — J.S.

JIM CAPALDI
★ ★ ★ **Daughter of the Night / RSO (NA)**
★ ★ ★ ★ **Short Cut Draw Blood / Is. (1976)**
★ ★ **Electric Nights / RSO (1979)**
Ex-drummer of Traffic is a more-than-credible rock singer, particularly on the oldie "Love Hurts" and the brief originals that comprise the rest of side one of *Short Cut.* Side two, four more extended compositions, has some of the tone and much of the blandness of Traffic. *Daughter* is idiosyncratic but worthwhile, *Electric Nights* less so. — D.M.

THE CAPTAIN AND TENNILLE
★ **Love Will Keep Us Together / A&M (1975)**
■ **Por Amor Vivremos / A&M (1976) ¶**
■ **Song of Joy / A&M (1976) ¶**
■ **The Captain and Tennille's Greatest Hits / A&M (1977)**
■ **Come in from the Rain / A&M (1977) ¶**
■ **Dream / A&M (1978)**
■ **Make Your Move / Casa. (1980)**
One good hit, "Love Will Keep Us Together," written and performed better by Neil Sedaka; smiley, mechanical pop for the rest. The Captain (Daryl Dragon) has been a Beach Boys sideman; Toni Tennille looks like a toothpaste-commercial reject, and acts the part. As sanctimonious as they are banal. — K.T.

CAPTAIN BEYOND
★ **Captain Beyond / Capri. (1972)**
★ **Sufficiently Breathless / Capri. (1973)**
Sorta like the Eagles with an organ, only wimpier. The American Moody Blues? — D.M.

CARAVAN
★ ★ ★ **If I Could Do It All Over Again / Lon. (1970) ¶**
★ ★ ★ **In the Land of Grey and Pink / Lon. (1971)**
★ ★ ★ ★ **Waterloo Lily / Lon. (1972) ¶**
★ ★ ★ **For Girls Who Grow Plump in the Night / Lon. (1973) ¶**

★ ★ **Caravan and the New Symphonia /
Lon. (1974)** ¶
★ **Better by Far / Ari. (1977)** ¶
There are passages on *Waterloo Lily* and *For
Girls* that careen with big-band swinging
presence reminiscent of Gil Evans. Caravan
has that rare ability to play orchestrated
rock that *rocks*. At the group's most symphonic, Caravan's odes to joy can be downright chilling. As for harmonies, it's *Wild
Honey* perfection personified.

Caravan materialized out of the Early
Canterbury Underground (England's unreal-
ized answer to our 1968 mythology of the
Haight), which also spawned Kevin Ayers,
Pink Floyd and Soft Machine; Caravan's Pye
Hastings (guitar) and David Sinclair (key-
boards) were in Wildflower, which became
Soft Machine.

As romantic as they are futuristic, Caravan's strong suit is the ability to sing sailing
harmonies over complex-yet-linear musical
settings while avoiding the Yes/Genesis
overpomp trap. — B.M.

CARESS
★ ★ ★ **Caress / RFC (1979)**
Very high-tech version of the standard disco
concept album formula: flatulent bass, metronomic strings, relentless bass drum, disembodied female vocals. Like most such, this is
most prominently attributed to its producer
(also writer, engineer and arranger), Boris
Midney, who plays all the horns and keyboards too. Cosmopolitan and not without
excitement. — D.M.

CARILLO
★ **Rings around the Moon / Atl. (1978)** ¶
★ **Streets of Dreams / Atl. (1979)**
Premature attempt to merge rock (pomp di-
vision) and Eurodisco (or at least post–
Giorgio Moroder production) proves that a
great idea poorly executed still stinks.
— D.M.

GEORGE CARLIN
★ ★ ★ **Class Clown / Li. Dav. (1972)**
★ **FM and AM / Li. Dav. (1972)**
★ ★ ★ **Occupation: Foole / Li. Dav.
(1973)**
★ **Toledo Windowbox / Li. Dav. (1974)**
★ **An Evening with Wally Londo / Li. Dav.
(1975)**
★ ★ **On the Road / Li. Dav. (1977)**
★ **Indecent Exposure / Li. Dav. (NA)**
★ **Original George Carlin / ERA (NA)** ¶
★ **Place for My Stuff / Atl. (1981)**
Carlin was an imaginative if traditional
stand-up comic (as recorded on the forgettable ERA album) till he got high and freaked
out in the early Seventies. He then evolved a
more personal style (autobiography replaced
characters and dialects), with an emphasis
on druggy jokes and a willfully naive viewpoint. His high point is *Class Clown,* a wonderfully vulgar and accurate remembrance of
high school and the Catholic church, leav-
ened by Lenny Bruce moralism (a profound
and bad influence). Carlin remains obsessed
with dope, though, and his approach is already embarrassingly dated. — K.T.

ERIC CARMEN
★ ★ **Eric Carmen / Ari. (1975)**
★ **Boats against the Current / Ari. (1977)**
★ **Change of Heart / Ari. (1978)**
★ ★ **Tonight You're Mine / Ari. (1980)**
A strong, intelligent pop-ballad singer, *Eric
Carmen* was his solo debut after leaving the
Raspberries in 1975. But one couldn't help
feeling he was more convincing as a rocker
in his original band, despite the two hits
("Never Gonna Fall in Love Again" and
"All by Myself"). *Boats* sank in a sea of
corny syrup. The rest were more of the
same. — D.M.

JEAN CARN
★ ★ **Jean Carn / Phila. (1976)**
★ ★ **Happy to Be with You / Phila. (1978)**
★ ★ **When I Find You Love / Phila. (1979)**
★ ★ **Sweet and Wonderful / TSOP (1981)**
Carn has such an outstanding voice, like a
more relaxed Gladys Knight, sweeping her
way from grit to gloss, that it's a shame that
none of her producers has been able to figure out how to present it effectively. Great
singer, dull discs. — D.M.

KIM CARNES
★ **Kim Carnes / A&M (1975)**
★ ★ **Sailin' / A&M (1976)** ¶
★ ★ **St. Vincent's Court / EMI (NA)**
★ ★ **Romance Dance / EMI (1980)**
★ ★ ★ **Mistaken Identity / EMI (1981)**
L.A. singer/writer sings white country soul à
la Dusty Springfield and Jackie DeShannon
but with a more impersonal Hollywood
gloss. *Sailin'* has the distinction of a classic
Jerry Wexler coproduction and contains the
1976 American Song Festival winner, "Love
Comes from Unexpected Places," which
Carnes cowrote with husband Dave Elling-
son. *Mistaken Identity* yielded Carnes' big-
gest hit, "Bette Davis Eyes." — S.H.

THE CARPENTERS
■ **Close to You / A&M (1970)**
■ **Carpenters / A&M (1971)**

- Ticket to Ride / A&M (1971)
- Song for You / A&M (1972)
- Now and Then / A&M (1973)
★ ★ Singles 1969–1973 / A&M (1973)
★ Horizon / A&M (1975)
- Kind of Hush / A&M (1976)
- Passage / A&M (1977)
- Christmas Portrait / A&M (1978)
This brother-sister duo from New Haven
epitomized early-Seventies MOR. By the re-
lease of *Horizon,* Karen Carpenter's con-
tralto had acquired ripe overtones while re-
maining serenely inexpressive. *Singles,* a
greatest-hits collection, says it all. Bubbly
and bland. — S.H.

IAN CARR'S NUCLEUS
★ ★ Out of the Long Dark / Cap. (1979) ¶
British jazz-rock group led by trumpeter
Carr. — J.S.

JAMES CARR
★ ★ ★ James Carr / P-Vine 3001 (NA), Jap.
imp.
★ ★ ★ James Carr / P-Vine 3004 (NA), Jap.
imp.
★ ★ ★ James Carr / P-Vine 3006 (NA), Jap.
imp.
Journeyman Sixties Southern soul singer,
mostly derived his inspiration from Percy
Sledge and Otis Redding—he can be a dead
ringer for either or both. Carr's best-known
hits are "Dark End of the Street" and "Pour-
ing Water on a Drowning Man," which
(along with his other Gold Wax singles) are
still available on 45 at oldies shops. The singles are a better investment by far than these
inevitably overpriced imports. — D.M.

LEROY CARR
★ ★ ★ ★ 1934 / Bio. (1973)
Carr was one of the most influential Chicago
bluesmen of the Thirties. His 1928 version of
"How Long, How Long Blues" was quite
popular and widely admired by other musicians, and Carr's reedy, cynical voice carried
the themes of loneliness and desperation convincingly. The Biograph session captures him
at the height of his powers, a year before his
death in 1935. — J.S.

LEROY CARR AND SCRAPPER BLACKWELL
★ ★ ★ ★ Naptown / Yazoo (1973)
Accompanied by the equally sophisticated
guitar playing of Scrapper Blackwell, Leroy
Carr put across an impressive array of blues
from 1928 to 1934, some of the best of
which is included here. — J.S.

PETE CARR
★ ★ ★ Not a Word on It / Big (1976)
★ ★ ★ Multiple Flash / Big (1978)
The precision and understatement of Muscle
Shoals, with a debt to the Allmans and a
taste of jazz. Guitarist Carr is a superb, sub-
tle technician, reminiscent of Roy Bucha-
nan and Jeff Beck. Chips off the latter's *Blow
by Blow* perhaps, but no bad ones.
 — C.W.

KEITH CARRADINE
★ I'm Easy / Asy. (1976) ¶
- Lost and Found / Asy. (1978)
Moody-voiced son of actor John Carradine
scored with the title track from *I'm Easy* in
Robert Altman's 1976 film, *Nashville.* Its
machismo sentiments and croaked vocal are
unfortunately echoed throughout that album.
And yet *Lost and Found* had even less to
recommend it. — D.M.

JOE "KING" CARRASCO
★ ★ ★ ★ ★ Joe "King" Carrasco and the
Crowns / Hann. (1981)
★ ★ ★ Synapse Gap (Mundo Total) / MCA
(1982)
The 1981 set is a great dance party record in
the tradition of the Sir Douglas Quintet by a
Tex-Mex new-wave quartet led by Carrasco's
tireless singing/guitar playing and the excel-
lent Farfisa keyboards of Kris Cummings.
Carrasco's songwriting is tremendous, from
the melodic pop of "Houston El Mover" and
"Buena" to the psychedelic story-songs of
"Caca de Vaca" to the bandido heartbreak
of "Federales" and finally to the apocalyptic
dance mania of "Don't Bug Me Baby" and
"I Get My Kicks on You." The second LP
sounds cluttered in comparison. — J.S.

JIM CARROLL BAND
★ ★ ★ Catholic Boy / Atco (1980)
★ ★ Dry Dreams / Atco (1982)
Jim Carroll is a writer with a solid reputation among the new poets and a small popular following thanks to his autobiographical
book, *The Basketball Diaries.* Correspond-
ingly, his lyrics are unusually crisp and
vivid, alive with street imagery and charged
with a truly dynamic sense of meter. Unfortunately, great verse does not a singer make,
and Carroll's delivery is little more than a
chant—which would be fine if backed by
something a bit more imaginative than the
punkish drone of his band. *Catholic Boy* is
worth hearing for "People Who Died," an
impassioned threnody to (literally) lost
youth. — J.D.C.

JOHNNY CARROLL
★ ★ **Black Leather Rebel / Roller C. (NA)**
Mediocre Fifties rock 'n' roller. — D.M.

THE CARS
★ ★ ★ ★ **The Cars / Elek. (1978)**
★ ★ ★ **Candy-O / Elek. (1979)**
★ ★ **Panorama / Elek. (1980)**
★ ★ **Shake It Up / Elek. (1981)**
Shrewd, witty Boston-area band whose 1978 debut album gets better and better with repeated listenings. Influences range from Beatle-esque song structures to mid-Sixties, punk-rock elements. The playing is competent, the songs catchy and hook-ridden, the production (Roy Thomas Baker) superbly calculated. "Just What I Needed" and "My Best Friend's Girl" became minor hits on the strength of some of the most efficient harmony vocal arrangements since the Beatles. *Candy-O* saw the formula wear a bit thin except for the amazing hit single "Let's Go." By *Panorama,* though, the band had descended to cliché pandering. — J.S.

BO CARTER
★ ★ ★ ★ ★ **Greatest Hits 1930–40 / Yazoo (1968)**
★ ★ ★ ★ ★ **Twist It Babe / Yazoo (1972)**
★ ★ ★ ★ ★ **Banana in Your Fruit Basket / Yazoo (NA)**
Carter popularized the Mississippi hokum blues in the Thirties on his own and with his band, the Mississippi Sheiks. He was a humorous and raunchy, if limited, vocalist, but a superb guitarist and violinist with an exemplary arrangement sense that enabled him to codify a lot of the white string-band and standard country-blues ideas others (notably Tommy Johnson and John Hurt) used, while still maintaining his own distinctive style.

Greatest Hits, Banana and *Twist It Babe* collect his best work from the Thirties and give a really good indication of what the locals were digging back in those days. On *Twist It Babe,* Carter accompanies his own singing on a National steel guitar. Other members of the Sheiks double on guitar and violin on various songs in the *Greatest Hits* set, which shows Carter in his best boasting, bawdy and drinking attitude. He even dabbles in humorous political protest here on "Sales Tax," with a hilarious intro that has Carter and a pal going in to buy a pack of cigarettes. When they find out about the sales tax, Carter's pal observes that there's a lot of things being sold that the government doesn't know anything about. *Banana* is an album of bawdy songs. — J.S.

CARLENE CARTER
★ ★ ★ **Carlene Carter / War. (1978)**
★ ★ **Two Sides to Every Woman / War. (1979)**
★ ★ ★ **Musical Shapes / War. (1980)**
Carlene Carter—daughter of June, granddaughter of Mother Maybelle and A.P.—has expanded the horizons of the Carter Family/Johnny Cash empire further into unfamiliar territory than any other member of the clan.

Her first and best album was a collaboration with the Rumour, who provide just the right combination of firmness and sweetness. The album was produced by Rumour guitarist Brinsley Schwarz and keyboard player Bob Andrews. Carter's intelligent, straightforward singing is at its best with the medium tempo and lyrical substance of songs like her own "Slow Dance" and "I Once Knew Love," Rodney Crowell's "Never Together but Close Sometimes" and Graham Parker's "Between You and Me."

Carter's second album, *Two Sides to Every Woman,* was produced in New York. Of its uninspired hard-rock arrangements, lifeless overproduction and songs that never quite jell either individually or en masse, the less said the better.

In *Musical Shapes* Carter is thankfully back in the crossover territory she's staked out for herself, this time supported on most tracks by the good-timey post-rockabilly energy of Rockpile. Produced by husband Nick Lowe, the combination of country and rock songs is effectively light, bright and sharp-edged. The album's good-humored tone makes Carlene's occasional tough-girl stance both more convincing and more entertaining than on the preceding record, and her duet with Dave Edmunds, "Baby Ride Easy," is an instant classic of rockabilly kitsch. — S.M.

CLARENCE CARTER
★ ★ ★ **Loneliness and Temptation / ABC (1975)** ¶
★ ★ **A Heart Full of Song / ABC (1976)** ¶
★ ★ ★ **Let's Burn / Ven. (1980)**
★ ★ ★ **Mr. Clarence Carter in Person / Ven. (1981)**
Blind singer/guitarist Clarence Carter's best work has inevitably been produced by Muscle Shoals entrepreneur Rick Hall. Unfortunately, all of the records they made for Atlantic, which include Carter's biggest hit, "Slip Away," are cut out. So is their final album, 1973's *Sixty Minutes With,* which successfully blended influences as diverse as the Doobie Brothers and C&W with Carter's own down-home oeuvre.

Both *Loneliness and Temptation* and *A Heart Full of Song,* like the Venture albums, were self-produced and recorded in Atlanta. Clarence Carter's country-bumpkin persona continually straddles the line between successful melodrama and farce. Without Hall's direction, the uptempo tracks fall flat (often they're rehashes of "Slip Away"), and the lyrics fall just this side of soap-opera mawkishness. — J.MC.

THE CARTER FAMILY
★ ★ ★ **The Carter Family Album** / **Lib. (1962)** ¶
★ ★ ★ **Best of the Carter Family** / **Col. (1965)**
★ ★ **World's Favorite Hymns** / **Col. (1973)**
★ **Three Generations** / **Col. (1974)** ¶
★ ★ **Fifty Years of Country Music** / **Camd. (1975)**
★ ★ ★ ★ **Happiest Days of All** / **Camd. (1975)**
★ ★ ★ ★ **Lonesome Pine Special** / **Camd. (1975)**
★ ★ ★ ★ **'Mid the Green Fields of Virginia** / **RCA (1975)**
★ ★ ★ ★ **More Golden Gems from the Original Carter Family** / **Camd. (1975)**
★ ★ ★ **My Old Cottage Home** / **Camd. (1975)**
★ ★ ★ ★ **The Original and Great Carter Family** / **Camd. (1975)** ¶
★ ★ **Country's First Family** / **Col. (1976)** ¶
★ ★ ★ **Smoky Mountain Ballads** / **Camd. (1976)**
★ ★ ★ ★ **Legendary Performers** / **RCA (1979)**

The Carter Family, with Jimmie Rodgers (The Singing Brakeman), virtually invented country music as we now know it. First emerging from the Virginia-Tennessee border country in 1927, the same region and era that produced Rodgers, the Carters' effect on the development of both American country and folk music was immediately pervasive. This trio of singers from the Blue Ridge region—A.P., Maybelle and Sara—established country and folk's basic close-harmony singing style, and a great many of the songs that both traditions share. (Woody Guthrie often borrowed Carter melodies for his songs; his "It Takes a Worried Man" is a direct rewrite of their scarifying "Worried Man Blues," for instance.) More recently, Maybelle (Sara's cousin and A.P.'s sister-in-law), now known as Mother Maybelle, had a heavy influence on the city folk revival of the early Sixties through her appearances at folk festivals and the like. Maybelle's flat-picking guitar style was also enormously in-

fluential on the development of both country and folk. The Carters' best-known material includes "My Clinch Mountain Home," "Worried Man Blues," "Keep on the Sunny Side," "Bury Me beneath the Weeping Willow," "Foggy Mountain Top," "Can the Circle Be Unbroken" and "Wildwood Flower."

The family's second generation, alternatively known as the Carter Sisters, is more inclined toward standard Nashville pop country, with a particularly sanctimonious evangelical religious bent. (June Carter, one of the Carter Sisters, later married Johnny Cash.)

The Carters recorded for many labels; the best of what remains catalogued is contained on the sides currently released on Camden, RCA's budget label. The Columbia material often features the Carter Sisters, and is consequently rated lower. A ten-disc retrospective assembled by RCA's subsidary is long overdue for U.S. release. — C.F.

VALERIE CARTER
★ ★ ★ ★ **Just a Stone's Throw Away** / **Col. (1977)**
★ ★ ★ **Wild Child** / **Col. (1978)**
Impressive debut album by California interpretive singer who brings to the genre more funkiness and rock spirit than anyone since Bonnie Raitt. Highlight is a remake of "Ooh Child." Star-studded cast, production by a variety of heavies, including Little Feat's Lowell George and Earth, Wind and Fire's Maurice White. *Wild Child,* the followup, was less successful. — D.M.

MARTIN CARTHY
★ ★ ★ ★ **Sweet Wivelsfield** / **Roun. (1974)**
★ ★ ★ ★ **Crown of Horn** / **Roun. (1976)**
★ ★ ★ ★ **Because It's There** / **Roun. (1979)**
Tremendous British Isles guitarist/vocalist, formerly of Steeleye Span, interprets a wide range of traditional material in old English, Celtic, Scottish and Welsh. *Second Album, Byker Hill, But Two Came By* and *Prince Heathen* (all imports) include performances by Fairport Convention's fiddler Dave Swarbrick, and Fairport's Ashley Hutchings is Carthy's producer. *Sweet Wivelsfield* showcases his guitar accompaniment and singing (including a traditional reading of "John Barleycorn"). *Because It's There* features a wide stylistic and instrumental range using accordion, trumpet, drums and mandolin. — J.S.

JOHNNY CASH
★ ★ **Original Golden Hits, Vol. 1** / **Sun (1969)**

★ ★ **Original Golden Hits, Vol. 2 / Sun (1969)**
★ ★ **Showtime / Sun (1969)**
★ ★ ★ **Story Songs of the Trains and Rivers / Sun (1969)**
★ ★ ★ ★ **Johnny Cash: The Legend / Sun (1970)**
★ ★ **The Rough-Cut King of Country Music / Sun (1970)**
★ ★ **The Singing Story Teller / Sun (1970)**
★ ★ ★ **Johnny Cash and Jerry Lee Lewis Sing Hank Williams / Sun (1971)**
★ ★ ★ **Johnny Cash: The Man, the World, His Music / Sun (1971)**
★ ★ ★ **Original Golden Hits, Vol. 3 / Sun (1971)**
★ ★ ★ **The Original Johnny Cash / Sun (NA)**

In 1955, when twenty-three-year-old Johnny Cash signed with Sun Records, only Hank Williams had managed to break through the restrictions of "hillbilly music" to sell country records to a pop audience. Cash did it with his first single, "I Walk the Line," and kept on for six Sun LPs and several extended-play 45s. Thus the rockabilly Cash was an influential figure in the blues-country fusion that led to rock & roll.

Rock fans will be most interested in the Sun records, available through reissues packaged by Shelby Singleton. Of the eleven albums listed above, however, only three are of more than passing interest. *Johnny Cash: The Legend,* a two-record set incorporating the first two *Golden Hits* LPs, is the one Johnny Cash record to own. With the late Luther Perkins on guitar, Marshall Grant on bass, and possibly either Jerry Lee Lewis or Charlie Rich on piano, this is the only Cash backup band worth mentioning. The album contains most of his classics—"Folsom Prison Blues," "Hey Porter," "Cry, Cry, Cry," "Ballad of a Teenage Queen," "I Walk the Line," "Get Rhythm," "Big River" and the great "Luther's Boogie." The arrangements are clear and simple; the production is crisp. *Original Golden Hits, Volume 3* will just about complete the Cash Sun collection; it contains "The Wreck of the Old 97," "Rock Island Line" and "Katy Too." Production here is uneven, and arrangements are more elaborate (backup vocals, more instruments).

Cash's lifelong preoccupation with American history, folklore, freedom and confinement are abundantly evident on these two albums. It is significant to note, also, that Cash's pop tunes were generally written by

Jack Clement or Cash; but all the folk tunes were written by Cash.

Aside from the *Hank Williams* set (which is more notable for the Jerry Lee Lewis sides), most of the rest of these LPs are expendable, some because they are repetitious of the material on the two collections above, some because of weak material.

★ **Hymns by Johnny Cash / Col. (1959)**
★ ★ ★ **Ride This Train / Col. (1960)**
★ **Hymns from the Heart / Col. (1962)** ¶
★ ★ ★ **Blood, Sweat and Tears / Col. (1963)** ¶
★ ★ ★ **Ring of Fire / Col. (1963)**
★ ★ **I Walk the Line / Col. (1964)**
★ ★ **Johnny Cash Sings the Ballads of the True West / Col. (1965)**
★ ★ ★ **Orange Blossom Special / Col. (1965)**
★ **Mean as Hell! / Col. (1966)**
★ ★ **Everybody Loves a Nut / Col. (1966)** ¶
★ ★ **Greatest Hits, Vol. 1 / Col. (1967)**
★ **The World of Johnny Cash / Col. (1970)**

Here is Johnny Cash the folksinger. While many of the songs are interesting and Cash's narratives show painstaking research, the series is flawed because it's stronger on folklore than on music. "Ring of Fire" is almost the only Cash song from this period that has survived.

Ride This Train is a particularly ambitious project, in which Cash as narrator assumes the role of American Everyman, taking the listener to coal miners and lumberjacks, cowboys and outlaws—including John Wesley Harding. This is one of the first pop concept albums, and, one suspects, the beginning of the Johnny Cash/Bob Dylan mutual admiration society. Cash's recitation of American place names (particularly Indian ones) and "Lorraine of Pontchartrain," an original song, are the stand-outs. The problem is that the album contains too much talking—every song is prefaced by a windy narrative.

Blood, Sweat and Tears, a similar concept, works better because its scope is narrower: specifically, the legend of John Henry; more generally, the American workingman. "Tell Him I'm Gone" and "Another Man Done Gone" are beautiful country-blues songs, and "Busted," the Harlan Howard classic, made its first appearance here. *Ballads of the True West,* a third concept album, is marred by its tendency to sound like a high school history lesson—a fault shared to a lesser degree by the other two.

Orange Blossom Special is the most musically satisfying album of this series. In addition to the ever-popular title song, the album includes three Dylan songs—"It Ain't Me Babe," "Don't Think Twice" and "Mama,

You Been on My Mind"—plus the country classics "Long Black Veil" and "Wildwood Flower." The problem is that Dylan sings Dylan better than Cash.

I Walk the Line and *Ring of Fire* are collections. Most of the former is available on Sun, and the material is superior to the *Ring of Fire,* which includes the title song and "I Still Miss Someone." *Greatest Hits* and *The World of* are also collections from this period, which culminated in the Cash/Dylan duet on *Nashville Skyline; Greatest Hits* is superior.

★ ★ ★ ★ ★ **Johnny Cash at Folsom Prison / Col. (1968)**
★ **The Holy Land / Col. (1968)** ¶
★ ★ ★ **Johnny Cash at San Quentin / Col. (1969)**
★ ★ ★ **Man in Black / Col. (1971)**
★ ★ **His Greatest Hits, Vol. 2 / Col. (1971)**
★ ★ **Johnny Cash Sings Precious Memories / Col. (1971)**
★ ★ **Christmas: The Johnny Cash Family / Col. (1972)**
★ ★ **Any Old Wind That Blows / Col. (1973)**
★ **Sunday Morning Coming Down / Col. (1973)**
★ **The Gospel Road / Col. (1973)**
★ ★ **Johnny Cash and His Woman (with June Carter Cash) / Col. (1973)**
★ ★ **Ragged Old Flag / Col. (1974)** ¶
★ ★ **Five Feet High and Rising / Col. (1974)** ¶
★ ★ **The Junkie and the Juicehead Minus Me / Col. (1974)** ¶
★ ★ ★ **Johnny Cash at Folsom Prison and San Quentin / Col. (1975)** ¶
★ ★ **Look at Them Beans / Col. (1975)** ¶
★ ★ ★ **One Piece at a Time / Col. (1976)** ¶
★ ★ **The Last Gunfighter Ballad / Col. (1976)** ¶
★ ★ ★ ★ **The Rambler / Col. (1977)**
★ ★ ★ **Gone Girl / Col. (1978)**
★ ★ ★ **Greatest Hits, Vol. 3 / Col. (1978)**
★ ★ ★ **I Would Like to See You Again (1978)**
★ ★ **A Believer Sings the Truth / Cadet (1979)**
★ ★ ★ **Johnny Cash Silver / Col. (1979)**
★ ★ ★ ★ **Rockabilly Blues / Col. (1980)**
★ ★ ★ **Encore (Greatest Hits, Vol. 4) / Col. (1981)**
★ ★ ★ **The Baron / Col. (1981)**

These albums, representing Cash's output for the past thirteen years, contain some of his best work since Sun and some of the most embarrassing. At times Cash is anti-establishment, at others as conventional as Hubert Humphrey. Sometimes he is both on the same record.

Folsom Prison (1968) is Cash's best album since he left Sun. Musically, it's lively, committed and exciting. There isn't a bad song here, but among the best are "Folsom Prison Blues"—better than on Sun—"Cocaine Blues," "25 Minutes to Go," "Jackson," "Give My Love to Rose" and "Send a Picture of Mother." In addition, *Folsom Prison* comes as close to being a documentary about prison life as one can come without a camera. Rather than being about history, this album *is* history.

San Quentin (recorded at a performance in that prison) is also live and lively. Although it misses a bit of *Folsom*'s vitality, *San Quentin* contains the hit "A Boy Named Sue." Columbia followed up with the two-record set that combines both prison albums.

Man in Black is the first of Cash's weird albums. It contains "Singin' in Viet Nam Talkin' Blues," done Bob Dylan style, a song about Johnny's trip to Vietnam; intentionally or not, it's an antiwar song. But this album has another song, "The Preacher Said, 'Jesus Said,' " a duet with Reverend Billy Graham. Then there's "Man in Black," Cash's famous declaration of mourning for the world.

Holy Land is like a home slide show of Cash's trip to Israel, replete with lots of talking and lots of religion; it contains "Daddy Sang Bass." *The Gospel Road* is a more sophisticated version of *Holy Land,* the soundtrack to Cash's movie about the life of Jesus. More talking; not much music. *Precious Memories* is a fine collection of country hymns.

Several of these albums are collections of country songs—*Any Old Wind That Blows* (mostly mediocre); a duet with wife June Carter Cash on *Johnny Cash and His Woman* (simpler and better); and *The Junkie and the Juicehead Minus Me* (strange, strange, strange). All are corny country curiosities that are eventually nerve-racking. Or collections of older Cash material recycled: *Sunday Morning Coming Down,* the second *Greatest Hits* LP, *Five Feet High and Rising* (one of the best).

One Piece at a Time made some sense out of this jumble. The title song, the story of an auto worker who steals a Cadillac from a factory over the course of several years, is actually funny. "Committed to Parkview," a song about commitment to a mental institution, rings true; and "Mountain Lady," a song about Mother Maybelle Carter (a seminal country influence and Johnny's mother-in-law) is beautiful.

The Last Gunfighter Ballad backslides

with outlaw imagery but is saved by the incredible "Far Side Banks of Jordan." *The Rambler,* on the other hand, harks back to *Ride This Train,* but isn't pedantic. Rather than narrated prefaces, a story in the form of a dialogue weaves through the record and the songs are logically linked. There are several stand-out numbers here, including "Lady," "After the Ball," "No Earthly Good," "My Cowboy's Last Ride," and "Calilou." — M.H.

JOHNNY CASH AND JUNE CARTER CASH
★ ★ **Johnny Cash and His Woman / Col. (1973)**
The attraction here is Johnny Cash, not June Carter Cash's consistently off-key, strained vocals, and nothing here measures up to their inspired reading of "Jackson." But thankfully, only six of the ten cuts feature June, and the four songs rendered solo by Cash are the best work here—especially a nice rendition of Steve Goodman's "City of New Orleans." — R.P.

ROSANNE CASH
★ **Rosanne Cash / Ari. (1978)** ¶
★ ★ ★ **Right or Wrong / Col. (1980)**
★ ★ ★ **Seven Year Ache / Col. (1981)**
When it came to infidelity, Hank Williams was convinced that your cheatin' heart would tell on you; Rosanne Cash wonders if adultery is right or wrong. Unless you recognize that as a question, you're going to have a hard time addressing the emotional issues of the modern world. In that sense, Rosanne Cash's *Right or Wrong* is the first real country album for the Eighties.

A collaboration with her producer/husband Rodney Crowell, who wrote many of the songs, the record is restrained without being innocuous, quiet without being laid-back. The tailored production uses bass and drum sounds that are closer to contemporary pop-disco than traditional country, and guitarist Frank Reckard, on leave from Emmylou Harris' Hot Band, plays with crispness and delicacy. Rosanne Cash (Johnny's daughter) has a clear, sweet, strong voice that makes her one of the best contemporary female vocalists, and she brings a rare degree of intelligence and personality to her phrasing and delivery. She is magnificent in the aching ambiguity of a song like Crowell's "Seeing's Believing," a reflection on finding yourself sadder and wiser but no closer to the answers than when you started out. The singer's lack of resolution is echoed in the melody and structure of the song, one of

Crowell's best. And unlike many country singers who shine in ballads, Cash is entirely convincing in rollicking gutsier numbers like "Big River."

Her first album is a naive embarrassment; her third, *Seven Year Ache,* includes several good songs (her own "Seven Year Ache" and "Blue Moon with Heartache" among them) and has brought her considerably closer to real commercial success. But the latter album teeters dangerously close to the edge of blandness and predictability, and Crowell's increasingly slick production has all but erased the intimacy, personality and wryness that were what made *Right or Wrong* so special. — S.M.

TERRY CASHMAN
★ ★ **Terry Cashman / Lifes. (1976)**
Cashman is best known for producing with Tommy West, Jim Croce. This solo debut does nothing to change that. — D.M.

CASINO
■ **Casino / MCA (1976)** ¶
Absolutely despicable rock band attempts a mid-Seventies revision of some Mott the Hoople ideas. — J.S.

THE CASINOS
★ **Then You Can Tell Me Goodbye / Frat. (NA)**
Further proof that not all fondly remembered hits of the Sixties are remembered with great clarity—or were made by groups that deserved longevity. — D.M.

SHAUN CASSIDY
★ **Shaun Cassidy / War. (1977)**
★ ★ **Born Late / War. (1977)**
★ ★ **Under Wraps / War. (1978)**
★ **Room Service / War. (1979)**
★ **That's Rock 'n' Roll—Shaun Cassidy Live / War. (1979)**
★ **Wasp / War. (1980)**
David Cassidy's younger brother follows a familiar pattern—hit TV show (*The Hardy Boys*) yields pop hits, most notably "Da Doo Ron Ron," from the first album, and "Hey Deanie," from *Born Late.* The former, like all of Cassidy's oldies covers, is horrid; the latter and some of the originals on *Born Late* (particularly "Teen Dream") are first-rate pop rock, not quite as good as the Raspberries, but in contention. Subsequent albums have made no noticeable progress. The best teen idol of the decade, if that's progress. — D.M.

JIMMY CASTOR BUNCH
★ **The Everything Man** / Atco (1974) ¶
★ **Butt of Course** / Atco (1975)
★ **Supersound** / Atco (1975)
★ **E-Man Groovin'** / Atco (1976)
★ **Maximum Stimulation** / Atco (1977)
Castor made a name for himself with the 1966 Latin pop hit "Hey, Leroy, Your Mama's Callin' You." He resurfaced in 1972 with the heavy-metal funk vamp "Troglodyte," on RCA. His albums for Atco are banal attempts to parlay his latter-day funk success into the Seventies disco market. These records are failures—the only single to get chart action during this period was the wretched "Bertha Butt Boogie Part 2," a ribald sequel to "Troglodyte." — J.S.

CATE BROTHERS
★ ★ ★ **Cate Brothers** / Asy. (1976)
★ ★ **In One Eye and Out the Other** / Asy. (1976)
★ ★ **Cate Brothers Band** / Asy. (1977)
★ ★ **Fire on the Tracks** / Atl. (1979)
Pulsating Memphis-style blue-eyed soul produced by Steve Cropper. Brothers Ernie and Earl Cate perform original material in the tradition of Sam and Dave. Their first album, *Cate Brothers,* contains their best songs, "Time for Us" and the hit, "Union Man." — S.H.

CATES SISTERS
★ ★ **Cates Sisters** / Capri. (NA)
★ ★ **Stepping Out** / Ova. (NA)
Post-Allmans singer/songwriter duo departs from the Southern rock formula without noticeably improving on the concept. — J.S.

CRAZY CAVAN
★ **Crazy Rhythm** / Boot (NA)
★ **Our Own Way of Rockin'** / Charly (NA), Br. imp.
★ **Rockability** / Charly (NA), Br. imp.
★ **Live at the Rainbow** / Charly (NA), Br. imp.
★ **Red Hot 'n' Rockabilly** / Charly (1979), Br. imp.
Rockabilly revivalism at its most straightfaced and dullest: Cavan has no idea that rockabilly has limits, so why should he be bothered by his own lack of talent and imagination? — D.M.

C.D. BAND
■ **HooDoo VooDoo** / Casa. (1979)
Dance to the Muzak? — D.M.

CECILIO & KAPONO
■ **Cecilio & Kapono** / Col. (1974)

■ **Elua** / Col. (1975)
■ **Night Music** / Col. (1977)
Hawaii Five-O meets Brewer and Shipley. Nice shirts. — J.S.

CERRONE
★ ★ **Love in C Minor** / Coti. (1977)
★ **Cerrone's Paradise** / Coti. (1977)
★ **Cerrone 3: Supernature** / Coti. (1978)
★ **Cerrone IV: The Golden Touch** / Coti. (1978)
★ **Cerrone V: Angelina** / Atl. (1979)
The last and most dreadful word in late Seventies European disco production. "Love in C Minor" was the hit. — J.S.

CHAD AND JEREMY
★ **The Best of Chad and Jeremy** / Cap. (1980)
What a pair of duds. This earnest, sensitive, university-type duo sang wretched string-laden ballads without being able to muster more than whispers. Their handful of British Invasion–era hits, ("Yesterday's Gone," "Summer Song" and "Willow Weep for Me") display a blandness and soullessness so profound that Peter and Gordon sound like Sam and Dave in comparison. — D.G.

THE CHALLENGERS
★ **Light My Fire with Classical Gas** / GNP (NA)
★ ★ **Sidewalk Surfin'** / GNP (NA)
★ ★ **Twenty-five Great Instrumental Hits** / GNP (NA)
★ **Vanilla Funk** / GNP (NA)
★ ★ **Wipe Out** / GNP (1967)
Surf instrumentals go MOR. Early indication that album rock was not always going to be superior to (or even smarter than) 45 rpm versions. — D.M.

CHAMBERS BROTHERS
★ **Groovin' Time** / Folk. (1966)
★ **The Time Has Come** / Col. (1968)
★ **A New Time, A New Day** / Col. (1968) ¶
★ **Love, Peace and Happiness** / Col. (1969) ¶
■ **The Chambers Brothers' Greatest Hits** / Col. (1971)
★ ★ **Best of the Chambers Brothers** / Fan. (1973)
★ **Chambers Brothers and Barbara Dane** / Folk. (NA)
★ **Our Best to You** / Stax (NA)
When the Chambers Brothers switched in the late Sixties from being a "gospel family" (as represented on the Fantasy, Stax and Folkways LPs) to a funk and soul outfit (picking up white drummer Brian Keenan),

they served as forerunners of black bands with large white audiences. Avoiding the soul studio systems of Motown, Stax or Philadelphia, they chose to psychedelicize their gospel sound. That is, they played crude, guitar-based rock and sang sloppy, spirited group vocals over the drone. The result was "Time Has Come Today," a lengthy hit in 1968.

The Chambers Brothers never evolved far from this primordial formula; they neither rocked nor, once they gave up gospel, brought their sound back home. The only really listenable tracks they produced are the smoother tunes like "People Get Ready" and sections of their "suite," "Love, Peace and Happiness," where the instinctive cohesion of the Brothers' vocals is given a chance.

Time Has Come is now a mere historical curio, *Love, Peace and Happiness* only a document (half of it is live), and the *Greatest Hits* package is of no use whatsoever.
— B.T.

CHAMELEON
★ ★ **Chameleon / Elek. (1979)**
Fusion-disco band led by ex–McCoy Tyner jazz saxophonist Azar Lawrence and ex–Stevie Wonder keyboardist Michael Stanton.
— J.S.

CHAMPAIGN
★ ★ **How 'Bout Us / Col. (1981)**
If Chicago were a middle-of-the-road R&B band instead of an MOR pop band, they'd probably sound just as tepid and predictable as Champaign. — J.D.C.

THE CHAMPS
★ ★ **Everybody's Rockin' / Lon. (1960), Belg. imp.**
★ ★ **The Best of the Champs / Lon. (1977), Br. imp.**
★ ★ **The Champs / Lon. (NA), Br. imp.**
★ ★ **Go Champs / Lon. (NA), Belg. imp.**
"Tequila" notwithstanding, the Champs weren't one of the great rock & roll instrumental groups, as everyone who's heard more than their hit can testify. After all, what can you expect from a band named after Gene Autry's horse? — D.M.

JAMES CHANCE
■ **Buy the Contortions / Ze (1979)**
■ **Off White / Ze (1979)**
Egomaniacal New York City sax player who has led various groups (the Contortions, James White and the Blacks, the Flaming Demonics) through a "no wave" mixture of funk and free-form jazz that can clear any room at any time. Although Chance (who during one period made it a habit to jump offstage and physically abuse the audience) decries the pseudo-intellectualism of avant-garde jazz, it is only through the revisionist posturing of a trendy, relentlessly "hip" art crowd that this noise could find encouragement at all. The hipster pose of Chance and his cult reeks, in its way, of the beatnik Fifties, which is probably the last time such cold, tuneless music was regarded by anybody as expressing certain truths about the urban environment. — W.K.

GENE CHANDLER
★ ★ ★ **The Girl Don't Care / Bruns. (1967)**
★ ★ **There Was a Time / Bruns. (1968)**
★ **The Two Sides of Gene Chandler / Bruns. (1969)**
★ **Get Down / 20th Cent. (1978)**
★ ★ **When You're Number One / 20th Cent. (1979)**
★ ★ **'80 / 20th Cent. (1980)**
★ ★ ★ **Just Be True / Charly (1980), Br. imp.**
★ ★ **Here's to Love / 20th Cent. (1981)**
★ ★ **Gene Chandler / 20th Cent. (NA)**
★ ★ **Two Sides of Gene Chandler / 20th Cent. (NA)**
Like so many Chicago soul stars of the Fifties and Sixties, Gene Chandler was almost entirely a creation of the songwriting and production skills of Curtis Mayfield. Under Mayfield's direction, Chandler's mid-Sixties persona was one of vulnerability. Chandler drenched Mayfield's songs with a believable desperation, like a man on the edge, phrasing each line with an exaggerated deliberateness. Chandler was able to step outside the melancholy on "Good Times," a finger-popping, Saturday-night high school classic. The three Mayfield/Chandler songs on *The Girl Don't Care* marked the end of their collaboration, but producer Carl Davis was able to effectively duplicate Mayfield's approach for a time. Unfortunately Davis was not able to maintain his grip on the singer's style, and Chandler's career—overburdened by standards and uncomfortable attempts at up-tempo dance material—quickly declined. (There was a brief comeback during the late-Seventies disco boom, but nothing really memorable came of it.) The Charly LP is Sixties material from the "Duke of Earl" era. — J.MC.

CHANGE
★ ★ ★ **The Glow of Love / War. (NA)**
★ ★ **Miracles / Atl. (1981)**

Exceptionally melodic pop-disco studio group produced by Jacques Fred Petrus with arranger/composers David Romani and Mario Malavasi struck a highly listenable balance between the cheerful escapism of Eurodisco and the hipper pop-funk of Chic. Their first and best album featured two creamy lead vocals ("The Glow of Love" and "Searching") by ace session singer Luther Vandross. — S.H.

CHANSON

★ ★ ★ **Chanson / Ario.-Amer. (1978)** ¶
★ ★ **Together We Stand / Ario.-Amer. (NA)** ¶
Solid dance group hit soul Top Ten in 1978 with "Don't Hold Back" (from *Chanson*), but was only able to follow with two minor hits in 1979. — D.M.

HARRY CHAPIN

★ ★ **Heads and Tales / Elek. (1972)**
★ **Sniper and Other Love Songs / Elek. (1972)**
★ **Short Stories / Elek. (1973)**
★ **Verities and Balderdash / Elek. (1974)**
★ **Portrait Gallery / Elek. (1975)**
★ ★ **Greatest Stories—Live / Elek. (1976)**
★ **On the Road to Kingdom Come / Elek. (1976)**
★ **Dance Band on the Titanic / Elek. (1977)**
★ **Living Room Suite / Elek. (1978)**
★ **Legends of the Lost and Found / Elek. (1979)**
★ **Sequel / Bdwalk (1980)**
Late singer/songwriter with avid cult devised short-story song format combining moral fables and melodramas. *Heads and Tales* contains Chapin's first hit, the archetypal ballad, "Taxi." The centerpiece of *Sniper* is a tasteless Freudian interpretation of the Texas tower murders. *Verities* contains Chapin's biggest hit and best song, "Cat's in the Cradle," cowritten with his wife. *Greatest Stories—Live* is a live greatest-hits album that shows Chapin's febrile entertaining style. Despite fine craftsmanship, all of Chapin's work tended to be as emotionally overwrought as it was simplistically preachy. — S.H.

TOM CHAPIN

★ ★ **Life Is Like That / Fan. (1976)**
Tom Chapin is a pleasant enough run-of-the-mill singer/songwriter of the semi-folk variety. At his worst he's nowhere near as irritating as his late brother, Harry Chapin; neither is he anywhere near as interesting at his best. David Spinozza's production is as low-key as the rest of this eminently forgettable affair. — R.P.

BLONDIE CHAPLIN

★ ★ ★ **Blondie Chaplin / Asy. (1977)**
Solo debut of "So Tough"/"Sail On Sailor"–era Beach Boys vocalist Blondie Chaplin. Invigorating set of soulish rockers marred by lush Seventies production hallmarks (droning guitars, leaden backing chorus); Chaplin's affecting voice and a not-bad collection of self-penned tunes have worn well since LP issued. Musicians include another Beach Boys hired hand, drummer Ricky Fataar, pianist Richard Tee and the Band's keyboardist Garth Hudson. — G.A.

MARSHALL CHAPMAN

★ ★ ★ **Me I'm Feelin' Free / Epic (1977)**
★ ★ ★ **Jaded Virgin / Epic (1978)**
★ ★ ★ **Marshall / Epic (1979)** ¶
Fine woman singer/songwriter/guitarist fronts a crack band and handles country and rock genres deftly. — J.S.

MICHAEL CHAPMAN

★ **Fully Qualified Survivor / Harv. (1969)** ¶
★ **Life on the Ceiling / PFA (1978)**
Pseudo-cosmic English folkie, kind of like Nick Drake without the chops (or intensity). *Fully Qualified* was produced by Gus Dudgeon. — D.M.

CHAPTER 8

★ ★ **Chapter 8 / Ario.-Amer. (1979)** ¶
So-so soul. "Ready for Your Love" came close to being a hit, but that's about it, unless you're obsessed with overly mellow funk groups. — D.M.

CHARISMA

★ **Beasts and Friends / Rou. (1970)**
★ **Charisma / Rou. (1972)**
A totally-out-of-it record company's attempt to keep up with the times in rock & roll. — D.M.

RAY CHARLES

★ ★ ★ ★ **The Great Ray Charles / Atl. (1957)**
★ ★ ★ **Soul Brother (with Milt Jackson) / Atl. (1959)**
★ ★ ★ ★ **Genius of Ray Charles / Atl. (1960)**
★ ★ ★ ★ ★ **The Greatest Ray Charles / Atl. (1961)**
★ ★ ★ **Soul Meeting (with Milt Jackson) / Atl. (1962)**
★ ★ **The Best of Ray Charles / Atl. (1971)**
★ ★ ★ ★ ★ **A Twenty-fifth Anniversary in Show Business Salute to Ray Charles / Atl. (1973), Jap. imp.**
★ ★ ★ ★ ★ **Ray Charles Live / Atl. (1973)**
★ ★ ★ **Come Live with Me / Cross. (1974)**

★ ★ **My Kind of Jazz, Part 3 / Cross. (1975)**

★ ★ ★ **Renaissance / Cross. (1975)**

★ ★ ★ ★ **True to Life / Atl. (1977)**

★ ★ **Fourteen Hits/The Early Years / King (1977)**

★ ★ ★ **Love and Peace / Atco (1978)**

★ ★ ★ **Ain't It So / Atl. (1979)**

★ ★ ★ ★ **Brother Ray Is at It Again / Atl. (1980)**

★ ★ ★ ★ **The Right Time / Atl. (1980), Jap. imp.**

★ ★ **Rockin' with Ray / Ev. (1980)**

★ ★ ★ ★ **A Life in Music / Atl. (1982)**

★ ★ **Ray Charles / Ev. (NA)**

★ ★ **Ray Charles, Vol. 2 / Ev. (NA)**

Ray Charles helped change the face of American popular music. Born in Georgia, blind since age six, he began recording in Los Angeles in the late Forties, as an acolyte of Nat "King" Cole. These records, now available on the two Everest LPs, are impressive mostly for their mastery of another man's form.

When he came to Atlantic and producers Jerry Wexler and Ahmet Ertegun, Charles changed his style. Although he still made jazz records, he also aimed for the rock and R&B market. His great breakthrough was to add elements of gospel music to both his singing and piano playing. The result was a series of hits, including "I've Got a Woman," "What'd I Say" and "Hallelujah I Love Her So," which were enormously popular as well as fundamentally influential. More than twenty years later, they still sound startlingly fresh.

As great a blues and jazz singer and player as he was, Charles never shied away from pop. Even at Atlantic, he experimented with country & western and Big Band. But when he left Atlantic for ABC-Paramount in 1959, Charles headed straight for the middle of the road, almost deserting his R&B and jazz following. Several of his hits there, particularly "Let's Go Get Stoned," "Your Cheating Heart" and "Hit the Road Jack," retain the spirit of the early music, but most of what he did as a pure pop singer was an unfortunate waste of his immense talent.

Charles controls the ABC material, so it is his own fault that it is unrepresented in this country, except for the very late material recorded for his own Crossover label. (Some of the ABC records were issued on Charles' Tangerine label.) Of the Crossover releases listed here, only *Renaissance* has flashes of his old wit.

Atlantic's policy, as with all of its historic material, is much more haphazard. It would be splendid to see a return to print of the four-volume *The Ray Charles Story,* a far more intelligent (and more intelligently annotated) selection than the four-record boxed set *A Life in Music,* which at least has the bare essentials. While his recordings with Milt Jackson are only middling jazz (including the so-called *Best of*), Charles mastered virtually every musical form in America, during the Fifties, and some sampling of each style is here.

True to Life, Ain't It So and *Brother Ray Is at It Again* were recorded during Charles' return to Atlantic, from 1977 through 1980. While they contain no hits, they are his most consistent pop recordings in many years, especially his version of "Drift Away" from *Ain't It So,* and "Ophelia," from *Brother Ray.*

The King album duplicates the Everest material. *The Right Time* is a combination of material from Fifties Charles albums with a fine song selection ("Leave My Woman Alone," "Lonely Avenue," "The Right Time," "I Believe to My Soul," "Let the Good Times Roll," "Talkin' 'Bout You") and extensive annotation, if you can find a Japanese translator.

The prize of all this is the *Twenty-fifth Anniversary* set, a two-disc collection that will run you about $25 retail, but is well worth it, for it collects not only Charles' best Atlantic but also his best ABC recordings. For "Crying Time" and "Booty Butt" alone (and despite an absence of proper annotation), this is a great recording, and proves the case for Charles convincingly.   — D.M.

CHARLIE

★ **Fantasy Girls / Col. (1976)**

★ ★ ★ **No Second Chance / Janus (1977) ¶**

★ **Lines / Janus (1978) ¶**

★ **Fight Dirty / Ari. (1979)**

The guitars flash, and Terry Thomas can write and sing with some ability, but there's little variation or originality in the quartet's debut for Columbia. *No Second Chance,* however, relied less on guitars than keyboards, and the arrangements were more than jams.   — C.W.

CHEVY CHASE

■ **Chevy Chase / Ari. (1980) ¶**

No matter how unendurably overbearing and smarmy you thought Chevy was on TV, his album will surprise you. To his preppie leer, he's added one of the lamest singing styles in human history. Why is this man smirking?   — D.M.

CHASE
- Chase / Epic (1971)
- Ennea / Epic (1972)
- Pure Music / Epic (1974)

Flee. — D.M.

SAM CHATMON
★ ★ ★ ★ ★ The Mississippi Sheik / Blue G. (1971)

★ ★ ★ Sam Chatmon and His Barbecue Boys / Fly. Fish (1980)

Part of the famous Chatmon family that included Bo Carter, and Lonnie Chatmon of the Mississippi Sheiks, Sam is a living embodiment of the Mississippi blues tradition. His singing remains excellent and his fingerpicking guitar style on these records (recorded while he was well past sixty), which is in opposition to the playing that characterized the Sheiks records, sounds very good. — J.S.

CHEAP TRICK
★ ★ ★ Cheap Trick / Epic (1976)
★ ★ ★ ★ In Color / Epic (1977)
★ ★ ★ ★ Heaven Tonight / Epic (1978)
★ ★ ★ ★ ★ Live at Budokan / Epic (1979)
★ ★ ★ Dream Police / Epic (1979)
★ ★ All Shook Up / Epic Nu-Disc (1980)
★ ★ Found All the Parts / Epic (1980)
★ ★ One on One / Epic (1982)

A heavy-metal highlight of the late Seventies, this Chicago quartet was also the least likely *looking* combo of the day: vocalist Robin Zander and bassist Tom Petersson were rock-star slim and blown-dry, but guitarist/songwriter Rick Neilsen was a ringer for Huntz Hall of the Bowery Boys and drummer Bun E. Carlos looked like an overweight war criminal on the lam.

The self-titled debut album was produced by Jack Douglas (Aerosmith), and only a hint of the band's power and Neilsen's compositional flair came through. But Tom Werman, who produced the second and third records, understood them perfectly: his settings and the clarity with which the songs were recorded have some of the edge Glyn Johns gives the Who. Neilsen's songs were ridiculous arabesques designed to set off his astonishing guitar work—which does powerchorded tricks in an individual yet mainstream rock style—and the group's ability to execute perfect Beatle-esque harmonies behind Zander. The tone was always light and often wryly humorous: it's hard to say what "Big Eyes" or "Clock Strikes Ten" from *In Color* are about, but "Surrender," from *Heaven,* is a gem: Neilsen's parents wig out behind their own advice to him and make

out on the couch while listening to Kiss records. If that isn't your idea of surrender, you've wandered into the wrong book by mistake. *Budokan* is a live set that surpasses the studio records.

With *Dream Police,* however, a decline began to set in, as Neilsen's jokes began to fall flat and the band's power-pop intensity disintegrated into pure FM-radio formula. This process was emphasized on *All Shook Up,* in which the band replaced Werman with George Martin and promptly ran out of ideas, sinking into the kind of hard rock they'd parodied in their best work. *Found All the Parts,* one of Epic's Nu-Disc mini-albums is a collection of outtakes from the early sets and a live version of "Day Tripper," not much worse or better than what you'll hear there—totally superfluous product, released with the band's endorsement. *One on One* is pure, pointless formula. — D.M.

CHUBBY CHECKER
★ Chubby Checker's Greatest Hits / Abkco (1972)

A former chicken plucker with a stage name clownishly aped from Fats Domino, Checker was a below-average R&B singer who hooked on to Hank Ballard's "The Twist," which subsequently became the hottest dance craze of the past twenty years. Checker even did instructional spots on television—"Just pretend you're grinding out cigarette butts with each foot." For nostalgia buffs and cultural historians only. — J.S.

CHEECH AND CHONG
★ Cheech and Chong / War. (1971)
★ ★ Big Bambu / War. (1972)
★ Los Cochinos / War. (1973)
★ Cheech and Chong's Wedding Album / War. (1974)
★ Sleeping Beauty / War. (1976)
★ Let's Make a New Dope Deal / War. (1980)

The Rise and Fall of Drug Humor—mostly its fall. Good mimics but strictly miniaturists of a boring, dated subculture. Abundant vulgarity that is extremely amusing to sixth-graders. — K.T.

CHELSEA
★ ★ ★ ★ No Escape / IRS (1980)

"Right to Work" is one of the truly memorable scorched-earth anthems of punk circa 1978. It's by far the best thing on this album of similarly hard-core punkitude with a socialist bent. Even though there's more bleat than beat in its message, Chelsea remains

one of the last unmodified punk bands.
— D.M.

CLIFTON CHENIER

★ ★ ★ **Louisiana Blues and Zydeco** / Arhoo.
(1966)
★ ★ **Bon Ton Roulet** / Arhoo. (1967)
★ **Black Snake Blues** / Arhoo. (1969)
★ ★ ★ ★ **Bayou Blues** / Spec. (1971)
★ ★ **Live** / Arhoo. (1972)
★ ★ **Out West** / Arhoo. (1974)
★ ★ ★ ★ ★ **Bogalusa Boogie** / Arhoo. (1976)
★ ★ ★ **Boogie in Black and White** / Jin
(1976)
★ ★ ★ **Frenchin' the Boogie** / Bar. (1976),
Fr. imp.
★ ★ ★ **Boogie 'n' Zydeco** / Maison de Soul
(1977)
★ ★ ★ **Red Hot Louisiana Band** / Arhoo.
(1978)
★ ★ ★ **New Orleans** / Cres. (1978)
★ ★ ★ **King of Zydeco** / Home C. (1980)
★ ★ ★ **Clifton Chenier on Tour** / Paris
Album (1980), Fr. imp.
★ ★ ★ ★ **Classic Clifton** / Arhoo. (1981)
★ ★ ★ **The King of Zydeco** / Arhoo. (1981)
★ ★ **Live Together (with Big Mama
Thornton)** / Crazy C. (1981)
★ ★ ★ **King of the Bayous** / Arhoo. (NA)
★ ★ ★ **Bayou Soul** / Crazy C. (NA)
Chenier is an accordionist. Born in Opelou-
sas, Louisiana, in 1925, he is the best-known
exponent of zydeco—a dance music composed of traditional French, Acadian (popularly known as Cajun), and rhythm & blues
elements. Chenier and his band—including
brother Cleveland on rub board, a variant of
the washboard—play everything from waltzes
to two-steps to 12-bar blues to local pop hits.
Obviously this is a very rhythmic music,
though as *Bogalusa Boogie* in particular reveals, it is also a good showcase for a strong
soloist—for instance, Chenier's imaginative
accordion or John Hart's tenor sax. *Bogalusa
Boogie* is also the best-recorded and most
naturally mixed of these sets.
The lyrics are frequently in French, but it
doesn't matter much, for this isn't really
music for listening in a strict sense. And although zydeco's popularity is largely regional, it has influenced a variety of nationally
known artists such as Doug Kershaw, Elvin
Bishop, Ry Cooder and Taj Mahal, although
none perform it as purely as Chenier.
Bogalusa Boogie, as stated, is Chenier's
strongest LP to date, but if the sound is at
all appealing—the accordion has been unduly maligned by Mel Bey and Lawrence
Welk—you're likely to want to hear the entire catalogue.

One cautionary note: the Steve Miller
listed in the liner credits of *Out West* is not
the same Steve Miller of "The Joker" or
"Fly Like an Eagle" fame; the Elvin Bishop
on that LP, however, is indeed the "Travel-
lin' Shoes" man.
The proliferation of Chenier recordings in
recent years is not altogether justified;
granted that he looms head and shoulders
over the rest of Cajun/zydeco music, the
genre is ultimately limited. Some of these records—particularly the various live albums,
including the one on Arhoolie—are pretty
spotty, some are more straight blues than zydeco (the Home Cooking set for one). On
the other hand, *Classic Clifton,* the Arhoolie
anthology of his best for the label, is definitive proof that Chenier is a major artist. It's
as good as any newly recorded blues record
of the last fifteen years. — I.M./D.M.

CHER

★ **Cher** / U.A. (1971) ¶
★ **Cher** / U.A. (1972) ¶
★ **Cher's Greatest Hits** / Sp. (1974) ¶
★ **Cher/Greatest Hits** / MCA (1974)
■ **Stars** / War. (1975) ¶
★ ★ **I'd Rather Believe in You** / War.
(1976) ¶
★ ★ **Cherished** / War. (1977) ¶
★ **Cher** / MCA (1977) ¶
★ **Take Me Home** / Casa. (1979)
■ **Prisoner** / Casa. (1979)
★ **Cher Sings the Hits** / Sp. (NA) ¶
★ **Black Rose** / Casa. (1980)
★ ★ **I Paralyze** / Col. (1982)
Although she was the lead voice on one of
rock's supreme trash classics, Sonny and
Cher's "I Got You Babe," Cher has neither
the spark of intelligence required of the competent interpretive singer nor sufficient vitality and expressiveness ("Gypsies, Tramps
and Thieves" notwithstanding) to serve as a
full-blown producer's ingenue. She remains
that oddest of artistic breeds, the TV celebrity, famous for *being* rather than doing. She's
perfect for the role, which requires the degree of narcissism revealed by the list of
album titles above. — D.M.

CHIC

★ ★ **Chic** / Atl. (1978)
★ ★ ★ **C'est Chic** / Atl. (1978)
★ ★ ★ ★ **Risqué** / Atl. (1978)
★ ★ ★ ★ **Les Plus Grands Succès de Chic/
Chic's Greatest Hits** / Atl. (1979)
★ ★ ★ **Real People** / Atl. (1980)
★ ★ **Take It Off** / Atl. (1981)
Bassist Bernard Edwards and guitarist Nile
Rodgers, veteran players on the New York

rock circuit, put together the Chic concept (musicians and singers decked out in high-fashion threads) at the height of the disco craze and made some of the era's most durable music. The first album's "Dance, Dance, Dance" broke the group in New York, but *C'est Chic,* with its novelty hit, "Le Freak" (the best-selling single in Atlantic Records' history), made Edwards and Rodgers the writer/producers of the hour and established their signature sound, a haunting, minimalist pop-funk built around the guitar and bass with a wash of strings and detached female voices carrying the lyrics. *Risqué,* Chic's most fully realized album, contained their end-of-the decade masterpiece, "Good Times" (also the basis of the Sugarhill Gang's "Rapper's Delight"). *Les Plus Grands* compiled the best of the first three albums. On *Real People* and *Take It Off,* Edwards and Rodgers shifted to a a tougher dance-rock style that featured Rodgers' spiky guitar; though interesting, the magic wasn't the same. — S.H.

CHICAGO
★ ★ ★ **Chicago Transit Authority / Col. (1969)**
★ ★ **Chicago II / Col. (1970)**
★ ★ **Chicago III / Col. (1971)**
★ **Chicago IV—Live at Carnegie Hall / Col. (1971)**
★ ★ **Chicago V / Col. (1972)**
★ ★ **Chicago VI / Col. (1973)**
★ ★ **Chicago VII / Col. (1974)**
★ ★ **Chicago VIII / Col. (1975)**
★ ★ ★ **Chicago IX—Greatest Hits / Col. (1975)**
★ **Chicago X / Col. (1976)**
★ **Chicago XI / Col. (1977)**
★ ★ ★ **Hot Streets / Col. (1978)**
★ **Chicago XIII / Col. (1979)**
★ **Chicago XIV / Col. (1980)**
★ **Greatest Hits, Vol. II / Col. (1981)**
★ **Chicago XVI / War. (1982)**
The point of Chicago Transit Authority's debut album was that a big rock band had managed to play with some funk. But succeeding installments, as producer James William Guercio took more and more control, were about as imaginative as the group's album titles. Now and then, though, the group would come up with a pleasant hit single (1974's "Wishing You Were Here," a collaboration with the Beach Boys, is the best example), which makes *IX* worth looking into. The bizarre death of guitarist Terry Kath (he shot himself while toying with a pistol) forced the group to add session guitarist/vocalist Donnie Dacus for *Hot Streets,*

and then, well-traveled Bill Champlin on *XVI.* Both albums were hits; neither was an improvement. — D.M.

THE CHIEFTAINS
★ ★ **The Chieftains 1 / Is. (1965)**
★ ★ ★ ★ **The Chieftains 2 / Is. (1969)**
★ ★ ★ **The Chieftains 3 / Is. (1971)**
★ ★ **The Chieftains 4 / Is. (1974)**
★ ★ ★ **The Chieftains 5 / Is. (1976)**
★ ★ **Bonaparte's Retreat / Is. (1976)**
★ ★ ★ **The Chieftains 7 / Col. (1978)**
★ ★ ★ **The Chieftains 8 / Col. (1979)**
★ ★ ★ **The Chieftains 9—Boil the Breakfast Early / Col. (1980)**
While the Chieftains' music is not strictly traditional—they play harmony passages and compose some tunes themselves—it does have a clarity and authenticity that has made them the best-known source of Irish folk music. The band's chief virtuosos—fiddler Sean Keane and composer/piper/tin whistler Paddy Maloney—weave their instruments through a beautifully spare mix that includes a goatskin drum, bagpipes, concert flute, wire-strung harp, concertina, bones and an occasional oboe or hammer dulcimer.

Moloney and three others of the band's seven members came out of Sean O'Raida's folk orchestra in the late Fifties and made *Chieftains 1.* That record promised much, but it was four years before the band members forsook their day jobs long enough to join with fiddler Keane to make the landmark *Chieftains 2.* While both records contain jigs, reels, hornpipes and polkas, the slow airs seem to ache with the beauty of the stories underlying them.

By the release of *Chieftains 4,* Moloney had begun to compose an occasional tune, and this rich recording contains an air that became "The Love Theme from *Barry Lyndon*" (Women of Ireland)." Perhaps more striking is the grimly martial "The Battle of Aughrim" or Keane's fiddle workout on a reel called "The Bucks of Oranmore." *Chieftains 5* is assured and lyrical, but *Bonaparte's Retreat* is seen by purists as a tricked-up commercial effort that leaves the band at a crucial crossroads. Despite appearing before one of the largest audiences in history when they played support for the Pope in Ireland, the Chieftains have not managed to avoid sounding clichéd on subsequent albums. — F.S.

THE CHIFFONS
★ ★ **Sweet Talkin' Guy / Laur. (1966)**
★ ★ ★ **Everything You Always Wanted to**

Hear by the Chiffons But Couldn't Get /
Laur. (1973)
The Chiffons were one of the greatest of the
early-Sixties girl groups (as well as one of
the few not produced by Phil Spector). Their
hits were in the jive-talking, street-
swaggering style of the time and included
the mesmerizing "One Fine Day," "He's So
Fine" and "Sweet Talkin' Guy" among others. But they hardly had enough to sustain
twenty tracks, as even the best of this pair of
LPs tries to do, and their remaining non-
anthology album is a simple period piece—
the title hit and some throwaway junk. You
ought to own this music, but not in this
form, unless you don't have a 45 spindle.
— D.M.

DESMOND CHILD AND ROUGE
★ ★ ★ Desmond Child and Rouge / Cap.
(1979)
★ ★ ★ Runners in the Night / Cap. (1979)
Child virtually defines fey white soul, with
the accent on *fey*. But Rouge was one of the
least histrionic female backup trios in the
history of white popular music, and on occasion Child's songwriting just got the better
of him: "Our Love Is Insane," the group's
near hit from the first album, was a bit jive,
but the title track of the second album has a
certain nice urban density, and some of the
rest is pleasurable in a sub-Springsteen (but
über–Meat Loaf) fashion. Unfortunately, the
best thing the group ever did, "Last of an
Ancient Breed," is included on neither of
these—it's on the soundtrack to the film *The
Warriors*. — D.M.

THE CHI-LITES
★ ★ Half a Love / Bruns. (1961)
★ ★ ★ Give It Away / Bruns. (1969)
★ ★ ★ ★ ★ Give More Power to the People
/ Bruns. (1971)
★ ★ ★ ★ Lonely Man / Bruns. (1972)
★ ★ ★ ★ Greatest Hits/Chi-Lites / Bruns.
(1972)
★ ★ ★ Letter to Myself / Bruns. (1973)
★ ★ The Chi-Lites / Bruns. (1974)
★ ★ ★ Toby / Bruns. (1974)
★ ★ ★ Greatest Hits, Vol. 2 / Bruns.
(1976) ¶
★ ★ ★ ★ Happy Being Lonely / Mer.
(1976) ¶
★ ★ ★ The Fantastic Chi-Lites / Mer.
(1977) ¶
★ ★ Heavenly Body / 20th Cent. (1980)
★ ★ Me and You / 20th Cent. (1981)
★ ★ I Like Your Lovin' / Bruns. (NA)
The Chi-Lites were among the leaders of a
group soul renaissance—termed "neoclassi-

cal" by Vince Aletti—that took place at the
beginning of the Seventies. The group's early
records hardly distinguished them from the
glut of others in the field who looked to the
early Temptations for inspiration. But gradually a distinct—and for soul music, unique—
persona began to emerge. Headed by lead
singer/songwriter/producer Eugene Record,
the Chi-Lites' stark portrait of excessive
male vulnerability was unlike that of even
the Moments and Delfonics, two other
groups who exercised melancholy with great
effect. Record highlighted his thin tenor with
the most plaintive production gimmicks: a
forlorn harmonica on "Oh Girl," windstorms
on "Coldest Days of My Life." While this
type of pathos was occasionally overwrought,
often it was quite dramatic and effective, and
Power to the People is a surprisingly first-rate
mixture of soul-music populism and quiet
desperation. After *Lonely*, the Chi-Lites lost
their bass singer, and subsequent records
found a retreat from starkness into simple
prettiness. In 1976, Eugene Record left and
the Chi-Lites were forced to regroup. Produced by long-time member Marshall
Thompson, the re-formed Chi-Lites debut,
Happy Being Lonely, contains a crop of very
good songs, mostly in the old vein, in a wide
variety of delicate, nondisco harmonic settings. The group's 20th Century-Fox
album belies that promise, unfortunately.
— J.MC.

CHILLIWACK
★ All Over You / A&M (1973)
★ ★ ★ Dreams, Dreams, Dreams / Mush.
(1977)
★ Lights From the Valley / Mush. (1978)
★ Breakdown in Paradise / Mush. (1979)
★ Wanna Be a Star / Millen. (1981)
At their best, Chilliwack was the finest Canadian rock band, outrocking B.T.O. and
outwriting Burton Cummings. But a lack of
consistency kept it from international success, and only these albums remain in print.
The A&M is one of the least successful, because it's the least diverse, though it does
have "Ground Hog," a Canadian hit.
Dreams, toned down from the band's usual
hard rock, with bright melodies and harmonies, remains their best effort. *Wanna Be a
Star* includes the hit "My Girl." — A.N.

CHILLY
★ For Your Love / Poly. (1979)
★ Come to L.A. / Poly. (NA)
German disco quartet adapted the Yard-
birds' "For Your Love" to disco. — J.S.

THE CHIPMUNKS
■ **Chipmunk Punk / Excel. (1980)**
■ **Urban Chipmunk / RCA (1981)**
When recording technology was in its relative infancy, the Chipmunks' speeded-up voices were perhaps excusable, at least as a Christmas novelty. But the fact that the Chipmunks enjoyed Top Forty success in the Eighties, when they were recycled and sold as part of a specious corporate "rock & roll heritage," serves as an indictment of the bankruptcy of ideas then prevalent within the music industry. That the industry was *proud* of this shit says less about its vulgarity than its greed. — D.M.

CHOCOLATE JAM COMPANY
★ **Spread of the Future / Epic (1979)**
Unappetizing. — D.M.

CHOPPER
★ **Chopper / Ario.-Amer. (NA)**
Is this supposed to be biker-oriented hard rock? Or just loud and awful? Bring back Blue Cheer. — D.M.

CHORDS
★ ★ ★ **So Far Away / Poly. (1980), Br. imp.**
Next to the Jam, who really transcended the classification anyway, the Chords were the best of the short-lived Mod revival that marked the period between the decline of punk and the ascendance of ska—or was it the decline of power pop and the ascendance of rockabilly?—as Britain's Next Big Thing. Whatever, the group had a couple of topnotch singles in "Maybe Tomorrow" and "Something's Missing," but by the time its only album was released, neo-Mod had begun to f-f-f-fade away, and the Chords themselves did so shortly after. (Not to be confused with the Chords of Fifties "Sh-Boom" fame.) — D.S.

RANDLE CHOWNING BAND
★ ★ **Hearts on Fire / A&M (1978)**
Innocuous pop singer/songwriter; years ago, guys like this never bothered billing their bands, which was more fair. The title could confuse you into thinking Chowning has something to do with rock. — D.M.

CHRIST CHILD
■ **Christ Child / Bud. (1977) ¶**
Inane attempt to cash in on punk by band that developed "their expression in the hills of Malibu and Topanga Canyons," according to the liner notes, which conclude, "You will love it—you will hate it—you *will not* ignore it!" We haven't, but it's our job. The rest of the world has, quite wisely, resisted more successfully. A truly putrid artifact. — D.M.

CINDY AND ROY
★ **Feel It / Casa. (1979)**
Dismal disco duo backed by bland beat. Album title must be ironic. — J.D.C.

CIRCUS MAXIMUS
★ ★ ★ **Circus Maximus / Van. (1967)**
★ ★ **Neverland Revisited / Van. (1968)**
Circus Maximus was New York's answer to San Francisco's psychedelic boom, combining Country Joe's tacky Farfisa organ sound with the fuzzy social leanings of the Airplane. Predictably, most of its music sounds absurdly dated, though a few melodies linger. The best one, "Wind," was contained on the debut album, *Circus Maximus.* An out-of-character, jazzy piece dominated by piano and an irresistible chorus, the song is still a progressive FM staple. Mostly though, the most interesting thing about the band is that Jerry Jeff Walker was a member. I mean, can you imagine Jerry Jeff in a band that called itself "the circus of the mind, theatred in a tent of imagination"? — J.B.M.

CHUCK CISSEL
★ ★ **Just for You / Ari. (1980)**
Bland soul man. — D.M.

CITIZEN
★ **Sex and Society / Ova. (1980)**
Inept Cars clones. — J.D.C.

CITY BOY
★ **City Boy / Mer. (1976)**
★ **Dinner at the Ritz / Mer. (1976)**
★ ★ **Young Men Gone West / Mer. (1977)**
★ **Book Early / Mer. (1978)**
★ **The Day the Earth Caught Fire / Atl. (1979)**
★ **Heads Are Rolling / Atl. (1980)**
Similar to though not as clever as 10cc's work, *City Boy* thrived on bright harmonies, gay melodies, crisp guitars and mischievous humor—energetic, though the arrangements lacked spice. *Dinner at the Ritz* relied less on 10cc but still lacked individuality. The scoring improved but the compositions lagged; blurry engineering worsened matters. *Young Men Gone West* provided the group's finest, liveliest playing and writing, and made tentative steps toward a unique style. — C.W.

C.J. AND COMPANY
★ ★ ★ **Devil's Gun / Westb. (1977) ¶**
★ ★ **Deadeye Dick / Westb. (NA) ¶**

The debut album's opening track, "Devil's Gun," is an interesting extension of black movie music, circa *Superfly* and *Trouble Man*. Problem is, there's no movie to go with it, although this lyric suggests a more interesting scenario than, say, *Superfly T.N.T.* or *The Mack*. Although produced by session guitarist Dennis Coffey, the group couldn't sustain this level of interest, but even the falsetto harmony stuff they fill out the rest of that LP with isn't bad. The second, unfortunately, sticks with the harmony.
— D.M.

CLANCY BROTHERS AND TOMMY MAKEM

★ ★ ★ In Person at Carnegie Hall / Col. (1963)
★ ★ Freedom's Sons / Col. (1967)
★ Home Boys Home / Col. (1968)
★ ★ The Best of the Clancy Brothers and Tommy Makem / Trad. (NA)

CLANCY BROTHERS WITH LOU KILLEN

★ ★ ★ Greatest Hits / Van. (1974)
Not one of these sets gives the Clancys their due. Irish tradition is boisterous and sentimental, openly revolutionary and mightily respectful of the past. "The Rising of the Moon," "Jug of Punch," "The Patriot Game," "Red-Haired Mary" and "The Leaving of Liverpool" are familiar because the Clancys have made them so at festivals and concerts since the early Sixties. But the rousing spirit of their music, even on the live *Freedom's Sons* (recorded in Dublin on the occasion of the fiftieth anniversary of the uprising of 1916) doesn't make the transition to disc vibrantly enough.

Other Tradition and Stinson recordings are theoretically still available, and the entire Columbia catalogue remains in print. The Vanguard "twofer," however, is the most recently recorded (June 1973) and finds the group in strong voice and with a good sampling of the overall repertoire. The *Carnegie Hall* LP is also representative, featuring "Patriot Game" (not on the Vanguard release), a twelve-minute children's medley, and Tom Clancy's reading of W. B. Yeats' "O'Driscoll (The Host of the Air)." — I.M.

CLANNAD

★ ★ ★ Clannad Two / Shan. (1979)
★ ★ ★ Dulaman / Shan. (1979)
★ ★ ★ Clannad in Concert / Shan. (1980)
★ ★ ★ Crann Ull / Tara (1980)
An Irish traditional group that sticks close to the older arrangements and performances of the music. The average listener would find them more difficult to listen to than a DeDanann or Bothy Band, as their rhythms are understated and all singing is in Gaelic.
— D.D.

ERIC CLAPTON

★ ★ ★ On Tour / Atco (1970)
★ ★ ★ ★ History of Eric Clapton / Atco (1972)
★ ★ ★ ★ 461 Ocean Boulevard / RSO (1974)
★ ★ There's One in Every Crowd / RSO (1975) ¶
★ ★ ★ No Reason to Cry / RSO (1976)
★ ★ ★ Eric Clapton / Poly. (1977)
★ ★ ★ Slowhand / RSO (1977)
★ ★ ★ Backless / RSO (1978)
★ ★ ★ Just One Night / RSO (1980)
★ ★ ★ Another Ticket / RSO (1981)
With the exception of his brief stint as Derek with the Dominos, Eric Clapton's solo career often seemed as much a reaction against his past as an extension of it. Between proclamations of "Clapton Is God" and the superstar guitarist persona that he invented with Cream, Clapton was often at odds with his fan's expectations. Predictably, his surroundings often defined the forms his music took.

Coming off the road with Delaney and Bonnie, Clapton's first solo record was influenced by their tambourine-shaking sound while displaying a stronger voice and songwriting talent than had earlier been apparent. This super-session aggregation centered around what was to become the Dominos.

Following *Layla* and his heroin nightmares, Clapton returned in more subdued tones with *461 Ocean Boulevard,* which featured his pop hit of the Wailers' "I Shot the Sheriff" as well as a first-class shuffling blues in Elmore James' "I Can't Hold Out." While dominated by quieter tunes, the album contained more spirit than the lackluster followup *No Reason to Cry,* where Clapton's gentle touch revealed a soft middle.

The super-session shenanigans of *No Reason to Cry* put together a predictably tasty menu that'll leave you hungry in an hour. The heavyweights—Dylan and members of the Band—brought along their minor songs, while Clapton was left holding the bag. Pleasant, but somewhat disorienting, it pictured Clapton still looking for an appropriate niche.

Wisely he retrenched on *Slowhand* and created an album with something of the homey ambiance of *461 Ocean Boulevard,* though without tunes to match that album's highlights. But the record's relaxed feel, along with Clapton's inclination to let his guitar do a little more of the talking, puts him back in solid journeyman terrain. *Backless* and its successors continued this trend. — J.B.M.

RICHARD CLAPTON
★ ★ ★ **Prussian Blue** / Inf. (1973), Aust. imp.
★ ★ ★ ★ **Girls on the Avenue** / Inf. (1975), Aust. imp.
★ ★ **Mainstreet Jive** / Inf. (1976), Aust. imp.
★ ★ **Highway One** / Inf. (1976), Aust. imp.
★ ★ ★ ★ **Goodbye Tiger** / Inf. (1977), Aust. imp.
★ ★ ★ **Past Hits and Previews** / Inf. (1978), Aust. imp.
★ ★ **Hearts on the Nightline** / Inf. (1979), Aust. imp.
★ ★ ★ **Dark Spaces** / Inf. (1980), Aust. imp.
Clapton is a singer/songwriter who succeeded in capturing moods of the Seventies in Australia with a convincing lyricism rare in that country's music. He clearly owes a lot to Bob Dylan, Van Morrison and Jackson Browne, and while these influences intrude a little too obviously in the first few albums, by 1977's *Goodbye Tiger* he had found a distinctive and appealing voice of his own. The best evocation on record of summer on the east coast of Australia, the songs on *Goodbye Tiger* have a melodic and lyrical integrity that have survived changing musical fashions, and their reflective tone never sounds mawkish or self-indulgent.

In 1978 Clapton went to Los Angeles assisted by a grant from the government's cultural foundation, the Australia Council, who probably didn't expect him to produce an album *(Hearts on the Nightline)* that owes more to funk rhythms and the L.A. session style than to his Australian roots. He has continued to develop a tougher, more electric sound. *Dark Spaces* reflects more brooding existential concerns—a prelude perhaps to Clapton's recent embrace of Christianity. — S.M.

GENE CLARK
★ ★ **White Light** / A&M (1971)
★ ★ ★ **Collector's Series: Early L.A. Sessions** / Col. (1972) ¶
★ **Two Sides to Every Story** / RSO (1977)
Although he has been making records on and off since leaving the Byrds after their second album, it's hard to avoid the fact that Clark's contributions to that band remain the best things he's ever done. The Columbia album, done not long after his split from the Byrds, had a Byrds-ish feel when originally released, but it was remixed when reissued and suffers terribly because of that. It now sounds like a bland country-rock album. Actually, for the best of Clark's post-Byrds work, one should seek out either of the Dillard and Clark Expedition LPs on A&M (both now out of print). — B.A.

GUY CLARK
★ ★ ★ ★ **Old No. 1** / RCA (1975)
★ ★ **Texas Cookin'** / RCA (1976) ¶
★ ★ **Guy Clark** / War. (1978)
Perhaps the best songwriter to come out of the Austin, Texas, progressive country scene. Influenced a great deal by Townes Van Zandt, Clark has a superb sense for the dramatic flourish and the keen detail. There's a modesty to his songs that allows his romantic ballads to balance hard-edged toughness with wry sentimentality, which is more evident on his first album, *Old No. 1,* than on his second and third. — K.R.

MICHAEL CLARK
★ **Save the Night** / Cap. (1979)
Undistinguished pop with contemporary rhythms (disco, rock, etc.). This Michael Clark is not to be confused with the former drummer of the Byrds, now with Firefall. — D.M.

ROY CLARK
★ ★ **Tip of My Fingers** / MCA (1963)
★ **Yesterday When I Was Young** / MCA (1969)
★ ★ **Superpicker** / MCA (1973)
★ ★ ★ **Pair of Fives** / MCA (1975)
★ ★ **Roy Clark's Greatest Hits, Vol. 1** / MCA (1975)
★ ★ **Heart to Heart** / MCA (1975)
★ ★ **Roy Clark in Concert** / Cap. (1976)
★ ★ **My Music and Me** / MCA (1977) ¶
★ ★ ★ **Hookin' It** / MCA (1977)
★ ★ **Labor of Love** / MCA (1978)
★ ★ **Banjo Bandit** / MCA (1978)
★ ★ **Roy Clark Live** / MCA (1978)
★ ★ ★ ★ **Makin' Music** / MCA (1979)
★ ★ **My Music** / MCA (1980)
★ ★ **Best of** / MCA (NA)
★ ★ **Roy Clark's Greatest** / Cap. (NA)
★ ★ **Guitar Spectacular** / Cap. (NA)
★ **Roy Clark Sings Gospel** / Word (NA)
★ ★ **The Lightning Fingers of Roy Clark** / Cap. (NA)
★ ★ **Meanwhile, Back at the Country** / MCA (NA)
Clark is a dexterous guitarist with decent chops and excellent accompaniment sense.

His singing is less interesting, however, and his cornpone humor, which is the trait he's known best for due to his exposure on *Hee Haw*, is often distracting and sometimes downright annoying. Clark is at his best on the instrumental set *Hookin' It* and when he's paired with a costarring musician, as on *Pair of Fives* (Buck Trent) and *Makin' Music* (Clarence "Gatemouth" Brown).
— J.S.

ALLAN CLARKE
★ ★ **I've Got Time** / Asy. (1976)
★ **I Wasn't Born Yesterday** / Atl. (1978) ¶
★ **Legendary Heroes** / Elek. (1980)
When Allan Clarke left the Hollies, he entered the sphere of anonymity. His first solo album for Asylum finds him interpreting a variety of fashionable writers, from Bruce Springsteen to Gavin Sutherland, without challenging the originals. On subsequent albums the material isn't that good. On all his records you keep waiting for those Hollies harmonies, but they never arrive. — J.B.M.

JOHN COOPER CLARKE
★ ★ ★ **Disguise in Love** / CBS (1978), Br. imp.
★ ★ ★ **Walking Back to Happiness** / Epic (1979), Br. imp.
★ ★ **Live** / Epic (1979), Br. imp.
★ ★ ★ **Snap Crackle and Bop** / Epic (1980), Br. imp.
★ ★ ★ **Ou Est La Maison de Fromage** / Rabid (1980), Br. imp.
★ ★ ★ **Me and My Big Mouth** / Epic (1981), Br. imp.
The wizard of wit, the doyen of the double entendre, Clarke hails from the north of England and his thick accent greatly contributes to the dry humor and cynicism of his poetry. Apart from *Live*, where he recites alone, he is usually assisted by the soft electronic funk of the Invisible Girls. Whether his subject is terminal working-class-ness (in "Cycle Sluts") or politics (in "Suspended Sentence"), Clarke can never resist a grin—or a pun: "Suspended Sentence" concerns hanging. Get it? — ML.H.

THE CLASH
★ ★ ★ **Give 'Em Enough Rope** / Epic (1978)
★ ★ ★ ★ ★ **The Clash** / Epic (1979)
★ ★ ★ **Black Market Clash** / Epic (1980)
★ ★ ★ ★ ★ **London Calling** / Epic (1980)
★ ★ ★ ★ **Sandinista!** / Epic (1981)
★ ★ ★ ★ **Combat Rock** / Epic (1982)
The most audacious, committed, imaginative, politically sophisticated and smartest rock band to emerge from England's punk movement, the Clash are also the only band from that revolt into style guaranteed to be around for the third edition of this book.

Their debut album (available in pristine form only as a British import—rated four stars in our first edition) was reassembled here as *The Clash*, two years after the fact, and incorporating a number of the remarkable singles the band had released in the interim: "White Man in Hammersmith Palais," "Complete Control" and "Clash City Rockers" are hard-edged punkers, relentless and speedy, far superior to what they replace, but even more informed by reggae rhythm and sensibility than "Police and Thieves," the highlight of the British issue. *This* is the definitive punk album. If the Clash have never done a single track as awesomely powerful as the best Sex Pistols' singles, the breadth and consistency of the band's music nonetheless marks it as the premier artistic entity to emerge from Britain in the Seventies.

However, there is no avoiding the disappointing *Give 'Em Enough Rope*, a half-hearted attempt to compromise the band's sound for American audiences (through the vehicle of producer Sandy Pearlman, best known for his work with Blue Oyster Cult). *Rope* reduced the Clash's intensity to the status of gesture, and though this may appeal to Malcolm McLaren/Marshall McLuhan advocates, the truth remains that the album's most effective tracks—"Stay Free," "English Civil War," "Safe European Home"—are those in which the band's persona effectively rubs out Pearlman's heavy-metal murk.

London Calling was, if not a complete reversal of form, at the very least the band's vindication, a record so shatteringly potent that it simply steamrollered skepticism. "Wrong 'Em Boyo," "London Calling," "Spanish Bombs," "Lost in the Supermarket," "Clampdown" and "The Guns of Brixton" established once and for all the imaginativeness of Mick Jones as a guitarist and of Joe Strummer and Jones as composers. Although the band's major limitation—Strummer's voice—has yet to be conquered, "Train in Vain," with Jones singing, finally snuck these hardest-core punks into the U.S. Top Thirty.

Black Market Clash, a ten-inch LP featuring as much music as most bands put on a 12-inch one, is an assortment of oddments that nonetheless spanned the group's rock and reggae approaches.

Sandinista! is more problematic. Its best songs—"The Call Up," "Junco Partner,"

"The Magnificent Seven" and "Charlie Don't Surf"—are almost of a piece with *London Calling,* but the group also indulges itself with spacier pop courtesy of associate members Tymon Dogg and Mickey Gallagher, and some excursions into the netherworld reggae style, dub. The dub (particularly "One More Dub") is evocative, and suggests an effective solution to the limitations of Strummer's singing. Gallagher and Dogg's material is primarily an indulgence, however, as is the album's three-disc length. *London Calling* was the rare two-record set that deserved little, if any, pruning—even its filler was purposeful—but *Sandinista!* is nonsensically cluttered.

Or rather, *seems* nonsensically cluttered. One of the Clash's principal concerns, both in England, where they are stars of the first order, and in America, where their cult following is just now expanding into a broad-based audience, is to avoid being stereotyped. In any event, *Combat Rock* streamlined their political funk-reggae-rock, and this focused album earned the group its first U.S. gold LP and another pair of hit singles. Now that they have broken through worldwide, it remains to be seen what the Clash can do with their prosperity. — D.M.

CLASSIX NOUVEAU
★ **Classix Nouveau / Lib. (1981)**
A cross between synthesizer-rock and Eurodisco that manages to sound flatter and colder than either genre individually.
— J.D.C.

OTIS CLAY
★ ★ ★ **I Can't Take It / Hi (1977)**
★ ★ ★ **Got to Find a Way / P-Vine (NA), Jap. imp.**
Journeyman Southern soul singer: more rootsy than Al Green, slicker than Otis Redding, less inspired than either. *I Can't Take It* features fine Willie Mitchell production and Hi's hard-driving house band. *Got to Find a Way* is a collection of earlier, small-label singles. Unfortunately, neither includes "Tryin' to Live My Life without You," which was a major hit for Bob Seger in 1981, and provided the melodic idea on which the Eagles based their 1980 smash "The Long Run." — D.M.

LEE CLAYTON
★ ★ ★ **Border Affair / Cap. (1978)**
★ ★ ★ **Naked Child / Cap. (1979)**
★ ★ ★ **The Dream Goes On / Cap. (1981)**
When he avoids subpoetic sensitivity and tells tales in the Tom T. Hall manner, Clay-

ton's gravelly voice and country-musical accents are a pleasure, if never a revelation.
— D.M.

MERRY CLAYTON
★ **Gimme Shelter / Ode (1970) ¶**
★ **Celebration / Ode (1971) ¶**
★ **Merry Clayton / Ode (1971) ¶**
★ **Keep Your Eye on the Sparrow / Ode (1975) ¶**
★ **Emotion / MCA (1980) ¶**
Merry Clayton was the powerful backup vocalist on the Rolling Stones' classic "Gimme Shelter" from *Let It Bleed.* None of her solo LPs approximate that moment. — J.S.

PAUL CLAYTON
★ ★ **Whaling Songs and Ballads / Stin. (1954)**
★ ★ **Foc'sle Songs and Shanties / Folk. (1959)**
★ ★ **Whaling and Sailing Songs / Trad. (NA)**
★ ★ ★ **American Folk Tales and Songs / Trad. (NA)**
The late singer of traditional folk music was heavily influential in the pre-Dylan Sixties folk revival. — D.M.

DAVID CLAYTON-THOMAS
★ **Clayton / ABC (1978)**
Ex–Blood, Sweat and Tears lead singer's only in-print solo album. Nothing to recommend. — J.S.

CLEAN LIVING
★ **Clean Living / Van. (1972)**
★ **Meadowmuffin / Van. (1973)**
Truth in packaging: squeaky folkie wholesomeness, even if they sing a lot about, and look as if they do a lot of, beer drinking.
— K.T.

EDDIE CLEARWATER
★ ★ ★ **Two Times Nine / Charly (NA), Br. imp.**
★ ★ **The Chief / Roos. (1980)**
Young Chicago guitarist/singer's principal claim to fame is his uncanny ability to replicate Chuck Berry's sound. He also replicates a good many of Chuck's themes, without much more than a glancing attempt at rewriting them, which can become annoying (especially on the *Two Times Nine* title track, which is nothing more than rehashed "Sweet Little Rock 'n' Roller"), especially since Clearwater has no special proficiency at any other variety of blues or rock & roll. On the Rooster album, he demonstrates to wearying effect. — D.M.

JACK CLEMENT

★ **All I Want to Do in Life / Elek. (1978)**
Former wild man engineer of Sun studios
(he taped the better part of the label's post-
Presley hits, and wrote a couple of the better
ones), Clement is no performer. Clement
does exist somewhere in the boasting netherworld of Jerry Lee Lewis and Bo Diddley,
so traditionalists may wish to remain alert to
this. — D.M.

VASSAR CLEMENTS

★ ★ ★ **Crossing the Catskills / Roun. (1973)**
★ ★ ★ **Hillbilly Jazz / Fly. Fish (1974)**
★ ★ ★ **Vassar Clements / Mer. (1975)**
★ ★ ★ **Superbow / Mer. (1975)**
★ ★ ★ **Vassar Clements Band / MCA (1977)**
★ ★ ★ **Vassar Clements: The Bluegrass
Sessions / Fly. Fish (1977)**
★ ★ ★ **Vassar / Fly. Fish (1980)**
Clements is probably Nashville's best-known
contemporary fiddler. These albums suffer
somewhat from that typical sideman's bane:
the inability (or refusal) to take over the sessions. Otherwise they are quite different,
though of about equal quality. *Vassar Clements* is the most varied and contains a couple
of modern, experimental cuts. *Superbow* is
mostly country boogie and Western swing,
and is the most cohesive. The musicianship
is technically excellent, but none of these albums really catches fire. — J.MO.

GINNI CLEMMENS

★ ★ ★ **Sing a Rainbow / Folk. (1965)**
An earth-motherish singer with a warm, full
and sweet bluesy voice, Clemmens is a commanding and wide-ranging stylist. Her emotional approach succeeds due to an evident
and appealing sincerity. — R.P.

GREGG CLEMONS

★ **Gregg Clemons / Nemp. (1980)**
AOR schlock. — D.M.

REVEREND JAMES CLEVELAND

★ ★ ★ ★ **Rev. James Cleveland with the
Gospel All-Stars: Out on a Hill / Savoy
(1959)**
★ ★ ★ **This Sunday in Person: James
Cleveland with the Angelic Gospel Choir /
Savoy (1961)**
★ ★ ★ **Rev. James Cleveland with the
Angelic Choir, Vol. 2 / Savoy (1962)**
★ ★ ★ ★ **Rev. James Cleveland and the
Angelic Choir, Vol. 3: Peace Be Still /
Savoy (1963)**
★ ★ ★ **Songs of Dedication / Savoy (1968)**
★ ★ **Rev. James Cleveland and the Angelic
Choir, Vol. 7 / Savoy (1969)**
★ ★ ★ **Rev. James Cleveland and the
Southern California Community Choir /
Savoy (NA)**
★ **Rev. James Cleveland with the Voices of
Tabernacle: God Has Smiled on Me /
Savoy (1972)**
★ ★ **Rev. James Cleveland and the Southern
California Community Choir: In the
Ghetto / Savoy (1973)**
★ ★ **Rev. James Cleveland with the Southern
California Community Choir: Give It to
Me / Savoy (1973)**
★ ★ **Rev. James Cleveland Presents the
Charles Fold Singers Recorded Live;
Jesus Is the Best Thing That Ever
Happened to Me / Savoy (1975)**
★ ★ **Rev. James Cleveland with the Greater
Metropolitan Church of Christ Choir: The
Lord Is My Life / Savoy (1976)**
Many would argue that Cleveland took mod-
ern gospel music as far as it could go, that
the only way a gospel artist could extend
Cleveland's innovations would be to abandon
some gospel conventions altogether (which of
course is what eventually happened). Certainly, Cleveland has been influenced by such
secular artists as Ray Charles, though not to
the extent that he was shaped by gospel pioneers like Robert Martin. Cleveland's vocals
are most conspicuously pop-tinged, though
even his arrangements (and piano playing)
showed he was quite aware of jazz. This was
true *despite* the fact that Cleveland didn't
stray from gospel for years. His voice, at its
peak, was a sandpapery baritone that would
have been an ideal blues vehicle.

Cleveland has recorded prolifically in a variety of settings; the albums listed above represent a cross section. The first, *Out on a
Hill,* shows him to be a well-developed gospel singer, though his style is not quite as
personal as it would become. Whatever technical niceties his voice lacks, he is a warm,
robust and versatile singer, and some of his
best compositions are here. The next two
LPs, *This Sunday* and *Volume 2,* show him
moving closer to his trademark sound, but
the tempos are still a little too rigid; the vocals aren't quite there. (These LPs also mark
the introduction of the teenage Billy Preston
as Cleveland's organist, a position Preston
maintained through several of Cleveland's
most productive years. Preston's "sound effects" organ proved something of a gospel
novelty.)

"Peace Be Still" (song and album) represents Cleveland's big breakthrough. It is an
eighteenth-century madrigal that Cleveland
arranges and sings like a perfect soul ballad.

Tension builds and builds without release until the end; the choir answers him in traditional call-and-response, or embellishes his vocal lines. The entire album is a supreme example of slow gospel singing. (Cleveland sang slow ones almost exclusively, which may hinder some from hearing even his best albums all the way through.)

Songs of Dedication presents him without choir or group. It's just his voice and piano plus organ. Still, it's a satisfying album. However raucous his voice, Cleveland sings with great taste, subtlety and conviction, and the high choral voices he usually used to set himself off are hardly missed.

By the time he began working with the Southern California Community Choir, Cleveland's voice had taken on even more resonance, but it had also mellowed (or faded, some might argue). Still, this was a hip, vibrant choir, and it worked well with Cleveland. About half the cuts were given over to other soloists, and they are usually at least as compelling as Cleveland himself. (In contrast, the Voices of Tabernacle is a thoroughly pedestrian choir.)

Of the three albums with this choir, the first is probably the best, owing to its ebullient feel and some of the freshest material Cleveland had cut in years. But the pairing also produced one of Cleveland's weakest albums. "In the Ghetto" is is an awkward stab at pop gospel, the stuttering bass of "When the Saints Go Marching In" an embarrassment. (The rest of the *Ghetto* LP is more typical gospel fare.)

For all its unevenness, the LP with the Church of Christ Choir is perhaps the most interesting pop-gospel fusion Cleveland has ever accomplished. And while his own voice has become rather ghostly, the album introduces an exciting new vocal soloist in the Reverend Isaac Whittmon. The album with the Fold Singers, like those with the Angelic Choir, benefits from being recorded live before an enthusiastic congregation, but the Folds themselves are an unnerving combination of the stately and the pointlessly hysterical.   — J.MO.

JIMMY CLIFF

★ ★ ★ ★ **Wonderful World, Beautiful People** / A&M (1970)
★ ★ **Reggae Spectacular** / A&M (1972) ¶
★ ★ ★ ★ **The Harder They Come** / Mango (1972) ¶
★ ★ ★ **Jimmy Cliff/Unlimited** / Rep. (1973)
★ **Music Maker** / Rep. (1974)
★ ★ **Struggling Man** / Is. (1974)
★ ★ **Follow My Mind** / Rep. (1975)
★ ★ ★ **In Concert: The Best of Jimmy Cliff** / Rep. (1976)
★ ★ ★ ★ **Jimmy Cliff** / Troj. (1976)
★ ★ **Give Thanx** / War. (1978)
★ ★ ★ **I Am the Living** / MCA (1981)
★ ★ **Give the People What They Want** / MCA (1981)

Jimmy Cliff's performance as Outlaw Ivan in a film called *The Harder They Come* almost single-handedly turned Jamaica and reggae into hippie-chic. (His singing on the album of the same name is inspired.) But—and this is the unfortunate contradiction that has plagued his recording career—he has since been rapped as a musical and cultural sell-out.

Some of the criticisms might be deflected if more people realized that Cliff is not a Rastafarian but a Muslim, and that his musical roots are just as much in R&B (e.g., Dee Clark) as reggae. Still, Cliff must account for the kind of musical schizophrenia that led him to record his *Follow My Mind* by cutting rhythm tracks in Jamaica, then heading to L.A. for extensive overdubs.

Cliff's first album, *Wonderful World, Beautiful People,* is mostly composed of songs he wrote in London between 1965 and 1968. It is a gritty, insistent record, full of songs he would later fall back on, particularly "Vietnam," his statement of anger about the war.

Unlimited, made in Kingston, is probably Cliff's most fervently political record. (Politically, Cliff is a true Muslim, emphasizing black cultural expression above all else.) On cuts like "Oh Jamaica" and "Under the Sun, Moon and Stars," lilting choral parts and a moving resignedness in the lyrics help lift Cliff's strong singing over poppish overdubs and easy calypso beats.

But *Struggling Man,* a 1974 Island compilation, was tepid; *Music Maker,* cut in New York that same year, was overproduced (full of prissy singing and vapid lyrics). *Follow My Mind,* despite its confused assembly, showed a strengthened vocal attack.

Cliff's version of "No Woman, No Cry" didn't stand up next to author Bob Marley's. Cliff's cover of "Dear Mother," a tune written by his talented collaborator, Joe Higgs, is good, but "Look at the Mountains" is an even better example of Cliff's recurring themes—family, God and country—twining through a homemade folk song.

In Concert: The Best of Jimmy Cliff is a 1976 release that had Cliff fronting an honest reggae band. His renewed passion and the interplay with an enthusiastic (console-boosted?) audience on songs like "Vietnam" keeps things bubbling. But almost every song dates back to 1972 or earlier—a worrisome indication that Cliff's formidable gifts have been sitting in limbo for several years now. *Jimmy Cliff,* his U.K. debut, may be his best—much of Cliff's concert material is still drawn from this LP—but it is not devoid of pop pap. *I Am the Living* tried for black American audience, yielding a couple of excellent pop tracks. *Give the People* finds him returning to straight reggae but devoid of fresh ideas. — R.F.G.

LINDA CLIFFORD
★ **Linda / Cur. (1977)**
★ **If My Friends Could See Me Now / Cur. (1978)**
★ **Here's My Love / RSO (1979)**
★ **Let Me Be Your Woman / RSO (1979)**
★ **I'm Yours / Cap. (1980)**
★ **Right Combination / RSO (1980)**
What, pray tell, is the point of Curtom (or anybody) recording mediocre black pop singers if label owner Curtis Mayfield isn't even going to produce them? — D.M.

CLIMAX BLUES BAND
★ ★ **A Lot of Bottle / Sire (1970)** ¶
★ ★ **Climax Chicago Blues Band Plays On / Sire (1970)** ¶
★ ★ **Tightly Knit / Sire (1972)** ¶
★ ★ **FM Live / Sire (1973)**
★ ★ ★ **Stamp Album / Sire (1975)** ¶
★ ★ **Shine On / Sire (1978)** ¶
★ ★ **Real to Reel / War. (1979)**
★ ★ **Flying the Flag / War. (1980)**
The basic sound is jazz-rock-blues, and it has changed only in minor ways since Climax formed in 1968. The early records are blues-dominated (as is *FM Live*), but on recent LPs Colin Cooper's reeds begin to assume parity with the guitars. — A.N.

PATSY CLINE
★ ★ ★ **Patsy Cline—Sentimentally Yours / MCA (1962)**
★ ★ ★ **Portrait of Patsy Cline / MCA (1964)**
★ ★ ★ **Patsy Cline Showcase / MCA (1966)**
★ ★ ★ **Patsy Cline's Greatest Hits / MCA (1967)**
★ ★ ★ ★ **The Patsy Cline Story / MCA (1968)**
★ ★ **Gone But Not Forgotten / Star. (NA)**
★ ★ **Here's Patsy Cline / Voc. (NA)**
Cline was on the charts only from 1957 until her death in the 1963 plane crash that also killed Cowboy Copas and Hawkshaw Hawkins. But her influence is still felt today and

her records remain startlingly contemporary. In part this is because Cline was the decisive influence on country queen Loretta Lynn, but in the main it is because she pioneered the countrypolitan style, in which strings and other pop arrangements are added to basic country songs.

In clumsier hands, this can be a disastrously banal mix. Cline, however, was such a soulful singer and pianist that she transcended platitude. "Walkin' after Midnight," "She's Got You," "I Fall to Pieces," "Crazy," even "Back in Baby's Arms" have a gentle splendor and a bemused detachment from romantic agony generally associated with soul music. On their evidence, Cline is one of the best popular singers of the post–World War II era. — D.M.

CLINIC
★ **Now We're Even / Rou. (NA)**
Not after listening to this. — J.S.

CLOUT
★ **Clout / Epic (1979)**
★ **Six of the Best / Epic (1980)**
Clout are somebody's answer to Abba. Who asked any questions? — R.P.

THE COASTERS
★ **Sixteen Greatest Hits / Trip (NA)** ¶
★ ★ ★ ★ **The Coasters' Greatest Hits / Atco (NA)**
★ ★ ★ ★ **Their Greatest Recordings: The Coasters' Early Years / Atco (1971)**
★ **The Coasters / Power. (NA)**
★ ★ ★ ★ **Wake Me, Shake Me / Atl. (1980), Jap. imp.**
★ ★ ★ ★ **The Coasters / Atl. (1980), Jap. imp.**
The funniest group in rock & roll history. In the Fifties, Jerry Leiber and Mike Stoller wrote a series of mini-situation comedies—"Charlie Brown," "Yakety Yak," "Little Egypt"—that defined the lighter side of the teenage dilemma. The Coasters were their vehicle, and a fine one, also capable of a fine, straight R&B harmony number like "Smokey Joe's Cafe."

The classic era is well represented by the Atcos, though each contains a couple of important songs not on the other. (Barrett "Dr. Demento" Hansen's liner notes probably give a slight nod to the *Greatest Recordings.*) The Trip is much later—a re-formed version of the group that Leiber-Stoller produced in the Seventies. The versions of the classics are inept, the new material mostly vulgar. The Japanese imports are beautiful reissues of original Atlantic LPs. Unfortunately, the contents differ from what's listed on the sleeves. But these albums contain some of the best of the Coasters' more obscure material. — D.M.

DOROTHY LOVE COATES AND THE GOSPEL HARMONETTES

★ ★ ★ ★ **The Best of Dorothy Love Coates and the Original Gospel Harmonettes / Spec. (NA)**

★ ★ ★ **The Best of Dorothy Love Coates and the Original Gospel Harmonettes, Vol. 2 / Spec. (NA)**

★ ★ **The Gospel Harmonettes / Savoy (NA)**

Dorothy Love Coates had a pleasingly raw voice and a sassy style that was later adapted by such soul singers as Aretha Franklin and Millie Jackson. More importantly, she was one of the great writers of gospel's golden era. Her imagery was rich and vivid, sometimes even surreal; she often referred pointedly to social and political issues, a gospel taboo at the time.

The first Specialty album is a gem, featuring "You Better Run," which has the feel of a jump blues à la Wynonie Harris, and "Ninety-Nine and a Half," which Wilson Pickett later rewrote for a secular hit. *Volume 2,* while hardly mediocre, suffers slightly by comparison. The Harmonettes broke up and regrouped several times; the Savoy album is neither the best nor the worst of their later work, but it is representative. Vocals are uncomfortably frayed, and the semiclassical and operatic arrangements incongruous. — J.MO.

EDDIE COCHRAN

★ ★ ★ **My Way / Lib. (1964), Fr. imp.**

★ ★ ★ **Singing to My Baby / Lib. (1968)**

★ ★ ★ **C'mon Everybody / Suns. (1970), Br. imp.**

★ ★ ★ ★ ★ **The Legendary Masters Series, Vol. 4: Eddie Cochran / U.A. (1972)**

★ ★ ★ **Cherished Memories / Suns. (1972), Br. imp.**

★ ★ ★ **The Many Sides of Eddie Cochran / Rocks. (1979), Br. imp.**

★ ★ ★ ★ **The Eddie Cochran Singles Album / U.A. (1979), Br. imp.**

★ ★ **A Legend in Our Time / Un. Pac. (NA)**

★ ★ ★ **The Eddie Cochran Memorial Album / U.A. (NA), Fr. imp.**

★ ★ ★ **The Legendary Eddie Cochran / U.A. (NA), Br. imp.**

★ ★ ★ **Eddie Cochran / Suns. (NA), Br. imp.**

★ ★ ★ **Eddie Cochran / U.A. (NA), Fr. imp.**

Another great Fifties rock & roller more honored abroad than at home, Eddie Cochran was virtually the prototype of the angelic punk, the hard fighter and partyer who went all soft inside when confronted with his sweetheart's charms. Together with cowriter Jerry Capehart, Cochran created a series of teenage fictions nearly as captivating and utterly as accurate in their details as Leiber and Stoller's for the Coasters. "C'mon Everybody," "Summertime Blues," "Something Else," "20 Flight Rock" and "Pink Pegged Slacks" are classics that deserve their stature, and almost without exception, Cochran's originals are at minimum a match for the contemporary versions sung by the Who, Blue Cheer, the Rolling Stones and others. Cochran was a powerful, raspy singer, and his guitar work cuts and stings.

(To perfectly fulfill the requirements of rock myth, Cochran died in April 1960 in a car crash on his way to Heathrow Airport, London, the day after completing a U.K. tour that was the apex of his short-lived career. Gene Vincent was mangled in the same wreck.)

Of these albums, only *The Legendary Masters Series* is indispensable, even for hard-core Fifties fans. This two-disc compilation of everything essential, plus a few rarities, is complete with liner notes by guitarist/critic Lenny Kaye, who has done a truly superb job. (The notes are also included with the five-record boxed set *Eddie Cochran* available as a French import, but missing some of the better selections on *The Legendary Masters Series.* Those five LPs are also available individually, but if you're devout enough to want one, you might as well invest in 'em all.) The preferred alternative is the *Singles Album,* but this is much more of a gloss on Cochran's career.

Cochran recorded a great deal, not only under his own name but also as an occasional sideman, and he cut a mine of demos for American Music, the publishing company that gave him his start. Almost every album listed here thus has something not on any of the others, though how much of Cochran's vast and not always consistent repertoire you'll really want to hear and hang on to is another question. But the basics are a fundamental part of rock & roll lore, and if only for their wit and later influence ought to be heard by anyone who's even a little bit serious about the music. — D.M.

HANK COCHRAN

★ ★ **Make the World Go Away / Elek. (1980)**

Journeyman country singer whose chief distinction is (a) having married fellow vocalist

Jeannie Seely, or (b) having performed in a pre-rock & roll duo with Eddie Cochran (no relation), depending upon whom you ask. (Those who choose Eddie are correct.) — D.M.

BRUCE COCKBURN
★ ★ ★ ★ **In the Falling Dark** / Is./True **(1976)**
★ ★ ★ **Circles in the Stream** / Is./True **(1977)**
★ ★ ★ **Further Adventures of** / Is. **(1978)**
★ ★ ★ **Dancing in the Dragon's Jaws** / Millen. **(1979)**
★ ★ ★ ★ **Humans** / Millen. **(1980)**
★ ★ ★ ★ **Résumé** / Millen. **(1981)**
★ ★ ★ ★ **Inner City Front** / Millen. **(1981)**
This gifted Toronto-based singer/songwriter (b. 1945) has yet to receive the recognition he deserves in the United States, though he's long been accepted in Canada as an important folk-pop voice. Cockburn started out as a Dylan-influenced acoustic singer/songwriter with an interest in impressionistic guitar effects and a metaphysical turn of mind. In the mid-Seventies he became a Christian mystic, and this spiritual revitalization suffused *In the Falling Dark,* his first U.S. release since two obscure, out-of-print Epic Records in the early Seventies. *In the Falling Dark* introduced a folk-jazz style that the live retrospective, *Circles in the Stream,* solidified.

Cockburn's mild-mannered singing style subsequently assumed a rockier edge, and his incorporation of reggae on *Dancing, Humans* and *Inner City Front* underscored an increasingly explicit leftist political viewpoint. *Dancing* contains Cockburn's one and only U.S. hit, "Wondering Where the Lions Are." *Résumé* is a well-selected best-of. *Humans* and *Inner City* mix up sexual and political anger and cosmic consciousness with an intuitive spontaneity that sometimes recalls Neil Young. Cockburn, however, is both folkier and jazzier than Young, and his painterly lyrics more detached. — S.H.

JOE COCKER
★ ★ ★ ★ **With a Little Help from My Friends** / A&M **(1969)**
★ ★ ★ ★ ★ **Joe Cocker!** / A&M **(1969)**
★ ★ ★ ★ **Mad Dogs and Englishmen** / A&M **(1970)**
Joe Cocker first emerged in 1969 as a novelty; an English Ray Charles soundalike singing a somewhat hysterical version of the Beatles' "With a Little Help from My Friends." The debut album *(Friends)* is in that spirit—not quite serious, but Cocker

wails, ignoring the girl choruses and patronizing accompanists. The second album, *Joe Cocker!,* has the Cocker trademarks—a nose for good material, a mix of ballads and straight-ahead rockers that show both his fragility and barroom growl—in spades. The sidemen are adept but occasionally lumbering, but who cares when you've got "Delta Lady," "She Came in through the Bathroom Window" and "Hitchcock Railway." *Mad Dogs,* cut on the 1970 tour led by Leon Russell, captures the frenzy of one of rock's most exciting shows. Although it's preferred by some to *Joe Cocker!,* the insistent raucousness can be grating—it probably was to Cocker, who didn't make another record until a couple of years later.
★ ★ **Joe Cocker** / A&M **(1972)**
★ ★ ★ **I Can Stand a Little Rain** / A&M **(1974)**
★ ★ **Jamaica Say You Will** / A&M **(1975)**
★ ★ ★ **Stingray** / A&M **(1976)**
★ ★ ★ ★ **Joe Cocker's Greatest Hits** / A&M **(1977)**
★ ★ ★ **Luxury You Can Afford** / Asy. **(1978)**
★ ★ ★ **Sheffield Steel** / Is. **(1982)**
Cocker's reemergence was stumbling. On *I Can Stand* and *Joe Cocker,* he sounded a little unsure. The slick production on the former and original material on the latter didn't help either. *Jamaica* and *Stingray* suffer from an excess of mediocre material, although the latter shows signs of renewal, particularly because of the support Cocker gets from the agile pop-soul band, Stuff, and his material, which is better than average and includes Dylan-Levy's "Catfish."

Sheffield Steel was yet another comeback. (Cocker has now made at least as many as Sly Stone.) Recorded in Jamaica, with producers Sly Dunbar and Robbie Shakespeare, it was fairly stiff and can't compare with his best. His duet with Jennifer Warnes, "Up Where We Belong," got him another hit, but the bathetic ballad was hardly worth the effort. — P.H./D.M.

COCKNEY REJECTS
■ **Greatest Hits, Vol. 1** / EMI **(1980), Br. imp.**
■ **Greatest Hits, Vol. 2** / EMI **(1980), Br. imp.**
■ **Greatest Hits, Vol. 3** / EMI **(1981), Br. imp.**
★ ★ **The Power and the Glory** / EMI **(1981), Br. imp.**
Unreconstructed British punk rockers, the Cockney Rejects made three predictable genre albums of nonmusical rabble-rousing before attempting to make a listenable record. *The Power and the Glory* ain't great, but at least it tries. — I.R.

CODE BLUE
★ ★ **Code Blue / War. (1980)**
Code Blue is a tight, poppish trio with new-wave smarts and an affinity for British Invasion–era rock. As promising as the combination sounds, it's the latter that sinks them, because Code Blue rarely ventures beyond enthusiastic nostalgia. Sure, they're witty enough to toss off a line like "Where are Freddie and the Dreamers? They're all selling shoes," but hardly wise enough to see the irony in their singing it. — J.D.C.

DAVID ALLAN COE
★ ★ ★ **Penitentiary Blues / SSS (1970)**
★ ★ **Mysterious Rhinestone Cowboy / Col. (1974)**
★ ★ ★ **Once Upon a Rhyme / Col. (1975)**
★ ★ ★ **Longhaired Redneck / Col. (1976)**
★ ★ ★ **David Allan Coe Rides Again / Col. (1977)**
★ ★ **Tattoo / Col. (1977)**
★ ★ ★ **Texas Moon / Plant. (1977)**
★ ★ **Family Album / Col. (1978)**
★ ★ **Human Emotions / Col. (1979)**
★ ★ **I've Got Something to Say / Col. (1980)**
★ ★ **Invictus Means Unconquered / Col. (1981)**
Coe's debut, a collection of prison songs, is country-flavored white blues, so there's a certain sameness to the music, and some of the lyrics are overly derivative. Still, it's full of fine harp work, and some stinging bottleneck guitar.

It's with the Columbia albums that a personal sound and stance evolves: the music is country with a beat, often heavily orchestrated with strings and background voices. He likes parody and seethes with a braggadocio that becomes increasingly overbearing. *Cowboy* is the weakest group of songs, and is mostly expendable. *Rhyme* has strong, imaginative material, and Coe's melodic sense is by now fully developed. *Longhaired Redneck* features a couple of his best songs, but here his braggadocio has turned into a distasteful (and potentially dangerous) megalomania that undercuts the whole album. The effect continues through the later records.
— J.MO.

LEONARD COHEN
★ ★ ★ ★ **Leonard Cohen / Col. (1968)**
★ ★ ★ ★ **Songs from a Room / Col. (1969)**
★ ★ ★ **Songs of Love and Hate / Col. (1971)**
★ ★ ★ **New Skin for the Old Ceremony / Col. (1974)**
★ ★ ★ **Best of Leonard Cohen / Col. (1976)**
★ **Death of a Ladies' Man / War. (1977)**
★ ★ ★ **Recent Songs / Col. (1979)**

Cohen is best known as Canada's poet laureate of outrage and existential despair; his novel, *Beautiful Losers,* was a Sixties classic. He is not much of a singer, but a couple of his songs, notably "Suzanne" (from *Leonard Cohen,* 1968) and "Bird on a Wire" (*Songs from a Room,* 1969), have been widely covered and occasionally have made a chart success. Although often overwrought in a pop context, his lyrics are invariably fascinating for lovers of terminal depression and morbid imagery, and his Columbia albums are well worth seeking for aficionados of gloom.

Unfortunately, when he made the switch to Warner Bros. in 1977, after a recording hiatus of a couple of years, he worked with former genius producer Phil Spector, who managed to botch the best set of lyrics that Cohen had written since his debut album by recording them with completely irrelevant musical arrangements. Nonetheless, the record might be worth searching out, if only because of its fascinatingly elliptical attack on feminist values, "Death of a Ladies' Man." *Recent Songs* is what Cohen does best; if you like him, you'll like it. — D.M.

MARGERY COHEN
★ **Starting Here, Starting Now / RCA (1977)**
If I'm not there in five minutes, start without me. — J.S.

MICHAEL COHEN
★ **What Did You Expect / Folk. (1973)**
★ **Some of Us Had to Live / Folk. (1976)**
★ **Everybody's Gotta Be Someplace / RCA (1978) ¶**
Gay troubadour with singing/writing style like Leonard Cohen's but much cruder.
. — S.H.

MIKE COHEN
★ **Moments / Pac. A. (1979)**
Unfortunately, only bad ones. — J.S.

COLD CHISEL
★ ★ ★ **Cold Chisel / WEA (1978), Aust. imp.**
★ ★ ★ **Breakfast at Sweethearts / WEA (1979), Aust. imp.**
★ ★ ★ ★ **East / Elek. (1980)**
★ ★ ★ **Swingshift / WEA (1981), Aust. imp.**
A competent blues-based rock & roll band, Cold Chisel are one of Australia's most successful acts. Guitarist Ian Moss and singer Jimmy Barnes are both well-versed in the traditions of R&B, but there's a sense that you've heard it all before. What you haven't

heard before are pianist Don Walker's lyrics, intelligent and convincing visions of a range of modern situations, written from the inside looking out. "Khe Sanh," about a Vietnam vet, is one of the best. The band's first single, the song was re-recorded for issue on the U.S. release of *East,* the best-realized of Cold Chisel's albums. Also included are "Star Hotel," about 1979 youth riots in Newcastle, New South Wales; "Choirgirl," a sentimental ballad with considerable melodic flair and some good guitar playing; and "My Baby," the band's biggest hit. *Swingshift* is a double live set of only average quality that reached No. 1 in Australia. — S.M.

COLD FIRE
★ Too Cold / Cap. (1981)
Title says it all. — D.M.

MOLKIE COLE
★ Molkie Cole / Janus (1977) ¶
With their clown makeup, this Cleveland band looked like the Hello People. On record, their cartoon pop was Sparks without the fire. — D.F.

NATALIE COLE
★ ★ ★ ★ Inseparable / Cap. (1975)
★ ★ ★ Natalie / Cap. (1976)
★ ★ ★ Unpredictable / Cap. (1977)
★ ★ ★ Thankful / Cap. (1977)
★ ★ Natalie Live / Cap. (1978)
★ ★ I Love You So / Cap. (1979)
★ ★ We're the Best of Friends / Cap. (1979)
★ ★ Don't Look Back / Cap. (1980)
★ ★ Happy Love / Cap. (1981)
With her debut album, *Inseparable,* Natalie Cole proved herself a first-class stylist who borrowed heavily from two diverse sources: Aretha Franklin and Chaka Khan. Marvin Yancy and Chuck Jackson wrote and produced, showing an admirable ear for restraint and conciseness. Cole is molded into a variety of soul and pop styles: bar-band funk, gospel-soul and torchy ballads. The highlight: the triumphant, midtempo "This Will Be." *Natalie* aimed at a similar standard, but this and later LPs were attempts at glossy, Las Vegas versatility and left one with a feeling that Cole was unable to develop a personal style. — J.MC.

NAT "KING" COLE
★ ★ ★ ★ Love Is the Thing / Cap. (1957)
★ Cole Español / Cap. (1958)
★ ★ Nat "King" Cole Sings George Shearing Plays / Cap. (1962)
★ More Cole Español / Cap. (1962)

★ Ramblin' Rose / Cap. (1962)
★ My Fair Lady / Cap. (1964)
★ ★ Unforgettable / Cap. (1965)
★ Nat "King" Cole Live at the Sands / Cap. (1966)
★ ★ The Best of Nat "King" Cole / Cap. (1968)
★ ★ Capitol Jazz Classics, Vol. 8 / Cap. (1972)
★ ★ Love Is Here to Stay / Cap. (1974)
★ The Christmas Song / Cap. (1975)
★ ★ ★ The Nat "King" Cole Story, Vol. 1 / Cap. (1975)
★ ★ The Nat "King" Cole Story, Vol. 2 / Cap. (1975)
★ A Mis Amigos / Cap. (1979)
★ ★ The King Cole Trio / Jazz T. (NA)
★ Walkin' My Baby Back Home / Cap. (NA)
★ A Blossom Fell / Cap. (NA)
This Earl Hines–influenced pianist-turned-crooner became the first black male singer to gain total pop mainstream acceptance and his own TV show in the early Fifties. Cole specialized in romantic ballads; his most consistent album, *Love Is the Thing* (1957), with luscious Gordon Jenkins arrangements is still a delightful dream and smooch record. An excellent technician but a bland interpreter, Cole was always indiscriminate in his choice of material. About half of the Cole in print is singles anthologies, and many of the songs are laughably trite. In the Sixties, Cole made the mistake of rerecording his early hits—"Nature Boy," "Mona Lisa," "Too Young" et al.—with arrangements that duplicated the originals. But these remakes, which comprise the bulk of the anthologies, capture little of the magic of the originals. For by the Sixties, Cole's voice had lost its smoothness and could evoke no longer these songs' innocent romanticism. — S.H.

JUDY COLLINS
★ A Maid of Constant Sorrow / Elek. (1962)
★ ★ Golden Apples of the Sun / Elek. (1963)
★ Judy Collins #3 / Elek. (1963)
★ ★ The Judy Collins Concert / Elek. (1964)
★ ★ ★ Judy Collins Fifth Album / Elek. (1965)
★ ★ ★ In My Life / Elek. (1967)
★ ★ ★ Wildflowers / Elek. (1968)
★ ★ ★ ★ Who Know Where the Time Goes / Elek. (1968)
★ ★ Recollections / Elek. (1969)
★ ★ Whales and Nightingales / Elek. (1971)
★ ★ Living / Elek. (1972)

★ ★ ★ Colors of the Day/The Best of Judy Collins / Elek. (1972)
★ ★ True Stories and Other Dreams / Elek. (1973)
★ Judith / Elek. (1975)
★ Bread and Roses / Elek. (1976)
★ ★ ★ The First Fifteen Years / Elek. (1977) ¶
★ ★ ★ So Early in the Spring / Elek. (1977)
★ Hard Times for Lovers / Elek. (1979)
★ Running for My Life / Cap. Elek. (1980)
★ ★ ★ ★ Times of Our Lives / Elek. (1982)

Judy Collins has always brought a sense of classical decorum to whatever songs she sang, be they traditional folk, art song, or MOR pop. On her first album, the crystal-voiced Colorado-reared singer turned in dignified versions of Anglo-American folk classics like "Wild Mountain Thyme" and "I Know Where I'm Going." With #3, she began to perform the work of contemporary songwriters, including Bob Dylan, and her first concert album included a stunning version of Dylan's "Lonesome Death of Hattie Carrol." Collins's fifth album was as emotionally rich as it was discriminating in its song choices—e.g., "Pack Up Your Sorrows," "Thirsty Boots" and "Tomorrow Is a Long Time."

On *In My Life* and *Wildflowers,* Collins moved beyond folk rock into art song. Besides a glowing version of the Lennon and McCartney title song, "In My Life," the material on the first included Jacques Brel's "La Colombe," Brecht-Weill-Blitzstein's "Pirate Jenny," and the declamatory "Marat/Sade." Where *In My Life* was both theatrical and political, *Wildflowers,* which included Collins' first major original song, "Since You Asked," was more dreamy and impressionistic, and it gave Collins the singer and Joni Mitchell the writer their first big hit in "Both Sides Now." Collins hit her artistic peak with *Who Knows Where the Time Goes,* a folk-rock album made with country-rock musicians. Ian Tyson's "Someday Soon," Rolf Kempf's "Hello, Hooray," Sandy Denny's title song, Robin Williamson's "First Boy I Loved" and Collins' own "My Father" were stand-outs.

After *Who Knows,* Collins assumed a cooler, artier stance. *Recollections* is an anthology. The ethereal *Whales and Nightingales* gave Collins a hit with "Amazing Grace." *Living* features Collins' quietly stirring renditions of Leonard Cohen's "Famous Blue Raincoast" and "Joan of Arc." *Colors* is a second, well-selected anthology. With five original songs, *True Stories* highlighted Collins' songwriting skills as no other album had before; its centerpiece was the autobiographical Debussy-inspired "Secret Gardens."

With *Judith,* Collins moved more toward MOR pop and scored another hit with Stephen Sondheim's "Send in the Clowns." But on both *Judith* and *Bread and Roses,* her voice sounded somewhat thinner and more strained than before. The two-record *First Fifteen Years,* was her third and most far-reaching anthology. With producer Gary Klein, Collins made her weakest album, *Hard Times for Lovers,* though her version of Sondheim's "I Remember Sky" stands out as impressive. *Running for My Life,* in which Collins had regained some of her vocal strength, included two songs from *Sweeney Todd* and a passionate remake of Jacques Brel's "Marieke." Clearly, Collins was the on the way toward finding the right personal balance between adult pop and art songs. *Times of Our Lives,* with five original songs, clinched Collins' artistic comeback. Perhaps her finest record in more than a decade, it found her in an urban pop-country groove that was sophisticated enough to accommodate art songs as well as pop, and Collins' voice, which had sounded damaged in the late Seventies, had regained most of its warmth and sureness. — S.H.

PHIL COLLINS
★ ★ ★ Face Value / Atl. (1981)
The big news here was that the Genesis drummer/vocalist's first solo LP didn't sound at all like a Genesis solo LP. Instead of the expected grand art-rock gestures, Collins opted for a seductively groomed collection of Eno-esque tone poems, bright vanilla R&B flash, romantic balladry, and a nearly one-man super-psychedelicized remake of the Beatles' "Tomorrow Never Knows." — D.F.

SHIRLEY COLLINS AND THE ALBION COUNTRY BAND
★ ★ ★ ★ No Roses / Ant. (1971) ¶
Collins sings traditional British Isles folk music, accompanied by acoustic and electric instruments. The "Band" is actually an all-star lineup of twenty-five British folk-rock players, gathered and coproduced by Ashley Hutchings. The atmosphere and emotion of the old receive tasteful framing with the energy of rock. — C.W.

COLLINS AND COLLINS
★ ★ Collins and Collins / A&M (1980)
Slickly produced but undistinguished broth-

er-and-sister disco act from Philadelphia.
— J.S.

COLOSSEUM

★ ★ ★ ★ **Those Who Are About to Die Salute You** / Dun. (1969)
★ ★ **Daughter of Time** / Dun. (1970)
Colosseum was one of the first successful British blues-rock bands to turn directly to jazz. The core of the group—drummer Jon Hiseman, tenor/soprano saxophonist Dick Heckstall-Smith and bassist Tony Reeves—was formed immediately after recording together on John Mayall's landmark *Bare Wires* album. Hiseman and Heckstall-Smith had also worked with Graham Bond and were well-schooled jazz musicians. Colosseum was augmented by organist David Greenslade and guitarist/vocalist James Litherland. Their debut, *Those Who Are About to Die Salute You,* stands as a high point in the peculiarly British synthesis of jazz, rock, R&B and classical elements. The extended track on side two, "Valentyne Sweet," demonstrates a conceptual link between John Coltrane and Procol Harum.
Unfortunately, subsequent Colosseum ventures, including *Daughter of Time,* fail to live up to the promise of their first record.
— J.S.

COLOSSEUM II

★ ★ ★ **Electric Savage** / MCA (1977) ¶
★ ★ ★ **Wardance** / MCA (1978) ¶
Colosseum-founder/drummer Jon Hiseman assembled this band in late 1976 around guitarist Gary Moore, bassist John Mole and multi-keyboardist Don Airey. These two fiery LPs present the band in fine form on a number of jazz-rock-fusion instrumentals in a style similar to Jeff Beck's landmark *Blow by Blow* album. — J.S.

JESSI COLTER

★ ★ ★ **I'm Jessi Colter** / Cap. (1975)
★ ★ ★ **Jessi** / Cap. (1975)
★ ★ ★ **Diamond in the Rough** / Cap. (1976)
★ ★ ★ **Mirriam** / Cap. (1977)
Jessi Colter's first three albums present her as a tough-voiced country-rock singer, something like Linda Ronstadt. The stance was easier to maintain as Waylon Jennings' wife—Jessi was even included in RCA's *Outlaws* anthology with Jennings and Willie Nelson. All of her records were coproduced by Jennings and featured his guitar playing as well as instrumental contributions from his backing band, the Waylors.
Colter writes all her own songs, some of which, like "Who Walks through Your Memory (Billy Jo)" and "The Hand That Rocks the Cradle," are very good. She scored a hit single with "I'm Not Lisa," a ballad from *I'm Jessi Colter.*
Mirriam is a complete departure from Colter's country rock image, a pristine, deadly sincere near-gospel album dedicated to her mother and rife with songs about God. Her singing is much starker here, and the overall effect, though different, is as striking as her other material. Jennings once again supplies instrumental support and a backup vocal appearance with Roy Orbison on "I Belong to Him." — J.S.

CHI COLTRANE

★ **Chi Coltrane** / Col. (1972) ¶
★ **Road to Tomorrow** / CLD (1977)
No, this is not the daughter of Alice Coltrane and Eugene Record. Actually, Chi Coltrane sounds like Carly Simon after an attack of soul. "Thunder and Lightning," Coltrane's one departure from the "sensitive" song, was a fluky one-shot hit in 1972. *That* must be the reason these albums are still in the catalogue. — A.S.

JEFFREY COMANOR

★ ★ ★ **A Rumor in His Own Time** / Epic (1976) ¶
Although Comanor weighs in at the light-to-welter end of the California-mellow scale, his singing and some of his songs reveal an adolescent eagerness unusual for the land of laid-back. For the rest—their lack of substance is balanced by pleasing melodies and tasteful, Eagles-style production. — A.S.

COMATEENS

★ ★ ★ **Comateens** / Cach. (1981)
This New York trio and its drum machine Rollo offer a lightweight, good-humored brand of Eighties dance music mostly characterized by skating-rink synthesizer and scrubbed rhythm guitar. The group's first single, a delightful stripped-down reading of Bowie's "TVC 15," is redone here, and similar arrangements are accorded "Summer in the City" and the "Munsters' Theme," both of which are good fun. Still, the best moments come on the group's own material, especially "Late Night City," an infectious harmony-pop concoction, and "Ghosts," eerie lovelorn disco. The rest falls somewhere in between these two extremes, but isn't nearly as memorable. — D.S.

COMMANDER CODY

★ ★ **Midnight Man** / Ari. (1977) ¶
★ ★ **Flying Dreams** / Ari. (1978)

These solo albums by George Frayne, the Commander himself, minus the Lost Planet Airmen, maintain the group's sense of fun but miss its musical adventurousness. For boogie-woogie stalwarts only.
— D.M.

COMMANDER CODY AND HIS LOST PLANET AIRMEN
★ ★ ★ Lost in the Ozone / Para. (1971)
★ ★ ★ Hot Licks, Cold Steel and Trucker's Favorites / Para. (1972)
★ ★ ★ ★ Live from Deep in the Heart of Texas / Para. (1974)
★ ★ ★ Country Casanova / Para. (1973)
Hot Licks features classic old and new truck-driving songs, including the epic yarn "Mama Hated Diesels." There's also the typically tongue-in-cheek country ballad, "Kentucky Hills of Tennessee," and a lively "Diggy Diggy Low." Billy Kirchen gets off on some state-of-the-art modern rockabilly guitar on the two Little Richard songs. The live album captures the Cody crew in their natural habitat—before a well-oiled crowd—and the band responds with some exemplary beer-drinking music in a variety of styles, all done with abundant good spirits. *Lost* reflects their uncertainty in the studio, but contains several of their trademark tunes— "Seeds and Stems (Again)," "Lost in the Ozone" and "Hot Rod Lincoln." *Casanova* swings a little more than on previous albums. But the selection of material is beginning to seem like a formula. All four of these sound like the work of a band that enjoys playing, whatever its technical shortcomings.
★ ★ Commander Cody and His Lost Planet Airmen / War. (1975) ¶
★ Tales from the Ozone / War. (1975) ¶
★ ★ We've Got a Live One Here! / War. (1976)
For the group's first Warner's LP, producer John Boylan attempts to slow down the tempo, standardize the material, smooth off the rough edges and generally strip Cody of all the human elements that made the group stand out. He nearly succeeded, but a little personality crept through anyhow. It took producer Hoyt Axton (on *Tales*) to reduce the group to what could be any faceless would-be L.A. country-rock band playing retreads and ready-mades. By *Live One,* the group has clearly given up. Though they lean heavily on their earlier, more inspirational material, the band's performance is perfunctory, its humor forced, and little is left but the raggedness, which has no charm by itself. — J.MO.

COMMODORES
★ ★ ★ ★ Machine Gun / Mo. (1974)
★ ★ ★ Caught in the Act / Mo. (1975)
★ ★ ★ Movin' On / Mo. (1975)
★ ★ ★ Hot on the Tracks / Mo. (1976)
★ ★ ★ Commodores / Mo. (1977)
★ ★ ★ Commodores Live / Mo. (1977)
★ ★ ★ Natural High / Mo. (1978)
★ ★ ★ ★ Greatest Hits / Mo. (1978)
★ ★ ★ Midnight Magic / Mo. (1979)
★ ★ ★ Heroes / Mo. (1980)
★ ★ ★ In the Pocket / Mo. (1981)
The Commodores took black rock to a kind of plateau in the late Seventies. They began in 1974 as a fairly nondescript but essentially powerful post-Sly revue act, but as the guitars and percussion stepped forward more boldly, they began to seem more like black music's answer to heavy metal. This came home most forcefully with *Machine Gun,* although succeeding records would be more popular. — D.M.

JEFF CONAWAY
★ Jeff Conaway / Col. (1980)
Conaway, a regular on the TV series *Taxi,* demonstrates why he made his mark in acting. — J.D.C.

CON-FUNK-SHUN
★ Con-Funk-Shun / Mer. (1977)
★ Secrets / Mer. (1977)
★ Loveshine / Mer. (1978)
★ Candy / Mer. (1979)
★ Spirit of Love / Mer. (1980)
★ Touch / Mer. (1980)
Boogie by the pound. — D.M.

THE CONGOES
★ ★ ★ ★ Heart of the Congoes / Beat 2 (1981)
An unholy alliance between the intergalactic voodoo of producer Lee Perry and the doomed-spirit wails of the Congoes make this a reggae classic. "Congo Man" takes African chant to an electronic frontier, while "Row Fisherman" evokes the sea in swirls of electronic effects. None of their other recordings without Perry have matched this, although "At the Feast," a single on New York's 99 label, is mighty fine.
— R.F.G.

CONGRESS OF WONDERS
■ Revolting / Fan. (1971)
■ Sophomoric / Fan. (1972)
Absolutely moronic hippie humor. Not a single laugh in more than ninety minutes of nonsense. — D.M.

EARL THOMAS CONLEY
★ ★ ★ **Blue Pearl / Sunbird (1980)**
★ ★ ★ ★ **Fire and Smoke / RCA (1981)**
Conley is a real country comer—a singer,
writer and performer of the first order whose
style is carved from the rough-hewn tradition, but who displays modernity in both
production and energy. A blue-collar man
with a more-than-canny eye for the essence
of a situation, Conley could be the commercial fulfillment of Kris Kristofferson's promise. That is, he's an unusually intelligent
country singer, albeit less Oxford and more a
singer than Kris. Conley can effectively
apply the simple country music form to contemporary complexities, among which are
Conley's first two albums. After a series of
semi-successful singles, Conley and coproducer Nelson Larkin cut the modern and
muscular *Blue Pearl* for Sunbird Records; it
so impressed RCA that they signed Conley,
combined tracks from *Blue Pearl* with newer
cuts and put out *Fire and Smoke*. Conley's
so good that both are worth having. — R.P.

DEAN CONN
★ ★ **Dean Conn / A&M (1980)**
Sweet-voiced, bluesy and boring. — D.M.

BILL CONNORS
★ ★ ★ **Theme to the Guardian / ECM/Poly.
(1975)**
Bill Connors' searing, pinpoint guitar playing
in the original heavily arranged electric version of Return to Forever helped define a
jazz-rock-fusion guitar style. Fans of his intense delivery will be surprised at this subdued, classically influenced record of acoustic guitar solos. Connors' compositional
sense and shrewdly calculated, multiple-
overdub technique suits the pristine recording style employed by ECM's Manfred Ei-
cher. — J.S.

NORMAN CONNORS
★ **Love from the Sun / Bud. (1972)** ¶
★ **Dance of Magic / Bud. (1972)** ¶
★ **Slew Foot / Bud. (1974)** ¶
★ **Dark of Light / Bud. (1974)** ¶
★ ★ **Saturday Night Special / Bud. (1975)** ¶
★ ★ **You Are My Starship / Bud. (1976)**
★ **Romantic Journey / Bud. (1977)**
★ ★ **This Is Your Life / Ari. (1978)** ¶
★ ★ **Best of Norman Connors / Bud. (1978)**
★ ★ **Invitation / Ari. (1979)**
★ ★ **Take It to the Limit / Ari. (1980)**
Since the advent of Sly Stone and Jimi Hen-
drix, black popular-music taste has expanded
to encompass a kind of middling jazz that
borrows ideas and sometimes songs from the

post-Coltrane innovators, but adapts them
for purposes of seduction and/or boogie.
What was once transcendent has now become shallow, and Connors is a principal exponent of this lack of depth—he's gathered a
couple of pop hits ("You Are My Starship"
is the most notable), and seems to record as
often as possible. All of these records were
made since 1972. Their most significant contribution was the introduction of the talented
bassist and vocalist Michael Henderson.
 — D.M.

THE CONTINENTALS
★ ★ **Fizz! Pop! (Modern Rock) / Epic
(1980)** ¶
A four-song, ten-inch record issued as part
of Epic's apparently abortive Nu Disk series
with not much to recommend it beyond its
packaging. "Walking Tall" is a total Costello
clone and "Two Lips from Amsterdam" is
as self-consciously cute as the pun that is its
main feature. An oddity for collectors.
 — G.A.

THE CONTOURS
★ ★ ★ ★ **The Contours / Mo. (1981)**
Reissue of their classic 1962 album includes
all the important hits—"Do You Love Me"
(later massacred by the Dave Clark 5),
"First I Look at the Purse" (damaged by J.
Geils), "Shake Sherrie," which may have the
greatest drum track of any pre–Keith Moon
rock record and "Can You Jerk Like Me."
This is Motown at its rawest, the rasping vocals seeming to belong more to the Atlantic/
Stax school than the sound of Young America. — D.M.

**BRIAN CONWAY AND TONY
DEMARCO WITH CAESAR PACIFICI**
★ ★ ★ **The Apple in Winter—Irish Music in
New York / Green L. (1981)**
A straightforward compilation of traditional
jigs, reels and hornpipes by native New
Yorkers Brian Conway, Tony DeMarco and
Caesar Pacifici. — D.D.

RY COODER
★ ★ ★ **Ry Cooder / Rep. (1970)**
★ ★ ★ ★ **Into the Purple Valley / Rep.
(1972)**
★ ★ ★ **Boomer's Story / Rep. (1972)**
★ ★ ★ ★ **Paradise and Lunch / Rep.
(1974)**
★ ★ ★ **Chicken Skin Music / Rep. (1976)**
★ ★ ★ **Show Time / War. (1977)**
★ ★ ★ **Jazz / War. (1978)**
★ ★ ★ ★ **Bop Till You Drop / War. (1979)**
★ ★ ★ **Borderline / War. (1980)**

Cooder's albums bring forgotten songs to life and reclaim vanishing traditions. If that sounds more like a Smithsonian project than rock & roll, it's worth mentioning that Cooder has played with the Rolling Stones, recorded songs by Burt Bacharach and Bobby Womack, and knows the value of brilliant drum tracks and impassioned guitar solos as well as any rocker. *Paradise and Lunch* is his masterpiece. From the Salvation Army–style cornet on "Jesus on the Mainline" to the gospel quartet that answers him on "Married Man's a Fool," the inspired arrangements are arguably perfect. Upbeat, bristling with tricky syncopation and his own dazzling guitar (especially "Tattler"), the album makes traditional music contemporary and turns modern songs (like "Mexican Divorce") into classics. *Chicken Skin Music* is an equally polished, less lively production. It bogs down among the Hawaiian instrumentals but comes to life again with snappy street-corner harmonies and lilting bolero rhythms. The arrangements on *Into the Purple Valley* and *Boomer's Story* are not as dramatic as those on Cooder's recent albums: they use fewer voices and the instrumentation is more conventional. Still, "Teardrops Will Fall" (on the former) and the magnificent slide-guitar rendition of "Dark End of the Street" *(Boomer's Story)* are worthy of his later work. And like all Cooder's albums, these discover and preserve songs that are delights in themselves. Cooder's first album is no different in that respect, featuring songs like "Alimony" and "Goin' to Brownsville," although their presentation is primitive compared to *Paradise and Lunch.* — A.S.

PETER COOK AND DUDLEY MOORE
★ **Good Evening / Is. (1974)**
★ ★ **Beyond the Fringe / Cap. (NA)** ¶
★ **Derek and Clive (Live) / Is. (NA)** ¶
Cook and Moore were part of Britain's pre-Beatles comedy renaissance. *Beyond the Fringe* and *Good Evening* are Broadway soundtracks. While *Fringe* is helped considerably by the real brains, Jonathan Miller and Allen Bennett, both albums consist of brittle, dotty sketches without bite: one-listen affairs. *Derek and Clive* is *all* bite: an extended impersonation of the British working class. The slang is lost on us, and the unremitting obscenity is unequaled in its inaccuracy and humorlessness—at least, to American ears. — K.T.

COOK COUNTY
■ **Pinball Playboy / Mo. (1979)** ¶

I love the idea of Hugh Hefner and Berry Gordy Jr. meeting in some dimly lit arcade. But even I could fall asleep with this insipid tripe as the encounter's soundtrack. Sounds like a cheapskate restaurant commercial. — D.M.

SAM COOKE
★ ★ ★ ★ ★ **The Best of Sam Cooke / RCA (1962)**
★ ★ ★ ★ **Ain't That Good News / Spec. (1964)**
★ ★ **Sam Cooke at the Copa / RCA (1964)**
★ ★ ★ ★ **This Is Sam Cooke / RCA (1970)**
★ ★ ★ **You Send Me / Camd. (1975)**
★ ★ ★ **The Golden Sound of Sam Cooke / Trip (NA)** ¶
★ ★ ★ ★ ★ **The Gospel Soul of Sam Cooke / Spec. (NA)** ¶
★ ★ ★ ★ **The Gospel Soul of Sam Cooke, Vol. 2 / Spec. (NA)** ¶
★ ★ ★ **Sam Cooke Sings the Billie Holiday Story / Up Fr. (NA)** ¶
★ ★ ★ **Sixteen Greatest Hits / Trip (NA)** ¶
★ ★ ★ ★ **That's Heaven to Me / Spec. (NA)**
★ ★ ★ ★ **Two Sides of Sam Cooke / Spec. (NA)**
Sam Cooke was not only one of the great founders of modern soul music, but also one of the premier black gospel singers of his era. The Specialty discs here, recorded in the early Fifties (some while Cooke was still a teenager), are among the best records he ever made, and contain all the elements of the style that, applied to secular material, made him a pop giant before his tragic murder in 1964.

Cooke's best-known songs are, of course, his pop hits—"You Send Me," "Having a Party," "A Change Is Gonna Come," "Another Saturday Night," "Bring It On Home to Me" and "Twistin' the Night Away"—which are well-represented on the RCA *Best of.* Cooke's style—a soaring tenor that could capture both the exultingly joyful and the painfully tragic aspects of a song—is one of the most influential in modern music: Rod Stewart, among many others, would be lost without him. Unfortunately, his voice was often applied to rather trivial material—a problem that plagues the *Copa* set, of course, but also the *Best of* collection. There simply wasn't any reason for Cooke to sing excerpts from "Porgy and Bess," rendered meaningless by continued trivialization over the years, when he could break hearts with a song like the great "A Change Is Gonna Come," his first posthumous release and one that ranks with Martin Luther King's best speeches as a verbal encapsulation of the changes black perspective underwent in the Sixties. — D.M.

SPADE COOLEY
★ ★ ★ **Columbia Historic Edition** / Col. (1982)

The "other" great Western swing band-leader, Spade Cooley, is well represented on this fine selection of his Okeh and Columbia sides from 1944–1946. Cooley was both a great fiddle player and a fine singer, and had he not been given a life sentence for the 1961 murder of his wife, he might be as fondly regarded today as Wills. Cooley was by no means as musically inventive a band-leader as Wills, but he was a great popular-izer, with his late-Fifties L.A. TV show and several movie appearances. This album, with a pair of previously unissued sides and notes by Jimmy Wakely, has excellent sound given the fairly primitive masters from which it was cut. — D.M.

RITA COOLIDGE
★ ★ ★ **Rita Coolidge** / A&M (1971)
★ **Nice Feelin'** / A&M (1971)
★ **The Lady's Not for Sale** / A&M (1972)
■ **Full Moon** / A&M (1973) ¶
★ **Fall into Spring** / A&M (1974)
★ **It's Only Love** / A&M (1975)
★ **Anytime . . . Anywhere** / A&M (1977)
★ **Love Me Again** / A&M (1978)
★ **Satisfied** / A&M (1979)
★ **Heartbreak Radio** / A&M (1981)
★ ★ **Greatest Hits** / A&M (1981)

Coolidge did credible stints as a session vo-calist with Joe Cocker and Delaney and Bonnie before making a fairly promising solo debut, *Rita Coolidge*, that owed much of its charm to the all-star session cast that backed her on it. Since then, her marriage to Kris Kristofferson (now ended) has provided sev-eral duets with hubby as well as film roles, and she's even had a couple of hit singles, but the content has been all downhill since the first LP. — J.S.

PRISCILLA COOLIDGE-JONES
★ ★ **Flying** / Capri. (NA)

Booker T. Jones' wife and Rita Coolidge's sister has little else to recommend her. — J.S.

MICHAEL COONEY
★ ★ **The Cheese Stands Alone** / Folk-Leg. (1969) ¶

Cooney is a storehouse of songs and lore from a variety of American traditions and an interpreter of selected folk-based writers— i.e., Malvina Reynolds and John Prine. This

doesn't sport a winning personality, but a sense of breadth is there. — I.M.

ALICE COOPER
★ ★ **Pretties for You** / War. (1969) ¶
★ ★ **Easy Action** / War. (1970)
★ ★ ★ ★ **Love It to Death** / War. (1971)
★ ★ ★ **Killer** / War. (1971)
★ ★ ★ **School's Out** / War. (1972)
★ ★ **Billion Dollar Babies** / War. (1973)
★ **Muscle of Love** / War. (1974) ¶
★ ★ ★ ★ ★ **Alice Cooper's Greatest Hits** / War. (1974)
★ ★ ★ **Welcome to My Nightmare** / Atco (1975)
★ **Alice Cooper Goes to Hell** / War. (1976)
■ **Lace and Whiskey** / War. (1977)
★ ★ **The Alice Cooper Show** / War. (1977)
★ **From the Inside** / War. (1978)
■ **Flush the Fashion** / War. (1980)
■ **Special Forces** / War. (1981)

Alice Cooper started out as just another bunch of weirdos who caught Frank Zappa's attention. The Zappa-influenced first album, *Pretties for You*, featured the band members in ludicrous drag, a humorous reproduction of the Mothers of Invention pose on *Absolutely Free*. Like many other Detroit bands of the early Seventies, Alice Cooper played high-energy hard rock, crudely at first, but the band improved fast and cut a great re-cord on its third try, *Love It to Death*. That record included "I'm Eighteen," the first of a string of excellent hit singles. Although it never made another album as consistent as *Love It to Death*, the band's singles formula sharpened, producing two classics: "School's Out" and "Elected." The name Alice Cooper originally applied to the whole group but was assumed eventually by the lead singer, who fired the other members and went Hol-lywood in 1975, teaming up with producer Bob Ezrin and guitarists Steve Hunter and Dick Wagner for *Welcome to My Nightmare*, which turned out to be his last gasp as a rocker. Now he's a *Tonight Show* guest and a hack L.A. entertainer, and the albums sound accordingly empty. — J.S.

D. B. COOPER
★ ★ ★ **Buy American** / War. (1980)
★ ★ ★ **Dangerous Curves** / War. (1981)

Marginally interesting American new-wave singer/writer; has more energy than early Seventies singer/songwriter types, but noth-ing more to say. Still, the music has a rois-tering joyousness that makes it appealing. And Cooper has a certain audacity that rec-ommends him: his stage namesake is the

first—and only—successful parachuting airline hijacker. — D.M.

DON COOPER

★ Don Cooper / Rou. (NA) ¶
★ Bless the Children / Rou. (1970) ¶
★ Ballad of C.P. Jones / Rou. (1971) ¶
★ What You Feel Is How You Grow / Rou.
   (NA) ¶

In the Seventies, every record company had
to have one lightweight country-folkish sing-
er/songwriter to record stuff like "Something
in the Way She Moves," and Roulette's was
Cooper. — D.M.

THE COOPER BROTHERS

★ The Cooper Brothers / Capri. (1978)
★ Pitfalls of the Ballroom / Capri. (1979)
Southern rock with Eagles overtones—
perfectly insipid. — D.M.

JOHNNY COPELAND

★ ★ ★ ★ Copeland Special / Roun. (1981)
Copeland has been a Texas blues legend
since the Fifties, when he recorded a series
of obscure but great singles for Atlantic. His
powerful voice and his sleek, burning,
post–T Bone Walker guitar playing are featured to good effect on this debut LP, which
boasts a horn section that includes Arthur
Blythe, Byard Lancaster and George Adams
as well as regular sidemen Joe Rigby and
John Pratt. "Claim Jumper," which was released as a single, shows off the hard-rocking
intensity of Copeland's outfit, while his beautiful rendition of W.C. Handy's "St. Louis
Blues" reveals Copeland as a master vocalist.
The Eighties blues revival is being spearheaded by Copeland's band, which has found
an audience not only in the roadhouses and
clubs where blues usually flourishes but also
in new-wave venues, where their deft rendition of the essential blues and early rock patterns is recognized as the elemental force
many new-wave bands have strived to duplicate. — J.S.

CORTINAS

★ ★ True Romance / CBS (1978), Br. imp.
True Romance is the sole album from this
early British new-wave quintet. The Cortinas
are polished but without style or grit, and as
a result, despite some cute pop culture
touchstones and anomalous glints of the
band's R&B beginnings, the LP is fairly
tepid. — I.R.

BILL COSBY

★ Bill Cosby Is a Very Funny Fellow Right!
   / War. (1964)

★ "I Started Out as a Child" / War. (1964)
★ Why Is There Air? / War. (1965)
★ ★ Wonderfulness / War. (1966)
★ Revenge / War. (1967)
★ ★ ★ To Russell, My Brother, Whom I
   Slept With / War. (1968)
★ 200 M.P.H. / War. (1968)
★ It's True! It's True! / War. (1969) ¶
★ ★ ★ The Best of Bill Cosby / War. (1969)
★ ★ More of the Best of Bill Cosby / War.
   (1970)
★ "When I Was a Kid" / MCA (1971)
★ For Adults Only / MCA (1972)
★ Inside the Mind of Bill Cosby / MCA
   (1972)
★ Fat Albert / MCA (1973)
★ Bill / MCA (1973)
★ Is Not Himself These Days / Cap.
   (1976)
★ Disco Bill / Cap. (1977)
★ Bill's Best Friend / Cap. (1978)

Along with Lenny Bruce and Woody Allen,
Bill Cosby has had the greatest influence on
American comedy in the past twenty years.
His tightly constructed routines contained no
formal "jokes": the humor was in his multitude of voices and elastic faces, and the inviting universality of the tales of his childhood in Philadelphia. Where Bruce and
Allen appealed almost exclusively to a white,
urban, college-educated audience, Cosby, at
the height of his nightclub and recording career (about 1968–1971), was probably the
best-known and loved comedian in the country. When he emerged in the early Sixties,
part of his attraction lay in the fact that he
was a friendly, apolitical black person. His
extraordinary ability to evoke common childhood experiences—their pleasures and anguish—transcended race and, because of
Cosby's pervasive presence on television, records and stage, is a vastly underestimated
contribution to the acceptance of black culture and attitudes by the white middle class.
However, his other material, especially that
having to do with marriage, is seriously
marred by a sexism all the more insidious
for its gentle guilelessness. The kid routines
remain his best stuff, with the side-long "To
Russell, My Brother, Whom I Slept With" a
marvelous work that says as much about an
American childhood as Henry Roth's *Call It
Sleep. For Adults Only* is only mildly racy,
but is his worst in its nasty view of marriage
as one long nag. Recently Cosby is either
barren of sufficient material to fashion solid
routines and stories, or desirous of breaking
away from the monologue set piece. In either
case, he has taken to uneven improvisation
and slapstick pantomime onstage. He makes

infrequent, arch and amusingly arrogant talk-show appearances (the arrogance is partially justified: he *is* a genius) and wry parodies of popular black music, the latter collected on the most recent album. This cannot last long; Cosby is certainly capable of anything and is not to be counted out.
— K.T.

COSMOLOGY

★ ★ **Cosmology** / Van. (1977)
Cosmic in intent but cluttered in impact, Cosmology attempt to fuse pseudo-poetry and big-band jazz-rock, striving for profundity but sounding like a hippie-dippy version of Blood, Sweat and Tears.   — R.P.

ELVIS COSTELLO

★ ★ ★ ★ **My Aim Is True** / Col. (1977)
★ ★ ★ ★ **This Year's Model** / Col. (1978)
★ ★ ★ ★ ★ **Armed Forces** / Col. (1978)
★ ★ ★ ★ **Get Happy** / Col. (1979)
★ ★ ★ **Taking Liberties** / Col. (1980)
★ ★ ★ **Trust** / Col. (1981)
★ ★ **Almost Blue** / Col. (1981)
★ ★ ★ ★ **Imperial Bedroom** / Col. (1982)
He looks like Buddy Holly after drinking a can of STP Oil Treatment, but this Elvis (who first appeared just before the original's death) is actually one of the better results of Britain's 1976–78 new-wave revolution. He is a burning and committed, if ultimately limited, guitarist and singer whose passion can be utterly overwhelming; should Costello reacquire the discipline he seemed to be gaining on each of his first three LPs, he may yet eclipse all the competition.

His debut LP, *My Aim Is True,* is highlighted by "Less Than Zero," a raging attack on British fascist leader Oswald Mosely and his nation's increasing fascination with right-wing solutions, and "Alison," a complex love song in which Elvis first expressed his bittersweet fascination with blame, guilt and seductions, conscious and unwitting. The music, played by an expatriate American ensemble called Clover, is stinging and taut, if not quite so fine as what would come later, but the sheer quality of the songs—and the intensity of Costello's commitment to putting them across—makes the record work.

This Year's Model and *Armed Forces,* Costello's most fully realized albums, are opposite sides of a coin. Each concentrates on matters of fidelity and honesty and events construed in passion, but *Model* centers on personal (and especially sexual) issues, while *Armed Forces* is Costello's most social and political record. (This is not to say that either album altogether ignores the issues

raised by the other—the question is one of concentration of Costello's intricate imagery.) Musically, these albums are equally contrasting. By now Costello had acquired the band he'd keep for succeeding tours and LPs—the Attractions, a feisty unit led by Steve Naive's scorching organ fills. On *This Year's Model,* the band plays flat-out, densely structured rock & roll; *Armed Forces* opens up the sound a great deal, with shimmering surfaces that bespeak Costello and producer Nick Lowe's fascination with pop production.

Costello's next album, however, backslid considerably. *Get Happy* is an album of soul-based music, hard-edged as Stax/Volt's finest hour, but crammed full of tiny tunes—twenty in all—which creates two problems. First, Costello tosses in the banal along with the beautiful, his best ideas right alongside his silliest. The result is a jumble that draws attention to Costello's obsessiveness without suggesting that it can lead him anywhere significant. Second (despite producer Lowe's disclaimer), the extra time muddies up the sound, an issue not so important when dealing with the densely mixed music on earlier Costello albums, but of the essence when trying to re-create the spaciousness and expansiveness of soul. The result is a failure, albeit one not unredeemed by some very good songs: "Motel Matches," "High Fidelity" and "Love for Tender," among the originals, plus the remakes of "I Can't Stand Up for Falling Down" and "I Stand Accused."

Taking Liberties is a compilation of songs Costello had released as B sides, or on the British (but not U.S.) editions of his albums. It too contains some fine material, notably "Getting Mighty Crowded," "Girls Talk," "Night Rally," "Stranger in the House" and "I Don't Want to Go to Chelsea," but *Liberties* inevitably lacks the unity of sound and theme that makes Costello's other records so outstanding.

Trust presents an entirely different set of problems. It is his first album in a truly personal style since *Armed Forces,* and while the songs' lyrics have his old devastating ability to get at the heart of complex romantic and sexual conundrums, the sound is a step backwards: cluttered, claustrophobic, the attack obtuse, the singing strained, lacking the ease of his best early work. While some think *Trust* an essential Costello work, it seems more likely to be remembered as the record that encapsulates his limitations: an inability (or unwillingness) to deal with production or to truly lead (i.e., galvanize) his band.

Trust left a number of questions—including his commercial future—utterly unresolved. Costello was the first new-wave artist to go gold in America, with *This Year's Model,* but since *Get Happy* (a record possibly made as much to dispel charges of racism as from creative impulse), he had been moving in circles, perhaps even retreating. *Armed Forces* in particular seemed to suggest a possible resolution of the gap between Costello's emotional distancing mechanisms and his political passion, but except in the sexual arena, his social concerns have largely been left dormant since then. And musically he had certainly not grown much, nor were his experiments particularly fruitful. His successful songs continued to sound very much the same as those on his first three albums.

Almost Blue did not bother to address any of these problems. It is an album of country songs, most of them standards, which in their original versions are characterized by great vitality. Costello has arranged them lifelessly and his singing is almost utterly without affect. The meaning of this is unfathomable. Either Costello had completely misunderstood the import of country conservatism or he had moved in only six years from an apostle of passion and an exemplar of the human spirit at its raging finest to just another posing aesthete.

Imperial Bedroom solves many of Costello's musical problems; it may have the finest use of aural montage technique of any pop album since *Sgt. Pepper's.* Geoff Emerick's production is brilliant, and the sound is the most detailed and exciting of any Costello record in years. Unfortunately, the songs have an insularity that's ultimately restrictive: Costello has managed to invert the Beatles by making every universal problem assume a private dimension. The results can be fascinating, but only to the previously committed. Whether Costello will ever decide that reengagement with the world at large is worthwhile is now the most interesting question of a marginal, but never uninteresting, career. — D,M.

ELIZABETH COTTEN
★ ★ ★ **Folksongs and Instrumentals with Guitar / Folk. (1958)**
★ ★ ★ **Elizabeth Cotten, Vol. 2: Shake Sugaree / Folk. (1967)**

Anyone who has learned three-finger guitar picking has probably played "Freight Train," a song Cotten composed when very young and which was later popularized by Peter, Paul and Mary. That tune and "Shake Sugaree" are the most commonly associated with her. She plays guitar and banjo left-handed, although strung as usual. She is that rare folk artist for whom the distinction between professional and traditional musician is meaningless. Both albums display her blues and ragtime-based style well.
— I.M.

GENE COTTON
★ **Save the Dancer / Ario. (1978)**
★ **No Strings Attached / Ario. (1979)**

Gene Cotton is one of those sincere and sensitive types whom housewives love to hear on their local Muzak station. So if he's such a nice guy, why do I want to punch him? Listen to his albums and discover for yourself. — R.P.

JAMES COTTON
★ ★ **Cut You Loose / Van. (1968)**
★ ★ ★ **100 Per Cent Cotton / Bud. (1974)**
★ ★ ★ **Super Harp—Live and on the Move / Bud. (1974)**
★ ★ ★ **High Energy / Bud. (1975)**
★ ★ **Taking Care of Business / Cap. (NA)**
★ ★ ★ **Chicago Breakdown / TKM (NA)**

Cotton's story is the stuff of blues legend. He ran away from home when he was nine to find blues harmonica player Sonny Boy Williamson, met up with him in Arkansas and was taken in as a member of the family. When he was thirteen, Cotton became (along with Junior Parker) one of two blues harpists in Howlin' Wolf's Arkansas band. Cotton was the harpist on Wolf's first sessions for Chess Records, and went on to play for over a decade with Muddy Waters in Chicago before forming his own group in 1965.

Cotton's earliest recordings with his own band on Verve/Forecast are now out of print. What remains is uneven, often more pop-oriented than blues-rooted, and mostly recorded with a series of session players. Oddly, the two more commercial Buddah albums stand out—Cotton's playing, singing and instrumental backup are in good form, though not always classic blues.

100 Per Cent Cotton was recorded with his band at the time; *High Energy* was produced by Allen Toussaint at his New Orleans studio and blends Cotton's sophisticated Chicago blues style to good effect with the steamy funk of New Orleans R&B. — J.S.

COTTONWOOD SOUTH
★ **Cottonwood South / Col. (1974) ¶**

A directionless set, flirting weakly with both hard rock and MOR, unimaginatively produced by Paul Rothchild. Three of the seven members do nothing but sing, and they do have their moments, but the playing is as plain as it is spare. — C.W.

COUCHOIS
★ **Couchois / War. (1979)**
★ **Nasty Hardware / War. (1981)**
Aggravatingly lame soft-rock quintet that sports three brothers and zero talent.
— D.M.

JOHN COUGAR
■ **Johnny Cougar / Riva (1979)**
■ **Nothing Matters and What If It Did / Riva (1980)**
★ ★ **American Fool / Riva (1982)**
Heretofore, Meat Loaf represented the nadir of what Bruce Springsteen's influence has wrought in the rock world. John Cougar's success in 1982 with "Jack and Diane" represents a new low: think of him as Meat Head, a boy from Indiana with a chip on his shoulder, but without any of Springsteen's sense of humor and with an actively misanthropic animus towards humanity replacing the Boss's compassion. Musically, Cougar's sometimes fun to hear, in the background—but brought forward, where the part of your mind that thinks must deal with him, his cynicism sours whatever good will his melodies might establish. — D.M.

COULSON, DEAN, MCGUINNESS, FLINT
★ ★ ★ **Lo and Behold / Sire (NA)** ¶
A collection of Bob Dylan songs, many of them extremely obscure ("Sign on the Cross," "Odds and Ends"), produced by Dylan's favorite interpreter, Manfred Mann, and excellently performed (by a group originally known as McGuinness-Flint). — D.M.

CLIFFORD COULTER
★ ★ **The Better Part of Me / Col. (1980)**
Mediocre soul-jazz keyboardist/vocalist.
— D.M.

COUNT BISHOPS
★ ★ ★ **The Count Bishops / Chis. (1977), Br. imp.**
★ ★ **Cross Cuts / Chis. (1979), Br. imp.**
The Count Bishops (later the Bishops) emerged with the first crop of British new-wave bands, but their idea of punk had a lot more to do with early Rolling Stones than Sex Pistols. Their self-titled debut LP includes the R&B standard "Down the Road Apiece" (unsurprisingly similar to the version on the Stones' third album) and songs by Willie Dixon and Elmore James besides choice material from the Kinks ("I Need

You") and Standells ("Good Guys Don't Wear White"). The band's rough-and-tumble spirit is engaging, but there's little to separate them from hordes of other white blues-rockers except their anomalous appearance and Dave Tice's gruff vocals—and the latter grow wearying after a while.

Two years later the Bishops were still mixing R&B with Sixties punk (Strangeloves and Easybeats this time around), and the result was still more lifelike than lively. *Cross Cuts* nonoriginals sound like it, while the few in-house compositions are almost nondescript. Unvarying guitar textures and lack of pacing don't help either. Well, they probably sounded great in the pubs. — S.I.

COUNT OSSIE AND MYSTIC REVELATION OF RASTAFARI
★ ★ ★ ★ ★ **Grounation / Grounation (1974)**
★ ★ ★ ★ **Tales of Mozambique / Dynamic (1975)**
Back in the early Sixties, before it was fashionable to be Rastas, Count Ossie's communal group of artisans, musicians, dancers, singers and poets perpetrated African consciousness as a wandering performance troupe in Jamaica. Ska, rocksteady and reggae musicians have traipsed up into the hills behind Kingston to partake of the feast, even after Count Ossie's death. *Grounation* offers three records' worth of authentic Rasta music ("grounation" refers to a Rastafarian ceremony) including poetry, jazz-inflected horn solos, group chanting and lots of African-style drumming, origin of the reggae pulse. *Mozambique* supplants *Grounation's* field recording with a recording studio and a more self-conscious, less inspirational historical perspective. — R.F.G.

COUNTRY COOKING
★ ★ ★ **Country Cooking / Roun. (1971)**
★ ★ ★ **Country Cooking with the Fiction Brothers / Fly. Fish (1971)**
★ ★ ★ **Frank Wakefield with Country Cooking / Roun. (1972)**
★ ★ ★ **Country Cooking / Roun. (1974)**
A stellar Northern "newgrass" outfit whose style incorporates urban and even European influences. Their variegated approach suggests that bluegrass grows well, with a little careful tending, in many different climes and regions. — R.P.

COUNTRY GAZETTE
★ ★ **A Traitor in Our Midst / U.A. (1972)** ¶
★ ★ **Out to Lunch / Fly. Fish (1976)**
★ ★ ★ **Live / Ant. (1976)** ¶
Country Gazette consisted primarily of L.A.

musicians who were key figures in the early-Sixties folk revival, then moved into folk rock and later became stalwarts in the floating crap game of early-Seventies country rock. Several had also worked with more traditional bluegrass groups such as Flatt and Scruggs' Foggy Mountain Boys or Bill Monroe's Bluegrass Boys. Though the most tradition-oriented of all the L.A. country rockers, they were not bluegrass purists. The problem was that while the group was full of exceptional pickers (especially fiddler Byron Berline and banjo player Alan Munde), the singing was usually barely acceptable. They also did bluegrass arrangements of some fairly dubious pop material (would you believe "Honky Cat"?). The live album is superior to the two studio efforts, if only because the songs are generally more congruous and there is more emphasis on instrumentals.
— J.MO.

THE COUNTRY GENTLEMEN

★ ★ ★ The Country Gentlemen, Vol. 1 / Folk. (1960)
★ ★ ★ The Country Gentlemen, Vol. 2 / Folk. (1961)
★ ★ ★ The Country Gentlemen, Vol. 3 / Folk. (1963)
★ ★ ★ The Country Gentlemen, Vol. 4 / Folk. (1973)
★ ★ The Country Gentlemen / Van. (1973)
★ ★ Remembrances and Forecasts / Van. (1974)
★ ★ The Award-Winning Country Gentlemen / Rebel (NA)
★ ★ Bringing Mary Home / Rebel (NA)
★ ★ ★ The Gospel Album / Rebel (NA)
★ ★ Joe's Last Train / Rebel (NA)
★ ★ Live at Roanoake / Zap (NA)
★ ★ New Look—New Sound / Rebel (NA)
★ ★ Play It Like It Is / Rebel (NA)
★ ★ Songs of the Pioneers / Pine M. (NA)
★ ★ Sound Off / Rebel (NA)
★ ★ The Traveller / Rebel (NA)
★ ★ Yesterday and Today, Vol. 1 / Rebel (NA)
★ ★ Yesterday and Today, Vol. 2 / Rebel (NA)
★ ★ Yesterday and Today, Vol. 3 / Rebel (NA)
★ ★ Young Fisherwoman / Rebel (NA)
Longtime bluegrass-circuit favorites, the Country Gentlemen play with an impressive, if clinical, efficiency. Known especially for on-the-mark triple harmonies and consistently high-quality live performances, the Gentlemen have always flirted with the periphery of the rock/pop audience without ever truly capturing it. The definitive works are on Folkways, though any of the Rebel/Zap LPs might be equally appealing to the initiated, and *The Gospel Album* is especially notable for its vocal tapestries. — R.P.

COUNTRY JOE AND THE FISH

★ ★ ★ ★ Electric Music for the Mind and Body / Van. (1967)
★ ★ ★ Feel Like I'm Fixin' to Die / Van. (1967)
★ ★ Together / Van. (1968)
★ ★ Here We Are Again / Van. (1969)
★ ★ ★ Greatest Hits / Van. (1970)
★ ★ C.J. Fish / Van. (1970)
★ ★ ★ The Life and Times of Country Joe and the Fish / Van. (1971)
★ Reunion / Fan. (1977)
It would have been nearly impossible in 1967 to find people who considered themselves card-carrying freaks without a wellworn copy of the first Country Joe and the Fish album. In many ways, *Electric Music for the Mind and Body* captured the essence of a mind-expanded counterculture lifestyle: the songs deal with the three main topics of the day: dope ("Flying High"), sex ("Not So Sweet Martha Lorraine") and politics ("Super Bird"). It's an infectious blend of blues, ragaish guitar-dominated rock and good old good time music. And coming from the wilds of Berkeley, the Fish added an often sardonic sense of humor to their energetic and politically aware music; the title track of *Feel Like I'm Fixin' to Die* is a romping mock celebration of death in Vietnam set to the tune of the old rag classic, "Muskrat Ramble." The album also shows Country Joe McDonald's growth as a balladeer, with the haunting "Janis" (written for Joplin) and the mystical "Who Am I." Though a bit more subdued than the debut LP, it's a worthy successor, demonstrating the band's maturity and willingness to explore different approaches and genres.

With *Together,* unfortunately, much of the energy and resourcefulness of the band seems dissipated. Other than the sublimely ridiculous "Rock and Soul Music" and the classic "Good Guys/Bad Guys Cheer," *Together* most assuredly isn't. McDonald's contributions are slim, leaving guitarist Barry Melton and drummer Chicken Hirsch to carry the songwriting burden, which they just weren't equipped to do. The last two albums, with keyboard player David Cohen, bassist Bruce Barthol and Hirsch all departed, are rather undistinguished, though *C.J. Fish* does feature one great song, "Rockin' Round the World," in which McDonald pulls off one of the best Mose Allison imita-

tions ever attempted. Not surprisingly, both best-of-collections lean heavily on the first two albums. The late Seventies *Reunion* is a sad, faint echo of the early material.
— B.A.

JAYNE (WAYNE) COUNTY
★ ★ **Blatantly Offensive / Attack (NA)**
★ ★ **Rock and Roll Resurrection / Attack (NA)**
★ **Storm the Gates of Heaven / Safari (1978)**
★ ★ **Wayne County and the Electric Chairs / Safari (1978)**
★ **Things Your Mother Never Told You / Safari (1978)**
In the New York glitter-rock circuit, whose flagship band was the New York Dolls, Wayne County represented the erotic left wing: a Georgia transvestite whose act featured the lewd, the rude and the crude, the latter a reference to music as hard-boiled as any prepunk sound in existence. Unfortunately, County was more interesting even then as a schematic for rock radicalism than as something to listen to. Shorn of visuals, among other things, neither his early nor his later (Jayne) works are much more than rabid noise. Still, there's no doubt that by taking androgyny to its absolute outer limit, County had his share of influence on the punk and new-wave scenes that glitter helped spawn. — D.M.

DON COVAY
★ **Travelin' in Heavy Traffic / Phil. (1976)**
A promising marriage between Don Covay and the Sound of Philadelphia resulted in a near-disastrous set. Covay, once one of soul's most righteous storytellers, is clearly floundering in his attempt at coming to grips with black pop music in the Seventies. His body of work on Atlantic though, available only on cutouts, is remarkably personal—the Sixties soul man as a rough and rugged individualist. — J.MC.

COWBOY COPAS
★ ★ ★ **The Best of Cowboy Copas / Star. (NA)**
★ ★ **Radar Blues / King (NA)**
Copas was a journeyman country singer whose career started with "Filipino Baby," in 1945, included an appearance on Pee Wee King's original "Tennessee Waltz" and ended in the 1963 plane crash that also killed Patsy Cline and Hawkshaw Hawkins. Copas made his earliest records for King, in the Forties and early Fifties. He then endured a long stretch without recording until

his career revived in 1959 with "Alabam," "Flat Top" and "Signed Sealed and Delivered," for Starday. Along with "Tennessee Waltz," Copas also had a hit with "Candy Kisses," earlier a major hit for George Morgan, but he's felt today more as a minor influence than as a surviving artistic presence.
— D.M.

COWBOYS INTERNATIONAL
★ ★ ★ ★ **The Original Sin / Virgin/Atl. (1979)**
More a vehicle for singer/songwriter Ken Lockie than an actual band, Cowboys International has included ex-Clash drummer Terry Chimes and Public Image Ltd. guitarist Keith Levene, among others, at times. With glimmers of influence ranging from David Bowie to the Velvet Underground and Roxy Music, *The Original Sin* is a taut, thrilling record that establishes Lockie as a talented and literate auteur. The use of dance-oriented drumming, cool synthesizers, and occasionally deadpan vocals presages the new romantic bands of 1981, but lacks the haughty pretension that discredits groups like Spandau Ballet and Visage. — I.R.

KEVIN COYNE
★ ★ ★ **Babble / Virgin (1979)**
★ ★ ★ **Millionaires and Teddy Bears / Virgin (1978)**
Coyne is a delightfully offbeat singer/songwriter/guitarist with a gravelly-voiced delivery and a penchant for bizarre imagery. For a real treat, find his out-of-print classics, *Marjory Razorblade* and *Matching Heads and Feet.* — J.S.

BILLY "CRASH" CRADDOCK
★ ★ ★ **Billy "Crash" Craddock's Greatest Hits / MCA (1974)**
★ ★ ★ **Live / MCA (1977)**
★ ★ ★ **Billy "Crash" Craddock Sings His Greatest Hits / MCA (1978)**
★ ★ ★ **Billy "Crash" Craddock / Cap. (1978)**
★ ★ ★ ★ **Turning Up and Turning On / Cap. (1978)**
★ ★ ★ **Laughing and Crying / Cap. (1979)**
★ ★ ★ ★ **Changes / Cap. (1980)**
★ ★ ★ **"Crash" Craddock / Cap. (1981)**
★ ★ ★ **I'm Tore Up / Power (NA)**
★ ★ ★ ★ **Sixteen Greatest Hits / Star. (NA)**
★ ★ ★ **Easy as Pie / MCA (NA)**
★ ★ ★ **Just Fine / MCA (NA)**
Despite an unsuccessful try at a career in rockabilly at the end of the Fifties, Craddock was an unknown knockabout until the early Seventies, when he recorded the first of a

long string of country hits, "Knock Three Times." Other hits from the MCA LPs were "Dream Lover," "Ruby Baby," "Sweet Magnolia Blossom," "Easy as Pie" and "Broken Down in Tiny Pieces." He continued his single success on the Capitol LPs with "I Cheated on a Good Woman's Love," "I Just Had You on My Mind," "I've Been Too Long Lonely Baby" and "You Say You're a Real Cowboy." Craddock handles ballads and rockers with equal dexterity; *Changes* is a particularly good example of his eclecticism. — J.S.

FLOYD CRAMER

★ ★ **Last Date / RCA (1960)**
★ ★ **Best of Floyd Cramer / RCA (1964)**
★ **This Is Floyd Cramer / RCA (1970)**
★ **Sounds of Sunday / RCA (1971)**
★ **Good Old Country Gospel / RCA (1972)** ¶
★ **Floyd Cramer in Concert / RCA (1974)**
★ **Wishing You a Merry Christmas / RCA (1976)** ¶
★ **Floyd Cramer Country / RCA (1976)**
★ **Floyd Cramer and the Keyboard Kick Band / RCA (1977)** ¶
★ **Floyd Cramer Country Hall of Fame / RCA (1977)**
★ **Super Hits / RCA (1979)**
★ **Dallas / RCA (1980)**
★ **Almost Persuaded / Camd. (NA)**
★ **Date with Floyd Cramer / Camd. (NA)**
★ **Floyd Cramer Plays the Big Hits / Camd. (NA)**
★ **Piano Masterpieces / RCA (NA)**
★ **Spotlight on Floyd Cramer / Camd. (NA)**
Nashville's leading country-pop session pianist made only one decent record on his own, "Last Date," which made Top Ten on the pop charts in 1960. ("On the Rebound" and "San Antonio Rose," not nearly so imaginative, also made the Top Ten in 1961.) Cramer's tours with Chet Atkins and Boots Randolph were where he gained his chief notoriety, but all in all, his playing is a prime example of the worst that happens when country goes to the city. — C.F.

THE CRAMPS

★ ★ ★ ★ **Gravest Hits / IRS (1979)**
★ ★ ★ ★ **Songs the Lord Taught Us / IRS (1979)**
★ ★ ★ **Psychedelic Jungle / IRS (1981)**
When it came to pop culture, the Cramps were just about the only new-wave band who really walked it like they talked it: all three of these records are literally infested with a passion for surf instrumentals, wild-hair rockabilly, science fiction flicks, late-night TV, garage psychedelia, bad jokes and primordial punk, what the liner notes to the band's first release, the five-song EP *Gravest Hits,* call "the psychotic debris of previous rock eras."

The core of the band—drummer Nick Knox, guitarists Ivy Rorshach and Bryan Gregory, singer Lux Interior—were able to sustain an aesthetic based primarily on the sort of trash antecedents they displayed on *Gravest Hits:* from the sublimely ridiculous "Surfin' Bird" to the merely ridiculous "Domino" to the quintessentially swaggering "The Way I Walk." The blend seemed fresh because it was filtered through musicians aware of, affected by, but distanced from the new-wave avant-garde; it remained powerful because of the tenacity with which the Cramps clung to such artless art. Indeed, on the debut LP, *Songs the Lord Taught Us,* they were better than ever, if only because "Drug Train," "I Was a Teenage Werewolf" and "Mystery Plane" were original songs that synthesized their influences and methods of artsy avoidance better than oldies ever could (or at least better than *most* oldies: somewhere they found one called "Strychnine").

Unfortunately, when science fiction became science fact, and Bryan Gregory up and split one day to devote himself full-time to the investigation of the occult, some damage was done. *Psychedelic Jungle* was produced by the band itself, and they did a better job than Alex Chilton had on the first album, but the passionate edge was gone, some of the tension between artiness and trashiness was missing. It was nothing the Cramps couldn't recover from, but it was going to be curious to watch them do it. Or would they simply fade away, after a moment of genius, like ? and the Mysterians or the Gants? — D.M.

LAMONT CRANSTON BAND

★ ★ **El-Ce-Notes / Waterh. (1979)**
★ ★ **Up from the Alley / Waterh. (1980)**
★ ★ **Shake Down / Waterh. (1981)**
Passable bar band from Minneapolis; the blues, not so much revived as defrosted and trotted out, not without the obeisance due them, but not with the imagination they deserve, either. — D.M.

DAN CRARY

★ ★ ★ **Lady's Fancy / Roun. (1977)**
Formerly of Sundance (of "Byron Berline and" fame), Dan Crary is simply one of America's best flat-picking acoustic guitarists. His album allows Crary to display his

flashy chops on an engagingly odd range of material. — R.P.

CAROLINE CRAWFORD
★ ★ **My Name Is Caroline / Mer. (1978)**
★ ★ **Nice and Soulful / Mer. (1979)**
"Coming On Strong" was Crawford's best moment, a 1979 close call on the soul chart. Nothing else here is up to that standard.
— D.M.

CRAWLER
★ ★ ★ **Crawler / Epic (1977)**
★ ★ **Snake, Rattle and Roll / Epic (1978)**
Back Street Crawler's continuation was more bluesy hard rock using Claptonesque guitar (Geoff Whitehorn) but less subtly crafted keyboards from Rabbit. Close but inferior to the Paul Kossoff–led original group.
— C.W.

CRAZY HORSE
★ **At Crooked Lake / Epic (1972)**
★ **Crazy Moon / RCA (1979)**
A good if unspectacular California rock & roll band, Crazy Horse got the break it needed backing Neil Young on *Everybody Knows This Is Nowhere.* The group went on to record several albums, the best of which, *Crazy Horse,* is unavailable despite the inclusion of the classic "Downtown" and the presence of Ry Cooder, Nils Lofgren and Jack Nitzsche. After guitarist Danny Whitten died, the Crazy Horse rhythm section kept going without him and recorded the sappy *At Crooked Lake,* but Neil Young didn't forget his friend and eulogized Whitten with his weirdest and in some ways most powerful album, *Tonight's the Night. Crazy Moon* was a miserable 1979 comeback attempt. — J.S.

PAPA JOHN CREACH
★ ★ **Papa John Creach / Grunt (1971)** ¶
★ ★ **Filthy / Grunt (1972)** ¶
★ ★ **Playing My Fiddle for You / Grunt (1974)** ¶
★ **I'm the Fiddle Man / Bud. (1975)** ¶
■ **Rock Father / Bud. (1976)** ¶
★ **Cat and the Fiddle / DJM (1977)**
★ **Inphasion / DJM (1978)**
★ ★ **Best of Papa John Creach / Bud. (NA)** ¶
This hoary fiddler was resurrected by the Jefferson Airplane toward the end of its career; the Grunt albums were part of the Airplane's solo deal with RCA/Grunt. The first was made while Creach was still in the band, and features the usual cameos from members of the Airplane clan. The other two Grunt records, recorded with an anonymous backup group called Zulu, and the subsequent Buddah records show Creach's thinness, both conceptually and musically. His only dramatic move is the hokey glissando that is repeated endlessly over the course of these albums. — J.S.

CREAM
★ ★ ★ ★ **Fresh Cream / RSO (1967)**
★ ★ ★ **Disraeli Gears / RSO (1967)**
★ ★ ★ **Wheels of Fire / RSO (1968)**
★ ★ ★ **Goodbye / RSO (1969)**
★ ★ **Live Cream / RSO (1970)**
★ ★ **Live Cream, Vol. 2 / RSO (1972)**
■ **Early Cream / Sp. (NA)** ¶

Cream was the pioneer of the power trio: guitar, bass and drums playing loud, largely improvised blues-based rock. Its influence was and still is enormous, even fourteen years after the group disbanded. Probably best remembered for concert work, guitarist Eric Clapton, bassist Jack Bruce and drummer Ginger Baker were actually most successful in the studio, where they could ignore the limitations of a trio.

Fresh Cream introduced their styles: Eric Clapton's distorted, alternately smooth and biting guitar, sporting vibrato, quickness and a thorough knowledge of B. B. King; Jack Bruce's thick-punching bass guitar, his strong tenor voice, but oddly inferior harmonica; and Ginger Baker's overpowering, technically awesome drums, complete with twin basses. The electrified country blues were excellent, but the original material was little more than a vehicle for virtuosity. Clapton was especially brilliant on his solos, as was Baker during his "Toad." Nevertheless, the guitarist overdubbed himself throughout, making up for the lack of another instrument.

Disraeli Gears switched producers (Robert Stigwood to Felix Pappalardi, with whom they stayed), resulting in more rock and less blues, "Sunshine of Your Love" (their first pop hit) being a prominent example. Bruce's collaboration with myth-inspired lyricist Pete Brown became more pronounced. It was a workable change, even considering Clapton's curious restraint during the record.

The two-record *Wheels of Fire* epitomized Cream's schizophrenia. It demonstrated increasingly varied and sophisticated studio work—Pappalardi's hand became more evident and accomplished; playing on many cuts, he amounted to a fourth member—and more acoustic instrumentation (cellos and bells even), but the firm electric blues base was still apparent on several cuts where Clapton let loose and played some of his most exotic solos.

In the studio Cream realized that everyone needn't go full tilt at once to show the group's considerable talents—a marked contrast to the album's live sides. The disciplined and comparatively brief "Crossroads" worked, but the other live numbers were too long and too wild. The formula was easy and deceptively limiting: start off simply, explode into a lengthy free-for-all, and end as begun. The brilliant moment occasionally surfaced, but self-indulgence was the general rule.

Goodbye had three more live cuts, and three from the studio, one from each player: all of the latter sounded less and less like Cream. Bruce's song, relying primarily on keyboards, recalled early Traffic, and Baker's was an equally tuneful rhythmic exercise. But the highlight was the Clapton-George Harrison collaboration, "Badge," with the Beatle handling rhythm guitar. A catchy rocker, Clapton gave it one of his most stunningly pretty solos.

Live and *Live, Volume 2* reiterated earlier misjudgments. (*Live* included one obscure studio cut.) *The Best, Rock Sensation* and the double *Heavy* LP (now deleted) remain excellent compilations. — c.w.

CREED
■ Creed / Asy. (1978)
Ten Years After, ten years after. Pathetic. — D.M.

CREEDENCE CLEARWATER REVIVAL
★ ★ ★ Creedence Clearwater Revival / Fan. (1968)
★ ★ ★ ★ Bayou Country / Fan. (1969)
★ ★ ★ ★ ★ Green River / Fan. (1969)
★ ★ ★ ★ ★ Willy and the Poor Boys / Fan. (1969)
★ ★ ★ ★ Cosmo's Factory / Fan. (1970)
★ ★ ★ Pendulum / Fan. (1970)
★ ★ ★ Mardi Gras / Fan. (1972)
★ ★ ★ Creedence Gold / Fan. (1972)
★ ★ Live in Europe / Fan. (1973)
★ ★ ★ More Creedence Gold / Fan. (1973)
★ ★ ★ ★ Chronicle / Fan. (1976)
★ ★ ★ ★ ★ Creedence 1969 / Fan. (1978)
★ ★ ★ ★ ★ Creedence 1970 / Fan. (1978)
★ ★ ★ ★ Royal Albert Hall Concert / Fan. (1981), later renamed *The Concert*
★ ★ ★ Creedence Country / Fan. (1981)
Creedence Clearwater Revival was probably the greatest American singles band, one of the hardest-rocking American groups of any genre, and almost the only exponent of working-class sensibility in American rock & roll—particularly California rock & roll—after the advent of Haight-Ashbury and before the rise of punk.

Led by guitarist/vocalist/writer John Fogerty, the group simply pumped out classic rock singles, one after another, in much the same rockabilly spirit as Elvis Presley and Jerry Lee Lewis, adding some touches of New Orleans R&B and other relatively antediluvian sources. On its first album *(CCR)*, the band attempted to stretch out, as was then the fashion, but though the approach garnered a hit with "Suzie Q," an extended version of the Dale Hawkins classic, Creedence didn't really hit its stride until Fogerty tightened up some three-minute songs. Then began the flood: "Bad Moon Rising," "Born on the Bayou," "Commotion," "Down on the Corner," "Green River," "Have You Ever Seen the Rain," "I Heard It through the Grapevine" (an extended song that worked), "Proud Mary," "Travelin' Band" and "Who'll Stop the Rain." All of this occurred between 1968 and 1973, when the group fell apart.

Perhaps best of all were "Lodi," the story of a working rocker's depression at being stuck in another out-of-the-way gin mill and his determination to beat everyone, and "Fortunate Son," a stab at the privileged that only kids from the wrong side of the ultra-hip San Francisco area could have felt so sharply. (Creedence arose from roughly the same town as the psychedelic bands, but came from much poorer families.) And after a time Fogerty burned to prove that he was as much an artist as anyone in the Grateful Dead—he apparently did not know that he was already more—and the group tried to stretch out, to make nominally "progressive" music. Not all of this was unsuccessful, by any means—"I Heard It through the Grapevine" is more intense than any six minutes of Grateful Dead music on record—but still, his métier was the single. Eventually, the group tried to achieve a communal balance, the other members of the quartet contributing songs to the final studio record, *Mardi Gras*, a noble but disappointing affair. Since then, it's all been repackages, except for the lamentable *Live in Europe*. The Royal Albert Hall Concert—which is *not* a recording from the Royal Albert Hall, but from an Oakland Coliseum show—is a fine representation of the band's live sound, which turned up unexpectedly in 1981. Originally released as *Royal Albert Hall Concert*, the title was changed to *The Concert*

Chronicle is a fine singles anthology, but

Green River and *Willy and the Poor Boys* are great rock records in their own right. — D.M.

LOL CREME AND KEVIN GODLEY
★ ★ Consequences / Mer. (1977) ¶
★ ★ ★ L / Poly. (1978) ¶
★ ★ ★ Freeze Frame / Poly. (1979) ¶
★ ★ ★ Ismism / Poly.-Del. (1981)
One-half of the original 10cc, Creme and Godley left the group in 1976, ostensibly to experiment with a new guitar synthesizer they called the Gizmo. The unexpected result was *Consequences,* a noble but failed rock opera, spread over three records with an overambitious storyboard, lots of spectacular sound effects, a guest appearance by British comedian Peter Cook, but no memorable tunes. *L* and *Freeze Frame* are easier to digest—single LPs on which the pair again overindulge their art school wit but within tighter song formats, much like recent Frank Zappa but without the scatology. All sonically impressive, but there's little here you'll go home humming. Notably, Creme and Godley have since gone on to produce videos for other recording artists. — D.F.

THE CRETONES
★ ★ ★ Thin Red Line / Planet (1980)
★ ★ ★ Snap! Snap! / Planet (1981)
Quartet including Mark Goldberg, songwriter much favored by Linda Ronstadt during the new-wavings of her *Mad Love* LP. Neat lyricizing and chiming guitars, but not gaudy enough to be much beyond one more from the California scene that produced Knack, 20/20 and Plimsouls. Good enough, though, to be someone's favorite of that place and time. First LP includes "Justine," "Mad Love" and others waxed by La Ronstadt. Second features cover art by Neon Park, Little Feat's house artist and keyboardist Bill Payne of that band on a good cut ("Swinging Divorcee"). — G.A.

BOB CREWE
★ Motivation / Elek. (1977)
Crewe has had moments of real inspiration as producer of the Four Seasons and of Mitch Ryder and the Detroit Wheels, and most recently, cowriter of Labelle's "Lady Marmalade." But on his own, both here and as proprietor of the Bob Crewe Generation (B.C.G.), he reveals himself as more of a purveyor of schlocky pop product, rather than the Spector doppelgänger he'd have you believe when he's Svengali-ing away. This is dreck. — D.M.

CRIMSON TIDE
★ Crimson Tide / Cap. (1978) ¶
★ Reckless Love / Cap. (1979) ¶
Southern funk/boogie band has little of the momentum they hoped to gain by borrowing the Alabama football team's nickname. Features sometime Rolling Stones sidekick Wayne Perkins on guitar. — J.S.

PETER CRISS
★ ★ Peter Criss / Casa. (1978)
★ Out of Control / Casa. (1980)
In which the former Kiss drummer reveals that in his heart of hearts, he'd rather be Barry Manilow. — J.D.C.

CRITICAL MASS
★ It's What's Inside That Counts / MCA (1980)
Critical mess, is more like it. — D.M.

JIM CROCE
★ ★ ★ You Don't Mess Around with Jim / Lifes. (1972)
★ ★ ★ Life and Times / Lifes. (1973)
★ ★ ★ I Got a Name / Lifes. (1973)
★ ★ Faces I've Been / Lifes. (1975)
★ ★ ★ Time in a Bottle—Jim Croce's Greatest Love Songs / Lifes. (1977)
In the middle of a popular craze for inflated, neurotic songwriters like Cat Stevens and James Taylor, Jim Croce's "Don't Mess Around with Jim," a brag, came as a refreshing intrusion. When followed by songs like "Time in a Bottle," "I Got a Name," "Operator" and "I'll Have to Say I Love You in a Song," it became apparent that Croce's modest, craftsman's sensibility could communicate certain feelings even better than the "sensitive" outpourings of the wounded-soul school.

Croce's singles fit in well both on AM and FM radio. Perfectly at ease with highly standardized pop-folk song forms, Croce's tactful melodies and subtly driven acoustic guitar arrangements carry his carefully crafted lyrics through clever hooks into surprisingly moving music. His accomplishments might have matured into something more imposing had he not died in a 1974 plane crash.

Croce's first album, *You Don't Mess Around with Jim,* set his permanent pattern: several gemlike love songs, two story tunes, a dollop of nostalgia and a few pleasant throwaways. The Cashman/West production formula had fully stabilized by *Life and Times,* Croce's second LP, and never varied during his short recording career. While strings and other sweetenings nudged Croce's songs into perfect commerciality, the singer himself usually sounds casually unfinished.

Simultaneously with *Life and Times,* Croce's nostalgic side began to take over and he started to produce strikingly impersonal experiments in the craft of sentiment. It fits him well. Aside from a rare embellishment in a fade-out chorus, Croce's voice was as musically laconic as it was restlessly verbal. So, while forever mawkish in his writing, the restraint of his style just manages to hover over a slough of complete sentimentality.

On *I Got a Name* there is a slight modulation into a tone of urgency, particularly with songs like "Lover's Cross," and it is probably his most emotional whole album. But the anthology of love songs, *Time in a Bottle,* contains his best moments overall. — B.T.

STEVE CROPPER
★ ★ **Playin' My Thang** / MCA (1980)
With Booker T. and the MGs, Cropper defined the perfectly understated guitar style and placed renewed emphasis on the instrument as a central part of the rhythm section, at a time when its soloing possibilities were getting way out of hand. Unfortunately, all the restraint and precision he showed as an ensemble player (and as occasional writer and producer at Stax Records) is dissipated in the laid-back indulgence of this solo bust. — D.M.

DAVID CROSBY
★ **If I Could Only Remember My Name** / Atl. (1971)
Interesting only as Crosby's first and only solo attempt. Otherwise a washout. — S.H.

CROSBY AND NASH
★ ★ **Crosby and Nash** / Atl. (1972)
★ ★ ★ **Wind on the Water** / ABC (1975)
★ **Whistling Down the Wire** / ABC (1976) ¶
★ ★ ★ **Live** / ABC (1977) ¶
★ ★ ★ **Best of Crosby and Nash** / MCA (1978)
These two usually function better together than separately. *Crosby and Nash* contains Nash's best acoustic ballad, the Dylan-esque "Southbound Train." The surprisingly rocking *Wind on the Water* was recorded with a fine touring band, and mixes political themes with intimations of old age and death. But what seemed like a creative renascence was only a one-shot. *Whistling Down the Wire* is at once smug, elitist and dull. The live album is notable mainly for featuring session stalwarts Danny Kortchmar, David Lindley,

Russ Kunkel, Tim Drummond and Craig Doerge at their onstage best. — S.H.

CROSBY, STILLS AND NASH
★ ★ **Crosby, Stills and Nash** / Atl. (1969)
★ ★ **CSN** / Atl. (1977)
★ ★ ★ **Replay** / Atl. (1980)
★ ★ **Daylight Again** / Atl. (1982)
Limpid "adult bubblegum" rockers and ballads of numbingly ersatz sensitivity. The music is slick and efficient, if soulless. The vocal harmonies that were supposed to be the trio's forte are so static when played at anything near a loud volume that they actually feel like needle pricks on the brain. The trio's reunion albums *(CSN, Daylight)* suffer from the same problems. — J.MO.

CROSBY, STILLS, NASH AND YOUNG
★ ★ ★ **Déjà Vu** / Atl. (1970)
★ ★ **Four Way Street** / Atl. (1971)
★ ★ ★ **So Far** / Atl. (1974)
The addition of Neil Young for *Déjà Vu* brought a quantum leap in songwriting ability. Young's chunky guitar and brooding vocals also picked things up a little. But there is still something hollow about this music. The aptly titled live LP (half acoustic, half electric) *Four Way Street* reveals a disturbing narcissism as each member does his solo numbers, though it does offer a few new songs and a couple of minutes of electric guitar dueling between Stills and Young. But most of it is sloppy, out-of-tune versions of songs already available in superior studio takes. *So Far* is a best-of collection that is questionably programed, but still offers a reasonable overview. — J.MO.

CHRISTOPHER CROSS
★ **Christopher Cross** / War. (1980)
Multi-Grammy winner Cross spins pabulum AOR fare characteristic of the vapidity of Eighties rock. Nicolette Larson, Don Henley, J.D. Souther, Michael McDonald and Larry Carlton add session help. — J.S.

THE CROSSFIRES
★ ★ ★ **Out of Control** / Rhino (1981)
The Crossfires are a surf band with a difference: the dementia of Mark Volman and Howard Kaylan, a.k.a. Flo and Eddie. While *Out of Control* is mostly twangy examples of the usual surf fare, there's also some insane (and occasionally inane) trash-pop reminiscent of vintage Turtles. This record is more than just an archivist's glimpse at the origins of a band, but a true document of budding musical madness. Fun, fun, fun. — R.P.

J.D. CROWE AND THE NEW SOUTH
★ ★ ★ **The New South / Roun. (1975)**
★ ★ ★ **You Can Share My Blanket / Roun. (1977)**
★ ★ ★ **My Home Ain't in the Hall of Fame / Roun. (1979)**
Crowe is a legendary banjo player whose best record, *The New South,* combines him with the great Tony Rice on guitar and vocals and Ricky Scaggs on fiddle and mandolin. — J.S.

RODNEY CROWELL
★ ★ ★ ★ **I Ain't Living Long Like This / War. (1978)**
★ ★ **But What Will the Neighbors Think / War. (1980)**
★ ★ ★ **Rodney Crowell / War. (1981)**
Rodney Crowell is one of that group of progressive country songwriters who realized that there was life outside Nashville in the middle Seventies and began to write about it. First noticed as songwriter and acoustic guitarist in early incarnations of Emmylou Harris' Hot Band, Crowell wrote many of Harris' best songs, including "Till I Gain Control Again" and "Ashes by Now." Emmylou Harris' versions show these songs at their best: Crowell's pleasant but light voice lacks the strength to give the songs the sort of emotional intensity they deserve.

His first album, *I Ain't Living Long Like This,* is a charmer, and includes Crowell's own deft version of "Voilà, an American Dream," later a hit for the Dirt Band. *But What Will the Neighbors Think* is an ill-advised attempt to update the sound with an injection of rock & roll toughness that merely sounds limp. *Rodney Crowell* sees him back where he belongs, sounding warm and confident with smart country-style songs that frequently strike the sort of emotional resonance they're meant to.

As a producer Crowell has become progressively slicker and more polished, and his albums suffer in the process—the arrangements often are just too easy. He is, however, a fine songwriter. Both the upbeat songs and the ballads manage to deal intelligently with modern relationships in a country-verging-on-pop form. — S.M.

CROWN HEIGHTS AFFAIR
★ ★ ★ **Foxy Lady / De-Lite (1976)**
★ ★ **Do It, Do It Your Way / De-Lite (1974)**
★ ★ **Crown Heights Affair / RCA (1978)** ¶
★ **Saturday Night Disco / De-Lite (1978)**
★ ★ **Dream World / De-Lite (1978)**
★ ★ **Dance Lady Dance / De-Lite (1979)**

★ ★ **Sure Shot / De-Lite (1980)**
Uninspired black octet managed to hit a couple of times during the mid-Seventies disco era, first with "Dreaming a Dream" in '75, then with "Foxy Lady" in '76. Both are contained on *Foxy Lady.* — D.M.

ARTHUR "BIG BOY" CRUDUP
★ ★ ★ **Look on Yonder's Wall / Del. (1968)**
★ ★ **Mean Ol' Frisco / Trip (1969)**
★ ★ ★ **Crudup's Mood / Del. (1970)**
Country-blues singer best known for providing Elvis with his debut song, "That's All Right." Crudup was never more than a journeyman bluesman—Elvis cut him to bits, however scandalous the royalty arrangements—but his late-Sixties Delmark recordings are interesting for a lightness of tone that neither the Trip nor a deleted RCA guilt anthology (*The Father of Rock and Roll*) possesses. — D.M.

CRUSADERS
★ ★ ★ ★ **Crusaders 1 / Blue Th. (1972)**
★ ★ ★ ★ **2nd Crusade / Blue Th. (1973)**
★ ★ ★ **Best of the Crusaders / Mo. (1973)** ¶
★ ★ ★ **Unsung Heroes / Blue Th. (1973)** ¶
★ ★ ★ **Scratch / MCA (1974)**
★ ★ ★ **Southern Comfort / Blue Th. (1974)**
★ ★ ★ ★ **Chain Reaction / Blue Th. (1975)** ¶
★ ★ **Those Southern Knights / Blue Th. (1976)** ¶
★ ★ ★ ★ **Best of the Crusaders / Blue Th. (1976)**
★ ★ ★ **Free As the Wind / Blue Th. (1977)**
★ ★ ★ **Images / Blue Th. (1978)**
★ ★ ★ **Street Life / MCA (1979)**
★ ★ ★ **Rhapsody and Blues / MCA (1980)**
These guys lay out the funkiest groove west of Rampart Street in New Orleans. Twenty years ago they were a knife-edged Texas R&B band sweating it out nightly in the bars where their kind of music lives its life. After making their Sixties migration to L.A. for survival, they switched to playing straight jazz under the name Jazz Crusaders. None of this material remains in print, but the Motown package gives the best remaining account of what they sounded like then. The quartet consisted of tenor sax player Wilton Felder, trombonist Wayne Henderson, Stix Hooper on drums and blues doctor Joe Sample on piano. Their rough-hewn yet virtuosic mix of precipitous soloing over rock-hard rhythm structures made them a particularly engaging jazz band.

It didn't take all that much for them to switch over to pure funk. All they really did was tighten up and simplify their arrangements, occasionally add a session bassist and sign up L.A. session guitarist extraordinaire Larry Carlton. The move was a success both commercially and aesthetically—hit singles like "Put It Where You Want It" gave them a mass audience, and they've become some of the most sought-after session players on the West Coast. Their own records are consistently fine, the best grease in the area. — J.S.

R.L. CRUTCHFIELD'S DARK DAY
★ **Exterminating Angel / In-Fi. (1981)**
For white boys who considered suicide when aspirin would have been enough. Minimal pleasures. — D.S.

THE CRYERS
★ ★ ★ **The Cryers / Mer. (1978)**
One of a thousand pop bands who crawled out of the woodwork after new wave made pop cool again, the short-lived Cryers had a catchy quality to their work most bands barely understand. — R.P.

CULTURE
★ ★ ★ ★ ★ **Two Sevens Clash / Joe G. (1977)**
★ ★ ★ **Baldhead Bridge / Joe G. (1978)**
★ ★ ★ ★ **Africa Stand Alone / April (1978)**
★ ★ ★ ★ ★ **Harder Than the Best / V.F.L. (1978)**
★ ★ ★ ★ ★ **Cumbolo / V.F.L. (1978)**
★ ★ ★ ★ **International Herb / V.F.L. (1979)**
★ ★ ★ ★ **Vital Selection / Virgin Int'l (1981)**
Rough country harmonies underpin Joseph Hill's chantlike lead vocals for reggae's premier roots vocal group. Hill's perfectionist streak and composing talent yields flawless productions and arrangements when he has his way. The haunting metaphors of his lyrics ("Iron Sharpen Iron," "Innocent Blood") give them a stark appeal beyond their essentially conventional Rastafarian content. *Two Sevens Clash* meshes these elements brilliantly to create a momumental work. *Africa Stand Alone* and *Baldhead Bridge* were mixed without Hill's supervision but retain considerable power nonetheless. *Cumbolo* and *Harder* are diamond-hard, polished masterpieces, but *International Herb* has fewer top-quality songs. *Vital Selection* compiles the high points from Virgin, but these are less satisfying out of context. — R.F.G.

BURTON CUMMINGS
★ ★ **Burton Cummings / Por. (1976)**
★ ★ **My Own Way to Rock / Por. (1977)** ¶
★ ★ **Dream of a Child / Por. (1978)** ¶
As strategist for the Guess Who and pop

poet laureate of Canada, Cummings feigned the Las Vegas crooner when he wasn't doing his Jim Morrison bit. So his solo debut, *Burton Cummings,* is an MOR crusade produced by Richard the Lionhearted Perry and led into battle under Cummings' histrionic anthem, "Stand Tall." The apparent enemy is Guess Who nemesis Randy Bachman, whose "You Ain't Seen Nothing Yet" gets the suave treatment, right down to Cummings' vocal parody of the guitar solo. The subsequent records have fewer highlights but less garish filigree. — J.S.

THE CURE
★ ★ ★ ★ **Boys Don't Cry / PVC (1980)**
★ ★ ★ ★ **. . . Happily Ever After / A&M (1981)**
The Cure's post-punk music ranges from catchy but odd pop ditties to slow ponderings to jagged outbursts of emotion. These American releases represent revisions of the Cure's three British albums. *Boys Don't Cry* is most of 1979's *Three Imaginary Boys* with the addition of essential singles; . . . *Happily Ever After* merely packages 1980's *Seventeen Seconds* and *Faith* in one sleeve. Both of these albums, though drastically dissimilar, are excellent and worthwhile. — I.R.

CHERIE CURRIE
★ **Beauty's Only Skin Deep / Mer. (NA)** ¶
Currie was the central figure in the Runaways, and the reason that that band failed may best be determined by a simple comparison of the dull sluttiness of this endeavor with Joan Jett's fairly inspired solo work. — D.M.

CHERIE AND MARIE CURRIE
★ **Messin' with the Boys / Cap. (1980)**
Bland heavy-metal pop featuring ex-Runaway Cherie Currie and kid sister Marie backed by most of Toto. Sounds like two fourteen-year-olds imitating Pat Benatar. — J.D.C.

TIM CURRY
★ **Read My Lips / A&M (1978)**
★ **Fearless / A&M (1979)**
★ **Simplicity / A&M (1981)**
Curry's an actor, and unless you're meathead enough to worship Meat Loaf (or *The Rocky Horror Picture Show* that produced both Loaf and Curry), you don't need to hear this drivel. Curry spars futilely with a few rock classics, but there's nothing interesting here that isn't better done elsewhere. (Try Murray Head, if you must indulge.) And since by listening to Curry, you're promoting the kind of preppy pothead smugness

Rocky Horror epitomizes, these albums are better off where they will be in only another year or two—deleted and forgotten. — D.M.

CURTIS BROS.
★ ★ ★ **The Curtis Bros. / Poly. (NA)**
Competent California rock in the Buffalo Springfield/Eagles tradition.
— D.M.

KING CURTIS
★ ★ ★ **The Best of King Curtis / Prest. (NA)** ¶
★ ★ ★ **The Best of King Curtis/One More Time / Prest. (1961)**
In the Fifties, King Curtis was an emerging star as a session saxophonist. His honking, dirty solo on the Coasters' "Yakety Yak" was the trademark of his early style, as well as providing a definitive rock & roll performance. These two albums mark the best of his early sessions as a featured soloist. At the time, Curtis' tone, a lowdown, guttural growl, was very much in the mold of the then-popular Willis "Gatortail" Jackson. With sidemen like Brother Jack McDuff, Billy Butler and Eric Gale, King Curtis works his way through R&B standards like "Honky Tonk," "Fever" and "The Huckle-buck." The twist novelties are cloying, but a smoky reading of "Harlem Nocturne" is a stand-out.
★ ★ ★ **King Soul / Prest. (1960)**
★ ★ ★ **Soul Meeting / Prest. (1960)**
★ ★ ★ **Jazz Groove / Prest. (1973)**
As leader of a session that included jazz notables like Nat Adderley, Wynton Kelly and Paul Chambers, King Curtis didn't venture far from the brawling saxophone style he brought to R&B sessions. *Soul Meeting* and *King Soul* were combined in the reissue, *Jazz Groove*. And though King was not out of his league playing blues and bop with such a formidable lineup, he proves to be a jazz frontman of only marginal interest.
★ ★ ★ ★ **The Best of King Curtis / Atco (1968)**
★ ★ ★ ★ **Live at the Fillmore West / Atco (1971)** ¶
★ ★ ★ **Soul Serenade / Ember (1972)**
★ ★ ★ **Twenty Golden Pieces of King Curtis and the Noble Knights / Bull. (NA)**
But if King Curtis was merely a competent jazz musician, he was a master at a simpler form. By the mid-Sixties, Curtis had few peers as a soul saxophonist and bandleader. His tone had broadened, and though the rough, muscular edges were still very much in evidence, he displayed an increased lyrical sense that sparkled on the wafting, self-composed "Soul Serenade" and ballads like

"Something on Your Mind" and "You've Lost That Lovin' Feeling'."
The Fillmore album shows King Curtis as a fully matured R&B master, fronting an awesome, powerhouse band that included stalwarts Cornell Dupree, Bernard Purdy and Gerald Jemmott. Though at times one wishes for more judicious material ("Mr. Bojangles"?), there's no arguing with the performance. Curtis and the band simply erupt on potboilers "Memphis Soul Stew" and "Them Changes." It was the supreme soul band of its time. — J.MC.

LITTLE JOE CURTIS
★ ★ **Soul / Als. (NA)**
The Miami disco version of soul—that is, more reliance is placed on rhythm grooves than on singers, who are usually just about as average and anonymous as this. — D.M.

SONNY CURTIS
★ ★ **Sonny Curtis / Elek. (1979)**
★ ★ **Love Is All Around / Elek. (1980)**
★ **Rollin' / Elek. (1981)**
Curtis was one of the Crickets, and he wrote the Bobby Fuller Four hit, "I Fought the Law," as well as "Love Is All Around," which provided *The Mary Tyler Moore Show* with its theme song (as well as his second album with a title). Curtis is not a strong singer, but he occasionally comes up with a good song idea: witness the above. Curtis is most interesting, though, when he's ruminating on his own (and rock's) history, as on "Do You Remember Roll Over Beethoven," from *Sonny Curtis*, and "The Real Buddy Holly Story," his review of the film *The Buddy Holly Story*, contained on *Love Is All Around*. *Rollin'* unfortunately offers nothing so personal; it's country pop at its most trite. (And Sonny ought to abstain from covering such songs as "Fifty Ways to Leave Your Lover" in the future, too.) — D.M.

CURTISS A
★ ★ ★ ★ **Courtesy / Twin T. (1981)**
Minneapolis's Curt Almsted comes across a bit like a white James Brown—regularly punctuating his powerful singing with even more powerful screams—but although he subtly incorporates an R&B flavor on a number of tunes, he's no way just another honky copping licks from the Godfather. Instead, *Courtesy* also mixes doses of rockabilly and raunchy, fast-paced rock into an unflaggingly energetic brew. Given time to develop Curtiss could turn into a rock & roll singer of the caliber of Mitch Ryder—but even wilder and without the schmaltz. One to watch. — D.S.

DADDY COOL
★ ★ ★ ★ **Daddy Who? Daddy Cool! / War. (1971)**
★ ★ ★ **Teenage Heaven / War. (1972)**
Emerging from the strangeness of the late Sixties rather than prefabricated TV nostalgia, Daddy Cool were one of the most engaging and original of Fifties revivalists. Performing largely their own songs, high-spirited reworkings of Fifties themes rather than direct copies, they achieved considerable success in their native Australia as well as some popularity in the U.S.

The first album, *Daddy Who? Daddy Cool!*, which contains early hits like "Eagle Rock," still sounds energetic and cheerful. Their strength came from the combination of Ross Wilson's singing, writing and onstage charm, and Ross Hannaford's clear, inventive guitar playing.

Ross Wilson became a major figure in the Australian rock world during the Seventies, principally as a songwriter and producer for bands such as Skyhooks and Jo Jo Zep and the Falcons. While he maintained an involvement in performance, it has been only with the 1979 lineup of his band Mondo Rock that Wilson has had any real success. The 1981 album *Chemistry* includes "State of the Heart," a wonderful moody ballad that initiated Mondo Rock's chart success. — S.M.

DAKOTA
★ **Dakota / Col. (1980)**
You don't even have to listen to this album to get an idea of what the music is like. Just use the geographical reference. Like Boston, Kansas, New England and the like, Dakota is AOR rock pablum, although like their state, they are also a little woolier and more backwoodsy than their more sophisticated and urbane cousins. — R.P.

LISA DAL BELLO
★ ★ ★ **Pretty Girls / Tal. (1979) ¶**
★ ★ **Drastic Measures / Tal. (1981)**
Beautiful dal Bello is being encouraged to go for the slavering MOR market. Pity, because her voice is spectacular. And on *Pretty Girls* she exhibits some possibilities as the songwriter for the smarter ladies in the singles complex. Melissa Manchester covered "Pretty Girls." — L.F.

LACY J. DALTON
★ ★ ★ **Lacy J. Dalton / Col. (1980)**
★ ★ ★ **Hard Times / Col. (1980)**
★ ★ ★ **Takin' It Easy / Col. (1981)**
Husky-voiced female vocalist swamped country charts in 1979 with the blockbuster single "Crazy Blue Eyes." The self-styled "country Janis Joplin" has a powerful stage presence and costarred in the film *Take This Job and Shove It.* — J.S.

ROGER DALTREY
★ ★ ★ **Daltrey / MCA (1973)**
★ **Ride a Rock Horse / MCA (1975)**
★ ★ ★ **One of the Boys / MCA (1977)**
Lead singer of the Who. *Daltrey,* produced and written by ancient British pop star Adam Faith, Leo Sayer and young newcomer David Courtney, uses the Who vocalist's limited voice to excellent advantage. "Giving It All Away," a minor hit, is as good a song as Daltrey has ever done. *Rock Horse,* produced and mostly written by Russ Ballard, makes a variety of errors, primarily in material selection. *One of the Boys* is nearly as hard-rocking as a Who LP; it contains a fine version of Andy Pratt's "Avenging Annie." — D.M.

THE DAMNED
★ ★ ★ **Damned, Damned, Damned / Stiff (1977), Br. imp.**
★ **Music for Pleasure / Stiff (1978), Br. imp.**

★ ★ ★ **Machine Gun Etiquette** / **Chis. (1979), Br. imp.**
★ ★ **The Black Album** / **IRS (1981), Br. imp.**

The most disposable and comic group in Britain's first punk thrust, the Damned committed the cardinal sin of such planned obsolescence: they stuck around. By trying to make a career out of music that would have been mildly charming as a one-shot affair, they inevitably draw comparisons with bands whose every move is plotted out. And although some progress in musicianship and songwriting is evident through the years, that's hardly where their appeal lies.

— W.K.

BARBARA DANE

★ ★ ★ **Barbara Dane and the Chambers Brothers** / **Folk. (1964)**
★ ★ **Barbara Dane Sings the Blues** / **Folk. (1965)**

Dane was a staple on UAW picket lines, in civil-rights marches and at antiwar rallies, her musical approach being: "The more serious the content, the more appealing the form should be." The intermingling of politics and music is a major concern of her own Paredon label, best exemplified here as the Chambers Brothers join her for a cappella renditions of "Go Tell It on the Mountain" and "Freedom Is a Constant Struggle," among other civil-rights anthems. The blues set is heartfelt, the kind of work that opened the way for Bonnie Raitt. — I.M.

RODNEY DANGERFIELD

★ ★ ★ **The Loser** / **Rhino (1980)**
★ ★ ★ ★ **No Respect** / **Casa. (1980)**

On *The Loser,* the early Dangerfield is vulgar, lewd, sexist, smirking and clichéd, but funny as hell. On *No Respect,* he is more of the same, but also (after Richard Pryor) the funniest stand-up comic of our times, relentless and hilarious. — D.M.

CHARLIE DANIELS BAND

★ ★ **Charlie Daniels** / **Cap. (1970)**
★ ★ ★ **Uneasy Rider** / **Epic (1976)**

The first phase of Charlie Daniels' solo career finds him grasping for his own identity as one of the first Southern rockers to follow in the wake of the Allman Brothers. That group's influence on him is transparent, though Daniels has a penchant for novelty songs ("Uneasy Rider" was even a freak hit) that the Allmans never displayed. The Capitol LP is both his most eclectic and least self-conscious effort. *Uneasy,* a reissue of one

of his early LPs for Kama Sutra, has more consistently focused performances; even the two long guitar jams almost sustain themselves.

★ ★ ★ **Fire on the Mountain** / **Epic (1974)**
★ ★ **Night Rider** / **Epic (1975)**
★ ★ **Saddle Tramp** / **Epic (1976)**
★ ★ **High Lonesome** / **Epic (1977)**
★ ★ **Whiskey** / **Epic (1977)**
★ ★ **Midnight Wind** / **Epic (1977)**
★ ★ **To John, Grease and Wolfman** / **Epic (1978)**
★ ★ **Million Mile Reflections** / **Epic (1979)**
★ ★ **Full Moon** / **Epic (1980)**

Here, a more distinctive Daniels Band sound emerges. *Saddle Tramp* shows him moving toward Western swing (but with his own, much harder arrangements) and country boogie-woogie. *Fire* is even more Western-oriented; the fiddle is finally as prominent as the guitar and the country-boy persona is more pronounced. *Fire* also contains the Daniels' rallying cry, "The South's Gonna Do It." The album represents Daniels' best effort in this phase, but it's already tipping his hand toward the extended Southern boogie, which he usually does to death. On succeeding albums he comes close to doing just that, despite more economical songwriting; also, his Southern pride is sounding more like trendy, empty-headed chauvinism. Some of his good-old-boyisms could embarrass even Billy Carter. — J.MO.

RICK DANKO

★ ★ ★ ★ **Rick Danko** / **Ari. (1977)**

This solo outing from the Band's bassist and co-lead singer is a moving and surprisingly fine record that approximates the ambiance of the Band's best moments without complacency or nostalgia. Danko's vulnerable vocal persona was the perfect expression of the plaintive emotion characteristic of much of Robbie Robertson's writing, and he makes the transition to fronting his own record without faltering. Despite the fact that Danko contributed little in the way of songwriting to his old group (though he did co-write the classic "This Wheel's On Fire" with Bob Dylan), his songs for this record are tremendous. Several tunes ("Brainwash," "Java Blues," "Sip the Wine") could well have been recorded by the Band.

The instrumental support, led by cameos from his former group mates, is also superb. Robertson handles lead guitar on "Java Blues," Richard Manuel electric piano on "Shake It," Levon Helm adds harmony vocals on "Once upon a Time" and Garth Hudson plays accordion on "New Mexico."

Guest appearances by Eric Clapton and Ronnie Wood and extensive collaboration on horn charts and guitar from Doug Sahm flesh out the impressive list of sidemen. — J.S.

BOBBY DARIN
★ ★ ★ The Bobby Darin Story / Atco (1961)
★ ★ Bobby Darin 1936–1973 / Mo. (1974)
★ Darin at the Copa / Bain. (1981)

Bobby Darin's first record, "Splish Splash" (1958), was the first white hit for Atlantic Records. Produced by Ahmet Ertegun, Darin's record helped touch off the Italian-American rock 'n' roll craze of the late Fifties, and his influence can be heard on Dion, Fabian, Frankie Avalon and even the young Rascals. Aside from "Dream Lover," a mopey ballad, and the finger-popping "Mack the Knife," however, Darin never quite lived up to the potential of his talent. He went to Hollywood and Vegas, tried folk rock in the late Sixties and came up with a nice hit in "If I Were a Carpenter." He then went straight pop once more at Motown in the early part of the Seventies. He died of a heart ailment in 1973, unrealized but also unrecognized for what he did accomplish. The Atco sides are pretty fine records, and hold some pleasant surprises for those who haven't heard them. — D.M.

DARLING AND STREET
★ The Possible Dream / Van. (1975) ¶

Erik Darling, a one-time member of the Weavers and Rooftop Singers and an itinerant banjo and guitar ace, teams up here for forgettable pop-folk mishmash. Darling is better than this, though it's hard to find supportive evidence on records. — T.S.

CHRIS DARROW
★ ★ ★ Chris Darrow / U.A. (1973) ¶
★ ★ ★ Fretless / Pac. A. (1979)
★ ★ ★ Eye of the Storm / Tak. (1981)

Darrow, formerly a founding member of Kaleidoscope with David Lindley, shares Lindley's light touch with anything stringed, has a fine cracked countryish voice, and a sensibility capable of synthesizing any sound from the Middle Eastern to the Middle Western into a unique, if self-consciously eccentric blend. None of these records are what you'd call pop, and their appeal is probably more folk than pop, but if you don't find those restrictions off-putting, all of them are worth hearing. — D.M.

PHILIP D'ARROW
★ ★ Philip D'Arrow / Poly. (1979)
★ Sub Zero / Poly. (NA)

On his self-titled debut album, D'Arrow almost gets away with expropriating all of Bruce Springsteen's least captivating mannerisms. On his second record, he doesn't even come close. — D.M.

COW COW DAVENPORT
★ ★ ★ ★ Cow Cow Davenport / Mag. (1976)
★ ★ ★ ★ Cow Cow Blues / Oldie B. (1977)

Singer/piano player is generally described as one of the first practitioners of boogie-woogie. But his style is radically different from the Albert Ammons/Meade Lux Lewis school that has come to define the genre. Davenport was closer to a style that predates the New Orleans piano playing of Smiley Lewis and Professor Longhair, although ironically Davenport was from Alabama and rarely worked in New Orleans. — J.S.

DAVE DAVIES
★ ★ ★ ★ AFLI-3603 / RCA (1980)
★ ★ Glamour / RCA (1981)

The younger brother of Kinks leader Ray Davies and cofounder of that band, Dave is responsible for the monster guitar riffs that powered the earliest Kinks tunes, "You Really Got Me" and "All Day and All of the Night," as well as the high harmonies that add an ethereal touch to the Kinks' vocal arrangements. Dave also penned such Kinks standards as "Death of a Clown," and his solo debut had been rumored since the late Sixties. The first solo LP proved to be a strident and haunting set pinned around Dave's banshee vocals and stinging blues-rock soloing. The followup featured more of the same but with weaker material. — J.S.

GAIL DAVIES
★ ★ ★ ★ The Game / War. (1979)
★ ★ ★ ★ I'll Be There / War. (1980)

Davies deserves more than just the respect she's due as a woman who writes, sings and produces her own country albums—*good* country albums, too. A clear-voiced, commanding singer, she's a stellar example of the best of the new country. — R.P.

BETTY DAVIS
★ ★ ★ Nasty Gal / Is. (1975)

Almost as if she were a black Marlene Dietrich, Betty Davis defines herself by unusual sexual posturing. On *Nasty Gal* she growls and snarls, taunts lovers, reveals bedroom secrets and challenges the familiar roles of female vocalists. The insistent funk tracks may become wearying, but the songs never fail to titillate. — J.MC.

REVEREND GARY DAVIS

★ ★ ★ **The Singing Reverend / Stin. (1963)**
★ ★ ★ ★ **Reverend Gary Davis, 1935–1949 /
Yazoo (1970)**
★ ★ **Lord I Wish I Could See / Bio. (1971)**
★ ★ ★ **Reverend Gary Davis / Bio. (1971)**
★ ★ ★ **When I Die I'll Live Again / Fan.
(1972)**
★ ★ **In Concert: Children of Zion / Kick.
(1972)**
★ ★ **Ragtime Guitar / Kick. (1973)**
★ ★ ★ **The Sun Is Going Down / Folk.
(1976)**
★ ★ ★ ★ **Pure Religion and Bad Company /
77 (NA)**
★ ★ ★ **The Guitar and Banjo of Reverend
Gary Davis / Prest. (NA)**
★ ★ ★ **Pure Religion / Prest. (NA)**
★ ★ ★ **Rev. Gary Davis at Newport / Van.
(NA)**

Davis, who became an ordained minister in
1933 at age thirty-seven thereupon banished
all sinful material from his repertoire, turning to gospel blues exclusively (and with as
lovely a touch as anyone since Blind Willie
Johnson). Davis, who was also blind, fortunately did not abandon his devilishly intricate six- and twelve-string guitar playing.
Davis recorded through the Forties—the best
of his vintage material is on the Yazoo set—
then was rediscovered during the folk-blues
revival of the Sixties. He spent the remainder
of his life teaching and performing, widening
his influence (musical if not religious).

Of his Sixties recordings, the loveliest are
on *Pure Religion and Bad Company*. The
rest are more run-of-the-mill, though nothing
here is less than listenable. (The instruction-
oriented Kicking Mule sets can be pretty
wearing, however.) — D.M.

MAC DAVIS

■ **I Believe in Music / Col. (1971)**
■ **Baby Don't Get Hooked on Me / Col. (1972)**
■ **Mac Davis / Col. (1973)**
■ **Song Painter / Col. (1974)**
■ **Stop and Smell the Roses / Col. (1974)**
■ **All the Love in the World / Col. (1975)**
■ **Burning Thing / Col. (1975)**
■ **Forever Lovers / Col. (1976)**
■ **Thunder in the Afternoon / Col. (1977)**
■ **Fantasy / Col. (1978)**
■ **It's Hard to Be Humble / Casa. (1980)**
■ **Texas in My Rear View Mirror / Casa.
(1980)**
■ **Mac Davis / Sp. (NA)**

Singer/songwriter Davis has done more to
set back the cause of popular music in recent
years than any other single figure. His execrable pop-morality pseudo-country hits, "I

Believe in Music" and "Stop and Smell the
Roses," encouraged a wholesale run to sententious Muzak that makes movie director
Robert Altman's vision of Nashville's self-
righteousness and pomposity look like humility. His one legitimate claim to rock foot-
notoriety was writing "In the Ghetto" for
Elvis. — J.S.

PAUL DAVIS

★ **Little Bit of Paul Davis / Bang (NA)**
★ ★ **Paul Davis / Bang (NA)**
★ ★ ★ ★ **Ride 'Em Cowboy / Bang (1974)**
★ ★ ★ **Southern Tracks and Fantasies /
Bang (1976)**
★ ★ ★ **Paul Davis / Bang (1977)**
★ ★ ★ **Singer of Songs, Teller of Tales /
Bang (1978)**
★ ★ ★ **Davis / Bang (1981)**

Davis is a Southern singer/songwriter of
some talent who began recording in the early
Seventies as a neo-folkie. *Little Bit* and *Paul
Davis* (Bang 226) featured original songs of
love and social protest, and while his sentiments were all too often saccharine and his
instrumental backing plain, his singing
showed definite promise. His popularity in
Atlanta and the small-label ethics at Bang
enabled Davis to continue recording. He
found his stride with *Ride 'Em Cowboy*. The
ambiance here leaned more toward country
rock, with some fine songwriting (the title
track, "You're Not Just a Rose," "Midnight
Woman," "Bronco Rider" and "Make Her
My Baby"), and excellent instrumental backing from guitarists Barry Bailey and Auburn
Burrell, steel guitarist Charlie Owen, drummer Roy Yeager and bassists Tom Robb and
Chris Ethridge. *Southern Tracks and Fantasies* was slickly contemporary pop, well produced and featuring some fine instrumental
backing from the Muscle Shoals crew (drummer Roger Hawkins, keyboardist Barry
Beckett and guitarist Jimmy Johnson). But
Davis' searching-for-a-hit songwriting here is
too formularized, which makes the album ultimately disappointing. *Singer of Songs* and
Davis suffered the same fate. — J.S.

TYRONE DAVIS

★ ★ ★ ★ **Tyrone Davis' Greatest Hits /
Dakar (1972)**
★ ★ ★ **Tyrone Davis / Dakar (1973)**
★ ★ ★ **It's All in the Game / Dakar (1973)**
★ ★ ★ **Home Wrecker / Dakar (1975)**
★ ★ **Love and Touch / Col. (1976) ¶**
★ ★ **Let's Be Closer Together / Col.
(1977) ¶**
★ ★ **I Can't Go This Way / Col. (1978) ¶**
★ ★ **Can't You Tell It's Me / Col. (1979)**

★ ★ **In the Mood with Tyrone Davis / Col. (1979)**
★ ★ **I Just Can't Keep Going On / Col. (1980)**
★ ★ **Everything in Place / Col. (1981)**
As a modishly romantic Seventies soul singer at Dakar, Davis used his big, Joe Simon–like voice on a variety of ballads to turn in some refreshingly moody hits, all of which fit into a single stylistic pattern set by "Can I Change My Mind?" the first and best. His *Greatest Hits* album is great make-out music, more sincere and less erect than Barry White's mumbles. At Columbia, he has been pushed into modern rhythm patterns, subordinated to the backing tracks, and generally washed out. — D.M.

SPENCER DAVIS GROUP
★ ★ ★ ★ **The Spencer Davis Group featuring Stevie Winwood / Is. (1981), Br. imp.**
★ ★ ★ ★ **Gimme Some Lovin' / Is. (1981), Br. imp.**
The first two albums by the great U.K. white soul group in which Winwood won his spurs as a Ray Charles soundalike while still in his teens. *Gimme Some Lovin'* includes the marvelous hits "Gimme Some Lovin'," "I'm a Man" and "Keep On Running." Some of the best British R&B ever waxed. — D.M.

JIMMY DAWKINS
★ ★ ★ **Jimmy "Fast Fingers" Dawkins / Del. (1974)**
★ ★ ★ **All for Business / Del. (1975)**
★ ★ ★ **Blisterstring / Del. (1976)**
Very good, though not exceptional, samples of contemporary Chicago blues guitar. One ought to be enough for anyone but fanatics—start with *Fast Fingers*. — D.M.

STU DAYE
★ ★ **Free Parking / Col. (1976)** ¶
Sharp wordsmith with enough rock & roll in him to sustain the imagery over the length of a song. Decent cover of Paul Simon's "The Boxer." — J.S.

DAZZ
★ **Kinsman Dazz / 20th Cent. (1979)** ¶
Another nine-piece funk band. Sometimes it seems like this kind of group gets less efficient the bigger it gets. I mean, Sly Stone never needed more than six other people, and his records were *alive*. — D.M.

THE DAZZ BAND
★ ★ ★ **Invitation to Love / Mo. (1980)**

★ ★ ★ **Let the Music Play / Mo. (1981)**
Slick funk octet scored with "Shake It Up" from *Invitation* and title track of *Let the Music Play* without quite crossing over. — D.M.

THE dB's
★ ★ ★ **The dB's / Albion (1981), Br. imp.**
★ ★ ★ **Repercussion / Albion (1981), Br. imp.**
Willfully lightweight but always engaging pop rock from a marginally new-wave band with roots in the coastal South and New York City. Naturally, no American label would touch this straightforwardly Beatles-influenced rock, so they had to cross the pond to record. Whether the band will ever expand its ambition enough to make a record of consequence, or find a trend it can ride to commercial success, remains to be seen. But for sheer craftsmanship, very little that has come along in the past few years can touch songwriters Chris Stamey and Peter Holsapple. — D.M.

THE DCA EXPERIENCE
★ ★ ★ **Bicentennial Gold / Priv. (NA)** ¶
That's right—a disco record of patriotic songs. Coproducer Tony Bongiovi and his band of merrily hard-working disco all-stars prove that the genre was a rich medium for novelty records. — J.S.

DEAD KENNEDYS
★ ★ ★ ★ **Fresh Fruit for Rotting Vegetables / IRS (1981)**
From their offensive name through the unchecked venom of the song titles ("Stealing People's Mail," "Drug Me," "Chemical Warfare," "Kill the Poor"), the one punk group to succeed since 1977 did it by heading in the only direction left: pure, hateful excess and overkill. The ripsaw guitar and lead singer Jello Biafra's malevolent delivery almost match the bite and sneer of vintage Sex Pistols. The real kicker is a political sensibility and "wit" that far surpasses anything dreamed of by Pistols potentate Malcolm McLaren, best expressed in the put-down of Jerry Brown and his "Zen fascists" in "California uber Alles." This document will probably hold up best as a one-shot; after all, the apocalypse is only coming once. — W.K.

DEADLY ERNEST
★ ★ **Deadly Ernest and the Honky-Tonk Heroes / Pac. A. (1979)**
Deadly dull. — W.K.

DEADLY NIGHTSHADE
★ **Deadly Nightshade / RCA (1975)** ¶
★ **F&W / RCA (1976)** ¶
Strident feminist folk rock. — J.S.

PETER DEAN
★ ★ **Four or Five Times / Bud. (1974)**
Fifty-ish jazz singer, notable mostly because he covers James Taylor's "Don't Let Me Be Lonely Tonight" and uses Taylor's wife (and Dean's cousin), Carly Simon, as a backing singer on both the title track and "So the Bluebirds and the Blackbirds Got Together." — D.M.

DEARDORFF AND JOSEPH
■ **Deardorff and Joseph / Ari. (1976)**
Singer/songwriter duo, who share management and the Bahai faith with Seals and Crofts, were notable mostly because Danny Deardorff was a paraplegic who had to be carried onstage. Great suffering has not, in this case, produced great art. — D.M.

CHRIS DE BURGH
■ **Far Beyond These Castle Walls / A&M (1975)**
■ **Spanish Train and Other Stories / A&M (1976)**
Chris de Burgh is a troubadour who has adopted and expanded the early Bee Gees' most insipid mistakes while incarnating all of Donovan's medieval fantasies. He even lives in a crumbling castle whence he issued *Far Beyond These Castle Walls,* which has no less than four tracks with spoken verses.

Apparently having read Borges, de Burgh comes back stronger with *Spanish Train and Other Stories.* Tighter piano/string arrangements make it sound almost like the Cat Stevens score to Ingmar Bergman's first rock musical. — B.T.

BERT DE COTEAUX
■ **Bert de Coteaux Plays a Stevie Wonder Songbook / RCA (1975)** ¶
Stiff instrumental versions of Wonder's hits, under the direction of noted disco arranger/producer de Coteaux. — S.H.

DE DANANN
★ ★ ★ **De Danann / Boot (1975)**
★ ★ ★ **The Mist-Covered Mountain / Shan. (1980)**
★ ★ ★ ★ **Selected Jigs and Reels / Shan. (1980)**
★ ★ ★ ★ **The Star-Spangled Molly / Shan. (1981)**
The best band of the second wave of Irish traditional music, De Danann shows wider influences on its repertoire than such strictly traditional groups as Clannad. *The Star-Spangled Molly* even includes "My Irish Molly," a sixty-year-old American tune which reached No. 5 on the Irish charts in 1981. Frankie Gavin, the leader of the group, is called by many the best musician of his generation as he plays the range of traditional Irish instruments. — D.D.

KIKI DEE
★ ★ **I've Got the Music in Me / R. (1974)**
★ ★ **Kiki Dee / R. (1977)**
★ ★ **Stay with Me / R. (1978)**
★ ★ **Loving and Free / R. (1978)**
These albums yield one fine single, "I've Got the Music in Me," and hardly anything else. The problem? Dee is a coward when it comes time to reach for the deeper emotions inherent in the material. Some scintillating pop arrangements are wasted as a result, much as her single with Elton John, "Don't Go Breaking My Heart," also spent time and talent frivolously. — D.MC.

DEEP PURPLE
★ **Book of Taliesyn / Tetra. (1969)** ¶
★ **Deep Purple / Tetra. (1969)** ¶
★ ★ **Deep Purple and the Royal Philharmonic / War. (1970)** ¶
★ ★ ★ **Deep Purple in Rock / War. (1970)**
★ ★ ★ **Fireball / War. (1971)**
★ ★ ★ ★ **Machine Head / War. (1972)**
★ ★ ★ **Purple Passages / War. (1972)**
★ ★ ★ ★ **Made in Japan / War. (1973)**
★ ★ ★ **Who Do We Think We Are! / War. (1973)**
★ ★ **Stormbringer / War. (1974)**
★ ★ **Come Taste the Band / War. (1975)**
★ ★ **Burn / War. (1976)**
★ ★ **Made in Europe / War. (1976)**
★ ★ ★ **When We Rock, We Rock and When We Roll / War. (1978)**
★ ★ ★ **Deepest Purple / War. (1980)**
The Deep Purple catalogue gives one, besides an often painful headache, a fairly clear picture of the disjointed meanderings of the hard-rock trail from the demise of the Yardbirds to the first stirrings of punk rock. *Purple Passages,* a compilation of selections from the band's first three albums, established its capability of drawing buckets of inspiration from any of the musical streams running into the main current of 1968 rock. Led by guitarist Ritchie Blackmore and keyboard player Jon Lord, Deep Purple used flashes of psychedelia, classical touches and (perhaps most significantly in trying to understand the band's longevity and rather sur-

prising consistency) plenty of bar-band, kick-out-the-stools consciousness.

Prone to self-indulgence, early Deep Purple plunged headlong into anything and everything that struck its fancy, making even their most glaring failures (most notably Jon Lord's out-of-print *Concerto for Group and Orchestra*) almost excusable.

The departures of original vocalists Rod Evans and bassist Nic Simper and the entrance of Ian Gillan and bassist Roger Glover proved to be the turning point for the band. *Deep Purple in Rock,* the fourth album, was a hodgepodge of power chords and psychedelic noodling, but with *Fireball,* the group began upping the wattage and leaving the thinking to art rockers. Blackmore, always a respected guitarist but until then never more than the sum of his influences, began to pull feverish and original solos out of nowhere, as he and Lord began to serve as counterpoints to each other. *Machine Head* was a crowning achievement, with "Highway Star," "Smoke on the Water" and the mind-melting "Space Truckin' " leading the way through two sides of mania that left one not only battered but begging for more. *Made in Japan,* a double live recording originally released only in Japan, was hastily released in the United States soon afterward as Deep Purple began to challenge Led Zeppelin for the sonic-overload throne.

The glory period was short-lived, however. *Who Do We Think We Are!* sported only one real gem, "Woman from Tokyo," and within two years, both Gillan and Blackmore had bowed out because of internal squabbling. Lord carried on with singer David Coverdale and American guitarist Tommy Bolin, but as the Seventies entered middle age, metalloid bombardments on the eardrums were no longer the favorite pastime of the maturing audience that had been Purple's. The band died an almost unnoticed death in 1976, and *Made in Europe,* recorded in '75 and released posthumously, with Blackmore on guitar, displays only the echoes of the power that once was Deep Purple. *When We Rock* and *Deepest Purple* are greatest-hits collections. — B.A.

RICK DEES
★ **Original Disco Duck / RSO (1976)**
"Disco Duck," a hit in the summer of '76, gave disco what it deserved while at the same time pointing out the genre's utility for novelty singles. Imagine Donald Duck singing Barry White songs and you'll get the idea. — J.S.

SAM DEES
★ ★ ★ **The Show Must Go On / Atl. (1975)** ¶
Sam Dees is a more than creditable songwriter, but his singing lacks distinction. His only album is professional, if none too varied, centering mostly on similarly constructed soul ballads. "Claim Jumping" is the best, a hard-hitting Southern funk song modeled after early Johnnie Taylor hits. — J.MC.

DEFUNKT
★ ★ ★ ★ **Defunkt / Hann. (1981)**
This New York-based outfit produces heavy, heavy funk with a jazz tinge, featuring sterling guitar interplay between Kelvyn Bell and Martin Aubert and an abundance of bounce to the ounce. Urban dance music with bite and substance. — D.S.

DÉJÀ VU
■ **Get It Up for Love / Cap. (NA)** ¶
This gruesome Toronto band is the brainchild of Skip Prokop, founding member and self-proclaimed auteur of Déjà Vu's immediate stylistic predecessor, Lighthouse. Although unburdened by a horn section, much less a string quartet, as was Lighthouse, Déjà Vu suffers fatally from the same problem: the band's components have yet to be introduced to each other. Consisting of an industrial-weight instrumental unit fronted by three singers intending to be the new Three Dog Night, Déjà Vu flounders on inane material ground into hash by heavy-metal R&B. The singers, never less than shrill, often sound like they are being emasculated. — B.T.

DESMOND DEKKER
★ ★ ★ ★ **Sweet Sixteen Hits / Troj. (1978)**
★ **Black and Dekker / Stiff (1980)**
★ ★ **Compass Point / Stiff (1981)**
Desmond Dekker's sweet, high singing is somewhat one-dimensional, but he's responsible for two Sixties rocksteady classics ("Israelites," one of the first reggae records to hit in America, and "Shanty Town," a rudie anthem). All the good Leslie Kong–produced stuff is on *Hits*. The Stiffs are an unsuccessful attempt to update Dekker's rocksteady and reggae with neo-ska British rock. — R.F.G.

DELANEY AND BONNIE AND FRIENDS
★ ★ **Genesis / GNP (1970)**
★ ★ ★ ★ **On Tour / Atco (1970)**
Delaney and Bonnie Bramlett were

Oklahoma-bred musicians who made mid-Sixties reputations in the Hollywood session scene (Delaney was a member of the Shindogs, who appeared on ABC's *Shindig*). They made their first album—not the GNP outtakes above—for Stax in 1968, in a kind of white gospel-funk mode to which Eric Clapton, among others, owes a great deal. In 1969, they formed a band to tour with Blind Faith that included Carl Radle, Leon Russell, Jim Price and Bobby Keys, all of whom went on to tour with Joe Cocker's Mad Dogs and Englishmen, an act of desertion that took the backbone from the duo's career. Before that, however, they made a couple of influential, laid-back tours of Europe (from which the live Atco LP, which features Clapton, is drawn) and the States.

The deleted LPs Delaney and Bonnie made for Elektra and Atlantic are all worthwhile listening for anyone interested in moderately impassioned white soul. The couple split up—artistically and maritally—in 1972 and both have since pursued solo careers.
— D.M.

THE DELEGATES
★ The Delegates / Mile. (NA) ¶
Heavy early-Seventies R&B verging on funk; "Funky Butt" was the single. — J.S.

DELEGATION
★ ★ ★ Promise of Love / Shady. (1979)
★ ★ Delegation / Mer. (1980)
★ ★ Delegation 2 / Mer. (1981)
Funksters managed a Top Ten R&B hit (which nearly crossed over) in 1979 with "Oh Honey." Since moving to Mercury, however, they've had no such luck. — D.M.

DELILAH
★ Dancing in the Fire / ABC (1978) ¶
Title track, a minor disco hit of 1978, characterizes the numbing mindlessness of the rest. How about a "Showbiz Medley" that includes "The Stripper," "Showbiz" and "Night Train"? Proof that a good beat and danceability are outdated criteria of quality.
— D.M.

THE DELLS
★ ★ They Said It Couldn't Be Done, But We Did It / Mer. (1977) ¶
★ ★ ★ Love Connection / Mer. (1977) ¶
★ ★ ★ Face to Face / ABC (1978)
★ ★ ★ New Beginnings / MCA (1978)
★ ★ ★ I Touched a Dream / MCA (1980)
★ ★ ★ Whatever Turns You On / MCA (1981)
★ ★ ★ ★ Oh, What a Night / VJ (NA)

The Dells, with the Isley Brothers, are probably the oldest remaining group in rock. Their first hit, "Oh, What a Night," made in a Chicago version of doo-wop harmony, appeared in 1956, and at least on the R&B charts, their success has continued virtually unbroken, with occasional appearances on the pop charts as well. Surprisingly, the best overview of their career can be found on a now-deleted Trip album, *The Dells' Greatest Hits* (Trip X-9503). The Vee Jay LP, while of Fifties origin, is much more spotty.

In the Sixties, the Dells became a Temptations/Impressions-style vocal group, and most of the now-deleted Cadet/Chess albums represent that phase of their career. Aside from the driving "There Is," perhaps the best record they ever made, and the remakes of the first two hits ("Oh, What a Night" and "Stay in My Corner"), they rarely dented the pop charts, although they always remained important in the soul field. Since 1975 they have become more modern still, but since today's soul formulas place more of a premium on rhythm and less on singing, the records aren't as interesting. Still, on some of the MCA material, lead singer Marvin Junior cuts loose with enough power to remind you that Teddy Pendergrass was perceptive in basing his style on Junior's.
— D.M.

THE DELMORE BROTHERS
★ ★ ★ ★ The Best of the Delmore Brothers / Star. (NA)
Vintage Forties country by one of the Grand Ole Opry's seminal duos. The Delmores are worth hearing if only for their "Blues Stay Away from Me," a classic that hit the Top Ten in 1949. The harmonies are achingly pure and intense. — D.M.

MAX DEMIAN
★ ★ ★ Call of the Wild / RCA (1978) ¶
Wacky science fiction-cum-hard rock band from Florida led by singer/songwriter/guitarist Paul Rose. — J.S.

SANDY DENNY
★ ★ ★ The North Star Grassman and the Ravens / A&M (1971)
★ ★ ★ ★ Sandy / A&M (1972)
Sandy Denny was a member of Fairport Convention, the landmark late-Sixties British group that combined elements of traditional English music with rock instrumentations. Denny's strong singing has its roots in plainsong, and Fairport Convention's stolid, dirgelike march beat is derived from the music of the Church of England. Denny's solo al-

bums, two of which are still in print, feature members of Fairport Convention in backup roles (notably the superb guitarist Richard Thompson) and give a good account of what Denny's music is about. Each album contains a magnificent interpretation of a Bob Dylan song ("Down in the Flood" on *Grassman,* "Tomorrow Is a Long Time" on *Sandy*). *Grassman* is sparser, while *Sandy* includes intriguing horn arrangements by Allen Toussaint, one of which works a wondrous, Band-like effect in a dialogue with Thompson's guitar toward the end of "For Nobody to Hear." Denny died in 1978 after a tragic fall down a flight of stairs. — J.S.

JOHN DENVER

★ Rhymes and Reasons / RCA (1969)
★ Take Me to Tomorrow / RCA (1970)
★ ★ Poems, Prayers and Promises / RCA (1971)
★ Aerie / RCA (1971)
★ Rocky Mountain High / RCA (1972)
■ Spirit / RCA (1972)
★ ★ Greatest Hits, Vol. 1 / RCA (1973)
■ Farewell Andromeda / RCA (1973)
■ Back Home Again / RCA (1974)
★ Beginnings / Mer. (1974)
■ An Evening with John Denver / RCA (1975)
■ Windsong / RCA (1975)
■ Rocky Mountain Christmas / RCA (1975)
■ Greatest Hits, Vol. 2 / RCA (1977)
■ I Want to Live / RCA (1977)
★ Whose Garden Was This / RCA (1977)
■ John Denver / RCA (1979)
★ A Christmas Together with the Muppets / RCA (1979)
■ Autograph / RCA (1980)

John Denver was one of the many pastoral singer/songwriters who proliferated in the early Seventies in the wake of James Taylor's initial impact. His thin, whiny voice, sophomoric writing and extremely limited instrumental facility made him far from the most interesting practitioner of the style, but his tenacity paid off. He reached a sort of creative highpoint with *Poems, Prayers and Promises,* then shortly after scored massive success with the single "Rocky Mountain High," a good song that far outshines Denver himself as well as anything else he's recorded. After the single, Denver was packaged as the latest TV star commodity, doing a double bill with Frank Sinatra and generally hamming it up on and off record. If his writing and performance left much to be desired before he made it, it positively festered once he became popular enough to stop trying. And he has. — J.S.

EUMIR DEODATO

★ ★ 2001: Also Sprach Zarathustra / CTI (1972)
★ Artistry / MCA (1974)
★ In Concert / CTI (1974)
★ ★ ★ The First Cuckoo / MCA (1975)
★ Very Together / MCA (1976)
★ Love Island / War. (1978)
★ Knights of Fantasy / War. (1979)
★ Night Cruiser / War. (1980)
★ Something Special / War. (1981)

Although wholly obedient to the laws of homogeneity, arranger/keyboardist/composer Eumir Deodato has written a new chapter in the history of elevator music. His albums consist of disco-charged orchestral pop/ rock/jazz/TV theme/classical swirling. Deodato has drawn melodic structures from Ravel, Page, Marley and Mancini on which to hang striding and rather chichi production formulas.

Because they are so environmental in strategy, Deodato's records are particularly hard to distinguish one from another. His version of Richard Strauss' "Zarathustra" was a hit, but the best-defined LP is *The First Cuckoo,* which contains a pair of lesser pop successes, "Black Dog" and "Caravan/ Watusi Strut." — B.T.

DEPECHE MODE

★ ★ Speak and Spell / Sire (1982)

British band's electronic dance music is all robot-pop product. Exception is "Just Can't Get Enough," a droll, catchy single. — J.F.

DEREK AND THE DOMINOS

★ ★ ★ ★ ★ Layla / RSO (1970)

Derek and the Dominos—particularly because of the extensive participation of Duane Allman—gave Eric Clapton the context in which to demonstrate his prowess without unnecessarily calling attention to it. Clapton and Allman battled neck to neck (sometimes it's tough to figure out who is playing which guitar), and the sessions brought out the best in each player, with Clapton's rumbling leads segueing perfectly into Allman's lightning runs. The guitar call and response on "Why Does Love Got to Be So Sad?" and the molten-metal exorcism of "Layla" alone make this one of the premier guitar albums of all of rock & roll. The group (sans Allman) also made a live recording (deleted), which, while featuring some attractive, stretched-out soloing by Clapton, pales next to Siren *Layla.* — J.B.M.

RICK DERRINGER

★ ★ ★ ★ All-American Boy / Blue S. (1973)

★ Spring Fever / Blue S. (1975) ¶
★ ★ Guitars and Women / Blue S.
   (1979)
★ ★ Face to Face / Blue S. (1980)
Rick Derringer's first solo album, *All-American Boy,* released in 1973, is a fine showcase of his often-inspired guitar playing and features, besides a fine rendition of "Rock and Roll Hootchie Koo" (originally done while he was with Johnny Winter And), such straight-ahead movers as "Teenage Love Affair" and "Slide on Over Slinky" and two fine ballads, "The Airport Giveth" and "Jump, Jump, Jump." The less said about *Spring Fever,* from its androgynous cover photo on down, the better. — B.A.

DERRINGER
★ ★ ★ Derringer / Blue S. (1976)
★ ★ Sweet Evil / Blue S. (1977) ¶
★ ★ ★ Derringer Live / Blue S. (1977) ¶
★ ★ If I Weren't So Romantic, I'd Shoot
   You / Blue S. (1978)
The first band Rick Derringer has led since the demise of the McCoys at the end of the Sixties, Derringer showed fine potential on its first LP, with a twin guitar attack (newcomer Danny Johnson played second guitar), a fine rhythm section (Kenny Aronson, formerly of Dust and Stories, on bass and Vinny Appice on drums) and some tough, sturdy songs ("Beyond the Universe," "Sailor"). *Sweet Evil* and *If I Weren't So Romantic,* though, suffered from rather weak material. *Derringer Live,* a set of tracks from the first two LPs done in concert, is a fairly successful picture of a band apparently more at home in front of an audience than in a studio. — B.A.

TERI DESARIO
★ Pleasure Train / Casa. (1978)
★ Caught / Casa. (NA)
★ Moonlight Madness / Casa. (NA)
Pleasant-voiced pop-disco vocalist had 1979 smash, "Yes I'm Ready," duet with K.C. of the Sunshine Band. That made No. 2, but it's hardly anything to get excited about at this late date, especially since it didn't pan out as a career. — D.M.

MICHAEL DES BARRES
★ I'm Only Human / Dream. (1980)
Des Barres is best known for appearing in the early L.A./London power pop band Detective, signed by Jimmy Page to his Swan Song label. Unfortunately, working here with British producer Michael Chapman, Des Barres is far more Hollywood than Anglo in execution, if not aspiration. Beneath the tin-

sel, that is, there is only more tinsel, and beneath that, a hollowness to chill the soul of any listener who has one. — D.M.

JACKIE DeSHANNON
★ ★ ★ ★ New Arrangement / Col. (1975) ¶
★ ★ You're the Only Dancer / Amh. (1977)
DeShannon was something of a star during the Sixties, a gentle blond folk rocker whose authorship of songs like "When You Walk in the Room," for the Searchers, and "Don't Doubt Yourself, Babe," for the Byrds, supplanted that image with real resilience. Her own hits, all deleted (on Imperial or United Artists), included Burt Bacharach's "What the World Needs Now Is Love" and "Needles and Pins." The Columbia album is first-rate singer/songwriter stuff; DeShannon has a better voice than Joni Mitchell, at least to these ears, and she gets more distance on her material. (This album includes the original version of "Bette Davis Eyes," cowritten by DeShannon.) The Amherst album, on the other hand, is a dismal disappointment, in which DeShannon's writing and performing are both reduced to contemporary singer/songwriter clichés. — D.M.

DESTINATION
★ ★ From Beginning to End / Butter.
   (1979) ¶
Unfortunately, this disco group's most intelligent move—a cover of Smokey Robinson's "I Gotta Dance to Keep from Cryin' "—was cut before they joined up with Butterfly. You're left with dance obsessiveness, competently done but without inspiration. — D.M.

JIMMY DESTRI
★ ★ ★ Heart on a Wall / Chry. (1981)
Oddly, the shadow of Talking Heads seems to hang over this solo album from Blondie keyboardist Jimmy Destri. The opening cut, "Bad Dreams," finds Destri sounding like David Byrne in his less manic phases, while "Don't Look Around" echoes the alienated theme of the Heads' "The Big Country." Chris Stein and Debbie Harry make cameo appearances, but the LP seems to be the essence of what Destri has contributed to Blondie: a warmth and cleverness not at all inappropriate to a pop enterprise, which finally makes it hard to mistake Destri's work for the postgrad angst of the Heads to which he obviously aspires. — G.A.

JONNY DESTRY AND DESTINY
★ Girls, Rock 'n' Roll and Cars / Mil.
   (1980)
This kid plays, sings, and acts like his des-

tiny is to be a star. And that's the problem.
— R.P.

DETECTIVE
★ ★ **Detective / Swan (1977)** ¶
★ ★ **It Takes One to Know One / Swan
(1978)** ¶
Credible but uneventful late-Seventies hard
rock from a band led by ex-Yes keyboardist
Tony Kaye.   — J.S.

DETROIT EMERALDS
★ ★ ★ ★ **Feel the Need / Westb. (1977)**
★ ★ **Let's Get Together / Westb. (1978)**
The best of what Detroit soul had left after
Motown moved to L.A. in 1970 is reissued
on the 1971 LP (original title: *You Want It,
You Got It, Feel the Need*). The style is basi-
cally neoclassic soul (the Temptations and
the Four Tops are reference points), and it
produced a pair of Top Forty records in
"You Want It, You Got It" and "Do Me
Right." But the real gem here is "Feel the
Need," one of the first records "made" by
discos, which propelled the album track into
semiclassic status. *Let's Get Together* is not
up to that standard.   — D.M.

MINK DEVILLE
★ ★ ★ **Mink DeVille / Cap. (1977)**
★ ★ ★ **Return to Magenta / Cap. (1978)**
★ ★ ★ ★ **Le Chat Bleu / Cap. (1980), Fr.
imp.**
★ ★ ★ **Coup de Grace / Atl. (1981)**
Willie DeVille emerged from the same Bowery bar that produced Blondie, the Ramones,
Talking Heads and Television, but has even
less connection with any of them than they
do with each other. What he really is, is a
sort of (too?) late-Seventies Mitch Ryder,
with tripled angst. Good voice, bad attitude—the same old story, but a good one.
The down-and-out in Paris *Le Chat Bleu* is
a near masterpiece.   — D.M.

DEVO
★ ★ **Q: Are We Not Men? A: We Are Devo
/ War. (1978)**
★ **Duty Now for the Future / War. (1979)**
★ ★ **Freedom of Choice / War. (1980)**
■ **Devo Live / War. (1981) (EP)**
★ **New Traditionalists / War. (1981)**
★ **Oh No, It's Devo / War. (1982)**
Devo updates the smart-ass smarminess of
Frank Zappa for college kids, which is prob-
ably what Robert Christgau meant when he
called the group "Meat Loaf for college
kids." But Devo does not possess an instru-
mentalist of Zappa's caliber, and the result is
an ideological mediocrity, in which only the

most obvious targets are ever poked and
prodded, that corresponds to the band's
music, which manipulates the minimalist and
abstract ideas associated with new wave into
a series of complete clichés. The exception is
"Whip It," which manipulates black street
clichés, both musical and lyrical, ably
enough to have become a hit.
   Devo's most odious quality is its quasi-
libertarian rhetoric, which is used as a basis
for elitist put-downs of everything "normal"
(including its audience, but excluding itself).
The puerility of most of its ideas, founded in
an unearned contempt for mass culture,
makes it impossible to take the quasi-
totalitarian flavor of its album titles (*Duty
Now, Freedom of Choice, New Traditionalists*)
seriously, even as satire. If there is anything
frightening about Devo's social vision, it's
that so many fans are willing to scoop up
this kind of nonsense.
   The records are to be avoided by all but
the most sententious. Especially to be missed
are the band's cover versions of rock classics
("Secret Agent Man," "Satisfaction"), which
are not only badly performed but ill conceived.   — D.M.

DEXY'S MIDNIGHT RUNNERS
★ **Searching for the Young Soul Rebels /
EMI (1980)**
Well, you won't find 'em listening to this
tripe. These snotty young Brits perform like
knowing the licks is the same thing as having soul, and as if a chip on your shoulder
will pass for artistic vision. Shortly after releasing this album, the band suffered a
schism, with several Dexies splitting to form
Bureau.   — J.D.C.

JOEL DIAMOND EXPERIENCE
★ **The Joel Diamond Experience / Casa.
(NA)**
Disco producer responsible for albums by
Engelbert Humperdinck, Telly Savalas, Britt
Ekland, Helen Reddy and David Clayton-
Thomas, plies his banal trade on his own be-
half.   — J.S.

NEIL DIAMOND
★ ★ **The Feel of Neil Diamond / Bang
(1966)**
★ ★ **Just for You / Bang (1967)**
★ **Velvet Gloves and Spit / MCA (1968)**
★ **Touching You, Touching Me / MCA
(1969)**
★ ★ **Sweet Caroline / MCA (1969)**
★ ★ **Shilo / Bang (1970)**
★ ★ **Tap Root Manuscript / MCA (1970)**
★ **Neil Diamond Gold / MCA (1970)**

★ ★ **Do It / Bang (1971)**
★ **Stones / MCA (1971)**
★ ★ ★ **Hot August Night / MCA (1972)**
■ **Moods / MCA (1972)**
■ **Jonathan Livingston Seagull / Col. (1973)**
★ ★ ★ **Double Gold / Bang (1973)**
■ **Rainbow / MCA (1973)**
★ ★ ★ **His Twelve Greatest Hits / MCA (1974)**
★ **Serenade / Col. (1974)**
★ ★ **Beautiful Noise / Col. (1976)**
★ **And the Singer Sings His Song / MCA (1976)**
★ **Love at the Greek / Col. (1977)**
★ **I'm Glad You're Here with Me Tonight / Col. (1977)**
★ ★ **You Don't Bring Me Flowers / Col. (1978)**
★ **September Morn / Col. (1979)**
★ **The Jazz Singer / Cap. (1980)**
★ **Love Songs / MCA (1981)**
★ ★ **On the Way to the Sky / Col. (1981)**
★ ★ **Yesterday's Songs / Col. (1981)**

A moody singer/songwriter, blander than Dylan, darker than Bacharach. Diamond's pop hits are numerous—more than twenty singles in the Top Forty—but he has never established himself as a "serious" artist in the manner of Dylan, although that's obviously his deepest wish.

At Bang from 1966 to 1968, Diamond was produced by Jeff Barry and Ellie Greenwich, who cowrote many of the Phil Spector hits. These records have a bright freshness: "Cherry Cherry," "Thank the Lord for the Nighttime" and "Kentucky Woman" are a definition of late-Sixties pop, as is "I'm a Believer," a hit for the Monkees.

At MCA (originally with the now-defunct subsidiary Uni), Diamond worked with a variety of producers before settling in with Tom Catalano, with whom he made his biggest hits, and worst music. His basic style hardly changed. A pleasant exuberance might give way to a brooding growl, depending on the lyric, but he was always accompanied by spare, driving rhythm sections, and additional elements—choruses, horns, rarely strings—were kept to a minimum. Few of these records had the excitement of those early ones, though "Brother Love's Traveling Salvation Show" is a nice twist on the *Elmer Gantry* theme. But Diamond was writing potboilers, and his thirst was for Pulitzer-level poesy. Unfortunately, his imagination and the very blandness of his voice condemned him to setting a model for the radical-MOR singer/songwriter style of the Seventies. In this sense, he has superficially

influenced everyone from James Taylor to Jim Croce.

Double Gold is an excellent representation of the Bang days, and of Sixties pop in general. (A caution, however: in the Sixties, pop was not always coincidental with rock.) *His Twelve Greatest Hits* is a fair retrospective of the era, and the one that followed. Avoid *Neil Diamond Gold,* an execrable live album, and *Rainbow,* a pathetic attempt to interpret songs written by others. *Hot August Night* is, on the other hand, a classic live set— Diamond summoned up passion and charisma from somewhere, though for pretty hokey material.

The later MCA period was marked by an identity crisis. Like many commercially successful, artistically disdained pop singers in the rock era, Diamond longed for another kind of success. *Tap Root Manuscript,* his first attempt to break through to the realm of Dylan and Paul Simon, is almost comic—side two consists of a quasi-African "folk ballet," which sounds like ordinary AM pop extended to twenty minutes. Strangely, however, the record contains one of Diamond's biggest (and best) hits, the marvelous "Cracklin' Rosie."

At Columbia, where Diamond was given a multi-million-dollar contract, his quest for artistic credibility reached absurd heights. His tenure there began with the soundtrack to the flop movie, *Jonathan Livingston Seagull*; Diamond's music was not quite as insipid as the film and the book, which does not excuse its vapidity or its commercial success. There's nothing to justify the pretensions of his succeeding albums, either. *Serenade* takes on Longfellow and is thrown for a loss; *Beautiful Noise* was produced by Robbie Robertson of the Band, and did more to make Robertson seem a mere hired gun than to make Diamond look like an artist (and his appearance in *The Last Waltz* should have been a death knell to any such aspirations); the soundtrack to *The Jazz Singer,* a film in which Diamond starred, is mere narcissism. His only hint of pop competence in the past five years is his duet with Barbra Streisand on "You Don't Bring Me Flowers," a record that owes all of its charm to her and all of its plodding sensitivity to him, and thus serves as the most fitting epitaph of talent squandered through a lack of any sense of proportion. — D.M.

MANU DIBANGO
★ ★ ★ **Afrovision / Is. (1978) ¶**
★ **Gone Clear / Mango (1980)**
★ ★ **Ambassador / Mango (1981)**

On the Mango albums, Dibango continues his experiments in global fusion. *Gone Clear* manages to dilute ingredients of reggae, disco and Afro-funk, but *Ambassador* has a few tasty moments that suggest his goal may be within reach. — R.F.G.

HAZEL DICKENS
★ ★ ★ **Come All Ye Coal Miners / Roun. (1975)**
★ ★ ★ **Hard-Hitting Songs for Hard Hit People / Roun. (1981)**
West Virginia folksinger, best known for her appearance on the soundtrack of the award-winning documentary film *Harlan County, U.S.A.* "They'll Never Keep Us Down," which closes the film, is included on *Hard-Hitting Songs*; as these titles indicate, Dickens isn't a folk preservationist, but a contemporary activist putting her concerns into song. What makes Dickens exceptional is her gift for writing and singing melodies and lyrics that sound like they were torn from the heart of the coal country in which she was raised. These records are important both because they are political and because they are beautiful—ultimately, that is, because their political and aesthetic concerns are inseparable. — D.M.

HAZEL DICKENS AND ALICE GERRARD
★ ★ **Won't You Come and Sing for Me? / Folk. (1967)**
★ ★ ★ ★ **Hazel and Alice / Roun. (1973)**
★ ★ ★ **Hazel Dickens and Alice Gerrard / Roun. (1976)**
Hazel and Alice are two women who, in the early Sixties, formally entered the male-dominated bluegrass scene as singers, instrumentalists and, later, composers. The 1973 Rounder album is their best, encompassing a slightly broader country music range, their themes running from traditional mining songs to latter-day statements on women's consciousness. The 1967 Folkways set is more straightforwardly bluegrass/old-timey-oriented. — I.M.

TOM DICKIE AND THE DESIRES
★ ★ **Competition / Mer. (1981)**
Full-bore hard rock, with new-wave aspirations, doesn't quite make it. Dickie was an interesting occasional vocalist with his original band, Susan, but not powerful enough to carry this set on his own. The songs are well written but their arrangements lack imagination: everything is simply hammered out. Still, if you like it raw . . . — D.M.

THE DICKIES
★ ★ **Dawn of the Dickies / A&M (1979)**
★ ★ **Incredible Shrinking Dickies / A&M (1979)**
One of the best of the L.A. new-wave bands, the Dickies took nothing, including themselves, seriously, covering Black Sabbath's "Paranoid" at 78 rpm among other moves, and attracted the keen attention of none other than the cultural sanitation man *par extraordinaire* Richard Meltzer, who contributed a pseudonymous biography entitled "A Sworn Testimonial to the Dickies" that is more interesting to read than the band is to listen to. 'Nuff said. — J.S.

LITTLE JIMMY DICKINS
★ ★ **Music to Park By / Power (NA)**
★ ★ **Picks on Big Johnny Cash / Plant. (NA)**
★ ★ ★ **The Best of the Best of Jimmy Dickins / Gusto (NA)**
Great novelty country songwriter best known for his version of the surrealist anthem, "May the Bird of Paradise Fly up Your Nose." — J.S.

BARBARA DICKSON
★ **The Barbara Dickson Album / Col. (1980)**
★ **Morning Comes Quickly / RSO (1981)**
British glitz/pop singer sports new-wave fashion (skinny ties, black shirt, baggy white overcoat), but poses as if she were in a bathing suit or evening gown. Sings that way, too. — J.S.

THE DICTATORS
■ **The Dictators Go Girl Crazy / Epic (1975)** ¶
■ **Manifest Destiny / Asy. (1977)**
■ **Bloodbrothers / Asy. (1978)**
A new low—rock songs about wrestling and contempt, not just for the music and the audience, but even for themselves. Witlessly performed. — D.M.

BO DIDDLEY
★ **Bo Diddley / Chess (1962)** ¶
★ ★ ★ ★ **Bo Diddley—Sixteen All Time Greatest Hits / Check. (1967)** ¶
★ ★ ★ ★ **Got My Own Bag of Tricks / Chess (1971)** ¶
Bo Diddley was one of the great fathers of rock & roll, ranking with such transitional blues artists as Fats Domino and Chuck Berry in both importance and influence. His most important songs included "I'm a Man/Bo Diddley," "Who Do You Love," "Mona" and "Road Runner"; these were among the building blocks of the English rock of the next decade, both in their eccen-

tric rhythmic sense and in their often bizarre sense of humor. (One English blues group, the Pretty Things, went so far as to name themselves after one of his songs.)

Diddley (born Ellis McDaniel) was raised in the Mississippi delta tradition, steeped in both blues and church music, but found his real place in Chicago, where he moved as a child. By 1955 he was ready to record for Chess, and his first record, "I'm a Man/Bo Diddley," became one of that year's major R&B hits, although it did not dent the pop charts. The biggest pop hit he ever had was "Say Man," which made the Top Twenty in 1959. No other Diddley single (there were dozens, many of them masterful) cracked the Top Fifty.

A great deal of this was due to his sensibility, based on outrage at a time when the vogue was relative conformity. If Chuck Berry had a vision of America as a comic-book paradise, Diddley—his nearest competitor at Chess—countered it with a view of all of life, but particularly sex, as a profound cosmic joke, played out at the expense of everyone, but particularly the solemn and pompous. So he wisecracked and cackled his way through songs with themes that bordered on the absurd: a botched stickup in "Cops & Robbers," and a series of crazed, sometimes demonic, love affairs, culminating in "Who Do You Love," the outlandish Willie Dixon song.

The music set it all up perfectly. The rhythmic attack was less sharp and direct than most other rock & roll and R&B of the era, but Diddley's strange beat—the Bo Beat, it was termed, though you know it as "Shave and a haircut/Two bits" electronified—made physical drive irrelevant, not that it couldn't be called upon when needed. A constant feature, in addition to Diddley's whipping guitar, was a pair of jiggling maracas, played by bassist Jerome Green, who was also a frequent verbal sparring partner ("Bring It to Jerome," "Say Man," "Hey Bo Diddley"). But as much as anything else, Bo's singing told the story. Cracking up, biting, sarcastic, jive and angry by turns, that voice often seemed to be putting on everything in the world, including itself.

Without Bo's beat, it is impossible to imagine the Rolling Stones, the Yardbirds or the Animals (whose "Story of Bo Diddley" is a perfect nutshell tribute to the man and a great history of the music). The best of it is contained on *Got My Own Bag of Tricks,* which includes all the familiar tunes from *16 Greatest Hits,* plus such rarities as "Cops and Robbers" and the hilarious "Bo Diddley

Is Loose." The other two records are, unfortunately, of more recent vintage. The early LPs (at least a dozen) can still sometimes be found as cutouts: especially recommended are *Go Bo Diddley, Bo Diddley Is a Gunslinger,* either of the records titled *Bo Diddley* on Checker (*not* the Chess above) and *Have Guitar Will Travel.* The titles say it all. — D.M.

DIESEL
★ **Watts in a Tank / Regency (1981)**
Includes their hit "Sausalito Summernight," but Watts the difference? — D.G.

CHERYL DILCHER
★ **Blue Sailors / BTF (NA)**
A leggy but terminally lame female singer from Allentown, Pennsylvania, Dilcher graduated from the New York coffeehouse circuit to the slick world of L.A. productions. Maybe she should have tried movies. — J.S.

DOUG DILLARD
★ ★ **Douglas Flint Dillard / You Don't Need a Reason to Sing / 20th Cent. (1974) ¶**
★ ★ ★ **Heaven / Fly. Fish (1979)**
★ ★ ★ **Jackrabbit / Fly. Fish (NA)**
Doug Dillard is the eldest of the brothers who made up the bluegrass/rock Dillards. On the Twentieth Century LP, he's stuck in a production mold more suitable to James Taylor (whom his voice vaguely resembles) than himself. The Flying Fish albums hew closer to the folkie outlines of Dillard's skills, but Dillard may be heard to much better advantage on recordings by the group. — D.M.

DILLARD AND CLARK
★ ★ ★ ★ **The Fantastic Expedition of Dillard and Clark / A&M (1968) ¶**
★ ★ ★ **Through the Morning through the Night / A&M (1969)**
Teamed with bluegrass banjo picker and harmonizer Doug Dillard and a group of musicians drawn from the best of the Sixties folk/country/rock circle for these two albums, Gene Clark is at his best since his days with the early Byrds. These records—especially *Fantastic Expedition*—successfully combine Dillard's iconoclastic bluegrass sensibilities with Clark's wonderfully warm singing. The Dillard and Clark albums rank with the Byrds' *Sweetheart of the Rodeo* and the first two Flying Burrito Brothers records as country-rock pioneers that still sound better than almost anything that's followed them. — S.M.

THE DILLARDS
★ ★ ★ **Back Porch Bluegrass** / Elek. (1963)
★ ★ ★ **Live . . . Almost!** / Elek. (1964)
★ ★ ★ **Pickin' and Fiddlin'** / Elek. (1965)
★ ★ ★ **Copperfields** / Elek. (1970)
★ ★ **Roots and Branches** / Anth. (1972) ¶
★ ★ ★ **Tribute to the American Duck** /
    Poppy (1973) ¶
★ ★ ★ **Glitter Grass from the Nashwood**
    Hollyville Strings / Fly. Fish (1977)
★ ★ ★ **The Dillards vs. the Incredible Flying**
    L.A. Time Machine / Fly. Fish (1977)
★ ★ **Decade Waltz** / Fly. Fish (1979)
★ ★ ★ **Homecoming and Family Reunion** /
    Fly. Fish (1981)
The Dillards hold a unique position in the
genealogy of West Coast folk rock. Unlike
the young folksingers who turned to rock because it was more familiar turf, the Dillards
were dyed-in-the-wool country musicians
from Missouri who met rock on their own
terms and took only what they wanted from
it. Originally made up of Douglas Dillard on
banjo, Rodney Dillard on guitar, banjo and
dobro, Dean Webb on mandolin and Mitch
Jayne on bass, the Dillards were a souped-up
bluegrass band featuring Doug as the fast-
fingers virtuoso, and they charged their vibrant live performances with a healthy dose
of corn-pone yokel humor.

In 1963, while shopping around for a foothold in the booming folk scene, they were
outcasts from both mainstream factions.
Their country irreverence irritated the puritanical folk traditionalists and the serious social protest singers, yet their act was too
"cracker" for the folk entertainers.

So the band was forced to find its own
level, which it did brilliantly. The Elektra albums are lively and enjoyable sets that have
held up. After *Back Porch Bluegrass,* their
straightforward introductory album (which
included a version of "Duelin' Banjos" a decade too early for *Deliverance*), the Dillards
let it all hang out with a live recording, *Live
. . . Almost!,* which showed them at their
zaniest, cracking slick jokes and poking fun
at Joan Baez (practically heresy at the time)
between greased-lightning cutting matches
and pristine country harmony vocals. They
even included a version of Dylan's "Walkin'
down the Line."

When the folk-rock style surfaced in 1965,
the Dillards were midwife to its vocal arrangements. Rodney Dillard had been thinking of recording Beatles songs and was already arranging Dylan material for the band.
The Byrds were well aware of the Dillards,
and even toured with them in 1965. Rodney
and Mitch helped out on the vocal arrange-

ments for the Byrds' demo, and Dean sang
with Roger McGuinn on the "Mr. Tambourine Man" demo. The close relationship enjoyed by the early folk-rock bands with the
comparatively veteran Dillards didn't end
there. Drummer Dewey Martin went from
working with the Dillards to completing the
original Buffalo Springfield lineup.

After the third album, *Pickin' and Fiddlin',* recorded with fiddler Byron Berline,
Doug left the band to hook up with the
Byrds' Gene Clark. Ironically, the Dillards
went on to make their most durable recording; *Wheatstraw Suite,* a now-deleted 1968
classic (Elektra), introduced Doug's replacement on banjo, Herb Pederson, and added a
couple of drummers, an electric bass and a
pedal steel guitar to their traditional instrumentation. The record is a brilliant rush of
fierce playing and beautifully precise vocal
harmonies with several excellent originals
("Nobody Knows," "Listen to the Sound")
and covers of the Beatles' "I've Just Seen a
Face" and Tim Hardin's "Reason to Believe." The next album, *Copperfields,* moved
further away from the traditional roots and
included covers of "Yesterday" and Eric Andersen's "Close the Door Lightly."

On *Roots and Branches,* Billy Ray Latham
replaced Pederson and the band moved more
completely into country-rock style, recording
Shel Silverstein's "Last Morning" and the
energetic "Get Out on the Road." The following year's *Tribute to the American Duck*
continued to mix rock and country material
and featured the rousing spiritual "You've
Gotta Be Strong." *Family Reunion* is just
that, an excellent live collection recorded in
1979. — J.S.

DILLINGER
★ ★ **C.B. 200** / Mango (1976)
★ ★ **Bionic Dread** / Mango (1977)
★ ★ **Babylon Fever** / U.A. (NA) ¶
Middling reggae group, which is not terribly
clever vocally or instrumentally. Regarded as
one of the giants of dub. — D.M.

THE DILLMAN BAND
★ **Lovin' the Night Away** / RCA (1981)
Title track, group's bid for hit single (apparently), sounds kind of like the Eagles singing
the *Saturday Night Live* theme song. Despite
production by Muscle Shoals honcho Rick
Hall, that's about the highlight. — D.M.

THE DINGOES
★ ★ ★ ★ **The Dingoes** / Mush. (1974), Aust.
imp.
★ ★ ★ **Five Times the Sun** / A&M (1977) ¶

★ ★ **Orphans of the Storm / Fest. (1978), Aust. imp.**

Encompassing both toughness and lyricism gave the Dingoes their almost legendary status in Australian rock. With the eclecticism of the best Australian music, they created an original fusion of R&B, country and rock, and gave it a distinctively local flavor.

Singer Broderick Smith shifts easily from blues shouting to ballads, and Kerryn Tolhurst's mandolin provides a sweet counterpoint to Chris Stockley's more abrasive guitar. On songs like Tolhurst's "Goin' Down Again" and "The Last Place I Wanna Be" from *The Dingoes,* their first album, the band is totally assured and passionate without ever losing the delicacy of its quieter moments. And in "Payday Again" and "Way Out West" there are traces of the Australian folk tradition that seem perfectly comfortable in this relatively unexpected setting.

The Dingoes recorded output is a sadly limited testimonial—a few tracks on the compilation *Live at the Station* (recently re-released on Missing Link records), the wonderful Australian debut, and the disappointingly anonymous U.S. release *Five Times the Sun,* which despite input from the Band's Garth Hudson only occasionally rises above mediocrity. The Dingoes split in 1978. Among the band's offshoots is Broderick Smith's Big Combo, a band with a sizable Australian following and an excellent 1981 album. — S.M.

MICHAEL DINNER
★ **The Great Pretender / Fan. (1974)**
★ ★ **Tom Thumb the Dreamer / Fan. (NA) ¶**

Dinner's albums are polished products full of sweet harmony and tasteful guitar, but no amount of studio pizzazz can pump life into his relentlessly predictable tunes. At best, the four-part harmony and intermittent reggae beat of *Tom Thumb the Dreamer* provide some diversion. With his twang, his finger-picking and his smug, earnest lyrics, Dinner is reminiscent of Don McLean. His mood is less sunny: he sees himself as a victim of women and includes a variety of social outcasts in his songs. But Dinner's visions, like his melodies, are secondhand. — A.S.

DION
★ ★ ★ **Dion Sings the 15 Million Sellers / Laur. (1966)**
★ ★ ★ **Sixty Greatest of Dion and the Belmonts / Laur. (1971) ¶**

★ ★ ★ ★ **Dion's Greatest Hits / Col. (1973)**
★ ★ ★ ★ ★ **Everything You Always Wanted to Hear by Dion and the Belmonts / Laur. (1973)**
★ ★ **Streetheart / War. (1976) ¶**
★ ★ ★ **Return of the Wanderer / Lifes. (1978) ¶**
★ ★ **Ruby Baby / Col. (1978)**
★ ★ **Donna the Prima Donna / Col. (1979)**
★ ★ ★ **Dion / Laur. (NA)**
★ ★ ★ **More of Dion's Greatest Hits / Laur. (NA)**

Dion DiMucci emerged from the Bronx in 1958. At first he appeared with a vocal trio called the Belmonts; together they made some of the greatest records of their era, beginning with "I Wonder Why" and including "A Teenager in Love." On his own, Dion hit with "A Lover's Prayer," "The Wanderer," "Runaround Sue" and "Lonely Teenager," and he also made some rare but mysteriously magnificent misfires, such as "Born to Cry" and "Sandy." He even attempted to create a dance craze with "The Majestic." Often dismissed as just another pretty face, Dion was much more accomplished than that. He was heavily influenced by Bobby Darin and black vocal groups, and only the nasality of his early records places him in the Fabian/Frankie Avalon league. In fact he belongs with Darin as one of the first white R&B singers—smooth, cool, but committed.

Good selections of his greatest hits can be found on the Columbia LP and the Laurie *Everything* package. *Sixty Greatest* is more than anyone but the most rabid fan wants to hear.

After a nasty bout with heroin, Dion re-emerged in 1968 as a kind of folk-rock singer/songwriter. He scored an immediate hit with the haunting "Abraham, Martin and John," perhaps the best, and certainly the best-received, protest song of all. The *Abraham* LP revealed enormous artistic growth, particularly a fascination with Robert Johnson–styled country blues; it is deleted but definitely worth seeking out. He signed with Warner Bros. in 1969 and cut a terrific first album, featuring the antidrug classic "Clean Up Your Own Back Yard," but he was soon trapped in the company's pop-rock production mill. *Streetheart,* released in 1976, was meant to reestablish him as a writer and performer of importance. But hack production and arrangements buried several good songs, particularly the title track (inspired by the Richard Price novel *The Wanderers,* which had in turn been inspired by his earlier hit) and "Queen of '59." Yet Dion remains one of the great underdeveloped talents in rock history. A third comeback would not be at all surprising, though, especially given the pleasures of the 1978 Lifesong LP, which includes the haunting "I Used to Be a Brooklyn Dodger." — D.M.

DIRE STRAITS
★ ★ ★ ★ **Dire Straits / War. (1978)**
★ ★ **Communique / War. (1979)**
★ ★ ★ **Making Movies / War. (1980)**
This monochromatic British blues group became one of the most celebrated bands of the late Seventies merely for championing Sixties musical values at a time when rock was in the violent throes of self-analysis. Group leader Mark Knopfler is a poor singer, an adequate guitarist out of the Peter Green/Eric Clapton school of British blues players, and a powerful songwriter. The stark, romantic visions expressed in songs like "Water of Love" and "Down Along the Waterline" contrast eerily with songs of bitterness and persecution like "In the Gallery" and the hit "Sultans of Swing." Knopfler is probably too bitter for his own good, but he's calculating enough to understand the key to Fleetwood Mac's lifelong success— their supple and driving rhythm section. "Sultans" made it on that same rhythmic solidity. *Communique* was a dead-sounding followup, but on *Making Movies* Knopfler recaptured some of his songwriting prowess with "Tunnel of Love" and "Romeo and Juliet." — J.S.

DIRTY ANGELS
★ ★ **Kiss Tomorrow Goodbye / Priv. (1977)**
★ ★ **Dirty Angels / A&M (1978)**
Despite production by the new-wave-associated Richard Gottehrer (*Blondie*), this is just more of the thump of standard American dumbbell hard rock. — D.M.

DIRTY LOOKS
★ ★ **Dirty Looks / Stiff (1980)**
★ ★ **Turn It Up / Stiff (1981), Br. imp.**
Staten Island new-wave band with a tight, aggressive sound but unimpressive material. Bassist Marco Sin is worth the price of admission. — J.S.

DIRTY TRICKS
★ ★ **Night Man / Poly. (1976)**
★ ★ **Hit and Run / Poly. (1977)**
Typically rudimentary British hard-rock band relied on fuzzy-toned guitars, hoarse blues-based vocals and production by Tony

Visconti. If that makes you curious, though, you probably already own a half-dozen records of this quality or better. — D.M.

DIXIE DREGS
★ ★ ★ **Free Fall / Capri. (1977)**
★ ★ ★ **What If / Capri. (1978)**
★ ★ ★ **Night of the Living Dregs / Capri. (1979)**
★ ★ ★ **Dregs of the Earth / Ari. (1980)**
Experimental Southern rock group noted for its virtuosic instrumental technique and its debt to the Mahavishnu Orchestra and Jeff Beck. — J.S.

DIXIE HUMMINGBIRDS
★ ★ ★ ★ ★ **The Best of the Dixie Hummingbirds / Pea. (NA)**
★ ★ ★ **A Christian Testimonial / Pea. (NA)**
★ ★ ★ **Everyday Every Hour / Pea. (NA)**
★ ★ ★ **The Gentlemen of Song / Pea. (NA)**
★ ★ ★ ★ **In the Morning / Pea. (NA)**
★ ★ ★ **Prayer for Peace / Pea. (NA)**
★ ★ ★ **Your Good Deeds / Pea. (NA)**
Long before Paul Simon introduced them to a pop audience via "Loves Me Like a Rock," the Hummingbirds were well known on the black gospel circuit as one of the best groups, if not *the* best. Gospel's vocabulary may be limited in words *and* music, but no group exploited it more fully than the 'Birds. Ira Tucker's lead vocals define the gospel style, and coleader James Walker is almost his equal. (Tucker's influence is apparent in such soul singers as Jackie Wilson, and he's coached Bobby Bland, too.) The other 'Birds (baritone James Kavis, tenor Beachey Thompson, bass William Bobo) provide fine support, while guitarist Howard Carroll is the most bracing in the field.

The 'Birds came along just as the jubilee singing style, with its blue notes and emphasis on close harmonies, was fading. As prime exponents of the modern quartet style, with its bent notes, moaning and more frenetic vocals, they were a major influence on soul music—especially Tucker, who is also a top songwriter with a flair for novelty songs ("Christian Automobile," covered by the Persuasions, and "Let's Go Out to the Programs," for example).

Christian Testimonial is a good enough introduction to their style. All emphasis is on vocals, though Carroll slips easily into jazzy guitar modes. The 'Birds are fairly rural-sounding, and the instruments are recorded poorly enough that the singing might as well be a cappella. The piano is heard almost subliminally, as it is on most of the group's early recordings. But *In the Morning,* which appropriately begins with the title song and ends with "This Evening," is the 'Birds at their absolute peak. The scatting lead on "In the Morning" is only one of several outstanding vocal efforts ("Bedside of a Neighbor," the moaning "This Evening" and the heavily syncopated "Jesus Walked the Water" are others). Also of special interest are "My Prayer," with its preaching vocal and orchestral arrangement, and "Let the Holy Ghost Fall on Me," which has the feel of a rock ballad. The rest of the 'Birds prepop albums follow the mode of these two, and show an enviable consistency in quality. *Best of* is just what it says; this is one of the most essential gospel albums in print.

★ ★ ★ **Live / Pea. (NA)**
★ ★ **Thanks to Thee / Pea. (NA)**
★ ★ ★ **We Love You Like a Rock / Pea. (NA)**
★ ★ **Wonderful to Be Alive / Pea. (NA)**

Like a Rock is their first excursion into secular material and styles. It contains the Simon song and Stevie Wonder's "Jesus Children of America," on which Stevie plays; there's still straight gospel material here, though the secular songs are quite good. Instrumentation runs from tuba to synthesizer, and one song even has a quasi-reggae beat. Other excursions into alien modes aren't quite as successful. The country instrumentation on *Thanks* is at first interesting (and also reaffirms the Hummingbirds' rural ties), but it's not very effective in the long run and the singing sounds like parody. *Wonderful* contains plenty of public-domain gospel material, but also a truly foolish novelty song; emphasis here is on lead singing rather than harmonies, and it sounds a bit tired. *Live,* with its mixture of previously unrecorded songs and 'Birds standards, is a slight disappointment, as the singing is a little off—age must be catching up with them—but there are some superb performances here, and it's as atmospheric as a live gospel album should be. — J.MO.

WILLIE DIXON

★ ★ **I Am the Blues / Col. (1970)**
★ ★ **Catalyst / Ova. (1973)**
★ ★ **What Happened to My Blues / Ova. (1976)** ¶
★ ★ **Willie Dixon and His Chicago Blues Band / Spivey (NA)**

Dixon is one of R&B's most important songwriters. He composed some of Bo Diddley's best songs, including "I'm a Man" as well as a number of important Muddy Waters and Howlin' Wolf numbers, such as "Hoochie Coochie Man" and "Wang Dang Doodle."

As a performer, he is definitely less interesting. — D.M.

BONNIE DOBSON

★ ★ ★ **Dear Companion / Prest. (NA)**

Dobson was one of those ethereal-voiced young women who popularized Child ballads in the early Sixties. More traditional than Judy Collins, more down to earth than the gloriously tragic Baez, Dobson never captured public imagination as firmly. Still, *Dear Companion* endures as pleasant, earnestly performed folk music. — A.S.

DR. BUZZARD'S ORIGINAL "SAVANNAH" BAND

★ ★ ★ ★ **Dr. Buzzard's Original "Savannah" Band / RCA (1976)**
★ ★ **Dr. Buzzard's Original "Savannah" Band Meets King Pennett / RCA (1978)** ¶
★ ★ **Dr. Buzzard's Original "Savannah" Band Goes to Washington / Elek. (1979)**

The most popular disco album of 1976, *"Savannah"* introduced a fresh approach to the idiom by reprising Big Band and earlier R&B in a sassy, arch Kurt Weill-influenced style. It contains the disco classics "I'll Play the Fool" and "Cherchez la Femme." But *King Pennett* and *Goes to Washington* show much less flair. — S.H.

DR. FEELGOOD

★ ★ **Malpractice / Col. (1976)** ¶
★ ★ **Sneakin' Suspicion / Col. (1977)** ¶

Simple to an extreme, these Britons emulate but fail to match the early R&B-influenced exploits of groups like the Rolling Stones. Their LPs sound like sparse backing for a lead musician who never appears. — C.W.

DR. HOOK

★ **Dr. Hook and the Medicine Show / Col. (1972)**
★ **Sloppy Seconds / Col. (1972)**
★ **Belly Up! / Col. (1973)**
★ ★ **Bankrupt / Cap. (1975)**
★ **A Little Bit More / Cap. (1976)**
★ **Dr. Hook and the Medicine Show Revisited / Col. (1976)**

Hook's oeuvre is dominated by the songwriting of nonmember Shel Silverstein: cutsey, mannered crypto-country rock. The band itself is competent in a spunky bar-band way, and *Bankrupt* is its best because it contains the most non-Silverstein material. The group seems to pride itself on being vulgar, but it works against the music. *Revisited* is an all-Silverstein best-of package, and Dr. Hook's worst. — K.T.

DR. JOHN

★ ★ ★ ★ ★ **Gris-Gris** / Atco (1968) ¶
★ ★ ★ ★ ★ **Gumbo** / Atco (1972) ¶
★ ★ ★ **In the Right Place** / Atco (1973) ¶
★ ★ ★ **City Lights** / Hori. (1979)
★ ★ ★ **Tango Palace** / Hori. (1979)
★ ★ ★ ★ **Dr. John Plays Mac Rebennack** /
  Clean Cuts (1981)
■ **Dr. John** / Trip (NA) ¶
★ **Dr. John** / Sp.
  (NA) ¶
★ ★ **Sixteen Greatest Hits** / Trip (NA) ¶
After a healthy and respected career as a
songwriter/arranger/pianist in New Orleans
in the early Sixties, Mac Rebennack burst on
the scene as a solo artist under the alias of
Dr. John Creaux, the Night Tripper. *Gris-
Gris,* his first album, features most of his fel-
low Bayou associates, albeit under voodoo-
ized masks: Jesse Hill is Dr. Poo Pah Doo
of destine tambourine and Harold Battiste is
Dr. Battiste of Scorpio of bass clef. The entire crew is "dregged up from . . . under the
eight visions of Professor Longhair rein-
canted in the charts of now." The record is
a wild celebration of New Orleans' Magnolia
Street mayhem, with such charmers as "I
Walk on Gilded Splinters," "Gris Gris
Gumbo Ya Ya" and "Croker Courtbouil-
lion," and was easily one of the most bizarre
LPs of the late Sixties, which is saying a
lot

The good Doctor's next few releases, however, did not match the spontaneity or excitement of *Gris-Gris. Remedies* (now deleted) includes a full-sided "Angola Anthem"
which is unfocused and seemingly endless;
The Sun, Moon & Herbs (now deleted), recorded in England with a host of guest stars
(Eric Clapton, Mick Jagger), is also disappointing. With *Gumbo,* though, all is forgiv-
en. Rebennack's piano playing, far too understated on previous albums, becomes the
focal point as he pays tribute to Huey Smith,
"Sugarboy" Crawford, Longhair and the entire New Orleans R&B sound through versions of its classic songs. This impeccable
strutting tour of New Orleans music features, besides Rebennack's impeccable piano
playing and his best recorded vocals, marvelous horn arrangements from Battiste. *In the
Right Place* is a record that on paper looked
great—Dr. John hooked up with Allen Toussaint as producer and the Meters as backing
musicians. But aside from the title track, Dr.
Johns's only big hit single, it's a failure:
much too slick and exacting. *Sixteen Greatest Hits* is certainly not that; it's a jumble of
demos from Rebennack's earlier years, some
sung by him and others by unidentified artists. This is for diehards only. *Dr. John Plays
Mac Rebennack* is an excellent record of
piano solos. — B.A.

DOCTORS OF MADNESS

★ ★ ★ **Late Night Movies, All Night
  Brainstorms** / Poly. (1976), Br. imp.
★ ★ ★ **Figments of Emancipation** / Poly.
  (1976), Br. imp.
★ ★ ★ **Sons of Survival** / Poly. (1978), Br.
  imp.
A bizarre British quartet given a big launch
by music and fashion bigwigs in 1976, the
Doctors of Madness were doomed from the
start due to their unfortunate timing. Just as
safety-pinned simplicity and straightforward-
ness were becoming the style, the Doctors
were suitably rebellious, but elitist and too
pretentious to be appealing. By the time
pomposity and style came back into vogue,
the Doctors had finally folded. Removed
from the times, their three LPs are powerful
and original, fueled by the arty songs of
"Kid Strange" and lead violin provided by
"Urban Blitz." The first two albums were released as a double package in America, but
that has been deleted. — I.R.

DR. STRUT

★ ★ **Dr. Strut** / Mo. (1979)
★ ★ **Struttin'** / Mo. (1980)
Passable funk 'n' fusion quintet. — J.S.

THE DODGERS

★ ★ **Love on the Rebound** / Poly. (1978)
Two former members of Badfinger formed
this band in 1976; one of them left in 1977.
This album of slick pop-rock vocals was issued in 1978. — I.R.

FATS DOMINO

★ ★ ★ ★ ★ **This Is Fats Domino!** / Imper.
  (1956), Fr. imp.
★ ★ ★ ★ **Let's Play Fats Domino** / Imper./
  U.A. (1959)
★ ★ ★ ★ **Cooking with Fats** / Lib. (1966)
★ ★ ★ ★ **Rare Dominoes, Vol. 1** / Imper./
  U.A. (NA), Fr. imp.
★ ★ ★ ★ **Rare Dominoes, Vol. 2** / Imper./
  U.A. (NA), Fr. imp.
★ ★ ★ ★ ★ **Fats Domino—Legendary Master
  Series** / U.A. (1972)
★ ★ ★ ★ **Play It Again Fats** / U.A. (1973),
  Br. imp.
★ ★ ★ ★ **Fats Domino Live at Montreux** /
  Atl. (1974), Br. imp.
★ ★ ★ ★ **Twenty Greatest Hits** / U.A.
  (1976), Br. imp.
★ ★ ★ ★ **The Fats Domino Story, Vol. 1** /
  U.A. (1977), Br. imp.

★ ★ ★ ★ **The Fats Domino Story, Vol. 2 /**
U.A. (1977), Br. imp.

★ ★ ★ ★ **The Fats Domino Story, Vol. 3 /**
U.A. (1977), Br. imp.

★ ★ ★ ★ **The Fats Domino Story, Vol. 4 /**
U.A. (1977), Br. imp.

★ ★ ★ **The Fats Domino Story, Vol. 5 /**
U.A. (1977), Br. imp.

★ ★ ★ **The Fats Domino Story, Vol. 6 /**
U.A. (1977), Br. imp.

★ ★ ★ **The Best American Music / ABC**
(NA), Fr. imp.

★ ★ ★ ★ ★ **Cooking with Fats / Imper.**
(NA), Fr. imp.

★ ★ ★ ★ **The Fabulous Mr. D. / Lib. (NA),**
Fr. imp.

★ ★ ★ ★ ★ **The Fabulous Mr. D. / Imper.**
(NA), Fr. imp.

★ ★ ★ **Fats Domino / Ev. (NA)**

★ ★ ★ **Fats Domino, Vol. 2 / Ev. (NA)**

★ ★ ★ **Fats Domino in Concert / Mer. (NA),**
Fr. imp.

★ ★ ★ **Fats Domino Live in Europe / U.A.**
(NA), Br. imp.

★ ★ ★ ★ ★ **Let's Dance with Domino /**
Imper. (NA), Fr. imp.

★ ★ ★ ★ ★ **Let's Play Domino / Imper.**
(NA), Fr. imp.

★ ★ **My Blue Heaven / Pick. (NA)**

★ ★ ★ ★ ★ **Rock and Rollin' / Imper. (NA),**
Belg. imp.

★ ★ ★ ★ ★ **Rock and Rollin' with Fats**
Domino / Imper. (NA), Fr. imp.

★ ★ ★ **Star Collection / WEA (NA), Ger.**
imp.

★ ★ ★ ★ **Two Sensational Albums / Pick.**
(NA), Br. imp.

Fats Domino is more than just one of the
names evoked when rock's Founding Fathers
are discussed. Domino is the renaissance
man among them—if not the Jefferson, at
least the Franklin of the bunch—able to do
what he does so well that he has been doing
it, consistently and nearly effortlessly, for
more than three decades. A great singer, an
absolutely enthralling pianist, a witty composer and a fine bandleader, it does him no
disservice to say that Domino's records are
often nearly indistinguishable: what is meant
is that they are *so* seamless that there are
few bad ones to eliminate.

Domino's hits—"My Girl Josephine,"
"Ain't That a Shame," "Blueberry Hill,"
"Let the Four Winds Blow," "I'm Ready,"
"The Fat Man," "Please Don't Leave Me,"
"Blue Monday," "When My Dreamboat
Comes Home" and many dozens more—are
beautiful, intensely rhythmic, humorous and
the essence of rock & roll, New Orleans divi-

sion. They have influenced almost everybody
worth talking about (Van Morrison so much
so that Van's best songs sometimes seem like
love letters to Fats). And of course there is
only one decent American sampler of his
music—*Legendary Masters*—while in Europe
almost everything he has recorded is obtain-
able.

In 1981, American Liberty reissued a
number of Fats' original albums, with their
old covers but with two songs per disc deleted; all these records are invaluable, and none
of them is less than terrific. Even though the
omissions from the American Liberty albums
aren't major, the imports are pristine and
well worth the extra dough, since they're
pressed more carefully than U.S. budget
discs.

The six-volume British *Fats Domino Story*
chronicles his career at Imperial Records
from 1949 to 1962 in basically two-year
chunks (Volumes 1 and 2 may now be out of
print). Because it is organized chronologically it may be a more coherent way to
catch up to his music (though it's not necessarily more fun than stumbling across the
delights of *Cooking with Fats*). *Rare Dominoes* collect some material from the Imperial
period that slipped through the cracks in
Britain, proving primarily that, discographi-
cally, Germans are more obsessive than Englishmen, and that Fats remains Fats even on
the slightest songs, no mean achievement.

The Everest, Pickwick (domestic) and remaining U.A. albums are primarily anthologies of Imperial material. The ABC set collects material from the early Sixties, right
after Fats finally left Imperial—it is very
fine. So is the Mercury *Concert* LP, surprisingly enough (since it was recorded in New
York and Las Vegas, not exactly hot spots
for this sort of music). *Star Collection* reissues his very fine Richard Perry–produced
album of the late Sixties, which produced a
final, minor hit in "Lady Madonna." The
imported Pickwick set, *Two Sensational Albums,* is the Mercury live set coupled with
some ABC material. Finally, *Fats Domino
Live at Montreux* captures him at the blues
and jazz festival in the mid-Seventies, still
playing his heart out. A genuine American
musical genius. — D.M.

THE DOMINOES

★ ★ ★ ★ **Billy Ward and the Dominoes**
Sixteen Greatest Hits / King (NA)

★ ★ ★ ★ **The Dominoes (Featuring Jackie**
Wilson), Vol. 3 / King (1977)

★ ★ ★ ★ **The Dominoes, Vol. 4 / King**
(1977)

Assembled by New York singing coach and composer Billy Ward from among his students, the Dominoes were one of the seminal gospel-to-R&B groups of the early Fifties. Best known for "Sixty Minute Man" and beginning the career of Clyde McPhatter ("Have Mercy Baby"), the Dominoes ranged much further from conventional pop than such established black harmony groups of the time as the Platters and the Ink Spots, adding both sacred ecstasies and street-level raunch to their blend. In addition to McPhatter, the Dominoes also gave Jackie Wilson his start, though the material he did with that group is less important than the McPhatter-led group's. — D.M.

DON AND DEWEY
★ ★ ★ Don and Dewey / Spec. (NA)

Fifties R&B. Don is "Sugarcane" Harris, who in the Sixties joined up with John Mayall for a brief spell, and Dewey is Dewey Terry, who handled most of the lead vocals. Their style was more lighthearted than raucous, more novelty than straightforward. The duo is a footnote in R&B history—and a thoroughly enjoyable one. This contains their essential hits. — K.R.

DONOVAN
★ ★ ★ Sunshine Superman / Epic (1966)
★ ★ ★ A Gift from a Flower to a Garden / Epic (1968)
★ ★ ★ ★ Donovan in Concert / Epic (1968)
★ ★ ★ Hurdy Gurdy Man / Epic (1968)
★ ★ ★ Barabajagal / Epic (1969)
★ ★ ★ ★ Donovan's Greatest Hits / Epic (1969)
★ Essence to Essence / Epic (1974)
★ ★ Seven Tease / Epic (1974) ¶
★ ★ Slow Down World / Epic (1976) ¶
★ Donovan / Ari. (1977)

Listening to Donovan's albums is like being consigned to relive the most insipid parts of the Sixties. But although the medieval-minstrel-flower-power-spiritual conceits have worn thin, Donovan's music from that era sounds remarkably pleasant, at least as background. So pleasant in fact that viewed from a jaded Seventies' perspective, it makes all the pretentious folderol charming.

Except for *Sunshine Superman,* the albums with a three-star rating are from Donovan's late-Sixties period of fancy bathrobes and peacock feathers. They each contain one or two memorable songs, but are worth the purchase only for aging nostalgics or students of cultural history (the latter will find them especially interesting as a type of laid-back music that didn't come from Los Angeles).

Greatest Hits and *Concert* are rated more highly because they have a higher concentration of hits. Even so, unless "Sunshine Superman" or "Mellow Yellow" are particularly important to you, you can easily get along without them. Unfortunately, Donovan's pre-electric, Dylan-influenced material ("Universal Soldier") is not available on LP in the U.S. Pye has a selection of that material, however, in its Golden Hour series, which is easily spotted in import bins.

The rest of the LPs are from Donovan's various comebacks in the Seventies. Oddly, most of them sound cynical; it's interesting that the Great Innocent may have turned sour, but so far it hasn't made for very interesting music. *Mellow Yellow,* Donovan's best Sixties album, is worth seeking out as a cut-out—it was recorded just at the moment when folkies were all smoking pot and just going electric and when the economy of England was still in good shape. That is, before Donovan was either innocent or cynical, and after he was political. — T.S.

THE DOOBIE BROTHERS
★ ★ The Doobie Brothers / War. (1971)
★ ★ ★ Toulouse Street / War. (1973)
★ ★ ★ The Captain and Me / War. (1973)
★ ★ What Were Once Vices Now Are Habits / War. (1974)
★ ★ ★ Stampede / War. (1975)
★ ★ ★ Takin' It to the Streets / War. (1976)
★ ★ ★ ★ Best of the Doobies / War. (1976)
★ ★ ★ Livin' on the Fault Line / War. (1977)
★ ★ ★ ★ Minute by Minute / War. (1978)
★ ★ One Step Closer / War. (1980)
★ ★ ★ ★ Best of the Doobies, Vol. 2 / War. (1981)

Probably no other band more perfectly epitomizes Seventies corporate rock than the Doobie Brothers, who formed in 1969 in San Jose and remained a profitable musical entity into the Eighties, despite numerous personnel changes and stylistic shifts. Originally a bikers' rock band headed by singer/guitarist Tom Johnston, percussionist John Hartman, and folksinger/songwriter Patrick Simmons, their hard-driving bluesy street rock suggested a lighter, more streamlined version of the Allman Brothers. After their first album, bassist Tiran Porter replaced Dave Shogren, and the band began working with Warner's staff producer Ted Templeman, who produced all their subsequent albums.

Toulouse Street, with its smash hit, "Listen to the Music" (written by Johnston), broke the Doobies commercially. Johnston also wrote and sang the two whooping-it-up hits from *Captain,* "China Grove" and "Long Train Runnin'." Patrick Simmons' Southern-style folk-rock song, "Black Water," highlighted *Vices.* With *Stampede,* which featured new guitarist and ex–Steely Dan member Jeff Baxter (since departed from the Doobies), they began incorporating jazz and R&B and scored with the Holland-Dozier-Holland tune, "Take Me in Your Arms (Rock Me a Little While)."

Takin' It to the Streets featured another new face in the keyboardist/vocalist/writer Michael McDonald, who joined the group around the time Tom Johnston departed. With his syncopated R&B-inflected pop tunes and rich, romantic Ray Charles–influenced vocals, McDonald quickly became the artistic focus of the group. He wrote and sang *Streets'* title song and "It Keeps You Runnin'," among other gems. But it wasn't until the runaway success of "What a Fool Believes," on *Minute* that McDonald was widely recognized as a major pop talent. As his star ascended, the contributions of the other Doobies sounded increasingly incidental. There were pressures on McDonald to go solo, and the resulting tensions showed in their music. McDonald's "Real Love" was the only first-rate song on *One Step Closer.* The second Doobies anthology is a better buy, since it contains most of McDonald's best work and less of Simmons' comparatively lightweight filler. — S.H.

THE DOORS
★ ★ ★ **The Doors** / Elek. (1967)
★ ★ **Strange Days** / Elek. (1967)
★ ★ **Waiting for the Sun** / Elek. (1968)
★ ★ **The Soft Parade** / Elek. (1969)
★ ★ ★ **Morrison Hotel** / Elek. (1970)
★ ★ **Absolutely Live** / Elek. (1970)
★ ★ **Thirteen** / Elek. (1970)
★ ★ **L.A. Woman** / Elek. (1971)
★ ★ **Weird Scenes inside the Gold Mine** / Elek. (1972)
★ ★ **Best of the Doors** / Elek. (1973) ¶
★ ★ **American Prayer** / Elek. (1978)
★ ★ ★ **The Doors Greatest Hits** / Elek. (1980)

Unlikely as it may seem, given the obnoxious and insipid cult that now surrounds Jim Morrison, he and his band did make an important contribution to the popular culture of the Sixties. While comparing the Doors to any of rock's greatest artists—from Chuck Berry and Buddy Holly to Creedence Clearwater Revival and the Clash—is clearly absurd, Morrison was in fact an important, if banal, erotic politician, adolescent eye-opener

and a genuinely dangerous teen idol. In this way, the Doors take their place in pop history as the progenitors of a whole wave of teenybopper anti-icons, the genuine precursors of Alice Cooper and Kiss.

Thus, the group's dabblings with Brechtian commentary, Artaudian reality inversions and sub-Langian psychology are perfectly appropriate expressions for an age dominated by *serious* adolescence. It should then go without saying that the Doors' best album (notwithstanding the aberration of *Morrison Hotel*) is its schematic first, which enlists Kurt Weill in pursuit of a hit single, stumbles across a tumescently pubescent classic in "Light My Fire," and concludes with the ultimate confusion of *dementia praecox* and profundity ("The End").

For the rest (again with the exception of *Morrison Hotel,* which is, even a doubter must confess, a fairly effective method of dealing with the specter of real American rock & roll that the Band and Creedence had re-created), the Doors were a singles act, more alluring (maybe) and more shrewdly marketed than Tommy James and the Shondells and the Guess Who, but not necessarily better. In fact, arguably not as good, since the band possessed a drummer too laid-back to really kick out the jams, an organist who sounded like he had been laid off from a cocktail lounge and a singer whose notion of the best way to express passion was to belch and grunt. Guitarist Robbie Krieger actually managed to get off some fairly listenable lines, but then he also wrote the band's only really humane song ("Running Blue," a tribute to Otis Redding, which is puppy-dog-charming in its clumsiness and lack of anything approaching genuine soulfulness). If Elektra ever has the courage to create a package that is nothing but singles—including stuff like "Five to One," and forgetting that "The End" ever existed except as a mistaken plunge into pomposity—the Doors might yet look like a modestly successful act. Lacking such confirmation of a limited but effective talent, we are left with the spectacle of such ephemera as *Absolutely Live,* a travesty of music and stand-up comedy, long ago eclipsed by Iggy Pop (among others) on nights when he wasn't even half trying. It hardly matters that Morrison originated the concept; others have done more with it, not that there was all that much to do with it in the first place.

Is this the most overrated group in rock history? Only a truly terminal case of arrested adolescence can hold out against such a judgment for very long. — D.M.

ROCKIN' DOPSIE AND THE TWISTERS
★ ★ ★ ★ ★ **Rockin' Dopsie and the Twisters / Roun. (1977)**
The hottest zydeco band in the land, led by Dopsie's great accordion and soulful vocals. Produced by Sam Charters for the Swedish label Sonet and licensed for release here by Rounder. This is a must. — J.S.

CHARLIE DORE
★ ★ ★ **Where to Now / Is. (1979)**
★ ★ **Listen! / Chrys. (1981)**
There was a time when Charlie Dore was the great white female hope of the English pub-rock scene—a kind of Britpop Emmylou Harris—and her debut album *Where to Now* was an encouraging demonstration of her vocal grace and winning songwriting. "Pilot of the Airwaves" still stands as one of pop's best unknown DJ tributes. But Dore has always had one foot in MOR never-never land and *Listen!*, on which two members of the faceless, soulless Toto crew do backup honors, is notable only for the talent so obviously gone to waste. — D.F.

GEORGIA TOM DORSEY
★ ★ ★ ★ **Come On Mama / Yazoo (1974)**
As the Reverend Thomas Dorsey, this man would become the greatest songwriter black gospel music has known. Here he is found in his sinful incarnation of the Twenties, performing first-rate country blues. — D.M.

DOUBLE EXPOSURE
★ ★ ★ **Ten Percent / Sals. (1976)**
★ ★ ★ **Four Play / Sals. (1978)**
Slick Spinners-like disco-soul group, great emphasis on harmonies but featuring terrific Philadelphia session playing. Excellent material includes contributions by Bunny Sigler and Holland-Dozier-Holland. — D.M.

DOUCETTE
★ ★ ★ **Mama Let Him Play / Mush. (1977)**
★ ★ ★ **Douce Is Loose / Mush. (1979)**
A versatile, hard-working Canadian act spearheaded by guitarist Jerry Doucette, this band offers plain old rock that's far more tolerable than most of its practitioners make it. — R.P.

DOUG AND THE SLUGS
★ ★ ★ **Cognac and Bologna / RCA (1980)**
Doug and the Slugs are a quirky Vancouver B.C. band which on its debut album explored vicissitudes of provincial bohemia via Doug Bennett's sardonic and slightly twisted tunes. Bennett (who looks like a cross between Alan Ladd and Dan Duryea) writes lyrics which owe as much to B movies and pulp fiction as to rock & roll. The Slugs' lightweight sound is partially redeemed by witty expropriation of the appropriate pop-rock quote for the right original song. Yet the LP only dimly captures appeal that made the group's "Slugfests" Vancouver's most unpredictable musical events. — G.A.

JERRY DOUGLAS
★ ★ ★ ★ **Fluxology / Roun. (1979)**
A tremendously influential dobro player, Douglas played with the landmark acoustic bluegrass New South group with Tony Rice, J.D. Crowe and Ricky Scaggs, who all appear on this fine acoustic instrumental set. — J.S.

DANNY DOUMA
★ ★ ★ **Night Eyes / War. (1979)**
Danny Douma is a better-than-average singer/songwriter whose El-Lay sessions on *Night Eyes* are less slick and rote than the average West Coast crooner fare. A nephew of the Fleetwood Mac clan, he's aided by John and Christine McVie, Mick Fleetwood, Eric Clapton, and Garth Hudson, and consequently there are tinges of the big Mac throughout, albeit pleasant ones. But Douma is most affecting when his vocalizing and material touches on a sound not unlike James Taylor. — R.P.

RONNIE DOVE
★ **Ronnie Dove Sings / Power (NA)**
Dove's hits ("One Kiss for Old Times Sake," "Say You," "When Liking Turns to Loving") were bathwater when they were popular around 1964–1966. God knows what anyone would want with them now. Even nostalgia has its limits. — D.M.

DOWNLINERS SECT
★ **Showbiz / Raw (1979)**
The Downliners Sect, mark one, was about the bottom of the barrel of London blues bands at the time of the British Invasion. Their ineptitude earned them a reputation as protopunk, which explains, but doesn't excuse, this late-Seventies punk-epoch revival of the outfit, which is all noise and no substance. — D.M.

DRAGON
★ ★ ★ **Sunshine / CBS (1977), Aust. imp.**
★ ★ **Running Free / Por. (1977), Aust. imp.**
★ ★ **O Zambesi / Por. (1978), Aust. imp.**
★ **Powerplay / Por. (1978), Aust. imp.**
★ ★ ★ **Greatest Hits / Por. (NA), Aust. imp.**

Jettisoning their early psychedelic predilections in the trip across the Tasman from New Zealand to Australia, Dragon produced a series of well-crafted pop hits in Australia between 1977 and 1979. Several of the best (including "Sunshine," the first) were on *Dragon,* their first U.S. release (now deleted), which was a compilation of their first two Australian albums.

Despite being a band of uniformly accomplished players, on record Dragon remained locked into a competent Top Forty anonymity. The cleanness and clarity of Peter Dawkins' production, though, laid the groundwork for a distinctive studio sound that has been adopted by a number of contemporary Australian bands, among them Matt Finish and InXS.

After an erratic U.S. and Australian tour in 1978, at the end of which, charismatic singer Marc Hunter parted ways with brother Todd and the band. The reconstituted Dragon included an unusual saxophone-and-violin combination, but with only moderately successful results (*Powerplay,* for example). Marc Hunter went on to a characterless pop solo career. — S.M.

THE DRAMATICS
★ ★ ★ ★ **Whatcha See Is Whatcha Get / Stax (1972, 1978)**
★ ★ ★ **Joy Ride / ABC (1976)** ¶
★ ★ ★ ★ **Shake It Well / ABC (1977)**
★ ★ ★ **Do What You Wanna Do / ABC (1978)**
★ ★ ★ **Anytime, Anyplace / MCA (1979)**
★ ★ ★ **The Dramatic Way / MCA (1980)**
★ ★ ★ **10½ / MCA (1980)**
★ ★ ★ **A Dramatic Experience / Stax (NA)**
Post-Motown Detroit soul quintet, led by singer Ron Banks, heralded something of a soul renaissance for that city, first in 1971–1972 with a pair of hits for Stax, "In the Rain" and "Whatcha See Is Whatcha Get" (reissued on *Whatcha See*), later with *Shake It Well.* These are uniformly good records, though *Shake* seemed to lift them to a new plateau. The Stax LPs, which like the ABC discs were done with producer Don Davis, are well worth investigating for lovers of neoclassicism in soul. The group's first LPs for Cadet (many of which are now deleted) aren't quite as good, though *Dells vs. the Dramatics* is worth hearing. The MCA LPs are showcases for Banks, but merely show him keeping current on trends. — D.M.

DUSTY DRAPES AND THE DUSTERS
★ ★ **Dusty Drapes and the Dusters / Col. (NA)**
Fails the white-glove test. — W.K.

MIKEY DREAD
★ ★ ★ ★ **At the Controls / Troj. (1979)**
★ ★ ★ ★ **World War III / Dread at the Controls (1980)**
★ ★ ★ ★ **Beyond World War III / Heartb. (1981)**
Formerly an innovative radio DJ in Jamaica, Mikey Dread began his rapping and producing career with two lyrically incisive, rhythmically tough hits: "Proper Education" and "Step by Step." After opening for the Clash on an American tour and working with them as a producer, he came up with the texturally interesting (gurgling, whining electronics) but less incisive *World War III.* The Trojan includes his first hits, while *Beyond* duplicates *World War III* except for two tracks discarded in favor of newer, stronger singles. — R.F.G.

THE DRIFTERS
★ ★ ★ ★ **Drifters' Golden Hits / Atl. (1968)**
★ ★ ★ ★ **The Early Years / Atco (1971)**
★ ★ ★ **The Drifters Twenty-four Original Hits / WEA (1975), Br. imp.**
There were actually two different groups who recorded for Atlantic under the name Drifters. Each has its own anthology; taken together they account for the early history of soul music. *Early Years,* showcasing Clyde McPhatter, provides one of the few observable transitions from post–World War II gospel singing through mid-Fifties R&B and, after widespread commercial success, pop styles. McPhatter was a giant among R&B singers, a strong influence on Smokey Robinson.

Golden Hits is closer to pop music. When producers Jerry Leiber and Mike Stoller added strings, a breakthrough sound— "soul"—resulted. The album features a number of lead singers, most notably Ben E. King, and some of the finest tunes ever to emerge from the Brill Building—"On Broadway," "Save the Last Dance for Me," "Under the Boardwalk" and "Up on the Roof." The British compilation includes songs from both groups and some material by a revived mid-Seventies version of the group, which is mildly horrid. — R.G.

DUCKS DELUXE
★ ★ ★ **Don't Mind Rockin' Tonite / RCA (1978)** ¶
One of the toughest outfits from the late lamented British pub-rock scene, the Ducks released one U.S. album with enough minor triumphs on it ("Coast to Coast," "Daddy Put the Bomp," "Fireball," "Hearts on My Sleeve," "West Texas Trucking Board") to

ensure them a small niche in rock history. Amen. — J.S.

LES DUDEK
★ ★ ★ **Les Dudek / Col. (1976)**
★ ★ ★ **Say No More / Col. (1977)**
★ ★ ★ **Ghost Town Parade / Col. (1978)**
Dudek is an extremely talented session guitarist noted for his work with Steve Miller and the Allman Brothers (he "ghosted" a Duane Allmanish lead on "Ramblin' Man"). But his solo albums, while featuring some fine playing, suffer from the characteristic sideman's dilemma. In this case, it sounds like fusion jazz and the standard Southern boogie, well turned but unadventurous. — J.S.

RICK DUFAY
★ **Tender Loving Abuse / Poly. (NA)**
Angry young wimp produced by Aerosmith mentor Jack Douglas. — J.S.

GEORGE DUKE
★ ★ ★ ★ **The Aura Will Prevail / Paula (1975)**
★ ★ ★ **I Love the Blues, She Heard My Cry / Pac. J. (1975)**
★ **Live on Tour in Europe / Atco (1976)**
★ ★ ★ **From Me to You / Epic (1977)**
★ ★ ★ **Reach for It / Epic (1977)**
★ **Don't Let Go / Epic (1978) ¶**
★ ★ ★ **George Duke / Pac. J. (1978)**
★ **Follow the Rainbow / Epic (1979)**
★ ★ ★ **Brazilian Love Affair / Epic (1980)**
★ ★ **A Taste of Jazz / CCJ (NA)**
★ ★ **After You've Gone / CCJ (NA)**
After a number of years jamming in West Coast clubs, Duke began his recording career as a jazz keyboardist with Jean-Luc Ponty in the early Seventies. Later, Duke joined Frank Zappa's band, where he started playing synthesizer, the instrument he's become known for. During and immediately following his Zappa stint, Duke recorded his first solo records (George Duke, Aura, I Love). He switched to a straight-ahead R&B style on joining up briefly with Billy Cobham in 1976, playing some heavy funk influenced by James Brown and Sly Stone. The combination of players should have been fruitful, but it wasn't, as the Live in Europe album painfully demonstrates. His Epic albums extend the funk strategy to much better effect. Duke finally achieved his goal—a hit single—with "Reach for It," a chanting, danceable blues funk pattern strongly reminiscent of Sly Stone's "Stand." He broke from the formula to make Brazilian Love Affair, an album that recalls his greatest talents. — J.S.

THE DUKES
★ ★ **The Dukes / War. (1979)**
This ensemble of British blues-rock veterans is unfortunately the last recorded effort of its most worthy member, guitarist Jimmy McCulloch (Wings, Thunderclap Newman, Speedy Keen), who died shortly after its release. Notwithstanding McCulloch's presence and talent, this is thoroughly pedestrian hard rock, unredeemed by imagination. — D.M.

CHAMPION JACK DUPREE
★ ★ ★ ★ **Women Blues of Champion Jack Dupree / Folk. (1961)**
★ ★ ★ ★ **Tricks / Cres. (1973)**
★ ★ ★ ★ **Happy to Be Free / Cres. (1973)**
★ ★ ★ ★ **Blues at Montreux / Atco (1973)**
★ ★ ★ ★ **Champion Jack Dupree / Ev. (NA)**
Dupree is more interesting as a stylist than a virtuoso, but he got the most out of his talent, and his records provide fine listening. A New Orleans native, Dupree learned to play barrelhouse piano as a kid from a guy named Drive 'Em Down, began playing on his own in the Thirties and supported himself by boxing, which is how he picked up his nickname. His postwar Forties recordings are notable for the drive and energy of his piano playing and powerful singing. The Everest and Crescendo recordings are not marked with dates, but the recording quality suggests they are sides from the late Fifties or Sixties. Fortunately, Dupree's powers did not wane with age, as the fine recording for Atco (saxophonist King Curtis is also on it) proves. — J.S.

CORNELL DUPREE
★ ★ ★ ★ **Teasin' / Atl. (1974)**
Cornell Dupree melts the blues into dripping caramel; sweet and thick, it should cover the earth. The guitarist from King Curtis' rhythm section, who laid down the lines on Aretha's early Atlantic tracks with cohorts Richard Tee and Bernard Purdie, later earned a little more fame with Stuff, but I prefer this album to both of that group's efforts. — A.G.

ROBBIE DUPREE
★ ★ **Street Corner Heroes / Elek. (1981)**
Sub-Springsteen mannerisms from a singer who could probably more profitably (though not much more interestingly) ape Billy Joel. Suitable for playing on FM radio stations in order to give the listenership an ideal excuse to switch channels. — D.M.

DURAN DURAN
★ ★ **Duran Duran / Harv./Cap. (1981)**

"Planet Earth" was an effective dance-rock single for these up-country British new romantics, but it's more of a song to shake your ass to than to consider seriously. Anyhow, serious consideration of Duran Duran is difficult indeed, because cleverly chopped coifs and daringly draped dress notwithstanding, they offer little of consequence beyond a beat. Their "progressive and fashionable" stance finally sounds like David Bowie filtered through cocktail-lounge consciousness. — R.P.

DÜROCS
★ ★ Dürocs / Cap. (1979) ¶
Dürocs majordomo Ron Nagle once made a very fine solo album for Warners, *Bad Rice*, but on this record, despite a cute remake of Gene Pitney's "It Hurts to Be in Love," he's simply too smarmy for his own good: pig jokes and randomized pop hooks fall flat. — D.M.

IAN DURY
★ ★ ★ ★ New Boots and Panties / Stiff (1977) ¶
★ ★ ★ Do It Yourself / Stiff (1978)
★ ★ ★ Laughter / Stiff (1980)
★ ★ ★ Lord Upminster / Poly. (1981)
The brilliant wit of Ian Dury blossomed in the mid-Seventies with the pub-rocking Kilburn and the High Roads. On his own, Dury scored immediately with the huge hit "Hit Me with Your Rhythm Stick" (not included on any of these LPs) and the great *Panties,* which included his other anthem, "Sex and Drugs and Rock and Roll." Chaz Jankel, Dury's colyricist, left after *Do It Yourself,* but the inclusion of ex–Dr. Feelgood guitarist Wilko Johnson on *Laughter* more than made up the slack. *Lord Upminster* saw Jankel and Dury reunited and set their songs against the stark rhythmic accompaniment of reggae masters Sly Dunbar and Robbie Shakespeare. — J.S.

AMON DUUL II
★ Hijack / Atco (1975)
★ ★ ★ Made in Germany / Atco (1975)
Hijack is pretentiously weird. The strings, reeds, brass and guitars are deliberately dark and cold, but finally leaden as well. Though it is German, the group sings in English, resulting in frequently awkward lyrics, and the low-pitched vocals are an unwise idea. The record does contain a few spirited passages, and these become the base for the far superior *Made in Germany.* Lively beat, colorful instrumentation and, most importantly, no impulse to be overly arty or bizarre. — C.W.

RICHARD DYER-BENNETT
★ ★ Richard Dyer-Bennett, Vol. 4 / Dyer-Bennett (1957)
★ ★ Richard Dyer-Bennett, Vol. 5 / Dyer-Bennett (1958)
A classically trained tenor, Dyer-Bennett uses simple Spanish guitar accompaniment to render old ballads ("Greensleeves," "Barbara Allen," and others). Considered a minstrel in the traditional sense of the term, he has recorded dozens of songs for his own label in addition to earlier efforts for others. Although few folksingers attempt this kind of formal presentation today, Judy Collins and Joan Baez can be cited as examples of contemporary artists who grew out of this stylized milieu. — I.M.

DYKE AND THE BLAZERS
★ ★ ★ ★ Dyke's Greatest Hits / Orig. Sound (NA)
★ ★ ★ ★ Funky Broadway / Orig. Sound (1967)
Dyke (Arlester Christian) and the Blazers predated the Seventies funk explosion with a series of raw, gutbucket dance hits. Their first smash, "Funky Broadway" (covered by Wilson Pickett), brought the word "funky" into the popular vocabulary, and subsequent singles were among the raunchiest soul records of the late Sixties. Dyke was shot to death in 1970. — J.MC.

BOB DYLAN
★ ★ ★ ★ ★ Bob Dylan / Col. (1961)
★ ★ ★ ★ ★ The Freewheelin' Bob Dylan / Col. (1962)
★ ★ ★ The Times They Are a-Changin' / Col. (1964)
★ ★ ★ ★ Another Side of Bob Dylan / Col. (1964)
When Bob Dylan (originally Robert Zimmerman) arrived in New York from Minnesota in 1960, he was little more than the latest in the line of Woody Guthrie imitators. By the time he made his first album, *Bob Dylan,* however, he was far beyond that, an amazingly original singer of traditional blues tunes (Blind Lemon Jefferson's "See That My Grave Is Kept Clean," for instance), country classics ("Highway 61") and his own original songs in the Guthrie talking-blues tradition: "Song to Woody" is stark and beautiful, "Talking New York" hilarious.

Freewheelin' contained some material in these veins, but was more notable for Dylan's emergence as the most inspired talent of the entire folk revival. His original love songs, particularly "Don't Think Twice,

It's All Right" and "Girl from the North Country," were lyrically far beyond anything any other popular or folk writer had attempted, and while some of his "protest" songs were jejune ("Masters of War"), others were lovely affirmations of humanity, like the immediate classic "Blowin' in the Wind," or frankly sardonic but nonetheless perfect ridicules of the cold war mentality ("Talking World War Three Blues" and "I Shall Be Free"). Peter, Paul and Mary's pop hit with "Blowin' in the Wind" established Dylan as a cult figure.

The Times They Are a-Changin' is Dylan's most topical, or protest-oriented, record, and its temporal concerns make it in many ways his most dated. The title song particularly suffers from age—it now sounds self-righteous—though there is a maturity of political analysis in "Only a Pawn in Their Game" and "The Lonesome Death of Hattie Carroll" that helps them hold up. Still, the best songs here are more personal, less tied to issues, such as "One Too Many Mornings" and "Restless Farewell," in which Dylan indicates that he may not be around the protest scene anymore; the haunting love song "Boots of Spanish Leather"; and his reminiscence about his childhood in the Minnesota copper country, "North Country Blues."

Perhaps the most prophetic song on the record, however, is "When the Ship Comes In," in theory a protest song, as chastising as an Old Testament sermon, but in fact an example of the surreal outpouring of imagery that would characterize Dylan's next period and the birth of folk rock. Although the next album, *Another Side of Bob Dylan,* retained the simple instrumentation—Dylan accompanying himself on guitar, piano and/or harmonica—it opted for far less topical material, and instead painted a series of fecund portraits of urban street life. "Chimes of Freedom," "Spanish Harlem Incident," "I Shall Be Free No. 10," "My Back Pages" and "I Don't Believe You" were all fragments from an entirely new breed of songwriting, not romantic or topical but rather philosophic or purely emotive. There were definite themes to some of them—as well as to "All I Really Want to Do," a hit for Cher, and "It Ain't Me Babe," a smash for the Turtles—but the levels of meaning accelerated; if they can be given any definition at all, these songs are visionary. And Dylan's entire early work must be seen as a process of development that led inevitably to this uniquely personal vision, whose accessibility and applicability in the lives of his genera-

tional peers was none the less potent for all its abstraction.

★ ★ ★ ★ ★ **Highway 61 Revisited / Col. (1965)**

★ ★ ★ ★ ★ **Bringing It All Back Home / Col. (1965)**

★ ★ ★ ★ ★ **Blonde on Blonde / Col. (1966)**

★ ★ ★ ★ ★ **John Wesley Harding / Col. (1968)**

★ ★ ★ ★ **The Basement Tapes / Col. (1975)**

At the Newport Folk Festival in the summer of 1965, Dylan unveiled a new, electric approach, appearing onstage with members of the highly amplified Paul Butterfield Blues Band. Folk purists were enraged that Dylan had "sold out" to commercial rock & roll, but when *Bringing It All Back Home* was released that fall, most seemed to stay with him, and he added a horde of new fans. Dylan's imagery got really wild here, though it still maintained links—sometimes melodic, sometimes lyric—to the folk tradition and still festered with elliptical protest. "Maggie's Farm," the minor hit "Subterranean Homesick Blues" and the abstract ballads "Mr. Tambourine Man," "Love Minus Zero/No Limit" and "She Belongs to Me" were peppered with lines that became slogans for the emerging youth culture: "You don't need a weatherman to know which way the wind blows," "Don't look back," and a dozen more. More importantly, by fusing the Chuck Berry beat of the Rolling Stones and the Beatles with the leftist, folk tradition of the folk revival, Dylan really had brought it back home, creating a new kind of rock & roll (dubbed folk rock but soon pervasive everywhere, inspiring in part the Beatles' *Rubber Soul* and *Revolver* and the Stones' *Between the Buttons*) that made every type of artistic tradition available to rock. The message was libertarian and it was seized and spread by cover versions (the Byrds had a No. 1 hit with "Mr. Tambourine Man") and imitators like the Turtles and P. F. Sloan, who wrote slangy West Coast approximations of Dylan's "message" lyrics, such as "Eve of Destruction," and plain rock bands. Dylan opened up new country for everyone in popular music, because his songs were unrestricted in meter, because his lyrics were so untamed and because his singing voice, once described as sounding like "a cow with its leg caught in a fence," made it clear that there was a difference between the great voice and the great rock & roll voice.

Highway 61 Revisited and *Blonde on Blonde,* released within six months of each other, are Dylan's two best albums, and two of the greatest in the history of rock & roll. *Highway 61* is a series of parables and tall tales, founded on tough rock guitar lines and crashing, dense keyboards. Its highlight was "Like a Rolling Stone," a six-minute hit single that said everything that needed to be said about the social revolution of the Sixties in simple terms. For that alone, the album would be essential; with the addition of "Ballad of a Thin Man," "Just Like Tom Thumb's Blues" and the title song, among others, it was an immediate hit and major Sixties classic. *Blonde on Blonde,* recorded in Nashville, is a two-record set that stakes out much the same turf and takes it, if anything, even further. Dylan's songs, some of them ostensibly about love affairs but all possessed of a barbed wit and some imponderably profound aphorisms, hit their peak with "I Want You" (a Top Twenty hit), "Just Like a Woman" and "Visions of Johanna." This was rock & roll at the farthest edge imaginable, instrumentalists and singer all peering into a deeper abyss than anyone had previously imagined existed.

Not surprisingly, what followed was withdrawal. In July 1966, Dylan had a motorcycle accident that forced him to withdraw from public appearances for the next year and a half. While recuperating, he and his backup band (the Hawks, later to become the Band) worked on new material, released a decade later as *The Basement Tapes,* which included some formidable songs, including "This Wheel's On Fire," "Too Much of Nothing" and "Tears of Rage"; some flat-out rock & roll, such as "Please Mrs. Henry" and "Odds and Ends"; and dozens of others, some sketchy, many brilliant. The two-record set that finally appeared isn't even all-inclusive, and includes many songs that feature the Band without Dylan, but it is a brilliant document nonetheless, made more legendary because of the long delay between creation and release. (Bootleg copies surfaced throughout this period, of course.)

The record that did appear was Dylan's quietest, most modest in years. "John Wesley Harding" is an outlaw tale, similar in theme to Guthrie's "Pretty Boy Floyd." The rest of the record has a kind of acceptance of bizarre phenomena—"I Dreamed I Saw St. Augustine" and "All Along the Watchtower," for instance—that indicated that Dylan had made some kind of reconciliation with the terms of his vision. *John Wesley Harding* is an intensely religious record, one that owes almost as much to country music as to rock. It is a lovely album, with a spirit of resilience beneath its placid surface.

★ ★ ★ **Nashville Skyline** / Col. **(1969)**
★ **Self-Portrait** / Col. (1970)
★ ★ ★ **New Morning** / Col. (1970)
★ ★ ★ ★ **Pat Garrett and Billy the Kid** / Col. (1973)
■ **Dylan** / Col. (1973)

Dylan's diminished energy cost him almost nothing in the way of adulation, but *Nashville Skyline,* which painted a picture of a blissfully romantic, decidedly uninteresting fool, nearly did. (The legions of admirers would hold on, though not forever.) *Nashville Skyline* contained a couple of striking songs, notably the great ballad "Lay Lady Lay" and a charming duet on the early "Girl from the North Country" with Johnny Cash. But in general, the album succumbed quickly to the vices of country music, its central idiom, without much awareness of C&W's strengths. It is typified by such babble as "Country Pie."

If *Nashville Skyline* was failed country, *Self-Portrait* was a disaster that crossed all generic boundaries. For the first time, Dylan attempted to interpret the songs of some of the writers who had followed him in the folk-rock movement, making himself ridiculous with versions of Paul Simon's "The Boxer" and Gordon Lightfoot's "Early Mornin' Rain," surrounding these with a batch of wholly uninspired originals. As Greil Marcus put it at the time, "I once said I'd buy an album of Bob Dylan breathing hard. But I never said I'd buy an album of Dylan breathing softly." *Blonde on Blonde* is probably the best two-record set in the history of rock & roll; *Self-Portrait* is almost certainly the worst double set ever done by a major artist.

Dylan, released a couple of years later, is an act of vengeance, with outtakes from *Self-Portrait,* put out by Columbia while Dylan was recording for Asylum in 1974. It features Joni Mitchell's "Big Yellow Taxi" and a version of "A Fool Such as I," the Presley hit, both guaranteed to net only horselaughs. Dylan had lost his sense of humor in the Seventies; this is as close to a joke as has been available from him in the last decade.

Dylan's immediate response to the negative critical and commercial reception of *Self-Portrait* was *New Morning,* released only three months later. While the songs are occasionally exceptional—particularly "Went to See the Gypsy," an obvious Elvis parable—the music is too diffuse to be really effective. Far better is his soundtrack to *Pat Garrett and Billy the Kid,* the Sam Peckinpah film in which Dylan had a minor role.

The title song isn't much, but "Final Theme" and "Knockin' on Heaven's Door" have an epic grandeur reminiscent of Dylan's best electric work, though they are much more modestly presented.

★ ★ **Planet Waves / Asy. (1974)** ¶
★ ★ ★ **Before the Flood / Asy. (1974)** ¶
★ ★ ★ **Blood on the Tracks / Col. (1975)**
★ ★ ★ **Desire / Col. (1975)**
★ ★ ★ **Hard Rain / Col. (1976)**
★ ★ **Street Legal / Col. (1978)**

In 1974, Dylan signed with David Geffen's Asylum Records; the company was then in the forefront of recording the singer/songwriter movement that was the most obvious inheritor of the songwriting tradition he'd founded in the Sixties. But his initial release there, *Planet Waves,* sounded hasty, unfinished. He was once more recording with the Band, something he had not done for a full album (except for the still mysterious—at that point—*Basement Tapes*), but there simply was not enough good material to produce the sort of major work expected from a performer of Dylan's stature. The best songs—"You Angel You," "Wedding Song," "Forever Young"—were simply adequate, and the rest were far less than that. *Before the Flood* is a two-record live set from the tour that followed the release of *Planet Waves.* Dylan reinterprets all of his old material drastically, singing the lyrics as though they either mean nothing at all or something very different from what we've always understood them to signify. This can be discomforting, but it is at least interesting, and with the able support of the Band, always at its best onstage, the record can reach the point of fascination.

Blood on the Tracks and *Desire* are the two best records Dylan has made since *John Wesley Harding.* The former is a bitter chronicle of love affairs gone wrong, whose best songs—"Tangled Up in Blue" and "Simple Twist of Fate"—might have been as great as anything he'd ever done if his band had offered him adequate support. Unfortunately, the playing was ragged and perfunctory; Dylan has never liked the strictures of modern recording technique, and spontaneity has worked well for him in the past, but working with relative amateurs has kept his work from greatness here. Similarly, *Desire,* much more ambitious in scope, lacks only a great band. With love songs like "Sara," such topical numbers as "Hurricane" and "Joey" (about the imprisoned boxer Rubin "Hurricane" Carter and gangster Joey Gallo, respectively) and simple rockers like the ironic "Mozambique," it could have been a masterpiece. Still, these remain his best recent works. *Hard Rain,* the live album from Dylan's 1976 tour, the Rolling Thunder Revue, is simply inconsequential, without the differences of interpretation that make *Before the Flood* fascinating. *Street Legal* was completely steeped in Cabala and Tarot imagery; it's a quasi-mystical odyssey whose purpose seems to be the concealment of Dylan's real feelings—even when the symbology is penetrated, all the record turns out to be about is the manipulation of symbols. These devices didn't add up to much, and they certainly failed to communicate anything of importance to even the most ardent listener.

■ **Live at Budokan / Col. (1978)**
Here Dylan attempted to do his version of Elvis Presley's Las Vegas shows. Like *Street Legal,* *Budokan* is all form and no content, but in an even more drastic way. The performances on *Before the Flood* disrupted conventional meaning, and served to open the songs up for a new audience and to reinterpret them for an old one. The versions of Dylan's songs on *Budokan* sabotage meaning, reduce it to rubble and walk blithely away, snapping their fingers like so many little hipster hitmen. It was as though Dylan were daring his audience to continue to pay attention—or even to respect him. This is his worst record by such a wide margin it's hard to fathom it.

★ ★ **Slow Train Coming / Col. (1979)**
★ **Saved / Col. (1980)**
★ ★ **Shot of Love / Col. (1981)**

In 1978, Dylan made the sudden and startling announcement that he had been converted to fundamentalist Protestantism; the specific source of his attraction to the least mystical form of Christianity remains more mysterious than his turn to that religion, which has always had an appeal to romantics. On the one hand, Dylan's conversion seemed the result of a desperate personal and artistic floundering symbolized by the self-destructiveness of the *Budokan* performances; on the other, given the lyrical biases of the initial Christian LP, *Slow Train Coming,* Dylan also seemed to be using religion to front for some newfound right-wing political views.

Slow Train was produced by Jerry Wexler and Barry Beckett, who recorded Dylan in Muscle Shoals, with members of the house band and some additional help from guitarist Mark Knopfler of Dire Straits (whose first album sounds like mini-Dylan impressionism). If the songs weren't so utterly devoid of Christian charity, the project might have succeeded; but with Dylan simply ranting ceaselessly about the perils of unbelief, the result is sterile and unsoulful. *Saved* was, if anything, worse, a caricature of fundamentalist cant—it prevents anyone else ever doing an effective satire of the Christian Dylan, because he's satirized himself.

Shot of Love is a different matter. Produced by Charles Plotkin (for the most part), it is close to the rock & roll of vintage Sixties Dylan, and the songs, although frequently as bitter and hostile as classic Dylan, are also more forgiving. For the first time, one begins to sense the strength Dylan draws from Christianity—and the deep need he felt for some humility to balance his life. This mood is made explicit in the album's finest song, "Every Grain of Sand," which closes the record with the first overtly emotional statement of belief that Dylan has made in many years. "Every Grain of Sand" is an indisputably great song, like a more poetic version of "Chimes of Freedom" or a more mature "It's All Over Now, Baby Blue." Whether it was a last gasp or a portent remains to be discovered, but at least one leaves *Shot of Love* feeling that Dylan is an artist with creative potential again.

★ ★ ★ ★ **Bob Dylan's Greatest Hits / Col. (1967)**
★ ★ ★ ★ ★ **Bob Dylan's Greatest Hits, Vol. 2 / Col. (1971)**
★ ★ ★ **Masterpieces / CBS (1978), Aust. imp.**

Dylan's first *Greatest Hits* package was assembled by Columbia while he was recuperating from the motorcycle accident: it contains all the obvious pre-*John Wesley Harding* material and is distinguished only because it marks the only LP appearance of "Positively 4th Street," the followup to "Like a Rolling Stone," and because the package contains a really horrible Milton Glaser poster of Dylan with rainbow-colored hair—a true psychedelic relic.

Masterpieces, an Australian only compilation, contains some rare and alternate takes that Dylan fanatics may find indispensable. It includes his version of "Tomorrow Is a Long Time," among others.

The second *Greatest Hits,* a two-record set, was compiled in 1971, this time with Dylan's cooperation. It's a model of the best of form, with unreleased tracks, a live cut, several previously uncollected singles and a smart selection of the most representative songs not included on the other set. In a way, *Greatest Hits, Volume 2* is the album that gives the best representation of what Bob Dylan has wrought in popular music, as a composer, lyricist and performer. Whatever his recent failures, he remains one of the greatest rockers of all time.   — D.M.

DYNASTY
★ ★ **Your Piece of the Rock / Solar (1978)**
★ ★ **Adventures in the Land of Music / Solar (1980)**
Leon Sylvers III–produced disco project is marginally interesting at best.   — J.S.

THE EAGLES
★ ★ **Eagles** / Asy. (1972)
★ ★ ★ **Desperado** / Asy. (1973)
★ ★ **On the Border** / Asy. (1974)
★ ★ ★ **One of These Nights** / Asy. (1975)
★ ★ ★ ★ **Their Greatest Hits** / Asy. (1976)
★ ★ ★ **Hotel California** / Asy. (1976)
★ ★ ★ **The Long Run** / Asy. (1979)
★ **Eagles Live** / Asy. (1980)

As auteurs of laid-back sexism, courtesy of Jackson Browne ("Take It Easy") and of cowboy-outlaw fantasy concept LPs *(Desperado)*, the Eagles seemed fairly harmless, notable mostly for some slick Glyn Johns production and even slicker country-pop harmonies. When Bill Szymczyk took over the production helm with *On the Border,* however, the harmonies were offset by rich-boy whines of sensual suffusion, the laid-backness was abetted by some paltry and inept attempts at rock & roll, and the sense of harmlessness was supplanted by a sense of spoiled-brat vengeance. The Eagles, to their credit, wanted to be not only one of the biggest-selling bands in the world (which they became, with *One of These Nights*) but also the best band (which is a title they could never have hoped to attain).

The result is some fairly punchy pop, highlighted by "Already Gone" (from *Border*), "One of These Nights," "Lying Eyes," "The Best of My Love" and "New Kid in Town." That their sexism had curdled into viciousness and that their whining became more and more dominant was irrelevant when the songs were heard one at a time on the radio. Taken as an ouevre, however, these qualities are both unavoidable and utterly unpalatable: While there are many less competent popular bands, it is hard to think of any so mean-spirited as the Eagles.

This is not to deny them their occasional moments of inspiration and insight (especially on *Hotel California*). The band's principal writers, Don Henley and Glenn Frey, have an exceptional gift for melody, and with the addition of guitarist Joe Walsh (for *Hotel California* and those following), the Eagles actually began to learn to rock (and laugh at themselves). But Henley's drumming has never been as strong as his singing: on the alleged *Live* set, which was perhaps the most heavily overdubbed such LP in history, Henley is supported by a real rock drummer, Joe Vitale which is an insurmountable limitation. And the group's wisdom is more likely to be Castaneda jive than incisive.

The Long Run is a smug attempt to prove the band's rock credentials once and for all. It falls pretty flat—the areas of success and failure are precisely those one would have predicted from listening to earlier Eagles efforts. The title song, however, is an interesting, if covert, plea to be taken seriously as artists: "we'll find out in the long run" is a message to critics. But if longevity determined greatness, Harold Stassen might be Emperor of the United States.   — D.M.

SNOOKS EAGLIN
★ ★ ★ **Possum up a Simmon Tree** / Arhoo. (1971)
★ ★ ★ **Down Yonder** / Sonet (NA), Br. imp.
★ ★ ★ **New Orleans Street Singer** / Folk. (NA)
★ ★ ★ **Legacy of the Blues, Vol. 2** / Sonet (NA), Br. imp.

Eclectic Louisiana blues performer, uses tom-toms and washboard in addition to guitar. Material ranges from spirituals to shoe-shine-boy chants to bad-man ballads. The Arhoolie set, his best, includes two Arthur Crudup songs, Elvis' first record, "That's All Right" and "Rock Me Mama," the hillbilly standard "This Train" and "John Henry."
— D.M.

EARTH, WIND AND FIRE

★ ★ ★ **Earth, Wind and Fire / War. (1971)** ¶
★ ★ ★ ★ **The Need of Love / War. (1972)**
★ ★ ★ ★ **Last Days and Time / Col. (1972)**
★ ★ ★ **Head to the Sky / Col. (1973)**
★ ★ ★ **Open Our Eyes / Col. (1974)**
★ ★ ★ **Another Time / War. (1974)**
★ ★ ★ ★ ★ **Gratitude / Col. (1975)**
★ ★ ★ ★ **Spirit / Col. (1976)**
★ ★ ★ **All 'n' All / Col. (1977)**
★ ★ ★ ★ **That's the Way of the World / Col. (1978)**
★ ★ ★ ★ **The Best of Earth, Wind and Fire, Vol. 1 / (1978)**
★ ★ ★ **I Am / Col. (1979)**
★ ★ ★ **Faces / Col. (1980)**
★ ★ ★ **Raise / Col. (1981)**

Maurice White, the vocalist/percussionist who is the energy behind EW&F, put this band together from a bunch of Chicago slum kids. When it started back in 1971, its music was closer to the street than it has become over the years. At first impression the group was like a straighter R&B version of the Art Ensemble of Chicago. Mystic and celebratory, the songs bridged into loose, jazzlike horn colors and elongated rhythms the likes of which recent EW&F fans probably wouldn't recognize.

When EW&F switched labels, it changed personality. White has reworked the personnel, expanded the fold and turned EW&F into one streamlined hit-cutting factory. All the while that same religious spirit not only maintained but came through even more strongly, if only because the size of its audience grew. To see EW&F on stage was to behold a gospel experience that was an existential hosanna guaranteed to heal your ills. *Gratitude,* a two-disc set (one disc recorded live), presents the band in its truest environment. The latter Seventies have grown up with EW&F hits like "Shining Star," "Celebrate" and "Sing a Song," some of the most joyous moments in modern music. Since then, White has indulged in both pompous spirituality and slick pop with banal results. On the other hand, as Maurice White confronts the Eighties, his be-all and end-all, the cosmic lyric mingled with the pop melody, seems an increasingly flimsy basis on which to base a significant career. The question remains whether White can—or rather, will—write songs that are memorable as something more than hip little jingles. — D.M.

SHEENA EASTON

★ ★ **Sheena Easton / EMI (1981)**
★ **You Could Have Been with Me / EMI (1981)**

Latter-day Olivia Newton-John, only more stilted—the only significant change is that instead of using *Mademoiselle* as a model, Easton goes after that *Cosmo* girl. That's progress for you. — J.D.C.

EASTSIDE CONNECTION

★ ★ **Brand Spanking New / Ramp. (1979)**

This seven-piece California outfit calls their music new-wave funk, but it sounds more like Chicago. — J.S.

THE EASYBEATS

★ ★ ★ ★ ★ **The Absolute Anthology 1965–1969 / EMI (1980), Aust. imp.**

A group of five migrant teenagers from England and Holland meet in Sydney in 1964 and form a band that will produce the greatest pop music to come out of Australia. The melodic and lyrical hooks, the reedy but powerful voice of singer Stevie Wright (or Little Stevie, as he was known at the time), and the dual guitars of Harry Vanda and George Young make for classic Sixties rock that has survived the years with all its freshness and excitement intact.

The distinctive urgent guitar rhythms that underlie their music have become a characteristic feature of a lot of the Australian rock that has followed. Vanda and Young, who were the band's principal songwriters, went on to become major producers of Seventies rock in Australia, and to record as Flash and the Pan in the Eighties. Young was the first of an illustrious rock & roll family to top the charts—younger brothers Angus and Malcolm make up the better half of AC/DC.

That edgy, driving rhythm is evident in early classics such as "Sorry" and "Wedding Ring," as well as in their masterpiece, the irresistible "Friday on My Mind." One of the greatest of all rock & roll songs about the weekend-as-transcendence-and-escape, the song was originally released late in 1966, and has since resurfaced in numerous cover versions in the wake of the new wave in the late Seventies.

In the Sixties it seemed that all popular Australian bands were obliged to make a pilgrimage to England, and tickets to London were first prize in Australia's biggest rock contest, Hoadley's Battle of the Sounds. Winners of the 1966 contest, the Easybeats left for England, but apart from "Friday on My Mind" they met with only limited success overseas. Their early records were the best, the English output progressively worse. This is reflected in the chronologically ordered anthology, which moves from the sheer pop brilliance of sides 1 and 2 to the relative mediocrity of side 4.   — S.M.

EATER
★ **The Album / The Label (1977), Br. imp.**
Despite their tender age (average fifteen) and their early entry into the British punk scene, nothing can excuse the wretched awfulness of this lot. Their originals are terrible; their covers ("Sweet Jane," "Queen Bitch") are worse. Not quite bad enough to be funny.
   — I.R.

ECHO AND THE BUNNYMEN
★ ★ ★ ★ ★ **Crocodiles / Sire (1980)**
★ ★ ★ **Heaven up Here / Sire (1981)**
At the turn of the decade, a spate of bands from Liverpool codified a new sound almost overnight. It was consistent with the stark themes of post-punk pop but championed a much more sophisticated and historically influenced musical sense. Along with The Teardrop Explodes, Echo and the Bunnymen spearheaded this movement, which was soon called (aptly but deceptively) the New Psychedelia. Echo's vocalist/lead guitarist Ian McCulloch left Teardrop to pursue a sound rooted in the late Sixties experimentation of West Coast U.S. bands like the Doors ("Rescue") and Love ("Villiers Terrace"). Drug references and decidedly surrealistic imagery led to the psychedelic tag. *Crocodiles* is an album of strong songwriting and excellent playing. *Heaven up Here* is still good if not quite as impressive.   — J.S.

BILLY ECKSTINE
★ ★ ★ ★ **Mr. B and the Band / Savoy (NA)**
★ ★ **The Modern Sound of Mr. B / Trip (NA)** ¶
★ ★ ★ ★ **Billy E / Savoy (1976)**
Billy Eckstine was at one time America's premier baritone crooner. His rococo phrasing on songs like "Cottage for Sale" and "Jelly Jelly" influenced a score of later singers. Eckstine also carried a formidable bop showcase band that featured at various times Charlie Parker, Dizzy Gillespie, Dexter Gordon and Gene Ammons (to name but a few). The notables on the first Savoy LP include Art Blakey, Sonny Stitt, Gordon and Ammons, and this double album covers Eckstine's career from 1945 through 1947—his peak years. The Trip album is a so-so ballad collection, a reissue of a 1964 Mercury set. Eckstine's voice had already frayed and the record is only of marginal interest.
   — J.MC.

ECLIPSE
■ **Night and Day / Casa. (1978)**
Sluggish late glitter-rock cover band; roots extend to wretched covers of such classics as "Born to Be Wild," "Sunshine Superman," "You Really Got Me." Original material *much* worse. And a glance at the overage, bare-chested, flabby dudes on the cover will give you a pretty clear picture of why bands like Kiss insist on lots of dry-ice smoke and heavy makeup.   — D.M.

ECSTASY, PASSION AND PAIN
★ ★ ★ ★ **Ecstasy, Passion and Pain / Rou. (1974)**
Long-lasting Seventies soul vocal group hit its stride with this album, including three Top Twenty R&B hits: "I Wouldn't Give You Up," "Good Things Don't Last Forever" and "Ask Me."   — D.M.

THE EDDIE BOY BAND
★ ★ **The Eddie Boy Band / MCA (1975)** ¶
When your better-than-average bar band sets out to play in the styles of the current Top Ten FM playlist, they are usually pleasing. When they have Josh Leo's good spirits and a fresh, modest instrumental lineup, as does Eddie Boy, they can even make good derivative records.   — B.T.

DUANE EDDY
★ ★ **Duane Eddy's Sixteen Greatest Hits / Jamie (1965)**
★ ★ **Pure Gold / RCA (1978)**
★ ★ ★ **The Vintage Years / Sire (NA)** ¶
Unless you're a student of Fifties and Sixties rock guitar, these don't hold up well. Eddy's low, "twangy" guitar style imbued the instrumental single with Top Ten power, but most of his subsequent hits sound like reworkings of his first big one, "Rebel Rouser." The Sire LP has an interesting liner note by Greg Shaw, but its four sides of twang are numbing.   — K.T.

RANDY EDELMAN
★ **If Love Is Real / Ari. (1977)**
★ **You're the One / Ari. (1979)**
Despite guest appearances from all-star session casts, Edelman never gets past the bad habits picked up from Elton John and Harry Chapin.   — J.S.

THE GRAEME EDGE BAND
★ ★ **Kick Off Your Muddy Boots / Thresh. (1974)**
★ ★ **Paradise Ballroom / Lon. (1977)** ¶
The Moody Blues drummer's seasoned outfit, including Adrian and Paul Gurvitz, plays

lukewarm pop. The frequent orchestration damages matters further. There are some good chord changes and melodies, but the bulk is surprisingly unmemorable chaff.
— C.W.

EDIKANFO
★ ★ ★ **The Pace Setters / EG (1981), Br. imp.**
This eight-piece Ghanaian band was recorded and produced by Brian Eno in Accra. Not as exciting or exotic as it should be. — ML.H.

DAVE EDMUNDS
★ ★ ★ **Rockpile / Mam. (1972)**
★ ★ ★ ★ **Dave Edmunds and Love Sculpture—The Classic Tracks—1968/ 1972 / One Up/EMI (1974), Br. imp.** ¶
★ ★ ★ **Subtle as a Flying Mallet / RCA (1975, rereleased 1978)** ¶
★ ★ ★ **Get It / Swan (1977)**
★ ★ ★ **Tracks on Wax 4 / Swan (1978)**
★ ★ ★ ★ **Repeat When Necessary / Swan (1979)**
★ ★ ★ **Twangin' / Swan (1981)**
★ ★ ★ **D.E. 7th / Col. (1982)**
Edmunds is a sort of Welsh rock wunderkind, noted as a guitarist, producer and minor pop-rock guru, whose work with Nick Lowe, Graham Parker, the Flamin' Groovies and others has helped keep the heart of the matter alive through a dolorous decade.

The EMI import includes not only much of the best from Love Sculpture, Edmunds' Sixties band, a power trio which specialized in frantically paced urban blues and electrified versions of Bizet and Khachaturian, but also tracks from his excellent solo debut, *Rockpile.* The early American LPs show Edmunds to slightly less advantage, as his obsession with recapturing the magic of the Sun records and Phil Spector productions of previous years becomes a mania for imitating them. Quite simply, these lack the bite of the earlier solo tracks. But beginning with *Repeat When Necessary,* Edmunds has grown much more ambitious, and the albums issued since then are a genuine extension of traditional rock, not a simple parody of it.
— M.G.

DEE EDWARDS
★ ★ **Two Hearts Are Better Than One / Coti. (1980)**
★ ★ **Heavy Love / Coti. (NA)**
Fairly pleasant soul voice drowned by Michael Zager's typically overdone production.
— D.M.

HONEYBOY EDWARDS
★ ★ **I've Been Around / Trix (NA)**
★ ★ ★ **Mississippi Delta Bluesman / Folk. (NA)**
★ ★ **Blues, Blues, Blues / Roots (NA), Br. imp.**
Mississippi country bluesman who settled in Chicago late (1954) never adopted urban style. His best material is from the Forties and early Fifties, and while fairly widely anthologized, is not represented above.
— D.M.

JONATHAN EDWARDS
■ **Have a Good Time for Me / Atco (1973)**
■ **Lucky Day / Atco (1974)**
■ **Rockin' Chair / Rep. (1976)**
■ **Sailboat / War. (1977)**
The most unctuously dumb of all the hippie singer/songwriters. His hit, "Sunshine" (on a now-deleted Atco LP), sells what he usually does—peace and bliss in the country, contempt for anyone who's not following along. It is the best of a truly miserable body of work. — D.M.

STONEY EDWARDS
★ ★ ★ **Mississippi You're on My Mind / Cap. (1975)** ¶
★ ★ **Blackbird / Cap. (1976)** ¶
★ ★ **No Way to Drown a Memory / MCA (1981)**
Edwards' intense, grainy, Haggard-like voice is heard to best effect on *Mississippi,* which is marred only by his overly sentimental reading of the title song. Most of these tunes are quite sentimental, in fact, but Edwards has an unerring melodic flair that compensates handsomely—and "Jeweldene Turner (The World Needs to Hear You Sing)" is a brilliant slice of country life. While *Mississippi* is mainstream country, *Blackbird* is "progressive"; it's an interesting group of songs, but Chip Taylor's production is distractingly cute. *No Way* is aptly titled.
— J.MO.

JOE EGAN
★ ★ ★ **Out of Nowhere / Ario. (1979)** ¶
Actually, Egan's antecedents couldn't be easier to discern: He was half of Stealer's Wheel with Gerry Rafferty, and this pleasant Anglo-pop record got made after Rafferty's "Baker Street" topped the charts in the land of AOR/MOR. Despite credible support (Gallagher and Lyle, Henry Spinetti, Alan Parker), Egan remains just another Garfunkel searching for a Simon, a pleasant-voiced lightweight with zero to say on his own.
— D.M.

WALTER EGAN

★ ★ ★ **Fundamental Roll** / Col. (1977)
★ ★ **Not Shy** / Col. (1978)
★ ★ **Hi Fi** / Col. (1979)
★ ★ **Last Stroll** / Col. (1980)

Fleetwood Mac's Lindsey Buckingham and Stevie Nicks produced *Fundamental* and Buckingham did *Not Shy* alone, and there's enough of his guitar and her voice on both to make Egan's rather puerile songs seem an East Coast equivalent of the everyday California teen dream, from the backseat romance to the call of the freeway . . . almost. Finally, both crash under the weight of Egan's postured immaturity. Still, for *Rumours* fans, useful accessories. Subsequent releases lack Lindsey and thus any interest to those not completely callow.   — D.M.

801

★ ★ ★ ★ **801 Live** / Poly. (1976)
★ ★ ★ **Listen Now** / Poly. (1978)

An occasional group led by Roxy Music guitarist Phil Manzanera with Brian Eno and various other musicians, 801 was a progressive jam band. The two LPs are strikingly different. *Live* captures a concert appearance from 1976 at which 801 played songs from Manzanera's excellent *Diamond Head* solo album as well as a trio of Eno tunes and even the Kinks' "You Really Got Me" and the Beatles' "Tomorrow Never Knows." The playing is ace and the loose feel energizing, making it a great LP. *Listen Now,* done in three studio sessions with a different lineup for each cut, displays skilled musicianship but generates less excitement; it's really a Manzanera solo effort with outside help.   — I.R.

DONNIE ELBERT

★ ★ ★ **From the Gitgo** / Sugar. (1981)

Veteran soul singer with incredible falsetto (his 1971 version of "Where Did Our Love Go" sounds like transvestite Diana Ross) turns his hand to the rap/funk explosion. Eccentric, interesting, anything but essential.   — D.M.

EL CHICANO

★ **Viva Tirado** / MCA (1970)
★ ★ **El Chicano** / MCA (1973)
★ ★ ★ **Cinco** / MCA (1974) ¶
★ **The Best of Everything** / MCA (1975)
★ ★ ★ **Pyramid of Love and Friends** / MCA (1975) ¶
★ ★ **This Is El Chicano** / SHB (NA)

El Chicano mixes heavy traces of Latin heritage with equally strong North American Top Forty influences. Technically excellent, but too often overcome by filler that's mostly movie music with a Latin beat. *Cinco* is probably their best; *Pyramid* their most successful.   — A.N.

FRANKIE ELDORADO

★ **Frankie Eldorado** / Epic (1980)

Dreary synthesizer-laden attempt at pop rock.   — J.D.C.

ELECTRIC FLAG

★ ★ ★ ★ **A Long Time Comin'** / Col. (1968)
★ **The Electric Flag** / Col. (1969) ¶
★ ★ **The Best of the Electric Flag** / Col. (1970) ¶

Electric Flag pioneered the rock-horn-band style, but never seemed to know whether they were playing blues, pop or rock. The first album, *A Long Time,* is an inspired failure, with the four key members, guitarist Michael Bloomfield, singer Nick Gravenites, drummer/vocalist Buddy Miles and bassist Harvey Brooks, at the top of their form. *Electric Flag* loses Bloomfield, as well as inspiration. *Best of* is unnecessary, since the three tunes from the second album are turkeys. Get *A Long Time Comin'* instead.   — P.H.

ELECTRIC LIGHT ORCHESTRA

★ ★ ★ **No Answer** / Jet (1972)
★ ★ ★ **ELO II** / Jet (1973)
★ ★ **On the Third Day** / Jet (1973)
★ ★ ★ **Eldorado** / Jet (1974)
★ ★ **The Night the Lights Went On in Long Beach** / U.A. (1974)
★ ★ ★ **Face the Music** / Jet (1975)
★ ★ ★ **Olé ELO** / Jet (1976)
★ ★ ★ **A New World Record** / Jet (1976)
★ ★ **Out of the Blue** / Jet (1977)
★ ★ **Discovery** / Jet (1979)
★ ★ **Time** / Jet (1981)

What started off as a splinter group of the Move concerning itself with a late-period Beatles mixture of orchestral sound and rock riffs has become an institution delivering one of rock's most commercial and empty pop sounds.

Move leader Roy Wood, seemingly the main force behind the original idea, inexplicably left after the first record. Control was then firmly in the hands of Jeff Lynne, who at first displayed the usual penchant of a classical rocker (as practitioners of any hybrid of classical music and rock were being called) for stretching out each and every song. On *ELO II* this tendency was mitigated by the strengths of the compositions (notably "Kuiama"); *On the Third Day* suffers by comparison, its side one suite coming off as undeveloped.

With *Eldorado,* Lynne decided to tie together a vaguely defined fairy tale/fantasy with shorter pop songs, and the effect was tremendous. With the sound finally gaining dimension, *Eldorado* flowed the way no other Electric Light Orchestra album had, and there was none of the jarring contrast between ballads and rockers that would mar subsequent records. *Face the Music,* with its pseudo-disco hit "Evil Woman," was hurt by an alternating of loud and soft numbers and by Lynne going overboard in reducing his songwriting to fit commercial norms. *A New World Record* demonstrated a style that was rapidly becoming formulaic: the attempt at a crossover single, the Chuck Berry-inspired rocker, the string-laden slow-motion tune. After that, it was all downhill. The prospect of across-the-board respect as a pop star seemed to be the motivating factor behind Lynne's every effort, and the promise once held by a vision of infusing rock with orchestral textures and dynamics faded away like the sound of strings on any ELO ballad. — W.K.

ELEKTRICS
★ ★ **Current Events / Cap. (1980)**
★ ★ **State of Shock / Cap. (1981)**
New wave without zap. — D.M.

YVONNE ELLIMAN
★ ★ **Love Me / RSO (1977)**
★ ★ **Night Flight / RSO (1978)**
Elliman played Mary Magdalene in *Jesus Christ Superstar,* and her version of "I Don't Know How to Love Him" was probably the best that befuddled gospel produced. Later, she toured as guitarist and singer with Eric Clapton, cutting several soul- and rock-influenced solo records that were better than these, which are straight out of the Bee Gees' breathless pop-disco mold. Although they squander her resources—at her best, Elliman's a belter—they did earn her a couple of hits, with a remake of Barbara Lewis' "Hello Stranger," and "If I Can't Have You," one of the soundtrack highlights from *Saturday Night Fever.* — D.M.

RAMBLIN' JACK ELLIOTT
★ ★ **Ramblin' Jack Elliott Sings Woody Guthrie and Jimmie Rodgers / MTR (1962)**
★ ★ ★ **Essential Ramblin' Jack Elliott / Van. (1976)**
★ ★ ★ **Hard Travelin' / Fan. (NA)**
★ ★ **Jack Elliott / Ev. (NA) ¶**

★ ★ ★ **Jack Elliott / Prest. (NA)**
★ ★ ★ **Ramblin' Jack Elliott / Prest. (NA)**
★ ★ ★ ★ **Songs to Grow On / Folk. (NA)**
Elliott was one of the most colorful figures in folk music in the Fifties and Sixties, a traveling companion of Woody Guthrie shortly before the latter was hospitalized, and a great influence upon the early Bob Dylan. The self-styled "last of the Brooklyn cowboys" (he was raised there) traded on an outlaw persona that was pure invention, but his singing is among the best the genre's recent adherents have to offer. *Hard Travelin'* is all Guthrie songs, the *Essential* a fine survey of his work on traditional material, while *Songs to Grow On* is a set of Guthrie's children's songs. All are affecting, but only a bit more so than his work on the other albums listed here, which contain more traditional material. Many other Elliott records are out of print, and worth seeking out, except perhaps for the final flawed few he made for Warners in the late Sixties. — D.M.

ELUSION
★ **All Toys Break / Coti. (1981)**
Passable soul harmony trio, not helped much by producer/arranger/conductor Michael Zager, who also contributes a good deal of the impoverished original material. One presumes that Zager is also responsible for the fifteenth-rate version of Sly Stone's "I Want to Take You Higher," done with so little enthusiasm and vigor that the rating above has been docked one star for its inclusion. — D.M.

JOE ELY
★ ★ ★ ★ **Joe Ely / MCA (1977)**
★ ★ ★ ★ **Honky Tonk Masquerade / MCA (1978)**
★ ★ ★ **Down on the Drag / MCA (1979) ¶**
★ ★ ★ **Musta Notta Gotta Lotta / MCA (1981)**
★ ★ ★ ★ **Live Shots / MCA (1981)**
Terrifically talented Texas singer/songwriter/bandleader gives a pretty good approximation of the excitement his band can generate in a live performance on the late Seventies records. Ely's powerful voice handles honky-tonk stompers, ballads and Tex-Mex ranchero tunes with equal facility, and producer Chip Young gets it all down cold. This is about as good as country-rock playing gets, combining the bite and release of rock emotion with the rich musical foundation of country (Ely's band includes accordion and steel guitar).

The albums also present two fine songwriters in Ely ("I Had My Hopes Up High," "Gambler's Bride") and Butch Hancock ("She Never Spoke Spanish to Me," "Suckin' a Big Bottle of Gin," "Tennessee's Not the State I'm In").

Musta Notta and *Live Shots* show that Ely has developed into one of the best country-rock performers today. The live album is by far the best work he has done. — J.S.

BILLY THE KID EMERSON
★ ★ ★ **Little Fine Healthy Thing / Charly (NA), Br. imp.**
Memphis-bred, Chicago-based rhythm & blues shouter best known for "When It Rains, It Really Pours," brilliantly covered by Elvis in the Sixties, and "My Gal Is Red Hot," demolished by Billy Lee Riley. Emerson was nonetheless one of the most talented and eclectic figures with whom Sam Phillips worked at Sun. This set of his material for that label is wide-ranging and worthwhile. — D.M.

EMERSON, LAKE AND PALMER
★ ★ ★ **Emerson, Lake and Palmer / Atl. (1971)**
★ ★ **Tarkus / Atl. (1971)**
★ **Pictures at an Exhibition / Atl. (1972)**
★ ★ ★ **Trilogy / Atl. (1972)**
★ ★ ★ **Brain Salad Surgery / Atl. (1973)**
★ **Welcome Back My Friends to the Show That Never Ends / Mant. (1974)**
★ **Works, Vol. 1 / Atl. (1977)**
■ **Works, Vol. 2 / Atl. (1977) ¶**
■ **Love Beach / Atco (1978) ¶**
■ **In Concert / Atl. (1979)**
★ ★ **Best of Emerson, Lake and Palmer / Atl. (1980)**
When Keith Emerson, Greg Lake and Carl Palmer got together in 1969, they were the product of two of rock's then-current trends: the idea of the supergroup, and the growing fascination with coupling rock's power to the classics. Despite their undeniable talents, they ultimately became the symbol of the problems inherent in those trends.

Carl Palmer was a relative unknown at the group's formation; Greg Lake had been on King Crimson's first, influential art-rock record. The star of the show was Keith Emerson, fresh from occasionally mangling the classics, burning American flags and stabbing his organ onstage with the Nice. He became the focal point of the debut, *Emerson, Lake and Palmer,* which was a relatively re-strained record.

The followup, *Tarkus,* opened the floodgates. The title song is an extended piece, of the vaguest possible concept, and featured as many farting, belching, and grunting sounds as Emerson could coax from a synthesizer. Unlike Pete Townshend, who used synthesizers subtly and to great effect, Emerson quickly tried for pure overkill. *Pictures at an Exhibition* signaled the nadir of the approach with its speeded-up trashing of Mussorgsky's work. *Trilogy* and *Brain Salad Surgery* are the only real group efforts. *Surgery's* "Karn Evil 9" is probably the masterpiece of ELP's hybrid form: yet another lengthy work that staggers under a burden of technical excess and an incomprehensible sci-fi theme.

At this point, the egos implicit in the band's name took over and put the act on ice for three years. The only release during that time was *Welcome,* a three-record live package with the most apt title in the field until Led Zeppelin's *The Song Remains the Same.* When all the various solo endeavors petered out, a reunion took place for *Works, Volume 1.* The two-record set is a bit of a cheat, since the first three sides are split into solo material that might never have found an audience on its own, but was guaranteed a listen because of the ELP name. The fourth side is barely a collaboration, just a version of an Aaron Copland work and another overdone number, this time performed with orchestra. An attempt to take a sixty-piece orchestra on tour following *Works* failed miserably, and that was the end of it. *Volume 2* was more solo stuff, and outtakes; *Love Beach* a last gasp that probably took no more than a day to complete; *In Concert* a useless document; *The Best of* simply product.

The failures of ELP show that egotism run rampant is no way for a group to function, and that mixing classical music and rock & roll can never work merely by harnessing the forms of one to the wattage of the other. ELP's real legacy was proving to a generation of punks that virtuosity is meaningless by itself. — W.K.

EMIGRÉ
★ **Emigré / Chrys. (1979)**
Canadian duo of ex-session player/producers in pointless solo effort. — J.S.

BUDDY EMMONS
★ ★ ★ **Steel Guitar / Fly. Fish (1975)**
★ ★ ★ **Buddy Emmons Sings Bob Wills / Fly. Fish (1976)**
★ ★ ★ **Buddies (with Buddy Spicher) / Fly. Fish (1977)**
★ ★ ★ **Minors Alloud / Fly. Fish (1979)**

Excellent steel guitarist on records that feature some of the best Nashville players in a less commercialized context than usual, and material including (besides the great Bob Wills hits) songs as diverse as Dylan's "Nothing Was Delivered," Ben E. King's "Spanish Harlem" and seventeenth-century German classical music. — D.M.

EMOTIONS

★ ★ ★ **Flowers / Col. (1976)**
★ ★ ★ **Rejoice / Col. (1977)**
★ ★ ★ **Sunshine / Stax (1977)**
★ ★ ★ **Sunbeam / Col. (1978)**
★ ★ ★ **Chronicle / Stax (1979)**
★ ★ ★ **Come into Our World / Col. (1979)**
★ ★ ★ ★ **Best of the Emotions / Stax (1979)**
★ ★ ★ **Untouched / Volt (NA)**

Flowers is a first-rate album, conceived by Earth, Wind and Fire's Maurice White who provides sparse and imaginative instrumental direction for the former Stax-Volt female trio. Lead singer Wanda Hutchison wrote the bulk of the songs, and her lead vocals add a moody, dark undercurrent to the album's flowery romanticism. *Rejoice* continues in that mold, though with less spectacular results; *Sunshine* is a collection from the group's work at Stax, released after "Best of My Love" (from *Flowers*) became a pop hit. *Untouched* has the group's earliest material; the more recent Columbia LPs are products of White's production mill. — J.M.C.

ENGLAND DAN AND JOHN FORD COLEY

★ **Fables / A&M (1972)**
■ **I Hear the Music / A&M (1976)**
★ **Nights Are Forever / Big (1976)**
★ ★ **Dowdy Ferry Road / Big (1977)** ¶
★ ★ **Some Things Don't Come Easy / Big (1978)** ¶
★ **Best of England Dan and John Ford Coley / Big (1979)**
★ **Just Tell Me You Love Me / MCA (1980)**

Their thin, tightly harmonized voices slide neatly over their acoustic guitar/piano mix, the neat hooks highlighted by cautious studio players. Few have had the laid-back FM radio formula down quite so well as England Dan and John Ford Coley. If they sound like watered-down Eagles suffering from chronic car-radio ennui, this may be only appropriate to their obsessive theme: return. A whole army of traveling salesmen would be unlikely to spend so much time preparing for homecomings.

In sound, their albums have evolved steadily from a nearly folk lightness to full pop production (on *Nights Are Forever*) with elements derived from Southern rock bands (reflecting their touring experience). But there is no noticeable change in the quality of their very limited writing and performing.
— B.T.

ENCHANTMENT

★ ★ ★ **Enchantment / U.A. (1976)**
★ ★ ★ **Once Upon a Dream / U.A. (1977)**
★ ★ **Soft Lights, Sweet Music / RCA (1980)**

Fine mid-Seventies soul harmony from Detroit quintet. *Enchantment*'s midtempo ballad hits, "Gloria" and "Sunshine," helped create the transition between Philadelphia International group concepts and the Solar groups of stars (Whispers, Shalamar) who followed. Being slightly ahead of and behind the vogue for such sweet singing didn't help them, but *Enchantment* still sounds fine in retrospect, a lot more than can be said for the funk groups by which they were surrounded when they first showed up on the scene. — D.M.

ENGLISH BEAT

★ ★ ★ ★ ★ **I Just Can't Stop It / Sire (1980)**
★ ★ ★ **Wha'ppen / Sire (1981)**

The English Beat is the only ska revival band whose melodies are as exhilarating as its beat—no mean feat in a movement that is defined by its rhythms. There are several reasons for this, but they boil down to a resolve to highlight melody over the beat wherever possible, and the wisdom to borrow from dub when grooving for its own sake. *I Just Can't Stop It* is everything a modern British pop album should be—relentlessly danceable, tuneful and socially conscious, as well as soulful and swinging. *Wha'ppen*, on the other hand, abandons its predecessor's exuberance for introspection and social commentary, an approach that is no less impressive, but far from compelling.
— J.D.C.

BRIAN ENO

★ ★ ★ ★ **Taking Tiger Mountain by Strategy / Is. (1974)**
★ ★ ★ **Here Come the Warm Jets / Is. (1974)**
★ ★ ★ ★ **Another Green World / Is. (1976)**
★ ★ ★ ★ **Before and After Science / Is. (1978)**
★ ★ **Music for Films / Poly. (1978)**
★ ★ **Music for Airports / Ed. EG (1979)**
★ ★ ★ ★ **My Life in the Bush of Ghosts (with David Byrne) / Sire (1981)**

After breaking with Roxy Music in 1972, Eno's solo albums earned him critical acclaim, a small cult following and an avant-garde reputation that has kept him away from the larger audience. His rock albums, comprising the third of his records still in print, reveal a fascination with lead-background relations and the more curious uses to which melody can be put. *Here Come the Warm Jets* redefined the Roxy style as a fantastic vehicle for Eno's surreal unsentimental irony. The electronically altered guitars of Robert Fripp and Ray Manzanera are devastating and Eno's vocals are a magical tour de force. *Taking Tiger Mountain by Strategy* is the perfection of Eno's rock mannerism, with guitars imitating machinery over a rhythm section of mesmerizing force and insistence.

Another Green World, a far more personal record, is the fruit of a series of experimental albums Eno made with Robert Fripp, including the deleted *Discreet Music.* On *Green World,* Eno's almost motionless settings become a kind of dreamlike pastorale meditation. Much of the music uses a well-ordered, though exotic, rhythm track under beautiful melodic fragments or wide washes of organ and synthesizer. But the wholly static piano-synthesizer duets (continued on *Low* and *Heroes,* Eno's collaborations with David Bowie) are what make *Green World* Eno's masterpiece.

Eno's ambient music experiments are, according to his own description, a kind of avant-garde Muzak. After all, even artists must go to the dentist's office sometime. The subtle background hum of *Music for Airports* and *Music for Films* certainly beats Mantovani hands down, but in the end that's not really saying much.

My Life, on the other hand, is a spectacular adaptation of Eno's pattern music collages. Using a crack band led by himself and David Byrne, and featuring bassist Busta Jones and an assortment of percussionists, Eno builds a dense and beautiful program of trance-music backgrounds for a series of found objects that consist of voice patterns chosen from radio broadcasts and ethnic music albums. — B.T.

JOHN ENTWISTLE
★ ★ ★ **Smash Your Head against the Wall** / MCA (1971)
★ ★ ★ **Whistle Rhymes** / MCA (1972) ¶
★ ★ ★ **Mad Dog** / MCA (1975) ¶
★ ★ ★ **Too Late the Hero** / Atco (1981)
Who bassist John Entwistle had the misfortune to be a good songwriter in a group (the Who) with a great one. *Smash Your Head against the Wall* showcased his instrumental talents (bass, keyboards, trumpet, trombone, fluegelhorn) and proved that his ballads were as good as his hard-rock songs. Unfortunately his second and best solo album, *Whistle Rhymes,* is now out of print, as is *Mad Dog,* a witty and eclectic collection ranging from the early-Sixties girl-group parody of the title track to "Cell Number Seven," Entwistle's homage to the Montreal jail where the Who spent a night during their 1974 tour. *Too Late the Hero* pits Entwistle against ex–James Gang crony Joe Walsh with predictably hot results. — J.S.

EON
■ **Eon** / Ario. (NA)
Time is definitely not on this outfit's side. — J.S.

EQUALS
★ **Unequaled Equals** / Laur. (1967)
Pop-soul group struck in 1968 with "Baby Come Back," which is not included here (probably because it was recorded for RCA). — D.M.

EQUATORS
★ ★ **Hot** / Stiff (1981)
Pleasantly competent English reggae, midway between Steel Pulse and new ska. Hot it's not, but warm maybe. — ML.H.

ROKY ERICKSON AND THE ALIENS
★ ★ ★ ★ **The Runes** (a.k.a. Roky Erickson and the Aliens) / CBS (1980), Br. imp.
★ ★ ★ ★ **The Evil One** / 415 (1981)
Erickson isn't just eccentric, he's downright bizarre. Once leader of the 13th Floor Elevators ("You're Gonna Miss Me" and other seminal Texas punk-psychedelia), Erickson not only believes he's a Martian but writes songs about all manner of occult and demonic beings. Such titles as "Two-Headed Dog," "Creature with the Atom Brain" and "Don't Shake Me Lucifer" might be just silly if they weren't backed up by some tremendously hard-hitting rock & roll, densely produced by former Creedence drummer Stu Cook to sound like sort of a cross between the Stones at their nastiest and Black Sabbath at their most ominous. The 415 album takes five tracks from the earlier British collection and adds five new ones. Either LP is fine, especially for horror and sci-fi buffs. — D.S.

ERUPTION
★ **Eruption** / Ario. (1978) ¶

Slick, anonymous disco. The cover of Ann Peebles' "I Can't Stand the Rain" proves how rhythmically sterile disco can become. — J.S.

ESSENTIAL LOGIC

★ ★ **Beat Rhythm News / Rough T./Logic (1979), Br. imp.**
Young singer/songwriter/saxophonist Lora Logic would benefit from musical if not corporal discipline. Her gritty sax playing is primal enough, but her portentous songs suffer from tunelessness, formlessness and—as the title of her group's LP warns—an advanced case of lyrical obtuseness masquerading as beatnik expressionism. Sax and twangy bass dominate Essential Logic's sound; the strident music has its moments (the moody intro to "The Order Form," the asymmetrical thrust of "Wake Up") so long as Lora sticks to her reed. Her high-pitched vocal vibrato unfortunately brings Marc Bolan to mind. Now *there* was someone with a sense of humor. — S.I.

SLEEPY JOHN ESTES

★ ★ ★ ★ **1929–40 / Folk. (1961)**
★ ★ **Legend / Del. (1962)**
★ ★ **Broke and Hungry / Del. (1964)**
★ ★ **Brownsville Blues / Del. (1965)**
★ ★ **Electric Sleep / Del. (1969)**
Estes was a fair guitarist and a good moaning-style singer from Brownsville, Tennessee, whose technique was similar to delta players. His best recorded work, done in the Thirties, is collected on the *1929–40* reissue. Despite stories he cut records with Sam Phillips in the Fifties that were never released, Estes was believed lost until Delmark got hold of him to make a generally uninspired series of comeback LPs in the Sixties. — J.S.

RICHARD EVANS

★ ★ ★ **Richard Evans / A&M (1979)**
Veteran jazz instrumentalist and producer Evans pulls out all the production stops on this jazz/funk solo effort that includes cameos from Eddie Harris and the Tower of Power horn section. — J.S.

BETTY EVERETT

★ ★ **Betty Everett Starring . . . / Trad. (NA)**
★ **Happy Endings / Fan. (1975) ¶**
Neither of Betty Everett's two best-known hits, "You're No Good" and "It's in His Kiss," are included on the Tradition album, a collection of early-Sixties Vee Jay material. The record is a mixed bag: blues, novelties,

ballads and three duets with Jerry Butler. Though they had a few hits, Butler and Everett don't really mesh as a vocal team and schmaltzy big-band arrangements mar all but a handful of songs. *Happy Endings* was done in conjunction with arranger Gene Page. Unfortunately some faceless charts and a rather nondescript choice of songs fail to give Everett much to work with. — J.M.C.

LEON EVERETTE

★ ★ **I Don't Want to Lose / Orlando (1979)**
★ ★ ★ **Hurricane / RCA (1980)**
★ ★ **If I Keep On Going Crazy / RCA (1980)**
Poor man's Johnny Lee—big voice and no idea where to go with it. "Hurricane" is almost an interesting ballad, though. — D.M.

PHIL EVERLY

★ ★ **Living Alone / Elek. (1979)**
Great argument for the idea that the best things come in pairs. — D.M.

THE EVERLY BROTHERS

★ ★ ★ ★ ★ **The Everly Brothers' Greatest Hits / Barn. (NA) ¶**
★ ★ ★ **Golden Hits of the Everly Bros. / War. (1962) ¶**
★ ★ **Very Best of the Everly Bros. / War. (1964)**
The Everly Brothers took Fifties rock 'n' roll nearest to country, but also nearest to the deadly soft rock of the Sixties and Seventies. An important influence on such folk rockers as Simon and Garfunkel, a few of the hits they cut from 1957 to 1962 are among the best of rock's first era: "Bye Bye Love," "Wake Up Little Susie," "Bird Dog," "All I Have to Do Is Dream," "Problems," "('Til) I Kissed You," all cut for Cadence and included on the Barnaby collections. The Warner material, cut from 1962 to 1967, is thinner, but still includes a few good songs, notably "Cathy's Clown," "Walk Right Back" and "Crying in the Rain." The Barnaby LP is a must; the Warner LPs are a luxury. — D.M.

EXILE

★ ★ **Mixed Emotions / War. (1978)**
★ **All There Is / War. (1979)**
★ **Don't Leave Me This Way / War. (1980)**
★ **Heart and Soul / War. (1981)**
Eurodisco act whose sole claim on anyone's attention is their 1978 No. 1 hit, "Kiss You All Over." You'd be much better off with the 45. — D.M.

FABIAN
★ **Sixteen Greatest Hits / Trip (NA)** ¶
Fabian's three 1959 hits ("Turn Me Loose," "Tiger" and "Hound Dog Man") are on one side of this collection. Along with such matter as the egregiously tacky "Kissin' and Twistin'," they provide a time-capsule memoir of this instant asphalt Elvis from Philadelphia. — F.S.

FABULOUS POODLES
★ ★ ★ ★ **Mirror Stars / Epic (1978)**
Witty, energetic and a little absurd, the Poodles combine elements from Ventures and Yardbirds guitar lines to Kinks/Who chord structures in the service of cleverly written cameo songs. "Mirror Stars" was a minor hit in early 1979. — J.S.

FACE DANCER
★ ★ **This World / Cap. (1979)**
★ ★ **About Face / Cap. (1980)**
This Washington, D.C.-area band took its name from the face-changing beings in Frank Herbert's *Dune.* They play hard rock faceless enough to deserve the reference. — J.S.

FACES
★ ★ **Ooh-La-La / War. (1973)**
★ ★ ★ ★ **Snakes and Ladders: The Best of Faces / War. (1976)** ¶
This is the Faces with Rod Stewart and Ron Wood. Beginning in 1971, the group originally known as the Small Faces (Ian MacLaglan, Ronnie Lane and Kenney Jones) began touring and recording with the taller Stewart and Wood, making some of the hardest-driving (albeit sloppiest) rock of the decade. The group had an enormous cult following, but its rather loose spirit could hardly be contained on record. Distressingly, only the group's least successful original recording, *Ooh-La-La,* remains in print, while the more

creative *Long Player* and *A Nod's as Good as a Wink* are no more. *Snakes and Ladders* is, for now, the definitive document: it includes the Top Forty hit "Stay with Me" and most of what was best and brashest from their other discs. — D.M.

FACTS OF LIFE
★ ★ **Sometimes / Kayv. (1977) (NA)**
★ ★ **Matter of Fact / Kayv. (1978) (NA)**
Pedestrian disco-funk unit nonetheless managed to land "Sometimes" 45 in Top Forty in 1977. — D.M.

JOHN FAHEY
★ ★ ★ ★ **Death Chants, Breakdowns and Military Waltzes / Tak. (1962)**
★ ★ ★ ★ **Dance of Death and Other Plantation Favorites / Tak. (1964)**
★ ★ **John Fahey Guitar / Van. (1967)**
★ ★ ★ ★ ★ **Blind Joe Death / Tak. (1967)**
★ ★ ★ **The Yellow Princess / Van. (1969)**
★ ★ ★ ★ **The New Possibility (Xmas Album) / Tak. (1969)**
★ ★ ★ ★ **Fare Forward Voyagers / Tak. (1973)** ¶
★ ★ ★ **Essential John Fahey / Van. (1974)**
★ ★ ★ ★ **John Fahey/Leo Kottke/Peter Lang / Tak. (1974)**
★ ★ ★ **Old Fashioned Love / Tak. (1975)**
★ ★ ★ **Christmas with John Fahey, Vol. 2 / Tak. (1975)**
★ ★ ★ ★ ★ **Best of John Fahey (1959–1977) / Tak. (1977)**
★ ★ ★ **Live in Tasmania / Tak. (1981)**
A native of Takoma Park, Maryland, Fahey is a self-taught guitarist who picked up his encyclopedic knowledge of rural blues and folk forms from field excursions and intensive study in the Library of Congress. His early work was culled from a variety of influences, including Elizabeth Cotten, Blind Willie Johnson, Charley Patton and Mississippi John Hurt. In 1958, Fahey borrowed

money to form his own record company, named it after his hometown and proceeded to record the most famous obscure album of recent times, *Blind Joe Death*. Even though there were only ninety-five copies of the record available for distribution, the album was extraordinary enough to plant the seeds of a worldwide reputation for the guitarist. Fahey later re-recorded the songs from that LP as *Death Chants*.

As he continued recording, Fahey began to extend his performance and composition under the influence of classical composers (especially the Russian romantics) and film soundtracks (he cites *The Thief of Baghdad* as a major influence). His catalogue, aside from the two rather uninspired attempts for Vanguard (which are repackaged as *Essential*), remains a magnificent selection of revitalized and experimental blues forms.

As if his exacting musical contribution weren't enough, Fahey has played an important entrepreneurial role as well. On successive field trips in the South, he rediscovered Bukka White (whom he recorded for his own label) and Skip James. He also discovered guitar prodigy Leo Kottke and sponsored Kottke's recording career on Takoma. In the process of writing his master's thesis on bluesman Charley Patton, Fahey collaborated with the late musicologist/guitarist Al Wilson, whom he subsequently introduced to blues collector Bob Hite, inadvertently spawning the late-Sixties blues and boogie band, Canned Heat. — J.S.

FAIRPORT CONVENTION
★ ★ ★ ★ ★ **Fairport Convention** / **A&M (1969)**
★ ★ ★ ★ ★ **Unhalfbricking** / **A&M (1969)**
The most distinctive and satisfying folk-rock LPs since the Byrds' first. Emerging in the late Sixties, the English Fairports were built around singer Sandy Denny and guitarist/vocalist Richard Thompson; they combined a timeless lyricism, an archivist's purism, rock & roll punch, Cajun good times, superb original songs and a sense of humor that led to marvelously idiosyncratic readings of obscure Dylan tunes. Their emotional commitment to their material was extraordinary. Had the Band been British, this is what it might have sounded like.
★ ★ ★ **Liege and Lief** / **A&M (1970)**
Well-thought-out traditional fare, but save for Denny's astonishingly passionate "Matty Groves," lacking in excitement.
★ ★ **Full House** / **A&M (1970)**
★ **Nine** / **A&M (1974)**
Denny had left the group (Thompson would

leave after *Full House*); she later made decent LPs with Fotheringay and the Bunch, plus two inconsistent solo discs, rejoining an in-name-only Fairport in 1975 for two desultory sets on Island (her best performance after *Liege and Lief* came with "The Battle of Evermore," on Led Zeppelin's *Zo-So* LP). Only Thompson's haunted "Sloth" rescues *Full House* from tedium; *Nine*, which followed other forgettable Fairport albums, is tedium itself.
★ ★ ★ ★ **Fairport Chronicles** / **A&M (1976)**
Two discs that collect much of the best of the first three albums, plus highlights of later LPs ("Sloth") and solo projects. Eminently listenable and enduring. — G.M.

ANDY FAIRWEATHER-LOW
★ ★ ★ **Spider Jiving** / **A&M (1974)** ¶
★ ★ **La Booga Rooga** / **A&M (1975)** ¶
★ ★ **Be Bop 'n' Holla** / **A&M (1977)** ¶
★ ★ **Mega-Shebang** / **War. (1980)**
English cult figure writes and sings hard rock and an occasional ballad. Primitive singing, sophisticated writing. Boozy, desperate, buffoonish. — S.H.

GEORGE FAITH
★ ★ ★ ★ **To Be a Lover** / **Mango (1977)**
On this Lee Perry–produced LP, reggae vocalist Faith reinterprets such soul classic as "Midnight Hour," "Ya Ya" and "Turn Back the Hands of Time," with emphasis on Jamaican rhythm and gospel emotion. The mix is perfect for light listening. — D.M.

MARIANNE FAITHFULL
★ ★ ★ ★ **Broken English** / **Is. (1979)**
★ ★ ★ **Dangerous Acquaintances** / **Is. (1981)**
There's nothing secret about Marianne Faithfull's past. As Mick Jagger's beautiful blond girlfriend during his most charismatic days, her bouts with drug addiction, comas, and chocolate bars are the stuff of which great Sixties legends are made. Her musical past is less memorable, her most notable contribution being the lugubrious "As Tears Go By." The rest of her recorded work consists of the dreariest of pop ditties that she sang in a voice that was catatonic at its most expressive.

After a public disappearance of almost ten years, Marianne Faithfull's comeback album, *Broken English*, is such a radical departure from anything that could have been expected that it is almost a revelation. With shocking honesty, Faithfull refuses to deny or gloss over her notorious past. Backed by exceptional musicians, including Steve Winwood, she warbles and cracks her way through songs about guilt, lost dreams, and political and personal violence that don't measure up to the emotional intensity she gives them, yet are consistently moving and compelling. The album's tour de force, "Why'd You Do It," is a song so obscene and angry that it makes any other musical expression of sexual jealousy paltry and insignificant.

Dangerous Acquaintances is the conventionally better album. The erratic herky-jerkiness of the debut is replaced by songs that are tuneful and consistent. Faithfull wrote or cowrote most of the songs on the album, and that involvement gives this material an authenticity that is missing when she relies on other writers to provide her with emotional catharsis. But what the album makes up for in consistency, it loses in intensity: *Dangerous Acquaintances* has a meditative maturity that is ultimately less satisfying than the fury and excess of the first album.

Clichés about courage and bravery are easily come by. But Marianne Faithfull has shown remarkable resiliency and, yep, courage, in transforming herself from a joke to one of the most creative and vital women currently working in rock. — D.G.

THE FALL
★ ★ ★ **Live at the Witch Trials** / IRS (1979)
★ ★ **Dragnet** / Step Forward (1979), Br. imp.

One of the more interesting bands to come out of the post-punk spate of experimentation in late-Seventies England. The Fall fool around enough to be considered forward-looking, play with enough energy to fire up an audience of Anglo-punks, and handle their instrumental concepts deftly enough to prevent boredom, which is a good trick. Mark E. Smith sings as flatly as anyone in the genre, but with enough passion and interest to be listenable. Epic-length "Music Scene" (from *Trials*) is worth a listen. — J.S.

FANDANGO
★ **Last Kiss** / RCA (1978) ¶
★ **One Night Stand** / RCA (1979) ¶
★ **Cadillac** / RCA (1980) ¶

This group is further confirmation of the more-is-less theory of rock-band size: a seven-piece group that outwimps the Eagles, displays less creative tension than a clothespin and could earn high points in a vocal anonymity contest. We won't go into the songwriting. Their principal justification for recording three albums is that a whole bunch of 'em can sing together at one time without getting all tangled up. Spare us more, oh great Nipper in the Sky. — D.M.

FANIA ALL STARS
★ ★ ★ ★ **Live at the Cheetah, Vol. 1** / Fania (1972)
★ ★ ★ ★ **Live at the Cheetah, Vol. 2** / Fania (1972)
★ ★ ★ ★ **Our Latin Thing** / Fania (1972)
★ ★ ★ ★ **Latin-Soul-Rock** / Fania (1973)
★ ★ ★ ★ **Salsa** / Fania (1976)
★ ★ ★ **Delicate and Jumpy** / Col. (1976) ¶
★ ★ ★ **Rhythm Machine** / Col. (1977)
★ ★ ★ ★ **Greatest Hits** / Fania (1977)
★ ★ ★ ★ **Live at the Red Garter, Vol. 1** / Fania (NA)
★ ★ ★ ★ **Live at the Red Garter, Vol. 2** / Fania (NA)
★ ★ **Crossover** / Col. (NA)

Fania Records has traditionally featured most of the best salsa artists, and the All Stars combine the top names in salsa in massive, swinging sessions that are an excellent jumping-off point for neophyte salsa lovers. Featured artists include Ray Barretto, Joe Bataan, Willie Colon, Larry Harlow, Mongo Santamaria, Johnny Pacheco, Louie Ramirez, Tito Puente, Eddie Palmieri, just to name a few. By all means get the Fania releases over the Columbias, which are a half-hearted attempt to slick up the idea and make it more commercial. — J.S.

FANTASTIC JOHNNY C.
★ ★ **Boogaloo Down Broadway** / Phil.-L.A. (1968)

Johnny is another one-hit wonder, "Boogaloo Down Broadway," a chunky soul shuffle, broke into the Top Ten in late 1967, so Johnny went into the studio and filled out an album's worth of cuts, most of which sound like attempts at remakes. He charted three other singles before disappearing altogether, but none of them made it past the Top Thirty, which means they didn't get much airplay and were quickly forgotten, as was Johnny. — J.S.

FANTASY
★ **Fantasy** / Pav. (NA)

I'll stay out of yours if you don't bother mine. — D.M.

FARAGHER BROTHERS
■ **Faragher Brothers** / ABC (1976)
■ **Family Ties** / ABC (1977) ¶
■ **Faragher Brothers** / Poly. (1979)
■ **Open Your Eyes** / Poly. (1981)

Tepid blue-eyed soul, poorly produced. — S.H.

DON FARDON
★ ★ **The Lament of the Cherokee Indian Reservation / GNP (1968)**

The Raiders picked up on the title track and made it a big hit—having done it first (and better) is Fardon's chief claim to fame. The rest of the album is similarly oriented to pop blues, about halfway between Eric Burdon and Tom Jones—sometimes an interesting place but more often precisely nowhere.
— D.M.

MIMI AND RICHARD FARIÑA
★ ★ ★ **Celebrations for a Grey Day / Van. (1965)**
★ ★ ★ **Reflections in a Crystal Wind / Van. (1966)**
★ ★ **Memories / Van. (1968)**
★ ★ **Best of Mimi and Richard Fariña / Van. (1971)**

Richard Fariña's novel, *Been Down So Long It Looks Like Up to Me,* is a slightly surreal classic of the transitional period between beatniks and hippies. His marriage to Joan Baez' sister, Mimi, was a folk-revival fairy tale; so was his death, on his birthday, in a motorcycle crash.

The albums are the relics of the first flowering of rock's self-conscious poesy, and they suffer from it. But Fariña's best songs ("Pack Up Your Sorrows" on *Celebrations,* for instance) could be as chilling as any of the other Dylan-inspired folk-rock singers, and he used rock rhythm sections more effectively on *Reflections* than any folk rocker except Dylan and the Byrds. *Memories* is a collection of leftovers, however, and the *Best of* doesn't hold up very well. The original albums, cut in 1964 and 1965, are interesting if dated period pieces. — D.M.

MIMI FARIÑA AND TOM JANS
★ ★ **Take Heart / A&M (1971)**

Mimi Fariña married Jans, who was then a disc jockey, after the death of her first husband, Richard Fariña. Jans has had a fairly successful solo career since then as a kind of country-rock writer and singer. This collaboration lasted only about as long as their marriage, which was exceedingly brief; if *Take Heart* is any indication, neither element of their relationship amounted to much more than a forgettable incident.
— D.M.

SANDY FARINA
■ **All Alone in the Night / MCA (1980) ¶**

Pointless pop singer; docked one star for appearing in *Sgt. Pepper's Lonely Hearts Club Band* movie. — D.M.

MARK FARNER
★ **Mark Farner / Atco (1977)**
★ **No Frills / Atl. (1978) ¶**

Ex–Grand Funk Railroad guitarist/singer/songwriter extends his penchant for naive politics ("Ban the Man") and cheap hedonism ("Dear Lucy") into solo album territory with predictably rotten results. Outside the inspired amateur context of Grand Funk, Farner is just another misguided and overly sentimental hippie songwriter. — J.S.

FATBACK BAND
★ ★ **Night Fever / Sp. (1976) ¶**
★ ★ ★ **Raising Hell / Event (1976) ¶**
★ ★ ★ **Yum Yum / Event (1976) ¶**
★ ★ **Brite Lites/Big City / Sp. (1979)**
★ ★ **Fatback XII / Sp. (1979)**
★ ★ **Hotbox / Sp. (1980)**
★ ★ **14 Karat / Sp. (1980)**
★ ★ **Tasty Jam / Sp. (1981)**
★ **Man with the Band / Sp. (NA) ¶**

Better-than-average disco funk outfit. — J.S.

FATHER'S CHILDREN
★ **Father's Children / Mer. (1979)**

One listen will demonstrate why Mom's not campaigning for equal time. — D.M.

FAT LARRY'S BAND
★ ★ **Feel It / WMOT (NA)**
★ ★ **Off the Wall / Stax (1977)**
★ ★ **Lookin' for Love / WMOT (1978)**
★ ★ **Spacin' Out / WMOT (1979)**
★ ★ **Stand Up / Fan. (1980)**

Pedestrian disco-funk takeoffs on Bill Cosby's TV hero Fat Albert, who is both more naturally cool and more bearable (on Saturday-morning TV, at that, which is saying a lot). — D.M.

FAUST
★ ★ ★ ★ **Faust / Rec. (1972), Br. imp.**
★ ★ ★ ★ **So Far / Rec. (1972), Br. imp.**
★ ★ **Outside the Dream Syndicate (with Tony Conrad) / Caro. (1973), Br. imp.**
★ ★ ★ **The Faust Tapes / Rec. (1973), Br. imp.**
★ ★ ★ **Faust IV / Virgin (1973), Br. imp.**

There is something very intimidating in the way this mysterious early-Seventies German group has been lionized by progressive rock and new-music critics. Yet the evidence on their extraordinary first two albums makes it hard to name another band, German or otherwise, that uprooted rock during that period with such dramatic force and radical imagination. But it is somehow appropriate that Faust, coming from a country with no rock & roll tradition, should create a revolutionary music that was rock only by association.

You can hear elements of Zappa, early acid Pink Floyd, the white-noise Velvet Underground (particularly on the live side-long "Miss Fortune" on *Faust*), and even snatches of psychedelic Beatles lyricism, but they come together in startling combinations with the group's seemingly anarchic tape-editing actually creating a refreshing new order of its own. Rock, jazz, electronics and musique concrète all come into play and yet come out sounding like no one thing except Faust music. Maybe the reason critics spent most of their time praising Faust—see, if you can, the original liner notes for the Virgin Records issue of *The Faust Tapes*—was because their music was so damn indescribable. Nevertheless, for a group no one knows much about, they have had a considerable influence on the post-punk industrial sounds of groups like Cabaret Voltaire in England and Pere Ubu and Chrome in America.

The British Recommended label has rereleased the first two albums in their original German packaging—*Faust* with clear vinyl and a clear plastic sleeve, *So Far* with an all-black motif and a collection of color prints based on the songs. *The Faust Tapes,* another Recommended reissue, is a collection of undoctored rehearsal tapes released to mark their signing to Virgin Records in 1973. — D.F.

ALMA FAYE
★ ★ **Doin' It** / Casa. (1979)
Competent dance chanteuse. — D.M.

FAZE-O
★ ★ ★ **Riding High** / She (1977)
★ ★ ★ **Good Thang** / She (1978)
★ ★ ★ **Breakin' the Funk** / She (1979)
Funk quintet produced by Ohio Players' Clarence "Satch" Satchell has had its moments, most notably "Riding High," which made the R&B Top Ten in 1978. In fact the title tracks from all three albums have made the soul charts. Not terribly distinguished, but a lot less like hackwork than most such. — D.M.

THE FEELIES
★ ★ ★ ★ **Crazy Rhythms** / Stiff (1980)
Excellent instrumental-based group from New Jersey incorporates the sophisticated rhythmic concepts of the new-wave experimentalists without making it sound coy or contrived. Interesting cover of "Everybody's Got Something to Hide (Except Me and My Monkey)." — J.S.

FONDA FEINGOLD
★ **Fonda Feingold** / Mer. (1978)
Classically trained singer/songwriter came up from the lounge circuit to make this record and probably returned there. — J.S.

FELA AND AFRIKA 70
★ ★ ★ ★ **Zombie** / Mer. (1978)
Multi-instrumentalist (tenor and alto sax, piano) Fela leads a hot fourteen-piece band in a blend of African rhythms with Western melodic and harmonic elements. The side-long title track shows the band at its best. — J.S.

JOSE FELICIANO
★ ★ **Feliciano!** / RCA (1968)
★ **Feliciano/10 to 23** / RCA (1969)
★ **Fireworks** / RCA (1970)
★ **Encore! José Feliciano's Finest Performances** / RCA (1971)
★ **José Feliciano** / RCA (1971) ¶
★ **Compartments** / RCA (1973) ¶
★ **For My Love . . . Mother Music** / RCA (1973) ¶
★ **And the Feeling's Good** / RCA (1974)
★ **Just Wanna Rock 'n' Roll** / RCA (1975) ¶
★ ★ **Sweet Soul Music** / Priv. (1976) ¶
This blind Latino's records are very uneven collections of indiscriminately selected material, some of it in Spanish. A virtuoso twelve-string guitarist and fiery singer, Feliciano puts his heart on his sleeve for a ballad, but his rockers are embarrassingly stiff. *Feliciano!* contains his first and biggest hit, "Light My Fire," and is a classic make-out album. *Sweet Soul Music,* coproduced by Jerry Wexler, almost succeeds in establishing an R&B base. — S.H.

DICK FELLER
★ ★ ★ **No Word on Me** / Asy. (1974) ¶
★ ★ ★ **Some Days Are Diamonds** / Asy. (1975)
A populist in the extreme, Dick Feller worries about the common man—about his foibles and follies, his triumphs and tragedies—and is quick to spot a phony. Feller's most famous song is "Abraham, Martin and John," a 1970 Dion hit, and like that one, his tales have real power ("Daisy Hill" on the deleted *Dick Feller Wrote* and "Cry for Lori" on *No Word on Me* are devastating chronicles of wasted lives). Feller, who surely checks his wallet when he encounters such praise, is careful to maintain a neat balance between the poignant and the humorous in his repertoire. Charlie McCoy, Johnny Gimble, Pete Drake and other redoubtable

players lend to each record a superior quality of musicianship; but it's Feller's rich baritone voice, his haunting melodies and his compelling lyrics that endure and place him several cuts above the Harry Chapins of this world. — D.MC.

SUZANNE FELLINI

★ **Suzanne Fellini / Casa. (1980)**
New York cabaret singer had her hit with "Makin' Love on the Phone." Which only goes to prove that "new wave" can be as formulized and faceless as anything else. — D.G.

NARVEL FELTS

★ ★ ★ ★ **Greatest Hits / MCA (1975)**
★ ★ ★ **Narvel the Marvel / MCA (1976)** ¶
★ ★ ★ **Touch of Felts / MCA (1977)**
★ ★ ★ **Narvel / MCA (1977)**
★ ★ ★ **Inside Love / MCA (1978)**
★ ★ ★ **One Run for the Roses / MCA (1979)**
★ ★ ★ **This Time / Hi (NA)** ¶
Felts is a melodramatic country singer strongly influenced by Roy Orbison and Charlie Rich. His quavering, strangely intoned singing makes for some flashy histrionics, especially on his ballads, and he covers a wide range of pop, soul and country material, but with formula country-pop productions. His version of "Drift Away" introduced him in 1973 to the country audience; his subsequent country hits have been "Reconsider Me," "Somebody Hold Me (Until She Passes By)" (1975) and "Lonely Teardrops" (1976). — J.S.

FREDDY FENDER

★ **Merry Christmas from Freddy Fender / ABC (1971)**
★ **Before the Next Teardrop Falls / Dot (1974)**
★ **Are You Ready for Freddy / Dot (1975)**
★ **Rock 'n' Country / ABC (1976)** ¶
★ **If You're Ever in Texas / Dot (1976)** ¶
★ ★ **Best of Freddy Fender / Dot (1977)**
★ **If You Don't Love Me / Dot (1977)**
★ **Swamp Gold / ABC (1978)**
★ **Texas Balladeer / Starf. (1979)**
★ **Together We Drifted Apart / Starf. (1980)**
★ **Since I Met You Baby / Acc. (NA)**
★ **Tex-Mex / MCA (NA)**
Freddy Fender (formerly Baldemar Huerta) is a classic example of a man ahead of his time. Long a legend in South Texas, he was the typical Mexican-American rock & roller

in the heyday of the Gulf Coast Sound, when Huey Meaux' productions of such people as Cookie and the Cupcakes and B. J. Thomas and the Triumphs set a standard for sentimental triplet-laden rock & roll. That Fender was in and out of prison only added to his stature. He was widely regarded— especially with Doug Sahm perpetuating his myth by constantly performing Fender's superlative "Wasted Days and Wasted Nights"—as the big contender from Texas, if ever his energy could be harnessed by a major record company. His Texas records—in both Spanish and English, on small local labels—were brilliant, if erratic, examples of Tex-Mex rock & roll. His vibrato vocals (especially in person, since his records always sounded as if they were cut in a garage) were unmatched.

Then Meaux got Fender a deal with a major record company and turned him into not only a country singer but an overworked goose that strained to lay golden eggs. Even "Wasted Days and Wasted Nights" sounded weak and exhausted. His biggest hits— "Before the Next Teardrop Falls" and "Roses Are Red," from the *Teardrop* album—are good country songs but thin Freddy Fender. The entire series of albums above shows Fender to have turned into a competent if unexciting country singer, but that is not saying a great deal given the usual level of country albums. — C.F.

JAY FERGUSON

★ ★ ★ **All Alone in the End Zone / Asy. (1976)**
★ ★ ★ **Thunder Island / Elek. (1977)**
★ ★ ★ **Real Life Ain't This Way / Asy. (1979)**
★ ★ ★ **Terms and Conditions / Cap. (1980)**
Ex–Spirit and Jo Jo Gunne leader Ferguson spices these more pop-oriented albums with all the things that made Jo Jo Gunne a fine band, albeit unsuccessful: short, high-energy pieces with great rock melodies, highlighted by appealing vocals. Guest appearances by Joe Walsh, Vitale and Lala. — A.N.

FERRARA

★ **Wuthering Heights / Mid. Int. (NA)**
Not a classic. — D.M.

BRYAN FERRY

★ ★ ★ ★ **"These Foolish Things" / Atl. (1974)**
★ ★ ★ **Another Time, Another Place / Atl. (1974)**
★ ★ ★ **Let's Stick Together / Atl. (1976)**

★ ★ **In Your Mind** / Atl. (1977)
★ ★ ★ **The Bride Stripped Bare** / Atl.
  (1978) ¶

Bryan Ferry's records are virtually answer discs to questions posed by the band he leads, Roxy Music. Where Roxy's rock amounts to a forced march on modernism, Ferry's solo albums are a continuing internal dialogue about the value of such old-fashioned concepts as romance and fidelity, tradition and the pop heritage. Ferry's so superficially debonair, he can seem as muddle-minded and perversely decadent as Dirk Bogarde, but that's just the stereotype he favors. In reality he's up to something more compelling.

"These Foolish Things" pits Lesley Gore against Bob Dylan, and not just for effect. Ferry views pop as a kind of continuum, extending through all sorts of Tin Pan Alley and Brill Building craftsmanship and incorporating visions as radical as Dylan's and as banal as Gore's. Within such a sensibility discerning what deserves to be dismissed as "trash" and what deserves elevation as "art" is not a simple problem. And such designations are so often determined by context that their order can be reversed almost at will. By altering tempos and singing every song with the deadpan emotional blankness he largely *avoids* with Roxy, Ferry exposes these issues as effectively as any pop singer in history.

Another Time, Another Place merely recycles this idea; only a spooky "The 'In' Crowd" saves it from mediocrity. *Let's Stick Together,* assembled from British B sides, is better, larger because it rocks harder, but *In Your Mind* is a failed attempt to present a set of all original material. Without the skilled instrumentals of Roxy Music to flesh out his lyrics, however, Ferry seems merely fey. *The Bride Stripped Bare* balances Ferry's approaches much more effectively, allowing him to cover such romantic soul standards as "That's How Strong My Love Is" alongside his despondently modern "When She Walks in the Room." The result might have been a triumph, if it weren't for the misconceived production, largely the product of this quintessentially British singer working with such Los Angeles session musicians as Rick Marotta and Waddy Wachtel, who also coproduced. (Ferry's lack of commercial success in America was probably the reason for this inappropriate matchup.) Still, *Bride* suggests that Ferry's solo work still has much undeveloped potential; it's unfortunate that he has devoted all of his time since then to the re-formed version of Roxy Music. — D.M.

FEVER
★ **Fever** / Fan. (1979)
Disco-funk trio with enough sidemen and vocalists to qualify as an orchestra, or for federal aid as a disaster area. The sort of group that figures the height of hip is adding Space Invaders noises to the usual grunt-and-grind funk clichés. You can dance to it, but it's hard to say why you'd want to. — D.M.

FEVER TREE
★ ★ **Fever Tree** / MCA (1968)
Houston band had one great hit ("Where Do You Go?" popularly known as "San Francisco Girls"), which stands as a nostalgic testament to the Summer of Love, and is included here. The rest is 1968's version of eclectic padding (Beatles, Buffalo Springfield, Wilson Pickett). — A.N.

W. C. FIELDS
★ ★ **W.C. Fields—Original Voice Tracks from His Greatest Movies** / MCA (1968)
★ ★ **Further Adventures of Larson E. Whipshade** / Col. (1974) ¶
★ ★ **Best of W. C. Fields** / Col. (1976)
If you don't know his films, these bits seem funny in their incongruity, but not as funny in their intended way: a consummate blast of misanthropic sarcasm. Fields could do something no other comedian has ever done, which is to despise amusingly. The records never even suggest this ability. — K.T.

THE FIFTH DIMENSION
★ ★ ★ **Greatest Hits on Earth** / Ari.
  (1972) ¶
■ **Star Dancing** / Mo. (1978) ¶
■ **High On Sunshine** / Mo. (NA)
■ **Everybody's Got to Give It Up** / Mo. (1981)
Choreographed bionic sepia. *Greatest Hits* contains the "essential" Sixties hits, "Aquarius," "Up Up and Away," etc. The Motown albums feature the group without its lead vocal team, Marilyn McCoo and Billy Davis, Jr., and are completely lackluster. — S.H.

FINGERS
★ **Fingers** / RCA (1979) ¶
Well-played but essentially banal disco funk. — J.D.C.

FIRE AND ICE
★ ★ **Fire and Ice** / Butter. (NA)
Another one of those faceless disco bands. Good groove, though. — D.M.

FIREFALL
★ ★ **Firefall** / Atl. (1976)

★ ★ **Luna Sea / Atl. (1977)** ¶
★ ★ **Elan / Atl. (1978)**
★ ★ **Clouds across the Sun / Atl.
(1980)**
★ ★ **Undertow / Atl. (1980)**
★ ★ **Best of Firefall / Atl. (1981)**
Firefall, the debut of this package of country-rock middleweight, presented a blandly
smooth electric/acoustic pop: pleasant but
dull, predictable melodies, chords and harmonies with the barest hint of a country
background. Some of Larry Burnett's songs
managed a rockish edge, but former Flying
Burrito Brother Rick Roberts' were sugary
and MORish. The electric guitar parts were
surprisingly refreshing, but the saxophone
awkward. The others offer a few catchier instances but otherwise repeat those shortcomings. — C.W.

FIRESIGN THEATRE

★ ★ **Waiting for the Electrician or Someone
Like Him / Col. (1968)**
★ ★ ★ ★ **How Can You Be in Two Places
at Once When You're Not Anywhere at
All? / Col. (1969)**
★ ★ ★ ★ ★ **Don't Crush That Dwarf, Hand
Me the Pliers / Col. (1970)**
Peter Bergman, Philip Proctor, David Oss-
man and Philip Austin first appeared in
1967 as a mutant hybrid of James Joyce,
Monty Hall, Douglas MacAuthur and Flash
Gordon. They were the first, and remain
the only, comedy group whose primary
medium was the stereo phonograph record
itself; thus, their best albums stand
up to literally hundreds of listenings. Multi-
tracked, multileveled, multidimensional—
one never gets to the bottom of them.
Consistent themes recur from LP to LP: that
changing TV channels is the fundamental
aesthetic and political experience of modern
times; that aliens long ago took over
California; that the U.S.A. lost World
War II (we were *fighting* fascism, remember).

Electrician, their first outing, is only fair,
but contains the incredible "Beat the Reaper," the first of several game-show parodies
("Hawaiian Sellout," "Give It Back"). *Two
Places* features an excellent if limited Sam
Spade satire, backed with the first full flowering of Firesign genius, a time trip involving
a used-car salesman, W.C. Fields and the
aforementioned author of *Ulysses,* who is liberally quoted. *Dwarf,* a complete work,
scrambles a fascist future, high school madness, old movies, the Korean War, ethnic
humor and uncontrolled paranoia to emerge
as the ultimate answer record to *Catcher in*

the Rye; it is also the greatest comedy album
ever made.
★ ★ ★ **I Think We're All Bozos on This Bus
/ Col. (1971)**
An ambitious, overly rational work about a
future run by machines and populated by
clones. Spooky, but a little too obvious. And,
as the Firesigns would later claim, not in-
sane, and that hurts.
★ ★ **Dear Friends / Col. (1972)** ¶
Transcriptions from the Firesign radio show.
Sometimes funny, but very conventional.
★ **Not Insane or Anything You Want To /
Col. (1972)**
Further decline: witless, noisy, unfocused.
★ ★ **The Tale of the Giant Rat of Sumatra /
Col. (1974)**
A halfassed comeback containing only one
good joke in the course of a meandering,
pointless Sherlock Holmes parody.
★ ★ ★ ★ ★ **Everything You Know Is Wrong
/ Col. (1974)**
The real comeback, in which daredevil
Rebus Cannebus attempts to put out the sun
in the center of the earth; slaves seize power;
Erich von Daniken gets his; aliens get us;
Nazis emerge from the South American jun-
gles to eat moss; and the lights go out all
over the world.
★ ★ ★ ★ **In the Next World, You're on Your
Own / Col. (1975)**
Based loosely on the popularity of Billy Jack
Dog Food ("The kind Billy Jack eats") and
Marlon Brando's refusal to accept an Acad-
emy Award; terrestrial destruction continues
as media pigs eat flaming death; cop shows
take over TV; aliens retreat into the central
cortex; and the hero knocks over a floor display of P. J. Probé wine. A triumph.
★ ★ ★ ★ ★ **Forward into the Past / Col.
(1976)**
Two LPs of Firesign's best over the years,
brilliantly selected and programmed. Horri-
fying, death-dealing, life-enhancing.
★ ★ **Just Folks . . . A Firesign Chat /
Butter. (1977)**
In the ups and downs of Firesigniana, another down: mostly pallid, single-tracked
parodies of Jimmy Carterland, though there
is that commercial for "Confidenz in the
System," a new wonder drug, and a few random lines are inexplicably hilarious.
★ ★ **Roller Maidens from Outer Space /
Epic (1979)**
★ ★ **Fighting Clowns / Rhino (1979)**
★ ★ **Carter/Reagan / Rhino (1980)**
In later years various members of the origi-
nal group (chiefly Proctor and Bergman)
have investigated such mundane topics as
the Carter-Reagan farce (*Fighting Clowns* as

well as *Carter/Reagan*), a long step down from the more cosmic concerns of Firesign's best. — G.M./D.M.

FIRST CHOICE
★ ★ ★ **So Let Us Entertain You / War. (1976)** ¶
★ ★ ★ **Delusions / Gold M. (1978)**
★ ★ ★ **Hold Your Horses / Gold M. (1979)**
★ ★ ★ **Breakaway / Gold M. (1980)**
A female trio, First Choice scored heavily on the R&B charts with three of the greatest hits of early disco, "Armed and Extremely Dangerous" and "Smarty Pants" in 1973 and "The Player, Part 1" in 1974. Somehow, the Philly Groove LPs that contained those songs (*Armed and Extremely Dangerous*; *Smarty Pants*—both with gloriously glitzy covers) have never been reissued. The rest of the music the group has made isn't bad, but there's nothing nearly so hot and danceable on any of these albums, despite occasional soul-chart action. — D.M.

FIRST CLASS
★ ★ **Going First Class / All Pl. (NA)**
Undistinguished disco group, not to be confused with the British act of the same name who hit with "Beach Baby." — D.M.

FISCHER-Z
★ **World Salad / U.A. (1979)**
★ **Going Deaf for a Living / U.A. (1980)**
British synthi-pop group couldn't figure out if they were new wave or art rock. If they'd waited a bit longer they could have tried for new romantic. — J.S.

FIVE BLIND BOYS
★ ★ ★ **Best of the Blind Boys, Vol. 2 / Pea. (NA)**
★ ★ ★ **Best of the Five Blind Boys / Pea. (NA)**
★ ★ ★ **Father, I Stretch My Hands to Thee / Pea. (NA)**
★ ★ **Precious Memories / Pea. (NA)**
★ ★ ★ ★ **The Original Five Blind Boys / Exo. (NA)**
Under Archie Brownlee, the Five Blind Boys were one of the first gospel groups to register in *Billboard*'s record-charts race. Judging from good-natured, uptempo shouters like "I'm a Soldier" and poppish ballads like "Oh Why," Brownlee should be considered one of the direct inspirations for rock & roll. Ray Charles' style was a distillation of Brownlee and Professor Alex Bradford; some twenty years after Brownlee cut "Where There's a Will There's a Way," Lonnie Mack had to change only a few words to re-

cord his pop version. Sam Cooke's highly effective "yodel" also derives from Brownlee.

All the above-named songs are on the Exodus LP, a must for any basic gospel collection. The Peacock albums often invoke Brownlee's name, but he had died before they were cut. The two *Best of* albums are hence slightly misleading, in that they include many songs associated with Brownlee. But they aren't Brownlee's versions. They're cut with Henry Johnson singing lead for the *Memories* set, which was a Brownlee tribute. Still, Johnson matured into one of the more solid and versatile lead singers of the Sixties, and the group's arrangements made better use of rock and soul technique than did most gospel groups evolving along that course. So the Peacock sides aren't without interest. — J.MO.

THE FIVE DU-TONES
★ ★ **Shake a Tail Feather / P-Vine (NA), Jap. imp.**
Group that originated the raunch & blues classic in an otherwise pedestrian set of late Fifties R&B. — D.M.

THE FIVE KEYS
★ ★ ★ ★ **Connoisseur Collection / Harlem Hit Parade (NA)**
★ ★ ★ **The Fantastic Five Keys / Cap. (NA)**
★ ★ ★ **The Five Keys / King (NA)**
★ ★ ★ **Fourteen Original Greatest Hits / King (NA)**
The Keys were one of the more important vocal groups in R&B during the pre–Presley Fifties. "Glory of Love" topped the charts in 1951; it was on Aladdin, and the original is not on any of these albums. The group then moved to Capitol, where its approach leaned closer to conventional Ink Spots pop, actually doing a cover version of the Charms' "Ling Ting Tong," a role usually reserved for white groups only. The group also scored with "Close Your Eyes," "Out of Sight, Out of Mind" and "Wisdom of a Fool," the latter two making the Top Forty during 1956. The group has continued to record sporadically until very recently, mostly for oldies and collector's labels. The King material is from way past the Keys' peak. — D.M.

THE FIVE ROYALES
★ ★ ★ ★ **Seventeen Original Greatest Hits / King (NA)**
★ ★ ★ ★ **Down Home with the Five Royales / Apollo (NA), Fr. imp.**
Led by guitarist/writer Lowman Pauling, the Royales were one of the definitive Fifties black harmony groups. Best known for origi-

nating such standards as "Think" and "Dedicated to the One I Love," almost everything the group ever recorded has genuine grandeur. The Royales recorded as early as 1953 (for Apollo) and as late as 1961, they hit the Top Forty (with "Dedicated"). Lead singer Johnny Tanner's gritty voice ranks with the greatest of R&B and rock & roll. — D.M.

THE FIVE SATINS
★ ★ ★ ★ **The Five Satins' Greatest Hits, Vol. 1 / Ember (NA)**
★ ★ ★ ★ **The Best of the Five Satins / Celebrity Showcase (NA)**
"In the Still of the Night," the Satins' definitive doo-wop hit of 1956, is as stark and poetic as any rock & roll ballad before or since. Writer/lead vocalist Fred Parris continued to make fine music with the Satins: "Oh Happy Day" is yet another doo-wop classic, for instance. After 1958, the Satins were not so scintillating.

The Ember album is perhaps preferable, containing eighteen tracks, including those by the re-formed group with Parris, but both have the basic goodies. — D.M.

ROBERTA FLACK
★ ★ ★ **First Take / Atl. (1969)**
★ ★ ★ **Chapter Two / Atl. (1970)**
★ **Quiet Fire / Atl. (1971)**
★ ★ ★ **Roberta Flack and Donny Hathaway / Atl. (1972)**
★ ★ **Killing Me Softly / Atl. (1973)**
★ ★ **Feel Like Makin' Love / Atl. (1975)**
★ ★ **Blue Lights in the Basement / Atl. (1977)**
★ ★ **Roberta Flack / Atl. (1978)**
★ ★ ★ **The Best of Roberta Flack / Atl. (1981)**
In the early Seventies, Roberta Flack brought a certain refinement and gentility to popular black music that helped pave the way for the achievements of Stevie Wonder, Marvin Gaye and Maurice White, among others. These artists owe her a genuine debt for her success in freeing contemporary black music from the stranglehold of soul conventions. Additionally, of course, there are moments of genuine beauty in "First Time Ever I Saw Your Face," "Hey That's No Way to Say Goodbye" (from First Take), "Reverend Lee" (on Chapter Two) and "Be Real Black for Me" on her collaboration with Donny Hathaway. Unfortunately, more often than not Flack substitutes artifice for feeling, and as a whole her recorded career is terribly dull and dreary.

A classic example is her cover of Aretha Franklin's "Baby I Love You," on the Hathaway duet album, where she and Hathaway decide to add a little pizzazz by vamping on the final "goodbye." The only problem is that "goodbye" is the one word that an intelligent interpretation would not emphasize—it destroys the meaning and thrust of the story line. The point seems trivial, but it helps explain why their version is so tedious. Flack's work is often tedious more from carelessness than anything else.

First Take and Chapter Two had a certain folk-and-funk verve that make them her best, but the success of "First Time Ever" destroyed Flack as an LP artist. From then on, her focus became smart, stylish singles and the albums became bloated, lifeless afterthoughts. — R.G.

FLAKES
★ ★ **Flakes / Sals. (1980)**
Dull late disco, notable (if at all) only for its remake of Freddie Scott's "Hey There Lonely Girl," which stumbled into the soul charts briefly. — D.M.

FLASH AND THE PAN
★ ★ **Flash and the Pan / Epic (1979)**
★ ★ **Lights in the Night / Epic (1980)**
Studio-wiz-turns-performer is a rock & roll syndrome of which many people are justifiably suspicious. Flash and the Pan is Harry Vanda and George Young, who had pivotal roles as players in and writers for the inspirational Sixties Australian band the Easybeats. But years in Sydney recording studios producing some of Australia's major rock acts of the Seventies, such as MOR popster John Paul Young and the AC/DC juggernaut (which includes two of George's younger brothers), seem to have erased the spontaneity that gave life to the Easybeats' pop gems.

Lacking the virtuosity and experimental bent of Steely Dan, or the deftness and whimsy of 10cc, these pop parodists rarely sound more than plodding and literal. Some of their songs have an undeniable novelty appeal ("Down among the Dead Men" from the 1979 album, for instance), and that's reflected in their commercial success both in America and at home. But their rhythms generally seem to have been turned out by a computer, and while the lyrics are occasionally clever, Vanda and Young have an unfortunate propensity for apocalyptic themes without the passion and personality that might render these visions powerful instead of merely ponderous and overwrought.
— S.M.

FLASH CADILLAC

★ ★ ★ **Flash Cadillac and the Continental Kids / Epic (1972)**
★ **Sons of the Beaches / Priv. (1975)**
★ ★ **Rock & Roll Forever / Epic (1975)**

Flash Cadillac, like Sha Na Na, works under the burden of either covering oldies it can't really match in spirit or execution, or writing its own songs to compete with classic oldies. In each case, the attempt often fails, but Flash and the boys' introductory album is the best of the genre. Their cover of "Muleskinner Blues" is so rabid it works. The album's upbeat songs are randy and wry, the ballads full of reverb but free of coyness.

Their first producer was Kim Fowley. Later, producers Toxey French and Jerry Leiber, trying to sweeten the product, lost the essence. *Rock & Roll Forever* packages the first album with two additional sides of stolid remakes, and *Sons of the Beaches* offers one side of ersatz Beach Boying and another of petrified bubblegum. The group also appeared in *American Graffiti,* as the band at the hop. — F.S.

FLASHMAN

★ ★ **Flashman / Van. (1977)**
Forgettable British art-rock band. — R.P.

FLATT AND SCRUGGS

★ ★ ★ ★ **The World of Flatt and Scruggs / Col. (1972)**
★ ★ ★ **A Boy Named Sue / Col. (1973)**
★ ★ ★ **Hard Travelin' / Col. (NA)**
★ ★ ★ **Flatt and Scruggs at Carnegie Hall / Col. (NA)**
★ ★ ★ **The Fabulous Sound of Flatt and Scruggs / Col. (NA)**
★ ★ ★ **Changin' Times / Col. (NA)**
★ ★ ★ ★ ★ **Don't Get Above Your Raisin' / Roun. (1978)**
★ ★ ★ ★ ★ **Golden Era / Roun. (1978)**
★ ★ ★ **Doin' My Time / S&R (NA)**
★ ★ ★ **Flatt and Scruggs Greatest Hits / Col. (NA)**
★ ★ ★ **Golden Hits of Lester Flatt & Earl Scruggs / Power (NA)**
★ ★ ★ **Preachin' Prayin' Singin' / Star (NA)**

Lester Flatt (guitar) and Earl Scruggs (banjo) are two of the most important bluegrass players in history. Scruggs' three-finger technique redefined banjo capabilities in the Forties when the two were featured in Bill Monroe's Bluegrass Boys. They left Monroe to form the Foggy Mountain Boys in 1948 and continued to record brilliantly through the mid-Fifties (this period is covered well on the Rounder LPs). Ironically, the duo's greatest fame came as their powers were waning when their instrumental was used as the *Beverly Hillbillies* television theme song. — J.S.

FLEETWOOD MAC

★ ★ ★ **Then Play On / War. (1969)**
★ ★ ★ **Kiln House / War. (1970)**
★ ★ ★ **Fleetwood Mac in Chicago / Sire (1971)**

In its original incarnation, Fleetwood Mac was the best traditional band to arise from the late-Sixties British blues revival. The band was spearheaded by Peter Green, whose lean lead guitar cut with the precision of an Anglo B. B. King. Its first two albums on Epic (now deleted), and the sessions produced in Chicago with such great traditional bluesmen as Willie Dixon and Otis Spann, revealed more than a trendy affection for the blues. The second album, *English Rose,* put blues chops to invigorating use, with such highlights as "Black Magic Woman" (made famous by Santana, who duplicated Green's solo) and the haunting British instrumental hit "Albatross."

Then Play On was Green's last album with Fleetwood Mac, and its deviation from pure blues ("Oh Well" segued from a blistering blues boogie to a near-classical ending) and strong rock contributions from guitarist Danny Kirwan pointed toward new directions for Mac. Even more bizarre changes were in the offing, though—Peter Green renounced the rock life for menial-laboring ascetic Christianity, and guitarist Jeremy Spencer, whose work with Mac was characterized by his lecherous voice and slide guitar, played on *Kiln House* and then became a Child of God. Thus ended the first chapter of one of the strangest career patterns in rock & roll.

★ ★ ★ ★ **Future Games / War. (1971)**
★ ★ ★ ★ **Bare Trees / War. (1972)**
★ ★ **Penguin / War. (1973)**
★ ★ **Mystery to Me / War. (1973)**
★ ★ ★ **Heroes Are Hard to Find / War. (1974)**

This long stretch of Fleetwood history, from 1970 to 1975, is a jumble of personnel changes, with the quality of the releases fluctuating accordingly. The crucial addition was Christine Perfect from a blues band called Chicken Shack. Perfect found both a singing and marital role in Fleetwood Mac as she married bassist John McVie. Her solid piano and smoky voice proved to be an exciting contrast to Kirwan's rocking sense. The latter had been the saving grace of *Kiln House,* which, despite its smooth playing, displayed an overwrought Buddy Holly fixation. *Future Games* and *Bare Trees* saw Mac gaining its sea legs in the pop-rock field, with McVie supplying the feminine warmth to contrast with Kirwan's more austere moodiness. The combination made the two records Fleetwood Mac's best work until Phase Three.

Penguin, recorded after Kirwan's departure to a solo career, found guitarist/vocalist Robert Welch taking up the compositional slack. But Welch wasn't as consistent as either Kirwan or Green, leaving Fleetwood Mac with a trio of rather lackluster albums, with Christine McVie providing the best moments. While *Heroes Are Hard to Find,* Welch's final album with the group before founding the heavy-metal band Paris, showed definite improvement, his replacements prompted a change that almost nobody could have predicted.

★ ★ ★ **Fleetwood Mac** / War. **(1975)**
★ ★ ★ ★ **Rumours** / War **(1977)**
★ ★ ★ **Original Fleetwood Mac** / Sire **(1977)**
★ ★ ★ **Vintage Years** / Sire **(1977)**
★ ★ ★ **Tusk** / War. **(1979)**
★ ★ ★ **Fleetwood Mac Live** / War. **(1980)**
★ ★ ★ ★ **Mirage** / War. **(1982)**

Stevie Nicks, the bewitching vocalist, and Lindsey Buckingham, a muscular lead guitarist with a writing style influenced by California rock and Buddy Holly, were added in 1976, and it proved a magical catalyst. Suddenly possessing three strong writers and singers, the new Fleetwood Mac produced an album that spawned three singles and sold more than 4 million copies, becoming Warner Bros.' all-time best-seller. Drummer Mick Fleetwood and bassist John McVie, the respective Fleetwood and Mac of the group's name and the only founding members still in the band, suddenly found themselves recognized as one of the finest rhythm sections in rock. And Stevie Nicks found herself as rock's newest heartthrob and the voice of one of 1976's finest singles, "Rhiannon (Will You Ever)."

Rumours, which was recorded under typically bizarre circumstances (two romantic liaisons within the group broke up), proved that *Fleetwood Mac* wasn't a fluke. Rather, it showed what a formidable hit-making machine Mac had become, as their sound took on more of the characteristics of the best California rock without becoming stale or predictable. (The record was the runaway best-seller of 1977, selling more than 10 million copies.) McVie and Buckingham shine in particular, with her wonderfully seductive "You Make Loving Fun" and his tough-rocking "Go Your Own Way" as highlights.

Controversy continued to plague the band, and the next album, *Tusk,* was long overdue when it finally came out. *Tusk,* a dense, personal two-record set, had none of the simple melodicism of the hit single formula coined by the previous two albums, yet the title track was interesting and Lindsey Buckingham's contribution to the record was tremendous. *Live* was a pretty obvious attempt to tread water while the band assembled new ideas. *Mirage,* when it arrived, was simply solid Fleetwood pop, without a hint of risk. All the melodicism had returned but none of the adventure. — J.B.M./J.S.

FLIGHT
★ **Excursion Beyond** / Mo. **(NA)**
Right down here to grubby old earth with the rest of us. — D.M.

FLO AND EDDIE
★ ★ **Rocksteady with Flo and Eddie** / Epip. **(1981)**
A Flo and Eddie reggae LP? It's not as far-fetched as one might expect, since Flo and Eddie are good harmony singers conversant with R&B vocal styles drawn on by reggae singers. This LP, recorded with the cream of Jamaican session men, mixes reggae, R&B and rock oldies (yes, the Turtles' "Happy Together" is there) with varying doses of tongue-in-cheek humor, lameness and genuinely nice moments. — J.S./R.F.G.

FLOATERS
★ **Floaters** / ABC **(1977)** ¶
★ **Magic** / ABC **(1978)**
★ **Float into the Future** / MCA **(NA)** ¶
Imagine Barry White as a thin, four-piece group? Never mind—just remember that "Float On," the 1977 LP's hit single, is a leading contender in the Dumbest Popular Record in the Universe Sweepstakes, but it hums great. *Magic* has fewer charms, the MCA album still less. — D.M.

THE FLOCK
★ **The Flock** / Col. **(1969)**
Eclectic but disjointed jazz rock. Wooden blues-based riffing, too much pointless soloing. The horns play some interesting charts but sound cold next to the dexterous violin of Jerry Goodman (later of the Mahavishnu Orchestra). — C.W.

EDDIE FLOYD
★ ★ **Experience** / Mal. **(1977)**
★ ★ ★ ★ **Chronicle** / Stax **(1978)**
Floyd was one of the second rank of Stax stars, but his writing and singing were good

enough to collect a sizable body of Sixties R&B hits, most notably "Knock on Wood" and "Raise Your Hand." *Chronicle* collects the best of them, and includes what might be the definitive catalogue of Stax effects, "Big Bird." Floyd sang in a raw soul style (as he had been doing since he appeared with the Falcons, in the late Fifties) only a bit less agitated than Otis Redding's. His writing credits include not only his own hits, but several of Wilson Pickett's, notably "Ninety-nine and a Half (Won't Do)."

The Malaco album is a dismal attempt to go disco at the hands of the TK Productions organization. — D.M.

KING FLOYD
★ ★ ★ **Well Done** / **Chim. (1977)**
★ ★ **Body English** / **Chim. (1977)**
Well Done is notable for one magnificent song, "I Feel Like Dynamite," a tough slab of Southern funk honed from Floyd's biggest hit, "Groove Me" (1970). Mild reggae and less commanding funk songs make up the rest of that album and also *Body English*. — J.M.C.

THE FLYING BURRITO BROTHERS
★ ★ ★ ★ **The Gilded Palace of Sin** / **A&M (1969)**
★ ★ ★ ★ **Burrito Deluxe** / **A&M (1970)**
★ ★ ★ ★ **The Flying Burrito Bros.** / **A&M (1971)**
★ ★ ★ **Last of the Red Hot Burritos** / **A&M (1972)**
★ ★ ★ **Close Up the Honky Tonks** / **A&M (1972)**
★ ★ **Flying Again** / **Col. (1976)** ¶
★ ★ **Airborne** / **Col. (1976)** ¶
★ ★ ★ **Sleepless Nights** / **A&M (1976)**
The Gilded Palace of Sin is one of the earliest and best matchings of rock & roll and country & western, thanks to former Byrd Gram Parsons' achingly pretty and fragile tenor, tinged with a youthfully innocent Southern accent, and "Sneaky" Pete Kleinow's facile pedal steel, often enlivened with distortion effects.

Burrito Deluxe adds Bernie Leadon on guitar and a third ex-Byrd (joining Parsons and bassist Chris Hillman), Michael Clarke, on drums. The result is tougher, leaner, faster, more rocking music with Leadon and Kleinow in the forefront—less variety perhaps, but an improved group. *Sleepless Nights* (containing three non-Burrito tracks from Parsons and Emmylou Harris, recorded after the singer had left) has nine competent outtakes from sessions done at this time, and

shows the more country-derived side of the hybrid.

Rick Roberts then joined, and his melodic singing and more pop-oriented writing gives *The Flying Burrito Bros.* a workable new direction. Chris Hillman assumed more control, both as a singer and writer, but the country influence was not decreasing.

The live *Last of the Red Hot Burritos,* released after the group disbanded, is an odd mixture: fiddle virtuoso Byron Berline leads a new lineup through "The Orange Blossom Special," while Hillman and Roberts play spirited but thin rock & roll. Kleinow had been replaced by Al Perkins.

Close Up the Honky Tonks, a two-record set, is half material from the first two albums, and half passable outtakes spanning each phase of the group; it's adequate but unthrilling.

Flying Again marked a reassembling that had two originals (Kleinow and bassist Chris Ethridge) and another ex-Byrd, Gene Parsons. This record—along with the ensuing *Airborne,* with yet another ex-Byrd, Skip Battyn—gives only the barest hint of the earlier incarnations, instead offering faceless approximations of pop, rock and country: a weak shadow, possibly even an insult, to the pioneers of before. — C.W.

THE FLYING LIZARDS
★ ★ ★ **The Flying Lizards** / **Virgin (1980)**
A conceptual novelty record. Although most of the album is given over to dreadfully self-conscious irony and lame disco licks, two moments of genius flicker among the debris. Producer David Cunningham pokes a few well-deserved holes in the cover-band ethos by reducing Eddie Cochran's "Summertime Blues" to a dialect joke and giving Berry Gordy's "Money (That's What I Want)" a treatment bald enough to reveal all the meanness of the lyric. Good for a few highbrow yuks, but that's about all. — J.D.C.

THE FLYS
★ ★ ★ ★ **Waikiki Beach Refugees** / **EMI (1978), Br. imp.**
★ ★ ★ **Own** / **EMI (1979), Br. imp.**
Waikiki Beach Refugees is post-punk power pop at its rawest, which is to say that it retains a genuinely nasty sense of Top Forty song form. *Own* stumbles over its own ambitions, though, with much less pleasant results. — D.M.

DAN FOGELBERG
★ ★ ★ **Home Free** / **Col. (1972)**
★ ★ **Souvenirs** / **Epic (1974)**

★ **Captured Angel** / Epic (1975)
★ **Nether Lands** / Epic (1977)
★ **Twin Sons of Different Mothers** / Epic (1978)
★ **Phoenix** / Epic (1980)
★ ★ ★ **The Innocent Age** / Epic (1981)

Extremely successful Illinois-born singer/ songwriter and multi-instrumentalist (now Colorado-based) has refined the richly textured Crosby, Stills and Nash sound into an engaging, ersatz light classical style. It's an appropriately sentimental idiom for Fogelberg's earnest pseudo-Victorian lyrics and throaty crooning style. On *Home Free,* his simplest album, Fogelberg suggested the potential of Jackson Browne in the reflective ballads "Be On Your Way" and "To the Morning." Subsequently, however, Fogelberg's lyrics have become increasingly contorted and grandiose, even as his music gained in sophistication. Highlights of recent albums include a strong version of the Hollies' "Tell Me to My Face" on *Twin Sons* (a collaboration with flutist Tim Weisberg) and the schlock standard, "Longer," on *Phoenix. The Innocent Age,* a double-record concept album about the hard realities of growing up, is Fogelberg's grand statement and suggests Thomas Wolfe translated into stilted verse. Despite embarrassingly overwrought lyrics, the music is the best crafted of Fogelberg's career. — S.H.

JOHN FOGERTY
★ ★ ★ ★ **John Fogerty** / Asy. (1975)

Fogerty's second post–Creedence Clearwater project (the first was recorded as *The Blue Ridge Rangers*) offers the only new songs he has written in the best part of a decade. Two of them—"Almost Saturday Night" and "Rockin' All over the World"—are outstanding, more anthemic and nearly as passionate as the best of Creedence. "The Wall" is another solid song, but most of the other originals are a bit lumbering, and while one of the oldies (Louis Armstrong's "You Rascal You") works well, his versions of Frankie Ford's "Sea Cruise" and Jackie Wilson's "Lonely Teardrops" are far too slight. Fogerty remains a great and gifted rocker, one of the premier American artists of his generation, whenever he chooses to apply himself more fully again. — D.M.

TOM FOGERTY
★ ★ **Excalibur** / Fan. (1972) ¶
★ ★ **Deal It Out** / Fan. (1981)

Tom Fogerty, brother of John, was the first member to leave Creedence Clearwater, but his early exit hasn't helped. His songwriting is penny-dreadful, his singing not much better, and without Creedence's whiplash rhythm section, this music is just plain faceless. A nice guy winds up in the usual position. — D.M.

FOGHAT
★ ★ **Foghat** / Bears. (1972)
★ ★ **Foghat** / Bears. (1973)
★ ★ **Energize** / Bears. (1973)
★ ★ ★ **Rock and Roll Outlaws** / Bears. (1974)
★ ★ **Fool for the City** / Bears. (1975)
★ ★ ★ **Night Shift** / Bears. (1976)
★ ★ ★ **Foghat Live** / Bears. (1977)
★ ★ **Stone Blue** / Bears. (1978)
★ ★ **Boogie Motel** / Bears. (1979)
★ ★ **Tight Shoes** / Bears. (1980)
★ ★ **Girls to Chat and Boys to Bounce** / Bears. (1981)

Foghat owns one weapon that has made it a top Middle American rock attraction— Chuck Berry simplified and amplified into a bludgeoning torrent of chunky rhythms. The band's style hasn't really changed over the course of eleven albums; rather, its attacks have become more sharply defined and the songwriting has improved. The band's appeal, nonetheless, rests on its particularly strong tunes; other elements of their recordings invariably reveal a wide gap in quality, and the live show is a predictable batch of them, from *Night Shift's* "Driving Wheel" to the title tunes from *Fool for the City* and *Rock and Roll Outlaws.*

Foghat scored an instant FM hit with its whining wah-wah treatment of Willie Dixon's "I Just Want to Make Love to You," a tune that essentially defines the style. Like Savoy Brown, from which two of the players came, Foghat's method is comparable to a meat-and-potatoes fighter who aims for the gut. The emotions of the tune are inevitably subservient to the big, metallic beat that brings in the kids. Consequently, while Foghat lacks the sense of humor to be one of Chuck Berry's best interpreters, it'll never be the worst.

Rock and Roll Outlaws is the most successful LP here, yet the qualitative difference between the live show and the records is lost in translation to the stage album. The other albums have highlights, but there's just too much retread here and not enough inspiration. — J.B.M.

ELLEN FOLEY
★ ★ **Night Out** / Epic (1979)
★ ★ **Spirit of St. Louis** / Epic (1981)

Ellen Foley is another in a long line of experienced backup singers (most notably on Meat Loaf's "Paradise by the Dashboard") who have virtually no identity as solo performers. Foley likes to come on tough, like some female Springsteen or fifth Clash, but essentially she fails or prospers at the whim of her illustrious producers. Ian Hunter and Mick Ronson, the producers of *Night Out,* must have had visions of Phil Spector dancing in their heads: They put Foley up against a Wall of Sound style that just doesn't suit her. Other inappropriate choices include a cover of "Stupid Girl." On *Spirit of St. Louis* Foley's boyfriend Mick Jones and pal Joe Strummer go for the La Pasionaria sound, cluttering up songs about Dali, psychoanalysis and the cafés of Europe with mandolins and calliopes, as if trying to create a musical *New York Review of Books.* All in all, these records are lessons in how far women still have to go in rock & roll. — D.G.

FAST FONTAINE
★ ★ **Fast Fontaine** / EMI (1981)
Doug "Fontaine" Brown was Bob Seger's bar-band mentor in mid-Sixties Michigan, later moved to California and started Southwind, one of the more listenable cowboy-rock bar bands of the period (which also featured Moon Martin). On this set, however, Fontaine suffers from weak songs and sloppy, overaggressive performances. Better to check out the Southwind LPs, if you can find them. — D.M.

THE FOOLS
★ **Sold Out** / EMI (1980)
★ **Heavy Mental** / EMI (1981)
Titles self-descriptive, apparently meant to be taken literally. Group earns its star for playing heavy metal in Boston, just badly enough to torture the city's legions of rock intellectuals. — D.M.

STEVE FORBERT
★ ★ ★ ★ **Alive on Arrival** / Nemp. (1978)
★ ★ **Jackrabbit Slim** / Nemp. (1979)
★ ★ **Little Stevie Orbit** / Nemp. (1980)
★ ★ **Steve Forbert** / Nemp. (1982)
Steve Forbert seemed a likely prototype for the Eighties folkie. Although he had Tom Sawyer's sense of purpose, he tempered it with a good deal of Huck Finn savvy. Sure, there was more wordplay than insight to his songs, but his graceful, effortless sense of melody made meaningfulness almost irrelevant. Or so it seemed on Forbert's precocious debut, *Alive on Arrival.* But on *Jack-rabbit Slim,* Forbert developed a disturbing fondness for dense *Blonde on Blonde*–ish arrangements; he proceeded to turn slick. These days his folk roots amount to bits of acoustic guitar bubbling up the mix, and while his melodies remain hummable, their freshness seems as artificial as a loaf of Wonder bread. — J.D.C.

THE FORCE
★ ★ **The Force** / Phil. (1979)
Dull dance music, without even a *Star Wars* joke to alleviate it. — D.M.

ROBBEN FORD
★ ★ ★ **Inside Story** / Elek. (1979)
Blues-fusion guitarist distinguished himself as a session player with Joni Mitchell and Jimmy Witherspoon before making this good if unspectacular solo record. — J.S.

TENNESSEE ERNIE FORD
★ ★ **Sweet Hour of Prayer** / Cap. (1957)
★ ★ **Tennessee Ernie Hymns** / Cap. (1957)
★ ★ **Tennessee Spirituals** / Cap. (1957)
★ **Star Carol (Christmas)** / Cap. (1958)
★ **Nearer the Cross** / Cap. (1958)
■ **Story of Christmas** / Cap. (1963)
★ ★ **Book of Favorite Hymns** / Cap. (1963)
★ ★ **Great Gospel Songs** / Cap. (1964)
★ ★ **Faith of Our Fathers** / Cap. (1967)
★ ★ **America the Beautiful** / Cap. (1970)
★ ★ **Make a Joyful Noise** / Cap. (1974)
★ ★ ★ **Twenty-fifth Anniversary** / Cap. (1974)
★ ★ ★ **Country Hits . . . Feelin' Blue** / Cap. (1975)
★ ★ **Precious Memories** / Cap. (1975)
★ **Sing His Great Love** / Cap. (1976)
★ ★ **He Touched Me** / Word (1977)
★ ★ **Let Me Walk with Thee** / Cap. (1978)
★ ★ ★ ★ **Best of** / Cap. (NA)
Ford's growling bass voice is employed for the most part on devotional hymns and specialty projects, but two white R&B classics, "Mule Train" and "Sixteen Tons," insure him a niche in rock & roll history. The rest is pretty much competent but forgettable. — C.F.

FOREIGNER
★ ★ ★ **Foreigner** / Atl. (1977)
★ **Double Vision** / Atl. (1978)
★ ★ **Head Games** / Atl. (1979)
★ ★ **4** / Atl. (1981)
★ ★ ★ **Records** / Atl. (1982)
This group of British and American journeyman hard rockers, led by Spooky Tooth refugee Mick Jones, outdid most of its antecedents on its 1977 debut. It lacked all subtlety, but on that album, "Cold as Ice" and "Feels

Like the First Time" transcended their limitations enough to become sizable pop hits. Succeeding LPs, however, have myopically rehashed the debut album, a formula approach that suggests the group belongs in the ranks of the simply banal. *Records*, the greatest-hits LP, collects all the Foreigner you'll ever need to hear. — D.M.

FORTRESS
★ ★ **Hand in the Till / Atl. (1981)**
Title presumably describes feeling of anyone dumb enough to purchase this benumbed hard-rock travesty. — D.M.

FOTHERINGAY
★ ★ **Fotheringay / A&M (1970)**
Uneven, unfocused and loosely performed, this is the sole effort by the defunct offshoot of Fairport Convention. Mainly Sandy Denny's British folk, with bits from comember Trevor Lucas and covers of Dylan and Lightfoot. — C.W.

FOUR ON THE FLOOR
★ ★ ★ *Four on the Floor / Casa. (1979)*
Al Kooper/Skunk Baxter disco project covers "There Goes My Baby" and a Stones medley of "Let's Spend the Night Together," "Lady Jane," "Paint It Black" and "Under My Thumb." Annoys as it works. — J.S.

FOUR OUT OF FIVE DOCTORS
★ **Four out of Five Doctors / Nemp. (1981)**
Pointless power pop. — D.M.

THE FOUR SEASONS
★ ★ ★ ★ **Four Seasons Story / Priv. (1975)** ¶
★ **Who Loves You / War. (1975)**
★ **Helicon / War. (1977)**
★ **Motown Super Star Series, Vol. 4 / Mo. (1981)**
★ **Reunited Live with Frankie Valli / War. (1981)**
In the early Sixties, the Four Seasons battled it out with Motown, the Beach Boys and the Beatles for supremacy on the pop charts. Led by the piercing falsetto of vocalist Frankie Valli, they scored repeatedly with hits like "Sherry," "Walk Like a Man," "Big Girls Don't Cry," "Dawn," "Rag Doll" and "Stay." The songs epitomized the Fifties hangover era before a Sixties style developed, the era invoked by *American Graffiti*. The Private Stock collection includes all relevant Four Seasons material. The Motown and Warner Bros. albums are lame attempts at reviving the group. — J.S.

THE FOUR TOPS
★ ★ ★ ★ **Four Tops: Greatest Hits / Mo. (1967)**
★ ★ ★ **Keeper of the Castle / Dun. (1972)** ¶
★ ★ **Main Street People / Dun. (1973)** ¶
★ ★ **Live and in Concert / Dun. (1974)** ¶
★ ★ ★ ★ ★ **Anthology / Mo. (1974)**
★ ★ **Night Lights Harmony / ABC (1975)** ¶
★ ★ **Catfish / ABC (1976)** ¶
★ ★ **The Show Must Go On / ABC (1977)** ¶
★ ★ **At the Top / MCA (1978)**
★ ★ ★ ★ **Motown Super Star Series, Vol. 14 / Mo. (1981)**
★ ★ **Four Tops Tonight / Casa. (1981)**
★ ★ ★ **Still Waters Run Deep / Mo. (1982)**
★ ★ ★ ★ ★ **Reach Out / Mo. (1982)**
★ ★ ★ ★ **The Four Tops / Mo. (1982)**
From their first hit, 1964's "Baby I Need Your Loving," the Four Tops were one of the grandest things about Motown. Lead singer Levi Stubbs had a huge, smoldering voice that set the group apart from the often airy music most other Motown acts made. But if the Tops' sound was not definitive, it was one of the best in Sixties soul music, as their long string of hits confirmed: "I Can't Help Myself," "It's the Same Old Song," "Standing in the Shadows of Love," "Bernadette" and half a dozen others. The best of all was the terrifying melodrama, "Reach Out, I'll Be There," which Phil Spector called "black Dylan." Stubbs has been criticized for overemoting, but here his histrionics matched the material and the incredible production of Holland-Dozier-Holland perfectly. There are few more transcendent moments in American music.

As the Sixties waned, however, the Tops were unable to keep up with the accelerating changes fostered by the emergence of black stars like Sly and the Family Stone and Jimi Hendrix, or with the new production values brought to Motown by Norman Whitfield and Barrett Strong. Although they scored an occasional chart success, such as "Still Water (Love)" in 1970 and "MacArthur Park," of all things, in 1971, time had clearly passed them by. Moving to ABC/ Dunhill in 1972 helped a bit—"Keeper of the Castle" was a Top Ten hit, and much less forced than their last few Motown discs—but soon attempts to remain contemporary or to go pop, and confusion between the two, took a toll. While the group remains intact, with Stubbs still a distinctive singer, their recent albums have grown more and more irrelevant. *Still Waters, The Four Tops,* and *Reach Out* are trimmed-down reissues of Sixties Tops LPs. — D.M.

KIM FOWLEY
■ **International Heroes / EMI (1973), Br. imp.**
■ **Living in the Streets / PVC (1978)**
■ **Sunset Boulevard / PVC (1977)**
Living proof of the Shangri-Las' "good bad but not evil" theory, but that doesn't mean that you have to listen to these conceptual anti-masterpieces to get the point. In fact, if you *do* listen, you've probably missed it.
— D.M.

FOXY
★ ★ **Foxy / Dash (1976)**
★ ★ **Get Off / Dash (1978)**
★ ★ **Foxy Live / Dash (NA)**
★ ★ **Hot Numbers / Dash (1979)**
★ ★ **Party Boys / Dash (1981)**
Typically aimless funk from the Miami mill of T.K. Productions. — D.M.

PETER FRAMPTON
★ ★ ★ ★ **Wind of Change / A&M (1972)**
★ ★ ★ **Frampton's Camel / A&M (1973)**
★ ★ ★ **Somethin's Happening / A&M (1974)**
★ ★ **Frampton / A&M (1975)**
★ ★ **Frampton Comes Alive / A&M (1975)**
★ **I'm in You / A&M (1977)**
★ ★ **Where I Should Be / A&M (1979)**
★ ★ **Breaking All the Rules / A&M (1981)**
Armed with several years of rock apprenticeship in the Herd and Humble Pie, a pretty face and an unusually seductive electric guitar style, Peter Frampton leaped into a solo recording career with the kind of confidence that comes from knowing you have *all* the attributes to make it big. *Wind of Change,* his first—and still his best—solo effort, amply demonstrates that confidence, mingled with a sense of exhilaration at being freed from the heavy-metal exigencies of Humble Pie. The first, airy chords of "Fig Tree Bay" announce the arrival of an above-average melodist but lightweight lyricist, and although the album is replete with fiery guitar work and some of Frampton's better songs ("It's a Plain Shame," "All I Want to Be," "The Lodger"), this unfortunate dichotomy was to persist in varying degrees on subsequent recordings.
Frampton's Camel featured the first Frampton group per se, and the music was uncharacteristically dense and hard-edged. Troubled and autobiographical, *Camel* contains one of Frampton's most touching and durable ballads, "Lines on My Face" (to him, it *mattered*); "White Sugar"; and "Do You Feel Like We Do," a typically friendly song that would become a staple in live performance.
Somethin's Happening was directionless,

with little more than the gleaming title tune and some pleasant moments to recommend it. A growing Frampton trend toward one to three strong, commercial rock songs mingled in with elegant filler was becoming more apparent.
Kicking off along and arduous American campaign of road trips, *Frampton* was infused with a languid, spacious feeling that harkened back to the first album and revitalized FM programmers' flagging interest.
Frampton Comes Alive, a double LP set complete with Frampton's best material, a *lot* of lead guitar and an adoring audience responding enthusiastically to his "nice" stage personality, did in fact capture the imagination of the listening populace and sold well over 8 million copies.
And, except for two passable Motown covers—"Signed, Sealed, Delivered (I'm Yours)" and "Roadrunner"—*I'm in You* merely confirmed the fact that Peter Frampton has little to say, but a very "pretty" way of saying it. Subsequent records did nothing to change that. — J.C.C.

CONNIE FRANCIS
■ **Very Best of Connie Francis / MGM (1963)**
■ **I'm Me Again / MGM (1981)**
People who missed the late Fifties may not know the answer to the question: "What's less funky than a Connie Francis movie?" The answer, in all its glitzy, depressing splendor, is right here. — D.M.

BOB FRANK
★ ★ ★ **Bob Frank / Van. (1972)**
Frank's a weedy songwriter/guitarist whose album is rife with bluesy folk tunes of boozers and dopers. Aside from his guitar playing, the only accompaniment to his singing is an occasional harmonica part. — J.S.

JIMMY FRANK
★ ★ **Such a Pity / Ario. (1980)**
East Coast singer/writer has advantage over early-Seventies types in a couple of areas: because of Bruce Springsteen's success, he gets to use a saxophone, and because of Paul Simon's hits, he can import drummer Roger Hawkins from Muscle Shoals to New York. Aside from that, and the fact that Frank isn't related to James Taylor, this isn't anything that you should not have already disregarded as having potential in about 1972.
— D.M.

STANLEY FRANK
★ ★ ★ **Play It Till It Hurts / A&M (1981)**

Peppy, light rock vigor, without much substance, but skillfully pieced together.
— D.M.

FRANKE AND THE KNOCKOUTS
★ ★ Franke and the Knockouts / Millen. (1981)
Bad imitations of Journey, Hall and Oates, and the Doobie Brothers. — J.D.C.

ARETHA FRANKLIN
★ ★ ★ Laughing on the Outside / Col. (1963) ¶
★ ★ ★ The Great Aretha Franklin / Col. (1964) ¶
★ ★ ★ ★ Unforgettable / Col. (1964)
★ ★ ★ ★ Songs of Faith / Check. (1964) ¶
★ ★ ★ ★ ★ I Never Loved a Man (The Way I Love You) / Atl. (1967)
★ ★ ★ Aretha Franklin's Greatest Hits, Vol. 2 / Col. (1968)
★ ★ ★ ★ Aretha's Gold / Atl. (1969)
★ ★ ★ ★ Spirit in the Dark / Atl. (1970) ¶
★ ★ ★ Aretha Live at Fillmore West / Atl. (1971) ¶
★ ★ ★ ★ Aretha's Greatest Hits / Atl. (1971)
★ ★ ★ ★ Young, Gifted and Black / Atl. (1972) ¶
★ ★ ★ ★ Amazing Grace / Atl. (1972)
★ ★ ★ All-Time Greatest Hits / Col. (1972) ¶
★ ★ ★ Best of Aretha Franklin / Atl. (1973) ¶
★ You / Atl. (1975) ¶
★ ★ Sparkle / Atl. (1976) ¶
★ ★ ★ ★ Ten Years of Gold / Atl. (1977) ¶
★ ★ Sweet Passion / Atl. (1977) ¶
★ ★ Almighty Fire / Atl. (1978) ¶
★ ★ ★ Aretha / Ari. (1980)
★ ★ ★ ★ Love All the Hurt Away / Ari. (1981)
★ ★ ★ ★ Jump to It / Ari. (1982)
Aretha Franklin is the greatest female singer of her generation, perhaps the greatest all-around musical talent in black music since Ray Charles. Not only as a singer, but also as a pianist, Franklin's work is as impressive and influential as any artist's of the past two decades.

Franklin was already famous on the black gospel circuit in the late Fifties, mostly as a result of her singing at the Detroit church where her father, the Reverend C. L. Franklin (himself the author of more than two dozen preaching LPs), was pastor, but also partly as a result of the Checker LP above. In 1959, John Hammond, the legendary CBS talent scout, signed her to a pop recording contract with Columbia. Franklin's first sides there, produced by Hammond and included on *The Great Aretha Franklin,* present her as a jazz singer and sometime pianist, a limited approach given the range of her talents, but one that had excellent results. Unfortunately, almost all of her other Columbia sides were produced by a series of white pop producers, who tried to make her a black version of Barbra Streisand. This approach was generally disastrous, with an occasional thrilling exception, like "Lee Cross."

In 1967, Franklin moved to Atlantic, where she entered a long and profitable association with producer Jerry Wexler (later assisted by Arif Mardin and Tom Dowd). Her first record there, *I Never Loved a Man (The Way I Love You),* was an immediate success, not only on the R&B charts, where she had had occasional success before, but also on the pop charts, where it made the Top Ten. It was followed by a string of winners, including "Respect," a No. 1 hit, and the immediate followups (all of them Top Ten): "Baby I Love You," "Chain of Fools," "A Natural Woman," "Think," "(Sweet Sweet Baby) Since You've Been Gone," "The House That Jack Built" and "I Say a Little Prayer." Wexler produced Franklin in Muscle Shoals with the tremendously propulsive rhythm section he had developed while working with Wilson Pickett, capitalizing not only on her feeling for blues but also on her gospel roots, and giving her remarkable piano-playing skills more prominence. The pattern, in fact, was similar to what Ahmet Ertegun and Wexler had done with Ray Charles (another gospel-based R&B singer/ pianist) in the late Fifties.

With the album *Soul '69,* Franklin began to expand her horizons ever further, into a variety of pop jazz that was tremendously emotional and as singular as anything recent popular music has produced. Beginning in 1971, she created another series of Top Ten hits, including a brilliant gospel version of "Bridge over Troubled Water," a remake of Ben E. King's "Spanish Harlem," the driving "Rock Steady" and "Day Dreaming." But after 1974, the Wexler-Mardin-Dowd production team was discarded, first for a confusing album with Quincy Jones, *Hey Now Hey (The Other Side of the Sky),* which shared many of the flaws of her Columbia work despite the inclusion of her sister Carolyn's wonderful "Angel," and later for a series of contemporary, disco-oriented producers, including Lamont Dozier and Curtis Mayfield. The hits became much more minor and much less frequent, and Franklin, always an eccentric, spent most of her time in the late Seventies floundering in search of a focus for her own genius.

Virtually everything Franklin has recorded is worth hearing, if only for the quality of her voice, which is too remarkable for capsule description. The great bulk of her Columbia work remains in print, but as is usual for that company, Atlantic has allowed her catalogue to fall into disrepair. Of the first few albums she did for that label, only *I Never Loved a Man* remains in print. Now lost are such gems as *Aretha Now, Aretha Arrives* and the record that remains her supreme achievement, *Lady Soul,* which includes "Respect," "Chain of Fools," "Good to Me as I Am to You" (featuring a guitar obbligato by Eric Clapton), "Since You've Been Gone," "Ain't No Way" and Ray Charles' "Come Back Baby." All of these records are musts for soul fans, if only they can find them. Lacking that, settle for the various greatest-hits collections: *Gold* includes all the early hits, up to "The House That Jack Built"; *Greatest Hits* contains much of the best of the "Spanish Harlem" period, as well as some of the earlier records, while *Ten Years of Gold* includes the most prominent early hits and such recent near misses as "Angel," "Until You Come Back to Me" and "Something He Can Feel."

Of the more sophisticated recent records, the best are the classic *Spirit in the Dark* and the more moderately successful *Young, Gifted and Black,* the adventurous and underrated *Soul '69,* and her two final albums with Wexler-Mardin-Dowd, *With Everything I Feel in Me* and *Let Me in Your Life. You* is a complete disaster—unredeemed even by her voice—while *Sparkle,* a Mayfield-produced soundtrack for a black-exploitation film, and the Lamont Dozier–produced *Sweet Passion* court catastrophe by not providing suitable channels for Franklin's occasionally wandering attention.

Live at Fillmore West features the only recorded collaboration between Franklin and Ray Charles, which makes it worthwhile, even though the band lacks focus; King Curtis' session with them, recorded at the same time and released as *King Curtis and the Kingpins Live at Fillmore West,* is better if less spectacular. Finally, *Amazing Grace,* a two-record set of gospel songs recorded live in Los Angeles in 1972, is a marvel in which the great star returns to her deepest roots and shines in total triumph over songs she has sung all her life. It is a perfect climax to any Franklin collection.

Franklin's three Arista albums have all been steps in a more controlled pop direction. "Jump to It," from the Luther Vandross-produced album, took Aretha back to the top of the soul and pop charts.
— D.M.

ERMA FRANKLIN
★ ★ **Soul Sister / Bruns. (1969)**
Erma Franklin's real claim to fame, besides being the sister of Aretha and Carolyn, is the pioneering version of "Piece of My Heart," not available on LP, which Janis Joplin turned into a Sixties anthem. On *Soul Sister,* Franklin essays late-Sixties standards, from soul numbers like "Hold On I'm Comin' " and "Son of a Preacher Man" to such instantly dated efforts as "By the Time I Get to Phoenix" and "Light My Fire."
— D.M.

MICHAEL FRANKS
★ ★ **The Art of Tea / Rep. (1976)**
★ ★ ★ **Sleeping Gypsy / War. (1977)**
★ ★ **Burchfield Nines / War. (1978)**
★ ★ **Tiger in the Rain / War. (1979)**
★ ★ **One Bad Habit / War. (1980)**
Affectingly light, jazzy pop—smooth but not slick. Franks possesses a casual, slow, almost talking style of singing; his melodies and tempos are leisurely without dragging. The albums center on Joe Sample's relaxed electric piano, with generally only guitar, bass and drums accompanying. Occasional sax and string arrangements are handled judiciously. *Sleeping Gypsy* is slightly more spacious and less restricted, though many of the same musicians appear on all of the records.
— C.W.

FRANTIQUE
★ **Frantique / Phil. (1979)**
Anonymous, slick group that epitomizes decline of the Gamble-Huff production mill into strained facelessness. — D.M.

STAN FREBERG
★ ★ ★ **Stan Freberg Presents the United States of America / Cap. (1961)**
★ ★ **The Best of Stan Freberg / Cap. (1963)**
★ **Freberg Underground Show No. 1 / Cap. (1966)** ¶
★ **Stan Freberg with the Original Cast / Cap. (1969)**
These unfunny records almost conceal Freberg's small, arch sense of humor. Raised on radio, he never really overcame his contempt for television (as expressed overtly in "Tele-Vee-Shun" on *Best of* and embodied by *Underground,* half seriously intended to bring back radio via record, or in Freberg's phrase,

"pay radio"). Nowadays, this makes him sound petty and shortsighted. *Freberg Presents* is easily the best thing here, with Freberg populating the touchstones of American history (Columbus' voyage, the Boston Tea Party, etc.) with sarcastic puns in thick Jewish accents. He must be seen as an important precursor to the sublime self-consciousness of the Firesign Theatre.

These recordings do not preserve Freberg's more important and much funnier stuff: his TV commercials and ad compaigns. It was he who set Ann Miller to tap-dancing atop a Campbell's soup can, and he who wrote the Sunkist prune ads featuring Freberg as an off-camera interviewer pressing the new pitted prune on a disdainful fat man who, after munching one, acknowledges their deliciousness but then picks another one up and sniffs, "Still haven't gotten rid of those nasty wrinkles, though, have you?" — K.T.

JOHN FRED
★ ★ ★ **Judy in Disguise with Glasses/Agnes English** / Paula (1967)

A genuine eccentric, Fred gathered a bunch of Louisiana sessionmen to fashion a sublimely commercial pop group called the Playboy Band in the late Sixties and early Seventies. "Judy in Disguise (with Glasses)" was their fluke hit single; for the rest, they purveyed a catchy white R&B sound that really rocked. Fred's immaculate taste led them to cover terrific songs by everyone from Mann and Weil to Willie Dixon, but it was on the all-original and unfortunately final album, *Permanently Stated* (now deleted), that Fred hit his peak: delicate wit, immature romance and the purest American rock & roll. — K.T.

JEFFREY FREDERICK AND THE CLAMTONES
★ ★ ★ **Spiders in the Moonlight** / Roun. (1977)

Part of the *Have Moicy* mafia. Frederick's smoky voice and irreverent lyrics make him one of the great practitioners of apocalyptic C&W. The heretically funny "Let Me Down," a very different look at the Jesus story, got the Clamtones run out of a certain Southern state one fateful night. The great instrumental accompaniment here includes several members of the legendary Holy Modal Rounders Big Band—keyboardist Richard Tyler, saxophonist Ted Deane, bassist Dave Reisch and multi-instrumentalist Robin Remailly. — J.S.

FREDDY AND THE DREAMERS
★ ★ **The Best of Freddy and the Dreamers** / Cap. (1979)

Freddy and the Dreamers are noteworthy only because they were the first of the British Invasion groups not to come from Liverpool. A true case of being in the right place at the right time, this group was the most unlikely assortment ever to become the object of teen libidinal fancy. Freddy was a hyped-up Buddy Holly lookalike with a castrato's voice who liked to do jumping jacks while he sang. (This was the alleged "dance," the Freddy.) The Dreamers were a thuggish group whose interest in the silly ballads and novelty numbers they performed was minimal. All their unmemorable hits like "I'm Telling You Now" and "Do the Freddy" are included on this album. — D.G.

FREE
★ ★ **Tons of Sobs** / A&M (1969) ¶
★ ★ **Free** / A&M (1970)
★ ★ ★ ★ **Fire and Water** / A&M (1970)
★ ★ **Free Live** / A&M (1971)
★ ★ **Heartbreaker** / Is. (1971)
★ ★ ★ ★ **Highway** / A&M (1973)
★ ★ ★ ★ **Best of Free** / A&M (1975)

At its best, Free walked on a tightrope of rolling drums—a voice skirting round and about the beat—and a dramatically sustained lead guitar. The music was taut and jaggedly rhythmic, with a much simpler production than most hard rock of the late Sixties—"All Right Now" squawked out of the box with raw bravado. Singer Paul Rodgers and drummer Simon Kirke brought some of these sensibilities to Bad Company, but they rarely matched the tastefully tense edge of the best Free music.

The debut album, *Tons of Sobs*, was standard British heavy blues, and the second showed potential, particularly on the slithery "I'll Be Creeping." But it wasn't until *Fire and Water*, which began with the stormy title cut and ended with "All Right Now," that Free hit its stride. Paul Kossoff established a guitar style that was simple in conception but inherently dramatic in execution, making Free an instant stand-out from much of the overplaying hard-rock competition. *Fire and Water* shows off Kossoff and Rodgers' burgeoning talents in their best hard-rock light; Rodgers' light, flexible blues voice took similar improvisational jumps that played off the other rhythms. *Highway* cooled down the burners, concentrating on rhythmic cohesion with a bit more of a pop feel. With bassist Andy Fraser and Rodgers' best tunes yet ("The Highway Song," "Bodie") and the tough-riffing "The Stealer," it was probably their most consistent album.

Free subsequently lost its bearings, with a routine live album and a fairly heartless *Heartbreaker,* whose best song, the awfully hippie but nicely rocking "Little Bit of Love," is included on the *Best of Free.* Bad Company's success dwarfed Free, and Paul Kossoff died while playing with Back Street Crawler. — J.B.M.

MICHELE FREEMAN
★ **Michele Freeman / Poly. (NA)**
Ex-airline stewardess began her musical career when she was discovered by Dick Clark, and if we're lucky, finished it after making this LP under the direction of "premier French disco composer" Don Ray. — J.S.

ACE FREHLEY
★ ★ ★ **Ace Frehley / Casa. (1978)**
Kiss guitarist put together the best solo outing from that group, including the hit single, "New York Groove." — J.S.

JEANNE FRENCH
★ ★ ★ **Diamond in the Rough / Col. (1981)**
Fairly talented woman vocalist fronts a good-sounding white R&B band led by guitarist Bobby Keyes and produced by Rick Hall at Muscle Shoals' Fame studios. — J.S.

KINKY FRIEDMAN
★ ★ ★ ★ **Sold American / Van. (1973)**
★ ★ ★ ★ **Lasso from El Paso / Epic (1976)**
Friedman made a big splash with his debut, *Sold American,* as much for his outrageous C&W stage persona, the "Texas Jewboy," as for his tremendous songwriting talents. His songs played off the self-depreciation of his ethnic joke for all it was worth, sometimes to riotous effect and sometimes into tasteless endgroove. "We Reserve the Right to Refuse Service to You" is a raucous tune that has him caught in the middle of the rednecks and Jews, a joking yokel outcast in both worlds, but "The Ballad of Charles Whitman" shows how tasteless he can be when he has a mind. The title cut is a no-nonsense classic, though, a poignant look at a washed-out cowboy star looking for a cheap rush and wondering where the glory went.

After a failed and now out-of-print second album for ABC, Friedman resurfaced on Epic with the happily indulgent smorgasbord *Lasso from El Paso.* It includes a live version of "Sold American," recorded in Colorado with Bob Dylan's Rolling Thunder

Revue, and an excellent version of Dylan's "Catfish." Texas producer Huey P. Meaux collaborated on several of the album's best tracks, such as the astoundingly funny bad-taste parable "Men's Room, L.A.," which presents Ringo Starr in a cameo appearance as Jesus. — J.S.

ROBERT FRIPP
★ ★ ★ ★ ★ **Exposure / Poly. (1979)**
★ ★ ★ **God Save the Queen/Under Heavy Manners / Poly. (1980)**
★ ★ ★ ★ **Let the Power Fall / Ed. EG (1981)**
★ ★ **The League of Gentlemen / Poly. (1981)**

ROBERT FRIPP AND BRIAN ENO
★ ★ ★ ★ **No Pussyfooting / Ed. EG (1981)**
★ ★ ★ **Evening Star / Ed. EG (1981)**
Guitarist/ideologue Robert Fripp is best known as the guiding force behind King Crimson, a band he dissolved in 1974 and reorganized (with revamped personnel) in 1981. These recordings cover Fripp's activities as a solo artist during the interim period.

No Pussyfooting and *Evening Star,* recorded in 1974 and 1976 respectively for British Island, are collaborations with Brian Eno; they utilize a tape loop to layer guitar textures over Eno's electronic drones. That approach was later scaled down to Frippertronics, in which the tape loop was provided by two tape decks in sequence, and the additional electronics were abandoned. *Let the Power Fall* is a wonderful display of the possibilities and limits of Frippertronics—alternately contemplative, static and elegiac, it's like listening to Matthew Arnold (and requires about the same attentiveness). *God Save the Queen/Under Heavy Manners* matches a side of good-to-excellent Frippertronics with a dreadful farce called "discotronics": Frippertronics with a dubbed-on funk rhythm section. Talking Head David Byrne contributes vocals under an assumed name, which ought to tell you something.

Exposure avoids the burden of a formal concept and finds Fripp in the role of songwriter, intellectual and wit. He wears the first role with aplomb, thanks to cameo vocals by Terre Roche, Daryl Hall and Peter Gabriel; the second by proxy, thanks to the taped wisdom of J. G. Bennett; and the third with malice, since most of the jokes concern the stupidity of record-company executives and elected politicians. In all, a remarkably human record.

Sadly, *The League of Gentlemen* found Fripp back in concept-land, this time fronting an alleged dance band, with "found" conversation interspersed as commentary. Thankfully, the failure of the *League* album led Fripp back to King Crimson, and some of his freshest music in years. — J.D.C.

FRISKY
★ **Frisky / Van. (1979)**
Listless. — D.M.

LEFTY FRIZZELL
★ ★ ★ ★ **Lefty Frizzell's Greatest Hits /
  Col. (1966)**
★ ★ ★ ★ **Remembering . . . / Col. (1975)**
★ ★ ★ **The Classic Style of Lefty Frizzell /
  ABC (1975)** ¶
★ ★ ★ **ABC Collection / ABC (1977)** ¶
Frizzell was a great honky-tonk country singer, influenced as a youngster by Jimmie Rodgers and later by Hank Williams. He emerged from the Texas oil country in the late Forties and had an immediate hit with his first record, "If You've Got the Money I've Got the Time." A string of country successes for Columbia followed, highlighted by "Long Black Veil" in 1959 and "Saginaw Michigan," a No. 1 hit in 1964. But honky-tonk singing fell out of commercial favor in the mid-Sixties (although Frizzell remained a favorite of such formidable C&W figures as Willie Nelson and Merle Haggard). Particularly after his move to ABC, Frizzell never again had much recording luck. He died in 1975. — C.F.

THE FUGS
★ ★ ★ ★ **The Fugs / ESP (1966)**
★ ★ ★ ★ **The Fugs' First Album / ESP
  (1966)**
★ ★ ★ ★ **Virgin Fugs / ESP (1966)**
★ ★ ★ ★ **Golden Filth / Rep. (1970)**
★ ★ ★ ★ **Fugs 4, Rounders Score / ESP
  (1975)**
Only the Sixties could have produced high-quality pornographic rock. The Fugs were led by a pair of leftovers from the beat generation, poets Ed Sanders and Tuli Kupferberg, which accounts for the high-art eroticism of their first two albums (*The Fugs* and *The Fugs' First Album*), which include selections from the poetry of William Blake and A. C. Swinburne. But it was the full flowering of mass bohemia—hippiedom, if you like—that produced such carnal comedies as "Slum Goddess," "Coca-Cola Douche" and "Kill for Peace."

What's involved here is nothing less than a perfect mixture of sacrilege, scatology, politics and rock. (Among the players: Richard Tee, Danny Kortchmar, Charles Larkey,

Peter Stampfel.) The early records on ESP—all except *Fugs 4*—are a bit cruder but contain the best songs. *Golden Filth* features live re-recordings of many of them, with an all-star New York band. *Fugs 4* is the result of a liaison with the similarly mad Holy Modal Rounders.

The sound wanders from brutal, straight-ahead rock to countryish rags (particularly on the Rounders LP) to effective and affecting folk rock. But this isn't the pandering to tradition of Oscar Brand, with his "bawdy songs." The Fugs meant to be offensive in every way imaginable, from the political to the poetic, and they succeeded gloriously. If they haven't all been melted, it's worth looking for the several deleted LPs on Reprise, including *Tenderness Junction, It Crawled into My Hand, Honest* and Ed Sanders' deleted solo LPs for that label. — D.M.

THE BOBBY FULLER FOUR
★ ★ ★ ★ **The Best of the Bobby Fuller Four
  / Rhino (1981)**
Best known for their only hit, "I Fought the Law," the Fuller quartet were one of the best American bands of the mid-Sixties, a throwback to the Southwestern rock styles of Buddy Holly and Roy Orbison. This collection of vintage 1965–66 material has consistent verve and rocks harder than almost any of its contemporaries. Had Fuller lived this would surely have been a much longer entry. — D.M.

BLIND BOY FULLER
★ ★ ★ **1935–40 / Blues C. (1966)**
Fuller was a Carolina blues player whose singing was meant to be backed up by his guitar playing rather than a central element of the music, as it was for most Tennessee and Mississippi players. The ragtime-influenced picking style is heard to good effect on this reissue, which includes his essential recordings during the period. — J.S.

JESSE FULLER
★ ★ ★ **The Lone Cat / GTJ (1961)**
★ ★ ★ **Brother Lowdown / Fan. (1972)**
Known primarily as the composer of "San Francisco Bay Blues," which was popularized by Peter, Paul and Mary, among others, Fuller was a vaudeville-like one-man band who was capable of playing guitar, cymbal, fotdella (a foot-controlled bass contraption he invented) and harmonica-kazoo at the same time. He sang in a blues style, but his music was also influenced by jazz and gospel forms. Both sets (the Fantasy is a repackage

of two Prestige LPs) were recorded in the early Sixties and are appropriately annotated and moderately well recorded. — I.M.

LOWELL FULSOM
★ ★ ★ ★ **Lowell Fulsom / Chess (1977)**
★ ★ ★ **Hung Down Head / Chess (1977)**
★ ★ ★ **Soul / Kent (NA)**
★ ★ ★ **The Tramp / Kent (NA)**
★ ★ ★ **Let's Go Get Stoned / Kent (NA)**
★ ★ ★ **Lowell Fulsom . . . Now / Kent (NA)**
Lowell Fulsom (often spelled Fulson) is a hard R&B performer, verging closer to pure blues than almost any other well-known singer of the Sixties except Bobby Bland. His guttural voice and twanging guitar can be charming but lack the resonance or depth of Bland and his material. Fulsom's best-known songs include "Tramp," which Otis Redding and Carla Thomas converted into a soul hit in 1966, and "Reconsider Baby." *Lowell Fulsom* (Chess), despite an ugly cover, contains the best of his work. — D.M.

FUNKADELIC
★ ★ **Hardcore Jollies / War. (1976)** ¶
★ ★ ★ **Best of the Funkadelic Early Years /
    Westb. (1977)** ¶
★ ★ ★ ★ **One Nation under a Groove / War.
    (1978)**
★ ★ ★ **Uncle Jam Wants You / War. (1979)**
★ ★ ★ **Connections and Disconnections /
    LAX (1981)**
Best of the Funkadelic Early Years combines tracks from the first eight Funkadelic albums. The band, George Clinton's original spinoff from Parliament, was one of the first black bands to fuse Sly Stone and Jimi Hendrix, incorporating horn players, backing voices, strings, social science, science fiction song titles and Pedro Bell's sleazy mutant psychedelic covers. The combination is daft but fascinating—the deleted LPs are well worth seeking out, particularly *Let's Take It to the Stage* (the title track of which blasts more earnest funk competitors) and *Standing on the Verge. Hardcore Jollies* is a momentary lapse, coinciding with a change in record label affiliation. The music of Funkadelic is an urban soundscape—not always pretty or appealing but perhaps the truest representation of urban life offered in black music.

One Nation and *Uncle Jam* are the albums on which Clinton perfected his visionary funk fusion. They are among the finest albums in the genre and are certainly its most ambitious. *Connections* is another, perhaps final, lapse. — J.M.C.

FUNKY COMMUNICATIONS COMMITTEE
★ ★ **Baby I Want You / Free Flight/RCA
    (1979)**
★ ★ **Do You Believe in Magic / RCA (1980)**
Ersatz Southern-fried Doobie Brothers-type band spawned from the second-string Muscle Shoals studio scene. They try so hard to live up to their initials—FCC—by getting on the radio that this band all but buries what could be some appealing qualities.
— R.P.

RICHIE FURAY BAND
★ **I've Got a Reason / Asy. (1976)**
★ **Dance a Little Light / Asy. (1978)**
★ **I Still Have Dreams / Asy. (1979)**
Furay possesses a most engaging voice, perfectly suited to the melancholy country-rock love songs he wrote and sang while a member of Buffalo Springfield, Poco and the Souther-Hillman-Furay Band. But his lyrics have deteriorated with each successive group, and on his solo LPs he hits rock bottom. His songs are so flighty and devoid of any substance that the voice ceases to be sorrowful and becomes pitiful. "I've Got a Reason" is the only redeeming item. — G.K.

FUSE
★ **Fuse / Epic (1969)** ¶
Forgettable Seventies hard rock featuring Cheap Trick's Rick Nielsen. — D.M.

THE FUTURES
★ ★ **Past, Present and the Futures / Phil.
    (1978)**
★ ★ **Greetings of Peace / Phil. (1981)**
This nondescript modern soul quintet would like to give Harold Melvin and the Bluenotes a run for their money, but it just doesn't have the chops. — D.M.

GABRIEL

■ **This Star on Every Heel / ABC (1975)**
■ **Sweet Release / ABC (1976)**
The only mystery about this horrible Seattle-area rock band is how it ever got to make *two* albums. — J.S.

PETER GABRIEL

★ ★ ★ ★ **Peter Gabriel / Atco (1977)** ¶
★ ★ ★ ★ **Peter Gabriel / Atl. (1978)**
★ ★ ★ ★ ★ **Peter Gabriel / Mer. (1980)**
★ ★ ★ ★ **Security (Peter Gabriel) / Gef. (1982)**
The former Genesis vocalist's identically ti-tled series of solo LPs is far superior to his work with the progressive rock band. Gabri-el's hardly less arty on his own, but his am-bitions are much more fully realized and his stance a good deal less pompous. At his best, Gabriel actually achieves a kind of stylized accessibility. The Atco album (the first) in-cludes "Solsbury Hill," a wonderfully spir-ited allegory of his breakup with Genesis, and "Modern Love," a wild, Who-like rock-er. "Here Comes the Flood," reminiscent of Randy Newman in its keyboard melodicism and temper of doom, suggests Jackson Browne's apocalyptic vision. Producer Bob Ezrin focused Gabriel's rather diffuse songs perfectly, which is much more than Robert Fripp, who produced Gabriel's second in-stallment, was able to achieve. On the other hand, the Fripp-produced album is more ad-venturous: the best songs ("D.I.Y.," "On the Air," "Home Sweet Home") are lucid, al-though Gabriel's personality seems subordi-nate to Fripp's experimentation with guitars and electronics.

The Mercury album, however, is Gabriel's triumph. In these songs of stark horror, Ga-briel expresses his revulsion at the conse-quences of the very modernity that makes his electrified music possible—needless to say, his despair over what comes next is

total. "Games without Frontiers," "And through the Wire," "Lead a Normal Life," "I Don't Remember" and the finale, "Biko," about the murdered South African poet Steve Biko, are more than an intellectual/mystic's version of hellfire and brimstone: they're an attempt to do something about the chaos in the world. So are the best songs on *Security,* especially "Shock the Monkey," a hit. Gabriel has established a sound to sus-tain us in the Eighties, no matter how cold the world may get: he's envisioned the worst of it already. — D.M.

GALLAGHER

★ ★ **Gallagher / U.A. (1980)**
Gallagher is a so-called comedian who fre-quently appeared on *Don Kirchner's Rock Concert.* His jokes are the product of a truly banal mentality, and Gallagher's delivery is that of a precious twit. — R.P.

RORY GALLAGHER

★ ★ **Live in Europe / Poly. (1972)** ¶
★ ★ ★ **Tattoo / Poly. (1973)** ¶
★ ★ **Sinner . . . and Saint / Poly. (1973)**
★ ★ ★ **Against the Grain / Chrys. (1975)**
★ ★ **Photo-Finish / Chrys. (1975)**
★ ★ **The Story So Far / Poly. (1976)** ¶
★ ★ ★ **Calling Card / Chrys. (1976)**
★ ★ **Top Priority / Chrys. (1979)**
★ ★ **Stage Struck / Chrys. (1980)**
Gallagher is an Irish guitarist who has gained international (though not American) stardom as a blues/boogie shouter since the breakup of his original group, Taste, in 1971. Aside from *Live,* most of this is springy blues; the addition of piano on *Tattoo* adds depth. *Story* and *Sinner* are repackages of import LPs never or no longer available here. *Against* is standard stuff, but *Calling Card* attempts to diversify with notable suc-cess, partially because it is better crafted than Gallagher's usual energetic spontaneity.

Stage Struck and *Top Priority* lose the spark. Here Gallagher is simply trudging through a formula. — A.N.

GAMMA
★ ★ ★ **Gamma / Elek. (1980)**
★ ★ ★ **Gamma 2 / Elek. (1980)**
Solid hard-rock group led by former Van Morrison guitarist Ronnie Montrose (chronologically, after his first solo band Montrose). A lead singer shy of success; terrific cover art. — D.M.

GAMBLER
★ ★ **Gambler / EMI (NA)**
Good example of the thin, unfocused attempts at formulized radio rock in which basically second-rate Midwestern bands seem to specialize. — R.P.

GANG OF FOUR
★ ★ ★ ★ ★ **Entertainment! / War. (1979)**
★ ★ ★ **Gang of Four / War. (1980)**
★ ★ ★ **Solid Gold / War. (1981)**
★ ★ ★ ★ **Another Day, Another Dollar /**
   War. (1981)
Gang of Four sprang up around England's Leeds University community at the same time as such bands as the Au Pairs, the Mekons and Delta 5, and exhibits the same fondness for brittle, simplistic funk riffs and dialectic lyrics. What has kept the Gang of Four from slipping into the postgraduate tedium the combination suggests is a flair for propulsive music with implicit pop hooks and an understanding that the band's ideology should never supersede its musical values. Even their radicalism has its light moments; the name Gang of Four is as much a pun on the band's status as a four-piece as a reference to Mme. Jiang and her counterrevolutionary cohorts. *Entertainment!* is highlighted by the brash insistence of Andy Gill's Hendrix-like rhythm guitar, which cauterizes the beat and gives the music a much-needed edge. It's the absence of that edge that makes *Solid Gold* a disappointment, despite some sturdy rhythm work. Both *Gang of Four* and *Another Day* are EPs, the former including some pre–*Entertainment!* tracks as well as two songs from *Solid Gold*, the latter featuring two live recordings and the band's most incendiary single, "To Hell with Poverty." — J.D.C.

CECIL GANT
★ ★ ★ **Killer Diller Boogie / Mag. (NA), Br.**
   imp.
Army private Gant recorded "I Wonder" in Los Angeles in 1944; it became a massive hit, touched off a trend toward black crooners (what historian Arnold Shaw calls "sepia Sinatras," though Bing Crosby is the operative reference point), and was Gant's last important musical contribution. By 1951, Gant was dead, at age thirty-seven. This album collects most of what the singer/pianist recorded in between. — D.M.

THE GAP BAND
★ **The Gap Band / Tattoo (1977)**
★ **Gap Band 2 / Mer. (1979)**
★ **Gap Band 3 / Mer. (1980)**
The gap this seven-piece, multiracial, post-R&B band would like to fill is the one left by the demise of Sly and the Family Stone. Unfortunately, these LPs (while recently popular) don't have anything close to Sly's eccentric ambition. — D.M.

JERRY GARCIA
★ ★ **Garcia / War. (1972)** ¶
★ ★ **Garcia / Round (1974)** ¶
★ **Merl Saunders, Jerry Garcia, John Kahn,**
   Bill Vitt: Live at the Keystone / Fan.
   (1973)
★ ★ ★ **Reflections / Round (1976)** ¶
★ ★ **Cats under the Stars / Ari. (1978)**
★ ★ ★ **Run for the Roses / Ari. (1982)**
Like other members of the Grateful Dead, when Jerry Garcia makes a solo album, it usually sounds like a mediocre Dead record. But since so much of the Dead's sound is keyed to his guitar, Garcia's LPs are generally the most interesting of the group's individual efforts.

His vocal range cracks at either end and shows all the expressiveness of a loaf of bread, so Garcia's charm clearly isn't his voice. The cover of *Reflections* depicts a body with the head of a guitar, and this neatly encapsulates his appeal. But most of these are only fodder for Dead fanatics. *Run for the Roses* features an interesting cover of Bob Dylan's "Knockin' on Heaven's Door." — J.B.M./J.S.

ART GARFUNKEL
★ **Angel Clare / Col. (1973)**
★ ★ **Breakaway / Col. (1975)**
★ ★ **Watermark / Col. (1977)**
★ **Fate for Breakfast / Col. (1979)**
Expensively produced but chilly artifacts from the choirboy half of the immortal duo. "Breakaway" was a 1976 hit single (it's Gallagher and Lyle's song, not the Beach Boys'), and that LP also includes the Simon and Garfunkel reunion song, "My Little Town." *Watermark* includes Garfunkel's "Wonderful World," a rehash of the Sam

Cooke tune that was a 1978 hit, but it's interesting mostly for the backing harmonies of Paul Simon and James Taylor. — D.M.

AMOS GARRETT
★ ★ ★ **Go Cat Go / Fly. Fish (1980)**
Good solo outing from the hot-licks guitarist famous for his session work with Paul Butterfield and Geoff and Maria Muldaur.
— J.S.

LEIF GARRETT
■ **Leif Garrett / Atl. (1977)**
■ **Feel the Need / Scotti (1978)**
■ **The Same Goes for You / Scotti (1979)**
■ **I Can't Explain / Scotti (1980)**
Okay, so Shaun Cassidy's versions of the Beach Boys aren't as bad as they seem. But that doesn't excuse *cloning* him. — D.M.

GARY'S GANG
★ ★ ★ **Keep On Dancin' / Col. (1979)**
★ ★ ★ **Gangbusters / Col. (1980)**
Above-average disco outfit hooked the excellent single "Keep On Dancin' " with a lively salsa beat and sharp soloing. — J.S.

DAVID GATES
★ ★ **First / Elek. (1973)**
★ ★ ★ **Never Let Her Go / Elek. (1975)**
★ ★ ★ **Goodbye Girl / Elek. (1978)**
★ ★ **Falling in Love Again / Elek. (1980)**
If David Gates' music is predictable, it is also impressive in its own way. Above all, Gates displays a concern for lyrics and melody (indeed, for song structure) that is nothing if not admirable and praiseworthy. But he can also be totally insipid: side two of *First* is an emotional wasteland. If his tendency for romantic overkill is checked, Gates, as *Never Let Her Go* indicates, can be convincing both as a rocker and a balladeer. What all of this means is that it's hard to knock a guy who once had the audacity to write Bread's brilliantly sugary hits.
— D.MC.

LARRY GATLIN
★ **The Pilgrim / Monu. (1974)**
★ **Rain-Rainbow / Monu. (1974)**
★ ★ **Larry Gatlin with Family and Friends / Monu. (1976)**
★ ★ **High Time / Monu. (1976)**
★ **Love Is Just a Game / Monu. (1978)**
★ **Oh, Brother / Monu. (1978)**
★ ★ **Larry Gatlin's Greatest Hits / Monu. (1978)**
★ **Straight Ahead / Col. (1979)**
★ **Help Yourself / Col. (1980)**
Gatlin began as a folkish country writer/

singer, much like a younger version of his initial sponsors, Johnny Cash and Kris Kristofferson. His debut album, *The Pilgrim,* contained a pair of fine songs, "Sweet Becky Walker" and "Penny Annie," plus notes by Cash, written in his Dylan-esque, half-poetic style. Since the debut, however, he has treaded ever nearer the most saccharine banalities of Nashville country pop, something for which his rough-edged voice is hardly suited. — D.M.

MARVIN GAYE
★ ★ ★ ★ **Marvin Gaye's Greatest Hits / Tam. (1964)**
★ ★ ★ ★ **Super Hits / Tam. (1970)**
★ ★ ★ ★ ★ **What's Going On / Tam. (1971)**
★ ★ ★ ★ ★ **Let's Get It On / Tam. (1973)**
★ ★ ★ ★ ★ **Anthology / Mo. (1974)**
★ ★ ★ **Live / Tam. (1974)** ¶
★ ★ ★ **I Want You / Tam. (1976)** ¶
★ ★ ★ ★ **Greatest Hits / Tam. (1976)**
★ ★ ★ **Marvin Gaye Live at the London Palladium / Tam. (1977)** ¶
★ ★ ★ ★ **Here My Dear / Tam. (1978)**
★ ★ ★ **In Our Lifetime / Tam. (1981)**
★ ★ ★ ★ **Motown Super Star Series, Vol. 15 / Mo. (1981)**
★ ★ **A Tribute to the Great Nat King Cole / Mo. (1981)**
★ ★ ★ **That Stubborn Kind of Fellow / Mo. (1981)**
★ ★ ★ ★ **M.P.G. / Mo. (1981)**
★ ★ ★ ★ ★ **Midnight Love / Col. (1982)**
Marvin Gaye is perhaps the most underrated soul singer of the Sixties. He was by far the toughest and grittiest of all the male Motown singers, and he has influenced everyone from Mick Jagger to Rod Stewart and Stevie Wonder. His early hits—"Hitch Hike," "Ain't That Peculiar," "Can I Get a Witness" and "I'll Be Doggone"—rank with Otis Redding's for sheer power.

Those songs are collected on the various greatest-hits collections, of which the best is *Anthology,* which includes the duet recordings he made with Tammi Terrell, Kim Weston and Mary Wells. Of the others, *Super Hits* is the most interesting. But all of Gaye's deleted early Tamla albums had something to recommend them, and are worth seeking out in bargain centers.

His last hit in the standard Motown fashion was the 1968 blockbuster "I Heard It through the Grapevine." Beginning in 1970, he began to record on his own initiative, away from the company's production mill. *What's Going On* opened the company's music up, both in terms of lyrics and music (long, elliptical tracks with fluid grooves replaced the precision-molded songs of the past). "Mercy Mercy Me" and "Inner City Blues" were hardheaded but hopeful songs about black urban life that discarded the romanticism of Gaye's (and Motown's) past. In this respect, *What's Going On* was a couple of years ahead of its time, and obviously influential on such records as Stevie Wonder's *Innervisions* and Curtis Mayfield's *Superfly.*

After *What's Going On,* however, Gaye slipped back into the role of black sex idol. *Let's Get It On* is perhaps the best overtly sensual music anyone in rock has ever made; the title song was an enormous hit and its groove tells the whole story. Unfortunately, Gaye has yet to match its consistency, although "Got to Give It Up," from the *London Palladium* album, was a hit in 1977 and demonstrated that Gaye still had the knack. *Here My Dear,* released in late 1978, is an epic two-disc chronicle of his divorce, whose theme is alimony. While it doesn't have the focus of Gaye's best music, it is fascinating because black popular music is rarely so frankly personal.

The three 1981 releases on Motown are reissues of Sixties vintage material. *Tribute* is a little less bloated than most Motown pop attempts, *M.P.G.* neatly balances Gaye's harder R&B shouting and slicker soul crooning and *That Stubborn Kind of Fellow* (a very early album, from 1963) is very tough and exciting, featuring three hits: "Pride and Joy," "Hitch Hike" and the title track.

Midnight Love is Gaye's 1982 comeback album, his first completely successful new music in almost a decade. It does not so much balance its contradictions—especially the tension between total immersion in hedonistic sensualism and an apparently equally fundamentalist Christianity—as overwhelm them. Gaye plays and sings almost every part here, climaxing (almost literally) with the hit "Sexual Healing," which juggles sexuality and spiritual conviction effortlessly. While not as lyrically important as *What's Going On, Midnight Love* exhibits in plenitude all the skills that have made (and continue to make) Marvin Gaye a top-rank artist of popular music. — D.M.

MARVIN GAYE AND TAMMI TERRELL
★ ★ ★ ★ ★ **Superstar Series, Vol. 2—Marvin Gaye and Tammi Terrell / Mo. (1980)**
★ ★ ★ ★ **You're All I Need / Mo. (1981)**
★ ★ ★ ★ **United / Mo. (1981)**
★ ★ ★ ★ ★ **Greatest Hits / Mo. (1981)**
Not just the greatest duet team in soul music history, possibly of the greatest in the history

of pop. From 1967 to 1970, Gaye and Terrell did a series of records together that were one of the central glories of Motown. The best of them ("Your Precious Love," "You're All I Need to Get By," "Ain't Nothing Like the Real Thing," "If I Could Build My Whole World around You" and the climactic "Ain't No Mountain High Enough") were also big hits. Had Terrell lived, they might still be going strong. Anyone with any interest in soul music, Motown or the artistry of harmony singing needs to hear at least one of their hits sets. *United* and *You're All I Need* are trimmed-down reissues of vintage LPs. — D.M.

CRYSTAL GAYLE
★ **Crystal Gayle / U.A. (1975)**
★ **Somebody Loves You / U.A. (1975)**
★ **Crystal / U.A. (1976)**
★ ★ **We Must Believe in Magic / U.A. (1977)**
★ **When I Dream / U.A. (1978)**
★ **I've Cried the Blue Right Out of My Eyes / MCA (1978)**
★ **Miss the Mississippi / Col. (1979)**
★ **Classic Crystal / U.A. (1979)**
★ **We Should Be Together / Col. (1979)**
★ **Favorites / U.A. (1980)**
★ **These Days / Col. (1980)**
★ **A Woman's Heart / Lib. (1981)**
Loretta Lynn's younger sister records in Nashville, but that's about all they have in common: where Loretta resists country formulas, or explodes them from the inside, Crystal just succumbs. As a result, "Don't It Make Your Brown Eyes Blue," a 1977 pop hit from . . . *Magic,* sounds mostly like Cher. — D.M.

GLORIA GAYNOR
★ ★ ★ ★ **Never Can Say Goodbye / MGM (1974)**
★ ★ **Experience Gloria Gaynor / MGM (1975)** ¶
★ ★ **I've Got You / Poly. (1976)** ¶
★ ★ **Glorious / Poly. (1977)** ¶
★ ★ **Steppin' Out / Poly. (1978)** ¶
★ ★ **Gloria Gaynor's Park Avenue Sound / Poly. (1978)**
★ ★ ★ **Love Tracks / Poly. (1978)**
★ ★ **I Have a Right / Poly. (1979)**
★ ★ **Stories / Poly. (1979)**
Gaynor is really only an average disco singer, but 1974's *Never Can Say Goodbye* scored a remarkable breakthrough in disco production by treating the three songs on side one ("Honey Bee," "Never Can Say Goodbye," "Reach Out I'll Be There") as one long suite, delivered without interrup-

tions of the dance beat that drove them. This has since become a standard disco format, but Gaynor's record not only did it first, it was one of the greats: all three of those songs are performed with shattering intensity, and the Tony Bongiovi/Meco Monardo/Jay Ellis production screams to be repeated again and again. Gaynor finally regained the touch with the 1979 hit "I Will Survive," and the excellent album containing it, *Love Tracks,* but subsequently returned to disco diva mediocrity. — D.M.

PAUL GAYTEN AND ANNIE LAURIE
★ ★ ★ ★ Creole Gal / Route 66 (NA), Swed. imp.
Gayten was one of the two most important New Orleans bandleaders of the Forties (second only to Dave Bartholomew), but he also made his mark as a singer ("True" was one of the first New Orleans records to become a national hit), pianist and producer (he worked with Clarence "Frogman" Henry, Bobby Charles, Etta James and Larry Darnell). His band was a breeding ground for musicians and singers, the most notable alumni being saxman Lee Allen and singer Laurie. The Route 66 album collects seventeen important sides from 1947 to 1957, most featuring Allen and a dozen spotlighting Laurie. Hunt this one down. — D.M.

THE J. GEILS BAND
★ ★ ★ ★ The J. Geils Band / Atl. (1970)
★ ★ ★ The Morning After / Atl. (1972)
★ ★ ★ Full House / Atl. (1972)
★ ★ ★ Bloodshot / Atl. (1973)
★ ★ ★ ★ Nightmares (and Other Tales from the Vinyl Jungle) / Atl. (1974)
★ ★ Blow Your Face Out / Atl. (1976)
★ ★ ★ ★ Monkey Island / Atl. (1977)
★ ★ ★ ★ Sanctuary / EMI (1978)
★ ★ ★ The Best of the J. Geils Band / Atl. (1979)
★ ★ ★ ★ Love Stinks / EMI (1980)
★ ★ ★ ★ Freeze-frame / EMI (1981)
★ ★ ★ The Best of the J. Geils Band, Vol. 2 / Atl. (1981)
★ ★ ★ Showtime! / Atl. (1982)
In the perennial quest for an American equivalent to the Rolling Stones, the best work of the J. Geils Band ranks at the top of the heap; along with Lynyrd Skynyrd, the Geils group perhaps came closest to the Stones' synthesis of rhythm & blues, bravado and a strong sense of outrage. The dominant instrumental voices are the brilliant harp playing of Magic Dick, perhaps the best white player on that instrument, and the volatile guitar work of J. Geils himself. But the

group's real leader (and with keyboardist Seth Justman, principal writer) is former Cambridge disc jockey and master of jive double-talk Peter Wolf.

Geils burst full grown from the Boston rock scene with a 1970 debut LP *(The J. Geils Band)* that was its most Stones-like, incorporating several blues covers (notably John Lee Hooker's "Serve You Right to Suffer" and Otis Rush's "Homework"), some hard-edged soul (Smokey Robinson's "First I Look at the Purse," a wonderful early example of Wolf's ability to mock black dialect) and a handful of similarly oriented originals. Both there and on *Morning After* the approach is tough and direct, and Geils had a rhythmic base so eager to find a groove and keep it that almost everything worked almost all of the time.

With *Full House,* however, the focus began to shift: on this live set, the group's stage show has begun not just to jell but to ossify. Wolf had developed a stage persona that mixed the witty with the obnoxious, and the group was slamming out riffs as close to boogie as blues. There was still more intelligence at work here than in a band like Foghat, but the balance between flair and respect for one's sources had begun to tilt, dangerously. Still, *Full House* is an enjoyable set, the band's first commercial success and a first-rate document of rock & roll in the early Seventies.

Bloodshot contained the group's first single hit—a modified reggae, "Give It to Me"— but aside from that song, the Show Stoppers' venerable funk classic "Ain't Nothin' but a House Party" and "Southside Shuffle," a good blues jam, the material was weaker than on any of the preceding records. Yet the album that followed, *Ladies Invited* (now deleted), began to turn the corner for the group: it successfully mixed R&B with more pop-oriented rock tunes. Unfortunately, the boogie following the group had developed rejected the album, and this commercial failure put Geils on the defensive. *Nightmares* contained another hit, the eerie "Must of Got Lost," but with far too much hammerheaded fooling around. *Hotline* (also deleted) deteriorated completely into an obviously condescending throwaway designed to placate the most elementary instincts of the band's followers. *Blow Your Face Out,* a two-disc live set, continued the process; only Eddie Floyd's "Raise Your Hand" and the Supremes' "Where Did Our Love Go" showed any of the old spark.

Monkey Island, then, came as a complete surprise, an album of very mature hard rock that revealed Justman and Wolf to be a trenchant songwriting team with a dark vision behind all the good times. It contains sufficient R&B to keep it rooted firmly in the Geils style, but allows the group considerable artistic latitude. The final song, "Wreckage," seems both a metaphor for a career gone awry (but not lost altogether) and a statement of purpose. It ends in a welter of heavy-metal guitar that ought to be the envy of Led Zeppelin; an inspired and melodic conception, *Monkey Island* hinted that Geils might yet find a workable alternative to pandering to its audience, without sacrificing any of its manic energy. (The two best-of collections Atlantic has released collect some of their more interesting oddments, but almost any of the originals are more worthwhile.)

Since moving to EMI-America, Geils has fully lived up to the potential suggested by *Monkey Island.* With each album, keyboardist, songwriter and now producer Seth Justman has come into his own to a greater degree. *Sanctuary,* done with the production aid of Joe Wissert, is a streamlined version of the concepts outlined on *Monkey Island.* But *Love Stinks* was a breakthrough for the band; the title song is one of the greatest things Geils has done, and its lyric is a hilarious spoof of new-wave nihilism as well as soul cliché. "Night Time" has the gunshot precision that the Strangeloves' original lacked, and "Come Back" and "Just Can't Wait" are full-scale showcases for the group, particularly Magic Dick. *Freeze-frame* sustained the band's enthusiasm, with Justman's clearheaded production and arrangement balancing new-wave influence and doo-wop roots, blues progressions and pop melodies, Wolf's passion for fashion and surfaces and the integral grit of the group. *Showtime!,* yet another live LP, documents the band's hysterical 1982 U.S. tour.

As few other rock bands can, J. Geils may claim to have grown artistically throughout its career. On the basis of its most recent work, the best is yet to come, something that might be said about even fewer groups who have recorded for more than a decade.
— D.M.

GENERATION X
★ ★ ★ Generation X / Chrys. (1978)
★ ★ Valley of the Dolls / Chrys. (1979)
British punk band had one bright idea, "Your Generation," a barbed rewrite of the Who's "My Generation," in which we are acerbically informed that the old wave is spent. Be that as it may, Billy Idol, the group's singer and central figure, was never able to come up with anything so inspired again, either here or in his solo career. So much for rock & roll regicide. — D.M.

GENESIS
★ ★ ★ Trespass / ABC (1970)
★ London Collector—In the Beginning / Lon. (1974)
★ ★ ★ The Lamb Lies Down on Broadway / Atco (1974)
★ ★ A Trick of the Tail / Atco (1976)
★ ★ ★ ★ The Best of Genesis / Bud. (1976) ¶
★ ★ Wind and Wuthering / Atco (1977)
★ ★ ★ Seconds Out / Atl. (1977)
★ ★ And Then There Were Three . . . / Atl. (1978)
★ ★ ★ ★ Duke / Atl. (1980)
★ ★ ★ ★ Abacab / Atl. (1981)
One of the most adventurous and eventually most accomplished of the British art-rock groups to come into prominence in the early Seventies, Genesis featured the songwriting and singing direction of Peter Gabriel; the studied, classically inspired arrangements of keyboardist Tony Banks; and the alternately angular and dulcet guitar playing of Michael Rutherford and Steve Hackett. The London album is made up of the earliest (1969) material, short tunes that are really failed pop songs and of interest only to the group's most ardent followers.

A characteristic sound that stretched out over complex arrangements began to emerge with *Trespass,* highlighted by a bizarre and frightening epic of conquest and betrayal called "The Knife," which would later become the climax to the band's live performances.

Hackett joined up after *Trespass* and the group went on to record its best albums for Charisma Records. These are now out of print, but the *Best of* collection on Buddah is an excellent representation of that period.

The Lamb Lies Down on Broadway is the conceptual "masterpiece" Genesis had always been pointing toward, but it was predictably dense and overblown. Still, it did mark the group's commercial high point. Gabriel's fractured narrative style works to good effect on the extended poetics of such cameo songs as "Supper's Ready," "Watchers of the Sky" or "The Musical Box," but over a two-record set his obscurantism swamps the project.

Gabriel was not with the band for ensuing albums, and his place was not adequately filled at first by drummer Phil Collins. The live *Seconds Out* is much more effective due to the addition of drummers Bill Bruford and Chester Thompson, leaving Collins free to sing. *And Then There Were Three,* however, features the group without Hackett, where they seemed to reach a turning point. Collins, Rutherford and Banks became a straightforward, melodic pop group for the first time, coining a simple sound on *Duke* and following it with the brilliant *Abacab,* on which Collins found his niche fronting the new lineup.   — J.S.

GENTLE GIANT
★ ★ **Acquiring the Taste** / Vert. (1971)
★ ★ **Three Friends** / Col. (1972)
★ **Octopus** / Col. (1973)
■ **The Power and the Glory** / Cap. (1974)
★ ★ ★ **Free Hand** / Cap. (1975)
★ ★ **Interview** / Cap. (1976)
★ ★ **Playing the Fool** / Cap. (1977) ¶
★ **Missing Piece** / Cap. (1977)
★ **Giant for a Day** / Cap. (1978)
★ ★ **Civilian** / Col. (1980)
★ ★ **Official "Live" Gentle Giant** / Cap. (1981)
Gentle Giant has never acquired more than a cult following since the group's inception in 1970. What support it does have is hardcore, attracted largely by the band's insistence on highly innovative song structures, superb musicianship and diverse styles. Weird but creative, this music demands active involvement from the listener.

Acquiring is historically their second album (the first is available only on import). Like the rest, it's a combination of contrasting classical, jazz and progressive rock (notably King Crimson) influences. It's probably their most accessible. *Three Friends* is ostensibly a concept album, though it's more instrumental than vocal. This one stars Kerry Minnear's keyboards, which compare stylistically with Keith Emerson's. It's uncharacteristically melodic. *Octopus* is based on the work of psychiatrist R. D. Laing and novelist Albert Camus, albeit with a medieval bent. Totally bizarre time signatures make it eclectic, intricate and showy, but not necessarily pleasant. *The Power and the Glory* is the band's most irritating, least listenable record, but *Free Hand* is Gentle Giant's answer to Yes' *Tales from Topographic Oceans.* It displays Jon Anderson's vocal shrieks, similarly complex time structures and the same unmelodious pitterpat music, yet it's probably their best record. *Interview* is similar, but not as accessible. *Playing the Fool* and *Official "Live" Gentle Giant* are good examples of the band's live sound. In sum: an acquired taste.   — A.N.

THE GENTRYS
★ **The Gentrys** / Sun (1970)
Name that tune time. These Gentrys (only vocalist Larry Hart remaining from the "Keep on Dancing" group of 1965) are adept at flabby and unimaginative rewrites of Rolling Stones, Yardbirds and Grass Roots songs, but they usually throw in a country ballad to keep you off balance. For lovers of elevator music only.   — D.MC.

LOWELL GEORGE
★ ★ ★ **Thanks I'll Eat It Here** / War. (1979)
Leader of the much-loved Little Feat, writer of the country-rock standard "Willin'," noted singer and slide guitarist George died shortly after this long-awaited solo album was released. In retrospect the album is disappointing and certainly wasn't meant to be his final say, but that's the way it goes. George's version of the Little Feat standard "Two Trains" is the high point.   — J.S.

PAUL GEREMIA
★ ★ ★ **Just Enough** / Folk. (1968)
Geremia's wry approach to blues and original folk-oriented material makes him much more attractive than the run-of-the-coffeehouse white folkie. It helps that this approach is directed more toward East Coast ragtime blues than the standard Mississippi delta variety.   — K.R.

THE GERMS
★ ★ ★ ★ **GI** / Slash (1979)
★ ★ **What We Do Is Secret** / Slash (1981)
Contrary to any of the mythology surrounding them, the Germs were not the great lost American band. Once you get past the tragic life and suicide of Darby Crash, and the wistful tales of L.A. slam-dancing, what you've got here is unreconstructed punk, circa 1977, with lyrics that are more crazily poetic than other would-be American Sex Pistols.

GI, produced by Joan Jett, has the amateurish breakneck instrumentation and garbled singing established by the Pistols. It's as frantic and charged up as punk gets. But wasteland of Los Angeles is not the housing projects of London, so ultimately the Germs' expressions of uniquely American experience are diminished by such strict imitation.

What We Do Is Secret, released as a posthumous tribute to lead singer and writer Crash, is a frightening document of degeneration, the aural equivalent of a rotting corpse.   — D.G.

GERRY AND THE PACEMAKERS
★ **Don't Let the Sun Catch You Crying /**
Laur. (NA)
★ **I'll Be There / Laur. (NA)**
★ **Second Album / Laur. (NA)**
★ **Girl in a Swing / Laur. (NA)**
★ ★ **Gerry and the Pacemakers' Greatest**
Hits / Laur. (NA)
★ ★ **The Best of Gerry and the Pacemakers**
/ Cap. (1979)
Despite the seeming wealth of British Invasion material listed above, this is really much ado about nothing, since even at their best—"Don't Let the Sun," "Ferry Cross the Mersey"—Gerry and the Pacemakers were the most fey of all Liverpudlian rockers. This is wimp rock before its vogue, and only terminal Anglophiliacs need dig any deeper than a couple of singles can take them. — D.M.

GET WET
■ **Get Wet / Bdwalk (1981)**
If this is producer Phil Ramone's idea of new wave, no wonder Billy Joel thought it was still rock & roll. — J.D.C.

ANDY GIBB
★ ★ **Flowing Rivers / RSO (1977)**
★ ★ **Shadow Dancing / RSO (1978)**
★ ★ **After Dark / RSO (1980)**
★ ★ **Andy Gibb's Greatest Hits / RSO**
(1980)
The young brother of the Bee Gees, Andy Gibb clicked commercially with these, mostly when his siblings were around for support, as writers or harmonizers. Anyway, couldn't he at least have had the sense of humor to record Dylan's "Watching the River Flow"? (Would that have made his debut LP a schlock-rock concept LP?) — D.M.

STEVE GIBBONS
★ ★ ★ **Any Road Up / MCA (1976) ¶**
★ ★ ★ **Rollin' On / MCA (1977) ¶**
★ ★ ★ **Caught in the Act / MCA (1977) ¶**
★ ★ ★ ★ **Down in the Bunker / Poly. (1978)**
★ ★ ★ **Street Parade / Poly. (1980)**
Veteran Birmingham rocker Steve Gibbons has a knife-edged voice and a cunning wit sharpened by years of slumming in the British Motor City's dank pubs before his discovery by the Who's Pete Townshend. His all-Birmingham group includes ex-Move bassist Trevor Burton, and his two studio albums include several minor successes ("Take Me Home," "Spark of Love," "Standing on the Bridge," "Please Don't Say Goodbye" and a cover of Chuck Berry's "Tulane"). *Caught in the Act* is a live set that proves

Gibbons' journeyman credentials without extending them. But *Down in the Bunker* is a small triumph of old-fashioned rock, driving and concise; it marks Gibbons as a sort of British Bob Seger, with a future potentially just as bright. — J.S.

JOE GIBBS AND THE
PROFESSIONALS
★ ★ ★ ★ ★ **African Dub Almighty / J.**
Gibbs (NA)
★ ★ ★ **African Dub Chapter Two / J. Gibbs**
(NA)
★ ★ ★ ★ **African Dub Chapter Three / J.**
Gibbs (NA)
★ ★ ★ **African Dub Chapter Four / J. Gibbs**
(NA)
This is primal dub, recorded before Jamaican producers gained access to the full range of studio effects. Consequently they had to rely on instrumental subtlety and rhythmic innovation. *African Dub* succeeds well on these counts in every chapter. — R.F.G.

TERRI GIBBS
★ ★ **Somebody's Knockin' / MCA (1981)**
★ ★ **I'm a Lady / MCA (1981)**
Although she's been promoted as a country singer, Terri Gibbs, much like Anne Murray (whom she resembles vocally), is really a singer, pure and simple, but one still searching for the right songs. Her albums have moments when all the elements come together, but her performances are largely tentative and unsettling, as is usually the case when an artist is uncomfortable with material. When she's on, however, she's very good. The evocative title track of her first album is a dark, brooding number with an uncluttered arrangement well suited to Gibbs' low-key, bluesy reading. On *I'm a Lady* she surveys a couple of popular standards, "I Wanna Be Around" and "Georgia on My Mind," to spectacular effect. These interpretations have a resonance that's missing from her upbeat but decidedly MOR-ish songs. Interesting records, but more for what they imply about Gibbs than for what's on the vinyl. — D.MC.

NICK GILDER
★ ★ **You Know Who You Are / Chrys.**
(1977)
★ ★ ★ **City Nights / Chrys. (1978)**
★ ★ **Frequency / Chrys. (1979)**
★ ★ **Rock America / Casa. (1980)**
Frail British pop singer scored with oddly erotic "Hot Child in the City," from *City Nights,* in 1978. But the rest of his material is hardly up to that standard. — D.M.

MICKEY GILLEY

★ ★ ★ **City Lights** / Play. (1974)
★ ★ ★ ★ ★ **Mickey Gilley's Greatest Hits, Vol. 1** / Play. (1976)
★ ★ ★ ★ **Gilley's Smokin'** / Play. (1976)
★ ★ ★ **First Class** / Play. (1976)
★ ★ ★ ★ **Mickey Gilley's Greatest Hits, Vol. 2** / Play. (1977)
★ ★ ★ **Flyin' High** / Play. (1978)
★ ★ ★ **Gilley** / Epic (1979)
★ ★ ★ **Encore** / Epic (1979)
★ ★ ★ **The Songs We Made Love To** / Epic (1979)
★ ★ ★ **That's All That Matters to Me** / Epic (1980)
★ ★ ★ **Lonely Hearts** / Epic (1981)
★ ★ ★ **Christmas at Gilley's** / Epic (1981)
★ ★ **Mickey Gilley at His Best** / Play. (NA)

Gilley is Jerry Lee Lewis' cousin, and the two played together extensively when they were kids, but when Jerry Lee made the move to big-time entertainment in 1956, Mickey went to work as a laborer. It wasn't until twenty years later, after Gilley opened a Houston club featuring himself as the main performer and clicked with a beautifully relaxed version of "Roomful of Roses," that he caught up with his cousin's musical notoriety.

Since then, Gilley has become the voice of honky-tonk. His smooth vocal delivery and plunking piano playing engendered an impressive string of hit singles—"I Overlooked an Orchid," "City Lights," "Window Up Above," "Bouquet of Roses," "Overnight Sensation," "Don't the Girls All Get Prettier at Closing Time," "She's Pulling Me Back Again," "How's My Ex Treating You." Gilley is equally at home singing a maudlin tearjerker or pounding up a rockabilly storm. He'll never make people forget about Jerry Lee Lewis, but he more than holds his own. — J.S.

IAN GILLAN BAND

★ **Ian Gillan Band** / Oy. (1976)
★ **Scarabus** / Is. (1978)
★ **Glory Road** / Virgin (1980) ¶

As the melodramatic Deep Purple lead singer and star of the original *Jesus Christ Superstar,* Gillan screeched with the best of them, but these solo outings leave it all behind. — J.S.

DAVE GILMOUR

★ ★ ★ **Dave Gilmour** / Col. (1978)

Pink Floyd's guitarist goes the solo album route with results that are fairly impressive as these things go. Gilmour works better in the more balanced atmosphere of the band, but his compositions retain enough rock influence to make their jazz and avant-garde pretensions palatable. — D.M.

GIORGIO

★ **Knights in White Satin** / Casa. (1977)
★ ★ **From Here to Eternity** / Casa. (1977)
★ **Battlestar Galactica** / Casa. (1978)
★ **E Equals MC²** / Casa. (NA)

Disco theoretician Giorgio Moroder is the man responsible for producing the electronic dance band called the Munich Machine, four Donna Summer albums and her computerized hit singles, "Love to Love You Baby" and "I Feel Love." Moroder's solo albums are comprised of nonstop synthesizer programs bleating narcotic trance patterns into infinity while disembodied voices chant themes in front of the endless sound system. Very odd, very catchy and very empty, Giorgio's songs get appropriate titles, such as "Utopia—Me Giorgio" and "Lost Angeles." An Italian working in Germany, Moroder creates austere but otherworldly productions that sound like futurist soundtracks for Fritz Lang's *Metropolis.* — J.S.

GIORGIO AND CHRIS

★ ★ ★ **Love's in You, Love's in Me** / Casa. (1978)

That's Giorgio Moroder, of course. Chris isn't given the dignity of a last name. Indeed, her purpose seems basically to be to serve as as a white, blond imitation of Donna Summer. Though the results are surprisingly listenable, they only go to show that Moroder and coproducer Pete Bellotte aren't the only masterminds involved in Summer's hits. They are here, though, and the limited results prove it. — D.M.

GIRL

★ ★ **Sheer Greed** / Jet (1980)

Heavy-metal fans love it. For the rest of us, hypersludge surprisingly light on its feet and deliberately, condescendingly illiterate. The band members all look like Lolita. — L.F.

THE GLADIATORS

★ ★ ★ ★ **Trenchtown Mix-up** / V.F.L./Jam Rock (1976)
★ ★ ★ ★ **Proverbial Reggae** / V.F.L./Jam Rock (1977)
★ ★ ★ ★ **Naturality** / V.F.L./Jam Rock (1978)
★ ★ ★ **Sweet So Til** / Virgin (1979)
★ ★ **Gladiators** / Virgin (1980)
★ ★ ★ ★ **Symbol of Reality** / Nighth. (1982)

So how come the Gladiators didn't become as well known as the Mighty Diamonds during the first great international reggae push in 1976? Their harmonies are just as full and sweet, their tunes equally catchy and the rhythms nearly as hard. They double as Jamaican sessionmen, so they can play their own instruments too. That lack of success may have led to the late-Seventies bland-out but in no way diminishes the joy-inspiring singing on the first three Virgin Front Line LPs and a very satisfying but hard-to-find Studio One LP. *Symbol of Reality* is a return to form. — R.F.G.

ROGER GLOVER
★ ★ **Roger Glover** / Oy. (NA)
★ ★ **Elements** / Oy. (1978)
Two undistinguished solo LPs from the Deep Purple bassist. Stick with the original band. — D.M.

TONY GLOVER
★ ★ ★ ★ **Blues-Harp** / Folk. (NA)
This is essentially an instruction record, but Glover's basso voice and deadpan delivery, plus his mastery of blues harmonica playing, make it something special. Not up to his work with the occasionally inspired Koerner, Ray and Glover trio, but worth hearing anyway. — D.M.

THE GODZ
■ **The Godz** / Millen. (1978)
■ **Nothing Is Sacred** / Casa. (1979)
Miserable hard-rock quartet from Columbus, Ohio, epitomized the most wretched excesses of Seventies rock. — J.S.

RON GOEDERT
★ ★ **Breaking All the Rules** / Poly. (NA)
If only Goedert were half so ambitious as his album title, rather than the conventional pop singer he is. — D.M.

LOUISE GOFFIN
★ **Kid Blue** / Asy. (1979)
★ **Louise Goffin** / Elek. (1981)
Daughter of Carole King and Gerry Goffin seems to have inherited little of Mom's melodic and singing skills, and her father's knack for encapsulating teenage romance in a few deft lines escapes her utterly, despite the fact that the debut album was recorded while Louise was still sweet sixteen. Produced by Danny Kootch, a Los Angeles session guitarist who usually knows better. — D.M.

GO-GO'S
★ ★ ★ ★ **Beauty and the Beat** / IRS (1981)

Although it so happens that all five Go-Go's are female and their music is 100 percent pop, this isn't an updated girl group—not by a long shot. Their exuberance and pop optimism make the Go-Go's sound like the Ramones gone three-dimensional, while the often bittersweet lyrics suggest that these ladies aren't exactly the heard-it-in-a-love-song suckers their hook heaviness would imply. In short, the Go-Go's pull off one of rock & roll's best tricks: simple music that's never condescending. — J.D.C.

ANDREW GOLD
★ ★ ★ **Andrew Gold** / Asy. (1975)
★ ★ **What's Wrong with This Picture?** / Asy. (1976)
★ ★ **All This and Heaven Too** / Asy. (1978)
★ ★ **Whirlwind** / Asy. (1980)
The L.A. studio musician's debut, *Andrew Gold,* is a gorgeous collection reminiscent of mid-Sixties Anglo-rock: beautifully rich, ringing guitars and melodies. Gold plays nearly all instruments. The followups switch to glossy orchestration—less bounce and little edge, a step toward MOR. The second album, *What's Wrong,* has "Lonely Boy," a 1977 hit that tells a perfect pop-psychology fable about a psychotic teenager. — C.W.

FRANNIE GOLDE
★ **Frannie Golde** / Por. (1976)
★ **Restless** / Por. (1980)
Slick writer/singer has hooks, lacks heart. — D.M.

GOLDEN EARRING
★ ★ **Moontan** / MCA (1974)
★ **Switch** / MCA (1975)
★ **To the Hilt** / MCA (1976) ¶
★ **Mad Love** / MCA (1977) ¶
★ **Golden Earring Live** / MCA (1977)
★ **Grab It for a Second** / MCA (1979)
★ **No Promises, No Debts** / Poly. (1979)
★ **Long Blond Animal** / Poly. (1980)
Highly derivative Dutch band that finally got a break when "Radar Love" (from *Moontan*) became a big hit in 1974. "Radar" is a great radio song, a fusion of Canned Heat and Kraftwerk, but unfortunately atypical of Earring's other work, a well-produced bag of riffs borrowed from other European rock groups, notably Pink Floyd and Jethro Tull. The other LPs are energetic and competent but faceless progressive rock. — A.N.

GOLDEN GATE QUARTET
★ ★ ★ ★ **Negro Spirituals Anthologie, Vol. 6** / Pathe Marconi (1962), Fr. imp.

★ ★ ★ **Negro Spirituals Anthologie, Vol. 1 / Pathe Marconi (1964), Fr. imp.**
★ ★ ★ ★ **Thirty-five Historic Recordings / RCA (1977), Ger. imp.**
Led by the legendary Bill Johnson (known to rock fans for some work with Ry Cooder), the Golden Gate Quartet was the finest exponent of jubilee gospel singing, the harmonizing style on which doo-wop is founded. The RCA two-record set contains many of the best of the group's recordings from the Thirties to the Fifties, and the singing is among the most exalted on record. The French LPs feature traditional spirituals ("Wade in the Water," "Precious Memories") and some secular numbers ("St. Louis Blues") and, while less important, are almost equally gorgeous.   — D.M.

BOBBY GOLDSBORO
★ **Bobby Goldsboro's Greatest Hits / U.A. (1970)**
★ **Bobby Goldsboro's Tenth Anniversary Album / U.A. (1974)**
■ **Bobby Goldsboro / Curb (NA)**
★ **Best of Bobby Goldsboro / U.A. (NA)**
Goldsboro's onetime tenure in Roy Orbison's backup group is more than offset by his solo recordings of such treacly hits as "Honey," a song so gooey a listener could drown in its icky sentimentality.   — D.M.

THE GOLLIWOGS
★ ★ **Golliwogs Pre-Creedence / Fan. (1975)**
A collection of singles recorded by Creedence Clearwater Revival just before the band adopted that name and found success. The key difference is that Tom Fogerty, not brother John, sings almost everything here. When John sings a couple of numbers you can spot the increase in inspiration instantly. For hard-core devotees of CCR only.
   — D.M.

LEROY GOMEZ
★ ★ ★ **Gypsy Woman / Casa. (1978)**
★ ★ ★ **I Got It Bad / Casa. (NA)**
Gomez made his reputation doing disco-rock songs with Santa Esmeralda (whose "Don't Let Me Be Misunderstood" is a kind of classic). He's not up to that standard here, but these are serviceable dance discs.   — D.M.

RAY GOMEZ
★ ★ **Volume / Col. (1980)**
Gomez is a chops-conscious rock and fusion guitarist best known as the "listenable" member of Stanley Clarke's late-Seventies aggregations. *Volume* finds him in a variety of settings ranging from standard rock & roll to

fusion-flash and overwrought funk. Aside from a hideous "Summer in the City," most of the material suits him fine, but the album is marred by the most debilitating of all guitar-whiz diseases—terminal noodling.
   J.D.C.

IAN GOMM
★ ★ ★ **Gomm with the Wind / Stiff (1978)**
★ ★ ★ **What a Blow / Stiff (1980)**
Bright, tuneful LPs loaded with pop rock, R&B and rockabilly chestnuts from the former Brinsley Schwarz guitarist.   — J.S.

PHILLIP GOODHAND-TAIT
★ ★ **Oceans Away / Chrys. (1976)**
★ ★ **Teaching an Old Dog New Tricks / Chrys. (1977)**
A mediocre singer but a pretty and occasionally haunting pop melodist who could use more spirited and varied backup and production. But Robert Kirby's orchestrations on *Oceans* are nicely done.   — C.W.

STEVE GOODMAN
★ ★ **Steve Goodman / Bud. (1971) ¶**
★ ★ **Somebody Else's Troubles / Bud. (1973) ¶**
★ ★ **Jessie's Jig and Other Favorites / Asy. (1975) ¶**
★ **Words We Can Dance To / Asy. (1976)**
★ ★ ★ **The Essential Steve Goodman / Bud. (1976) ¶**
★ **Say It in Private / Asy. (1977)**
★ ★ **High and Outside / Asy. (1979)**
★ ★ **Hot Spot / Asy. (1980)**
Steve Goodman is the perfect master of the latter-day urban folk scene—and its perfect fool. From the effortless grace of his guitar work to the ingenious elegance of his lyrics, he radiates technique and taste—and they nearly choke him. As a songwriter (best known for "City of New Orleans"), Goodman has a gift for wry commentary, such as "Chicken Cordon Blues" *(Essential)*—a palate-rending tale of macrobiotic deprivation—or the caustic "Banana Republics" *(Words)*.
   As a singer he's most at home with the country-flavored songs that predominate his earlier albums for Buddah. Since *Jessie's Jig* (his Asylum debut) he's favored slicker, more contemporary songs and arrangements. But though Goodman doesn't sound like a folkie anymore, he's kept the insular aesthetics of the coffeehouse—topical references, in jokes ("Daley's Gone" to the tune of "Delia's Gone"). Technology is suspect in his lyrics and his choice of material suggests that the old is automatically good. Unlike

Arlo Guthrie (who successfully maintains both a folk and a pop audience), Goodman confuses taste with style and substitutes the accepted values of a small community for a personal voice. He's deservedly a cult figure selling small subtleties and limited perfections, though his cult may not be willing to follow him through the strings and studio singers he's using now. — A.S.

THE GOOD RATS
★ ★ ★ **From Rats to Riches** / Pass. (1978)
★ ★ ★ **Birth Comes to Us All** / Pass. (1978)
Long Island–based bar band still hasn't made it after fifteen years of trying. The main feature here is the singing of Peppi Marchello, whose raunchy timbre could shatter Memorex. *From Rats to Riches* is basically their live show translated to vinyl; *Birth* is an artier effort, with a vague concept centered around growing up. Better off looking for their long-deleted 1974 Warner Brothers album, *Tasty.* — W.K.

THE GOOD VIBRATIONS
■ **I Get Around** / Millen. (1978)
Disco Beach Boys—an idea that could curdle milk. — J.D.C.

GOOSE CREEK SYMPHONY
★ ★ **Goose Creek Symphony** / Cap. (1970)
★ ★ **Welcome to Goose Creek** / Cap. (1971)
★ ★ **Words of Ernest** / Cap. (1972)
Like many country-rock bands, Goose Creek Symphony can't be faulted on technical grounds, but can't be praised on emotional ones, either. These albums are continually promising but never quite deliver, leaving Goose Creek in the ranks of the perennial also-rans. — D.M.

ROBERT GORDON
★ **Robert Gordon with Link Wray** / Priv. (1977)
★ **Fresh Fish Special** / Priv. (1978) ¶
★ **Rock Billy Boogie** / RCA (1979) ¶
★ **Bad Boy** / RCA (1979)
★ ★ **Are You Gonna Be the One?** / RCA (1981)
Gordon would like to be a rockabilly revivalist, but since he understands none of the nuances of the genre, he is finally hopeless. Reducing some of the greatest American music ever created to a matter of mannerism insults it, and when Gordon attempts to interpret a modern song in the idiom (e.g., Bruce Springsteen's "Fire," on *Fresh Fish Special*), he simply sounds confused. Well-intentioned but inept. — D.M.

ROSCOE GORDON
★ ★ ★ **Roscoe Gordon** / Charly (1971), Br. imp.
★ ★ ★ **The Best of Roscoe Gordon, Vol. 1** / Chis. (NA), Br. imp.
★ ★ ★ **Keep On Doggin'** / Mr. R&B (NA), Swed. imp.
To say that Gordon was a seminal figure on the late Forties/early Fifties Memphis blues and R&B scene is not the same as saying that he was a major musician. Although Gordon's support was important both to peers such as Johnny Ace, Earl Forrest and B.B. King (the Beale Streeters) and to up-and-comers like Bobby Blue Bland (King's onetime chauffeur) and Junior Parker, his own recordings are not the equal of any of theirs (except Forrest's). All of these assemble his recordings for Sam Phillips, issued on labels including RPM, Chess, Sun and Duke, in varying configurations but the music, while competent enough, lacks inspiration. — D.M.

LESLEY GORE
★ ★ **The Golden Hits of Lesley Gore** / Mer. (1965)
"It's My Party (and I'll Cry If I Want To)" is as succinct a declaration of emotional independence as you can find. The followup, "Judy's Turn to Cry," shows how quickly petulance can turn to revenge. Lesley Gore didn't need assertiveness training ("You Don't Own Me" is a prefeminist anthem), but then she was a Sarah Lawrence girl. — A.S.

VERN GOSDIN
★ ★ **Til the End** / Elek. (1977)
★ ★ **Never My Love** / Elek. (1978)
★ ★ **The Best of Vern Gosdin** / Elek. (1979)
★ ★ **You've Got Somebody** / Elek. (1979)
★ ★ **Passion** / Ova. (1981)
Gosdin can't decide to go for Don Williams'–style basso sensuality or simply become a schlock weeper/crooner in the Kenny Rogers/Eddie Rabbitt mold. But guess which tendency looks like it's winning. — D.M.

BARRY GOUDREAU
★ ★ **Barry Goudreau** / Por. (1980)
Blather from Boston's second guitarist, aided by bandmates Brad Delp on vocals and drummer Sib Hashian. This tepid collection of clubfooted rockers and stadium pop just goes to show that group leader Tom Scholz is the whole show. — D.F.

GQ
★ ★ ★ DiscoNights/Ari.(1979)
★ ★ ★ GQTwo/Ari.(1981)
This rock-funk-disco group scored hits with "Disco Nights (Rock-Freak)" and a remake of Billy Stewart's "I Do Love You" from *Disco Nights* and "Sitting in the Park" from *GQ Two,* although only the first crossed over. Worth watching. — D.M.

LARRY GRAHAM
★ My Radio Sure Sounds Good to Me / War. (1978)
★ One in a Million / War. (1980)
★ Just Be My Lady / War. (1981)
With Sly and the Family Stone, Graham literally invented modern funk bass playing. With Graham Central Station, he nearly funked himself into the ground, reiterating what he'd done with Sly with a lack of imagination that makes his lack of commercial success somewhat mystifying. On his own, he's decided to become one of those lugubriously philosophizing soul crooners (à la Barry White and Teddy Pendergrass). Interminable unless you're hot for his bod. — D.M.

GRAHAM CENTRAL STATION
★ ★ ★ Graham Central Station / War. (1974)
★ ★ ★ Release Yourself / War. (1974)
★ ★ ★ Ain't No Bout-a-Doubt It / War. (1975)
★ ★ ★ Mirror / War. (1976)
★ ★ ★ Now Do U Wanta Dance / War. (1977)
★ ★ ★ Star Walk / War. (1979)
When it began recording in 1972, GCS was almost alone in carrying on and developing Sly Stone's visionary R&B invention of the late Sixties. But others have since caught up and left these guys in the dust. Three acts that quickly come to mind are George Clinton's Funkadelic/Parliament/Rubber Band school of mind-twisting funk; Earth, Wind and Fire, with its emotional and instrumental intensity; and ex–James Brown hornman/arranger Fred Wesley's brass adventurists, the JB's (now the Horny Horns). Which leaves ex–Sly bassist Larry Graham's congregation as merely an expert dance band. In the not-too-creative but professional footsteps of their fellow East Bay Oaklanders, Tower of Power, they do what they do well, but it just doesn't grow. — B.M.

GRAND FUNK RAILROAD
★ ★ On Time / Cap. (1969)
★ ★ Grand Funk / Cap. (1969)
★ ★ Closer to Home / Cap. (1970)
★ ★ Live Album / Cap. (1970)
★ ★ ★ Survival / Cap. (1971)
★ ★ E Pluribus Funk / Cap. (1971)
★ ★ Mark, Don and Mel 1969–1971 / Cap. (1972)
★ ★ Phoenix / Cap. (1972)
★ ★ ★ We're an American Band / Cap. (1973)
★ Shinin' On / Cap. (1974) ¶
★ Caught in the Act / Cap. (1975)
★ Good Singin', Good Playin' / MCA (1976) ¶
★ ★ Grand Funk Hits / Cap. (1976)
★ Grand Funk Lives / War. (1981)
★ What's Funk / War. (1983)
Grand Funk Railroad created an immediate and enormous following with its appearance at the 1969 Atlanta Pop Festival, then parlayed that popularity into national notoriety by exploiting the extraordinarily abrasive critical attacks on the band. It was really the first attack on the dichotomies that had lain dormant within the Sixties rock community, for all its vision of peace and hope, and as such, the anti-press campaign became a marvelous portent of things to come.

The group was a power trio, in some senses a surrogate for those who'd missed being bludgeoned by Cream's dissemblings upon blues themes. Drummer Don Brewer, bassist Mel Schacher and guitarist Mark Farner were archetypal Midwestern rock & rollers, long-haired, impolite and sweaty, with a kind of radical cheek orientation that was more naive and divisive than sophisticated or analytical. For Grand Funk, and many similar heavy-metal bands of the era, "Power to the People" was a slogan that justified rampant consumerism, as long as the consumer smoked pot, a perfect misunderstanding of populism.

Wretched was the word to describe Grand Funk's music. Although the group occasionally achieved an interesting song—"I'm Your Captain" was about the best of the early ones—the playing was never much more than energetic, always dull in its meter, and the singing was completely hopeless. The production of Terry Knight, formerly a recording artist in his own right, mostly took a back seat to some clever promotions.

By 1972, the group and Knight were embroiled in a nasty lawsuit, and Grand Funk rarely came up with anything quite so ingenious, despite a succession of producers that included Jimmy Ienner and Frank Zappa. Only Todd Rundgren could do much with them, producing a masterful hard-rock hit single in 1973 with *We're an American Band*'s title track. When the group left Capitol in 1976, it was obvious Grand Funk was near the end of the line; the group recorded one album for MCA and folded. (Farner, the band's frontman, has since recorded an awful Atlantic solo LP.)

Among the discs available, it is hard to choose; most are simply unlistenable without the cult fervor that once surrounded the band. *Survival,* however, contains a sledge-hammer version of the Rolling Stones' "Gimme Shelter." *Grand Funk Hits,* which has "We're an American Band," is about the best bet, although why anyone except professional nostalgists would still be interested is mystifying. This is one legend whose rehabilitation is highly unlikely. — D.M.

THE GRANDMOTHERS
★ ★ ★ **The Grandmothers / Rhino (1980)**
Good collection of odds and ends from ex–Mothers of Invention sidemen including Don Preston, Jimmy Carl Black, Buzz and Bunk Gardner, Motorhead James Sherwood and Elliot Ingber. — J.S.

GRAND TOUR
★ **On Such a Winter's Day / Butter. (NA)**
The Mamas and the Papas, discofied? Unh-unh. — D.M.

EDDIE GRANT
★ ★ ★ ★ **Living on the Front Line / Epic/ Ice (1979)**
★ ★ ★ **Can't Get Enough / Ice (1980)**
★ ★ **My Turn to Love You / Epic (1980)**
Eddie Grant's easy assimilation of rock, reggae, soca, African and funk styles places him among the new breed of global musicians. A West Indian living in England, he scored with "Baby Come Back," a Sixties smash, as a member of the rock group the Equals. Having fully mastered the studio as engineer and producer, he applied his knowledge in the late Seventies to his triumphant "Front Line Symphony," an ambitious, seamless fusion of the aforementioned styles. Recent releases haven't cut so deep, but Eddie Grant may well chart important musical directions in the Eighties. — R.F.G.

GRASS ROOTS
★ **Where Were You When I Needed You / Dun. (1966)** ¶
★ ★ ★ **Golden Grass / Dun. (1968)** ¶
★ **Lovin' Things / Dun. (1969)** ¶
★ ★ **More Golden Grass / Dun. (1970)** ¶
★ ★ ★ **Their Sixteen Greatest Hits / Dun. (1971)**
★ **Move Along / Dun. (1972)** ¶
Had the Grass Roots faded away after their first two pop-punk hits, "Let's Live for Today" (1967) and "Midnight Confessions" (1968), they might be fondly remembered. Unfortunately, the group stuck around through most of the Seventies, with records progressively more mediocre in the same half-rock, half-schlock manner. They finally gave up in 1975, after a career not nearly so interesting as the best pop groups of their day (Three Dog Night, for instance). — D.M.

THE GRATEFUL DEAD
★ **Grateful Dead / War. (1967)**
★ ★ **Anthem of the Sun / War. (1968)**
★ ★ **Aoxomoxoa / War. (1969)**
★ ★ ★ **Live Dead / War. (1970)**
★ ★ **American Beauty / War. (1970)**
★ ★ ★ **Workingman's Dead / War. (1970)**
★ ★ **The Grateful Dead / War. (1971)**
★ ★ ★ **Europe '72 / War. (1972)**
★ **Wake of the Flood / Grate. (1973)**
★ **History of the Grateful Dead, Vol. 1 / War. (1973)**
★ **The Grateful Dead from the Mars Hotel / Grate. (1974)**
★ ★ **Best of the Grateful Dead—Skeletons in the Closet / War. (1974)**
★ **Blues for Allah / Grate. (1975)**
★ **Steal Your Face / Grate. (1976)**
★ **Terrapin Station / Ari. (1977)**
★ **Shakedown Street / Ari. (1978)**
★ ★ **What a Long, Strange Trip It's Been / War. (1978)**
★ **The Grateful Dead Go to Heaven / Ari. (1980)**
★ **Dead Reckoning / Ari. (1981)**
The Grateful Dead epitomize hippie rock & roll, and if you're a hippie yourself, you might want to invert the judgments expressed in the ratings above. But unless you are, this is one assertedly major oeuvre that's virtually worthless except for documentary purposes. The Dead's long modal jams may be the stuff of mesmerism in concert (though even there, it's questionable), but they're simply self-indulgent and boring on disc. The band's attempts at pop, rock and country are rendered effortlessly irritating and stodgy by the band's lack of a crisp rhythm section and/or a single competent vocalist.

The Dead are worshiped for their image as hip patriarchs, which means that as long as Jerry Garcia has that acid twinkle in his eye, he'll never have to worry about his pedestrian set of chops. Truthfully, there simply isn't very much about this group that's impressive, except the devotion of its fans to a mythology created in Haight-Ashbury and now sustained in junior high schools across America. At its peak, the Dead has essayed competence: *Workingman's Dead* is third-rate next to *Sweetheart of the Rodeo,* much less anything Gram Parsons ever recorded on his own, but it has a sweet ingenuousness that renders it bearable. Similarly, *Live Dead* isn't much less interminable than any other Dead concert piece, but it has a freshness that feints toward vitality. But when the Dead attempt to rework rock and blues standards—as they did on their horrible debut album, and have sporadically since— they are a pox upon the face of pop. And the group's patchouli-oil philosophy, which does nothing more than reinforce solipsism and self-indulgence in its listeners, except when it's nurturing its Hells Angels fan club, is exactly the sort of stuff that gave peace 'n' love a bad name.

Since joining Arista, the Dead have basically relinquished any claim to being taken seriously except as nostalgia mongers. They essentially fulfill the same purpose as do the current Beach Boys: offering facile reminiscence to an audience with no memory of its own. This would be a tragic end, if there had been any genuine glory involved to begin with. — D.M.

CARL GRAVES
■ **Carl Graves / A&M (1976)**
Hopelessly lame arrangements of some fairly decent songs (notably "My Whole World Ended," and Neil Sedaka's "Breaking Up Is Hard to Do") aren't all that mar this first and only record by a singer who sounds like he's still auditioning. — D.M.

DOBIE GRAY
★ ★ **New Ray of Sunshine / Capri. (1975)** ¶
★ ★ ★ **Midnight Diamond / Inf. (1978)**
★ ★ **Dobie Gray / Inf. (1979)**
★ ★ **Greatest Hits of Dobie Gray / Power (NA)**
Dobie Gray is best known for his spectacular renditions of "Loving Arms" and "Drift Away," the title songs to two MCA albums that are unfortunately no longer in circulation. *New Ray, Midnight Diamond* and *Dobie Gray* can't sustain that earlier brilliance, mostly because of poor material. Gray's expressive baritone is wasted on standard country-rock songs, and when he does get something passable to sing, thin production robs him of much of his power. — C.F.

GREAT BUILDINGS
★ ★ **Apart from the Crowd / Col. (1981)**
Trite, predictable L.A. power pop. — J.D.C.

AL GREEN
★ ★ **Green Is Blues / Hi (1970)** ¶
★ ★ ★ ★ **Al Green Gets Next to You / Hi (1970)** ¶
Green Is Blues, Al Green's Hi debut and a so-so collection of soul and pop standards, caused little reaction on its release. Few predicted that his very next album would see the emergence of the heir to the Sam Cooke–Otis Redding throne. To the delight of those who favor Redding over Cooke, *Gets Next to You* is rough. The smoothing of style and delivery was yet to come, a fact evident from Green's hokey getup on the cover of his second LP.
★ ★ ★ ★ ★ **Let's Stay Together / Hi (1972)**
★ ★ ★ ★ **I'm Still in Love with You / Hi (1972)** ¶
★ ★ ★ ★ ★ **Call Me / Hi (1973)** ¶
Call Me and *Let's Stay Together* are surely the best Al Green records. He didn't turn out to be the next incarnation of Otis Redding, but rather a vocalist who flaunted a cuddly persona in the face of those who liked their soul rugged and harsh. *Let's Stay Together* is still closer to old-fashioned Stax-Volt soul than the followups would ever be. Both "Old Time Lovin' " and "It Ain't No Fun for Me" suggest Stax; the choked rhythm guitar on "Ain't No Fun" and the unwashed gospel of "Old Time Lovin' " are as pure as the rawest Redding or Sam and Dave record. *I'm Still in Love with You* finds few holes in producer Willie Mitchell's seam and one real moment of boredom: a six-and-a-half-minute version of "For the Good Times." But if *Let's Stay Together* recalls Stax, *Call Me* manages to distill Green's affection for Sam Cooke and Claude Jeter. The subtlety of both technique and mood change is as astounding as it is difficult to perceive.
★ ★ ★ ★ **Livin' for You / Hi (1973)** ¶
★ ★ ★ ★ **Al Green Explores Your Mind / Hi (1974)** ¶
★ ★ ★ ★ ★ **Greatest Hits / Hi (1975)**
Not only does *Livin' for You* mark the first evidence of creative decline, but it also contains the first of many Al Green songs that mix oblique sexual and religious metaphors ("Sweet Sixteen"). *Explores Your Mind* finds its true moment of greatness in such a song—the blues shuffle "Take Me to the River." While a gospel song had been included on previous records, Green's obsession with religion dominates *Explores Your*

Mind, as it would in albums to follow.
Greatest Hits was released almost simultaneously with *Explores Your Mind.* It includes a small but delightful bonus: two extra minutes of "Let's Stay Together."
★ ★ ★ ★ **Al Green Is Love** / Hi (1975) ¶
★ ★ ★ ★ **Full of Fire** / Hi (1976) ¶
★ ★ ★ **Have a Good Time** / Hi (1976)
Al Green Is Love is enigmatic and adventurous. Green and Mitchell attempt to loosen the formula: the crack Hi rhythm section is spotlighted on the thundering "Love Ritual," while at other times Green is seemingly caught in some private hell ("Love Sermon"). Both *Full of Fire* and *Have a Good Time* are a return to more conventional territory, and Green's paranoia becomes full-blown on "Keep Me Crying," a song from *Good Time.*
★ ★ ★ ★ **The Belle Album** / Hi (1977)
★ ★ ★ ★ **Truth 'n' Time** / Hi (1978)
★ ★ ★ ★ ★ **Greatest Hits, Vol. 2** / Hi (1977)
★ ★ ★ **Love Ritual** / Lon. (1978)
These albums, released in 1977 and 1978, are Green's most adventurous. Producer Mitchell was gone; Green now produced himself. And the music swung drastically from the straight soul of Mitchell's conception to smoldering funk, hot disco changes and intimations of pure blues. Green himself was sometimes featured on guitar. The songs are intimate and percussive and suggest an incomplete resolution of his previous religious and paranoid musings. "Belle," the first album's attempt for a hit, wasn't the chartbuster it deserved to be, but the approach of these records suggested that Green's eccentricities might have found a new focus.
★ ★ ★ **The Lord Will Make a Way** / Myrrh (1980)
★ ★ ★ **Higher Plane** / Myrrh (1981)
★ ★ ★ ★ ★ **Tokyo . . . Live** / Cream (1981), Fr. imp.
The nature of that focus, as it turned out, was gospel music. Green retired from live performances and secular singing, becoming a full-time preacher who made the two LPs of hymns released on Myrrh, neither as glorious as his best pop work but both pleasurable listening. *Tokyo* is from his late seventies Japanese tour and is a marvelous document of Green's greatness on stage. — J.MC./ D.M.

JACK GREEN
★ ★ **Humanesque** / RCA (1980)
★ ★ **Reverse Logic** / RCA (1981)
Green's claim to fame is that he was a member of one of the later versions of the Pretty

Things. His solo albums are slick power pop, designed to be played as background music on the radio, between cuts of more distinction. — D.M.

THE GREENBRIAR BOYS
★ ★ ★ **Ragged but Right!** / Van. (1964)
★ ★ ★ **Better Late Than Never** / Van. (1966)
★ ★ **Best of the Greenbriar Boys and John Herald** / Van. (1972)
The Greenbriar Boys paved the way for the city bluegrass scene of the Sixties. John Herald and Bob Yellin headed up the band, with a succession of members that included Eric Weissberg, Ralph Rinzler, Frank Wakefield, Jim Buchanan and Dian Edmondson. The various artists shared a sophisticated respect for the music, were accomplished musicians (bluegrass being a virtuoso form) and displayed an originality in material and its execution that was rarely paralleled.

Highlighted by Herald's unique high tenor, the music is as convincing today as then. And their scholarly quest for new sources made the Boys' own records sources for others. "Take a Whiff on Me," "Ragged but Right" and "Stewball" rapidly became staples of bluegrass and folk-rock groups. *Ragged* and *Better* are more representative of the group's talents than the Herald-dominated *Best of.* — I.M.

DENNY GREENE
★ **Denny Greene** / Mid. Int. (NA)
Predictably synthetic Sha Na Na sideman's solo album. — D.M.

RICHARD GREENE
★ ★ ★ ★ **Duets** / Roun. (NA)
★ ★ ★ **Ramblin'** / Roun. (1979)
Greene is an excellent fiddler known to many rock fans for his work with Seatrain, but whose best moments have come in an acoustic bluegrass format. *Duets* pits him against David Grisman's mandolin, Tony Rice's guitar, Tony Trischka's banjo, J.D. Crowe's banjo and David Nichtern's guitar. *Ramblin'* covers a variety of contexts in which he plays with Rice, Peter Rowan, Maria Muldaur, Andy Statman and others. — J.S.

ELLIE GREENWICH
★ ★ **Ellie Greenwich Composes, Produces and Sings** / U.A. (1968)
★ ★ ★ **Let It Be Written, Let It Be Sung** / Verve (1973)
Its title would lead you to believe *Composes, Produces and Sings* might be the Ellie

Greenwich album to own. But the songs, her own and others, are fairly ordinary, and Greenwich's performances sometimes lack enthusiasm. Not so on *Let It Be Written*. Here one of rock & roll's preeminent songwriters dares to offer a different viewpoint on some of the great songs she wrote for other artists. Greenwich's triumph is in making her mellow, introspective interpretations valid without discrediting the original recordings. Where Lesley Gore rages through "Maybe I Know," Greenwich's sangfroid is the resigned acceptance of a lover who's been anesthetized to faithless love; who, indeed, would be shocked by a show of loyalty. Similarly, Darlene Love's unrestrained glee on "Today I Met the Boy I'm Gonna Marry" becomes Greenwich's cool declaration of purpose—a goal not yet attained but clearly in sight, as opposed to Love's adolescent musings on something that may never come to pass. *Let It Be Written* is many things, but most of all it's certifiable proof that rock was, is and always will be about great songs sung with passion, commitment and intelligence. — D.MC.

GREEZY WHEELS
★ ★ ★ Romance / Lon. (NA)
Engaging combo updates Western swing in a manner reminiscent of Asleep at the Wheel but with a distinct personality. A group ahead of its time. — J.S.

GREY AND HANKS
★ ★ Prime Time / RCA (1980) ¶
Not-ready-for-prime-time funk. — J.D.C.

GLENDA GRIFFITH
★ ★ Glenda Griffith / Ario. (1977)
Glenda Griffith has a nice voice and covers listenable material. Nonetheless, the main interest of this record is the fact that it was produced by Eagle Don Henley. — R.P.

MARCIA GRIFFITHS
★ ★ ★ Sweet Bitter Love / Troj. (1974)
★ ★ ★ Naturally / High N. (1978)
★ ★ ★ ★ Stepping / High N. (1979)
Those who believe that female reggae singers are a recent phenomenon should check out I-Three Marcia Griffiths', fifteen hitmaking years as documented by these records (and the rarely available late-Sixties *At Studio One* LP). Her understated, pristine vocals achieve impact with sheer tonal beauty and subtle, soulful embellishments—maybe she's the Jamaican Roberta Flack. Much of her material has been unabashedly pop (half of *Bitter*

Love is straight soul balladry), but *Stepping* hits several peaks, making it one of the three best female reggae LPs thus far. — R.F.G.

ROB GRILL
★ ★ Uprooted / Mer. (1980)
Grassroots singer sounds engaging enough but just doesn't have the material to make this solo effort anything special. — J.S.

GRIN
★ ★ Gone Crazy / A&M (1974)
Grin (Nils Lofgren, guitar, keyboards and vocals; Bob Berberich, drums and vocals; Bob Gordon, bass and vocals; and, later, Tom Lofgren, guitar) was a first-class early-Seventies band that never achieved wide success; *Gone Crazy,* an eviscerated farewell made after the group left Spindizzy / CBS following three LPs, shows little of its talent. Their best work is on *1 + 1,* a lovely blend of tough hard rock ("Moon Tears," "End Unkind") and ironic teen-heartbreak ballads ("Lost a Number"). It can still be found in bargain bins, as can *Best of Grin,* an erratic collection of tracks from the slight *Grin, 1 + 1* and the overproduced, strained *All Out.* — G.M.

GRINDERSWITCH
★ ★ Honest to Goodness / Capri. (1971) ¶
★ ★ Macon Tracks / Capri. (1975) ¶
★ ★ Pullin' Together / Capri. (1976) ¶
★ ★ Redwing / Atco (1977)
★ Have Band, Will Travel / Robox (NA)
Fervid Southern boogie, performed thunderously and unfeelingly, just the sort of thing that gave the genre a bad name. Stick with the Allmans, Lynyrd Skynyrd or, at the outside, Wet Willie; this stuff is for Charlie Daniels addicts only. — D.M.

DAVID GRISMAN
★ ★ ★ ★ Hot Dawg / A&M (1976)
★ ★ ★ ★ David Grisman Quintet / Kal. (1979)
★ ★ ★ ★ David Grisman Quintet '80 / War. (1980)
★ ★ ★ ★ David Grisman Album / Roun. (1980)
★ ★ ★ ★ Mondo Mando / War. (1981)
Mandolin virtuoso Grisman spearheaded a new wave of acoustic bluegrass he has nicknamed "Dawg Music." Grisman's quintet costarred the extraordinary talents of fiddler Mark O'Conner and guitarist Tony Rice, both of whom went on to solo success. — J.S.

LARRY GROCE
■ **Junkfood Junkie / War. (1976)**
■ **Winnie the Pooh for President / RCA (1980)**
The fact that "Junkfood Junkie" (a 1976 hit about a closet burger freak in a vegetarian world) took the wind out of the sanctimonious health-food cult doesn't excuse an album that's the aural equivalent of a Big Mac diet. The RCA LP has even less reason to exist. — D.M.

HENRY GROSS
★ **Henry Gross / A&M (1973) ¶**
■ **Plug Me into Something / A&M (1975)**
■ **Release / Lifes. (1976) ¶**
★ **Show Me to the Stage / Lifes. (1977) ¶**
★ **Love Is the Stuff / Lifes. (1978) ¶**
★ **What's in a Name? / Cap. (1981)**
Working in realms far beyond the derivative, Gross takes Rolling Stones–type rockers, Beatle-esque ballads, Lou Reed–styled documentaries, songwriterish laments, Southern rock and phony C&W and turns them all into flavorless FM fodder. Gross does do a passable Beach Boys imitation ("Shannon," from *Release,* was a smash in 1976), but his idea of rock is facile doodling, and his love songs are gruesome propositions at best.

Cashman and West, who own Lifesong, are the ideal producers for Gross. Their obsessively tasteful and genuinely indifferent approach pulls the gutless whole together under a fine gelatin of functionalist studio technique. (They even disguise Gross' wholly dumb guitar playing—a good trick.)

Gross' music stays on the radio by means of his tunes' subliminal appeal to their half-remembered predecessors, making him a good bet for distracted listening. — B.T.

THE GUESS WHO
★ ★ **Shakin' All Over / Sp. (1968) ¶**
★ ★ ★ **Wheatfield Soul / RCA (1969) ¶**
★ ★ ★ ★ **Canned Wheat / RCA (1969) ¶**
★ ★ **American Woman / RCA (1970)**
★ ★ ★ **Share the Land / RCA (1970) ¶**
★ ★ ★ ★ ★ **Best of the Guess Who / RCA (1971)**
★ **Rockin' / RCA (1974) ¶**
★ **No. 10 / RCA (1977) ¶**
★ ★ ★ **Best of the Guess Who, Vol. 2 / RCA (1973) ¶**
★ **Road Food / RCA (1973) ¶**
★ **The Way They Were / RCA (1976) ¶**
★ ★ ★ **Greatest of the Guess Who / RCA (1977)**
★ **All This for a Song / HTK (1979)**
The title of the second Guess Who album *Wheatfield Soul* was a pun on the band's western Canadian roots, but even though the musicians were somewhat provincial, they were far from amateurish. Led by guitarist Randy Bachman and fronted by lead singer Burton Cummings, the Guess Who coined a fairly substantial, jazz-inflected R&B sound similar to contemporary Southern bands, such as the Classics IV.

Bachman's chord structures and Cummings' lyrics created the group's first hit, "These Eyes." And while the rest of the record was more experimental and included Cummings' blatant Jim Morrison imitation on the melodramatic "Friends of Mine," the follow-up album, *Canned Wheat,* paid more attention to the singles formula and produced a string of pop-rock hits— "Laughing," "No Time" and "Undun."

American Woman turned out to be the band's psychedelic LP, and was accordingly loud, fuzz-guitar drenched and repetitive. It sounds dated today, despite the title track's tremendous success as a hit single. Until that album, the Guess Who was a quartet with Bachman firmly in control of its musical direction. After Bachman left in 1970 to form Brave Belt and later Bachman-Turner Overdrive, Cummings took full control, added two guitarists to replace Bachman, and the Guess Who began to grind it out.

The title track of *Share the Land* was the band's last well-written hit, and it's all downhill from there. *Greatest* makes the most sense by culling the good moments from this group's erratic but occasionally brilliant career. *Shakin' All Over* is the pre-Cummings band; the title track, a 1965 hit, is first-rate, but everything else is filler.
— J.S.

GIB GUILBEAU
★ ★ **Gib Guilbeau / Als. (1973)**
★ ★ **Gib Guilbeau Sings / Als. (1973)**
★ ★ **Cajun Country / Als. (1975)**
Louisiana songwriter and (briefly) member of the Flying Burrito Brothers, best known for writing "Big Bayou," covered by both Rod Stewart and Ron Wood. — D.M.

GUITAR SHORTY
★ ★ ★ **Carolina Slide Guitarist / Flyr. (1973)**
The title doesn't begin to describe the talents of this mid-Atlantic songster. He's an East Coast resource much like Mance Lipscomb with a repertoire that ranges from gospel to boogie, including a rocking "Drinkin' Wine (Spo-de-o-dee)." *Carolina Slide Guitarist* was recorded in 1970, when Shorty was still relatively young (only thirty-eight) for an acoustic country bluesman. — D.M.

GUITAR SLIM

★ ★ ★ ★ **The Things I Used to Do** / **Spec. (NA)**
Very fine set of New Orleans rhythm & blues, circa 1954–1956, spotlighting the marvelous title track, as sensual as any hit of its era. — D.M.

GUITAR SLIM

★ ★ ★ **Greensboro Rounder** / **Flyr. (1979)**
Pleasant North Carolina country bluesman. Despite the poor annotation, don't be misled: this is not the same Guitar Slim of "The Things I Used to Do," the '54 rock & roll hit. These sides, recorded in 1974 and 1975, are listenable but hardly up to that standard. — D.M.

GUS

★ ★ **Convicted** / **Nemp. (1980)**
Noise-by-numbers AOR ick, save for one goodie ("She's Not Gonna Come to You") and the only known ode to a Japanese drug squad ("So You Busted Paul McCartney"). — L.F.

ARLO GUTHRIE

★ ★ ★ **Alice's Restaurant** / **Rep. (1967)**
★ ★ **Arlo** / **Rep. (1968)** ¶
★ ★ ★ **Running down the Road** / **Rep. (1969)**
★ ★ **Washington County** / **Rep. (1970)**
★ ★ ★ ★ **Hobo's Lullaby** / **Rep. (1972)**
★ ★ ★ ★ **Last of the Brooklyn Cowboys** / **Rep. (1973)**
★ ★ ★ **Arlo Guthrie** / **Rep. (1974)** ¶
★ **Together in Concert (with Pete Seeger)** / **Rep. (1975)**
★ ★ ★ ★ ★ **Amigo** / **Rep. (1976)**
★ ★ **The Best of Arlo Guthrie** / **War. (1977)**
★ ★ ★ **One Night** / **War. (1978)**
★ ★ ★ ★ **Outlasting the Blues** / **War. (1979)**
Arlo Guthrie's "Alice's Restaurant," an eighteen-minute underground hit in 1967, immediately established him as the inheritor, and perhaps the fulfillment, of the folk-music tradition pioneered by his father, Woody. "Alice" was funny, leftishly political as well as folk-based, but it was also up-to-date in a way that implied his absorption of those on whom Woody had had his greatest influence: Bob Dylan, Jack Elliott and other early Sixties folkies. And if Arlo's first attempts at serious material were weaker than his humorous songs, the lovely "Chilling of the Evening" indicated that that wouldn't always be so.

Yet *Arlo,* a live album that followed the success of "Alice," emphasized the hit novelty status, partly because it was framed by similar, shaggy, hippie story-songs, partly because the musical arrangements were too skeletal, partly because the original material was weak. The album's best track, in fact, is the Ernest Tubb country standard, "Try Me One More Time."

Perhaps this was obvious to the artist himself, for with *Running down the Road* almost everything shifted. Arlo began working with producer Lenny Waronker, whose roots were more pop than folk, and rather than writing all of his own material, he became an interpretive singer, recording songs by his father, Mississippi John Hurt, Pete Seeger and Gus Cannon, as well as originals. The latter are mostly dated, but the dope-smuggling anthem "Coming into Los Angeles" remains among his best-known work. In 1969, *Running* seemed a breakthrough; today it seems dated and slightly out of focus.

Hobo's Lullaby, released in 1972, was almost entirely interpretive, and contains Guthrie's best-known post-"Alice" number, Steve Goodman's "City of New Orleans," which immediately became a sort of singer/songwriter standard. "City" was brilliant, a song that extended rather than merely invoked the tradition Woody had founded, and it became Guthrie's first "serious" Top Twenty hit. This is a near-perfect interpretive folk-rock LP—listen to the rocking sax on Hoyt Axton's "Lightning Bar Blues"— and the folk-rock genre has produced the best interpretive singing in rock.

But with *Washington County,* Arlo once more attempted to write all his own material, and the project fell flat. Its best moments are instrumental, not exactly what we came for. To really fulfill the tradition, Guthrie needed a more direct approach. *Last of the Brooklyn Cowboys,* a designation swiped from Jack Elliott, provided just the remedy, opening with an Irish reel and including songs by Woody, plus country, ragtime, white gospel, Stephen Foster jazzlike waltz-time pop/blues, and even some Latin and cowboy/Mexican accents. This is Guthrie's most eclectic LP, and a great deal of its success is due to outside forces: coproducers Waronker and John Pilla and the cast of L.A. studio pros who played on it. The biggest flaw is Dylan's "Gates of Eden," perfect for Arlo's reedy voice but a truly bad song.

Arlo Guthrie was more uneven: "Presidential Rag" is perhaps the greatest and certainly the most vicious anti-Nixon song. Unlike most other topical songs of our era, it hasn't dated a bit, much like Woody's protest masterpiece, "Deportees," which is also included. More striking was "Children of Abraham," a song about the Arab-Israeli dispute that made sense of that political mess by relying on just the sense of tradition Guthrie had brought to *Brooklyn's* music. Most of the rest, however, was not nearly as strong.

The *Together in Concert* LP was a barely mitigated disaster. Guthrie's sense of folk tradition was too natural and free-flowing to jell with Pete Seeger's pedantic and sanctimonious approach, and the two-record set does little but expose the worst of both men's weaknesses.

But in 1976, Guthrie released an album that finally connected all the links of the chain: *Amigo* spanned the folk tradition with the same assurance that *Brooklyn* had, and by adding a piece of pure rock & roll in the Rolling Stones' "Connection," Guthrie brought it all back home as no one since early electric Dylan had been able to do. In this context, a song about the martyred Chilean poet Victor Jara meshed seamlessly with more personal concerns expressed in songs like "Manzanillo Bay" and "Massachusetts."

Amigo is a triumph Guthrie has not yet been able to recapitulate. On *One Night,* in fact, he really floundered, seeking a rapport with his band that just wasn't forthcoming. He returned to strength and produced perhaps his best set of original songs with *Outlasting the Blues,* which also reflects his conversion to Roman Catholicism. *Outlasting the Blues* is an almost frightening meditation upon mortality, Guthrie's most confessional album (only two songs weren't self-written), and while the music never jells as completely as on *Amigo,* most of the time it's effectively reminiscent of *Desire*-period Dylan. Rewriting "Which Side" as a new hymn, confronting his own fears of dying diseased (like his father) in "Prologue" (and "Epilogue"), myth-making in "Wedding Song," Arlo Guthrie begins to fashion for himself a powerful adult persona, linked to tradition but beginning to extend it both impressively and matter-of-factly. (Avoid the ill-chosen *Best of* and go for some of the four- and five-star material here, any of which offers a better perspective on Guthrie's talents and pleasures.) — D.M.

WOODY GUTHRIE

★ ★ ★ ★ Cowboy Songs / Stin. (1944)
★ ★ ★ ★ Folk Songs by Woody Guthrie and Cisco Houston / Stin. (1944)
★ ★ ★ ★ Songs to Grow On / Folk. (1951)
★ ★ ★ ★ Songs to Grow On, Vol. 2 / Folk. (1958)
★ ★ ★ ★ Songs to Grow On, Vol. 3 / Folk. (1961)
★ ★ ★ ★ Woodie Guthrie Sings Folk Songs / Folk. (1962)
★ ★ ★ ★ ★ Dust Bowl Ballads / Folk. (1964)
★ ★ ★ ★ Woody Guthrie Sings Folk Songs, Vol. 2 / Folk. (1964)
★ ★ ★ ★ ★ This Land Is Your Land / Folk. (1967)
★ ★ ★ ★ ★ A Legendary Performer / RCA (1977)
★ ★ ★ ★ Woody Guthrie / War. (1977)
★ ★ ★ ★ Immortal Woody Guthrie / Olym. (NA)
★ ★ ★ ★ Legendary Woody Guthrie / Trad. (NA)
★ ★ ★ ★ Early Years / Trad. (NA)
★ ★ ★ ★ Woody Guthrie / Ev. (NA)
★ ★ ★ ★ ★ Woody Guthrie: Library of Congress Recordings / Elek. (NA)

Woody Guthrie ranks with the half-dozen most important names in the history of American music. After his childhood in Oklahoma, he went west to California, the very incarnation of Steinbeck's Tom Joad (in *The Grapes of Wrath*), about whom he wrote a ballad. Throughout the Thirties and Forties, and into the Fifties until felled by Huntington's chorea, Guthrie was the most influential songwriter on the American political left, a remarkable, energetic figure whose creations include literally hundreds of songs, dozens of poems, exhaustive journals, novels and other autobiographical material as well as one of the classic hobo legends. All of this would serve to inspire not only his peers—particularly such singers as Lee Hays, Pete Seeger, Cisco Houston and Ramblin' Jack Elliott—but also the Beats and, of course, the folk and leftist movements that became the Sixties counterculture.

Guthrie's musical approach was raw and primitive, generally amounting to just a voice and acoustic guitar, sometimes adding a harmonica but never more. The naiveté he enjoyed projecting is totally belied by the quality of his songs and the intensity of his performances. It was no dumb Okie who wrote "Deportee," as subtle a picture of discrimination against migrant workers as has been done to date, or "This Land Is Your Land," as beautiful a portrayal of American natural glory as has been created in any medium. Throughout these songs, from the outlaw ballads like "Pretty Boy Floyd," to the depictions of the dust bowl in Guthrie's many songs about that catastrophe, to the children's tunes and the political calls-to-arms, there is a singular artistic vision at work, one of the greatest of its generation. No wonder the greatest American composer of our era, Bob Dylan, began his career in total, awestruck emulation of Guthrie.

The basic Guthrie document is the *Library of Congress Recordings,* which contains much conversation between Guthrie and Alan Lomax, as well as a good share of both original and traditional tunes. *Dust Bowl Ballads* and *This Land Is Your Land,* as well as the RCA *A Legendary Performer* (which was also previously known as *Dust Bowl Ballads*), are the best selections of his material, although there is no one record that presents all of Guthrie's best work; there's simply too much of it for that. The Stinson material is largely devoted to traditional songs, often featuring Guthrie accompanied by one of his many sidekicks—Cisco Houston, Leadbelly, Sonny Terry and Brownie McGhee, or Pete Seeger. The recordings on Tradition, Everest, Olympic, and Warner Bros. basically recapitulate the approaches above. (*Legendary Woody Guthrie* on Tradition repeats much of what's available on the Everest LP.) *Songs to Grow On,* finally, is a series of some of the greatest children's recordings ever made—both Guthrie's wonderfully amusing original children's songs and some of the folk tunes he grew up with. — D.M.

BUDDY GUY
★ ★ ★ ★ **Man and the Blues / Van. (1968)**
★ ★ ★ ★ **This Is Buddy Guy / Van. (1968)**
★ ★ ★ **Hold That Plane / Van. (1972)**
★ ★ ★ ★ **I Was Walking through the Woods / Chess (1977)**
★ ★ ★ ★ **In the Beginning / Red L. (NA)**
One of the younger Chicago bluesmen, Guy began recording for Chess in the Sixties after serving an apprenticeship in Muddy Waters' band. A flashy guitarist influenced by B. B. King and Elmore James and a good vocalist in the Bobby Bland style, Guy enjoyed a lot of crossover success with white audiences and covered a number of popular R&B songs ("Knock on Wood") in addition to blues staples. *This Is* is a fairly hot live set. Guy now tours jointly with harpist Junior Wells. — J.S.

STEVE HACKETT

★ ★ Voyage of the Acolyte / Chrys. (1976)
★ ★ Please Don't Touch / Chrys. (1978)
★ ★ Spectral Morning / Chrys. (1979)
★ ★ Defector / CMA (1980)

Genesis guitarist tries his hand at solo outings with middling success. Hackett is technically proficient, but his classically inspired
instrumental meanderings are bereft of any
dynamic focus.   — J.S.

SAMMY HAGAR

★ ★ Nine on a Ten Scale / Cap. (1976)
★ ★ ★ Sammy Hagar / Cap. (1977)
★ ★ ★ Musical Chairs / Cap. (1977)
★ ★ ★ Sammy Hagar Live / Cap. (1978)
★ ★ Street Machine / Cap. (1979)
★ ★ Danger Zone / Cap. (1979)
★ ★ Harder, Faster / Cap. (1979)
★ ★ Standing Hampton / Gef. (1981)
★ ★ ★ Three Lock Box / Gef. (1982)

Hagar was lead singer in Montrose before
leaving to form his own band in late 1975.
His first album, *Nine on a Ten Scale,* was
notable mostly for a version of Van Morrison's "Flamingos Fly." But Hagar is a capable hard rocker of the generation weaned on
Cream albums, and his brusque singing fits
well with the polished crunch of his band.
Backed by a group built around former
Montrose members, Hagar charges through
a variety of spotty material, including a
number of songs he claims are destined for
some future space opera, and covers items as
diverse as Donovan's "Catch the Wind" and
the Paul Revere and the Raiders' hit, "Hungry." The results are often pedestrian, but
just as often enjoyable. On *Three Lock Box*
Hagar collaborated with Journey keyboardist
Jonathan Cain.   — J.S.

NINA HAGEN

★ ★ Nina Hagen Band / Col. (1980)

Nina Hagen is considered a major artist in
continental Europe, but all this four-song
sampler proves is that some things just don't
translate. Between Hagen's theatrical vocals
and her band's slick, new-wave-derived
Sturm und Drang, this could almost pass for
Queen doing punk rock in German. Except
that even Queen would have better taste
than to cover "White Punks on Dope."
  — J.D.C.

MERLE HAGGARD

★ ★ ★ I'm a Lonesome Fugitive / Cap.
(1967)
★ ★ Pride in What I Am / Cap. (1969)
★ ★ Same Train, a Different Time / Cap.
(1969)
★ ★ ★ ★ Okie from Muskogee / Cap. (1970)
★ ★ ★ ★ The Fightin' Side of Me / Cap.
(1970)
★ ★ A Tribute to the Best Damn Fiddle
Player in the World / Cap. (1970)
★ ★ Sing a Sad Song / Cap. (1971)
★ ★ ★ Hag / Cap. (1971)
★ ★ ★ ★ The Best of Merle Haggard / Cap.
(1972)
★ ★ I Love Dixie Blues / Cap. (1973)
★ ★ Merle Haggard's Christmas Present /
Cap. (1973)
★ ★ ★ If We Make It through December /
Cap. (1974)
★ ★ ★ His Thirtieth Album / Cap. (1974)
★ ★ My Love Affair with Trains / Cap.
(1974)
★ ★ Keep On Movin' / Cap. (1975)
★ ★ It's All in the Movies / Cap. (1976)
★ ★ ★ ★ ★ Songs I'll Always Sing / Cap.
(1976)
★ ★ The Roots of My Raising / Cap. (1976)
★ ★ A Working Man Can't Get Nowhere
Today / Cap. (1977)
★ ★ ★ Eleven Winners / Cap. (1977)
★ ★ Ramblin' Fever / MCA (1977)
★ My Farewell to Elvis / MCA (1977)
★ ★ ★ The Way It Was in '51 / Cap. (1978)

★ ★ **Serving 190 Proof** / MCA (1979)
★ ★ ★ **High on a Hilltop** / Cap. (1980)
★ ★ ★ **The Way I Am** / MCA (1980)
★ ★ ★ **Back to the Barrooms** / MCA (1980)
★ ★ ★ **Big City** / Epic (1981)
★ ★ ★ **My Favorite Memory** / Epic (1981)
★ ★ ★ ★ **Songs for the Mama Who Tried** / MCA (1981)

Merle Haggard has been compared to Woody Guthrie (for the populist streak in his songwriting) and such country heroes as Bob Wills, Jimmie Rodgers and Lefty Frizzell. Both comparisons are correct, but beyond his inheritance and the notoriety that "Okie from Muskogee" brought him, Haggard has made consistently listenable (and sometimes classic) country music since he began recording in 1963.

Haggard's parents drifted from dust-bowl Oklahoma to Bakersfield, California, in the early Thirties. Born in 1937, he was only fourteen when his father died of a brain tumor; he soon ran away from home, and a year later landed in reform school. In 1957, after several years of odd jobs and jail visits, the nineteen-year-old Haggard was sentenced to one to fifteen years in San Quentin on a safecracking rap.

When he was released, Haggard played guitar for Wynn Stewart, who gave him "Sing a Sad Song" to record as a single. Released on the obscure Tally label, it went to No. 19 on the country charts in 1963. Two years later, "(All My Friends Are Gonna Be) Strangers" became a hit and won him a Capitol contract.

The early *Sing a Sad Song* and *High on a Hilltop* (sometimes found as a twofer) contain those first two hits and such classics as "Swinging Doors" and "The Bottle Let Me Down." But those two, and *I'm a Lonesome Fugitive,* are effectively boiled down to the fine selection found on *The Best of Merle Haggard.*

Haggard recorded "Okie from Muskogee" in late 1969; the song, framed by a Muskogee crowd's applause, appears on the record of that title, a concert disc that also has good treatments of several Hollywood cowboy anthems: "White Line Fever," "Silver Wings," "Mama Tried" and "Working Man Blues," among others. *The Fightin' Side of Me,* a second live LP, documents a sometimes-uproarious Philadelphia show from 1970. Haggard's ex-wife, Bonnie Owens, fluffs Woody Guthrie's "Philadelphia Lawyer," and Merle runs through parodies, tributes and hits; "I Take a Lot of Pride in What I Am," along with "Okie from Mus-

kogee" and "If We Make It through December," the 1975 recession anthem, are the songs that made him something of a standard bearer for the so-called silent majority.

Haggard's tribute records—to Bob Wills *(Fiddle Player),* Elvis and Jimmie Rodgers *(Same Train)*—are adept but often mawkishly narrated, and superfluous except as shills for the originals. *I Love Dixie Blues,* which features him live in New Orleans with a Dixieland brass section, joins these derivative efforts as a curio.

Such marginal albums as *My Love Affair with Trains* enabled Haggard to release *Thirtieth Album* in 1974, only eleven years after his recording career began. The latter contains the salty "Old Man from the Mountain" and "Honky Tonk Night Time Man," which join "Living with the Shades Pulled Down" (from *Movies*) as studies of fatheaded but funny redneck libertinism.

The pick of Haggard's formidable output is contained in the two-disc *Songs I'll Always Sing; Eleven Winners* has similar intentions but is only a passable sampling whose release coincided with his 1977 departure from Capitol. Since then Haggard has recorded for both MCA and Epic, with competent if unexciting results. The exception is the gospel set, *Songs for the Mama Who Tried.* Whether Haggard will ever put another great LP together remains to be seen. But his best songs reveal a composer/performer who is not only one of country music's glories but enduringly important on anyone's terms. — F.S.

BILL HALEY AND HIS COMETS
★ ★ ★ **Golden Hits** / MCA (1972)
★ ★ **Greatest Hits** / MCA (NA)
★ **Rock and Roll Is Here to Stay** / Gusto (NA)
★ **Rockin'** / Cor. (NA)
★ **Rock and Roll** / Cres. (NA)
★ **Rock around the Country** / Cres. (NA)

In 1954, Bill Haley assembled the bones of a synthesis of country swing, R&B, big band and Dixieland elements. He brought it all down on the second and fourth beats, and white rock & roll was born as a popular phenomenon.

It took Elvis to put flesh on those bones, but the freshness and danceability of the medium Haley had outlined was not lost on the white audiences that began boogieing to "Rock around the Clock." (And not only whites—Haley made two of the five records by white singers that made the R&B charts in 1950–1955.)

The reasons for his success are still audible. If his breakthroughs (technical and commercial) seem tame and quaint today, they are still very listenable period pieces. And occasionally a song like "Shake, Rattle and Roll" will ineluctably loosen up your legs. Except a few odds and ends, *Golden Hits* gets it all down in twenty-four quick doses. — F.S.

DARYL HALL
★ ★ ★ Sacred Songs / RCA (1980) ¶
The Robert Fripp–produced solo album by the first half of Hall and Oates. When it was recorded, it seemed so radical that the RCA brass tossed it in the vault and refused to release it until almost three years later. By that time, most of the ground it had broken had been rebroken on the Hall and Oates albums *Along the Red Ledge* and *X-Static*. — J.D.C.

DARYL HALL AND JOHN OATES
★ Whole Oates / Atl. (1972)
★ ★ ★ Abandoned Luncheonette / Atl. (1973)
★ ★ War Babies / Atl. (1974)
★ ★ Daryl Hall and John Oates / RCA (1975)
★ ★ ★ Bigger Than Both of Us / RCA (1976)
★ ★ No Goodbyes / Atl. (1977)
★ ★ ★ Beauty on a Back Street / RCA (1977)
■ Past Times Behind / Chel. (1977) ¶
★ ★ Livetime / RCA (1978)
★ ★ ★ Along the Red Ledge / RCA (1978)
★ ★ X-Static / RCA (1979) ¶
★ ★ ★ Voices / RCA (1980)
★ ★ ★ Private Eyes / RCA (1981)
★ ★ ★ H₂O / RCA (1982)

It may very well be true, as critic Paul Nelson has suggested, that Daryl Hall is so chic that, were he writing *Moby Dick,* he'd make the whale off-white. But this Philadelphia-based duo owes more to hard rock and streetcorner soul than any of its disco-based hits indicate; because their albums present such a decorative surface, songs sometimes blend together in an unnecessarily mellow mélange.

Their early records for Atlantic are erratic (the Chelsea sides include a goodly number of Daryl Hall demos and very little of his work with John Oates). The high point is, of course, the oft-recorded "She's Gone," an upbeat soul ballad worthy of the Spinners; it's included on both *Abandoned Luncheonette* and *No Goodbyes,* a collection released by Atlantic to cash in on the greater success the team has enjoyed with RCA.

With RCA, they've had better luck. Their biggest hit, "Sara Smile," is on *Bigger Than Both of Us,* but beginning with *Beauty on a Back Street,* hard rock reentered the mix in a more forceful way. *Livetime,* a concert LP, presented their pop soul in a most driving context, and *Red Ledge* has one side of tough soul songs somewhat in the Gamble and Huff mold and another side of flat-out rockers, which include guest appearances from Todd Rundgren, Robert Fripp, George Harrison and Cheap Trick's Rick Nielsen, all on guitar.

The group's lack of Top Forty success and its faltering album audience spurred a return to its soul basis exclusively on the four most recent albums. *X-Static* attempted to hold on to some of the rock elements, but the attempt was halfhearted. *Voices, Private Eyes* and *H₂O* focused almost exclusively on harmony, and with fine results, at least commercially: each produced several hit singles and recaptured Hall and Oates' audience. But these records also represented a withdrawal from anything challenging, and threatened to become the formula the group managed to avoid in its first success. While Hall and Oates certainly are more interesting singers than jammers, the retreat into safe harbors just at the point when their synthesis of rock & soul was beginning to mature is unfortunate. — D.M.

JIMMY HALL
★ ★ ★ Touch You / Epic (1980)
Wet Willie's lead vocalist sets out on his own, and puts his soul shoes on. Most of this works pretty well as a kind of Muscle Shoals pastiche, but there's no song sufficiently memorable to shake the project loose. The result is, like Wet Willie's records, some pleasant Southern rock but nothing new. — D.M.

JOHN HALL
★ John Hall / Asy. (1978)
★ Power / Col. (1979)
★ All of the Above / EMI (1981)
Exactly as unctuous, sanctimonious and solemn as his work with Orleans. The title song of the Columbia album approaches self-parody. — D.M.

TOM T. HALL
★ ★ ★ ★ In Search of a Song / Mer. (1971)
★ ★ ★ We All Got Together and . . . / Mer. (1972)
★ ★ ★ The Storyteller / Mer. (1972)

★ ★ ★ ★ ★ **Tom T. Hall's Greatest Hits /**
Mer. (1972)
★ ★ ★ ★ **Rhymer and Other Five and**
Dimers / Mer. (1973)
★ ★ **For the People in the Last Hard Town**
/ Mer. (1973)
★ **Country Is / Mer. (1974)**
★ ★ **Songs of Fox Hollow / Mer. (1974)**
★ ★ **I Wrote a Song about It / Mer. (1975)**
★ ★ ★ **Greatest Hits, Vol. 2 / Mer. (1975)**
★ ★ **Faster Horses / Mer. (1976)**
★ **Magnificent Music Machine / Mer. (1976)**
★ **New Train—Same Rider / RCA (1977)**
★ **About Love / Mer. (1977)**
★ **Places I've Done Time / RCA (1978)**
★ **Saturday Morning Songs / RCA (1979)**
★ **Soldier of Fortune / RCA (1980)**
★ **Ol' T's Back in Town / RCA (1981)**
Hall got his start as house songwriter for a
Nashville country music publishing firm in
the mid-Sixties and built a reputation for
writing controversial material after Jeannie
C. Riley turned his "Harper Valley P.T.A."
into a pop hit single in 1968. By the time he
started recording, Hall had already turned
out more than five hundred songs, and he
wasted no time getting as much of it onto
record as he could. A number of Hall's
songs, especially on his first four (now-
deleted) albums, are well-drawn dramas
about down-and-out and alienated characters. "Ballad of Forty Dollars," "Homecoming," "A Week in a Country Jail" and "Salute to a Switchblade" justify Hall's
reputation for incisive storytelling. But much
of the rest of his material is the hackneyed
observation and freeze-dried sentiment of
processed MOR country music.

Jerry Kennedy's excellent production of
Hall's albums brought together many of
Nashville's top session players (including
Bob Moore, Buddy Harman, Charlie McCoy
and Pig Robbins), and the earlier albums are
also hot instrumental sessions, unencumbered
by the ruthless country pop mixes of the
later LPs, where saccharine but militant
string sections drown out the backing band's
ambiance.

Hall and Kennedy continued their successful formula until *Last Hard Town,* but since
that record, Hall's writing has become more
and more gimmicky while the production
has turned to the maudlin strings and glossy
postures of standard country pop. Even at
his worst, Hall still has enough wit to turn
out an occasional gem like "Lying Jim"
(from *I Wrote a Song about It*). But lately
it seems he's more interested in selling
pickup trucks than writing good songs.
— J.S.

HALLOWEEN
★ **Come See What It's All About / Mer.**
(1979)
L.A. disco sextet tried to make it on the
post–Village People concept of dressing up
as ghoulish characters. Good only for a
laugh. — J.S.

DIRK HAMILTON
★ ★ ★ **You Can Sing on the Left or Bark on**
the Right / ABC (1976)
★ ★ ★ **Alias I / ABC (1977)**
★ ★ ★ **Meet Me at the Crux / Elek. (1978)**
★ ★ **Thug / Elek. (1979)**
A post-folk singer with a tenor that seems to
emanate from the core of his Adam's apple,
Hamilton has a gift for terse, evocative imagery that can be simultaneously bitter and
magnanimous. Also loony (progressively
more so with each album). Needless to say,
he isn't well known, but *Alias I,* with its
novel delineations of an ambitious, frustrated
loner, and *Crux,* which has an even crazier
cast, are hilarious and chilling albums. *You
Can Sing on the Left* is uneven, but "She
Don't Squash Bugs" juggles adoration and
fear of women with admirable frankness and
wit. But *Thug* placed Hamilton's aphoristic
wit at a dead end, largely because he hasn't
developed a sound to properly deliver the
message. — K.T./D.M.

HAMMER
★ **Hammer / Asy. (1978)**
★ **Black Sheep / Asy. (1979)**
The worst nightmares produced by fusion
feature the grinning face of ex–Mahavishnu
Orchestra keyboardist Jan Hammer, who's
responsible for these LPs under his name as
a leader. — J.S.

ALBERT HAMMOND
■ **My Spanish Album / Cay. (1977)**
■ **Album de Recuerdos / Cay. (1978)**
■ **Espinita / Cay. (1978)**
Hammond had a sort of junky singer/
songwriter hit in "It Never Rains in Southern California." These albums, then, must
have been recorded with the Spanish plains
in mind—which does not help. — D.M.

JOHN PAUL HAMMOND
★ ★ **John Hammond / Van. (1963)**
★ ★ **Big City Blues / Van. (1964)**
★ ★ ★ **So Many Roads / Van. (1965)**
★ ★ **Country Blues / Van. (1965)**
★ ★ ★ **The Best of John Hammond / Van.**
(1970)
★ ★ ★ **Southern Fried / Atl. (1970)**

★ ★ **John Hammond Solo** / Van. (1976)
★ ★ **Footwork** / Van. (1978)
Son of famed talent scout John Hammond, Sr., John Paul Hammond comes by his devotion to country blues honestly enough, and performs with a pedant's rectitude. But Hammond has never developed the individual performing personality that is the mark of the true bluesman, black or white, and the result is that his albums sound more like exercises than the real thing. The exceptions are *So Many Roads* and *Southern Fried,* where he is backed by excellent bands, including members of the Band and the Rolling Stones on the latter. — D.M.

LAWRENCE HAMMOND
★ ★ ★ **Coyote's Dream** / Tak. (1976)
Skillful latter-day folkie. — D.M.

ROY HARPER
★ ★ **Folkjokeopus** / World Pac. (1969)
★ ★ ★ **Flat Baroque and Berserk** / Chrys. (1970)
★ ★ ★ ★ **Stormcock** / Chrys. (1971)
★ ★ ★ **Lifemask** / Chrys. (1973)
★ ★ ★ **Valentine** / Chrys. (1974)
★ ★ ★ **Flashes from the Archives of Oblivion** / Chrys. (1974)
★ ★ ★ ★ **When an Old Cricketer Leaves the Crease** / Chrys. (1976)
★ ★ ★ **One of These Days in England (Bullinamingvase)** / Chrys. (1977)
★ ★ ★ ★ **1970–1975** / Chrys. (1978)
English singer/songwriter cult hero Roy Harper has made many friends throughout his career, which started in 1964 with a homemade album called *The Sophisticated Beggar.* Jimmy Page, Dave Gilmour of Pink Floyd, and Mr. and Mrs. Paul McCartney have all appeared on his records. Led Zeppelin recorded a tribute to him called "Hats Off to Harper" and Pink Floyd commissioned him to sing "Have a Cigar" on *Wish You Were Here.*

Although none of this has made him any more famous, Harper has nonetheless made a remarkable series of albums over the years. Linked with the British folk scene because of his predominantly acoustic beginnings, he is actually closer in spirit to maverick tunesmiths like Peter Hammill and Kevin Coyne in the provocative intensity of his lyrics (he can also write achingly beautiful love songs) and the matching drive of his performance. The organic grandeur of *Stormcock* and the deft fusion of magnum rock force and dramatic balladry in *Cricketer* (his only album still in print in America) are his finest achievements, although the *1970–1975* compilation is worth seeking out as an overview of the Harper oeuvre. — D.F.

SLIM HARPO
★ ★ ★ **Blues Hangover** / Flyr. (1976), Br. imp.
★ ★ ★ ★ **He Knew the Blues** / Sonet (1978), Br. imp.
★ ★ ★ **Got Love If You Want It** / Flyr. (1980), Br. imp.
★ ★ ★ ★ **Slim Harpo Knew the Blues, Vol. 1** / Ex. (NA)
★ ★ ★ **Slim Harpo Knew the Blues, Vol. 2** / Ex. (NA)
Little-known but influential Louisiana blues singer whose Fifties and Sixties recordings with entrepreneur Jay Miller included "I'm a King Bee" and "Baby Scratch My Back," laconic, raspy, harmonica-driven gutbucket R&B. "King Bee" and his "Hip Shake" were both recorded by the Rolling Stones; Mick Jagger patterned a good part of his approach to blues singing on Harpo's. The intense smoky eroticism of Harpo's singing is well represented everywhere above, but especially on the *Knew the Blues* sets. The Flyrights are alternate and unissued takes, part of the Legendary Jay Miller Sessions, and valuable mostly to collectors and fanatics (if there's a difference—I own them all). — D.M.

THE HARPTONES
★ ★ ★ ★ **The Harptones** / Emus (NA)
★ ★ ★ ★ **Love Needs** / Amb. (1982)
The Harptones were one of the most formally elegant and musically exciting of all doo-wop harmony groups. They were blessed with the most classic doo-wop lead voice of them all, Willie Winfield. His singing is everything the liner notes of these two sets call it: satiny, inimitable, clear, pure, sweet and innocent. The Emus set includes remastered versions of the original Fifties releases (ten tracks, including "The Shrine of St. Cecilia," "Cry Like I Cried" and "A Sunday King of Love"), slightly speeded up but still thrilling. *Love Needs* was recorded in early 1982 as part of Ambient's ambitious doo-wop revival program, and (along with the Jive Five set recorded around the same time) ranks as the finest doo-wop recorded in the past twenty years. The highlight is Winfield's wonderful reworking of the Jackson Browne/Lowell George/Valerie Carter love song, "Love Needs a Heart," which removes the Harptones from the ranks of nostalgia and places them among American musical history's greatest groups. — D.M.

DON "SUGARCANE" HARRIS
★ ★ ★ **Sugarcane / Epic (1970)**
As half of the venerable R&B duo Don and
Dewey, Harris has some claim to rock (well,
doo-wop) fame. But here he engages himself
as a violinist in a context closer to mood
jazz . . . nothing to scare Jean-Luc Ponty or
Jerry Goodman, or even a Cajun crazy like
Doug Kershaw, all of whom are more imagi-
native performers on the same instrument.
— D.M.

EMMYLOU HARRIS
★ ★ ★ ★ **Pieces of the Sky / War. (1975)**
★ ★ ★ **Elite Hotel / War. (1976)**
★ ★ ★ **Luxury Liner / War. (1977)**
★ ★ **Quarter Moon in a Ten-Cent Town /
War. (1978)**
★ ★ ★ ★ **Profile/The Best of Emmylou
Harris / War. (1978)**
★ ★ ★ **Blue Kentucky Girl / War. (1979)**
★ ★ ★ ★ **Roses in the Snow / War. (1980)**
★ ★ ★ **Light of the Stable / War. (1980)**
★ ★ **Evangeline / War. (1981)**
★ ★ **Cimarron / War. (1981)**
Though Harris recorded an obscure folk-pop
album for Jubilee in 1969, her duets with
country-rock pioneer Gram Parsons on *GP*
and *Grievous Angel* were what established
her as a demure honky-tonk angel. That
image was sharpened on her Warners debut
in 1975, produced (like all her subsequent albums) by husband Brian Ahern in a tasteful,
pedal-steel-inflected country-pop style that
appealed equally to country and rock fans.
Pieces contained a pair of genre classics—the
weepy "Boulder to Birmingham," and "If I
Could Only Win Your Love" (the first of
several memorable Harris remakes of Louvin
Brothers songs).

Harris' records have varied in quality depending on how formulaic they are. Though
lovely, her sweet, silvery soprano is not an
especially expressive instrument, and Ahern's
arrangements can become repetitive. On
Elite Hotel, Harris emphasized the Gram
Parsons connection with three touching
cover versions of his songs. The high points
of *Luxury Liner* are another Louvin Brothers cover ("When I Stop Dreaming") and
Townes Van Zandt's "Poncho and Lefty."
Quarter Moon contains a haunting version of
Dolly Parton's previously unrecorded "To
Daddy."

After *Profile* (a good, though far from definitive, anthology), Harris made two of her
finest albums, featuring the harmony vocals
and instrumental support of country music
traditionalist Ricky Skaggs. On *Roses,* her
best album, Harris and Ahern almost totally
foreswore conventional rhythm tracks in
favor of more traditional bluegrass-oriented
arrangements. The title cut of *Light of the
Stable,* a Christmas album, found Harris
harmonizing with Linda Ronstadt, Dolly
Parton, and Neil Young. With *Evangeline,*
Harris and Ahern returned to the same
pleasantly plodding formulas of earlier albums. *Evangeline*'s high point is a remake of
the Fifties novelty hit "Mr. Sandman." "If I
Needed You," a duet with the country
singer Don Williams, is the artistic cornerstone of the otherwise humdrum *Cimarron.*
— S.H.

JODY HARRIS/ROBERT QUINE
★ ★ ★ ★ **Escape / In-Fi. (1981)**
Best all-guitar album in years. Two Strato-
casters, a rhythm machine, ten million inspired overdubs that amazingly never sink to
empty showboating, and just enough tape
manipulations and other electronic effects
make for a truly heartening double entry in
the guitar-hero sweepstakes. Quine has also
played with Richard Hell, Brian Eno and
Lou Reed, and Harris has served time in the
Contortions and the Raybeats. One doubts
this will be either's pinnacle, but for now it
will certainly do as the record truest to the
spirit of Miles Davis in the year of his comeback. Also answers the question of where the
Hendrix legacy can go without being redundant or insulting. — L.B.

MAJOR HARRIS
★ ★ ★ **My Way / Atl. (1975)**
★ ★ **How Do You Take Your Love / RCA
(1978)** ¶
★ ★ **The Best of Major Harris, Now and
Then / WMOT (1981)**
Like many Philadelphia singers, Major Har-
ris has a limited range and a tendency to
sing flat. *My Way* includes "Love Won't Let
Me Wait," a hit whose selling point was the
orgiastic moaning of an anonymous female.
The album is a fair sampling of mid-
Seventies Philly soul, but subsequent LPs are
without distinguishable material or produc-
tion gimmicks. — J.M.C.

RICHARD HARRIS
★ ★ **A Tramp Shining / Dun. (1968)** ¶
★ **The Richard Harris Love Album / Dun.
(1970)** ¶
★ ★ **His Greatest Performances / ABC Dun.
(1973)** ¶
■ **The Prophet, by Kahlil Gibran / Atl. (1974)**
It's one thing for a breathless singer to rasp
his way through Jim Webb's pop baroque
pillow fights. There are compensations when

Webb's overripe melodies get the orchestral exploitation of *A Tramp Shining.* "Mac-Arthur Park," the hilarious masterpiece of the Webb-Harris collaboration, became a 1968 hit and revolutionized MOR by adapting John Lennon's "A Day in the Life" to the sentiments of an Erich Segal novel. Very effective.

However, it's another thing to try stretching such diva turns into a sustained musical enterprise. Which makes the rest of these simply embarrassing; Harris even makes *The Prophet* seem more pop-platitudinous than it was in print. — B.T.

WYNONIE HARRIS
★ ★ ★ ★ ★ **Good Rockin' Blues / Gusto (1977)**
★ ★ ★ ★ **Mr. Blues Is Coming to Town / Route 66 (NA), Swed. imp.**
★ ★ ★ ★ **Oh Babe / Route 66 (1982), Swed. imp.**

With Roy Brown, Harris was simply the hottest, most influential blues shouter/crooner of the late Forties. These sets feature him at his peak; the Gusto sides include his wild and intense "Good Rockin' Tonight," the model for Elvis' version, and much of his other work for Federal Records. The Route 66 material, more thoroughly annotated, ranges from 1945 to 1964, and includes lesser-known material released on Federal and King, often in settings where his small jump band predominates. — D.M.

THE DON HARRISON BAND
★ ★ ★ **The Don Harrison Band / Atl. (1976)** ¶
★ ★ **Red Hot / Atl. (1976)**

Clean, sharply focused, post–Creedence rock, courtesy of ex–Creedence drummer Doug Clifford and bassist Stu Cook, plus guitarist Russell Dashiell and Harrison himself—the latter an unreconstructed Southern rocker now based in California. The first album, *The Don Harrison Band,* is graced by "Living Another Day," Harrison's lovely, unassuming tale of the days he spent as a janitor in a recording studio, listening to everybody's music but his own.

Red Hot, unfortunately, is cooled off. — G.M.

GEORGE HARRISON
★ ★ ★ ★ ★ **All Things Must Pass / Apple (1970)**

A grand gesture—philosophically (check the title), musically (with Ringo Starr, Billy Preston, Dave Mason, Eric Clapton and Phil Spector), spiritually and morally. Coming at the end of 1970, the year the Beatles broke up, this three-record set established George as a heavy mystic and an ex-Beatle with a future. Cynics will note the presence of the same sanctimoniousness that has marred his later work; what saves this set is humility, respect for the audience and Phil Spector's typically Wagnerian production. A monumental album that makes a nice signpost for the Seventies.

★ ★ ★ ★ **The Concert for Bangladesh / Apple (1972)**

Harrison and friends (Clapton, Preston, Leon Russell, Ringo, Ravi Shankar and Bob Dylan, again with Spector producing) stage an overblown concert spectacular for the starving masses of Bangladesh, some of whom were to have benefited from the proceeds. Bob Dylan's is the best of the six sides.

★ ★ ★ **Living in the Material World / Apple (1973)**
★ **Dark Horse / Apple (1974)**
★ **Extra Texture (Read All about It) / Apple (1975)**
★ ★ **Thirty-Three and 1/3 / Dark (1976)**
★ ★ **Best of George Harrison / Cap. (1976)**
★ **George Harrison / Dark (1979)**
★ **Somewhere in England / Dark (1981)**
★ **Gone Troppo / Dark (1982)**

With few exceptions, Harrison's post-Bangladesh work has been preachy, sophomoric and dull. Is that because of his tendency to work with mediocrities like Tom Scott, Billy Preston and Gary Wright? Partly—but the real conclusion seems to be that his bout with Indian mysticism has simply been too much for what were always limited entertainment abilities at best. — F.R.

WILBERT HARRISON
★ ★ **Soul Food Man / Chel. (NA)** ¶

Harrison is best known as the most successful popularizer of "Kansas City," which he took to No. 1 in 1959 over competing versions by James Brown and Hank Ballard. His only other Top Forty hit in 1969 was the bouncy blues "Let's Work Together," and the album released under that name (on the now-defunct Sue label) is well worth finding. *Soul Food Man* is an ineffective mid-Seventies attempt to recapture his sound, an unfortunate sole remnant for such an interesting yet minor artist's career. — D.M.

DEBBIE HARRY
★ ★ **Koo Koo / Chrys. (1981)**

What should have been a meeting of modern musical minds—Debbie Harry and Chris Stein of Blondie with Nile Rodgers and Bernard Edwards of Chic—emerges as meandering mush. Harry's flat-toned voice makes an ideal vehicle for some hot urban rap, but the album never ignites, sounding more like an experiment, which it is. "Backfired," side two's first cut, makes an appropriate subtitle for this less-than-thrilling execution of what could have been an exciting cross-breeding. Ultimately, *Koo Koo* is ho hum. — R.P.

JOHN HARTFORD
★ ★ ★ **Aero-Plain / War. (1971)**
★ ★ **Tennessee Jubilee / Fly. Fish (1975)**
★ ★ **Mark Twang / Fly. Fish (1976)**
★ ★ **Nobody Knows What You Do / Fly. Fish (1976)**
★ ★ **Glitter Grass from the Nashwood Hollyville Strings / Fly. Fish (1976)**
★ ★ **All in the Name of Love / Fly. Fish (1977)**
★ ★ **Headin' down into the Mystery / Fly. Fish (1978)**
★ ★ **Slumberin' on the Cumberland / Fly. Fish (1979)**
★ ★ **You and Me at Home / Fly. Fish (1981)**
Glen Campbell's former banjo player claimed a half acre of Opryland for the freaks with the easygoing *Aero-Plain,* which features first-rate musicianship from Tut Taylor, Norman Blake and Vassar Clements. Since then he's developed that obscure but witty turf over the eight Flying Fish albums, which are samey but, taken one at a time, amusing. — A.E.G.

DAN HARTMAN
★ ★ ★ **Instant Replay / Blue S. (1978)**
★ ★ **Relight My Fire / Blue S. (1979)**
★ ★ **It Hurts to Be in Love / Blue S. (1981)**
Former Edgar Winter bassist (he wrote "Free Ride") turns to disco self-production with catchy if inconsequential results. — D.M.

ALEXANDER HARVEY
★ ★ **Preshus Child / Kam. S. (1976)**
★ ★ **Purple Crush / Bud. (1977)** ¶
Perhaps the most mild-mannered of all the country music outlaws, Harvey produced a series of albums for a variety of labels in the mid-Seventies.

At his best, Harvey sings exactly like Johnny Cash, a neat trick but hardly worth investment of time or money. His most well-known song, "Delta Dawn," was one of the outstanding numbers on Bette Midler's debut LP. — D.M.

THE SENSATIONAL ALEX HARVEY BAND
★ ★ ★ **Next / Vert. (1973)** ¶
★ ★ **The Impossible Dream / Vert. (1974)** ¶
★ ★ ★ **Live / Atl.(1975)**
★ ★ **Tomorrow Belongs to Me / Vert. (1975)** ¶

The penultimate (pre–Sex Pistols) British working-class-hero band, SAHB is almost unknown in the U.S. except to cultists. Prime resources: raunch, energy, sweat. SAHB (led by forty-three-year-old Alex Harvey) exemplified the punk attitude long before it was fashionable. Unfortunately, most of what it did was better seen live than endured on vinyl. *Tomorrow* includes a bizarre one-act play, "Tale of the Giant Stoneater." The Atlantic LP is definitive, including extended versions of their crowd-pleasers, "Vambo," "Tomahawk Kid" and "Delilah." Harvey died in 1982. — A.N.

FUZZY HASKINS
★ ★ **Radio Active / Westb. (1978)** ¶
Undistinguished solo set from minor member of George Clinton's Parliafunkadeliment troupe. Clinton's not here, but Jerome Brailey, Glen Goins and Bernie Worrell are, for what it's worth. No matter the names, they're going through pretty predictable paces here. — D.M.

HATFIELD AND THE NORTH
★ ★ **Hatfield and the North / Virgin (1973)**
In 1973 this stuff was the cat's progressive-rock pajamas—complex time signatures, fractured Zappa-esque melodies and tortuous fusoid riffing à la Soft Machine, Caravan, etc. This British quartet had more than just pedigree going for them (their credits included maverick avant-rock heavyweights like Gong, Egg and Matching Mole): on their one U.S. release they spiced their instrumental derring-do with bright absurdist humor. Would you believe "Lobster in Cleavage Probe" and "Gigantic Land-Crabs in Earth Takeover Bid"? There's more where that came from on their second U.K. album, *The Rotter's Club,* and on a 1981 compilation. — D.F.

DONNY HATHAWAY
★ ★ ★ **Everything Is Everything / Atco (1970)**
★ ★ ★ **Donny Hathaway / Atco (1971)**
★ ★ ★ **Donny Hathaway Live / Atco (1972)**
★ ★ ★ ★ **Extension of a Man / Atl. (1973)** ¶
Hathaway is a fairly accomplished singer/songwriter/keyboardist best known for his duets with Roberta Flack. On his own, he leans to the MOR side of the R&B axis. His first two early-Seventies albums present him as a glib interpreter of pop material from "I Believe in Music" to "He Ain't Heavy, He's My Brother" and a fairly good arranger. *Extensions of a Man* is his major work, a stylistic hodgepodge with autobiographical overtones. His version of Al Kooper's "I Love You More Than You'll Ever Know" is very good, and excellent instrumental support from guitarists David Spinozza and

Cornell Dupree, bassist Willie Weeks and percussionist Ralph MacDonald rounds things out. The live album is an unaffected and spirited set of recordings from the Troubadour in Hollywood and the Bitter End in New York. — J.S.

RICHIE HAVENS
★ ★ ★ **Mixed Bag** / MGM **(1968)**
★ **Mirage** / A&M **(1973)** ¶
★ **End of the Beginning** / A&M **(1976)** ¶
★ **Connections** / Elek. **(1979)**
Havens is one of the few singers who can handle depressing material without resorting to melodramatics or self-pity. "Morning, Morning" and "I Can't Make It Anymore," the best tracks on *Mixed Bag,* demonstrate this beautifully. In a sense they captured better than anything else the sadness behind the seeming ebullience of the Woodstock era, and it's no accident that it took a *black* folk-rock singer to do it.

In subsequent years, however, Havens has repeated this approach ad nauseum, and little of value has emerged. — R.G.

DALE HAWKINS
★ ★ ★ **Dale Hawkins** / Chess **(1977)** ¶
A solid set of Fifties rock & roll—the straight stuff—highlighted by the original big hit, "Suzie Q." Most notable for the driving guitar playing and Hawkins' overpowering vocals, which are an early prophecy of John Fogerty's. — D.M.

THE EDWIN HAWKINS SINGERS
★ ★ **The Best of the Edwin Hawkins Singers** / Bud. **(NA)**
Hawkins had an off-the-wall 1969 pop hit with "Oh Happy Day," which featured lead singer Dorothy Morrison over a surging, joyous choir. Then Morrison left and Hawkins began experimenting with pop, Vegas-like arrangements. Though mostly pedestrian, *Best* does contain a few exhilarating gospel cuts. — J.MO.

RONNIE HAWKINS
★ ★ ★ **The Best of Ronnie Hawkins** / Rou. **(1963)** ¶
★ ★ **Rockin'** / Pye **(1977),** Br. imp.
★ ★ **Hawk** / U.A. **(1979)**
★ ★ **Ron Hawkins Quartet** / Ozark **(NA)**
Early-Sixties (that is, latter-day) rockabilly, who is best remembered for singing a couple of minor hits, notably "Mary Lou," and for giving a name and a break to the Hawks, a backup band that later became famous as the Band. The Hawks make a prominent appearance on the unfortunately unavailable Rou-

lette LP. The Ozark album isn't that good, but it is vintage. The United Artists and Pye sets are more recent and mostly feature Hawkins bragging and growling, well within the rock tradition, but necessary listening only for obsessives. — D.M.

SCREAMIN' JAY HAWKINS
★ ★ ★ **Screamin' the Blues** / Red L. **(1979)**
Rhythm & blues weirdo. This album traces Hawkins' career from 1953 to 1970, but it misses his only really important song, "I Put a Spell on You." That track is so often anthologized that it's hard to say whether anything else he ever did is really necessary. But it was Screamin' Jay's crypt-kicking stage show that inspired George Clinton's maggot-brain extravaganza, and his hoodoo comedy has bite beneath its bravado. Inconsequential but fun, then, and a lesson that roots aren't always solemn. — D.M.

TED HAWKINS
★ ★ ★ ★ ★ **Watch Your Step** / Roun. **(1982)**
Hawkins is a strange cross between urban soul crooner and folk bluesman: his voice alternates between Sam Cooke gospel phrasing and Mississippi John Hurt country inflections, and his writing and playing have the same mixture of innocence and awareness. Bruce Bromberg originally recorded Hawkins in Los Angeles in 1971, but the singer's later incarceration in prison prevented their release for more than a decade. Yet such songs as "Watch Your Step," "Bring It Home Daddy," "Who Got My Natural Comb," "Stay Close to Me," "Stop Your Crying" and "Peace and Happiness" have dated hardly at all. As beautiful and easeful as any music recorded in the Seventies, Hawkins' reemergence is a powerfully hopeful sign for the return of natural music in the Eighties. Soul and blues fans need to hear this, if only to restore their faith in the dying art of emotional conviction. — D.M.

HAWKLORDS
★ ★ **Twenty-five Years On** / Char. **(1979)**
Hawkwind's last desperate gasp, this time as loopy futurist fantasy rock. Tuneful at times, but since when has that been an excuse? — J.D.C.

HAWKWIND
★ ★ **Hawkwind** / U.A. **(1971)**
★ **In Search of Space** / U.A. **(1972)**
★ **Doremi Fasol Latido** / U.A. **(1972)** ¶
★ **Space Ritual Live** / U.A. **(1973)**
★ **Quark, Strangeness and Charm** / Sire **(1977)**

England's answer to acid rock, Hawkwind is primarily the medium for Bob Calvert's visions of science-fiction apocalypse. Concept overshadows music pretty drastically throughout the Hawkwind opus, and whatever social importance the band might have been credited with has dissipated over the years. — J.S.

ISAAC HAYES
★ ★ ★ **Chocolate Chip / ABC (1975)** ¶
★ ★ **Disco Connection / ABC (1975)** ¶
★ **Groove-a-Thon / ABC (1976)** ¶
★ **Juicy Fruit / ABC (1976)** ¶
★ **Man and a Woman / ABC (1977)**
★ **New Horizon / Poly. (1977)**
★ ★ **Hotbed / Stax (1978)**
★ **For the Sake of Love / Poly. (1978)**
★ ★ **Isaac Hayes—Movement / Stax (1979)**
★ **Don't Let Go / Poly. (1979)**
★ **And Once Again / Poly. (1980)**
★ ★ ★ **Enterprise—His Greatest Hits / Stax (1980)**
★ **Lifetime Thing / Poly. (1981)**
Isaac Hayes first appeared, chains draped across his bare chest and calling himself Black Moses, as the last big-time proponent of the declining Memphis Sound. Though no heir to the tradition of Sam and Dave (for whom he wrote some great songs with partner David Porter), Hayes did gradually pick up steam by groaning long intros into truly gruesome ballads, which were expanded into huge workouts by his band, the Movement. Then in 1970, "Theme from *Shaft,*" aided by Curtis Mayfield's "Superfly," put the disco seal of fate on soul music. But most of the *Shaft* album was bad movie music, and Hayes' first full disco album *Chocolate Chip,* is alternately a lush and pushy party record, though Hayes unfortunately dropped his ballad intros just as Barry White picked up on the gimmick. The followup, *Disco Connection,* is so evenly programmed for dancing that Hayes is almost absent, except for the rare growl. He returns, however, to torpedo *Juicy Fruit* with already horrific self-parody, whether conscious or not no one has ever determined. Subsequent Hayes is nothing but factory simulacrum, easily ignored and rather dadaistic in his overblown obsequiousness to the disco style and scene he at least partly fathered. — B.T.

JUSTIN HAYWARD
★ ★ **Songwriter / Deram (1977)**
★ ★ **Night Flight / Deram (1980)**
The Moody Blues guitarist hits an acceptable if unspectacular balance between the sugary and the hard. Catchy tunes and instrumenta-

tion, good guitars—similar but finally inferior to the best of the group. — C.W.

JUSTIN HAYWARD AND JOHN LODGE
★ ★ **Bluejays / Thresh. (1975)**
Two ex–Moody Blues members make what sounds like a Moodies album, but a mediocre one. Lazy tempos, dull strings, syrupy lyrics, sameness. — C.W.

THE HEADBOYS
★ ★ ★ **The Headboys / RSO (1980)**
Recorded in Scotland, this LP blends psychedelic-futuristic mood, boys-on-a-spree spirit and keyboard-dominated instrumentation without finally delivering unified whole. Lyrics, when not playful, are a bit windy, but in that respect, the group borrows from high Sixties Brit rock. Maybe the Headboys wanted to be rock's philosopher kings? Unfortunately, position had been abolished in 1978. — G.A.

HEAD EAST
★ ★ **Flat as a Pancake / A&M (1975)**
★ ★ **Get Yourself Up / A&M (1976)**
★ ★ **Gettin' Lucky / A&M (1977)**
★ ★ **Head East / A&M (1978)**
★ ★ **Live / A&M (1979)**
★ ★ **Different Kind of Crazy / A&M (1979)**
★ ★ **U.S. 1 / A&M (1980)**
St. Louis hard rockers forced themselves into the national spotlight after phenomenal regional popularity in the mid-Seventies. Though the band tends to be flatulent, there are good moments on all of these records. — J.S.

ROY HEAD
★ ★ ★ **Head First / Dot (1976)** ¶
★ ★ ★ ★ **A Head of His Time / Dot (1976)** ¶
★ ★ ★ **Tonight's the Night / ABC (1978)**
★ ★ **In Our Room / Elek. (1979)**
★ ★ **The Many Sides of Roy Head / Elek. (1979)**
Once a fine vocalist in the blue-eyed soul vein ("Treat Her Right" was a '65 hit), Roy Head has reemerged a country singer—but of a different sort. The title of his second album is an ironic and intentional pun: a singer equally at home with country, rock, soul and Broadway show tunes—all of which are represented here—still waits his just due, critically and commercially. For its display of sheer vocal prowess, *A Head of His Time* stands as the definitive Roy Head album. — D.MC.

THE HEADHUNTERS
★ ★ **Survival of the Fittest** / Ari. (1975) ¶
★ ★ **Straight from the Gate** / Ari. (1977)
Herbie Hancock's electric backup band tried
its hand at disco funk with poor results.
— J.S.

HEART
★ ★ ★ **Dreamboat Annie** / Mush. (1976)
★ ★ **Little Queen** / Por. (1977)
★ ★ **Magazine** / Mush. (1978)
★ ★ ★ **Dog and Butterfly** / Por. (1978)
★ ★ ★ **Bebe Le Strange** / Epic (1980)
★ ★ ★ **Greatest Hits/Live** / Epic (1980)
The Heart sisters, singer Ann and guitarist
Nancy Wilson, have always suffered from
acute musical schizophrenia. On the one
hand they fancy themselves backwoods folk
sirens, all acoustic guitars and mystic sere-
nades, and on the other they pound it out
like heavy-metal tomboys (note their carbon
copy of Led Zep's "Rock and Roll" on
Greatest Hits/Live).

This ersatz Jethro Zeppelin concept, however, has only worked intermittently on record. The group's debut, *Dreamboat Annie,*
a Top Forty sleeper, is a pleasant if somewhat derivative surprise that yielded two hit
singles, "Magic Man" and "Crazy on You."
The followup, *Little Queen,* suffers from lack
of focus and even stooped to downright pla-
giarism—note the similarity between "Dream
of the Archer" and "The Battle of Evermore" on Zeppelin's "untitled" LP)—while
Magazine consists of half-baked demos released by Heart's old label during a contract
dispute.

Both *Dog and Butterfly* and *Bebe Le
Strange* are closer to the mark, but the two-
record *Greatest Hits/Live* has all the hits
and none of the dross, fleshed out with some
spirited live tracks and a seductive cover of
Aaron Neville's hit R&B ballad "Tell It Like
It Is." — D.F.

HEAT
★ ★ ★ **Heat** / MCA (1980)
★ ★ ★ **Still Waiting** / MCA (1980)
Contemporary funk competence. — D.M.

THE HEATERS
★ **Heaters** / Ario. (NA)
★ **Energy Transfer** / Col. (NA)
L.A. power-pop unit with all the impact of
stale bubblegum. — J.S.

THE HEATS
★ ★ ★ **Have an Idea** / Alb. (1980)
Ingratiating Pacific Northwest update of garage band/British pub essentials, fueled by
imaginative songwriting and playing. It ultimately languishes under alternately uncaring
and heavy-handed production, jointly credited to the Heats and Howard Leese of
Heart, whose management company backed
and distributed this regional LP. — G.A.

HEATWAVE
★ **Too Hot to Handle** / Epic (1977)
■ **Central Heating** / Epic (1978)
■ **Hot Property** / Epic (1979)
■ **Candles** / Epic (1980)
Despite the presence on *Too Hot* of a major
1977 hit single, "Boogie Nights," the most
fitting subtitle here would seem to be "Too
Boring to Be Believed." Much less listened
to for any length of time. — D.M.

HEAVEN AND EARTH
★ ★ ★ **Heaven and Earth** / Mer. (1978)
★ ★ ★ **Fantasy** / Mer. (1980)
This four-piece soul group from Chicago can
become overly lush or too discofied, but basically is a competent example of the way in
which falsetto harmony styles were revived
during this period. — D.M.

HEAVEN 17
★ ★ ★ **Penthouse and Pavement** / Virgin
(1981), Br. imp.
Half of Human League decamped to form
the electro-pop and funk backbone of
Heaven 17. While their first single, "We
Don't Need This Fascist Groove Thang,"
was simply marvelous, this record (with the
Penthouse side purely electronic, the *Pavement* mostly Linn drum computer) is disappointing. Too much like Travelogue—barely
boppy but not much more. — ML.H.

RICHARD HELL AND THE VOIDOIDS
★ ★ ★ ★ ★ **Blank Generation** / Sire (1977)
Seminal album that transcends the headbang
limitations of punk rock by melding the desolate slum screeds of one of the form's Seventies avatars with shattering assaults by a
band that prophesied the later No Wave
punk-jazz fusion. Hell is a true poet even
though he thinks so, and guitarist Robert
Quine in particular is shaping up as one of
the true Stratocaster titans of the Eighties.
Essential to any modern music collection or
anybody concerned about the dead-end quality of contemporary life in the West.
— L.B.

LEVON HELM
★ ★ ★ **Levon Helm and the RCO All
Stars** / ABC (1977)
★ ★ ★ **Levon Helm** / ABC (1978)

★ ★ ★ ★ **American Son** / MCA (1980)
★ ★ ★ **Levon Helm** / Cap. (1982) ¶
Former Band drummer Helm's first solo outing *(Levon Helm and the RCO All Stars)* is aptly named, providing a vital context for blues harpist Paul Butterfield, keyboardist/guitarist Mac "Dr. John" Rebennack, guitarists Steve Cropper and Fred Carter, Jr., bassist Donald "Duck" Dunn and a crack horn section led by Howard Johnson on baritone sax and tuba. Helm's Band cohorts Robbie Robertson and Garth Hudson also guest on the record. The session is a relaxed semi-jam with basic arrangements that give everybody a chance to blow to their heart's content. Helm's craggy vocals and Butterfield's harp pretty much steal the show, and the surprise inclusion of two of Rebennack's best tunes, "Washer Woman" and "Sing Sing Sing," flesh out a sturdy set of standards. *Levon Helm* is not as hot, but *American Son* is a great solo album. The Capitol album features backup from the Muscle Shoals Rhythm Section and Russell Smith of the now-defunct Amazing Rhythm Aces. — J.S.

HELMET BOY
★ ★ ★ **Helmet Boy** / Asy. (1980)
Despite the really stupid name, this marginally new-wavish quartet has its moments: a silly slowed-down mess-around on "Rebel (She's A)," and some solid hooks in the originals, even a moderately interesting "Pictures of Lily" update, "Poster Girl." But neither of the band's writers seems to understand how to use the love song as a metaphor for something bigger, which is what really makes for transcendent pop. The result is merely ephemeral pleasure; it'll pass, but barely. — D.M.

BOBBY HELMS
★ ★ ★ **My Special Angel** / Voc. (1969)
Helms had a Top Ten hit in 1957 with the title cut, a nicely crooned R&B ballad, and followed it up with the Christmas novelty "Jingle Bell Rock." He hasn't been heard of since, except between Thanksgiving and New Year's. — D.M.

MICHAEL HENDERSON
★ ★ ★ **Solid** / Bud. (1976)
★ ★ ★ **Goin' Places** / Bud. (1977)
★ ★ ★ **In the Night Time** / Bud. (1978)
★ ★ ★ **Do It All** / Bud. (1979)
★ ★ ★ **Wide Receiver** / Bud. (1980)
A genuinely great session bassist, Henderson helped pioneer funk 'n' fusion, that bizarre post–*Bitches Brew/There's a Riot Goin' On*

concoction for which George Clinton is usually granted (but doesn't deserve) sole credit. That said, it must be admitted that Clinton gets more attention because he has a sense of humor and some notion of how to structure a tune. Henderson's albums amount to funk wallpaper—not without their virtues as background music, but not exactly stimulating when you're paying full attention (unless you're a technician). — D.M.

JIMI HENDRIX
★ ★ ★ ★ ★ **Are You Experienced?** / Rep. (1967)
★ ★ ★ ★ ★ **Axis: Bold as Love** / Rep. (1967)
★ ★ ★ ★ **Electric Ladyland** / Rep. (1968)
★ ★ ★ ★ **Smash Hits** / Rep. (1969)
★ ★ ★ ★ **Band of Gypsys** / Cap. (1970)
★ ★ ★ **The Cry of Love** / Rep. (1971)
★ ★ ★ **Hendrix in the West** / Rep. (1971) ¶
★ ★ ★ **Soundtrack from** *Experience*, Vol. 1 / Ember (1971), Br. imp.
★ ★ **Soundtrack from** *Experience*, Vol. 2 / Ember (1971), Br. imp.
★ **Isle of Wight** / Poly. (1971), Br. imp.
★ ★ ★ **Loose Ends** / Bar. (1973), Fr. imp.
★ ★ **Soundtrack from the Film** *Jimi Hendrix* / Rep. (1973)
★ ★ ★ **Crash Landing** / Rep. (1975)
★ ★ **Midnight Lightning** / Rep. (1976)
★ ★ ★ **The Essential Jimi Hendrix** / Rep. (1978)
★ ★ ★ **The Essential Jimi Hendrix, Vol. 2** / Rep. (1979)
★ ★ **Nine to the Universe** / Rep. (1981)
★ **Jimi Hendrix, Vol. 1** / Trip (NA)
★ **Jimi Hendrix, Vol. 2** / Trip (NA)
★ **Jimi Hendrix in Concert** / Sp. (NA)
Jimi Hendrix was the most innovative instrumental genius the rock era produced, a wizard guitar player whose sense of technique never overwhelmed the blues and rock & roll spirit that was the underpinning of his genius.

Hendrix improvised with the fervor of a born jazzman; he philosophized like the most cosmic rocker; but ultimately he brought everything down to basics and built his most elaborate structures from the rudiments of soul, a reflection of his experiences on the chitlin circuit, where he cut his teeth. Although his public image suggested a frivolous playboy hippie, a druggie whose musical ability was 90 percent intuition and very little intelligence, the reality is far different. On the records released in his lifetime—the first three with the Jimi Hendrix Experience, *Band of Gypsys* and *Smash Hits*—every effect is deliberately placed, with an overriding vision that is simply as impressive as anything in pop history, easily the equal of the Beatles' on *Sgt. Pepper's.*

Hendrix recorded as a sideman with Little Richard, the Isley Brothers and Curtis Knight, but these sessions (which sometimes turn up as "Jimi Hendrix with . . ." exploitation packages) are basically pretty conventional soul music—although his machine-gun guitar solo on the Isleys' version of "Stagger Lee" is a kind of prophecy.

Still, *Are You Experienced?* was probably the most stunning debut album of all time. Hendrix had completely assimilated the avant-rock guitar vocabulary of Eric Clapton, Jeff Beck, Pete Townshend and Jimmy Page, and extended it past the breaking point. He took the implications of feedback and distortion devices to their farthest extreme, and more than anything made the most furious, *biggest* noise in the history of rock up to that time. *Are You Experienced?* is simply an explosion of talent, and while some of Hendrix's lyrical concerns now seem dated, the best of the songs on that album ("Purple Haze," "Fire," "Manic Depression," "I Don't Live Today") are classics. Mitch Mitchell's drumming is stunning and Hendrix's singing, while not conventionally proper and far from pretty, is intense and believable.

Axis: Bold as Love and *Electric Ladyland* extended Hendrix's penchant for pastiche; the latter is a tour de force of audio montage, so much so that except for a few moments ("All along the Watchtower," "Voodoo Chile (Slight Return)") it virtually abandons the pop song form altogether. Yet Hendrix had a method of building accessibility into even his most outrageous conceits. *Axis* contains some of the most memorable Hendrix ballads ("Little Wing," "Castles Made of Sand"), but while its individual tracks are outstanding, it must be seen as a transitional piece between *Are You Experienced?* and *Electric Ladyland.*

Hendrix then delved further into experimentalism, recording an immense quantity of unfinished music before his sudden death in 1970. The only other full-scale album project released in his lifetime (*Smash Hits* contains only a couple of songs that aren't on the first two albums) was *Band of Gypsys.* This is Hendrix's rebellion against the white audience's conception of him as Super Spade, a venture into funk futurism, abandoning psychedelia and taking off on propositions suggested by Sly Stone, Miles Davis and James Brown rather than the Yardbirds, Who and Dylan. "Machine Gun" is the essence of the funk style of the later Seventies, and while the rest isn't up to that standard, this is certainly his most underrated and overlooked album. The support by bassist Billy Cox and drummer Buddy Miles is solid, if unspectacular.

Posthumous Hendrix releases are a mess. The initial one, *The Cry of Love,* isn't bad, because it assembles those leftovers nearest completion. But the other material is a jumble, made worse by producer Alan Douglas, who as curator of the Hendrix musical estate has taken it upon himself to overdub new backing tracks and perform all of the other chicanery used to defile the legacy of musical masters. Douglas is far from a neutralist—he would like to establish Hendrix as primarily a fusion-jazz player, which is as inappropriate as labeling him a mere heavy metal/power trio virtuoso. In consequence, such Douglas issues as *Crash Landing, Midnight Lightning* and *Nine to the Universe* are mediocre and untrustworthy. The *Essential Jimi Hendrix* anthologies are also inadequate because they lack a comprehensive overview of Hendrix as both technical genius and inspired artist, opting for a seesaw look at the guitarist and the rocker, with no balance. If a sampler is what you want, *Smash Hits,* with the intense blues, "Red House," and representative tidbits of the first two LPs, is better than either. But really, the three Experience albums are indispensable, and *Band of Gypsys* isn't far behind.

The Trip and Springboard albums are old work tapes from Hendrix's pre-Experience days, which should never have been released in any form. The soundtrack material from *Experience* contains enough live work to make it interesting, but the Reprise soundtrack is a pointless reiteration of Experience material plus some interview comments. Indeed, with the exception of *Isle of Wight,* which was a bad show all around, almost any live Hendrix is worth hearing: any chance to pick up *Hendrix in the West,* which Douglas deleted, is to be seized immediately.

It is virtually pointless to speculate upon what Jimi Hendrix might have done had he lived because his music was never headed in a single, simple direction. Hendrix would certainly have done more rock and more fusion, and would have made some attempt to perfect the funk style suggested by *Band of Gypsys.* It's the reminder of his achievements, those we mere listeners in a way can't imagine, that makes his loss so enormous. — D.M.

NONA HENDRYX

★ ★ ★ ★ **Nona Hendryx / Epic (1977)** ¶
The former member of Labelle comes up
with a solo disc that is somewhere between
her old group's avant-garde R&B and heavy
rock, à la the Who. This is admirable, winning stuff, maybe the hardest rock ever made
by a woman (black or white), but it slipped
through the cracks of record marketing clichés—how to promote a black woman on
FM radio? how to promote hard rock on
black radio?—so naturally there hasn't been
a followup — D.M.

DON HENLEY

★ ★ ★ ★ **I Can't Stand Still / Asy. (1982)**
By far the best of the post-Eagles solo albums. Henley has managed to curb most of
his penchant for decadence (if not his taste
for sexism), and he's discovered a knack for
trenchant social comment: both the hit,
"Dirty Laundry" (marred only by some
misogynistic sideswipes), and "Johnny Can't
Read" are powerfully observed and delivered. And no one ever said Henley didn't
have a great voice, as he proves over and
over again here, especially on the album's
closing number, a reggae-influenced rendition
of the gospel standard "The Unclouded
Day." — D.M.

HENRY COW

★ ★ ★ **Henry Cow / Red (1973)**
★ ★ ★ **Unrest / Red (1974)**
★ ★ ★ **Desperate Straights (with Slapp
Happy) / Red (1975)**
★ ★ ★ **In Praise of Learning (with Slapp
Happy) / Red (1975)**
★ ★ ★ **Henry Cow Concerts / Caro. (1976),
Br. imp.** ¶
★ ★ ★ **Western Culture / Inter. (1980)**
Taking their name from the experimental
American composer Henry Cowell (who was
pounding his fist on the piano keyboard long
before Jerry Lee Lewis), Henry Cow were
among the most uncompromising of Britain's
mid-Seventies avant-garde rock bands. They
were certainly the most durable, lasting in
one form or another for nearly ten years.
   Recorded five years after guitarist Fred
Frith and drummer Chris Cutler first formed
the band in 1968, Henry Cow's debut album
(titled *Legend* in England) already put them
leagues ahead of their art-rock peers. Closer
to Soft Machine's free jazz inventions, *Henry
Cow* pushed rock's boundary even further
with Chris Cutler's expert hyper-rhythmic
drumming underscoring Frith's alien guitar
tangents and the complex scoring for reeds
and keyboards. If there was a bit of Zappa

here, there was also lots of jazz and a few
bows to the modern European composers.
Unrest found them becoming increasingly
abstract—just try and find the reference to
the Yardbirds' "Got to Hurry" in "Bittern
Storm over Ulm"—without outdistancing its
small but devoted audience.
   Desperate Straights and *In Praise of
Learning* were collaborations with an eccentric trio called Slapp Happy (also signed to
Virgin, Cow's British label), with German
singer Dagmar adding an element of Kurt
Weill to the group's already dense sound.
(Frith, Cutler and Dagmar have since recorded together as the Art Bears.) The
Henry Cow Concerts is a fascinating two-
record compendium of live performances, including a guest appearance by ex–Soft Machine vocalist/drummer Robert Wyatt, while
Western Culture is a collection of 1978 studio recordings. Fred Frith can also be heard
on his own series of solo pluck-scratch-and-
scrape guitar albums.
   The Red releases are all reissues of Cow's
original Virgin LPs. — D.F.

THE HEPTONES

★ ★ ★ ★ **Night Food / Is. (1976)**
★ ★ **Cool Rasta / Troj. (1976)**
★ ★ ★ ★ **Party Time / Mango (1977)**
★ ★ ★ **In Love with You / U.A. (1978)** ¶
★ ★ ★ **Good Life / Greens. (1980)**
★ ★ ★ ★ **On the Run / Shan. (1982)**
★ ★ ★ **Better Days / Third World (NA)**
The Heptones come closer than any other
reggae performers—even Toots and the May-
tals—to completely merging the Jamaican
idiom with American soul. Although the
rhythm has the characteristic hesitation beat,
the trio's vocals are patterned closely on the
model of Stax and Motown groups; as if in
tribute, they include the Four Tops' "Baby I
Need Your Lovin' " on *Night Food. Night
Food* also contains versions of some of their
earlier hits, including "Book of Rules" and
"Mama Say."
   Just as the Heptone's three-part singing
defined rocksteady harmony in the Sixties
(*On Top* is the preeminent document of that
era), their harmonic classicism has memori-
alized that era ever since, the records rising
and falling with the quality of the material.
Leader Leroy Sibbles left by *Better Days,* but
he was replaced by Naggo Morris, and to
the surprise of many, the Heptones have
continued to make excellent music.
   — D.M./R.F.G.

KEITH HERMAN

★ **The Next Song Is / Radio (1979)**

Lightweight writer/singer says hobbies are music and girls. On the basis of his music, he's a more likely celibate than Lothario. — D.M.

HERMAN'S HERMITS
★ **Herman's Hermits XX (Their Greatest Hits) / Abkco (1973)**
If you need conclusive evidence that not everything that followed the Beatles out of Britain in 1964–65 was brilliant, by all means hear this. The Hermits had plenty of hits—"No Milk Today" was about the best, the worst is a toss-up between "Henry the Eighth" and "Silhouettes"—all in a sort of sub-English-music-hall style. It would be cheaper, and no more unpleasant, to record yourself in the shower while holding your nose. Yecch. — D.M.

HERO
■ **Boys Will Be Boys / 20th Cent. (1978)**
Hard rock from the folks who brought you Shaun Cassidy and Debby Boone. Don't be deceived: this album's "The Kids Are All Right" is not a version of the Who's masterwork but some dumbbell's "original." — D.M.

JOHN HIATT
★ **Overcoat / Epic (1975)**
★ ★ **Slug Line / MCA (1979)**
★ ★ **Two-Bit Monsters / MCA (1980)**
★ ★ **All of a Sudden / Gef. (1982)**
Hiatt's strained soulfulness always overcomes his wise-guy charm, at least in these quarters. Indeed, if one weren't so certain of Ry Cooder's taste (and if Hiatt weren't a member of Cooder's recent bands), the temptation would be to dismiss this pompous posturing as a fairly vile example of post–Springsteen bombast. However, faith assures us something must be here. Possibly by the next edition it will be located in more than association. — D.M.

HICKORY WIND
★ ★ ★ ★ **Fresh Produce / Fly. Fish (1976)**
★ ★ ★ ★ **Crossing Devil's Bridge / Fly. Fish (1978)**
Excellent progressive bluegrass band. — J.S.

DAN HICKS AND HIS HOT LICKS
■ **Original Recordings / Epic (1969)**
★ ★ **Striking It Rich / Blue Th. (1972)**
★ ★ ★ **Last Train to Hicksville / Blue Th. (1973)**
★ ★ ★ **It Happened One Bite / War. (1978)** ¶

Is Dan Hicks Haight-Ashbury's answer to Jim Kweskin? No. Hicks and the Hot Licks have more up the sleeves of their seedy furs than hip camp and cabaret. The violin virtuosity of Sid Page, the spiffy harmonies of Maryann Price and Naomi Eisenberg and all those quotable sources, from Western swing to Fifties cool, serve Hicks' curmudgeon's-eye view of life in the breakdown lane. Hicks gives nostalgia a mordant, modern voice. His ear for a piquant idiom extends beyond the last fifty years of popular song to the stuff of conversation. Hicks has cultivated a twang, a yodel and an air of gum-chewing innocence that fools no one—if he can help it. Probe his sentimentality and you find a sneer.

Warning: the forgettable *Original Recordings* are pre-Price and Eisenberg. The live *Where's the Money* (now deleted), on the other hand, is their moment of glory—durable, original, as feverish as a speed rap, as wryly romantic as a sloe gin fizz. — A.S.

SENA AND SONIA HIGGS
★ ★ ★ ★ **Juvenile Delinquent / Clap. (1981)**
Here's a convincing rock-reggae synthesis—real punky reggae—played, produced, arranged and composed by the Wailers' Aston "Family Man" Barrett. The sole outside contribution is the youthful vocals of Sena and Sonia Higgs. You get hard-nosed, edgy playing stretched out dub-wise over four cuts, retaining the rhythmic complexity of reggae but substituting rock's drive for reggae's easy rolling. — R.F.G.

HIGH COTTON
★ ★ **High Cotton / Is. (1976)**
Discovered and produced (perhaps a bit prematurely in the group's development) in 1975 by the venerable Allen Toussaint and Marshall Sehorn. High Cotton is a seven-piece working-class band that plays Southern rock with a brassy edge. Despite a couple of hot white R&B originals (most notably "Ain't It a Shame") and a fine Allman-like ballad ("Meet Me at the Junction"), this debut LP fails to distinguish the band from the rest of the genre and was duly forgotten almost as soon as it was released. — G.K.

HIGH INERGY
★ ★ **Turnin' On / Gor. (1977)**
★ ★ **Steppin' Out / Gor. (1978)**
★ ★ **Shoulda Gone Dancin' / Gor. (1979)**
★ ★ **Frenzy / Gor. (1979)**
★ ★ **Hold On / Gor. (1980)**
Late-Seventies R&B group came up with a big pop hit, "You Can't Turn Me Off," in late 1977. — D.M.

HIGHWAY QC's
★ ★ Be at Rest / Pea. (NA)
★ Stay with God / Savoy (NA)
The QC's once served as a sort of farm team
for the Soul Stirrers: Sam Cooke, Johnnie
Taylor and Willie Rogers all started here before moving up to that group. But apparently there are no readily available recordings of the group from that era. The
Peacock album here has strangely cool and
restrained lead vocals (Spencer Taylor is responsible), but the album may be of interest
to fans of falsetto soul groups, since the
QC's lean heavily in that direction. The
Savoy set is a very uneasy fusion of soul and
gospel. — J.MO.

HIGHWOODS STRING BAND
★ ★ ★ ★ Fire on the Mountain / Roun.
(1972)
★ ★ ★ Dance All Night / Roun. (1974)
★ ★ ★ No. 3 Special / Roun. (1977)
Good old-timey and bluegrass quintet plays
mostly traditional material with spirit and
humor. The twin fiddles of Walt Koken and
Bob Potts provide their distinctive identity.
— J.S.

DAN HILL
★ Dan Hill / 20th Cent. (1975)
★ ★ Longer Fuse / 20th Cent. (1977)
★ ★ Hold On / 20th Cent. (1978)
★ Frozen in the Night / 20th Cent. (1978)
★ If Dreams Had Wings / Epic (1979)
★ Partial Surrender / Epic (1980)
This Canadian singer is a cloying but
(among young females) compelling performer
of adolescent love songs. The atavistic lyrics
and Hill's gasped vocals are complemented
by strings, which set the tone of lonely-boy-
in-the-woods romance. Hill's forte is using
Poetic Statements to puff up seductions in
pleasant surroundings. *Longer Fuse* (the title
is apparently meant to evoke Jackson
Browne's "The Fuse") is more of the same,
but without pop-song relief, making it Hill's
most self-important and confused LP, but
also his most commercially successful,
thanks to an Elton John–styled ballad,
"Sometimes When We Touch." — B.T.

Z. Z. HILL
★ ★ ★ Pure Soul / Kent (NA)
★ ★ ★ Soul Stirring Z. Z. Hill / Kent (NA)
★ ★ ★ Whole Lot of Soul / Kent (NA)
★ ★ ★ Dues Paid in Full / Kent (NA)
★ ★ ★ ★ The Brand New Z. Z. Hill /
Mank. (NA)
★ ★ ★ Let's Make a Deal / Col. (NA)
★ ★ ★ Mark of Z.Z. / Col. (1978)

★ ★ ★ ★ The Rhythm and the Blues / Mal.
(1982)
Z. Z. Hill is an underrated vocalist with a
lazy, relaxed singing style and a voice that
resembles Bobby Bland's. The Kent LPs are
collections of Kent singles recorded in mock-
Bland style; the arrangements are often less
than imaginative, and overbearing horns tend
to clutter many of the songs.
    After leaving Kent, Hill recorded with a
wide range of producers, each in a slightly
different and offbeat vein, usually successfully. *Brand New* sports a Jerry "Swamp
Dogg" Williams production; *Deal* and *Mark
of Z.Z.* are Philly-oriented disco material.
Williams offered Hill a standard Muscle
Shoals background with a catch: side one is
linked by a thematic concept called Blues at
the Opera, predating Millie Jackson's similar
concept recordings.
    What may be Hill's very best record, *Keep
On Lovin' You*, has been deleted by United
Artists. Production work is divided by Allen
Toussaint, Lamont Dozier and Matt Hill,
the singer's brother. Z.Z. proves to be a pliable stylist who fits well into the imaginative
settings offered by all three mentors.
    Oddly, Hill found his greatest commercial
success in 1982, with his most traditional recent album, *The Rhythm and the Blues*,
which is also one of his best. — J.MC./D.M.

HILARY
★ Just before After Hours / Col.
(1979)
An album by a female flutist of post-fusion
cocktail jazz, certainly right for listening to,
as the title says—that is, when you want to
sleep. So pleasant it's downright tiring.
— R.P.

CHRIS HILLMAN
★ Slippin' Away / Asy. (1976)
★ ★ Clear Sailin' / Asy. (1977)
In the context of the Byrds and the Flying
Burrito Brothers, Hillman sang harmonies,
wrote an occasional song and took the odd
lead vocal, but he simply does not possess
the vocal or lyrical talent to sustain interest
over an entire album. Even with the assistance of virtually every name session musician in Los Angeles, neither of Hillman's
solo albums really get off the ground. Typically, the two best cuts on *Slippin' Away*
have fatal flaws: "Step On Out" is a rocking
love story ruined by war metaphors, while
an otherwise affecting lament. "Falling
Again," is hampered by a gushy synthesizer.
Clear Sailin' is bouncier, which at least
makes it more listenable, and "Quits" is a

solid ballad. But on both albums Hillman is forced to cover his weakness as an emotive singer with harmonies on every chorus, thereby removing any tension or drama from the songs. As a luxury item in a group of greater talents, Hillman could be gratifying, but his solo career is strictly a mistake.
— G.K.

JUSTIN HINES
★ ★ ★ **Just in Time / Mango (1979)**
In much the same vein as *Jezebel* but with fewer peaks and less striking material.
— R.F.G.

JUSTIN HINES AND THE DOMINOES
★ ★ ★ **Jezebel / Is. (1976)**
Relatively slick Jamaican reggae group, which places more emphasis on horns than is customary. The lyrical concern is as sociological as is usual for reggae, though not as sharp as the best of the genre. — D.M.

HI RHYTHM
★ ★ ★ **On the Loose / Hi (NA)**
As a backup unit for Al Green, Syl Johnson and Ann Peebles, Hi Rhythm has developed a reputation as a crew of tasteful and first-rate soul session players. This solo album, however, is hardly tame. Here the band opts for a refreshingly wacky and adventurous sensibility (including a song called "Superstar" that sports a banjo solo and a lyric that pokes fun at Green). — J.MC.

HI-TENSION
★ **Hi-Tension / Is. (1978)**
Low energy. — D.M.

THE HITMEN
★ ★ ★ **Aim for the Feet / Col. (1980)**
★ ★ ★ **Torn Together / Col. (1981)**
Unlike many of their contemporaries in post-new-wave British rock, the Hitmen eschew self-conscious posturing in favor of a no-nonsense approach to churning out tight, R&B-influenced rock with an eye toward hit singles. Both records capture the strength of the band's very popular live sound. — J.S.

CATFISH HODGE
■ **For Free / 20th Cent./Westb. (1975)**
■ **Eyewitness Blues / Adel. (1979)**
■ **Bout with the Blues / Adel. (1981)**
Can blue men sing the whites? Hodge is as tedious as they come. — J.S.

ROSCOE HOLCOMB
★ ★ ★ ★ **The High Lonesome Sound / Folk. (1965)**

Holcomb was one of the greatest discoveries of the folk music revival of the early Sixties. This LP is the only recording still in print (he made two others), but it's a winner: Holcomb's voice is the essence of the title, and he's an adept banjo player as well. In addition, there's interview material—taped for the 1962 film of the same name—which gives a look at the sociology of the eastern Kentucky mountains. His answer about rock & roll is a classic—perhaps one reason why Bob Dylan was one of this album's enthusiasts back when it was first released. — D.M.

AMY HOLLAND
★ **Amy Holland / Cap. (1980)**
Thin-voiced protégée of Doobie Brother Michael McDonald put out a McDonald-coproduced debut album that spawned a forgettable medium-sized hit, "How Do I Survive." — S.H.

JOOLS HOLLAND
★ ★ **Untitled LP / IRS (1982)**
★ ★ **Jools Holland and His Millionaires / A&M 1981**
Holland went from the new-wave/avant-garde stylings of his first LP (plus guest spots with the likes of Alternative TV) to playing keyboards for Squeeze before breaking off on his own to form the Millionaires. With the Millionaires he netted the English hit "Bumble Boogie" (based on "Flight of the Bumblebee"), thus providing one of the best examples of new-wave cash-in on record. — J.S.

THE HOLLIES
★ **Words and Music by Bob Dylan / Epic (1969)**
★ ★ **Distant Light / Epic (1972)**
★ ★ ★ **Romany / Epic (1972)**
★ ★ ★ ★ ★ **Greatest Hits / Epic (1973)**
★ ★ **Hollies / Epic (1974)** ¶
★ ★ **Crazy Steal / Epic (1978)**
The Hollies never overcame the reputation they earned during the British Invasion as masters of finely crafted pop hits that made magic as singles but could make LPs tedious. In fact some of the group's early Imperial albums (all deleted) were fairly solid, but more recently, they have seemed pop stylists rather than pop artists. The difference is crucial, perhaps best expressed by Graham Nash's need to leave the group in the late Sixties to escape its frothy limitations. (Crosby, Stills and Nash owes a good deal of its more substantial froth to what Nash learned with the Hollies, however.)

The Hollies' bright instrumentation and

cheery harmonies thrive in catchy pop frameworks; when the formula was applied to more serious-minded interpretations, as on the Dylan album, the effect could be disastrous. The problem has never been performance—their harmonies are inevitably attractive and the instrumental accompaniment universally competent—but their material has often been at odds with their distinctly pop sound.

Greatest Hits, however, is a gem, even featuring versions of the Imperial hits ("Look through Any Window," "Bus Stop," "Carrie-Anne") along with the more recent "Long Cool Woman" and "The Air That I Breathe." This is undeniable proof that the two-minute-and-thirty-second single is the most potent rock & roll medium. Impeccably crafted, and as pleasurable as an ice cream cone on a blistering day, these songs hold a lot of teenage memories that are jogged and enlivened with each listening. — J.B.M.

BRENDA HOLLOWAY
★ ★ ★ **Every Little Bit Hurts / Mo. (1964)**
Another of Motown's fine reissues of original Sixties material at a budget price. Holloway is known only for "Every Little Bit Hurts," one of the great soul ballads of the period, but she also was one of the first female writer/performers in this area of pop. (Only two originals are here, however.) Holloway also turns in good work on three Smokey Robinson songs, "I've Been Good to You" "Who's Loving You," and "(You Can) Depend on Me." Soulful easy listening. — D.M.

LOLEATTA HOLLOWAY
★ ★ **Loleatta / Gold M. (1977)**
★ ★ ★ **Queen of the Night / Gold M. (1978)**
★ ★ **Love Sensation / Gold M. (1980)**
Strident disco chanteuse who's basically dull except when paired with Philadelphia eccentric Bunny Sigler, as she is on *Queen.*
— D.M.

BUDDY HOLLY
★ **The Great Buddy Holly / MCA/Coral (1967)**
★ ★ ★ ★ ★ **The Complete Buddy Holly / MCA (1969)**
★ **A Rock and Roll Collection / MCA (1972)**
★ ★ ★ **Twenty Golden Greats / MCA (1978)**
The Holly review in the first edition of this book begins by saying "If any major rock figure was ever worse served by his record company than Buddy Holly, I'd sure like to hear about it." The release in the United

States of *The Complete Buddy Holly* completely reverses that judgment. Thanks to the revival of interest in Buddy and his music kicked up by the acclaimed film *The Buddy Holly Story* in 1978, Holly's music now is readily available in model condition.

The Complete Buddy Holly is a six-record collection boxed with an extensively annotated booklet; extensive notes are printed on each LP sleeve. The collection was originally issued in the U.K., where Holly remains legendary. If we awarded six stars this album would deserve them, for it is close to perfect: It includes all of Holly's music, and in the case of songs producer Norman Petty later overdubbed, it includes the pristine version as well as the altered one. Additionally, the sound has been cleaned up without damaging the ambiance: there's no fake stereo here, but there is complete fidelity.

Holly, of course, is one of the great early figures of rock & roll, a masterly writer and singer, hard-driving bandleader and imaginative record maker. "Rave On," "That'll Be the Day," "Oh Boy," "Not Fade Away," "True Love Ways," "Raining in My Heart," "Maybe Baby" and others sound as hot today as when they were recorded. Holly's ability to sound innocent and suddenly switch to sounding tough, his wit and romanticism mark him as an important antecedent for all kinds of later figures, from John Lennon and Paul McCartney to Tom Petty and Waylon Jennings (with whom Buddy worked).

The notes to *The Complete Buddy Holly* tell the details of Holly's legend (and of course his untimely death, with the Big Bopper and Ritchie Valens in a 1959 plane crash) more clearly and completely than we can hope to do here. If you need to be convinced of Buddy's greatness, the *Twenty Golden Greats* is a good starter. But once you know, *The Complete Buddy Holly* alone will do. — D.M.

HOLLYRIDGE STRINGS
■ **Beatles' Song Book / Cap. (1964)**
■ **Beach Boys' Song Book / Cap. (1964)**
Instrumental cover versions, pure schmaltz for those who can still remember the good old days (pre-Elvis). — S.H.

RUPERT HOLMES
★ ★ **Rupert Holmes / Epic (1975) ¶**
★ **Singles / Epic (1976) ¶**
★ ★ **Widescreen / Epic (1977) ¶**
★ **Pursuit of Happiness / Priv. (1978)**
★ **Partners in Crime / MCA (1979)**

★ **Adventure / MCA (1980)**
★ **Full Circle / MCA (1981)**
Holmes—a bubblegum rocker turned pop revivalist—would probably like to be Barry Manilow with class. He started with something called "film rock," which was like ordinary rock except that it tried to be cinematic. Unfortunately he forgot that easy listening means the music must be easy to listen to. He got the message in time for *Singles,* but he still doesn't know what to do with it. — F.R.

JOHN HOLT
★ ★ ★ **1,000 Volts of Holt / Troj. (1975)**
★ ★ **2,000 Volts of Holt / Troj. (1976)**
★ ★ **Dusty Roads / Troj. (1976)**
★ **Twenty Golden Love Songs / Troj. (1980)**
★ ★ **Sugar / Clock. (NA)**
Those who dismiss John Holt as MOR reggae personified miss the point. As lead singer and composer of the Paragons, Holt made some of the great rocksteady sounds of the Sixties (Blondie's "The Tide Is High" was a late-Sixties Jamaican hit for the group). He still has a loyal following (his "Ghetto Queen" hit in 1981), and his later reggaefied remakes of pop and soul tunes should not diminish his excellent, soulful singing. He can still rise to the level of great material and production; unfortunately he has rarely gotten either. — R.F.G.

HOLY MODAL ROUNDERS
★ ★ ★ ★ **Indian War Whoop / ESP (1967)**
★ ★ ★ ★ **Holy Modal Rounders, Vol. 1 / Prest. (1968)**
★ ★ ★ ★ **Stampfel and Weber / Fan. (1972)**
★ ★ ★ **Alleged in Their Own Time / Roun. (1976)**
★ ★ **Last Round / Adel. (1979)**
★ ★ ★ **Going Nowhere Fast / Adel. (1981)**
Steve Weber (guitar and vocals) and Peter Stampfel (fiddle, banjo and vocals) were cocreators and lone practitioners of the genre known as acid folk. Stampfel, who has a working knowledge of almost every song ever written, and Weber, who only sometimes has a working knowledge of his own compositions, teamed up in the early Sixties and have produced such classics as "Boobs a Lot," "Half a Mind," "The I.W.W. Song" and "Bird Song" (one of the standouts on the *Easy Rider* soundtrack). *Indian War Whoop* has playwright Sam Shepard on drums, and its first side is a conceptual affair entitled "Jimmy and Crash Survey the Universe." Any of their albums are musts for lovers of out-of-control mind warp, although their best LP, *The Moray Eels Eat the Holy*

Modal Rounders (Elektra), is sadly out of print. It features Michael Hurley's legendary "Werewolf" and a fractured rendition of the old jug-band favorite "Mobile Line," not to mention "The STP Song" or "My Mind Capsized." — B.A.

MARCUS HOOK ROLL BAND
★ **Marcus Hook Roll Band / Cap. (NA)**
Forgettable heartland rock act. — D.M.

EARL HOOKER
★ ★ ★ **Two Bugs and a Roach / Arhoo. (1969)**
★ ★ ★ **Hooker and Steve / Arhoo. (1970)**
★ ★ ★ **There's a Fungus among Us / Red L. (1972), Br. imp.**
★ ★ ★ **First and Last Recordings / Arhoo. (1973)**
★ ★ ★ **Funk: The Last of the Great Earl Hooker / Ant. (1977)**
★ ★ ★ **The Leading Brand / Red L. (1977), Br. imp.**
★ ★ ★ ★ **Blues Guitar / P-Vine (NA), Jap. imp.**
A fine slide guitarist but weak singer, Hooker was at his best on instrumentals. Born in Mississippi, where he learned slide guitar from Robert Nighthawk, Hooker was a prominent Chicago sideman and leader throughout the Fifties and Sixties. *Hooker and Steve* features him with Steve Miller. The two Red Lightnin's and the P-Vine (on the latter he is aided by other singers) are his best, though. — D.M.

JOHN LEE HOOKER
★ ★ ★ ★ **The Real Folk Blues / Chess (1968), Fr. imp.**
★ ★ ★ **No Friend Around / Red L. (1970), Br. imp.**
★ ★ ★ **John Lee Hooker's Endless Boogie / ABC (1971)**
★ ★ ★ ★ **Mad Man Blues / Chess (1971)**
★ ★ ★ **The Best of John Lee Hooker / Cres. (1974)**
★ ★ ★ **Blues before Sunrise / Bull. (1976)**
★ ★ ★ **Black Snake Blues / Fan. (1977)**
★ ★ ★ ★ **This Is Hip / Charly (1980), Br. imp.**
★ ★ ★ ★ **Everybody's Rockin' / Charly (1981), Br. imp.**
★ ★ ★ **Drifting through the Blues / United (NA)**
★ ★ ★ **The Blues / United (NA)**
★ ★ ★ **Folk Blues / United (NA)**
★ ★ ★ **The Great Blues Sounds of John Lee Hooker / United (NA)**
★ ★ ★ **Original Folk Blues / United (NA)**

★ ★ ★ **John Lee Hooker / Chis. (NA), Br. imp.**
★ ★ ★ **Hooked on the Blues / Arc. Folk (NA)**
★ ★ **I'm in the Mood / Up Fr. (NA)**
★ ★ ★ **John Lee Hooker Gold / VJ (NA)**
★ ★ ★ ★ **I'm John Lee Hooker / VJ (NA)**
★ ★ ★ **Travelin' / VJ (NA)**
★ ★ ★ ★ **The Best of John Lee Hooker / VJ (NA)**
★ ★ ★ **Get Back Home in the U.S.A. / Black and Blue (NA), Fr. imp.**
★ ★ ★ **Boogie Chillun / Fan. (1972)**
★ ★ **Black Rhythm and Blues / Fest. (NA), Br. imp.**
★ ★ **Live and Well / Orna. (NA), Br. imp.**
★ ★ ★ **Boogie with Hooker 'n' Heat / Trip (NA)**
★ ★ ★ ★ ★ **Greatest Hits of John Lee Hooker / United (NA)**
★ ★ ★ **John Lee Hooker / United (NA)**
★ ★ ★ ★ **John Lee Hooker / Arc. Folk (NA)**
★ ★ ★ ★ **John Lee Hooker Alone / Spec. (NA)**
★ ★ ★ **The Real Blues / Trad. (NA)**
★ ★ ★ ★ **Whiskey and Wimmen / Trip (NA)**
Hooker was probably the most eccentric of the electric, urban bluesmen who emerged in the late Forties and early Fifties. First of all, he was based in Detroit, rather than Chicago; more importantly, he never restricted himself to strict 12-bar formats, treating blues more as a feeling than a form, more an emotional resource than a binding tradition.

Hooker began recording for Modern Records in 1948; he had an almost immediate, if moderate, success with "Crawling King Snake Blues," but his big breakthrough did not come until 1951, with "I'm in the Mood." Although he recorded prolifically for Modern and later Vee Jay throughout the Sixties, he did not have another big hit until "Boom Boom," in 1962. But his eccentric, thumping rhythms—a fundamental source of what rockers call "boogie"—and gravelly voice were enormously influential on early British R&B bands, particularly Eric Burdon and the Animals, who popularized both "Boom Boom" and Hooker's more obscure "I'm Mad Again" for white audiences. Later, Canned Heat would record his "Whiskey and Wimmen," first made for Vee Jay in the early Sixties. During that decade, Hooker recorded principally for ABC/Bluesway, although only *Endless Boogie,* an early Seventies affair, remains in print.

Because Hooker also recorded for a number of other labels, frequently under pseudonyms, and because all of his material has been licensed and relicensed in a bewildering pattern, there's hardly any way to make sense of the multitude of collections of his work available. The United material is mostly from his earliest, Modern period, as are the Red Lightnin', Chiswick, Everest and Tradition albums. His Vee Jay records are collected on the Archive of Folk, Trip, Bulldog, Charly, Up Front and of course Vee Jay sides were made for that company. Most of the rest was made for the company now issuing it, but there are literally dozens of out-of-print Hooker albums, too. The listings here offer only a rough guide—an album-by-album assessment of Hooker's quirky, prolific output would probably bog down in maddening minutiae without ever getting near completion. Suffice to say that in one way or another, all of this music had its share of influence—on the development of blues, rhythm & blues and white rock & roll and especially the white blues and R&B groups of the Sixties. Even more significantly, the bulk of Hooker's material, though undeniably repetitious, remains listenable (and the best of it revelatory) even today.
— D.M.

LIGHTNIN' HOPKINS
★ ★ ★ **Gotta Move Your Baby / Prest. (1960)**
★ ★ ★ **Blues / Prest. (1960)**
★ ★ ★ ★ **Best of Texas Blues Band / Prest. (1962)**
★ ★ ★ ★ **Hootin' the Blues / Prest. (1962)**
★ ★ ★ ★ ★ **Lightnin' Sam Hopkins / Arhoo. (1962)**
★ ★ ★ ★ **Greatest Hits / Prest. (1963)**
★ ★ ★ ★ ★ **Early Recordings / Arhoo. (1963)**
★ ★ **With Brothers and Barbara Dane / Arhoo. (1966)**
★ ★ ★ **Roots / Folk. (1968)**
★ ★ ★ ★ **Texas Blues Man / Arhoo. (1968)**
★ ★ ★ ★ **Talkin' Some Sense / Jewel (1971)**
★ ★ ★ **Early Recordings, Vol. 2 / Arhoo. (1971)**
★ ★ ★ ★ **Double Blues / Fan. (1972)**
★ ★ ★ ★ **In Berkeley / Arhoo. (1973)**
★ ★ ★ **Great Electric Show and Dance / Jewel (1973)**
★ ★ ★ ★ **A Legend in His Own Time / Blue Anthology (1976)**
★ ★ ★ ★ **Lightnin' / Toma. (1977)**
★ ★ ★ ★ **Autobiography / Trad. (NA)**
★ ★ ★ ★ **Best / Trad. (NA)**
★ ★ ★ ★ ★ **Blues / Main. (NA)**
★ ★ ★ **Country Blues / Trad. (NA)**
★ ★ ★ **Dirty Blues / Main. (NA)**
★ ★ ★ ★ **Lightnin' Hopkins / Arc. Folk (NA)**

★ ★ Lightnin' Hopkins / Trip (NA)
★ ★ ★ ★ Lightnin' Strikes / Trad. (NA)
★ ★ ★ Low Down Dirty Blues / Main. (NA)
★ ★ ★ ★ ★ Original Folk Blues / United
(NA)
★ ★ ★ ★ ★ The Rooster Crowed in England
/ 77LA (NA)
★ ★ ★ ★ Lightnin' Hopkins / Arhoo. (NA)
★ ★ ★ ★ Lightnin, Vol. 2 / Arc. Folk (NA)
★ ★ ★ Lightnin' Hopkins / Boul. (NA)
★ ★ ★ Blue Lightnin' / Jewel (NA)
★ ★ ★ Blues Giant / Olym. (NA)
★ ★ ★ ★ Soul Blues / Prest. (NA)
★ ★ ★ ★ Lightnin' / Soul Pa. (NA)
★ ★ ★ ★ Down Home Blues / Souffle
(NA)
★ ★ ★ ★ Lightnin' Blues / Up Fr. (NA)
The last of the great country-blues singers,
Hopkins didn't even start recording until
he'd been playing for over twenty years at
country picnics and parties in Texas. Hop-
kins learned to play watching Blind Lemon
Jefferson, who taught him a few tricks, as
did Hopkins' cousin, "Texas" Alexander.
Hopkins went to Houston to record in 1946
and did a series of duets with piano player
"Thunder" Smith. After a few tries, Hopkins
finally clicked when he recorded solo for
Gold Star Studio, accompanying himself on
guitar. A single, "Short Haired Woman"
backed with "Big Mama Jump," became a
huge regional hit.

Hopkins played around and built up a
reputation as a renegade who would accept
payment for recording only in cash and insisted on being paid after recording each
song before he'd go on to the next one. He
accumulated and spent plenty this way, because over the years the prolific Hopkins has
become the most frequently recorded bluesman in history. The remarkable thing is that
his records are of such consistently high
quality—his ragged, urgent voice and deft
guitar playing always come off well on the
rambling, autobiographical stories he spins
during sessions. Hopkins' glibness, his narrative force and smooth, relaxed delivery, provided an obvious model for much of Bob
Dylan's early style. Hopkins made his last
New York appearance at Tramps a few
months before his death in early 1982. He
had trouble moving his fingers well enough
to play, but even at that late date his vocals
were still strong and assured.   — J.S.

JIMMY "BO" HORNE
★ ★ ★ Dance across the Floor / Sunshine
(1978)
★ ★ ★ Going Home for Love / Sunshine
(1980)

Oft-successful on the dance-floor charts,
Horne finally crossed over to pop in disco's
big year, 1978, with "Dance across the
Floor," which made the Top Forty.
— D.M.

HORSLIPS
★ ★ The Book of Invasions / DJM (1977)
★ ★ Aliens / DJM (1978)
★ ★ The Man Who Built America / DJM
(1979)
★ Short Stories, Tall Tales / Mer. (1980)
★ Belfast Gigs / Mer. (1981)
Heavy-handed rock adaptations of traditional
Irish folk music: inappropriately dirty gui-
tars, muddy production and a general lack
of polish cover up the occasional inspired
passages.   — C.W.

BIG WALTER HORTON
★ ★ ★ Big Walter Horton with Carey Bell /
Alli. (1972)
★ ★ ★ An Offer You Can't Refuse / Red L.
(1972), Br. imp.
★ ★ Little Boy Blue / JSP (NA), Br. imp.
★ ★ ★ King of the Harmonica Players /
Delta (NA), Swed. imp.
Horton is one of the masters of blues har-
monica, ranking with the two Sonny Boy
Williamsons (John Lee Williamson, Rice
Miller), Little Walter and Junior Wells as
the instrument's major innovators. Horton
has recorded as a sideman for Willie Dixon,
Otis Rush, J. B. Hutto, Johnny Shines and
Muddy Waters (he replaced the great Junior
Wells), among others. (Other solo sides were
recorded for the Chicago-based States and
Cobra.) The Alligator record, which often
features Horton in harp duets with Bell, is
rugged, pure and free, although the constant
focus on harmonica, coupled with Horton's
nondescript vocal style, can make it a trifle
wearing. The other material suffers from the
same defects, but with less compensatory
value. Half of the Red Lightnin' LP features
Paul Butterfield; the JSP is a live set; the
Delta set is archival, featuring Horton solo
and as a leader and sideman from the Fifties
through 1970.   — D.M.

JOHNNY HORTON
★ ★ The Spectacular Johnny Horton / Col.
(1959)
★ Johnny Horton Makes History / Col.
(1960)
★ ★ Johnny Horton's Greatest Hits / Col.
(1960)
★ ★ ★ Honky-Tonk Man / Col. (1962)
★ ★ ★ The World of Johnny Horton / Col.
(1971)

★ ★ **Johnny Horton on the Louisiana Hayride / Col. (NA)**

Johnny Horton catapulted to national fame in May 1959 on the strength of the No. 1 hit "The Battle of New Orleans." He went on to quickly establish himself as the singer of history-oriented novelty songs, vignettes of life in Alaska and other oddities. But ironically he had little serious album success until several months after his death in an automobile accident in Texas on November 5, 1960.

Blessed with a rough-edged voice that slipped easily into falsetto, and an infectious enthusiasm that helped him pull off his historical narratives on record, Horton was an early example of an artist who attracted both the country and pop audiences. Interestingly, he seemed to be turning away from pop novelty items and settling into an unpretentious honky-tonk country vein when he died.

The Spectacular Johnny Horton, his debut Columbia album (after several singles for independent labels), found him with a strong voice but no direction. The country roots are there, but all the attention was garnered by "Battle of New Orleans" and "When It's Springtime in Alaska." Horton carried the musical chronicles genre to its furthest extreme on *Johnny Horton Makes History,* which, although it must be regarded as camp to be appreciated today, is indispensable for those patriots who thought the Bicentennial was the experience of their lifetimes. Subtitled "Action Tales of Battles, Heroes and Epic Events," the album did yield three hit singles, "Sink the Bismarck," "Johnny Reb" and "Johnny Freedom."

His successful string of singles continued with the irrepressible "North to Alaska," the theme song of the movie of the same name. All these 45s were thrown together to create Horton's first hit album, *Greatest Hits.* It was the next two singles, however, "Sleepy-Eyed John" and "Honky-Tonk Man," that represented a move into a more indigenous country territory for Horton, and the posthumously released *Honky-Tonk Man* is generally considered his best. *Louisiana Hayride* is good but not especially exciting material from Fifties radio broadcasts.

If you're looking for one package that summarizes Horton's short but trenchant career, the best bet is the *World of Johnny Horton.* This double album includes not only the earlier novelty hits, but also much of the later honky-tonk, quasi-rockabilly material. — G.K.

BILL HORWITZ
★ ★ **Lies, Lies, Lies / ESP (1975)**
Marxist—well, at least anticapitalist—folk-rock singer/songwriter, whose music was already an anachronism when released in 1975, but fine for those who like such things. — D.M.

HOT
★ ★ **Hot / Big (1977)**
★ ★ **If That's The Way You Want It . . . You Got It / Big (1978)**
★ ★ **Strong Together / Big (1979)**
One of the more interesting soul successes of 1977, Hot's hit single, "Angel in Your Arms," was a trashy mixture of girl-group nostalgia and contemporary rhythm that was only barely resistible. The rest of *Hot* and all the followups were just the trash. — D.M.

HOT CHOCOLATE
★ ★ **Every 1's a Winner / Inf. (1972) ¶**
★ ★ ★ **Greatest Hits / Big (1974)**
★ ★ **Cicero Park / Big (1975) ¶**
★ ★ **Hot Chocolate / Big (1975) ¶**
★ ★ **Man to Man / Big (1976) ¶**
★ ★ **Going Through the Motions / Inf. (1979)**
English pop group of the mid to late Seventies, with an interesting mix of black and white members and influences. Its most important achievement has probably been writing the pop-reggae gem, "Brother Louie," which Stories made a U.S. hit. Others included "You Sexy Thing" and "Don't Stop It Now." Because the group had nothing to say when it stretched out, *Greatest Hits* is by far the best bet. — D.M.

HOTEL
★ **Hotel / MCA (1979) ¶**
★ **Half Moon Silver / MCA (1979) ¶**
Lame late-seventies Southern outfit tried unsuccessfully to combine rock, jazz and classical elements. Claim to fame is being commissioned to write a ballet for the Birmingham (Alabama) Ballet Company. — J.S.

HOT ICE
★ ★ **Stone Disco / Radio (1979)**
Formula dance music. — D.M.

HOT RIZE
★ ★ ★ **Hot Rize / Fly. Fish (1979)**
★ ★ ★ **Radio Boogie / Fly. Fish (1981)**
Sparked by the fine tenor voice of Tim O'Brien, Hot Rize play clean-cut progressive bluegrass with an efficiency and emotiveness that make them one of the top outfits in the idiom. — R.P.

HOTT CITY
★ Ain't Love Grand / Butter. (NA)
Disco product. — D.M.

HOT TUNA
★ ★ Hot Tuna / RCA (1970)
★ First Pull Up, Then Pull Down / RCA (1971) ¶
★ ★ Burgers / Grunt (1972)
★ ★ The Phosphorescent Rat / Grunt (1973)
★ ★ America's Choice / Grunt (1975)
★ ★ Yellow Fever / Grunt (1975)
★ ★ ★ Hoppkorv / Grunt (1976)
★ ★ Double Dose / Grunt (1977)
★ ★ Final Vinyl / Grunt (1979)
When Jefferson Airplane guitarist Jorma Kaukonen and bassist Jack Casady conceived this band, they wanted to call it Hot Shit, but RCA wouldn't hear of it. Too bad. That endearing appellation was tailor-made for this band.

Kaukonen and Casady's blues excursions always seemed incongruous and circumscribed in the context of Airplane, and Hot Tuna was originated as an outlet for such fantasies. Although the first album came from a live session, it prescribed the two sources from which the band would obtain its material: country and gospel blues standards and Kaukonen's occasional romantic songwriting. With *First Pull Up,* also a live recording, drummer Sammy Piazza and Airplane violinist Papa John Creach signed on, and Kaukonen plugged in his guitar, but none of this helped dispel the band's innate dispassion. In particular, Kaukonen's nasal, taciturn vocals and the excessive, meandering jams belied the assertions of blues spirit.

In spite of the departure of Creach and the replacement of Piazza with Bob Steeler, little progress was made from *Burgers* to *Yellow Fever.* Hot Tuna's dirgelike blues rock became increasingly insular, and the musicianship, never to be faulted for technique, was now simply perfunctory. Kaukonen, once a biting, economical guitarist, now favored four-minute traipsing solos, and Casady's rumbling bass impeded the dynamics even more. *Hoppkorv* is unarguably the band's most aggressive LP, because its staggered layers of combative guitars, female harmonies and keyboard embellishments lend Hot Tuna a badly needed textural variety, something never approached (and rarely attempted) elsewhere in the band's work.
— M.G.

THE HOUNDS
★ Puttin' on the Dog / Col. (1979)

Woof. (That's a cheap shot, but then, that's just what they deserve.) — D.M.

THE DIXON HOUSE BAND
★ Fighting Alone / Inf. (1979)
★ Naked Madness / A&M (1980)
Dull keyboardist/vocalist leads lounge-rock group through perfunctory paces. — D.M.

SON HOUSE
★ ★ ★ Father of the Folk Blues / Col. (1965)
★ ★ ★ ★ Son House / Arhoo. (1973)
★ ★ ★ Real Delta Blues / Blue G. (1979)
★ ★ ★ ★ Son House/Blind Lemon Jefferson / Bio. (NA)
★ ★ ★ ★ The Legendary 1941/42 Recording / Folklyric (NA)
★ ★ ★ Son House and Robert Pete Williams / Roots (NA)
★ ★ ★ The Vocal Intensity / Roots (NA)
Although the Columbia and Blue Goose records were made in his dotage, Alan Lomax' field recordings for the Library of Congress (released on Arhoolie and Folklyric) mark House as one of the central figures in Mississippi blues. His stark, soulful singing and ringing open-tuned bottleneck guitar style made him a legend in the small Mississippi delta towns where he played house parties in the late Twenties and Thirties. He came to the attention of Charlie Patton, who set up House's first recording session with Paramount which is collected on the Biograph set. House took up performing with Patton's friend Willie Brown, and built up a following that included the young Robert Johnson. It's a tribute to his powers that House still sounds vibrant on Blue Goose material, recorded privately by Nick Perls in the Sixties.
— J.S.

CISCO HOUSTON
★ ★ ★ Cowboy Songs (with Woody Guthrie) / Stin. (1944)
★ ★ ★ Cowboy Ballads / Folk. (1952)
★ ★ ★ Railroad Ballads / Folk. (1953)
★ ★ ★ Hard Travelin' / Folk. (1954)
★ ★ ★ Cisco Houston Sings Songs of Woody Guthrie / Van. (1963)
★ ★ ★ I Ain't Got No Home / Van. (1967)
★ ★ Cisco Houston Sings American Folk Songs / Folk. (1968)
★ ★ Cisco Houston / Ev. (NA)
Cisco Houston's main claim to fame is as Woody Guthrie's sidekick; he recorded many other albums with Guthrie, although his equal billing on *Cowboy Songs* was rare. Houston's best recordings are of Guthrie songs, but his vocal prowess wasn't particu-

larly suited to the populist folk genre. He was halfway between a slick cowboy vocalist like Gene Autry and a pop singer of the late Forties/early Fifties era (when most of these sides were made). This made him a perfect vehicle for the pop-folk production on the Vanguard recordings, made during the Kingston Trio craze in the late Fifties. — D.M.

CISSY HOUSTON
★ ★ **Step Aside for a Lady** / Col. (NA)
★ ★ **Surprises** / Atl. (NA)
★ ★ **Warning Danger** / Col. (1979)
Houston is so outstanding as a backup singer, in the studio and onstage, and as a member of the Sweet Inspirations that it's a shame she's never made a solo album that was more than aimless. Maybe she's too blessed—these projects haven't been able to focus her talents on the one or two outstanding traits it takes to make distinctive solo vocal records. — D.M.

THELMA HOUSTON
★ ★ **Thelma and Jerry** / Mo. (1978)
★ ★ ★ ★ **Anyway You Like It** / Tam. (1976)
★ ★ ★ **The Devil in Me** / Tam. (1977)
★ ★ **Ready to Roll** / Tam. (1978)
★ ★ **Two to One** / Mo. (1978)
★ ★ **Never Gonna Be Another One** / RCA (1981)
★ ★ ★ **Super Star Series, Vol. 20** / Mo. (1981)
Thelma Houston is one of a handful of genuinely talented vocalists to emerge from the Seventies disco phenomenon. Before her big hit, "Don't Leave Me This Way," Houston had spent nearly a decade in obscurity, completing pop albums in Hollywood with Jimmy Webb and Joe Porter (now deleted) and turning in a perfunctory appearance on the soundtrack to Motown's *Bingo Long and the Traveling All-Stars.* All the while she was perfecting her own gospel-based pop style, which has a chilling precision and nuance of phrasing rare in soul music.

By the time "Don't Leave Me This Way" clicked in 1976, Houston was more than ready; the rest of *Anyway You Like It,* and much of *The Devil in Me,* is a bit too mechanical to be considered successful, but her handling of ballads and standards is masterful. *Thelma and Jerry* was conceived as a reprise of Marvin Gaye's duets with Tammi Terrell, but Jerry Butler's failing voice and talents don't couple well with Houston's skill and zest. The other albums are exercises in competence. — R.G.

FRANK HOVINGTON
★ ★ ★ ★ **Lonesome Road Blues** / Flyr. (1976)
Traditional Delaware-based blues guitarist, discovered by John Fahey. Hovington ranges through a variety of material, from "Mean Old Frisco" and "John Henry" to "Where Could I Go But to the Lord," which places him in the Mance Lipscomb songster tradition. Hovington is a fine singer (with experience in gospel quartets), but his guitar playing is so superb it overshadows everything else he does. — D.M.

CHUCK HOWARD
★ **Chuck Howard** / Cream (1977)
Los Angeles songwriter takes a turn at crooning. His C&W stuff is both clichéd and far too slick to be believed for even an instant ("Happy Birthday, Honey" is so unctuous it almost qualifies as honkie Barry White), and while his cover of Luther Ingram's "(If Loving You Is Wrong) I Don't Want to Be Right" is better, it isn't *that* much better. — D.M.

STEVE HOWE
★ ★ **Beginnings** / Atl. (1975)
★ ★ **Steve Howe Album** / Atl. (1979)
Rough drafts of Yes albums, from the group's guitarist. Howe is typically expert (except on bass). The backing is creditable, and an occasional passage shines, but most of the songs are too loose, his singing weak and the lyrics naive. — C.W.

DIANA HUBBARD
■ **Life Times** / Waterh. (1979)
L. Ron's daughter in a very extraneous effort awash with scientological platitudes. Goo-goo, without the ga-joob. — J.S.

R. B. HUDMON
★ ★ **Closer to You** / Coti. (NA)
Hudmon has occasionally made singles that indicate he has potential as a journeyman soul balladeer. Unfortunately he's given the big-noise contemporary treatment here, and the results are fairly dire. — D.M.

HUDSON
★ **Damn Those Kids** / Elek. (1980)
The Hudson Brothers drop the family tag and try to go it as a rock band. Admittedly these guys do make Top-Forty popsicles of a tantalizing flavor, but it's all as hokey and silly as the Brothers' former network TV show. Is it those kids that the Hudsons are damning, or themselves for rolling down a dead-end commercial road this album tries

(with some heart, at least) to back the boys out of? — R.P.

AL HUDSON AND THE SOUL PARTNERS
★ ★ **Especially for You** / MCA (1977)
★ ★ ★ **Cherish** / MCA (1977)
★ ★ ★ **Do Ya Feel Like Dancin'** / ABC (1978) ¶
★ ★ **Happy Feet** / MCA (1979) ¶
Especially and *Do Ya* aren't much, but *Cherish* is a highlight of recent Chicago soul—not disco, but not dated either. Hudson's appeal has been restricted to the soul market, but he's worth checking out by more than just cultists. — D.M.

LEON HUFF
★ **Here to Create Music** / Phil. (1980)
He certainly is, but not this fluff. Almost everything Huff has ever produced is better than the Muzak included here. — D.M.

HUMAN LEAGUE
★ ★ ★ **Reproduction** / Virgin (1979), Br. imp.
★ ★ ★ **Travelogue** / Virgin Int'l (1980)
★ ★ ★ **Dare** / A&M/Virgin (1982)
Human League's synthesizer-voice interplay has set the style for numerous post-punk bands. Their first two albums were recorded as a trio. *Reproduction* suffers from incomplete musical development and pomposity; *Travelogue* is much slicker and less self-conscious. Both offer provocative sounds and concepts for the open-minded futurist. *Dare,* done as an overhauled sextet, is thoroughly pop-oriented, and has some enchanting songs. — I.R.

HUMAN SEXUAL RESPONSE
★ **Figure 14** / Pass. (1980)
★ **In a Roman Mood** / Pass. (1981)
Silly, pretentious Boston-area group earned new-wave kudos for the precious lyrics of songs like "Jackie Onassis" and "What Does Sex Mean to Me" but traffics in the most vapid instrumental and performance styles. Cold fish. — J.S.

HUMBLE PIE
★ ★ ★ ★ **As Safe as Yesterday Is** / A&M (1969)
★ ★ ★ **Town and Country** / A&M (1969)
★ ★ ★ **Humble Pie** / A&M (1970)
★ ★ ★ **Rock On** / A&M (1971)
★ ★ ★ ★ **Performance: Rockin' the Fillmore** / A&M (1971)
★ ★ **Smokin'** / A&M (1972)
★ ★ ★ **Eat It** / A&M (1973)

★ ★ **Thunderbox** / A&M (1974)
★ ★ **Street Rats** / A&M (1975)
★ **On to Victory** / Atco (1980)
★ **Go for the Throat** / Atco (1980)
Formed in 1968 by ex–Small Face Steve Marriott and future superstar Peter Frampton, Humble Pie enjoyed massive popularity until its timely demise in 1975. *As Safe* is fantastically progressive, similar to the best work of the Small Faces. *Town and Country* is uneven—here they're clearly seeking direction. *Humble Pie* and *Rock On* mark the end of Frampton's studio contributions; both have a transitional feel, somewhere between intelligently crafted progressive rock and boogie excess. With *Rockin' the Fillmore,* the group exploded commercially; mainly because of its success, the Pie concentrated thereafter on boogie. "I Don't Need No Doctor" and "Rolling Stone" became FM-radio and beer-party favorites—unfortunately they also trace the decline of Marriott's voice, and simply bludgeoned the more melodically oriented Frampton.

Minus Frampton, *Eat It* had only Marriott's R&B perversions to rely on. Side four of this is live; the studio sides feature a black female chorus and a half-dozen R&B standards. The final albums simply play out the string, with numbers by Chuck Berry and the Beatles pasted in to finish up a project that was as over as they come. — A.N.

CLAY HUNT
★ ★ **Part One** / Poly. (1980)
One star added for sparing us part two. — D.M.

GERALDINE HUNT
★ **No Way** / Prism (NA)
Title is correct. — D.M.

IAN HUNTER
★ ★ ★ ★ **Ian Hunter** / Col. (1975)
★ ★ **All American Alien Boy** / Col. (1976)
★ ★ ★ ★ **Shades of Ian Hunter** / Col. (1978)
★ ★ ★ ★ **You're Never Alone with a Schizophrenic** / Chrys. (1979)
★ ★ ★ **Live: Welcome to the Club** / Chrys. (1980)
★ ★ ★ ★ **Short Back and Sides** / Chrys. (1981)
As lead singer and songwriter for Mott the Hoople, Hunter mined rock history for influences, looking for some mythic connection between Bob Dylan, the Kinks, Doug Sahm and Lou Reed. It turns out that Mott the Hoople *was* that connection, and though

Hunter's penchant for self-indulgence eventually doomed his association with that group, he took the band's identity with him when he left. *Ian Hunter,* his solo debut, stands as a personal high point, a rocking extravaganza that features some of Hunter's toughest songwriting (from such gut crunchers as "Once Bitten Twice Shy," "Who Do You Love" and "I Get So Excited" to the pensive "It Ain't Easy When You Fall"). Mick Ronson's production and guitar-playing support is the perfect complement to Hunter's approach. The alarming slide guitar solo on "The Truth, the Whole Truth, Nuthin' but the Truth" is one of Ronson's best moments on record.

All American Alien Boy seems to lack the desperation that charged *Ian Hunter,* and aside from several obligatory hot tracks (like the title cut), it's a forgettable album. *Shades* collects the pertinent Columbia tracks, including parts of *Overnight Angel,* which was never released as an LP proper in the U.S.

You're Never Alone marked a comeback for Hunter, with great stompers like "Cleveland Rocks" and "Just Another Night" and excellent ballads like "The Outsider" and "Ships," which was adaptable enough to become one of Barry Manilow's biggest hits. *Welcome* is a good live set. *Short Back and Sides* is a brash set in which the rocker in Hunter goes out of his way to outflank new wave. — J.S.

IVORY JOE HUNTER
★ ★ ★ ★ ★ **Seventh Street Boogie / Route 66 (1977), Swed. imp.**
★ ★ ★ ★ ★ **Jumping at the Dew Drop / Route 66 (1980), Swed. imp.**
★ ★ ★ **Ivory Joe Hunter / Arc. (NA)**
★ ★ ★ **I've Always Been Country / Para. (NA)**

Excellent stride piano player and smooth-voiced vocalist who grew up in Texas and played in a blues/jazz format, using saxophonists such as Illinois Jacquet and Arnett Cobb, who would later become jazz stars in their own right. Hunter moved to California in the Forties, where his compositions made him one of the most successful R&B writers and performers of the time, beginning with "Blues at Sunrise," on which he was accompanied by Johnny Moore's Three Blazers. Hunter's combination of jazz, blues, country and R&B styles was extremely influential, and his songs have been recorded by Elvis Presley, Nat King Cole, Pat Boone, Freddy Fender, Ruth Brown and Teresa Brewer. — J.S.

ROBERT HUNTER
★ **Tales of the Great Rum Runners / Round (1974)** ¶
★ **Tiger Rose / Round (1975)** ¶

Hunter is a Grateful Dead lyricist, and his solo album is similar to records by other spinoffs of that group: at its height, it comes in a tad below the best Dead; at its worst, it exaggerates the aspects that make the Dead notoriously inconsistent. Hunter sings his admirably varied set of tunes like Jerry Garcia trying to imitate Randy Newman. Not exactly easy listening. — J.B.M.

MICHAEL HURLEY
★ ★ ★ ★ **Long Journey / Roun. (1976)**
★ ★ ★ ★ **Snockgrass / Roun. (1980)**

Hurley comes from Bucks County, Pennsylvania, where he used to hang out with Jesse Colin Young. When Young put together Raccoon Records in the early Seventies, he released two Hurley solo albums, now out of print and highly prized collector's items. Hurley's songwriting provided the focal point for the great 1976 *Have Moicy* album, which debuted the Unholy Modal Rounders and Jeffrey Fredericks and the Clamtones. The surprising success of that record led Rounder to commission Hurley's third solo album, *Long Journey,* featuring his characteristic catalogue of bizarre songs about twisted characters. "Reconciled to the Blues," "Hog of the Forsaken" and "The 8-Ball Cafe" are brilliant descriptions of human acceptance of degradation as a neutral, even interesting, condition. The musicians include Peter Stampfel on banjo and stalwarts from Hurley's sometimes backup band, the Redbirds: Morgan Huber, Robert "Frog" Nickson and Al Zangler. *Snockgrass* adds another collection of Hurley gems like "Midnite Rounder," "I'm Getting Ready to Go," the autobiographical "Automatic Slim and the Fat Boys," and an excellent version of "Jole Blon." — J.S.

MISSISSIPPI JOHN HURT
★ ★ ★ ★ ★ **The Best of Mississippi John Hurt / Van. (1965)**
★ ★ ★ ★ **Mississippi John Hurt—Today / Van. (1966)**
★ ★ ★ ★ **The Immortal Mississippi John Hurt / Van. (1968)**
★ ★ ★ **Last Sessions / Van. (1972)**
★ ★ ★ **Mississippi John Hurt—His First Recordings / Bio. (1972)**
★ ★ ★ ★ **1928 Sessions / Yazoo (1975)**
★ ★ ★ ★ ★ **Monday Morning Blues / Flyr. (1981), Br. imp.**

John Hurt is the only Mississippi delta-blues

singer whose gift might be described as delicacy and gentleness. Though Hurt finally belongs to the songster tradition rather than the world of hard-core bluesmen (his repertoire included dance and party tunes, narrative ballads, spirituals and hymns), he is a singular figure even within that idiom, for his occasional ribaldry only enhances his complete and unshakable dignity, a dignity that is finally the opposite of, say, Howlin' Wolf, a performer who is Hurt's polar opposite. But where Wolf acquired his dignity by never disguising or hiding his bitterness, by granting it full expression, Hurt (who lived a much rougher life) achieved his by never denying hope or concealing his fundamental joy at the complexities and possibilities of life. In John Hurt's version, even the bad man "Stack o' Lee" has a future.

Hurt originally recorded in New York in 1928, and these sessions (available on both Yazoo and Biograph—the former has far superior sound) are among the highlights of vintage blues listening, Hurt fingerpicking with great dexterity and singing as sweetly as anyone who's ever drawn breath. These tracks are not only graceful, they seem to emerge from a state of grace. Hurt is a wise and witty observer of the scenes of which he sings. "Stack o' Lee Blues," "Candy Man Blues," "Nobody's Dirty Business" and "Got the Blues Can't Be Satisfied" are quiet, intense masterpieces of form and feeling.

Hurt then disappeared, going back to sharecropping until he was rediscovered in 1962 by Tom Askins, who made the gorgeous Library of Congress recordings found on *Monday Morning Blues.* Hurt was then seventy years old, but he still played with force and deep emotion, as he proved over the next several years, until his death in 1967, playing college campuses and at the Newport Folk Festivals, engaging everyone he met with a mixture of genuine Christian faith, incredible good humor, and sheer musical genius. A good picture of Hurt in this period is contained on *The Best of Mississippi John Hurt,* a two-disc recording of a 1965 college concert, which is virtually a survey of his staple repertoire. The other Vanguard recordings are somewhat less charming because they were made in a pure studio context, but while Hurt has lost some technical ability due to age, there are no more charming albums of American music in existence. Even *Last Sessions,* on which Hurt wheezes and rattles, clearly on his last legs, does not surrender his marvelous spirit. — D.M.

WILLIE HUTCH

★ ★ Color Her Sunshine / Mo. (1976) ¶
★ ★ ★ Havin' a House Party / Mo. (1977)
★ ★ In Tune / Whit. (1978)
★ ★ Midnight Dancer / Whit. (1979)

All of Hutch's albums have a stylistic similarity that can be traced to his first and best Motown record, the soundtrack to *The Mack.* Unfortunately, the best records by this limited vocalist/songwriter are out of print. These albums, like much of his other work, are too dependent on clichés to be of more than minor interest. — J.MC.

J. B. HUTTO

★ ★ ★ ★ Hawk Squat / Del. (1968)
★ ★ ★ Slidewinder / Del. (1973)
★ ★ ★ Hipshakin' / Flyr. (NA)
★ ★ ★ ★ Keeper of the Flame / Flyr. (NA)
★ ★ ★ Master of Modern Blues / Test. (NA)

Excellent contemporary Chicago blues guitarist whose rough-edged delta style is heavily influenced by Elmore James. *Hawk Squat* is with pianist Sunnyland Slim. — J.S.

PHYLLIS HYMAN

★ Phyllis Hyman / Bud. (1977)
★ ★ Somewhere in My Lifetime / Ari. (1978)
★ ★ You Know How to Love / Ari. (1979)
★ ★ Can't We Fall in Love Again / Ari. (1981)

Although Hyman has had some soul chart success, most notably with the title tracks from the first two Arista LPs, even as a contemporary ballad singer she's not noticeably modern in approach. She's still purveying the rather staid style of Nancy Wilson, not even grooving with as much chic sheen as Dionne Warwick. The result is so tasteful it gets on your nerves. On the Buddah LP, where she tries some uptempo dance tunes, the results are simply ludicrous. — D.M.

IAN AND SYLVIA

★ ★ ★ **Ian and Sylvia / Van. (1962)**
★ ★ ★ **Four Strong Winds / Van. (1963)**
★ ★ ★ **Northern Journey / Van. (1964)**
★ ★ ★ **Ian and Sylvia: Early Morning Rain / Van. (1965)**
★ **Nashville / Van. (1968)**
★ ★ ★ **The Best of Ian and Sylvia / Van. (1968)**
★ ★ ★ ★ **Greatest Hits, Vol. 1 / Van. (1970)**
★ ★ ★ ★ **Greatest Hits, Vol. 2 / Van. (1971)**
★ **The Best of Ian and Sylvia / Col. (1973)** ¶

Although they weren't nearly as well known as some of their peers in the early-Sixties urban folk movement, Ian and Sylvia were both a major force within it and deeply influential on the generation of rock and folk singers who followed them out of Canada. Much of Ian Tyson's phrasing can be heard in the work of Gordon Lightfoot, and in a less direct way, in Neil Young's. His wife, Sylvia, would seem to have had her share of influence on Joni Mitchell and the McGarrigle sisters.

The duo originally sang mostly traditional ballads, with voice and guitar occasionally augmented by autoharp or acoustic bass. But as early as their second album *(Four)* they recorded Dylan's "Tomorrow Is a Long Time," and Tyson wrote the title song. Sylvia's "You Were on My Mind"—from *Northern Journey*—became a pop hit for We Five during the folk-rock craze, and by *Early Morning Rain,* the duo was deeply into the day's leading folk-based songwriters, introducing the world to Lightfoot's classic title song and "For Lovin' Me," both hits for Peter, Paul and Mary, and making a bow to country & western with Johnny Cash's "Come In, Stranger."

Throughout, the pair's style was distinctive, the deep, rolling resonance of Ian's voice a perfect foil for Sylvia's soprano, often evoking Canada as a kind of successor to the Wild West. But when they tried to go fully country & western on *Nashville,* the results were dismal. The original songs weren't good, and even the pair of Dylan tunes ("The Mighty Quinn" and "Wheels on Fire") were better done elsewhere. (The deleted *Play One More* is a better exposition of this aspect.) They recorded briefly for Columbia (whence that label's *Best of*), with dire results.

The Vanguard *Best of* is a one-record collection that has some of their best work. But the *Greatest Hits* collections contain two discs each for the price of one. The first is an especially fine representation of their music. — D.M.

JANIS IAN

★ **Janis Ian / Poly. (1967)**
■ **Present Company / Cap. (1971)**
★ ★ **Stars / Col. (1974)**
★ ★ ★ **Between the Lines / Col. (1975)**
★ **Aftertones / Col. (1975)**
★ **Miracle Row / Col. (1977)**
★ **Night Rains / Col. (1979)**
★ **Restless Eyes / Col. (1981)**

Postadolescent sob sister is three parts Joan Crawford to one part T. S. Eliot. *Janis Ian* contains "Society's Child," the protest song that made her a teen sensation in 1967. Her Columbia albums are painstaking Rorschachs of bitter, humorless self-pity. *Between the Lines* contains Ian's best songs, "At Seventeen" and "Watercolors." — S.H.

ICE

★ ★ **Ice / Pass. (NA)** ¶
★ ★ **Import/Export / Pass. (NA)** ¶

The usual blips, squeaks and mechanical moans of European art rock, as manifested in the synthesizer effects of the late Seventies. — D.M.

ICEHOUSE
★ ★ ★ **Icehouse** / Chrys. (1981)
Australian band adopts many of the stylizations of late-Seventies British electronic rock,
but in a much more personable, gutsy and
intelligent fashion than is usual. A thorough-
going affection for pop music keeps Icehouse
on just the right side of the frigid pretentiousness of its electro-romantic mentors.
— S.M.

IF
★ ★ **Not Just Another Bunch of Pretty
Faces** / Cap. (1974) ¶
This talented English jazz-rock band released
about six albums between 1970 and 1975.
Not Just is one of their last, recorded after
personnel changes had altered the band almost completely. Still, worth a listen, mainly
on the strength of Dick Morrissey's reed
work. — A.N.

IJAHMAN
★ ★ ★ ★ **Haile I Hymn** / Mango (1978)
★ ★ ★ ★ ★ **Are We a Warrior?** / Mango
(1979)
Maybe they label Ijahman Levi's music reggae because he's Jamaican and uses reggae
rhythms as his medium, but he sounds like
no other reggae artist. Frequently strumming
an acoustic guitar in the midst of drums-
and-bass rhythms, he sings strangely sweet,
heartfelt hymns (many in major keys!) to
God and the Spirit of Love—both sacred
and romantic. The music's hypnotic effect
may come from the circular musical figures,
but listeners are more likely entranced by
Ijahman's transcendent, seemingly exalted
singing. — R.F.G.

THE IMAGINATIONS
★ ★ ★ **The Imaginations** / 20th Cent. (1974)
★ ★ ★ **Good Stuff** / 20th Cent. (1975)
Solid disco music with undistinguished vo-
cals but strong dance rhythms. — D.M.

THE IMPRESSIONS
★ ★ ★ **The Fabulous Impressions** / ABC
(1967) ¶
★ ★ ★ **We're a Winner** / ABC (1968) ¶
★ ★ ★ ★ **Best of the Impressions** / ABC
(1968) ¶
★ ★ ★ ★ ★ **Impressions Sixteen Greatest
Hits** / ABC (1971) ¶
★ ★ **First Impressions** / Cur. (1975) ¶
★ ★ **Loving Power** / Cur. (1976) ¶
★ ★ **It's about Time** / Coti. (1976) ¶
★ ★ ★ ★ **Vintage Years—The Impressions
featuring Jerry Butler and Curtis
Mayfield** / Sire (1976)

★ ★ **Come to My Party** / 20th Cent.
(1979)
★ ★ **Fan the Fire** / 20th Cent. (1981)
★ ★ ★ ★ **The ABC Collection—Curtis
Mayfield amd the Impressions** / ABC
(NA)
The Impressions were one of the greatest
harmony vocal groups of the soul era.
Formed in Chicago during the late Fifties,
their earliest recordings were made with a
group that included songwriter/guitarist/
vocalist Curtis Mayfield and the brilliant
singer Jerry Butler, resulting in beautifully
constructed songs like "For Your Precious
Love."
　　After Butler left, Mayfield gave the group
a socially conscious gospel style that would
remain unequaled until the Staples Singers
turned to secular material in the early Seventies. Mayfield's high falsetto came to dominate the sound, and his songwriting certainly
provided its most inspirational moments,
raising the Impressions to a level matched
only by the Temptations among Sixties black
vocal groups. "Amen," "We're a Winner,"
"Gypsy Woman," "I'm So Proud," "Keep
On Pushin' " and "People Get Ready" are
all classic hits from this era.
　　Mayfield went solo in 1970, and the remaining members have carried on with disappointing results, first at Curtom (Mayfield's own label) and later with Cotillion
and Twentieth Century-Fox, where attempts
to modernize their style have faltered.
　　The well-annotated Sire collection would
be the top choice even if it weren't the only
Sixties Impressions available—it has the
greatest historical scope. *The ABC Collection,*
the *Best of* and *Sixteen Greatest Hits* are all
adequate documents, however, and none of
the ABC material is less than respectable.
The Curtom, Cotillion and Twentieth
Century-Fox LPs ought to be avoided.
— D.M.

THE INCREDIBLE STRING BAND
★ **The Incredible String Band** / Elek. (1966)
★ ★ ★ **The 5000 Spirits or the Layers of the
Onion** / Elek. (1967)
★ ★ ★ ★ **The Hangman's Beautiful Daughter**
/ Elek. (1968) ¶
Like other mid-Sixties folkies, Robin Williamson and Mike Heron started out fitting
personal chronicles and self-righteous protests to blues and fiddle tunes, though by
their second Incredible String Band album
they'd begun to forge an original style from
a variety of traditions. Williamson favored
the rhythmic liberties of a cappella ballads
and the weird shading of Middle Eastern

quarter tones and used them brilliantly in "The First Girl I Loved." Heron preferred calypso accents and exuberant innocence. *The Hangman's Beautiful Daughter* is their most eclectic and most experimental album, a pattern (never equaled) for all the rest. Abstruse fantasies, reminiscences and parables are set to melodies that draw on everything from spirituals to Gilbert and Sullivan. Unlike the later albums, *Hangman*'s sweetness and light is balanced by humor and vestiges of protest.

★ ★ **Wee Tam / Elek. (1968)**
★ ★ **The Big Huge / Elek. (1969)**
★ ★ **Changing Horses / Elek. (1969)**
★ **I Looked Up / Elek. (1970)** ¶
★ ★ **Relics / Elek. (1970)**
■ **U / Elek. (1971)** ¶

Middle-period String Band records are a tribal love feast—the whole family playing and singing about reincarnation and nature's way. Female participants Rose and Licorice (as befits their subordinate positions, presumably) are never listed with last names, but their piccolo-thin, high harmonies add an awkward grace to Heron and Williamson's frantic display on every kind of stringed instrument. It's spirit, not technique or playing in tune, that counts, and the String Band doesn't sacrifice communalism to aesthetics—voices may shrill and fiddles screech, but they're never discreetly buried on a track. At their best—"You Get Brighter" *(Wee Tam),* "Greatest Friend" *(Big Huge),* "Sleepers, Awake!" *(Changing Horses)*—the group transcends spiritual propaganda in songs that have the spacious simplicity of folk hymns. And Heron and Williamson's lively, resonant melodies rescue more songs than deserve it from self-indulgence and vapid mysticism. It's a tribute to their obsessive antiformalism that even their most accessible songs—from *Hangman* on—lose something when strung together on *Relics* (a two-volume collection spanning all seven earlier albums). The String Band goes nowhere if not with the flow.   — A.S.

THE IN CROWD
★ ★ **Man from New Guinea / Mango (1979)**
Facile MOR reggae played by competent musicians without compelling material. Four Aces harmonies meet reggae rhythms!
— R.F.G.

INFINITE SOUND
★ **Infinite Sound / 1750 Arch (1975)**
Arty Bay Area band is a good deal less profound than it thinks it is.   — D.M.

LUTHER INGRAM
★ ★ ★ ★ **(If Loving You Is Wrong) I Don't Want To Be Right / Koko (1972)** ¶
★ ★ ★ **I've Been Here All the Time / Stax (1972)**
★ ★ ★ **Let's Steal Away to the Hideaway / Koko (NA)**

Ingram's biggest hit, "(If Loving You Is Wrong) I Don't Want To Be Right," is one of the classic soul ballads of the Seventies, and virtually the only one revived often enough to qualify as a standard. He has never come up with another disc quite as satisfying, but his soul-steeped style, less delicate than those of many of his peers, suffered less then most in the disco days.
— D.M.

THE INMATES
★ ★ ★ **First Offence / Poly. (1979)**
★ ★ ★ **Shot in the Dark / Poly. (1980)**

This umpteenth-generation British R&B that works off first-generation roots (Rolling Stones, Pretty Things) has the style but not the feeling that made the originals great. Despite a modest FM hit with their remake of the Standells' "Dirty Water" and producer Vic Maile's relatively full sound (as compared to the tinniness of his work with Dr. Feelgood, the band's most obvious antecedent), the Inmates' music lacks the drive that makes someone like Graham Parker (whose influences are roughly the same) so powerful.
— W.K.

INNER CIRCLE
★ ★ **Reggae Thing / Cap. (1976)** ¶
★ ★ **Ready for the World / Cap. (1977)** ¶
★ ★ **Everything Is Great / Is. (1979)**
★ ★ **New Age Music / Mango (1980)**

When reggae albums this mediocre began being released in the U.S., it was a sign that the Jamaican genre had come of age as a multinational commodity. Although they're said to be a big thing back home, Inner Circle's American releases have all the rhythm but none of the exhilaration of the best reggae.   — D.M.

INTERVIEW
★ ★ ★ **Big Oceans / Virgin (1979)**
★ ★ ★ ★ **Interview / Virgin (1980)**
★ ★ ★ **Snakes and Lovers / Virgin (1980)**

Along with such other British groups as Ultravox and Orchestral Maneuvers in the Dark, Interview set the sonic stage for the Group with No Name soundtrack that created the New Romantics' Frankenstein. Unlike those other bands, however, Interview's instrumental conceptions are rooted firmly in a mainstream rock tradition, and at certain points, as on *Interview*'s "Adventurers," they sound as good as anything made in the past five years. — J.S.

INTRUDERS
★ ★ ★ **Save the Children** / TSOP (1973)
One of the first vocal groups to get the Gamble-Huff Philly-soul-production treatment. This is the only Intruders LP remaining in print, and it's a good one, with hot rhythm tracks, wonderful harmonies and an utter absence of the sodden religious philosophizing that mars recent Gamble-Huff lyrics. There's even a hit on the disc: "I'll Always Love My Mama," sentiments that seem much more appropriate to pop music than today's mystical mumbo jumbo. — D.M.

DONNIE IRIS
★ ★ **Back on the Streets** / MCA (1980)
★ ★ **King Cool** / MCA (1981)
Pittsburgh rocker Donnie Iris is a terrific singer, but his brand of prepubescent pop rock is strictly low-grade stuff. "Ah! Leah" from the *Streets* album and "Love Is Like a Rock" off of *King Cool* are his best moments. Equipped with one of the more versatile voices in rock, Iris can pull off just about any style he wants, from Lennon-ish ballads to Devo-ish rockers, but his material is only marginally interesting. — O.C.

IRON BUTTERFLY
★ ★ **In-A-Gadda-Da-Vida** / Atco (1968)
■ **Iron Butterfly—Live** / Atco (1970)
Some might call the Iron Butterfly rock & roll semiologists for arriving at a mythic description of 1968's psychedelic heavy-metal zeitgeist with the side-long title track from the first album, *In-A-Gadda-Da-Vida*. Others might argue that the track is a mock-epic Eden analogue. But the album that at one point outsold everything else in the Atlantic/Atco catalogue quickly became as forgettable an artifact as the group itself, so speculation as to its worth is pointless. It's now garbage. — J.S.

THE IRON CITY HOUSEROCKERS
★ ★ ★ **Love's So Tough** / MCA (1979)
★ ★ ★ ★ **Have a Good Time (But Get Out Alive)** / MCA (1980)
★ ★ ★ ★ **Blood on the Bricks** / MCA (1981)
The strength of this gutsy Pittsburgh bar band resides in the songwriting ability of lead singer Joe Grushecky. Working the same (dark) side of the street as Bob Seger and Bruce Springsteen at their most blue-collar, Grushecky musters a lot more anger

than those two ever do. The titles of his best songs tell the story: "I Can't Take It," "This Time the Night (Won't Save Us)," "Watch Out," "Don't Let Them Push You Around," "We're Not Dead Yet," "Have a Good Time (But Get Out Alive)." There are also the obligatory songs dedicated to women offering salvation, which only come off when Grushecky's voice—not the most expressive instrument in the genre—conveys his need directly (as on "Be My Friend" from *Blood on the Bricks*).

Love's So Tough is a hit-and-miss affair, but *Good Time* and *Bricks* show the Houserockers hitting their stride. *Bricks* is probably their best, producer Steve Cropper delivering a full sound, but *Good Time* contains their finest moment. The singer in "Old Man's Bar" tells of Dom's Cafe, a fifty-cent beer joint that he hopes no one sees him in. His voice, however, barely able to make it over the delicate mandolin and accordion arrangement, betrays sympathy for the vets who haunt the place. When "Junior's Bar" comes crashing in next, the musical contrast is dramatic but the feeling stays the same; the singer, cruising now, is a veteran himself of a different type of conflict, one with its own desperation and horrors. The music's power overwhelms his conclusions and provides a transcendent escape that only Springsteen, in much the same way, has been able to achieve. — W.K.

IRONHORSE
★ ★ **Ironhorse** / Scotti (1979)
★ ★ **Everything Is Gray** / Scotti (1980)
Guitarist Randy Bachman's post-BTO project failed to capture the commercial spark that characterized his previous work with that band and the Guess Who. — J.S.

IRON MAIDEN
★ ★ ★ ★ **Iron Maiden** / Harv. (1980)
★ ★ ★ **Killers** / Harv. (1981)
★ ★ ★ **Maiden Japan** / Harv. (1981)
Unlike the rest of the "new wave of heavy metal," as Iron Maiden and their contemporaries were dubbed by the British press, there's no pretense to rock & roll revisionism here. Iron Maiden hasn't spurned the excesses of early-Seventies heavy metal, they've merely learned how to pull them off without sounding like clichés. Hence the guitar solos go on forever, but never quite become boring; the songs rarely amount to more than a hyperdrive blues riff with a vocal pasted on top, yet pack enough punch so you don't much mind. The self-titled debut is preferable to *Killers*, if only because it tends more

to hard-and-fast. *Maiden Japan* is a live EP, released largely to capitalize on the band's rapid success. — J.D.C.

I ROY

★ ★ ★ ★ **Presenting** / Troj. (1973)
★ ★ ★ **Hell and Sorrow** / Troj. (1973)
★ ★ ★ **Many Moods of** / Troj. (1975)
★ ★ ★ **Heart of a Lion** / V.F.L. (1978)
★ ★ ★ ★ **Crisus Time** / Caro. (1979)
★ ★ **Cancer** / V.F.L. (1979)
★ ★ ★ **Whap 'n Bap 'n** / V.F.L. (1980)

I Roy followed hot on the heels of DJ innovator U Roy to become one of the most consistent reggae rappers back when the lyrical message was supposed to have content as well as flash. As a result, he regularly turns out material worthy of repeated listening. His *Whap 'n Bap 'n* even has a couple of American funk-style rappers on which he beats the American rappers at their own game. — R.F.G.

WELDON IRVINE

★ **Cosmic Vortex** / RCA (1974) ¶
★ **Spirit Man** / RCA (1975) ¶
★ **Sinbad** / RCA (1976) ¶

Flaccid funk, marginally jazz rock, though not really adventurous enough to qualify as much more than aural wallpaper. *Cosmic Vortex* contains the unbelievably jive "Love Jones," parodied by Cheech and Chong as "Basketball Jones" (and done a hell of a lot more imaginatively by Brighter Side of Darkness). If you're in the market for deep background music, and I mean deep, this belongs. — D.M.

GREGORY ISAACS

★ ★ ★ ★ **Cool Ruler** / V.F.L. (1978)
★ ★ ★ **Soon Forward** / V.F.L. (1979)
★ ★ ★ ★ **Lonely Lover** / PRE (1980)
★ ★ ★ ★ **More Gregory** / Mango (1981)
★ ★ ★ ★ **Best of, Vol. 2** / Hit (1981)
★ ★ ★ ★ **The Early Years** / Troj. (1981)
★ ★ ★ ★ **Meets Ronnie Davis** / J. Gibbs (NA)
★ ★ ★ ★ **Mr. Isaacs** / Shan. (NA)
★ ★ ★ **Best of** / GG (NA)
★ ★ ★ **Extra Classic** / Shan. (NA)

It's doubtful whether Gregory Isaacs has ever cut a bad record in ten years of recording. His thoughtful lyrics eschew the clichés and his understated, sinous melodicism combines equally effectively on romantic message material. Yet a certain sameness of production and composition makes it difficult to single out one LP over another—there is no single essential Gregory Isaacs record and none undeserving of attention. — R.F.G.

ISLEY BROTHERS

★ ★ ★ **This Old Heart of Mine** / Pick. (1966) ¶
★ ★ ★ ★ **Forever Gold** / T-Neck (1972) ¶
★ ★ ★ ★ **3 Plus 3** / T-Neck (1973) ¶
★ ★ ★ **Live It Up** / T-Neck (1974)
★ ★ **Rock around the Clock** / Camd. (1975)
★ ★ **The Very Best of the Isley Brothers** / U.A. (1975)
★ ★ ★ **The Heat Is On** / T-Neck (1975)
★ ★ ★ **Harvest for the World** / T-Neck (1976)
★ ★ ★ **Go for Your Guns** / T-Neck (1977)
★ ★ ★ ★ **The Best of the Isley Brothers** / Bud. (1978)
★ ★ ★ **Showdown** / T-Neck (1978)
★ ★ ★ **Timeless** / T-Neck (1978)
★ ★ ★ **Winner Takes All** / T-Neck (1979)
★ ★ ★ **Go All the Way** / T-Neck (1980)
★ ★ ★ **Inside You** / T-Neck (1981)
★ ★ ★ ★ **Superstar Series, Vol. 6** / Mo. (1981)
★ ★ ★ **Doin' Their Thing** / Mo. (1981)
★ ★ ★ **This Old Heart of Mine** / Mo. (1981)
★ ★ ★ **Grand Slam** / T-Neck (NA)

One of the longest-lasting groups in rock history, the Isley Brothers have been making hits since the Fifties, and in a variety of styles. Their first records were raucous, sometimes delirious call-and-response affairs. "Shout," available on *Rock around the Clock,* provided the group with both its first hit and also a signature song for the frenzied gospel style. But despite an impressive number of single releases (including several that featured Jimi Hendrix as a session guitarist), the Isleys' early-Sixties output seemed a bit too raw for the marketplace; the exception was the remake of "Shout," now considered a rock classic, "Twist and Shout" (contained in the U.A. set), which is as often covered as any song of its era. (Perhaps the most notable version is the Beatles'.)

After shifting to Motown midway through that decade, the group had one other major hit, "This Old Heart of Mine" featuring Ronnie Isley's wild, barely controlled tenor lead vocal, which gave the group's sound an intensity rare for a Berry Gordy act. (The Pickwick LP is also a collection from the Motown period.)

The group was one of the first to form its own label, T-Neck, in the early Seventies, giving it greater artistic control just at the moment when soul was developing an expanded consciousness. The early records for

Buddah—T-Neck's first distributor—are typified by "It's Your Thing," a slice of simple, hard-edged funk that was a hit in 1973. Gradually, with the addition of younger Isleys (Ernie on guitar, Marvin on bass and keyboard player Chris Jasper) the conception broadened, and the influences of Sly Stone, Jimi Hendrix and white hard rock were incorporated. When T-Neck switched to CBS as its distributor, its first reward was a smash pop hit, "That Lady" (from *3 Plus 3*), which set the pace for most of the uptempo songs that followed: infectious, snaky funk, highlighted by Ernie Isley's sinewy guitar solo. Subsequent albums have shown the redundancy of the young Isley's guitar playing, and the group hasn't developed the sound much past the ideas presented on *3 Plus 3*. But such artistic conservatism has paid off: they may be the products of a formula, rather than a creative context, but all of the T-Neck/CBS LPs are also in the platinum and gold commercial range. — J.MC.

ISRAEL VIBRATION
★ ★ ★ ★ **The Same Song** / Top. R. (1979)
★ ★ ★ ★ **Unconquered People** / Gener. (1980)

Rough, country harmonies cast in a guileless singsong add up to peculiar magic, best captured on *The Same Song*'s title cut, an anthem that could be a hit in any time or place. The three paraplegic members of Israel Vibration grew up in institutions together before becoming a part of the Twelve Tribes Rastafarian organization—an expression of faith that fills much of the lyrics. — R.F.G.

THE ITAL
★ ★ ★ **Brutal Out Deh** / Nighth. (1982)

The Ital are a criminally underrecorded roots-reggae harmony group who serve up smooth country harmonies over lean, insidious rhythms. *Brutal* presents mostly new material that compensates for a certain laid-back consistency with unpretentious charm. It's addictive. — R.F.G.

BURL IVES
★ ★ ★ **The Best of Burl Ives** / MCA (1965)
★ ★ **Burl Ives' Greatest Hits** / MCA (1967)
▪ **The Times They Are A-Changin'** / Col. (1968)
★ **Song Book** / Cor. (1973)
★ **Burl Ives Sings** / Col. (1981)
★ **The Best of Burl Ives, Vol. 2** / MCA (NA)

Although his biggest hits—"A Little Bitty Tear," "Call Me Mr. In-Between" and "Funny Way of Laughin' "—came in the early Sixties, Ives' real contribution came in the post–World War II period. Having performed solo as he traveled around the country during the Thirties, and having sung with the Almanac Singers on occasion, his postwar solo outings helped develop a public consciousness of folk and folk-based material that would open the way for the Kingston Trio and the hootenanny craze. —I.M.

PAUL JABARA
★ ★ **Perils of Paul / Casa. (1977)**
★ ★ **Keeping Time / Casa. (1978)**
★ ★ **Third Album / Casa. (NA)**
An attempt to turn a white soul singer into
a male answer to Donna Summer. The beat's
right, but the stories don't match Summer's
Once upon a Time, and the singing's just
this side of wretched. — D.M.

CHARLES JACKSON
★ ★ ★ **Passionate Breezes / Cap. (1978)**
★ ★ ★ **Gonna Getcha Love / Cap. (1979)**
Solo efforts by slick soul producer (with
partner Marvin Yancey and arranger Gene
Barge, both of whom supervise here, this
team did Natalie Cole's first—and best—
albums). These are nothing to brag about,
but they're a whole lot less embarrassing
than most, despite an inclination toward
Barry White–style heavy breathing. Mostly
what you get are exceptionally competent
ballads sung with efficient determination, if
not much heart. — D.M.

CHUCK JACKSON
★ ★ ★ **Needing You, Wanting You / All Pl.
(1975)**
★ ★ ★ **Patty / Stang (1976)**
★ ★ ★ **I Wanna Give You Some Love /
EMI (NA)**
Chuck Jackson's early-Sixties hits, which included "Any Day Now" and "I Don't Want
to Cry," combined an "uptown" production
style (strings, heavy choral backups and nondescript band tracks) with his muscular baritone. Jackson is not the most flexible of vocalists; consequently the feel of those songs
(available on a deleted Wand *Greatest Hits*
album) is too homogeneous. But the quality
of the lyrics and the intensity of performance
lend them vitality. "Needing You," a 1975
soul hit, was a welcome re-creation of the
old style. The subsequent albums are anach-

ronistic and often crude, but not without
charm. — J.M.C.

JERMAINE JACKSON
★ **My Name is Jermaine / Mo. (1976)**
★ ★ **Feel the Fire / Mo. (1977)**
★ **Frontiers / Mo. (1978)**
★ **Jermaine / Mo. (1980)**
★ **Let's Get Serious / Mo. (1980)**
★ ★ **Superstar Series, Vol. 17 / Mo. (1981)**
★ **I Like Your Style / Mo. (1981)**
Despite his remaining loyal to Motown (out
of necessity, perhaps, since he's Berry
Gordy's son-in-law), Jermaine has never
risen above purely pedestrian boogie. The
brother you're looking for is Michael.
— D.M.

JOE JACKSON
★ ★ ★ ★ **Look Sharp / A&M (1979)**
★ ★ ★ **I'm the Man / A&M (1979)**
★ ★ ★ **Beat Crazy / A&M (1980)**
★ ★ ★ **Joe Jackson's Jumpin' Jive / A&M
(1981)**
★ ★ ★ **Night and Day / A&M (1982)**
Joe Jackson seemingly came from nowhere
to become the latest in a series of great
white Anglo hopes, following Graham Parker and Elvis Costello. His debut, *Look
Sharp,* is perhaps the most commercially
sharp release to come from the new wave; its
reggae-tinged ballads and rockers, laid down
with cutting rhythm guitar and Graham
Maby's thrusting bass work, met immediate
acclaim. *I'm the Man* and *Beat Crazy* are
variations on his angry-young-man themes,
but it was increasingly obvious that Jackson
was disillusioned and becoming disjointed.
(*Beat Crazy*'s inner sleeve describes the
album as "a desperate attempt to make some
sense of Rock and Roll . . . we knew it was
destined to failure . . . why did we try?")
With *Joe Jackson's Jumpin' Jive,* he sidesteps the whole issue of working out his ar-

tistic problems by releasing a record of swing-era remakes. It's difficult to see where these faithful but soulless updatings of various Forties numbers will lead him. — W.K.

MAHALIA JACKSON

Jackson is probably the best-known, and arguably the best, gospel singer in history, a path-breaker who drew from blueswomen Bessie Smith and Ma Rainey as well as from such influential gospel singers as Willie Mae Ford Smith and Roberta Martin.

With her pliable contralto, she preferred to sing slow hymns; they gave her plenty of room to stretch out, to repeat lines endlessly with the emphasis slightly different each time, to show off her full range of vocal slurs and bent notes. Because she did rely almost exclusively on slow hymns, her albums may appear sluggish to the casual listener; the trick is to listen for how many different things she could do with a group of songs so much alike.

What's most amazing is how effortless she makes it all sound. There's no sense of strain when Jackson reaches for a high note, as is often the case with gospel singers pushing their voices to the limit; she sounds relaxed even when she shouting.

For our purposes, her career divides neatly into two periods. There are the Apollo sides (now on Kenwood) from the late Forties and early Fifties. There are pure gospel, usually just Jackson with her extraordinary pianist Mildred Falls and an unidentified organist, with background voices or maybe a guitar also added on occasion. Then there are the Columbia sides, beginning in 1954, with a full rhythm section; here she is sometimes saddled with an orchestra, pop tunes and all manner of other encumbrances.

★ ★ ★ **In the Upper Room** / Ken. (NA)
★ ★ ★ ★ **Just as I Am** / Ken. (NA)
★ ★ ★ ★ **Christmas with Mahalia Jackson** / Ken. (NA)
★ ★ ★ ★ ★ **Best of Mahalia Jackson** / Ken. (NA)
★ ★ ★ **Sing Out** / Ken. (NA)
★ ★ ★ **Mahalia! Mahalia! Mahalia!** / Ken. (NA)
★ ★ ★ ★ **World's Greatest Gospel Singer** / Ken. (NA)
★ ★ ★ ★ ★ **1911–1972** / Ken. (1972)
★ ★ **God Answers Prayer** / Ken. (1973)
★ ★ ★ **How I Got Over** / Col. (1976)
There is much duplication of material from album to album here. There are also several that might well be called "best of," in addition to the one that has that title. For example, *Christmas,* despite its title, contains

hardly any Christmas songs; it does have "Silent Night" plus many more of her best-known songs, all of which are also spread out amongst the other Kenwood LPs. It is an excellent introduction to Mahalia, but better still are *Best of* itself and *1911–1972;* the latter contains her original version of "Move On Up a Little Higher," which is said to have sold an astounding 2 million copies in the small gospel market, and such other favorites as "I'm On My Way to Canaan," "In the Upper Room" and "How I Got Over." These are the two essential Mahalia albums, and all but the hard-core fan would be well advised to stop right there.

Besides the title song, *Upper Room* features several more top early efforts ("City Called Heaven," "His Eye Is on the Sparrow," "Walking to Jerusalem"), but *Just as I Am* is superior. "Go Tell It on the Mountain" demonstrates her immaculate phrasing (as well as her peculiar, old-time New Orleans accent); there's also the title song, the wailing "Prayer Changes Things," and the haunting "What Then."

Of the rest, *Mahalia!* is unbeatable on side two, especially the bounce (another legacy of her New Orleans heritage) of "He Said He Would." *Sing Out,* which has what sounds like an overdubbed live audience on some cuts, seems to have been compiled with an eye to the folkie market; *God Answers Prayer* is another posthumous album, made up mostly of cuts best left in the can. Though released on Columbia, *How I Got Over* is listed here because it's closer to the Apollo sides in spirit and sometimes even chronologically. It's also a posthumous LP, made up of 1954 radio performances and a few songs from a 1963 TV show shot in a black church. Inexplicably, these are the only sides available of Mahalia cut before a black church congregation, though there are several live concert albums.

★ ★ ★ **Great Gettin' Up Morning** / Col. (1959)
★ **The Power and the Glory** / Col. (1960)
★ ★ ★ **Bless This House** / Col. (1963)
★ ★ ★ **Mahalia Jackson: Greatest Hits** / Col. (1963)
★ **I Believe** / Col. (1964)
★ ★ **Garden of Prayer** / Col. (1966)
★ ★ **My Faith** / Col. (1967)
★ ★ ★ **In Concert** / Col. (1967)
★ ★ **A Mighty Fortress** / Col. (1968)
★ ★ **Sings the Best-Loved Hymns of Dr. Martin Luther King, Jr.** / Col. (1968)
★ **Christmas with Mahalia** / Col. (1968)
★ **What the World Needs Now** / Col. (1969)

★ ★ ★ **Right Out of the Church** / Col.
(1969)
★ ★ **Sings America's Favorite Hymns** / Col.
(1971)
★ ★ **The Great Mahalia Jackson** / Col.
(1972)
Here's where the going gets grimmer. There
was always pressure on Mahalia to sing jazz
especially, but also blues and pop. She resisted at first, but when she moved to Columbia in 1954, she compromised to some
extent by doing such "mainstream" hymns
as "Onward Christian Soldiers," "Rock of
Ages," "The Old Rugged Cross," etc. By the
end of her career, she had acquiesced and
was singing material like "Abraham, Martin
and John," "Put a Little Love in Your
Heart" and "What the World Needs Now."

Columbia recorded her some of the time
with a rhythm section and background
voices; often there were strings and even a
full orchestra. *The Power and the Glory*, for
example, features a full orchestra and choir
directed by hackmeister Percy Faith(!),
whose arrangements are so predicably bombastic that the album is barely listenable.
Too often, Mahalia herself became just a
pretty, operatic voice used to complement
the arrangement.

Indeed, much of what made her great was
stifled under Columbia in the interests of
reaching a mass audience. Her unique sense
of timing—the way she sang around the
beat—suffered most. The piano style of Mildred Falls, who stayed with Mahalia to the
end and is featured on many of these albums, was similarly ironed out.

Still, there is, to rework slightly the title
of one of Mahalia's favorite songs, some
wheat among the tares here; the following
evaluations separate the two. The highs and
lows are discussed; the in-betweens, which
dominate her Columbia years, are not. Unfortunately, they tend to represent her output too well, being depressingly unmemorable in any way despite her voice.

A small group accompanies Mahalia on
Great Gettin' Up Morning, and she is especially impressive on "How Great Thou Art."
Bless This House also features a simple
rhythm section, and while Mahalia is saddled with a "Summertime"/"Sometimes I
Feel like a Motherless Child" medley, she
pulls it off respectably; the bulk of the material is more fitting for her, especially "Standing Here Wondering Which Way to Go,"
"Trouble with This World" and "Precious
Lord." *Greatest Hits* features re-recordings
of some of her Apollo hits, plus newer
songs; her singing has become perceptibly

more stylized, but this will pass as an introduction to Mahalia for those who can't find
the Kenwood albums. The *In Concert* set
shows that out of the studio, she retained
many of her unique vocal characteristics;
though her voice is a little frayed, "He Was
Alone" is a superlative performance. *Right
out of the Church* marks a return to the
roots. With solid gospel material, a small
rhythm section and some reasonably unobtrusive backup singers, Mahalia achieves the
most vigorous album of the later stage of her
career.

Musts to avoid, besides *The Power and the
Glory: I Believe*, which is in a similar model
and sounds like bad movie music; *Christmas*,
which is a travesty of hokiness; and *What
the World Needs Now*, which is mostly pop
songs (some of which also appear on *The
Great Mahalia Jackson*, a double album).
— J.MO.

MICHAEL JACKSON
★ ★ ★ ★ **The Best of Michael Jackson** /
Mo. (1975)
★ ★ ★ ★ ★ **Off the Wall** / Epic (1979)
★ ★ ★ ★ **Motown Superstars Series, Vol. 7** /
Mo. (1980)
★ ★ ★ **One Day in Your Life** / Mo. (1981)
★ ★ ★ ★ **Got to Be There** / Mo. (1981)
★ ★ ★ ★ **Ben** / Mo. (1981)
★ ★ ★ ★ ★ **Thriller** / Epic (1982)
The Motown collections do a good job of re-
ducing Michael Jackson's early-Seventies
solo hits (soul trailing into disco) to discs
more serviceable than the albums from
which they came. Those hits include some of
the glories of Motown's period of Detroit-to-
Hollywood transition: "Ben," "Got to Be
There," "I Wanna Be Where You Are,"
"Rockin' Robin." Michael was still too
young to be quite as incandescent on his
own as with the Jackson Five, but *Ben, Got
to Be There*, and *One Day in Your Life* all
have their heady moments. (These are his
first Motown albums, recorded and issued in
the early Seventies, then deleted and restored
to the catalogue in 1981.)

Nothing, not even his groundbreaking
work with his family, quite prepared the
world for *Off the Wall*, a masterpiece of
modern record making. Jackson's voice—
adolescent breathiness crowding maturity—
was the perfect vehicle for music that broke
down stylistic and conceptual barriers with
casual cool. *Off the Wall* features disco beat
and rock guitar, soul intensity and good-time
jive, a triumphant merger of the mechanical
and the spiritual. Its hits ranged all over the
map—the ballad "She's Out of My Life,"

the dance-beat rockers "Off the Wall" and "Rock with You," and the relentless disco funk of "Off the Wall" all made the airwaves that much more invigorating in 1979 and 1980. *Off the Wall* is unquestionably one of the most important records of the past decade.

Jackson topped himself—or came close—with *Thriller*. Although producer Quincy Jones' contributions were increasingly flimsy, dragging down the excitement of Jackson's own self-discovery (musical and personal), the exotic whirl of "Betty Jean Is Not My Lover," the hard-rock flair of "Beat It" (featuring Edward Van Halen on guitar—so strong it broke the FM rock radio color line), the heartwarming duet with Paul McCartney on "The Girl Is Mine" were only the highlights of a record that is compulsively listenable and seems destined to be as popular and influential as *Off the Wall*.

Michael Jackson's importance as a singer was established with the very first Jackson Five singles. His importance as a record-making innovator is somewhat obscured by his collaboration with Quincy Jones (although the difference between the debacle of Jones' work with Donna Summer and the genius of his work with Jackson gives a clue as to who is really boss), but both his songwriting and his production and arranging chops have grown so mightily on this second album that he is now in the very top rank of rock artists measured from the beginning. Like Stevie Wonder, Jackson has been capable of sustaining an artistic persona from preadolesence into adulthood, and theorists of rock's eternal attachment to youth notwithstanding, his music has grown richer and more intelligent with each passing year. Michael Jackson is no longer an optional pleasure for those who pretend to know about American music. He has become a necessity. — D.M.

MILLIE JACKSON
★ ★ ★ It Hurts So Good / Spring (1973)
★ ★ ★ ★ Caught Up / Spring (1974)
★ ★ ★ ★ Still Caught Up / Spring (1975)
★ ★ ★ Free and in Love / Spring (1976)
★ ★ ★ Lovingly Yours / Spring (1976)
★ ★ ★ Feelin' Bitchy / Spring (1977)
★ ★ ★ Get It Out 'Cha System / Spring (1978)
★ ★ Moment's Pleasure / Spring (1979)
★ ★ Live and Uncensored / Spring (1979)
★ ★ For Men Only / Spring (1980)
★ ★ I Had to Say It / Spring (1980)
★ Just a Li'l Bit Country / Spring (1981)

Jackson first scored with a pair of fairly conventional soul singles in 1972: "My Man, a Sweet Man" and "Ask Me What You Want." Those records are no longer available on LPs. *It Hurts So Good,* which followed in 1973, was notable principally for containing a couple of songs from the blaxploitation flick *Cleopatra Jones,* but it was less than exceptional.

With *Caught Up,* released the next year, Jackson and producer Brad Shapiro hit their stride. *Caught Up,* and most of what followed it, was based on a simple concept: Jackson rapping her way through one side as a seductress, daring the wife to keep her man; and on the flip, as the wife, challenging the temptress to take him. *Caught Up* interspersed a revamped version of Luther Ingram's R&B adultery hit, "(If Loving You Is Wrong) I Don't Want to Be Right," with original material to achieve her best effect. *Still Caught Up* continues the story, with material only slightly less fine. *Free and in Love* features a first-rate version of "Feel Like Making Love," doubly impressive because Jackson is interpreting Bad Company's song, not Roberta Flack's.

Lovingly Yours and *Feelin' Bitchy* seemed to have taken the concept to its limit—the latter's contents were so explicit that the album required an airplay warning on the DJ copy. But Jackson has continued to plow this thin and narrow turf, with inevitably diminishing returns. The exception is *Just a Li'l Bit Country,* in which Millie discovers why there is no female Charley Pride.
— D.M.

PYTHON LEE JACKSON
★ ★ In a Broken Dream / Cres. (1972)
This obscure Australian group's sole album probably would never have been released in America had it not been that when it was recorded, the band lacked a vocalist for the title track. A then (1970) unknown singer named Rod Stewart stepped in, and the result, while not terribly impressive as part of Stewart's body of work, became a hit following the U.S. success of "Maggie May."
— D.M.

SHAWNE JACKSON
★ ★ ★ Shawne Jackson / RCA (1976)
Shawne Jackson was the singer in a short-lived mid-Seventies band led by ex–Mandala Soul Crusade, Bush and Guess Who lead guitarist Domenic Troiano. Troiano dominates the record, producing, arranging and writing most of the material, with his guitar the principal solo voice. The result is a kind

of high-water mark for the Toronto R&B scene. — J.S.

WALTER JACKSON

★ ★ **Feeling Good** / Chi-S. (1976)
★ ★ **I Want to Come Back as a Song** / Chi-S. (1977)
★ ★ ★ **Walter Jackson's Greatest Hits** / Epic (1977)
★ ★ **Good to See You** / Chi-S. (1978)
★ ★ **Send in the Clowns** / 20th Cent. (1979)
A moody baritone crooner, Jackson made his reputation in the early Sixties as part of Okeh's Chicago soul stable; those R&B hits are included on the Epic collection. Only "It's All Over," from 1964, made any substantial dent in the pop charts, however.

Feeling Good, Jackson's Chi-Sound debut, includes a re-recording of "Welcome Home," his 1965 hit. But the rest of that album, and the others on Chi-Sound and Twentieth Century-Fox, are marred by rather wooden arrangements. — J.M.C.

JACKSON HIGHWAY

★ ★ ★ **Jackson Highway** / Cap. (1980)
Local band shepherded by the Muscle Shoals Sound Studio players, and for good reason. Although Jackson Highway have yet to truly define a style, they display a plethora of writing and playing talent that should serve them well in the future. — R.P.

THE JACKSON FIVE

★ ★ ★ **Maybe Tomorrow** / Mo. (1981)
★ ★ ★ ★ **Anthology** / Mo. (1981)
★ ★ ★ ★ **Motown Superstar Series, Vol. 12** / Mo. (1980)
★ ★ ★ ★ **Diana Ross Presents the Jackson Five** / Mo. (1981)
★ ★ ★ ★ **ABC** / Mo. (1981)
★ ★ ★ ★ **Third Album** / Mo. (1981)
★ ★ ★ ★ **Greatest Hits** / Mo. (1981)
Restored to humanity, some of the most charming children's records known to man. Also some of the funkiest. Michael Jackson, the lead singer, grew up to become Michael Jackson, achievement enough for any man. — D.M.

THE JACKSONS

★ ★ ★ **The Jacksons** / Epic (1976)
★ ★ ★ **Goin' Places** / Epic (1977)
★ ★ ★ ★ **Destiny** / Epic (1978)
★ ★ ★ ★ **Triumph** / Epic (1980)
★ ★ ★ **Live** / Epic (1981)
After leaving Motown, the Jacksons were saddled with another faltering production-mill approach, this one Kenneth Gamble and Leon Huff's, for their first two Epic albums. Though no group that sports a vocalist as original and multitalented as Michael Jackson can be altogether dismal, *The Jacksons* and *Goin' Places* come a lot closer than necessary.

Destiny, which was the first self-produced album that the family had done, reversed the trend. Rather than Gamble and Huff's meandering dance music and stiff ballads, *Destiny's* groove was solid and focused, as epitomized by "Shake Your Body (Down to the Ground)," the group's biggest post-Motown hit. Although *Triumph* produced no hits that big, "Lovely One" and "Heartbreak Hotel" were important hits, and coming off "Shake Your Body," big enough to matter. Michael Jackson's burgeoning solo career has since stalled matters—the Jacksons may be the family that plays together, but they clearly would not be playing in the majors without Michael. *Live* is a holding action, not a bad record, but not especially interesting listening because the conventions of a Jacksons' concert don't translate particularly well to the living room. — D.M.

DEBBIE JACOBS

★ ★ **Undercover Lover** / MCA (1979)
★ ★ **High on Your Love** / MCA (1980)
Your typical soul shrieker and moaner. — D.M.

LITTLE WALTER JACOBS

★ ★ ★ ★ **Super Blues** / Check. (1967)
★ ★ ★ ★ ★ **Boss Blues Harmonica** / Chess (NA)
★ ★ ★ **Quarter to Twelve** / Red L. (1970), Br. imp.
★ ★ ★ **Thunderbird** / Syndicate Chapter (1971)
★ ★ ★ ★ **Confessin' the Blues** / Chess (1976), Br. imp.
★ ★ ★ ★ **Hate to See You Go** / Chess (NA)
★ ★ ★ ★ ★ **Little Walter** / Chess (NA)
★ ★ ★ ★ ★ **Southern Feeling** / Roi du Blues (NA), Can. imp.
★ ★ ★ ★ **Blue Midnight** / Roi du Blues (NA), Can. imp.
Little Walter's contribution to modern blues, rhythm & blues and rock is inestimable. For twenty years, from 1947, when he made his first recordings, until his death in a fight in 1968, he was known as the greatest harmonica player in history and was the most popular Chicago-based bluesman aside from Muddy Waters.

Jacobs got his training as blues harpist with Waters' band in the Forties and Fifties. When he put together his own group, it became apparent that Jacobs was not only a virtuoso instrumentalist but a first class singer and bandleader as well. He released relatively few records, but everything he recorded is of the highest quality as far as arrangement, vocal-instrumental performance and band sound go. There are no bad Little Walter albums. The Chess are reissues of his best and best-known sides; the Roi du Blues are beautiful rare outtakes, as strong as most of his famous material. The Red Lightnin' and Syndicate Chapter albums duplicate much of the above.

Every harmonica player after Little Walter has in some way been influenced by his style, especially rock players, from John Mayall to Magic Dick of the J. Geils Band. Jacobs was able to take hard bop melodic ideas from contemporary saxophonists and match them to a simpler but more forceful blues rhythm with heavily emphasized guitar parts, suggesting a further link between bop-era jazz players and rock & roll. The Little Walter harmonica style thus transposed saxophone ideas into terms compatible with and influential on guitars. — J.S./D.M.

JADE WARRIOR
★ ★ Jade Warrior / Vert. (1971)
★ ★ ★ Released / Vert. (1971)
★ ★ ★ Last Autumn's Dream / Vert. (1972)
★ ★ ★ Waves / Is. (1975)
★ ★ Kites / Is. (1976)
An intriguing, almost unknown English progressive rock band, heavily influenced by King Crimson, Jethro Tull and British jazz-rock. The LP covers are characterized by Chinese motifs that rarely carry over into the music. The Island albums, from the middle Seventies, are more experimental than the Vertigo ones of a few years earlier; *Kites* even manages "Teh Ch'eng," which finally realizes the group's Oriental flourishes.
— A.N.

THE JAGS
★ ★ ★ Evening Standards / Is. (1980)
★ No Tie Like a Present / Is. (1981)
British quartet's first album was reminiscent of Elvis Costello ("Back of My Hand" is a great tune), but the joke wore thin the second time around. — J.S.

JAH LION
★ ★ Columbia Colly / Mango (1976)
Available evidence suggests that Jah Lion is Lee Perry toasting to more-bizarre-than-usual Lee "Scratch" Perry remixes of some of his own better productions. Record-company sources, however, insist that although Perry cowrites and produces, he does not perform here. — R.F.G.

THE JAM
★ ★ ★ In the City / Poly. (1977)
★ ★ ★ This Is the Modern World / Poly. (1977)
★ ★ ★ ★ All Mod Cons / Poly. (1978)
★ ★ ★ ★ Setting Sons / Poly. (1980)
★ ★ ★ ★ Sound Affects / Poly. (1981)
The Jam was mod at a time when its new-wave compatriots were decidedly punk. The obvious musical reference was the early Who, but not the Who of "My Generation" that propelled the Sex Pistols. Rather, the Jam attached itself to the lighter Townshend vision of such songs as "The Kids Are Alright" and "So Sad About Us." *In the City,* as with most new-wave debut albums, is a raw translation of stage show into the studio, spiced with a few cover versions. *This Is the Modern World* displays a more individual style, but suffers from a muffled sound and leader Paul Weller's inconsistent vocals. After America turned a deaf ear to its very British sound, the group was generally given up as a lost cause.

Weller and company took their time making *All Mod Cons,* and it shows in the album's breakthrough power. The inner sleeve is an assembly of various mod artifacts, but now Weller has put some distance between himself and his obsessions. *Cons* contains a splendid cover of the Kinks' "David Watts," whose songwriter Ray Davies had developed a style of songwriting that often concerned itself with England's past. Weller proves himself an heir to that tradition, and to that of the great Sixties songwriters, with "Mr. Clean," "In the Crowd," and "The Place I Love." Although it's possible to sit around and dissect all the influences, the record is more than just a compendium of British beat styles. The last track, "Down in a Tube Station at Midnight," is a gripping tale of mindless racist violence; its personal focus and driving music give it a haunting strength.

On *Setting Sons,* Weller sets his sights even further back. He creates songs that evoke an England of military might and unity, and reveals a pessimistic streak in his observations of decay and failed promise. The music is dense and not nearly as charismatic or varied as *All Mod Cons,* but there is an undeniable force to a number like "Eton Rifles" that is an accomplishment.

Sound Affects is a return to diversity and finally brings a brightness and clarity to the Jam's sound on vinyl. The group's performances are at a peak, especially on "Set the House Ablaze," a tour de force of metal proportions. And although Weller occasionally opts for easy cynicism instead of digging deeper, *Sound Affects* is the mark of a man and a group who will rank with the Eighties' finest. — W.K.

ELMORE JAMES

★ ★ ★ **Whose Muddy Shoes (with John Brim) / Chess (1969), Fr. imp.**
★ ★ ★ ★ **Anthology of the Blues: The Resurrection of Elmore James / United (1976)**
★ ★ ★ ★ ★ **One Way Out / Charly (1980), Br. imp.**
★ ★ ★ ★ **Anthology of the Blues: Legend of Elmore James / United (NA)**
★ ★ ★ **Elmore James / United (NA)**
★ ★ ★ **History of Elmore James, Vol. 1 / Trip (NA)**
★ ★ ★ **History of Elmore James, Vol. 2 / Trip (NA)**
★ ★ ★ ★ ★ **Got to Move / Charly (NA), Br. imp.**
★ ★ ★ **The Best of Elmore James / Chis. (NA), Br. imp.**

Elmore James recorded for only eleven years, from 1952 until his death in 1963, but his influence was far greater than such a brief span would suggest. His slide-guitar style was perhaps the most important in the translation of that technique into rock's version of blues. A good number of his stinging, whiplash songs, from his signature tunes "It Hurts Me Too" and "Dust My Broom" to the dance number "Shake Your Moneymaker" and the spiritually ravaged "The Sky Is Crying," have been covered again and again, by Eric Clapton, Fleetwood Mac and dozens of others. The Charly LPs, which have material originally on Trumpet, Vee Jay, Fire, Enjoy and Chief, are the best introductions. Chances are, once you're familiar with James' brilliant slide playing and keening voice, you'll want to hear the rest as well. — D.M.

ETTA JAMES

★ ★ ★ **At Last / Cadet (1961)**
★ ★ ★ **Top Ten / Cadet (1963)**
★ ★ ★ ★ **Tell Mama / Cadet (1968)**
★ ★ ★ ★ ★ **Peaches / Chess (1971)**
★ ★ **Come a Little Closer / Chess (1974)**
★ ★ **Etta Is Betta Than Evah / Chess (1977)**
★ ★ ★ ★ **Deep in the Night / War. (1978)**

The *New York Times* called Etta James "a soul star who has been intense and intelligent about soul music for longer than anyone since Ray Charles." Others have called her one of the great ballad singers of the century on the basis of such classics as "At Last," "I'd Rather Go Blind" and recent treatments of Randy Newman's "God's Song" and her own "Moanin'."

Yet unlike Charles', James' recording career is an utter shambles, containing frequent confrontations with hack producers and some of the most unlikely, inappropriate material imaginable. Even *Peaches,* an anthology of her early work and the one indispensable James album, is a mess. Tracks were put together with complete disregard for both historical continuity and listenability. Revved-up neo-Motown material alternates with Southern soul ballads in completely chaotic fashion. Yet if you pick up and put down the needle at the right spots, you can hear one of the two or three deepest, most profound voices in rhythm & blues.

Of the other albums, *Tell Mama*—produced by Rick Hall in Muscle Shoals a couple of years after that studio's success with Aretha Franklin—is by far the best, but also the hardest to find. It has a touch of the flavor of Aretha's *I Never Loved a Man* and features James' most popular hit, "Tell Mama," as well as "I'd Rather Go Blind" and Otis Redding's "Security," *At Last* and *Top Ten,* two early albums consisting of almost identical material, are both better than one would expect. Both were recorded in the early Sixties and feature decent, down-home renderings of standards alongside some reasonably intelligent blues numbers. Both albums have more than their share of junk, though, particularly the Motown-inspired numbers.

Come a Little Closer is a comeback attempt engineered by former Three Dog Night producer Gabriel Mekler. It's an ambitious failure, with a stunning version of "St. Louis Blues" ruined by a Mitch Miller–style chorale background. But she does well by Randy Newman, and the self-penned, wordless "Moanin'" is a neglected soul classic. *Etta Is Betta Than Evah,* on the other hand, tries to be raunchy. It succeeds in that regard, but without much quality. There's something forced about a 1977 album trying to capture 1962 looseness, and too much is underdeveloped.

While the great Etta James album is yet to be made, *Deep in the Night,* produced by Jerry Wexler and released in 1978, is more intelligently assembled than anything else here. Her readings of such pop hits as "Only Women Bleed" and "Take It to the Limit" are superb, and the arrangements provided by Barry Beckett and Wexler are excellent.

James sings from the bottom of her soul and this time, at least, it pays off. — R.G.

FREDDIE JAMES
★ **Get Up and Boogie** / War. (NA)
Exactly as imaginative as its title. — D.M.

RICK JAMES AND THE STONE CITY BAND
★ ★ ★ **Come Get It** / Gor. (1978)
★ ★ ★ **Bustin' Out of L Seven** / Gor. (1979)
★ ★ ★ **Fire It Up** / Gor. (1979)
★ ★ ★ **Garden of Love** / Gor. (1980)
★ ★ ★ **In 'n' Out** / Gor. (1980)
★ ★ ★ **Street Songs** / Gor. (1981)
★ ★ ★ **The Boys Are Back** / Gor. (1981)
James comes on like a rocker, all flashy clothes, a guitar slung low at his hip. But he isn't really a part of the dance-rock sound that emerged in the wake of disco, so much as a very skillful bandleader whose hits—from "Mary Jane" to "Bustin' Out"—have incorporated slick modern soul production technique in a funk context. References to ganja and partyin' all night don't exactly make this stuff raw and street-level. Divorced from his rhetoric, though, James remains a skillful, if not terribly inspired, hitmaker. — D.M.

SKIP JAMES
★ ★ ★ **Skip James: Greatest of the Delta Blues Singers** / Melo. (1968)
★ ★ ★ ★ **Early Blues Recordings—1931** / Bio. (1971)
James (1902–1969) was one of the greatest guitarists, pianists and singers to work within the frame of Mississippi delta blues, but because he was also one of the more idiosyncratic, his formal influence has been much less than that of Robert Johnson, Charlie Patton, Son House or even Tommy Johnson. His impact has been as an *inspiration*—on hearing him play, either on his original recordings or, after his rediscovery in 1964, in live performance, any number of musicians were moved to deepen the passion and commitment of their own music.

Early Blues collects a number of James' original recordings for Paramount, including his magnificent "Devil Got My Woman" and "If You Haven't Any Hay," which features James' wild, almost absurdist piano work. It is one of the central documents of delta blues. *Greatest* was cut in 1964, and while it demonstrated that James had lost none of his powers over the years, the best was yet to come.
★ ★ ★ ★ ★ **Skip James Today!** / Van. (1966)
★ ★ ★ ★ ★ **Devil Got My Woman** / Van. (1968)

These two modern recordings are among the most important blues albums ever made. The sound is full of presence, and the performance full of life—charged with bitterness, love, desire and a sense of fun (most evident on *Today!* with "I'm So Glad," first recorded by James in the Thirties and later made famous by Cream). James' high, ghostly voice pierces the night air—it always seems like night when these albums are playing—and his guitar shadows the moon.

If one must choose, the edge here goes to *Devil*, if only for the staggering version of the title song, which delves as deeply into the heart of American mystery as any tune ever has—and seals James' status as one of the finest, most aware folk artists of all time. Perhaps the reason so few of his songs have been recorded by others is that most musicians understand that the original performances simply can't be topped. — G.M.

SONNY JAMES
★ ★ ★ ★ **The Best of Sonny James** / Cap. (1966)
★ ★ ★ **Traces** / Cap. (1972) ¶
★ **When the Snow Is on the Roses** / Col. (1972)
★ ★ **Sonny James Sings the Greatest Country Hits of 1972** / Col. (1973) ¶
★ ★ **If She Just Helps Me Get Over You** / Col. (1973)
★ ★ **Is It Wrong** / Col. (1974)
★ ★ ★ **Biggest Hits of Sonny James** / Cap. (1975)
★ ★ **Little Bit South of Saskatoon** / Col. (1975)
★ **The Guitars of Sonny James** / Col. (1975)
★ ★ ★ **Two Hundred Years of Country Music** / Col. (1975)
★ ★ ★ **When Something Is Wrong with My Baby** / Col. (1976) ¶
★ ★ **You're Free to Go** / Col. (1976) ¶
★ ★ **In Prison, in Person** / Col. (1977) ¶
★ ★ **Sonny James' Greatest Hits** / Col. (1978)
★ **This Is the Love** / Col. (1978)
★ ★ ★ **Best of Sonny James** / Cap. (NA)
★ **Sonny's Side of the Street** / Monu. (NA)
James' first hit was the soft-rock tear-jerker "Young Love," a 1956 rockabilly ballad smash, for Capitol. He has never repeated that pop success, but his country hits have been frequent, including a run of C&W No. 1s that lasted from 1967 to 1971. In 1972 he moved to Columbia, and in that label's production mill has produced more hits but less satisfactory ones. James' voice is now much deeper than when he cut "Young Love," so he sounds somewhat like Johnny Cash. At his best—or simply when he is given a chal-

lenging project, like *Something Is Wrong,* which includes some soul-based songs and some rockabilly, or on the collection of classic and traditional songs, *Two Hundred Years*—he is still a surprisingly affecting performer. — D.M.

TOMMY JAMES
★ ★ **Mony Mony / Rou. (1968) ¶**
★ ★ **Crimson and Clover / Rou. (1969) ¶**
★ ★ ★ **Cellophane Symphony / Rou. (1969) ¶**
★ ★ **Tommy James / Rou. (1969) ¶**
★ ★ **Travelin' / Rou. (1970) ¶**
★ ★ ★ ★ **The Best of Tommy James / Rou. (1971)**
★ **In Touch / Fan. (1976)**
★ **Midnight Rider / Fan. (1977)**
★ **Three Times in Love / Millen. (1980)**
★ **Easy to Love / Millen. (1981)**
★ ★ **My Head, My Bed and My Red Guitar / Rou. (NA) ¶**
Tommy James' late-Sixties pop hits, with his group the Shondells and on his own, were actually first-rate AM rock. "I Think We're Alone Now," "Crimson and Clover" and "Crystal Blue Persuasion," a transparent allegory about his involvement with amphetamines, were interesting, if totally lightweight, radio fare. Had James come along at a time when the rock audience was less self-conscious about the distinction between hit singles and concept albums, he might have turned himself into a precursor of Elton John and Neil Diamond. Unfortunately, Roulette's rather hidebound approach to marketing and his drug problem conspired against such respectability. His *Best of* album and *Cellophane Symphony,* where he does stretch out a fraction, remain worth hearing. But the rest, particularly the mid-Seventies Fantasy sets, in which he tries to become to Linda Ronstadt what Ford is to General Motors, are dull and dismal.
— D.M.

JAMES GANG
★ ★ ★ ★ **The James Gang Rides Again / ABC (1970)**
★ **Live in Concert / ABC (1971)**
★ **Straight Shooter / ABC (1972)**
★ ★ ★ **The Best of the James Gang/Joe Walsh / ABC (1973)**
This version of the James Gang featured guitarist/singer/songwriter Joe Walsh, a gifted interpolator of West Coast and British rock styles who mightily impressed the Who's Pete Townshend during a set in Cleveland, the band's hometown. The first album (*James Gang,* now deleted) shows their roots: a combination of Buffalo Springfield's

and the Yardbirds' guitar styles. *Rides Again,* the second LP, demonstrates what Townshend responded to in Walsh's playing. Walsh had figured out a rhythm/lead-guitar technique that became the most significant post-Cream power-trio strategy. As side one of *Rides Again* indicates, he picked up a lot of cues from Townshend and Jeff Beck.

But Walsh was bored with the trio format. Side two of *Rides Again* presents him as a songwriter, leading the band on keyboards for a more layered effect reminiscent of late-period Beatles recordings. His facility with country-rock modes anticipates the trademark sound of the Eagles, which Walsh joined in 1976. *Rides Again* is one of the most important rock records of the Seventies.

By the time of the live album, though, Walsh's heart was no longer in the material. And since the band didn't have this, the anthologies aren't particularly useful.
★ ★ ★ **Sixteen Greatest Hits / ABC (1973)**
★ **Bang / Atco (1973)**
★ **Newborn / ACO (1975)**
★ **Jesse Come Home / Atco (1976)**
Drummer Jim Fox continued the James Gang but was never really able to find a suitable replacement for Walsh. The result was turgid Midwestern heavy metal.
— J.S.

NICK JAMESON
★ ★ **Already Free / Bears. (1977)**
Another batch of unconvincing (because so dispassionate) love songs from another anonymous writer/singer (destined to remain all three), accompanied by electric piano, grunting funk bass, a few tasteful strings and (the only real mark of distinction) a few harp interjections by Paul Butterfield. Dismal.
— D.M.

JAN AND DEAN
★ ★ ★ ★ **Legendary Masters / U.A. (1971)**
★ ★ ★ **Gotta Take That One Last Ride / U.A. (1974)**
★ ★ ★ **Dead Man's Curve / U.A. (NA)**
Jan and Dean, of course, were the principal competitors of the Beach Boys (whose Brian Wilson helped write many of their hits) in the surf-and-hot-rod scene of the pre-Beatles Sixties. Their hits included "Dead Man's Curve," "Surf City," "Drag City" and scads more, most of them pretty wacky. Neither Jan Berry nor Dean Torrance was an accomplished singer—they *looked* right, though—but they got by on nerve and sheer madness, which is better than well represented on side four of *Legendary Masters.* That record also

includes the group's first hit, the pre-surf "Baby Talk." — D.M.

JANICE
■ Janice / Fan. (1970)
Nice girls finish last, too. — D.M.

BERT JANSCH
★ ★ ★ Jack Orion / Van. (1970)
Jansch is a central figure of the British folk-rock scene, both on his own and as a member of Pentangle. He is one of that genre's most accomplished guitarists, and *Jack Orion* is his best and most influential recording. It features almost exclusively folk music of the British Isles, most of it completely solo but with occasional assistance from John Renbourn. A wide selection of other Jansch albums is available on import. — C.W.

BERT JANSCH AND JOHN RENBOURN
★ ★ ★ ★ Stepping Stones / Van. (1968)
Two spirited, agile and subtle acoustic guitarists; no backing. Mostly original instrumentals incorporating blues, jazz, British Isles folk and Indian ragas. Occasional vocals from Jansch. — C.W.

JAPAN
★ ★ Adolescent Sex / Ario. (1978), Br. imp.
★ ★ Obscure Alternatives / Ario. (1978), Br. imp.
★ ★ Quiet Life / Ario. (1980), Br. imp.
★ ★ Gentlemen Take Polaroids / Virgin (1980), Br. imp.
★ ★ Tin Drum / Virgin (1981), Br. imp.
★ ★ Assemblage / Ario. (1981), Br. imp.
This band wants to branch out into sculpture, photography and films; their music doesn't excite even them. Atmospheric, though. — ML.H.

JEAN-MICHEL JARRE
★ ★ Oxygene / Poly. (1977)
★ ★ Equinoxe / Poly. (1978)
★ ★ Magnetic Fields / Poly. (1981)
Classical/electronic keyboardist produces interesting but bloodless space music. — J.S.

AL JARREAU
★ ★ ★ We Got By / Rep. (1975)
★ ★ ★ Glow / Rep. (1976)
★ ★ ★ Look to the Rainbow / War. (1977)
★ ★ ★ All Fly Home / War. (1978)
★ ★ ★ This Time / War. (1980)
★ ★ ★ Breakin' Away / War. (1981)
Often hailed as a jazz singer, Al Jarreau is a protean vocalist still in search of a personal style. He can simulate virtually any horn or reed instrument with disarming accuracy, and his breathing maneuvers are nearly enough to send even Al Green back to yoga school. But thus far his techniques surpass his skills. His scatting swings with all the dexterity of a lumberjack, and his songwriting is rarely more than a flashy weave of passable soul fundamentals. *We Got By* is all original Jarreau and flows better than *Glow,* with its misplaced emphasis on pop warhorses ("Fire and Rain," "Your Song"). *Rainbow* is live; *Breakin' Away* contains Jarreau's first hit single, "We're in This Love Together." — M.G.

SCOTT JARRETT
★ ★ Without Rhyme or Reason / Ari./GRP (1980)
Incredibly insipid folkie nonsense from Keith Jarrett's younger brother. — J.D.C.

WAYNE JARRETT
★ ★ ★ Showcase / Wac. (1980)
★ ★ ★ What's Wrong with the Youths? / Jah Life (1981)
A capable young roots reggae singer whose "Saturday Night Jamboree" anthem was a memorably anthemic hit in 1980. *Showcase* features ethereal production that enhances run-of-the-mill material, while *Youths* includes "Jamboree" in a harder-hitting but not necessarily more interesting set. — R.F.G.

JAVAROO
★ Out / Cap. (1980) ¶
Pleasant but pointless mainstream rock. Conceived more for radio programers than listeners of more amateurish persuasion, and thus a failure even on its own terms. — D.M.

JAY AND THE AMERICANS
★ Jay and the Americans Greatest Hits, Vol. 1 / U.A. (1965)
★ Jay and the Americans Greatest Hits, Vol. 2 / U.A. (1967)
From "She Cried" to "Cara Mia," about as aesthetically fulfilling as white-bread-and-margarine sandwiches. And someone ought to punish these boys for what they did to the beauty of "This Magic Moment." — D.M.

BLIND LEMON JEFFERSON
★ ★ ★ Black Snake Moan / Mile. (NA)
★ Master of the Blues, Vol. 1 / Bio. (1968)
★ Master of the Blues, Vol. 2 / Bio. (1971)
★ ★ ★ ★ Blind Lemon Jefferson / Mile. (1975)

★ ★ ★ Blind Lemon Jefferson, Vol. 2 / Mile. (NA)

★ ★ Blind Lemon Jefferson, Vol. 1 / Roots (NA)

★ ★ Blind Lemon Jefferson, Vol. 2 / Roots (NA)

★ ★ Blind Lemon Jefferson, Vol. 3 / Roots (NA)

Jefferson is probably the single most influential country-blues artist of the Twenties. Both his guitar and vocal styles were emulated by others immediately, and his impact continues to be felt today via such far-ranging blues-based musicians as John Hammond Jr., David Bromberg, Jerry Lee Lewis, B. B. King and any number of others.

All of the above recordings were originally made as 78s for Paramount between 1926 and 1929. The elimination of surface noises without distorting the tonal quality is best accomplished on the Milestone sets—guitar lines are readily discernible, lyrics generally comprehensible with little extra effort. The Biograph and Roots material is flatter sounding and less dynamic in its treble range, making it chiefly of historical rather than musical value. — I.M.

MORRIS JEFFERSON
★ ★ ★ Spank Your Blank Blank / Parach. (1978)

The centerpiece of a dance craze, believe it or not. Our copy includes a flyer with complete instructions for "Spank Your Blank Blank Dance Steps." Both disc and dance are pretty funky, too. A period classic, I guess. — D.M.

THE JEFFERSON AIRPLANE
★ ★ ★ Jefferson Airplane Takes Off / RCA (1966)
★ ★ ★ ★ Surrealistic Pillow / RCA (1967)
★ ★ ★ After Bathing at Baxter's / RCA (1967)
★ ★ ★ Crown of Creation / RCA (1968)
★ ★ ★ ★ Bless Its Pointed Little Head / RCA (1969)
★ ★ ★ ★ ★ Volunteers / RCA (1969)
★ ★ ★ Worst of the Jefferson Airplane / RCA (1970)
★ ★ ★ Thirty Seconds over Winterland / Grunt (1973)
★ ★ Early Flight / Grunt (1974) ¶
★ ★ ★ Flight Log 1966–1976 / Grunt (1977)

In the mid-Sixties an ambitious San Francisco artist/musician named Marty Balin decided to put together a band to play at his club, the Matrix. The band eventually became the Jefferson Airplane, the first of the San Francisco bands that would become famous in the 1967 acid-rock era. Initially the Airplane was a folk group, with Balin singing lead and a woman vocalist, Signe Anderson, backing him. *Jefferson Airplane Takes Off* is dominated by Balin's pensive ballads and a decidedly folk-rock feel.

Surrealistic Pillow established the band's subsequent sound and put the group over the top commercially. Anderson was replaced by Grace Slick, who brought two of her own songs from her former group, the Great Society, both of which became hit singles. "White Rabbit" and "Somebody to Love" became the Airplane's trademarks, and Slick took much of the attention away from Balin, despite his inclusion of songs like "3/5 of a Mile in Ten Seconds" and "Plastic Fantastic Lover."

After Bathing at Baxter's attempted to capture the psychedelic aura of the Airplane's live performances on record. The record was divided into sections, but everything ran together into a seamless whole. There were some great moments, such as "The Ballad of You, Me and Pooneil" and "Won't You Try"/"Saturday Afternoon." The density of the album's production was truly staggering, but it was an attempt doomed to ultimate, even if heroic, failure. You can't record an LSD trip, so the album ends up sounding like a bizarre indulgence.

The Airplane went back to single tracks for *Crown of Creation.* The band had already begun to fragment, and Balin's lyrics to "The House at Pooneil Corners" provided a chilling science-fiction metaphor for its disintegration. Slick contributed two strange and poetic songs, "Greasy Heart" and "Lather." But Kantner's title song was the most significant track because it indicated the band's future direction into science fiction.

The live album, *Bless Its Pointed Little Head,* did everything it was supposed to do, and a lot of what *Baxter's* couldn't. The band took a lot of chances live and consequently was not always very good, but when it was right, it was awesome; this record gets those moments down for posterity. Guitarist Jorma Kaukonen, bassist Jack Casady and drummer Spencer Dryden are the stars on this set, and they set up their post-Yardbirds, metal electro-attack with sublime logical frenzy.

Volunteers is the band's best studio album. It was also its last gasp as a group. The Balin/Kantner political anthem, "Volunteers," and its companion piece, Kantner's "We Can Be Together," were written and performed at the height of the Vietnam War resistance movement and provided a stirring tribute to the utopian idealism of the late Sixties. A lot of similar sentiments have dated badly since then, but these songs stand, if only for their naive realism and refusal to despair. The album also includes the definitive version of the apocalyptic "Wooden Ships," written by Kantner with help from David Crosby and Stephen Stills. Instrumentally, the band was never sharper, with Kaukonen and Casady playing up a firestorm, and Kaukonen's adaptation of the traditional "Good Shepherd" was terrific, a precursor of his best moments in his own band, Hot Tuna.

After Balin left, the group literally fell apart. A cursory listen to the wretched *Bark* (deleted) will prove the point. The band had added violinist Papa John Creach and replaced Spencer Dryden with Joey Covington, but there were major problems with material and overall focus. *Thirty Seconds over Winterland* was better because it was live and unburdened by the need for new material, but it wasn't as good as *Bless Its Pointed Little Head.* The greatest-hits collections are what you might expect, but this band is not best represented by such anthologies, although *Flight Log* is almost comprehensive enough to do the trick. — J.S.

THE JEFFERSON STARSHIP

★ ★ ★ ★ Blows against the Empire / RCA (1970)
★ ★ ★ Dragon Fly / Grunt (1974)
★ ★ ★ ★ ★ Red Octopus / Grunt (1975)
★ ★ Spitfire / Grunt (1976)
★ ★ ★ Earth / Grunt (1978)
★ ★ ★ ★ Gold / Grunt (1979)
★ ★ Freedom at Point Zero / Grunt (1979)
★ ★ Winds of Change / Grunt (1982)
The Jefferson Starship is the most obvious byproduct of the chemical breakdown of the Jefferson Airplane. When Airplane founder Marty Balin quit the group, the band splintered into two factions, the Paul Kantner/Grace Slick songwriting axis and the Jorma Kaukonen/Jack Casady instrumental duo (Hot Tuna). *Blows against the Empire* was really a Kantner solo album recorded while the Airplane was in its death throes. Jefferson Starship was the name Kantner used for the assemblage of San Francisco players on the album (including Slick; Jerry Garcia, Bill Kreutzmann and Mickey Hart from the Grateful Dead; and Kaukonen's brother, Peter), and the name stuck when the Airplane foundered and Kantner kept going.

Dragon Fly was really the first Starship album. Kantner and Slick fronted the group,

bringing only violinist Papa John Creach with them from the Airplane. Ex-Quicksilver Messenger Service member David Freiberg alternated on bass and keyboards with Pete Sears; John Barbata was the drummer; and Craig Chaquico played lead guitar. The instrumental personality of the Airplane was reduced to typical Seventies functional competence, making the band much less interesting but more disciplined than the Airplane. "Ride the Tiger" was as good a song as anything Kantner or Slick wrote for the Airplane, and "That's for Sure" was also good. But the rest was filler, with one major exception: Kantner's collaboration with Marty Balin, "Caroline," the album's best song, on which Balin performed a tremendous vocal.

When Balin agreed to lend a more complete hand to the making of *Red Octopus,* the Starship came into its own. Balin contributed to five songs and wrote a blockbuster ballad, "Miracles," which became the biggest hit single the Starship or Airplane ever produced. His presence inspired the rest of the band to excellence. Slick came up with two of her best songs in years, "Play on Love" and "Fast Buck Freddie." *Red Octopus* was a triumph for Balin, Kantner and Slick, one of the best albums of 1975 and proof positive that rock musicians can age gracefully.

Spitfire and *Earth* were disappointments after *Red Octopus.* They suffered not only by comparison, but from apparent fatigue. Slick sounds strained, Kantner overstuffed (on *Earth,* he's almost absent) and Balin either muzzled or uninterested. Creach was gone altogether. By *Freedom,* so was Balin. Mickey Thomas took over Balin's spot opposite Slick, completing the band's evolution into a fairly faceless echo of its former personality. *Winds of Change* did not bode well for the band's future. — J.S.

JEFFREE

★ ★ Jeffree / MCA (1979)
Middling soul group. — D.M.

GARLAND JEFFREYS

★ ★ ★ ★ Ghost Writer / A&M (1977)
★ ★ ★ ★ One-Eyed Jack / A&M (1978)
★ ★ ★ American Boy and Girl / A&M (1979)
★ ★ ★ ★ Escape Artist / Epic (1981)
★ ★ ★ Rock 'n' Roll Adult / Epic (1981)
A classic New York rocker—mulatto, theatrical, obsessed with themes of identity and rage—Jeffreys moves from rock to reggae to balladry on the edge of soft pop. He's perhaps a better writer than performer (and bet-

ter lyricist than melodist), but several tracks on these albums are genuine classics. *Ghost Writer* contains both "Wild in the Streets," his great 1973 near miss of a hit single, and the marvelous *hommage à cinéma,* "35 Millimeter Dreams," among others. *One-Eyed Jack* chronicles an obsession with Jackie Robinson and other emblems of American racial hostility and ambiguity, as seen by someone who's lived most of its difficulties. *American Boy and Girl* is a more difficult concept, dedicated to the runaways on New York's infamous Minnesota Strip, the kids who whore and hustle (and often die) while still in their teens. It doens't really come off, but its compassion lends the album a certain substance, anyhow.

Escape Artist is musically Jeffrey's most powerful recording, albeit his least eccentric one. "R.O.C.K.," "Graveyard Rock" and a brilliant cover of "96 Tears" establish Jeffreys' credentials as a hotshot rock & roller, and "Christine" and "True Confessions" are typically intricate and intriguing ballads. A live album, *Rock 'n' Roll Adult* covers much of the same ground, plus a selection of his best early work, but without adding much to the original versions.
— D.M.

JELLY
★ ★ ★ A True Story / Asy. (1977)
They look terribly unlikely—a pop vocal trio shouldn't contain a very plain woman, a tweedy John Le Carré type and a hirsute, bespectacled third party who could pass for an unfrocked minister—but they sound fairly swell. Now if only some wag at Asylum hadn't persisted in booking them with the company's other big pop act, Bread. Thank God the Peanut Butter Conspiracy folded during the psychedelic era. — D.M.

SNUFFY JENKINS AND PAPPY SHERRILL
★ 33 Years / Roun. (1971)
★ ★ ★ Crazy Water Barn Dance / Roun. (1976) ¶
★ ★ Snuffy and Pappy / Roun. (1976)
Basically a novelty act of exceptional technical competence, Jenkins (banjo) and Sherrill's (fiddle) second Rounder LP, *Crazy Water,* is a much livelier and more virtuoso set than their first or their third. Jenkins, though not as commercially successful as Earl Scruggs, is probably equally responsible for the development of the three-finger banjo style that became one of the backbones of bluegrass. — I.M.

WAYLON JENNINGS
★ ★ Waylon Jennings / Voc. (1969)
★ ★ The Best of Waylon Jennings / RCA (1970)
★ ★ ★ Singer of Sad Songs / RCA (1970)
★ ★ ★ The Taker/Tulsa / RCA (1971)
★ ★ ★ Good Hearted Woman / RCA (1972)
★ ★ ★ Ladies Love Outlaws / RCA (1972)
★ ★ ★ Lonesome, On'ry and Mean / RCA (1972)
★ ★ Heartaches by the Number / Camd. (1972)
★ ★ ★ Honky Tonk Heroes / RCA (1973)
★ ★ This Time / RCA (1974)
★ ★ The Only Daddy That'll Walk the Line / RCA (1974)
★ ★ The Ramblin' Man / RCA (1974)
★ ★ ★ Dreamin' My Dreams / RCA (1975)
★ ★ Ruby, Don't Take Your Love to Town / Camd. (1975)
★ ★ ★ Waylon Live / RCA (1976)
★ ★ Country Boy and Country Girl / RCA (1976) ¶
★ ★ Mackintosh and T.J. / RCA (1976) ¶
★ ★ ★ Are You Ready for the Country / RCA (1976)
★ ★ ★ Dark Side of Fame / Camd. (1976)
★ ★ ★ Ol' Waylon / RCA (1977)
★ ★ ★ Waylon and Willie / RCA (1978)
★ ★ I've Always Been Crazy / RCA (1978)
★ ★ ★ What Goes Around Comes Around / RCA (1979)
★ ★ ★ Waylon Jennings' Greatest Hits / RCA (1979)
★ ★ ★ Music Man / RCA (1980)

The central fact of Waylon Jennings' career is not his status, along with Willie Nelson's, as one of country music's outlaws, but the power and durability of his big, rolling voice. He can use that voice to belt and purr; sometimes, as on his two versions of "MacArthur Park," his gruff fervor seems almost ludicrous, but he can also convey enough passion and vulnerability to elevate such mediocre pop and country vehicles as "Sweet Caroline" or "Ruby, Don't Take Your Love to Town."

Born in West Texas in 1937, Waylon found work as a teenage disc jockey in Lubbock and became Buddy Holly's protégé. He became bass player for the Crickets in 1958, but Holly died the next year in the legendary Iowa plane crash (Jennings had given his seat on the fatal flight to the Big Bopper) and Waylon began working bars in Phoenix, where he first met Willie Nelson.

In 1965, Waylon signed with RCA and

moved in with Johnny Cash just outside of Nashville. The folk-tinged country albums he cut over the next four years are mostly out of print; *Heartaches by the Number* culls "country favorites" from that phase, but "Nashville Bum," from *The Only Daddy That'll Walk the Line,* makes early mock of the system he came to loathe.

The Best of Waylon Jennings marked the end of that period, and within a year Waylon said goodbye to the Opry shitkickers with *Singer of Sad Songs* ("Honky Tonk Woman") and *The Taker/Tulsa* ("Sunday Mornin' Comin' Down" was one of its four Kristofferson songs).

Waylon broadened his mystique with help from Willie Nelson on *Good Hearted Woman* and, still working with name sessionmen in Nashville, enlisted such quirky songwriters as Mickey Newbury and Billy Joe Shaver on his next three albums (all cut in one year of expanding crossover popularity). *This Time* and *The Ramblin' Man* showed Waylon retrenching, using sparer arrangements for sets of introspective songs. *Dreamin' My Dreams,* produced by Waylon with Jack Clement, completed his shift out of the RCA studio formula. The resolute beat of "Are You Sure Hank Done It This Way" and "Waymore's Blues" (in part a tribute to Jimmie Rodgers) joined with "Bob Wills Is Still the King" (live and fierce in Austin) to showcase a determinedly history-minded Waylon.

The first weeks of 1977 saw the release of *Outlaws,* an anthology on which Waylon joined with Willie Nelson, Tompall Glaser and his own wife, Jessi Colter, to affirm their collective image as outsiders—and to prove their marketability. The Waylon-Willie duet, "Good Hearted Woman," became a hit single.

As a result of the attention paid *Outlaws,* Waylon was ready to address a new audience with a Neil Young title song: *Are You Ready for the Country* is laced with rock guitar, but as with *Ol' Waylon,* the real message is that the singer need not concern himself with labels.

Waylon is still tugging up roots; *Are You Ready's* "Old Friend" celebrates Buddy Holly's enduring presence, and *Ol' Waylon* contains an Elvis medley and two tributes to the Willie/Waylon/Texas axis.

With *Waylon and Willie,* released early in 1978, the two veterans earned their credentials as reclusive pop stars. But the good news, as Waylon's cover of Stevie Nicks' "Gold Dust Woman" shows, was his easy

power on both rockers and ballads. Unfortunately, his work since then has mainly marked time, the highlight being a beautiful rendition of Bob McDill's "Amanda," on *Greatest Hits.*   — F.S.

JETHRO TULL

★ ★ ★ ★ **This Was** / Chrys. (1969)
★ ★ ★ ★ **Stand Up** / Chrys. (1969)
★ ★ ★ **Benefit** / Chrys. (1970)
★ ★ ★ **Aqualung** / Chrys. (1971)
★ ★ **Thick as a Brick** / Chrys. (1972)
★ ★ ★ ★ **Living in the Past** / Chrys. (1972)
★ ★ **Passion Play** / Chrys. (1973)
★ ★ **War Child** / Chrys. (1974)
★ ★ ★ **Minstrel in the Gallery** / Chrys. (1975)
★ ★ ★ **MU—The Best of Jethro Tull** / Chrys. (1976)
★ ★ **Too Old to Rock 'n' Roll; Too Young to Die** / Chrys. (1976)
★ ★ ★ **Songs from the Wood** / Chrys. (1977)
★ ★ ★ **Repeat** / Chrys. (1977)
★ ★ **Heavy Horses** / Chrys. (1978)
★ ★ ★ **Bursting Out** / Chrys. (1978)
★ ★ ★ ★ **A** / Chrys. (1980)
★ ★ ★ **Broadsword and the Beast** / Chrys. (1982)

Jethro Tull was originally, at best, a gut-busting fusion of jazz, R&B and progressive rock. Nothing the group has done since can equal the energy of the first album, *This Was,* a 1969 release that featured guitarist Mick Abrahams. *Stand Up* replaces Abrahams with Martin Barre, but like all subsequent Tull releases, it is dominated by flutist/vocalist Ian Anderson. *Stand Up* contains some of Tull's best music, but here is also the beginning of their characteristic diddling around.

Benefit finds Anderson still conceiving three- and four-minute songs, but *Aqualung* begins the slide into semi-autobiographical morality plays. Typically, *Aqualung* can be hummed, though it is not danceable. *Thick as a Brick* is a single song divided over two sides, with relatively undifferentiated movements. *Living in the Past* recapitulates the first five, adds some previously unavailable British singles and a live side from Carnegie Hall in 1970, which is based on "Dharma for One," off *This Was.* It is the essential package.

The rest are mostly interesting because of the pomposity of their themes. *War Child* is partially orchestrated and thoroughly eclectic; *Minstrel* has Anderson's most successful fusion of Elizabethan and rock structures; *Too Old* is a canard. *MU* spans their work

from 1972 to 1975, but the selections are poorly chosen, especially compared to the well-executed *Living. Songs from the Wood* abounds with unadulterated Elizabethan boogie; this album showed that Tull was moving toward the Fairport Convention/Steeleye Span school of British folk rock. The folk-rock move was underscored on *A* by the addition of ex-Fairport bassist Dave Pegg to the lineup, which was highlighted by the spectacular guest performance of Eddie Jobson on keyboards and electric violin.
— A.N.

JOAN JETT
★ ★ ★ ★ ★ **Bad Reputation / Bdwalk (1981)**
★ ★ ★ ★ **I Love Rock & Roll / Bdwalk (1981)**
Jett's sudden rise to fame is a success story that flies in the face of the record industry "recession." The ex-Runaways vocalist/guitarist released *Bad Reputation,* her first LP, in the States as an Ariola import and quickly sold 22,000 copies, at which point she and manager Kenny Laguna began paying for their own domestic pressings. Jett took to the road in part to help finance her record and became an overnight sensation, parlaying her sassy stage manner and no-nonsense hard-rock chops into one of the hottest stage shows of the time. *Bad Reputation* is a hard-rock masterpiece, reworking gems like Gary Glitter's "Do You Wanna Touch Me (Oh Yeah)," the Isley Brothers' "Shout" and Sam the Sham's "Wooly Bully" and adding catchy originals like the title track and "Let Me Go." The album also features session performances by Steve Jones, Paul Cook and Sean Tyla. *I Love* finds Jett backed up by her touring band, the Black-hearts, on another tight and jumping set highlighted by the title track (which became one of the surprise hits of 1982) and a remake of the Christmas classic "The Little Drummer Boy." — J.S.

JEZZREEL
★ ★ ★ **Great Jah Jah Showcase / Wac. (1979)**
One of the best reggae records to be recorded in America, *Showcase* offers extended dub-ups of roots songs awash in shimmering echo and crashing cymbals. The rhythms are hard, the vocals convincing. — R.F.G.

JILTED JOHN
★ ★ ★ **True Love Stories / EMI (NA) ¶**
Tongue-in-cheek soap opera songs about teenage life in England. Best moment is the hilarious "Baz's Party." — J.S.

THE JIVE FIVE
★ ★ ★ ★ ★ **Here We Are! / Ambient (1982)**
Best known for their 1961 hit, "My True Story," this doo-wop/soul group never scored significantly again until this remodeled record was issued. Vocalist Eugene Pitt is a warm and moving stylist, and when he attacks Steely Dan's "Hey Nineteen," he both creates a moving tribute to the soulmen and women of yore and establishes that there's still vitality in such styles. Simply beautiful. — D.M.

JIM AND JESSE
★ ★ ★ **Diesel on My Tail / Epic (1967)**
★ ★ ★ **Banjo in the Hills / Star. (NA)**
Country singing duo that's more interesting than most, because it has folk roots and a sense of history. — D.M.

THE JODIMARS
★ ★ ★ **Well Now Dig This / Bulld. (1970)**
Fifties trio rocks pretty well; includes some members of Bill Haley's Comets. Inessential except for period collectors. — D.M.

BILLY JOEL
★ **Piano Man / Col. (1973)**
★ **Streetlife Serenade / Col. (1974)**
★ ★ **Turnstiles / Col. (1976)**
★ ★ ★ **The Stranger / Col. (1977)**
★ ★ ★ **52nd Street / Col. (1978)**
★ ★ **Glass Houses / Col. (1980)**
★ ★ **Songs in the Attic / Col. (1981)**
★ ★ **The Nylon Curtain / Col. (1982)**
This Long Island singer/songwriter and virtuoso keyboardist has earned an avid cult following by wasting his talent with self-dramatizing kitsch. At least that's the story with the first three albums *(Piano Man, Streetlife Serenade, Turnstiles),* which together have one good song, "New York State of Mind," on *Turnstiles. The Stranger* was a considerable improvement. Joel's singing, which has often and aptly been compared to the monotone of Harry Chapin, was given more effective support, which gave him a pair of hits, "Just the Way You Are" and "Only the Good Die Young," which also seemed to reflect an increasingly mature lyrical perspective. *52nd Street* went further toward rock, though even its best numbers— "Big Shot," "52nd Street," "My Life"—were closer to Paul McCartney pop. *Glass Houses* is Joel's attempt to establish once and for all that he is a rocker to the core, which is a nearly disastrous error, not so much because he can't rock as because he is better at several other things. "It's Still Rock 'n' Roll to Me" may have redeemed the project com-

mercially, but artistically the album fails, and as a career move, it was pointless.

Songs in the Attic is a live set, focusing on songs written earlier in Joel's career, which serves mostly to demonstrate that (a) onstage he's no natural, and (b) he has become a better craftsman as his career progressed.

The Nylon Curtain is Joel's attempt to establish himself as a "meaningful" rock commentator in the continuum of (roughly) Dylan-to-Lennon-to-Browne-to-Springsteen. But he is neither musically or lyrically original enough to justify the banality of his "insights," and to the extent that these songs are meant to be political statements, they are cowardly. "Allentown" is about as defeatist as even a song about unemployment can be, the product of Joel's attempt to provide the kind of bogus objectivity that makes straight newspaper and TV journalism a bore. And "Saigon Nights," a Vietnam song that refuses to take sides, borders on obscenity. The concept that anyone, much less a major pop craftsman, lived through the war without ever acquiring an attitude about it (without ever understanding why that war was *not* a war like all others, even—especially—for the soldiers who fought it) says more about Joel's ultimate shallowness than anything else one needs to mention. Although *The Nylon Curtain* was Joel begging to be taken seriously, there simply isn't any way to deal with him except as a lightweight. — D.M.

DAVID JOHANSEN

★ ★ ★ David Johansen / Blue S. (1978)
★ ★ ★ ★ In Style / Blue S. (1979)
★ ★ ★ Here Comes the Night / Blue S. (1981)
★ ★ ★ ★ Live It Up / Blue S. (1982)
It seemed unlikely, after the breakup of the New York Dolls, that lead singer David Johansen would make records on his own that displayed both power and sensitivity. *David Johansen* retains some of his old group's heaviness without quite capturing its protopunk panache. Ably abetted by former Doll Sylvain Sylvain, the record does reveal a previously untapped (or drowned out) tenderness, as in "Lonely Tenement."

The last song on *David Johansen,* "Frenchette," supplies some clues for the direction of his next album. With its references to the Marvelettes, the Ronettes and "Levi Stubbs," the song anticipates the focus of most of *In Style:* a weird version of a modern-day soul record. From the opening Four Tops tribute, "Melody," through the beautifully rolling rhythms of "Swaheto Woman," Johansen sings with a passion and commitment un-

matched by anything else in his career. And "Flamingo Road," a slowly building epic, shows a maturing of the man's talents, which only makes the following effort, *Here Comes the Night,* that much more disappointing. Although the songwriting is still there (especially on "You Fool You" and "My Obsession"), the stripped-down metallic feel of the music seems like a step back after the liberating looseness of *In Style.* Johansen recovered his poise, however, with the live album, *Live It Up,* a wonderful medley of what he does best: pathos and comedy, oldies and originals. Worth it for the Animals medley and "Build Me Up Buttercup" alone.
— W.K.

ELTON JOHN

★ ★ ★ Elton John / MCA (1970)
★ ★ ★ Tumbleweed Connection / MCA (1971)
★ ★ ★ 11-17-70 / Uni. (1971)
★ ★ ★ Madman across the Water / MCA (1971)
★ ★ ★ Honky Chateau / MCA (1972)
★ ★ ★ Don't Shoot Me, I'm Only the Piano Player / MCA (1972)
★ ★ ★ ★ Goodbye Yellow Brick Road / MCA (1973)
★ ★ Caribou / MCA (1974)
★ ★ ★ ★ ★ Greatest Hits / MCA (1974)
★ Empty Sky / MCA (1975)
★ ★ ★ Capt. Fantastic and the Brown Dirt Cowboy / MCA (1975)
★ ★ ★ Rock of the Westies / MCA (1975)
★ Here and There / MCA (1976)
★ ★ Blue Moves / MCA (1976)
★ ★ ★ Greatest Hits, Vol. 2 / MCA (1977)
★ ★ ★ A Single Man / MCA (1978)
★ Victim of Love / MCA (1979)
★ 21 at 33 / MCA (1980)
★ ★ The Fox / Gef. (1981)
★ ★ Jump Up / Gef. (1982)
As one of the most massively popular stars of the Seventies, Elton John symptomized some of what was best and a great deal of the worst of that decade's pop music. John's hits reveal little personal style, but a great deal of musical personality. While the best of them are fresh-faced and innocent ("Rocket Man," "Daniel," "Your Song," "The Bitch Is Back"), or cheerfully stylized pastiches of his antecedents and superiors ("Burn Down the Mission," "Honky Cat," "Crocodile Rock"), the worst of them ("Bennie and the Jets," "Saturday Night's Alright for Fighting") are bathetic, wallowing in sentimentality and cliché. Always, John was burdened with Bernie Taupin's opaque and pompous lyrics, the most ambitious of which defy

comprehension, much less analysis, although at times ("Rocket Man") their quirks made them charming.

John seemed to be willing to sing almost any kind of pop, and although one might sometimes question his ability in some forms, he did pull off light soul with "Philadelphia Freedom" and a kind of country soul with "Country Comfort." But as often as John made his lust to cover the pop spectrum an effective tool, he was liable to fall back into utterly messy self-indulgence. In general, this made his singles much more successful than his albums, even the best of which are radically uneven, with good songs following bad in a hopelessly merry hodgepodge. As a live performer, John has a tendency to sabotage himself with campy cutesiness (displayed to an absolute extreme on *11/17/70*), coming on like the world's most idiotic ham. If this is charming, it leaves a lot of listeners wondering why. And it totally undercuts any claim John might have to being taken seriously as an artist, so no one remotely serious could miss this wildly when it was time to lighten up. John restrained himself from such comedy on the albums, but there a little madness was necessary, since the closer they came to being pure filler, the more overreaching Taupin's lyrics became.

John worked with extremely skillful bands, and Gus Dudgeon's production was extremely crisp and always to the point. The most outstanding musical characteristic of his records, however, tends to be Paul Buckmaster's lush string arrangements, which serve as lovely counterpoint to John's punchy rhythms. When John attempted to make straight rock records with a half English, half American band of sessionmen *(Caribou, Rock of the Westies),* the results were credible mostly when he achieved the same sounds he'd been getting in London. His hard rock was never credible, ironically enough, since he apparently only did hard rock to gain credibility with the one segment of the pop world that resisted him. After *Blue Moves,* John and Taupin split apart and Elton recorded little for some time. The final three MCA albums represent lame efforts to contemporize his music to disco standards, but in his heart John is either a light rocker or a straight pop singer. Funk is quite beyond him. Even Thom Bell's production on *Here and There* is wasted.

The Fox reunited Elton with Taupin at least part of the time, but while the pair were more interesting together than they ever could have been apart, the bubble had burst. Had he not become an international celebrity, Elton John's music would be recalled today as pleasant radio fodder, and nothing more would be expected of it. But in the artistic cult atmosphere of the Seventies, with its emphasis on the singer/songwriter, more pressure was brought to bear. If one accepts this as a false standard by which to judge most pop singers, then one may enjoy the first *Greatest Hits* album and perhaps some of the bright moments on a few of the more conceptual later records *(Capt. Fantastic, Goodbye Yellow Brick Road, Rock of the Westies).* But if one seeks meaning and genuine passion, one must move on. — D.M.

ROBERT JOHN
★ ★ **Back on the Street / EMI (NA)**
★ ★ **Robert John / EMI (1979)**
John's had a couple of Top Ten pop singles, notably "The Lion Sleeps Tonight" in 1972 for Atlantic, and "Sad Eyes" from *Robert John,* and he's made the charts a few other times as well. But he's mostly a stodgy vocalist, not even exciting enough to be labeled today's Brian Hyland. Second-rate Neil Sedaka is nearer the mark. — D.M.

SAMMY JOHNS
★ **The Van / War. (1977)**
Southern folk musician was transformed into a vapid Hollywood songwriter on the strength of "Chevy Van," a simpy song about sex in the back of a Chevy van. This led to *The Van,* a soundtrack for a film based loosely on that very concept. Phew! — J.S.

BLIND WILLIE JOHNSON
★ ★ ★ ★ **Blues / Folk. (1957)**
★ ★ ★ ★ **1927–30 / Folk. (1965)**
★ ★ ★ ★ **Praise God I'm Satisfied / Yazoo (1976)**
The greatest rural spiritual artist to record. Johnson's ability is riveting and revealing; Steve Calt's notes on the Yazoo LP, which claim that Johnson's playing is sometimes "so perfect that it cannot be improved upon, even in one's imagination," is only a slight exaggeration. Johnson may be the finest bottleneck guitarist in the country-blues tradition, and his voice—a growl that sounds like the hellhound Robert Johnson feared—is similarly exalted, a marvelous instrument whether speaking in the cadences of the pulpit or simply running free through his music.

Johnson is a completely apocalyptic writer, and his strangest songs sound like something Cotton Mather made up to frighten particularly backsliding parishioners. Every catastrophe is seen as an ominous working out of divine judgment, and a promise of worse to come. That is, Blind Willie preached Christian terror, not Christian love (for that, turn to Mississippi John Hurt), and it is a measure of his genius that he makes cynical New York sophisticates sit up and take notice nearly sixty years after his first music was recorded.

Johnson recorded a number of laments that would latter become standards—"If I Had My Way," "Dark Was the Night and Cold the Ground," "Motherless Children," "Jesus Make Up My Dying Bed," "You're Gonna Need Somebody on Your Bond," "Keep Your Lamp Trimmed and Burning," "I Just Can't Keep from Crying" and "Let Your Light Shine on Me." These songs have been covered by rock groups from the Grateful Dead to Led Zeppelin, from Hot Tuna to Taj Mahal, indicating the breadth of Johnson's influence. The Yazoo LP, which features the turbulent and frightening title track and other late-Twenties tracks, is one of the few rural black albums in existence. — D.M./J.S.

GENERAL JOHNSON
★ ★ ★ **General Johnson / Ari. (1976)** ¶
The former Chairman of the Board lead singer, General Johnson is also a creditable songwriter ("It Will Stand," "Patches"). This solo album is a bit limited in scope and includes some annoyingly stock arrangements, but it also has its share of nice moments—"All in the Family," for instance. — J.MC.

LINTON KWESI JOHNSON
★ ★ ★ ★ ★ **Dread, Beat, and Blood / Virgin/Heartb. (1979)**
★ ★ ★ ★ **Forces of Victory / Mango (1979)**
★ ★ ★ ★ **Bass Culture / Mango (1980)**
Proof of poetry's power: given the immediacy of headlines, fired by angry revulsion, but structured by rational analysis. Linton Kwesi Johnson is a U.K.-based poet and political activist who articulates the oppressive dark side of British life as experienced by minorities and the working class. He integrates poetry with reggae rhythms ("I write with a reggae bass in mind," he has said) and electric textures to produce records of unrelenting intensity. *Dread, Beat, and Blood* is a nightmarish, frightening record that drips with violence and inescapable menace. *Forces* and *Bass Culture* are more tuneful but still compelling examples of crushing rhythms intensifying vérité lyrics. — R.F.G.

LONNIE JOHNSON
★ ★ ★ ★ **The Blues of Lonnie Johnson / Swag. (NA)**
★ ★ ★ ★ ★ **Eddie Lang and Lonnie Johnson / Swag. (NA)**
★ ★ ★ ★ **Eddie Lang and Lonnie Johnson Vol. 2 / Swag. (NA)**
★ ★ ★ ★ ★ **Mr. Johnson's Blues / Swag. (NA)**
★ ★ ★ ★ ★ **Tomorrow Night / King (NA)**
★ ★ ★ **Lonnie Johnson / RCA (NA)**
★ ★ ★ **Losing Game / Prest. (1960)**
★ ★ ★ ★ **The Originator of Modern Guitar Blues / Blues B. (1980)**
Lonnie Johnson was the first great guitarist of the twentieth century. His originality and the breadth of his influence (Robert Johnson to Charlie Christian to B.B. King) are stunning. He recorded in a variety of contexts—on solo guitar, in guitar duets, as accompanist for country-blues singers, in jazz bands—and he also played piano, violin and mandolin. By 1912 his reputation as a master guitarist was already established. He accompanied Spencer Williams, Victoria Spivey, Louis Armstrong's Hot Five, Texas Alexander and Duke Ellington. His jazz playing was superb, and it was influential in the most unlikely places. Robert Johnson claimed to be related to him.

In 1929 he began to record guitar duets with Eddie Lang, vibrant and classic blues/jazz performances that are reissued on the Swaggie sides. Many collectors have expressed interest only in Johnson's early years, but he continued to mature as a guitarist and especially as a singer and recorded exceptional blues records in the Forties and Fifties. The Blues Boy and King albums are every bit the classics his earlier works were. — J.S.

ROBERT JOHNSON
★ ★ ★ ★ ★ **King of the Delta Blues Singers / Col. (1961)**
★ ★ ★ ★ ★ **King of the Delta Blues Singers, Vol. 2 / Col. (1970)**
These records document the work of a man universally regarded as the greatest practitioner of the country-blues genre identified with the Mississippi delta area, where so much of it was nurtured. Johnson synthesized the styles of Skip James, Henry Townsend, Son House and other blues greats before him. Johnson was undoubtedly at the height of his powers when these sides were recorded in 1935 to 1936, and he seems to make magic, his performance is so driven. His voice and slide-guitar playing complement each other perfectly as he provides a

running commentary on the troubles that plague him and would eventually lead to his violent death in 1937. Johnson's shadowy legend and brutal, dead-serious explication of it in song constitute one of the most emotional chapters in blues history, and it's all here in two neat packages. Even aside from the great songs, his bottleneck guitar playing alone is worth listening to, because it's influenced virtually everyone who's played in that style since. — J.S.

ROBERT JOHNSON
★ ★ **Close Personal Friend / Ens. (1978)**
★ **The Memphis Demos / Ens. (1980), Br. imp.**
Johnson suffers from session syndrome. Though he's worked with Isaac Hayes, Anne Peebles and even the Rolling Stones, a lack of strong original material cannot be rescued by any amount of dazzling guitar work. This Robert Johnson is not to be confused with the King of the Delta Blues. — ML.H.

SYL JOHNSON
★ ★ ★ ★ **Back for a Taste of Your Love / Hi (1973)** ¶
★ ★ ★ ★ **Total Explosion / Hi (1976)** ¶
★ ★ ★ **Uptown Shakedown / Hi (NA)**
Syl Johnson's music is one of the last soul styles to incorporate Southern soul with a bluesman's sensibility. His first Hi album, *Back for a Taste of Your Love,* is in an Al Green mold. "We Did It" and "Back for a Taste" are seamless and uptempo, like the Green hits of the period (1973), though "The Love You Left Behind" is brash and rugged—a Hi anomaly. *Total Explosion,* recorded three years later, is even rougher and more assertive; it shows scarcely a hint of Green's influence. *Explosion*'s two hit singles, "Take Me to the River" and "I Only Have Your Love," are blues shuffles with harmonica intros. — J.MC.

TOMMY JOHNSON AND ISHMAN BRACEY
★ ★ ★ ★ **Tommy Johnson and Ishman Bracey / Roots (NA), Br. imp.**
Two of the best of the Delta blues singers run through their stuff on these 1928 recordings. This is the bulk of each man's material, although some slightly later sides by each are collected on various country-blues anthologies. Of the two, Johnson is by far the more important: his "Canned Heat," "Maggie Campbell Blues" and others made him one of the most influential blues singers in the Mississippi region for more than thirty years, until his death in 1956. Traces of his

sound may be found in singers as various as Howlin' Wolf and Otis Spann—which is to say, bluesmen from the roughest to the slickest. Bracey's appeal is more limited, especially because his singing was so nasal, but he is a fine piano and guitar player. — D.M.

TOM JOHNSTON
★ ★ **Everything You've Heard Is True / War. (1979)**
Johnston was an original member of the Doobie Brothers, but when they went toward pop disco with Michael McDonald as lead vocalist, he split to go off on his own. This album has songs that sound a great deal like early Doobies, and vocals that do the same. But it lacks that band's drive and freshness, which is probably one reason why the rest of the group let Johnston go. — D.M.

JO JO GUNNE
★ ★ ★ ★ **Jo Jo Gunne / Asy. (NA)**
This band grew from the breakup of Spirit. Built around Jay Ferguson and Mark Andes, they released four superb albums between 1972 and 1974, all (except the second) excellent. High-energy tromp. — A.N.

JO JO ZEP AND THE FALCONS
★ ★ **Don't Waste It / Oz (1976), Aust. imp.**
★ ★ ★ **Whip It Out / Oz (1977), Aust. imp.**
★ ★ ★ **So Young / Oz (1978), Aust. imp.**
★ ★ ★ ★ **Jo Jo Zep and the Falcons / Rockb. (1979), Br. imp.**
★ ★ ★ **Screaming Targets / Mush. (1979), Aust./Br. imp.**
★ ★ ★ **Hats Off Step Lively / Mush. (1980), Aust./Br. imp.**
★ **Taking the Wraps Off / Rockb. (1980), Br. imp.**
★ ★ ★ **Screaming Targets / Col. (1980)**
★ ★ ★ **Step Lively / Col. (1981)**
★ ★ ★ **Dexterity / Mush. (1981) Aust. imp.**
The Falcons began as a dynamite rhythm & blues band, with a touch of Melbourne quirkiness. Their early recordings (the English release *Jo Jo Zep and the Falcons* compiles the best of them) have the good-humored rawness of the best pub rock. But like many riveting live bands, the Falcons suffered in the translation to vinyl, as the relative tedium of *Taking the Wraps Off* attests.

Singer and saxophonist Joe Camillieri led the band to moderate Oz pop success in the late Seventies with a slicker sound and a reggae flavor. A certain anonymity and blandness accompanied this transformation, although the band did produce some fine singles. "So Young" (covered but never released by Elvis Costello) and "Hit and Run" are both featured on the U.S. release of *Screaming Targets,* though in general this album suffers from the band's having listened too hard to English artists covering some of the same ground, Graham Parker and the ska bands from the Two Tone label in particular.

Step Lively combines the best of the 1980 and 1981 Australian releases. Through the routes of reggae and disco, Camillieri seems to be heading back toward the sources of black music, from which his original R&B strength was drawn. On *Step Lively,* with the big brass sound and lavish production of "Sweet Honey Sweet" and "Tighten Up," the band is closer than it has been on record to a truly effective and original variation on the pop-soul-ska themes they've been exploring. — S.M.

FLOYD JONES—EDDIE TAYLOR
★ ★ ★ **Masters of Modern Blues, Vol. 3 / Test. (1966)**

Jones and Taylor each have a side as featured vocalist-guitarist on this Chicago blues LP. They're only middling performers in the genre, but they've backed up some much bigger names. And with accompanists such as Big Walter Horton, the redoubtable Otis Spann and drummer Fred Below, this is almost a Muddy Waters session without the boss. — D.M.

GEORGE JONES
★ ★ ★ **Nothing Ever Hurt Me / Epic (1973)**
★ ★ ★ **Grand Tour / Epic (1974)**
★ ★ ★ **Best of George Jones / Epic (1975)**
★ ★ ★ **George Jones / Epic (1975)**
★ ★ ★ **I Wanta Sing / Epic (1975)**
★ ★ ★ ★ **Memories of Us / Epic (1975)**
★ ★ ★ **Picture of Me / Epic (1975)**
★ ★ ★ ★ ★ **The Battle / Epic (1976)**
★ ★ ★ **Alone Again / Epic (1976)**
★ ★ ★ **All Time Greatest Hits, Vol. 1 / Epic (1977)**
★ ★ ★ **Bartender's Blues / Epic (1978)**
★ ★ ★ **Encore / Epic (1981)**
★ ★ ★ **Country Gospel / Gusto (1981)**
★ ★ ★ **Still the Same Old Me / Epic (1981)**
★ ★ ★ ★ ★ **Double Gold George Jones / Musi. (NA)**
★ ★ ★ ★ **Sixteen Greatest Hits / Trip (NA)**
★ ★ ★ **Crown Prince of Country Music / Power (NA)**
★ ★ ★ ★ **Golden Hits / Star. (NA)**
★ ★ ★ **I Am What I Am / Epic (NA)**
★ ★ ★ **White Lightnin' / Chis. (NA)**

George Jones is known to the popular audience for his 1965 crossover country hit, "The Race Is On," and as Tammy Wynette's ex-husband. (He has recorded several duet LPs with Wynette, and another series with Melba Montgomery.) But Jones is really the last pure country singer. He still sings as he did when growing up in the Forties in East Texas honky-tonk territory; he is the most uncompromising of country artists, blithely ignoring every trend. His songs, which lean heavier to the romantic rather than boozing side of the honky-tonk tradition, are perhaps best known to concert audiences; he has never been a particularly huge record seller.

Jones' early-Sixties sides for Musicor are certainly his most consistent work. Such hits as "All I Have to Offer You Is Me," "White Lightning," "The Race Is On," "Window Up Above" and "Good Year for the Roses" established him as an influence among other country artists beyond his commercial stature. His Epic sides are much less raw, smoothed out by Billy Sherrill's formula productions. Still, he made his best album with Sherrill, *The Battle,* an album-long eulogy for his marital breakup with Wynette. The title song is a classic, as is the album's cover, which features framed portraits of Jones and Wynette on either side of a white bed, at the foot of which is a pair of empty boots. It seems to say everything, at least until he sings. — D.M.

GEORGE JONES AND GENE PITNEY
★ ★ ★ **It's Country Time Again / Musi. (1962) ¶**

This is just the kind of stuff Jones did with Melba Montgomery (and later, Tammy Wynette), but here Pitney's falsetto takes the female role—no small task for an Italian kid from the Bronx. It works, though. The material runs to country standards (a terrific "Mockin' Bird Hill") with one solo number apiece. A weird but often excellent record; worth digging up if you dig country, Pitney or both. — D.M.

GRACE JONES
★ **Portfolio / Is. (1977)**
★ **Fame / Is. (1978)**
★ **Muse / Is. (1979)**
★ **Warm Leatherette / Is. (1980)**
★ **Nightclubbing / Is. (1981)**

Jones, an ex-model, is better known for the elaborate stage settings of her live performances than for her singing. Her records are the least interesting part of her career. Buy the video instead. — J.S.

RICKIE LEE JONES

★ ★ ★ ★ ★ **Rickie Lee Jones** / War. (1979)
★ ★ ★ ★ **Pirates** / War. (1981)

Discovered by Warner Bros. honcho producers Lenny Waronker and Russ Titelman, this eccentric Beat goddess burst upon the pop scene in 1979 with a platinum debut album that presented her as the female answer to Van Morrison/Bruce Springsteen/Tom Waits, with a dash of Billie Holiday thrown in. Her slurred, madly romantic lyrics and torchy emotionality made for one of the most vivid debuts in years, with the hot bop hit, "Chuck E's in Love," going Top Five, and the wistful "Company" becoming a cabaret standard. It was probably the finest of all of Waronker and Titelman's production collaborations.

Pirates was more ambitious but more diffuse and strongly reminiscent in its free-form style and self-contained personal mythology of Laura Nyro's *New York Tendaberry.* Despite many moments of sheer brilliance, it suggested that Jones was possibly too confused to realize the full potential of her immense talents. — S.H.

SPIKE JONES

★ ★ ★ ★ ★ **Spike Jones Is Murdering the Classics** / RCA (1971)
★ ★ ★ ★ **The Best of Spike Jones** / RCA (1975)
★ ★ ★ **Spike Jones in Stereo** / War. (NA) ¶
★ ★ ★ **The Best of Spike Jones, Vol. 2** / RCA (NA)
★ ★ ★ **The Hilarious Spike Jones** / Camd. (NA)
★ ★ ★ **King of Corn** / Glen. (NA)

"Spike Jones made hundreds of records, nearly every one of them a total outrage," writes Dr. Demento in the notes to *Dr. Demento's Delights,* a collection of madcap recordings that includes Jones' hysterical gem from 1949, "Ya Wanna Buy a Bunny." Unlike Stan Freberg, whose parodies of rock & roll were born of hatred and misunderstanding, Jones loved the music he sent up—his aim was to take an honest poke at its pomposities.

Of the hundreds of records Jones and his City Slickers recorded, only a few are now in print, but all of them are terrific. Most outrageous and most indispensable: *Spike Jones Is Murdering the Classics,* which features the City Slickers' unforgettable interpretations of the "William Tell Overture" and "Dance of the Hours," complete with gargles, coughs, wheezes, sneezes and hiccups punctuated by shots from Jones' Smith & Wesson .22. The first *Best of* album includes such bits of inspired lunacy as "Cocktails for Two" and "Laura." *Spike Jones in Stereo* teams Jones with Dracula and Vampira, Frankenstein, the Mad Doctor, Alfred Hitchcock ("Poisen to Poisen") and, in a "Spooktacular Finale," the Entire Ghastly Cast. To explain further would be, like the music, sheer insanity. — D.MC.

TOM JONES

★ **Tom Jones Live** / Par. (1968) ¶
★ **Fever Zone** / Par. (1968) ¶
■ **Help Yourself** / Par. (1969) ¶
★ **This is Tom Jones** / Par. (1969)
★ **Tom Jones Live in Las Vegas** / Par. (1969)
★ **Memories Don't Leave Like People Do** / Par. (1973) ¶
★ ★ ★ **Tom Jones' Greatest Hits** / Lon. (1973)
★ **What a Night** / Epic (1977) ¶
★ **Say You'll Stay Until Tomorrow** / Epic (1977)
★ **Tom Is Love** / Epic (1977)
★ **Darlin'** / Mer. (1981)

Tom Jones is the missing link between Elvis Presley and middle-class sex-symbol clones like Engelbert Humperdinck and Mac Davis. But this hunky Welshman is a bit better than the rest of the pack: he pushes as hard as his awkward voice allows, never hitting a blue note in the process. But his triumphs in singles like "It's Not Unusual" and "Delilah" have earned him a permanent niche in the annals of nursing-home rock. — J.S.

THE JONES GIRLS

★ ★ ★ **At Peace with Woman** / Phil. (1980)
★ ★ ★ **Get As Much Love As You Can** / Phil. (1981)

With a little bit of Forties vocal jazz and a whole lotta Supremes, this Gamble/Huff progeny manages to add intelligence and resonance to every song they sing. The first LP in particular is a superb example of just how smart sweet soul music can be. — L.F.

JANIS JOPLIN

★ **I Got Dem Ol' Kozmic Blues Again, Mama** / Col. (1969)
★ ★ ★ ★ **Pearl** / Col. (1971)
★ ★ **Joplin in Concert** / Col. (1972) ¶
★ ★ ★ **Janis Joplin's Greatest Hits** / Col. (1973)
★ ★ **Janis** / Col. (1974)
★ ★ ★ ★ **Farewell Song** / Col. (1982)

The same air of desperation that kindled Janis Joplin's best performances left her screeching ineffectually through others.

These glories and excesses can often be found side by side in one song. Her work in 1967–68 with Big Brother and the Holding Company established Joplin as the type of culture hero whose death by overdose in 1970 would seem sadly logical.

Her first solo album *(I Got Dem Ol' Kozmic Blues Again, Mama)* is uneven. The studio band is sometimes listless and the album's three best songs—"Try," "Maybe" and "Kozmic Blues"—appear later in livelier versions. Her only other studio album, *Pearl,* benefits from the sympathy and chops of the Full Tilt Boogie Band. Even though four of its songs are included on *Greatest Hits,* the nicely paced *Pearl* is still a necessity for her urgent "A Woman Left Lonely" and "My Baby."

Joplin in Concert salvages the early, brutal "Down on Me," plus versions of "Piece of My Heart," "Summertime" and "Ball and Chain." All these are available as studio takes on *Greatest Hits,* and much of the rest on the live album is dreck.

The movie soundtrack *Janis* likewise draws heavily on earlier recordings; but it is worthwhile for snatches of her simultaneously funny and heartbreaking raps, and for two surprisingly warm and listenable sides of Janis singing country blues in a noisy bar in Austin, Texas, around 1963–64.

Greatest Hits is a bumpy ride through her best-known songs ("Me and Bobby McGee"). It boasts ten classic Joplin cuts, but the rich, mature *Pearl* is still the one indispensable item from this great-hearted singer who came and left so abruptly. *Farewell Song* is an amazing LP that documents Joplin's career in careful, loving strokes, with liner notes by Country Joe McDonald. — F.S.

LOUIS JORDAN

★ ★ **Rhythm and Blues Oldies, Vol. 1 / Blues Sp. (1972)**
★ ★ ★ ★ ★ **The Best of Louis Jordan / MCA (1975)**
★ ★ ★ **Louis Jordan's Greatest Hits / MCA (1975)**
★ ★ **I Believe in Music / Black and Blue (1975), Br. imp.**
★ ★ ★ **Louis Jordan's Greatest Hits, Vol. 2 / MCA (1981)**
★ ★ **Prime Cuts / Swing H. (NA), Br. imp.**
★ ★ **Good Times / Swing H. (NA), Br. imp.**

The great Forties jump-blues singer, saxman and bandleader, whose shouting and wild sense of humor was a major influence on many singers of the next generation—Chuck

Berry in particular. Jordan's best songs— "Saturday Night Fish Fry," "Choo Choo Ch'Boogie," "Ain't Nobody Here But Us Chickens," "Knock Me a Kiss," "Five Guys Named Moe" and the devastating "Caldonia"—are all on the modestly well-annotated MCA *Best of.* The other MCAs are redundant; the Swing House material is from Forties radio broadcasts, while the Black and Blue and Blues Spectrum recordings are remakes, the latter with a band led by Johnny Otis, but still nowhere near the quality of the originals. — D.M.

MARC JORDAN

★ ★ **Mannequin / War. (1978)**
★ ★ **Blue Desert / War. (1979)**
Marc Jordan makes a supposedly sophisticated brew of jazz, soul and rock. Steely Dan is the obvious reference point, and Donald Fagen guests on the Gary Katz–produced *Mannequin.* But it all sounds like cocktail music for some plush Holiday Inn lounge. Despite the presence of L.A.'s top studio talents on both LPs, Jordan's music is irritatingly undefined and far too mellow to hook the listener. — R.P.

JOURNEY

★ **Journey / Col. (1975)**
★ **Look into the Future / Col. (1976)** ¶
★ **Next / Col. (1977)**
★ **Infinity / Col. (1978)**
★ **Evolution / Col. (1979)**
★ **In the Beginning / Col. (1979)**
★ **Departure / Col. (1980)**
★ **Captured / Col. (1981)**
★ **Escape / Col. (1981)**
Journey was a dead end for San Francisco area rock. Led by two former members of Santana, keyboardist/singer Gregg Rolie and guitarist Neal Schon, the band made records perfectly calculated to be inserted into FM radio playlists: *Stepford Wives* rock, dead on its feet without any awareness of the utter triviality (not to mention banality) of such a scheme. Rolie may be the singer with the least character in pop history; he outstrips even Paul Anka and Pat Boone as an utter dullard, and the band's mixture of heavy-metal excess and fusion drone was not only a nitwit merger but plodding to boot. As of *Infinity* Rolie was replaced as lead singer by Steve Perry, an acetylene-torch vocalist with a penchant for strident Sam Cooke imitations. Rolie was eventually phased out altogether, with Jonathan Cain taking over keyboards. Journey gives the people what they want. Hopefully, the people will soon want something that doesn't reek of exploitive

cynicism. (They *are* more energetic than Pablo Cruise, though.) — D.M.

THE JOY
★ ★ ★ **The Joy / Fan. (1977)**
In 1977, Toni Brown and Terry Garthwaite attempted to re-form Joy of Cooking, with a slightly altered name but the same folkish funk sound. This album was the result; they didn't quite pull it off, but not for want of trying. The Joy was the first reasonably interesting rock group led by women, but that hardly justifies its aimlessness. — D.M.

JOY OF COOKING
★ ★ ★ **Joy of Cooking / Cap. (1971)**
★ ★ ★ **Closer to the Ground / Cap. (1971)**
★ ★ ★ **Castles / Cap. (1972)**
In the early Seventies, the Berkeley-based Joy of Cooking was a provocative blend of folk and rock, women and men. Toni Brown and Terry Garthwaite were not only the vocalists and songwriters of the group but also the instrumental leaders of a five-piece band.

What's surprising is how well these records hold up. Though the idea of a women-led band is no longer novel, Brown and Garthwaite's energy and air of delighted discovery survives and unites their sometimes fragmented intentions. As, well, foremothers, they touched most of the bases Fleetwood Mac, the McGarrigles and Heart now divvy up among themselves: personal commentary with a pop beat, sweet harmonies and hardheaded romanticism, a fusion of pastoral and urban visions. The sound on these albums is often thin (only *Castles* is enriched by horns and strings), the arrangements are more homey than honed, but the songs—proud without being preachy, woman-oriented but not exclusionary—transcend the times that produced them. — A.S.

J.T. CONNECTION
★ ★ **Bernadette / Butter. (NA)**
Group's good taste in choosing the Four Tops' fourth-greatest hit (No. 1 is "Reach Out, I'll Be There") as part of a medley is unfortunately unmatched by an ability to update it properly for disco format. — D.M.

JUDAS PRIEST
★ **Sad Wings of Destiny / Janus (1976)**
★ **Sin after Sin / Col. (1977)**
★ **Stained Class / Col. (1978)**
★ **Rocka-Rolla / Visa (1978)**
★ **Hell Bent for Leather / Col. (1979)**
★ **Unleashed in the East / Col. (1979)**
★ **British Steel / Col. (1980)**
★ **Point of Entry / Col. (1981)**

★ **Screaming for Vengeance / Col. (1982)**
Grunting, flailing hard rock, as vulgar as its name, but less euphonious. For lovers of recycled Led Zeppelin riffs only. — D.M.

JULES AND THE POLAR BEARS
★ ★ ★ ★ **Got No Breeding / Col. (1978)**
★ ★ ★ **Fenetics / Col. (1979)**
Got No Breeding showcases the extraordinary songwriting talents of Jules Shear. Virtually every song on the record is a masterful synthesis of cleverly turned melodies twisted around mouthfuls of offbeat imagery, all punctuated by the excellent guitar playing of Richard Bredice. *Fenetics* is almost but not quite as good. — J.S.

JUMBO
★ **Turn on to Love / Prel. (1976)**
No big deal. — D.M.

JUNIE
★ ★ ★ ★ **Bread Alone / Col. (1980)**
★ ★ ★ **Junie 5 / Col. (1981)**
Junie Morrison led the Ohio Players and cut three earlier solo albums before making his breakthrough with *Bread Alone*. This self-produced funk classic is highlighted by hot, uncredited bass and drums tracks (played by Junie himself, as are all of the other instruments), but what really makes this funk different from all others is Junie's soulful singing, which adds a warm dimension George Clinton and company have never come close to achieving (even with Philippé Wynne). Morrison's attention apparently wavered on side two, and *Junie 5* is a good deal more pedestrian, but for one side, and two-thirds of another, he made funk as solid, earthy and humane as anyone around. — D.M.

MICKEY JUPP
★ ★ ★ **Juppanese / Stiff (1978), Br. imp.**
British rocker/writer with a knack for Berry-esque humor. Jupp's only LP was produced by Nick Lowe and Gary Brooker of Procol Harum fame. Side one is Rockpile backing Jupp through jumping originals and two winsome ballads. On the second side, Brooker, Chris Spedding, Bruce Lynch and Dave Mattacks sound slightly more lubricious, reflecting odd production pairing. Dave Edmunds recorded a version of this LP's "You'll Never Get Me up in One of Those." Jupp's "Switchboard Susan," not included, was separately waxed by Lowe, Brooker and the Searchers. — G.A.

BILL JUSTIS
★ ★ ★ ★ **Raunchy / Sun (1969)**

One of Sam Phillips' ablest sessionmen during Sun Records' early days, Bill Justis is a prime example of a rock & roll saxophonist whose searing melodiousness is tempered beautifully by a craftsman's precision. Nowhere is this demonstrated better than on his landmark 1964 instrumental, "Raunchy," which is the cornerstone of his lively, first and sole in-print Sun album. — D.MC.

PATRICK JUVET
★ ★ **Got a Feeling / Casa. (1978)**
★ ★ **Lady Night / Casa. (1979)**
Pretty-boy vocalist of the Eurodisco set. Glamorous album-cover photos better setting for Juvet than anything inside sleeve. He and Amanda Lear are the twin totems of white disco-come-lately as jet-set pandering.
— G.A.

KALEIDESCOPE
★ **When Scopes Collide / PFA (1976)**
Semi-legendary late-Sixties San Francisco band is not well represented by this Seventies revival attempt. The earlier version of the group did several fine LPs on Epic, which merged blues, country and Middle Eastern music, and gave instrumentalist David Lindley his start. — J.S.

MADLEEN KANE
★ **Rough Diamond / War. (1978)**
★ **Cheri / War. (1979)**
Eurodisco chanteuse in the spirit of Andrea True Connection's "More More More," except there isn't a song on either of these albums that's as interesting as the former porno starlet's hit. — D.M.

KANSAS
★ ★ ★ **Kansas / Kir. (1974)**
★ ★ **Masque / Kir. (1975)**
★ ★ ★ **Song for America / Kir. (1975)**
★ ★ **Leftoverture / Kir. (1976)**
★ **Point of Know Return / Kir. (1977)**
★ **Two for the Show / Kir. (1978)**
★ **Monolith / Kir. (1979)**
★ **Audio-Visions / Kir. (1980)**
Arena-rockers with excessive British art-rock (circa early Seventies) obsession. Kansas came out of that peculiar period in rock's history when overwhelming technical proficiency was appreciated over such qualities as restraint, brevity and the simple communication of the human voice. Kansas didn't begin as badly as they (and all the other dinosaurs) ended up; the first three records, especially *Song for America,* had moments when the grasping for a space-age sound seemed likely to succeed. But the eternal road that a group like this must set out on for financial survival led to a retreat from any further innovation or experimentation, and they insisted on merely slinging out, in the same redundant form, their increasingly incoherent apocalyptic science-fiction mishmash. The breakthrough to the major leagues came with *Leftoverture*'s "Carry On Wayward Son"; if that wasn't harbinger enough of their rapid commercial ascent and speedy artistic descent, then the popular and vapid "Dust in the Wind" from *Point* certainly was. As with all other groups in the genre, the release of a follow-up double live album was the final clue to the hardening of their arteries. Subsequent releases were useless, as any future ones undoubtedly will be.
— W.K.

KAT MANDU
★ **Kat Mandu / Mar. (1980)**
Poor as the pun 'pon which it's based.
— D.M.

JORMA KAUKONEN
★ ★ ★ **Quah / Grunt (1975)**
★ ★ **Jorma / RCA (1979)**
★ ★ **Barbeque King / RCA (1981)**
Jefferson Airplane/Hot Tuna guitarist Kaukonen's first solo album is an all-acoustic guitar set. Kaukonen does some vocals, and some instrumental tunes and duets with guitarist Tom Hobson. Kaukonen was a folk guitarist before plugging in with the Airplane; his acoustic solo, "Embryonic Journey," on *Surrealistic Pillow* and the first acoustic Hot Tuna album are preparation for *Quah,* on which Kaukonen fares better than on the most recent Hot Tuna stuff. *Barbeque King* documents Jorma's odd venture into the world of punk rock. — J.S.

RYO KAWASAKI
★ ★ ★ **Juice / RCA (1976)**
Kawasaki is a virtuoso Japanese electric guitarist who justifies his reputation with his playing, writing and arrangements on this debut album. The instrumental support from

keyboardist Tom Coster is exemplary, but the rest of the accompaniment and production makes this sound like an ordinary fusion record. — J.S.

JOHN KAY
★ ★ **All in Good Time** / Mer. (1978)
The former Steppenwolf lead singer in a disappointing outing. Sounds more like "Born to Be Mild." — D.M.

KAYAK
★ **Royal Bed Bouncer** / Janus (1975)
★ **Starlight Dancer** / Janus (1977)
★ **Phantom of the Night** / Janus (1978)
★ **Periscope** / Mer. (1979)
Are these "concept" LPs by mid-Seventies European art rockers so lame because the Dutch quintet that made them doesn't understand its own English lyrics? Or is it just that pompous clowns like these had complete contempt for anyone who'd listen to this type of pop, which they were making only because the "serious music" they preferred wouldn't make them rich?
— D.M.

THE KAY GEE'S
★ ★ ★ **Keep On Bumpin' and Master Plan** / Gang (1975)
★ ★ **Find a Friend** / Gang (1975)
★ ★ **Burn Me Up** / De-Lite (1979)
The Kay Gee's are protégés of Kool and the Gang. Not surprisingly, their records sound markedly like their mentors'. *Keep On Bumpin'* has the Gang's burping vocals, loony atmosphere and staccato horn riffs. The successors are milder and reflect Kool and the Gang's preoccupation with the ethereal.
— J.M.C.

KC AND THE SUNSHINE BAND
★ ★ ★ **Do It Good** / TK (1974)
★ ★ ★ **KC and the Sunshine Band** / TK (1975)
★ ★ **Part** / TK (1976)
★ ★ **Who Do Ya** / TK (1978)
★ **Do You Wanna Go Party?** / TK (1979)
★ ★ **KC and the Sunshine Band's Greatest Hits** / TK (1980)
The Sunshine Band's early recordings, found on *Do It Good,* were ambitious and fresh. At the time, the group consisted of just two members, Rick Finch and H.W. Casey, who were given free rein in the TK studios to explore their eccentric funk vision. *Do It Good* is ragged, but the energy expounded borders on the maniacal. The best of it is "Queen of Clubs," runaway Miami funk that blends Finch's machine-gun bass line, surging Jun-

kanoo horns and George McCrae's falsetto banshee wail.

Pop success began with "Get Down Tonight," and since then Finch and Casey have whittled the music down to its lowest common denominator: a pile-driving, percussive groove and hook lines as simple as any in pop. The result: bubblegum funk. — J.M.C.

ERNIE K-DOE
★ ★ ★ ★ **Mother-in-Law** / Bandy (NA)
★ ★ ★ ★ **Ernie K-Doe, Vol. 2** / Bandy (NA)
Very fine New Orleans singer of the early Sixties had the city's characteristically light and soulful touch. K-Doe's only big hit was "Mother-in-Law," but such minor ones as "Wanted $10,000 Reward," "Te-Ta-Te-Ta-Ta" and "A Certain Girl" (covered by both the Yardbirds and Warren Zevon) make both these LPs splendidly listenable two decades after they were first recorded. — D.M.

THE KEANE BROTHERS
★ **The Keane Brothers** / 20th Cent. (1977)
★ **Taking Off** / ABC (1979)
Preteen pop singers who didn't learn the first and only important lesson the Osmonds had to teach: if you gotta fake it, steal from somebody as talented as the Jackson 5. The Keanes' fake Elton John moves aren't any better just because they aren't old enough to know that the originals are synthetics, too.
— D.M.

KEBEKELEKTRIK
★ **Kebekelektrik** / Sals. (1978)
Internationalized disco product. — D.M.

SPEEDY KEEN
★ ★ ★ **Y'Know Wot I Mean?** / Is. (1976)
Good rock & roll, though inferior to the Thunderclap Newman album on which Keen debuted. One side hard, the other introspective and reserved. He plays an assortment of instruments; his Who-like singing is better than ever. Backup includes half of Back Street Crawler. — C.W.

BILL KEITH
★ ★ ★ **Something Auld, Something New, Something Borrowed, Something Bluegrass** / Roun. (1976)
As banjoist for Bill Monroe, the Jim Kweskin Jug Band and others, Keith almost single-handedly expanded the scope of bluegrass banjo. Taking Earl Scruggs' work for starters, he added chromatic breaks, a new peg system and post-ragtime jazz to the idiom. — I.M.

ROBERTA KELLY
★ ★ **Trouble Maker / Oasis (1977)**
★ ★ **Zodiac Lady / Casa. (1977)**
★ ★ **Gettin' the Spirit / Casa. (1977)**
Roberta Kelly fronts for the disco beat of
the Musicland Studios of Munich, West Ger-
many, much as Donna Summer does in
America. Unfortunately, Kelly does not have
Summer's voice or her brilliant production.
This has a heavy beat, but that's about it.
— D.M.

EDDIE KENDRICKS
★ ★ ★ **All by Myself / Tam. (1971)**
★ ★ ★ **People . . . Hold On / Tam. (1972)**
★ ★ ★ **He's a Friend / Tam. (1976)**
★ ★ ★ **Goin' Up in Smoke / Tam. (1976)**
★ ★ ★ **Slick / Tam. (1977)**
★ ★ ★ ★ **Eddie Kendricks at His Best /
Tam. (1978)**
★ ★ ★ **Vintage '78 / Ari. (1978)**
★ ★ ★ **Something More / Ari. (1980)**
★ ★ ★ ★ **Superstar Series, Vol. 19 / Mo.
(1981)**
Kendricks was the higher pitched of the
Temptations' two lead vocalists—David Ruf-
fin was the other—and his leads on songs
like "Beauty Is Only Skin Deep" helped establish a certain type of soul singing. But
after leaving the Temptations, Kendricks has
operated in a very updated Philadelphia
rhythm style that uses the front man more
as a chant leader than as a crooner. Ken-
drick's first hit in this disco-oriented mode
came in 1973, with "Keep On Truckin'."
Since then, he's rarely been out of sight. In
late 1977 he signed with Arista, where he's
made a couple of adequate LPs. Only time
will tell whether his departure from the
Tamla/Motown rhythm mill will be productive. — D.M.

RAY KENNEDY
★ ★ **Ray Kennedy / Col. (1980)**
Kennedy, the K of KGB, trots out his two
hits—"Sail On Sailor," written with Brian
Wilson, and "Isn't It Time," a biggie for the
Babys—and bellows through several faceless
rockers. Big deal. — J.D.C.

CHRIS KENNER
★ ★ ★ ★ ★ **Land of 1,000 Dances / Atl.
(1966), Jap. imp.**
A beautiful reissue (in the original package)
of Kenner's only Atlantic LP. Kenner is best
known as a writer, and all his best-known
songs are here: "Land of 1,000 Dances" itself, "Come Back and See," "Packing Up,"
"Something You Got," "I Like It Like
That." What's surprising is that Kenner was

also one of the finest voices in New Orleans,
a thrilling tenor with true grit. Needless to
say, Allen Toussaint's arrangements are marvels of groove. One of the great unknown albums of rock & roll. — D.M.

GERARD KENNY
★ **Made It thru the Rain / RCA (1979)**
Boring Billy Joel type. — D.M.

THE KENTUCKY COLONELS
★ ★ ★ **Livin' in the Past / Tak. (1975)**
★ ★ ★ **The Kentucky Colonels / Roun.
(1976)**
★ ★ ★ ★ **The White Brothers (The New
Kentucky Colonels) / Roun. (1977)**
This seminal Southern California bluegrass
band yielded such low-profile L.A. stalwarts
as Clarence White (Byrds), Billy Ray
Latham (Dillards) and Roger Bush (Country
Gazette), as well as Roland White, who
made similar inroads in Nashville playing for
Bill Monroe and Lester Flatt. The first two
LPs are surprisingly good quality tapes of
the Colonels' snappy, almost scat-influenced
style while still plucky youths. Playing with
incredible speed and agility, the Colonels display a fresh ebullience and professional abandon rare in usually staid bluegrass bands.
The last LP is a live album from a 1973
Swedish reunion tour, where the instrumental facility and upbeat style of the Colonels
has matured like a vintage wine. Throughout
the three sets, the late Clarence White plays
superb guitar. If he had lived, the Colonels
would no doubt have gained their rightful
public acclaim in bluegrass circles. A footnote in rock history worth savoring. — R.P.

DOUG KERSHAW
★ ★ **The Cajun Way / War. (1969)**
★ ★ **Spanish Moss / War. (1970)**
★ ★ **Doug Kershaw / War. (1971)**
★ ★ **Swamp Grass / War. (1972)**
★ ★ **Devil's Elbow / War. (1972)**
★ ★ **Douglas James Kershaw / War. (1973)**
★ ★ **Mama Kershaw's Boy / War. (1974)**
★ ★ **Alive and Pickin' / War. (1975)**
★ ★ ★ **The Ragin' Cajun / War. (1976)**
★ ★ **Louisiana Man / War. (1978)**
★ ★ **Instant Hero / Scotti (NA)**
Kershaw is a white Cajun fiddle player who
in 1961 had two regional country hits that
also made the country charts, "Louisiana
Man" and "Diggy Diggy Lo." But he's
never attained a sizable following because
he's just too weird—with his wild shoulder-
length black hair atop a warlock's face that
houses a paranoid's eyes. Onstage, Kershaw
writhes, whoops and rips the strings of his

fiddle to shreds before settling down to any *serious* sawing. Thus he is offputting to, say, Johnny Cash's audience, and too exotically rural to open for, say, Jefferson Starship's. In this limbo between country and rock, Kershaw remains an erratic novelty in search of a style. His albums jump from genre to genre: *Douglas James Kershaw* features insipid string arrangements, *Swamp Grass* is quasi-rock, *Devil's Elbow* is crypto-psychedelia. They all contain one or two extraordinary, banshee-inspired numbers, and the rest are uniformly tedious mixes of progressive MOR and off-key yowling. It is only on *Ragin' Cajun,* easily the best of these, that he has abandoned this stylistic self-consciousness and just lets the music blare and moan as it will. As if to confirm the rightness of this decision, *Ragin'* yielded his first hit single since the Sixties, "It Takes All Day (To Get Over Night)," again heard only on country stations. — K.T.

THE KEYS
★ ★ ★ **Keys Album / A&M (1981)**
Tough British R&B quartet produced by Joe Jackson. Guitarist Steve Tatler and bassist Drew Barfield supported Bill Haley on his last British tour. — J.S.

CHAKA KHAN
★ ★ ★ **Chaka / War. (1978)**
★ ★ ★ **Naughty / War. (1980)**
★ ★ ★ ★ **What Cha Gonna Do for Me / War. (1981)**
Khan made her name with Rufus and possesses one of the most energetic, capable voices in R&B. The possibilities suggested by her singing are endless, which is what makes the bulk of these records so maddening— Khan and producer Arif Marden are content to go for easy hits, peddling her as the Aretha Franklin of the Eighties. *What Cha Gonna Do* finally breaks some new ground, romping through Dizzy Gillespie's "A Night in Tunisia," but doesn't deliver all that it promises. — J.D.C.

KID BLAST
★ **Kid Blast / Clar. (1977)**
A *Bye Bye Birdie* version of punk as viewed from Hollywood and Vine, perpetrated by the veteran Tacoma bar band Chinook and a record-label lyricist. Someone decided they should become Kid Blast because of original moniker's similarity to Yiddish term schnook. He was right. — G.A.

KID CREOLE AND THE COCONUTS
★ ★ ★ **Off the Coast of Me / Ant. (1980)**

★ ★ ★ **Fresh Fruit in Foreign Places / Sire/Ze (1981)**
Kid Creole and the Coconuts, the brainchild of prolific producer/writer August Darnell, turned out a zany Caribbean-style pop soul that in live performance suggested the Marx Brothers run amok in Bob Marley's Kingston. Dubbed "mulatto music" by Darnell (on-again, off-again partner of Stony Browder, the leader of Dr. Buzzard's Original Savannah Band), both albums were essentially madly eclectic movie fantasies translated into musical extravaganzas, with calypso the basic beat. While the songs on *Fresh Fruit* weren't as memorable as those on *Coast,* this amusing pop parody of Homer's *Odyssey* was optioned by theater impresario Joseph Papp for presentation at the New York Public Theater. It would be New York's first "rap musical." — S.H.

JOHNNY KIDD AND THE PIRATES
★ ★ ★ **Johnny Kidd, Rocker / EMI (1978), Fr. imp.**
Before the Beatles, English rock & roll was motley at best. Everybody had a gimmick: Kidd's was his eye patch. But Kidd had some real vocal power, and he wrote one perfect rock song, "Shakin' All Over." (For some reason, the definitive version was done by Randy Bachman's original Guess Who, but the one here is swell, too.) This two-record set (plus bonus 45) contains all the essentials of a career that began in 1959 and ended in a car crash in 1966, just as Kidd's kind of brash rock & roll was being swathed in beads and headbands. Listen for the guitar playing: Mick Green of the Pirates (who have also recorded on their own) influenced just about everybody from Pete Townshend on down in Britain's first rock generation. — D.M.

KID DYNAMITE
★ **Kid Dynamite / Cream (1976)**
Former Steve Miller Band members apparently didn't know when they had it good; wretched singing, material that's sheer stupidity, one awful cover version (Junior Walker's "Shotgun"). In a word, lame. — D.M.

GREG KIHN
★ ★ **Greg Kihn / Beserk. (1976)**
★ ★ **Greg Kihn, Again / Beserk. (1977)**
★ ★ **Next of Kihn / Beserk. (1978)**
★ ★ **With the Naked Eye / Beserk. (1979)**
★ ★ **Glass House Rock / Beserk. (1980)**
★ ★ ★ **Rockihnroll / Beserk. (1981)**
★ ★ ★ **Kihntinued / Beserk. (1982)**

In the context of San Francisco-area rock & roll, Greg Kihn is possibly one of the most exciting artists to come along in years—since Commander Cody, if not John Fogerty. But this says more about the pathetic state of West Coast rock—after all, what's Kihn's competition, Pablo Cruise and Journey? The Dead Kennedys?—than about Kihn's limited talents.

Kihn has been compared to Bruce Springsteen, Tom Petty and Buddy Holly, but his ideas aren't nearly so well-realized as theirs were, and are, nor are his ideas as good in the first place. If Kihn ought to be compared to anyone, it is probably Beserkley Records stablemate Jonathan Richman—both are eccentric, both have a genuine passion for rock & roll that's overwhelmed by wimpiness. But only Richman has a redemptive view of the world. Kihn sings about girls, cars and lighthearted, nonthreatening kicks because that's the limit of his vision. He has ruined at least one great pop song (Springsteen's "Rendezvous," on *With the Naked Eye*), and his covers of similar light pop rockers of the Sixties are invariably unimaginative and so forced that they pale next to the ease of the originals.

On the other hand, by 1981, the entire nation's pop-rock sensibility was so benumbed that when Kihn recorded his first competent tune in the genre, "The Breakup Song (They Don't Write 'Em)," he immediately went Top Twenty. *Rockinhroll,* from which "The Breakup Song" was drawn, is Kihn's most fully realized wimp-rock so far. *Kihntinued*, no less creampuff, is more engaging because it's just rock dance groove. When he's not making clunky versions of classics, Kihn has become a rather listenable lightweight.
— D.M.

ROCK KILLOUGH
★ **Highway 31 / Elek. (1980)**
Killough is an aspiring Nashville songwriter type, and this album is apparently designed to showcase his composing skills—it certainly doesn't reflect well on his performing abilities. The accompaniment is Nashville session adequate, which is fairly good, but the songs themselves—well, they haven't topped the charts yet, have they? (As for the Jimmie Rodgers song butchered here, the less said the better.) — D.M.

KILO
★ **Kilo / Stax (1979)**
Pedestrian funk outing. — D.M.

ALBERT KING
★ ★ ★ **Door to Door / Chess (1969)**
★ ★ ★ **Years Gone By / Stax (1969)**
★ ★ ★ **The Pinch / Stax (1976)**
★ ★ **Albert / Ut. (1976)**
★ ★ ★ **Albert Live / Ut. (1977)**
★ ★ ★ **Truckload of Lovin' / Ut. (1976)**
★ ★ ★ **King of the Blues Guitar / Atco (1977)**
Of the three blues-singing and guitar-playing (though unrelated) Kings, Albert was clearly the inferior, in both approach and influence, in comparison with either B.B. or Freddie. Indeed, his style was almost entirely derived from B.B.'s—although that could also be said of half the other blues guitarists, black and white, of the Sixties and Seventies.

King began recording for King Records in 1961, when he had a Top Twenty R&B chart hit, "Don't Throw Your Love on Me So Strong." But his two most familiar songs, "Born under a Bad Sign" and "Cross Cut Saw," were both cut in 1967. "Born under a Bad Sign," the best and most widely covered (notably by Cream and Creedence Clearwater Revival) of the two, was written by Booker T. Jones and William Bell, and recorded for Stax; it is now available, along with most of the best of King's work, on the Atco album. "Born under a Bad Sign" might have been a simple soul song, but King's straight 12-bar approach, rough-edged voice and raw guitar accented the tragedy, and minimized the self-pity, of the lyric's rather fantastic imagery.

King's series of albums for Stax, almost all of which are worthwhile, are slowly being reissued. There are also sets of new material released under Fantasy's Stax reissue program. The Utopia LPs were recorded in the Seventies and produced by Bert de Coteaux and Tony Silvestre, who attempt to modernize King's approach without taking him into straight modern black music. The result is interesting but not as effective as his pure blues playing. — D.M.

B.B. KING
★ ★ ★ ★ **Let Me Love You / Kent (NA)**
★ ★ ★ ★ ★ **Live, B. B. King on Stage / Kent (NA)**
★ ★ ★ ★ **Pure Soul / Kent (NA)**
★ ★ ★ ★ ★ **The Jungle / Kent (NA)**
★ ★ ★ ★ **Boss of the Blues / Kent (1969)**
★ ★ ★ ★ ★ **From the Beginning / Kent (NA)**
★ ★ ★ ★ ★ **Underground Blues / Kent (NA)**
★ ★ ★ ★ **Incredible Soul of B.B. King / Kent (NA)**
★ ★ ★ **Turn On with B. B. King / Kent (NA)**

★ ★ ★ ★ Greatest Hits of B. B. King / Kent (NA)

★ ★ ★ ★ Better Than Ever / Kent (NA)

★ ★ ★ Doing My Thing, Lord / Kent (NA)

★ ★ ★ ★ Original "Sweet Sixteen" / Kent (NA)

★ ★ ★ ★ ★ B. B. King Live / Kent (NA)

★ ★ ★ ★ Anthology of the Blues—B. B. King 1949–50 / Kent (NA)

★ ★ ★ ★ Mr. Blues / ABC (1963)

★ ★ ★ ★ Confessin' the Blues / ABC (1965)

★ ★ ★ ★ Blues Is King / ABC (1967)

★ ★ ★ ★ Lucille / ABC (1968)

★ ★ ★ ★ Live and Well / ABC (1969)

★ ★ ★ ★ Indianola Mississippi Seeds / ABC (1970)

★ ★ ★ ★ ★ B. B. King Live in Cook County Jail / ABC (1971)

★ ★ ★ ★ ★ B. B. King Live at the Regal / ABC (1971)

★ ★ ★ ★ L.A. Midnight / ABC (1972)

★ ★ ★ ★ Guess Who / ABC (1972)

★ ★ ★ ★ The Best of B. B. King / ABC (1973)

★ ★ ★ ★ To Know You Is to Love You / ABC (1973)

★ ★ ★ Electric B. B. King / ABC (NA)

★ ★ ★ ★ Together for the First Time / Dun. (1974)

★ ★ ★ Friends / ABC (1975)

★ ★ ★ ★ Completely Well / ABC (1975)

★ ★ ★ ★ ★ Back in the Alley / ABC (1975)

★ ★ ★ ★ Blues on Top of Blues / ABC (1975)

★ ★ ★ ★ Lucille Talks Back / ABC (1975)

★ ★ ★ ★ Together Again . . . Live / Imp. (1976)

★ ★ ★ ★ King Size / ABC (1977)

B. B. King is perhaps the greatest figure on the postwar urban blues scene, a powerful performer, a consolidator of blues styles, a great bandleader, an even greater singer and an innovative guitarist who's influenced virtually every blues guitarist to come after him. His clean, economical style can be heard quite clearly in the work of Eric Clapton and Michael Bloomfield, to use two stand-out examples among rock players.

King's intelligence and consummate professionalism have made him revered by a black audience that looks to his performance as the standard against which all else must be judged. Although King never made direct attempts to pander to a white audience, his reputation grew in the Sixties after his impact on rock players became obvious, and King played a series of enthusiastically received dates at the Fillmores East and West.

The key to King's success is the wide range of ideas he brings in very squarely under the umbrella of blues playing. As a child, he heard a great deal of gospel music and listened to recordings by Blind Lemon Jefferson; the Texas guitar style of Jefferson and T-Bone Walker became B.B.'s foundation. But King's musical exposure was extensive, and he appended many disparate elements to that base: Jimmy Rushing's singing with the Count Basie orchestra; Al Hibbler's singing with Duke Ellington; the guitar playing of jazz stars Django Reinhardt and Charlie Christian; other blues players like Bukka White, Lowell Fulsom, Elmore James and Johnny Moore and the Three Blazers.

In 1948 King became a Memphis disc jockey, quickly gained a reputation for playing great records that couldn't be heard elsewhere, and began to piece together ideas for his own recording career. King's ear for great material led him to cover a number of songs that did far better for him than for the original writers. His first hit, in 1950, was with Lowell Fulsom's "Three O'Clock Blues." Later in his career, he turned Memphis Slim's "Every Day I Have the Blues" and Robert Nighthawk's "Sweet Little Angel" into such personal statements that most people think King wrote them himself. King also successfully covered Arthur Crudup's "Rock Me Mama," Joe Turner's "Sweet Sixteen" and Roy Hawkins' "The Thrill Is Gone."

King's first Memphis band included vocalist Bobby Bland, who credits King as a major influence on his singing, pianist Johnny Ace and drummer Earl Forrest. Once King began touring behind the success of his first records, he developed a sophisticated band setup built around a solid rhythm backup and featuring tight horn sections to punctuate his highly emotional "crying" blues style and expressive guitar playing.

Over the years, King has recorded prolifically, yet he's kept his ideas varied and the emotional content well focused enough so that he never sounds stale. He has practically never cut a bad record.

His earliest available work is on the Fifties and Sixties Kent albums. Kent continued to release previously rejected material after King left for ABC, but in general the Kent records are very good. The ABC material is more far-ranging, as King expanded into using session musicians and augmented lineups. Some of these records, particularly several produced by Bill Szymczyk (Completely Well, Indianola Mississippi Seeds), show how many different things can be done within the seemingly tight restrictions of the blues.

King's best records, though, are the live sets, where the electricity of audience/performer interaction spurred King on to elaborate vocal and instrumental histrionics, and he demonstrated his total control over the concert experience. *Live at the Regal* is the generally acknowledged classic. — J.S.

BEN E. KING
★ ★ ★ ★ **Ben E. King's Greatest Hits** / Atco (1964)
★ ★ ★ **Supernatural** / Atco (1975) ¶
★ **I Had a Love** / Atco (1976) ¶
★ ★ ★ **Benny and Us (with the Average White Band)** / Atco (1977) ¶
★ ★ ★ **Let Me Live in Your Life** / Atco (1978)
★ ★ **Music Trance** / Atco (1980)
★ ★ **Street Tough** / Atl. (1981)
★ ★ ★ ★ **What Is Soul** / Atl. (1981), Jap. imp.
★ ★ ★ ★ **Stand by Me** / Atl. (1981), Jap. imp.

In the annals of soul music, Ben E. King ranks only slightly behind Smokey Robinson, Curtis Mayfield and Aretha Franklin. From his first single ("There Goes My Baby," with the Drifters), he left an indelible mark on the genre, and on rock in general. "There Goes My Baby"—cowritten by King—was the first soul hit to use strings, and his other Drifters' records were equally influential, partly because of the brilliant production by Jerry Leiber and Mike Stoller (and occasionally the young Phil Spector). On his own, King had a series of major hits, including "I (Who Have Nothing)" and "Don't Play That Song for Me." The most notable of them all was the brilliant "Stand by Me," one of the starkest love songs ever written—it too was self-penned; its opening bass solo alone is among rock's great moments. *Greatest Hits* collects his solo sides, and is invaluable to anyone who would understand early-Sixties soul. The imported discs are intact Atlantic LPs from this era, with excellent notes, if you can read Japanese.

The hits ran out in the latter part of that decade, but King returned, talent intact, with *Supernatural,* in 1975. The title track was a major hit in the early days of disco, and one of its best. But the rest of the album, as well as *I Had a Love, Benny and Us, Music Trance,* and *Street Tough,* buried King in an excess of production and rhythm. One is left wondering when his producers will stand aside and simply let the man sing again. — D.M.

CAROLE KING
★ ★ ★ **Carole King: Writer** / Ode (1970)
★ ★ ★ ★ ★ **Tapestry** / Ode (1971)
★ ★ ★ **Music** / Ode (1971)
★ ★ ★ **Rhymes and Reasons** / Ode (1972)
★ ★ ★ **Fantasy** / Ode (1973)
★ ★ ★ **Wrap Around Joy** / Ode (1974)
★ ★ ★ ★ **Really Rosie** / Ode (1975)
★ ★ ★ ★ **Thoroughbred** / Ode (1976)
★ ★ **Simple Things** / Cap. (1977)
★ ★ **Welcome Home** / Cap. (1978)
★ ★ ★ ★ **Her Greatest Hits** / Ode (1978)
★ ★ **Touch the Sky** / Cap. (1979)
★ ★ **Pearls** / Cap. (1980)

Carole King was one of the most important pop and rock songwriters of the Sixties, numbering among her hits (written with lyricist and first husband Gerry Goffin) the Drifters' "Up on the Roof" and "Some Kind of Wonderful," the Byrds' "Goin' Back," the Shirelles' "Will You Love Me Tomorrow," Aretha Franklin's "You Make Me Feel like a Natural Woman," and virtually numberless others. These were great songs, but after she and Goffin split, their teenage romantic fantasies ended, though they continued to write together. King moved to California, where she married bassist Charles Larkey and raised a family. In 1970 she returned to music as a performer.

Writer, her first solo album, attracted some critical notice but not much public acknowledgment, although in retrospect it contains some of her finest work, particularly the remodeled "Goin' Back." With *Tapestry,* however, King broke wide open—the record remains one of the half-dozen biggest sellers in history, and its major hits—"It's Too Late," "I Feel the Earth Move" and "You've Got a Friend," which scored biggest for friend James Taylor—are classics of their type.

The Taylor connection is not coincidental—he appeared on both records, and together Taylor and King defined what was quickly labeled the singer/songwriter school. The emphasis was on craftsmanship as much as artistry, but the focus was also much more intensely personal than earlier pop: a song like "Goin' Back" has much heavier emotional connotations if there is no distance between singer and writer. The music, too, was distinctly stylized; King emphasized piano, Taylor guitar, but otherwise the songs relied on light drums and acoustic guitars (with a bit of light electric) to create a homey "living room" feeling. The watchword was initimacy, and on that scale, *Tapestry* is one of the best LPs ever made.

But as the records that followed showed,

there were limits to what even King could do with the singer/songwriter approach. *Music* contained some fine songs—particularly "Sweet Seasons" and "Some Kind of Wonderful"—but as King exhausted her reserve of material, the new songs began to seem repetitious in their celebrations of the domestic virtues. King's voice was consistently pleasant, and each of the records has some striking moments, but what is most apparent is a kind of musical and lyrical redundancy. Toni Stern's lyrics predominated over Goffin's, and their addition of a female perspective, so rare in rock, could be revelatory, but only in a relative sense.

A kind of nadir was reached with *Wrap Around Joy,* in 1974. Saddled with an inferior lyricist in David Palmer, and much more adventurous settings, featuring horns and heavy vocal choruses, King turned in only one really outstanding song, "Jazzman." The rest is pretentious muck, unleavened with humor and overburdened with quasi-poetic metaphor.

King rebounded somewhat with *Really Rosie.* Written as the soundtrack to a TV special based on the Maurice Sendak story, it is the best children's rock album, and the music is so worthwhile that it is exceptionally appealing to adults as well. *Thoroughbred,* the record that followed her breakup with Larkey, was her best since *Tapestry.* The arrangements were a bit tougher—closer to rock—and Goffin once more became her principal collaborator, although King had turned to writing much more of her material herself. At least one song, the splendid "Only Love Is Real," seemed to capture the essence of King's entire body of work, both in its lyric and melody, which left one with the feeling—or at least the hope—that King's future work might regain the mass resonance of her pop hits and *Tapestry.* But her Capitol albums are guru-mad: King trying to sell her audience universal utopia. I liked her better when she offered only perfect romantic bliss.   — D.M.

EARL KING
★ ★ ★ ★ **Earl King: Those Lonely Lonely Nights / Ace/Vivid (1979), Jap. imp.**
★ ★ ★ **Street Parade / Charly (NA), Br. imp.**
★ ★ ★ **Good Old New Orleans Rock 'n Roll / Sonet (1977), Br. imp.**
The fine New Orleans singer and guitarist is shown to best advantage on his Fifties material contained on the Ace/Vivid replica of his original (1955) album. "Those Lonely Lonely Nights" is one of the classics of the

New Orleans music of the period, and the rest of the album is quite fine as well. *Street Parade* is a 1972 session, with Marshall Sehorn and Allen Toussaint at the production controls. The Sonet album, a 1977 session, is the least of what's here but still cuts quite a competent New Orleans groove.   — D.M.

EVELYN "CHAMPAGNE" KING
★ ★ ★ ★ **Smooth Talk / RCA (1977)**
★ ★ ★ **Music Box / RCA (1979)** ¶
★ ★ ★ **I'm in Love / RCA (1981)**
Philadelphia prodigy Evelyn "Champagne" King hit during Saturday-night fever with "Shame," a classic belonging to R&B more than to disco. It came from *Smooth Talk*'s roadhouse sass and smoky whisper, and set a standard of flesh-and-blood dance music that *Music Box* didn't live up to. *I'm in Love* is the slickest of the three; just as dance music is warming up, a potentially hot singer retros into cold, satin-pants shtick.   — L.F.

FREDDIE KING
★ **Burglar / RSO (1974)**
★ ★ ★ **Larger Than Life / RSO (1975)**
★ ★ **The Best of Freddie King / Shel. (1975)**
★ ★ **Freddie King (1934–1976) / RSO (1977)**
Freddie King's sudden death in December 1976 (he was forty-two) robbed blues and rock of an active cross-pollinator. He left his prophetically titled final release, *Larger Than Life,* as a barrelhousing live-in-Texas epitaph. *Burglar* and *Freddie King (1934–1976),* a posthumous collection, were both cut with British sessionmen and offer less. Freddie's brassy singing and speedy picking also survive on Shelter's *Best of* ("Palace of the King" is the peak of his late-Sixties collaboration with Leon Russell). But his out-of-print sides for King Records, which date from the Fifties, especially the Eric Clapton touchstone, *Hideaway* (containing Billy Myles' "Have You Ever Loved a Woman"), remain the best evidence of an electric guitar that roamed from Texas to Chicago. Unfortunately, the King albums are extremely difficult to find.   — F.S.

THE KINGBEES
★ ★ ★ ★ **The Kingbees / RSO (1980)**
★ ★ ★ **The Big Rock / RSO (1981)**
Smart update of big beat basics by L.A. trio led by Jamie James. On vinyl, the Kingbees shake it without the straitjacket self-consciousness of other contemporary rockabillyists. Songs are sparse, infectious and minus revivalist obscuranitism. Debut featured only two (well-chosen) oldies, including a rocked-up Don Gibson tune, "Sweet

Sweet Girl to Me." Second outing suffers from the dead hand of the past and originals not altogether up to Kingbees' standards. Fine performances from all three musicians on both LPs. — G.A.

KING BISCUIT BOY
★ ★ ★ **King Biscuit Boy / Epic (NA)** ¶
Ex–Ronnie Hawkins sideman Richard Newell (a.k.a. King Biscuit Boy), a local favorite blues shouter and harmonica player in Canada, meets Allen Toussaint and the Meters, and comes up on the short end. A good album, but more Toussaint's than Biscuit's—more funky New Orleans than bluesy Chicago. — A.N.

KING CRIMSON
★ ★ ★ ★ **In the Court of the Crimson King / Atl. (1969)**
★ ★ ★ **In the Wake of Poseidon / Atl. (1970)**
★ ★ **Lizard / Atl. (1971)**
★ ★ **Islands / Atl. (1972)**
★ ★ ★ **Lark's Tongue in Aspic / Atl. (1973)**
★ ★ ★ **Starless and Bible Black / Atl. (1974)**
★ ★ ★ **Red / Atl. (1974)** ¶
★ ★ ★ **USA / Atl. (1975)**
★ ★ ★ **Discipline / War. (1981)**
★ ★ ★ **Beat / War. (1982)**
In the Court of the Crimson King helped shape a set of baroque standards for art rock, merging angry frenetic guitars and saxophones, delicate woodwinds and other acoustic instruments, and the symphonic majesty of the Mellotron. It works, through the cohesive arranging and superb musicianship of guitarist/leader Robert Fripp and his ensemble. Ian McDonald was at the center, playing every instrument except guitar, bass (Greg Lake, who also sang) and drums (the nimbly, even melodically inventive Michael Giles). This is wonderfully colorful music, reaching a variety of moods, tones, volumes and tempos; Peter Sinfield's magical lyrics enhance the musical aura. The songs are long, but to worthwhile purpose.

McDonald then left, and much of *In the Wake of Poseidon* seems to be Fripp's attempt to rework the debut his way. Competent but finally inferior, the LP's color and breadth don't quite measure up. Elsewhere, there's Fripp's effectively dark Mellotron and Keith Tippet's fresh, jazz-tinged piano. *Lizard* is similar, despite more personnel changes (of the original lineup, only Fripp remained), but the more pronounced jazz influence is somewhat cold and aimless; the brass and reed solos tend to meander. *Islands* continues this icy abstractness, stress-

ing playing over composing at a time when more changes had left the group at its weakest: Fripp and saxist/flutist Mel Collins play well, but Boz Burrell (bass, vocals) and Ian Wallace (drums) lack the necessary precision. The arrangements are more spare and dull.

Larks' Tongues in Aspic emerged with a tight new quintet: Fripp, future Yes-man Bill Bruford on drums, John Wetton (later of Roxy Music) on bass and vocals, David Cross on violin and Jamie Muir on percussion; Sinfield was gone, replaced by Richard Palmer-James. The sound is less ornate; sharper and weightier, it deserved more than the mediocre compositions accorded it here. The same lineup, minus Muir, was intact for the far superior *Starless and Bible Black,* where the emphasis is less on ornamentation than on sheer power, abrasive but firmly controlled. The writing matches the playing, showing a subtle influence from such fusionists of rock and jazz as the Mahavishnu Orchestra. *USA,* from the same quartet, is a capable live set that improves on three of *Larks'* pieces, and includes one new cut. *Red* saw the group out in a blaze of glory: a tautly energetic finale and realization of their last directions, driven by Fripp's distorted guitar and Wetton's similarly aggressive bass. Bruford punctuates magnificently. Supplemented by the Mellotron, *Red* gives new meaning to the concept of a trio. *Discipline* is a credible comeback for Fripp, followed by the promising *Beat.* — C.W.

THE KINGS
★ ★ ★ **The Kings Are Here / Elek. (1980)**
★ ★ **Amazon Beach / Elek. (1981)**
This Toronto group's 1980 hit, "This Beat Goes On/Switchin' to Glide" has an undeniable catchiness that transcends its teen-dream silliness. It sets the pace for the rest of the debut album, Cars-influenced pop that occasionally recalls the least offensive moments of mid-Sixties garage rock. *Amazon Beach* aspires to meaningful social commentary on sexual politics and quickly becomes lost in its pretensions. — D.G.

THE KINGSMEN
★ **The Kingsmen / Picca. (1980)**
Before the beginning of time (or at least the Beatles), men made singles that (when slowed from 45 to 33 ⅓ rpm) contained all sorts of coded sexual garbage. Or so it was said. The Kingsmen never discouraged this interpretation of "Louie Louie," and until I was in my twenties, I took it as an article of faith, just like the one about the Lovers'

Lane couple who found the hook on their car door.

The Kingsmen actually made some good followups to "Louie Louie" (remember "Annie Fannie"? "Jolly Green Giant"?) and even some passable albums, which have a grungy, frat-house ambiance that helps define Sixties punk. (Their live album should especially be heard by fans of the Clash, who annexed the rudiments of "Should I Stay or Should I Go" from it.) Unfortunately, none of the good stuff is on this sole survivor among Kingsmen LPs, an actual LP's worth of outtakes and throwaways. Even if one believes in marginalia, this is taking it too goddamn far. — D.M.

KINGSTON TRIO
★ ★ ★ **The Best of the Kingston Trio, Vol. 1** / (1962)
★ ★ ★ **From the Hungry i** / Cap. (NA)
★ ★ ★ **Scarlet Ribbons** / Cap. (NA)
★ ★ ★ **Tom Dooley** / Cap. (NA)

With the demise of the Weavers in the early Fifties and the blacklisting of Pete Seeger in the McCarthy years, it was not until the Kingston Trio's 1959 hit, "Tom Dooley," that professional folk performance recaptured a hold on American pop music.

"Tom Dooley" was a traditional ballad from Frank Proffitt's repertoire, and represented one aspect of the Trio's work—carefully arranged, edited versions of traditional folk songs. The Kingston Trio, however, also found material from contemporary songwriters such as Seeger ("Where Have All the Flowers Gone"), Bob Dylan ("Blowin' in the Wind") and Will Holt ("Lemon Tree") as well as drawing on such commercially familiar sources as Lerner and Loewe ("They Call the Wind Maria") and the Julius Monk satirical revues ("Ballad of the Shape of Things").

This breadth gave Dave Guard, Nick Reynolds and Bob Shane's group broad appeal and opened the way for Peter, Paul and Mary, the Chad Mitchell Trio and a host of imitators, and for the songwriters whose work they performed. John Stewart replaced Guard in 1961, and although a group with Reynolds continues to tour under the name, the Kingston Trio can really be said to have disbanded in 1968. — I.M.

THE KINKS
★ ★ ★ **You Really Got Me** / Rep. (1964) ¶
★ ★ ★ **Kinks-Size** / Rep. (1965) ¶
★ ★ ★ ★ ★ **Greatest Hits!** / Rep. (1966) ¶
★ ★ ★ ★ **The Live Kinks** / Rep. (1967)
★ ★ ★ ★ **Something Else** / Rep. (1968)

★ ★ ★ ★ ★ **The Kinks Are the Village Green Preservation Society** / Rep. (1969)
★ ★ ★ ★ **Arthur** / Rep. (1969)
★ ★ ★ ★ ★ **Lola Versus Powerman and the Moneygoround** / Rep. (1970)
★ ★ ★ ★ **Kink Kronikles** / Rep. (1972)
★ ★ ★ **Everybody's in Showbiz, Everybody's a Star** / RCA (1972)
★ ★ ★ **Preservation, Act One** / RCA (1973)
★ ★ ★ **Preservation, Act Two** / RCA (1974)
★ ★ **Soap Opera** / RCA (1975)
★ ★ ★ **Schoolboys in Disgrace** / RCA (1975)
★ ★ ★ **Greatest Hits—Celluloid Heroes** / RCA (1976)
★ ★ ★ **Sleepwalker** / Ari. (1977)
★ ★ ★ **Misfits** / Ari. (1978)
★ ★ ★ **Low Budget** / Ari. (1979)
★ ★ ★ **One for the Road** / Ari. (1980)
★ ★ **Second Time Around** / RCA (1980)
★ ★ ★ **Give the People What They Want** / Ari. (1981)

There never had been a rock & roll sound like the one introduced by the Kinks with their first hit, "You Really Got Me." With one simple riff, Ray Davies and brother Dave Davies virtually invented power-chord rock. The furious sound of that record should be contrasted with the velvet-suit, ruffled-shirt outfits members of the band wore at the beginning of their career, which gave immediate notice that the Kinks were a complex unit. Their early albums contained, besides a few monumental hits like "All Day and All of the Night," "Tired of Waiting for You" and "I Need You," the usual blues reworkings common to the era. But by their fifth album, *Kink Konstroversey* (out of print), it was clear that songwriter Ray Davies was growing by leaps and bounds. Here, in addition to the chaos of "Till the End of the Day" and "Milk Cow Blues," were some poignant ("The World Keeps Going Round"), self-mocking ("I'm on an Island"), starkly beautiful ("Ring the Bells") compositions.

Davies' use of narrative came to full maturity on the classic *Face to Face* (out of print), arguably rock's first concept album. Looking around at the often drab, sometimes melodramatic day-to-day occurrences of average people, Davies concocted his own peculiarly English microcosm of the world, and proof of his brilliance and eloquence as a writer resides in such tracks as "Rosie Won't You Please Come Home," "Too Much on My Mind" and "Rainy Day in June." "Sunny Afternoon," a vaudevillian tune, was a hit for the band, their last for a long time.

Something Else continued Davies' masterful combination of rock and pop, with the ethereal "Waterloo Sunset" leading an album of uniformly excellent songs, among them "Afternoon Tea," "David Watts," "Situation Vacant" and brother Dave's "Death of a Clown." Another conceptual album, *Village Green*, followed, and again the group produced a very quiet and modest masterpiece. Davies zeroed in on the inhabitants of a sleepy English town and revealed their broken dreams and fading hopes through a collection of expertly assembled vignettes.

Although the group had been making uncannily fine albums, their audience had all but disappeared, heading for the psychedelic sounds of the late Sixties. With the band at its lowest point commercially in 1970, Davies was asked to write a score for a British television special about the decline of the British Empire. The album's soundtrack, *Arthur*, put the Kinks back on the map, and as the Kinks began to rock again, with songs like "Victoria," "Australia" and "Brainwashed," things began looking up. *Lola* gave them their first hit in five years, and with a song about a transvestite, at that. The band forged on, combining tough, tongue-in-cheek numbers like "Top of the Pops" and "Apeman" with haunting ballads such as "A Long Way from Home" and "Get Back in Line."

After *Lola*, the Kinks moved to RCA records; their initial LP for the label, *Muswell Hillbillies* (deleted), found them once again in softer territory. But Davies' songwriting talents helped produce an album that stands as his signature statement. There were splashes of the music hall ("Skin and Bones") and the legitimate theater ("Alcohol," "Holiday"); elements of rock ("Twentieth Century Man"), blues ("Acute Schizophrenia Paranoia Blues"), ballads ("Oklahoma U.S.A.") and country ("Holloway Jail"). Davies' infatuation with theatricality, however, soon began to dominate the group's records. *Everybody's in Showbiz*, while containing the lovely "Celluloid Heroes," was the first Kinks album in a long time with any truly weak tracks, and the live disc included in the set relies more on Davies' camp stage act than on good music for its success. (The earlier *Live Kinks*, recorded in 1966, has that *plus* some ferocious music.) From there, it was inevitable that Davies compose a full-bodied, plotted extravaganza. *Preservation*, a two-part, three-record affair (only half of which remains available) was hampered by its rather involved and self-absorbed plot. Another concept LP, *Soap Opera*, followed, but it too was a bit thin

and ineffective. The main problem with both works is that they contained no distinguished compositions. *Schoolboys in Disgrace* brought Davies back to straight unconnected song settings, with fairly good results. Dave Davies' reemergence on guitar helped quite a bit on *Schoolboys* and on the band's first record for Arista, *Sleepwalker*, which has, in "Juke Box Music," the best song Davies had composed in years. *Misfits* follows the same pattern, with similar success. *Low Budget* saw the Kinks at their greatest popularity since the days of their first hits. The obligatory live LP, *One for the Road*, consolidated this newfound strength as a top arena attraction, and *Give the People* lived up to its name as the band established a solid AOR radio formula. — B.A./J.S.

FERN KINNEY

★ ★ ★ **Groove Me / Mal. (1979)**
★ ★ **Fern / Mal. (1981)**

Kinney's a decent disco-blues performer whose biggest success came with "Groove Me," a middling soul hit that also made some crossover noise. — D.M.

DANNY KIRWAN

★ ★ **Second Chapter / DJM (1975)**
★ ★ **Danny Kirwan / DJM (1977)**
★ ★ **Hello There Big Boy / DJM (1979)**

Kirwan was the first addition to the basic lineup of Fleetwood Mac and one of the first members to leave; he helped make some of their early albums (particularly *Kiln House*) as good as they were. But without that group's fine rhythm section, his solo albums wander aimlessly, just another good guitarist in search of something to play and something to say. — D.M.

KISS

★ **Kiss / Casa. (1974)**
★ **Hotter than Hell / Casa. (1974)**
★ **Dressed to Kill / Casa. (1975)**
★ ★ ★ **Alive / Casa. (1975)**
★ ★ ★ ★ **Destroyer / Casa. (1976)**
★ **The Originals / Casa. (1976)**
★ ★ ★ **Rock and Roll Over / Casa. (1977)**
★ ★ **Love Gun / Casa. (1977)**
★ ★ **Alive II / Casa. (1977)**
★ ★ ★ **Double Platinum / Casa. (1978)**
★ ★ ★ **Dynasty / Casa. (1979)**
★ ★ **Unmasked / Casa. (1980)**
★ ★ ★ **Music from "The Elder" / Casa. (1981)**
★ ★ **Creatures of the Night / Casa. (1982)**

Solo Albums
★ ★ **Paul Stanley / Casa. (1978)**

★ ★ **Gene Simmons** / **Casa. (1978)**
★ ★ **Ace Frehley** / **Casa. (1978)**
★ ★ **Peter Criss** / **Casa. (1978)**

The power riffing, the exuberance, the innate humor—even the subtlety—marking such early Kiss classics as "Deuce," "Strutter" and "Nothin' to Lose" are lost in production so muddy it renders the group's first three albums, *Kiss, Hotter than Hell* and *Dressed to Kill* (and *The Originals* collection), unlistenable. When Kiss needed to establish itself on record, *Alive* was released. By capturing the real thunder of the group in concert, *Alive* justifies much of Kiss's popularity, and contains one of rock's indisputably great anthems in "Rock and Roll All Nite."

Destroyer was a logical step forward. Paired for the first time with a forceful producer in Bob Ezrin—who is both a master of studio technology and a classically trained musician—Kiss came forth with a concept album that explored the psychological ramifications of the members' stage personas via music that is by turns driving and dynamic, chilling and introspective. Moreover, *Destroyer* is sophisticated in a manner apart from standard heavy-metal fare: the intricate time signatures of "Detroit Rock City," for example, present a challenge to any rock musician.

Kiss's return to minimalism, *Rock and Roll Over,* produced by the passive Eddie Kramer, lacks *Destroyer*'s distinctive production and memorable material, save a quintessential Kiss song in "I Want You." The rest merely reworks the fire-breathing formula.

In 1978, the members of Kiss each released a solo album. These weren't great artistic achievements by any means, but did give fans an idea of what each musician brought to the band in terms of sensibility. There are plenty of surprises here: Frehley's is the hardest-rocking and best of the four LPs, with the fine "New York Groove," which was a hit single; Criss' blue-eyed soul stylings have a certain gruff charm, but the material is so-so; Stanley's is closest to the Kiss sound in all respects, but lacks the zip of Frehley's rock; Simmons' LP is mellow, almost middle-of-the-road rock, heavily orchestrated in some instances and only occasionally raunchy in the *Love Gun* style.

Dynasty and *Unmasked,* most notably the former, return to the raw style of Kiss's early albums, but are better produced and better written than any of those efforts. *The Elder* marks Kiss's reunion with Ezrin, and once again the combination clicked. The band hadn't been so adventurous since *De-*

stroyer; the high-caliber musicianship (new drummer Eric Carr is especially impressive), songwriting and singing indicate how well Kiss responds to Ezrin in the studio. Simmons' sensitive vocal on "World Without Heroes" displays a depth of feeling heretofore lacking on Kiss records. In fact, with the exception of the vengeful "Mr. Blackwell" (cowritten by Simmons and Lou Reed), *"The Elder"* is remarkable for the way it seeks to reach the heart rather than the crotch—and when's the last time anyone accused Kiss of being sentimental? *Creatures* adds nothing to the band's reputation.
— D.MC.

OSAMU KITAJIMA
★ ★ ★ ★ **Osamu** / **Is. (1977)**
Osamu Kitajima is a Japanese composer and instrumentalist whose sole American release reveals a talent with an intriguing cross-cultural vision and far more imagination than your average instrumental music artist. Laced through an intriguing jazz-rock mix are slices of such Japanese instruments as the koto, biwa, shakuhachi and nohkan. The stellar production adds a glistening veneer to this lovely and often impressive mating of Oriental thinking with a rock & roll consciousness. — R.P.

KLAATU
★ **Klaatu** / **Cap. (1976)**
★ **Hope** / **Cap. (1977)**
★ **Sir Army Suit** / **Cap. (1978)**
★ **Endangered Species** / **Cap. (1980)**
Named for a robot in a science-fiction movie, Klaatu's only claim to fame came through rumor: its self-titled first LP was reported to be the re-formed Beatles, a 1976 scam perpetuated by the group members' refusal to identify themselves. When word leaked out that it was only a batch of anonymous Canadian session players, reality asserted itself: mediocrity runs rampant through each of these discs, even the attempt to make *Sir Army Suit* a Northland *Sgt. Pepper's.* Good for a laugh—barely. — D.M.

KLEEER
★ **I Love to Dance** / **Atl. (1979)**
★ **Winners** / **Atl. (1979)**
★ **License to Dream** / **Atl. (1981)**
Highly undistinguished soul/funk outfit scored minor R&B chart successes with "Keep Your Body Workin' " and "Tonight's the Night (Good Time)" from *I Love to Dance* debut LP. Since then has tried everything from a bugle call to the post to Space Invaders computer noises without any luck,

a rare triumph of common sense in the recording/broadcasting industries. — D.M.

KLIQUE
★ ★ **It's Winning Time** / MCA (NA)
Not the in crowd. — D.M.

KLYMAXX
★ ★ ★ **Never Underestimate the Power of a Woman** / Solar (1981)
In the title cut, the eight women of Klymaxx boast of jamming just as hard as they can. And they do a credible job, too. Maybe next time their (male) producers will let them write more than one song. — J.D.C.

THE KNACK
■ **Get the Knack** / Cap. (1979)
■ **. . . But the Little Girls Understand** / Cap. (1980)
■ **Round Trip** / Cap. (1981)
It's hard to appreciate on how many levels the Knack offended people with the instant success of *Get the Knack* and the No. 1 "My Sharona." Musicians resented them for their obscenely rapid rise (although the new wave they supposedly came from wanted exactly such chart flexibility). Beatles lovers hated the *Meet the Beatles* imagery being used to sell the Knack as a new Fab Four. And feminists despised them for their misogynist, teenage-girls-as-objects attitude.

It's that last complaint that makes these records sickening and unlistenable. All females are prey for the Knack's mentality, but the younger the better. Of course, if for some reason the girl doesn't play nice for the boys, she's termed selfish and then discarded (which would have been the end result anyway). Maybe nobody really caught on the first time; after all, on the followup to "Sharona," "Good Girls Don't," the words "sitting on your face" are cut out.

Somehow all the negative feeling caught up with the Knack, because . . . *But the Little Girls Understand* was not the smash expected, despite a "Sharona" carbon copy (the despicable "Baby Talks Dirty") and modern-day marketing techniques which usually guarantee that success repeats itself. The band licked its wounds and finally came up with *Round Trip*, whose title bespoke of hope for a return to grace. Not in this lifetime, probably; the Knack seem destined to be a trivia question in the year 2000.
— W.K.

THE KNICKERBOCKERS
★ ★ **Lies** / Line (1965), Ger. imp.
A reissue of the album made by the famous guys from New Jersey whose only hit— "Lies," of course—sounds so much like the Beatles that it fooled my kids on the car radio in 1982. Unfortunately, the rest of the album, despite the hilarious testimonials on the sleeve (from Brian Wilson, many disc jockeys and Marvin Gaye to Ian Whitcomb and Glen Campbell) contains versions of the Fab Four sound considerably more strained and therefore less convincing. "Lies" is one of the reasons God invented singles, however. — D.M.

FREDERICK KNIGHT
★ ★ **Knight Kap** / Juana (NA)
★ ★ **Let the Sunshine In** / Juana (NA)
Best known for his 1972 crossover hit, "I've Been Lonely for So Long," Knight is a journeyman soul singer reduced here to not-unsympathetic (but not especially appropriate) disco settings. — D.M.

GLADYS KNIGHT AND THE PIPS
★ ★ ★ **Gladys Knight and the Pips' Greatest Hits** / Soul (1970)
★ ★ ★ **Standing Ovation** / Soul (1972)
★ ★ ★ ★ **Neither One of Us** / Soul (1972)
★ ★ ★ ★ **Imagination** / Bud. (1973)
★ ★ ★ ★ **Anthology** / Mo. (1974)
★ ★ ★ **Claudine** / Bud. (1974)
★ ★ ★ **I Feel a Song** / Bud. (1974)
★ ★ **Bless This House** / Bud. (1975)
★ ★ ★ **Second Anniversary** / Bud. (1975)
★ ★ ★ ★ **Gladys Knight and the Pips' Greatest Hits** / Bud. (1976)
★ ★ **Pipe Dreams** / Bud. (1976)
★ ★ ★ **Still Together** / Bud. (1977)
★ ★ ★ **Love Is Always on Your Mind** / Bud. (1977)
★ ★ **Miss Gladys Knight** / Bud. (1978)
★ ★ ★ ★ **Motown Superstar Series, Vol. 13** / Mo. (1980)
★ ★ ★ **Everybody Needs Love** / Mo. (1981)
★ ★ ★ **Nitty Gritty** / Mo. (1981)
★ ★ **Early Hits** / Sp. (NA)
★ ★ **Gladys Knight and the Pips** / Trip (NA)
★ ★ **Gladys Knight and the Pips** / Up Fr. (NA)
★ ★ **How Do You Say Goodbye** / Sp. (NA)
Gladys Knight and the Pips began singing together as teenagers. By 1961, they clicked twice on the pop charts with "Letter Full of Tears" and "Every Beat of My Heart," in a Fifty-ish vocal group mode. Those records, done for Fury, are classics, but what surrounds them—on repackages onto Trip, Up Front and Springboard—is mostly mush. The versions included on Motown's *Anthology*, however, are re-recorded and to be avoided.

At Motown's subsidiary, Soul, the group, beginning in 1967, recorded a batch of tough, gritty sides, closer to Martha and the Vandellas than to the frothy Supremes. The first of them was "Everybody Needs Love," and the series included what is perhaps the best version of "I Heard It Through the Grapevine," "The End of Our Road," "Nitty Gritty" and "Friendship Train" through 1969. In 1970 the group teamed up with producer Johnny Bristol for an adult soul ballad, "If I Were Your Woman," which set the mold for the rest of their career. Rather than the shouting histrionics that had characterized Knight's singing on her early records, these featured elaborate productions, more sentimental and sensual than in the past; "Woman" was the highlight, but "I Don't Want to Do Wrong" and "Neither One of Us (Wants to Be the First to Say Goodbye)" were in the same mold.

Knight was now the dominant force in the group, stepping ever more out front, and when they went to Buddah, she adopted an even more adult persona, much more like Dionne Warwick than the hoarse belter of the past. The group recorded songs by Barry Goldberg and Gerry Goffin, who contributed "I've Got to Use My Imagination," and Jim Weatherly, who penned several Knight hits (including her greatest, "Midnight Train to Georgia"); 1973 was probably their peak year. The hits continued through 1975, but a spiral of banality begun on *Second Anniversary* with a medley of "The Way We Were/ Try to Remember" reigned unchecked. A brief association with Curtis Mayfield (*Claudine,* a soundtrack) helped a bit but didn't really orient them. Since then the records have been more formulaic, though the beauty of Knight's performances can occasionally cut through.

Anthology is the ideal collection of the years at Soul; *Greatest Hits,* on Buddah, is a more-than-adequate retrospective of the Buddah syndrome, though *Imagination,* which contains both of her 1973 hits, is just about as definitive. *Pipe Dreams,* the soundtrack to the film in which Knight made her acting debut, is probably the weakest of the   post–Vee Jay discs. The Pips recorded on their own for a time, but reunited with Gladys when neither separate career panned out. Nonetheless, they've done little recording lately. The most recent LPs listed are reissues of Sixties and early-Seventies stuff.   — D.M.

TOMMY KNIGHT
★ ★ **Tommy Knight / Col. (1981)**
Machine-made pop-rock product.   — D.M.

FRED KNOBLOCK
★ ★ **Why Not Me / Scotti (1980)**
Mediocre pop singer nonetheless scored a pair of Top Thirty hits, the title track and "Killin' Time," the latter a duet with Susan Anton.   — D.M.

KOCKY
★ ★ **Kocky / Wind. (1979)** ¶
Pedestrian funk.   — J.D.C.

JOHN KOERNER
★ ★ ★ **Spider Blues / Elek. (NA)**
★ ★ ★ ★ **Running Jumping Standing Still (with Willie Murphy) / Elek. (NA)**
As a member of Koerner, Ray and Glover, John Koerner earned a reputation as a fine blues guitarist, whose approach involved the eccentricity of playing a seven- (rather than the usual six- or twelve-) string guitar. *Spider Blues* is a solo album of guitar work from the early-Sixties folk revival period. *Running* is the result of a late-Sixties collaboration with fellow Minnesotan Willie Murphy, and it rocks a lot harder—a fine example of white blues at its best.   — D.M.

KOERNER, RAY AND GLOVER
★ ★ ★ ★ **Blues, Rags and Hollers / Elek. (NA)**
★ ★ ★ **Lots More Blues, Rags and Hollers / Elek. (NA)**
John Koerner (seven-string guitar), Dave Ray (twelve-string guitar) and Tony Glover (harmonica) were from the same University of Minnesota folk scene that produced Bob Dylan in the early Sixties. They were the finest white blues group in the entire folk revival of that era, and these albums (along with the now-deleted *Return of Koerner, Ray and Glover*) were highly influential on aficionados of black American folk music. Ray was a formidable twelve-string stylist, the best of his era, and Koerner's approach to blues was fairly unbeatable, while Glover's emulation of Sonny Boy Williamson kept the rhythm going at a hot pace.   — D.M.

BONNIE KOLOC
★ ★ ★ **After All This Time / Ova. (1971)**
★ ★ ★ **Hold on to Me / Ova. (1972)**
★ ★ ★ **Bonnie Koloc / Ova. (1973)**
★ ★ ★ **You're Gonna Love Yourself in the Morning / Ova. (1974)**
★ ★ ★ ★ **Bonnie at Her Best / Ova. (1976)**
★ ★ ★ ★ **Close-Up / Epic (1976)**
★ ★ ★ **Wild and Reclusive / Epic (1978)**
Female interpretative singer who is commendable on all accounts: excellent production, sensitive playing and knowing, deeply

felt vocals. Koloc's values are traditionalist, in much the same way as Bonnie Raitt's, but she's also capable of moving toward pop without becoming as flimsy as Linda Ronstadt and her ilk. — D.M.

KOOL AND THE GANG
★ ★ ★ **Wild and Peaceful** / De-Lite (1973)
★ ★ **Open Sesame** / De-Lite (1976)
★ ★ **The Force** / De-Lite (1977)
★ ★ ★ ★ **Kool and the Gang Spin Their Top Hits** / De-Lite (1978)
★ ★ **Everybody's Dancin'** / De-Lite (1978)
★ ★ **Ladies' Night** / De-Lite (1979)
★ ★ ★ **Celebration** / De-Lite (1980)
★ ★ **Something Special** / De-Lite (1981)

As the first important funk and horn band of the Seventies, predating even James Brown's JB's, Kool and the Gang derived from the soul revues of the Sixties. Most of the major soul acts of the time carried large bands that verged on being orchestras, in which the most prominent solo instrument was the saxophone. While the crowd piled in, the band would often warm up by playing whatever pop-jazz pieces were then fashionable.

Kool and the Gang, with their obvious affection for jazz, added a party atmosphere to such instrumentals that gave their songs a deranged flavor; the horns sputter a staccato riff, while in the background band members whoop and holler in seemingly uncontainable delight. After the first few successful instrumentals, Kool (bassist Robert Bell) and the Gang added loose vocal lines. On "Who's Gonna Take the Weight," there is a short spoken intro about worldly responsibility that leads into a driving track punctuated periodically by shouts of the title. "Funky Man" was an even more crazed vision—a good-humored song whose principal character is a man whose clothes stink.

The group has made more than a dozen LPs, and what's left is hardly representative of more than a decade's work. The zenith of the approach is *Wild and Peaceful,* in which burping vocals and good-time horn charts are anchored by a metronomic beat. Songs like "Hollywood Swingin' " and "Funky Stuff" found an unexpected home with the white disco audience. Subsequent records have seen little variation from that formula; although spiritual concerns have seeped into the lyrics, the albums all revolve around similar sounding instrumentals—with an incessant rhythmic approach and horn charts that haven't altered in years.
— J.MC.

AL KOOPER
★ **I Stand Alone** / Col. (1967)
★ ★ ★ **Super Session** / Col. (1968)
★ **Live Adventures of Al Kooper and Mike Bloomfield** / Col. (1969)
★ **Kooper Session** / Col. (1970)
★ **Unclaimed Freight** / Col. (1975)

At first glance Al Kooper's solo career would seem to divide into two impulses: the "session" albums and the elaborate "pop" productions. On closer inspection, however, all of Kooper's albums collapse into a failure of the Grand Pop that Kooper first envisioned as leader of the original Blood, Sweat and Tears.

Despite their commercial success, the "session" albums manage to insult everyone involved. The most famous, *Super Session,* features Stephen Stills (guitar only) on one side and Mike Bloomfield on the other. Kooper took the finished "session" tapes and then added horns and production to highlights his amateurish vocals and organ playing. His psychedelicized production of the Stills side shoves Stills' feeble needles-and-pins guitar solos onto the rhythm track. Bloomfield's work (also in settings imposed by Kooper afterward) is sterling, perhaps the last great performance of Bloomfield's career. On this side, Kooper's contributions consist of inept Jimmy Smith imitations on the organ, horn charts to cover the dead spots, and his patented thin-pipe soul vocals.

Kooper's subsequent attempts to re-create the original session, *Live Adventures* and *Kooper Session* with Shuggie Otis, merely repeat the mistakes and stretch out the dead spots.

The Kooper pop canon is a hugely arrogant, incredibly inflated and totally misconceived version of Blood, Sweat and Tears' *Child Is Father to the Man* concept, using studio musicians in place of a stable band. The latest of these, *Act Like Nothing's Wrong* (United Artists; deleted), after a hiatus of several years, at least shows that Al Kooper is on to himself as a joke, but it is still lousy. — B.T.

THE KORGIS
★ ★ **The Korgis** / War. (1979)
★ ★ **Dumb Waiters** / Asy. (1980)

Self-consciously clever art-school pop, all form and no content. — J.D.C.

DANNY KORTCHMAR
★ **Innuendo** / Asy. (1980)

Extraordinary session guitarist (James Taylor, Crosby and Nash, etc.) makes extraordinarily wrong-headed solo album. Most side-

man solo albums are pointless because they are without a concept or purpose. Danny Kootch, as he's known, doesn't make that mistake, but his rock & roll is histrionic, and as for his attempts at eclecticism . . . just stay away. The star is for chops.
— D.M.

KORONA
★ **Let Me Be** / U.A. (1980)
The kind of music made to excite record-company employees, bedazzle radio pro-gramers and dull the public palate—incompetently put together. — D.M.

LEO KOTTKE
★ ★ ★ **Circle round the Sun** / Symp. (1969)
★ ★ ★ **Mudlark** / Cap. (1971)
★ ★ ★ ★ **Six- and Twelve-String Guitar** / Tak. (1972)
★ ★ ★ ★ ★ **Greenhouse** / Cap. (1973)
★ ★ ★ ★ ★ **My Feet Are Smiling** / Cap. (1973)
★ ★ ★ **Ice Water** / Cap. (1974)
★ ★ ★ **Dreams and All That Stuff** / Cap. (1974)
★ ★ ★ **Chewing Pine** / Cap. (1974)
★ ★ ★ **Leo Kottke 1971–1976/"Did You Hear Me?"** / Cap. (1976)
★ ★ ★ ★ **Leo Kottke** / Chrys. (1976)
★ ★ ★ ★ **Leo Kottke—The Best** / Cap. (1978)
★ ★ **Burnt Lips** / Chrys. (1978)
★ ★ **Balance** / Chrys. (1979)
★ ★ ★ **Guitar Music** / Chrys. (1981)
Although Kottke is often mentioned in the same breath with John Fahey, a more ap-propriate comparison is with the late coun-try-blues guitarist Sam McGee. Unlike Fahey, a highly idiosyncratic artist whose career has lately taken a turn away from American folk music, Kottke remains a staunch traditionalist. Like McGee's, his ca-reer bespeaks a profound commitment to the simple virtues of harmony, melody, and if you will, plain talk found in country, folk and blues songs. The bristling energy of Kottke's early albums is due in large part to a redoubtable and curious penchant for find-ing new possibilities within the oldest genres. This often culminates in beautiful surprises, foremost among them being his exquisite, moving rendition of Bach's "Jesu, Joy of Man's Desiring" (first heard on the Takoma album; repeated on *My Feet Are Smiling*). *My Feet Are Smiling*, a live album, signals the end of Kottke's musical free-spiritedness; subsequent recordings have found him striv-ing, most unsuccessfully, for a more com-mercial middle ground. As he does this he

sings less, which is unfortunate, despite Kott-ke's protests to the contrary. While not an adept singer technically, he is blessed with a deep, resonant voice capable of great emotive power. It is no accident that his best albums —*Greenhouse, My Feet Are Smiling, Ice Water*—contain his finest vocal perfor-mances. And of his post-live albums, only *Ice Water*, graced by a superb interpretation of Tom T. Hall's "Pamela Brown," ap-proaches vintage Kottke. However, a label change in 1977 proved fruitful. *Leo Kottke*, complete with orchestra and Jack Nitzsche arrangements, is, aesthetically speaking, Kottke's most fully realized work since *Greenhouse*.

Notable among his Chrysalis albums is 1981's *Guitar Music*, Kottke's first solo in-strumental album since 1969's *Circle round the Sun*. Producing himself, Kottke also wrote thirteen songs, including a dreamy suite on side one (titled, appropriately, "Side One Suite"), in addition to interpreting Bob Nolan's "Tumbling Tumbleweeds," Felice and Boudleaux Bryant's "All I Have to Do Is Dream," and Santo and Johnny's "Sleep Walk." Casual listeners may find *Guitar Music* lacking for energy in spots, but closer inspection reveals an LP interesting both for the choices Kottke makes as an instrumen-talist and for the spirit in his playing.
— D.MC.

KRACKER
★ ★ **Hot** / Dash (1976)
Cuban/American five-piece hard-rock band from Miami. No big deal. — J.S.

KRAFTWERK
★ ★ ★ ★ **Autobahn** / Mer. (1975)
★ ★ ★ **Radio-Activity** / Cap. (1975)
★ ★ ★ **Trans Europe Express** / Cap. (1977)
★ ★ ★ **Man Machine** / Cap. (1978)
★ ★ ★ **Computer World** / War. (1981)
This German band didn't invent the synthe-sizer, but *Autobahn*, a sonic portrait of a drive along the world's second most famous roadway (after Route 66), went a long way toward popularizing the instrument. Com-plete with whooshes resembling passing autos, repeated refrains and droning chorus-es, "Autobahn" is a 22-minute composition that encapsulates the hypnotic redundancy of a twelve-hour drive. Valuable as both a mu-sical oddity and background music for watching tropical fish sleep.

The other albums repeat the latter's musi-cal themes with varying motifs, and are hence unnecessary. — A.N.

BILLY J. KRAMER AND THE DAKOTAS
★ ★ ★ **The Best of Billy J. Kramer and the Dakotas / Cap. (1979)**
Poor Billy J. was always the poor relation in Brian Epstein's family of Liverpool stars. Troubled by a weight problem and an outdated teen idol's voice, he was given Lennon/McCartney rejects to sing and eventually faded into oblivion when the Beatles began to take up all of Epstein's time and affection.

Although not the most exciting music ever recorded, Kramer's hits—"Little Children," "Bad to Me," "From a Window," and others—still have an unassuming sweetness and charm that stand up to repeated listening and sound a lot better than today's equivalently tangential music. — D.G.

TIM KREKEL
★ ★ ★ **Crazy Me / Capri. (1979)**
Krekel's the kind of Southern rock & roller who pens tunes with real catfish hooks, then fries the results in a tasty batter. Krekel's rough-hewn quality and spunky country-boy energy are refreshing, especially since those elements flavor his songs with an almost immediate pop appeal. — R.P.

KRIS KRISTOFFERSON
★ ★ **The Silver-Tongued Devil and I / Col. (1971)**
★ ★ **Me and Bobby McGee / Col. (1971)**
★ **Border Lord / Col. (1972)**
★ **Jesus Was a Capricorn / Col. (1972)**
★ **Spooky Lady's Sideshow / Col. (1974)**
★ **Who's to Bless and Who's to Blame / Col. (1975)**
★ **Surreal Thing / Col. (1976)**
★ ★ **Easter Island / Col. (1978)**
★ **Shake Hands with the Devil / Col. (1979)**
★ **To the Bone / Col. (1980)**
Country rock's only Rhodes scholar and its best film actor (*A Star Is Born, Pat Garrett and Billy the Kid*) is also a key figure in the rejuvenation of Nashville. As a songwriter in the late Sixties, Kristofferson contributed tunes like "Help Me Make It through the Night," "Me and Bobby McGee" and "Sunday Morning Coming Down" to singers such as Roger Miller, Janis Joplin and Johnny Cash, opening new possibilities of sexual frankness and emotional honesty to the C&W field.

But as a performer, he is a questionable talent. Even when the material is as strong as it is on his first two albums, *Me and Bobby McGee* and *Silver-Tongued Devil*,

Kristofferson's aphoristic tales soon wear thin, as does his rough singing style—which is minimal, to put it charitably. — S.H.

KRIS KRISTOFFERSON AND RITA COOLIDGE
★ **Kris and Rita Full Moon / A&M (1973)**
★ **Breakaway / Col. (1974)**
★ **Natural Act / A&M (1978)**
The Nelson Eddy/Jeanette MacDonald of rock, except that he can hardly sing and she sounds like she's only half trying. — S.H.

DAVID KUBINEC
★ ★ ★ **Some Things Never Change / A&M (1979)**
British singer/songwriter with a strong debt to David Bowie. The songs here are good, but the reason this record works so well is the brilliant production of John Cale, who also plays keyboards. Guitarists Ollie Halsall and Chris Spedding play crucial session parts. — J.S.

LEAH KUNKEL
★ ★ **Leah Kunkel / Col. (1979)**
★ ★ **I Run with Trouble / Col. (1980)**
Cass Elliot's sister did the usual round of backup session vocals (credits include Art Garfunkel's *Watermark*) before making her own somewhat shapeless records with the L.A. session mafia. — J.S.

JIM KWESKIN
★ ★ ★ **Jim Kweskin and the Jug Band / Van. (1963)**
★ ★ **Jug Band Music / Van. (1965)**
★ ★ ★ **Relax Your Mind / Van. (1966)**
★ ★ **Jim Kweskin / Van. (1966)**
★ ★ **Jump for Joy / Van. (1967)**
★ ★ ★ **Best of Jim Kweskin / Van. (1968)**
★ ★ **Whatever Happened to the Good Old Days at Club 47 / Van. (1968) ¶**
★ ★ ★ **Greatest Hits / Van. (1970)**
This selection includes what remains from the heyday of the Jim Kweskin Jug Band, the early-Sixties folk revival and Kweskin's solo material from the same period. The solo stuff isn't worth much, but the Kweskin Jug Band, besides being Boston's major contribution to the folkie scene, was a formidable array of talent and by far the best of the short-lived jug-band revival. It included Maria Muldaur (whose "Woman" on *Relax* presages her Seventies approach); her husband, Geoff; bassist Fritz Richmond; and a then unknown, Mel Lyman, who later created a psychedelic dictatorship in Boston. — D.M.

SLEEPY LA BEEF
★ ★ **Bull's Night Out** / Sun (1976)
★ ★ ★ **1977 Rockabilly** / Sun (1977)
★ ★ **Beefy Rockabilly** / Charly (1978), Br.
imp.
★ ★ **Sleepy La Beef and Friends** / Ace
(1979)
★ ★ **Down Home Rockabilly** / Sun (1979)
★ ★ **Rockabilly Heavyweight** / Charly
(1979), Br. imp.
★ ★ ★ **Early Rare and Rockin'** / Baron
(NA)
★ ★ **It Ain't What You Eat (It's The Way
You Chew It)** / Roun. (1981)
La Beef has the soul of a rockabilly, I guess,
but even in the era of rockabilly revivals,
that makes him a bit out of date. And soul
isn't all there is to this stuff—most of the
time you'll have no trouble understanding
how La Beef earned his nickname. When he
essays rockabilly (as on his first Sun album
and the old sides collected on Baron), La
Beef can sometimes reach competence. When
he's trying to be expansive (i.e., sing pop and
country, too), he's simply a big-name bar
belter. — D.M.

PATTI LaBELLE
★ ★ ★ ★ **Patti LaBelle** / Epic (1977)
★ ★ ★ **Tasty** / Epic (1978)
★ ★ ★ **It's Alright with Me** / Epic (1979)
★ ★ ★ **Released** / Epic (1980)
★ ★ ★ ★ **Best of Patti LaBelle** / Epic (1981)
Patti LaBelle's triumphant solo debut marks
this singer's third career (in her first two she
led Patti LaBelle and the Bluebells and La-
belle). There are two instant classics here—
"Joy to Have Your Love" and "Dan Swit
Me"—a spunky version of Bob Dylan's
"Most Likely You'll Go Your Way and I'll
Go Mine" and an all-stops-out rendition of
"Since I Don't Have You." Producer David
Rubinson gives Patti the consistent pop R&B
setting that always just eluded her with La-

belle. *Tasty* and the rest are merely competent. — J.S.

LABELLE
★ ★ ★ ★ **Nightbirds** / Epic (1974)
★ ★ **Phoenix** / Epic (1975) ¶
★ ★ **Chameleon** / Epic (1976) ¶
A brilliant but erratic Seventies group, this
trio of magnificent women vocalists included
the high-pitched histrionics of Patti LaBelle,
the hard-edged belting of Nona Hendryx and
the sultry soul singing of Sarah Dash, who
had earlier performed as Patti LaBelle and
the Bluebells. In a way, their problem was
they were too good: they were capable of ac-
complishing so much that Labelle never developed a consistent, focused style. The deleted *Pressure Cookin'* was one peak,
fronting a relaxed but airtight R&B band
and covering an amazing range of material,
including a marvelous medley of "Something
in the Air" and "The Revolution Will Not
Be Televised." The commercial high point
was the Allen Toussaint–produced "Lady
Marmalade" from *Nightbirds,* but Toussaint
couldn't find the handle outside of that brilliant single, and subsequent attempts found
Labelle floundering through a number of un-
satisfactory strategies. Eventually this lack of
direction led to the trio's dissolution. — J.S.

CHERYL LADD
■ **Cheryl Ladd** / Cap. (1978)
■ **Dance Fever** / Cap. (1979)
Would that this former Charlie's Angel had
sufficient imagination to have created jiggle-
rock. Instead, she sounds like she recorded
after completing a stint in the lounge at the
Holiday Inn in Passaic, New Jersey.
— D.M.

PETER LA FARGE
★ ★ ★ **Peter La Farge Sings of Cowboys** /
Folk. (1963)

★ ★ ★ **Iron Mountain / Folk. (1963)**
★ ★ ★ **Peter La Farge, on the Warpath / Folk. (1965)**
★ ★ ★ **As Long as the Grass Shall Grow / Folk. (1968)**

The son of a sociologist who studied Native Americans, La Farge claimed to be a Pima Indian himself. Such self-mythologizing aside, before he died in 1965 at age thirty-four, La Farge wrote the poignant "Ballad of Ira Hayes" (among other songs), which was recorded by such artists as Bob Dylan, Patrick Sky and Johnny Cash. Although La Farge had written, performed and become familiar with folk music prior to his service in Korea, it was evidently that experience, combined with his own sense of heritage, that forged him into a writer who voiced the plight of American Indians as no other has done. These four (of five) Folkways sets express the anguish and strength of his music in its most basic form. — I.M.

DAVID LA FLAMME
■ **White Bird / Amh. (1976)**
■ **Inside Out / Amh. (1978)**

La Flamme's original group, It's a Beautiful Day, was easily the lamest band ever to emerge from Fillmore West and environs: all pretty hippie pretensions and a complete absence of energy. "White Bird," the title track of La Flamme's initial solo outing, was a hit for It's a Beautiful Day and serves as both warning and (one dreads to suppose) recommendation for the somnolent virtues of both these albums. — D.M.

CORKY LAING
★ ★ **Makin' It on the Streets / Elek. (1977)**

Apparently Laing knows nothing about the title subject, which figures: he used to be the drummer in Mountain and in West, Bruce and Laing, which only saw the street from the backseats of limousines. — D.M.

GREG LAKE
■ **Greg Lake / Chrys. (1981)**

Former bassist for King Crimson and Emerson, Lake and Palmer, Greg Lake cranks up his grandiose pipes and overloaded bass to sludge through another heaping pile of musical bullshit. Clarence Clemons must have been short on cash the week he agreed to play on this record. — R.P.

LAKE
★ **Lake / Col. (1977)**
★ **Lake 2 / Col. (1978)**
★ **Paradise Island / Col. (1979)**

Competent meld of German synthesizer and L.A. harmony Muzak, circa 1977–78: the Eagles meet Tangerine Dream. Bad idea nets the predictable result. — D.M.

LAKESIDE
★ ★ ★ **Shot of Love / Solar (1978)**
★ ★ ★ **Rough Riders / Solar (1979)**
★ ★ ★ **Fantastic Voyage / Solar (1980)**
★ ★ ★ **Your Wish Is My Command / Solar (1981)**

Nine-piece funk and harmony group that helped spearhead pioneer producer Dick Griffey's late Seventies/early Eighties revival of soul groups in disco context. Group has had several chart successes, beginning with "It's All the Way Live (Part 1)" in 1978, which made it to No. 4 on the R&B ledger. While not quite at the level of the best Solar groups, such as Whisper and Shalamar, Lakeside executes the formula well. — D.M.

KEVIN LAMB
★ ★ **Sailing down the Years / Ari. (1978)** ¶

Middling rocker's chief distinction is his associates: producer Gary Lyons, percussionist Ray Cooper, guitarists Andy Summers, Junior Marvin and B. J. Cole, vocalist Chris Thompson. All have shown lots more elsewhere. — D.M.

THE LAMBRETTAS
★ ★ **Beat Boys in the Jet Age / R. (1980)** ¶

Beat boys ought to have better rhythmic sense than these nouveau mod hacks. — J.D.C.

MAJOR LANCE
★ **Now Arriving / Soul (1978)** ¶

Does not contain "The Monkey Time" or other great hits. — D.M.

ROBIN LANE AND THE CHARTBUSTERS
★ ★ ★ ★ **Robin Lane and the Chartbusters / War. (1980)**
★ ★ ★ **Five Live / War. (1981)**
★ ★ ★ **Imitation Life / War. (1981)**

Robin Lane was a good singer/songwriter and sometime backup vocalist (Neil Young, Batteaux) who was energized and literally electrified by the emergence of the Sex Pistols and the Clash. In the late Seventies she put aside her acoustic guitar, assembled a crack band out of the best rock musicians in Boston and was signed to Warner Bros. after an independently released single ("When Things Go Wrong") became a regional hit. The first album was excellent: a punchy, guitar-driven sound reminiscent of Tom Petty and the Heartbreakers (as well as the best of the early San Francisco–based bands: Quicksilver Messenger Service, Jefferson Airplane, etc.) coupled with Lane's strong, emotive vocals. Despite critical acclaim, the group never gained widespread acceptance, and late in the summer of 1981 they broke up. It's expected that Robin Lane will continue to record on her own.   — B.C.

RONNIE LANE
★ ★ ★ **Any More for Any More / GM (1974), Br. imp.** ¶
★ ★ ★ **Ronnie Lane's Slim Chance / A&M (1975)** ¶
★ ★ ★ **Mahoney's Last Stand / Atco (1976)** ¶
★ ★ ★ ★ **One for the Road / Is. (1976), Br. imp.** ¶
★ ★ ★ **See Me / GM (1980), Br. imp.**
When Ronnie Lane left the Faces in 1973, it was carnival music he wanted to make—sprightly, spontaneous and exquisitely simple. He succeeded, but it cost him his audience, which is why only his first album, *Slim Chance,* was released in the States. The others are lovely, however.

Mahoney's Last Stand is blues and rock from the Faces (principally Ron Wood) and friends (Rick Grech, Pete Townshend) minus Rod Stewart. Much filler, sometimes sloppy, but can at least boil water.   — F.R.

PETER LANG
★ ★ ★ **The Thing at the Nursery Room Window / Tak. (1972)**
★ ★ **Lycurgus / Fly. Fish (1975)**
★ ★ **Back to the Wall / Waterh. (NA)**
★ ★ **Prime Cuts / Waterh. (NA)**
Lang is an interesting folk- and classical-based acoustic guitarist of the John Fahey school; the Takoma album lacks all of Fahey's warmth and invention but is still admirably soothing music. On the Flying Fish set, he makes the mistake of singing and stepping out on some relatively boogie-woogie tunes. The Waterhouse LPs are no improvement.   — D.M.

DON LANGE
★ ★ ★ **Natural Born Heathen / Fly. Fish (1978)**
★ ★ ★ **Don Lange Live / Fly. Fish (1981)**
Lange's a heartfelt, lyrical writer who is also clever, humorous and socially conscious, a rare mixture of formerly familiar quantities. *Natural Born Heathen* sets Lange in a jazz feel, but his firmly fashioned songs need few frills to stand out and be noticed.   — R.P.

NEIL LARSEN
★ **Jungle Fever / Hor. (1978)**
★ **High Gear / A&M (1979)**
Noodling jazz from keyboardist who is connected with rock only because he's also recorded with guitarist Buzzy Feiten (of minor Paul Butterfield renown), because he uses the R&B-style rhythm section of Willie Weeks and Andy Newmark, and because most of his best ideas have been put to ten times better use by Carlos Santana, among many others. Conservative and dull.
— D.M.

LARSEN-FEITEN BAND
★ **Larsen-Feiten Band / War. (1980)**
A couple of session hacks hole up together for tasteful (one supposes), unimaginative, unsubtle jazz-rock effort.   — D.M.

NICOLETTE LARSON
★ **Nicolette / War. (1978)**
★ **In the Nick of Time / War. (1979)**
★ **Radioland / War. (1980)**
A protégé of Linda Ronstadt's and a featured backing singer with Neil Young, Larson epitomizes the worst of L.A. Seventies pop rock. So laid-back it's a wonder she can stand up. Her debut album is a certified snore, and of course a commercial smash circa 1978–1979. Her subsequent releases are better only because they were less successful, and therefore easier to ignore. No, rock isn't dead, but anyone who remembers Little Eva may wish it were after hearing these.
— D.M.

DENISE LaSALLE
★ ★ ★ **Here I Am Again / Westb. (1975)** ¶
★ ★ **Second Breath / ABC (1976)** ¶
★ ★ **The Bitch Is Bad / ABC (1977)** ¶
★ ★ ★ **Under the Influence / MCA (1978)**
★ ★ ★ **Unwrapped / MCA (1979)**
★ ★ **I'm So Hot / MCA (1980)**
★ ★ ★ **Guaranteed / MCA (1981)**
Denise LaSalle is a sensitive Southern soul singer/songwriter whose style, like that of Candi Staton, occasionally suggests a heavy C&W influence. Though her best work, *Trapped by a Thing Called Love* (Westbound), is out of print, *Here I Am Again* is a fair representation: a sturdy collection of ballads and rugged midtempo Memphis soul. The ABC albums are less assured. LaSalle seems at a loss for direction, and the music is an uneasy collage of Motown, country and diluted Southern soul. But LaSalle's sass served her well on a couple of the MCA LPs, most notably *Unwrapped,* with disco remakes of "Trapped by a Thing Called

Love" and Rod Stewart's "Do Ya Think I'm Sexy." — J.MC./D.M.

DAVID LASLEY
★ ★ ★ ★ **Missin' Twenty Grand / EMI (1982)**
Lasley made his reputation as a background singer for James Taylor, but his real métier is blue-eyed soul, Motor City falsetto variant. This album of primarily self-written material is remarkable not only for the purity of Lasley's voice, however, but for the passion of his concerns, the matter-of-factness with which he deals with his gay lifestyle and the aggressive statements it makes about sexual, racial and other political matters. "On Third Street" is as good a confessional song as Joni Mitchell's ever written, and "Treat Willie Good" and "Roommate" are trenchant, funny statements of sexual dilemmas. Beautiful music in the best sense. — D.M.

LATIMORE
★ ★ ★ **Latimore / Glades (1973)**
★ ★ ★ **More, More, More / Glades (1974)**
★ ★ ★ ★ **Latimore III / Glades (1975)**
★ ★ ★ **It Ain't Where You Been . . . / Glades (1977)**
★ ★ ★ **Dig a Little Deeper / Glades (1978)**
Miami's Benny Latimore is an accomplished keyboard player and distinctive vocalist who evinces an intriguing persona, combining elements of storyteller Oscar Brown Jr. and cabaret blues singer Lou Rawls with the earthy sexiness of traditional soul singers. The sparsely produced *More, More, More* includes blues and soul ballads, highlighted by Latimore's biggest hit, the smoldering "Let's Straighten It Out." Its followup, *Latimore III,* shows a real evolution of style. Latimore had a hand in writing five of the eight songs, and the best, "Keep the Home Fire Burnin' " and "There's a Redneck in the Soul Band," show a real wit and originality. *It Ain't Where You Been* has the same type of fluid, seamless groove as *Latimore III,* but the songs, while attractive, are longer and tend to sound alike. — J.MC.

STACY LATTISAW
★ ★ ★ **Young and in Love / Coti. (1979)** ¶
★ ★ ★ **Let Me Be Your Angel / Coti. (1980)**
★ ★ ★ **With You / Coti. (1981)**
Lattisaw's debut album, produced by Van McCoy, was all girlish innocence, which figures—she was only twelve when it was made. By the time she was thirteen, she'd come up with a pair of Top Ten soul hits, "Dynamite!" and "Let Me Be Your Angel,"

and the latter crossed over, making the pop Top Thirty. Her pleasant, unhysterical voice and solid dance tracks make all three albums pleasurable, if slight, listening. — D.M.

THE LAUGHING DOGS
★ ★ **The Laughing Dogs / Col. (1979)**
★ ★ ★ **Meet Their Makers / Col. (1980)**
The Laughing Dogs made their debut on *Live at C.B.G.B.'s* with a slightly metalloid variation on the hyper-pop of the Shirts or Dirty Looks, a sound that was only slightly refined on these albums. — J.D.C.

LAURIE AND THE SIGHS
★ ★ ★ **Laurie and the Sighs / Atl. (1980)**
Pat Benatar clone with power-pop tendencies. — J.D.C.

BETTYE LAVETTE
★ ★ ★ ★ **Tell Me a Lie / Mo. (1982)**
The best album of this journeywoman soul singer's career is a pure piece of Memphis/Muscle Shoals groove, although it was recorded in 1982 in Nashville. From the hit, "Right in the Middle (of Falling in Love)" straight on through, Lavette runs through a series of tricks learned from about fifteen years of making minor and sometimes lovely soul and R&B singles. But this time it all clicks (thanks largely to the sensitivity of producer Steve Buckingham, who lets fashion come to Bettye rather than vice versa). There are even pleasant updates of a pair of Motown classics, "I Heard It through the Grapevine" and "If I Were Your Woman." — D.M.

BARBARA LAW
★ **Take All of Me / Pav. (NA)**
Wonderful, the impact of the women's movement on the music industry. — D.M.

LAWLER AND COBB
★ **Men from Nowhere / Asy. (1980)**
Back where you came from. — D.M.

KAREN LAWRENCE
★ ★ ★ **Girl's Night Out / RCA (1981)**
Ex-1994 lead vocalist makes the switch from HM/art rock to a new-wavish solo set deftly. Lawrence has a good voice and a penchant for melodic hooks (title track, "March of the Pins"). Only drawback is the obligatory remake, "Sealed with a Kiss." — J.S.

DEBRA LAWS
★ **Very Special / Elek. (1981)**
Guess again. — D.M.

LAZY RACER
★ ★ ★ **Lazy Racer / A&M (1979)**
★ ★ **Formula 2 / A&M (1980)**
British R&B band led by veteran session guitarist Tim Renwick (who plays some fine slide guitar here) and produced by the master of crisp, funky sound, Glyn Johns.
— J.S.

LEADBELLY
★ **Take This Hammer / Folk. (1950)**
★ **Easy Rider / Folk. (1953)**
★ ★ ★ ★ **Leadbelly's Last Sessions, Vol. 1 / Folk. (1953)**
★ ★ ★ ★ **Leadbelly's Last Sessions, Vol. 2 / Folk. (1953)**
★ ★ **Leadbelly Sings Folk Songs / Folk. (1968)**
★ **Leadbelly / Cap. (1969)**
★ ★ ★ **Leadbelly / Fan. (1973)**
★ ★ ★ **Good Mornin' Blues / Bio. (NA)**
★ ★ ★ **Leadbelly's Library of Congress Recordings / Elek. (NA)**
★ **Leadbelly's Legacy, Vol. 3 / Folk. (NA)**
Biographies of Leadbelly (Huddie Ledbetter) can be found with almost all of these albums, and in any number of books about blues and/or American folk music. For present purposes, it is most important to note his authorship of such songs as "Goodnight Irene" (a three-month No. 1 hit for the Weavers in 1950, a year after Leadbelly's death), "Rock Island Line," "Give Me Li'l Water Sylvie" and "Take This Hammer," plus literally hundreds of other ballads, shouts, hollers and blues that he either wrote or preserved through constant performance and recording.

A master of the twelve-string guitar, Leadbelly is additionally credited with developing the "walking bass" style of playing. His influence on such contemporaries as Woody Guthrie, Cisco Houston, Sonny Terry (all three sing with him on *Sings Folk Songs*), Pete Seeger, Oscar Brand and countless others is inestimable. And his songs, although sometimes appearing under the copyright of Alan Lomax (the man who first "discovered" and recorded Leadbelly, but who later wrote what many considered an offensive and inaccurate biography), are a part of the fabric of American folk tradition.

In 1933, Leadbelly made 78 rpm recordings of some 135 selections for the Library of Congress. The Elektra three-record set is drawn from these and later sessions, also cut by Alan and John Lomax. The difference the tape-recording process made is evident when comparing the Elektra set with Folkways' *Last Sessions,* recorded in 1948. On the latter collections (two discs each), Leadbelly's friend and folk-music enthusiast/scholar Frederic Ramsey, Jr., in whose apartment the recordings were made, speaks with the singer and encourages little monologues and asides. Although the Lomaxes tried to do the same for the Library of Congress, they had to contend with the time limitations of 78 rpm disc-cutting equipment (about five minutes per side).

Ramsey had originally hoped that the three nights of recording that became *Last Sessions* would be the first of a series, but Leadbelly died before further sessions could be arranged. Variations on given songs, sometimes in snatches used to illustrate a point, are left in, and both for quality of recording and range of material, *Last Sessions* constitutes the most highly recommended of Leadbelly's records.

The Biograph album is also of interest. It has been remastered with great care, and side one (circa 1940) features Woody Guthrie as a quasi-narrator for what is believed to have been an audition for a radio program featuring Leadbelly. Side two consists of half a dozen tunes recorded in 1935 that represent his first commercial efforts. None of this material has been previously available. The Fantasy set is made up of tracks variously recorded for Musicraft, Disc and Asch between 1939 and 1944.

Sings Folk Songs is spirited, what with its three-man backup team, and includes some lesser-known songs. As usual (and as with *Take This Hammer*), original mono versions are preferable to the stereo.

Easy Rider and *Legacy,* both ten-inch discs, date from the mid-Thirties. The Capitol set, recorded in Hollywood in 1944, lacks the warmth exuded on the later *Last Sessions,* but does have a few rare tracks that find Leadbelly playing piano instead of guitar. — T.M.

BERNIE LEADON
★ ★ **Natural Progressions / Asy. (1977)**
The former Eagle and Flying Burrito Brother turns in a solo LP that is the very model of washed-out California rock. Oh so country-funky, and oh so dull. Excesses exceeded only by fellow Eagle exile Randy Meisner's dismal affair. — D.M.

AMANDA LEAR
★ ★ **Sweet Revenge / Chrys. (1978) ¶**
Husky-voiced would-be disco chanteuse better known as model on cover of Roxy Music LP than for anything she's done in the studio. *Sweet Revenge* is slightly less ludicrous

than monumentally inane *I Am a Photograph.* — G.A.

DR. TIMOTHY LEARY
■ **The Psychedelic Experience** / Folk. (1966)
Look, when you grew up around people like this, you knew what to do: stay the hell away, because they'd only get you in trouble, and then dodge the blame (and the pain). There are more interesting ways to be conned, believe me. — D.M.

LED ZEPPELIN
★ ★ ★ ★ **Led Zeppelin** / Atl. (1969)
★ ★ ★ ★ **Led Zeppelin II** / Atl. (1969)
★ ★ ★ ★ **Led Zeppelin III** / Atl. (1970)
★ ★ ★ ★ ★ **Untitled** / Atl. (1971)
★ ★ ★ ★ **Houses of the Holy** / Atl. (1973)
★ ★ ★ **Physical Graffiti** / Swan (1975)
★ ★ ★ ★ **Presence** / Swan (1976)
★ ★ ★ **The Song Remains the Same** / Swan (1976)
★ ★ ★ **In through the Out Door** / Swan (1979)
★ ★ **Coda** / Swan (1982)
When Led Zeppelin's debut album appeared in 1969, the anticipation built up among knowledgeable music fans, excited over the prospects of Jimmy Page (the Yardbirds' last guitarist) leading his own group, was replaced by an equally king-sized disgust. Here was a band that, when not busy totally demolishing classic blues songs, was making a kind of music apparently designed to be enjoyable only when the listener was drugged to the point of senselessness. Page, a young veteran of the mid-Sixties guitar wars, had somehow made two very important discoveries: spaced-out heavy rock drove barely pubescent kids crazy; the Sixties were over. And so with virtually no critical support Led Zeppelin was soon the biggest new band on earth.

Led Zeppelin II was somewhat weaker than its predecessor, leaving skeptics optimistic that soon all the superhype (also the name of Page and singer Robert Plant's song-publishing company) would be over, and the minor commercial flop of *Led Zeppelin III* seemed to support that feeling. Yet there were some strange things going on there. While side one covered usual Zep territory, from the absurd ("Out on the Tiles") to the ridiculous ("Immigrant Song"), side two, done mostly acoustically, represented the band's turning point.

Plant's voice had come down from the hysteria range, and he was being backed by Page on everything from banjo ("Hangman") to mandolin ("That's the Way") to steel guitar ("Tangerine"); new directions were being followed. "Tangerine" formed the musical basis of "Stairway to Heaven," which would become to the Seventies what "Satisfaction" had been to the Sixties. The song was the centerpiece of *Untitled,* arguably Zeppelin's finest album (although one is tempted to give the band's initial LP an extra notch for sheer chutzpah value). That fourth album showed all sides of the group, with the indescribably chaotic "Black Dog," the stark and powerful "When the Levee Breaks" (the first Zep blues rework that didn't sound like a bizarre parody) and respites from the frenzy like "Going to California," on which Plant's hippie stance was finally bared.

Houses of the Holy was a fine successor, ranging from murky and foreboding ("No Quarter") to rollicking ("Dancing Days," "D'yer Mak'er") to idiotic ("The Crunge"). *Physical Graffiti,* a double set, has plenty of filler, but Page's "Kashmir" is a masterpiece of controlled tension, full of the Eastern influence that's been in his playing since the Yardbirds days. *Presence,* done quickly after a car accident prevented the band from touring for a while, is probably its most down-to-earth LP, with the band drawing on all their resources—a little soul ("Royal Orleans"), a little blatant macho ("Candy Store Rock"), a little heavy mania ("Achilles Last Stand") and a little guitar raveup ("Hots on for Nowhere"). *The Song Remains the Same* is a nice souvenir of the concert film, though nothing extraordinary. *In through the Out Door* was aptly named, as the band broke up in the wake of drummer John Bonham's death. *Coda* scrapes the bottom of the barrel after the band's official breakup. — B.A.

ALVIN LEE
★ ★ ★ ★ **In Flight** / Col. (1974) ¶
★ ★ **Pump Iron** / Col. (1975) ¶
★ ★ **Rocket Fuel** / RSO (1978)
★ ★ **Alvin Lee** / Col. (1978)
★ ★ **Free Fall** / Atl. (1980)
★ ★ **Ride On** / RSO (1981)
In Flight—two live records with most of the soul group Kokomo as backup—was largely vintage rock & roll led admirably by former Ten Years After guitarist Alvin Lee. His often Presley-like vocals and economic but spirited guitar—no Ten Years After–style showing off—resulted in short songs and neat playing, which wasn't a throwback or an imitation. *Pump Iron* used different musicians (some of Britain's better players) and retained the earlier records' approach in a studio setting—good but lacking the same verve. *Rocket Fuel* was much more disorga-

nized—more akin to Ten Years After's boogie excesses. Subsequent albums wavered between blues-ish rock and the typical exhausted English rock guitarist's countryish funk. Alvin's no J.J. Cale. Nor even Dave Mason. — C.W.

ALVIN LEE AND MYLON LEFEVRE
★ ★ ★ **On the Road to Freedom / Col. (1973)**
Good potpourri of American rock and rhythm & blues from mostly British rockers. (LeFevre, however, is American.) Traces of bluegrass and C&W. LeFevre's expressive voice resembled Dickey Betts'; Lee's guitar was agile and varied, avoiding the show-off tendencies of Ten Years After. Pleasingly pastoral and rustic. Steve Winwood, Ron Wood, Mick Fleetwood, George Harrison offer support. — C.W.

BRENDA LEE
★ **Sincerely, Brenda Lee / MCA (1962)** ¶
★ ★ ★ **Ten Golden Years / MCA (1966)** ¶
★ ★ **Here's Brenda Lee / Voc. (1967)**
★ ★ **Let It Be Me / Cor. (1968)**
★ ★ ★ **Brenda Lee Story / MCA (1973)**
★ **L.A. Sessions / MCA (1976)** ¶
★ **Even Better / MCA (1980)**
★ **Take Me Back / MCA (1980)**
Brenda Lee was the best white female rock singer of the Fifties. Such hits as "Sweet Nothin's," "Dum Dum," "Rockin' around the Christmas Tree" and "I'm Sorry" were as tough, if as sentimental, as the best of any male rock & roller, and far beyond the capacity of any of her peers (with the possible exception of Wanda Jackson). The evidence is on *Brenda Lee Story,* a two-record set, and *Ten Golden Years,* a single disc, both of which collect her best work of that period. (The Coral and Vocalion sets are unnecessary period curios. The singles were the essence of Lee.)

Her MCA albums unfortunately reflect the kind of artistic disintegration so many country-based white rockers of the Fifties went through in recent years. They are totally tame, formulaic country albums, with virtually nothing to recommend them except the odd pleasure of Lee's still-sobbing voice. — D.M.

BYRON LEE AND THE DRAGONAIRES
★ **Disco Reggae / Mer. (1975)**
It would be easy to dismiss Byron Lee as the Neil Hefti or Mantovani of reggae for his featherweight, effortless Jamaican records, among which only this LP was released in the U.S. But as a producer and creative

force behind Kingston's Dynamic Sounds Recording Studio, Lee is a seminal figure in reggae's development. Which doesn't excuse him for the false advertising here: it's all watered-down reggae except for one track, a reggae-ized version of "The Hustle." — G.K.

DICKEY LEE
★ ★ **Rocky / RCA (1975)** ¶
★ ★ **Angels, Roses and Rain / RCA (1976)** ¶
★ ★ **Again / Mer. (NA)**
★ ★ **Dickey Lee / Mer. (NA)**
Singer best known for early-Sixties soap-opera smash "Patches" became a competent, uninspired country singer with plenty of chart hits, none especially memorable (well, maybe "9,999,999 Tears") in the Seventies. Title track of *Rocky,* however, matches the morbidity of "Patches." — D.M.

JACK LEE
★ ★ **Jack Lee's Greatest Hits, Vol. 1 / Maid. (1981)**
Lee's claim to fame is writing two of the songs on Blondie's *Parallel Lines.* "Hanging on the Telephone," Lee's *real* greatest hit, is here, but pales in comparison to Blondie's rendition, partially because, like the rest of this set, it sounds like a demo (which it most likely is). Lee is a good songwriter but an unexceptional singer, and most of the performances here don't really do justice to the material. — D.S.

JOHN LEE AND GERRY BROWN
★ ★ **Mango Sunrise / Blue N. (1975)** ¶
No Caribbean accents here, despite the title. Mostly it's a mixture of heavy-rock guitar around electric piano jazz clichés, with Lee concentrating on bass and ARP synthesizer and Brown on drums. Guest appearances by guitarists Wah Wah Watson and Philip Catherine help, but not half enough. — D.M.

JOHNNY LEE
★ ★ ★ **Lookin' for Love / Asy. (1980)**
★ ★ ★ **Bet Your Heart on Me / Asy. (1981)**
As the romantic theme song of *Urban Cowboy,* "Lookin' for Love" was the most beautiful pop-country ballad of the early Eighties—and one of the best-selling. But Lee has been overlooked by country critics, probably because his approach is more oriented to love songs than honky-tonking, and because he doesn't write. Nonetheless, he has what may be the finest voice of any contemporary country vocalist, a mixture of gravel and innocence that is the perfect analogue to

Urban Cowboy's dreamy dance sequence between Debra Winger and John Travolta that "Lookin' for Love" kicks off.

Lookin' for Love has stronger material than *Bet Your Heart on Me,* backing up the title track with such winners as "Do You Love as Good as You Look" (which is *smooth* honky-tonk) and "Fool for Love." *Bet Your Heart*'s arrangements threaten to fall into Kenny Rogers treacle-land, but the strength of Lee's voice saves him from that calamity. But since then, he's foundered in exactly the kind of jello-mold pop-country arrangements his voice was born to undercut. Nothing wrong here that some ambition couldn't cure—see John Anderson. — D.M.

MYLON LEFEVRE
★ ★ **Rock & Roll Resurrection / Mer. (1979)**
Southern rocker Mylon has had his moments—the 1970 solo *Mylon* with most of the Atlanta Rhythm Section as backup, and the excellent *On the Road to Freedom* with Alvin Lee—but this is not one of them. — J.S.

LEGS DIAMOND
★ **Diamond Is a Hard Rock / Mer. (1977)**
★ **Legs Diamond / Mer. (1977)**
★ **Firepower / Cream (1978)**
Mindlessly metallic. — D.M.

LEMON
★ **Lemon / Prel. (1978)**
Appropriate name and title, even if you *like* disco. — D.M.

JOHN LENNON
★ ★ ★ ★ ★ **John Lennon/Plastic Ono Band / Apple (1970)**
An instinctively popular artist, Lennon was always an angry man, caught between a desire to please his audience and to assault it. This contradiction, muted in his Beatles days, surfaced immediately in his solo work and marked his career with desperation, smugness and confusion.

Lennon began his break from the Beatles well before the formal dissolution of the group in 1970. In 1969 he and Yoko Ono, his then-love-soon-to-be-wife, put out two so-called unfinished music tape-buzz LPs: *Two Virgins,* with the scandalous pre-fall Adam and Eve cover, and *Life with the Lions,* which commemorated Yoko's miscarriage of that year.

The Wedding Album (also 1969), a narcissistic boxed set, celebrated John and Yoko's marriage, after which the duo embarked on a worldwide crusade for "peace," which produced *Live Peace in Toronto 1969* (released 1970), featuring one side of first-class raving rock (Lennon's pickup band included Eric Clapton) and one side of Yoko's avant-garde ravings. Singles—notably "Give Peace a Chance," the stunning "Cold Turkey" and "Instant Karma"—also came out of this period.

But it was *John Lennon/Plastic Ono Band* (released in conjunction with the shattering "Lennon Remembers" interviews in *Rolling Stone*) that revealed Lennon as a new man, liberated by the fall of the Beatles. Primal scream therapy, which John had then recently undergone, now dates the LP, but it also inspired its vital extremism: the record was a full, blistering statement of fury, resentment and self-pity, and Lennon's proof that the true power of rock as music is to be found in stripping it as bare as primal therapy was supposed to strip the soul. Thus there was virtually no instrumentation beyond a primal rock band composed of Lennon on rough lead guitar, Ringo on drums, Klaus Voormann on bass and Billy Preston's occasional keyboards: the music didn't cut, it bit. Nearly a decade later, "Well Well Well" particularly holds its power, though "Working Class Hero" too remains a favorite; John's singing on the last verse of "God's Song" may be the finest in all of rock. A lot of people hated *JL/POB,* but few have really forgotten it; it stands as John's strongest, most sustained piece of work in the Seventies.

★ ★ ★ **Imagine / Apple (1971)**
If *JL/POB* was sparked by the cry "The dream is over," the message of *Imagine,* a much more accessible pop album, was "Long live the dream": as a popular artist, the angry man simply could not endure without a dose of utopianism in his music, his sense of romance and his politics. *Imagine,* despite its notorious attack on Paul McCartney ("How Do You Sleep?"), felt like a breath of fresh air in 1971; "Gimme Some Truth," a nasty rocker, "Oh Yoko," an almost girlgroupish ditty and the lovely "Jealous Guy" still do. At this point, John seemed to know where he was going, and to be going in a good direction.

★ **Some Time in New York City / Apple (1972)**
★ ★ **Mind Games / Apple (1973)**
★ ★ **Walls and Bridges / Apple (1974)**
It didn't seem that way after *Some Time,* a disastrous collaboration between John, Yoko and the leftish rock band Elephant's Memo-

ry. This was a two-LP set divided between horrendous Phil Spector–produced protest epics and live recordings (some with Frank Zappa): the politics were witless and the live jams mindless. After John's ideological flip-flops of the previous years (from the Maharishi to "peace" to primal therapy, each embraced as an absolute Answer), it was hard to take his new political commitments seriously; here the question of taking his music seriously never came up.

Both *Mind Games* and *Walls and Bridges* were drastic retreats from the anti-pop stance of *Some Time,* and both produced hits: "Mind Games," the trendy "Whatever Gets You thru the Night" and "#9 Dream." The sound was lush and conventional, the singing assured, but there was no real point of view at work—no point at all, in fact, save for continuing a career for its own sake; only "Going Down on Love" *(Walls)* recalled the gutty realism of *JL/ POB,* which seemed very far away. Like so many veterans of the Sixties trapped in the Seventies, Lennon (by then the subject of a brutal but accurate parody on the National Lampoon's *Radio Dinner* LP) had no idea of how to relate to his audience: with what appeared to be panic, he substituted production techniques for soul, building a bridge to his listeners with his sound but erecting a wall around himself with empty music.

★ ★ **Rock 'n' Roll / Apple (1975)**
Lennon knew it; he just didn't know what to do about it, and so, again like many others, he tried to escape a dead end by going back to his roots with an oldies album. *Rock 'n' Roll* (1975, a year that also saw John popping up on a couple of Elton John 45s) began as a collaboration with Phil Spector, who needed a shot of rhythm & blues as much as John did, but the partnership soon came to grief—as did most of the album. Remakes of "Stand by Me" and "Just Because" were deeply touching, but with the rest of the tunes—mostly classic hard rockers—John never found a groove. And so, no doubt tired of his helpless drift back and forth between adventure *(JL/POB, Some Time)* and retreat *(Imagine, Mind Games, Walls, R'n'R),* Lennon shut up, his battle with Paul McCartney apparently conceded.

★ ★ ★ **Shaved Fish / Apple (1975)**
A short-term epitaph: collected singles since 1969, omitting *R'n'R.* Highlights are still "Cold Turkey," "Instant Karma" and "Power to the People" (a nervy 45 from 1971). John's first solo LP remains his testament: divided, bitter and utterly uncompromising qualities.   — G.M.

JOHN LENNON/YOKO ONO
★ ★ ★ ★ ★ **Double Fantasy / Gef. (1980)**
It's easy to see *Double Fantasy,* the album released shortly before John Lennon's assassination, as the beginning of a musical renaissance when you realize what a well-focused expression of his collaborative venture with Yoko Ono it is. *Double Fantasy* alternates songs by John and Yoko in a way that coherently blends their visions. In fact Yoko's songs amplify Lennon's.

Lennon succeed in elevating his concern with domesticity to a work of art in itself. "Starting Over," the hit single, sounds as lush and beautiful as his characteristic post– "Strawberry Fields Forever" recordings. "Dear Yoko" compares favorably to "Oh Yoko" from *Imagine.* In "Watching the Wheels" Lennon describes his new outlook with the same chilling purpose and exacting logic that he brought to the Beatles kiss-offs, "Working Class Hero" and "The Dream Is Over."

The best example of the felicitous collaboration between the two comes when Lennon's pained lament, "I'm Losing You," segues into Yoko's answer, "I'm Moving On." The combination has astonishing power, perhaps because Yoko so obviously holds her own in John's medium—hypnotic medium-tempo rock & roll. When her characteristic broken-voiced squeals punctuate the end of the song, it's a genuinely expressive moment that climaxes the record.
   — J.S.

J. B. LENOIR
★ ★ ★ **Alabama Blues / L+R (1979), Ger. imp.**
★ ★ ★ **Down in Mississippi / L+R (1980), Ger. imp.**
★ ★ ★ ★ **J. B. Lenoir / Chess (NA), Fr. imp.**
★ ★ ★ ★ **Mojo Boogie / Flyr. (NA), Br. imp.**
The Samuel Fuller of Chicago blues, J. B. Lenoir was the most political commentator that genre produced, as well as one of the finest vocalists. His guitar playing was less distinctive, but "Korea Blues," "Eisenhower Blues" and "I'm in Korea" got at the heart of everyday experience in that gray era perfectly: they're a GI's foxhole view of society. Lenoir sang straight sex and party blues too, but he made his mark with his socially oriented music (so effectively that a White House representative allegedly attempted to get the Chess brothers to censor him).

The Chess album above, twenty-eight tracks originally made for Checker and Parrot, is definitive, but the Flyright also contains important Fifties recordings, these initially released on J.O.B. The L+R albums are acoustic, from the mid-Fifties and among his most politicized, though not as splendidly sung. — D.M.

BARRINGTON LEVY
★ ★ ★ **Bounty Hunter / Jah Life (1979)**
★ ★ ★ ★ ★ **Englishman / Greens. (1980)**
★ ★ **Robin Hood / Greens. (1980)**
By 1980 it seemed that you could hardly turn around without bumping into a Barrington Levy tune—he was reggae's boy wonder of 1979. It's amazing that a relatively inexperienced teenager could crank out so much product yet maintain a fairly consistent quality. *Bounty Hunter,* his debut, features stone-to-the-bone rhythms and urgent vocals. *Englishman* brings his melodic and rhythmic talent to a satisfying peak. — R.F.G.

JONA LEWIE
★ ★ ★ **On the Other Hand There's a Fist / Stiff (1978)** ¶
New-wave keyboardist with a penchant for memorable synthesizer rhythmic structures fields a tuneful and engaging set featuring session performances by Martin Belmont, Bob Andrews and Kirsty MacColl. Highlights are "(You'll Always Find Me in the) Kitchen at Parties" and the Nick Lowe/Ian Gomm–penned "God Bless Whoever Made You." — J.S.

GARY LEWIS AND THE PLAYBOYS
★ ★ **The Greatest Hits of Gary Lewis and the Playboys / Power (1978)**
Would you buy a used diamond ring from this man? Gary Lewis sang like his father acts—goofy—and without Dean Martin for a straight man. But that doesn't mean we can't treasure his handful of pathetic contributions to Sixties rock, generally written and arranged (in collaboration) by a ducktailed Leon Russell. "This Diamond Ring" is what you remember, but there's also "Everybody Loves a Clown," "She's Just My Style" and the rest of Lewis' Beatles-era pop hits, a high point in mainstream masochism.
— M.G.

BARBARA LEWIS
★ ★ ★ **Hello Stranger / Solid S. (1981)**
Sixteen fine early-to-mid-Sixties pop-soul hits, including the title track, "Baby I'm Yours" and "Make Me Your Baby." Lewis fits in somewhere between Dionne Warwick and Gladys Knight—too lightweight for

greatness but endlessly pleasurable nonetheless. — D.M.

FURRY LEWIS
★ **Furry Lewis Blues / Folk. (1959)**
★ ★ **Back on My Feet Again / Prest. (1961)**
★ ★ **Fabulous Furry Lewis / So. (1975)**
★ ★ ★ ★ **In His Prime / Yazoo (1975)**
★ ★ **Shake 'Em on Down / Fan. (1978)**
Lewis made some interesting recordings in the late Twenties, which are preserved on the Yazoo set. His singing was good if not spectacular, and he had a broad range of material, but it was his sloppy yet engaging slide-guitar work that set him apart from other Memphis-based blues figures of his time. Lewis was resurrected during the early-Sixties blues revival and subsequently became a character actor, appearing on the Johnny Carson TV show and in Burt Reynolds' films. At that point he was more of a comedian than a musician, but the Folkways and Fantasy sets are pretty good Sixties sets.
— J.S.

HUEY LEWIS AND THE NEWS
★ ★ **Huey Lewis and the News / Chrys. (1980)**
Attempt to create power pop/surf music merger, fumbled on both ends. No pop in their power, no sting to their harmonies, and this ain't the return of "Pipeline" either.
— D.M.

JERRY LEE LEWIS
★ ★ ★ **Golden Hits of Jerry Lee Lewis / Smash (1964)**
★ ★ ★ ★ **Jerry Lee Lewis' Original Golden Hits, Vol. 1 / Sun (1969)**
★ ★ ★ ★ **Jerry Lee Lewis' Original Golden Hits, Vol. 2 / Sun (1969)**
★ ★ ★ **Jerry Lee Lewis' Rockin' Rhythm and Blues / Sun (1969)**
★ ★ ★ **Jerry Lee Lewis' Golden Cream of the Country / Sun (1969)**
★ ★ ★ **A Taste of Country / Sun (1970)**
★ ★ ★ **Sunday Down South / Sun (1970)**
★ ★ ★ **Memphis Country / Sun (1970)**
★ ★ ★ **Ole Tyme Country Music / Sun (1970)**
★ ★ ★ ★ **Best of Jerry Lee Lewis / Smash (1970)**
★ ★ ★ ★ **Monsters / Sun (1971)**
★ ★ ★ ★ **Jerry Lee Lewis' Original Golden Hits, Vol. 3 / Sun (1971)**
★ ★ ★ **Country Class / Mer. (1975)** ¶
★ ★ ★ **Country Memories / Mer. (1977)**
★ ★ ★ ★ **Best of Jerry Lee Lewis, Vol. 2 / Mer. (1978)**
★ ★ ★ **Jerry Lee Lewis / Elek. (1979)**

★ ★ ★ **When Two Worlds Collide / Elek. (1980)**
★ ★ ★ ★ **Killer Country / Elek. (1980)**
★ ★ ★ ★ **The Original Jerry Lee Lewis / Sun (NA)**
★ ★ ★ **Jerry Lee Lewis / Ev. (NA)**

Of all the rock & roll singers who followed Elvis Presley into Memphis and Sam Phillips' Sun Records in the late Fifties, the greatest was undeniably Jerry Lee Lewis. He would tell you so himself, for Lewis is a master of the Bunyan-esque brag, a swaggering piano stomper whose arrogance is as legendary as his vanity, though neither is quite a match for the enormity of his talent.

Lewis' two biggest hits were his first, "Whole Lotta Shakin' Going On" and "Great Balls of Fire," both released on Sun in 1957. Those songs presented fundamentalist gospel imagery as sexual innuendo, and Lewis portrayed, through his romping, stomping, incessant piano backbeat and his heated singing, a kind of Elmer Gantry out for action and trouble be damned. Lewis was the very incarnation of what Northerners feared about the South—the most arrogant and unregenerate of the all the Fifties rockers. Compared to Lewis, Elvis Presley's humility seems absolutely overweening. And it was this triumph of the id, which has made so much of Lewis' music so forceful, that proved his undoing.

Lewis had only two other Top Forty hits in the rock & roll era: "Breathless" and "High School Confidential," both in 1958. After that, he virtually dropped out of sight, for he had married his fourteen-year-old third cousin, an irreparable violation of social taboo. He still made records, including some more than faintly great ones, covered everybody from Elvis to Chuck Berry and often cut them on their own songs—but few heard him, because the radio stations simply wouldn't play his music.

If Lewis' music of this period could be compared to anyone else's (besides Presley, to whom everything in rock is comparable), the most apt alter ego would be Little Richard. Like Lewis, Richard's focus was a pounding piano, with a kind of primitive boogie-woogie approach and more than a hint of the church in his vocals. But Lewis parted company as a vocalist; Little Richard shouted, but Jerry Lee sang like a demented choirboy, so that even the licentious lyrics of "Great Balls of Fire" got a properly rounded enunciation. This was part of Lewis' greatest implicit boast: that he could cut anybody at anything, and if necessary, when it came to

music, he could cut everybody all at once.

Banished from pop radio, Lewis turned to cutting country songs, where his natural instincts and his really quite exquisite voice already made him at home. By 1967 his excellent country records (made with producer Jerry Kennedy in Nashville for Mercury's country line, Smash), were beginning to become heavy factors on the country charts. Since then he has cut a number of the best country songs of the past twenty years, including "What Made Milwaukee Famous Has Made a Loser Out of Me," "She Even Woke Me Up to Say Goodbye," "You Belong to Me" and "Who's Gonna Play This Old Piano." He hardly ever sings rock & roll anymore, but whenever he wants to, he's still great at it. And even his country records are pretty untamed; Jerry Lee Lewis has never surrendered. — D.M.

LINDA LEWIS
★ **Not a Little Girl Anymore / Ari. (1975)**
Odd title for this squealing, histrionic London vocalist of West Indian descent who sounds like an R&B Shirley Temple. — J.S.

MEADE LUX LEWIS
★ ★ ★ ★ **Tell Your Story / Oldie B. (NA)**
★ ★ ★ **Meade Lux Lewis / Arc. Folk (NA)**
★ ★ ★ **Barrelhouse Piano / Story. (NA)**
Lewis was one of the best-known practitioners of barrelhouse piano, which he learned in his native Chicago under the tutelage of Jimmy Yancey. He hit his high point in 1927 with the hard-driving "Honky-Tonk Train Blues," which became his trademark. — J.S.

SMILEY LEWIS
★ ★ ★ ★ **I Hear You Knocking / U.A. (1978), Jap. imp.**
Lewis was a great New Orleans singer whose biggest hit, the title track, is typical of his Fats Domino–influenced, hard-edged R&B. These Fifties tracks are all exquisite. — D.M.

LORI LIEBERMAN
★ **Lori Lieberman / Cap. (1972) ¶**
★ **Becoming / Cap. (1973) ¶**
★ **Letting Go / Millen. (1978)**
Ineffectual Laura Nyro imitation. — J.S.

GORDON LIGHTFOOT
★ ★ ★ **Lightfoot / U.A. (1966)**
★ ★ ★ **The Way I Feel / U.A. (1968)**
★ ★ **Back Here on Earth / U.A. (1968)**
★ ★ ★ **Sunday Concert / U.A. (1969)**
★ ★ ★ ★ **If You Could Read My Mind / Rep. (1970)**

★ ★ ★ **Best of Gordon Lightfoot** / U.A.
(1970)
★ ★ **Summer Side of Life** / Rep. (1971)
★ ★ **Best of Gordon Lightfoot, Vol. 2** / U.A.
(1971) ¶
★ ★ ★ **Don Quixote** / Rep. (1972)
★ ★ **Old Dan's Records** / Rep. (1972)
★ ★ **Sundown** / Rep. (1974)
★ ★ **Cold on the Shoulder** / Rep. (1975)
★ ★ ★ **Gord's Gold** / Rep. (1975)
★ ★ ★ **Summertime Dream** / Rep.
(1976)
★ ★ **Endless Wire** / War. (1978)
★ ★ **Dream Street Rose** / War. (1980)
Born into a well-to-do family from the London, Ontario, area—English Canada's Tory stronghold—and brought up as a classically trained choirboy, singer/songwriter Gordon Lightfoot has had a long, successful career, first as a "folksinger," then in the Seventies as *the* Canadian musical institution. These two phases in Lightfoot's career are marked less by a change in style than by a switch of record companies, from United Artists to Reprise/Warner Bros., and by the increasing slickness of his producer, Lenny Waronker.

Lightfoot, his first album, introduced Lightfoot's style in a mature form: firm, fast strumming on guitar and a smooth baritone voice. It was a style that made Lightfoot one of the most engaging singers to come from the Sixties folk boom. This first album also contains several songs that have since become frequently recorded standards, notably "Early Morning Rain"; "For Lovin' Me," penned by Lightfoot; and "The First Time," by Ewan McColl. The subsequent U.A. albums may now seem more formulaic than they did when first released. Lightfoot's lyrical sophistication, forceful melodies and stolid posture remain admirable, but the major topical songs, "Black Day in July" and "Canadian Railroad Trilogy," sound glossy and overwritten. Too many of the ballads ("If I Could" and "Mountains and Marion") are so reflectively vague that they verge on being folkie Tin Pan Alley. This is, in fact, the tendency that overtakes Lightfoot on several of his Reprise/Warner albums.

Although beautifully produced and featuring Lightfoot's most consistent collection of songs, *If You Could Read My Mind* was a sleeper until the title song became a smash hit single in 1970 and Lightfoot was rediscovered by a public who remembered him only by way of cover versions of his early songs, such as Peter, Paul and Mary's "Early Morning Rain." Stylistically, *If You Could* recast Lightfoot's mixture of ballads and topical songs into a blend of elements

from both genres. Typically, "Sit Down Young Stranger" takes on a highly personal tone to welcome American draft dodgers and deserters to Canada. The song also points to Lightfoot's growing semi-official status in Canada. The "Railroad Trilogy," having led to a whole catalogue of Canadian songs, also led to Lightfoot's Seventies position as his country's songwriter laureate, with "Alberta Bound" and "Christian Island (Georgia Bay)" finally leading to the masterful epic "Wreck of the Edmund Fitzgerald" (on *Summertime Dream*).

Even when Lightfoot's ballads are tired and indulgent, which is often on *Summer Side of Life* and *Cold on the Shoulder,* Lenny Waronker's production has been able to screen the albums so pleasingly that even the most minor later Lightfoot is listenable. (But the converse is *Gord's Gold,* on which he rerecords his Sixties songs in a way that makes them sound minor as well.) On the most recent albums, *Endless Wire* and *Dream Street Rose,* Lightfoot seems at last aware of his gradual drift into well-crafted post-folk Muzak: the studio players are as strongly highlighted as his indifferent vocals, leaning heavily on medium-tempo tunes and strings. Now approaching middle age, Lightfoot is apparently satisfied with his role as a Canadian institution, writing one or two superior songs a year and gliding easily over the rest of his annual album and tour. In the off months, Lightfoot occasionally plays Las Vegas or Lake Tahoe; in midwinter he does a sold-out week at Toronto's Massey Hall.
— B.T.

LIGHTNING
★ **Lightning** / Casa. (NA)
Still waiting for first strike. — D.M.

LIGHTNIN' SLIM
★ ★ ★ **The Early Years** / Flyr. (1977), Br.
imp.
★ ★ ★ **Trip to Chicago** / Flyr. (1978), Br.
imp.
★ ★ **London Gumbo** / Sonet (1978), Br. imp.
★ ★ **The High and the Lonesome** / Sonet
(NA), Br. imp.
Slim's best recordings, guttural swamp-blues, were cut for Excello in a kind of Slim Harpo mode; they're collected on Flyright's albums. The Sonet LPs, recorded later, drop a notch in quality, due to slicker arrangements and less exciting bands. — D.M.

DENNIS LINDE
★ **Under the Eye** / Monu. (1977)
Linde's entire reputation rests on having penned Elvis Presley's last rock hit, "Burn-

ing Love," in 1972. Since then, he's recorded several times, but no one has done his work a similar favor. This is what's left, and it's not much. — D.M.

DAVID LINDLEY
★ ★ ★ ★ El Rayo-X / Asy. (1981)
★ ★ ★ Win This Record / Asy. (1982)
Celebrated guitarist/multi-instrumentalist, longtime Jackson Browne sidekick and founding member of Kaleidoscope didn't get around to making his solo album for more than a decade, and no wonder. It can't be easy to come up with such an unlikely mixture of reggae, blues, soul and folk: it's kind of like Ry Cooder, but funnier, though Lindley definitely isn't kidding. Steeped in funkiness, with enough bite for rock & roll, this is a cult classic that deserves its stature.

Win This Record is more cultish than classic, focusing on Jamaican and New Orleans rhythms but with sporadic success. Lindley wrote one good song. "Talk to the Lawyer," but the covers are more quirky than illuminating. — D.M.

LIPPS INC.
★ ★ ★ ★ Mouth to Mouth / Casa. (1980)
★ ★ ★ Pucker Up / Casa. (1980)
Lipps Inc. is the best kind of pop joke—one you can dance to. The hit was the wonderfully loopy "Funkytown," on *Mouth to Mouth;* although the rest of the Lipps Inc. repertoire was similarly danceable, it was never quite as inspired. — J.D.C.

MANCE LIPSCOMB
★ ★ ★ Texas Sharecropper and Songster / Arhoo. (1960)
★ ★ ★ Texas Songster, Vol. 2 / Arhoo. (1964)
★ ★ ★ You'll Never Find Another Man Like Mance / Arhoo. (1964)
★ ★ ★ Texas Songster in a Live Performance / Arhoo. (1966)
★ ★ ★ Texas Songster, Vol. 4 / Arhoo. (1967)
★ ★ ★ Texas Songster, Vol. 5 / Arhoo. (1970)
★ ★ ★ Texas Songster, Vol. 6 / Arhoo. (1974)
In 1960, when Arhoolie's Chris Strachwitz first recorded the Navasota, Texas, songster (the term Lipscomb himself used to describe the range of material he performed), the guitarist/singer was already sixty-five years old and had been a musician for more than fifty years. The first Arhoolie album marked the beginning of a semiprofessional career; Lipscomb was soon in great demand, along with

such contemporaries as Furry Lewis and Mississippi John Hurt, at folk festivals, coffeehouses and folk-music clubs, in addition to continuing to play for friends and relatives at parties and dances.

Almost all of the material Lipscomb recorded for Arhoolie was done solo, although an occasional cut features a second guitar, or as on *Volume 5,* two cuts that find him accompanied by drums and bass. Lipscomb was a bottleneck guitarist of great strength, and each of these LPs tends to distribute his attention among ballads, spirituals, blues, ragtime, jazz, children's songs and dance tunes. *Volume 6* was recorded when Lipscomb was seventy-seven years old, and stands as a remarkable testament to a man kept young by his music. — I.M.

LIQUID GOLD
★ ★ Liquid Gold / Parach. (NA)
Typical formula dance group had almost-hit in 1979 with "My Baby's Baby." — D.M.

LITTLE ANTHONY AND THE IMPERIALS
★ ★ ★ We Are the Imperials / End (NA) ¶
★ ★ ★ Forever Yours / Rou. (NA)
★ Daylight / Song. (NA)
★ ★ ★ Out of Sight, Out of Mind / U.A. (1969)
★ Best of Little Anthony and the Imperials / Lib. (1981)
From the late Fifties through the British Invasion era, Little Anthony and the Imperials scored with such hits as "Shimmy Shimmy Ko Ko Bop," "Goin' out of My Head," "Tears on My Pillow," "Hurt So Bad," and "I'm on the Outside (Looking In)." "Shimmy Shimmy" and "Tears" highlight the End and Roulette albums, which are compilations made while Anthony Gourdine led his group in typical New York City streetcorner doo-wop. The United Artists album has the other hits, which are bigger productions, slicker and less teenage, but all in all, more impressive recordings. The Songbird set is a disastrous attempt to go Christian (not gospel) by Anthony on his own.

The best Anthony and the Imperials hits are more important because the group survived so long than because they are great doo-wop singers; nothing Gourdine and company did really compares to the best of the Teenagers, Schoolboys or Students, to name just three superior doo-wop combos. But these records do establish the transition between the sweet rudiments of streetcorner harmony and the forthcoming slickness of Motown-era soul. And Gourdine's high vocal style is quite different—more articulate and mature—than almost any of his competitors. — D.M.

LITTLE BEAVER
★ ★ ★ ★ **Little Beaver** / Cat (1974)
★ ★ **Black Rhapsody** / Cat (1974)
★ ★ **When Was the Last Time** / Cat (1976)
★ ★ ★ **Party Down** / Cat (1977)
This Miami session guitarist's debut album has so far proved to be his most satisfying. Beaver's moody vocals and delicate guitar soloing are highlighted on *Little Beaver*—a set of sinewy blues songs. As a guitarist, he favors single-note playing with a clear tone reminiscent of Wes Montgomery. *Black Rhapsody* is Beaver's tribute to Montgomery; it even includes a song called "Tribute to Wes." Unfortunately, the rhythm section is a little stiff and the instrumentals are only mildly satisfying—excepting for a tough, funk number called "Hit Me with Funky Music." Little Beaver found commercial success in "Party Down," a sultry dance song. The *Party Down* album is filled with variations on the theme. The relaxed mood proves to be the perfect setting for his oozing solos. After a two-year hiatus, *When Was the Last Time* found the guitar mixed low and the emphasis on romantic crooning. — J.MC.

LITTLE EVA
★ ★ **Llllloco-motion** / Lon. (1962), Br. imp.
Granted, "The Loco-motion" is one of the three or four greatest recordings ever made. But you don't really need to hear Little Eva's album, unless: (a) you're willing to be disillusioned about what Eva had to do with her hit; (b) you're a terminal fanatic Carole King fan (she wrote the title track and six more); or (c) you've got a ton of dough to waste. In which case, go right ahead. (Does not contain either of Eva's other chartmakers, "Let's Turkey Trot" or the inspired "Keep Your Hands off My Baby.") — D.M.

LITTLE FEAT
★ ★ ★ ★ **Little Feat** / War. (1971) ¶
★ ★ ★ ★ ★ **Sailin' Shoes** / War. (1972)
★ ★ ★ ★ ★ **Dixie Chicken** / War. (1973)
★ ★ ★ ★ **Feats Don't Fail Me Now** / War. (1974)
★ ★ ★ ★ **The Last Record Album** / War. (1975)
★ ★ ★ **Time Loves a Hero** / War. (1977)
★ ★ ★ ★ **Waiting for Columbus** / War. (1978)
★ ★ ★ **Down on the Farm** / War. (1979)
★ ★ ★ ★ ★ **Hoy Hoy** / War. (1981)

One of the best-loved American bands of the Seventies, Little Feat continued the tradition of multiracial blues rock that thrived in the late Sixties and was a consistently tremendous live band during a period when American rock moved for the most part into the overstatement of arena performance. Group leader/vocalist/slide guitarist/songwriter Lowell George founded the band at the turn of the decade with fellow ex–Mothers of Invention member Roy Estrada on bass, the maniacal Ritchie Hayward on drums and virtuoso keyboardist Bill Payne. *Little Feat* was a much-heralded debut that saw the band at its weirdest, from the strange rumblings of "Hamburger Midnight" and "Snakes on Everything" to the acid country of George's classic song "Willin' " and the amazing dual guitars of George and Ry Cooder on "Forty-Four Blues/How Many More Years." With *Sailin' Shoes,* the group's sound came into focus with George firmly in control and delivering such songwriting gems as the title track, "Easy to Slip," "Teenage Nervous Breakdown" and the band's live showstoppers, "Cold, Cold Cold" and "Tripe Face Boogie."

On *Dixie Chicken* Estrada was replaced with black bassist Kenny Gradney and percussionist Sam Clayton. A lead guitarist, Paul Barrere, was added, and George's dream band was completed. This record was Little Feat at its best, as the title track, "Two Trains," "On Your Way Down" and "Fat Man in the Bathtub" prove. The supple multirhythms and the melodic interplay between Barrere and Payne gave the band a deliciously rich sound, and that pair began to overshadow George in the band on *Feats Don't Fail Me Now,* with Payne contributing "Oh Atlanta" and Barrere the superfunk vamp "Skin It Back," while George delivered "Spanish Moon" and "Rock and Roll Doctor."

By the time of the aptly named *Last Record Album,* George's role in the band had shrunk to lead vocalist, although two of his best songs, "Down below the Borderline" and "Long Distance Love," were used. Barrere and Payne continued to pick up the slack, Barrere with the great "All That You Dream" and Payne with "Day or Night," but without George's active direction, the band began to flounder. On *Time Loves a Hero,* they resorted to a semi-fusion stance. *Hero* showcased some great playing but lacked the material to back it up.

Waiting for Columbus, the long-awaited live Little Feat album, again provides a format for hot playing but seems overcome by glossiness. Little Feat had always been funky but loose and unpredictable, which gave a real sense of spontaneity to its performance, but now the group became slick. Nevertheless, this is as good a live album as you're ever likely to hear.

When Lowell George died in 1979, Little Feat was in the middle of recording *Down on the Farm*. Ironically, George had retaken the helm on this record, unexpectedly leaving the band to pick up the pieces and try to carry out his ideas. Though the results are somewhat uneven, the material is very strong, particularly George's "Kokomo" "Six Feet of Snow" and the heartbreaking love song "Be One Now."

Hoy Hoy is a retrospective view of the band's career—it's the only record to capture the amazing scope of Little Feat. Blues rock, country, R&B, jazz fusion and acoustic solo performance pop in and out of a wistful presentation that is a stirring tribute to Lowell George's beautiful and ultimately doomed musical conception. Bill Payne assembled it with the attention to little details that brings out the project's underlying poignancy: bits of a George practice track, on which he was working out a song; demos from the band's early days; an amazing blues, "Sweet China White," that George mysteriously chose not to include on his solo album. *Hoy Hoy* also includes live tracks recorded during the height of the band's career, thus providing that sense of perspective missing from *Waiting for Columbus*.   — J.S.

LITTLE STEVEN AND THE DISCIPLES OF SOUL
★ ★ ★ ★ **Men without Women** / EMI (1982)
Because Steven's alter ego is Miami Steve of the E Street Band, and because he sings in a scratchy-throated, soulful roar, the obvious comparisons are to Springsteen and Dylan. But the correct ones are to a line of descent that includes the Young Rascals (whose drummer, Dino Danelli, is a Disciple) Mitch Ryder, the Rolling Stones of *Exile on Main Street* (which is the real antecedent of those vocals—not to mention the horn arrangements) and the first three Asbury Jukes LPs (produced and largely composed by Miami Steve).

This is rough, raw white soul, as tough as its pretensions. But the biggest message here is in the combination of impassioned music and outstanding songs. "Until the Good Is Gone" is an anthem, and "Lyin' in a Bed of Fire," "Under the Gun" and "Forever" are perfect expressions of romantic soul's merger with rock idealism.   — D.M.

LITTLE WILLIE LITTLEFIELD
★ ★ ★ ★ **Little Willie Littlefield, Vol. 1** / Chis. (1981), Br. imp.
★ ★ ★ ★ **Little Willie Littlefield, Vol. 2** / Chis. (1981), Br. imp.
★ ★ **Paris Streetlights** / Paris Album (1981), Fr. imp.
★ ★ ★ ★ **It's Midnight** / Route 66 (NA), Swed. imp
Fine Texas-bred sophisticated blues vocalist and pianist on both boogie blues and smoky-room ballads. Littlefield's best recordings, from the Forties and through the Fifties, are collected on the Route 66 and Chiswick LPs (the Chiswicks are ten-inchers with ten songs apiece). Recorded in France in 1980, the Paris Album set isn't up to par.   — D.M.

LITTLE JOE BLUE
★ ★ **Don't Tax Me In** / Flyr. (NA) Br. imp.
B. B. King clone. Typical late-Seventies blues.   — D.M.

LITTLE MILTON
★ ★ ★ ★ **If Walls Could Talk** / Chess (1969), Fr. imp.
★ ★ ★ ★ **Greatest Hits** / Chess (1972) ¶
★ ★ ★ **Blues 'n' Soul** / Stax (1974)
★ ★ **Montreaux Festival** / Stax (1974)
★ ★ ★ ★ **Raise a Little Sand** / Red L. (1975), Br. imp.
★ **Friend of Mine** / Glades (1977)
★ ★ ★ **Walking the Back Streets** / Stax (1981)
One of the most gravel-voiced of Chicago rhythm & blues singers, Little Milton Campbell in fact owes more to Howlin' Wolf than Curtis Mayfield. Because he recorded for Chess and plays guitar as well as sings, Milton has often been described as a blues artist, but he managed to retain his popularity on the soul scene in the Sixties while most harder blues performers lost theirs. A good deal of this is due to his whimsically sensual material, notably the hits "Grits Ain't Groceries" and "We're Gonna Make It." The Chess greatest-hits album is masterful, presenting Milton as a sort of Northern equivalent to Bobby Bland. *If Walls Could Talk* is the best of the many albums that Milton cut for the label. The Red Lightnin' album collects the early sides he recorded before leaving Memphis, which were recorded for Sun and Meteor and are the most blues-laden material.

But in 1971 Milton left Chess, and began recording for Stax. He had some commercial success there, but after the label folded, he was left adrift, conceptually and contractually. Stax's revival by Fantasy has seen several

Milton albums issued; the best of these is *Walking the Back Streets,* which collects some singles not previously available on albums. His 1977 LP for TK's Glades subsidiary is perfunctory funk, far from the blues and gritty R&B Milton sings at his best. — D.M.

LITTLE RICHARD
★ ★ ★ ★ Little Richard / Spec. (1958)
★ ★ ★ ★ ★ The Fabulous Little Richard / Spec. (1959)
★ ★ ★ His Biggest Hits / Spec. (1959) ¶
★ ★ ★ ★ ★ Little Richard's Grooviest Seventeen Original Hits / Spec. (1959)
★ ★ ★ ★ ★ Well Alright! / Spec. (1959)
★ ★ ★ Little Richard's Greatest Hits / Trip (1967) ¶
★ ★ ★ The Best of Little Richard / Exact (1980)
★ ★ ★ Tutti Frutti / Accord (NA)

Little Richard's music remains among the most vital rock & roll two decades after it was first recorded. His wild pumping piano style (matched only by Jerry Lee Lewis in the annals of world history), his braggadocio singing, with its gospel-derived screams and hollers, and his manic songs—"Long Tall Sally," "Lucille," "Jenny Jenny," "Tutti Frutti" and the rest—are all models for later performers. But on record, Richard remains indubitably Richard.

His Specialty sides are the originals, recorded in the middle and late Fifties before he changed his name back to Richard Penniman and became a minister. *Grooviest Seventeen Original Hits* is the definitive collection, although *His Biggest Hits* is available in pristine monaural sound, which is preferable. *Well Alright!* and *The Fabulous Little Richard* are excellent compilations with some rare tracks; the latter includes the version of "Kansas City" on which the Beatles based theirs.

Little Richard's career as a gospel singer is unfortunately no longer represented on records. Nor is his Seventies comeback for Warners, although *The Rill Thing,* which contains the marvelous "Freedom Blues," an unrestrained rocker in the grand tradition, frequently shows up in bargain bins. The Trip collection is the re-recording of the Fifties hits that Richard cut for Vee Jay during the Sixties; they are vastly inferior. Better to look for Epic's *Cast a Long Shadow,* a reissue of a live-in-the-studio set for Okeh in the Sixties. A-wop-lop-a-loo-bop-a-wop-bam-boom. — D.M.

LITTLE RIVER BAND
★ ★ ★ Little River Band / Cap. (1975)
★ ★ After Hours / Cap. (1976), Aust. imp.
★ ★ Diamantina Cocktail / Cap. (1977)
★ ★ ★ Beginnings / Cap. (1978)
★ ★ Sleeper Catcher / Cap. (1978)
★ ★ First under the Wire / Cap. (1979)
★ ★ Backstage Pass / Cap. (1980)
★ ★ Time Exposure / Cap. (1981)

Competent but unoriginal guitar-based Australian band. That their music is undistinguishable from a hundred other slick-but-earnest West Coast music-industry products may account for their considerable U.S. success. LRB's earlier country-rock flavored material is probably artistically preferable to the more heavily orchestrated MOR pop ballads of the last three or four albums. But only just. — S.M.

LITTLE SONNY
★ ★ Black and Blue / Enterp. (NA)
★ ★ Hard Going Up / Enterp. (NA)

Detroit-based blues harp player is a fine instrumentalist and a decent singer, but his only two albums are overproduced. — D.M.

LIVE WIRE
★ ★ ★ ★ Pick It Up / A&M (1979)
★ ★ ★ No Fright / A&M (1980)
★ ★ ★ Changes Made / A&M (1981)

Excellent quartet of blues-rocking Britishers was at first lumped together with Dire Straits just because it used a traditional form at a time when experiment was rife. But producer/lead guitarist Simon Boswell (he produced *No Fright* and *Changes Made;* Glyn Johns produced *Pick It Up*) drew raves from Eric Clapton and proved himself to be an original talent as Live Wire continued to deliver the goods. — J.S.

LOBO
★ ★ The Best of Lobo / Big (1976)
★ Lobo / MCA (1979)

Lobo had a string of pop hits, most notably 1971's "Me and You and a Dog Named Boo" and 1972's "I'd Love You to Want Me." It is surprising that Lobo is of Spanish origin and sings in a gentle, José Feliciano style of folk pop. All the hits are on *Best,* for anyone who still cares. — D.M.

ROBERT JR. LOCKWOOD
★ ★ ★ Steady Rollin' Man / Del. (1973)
★ ★ ★ ★ Blues Live in Japan / Advent (1974)
★ ★ ★ Contrasts / Trix (NA)
★ ★ ★ Robert Jr. Lockwood Does Twelve / Trix (NA)

★ ★ ★ **The Baddest New Guitar** / P-Vine
(NA), Jap. imp.
Excellent twelve-string guitarist who often
appeared as sideman to better-known performers (Little Walter and Sonny Boy Williamson in particular). Lockwood came from
the delta (where Robert Johnson allegedly
was his stepfather—thus the Junior) but is
best known as a Chicago performer.
— D.M.

ROBERT JR. LOCKWOOD AND JOHNNY SHINES
★ ★ ★ **Hangin' On** / Round. (1980)
★ ★ ★ ★ **Dust My Broom** / Flyr. (NA), Br.
imp.
Two fine Southern-bred Chicago bluesmen
with intimate connections to Robert Johnson
chase his ghost across five decades—from
their own youth through the complete Fifties
sides recorded for J.O.B. (reissued on Flyright) and a Seventies reunion of duets (on
Rounder). — D.M.

JOHN LODGE
★ **Natural Avenue** / Lon. (1977)
From the Moody Blues bassist, sweet but
forgettably airy melodies, plain orchestration,
flat engineering; weak and precious.
— C.W.

NILS LOFGREN
★ ★ ★ ★ **The Best of Nils Lofgren and Grin**
/ Epic (NA)
★ ★ ★ ★ ★ **Nils Lofgren** / A&M (1975)
★ ★ **Cry Tough** / A&M (1976)
★ **I Came to Dance** / A&M (1977)
★ ★ **Night after Night** / A&M (1977)
★ ★ ★ ★ **Nils** / A&M (1979)
★ ★ ★ **Night Fades Away** / Backs.
(1981)
Nils Lofgren is the great lost rocker of the
Seventies. A good songwriter (when he
works at it), a great, flashy guitarist and a
tireless stage performer with winning charisma, Lofgren has created some very good, at
times classic, rock & roll. The reason for his
lack of success, though, is basic. For all this
undeniable talent he has never developed it
fully. All the qualities that still make him a
refreshing artist—sizable rock intuition, guitar chops second to none, spontaneous stage
ideas—hamper his efforts, especially on record, to assess his virtues and expand upon
them.

After four hit-and-miss attempts with Grin
(the successes are chronicled on *The Best of
Nils Lofgren and Grin*), Lofgren scored with
his first solo album, a tour de force of un-
quenchable vitality and disarming subtlety.

Adding acoustic guitar and piano onto a
power trio of himself, Wornell Jones and
Aynsley Dunbar, Lofgren offered tales of
teen love lost and recovered. On a record
filled with a wit and warmth he would never
again capture in full, three tracks stand out.
"Back It Up" is a perfectly constructed two-
minute-plus number that should have been
the AM breakthrough that always eluded
him, and his tribute to Rolling Stone Keith
Richard, "Keith Don't Go," swaggered with
a vibrancy that its subject hadn't mustered
in years, but the highlight was probably the
album-closing "Goin' Back." Lofgren's rendition may be the best the song ever received
because his persona was so perfectly summed
up in the song's wistful celebration of joyous
innocence.

Cry Tough, on the heels of that effort, was
a major disappointment. Producer Al
Kooper brought out the worst in Lofgren,
who seemed intent on becoming a boasting
guitar hero; also, the songwriting was fading.
But in comparison with *I Came to Dance,
Cry Tough* is a gem. Poised on the brink of
stardom mainly because of his dynamic stage
performances, Lofgren choked up. The self-
produced *I Came to Dance* is a total fiasco,
and undoubtedly the worst record ever put
out by an artist just about to hit the big
time. The only thing *Dance* accomplished
was banishing Nils to the bush leagues forever. The obligatory double live album, *Night
after Night,* followed, and couldn't save the
day. Inferior to the "official bootleg," *Back
It Up,* released by A&M two years earlier
(and worth paying collector's prices for),
Night's extended arrangements vitiated the
strength of his work. Lofgren seemed artistically spent, washed up at twenty-six.

Nils returned the man, no longer a boy,
from his self-imposed exile. Seemingly from
nowhere, Lofgren delivered a record that finally demonstrated artistic and personal maturity. He collaborated extensively with Lou
Reed and producer Bob Ezrin, and only
some cruel, misogynistic lyrics on side two
prevented *Nils* from being a comeback. With
a carefully assembled production showcasing
a renewed gift for composing ("Steal Away,"
"A Fool Like You," and "No Mercy"—the
powerful story of a young boxer's compassion for the champion whose dreams he is
about to end forever), Lofgren conjured up
the best ballad of his career. "Shine Silent-
ly," with its moving, almost hypnotic
rhythm, builds up a feeling of majesty that
contrasts poignantly with the world-weary
vocal.

The commercial damage to his career had

already been done, however, and *Nils* went nowhere on the charts. Leaving A&M, Lofgren hooked up with MCA-distributed Backstreet, but any change was invisible. *Night Fades Away* suffered from another strained production (courtesy of Jeff Baxter), and some of Nils' best performances in the studio are wasted by it and his usual inability to think the songs out a bit more. While live performances to support the disc showed old-time exuberance and skill, Lofgren had once again failed to show any consistency. Ultimately, that's the man's fatal flaw, and instead of his often lofty achievements, unfortunately what he may be most remembered for.   — W.K.

DAVE LOGGINS
★ **Personal Belongings / Van. (1972)**
★ **Apprentice (in a Musical Workshop) / Epic (1974)**
★ **Country Suite / Epic (1976)**
★ **One Way Ticket to Paradise / Epic (1977)**
★ **David Loggins / Epic (1977)**
Acoustical singer/songwriter whose only hit, "Please Come to Boston," is on *Apprentice.* Earnest schlock.   — S.H.

KENNY LOGGINS
★ ★ **Celebrate Me Home / Col. (1977)**
★ ★ **Nightwatch / Col. (1978)**
★ ★ **Keep the Fire / Col. (1979)**
★ ★ **Alive / Col. (1980)**
On his own, without Jim Messina to provide some effervescence, Loggins is as flat as a day-old open can of beer. This is to Loggins and Messina's lightweight MOR what the Art Garfunkel solo albums are to Simon and Garfunkel's heavyweight MOR: a sad reflection of a once enjoyable past.   — D.M.

LOGGINS AND MESSINA
★ ★ ★ **Loggins and Messina Sittin' In / Col. (1972)**
★ ★ ★ **Loggins and Messina / Col. (1972)**
★ **Full Sail / Col. (1973)**
★ ★ ★ **On Stage / Col. (1974)**
★ **Mother Lode / Col. (1974)**
★ **"So Fine" / Col. (1975)**
★ **Native Sons / Col. (1976)**
★ ★ ★ **The Best of Loggins and Messina/ Friends / Col. (1976)**
★ ★ **Finale / Col. (1977)**
Originally this was Jim Messina's laid-back escape hatch from Poco. But Poco virtually invented laid-backness, so there wasn't too much further to go by the time Messina decided to join forces with West Coast folkie Kenny Loggins. Messina's career high points were his marginal contributions to the Buffalo Springfield and the first two Poco albums, which were about as high energy as this peculiarly tired genre comes. Thus Loggins and Messina became spokesmen for the "easy" aesthetic.

There's no question that the first two duo LPs were warm and rocking. So it's little wonder that nearly 80 percent of the final *Best of* album was comprised of songs that originally appeared on those two LPs. "Vahavella" (even better in its broiling reincarnation on the live album), "Angry Eyes" and their most essential hit, "Your Mama Don't Dance," were infectious if unassuming pop. But the unassumingness snowballed over the years into total snore. Loggins and Messina didn't stop—they just faded away.   — B.M.

THE LOOK
★ ★ ★ **We're Gonna Rock / Pl. Rec. (1981)**
Yet another Midwestern journeyman hard-rock outfit, leaden lyrics celebrating the glories of rock over fleet if predictable guitar patterns. Cover of Animals' "Don't Let Me Be Misunderstood" is disc's most satisfying cut. Potentially as great a menace as R.E.O. Speedwagon.   — G.A.

LOOSE CHANGE
★ **Straight from the Heart / Casa. (NA)**
Dance group, nothing especially obnoxious, but docked one star for meretricious title.   — D.M.

LOST GENERATION
★ ★ ★ **Sly, Slick and Wicked / Bruns. (1970)**
★ ★ **Young, Tough and Terrible / Bruns. (1972)**
Modern soul group recorded these two albums in the early Seventies, after scoring a Top Forty pop hit with "Sly, Slick and Wicked." Moderate R&B, no pop success followed, and like most such items, this group disappeared.   — D.M.

LOST GONZO BAND
★ ★ **Lost Gonzo Band / MCA (1975)**
★ ★ **Thrills / MCA (1976)** ¶
★ ★ **Signs of Life / Cap. (1978)** ¶
Jerry Jeff Walker's backup band plays a credible version of the raucous country-rock bar-band music that Walker and his Austin cronies helped popularize in the Seventies. Unfortunately, the group lacks the personality or songwriting ability to make it on its own.   — J.S.

LOVE
★ ★ ★ ★ ★ **Forever Changes / Elek. (1968)**
★ ★ ★ ★ **Best of Love / Rhino (1980)**
Forever Changes is a light classic from the late psychedelic era. It is all that survives of almost a dozen Love LPs, most of them harder-rocking and less worthwhile. This is rather like a soundtrack from an LSD movie—lead singer Arthur Lee is a bizarre composer whose song titles tell a good deal of the story: "A House Is Not a Motel," "The Good Humor Man He Sees Everything Like This," "Bummer in the Summer," "You Set the Scene." Although it's similarly dated, the music has an exotic frothiness and the string settings are among the most gorgeous in rock history. Even the lyrics, while occasionally demented, were usually too inchoate to be anything but curiously passionate love songs. Indescribably essential.

The Rhino set collects odds and ends from all the group's albums. It's for fanatics, mostly. — D.M.

LOVE AND KISSES
■ **Love and Kisses / Casa. (1977)**
■ **How Much, How Much I Love You / Casa. (1978)**
■ **You Must Be Love / Casa. (NA)**
Really vile disco concept act—voices out of the Mormon Tabernacle, arrangements that sound like Enoch Light on speed. All the LP covers are a sexist mess, too. — D.M.

LOVE CHILD'S AFRO-CUBAN BLUES BAND
★ ★ ★ **Out among 'Em / Roul. (1975)**
Surprisingly lively—if cumbersomely monikered—dance group. — D.M.

LOVE DE-LUXE
★ ★ ★ **Here Comes That Sound / War. (1979)**
A dance record that gets on the good foot purposefully. Nothing special, but definitely listenable. — D.M.

LOVEJOYS
★ ★ ★ **Reggae Vibes / Top R. (1981)**
A relatively recent entry in the female reggae sweepstakes, the Lovejoys are two American women (though you'd never guess it) who write and sing their own material. Their warm harmonies and pleasing melodies more than compensate for the missing cutting edge. Hum away your day. — R.F.G.

LOVE OF LIFE ORCHESTRA
★ **Star Jaws / Lovely Music (1977)**
Sounds more like love of death. — J.S.

LOVERBOY
★ ★ ★ **Loverboy / Col. (1980)**
★ ★ **Get Lucky / Col. (1981)**
Although the hooks suggest a strong pop sensibility, the crushing inanity of Loverboy's guitar-heavy sound marks them for what they are—lightweight hard rock. — J.D.C.

LOVE UNLIMITED
★ **Under the Influence of Love Unlimited / 20th Cent. (1973)**
★ **In Heat / 20th Cent. (1974)**
★ **He's All I've Got / Unli. (1977)**
★ **Love Is Back / Unli. (1979)**
★ **Best of Love Unlimited / Unli. (1980)**
★ **Welcome Aboard / Unli. (1981)**
Barry White's subsidiary vocal group scored on the charts with a couple of tidbits, but mostly served as a kind of pretty fluff for White's macho-horny growl. He married one of 'em. And he can keep 'em. — D.M.

LOVE UNLIMITED ORCHESTRA
★ ★ **Rhapsody in White / 20th Cent. (1974)**
★ **White Gold / 20th Cent. (1974)**
★ **Music Maestro Please / 20th Cent. (1975)** ¶
★ **My Sweet Summer Suite / 20th Cent. (1976)**
★ **My Musical Bouquet / 20th Cent. (1978)**
★ **Let 'Em Dance / Unli. (1981)**
The Orchestra's hit, "Love's Theme," sounded like some dreamy movie music for a Diana Ross flick in 1974, but by now it's become as unbearably odious as the chubbo they back up. And Barry White is (you know, baby) pretty (uh-huh) goddamn lame. (All right, darlin'.) — D.M.

LENE LOVICH
★ ★ ★ **Stateless / Stiff/Epic (1978)**
★ ★ **Flex / Stiff/Epic (1979)**
★ **No-Man's Land / Epic (1981)**
Another American expatriate who came into national visibility by way of the early Be Stiff American tours. Lovich is a true eccentric whose Yugoslavian princess/swirling dervish appearance is the perfect visual complement to her quirky digital voice. *Stateless* has the best display of her idiosyncratic pop and contains her rock-as-disco hit, "Lucky Number." *Flex* strained trying to recapture the good-natured freneticism of *Stateless,* and Lovich began to sound shrill and self-parodying. Nothing on *No-Man's Land* is up to her earlier material. — D.G.

THE LOVIN' SPOONFUL
★ ★ ★ ★ ★ **Best of the Lovin' Spoonful /
Kam. S. (1967)**
It's a real shame that a group that contributed so heavily to folk rock and the general resurgence of the rock & roll spirit in the mid-Sixties should have all of its original albums out of print. The band produced such hits as "Do You Believe in Magic," "Summer in the City" and "Daydream," and had a fine songwriter in John Sebastian, plus a real rocker in Zal Yanovsky. The remaining anthology is recommended, but only as an introduction; any of the group's first five albums, especially *Daydream* and *Hums of the Lovin' Spoonful,* are worth hunting down.
— B.A.

NICK LOWE
★ ★ ★ ★ **Pure Pop for Now People / Col.
(1978)**
★ ★ ★ **Labour of Lust / Col. (1979)**
★ ★ **Nick the Knife / Col. (1982)**
★ ★ **The Abominable Showman / Col. (1983)**
The English title of Lowe's first album was *Jesus of Cool,* a serious overstatement even for a man who went on to marry Carlene Carter. Lowe won his spurs with Brinsley Schwarz as the band's principal songwriter, part-time singer and full-time bassist; he also appears as bassist/vocalist with Rockpile when that group is together. Here he's supported primarily by Rockpile.

Lowe's songs are always witty, and he's capable of reworking (or wrecking) Sixties-style pop textures quite imaginatively. *Pure Pop* is extraordinarily well-crafted: "Heart of the City," "Marie Provost" and "Rollers Show" are exciting and the latter pair is quite hilarious as well. *Labour of Lust* produced a No. 12 single in "Cruel to Be Kind," which plays off Lowe's sensibility quite nicely, though its shallowness might not have been entirely a pose. Like a great many previous pop dilettantes, Lowe is now confronted with the problem of having used up his most facile ideas. His third and fourth albums merely grind out pop-rock readymades. Chances are he'll now be recalled primarily as a quirky bassist and failed pop producer (his Elvis Costello and Graham Parker productions never broke through). One suspects Lowe's better than that, but the evidence on hand is mixed. — D.M.

THE LOW NUMBERS
★ **Twist Again with the Low Numbers /
Rhino (1978)**
At their best, as derivative of the Jam as the latter was of the Who; at their worst—which

is almost all the time—just barely listenable.
— W.K.

L.T.D.
★ ★ ★ **Love, Togetherness and Devotion /
A&M (1974)**
★ **Gittin' Down / A&M (1974)**
★ **Love to the World / A&M (1976)**
★ ★ **Something to Love / A&M (1977)**
★ **Togetherness / A&M (1978)**
★ **Devotion / A&M (1979)**
★ **Shine On / A&M (1980)**
Slick Seventies ensemble R&B group enjoyed disco crossover popularity. — J.S.

CARRIE LUCAS
★ ★ ★ **Carrie Lucas in Danceland / Solar
(1979) ¶**
★ ★ ★ ★ **Portrait of Carrie / Solar (1980)**
Lucas is a good singer and a better writer who could turn out to be the brightest star in the Solar galaxy. Unfortunately, neither of these albums ever compromise their production values long enough to let us know for sure. — J.D.C.

JON LUCIEN
★ ★ **Rashida / RCA (1973)**
★ ★ ★ **Mind's Eye / RCA (1974) ¶**
★ ★ ★ ★ **Song for My Lady / Col. (1975)**
★ ★ ★ **Premonitions / Col. (1976) ¶**
★ ★ ★ **I Am Now / RCA (1977) ¶**
★ ★ ★ **The Best of Jon Lucien / Col. (NA)**
Jon Lucien is a baritone singer who croons his spiritual and love songs in fashionably glossy pop-jazz settings. He is also sometimes an instrumentalist and songwriter capable of writing unashamedly mushy love songs. Arrangements differ little from album to album, and their lushness often gives his music an unnecessary MOR bent. On romantic ballads, Lucien's phrasing is reminiscent of Johnny Hartman's, but he tends to be at his most imaginative on uptempo songs. — J.MC.

LUCIFER'S FRIEND
■ **I'm Just a Rock 'n' Roll Singer / Bill.
(1974) ¶**
★ **Banquet / Pass. (1975) ¶**
■ **Mind Exploding / Janus (1976) ¶**
★ **Good Time Warrior / Elek. (1978)**
★ **Sneak Me In / Elek. (1980)**
★ **Mean Machine / Elek. (1981)**
Classic European hackwork, with influences acquired, but not absorbed, from Genesis, Led Zeppelin, Grand Funk and the nether world of jazz rock. The group is composed of a typical "progressive" rock mixture of Germans and Englishmen, whose artistic

pretensions consistently outrace their ability to sing a song. Real bad stuff. — D.M.

LYDIA LUNCH
■ Queen of Siam / Ze (1980)
Anyone who complains this much about inhumanity is obliged to display some humane emotion. Without that, this "punk-funk" screech is just so much avant-garde horseshit. — D.M.

BASCOM LAMAR LUNSFORD
★ ★ Smokey Mountain Ballads / Folk. (1953)
★ ★ Music from South Turkey Creek / Roun. (1976)
Lunsford, who wrote "Old Mountain Dew" about his brief tenure as a full-time lawyer, sings and plays banjo (two-finger style) on the first side of this LP. He is credited with several hundred items in the Archive of American Folksong, although relatively little has been recorded. George Pegram and Red Parham are on side two. — I.M.

CHERYL LYNN
★ Cheryl Lynn / Col. (1978)
★ In Love / Col. (1979)
★ In the Night / Col. (1981)
Because it is every white, middle-aged record executive's dream to discover a hot looker with a hook, the 1979 success of this wretched pop vocalist perhaps portends a trend. But that doesn't mean anyone ought to follow it. — D.M.

LORETTA LYNN
★ ★ ★ Hymns / MCA (1965)
★ ★ ★ You Ain't Woman Enough / MCA (1967)
★ ★ ★ ★ Don't Come Home A-Drinkin' / MCA (1967)
★ ★ ★ Who Says God Is Dead? / MCA (1968)
★ ★ ★ ★ ★ Loretta Lynn's Greatest Hits / MCA (1968)
★ ★ ★ Here's Loretta Lynn / Cor. (1968)
★ ★ ★ ★ Coal Miner's Daughter / MCA (1971)
★ ★ ★ Alone with You / Cor. (1972)
★ ★ ★ They Don't Make 'Em Like My Daddy / MCA (1974)
★ ★ ★ ★ Loretta Lynn's Greatest Hits, Vol. 2 / MCA (1974)
★ ★ ★ Back to the Country / MCA (1975)
★ ★ ★ Home / MCA (1975)
★ ★ ★ ★ When the Tingle Becomes a Chill / MCA (1976)
★ ★ ★ Somebody Somewhere / MCA (1976)

★ ★ ★ ★ I Remembered Patsy / MCA (1977)
★ ★ Out of My Head and Back in My Bed / MCA (1978)
★ ★ Loretta / MCA (1980)
★ ★ We've Come a Long Way Baby / MCA (1981)
Loretta Lynn is one of the most perplexing of all country women performers. A major star for the past decade, she seems torn between the raw roots of her Kentucky upbringing—"Coal Miner's Daughter" is her story—and the middle-class demands of modern Nashville. But within this series of contradictions (and with the exception of her often pallid duet work with Conway Twitty), Lynn has recorded some of the most consistently appealing music to come from Nashville in this decade.

Mostly this has meant her hits, which include tough-woman songs that are nearly female honky-tonk, like "You Aint' Woman Enough," such social commentary items as "The Pill" and "One's on the Way," both examples of instinctive working-class feminism; and country weepers like "When the Tingle Becomes a Chill" and "They Don't Make 'Em Like My Daddy." If Lynn were ever granted artistic rather than purely commercial production values, she might become the most important female singer of her generation. — D.M.

LORETTA LYNN AND CONWAY TWITTY
★ ★ We Only Make Believe / MCA (1970)
★ ★ Lead Me On / MCA (1971)
★ ★ Louisiana Woman, Mississippi Man / MCA (1973)
★ ★ Country Partners / MCA (1974)
★ ★ Feeling / MCA (1975)
★ ★ United Talent / MCA (1976)
★ ★ Dynamic Duo / MCA (1977)
★ ★ Honky-Tonk Heroes / MCA (1978)
★ ★ The Very Best of Loretta Lynn and Conway Twitty / MCA (1979)
★ ★ Diamond Duet / MCA (1979)
★ ★ Two's a Party / MCA (1981)
Loretta gets top billing here, but it is Conway's penchant for Nashville schlockapolitan that dominates. The entire C&W duet tradition is somewhat perverse—since the duets are usually forced marriages without any real aesthetic ground, as here, where what Loretta and Conway share is mostly some packaged tours and a mutual record label. I guess all the kissy-face and handholding, which ranges from the covers to the lyrics, are fine if you can stomach cutesiness

as a steady diet. If not, you'll agree that both partners are better off on their own. — D.M.

GLORIA LYNNE
★ **I Don't Know How to Love Him / ABC (NA)**
★ ★ **Gloria Lynne / Ev. (1966)**
Gloria Lynne is a relatively minor jazz singer with an unusually husky voice. She has seen better days. Esmond Edwards' production on *I Don't Know* is simultaneously garish and cloddish. It brings out the worst in her, when she isn't drowned out by his wah-wah effects and violins. The Everest LP is from her brief days of Top Thirty success with "I Wish You Love" in 1964. — R.G.

PHIL LYNOTT
★ ★ ★ **Solo in Soho / War. (1980)**
Thin Lizzy leader's solo try is more song-oriented, less heavy than his group's metallic work. "King's Call" is one of the most moving reminiscences of the night Elvis Presley died, "Ode to a Black Man," is Lynott's assertion of his racial priorities, and "Talk in '79" a biting commentary on the then-contemporary music scene, pillorying figures ranging from *The Rocky Horror Show* to Nina Hagen. Lynott's support includes the boys from Lizzy as well as Dire Straits' Mark Knopfler and Midge Ure of Ultravox. This is more controlled, musically and compositionally, than most of what Lizzy has churned out since *Johnny the Fox,* although Lynott doesn't always seem certain of his sonic direction. — D.M.

LYNYRD SKYNYRD
★ ★ ★ **Pronounced Leh-Nerd Skin-Nerd / MCA (1973)**
★ ★ ★ ★ **Second Helping / MCA (1974)**
★ ★ **Nuthin' Fancy / MCA (1975)**
★ ★ **Gimme Back My Bullets / MCA (1976)**
★ ★ ★ ★ **One More from the Road / MCA (1976)**
★ ★ ★ ★ **Street Survivors / MCA (1977)**
★ ★ ★ **Skynyrd's First . . . And Last / MCA (1978)**
★ ★ ★ ★ **Gold and Platinum / MCA (1979)**
Plugging in hard-rock influences, where most other Southern bands place country roots, a mix of British rock sensibilities and hard-drinking Southern boogie established Lynyrd Skynyrd as top contenders for the mid-Seventies Southern rock throne.

Second Helping is the band at its chunky best, with rhythm and lead licks fairly bursting from the seams of songs like "The Needle and the Spoon" and the tongue-in-cheek "Workin' for MCA." Lead singer Ronnie Van Zant's reputation as a rabble-rousing hero was solidified with "Sweet Home Alabama," Skynyrd's breakthrough single (and an ostensible reply to Neil Young's "Southern Man").

When producer Al Kooper was dumped for Tom Dowd's cleaner sound, after *Nuthin' Fancy,* Skynyrd also lost some of its distinction. While there were still some strong tunes—"Saturday Night Special" cracked like the gun it was named after—there wasn't the sort of combustion that drove the first two albums. *Gimme Back My Bullets* continued this trend with a few notable tunes and a clutter of well-executed but otherwise lackluster performances. The fact that the bulk of the tough-rocking live double album, *One More from the Road,* was drawn from the first two LPs indicates that while Skynyrd reached its commercial peak through incessant touring, it was at a critical point in its recording career—when creative growth was straining to match popular appeal. The soaring beauty of "Free Bird" was matched by its ascent as an FM standard, but Ronnie Van Zant's writing was suffering.

Skynyrd met the challenge with *Street Survivors,* the band's hardest-rocking studio album since *Second Helping.* But the victory was wrested from its grasp by a plane crash within weeks of the album's October 1977 release. (Van Zant, guitarist Steve Gaines and singer Cassy Gaines died in the wreck.)

"That Smell," a maniacally propulsive tune from *Street Survivors* dealing with the perils of the rock & roll trail, served as the band's epitaph. At least until the release of *First and . . . Last* a year later. That album, compiled from tapes made before Al Kooper discovered the band, contains some of Van Zant's best writing; it was far from a ploy to market the remains of a rock ghost. And Van Zant's true epitaph is contained in its best song, "Was I Right or Wrong," in which a singer, spurned by his family, finds success and returns home to find his parents dead. — J.B.M.

M

★ ★ ★ **New York, London, Paris, Munich /
Sire (1979)**
★ ★ **The Official Secrets Act / Sire (1980)**
M is Robin Scott, whose claim to fame is
"Pop Muzik," a bouncy paean to pop that
was the first workable fusion of new-wave
sensibility and the disco beat (a prelude to
dance-oriented rock). That's about all *New
York, London* has to offer, though; *Official
Secrets* is mostly droll agitprop that smacks
of Antmusic.   — J.D.C.

MARY MacGREGOR

★ ★ **Torn between Two Lovers / Ario.
(1977)**
★ **In Your Eyes / Ario. (1978)**
Kvetchy pop singer. "Torn between Two
Lovers" was the kind of self-indulgent ballad
that could only have been a hit during the
height of the Me Decade.   — D.G.

MACHINE

★ ★ **There But for the Grace of God Go I /
RCA (1979)** ¶
★ ★ **Moving On / RCA (NA)**
Disco band had a hit with the August Dar-
nell-penned title track of *There But,* which
sold on the strength of its popularity in gay
discos.   — J.S.

JIMMIE MACK

★ ★ ★ **Jimmie Mack / Big (1978)** ¶
★ ★ ★ **On the Corner / Big (NA)** ¶
★ ★ ★ **Jimmie Mack and the Jumpers /
RCA (1981)**
Hard rock that's high energy without being
heavy metal by the former Montrose lead
vocalist. This Jimmie Mack never met Martha and the Vandellas, but he's an above-
average white screamer. The RCA album
has the best songs, the tightest playing, and
production by Roy Bittan of the E Street
Band.   — D.M.

LONNIE MACK

★ ★ ★ **Lonnie Mack with Pismo / Cap.
(1977)** ¶
Semi-legendary rock guitarist Lonnie Mack
is best known for his 1963 instrumental hit
with Chuck Berry's "Memphis." *With Pismo*
is in a laid-back country vein that's pleasant
but does nothing to further his reputation
for hot licks, although it does include a
guest appearance by the able sessionman
David Lindley. Elektra's reissue of the original Mack album—*For Collectors Only* (now
deleted)—is more worth tracking down.
  — J.S.

UNCLE DAVE MACON

★ ★ ★ **Early Recordings / Coun. (NA)**
★ ★ ★ **Wait 'Til the Clouds Roll By / Hist.
(NA)**
★ ★ ★ **Laugh Your Blues Away / Roun.
(1979)**
A pioneer in the field of commercial country
music, Macon was a superb banjo player and
vocalist who surrounded himself with excellent backup musicians (Sam and Kirk
McGee, the Delmore Brothers) or performed
solo, whether on record, in concert or during
his twenty-seven years as a star on *The
Grand Ole Opry.* The first two albums contain remasters of Twenties and Thirties 78s,
drawn from the two hundred titles he cut
for various labels. All are technically well
handled and offer sufficient background information for a first-time listener.   — I.M.

MADCATS

★ **Madcats / Ari./Bud. (1978)** ¶
Relentlessly irritating AOR swill.   — D.M.

MADE IN U.S.A.

★ ★ **Made in U.S.A. / De-Lite (1977)**
The usual disco septet, this time with a supper-club female singer, offset by some grittier
male background singing.   — D.M.

MADNESS
★ ★ ★ ★ **One Step Beyond . . . / Sire (1979)**
★ ★ ★ ★ **Absolutely / Sire (1980)**
★ ★ ★ **Madness 7 / Stiff (1981)**
Of all the ska revival bands, Madness is perhaps the most popular in Britain, and it's not hard to understand why. Their approach to the ska beat is relentless and joyful, like the best R&B, but the band's repertoire overall owes as much to Cockney music-hall traditions as to classic bluebeat oldies. *One Step Beyond . . .* is more freewheeling, with a heavier R&B feel; *Absolutely* focuses more on the group's sense of social irony, which is as broad as it is acute. — J.D.C.

MAGAZINE
★ ★ ★ **Real Life / Virgin (1978), Br. imp.**
★ ★ ★ **Secondhand Daylight / Virgin (1979), Br. imp.**
★ ★ ★ **The Correct Use of Soap / Virgin (1980)**
★ ★ ★ **Play / IRS (1980)**
★ ★ ★ **Magic, Murder and the Weather / IRS (1981)**
Straightforward British new-wave band featuring lead singer Howard Devoto is mannered and polished in a style reminiscent of early Roxy Music, but not as good. High points: "Philadelphia" (from *Soap*) and "Shot by Both Sides" (from *Real Life*). — J.S.

MAGIC SAM
★ ★ ★ ★ **West Side Soul / Del. (1968)**
★ ★ ★ ★ **Black Magic / Del. (1969)**
★ ★ ★ **The Late Great Magic Sam / L+R (1980), Ger. imp.**
★ ★ ★ ★ **Magic Rocker / Flyr. (1980), Br. imp.**
★ ★ **The Other Takes 1956–1958 (with Otis Rush) / Flyr. (1980), Br. imp.**
★ ★ ★ **Out of Bad Luck / P-Vine (1980), Jap. imp.**
In the late Sixties, Magic Sam was perhaps *the* key figure in Chicago's West Side soul and blues bar scene, and his bands were never anything less than outstanding. If he hadn't died of a heart attack in 1969, at age thirty-two, Sam Maghett (his real name) would certainly be a formidable practitioner of third-generation Chicago blues. As it is, his recorded legacy is impressive, a body of work that bridges distinctions between blues and R&B.

Sam was a big-voiced shouter, not an especially subtle singer, but forceful and effective. His guitar style is never much more than adequate, and when pitted against Otis Rush on *The Other Takes,* he clearly comes off second best. For my money, his strengths are best shown on the Delmark albums, both of them issued during his lifetime. His band there includes Mighty Joe Young on second guitar, Lafayette Leake on piano and Odie Payne on drums, and it is outstanding.

Maghett was one of the last bluesmen to come to Chicago from Mississippi, and his roots in the original soil of the blues show. But he is unafraid of modernizing his sound, and "I Just Want a Little Bit" from *Black Magic* is simply B. B. King further (and fabulously) urbanized. Together with "Easy Baby," and *West Side Soul*'s "All of Your Love" and "Every Night and Every Day," these are the best of Sam's late-Sixties tracks, and indicate the direction he was moving in when he died.

The other outstanding set here is *Magic Rocker,* which features Sam with his uncle Shakey Jake (James Harris) as well as Payne, Mack Thompson, Willie Dixon, Harold Burrage, Little Brother Montgomery and Syl Johnson, all important middle-level Chicago talents. Recorded in 1957–58 and originally issued on Cobra, these tracks prove Sam's aptitude for pure blues playing. The P-Vine material is also fine, but unlike the Delmark and Flyright sides, it is not annotated, except for a notation that the tracks were originally issued on Jewel. (There are Japanese notes if you can translate them.) *The Other Takes* (one side by Sam, one by Rush) features more Cobra material, including five takes plus two false starts of "Easy Baby," and can be a bit wearing for nonfans. The L+R album contains mostly Cobra material from 1963–64 (including a fabulous "High Heel Sneakers") except for the final two tracks, recorded live in London in October 1969, just a week before Sam died. — D.M.

MAGMA
★ ★ ★ **Magma / Phi. (1971), Fr. imp.**
★ ★ ★ **1001 Degrees Centigrade / Phi. (1972), Fr. imp.**
★ ★ ★ **Mekanik Destruktiw Kommandoh / A&M (1973) ¶**
★ ★ ★ **Kohntarkosz / A&M (1974) ¶**
★ ★ ★ **Magma Live / Ut. (1975)**
★ ★ ★ **Udu Wudu / Ut. (1976)**
★ ★ ★ **Attahk / Toma. (1978)**
A sort of French whole earth orchestra, Magma is progressive European rock in the extreme. As if the dense avant-Wagnerian wall of oppressive percussion, dark jazz variations for guitar, violin and keyboards, and hellish operatic singing is not forbidding enough, leader/drummer/lyricist Christian

Vander invented his own Franco-German Esperanto in which to tell his apocalyptic stories. The first three albums deal with nothing less than the end of the world, an abbreviated version of what was supposed to be a nine-album oratorio. The rest of the records presumably pick up the tale—or what's left of it, anyway—from there.

But you don't have to understand Vander's alien gibberish to hear Magma's combustible strains of Bartók, Stravinsky, Stockhausen and Coltrane. The remarkable complexity and genuine excitement of much of this music is often obscured by the leaden repetition of the extended pieces and the overbearing seriousness of Vander's concept. Still, there are strange forces at work here, and listening to Magma in concentrated doses could put you through some altered states. For its more obvious jazz accents and shorter "songs," beginners are advised to start with *Attahk.* — D.F.

MAGNET
★ **Worldwide Attraction / A&M (1979)**
Homogenized pop rock. Nothing here draws you in. — D.M.

THE MAGNETICS
★ ★ ★ ★ **Rockabilly Fools / Roll. R. (1981)**
These Seattle neo-boppers split up after recording this debut; a record with the subtlety, command of nuance and conviction missing from a half-dozen other, more publicized big-beat redos. Here pompadour and posture are secondary to performance. All five Magnetics vocalize and four take songwriting credits. Not the least of this record's merits are exceptional originals and a selection of oldies as canny and surprising as the band's execution of them. Rolling Rock's production was up to snuff, though its distribution isn't. — G.A.

JAKOB MAGNUSSON
★ ★ **Special Treatment / War. (1979)**
Uninspired fusion quartet; superior lineup of sidemen includes Skunk Baxter, Ernie Watts and Michal Urbaniak. — D.M.

TAJ MAHAL
★ ★ ★ **Taj Mahal / Col. (1967)**
★ ★ ★ ★ **Giant Step / De Old Folks at Home / Col. (1969)**
★ ★ ★ **The Natch'l Blues / Col. (1969)**
★ ★ ★ **The Real Thing / Col. (1971)**
★ ★ **Happy Just to Be Like I Am / Col. (1972)**
★ **Recycling the Blues (and Other Related Stuff) / Col. (1972)**
★ ★ **Oooh So Good 'n' Blues / Col. (1973)**
★ ★ **Mo' Roots / Col. (1974)**
★ **Music Keeps Me Together / Col. (1975)**
★ **Satisfied 'n' Tickled Too / Col. (1976)**
★ ★ ★ **Anthology, Vol. 1 / Col. (1977)**
★ **Music Fuh Ya' (Música Para Tu) / War. (1977)**
★ **Brothers / War. (1977)**
★ ★ **Evolution (The Most Recent) / War. (1978)**

Few artists can boast a catalogue that so specifically chronicles changes in personal musical conception and social attitudes. Taj Mahal began as a blues interpreter, but his music has since encompassed rock, traditional Appalachian sounds, jazz, calypso, reggae and a general tendency toward experimentation and assimilation.

For example, take the four-man string section on the live *The Real Thing,* or Jesse Ed Davis' superbly complementary guitar work on any number of these albums. Mahal performs with bands, orchestras and as a soloist. Through his understanding of contemporary tastes, he has brought the music of his heritage to a mass audience. A self-taught musician who took it upon himself to explore the roots of his music academically, Mahal brings a rare historical perspective to his work, and while he is dedicated to educating his fans, he's never preachy about it.

His debut, *Taj Mahal,* is his least-defined LP. Although Davis and Ry Cooder are among the backup troupe, Taj sounds a bit lost in the recording studio. Musically, the set lacks the focus he was subsequently able to develop. But it does include his landmark, "The Celebrated Walking Blues." *Giant Step/De Old Folks at Home* is a two-record set that incorporates smooth country blues and understated rock rhythms. The second LP is a solo disc, on which Taj plays harmonica, guitar and banjo in addition to singing. The record suffers from poor production: fuzzy vocals and a severe stereo mix that places banjo completely on the left speaker, voice completely on the right.

The Natch'l Blues is just that, although rather than interpreting traditional bluesmen, Mahal himself is the principal songwriter, in addition to rearranging such tunes as "The Cuckoo" and "Corinna." *The Real Thing* is a two-disc live album that features little material from the earlier sets; the regular band is augmented by a tuba section that doubles on other brass. Rather than Mahal's usual three- to four-minute renditions of blues themes, this album includes a number of extended jams. The studio set, *Happy Just to*

Be, also includes the tuba/brass section and draws a clear picture of the relationship between blues and rock. Listen to what happens to "Oh Susanna" and the title track.

Oooh So Good 'n' Blues, Satisfied 'n' Tickled Too, Mo' Roots and *Recycling the Blues* represent various stages of Mahal's discovery of other blues forms and an increasing fascination with Caribbean music. *Mo' Roots* is the most ambitious in its variations on calypso and reggae themes.

Anthology was to be the first of a projected three-part series, which never materialized. The LP is concerned with his early blues and country-blues recordings, and it's excellent.

In addition to his own albums, Taj has done several film scores, the best known being *Sounder,* in which he also played a minor acting role. *Brothers,* based on the lives of George Jackson and Angela Davis, also features a score by Taj consisting of both background music and original songs. The two Warner Bros. albums continue his fascination with Caribbean sounds, with mixed results. But as always, his next step is unpredictable. — I.M.

MAHOGANY RUSH
★ **Maxoom / 20th Cent. (1971)** ¶
★ **Child of the Novelty / 20th Cent. (1971)** ¶
★ **Strange Universe / 20th Cent. (1975)** ¶
★ **Mahogany Rush IV / Col. (1976)**
★ **World Anthem / Col. (1977)**
★ **Live / Col. (1977)**
★ **Tales of the Unexpected / Col. (1979)**
★ **What's Next? / Col. (1980)**
Frank Marino, so the story goes, was involved in a serious car accident somewhere around 1970 or 1971 and lapsed into a deep coma for several days. A nonmusician before the crash, he was supposedly visited while in a coma by the spirit of the late Jimi Hendrix, who endowed the poor Canadian with a soupçon of his deceased talent. Marino awoke, picked up a guitar and started playing riffs in a very familiar style. He acquired a bassist and drummer and cut *Maxoom* for Montreal's tiny Kot'ai label (later reissued on Twentieth Century-Fox).

This is an interesting story, but unfortunately, listening doesn't support it. Marino is obviously a pretty fair guitarist and a devout, almost maniacal Hendrix fan, but unless Jimi regressed to his Curtis Knight days while crossing the Styx, his amalgamation with Marino's physical being is doubtful. Lots of *Axis: Bold as Love* feedback and

sound effects and a poignant Hendrix homage ("Buddy") make *Maxoom* a nifty curiosity, but not much more.

With *Child of the Novelty,* however, Marino lowers his voice an octave, and his songwriting and guitar are more accessible, in the fashion of *Electric Ladyland.* Since then, beginning with *Strange Universe,* Marino's playing has grown more fluid and varied, even taking a run at a jazz riff on occasion. But nobody tells the Hendrix tale much any more. After all these years it's apparent that Marino will never be an innovator, and at best he's just a competent mime. — A.N.

MAIN INGREDIENT
★ ★ **Afrodisiac / RCA (1973)** ¶
★ ★ ★ **Greatest Hits / RCA (1973)** ¶
★ ★ **Euphrates River / RCA (1974)** ¶
★ ★ **Rolling Down a Mountainside / RCA (1975)** ¶
★ ★ **Shame on the World / RCA (1975)**
★ ★ **Spinning Around / RCA (1976)**
★ ★ **Music Maximus / RCA (1977)** ¶
★ **Ready for Love / RCA (1980)**
★ **I Only Have Eyes for You / RCA (1981)**
Black MOR, a little tougher and funkier than the Fifth Dimension, but not by much. The hits—particularly "Everybody Plays the Fool"—were about the best of it, but in general this is a good example of how characterless black pop has become in the past decade. — D.M.

JAH MALLA
★ ★ ★ **Alive and Well / Clap. (1979)**
★ ★ **Jah Malla / Mod. (1981)**
Jah Malla, which includes sons of legendary Jamaican musicians Ernest Ranglin and Roland Alphonso (formerly of the Skatalites), have put on some of the most inspiring live shows of any American reggae band. On record, their potential is barely tapped. *Alive* sketches an interesting, energized jazz/reggae fusion. *Jah Malla* attempts to shoehorn the band into pop formulas, sacrificing energy for catchiness. — R.F.G.

MALLARD
★ ★ ★ **In a Different Climate / Virgin (1977)**
Mallard is a former Captain Beefheart backing band from the northern California town of Eureka. But they haven't quite found it, after all; this is derivative of Beefheart's innovations, all right, but of his less inspired later ones rather than the bizarrely brilliant early stuff. Some quirky pleasures here, but not quite enough. — D.M.

MAMA CASS
★ ★ **Dream a Little Dream** / Dun. (1968) ¶
★ ★ **Make Your Own Kind of Music** / Dun. (1969) ¶
★ ★ **Mama's Big Ones** / Dun. (1971)

As a member of the Mamas and the Papas, Cass Elliott was a highly visible star during the more complex and ethereal moments of folk rock. But these albums, made in the waning days of the group, are all too characteristic of her and their style: light, sentimental pop with a veneer of rock rhythm. Only for those who also miss Sopwith Camel. — D.M.

THE MAMAS AND THE PAPAS
★ ★ **The Mamas and the Papas** / Dun. (1966)
★ ★ ★ **Farewell to the First Golden Era** / Dun. (1967)
★ ★ **The Papas and the Mamas** / Dun. (1968)
★ ★ ★ **The Mamas and the Papas: Sixteen of Their Greatest Hits** / Dun. (1969)
★ ★ **A Gathering of Flowers** / Dun. (1970)
★ ★ ★ **The Mamas and the Papas' Twenty Golden Hits** / Dun. (1973)

The Mamas and the Papas mastered a very slick form of Sixties folk rock, a kind of West Coast version of Simon and Garfunkel, although this quartet's chief songwriter, John Phillips, lacked the sardonic edge of Paul Simon. The group was formed by four veterans of the Greenwich Village folk scene—Phillips; his wife, Michelle; Mama Cass Elliott; and Denny Doherty—while they were down and out in the Virgin Islands in 1965. After relocating to the Los Angeles area and hooking up with producer Lou Adler, the band scored a formidable series of hit singles from 1966 to 1968: "California Dreamin'," "Monday Monday," "Dedicated to the One I Love" (a sweet cover of a Shirelles hit), "Creeque Alley" (a sometimes hilarious parable of the band's career before stardom) and "Twelve Thirty."

The Mamas and the Papas represented folk rock's rapprochement with conventional pop music. Adler surrounded them with the best Hollywood sessionmen of the day, and while sometimes cloyingly sentimental, the records are always highly professional. By typifying hippies in the most harmless sort of way, the group reached a commercial peak of acceptability that more authentic practitioners were denied. And because their singing was so good, and because Phillips and Adler were astute commercially, the band acquired a considerable reputation in hippie-era music circles, helping organize the momentous Monterey International Pop Festival in 1967.

Since then, Phillips has gone on to a rather dissolute career as a pop aristocrat (his most notable achievement has been acting as producer for Robert Altman's *Brewster McCloud*). Michelle, who was divorced from John in 1968 around the time the group broke up, has engaged in a similar career, with spurts of acting (best in *Dillinger,* but not all that great at any time). Cass Elliott, the band's most visible symbol, died in London in 1971; she had a couple of hits on her own. Doherty is no longer present on the recording scene.

Of the albums still available, almost all are anthologies, and the original LPs are not the best the group made. (That honor goes to *If You Can Believe Your Eyes and Ears,* their first.) Any LP rated three stars is a decent sampler. — D.M.

MELISSA MANCHESTER
★ **Home to Myself** / Ari. (1973)
★ **Bright Eyes** / Ari. (1974)
★ ★ **Melissa** / Ari. (1975)
★ **Better Days and Happy Endings** / Ari. (1976)
■ **Help Is on the Way** / Ari. (1976)
■ **Singin'** / Ari. (1977)
★ **Don't Cry Out Loud** / Ari. (1978)
★ **Melissa Manchester** / Ari. (1979)
★ **For the Working Girl** / Ari. (1980)

At her best, this one-time backup singer for Bette Midler sounds like a cross between the Divine Miss M and Dionne Warwick. Her first two albums are intimate, if somewhat unsure. *Melissa,* her most outgoing set, contains the hit "Midnite Blue." From here on, Vini Poncia's inept, overblown productions undermine Manchester's charm. — S.H.

MANDRILL
★ ★ ★ ★ **The Best of Mandrill** / Poly. (1975) ¶
★ ★ **We Are One** / Ari. (1977)
★ ★ **The Greatest** / Ari. (1977)
★ ★ **New Worlds** / Ari. (1978)
★ ★ **Getting in the Mood** / Ari. (1980)

This septet originated in Brooklyn's Bedford-Stuyvesant section and played a streetwise amalgam of funk, salsa and rock elements organized around a loosely Latin-jazz format. On later albums, the range was extended to include disco and heavily arranged ballads, and the band's instrumental capability matured, especially on the now out-of-print *Mandrilland.* All the band's best work is on the cutout records done for Polydor and United Artists, and the *Best of* collection is the only set worth hearing. Mandrill's four Arista albums are fairly pointless compared to much of the band's earlier material.   — J.S.

THE MANHATTANS

★ ★ ★ ★ **There's No Me without You** / Col. (1973)
★ ★ **That's How Much I Love You** / Col. (1974)
★ ★ ★ **The Manhattans** / Col. (1976)
★ ★ ★ ★ **It Feels So Good** / Col. (1977)
★ ★ ★ **There's No Good in Goodbye** / Col. (1977) ¶
★ ★ **Love Talk** / Col. (1979)
★ ★ **After Midnight** / Col. (1980)
★ ★ ★ **Greatest Hits** / Col. (1980)
★ ★ ★ **Black Tie** / Col. (1981)
★ ★ ★ ★ **Follow Your Heart** / Solid S. (1981)
The Manhattans are a low-key group that rarely extends itself beyond what it does best: rumbling, old-fashioned soul ballads like "Kiss and Say Goodbye." Gerald Alston, the lead singer, has a tenor that is modest at best, yet the Manhattans' consistency and taste in the genre has few rivals. The records are packed with a real sincerity and soulfulness. The Columbia albums are produced by Philadelphia perennial Bobby Martin, with the exception of one side on *That's How Much,* which is filled with five mediocre songs from the group's De Luxe days. *It Feels So Good* is their strongest album yet, marred only by Blue Lovett's spoken, Barry White–style intros on just about every song. *Follow Your Heart* is a marvelous set including the best of the band's early recordings, made between 1964 and 1967.   — J.MC.

THE MANHATTAN TRANSFER

★ **Jukin'** / Cap. (1975)
★ ★ **The Manhattan Transfer** / Atl. (1975)
★ ★ **Coming Out** / Atl. (1976)
★ ★ **Pastiche** / Atl. (1978)
★ ★ **Extensions** / Atl. (1979)
★ ★ **Mecca for Moderns** / Atl. (1981)
★ ★ **Best of the Manhattan Transfer** / Atl. (1981)
Picking up where Bette Midler fell apart, the Manhattan Transfer lifts nostalgia out of the Continental Baths and into the Waldorf. Pert and debonair, these well-groomed exponents of recherché schmaltz may lack Midler's penchant for the outrageous, but that's okay; they sing effortlessly, and they distance themselves from their illusion without puncturing it.   — F.R.

BARRY MANILOW

★ ★ **Barry Manilow** / Ari. (1973)
★ ★ **Barry Manilow II** / Ari. (1974)
★ **Tryin' to Get the Feeling** / Ari. (1975)
★ **This One's for You** / Ari. (1976)
★ ★ **Barry Manilow Live** / Ari. (1977)
★ **Even Now** / Ari. (1978)
★ ★ **Barry Manilow's Greatest Hits** / Ari. (1978)
★ **One Voice** / Ari. (1979)
★ **Barry** / Ari. (1980)
★ **If I Should Love Again** / Ari. (1981)
Brooklyn-born singer/composer/arranger/ entertainer has had an extremely successful career belting old-fashioned, sentimental pop tunes against a hard-rock drum sound. A one-man urban melting pot, Manilow's personality blends Italo-American balladry with Jewish vaudeville shtick, a Brill Building song sense and a dash of cabaret camp. His first two albums suggested a more adventurous musical personality than the one that solidified after the success of "Mandy," his first No. 1 hit (from *Barry Manilow II*). In the wake of "Mandy," there followed a stream of carefully chosen formula ballads that Manilow and his coproducer Ron Dante arranged in the grandiose, impersonal style of deluxe TV commercials. Some of the biggest hits include "I Write the Songs" (1975), "Weekend in New England" (1976), "Looks Like We Made It" (1977), "Can't Smile without You" (1978), and the pop-disco "Copacabana" (1978). All are contained on the two-disc *Greatest Hits. Live* features Manilow's "Very Strange Medley," an amusing recap of the commercials he wrote and/or sang in his pre-pop days.   — S.H.

BARRY MANN

★ ★ **Survivor** / RCA (1975) ¶
★ ★ **Joyride** / U.A. (1977) ¶
★ ★ **Barry Mann** / Casa. (NA)
Solid if unexceptional albums by the male half of the legendary Mann/Cynthia Weil songwriting team.   — S.H.

MANFRED MANN

★ ★ **Glorified, Magnified** / Poly. (1972)
★ ★ ★ ★ **Manfred Mann's Earth Band** / Poly. (1972)
★ ★ ★ **Get Your Rocks Off** / Poly. (1973)
★ ★ ★ ★ **The Best of Manfred Mann** / Janus (1974)
★ ★ **Solar Fire** / Poly. (1974)
★ ★ **The Good Earth** / War. (1974)
★ ★ **Nightingales and Bombers** / War. (1975)

★ ★ The Roaring Silence / War. (1976)
★ ★ ★ The Best of Manfred Mann / Cap. (1977)
★ Watch / War. (1978)
★ ★ ★ Angel Station / War. (1979)
★ ★ Chance / War. (1980)

Manfred Mann's original band (represented on the essentially identical Janus and Capitol/EMI collections) was a late-blooming part of the post-Beatles British Invasion and less notable for keyboardist/arranger Manfred Mann himself than for the singing of Paul Jones, one of the best vocalists of that era.

The group's best-known American songs—"Do Wah Diddy," "Sha La La" (both 1964) and "Pretty Flamingo" (1966)—feature Jones' smooth but resonant vocals. On LP, Mann was known for his flirtation with jazz (on one early album, the group did a perfectly dreadful version of Herbie Hancock's "Watermelon Man") and as a frequent interpreter of Bob Dylan material. The later tendency reached its height in 1968, when Mann turned Dylan's "Mighty Quinn" into a splendid Top Ten hit. By then, however, Jones had been replaced by the more flexible but less enduring Mike D'Abo, who went on to write Rod Stewart's early signature song, "Handbags and Gladrags." And numerous other personnel shifts resulted in a drastic change of direction for the group, which was known (beginning with the eponymous 1972 LP on Polydor) as the Earth Band. The Earth Band specialized in extravagant reworkings of pop songs, including terrific versions of Randy Newman's "Living without You" and Dylan's "Please Mrs. Henry" on the *Manfred Mann's Earth Band* album, and John Prine's "Pretty Good" and Dylan's "Get Your Rocks Off" on *Get Your Rocks Off*. The result could be termed jazz rock, though all of it is much more oriented toward pop vocals than any of the other jazz-rock fusion attempts.

A switch to Warner Bros. in 1974 coincided with Mann's discovery of Bruce Springsteen as an artist equally susceptible to remodeling in this manner, and in 1976 Mann scored his most recent pop hit with "Blinded by the Light," a Springsteen song from *The Roaring Silence*. By then, however, a great deal of the novelty had worn off and, as Chris Hamlet-Thompson's vocals were none too endearing (they were rather emotion-starved, in fact), the Earth Band seemed simply a curiosity, and a shopworn one at that, by the time of 1980's *Chance*.
— D.M.

DARRELL MANSFIELD BAND
★ ★ Darrell Mansfield Band / Poly. (NA) ¶
★ ★ Get Ready / Poly. (NA)
Good-rocking blues; well done but nothing spectacular. — J.S.

PHIL MANZANERA
★ ★ ★ ★ Diamond Head / Atco (1975) ¶
★ ★ ★ Listen Now / Poly. (1978) ¶
★ ★ ★ K-Scope / Poly. (1978) ¶
The Roxy Music guitarist enlists Britain's best—John Wetton, Brian Eno and many others—for expert, proudly electric rock permutations. Manzanera's chords are sharp and silvery, his single notes thick with distortion and sustain. The material spans rock, R&B, electronics and an acoustic guitar/oboe arrangement. — C.W.

THE MARCELS
★ ★ Blue Moon / Epic (NA)
Granted, "Blue Moon" is as great a cover version of a Tin Pan Alley standard as any doo-wop group ever did. But why would you want a whole album by the Marcels, who never came close to that standard again? — D.M.

BENNY MARDONES
★ ★ Never Run, Never Hide / Poly. (1980)
★ Too Much To Lose / Poly. (1981)
Like Tom Petty, Bob Seger and Bruce Springsteen, Benny Mardones has a strong feel for rock & roll's traditions, and understands the workaday life of Middle America. Unfortunately, he understands it only as cliché, and rarely transcends that limitation with his music. — J.D.C.

MARK-ALMOND
★ ★ Rising / Col. (1972)
★ ★ Mark-Almond 2 / Blue Th. (1972)
★ ★ The Best of Mark-Almond / Blue Th. (1973)
★ ★ To the Heart / ABC (1976)
★ ★ Other People's Rooms / A&M (1978)
Guitarist Jon Mark and reed man Johnny Almond (alumni of John Mayall's group) play the most lightweight vocal jazz rock imaginable—mood music for the Valium set. This sort of sound has neither peaks nor valleys, just the same dull threnody, a passionless evocation of life's most minute pleasures. Despite a brief vogue in the early Seventies, this batch of easy-listening rock is probably as boring as any comparable catalogue in recorded history. — D.M.

BOB MARLEY AND THE WAILERS
★ ★ ★ ★ Catch a Fire / Is. (1972)
★ ★ ★ ★ Burnin' / Is. (1973)

★ ★ ★ ★ **African Herbsman** / Troj. (1974)
★ ★ ★ ★ **Rasta Revolution** / Troj. (1974)
★ ★ ★ ★ **Natty Dread** / Is. (1975)
★ ★ ★ ★ **Live** / Is. (1975)
★ ★ ★ **Rastaman Vibrations** / Is. (1976)
★ ★ ★ **Exodus** / Is. (1977)
★ ★ ★ **Birth of a Legend** / Calla (1977)
★ ★ ★ **Early Music** / Calla (1977)
★ ★ ★ **Babylon by Bus** / Is. (1978)
★ ★ ★ ★ **Kaya** / Is. (1978)
★ ★ ★ ★ **Survival** / Is. (1979)
★ ★ ★ **Soul Shakedown Party** / Ala (1980)
★ ★ ★ ★ **Uprising** / Is. (1980)
★ **Chances Are** / Coti. (1981)

The Wailers have been the most important group in reggae since the late Sixties; their only real challengers are Toots and the Maytals. Bob Marley, Peter Tosh and Bunny Livingston (who now records as Bunny Wailer) joined together in the mid-Sixties and recorded several primordial singles (collected on the Calla packages), including the brilliant "Trench Town Rock." Because they've only been available on import, *African Herbsman* and *Rasta Revolution* (Lee Perry productions featuring the greatest original Wailers recordings) have been overlooked. These late-Sixties, early-Seventies collaborations coupled Lee Perry's rhythmic genius with the Wailers' transcendent harmonies. *Soul Shakedown Party* looks like a bootleg but actually is a worthwhile collection of Leslie Kong–produced Sixties cuts. *Catch a Fire* was the group's first American release, but while it got excellent critical notices, it received little airplay or public attention. With *Burnin'*, Tosh and Livingston left the group and Bob Marley, who had been the group's principal guitarist, took the band over. Under his direction, it continued to make some of the most exciting music of the Seventies, climaxing with the London concert captured on *Live*.

Thereafter, as Marley became more prominent among white rock listeners, he took the band in the direction of superstar guitar-playing. Marley is an estimable guitarist, but many of his compositions are meandering (*Exodus* is a perfectly self-descriptive title), and he only rarely achieved the focus and effect of his earlier music in this period.

Even so, when Marley did manage to bring everything together—as on *Kaya*'s title track, "Wake Up and Live" from the brilliant, politicized *Uprising,* and the achingly beautiful "Redemption Song" from *Survival*—he was clearly one of the major music-makers of his time. If *Kaya, Exodus* and *Survival* retreat into the murk of Rasta "rea-

soning," then *Uprising* is certainly the most ambitious musical statement of black commitment, pride and courage anyone has made, and a concept album that comes within a hair of being fully realized.

These are the factors that make one mourn Marley's death from cancer in 1981 especially deeply. And they are what makes the release of the demos and work tapes on *Chances Are* especially repulsive. May this record gather dust—Marley's genuine work surely never will, for each record grows more interesting with the passage of time, each listening reveals some new facet. If he was not always successful, he was at least the boldest challenger in the pack.
— D.M./R.F.G.

RITA MARLEY
★ ★ ★ ★ **Who Feels It Knows It** / Tuff Gong (1980)
★ ★ ★ ★ **Who Feels It Knows It** / Shan. (1982)

Amazingly enough, after fifteen years of performing (most recently as an I-Three), Rita (yes, she was Bob's wife) Marley has only recorded one LP. *Who Feels It* meditates on simply expressed Rastafarian themes (God, peace, love, etc.) in the immensely appealing context of warm harmonies, understated sweet singing, and the top-flight musicianship of the Wailers and friends. The Shanachie version substitutes the loopy doper classic, "One Draw," for the sublime "Beauty of God's Plan." — R.F.G.

MARSEILLE
★ **Marseille** / RCA (1979) ¶

Derivative is generally okay in rock & roll, but you've gotta pick your sources more carefully than this; half a Beatles melody, Alice Cooper vocals and Kiss rhythm riffs ain't gonna cut it, even among the junior high school set. Here's proof. — D.M.

MARSHALL TUCKER BAND
★ ★ ★ **The Marshall Tucker Band** / Capri. (1973)
★ ★ ★ **A New Life** / Capri. (1974)
★ ★ ★ **Where We All Belong** / Capri. (1974)
★ ★ ★ ★ **Searchin' for a Rainbow** / Capri. (1975)
★ ★ ★ **Long, Hard Ride** / Capri. (1976)
★ ★ ★ **Carolina Dreams** / Capri. (1977)
★ ★ ★ **Greatest Hits** / Capri. (1978)
★ ★ ★ **Tenth** / War. (1980)
★ ★ ★ **Dedicated** / War. (1981)
★ ★ ★ **Tuckerized** / War. (1982)
★ ★ ★ **Just Us** / War. (1983)

The Marshall Tucker Band was one of the first of the so-called Southern boogie bands of the Seventies. Their music is indeed Southern, it definitely boogies (albeit quite sensitively at times), and it's a band in the strictest sense of the word.

Like other bands of this ilk, the music is heavy and riff-oriented, yet it depends more on melody and affected vocals than on jamming. The occasional use of Jerry Eubanks on alto sax and flute gives the band distinctive depth uncharacteristic of the genre. The constant instrumental highlight, though, is guitarist Toy Caldwell. His brother, bassist Tommy Caldwell, died in 1980.

Of these albums, *Where We All Belong* and *Greatest Hits* are the best introduction for the uninitiated. The latter includes the group's best-known songs, such as "Heard It in a Love Song," while *Where We All Belong* includes a live disc paired with a studio session, both of which feature Caldwell prominently, especially on the twelve-minute "Every Day I Have the Blues." But the band hit a creative apex with *Searchin'*, a comparatively laid-back affair featuring several solid country numbers; the albums since then have principally been repetitions of the formula established there. *Dedicated* was the first album after Tommy Caldwell's death, with Franklin Wilkie replacing him on bass. *Just Us* is their most country-music-influenced LP. — A.N.

MARTHA AND THE MUFFINS
★ ★ ★ ★ Metro Music / Dindisc (1980)
★ ★ ★ Trance and Dance / Virgin (1980)
★ ★ ★ Danseparc / Virgin (1983)
Stars of the Toronto new wave, this crisp six-piece band boasts two female vocalists/keyboardists named Martha, a hot saxophone player and a durable rhythm section. "Echo Beach," from *Metro Music,* epitomizes the irresistible melodicism that sets the band apart from its contemporaries on the new-wave beat. — J.S.

MARTHA AND THE VANDELLAS
★ ★ ★ ★ ★ Anthology / Mo. (1974)
★ ★ ★ ★ ★ Super Star Series, Vol. II / Mo. (1981)
Martha Reeves was the most blues-oriented of all of Motown's Sixties female singers, and her triumphs—"Dancing in the Streets" and "Heat Wave" particularly—are among that label's longest-lasting. The approach is brassy and rocking, and there isn't a clinker among the many hits collected on these albums, which include (in addition to the anthems listed above) "Livewire," "Quicksand"

and "Come and Get These Memories." Reeves has gone on to an undistinguished solo career in the Seventies, but these songs will outlive her as dance and party records and great examples of Motown's high-spirited Sixties vision. — D.M.

MOON MARTIN
★ ★ ★ Shots from a Cold Nightmare / Cap. (1978)
★ ★ ★ Escape from Domination / Cap. (1979)
★ ★ ★ Street Fever / Cap. (1980)
Martin's chief claim to fame is writing "Rolene" and "Cadillac Walk" for Mink DeVille, but there is more authentic toughness to these LPs than almost anything that has come from Los Angeles in years. Not exactly soulful, but definitely rocking. — D.M.

THE ROBERTA MARTIN SINGERS
★ ★ ★ Twelve Inspirational Songs / Savoy (NA)
★ ★ He's Done Great Things for Me / Savoy (NA)
★ ★ ★ Grace / Savoy (NA)
★ ★ God Is Still on the Throne / Savoy (NA)
As a composer, arranger, pianist and singer, Roberta Martin is one of the founders and giants of modern gospel. Her influence extends down through later generations of gospel artists—the Reverend James Cleveland, most significantly—and on into soul music. One could easily build a case for Martin as an early model for Aretha Franklin—perhaps more so for her piano than her singing, but even vocally to some extent.

Yet the Martin Singers might not have much appeal for rock fans. This is partly because the style she pioneered got filtered through too many artists before it hit the soul field. True, many fine singers passed through her ranks—Myrtle Scott, Eugene Smith, Robert Anderson ("the Bing Crosby of gospel"), Norsalus McKissick, Bessie Folk, Willie Webb, Deloris Campbell and others. But they tend to be quite smooth, as Anderson's nickname implies, and perhaps as essential to the evolution of black nightclub singers as to soul singers. A gospel fanatic will want to hear Martin's work, but for most others she is primarily of historical interest—except perhaps for that thick, rich piano style. — J.MO.

STEVE MARTIN
★ Let's Get Small / War. (1977)
■ A Wild and Crazy Guy / War. (1978)

One-liners are not enough to sustain a full album, even though Martin's smarm and charm are meant to be identical—for better or worse, maybe they are. But even at first glance, the smug routines of these in-concert comedy LPs are thin. *Let's Get Small* has the hit single, "King Tut," which gives Martin's work the more narrative context it requires. — D.M.

MARTIN BOGAN AND ARMSTRONG
★ ★ ★ **Barnyard Dance / Roun. (1972)** ¶
★ ★ ★ **Martin Bogan and Armstrong / Fly. Fish (1974)**
Founded in the Thirties, this black string band re-formed in 1970 to play precisely the same rags, pop songs, country blues and jazz. Mandolin, fiddle, guitar and bass constitute the instrumentation, and the style is untouched by age. The quartet has played the festival route in recent years, and has recorded with Steve Goodman. The infectious vitality of Carl Martin, Ted Bogan, and Howard and Joe Armstrong (father and son) is best witnessed in person, but these discs are rare chronicles of a nearly extinct form. — I.M.

JOHN MARTYN
★ ★ ★ ★ **So Far So Good / Is. (1977)** ¶
★ ★ ★ ★ **One World / Is. (1977)** ¶
After a few ordinary albums, Scottish folksinger John Martyn evolved an elliptical style of writing and playing in the mid-Seventies and started singing in a sensuous, low-key rock-blues voice. Pentangle bassist Danny Thompson lends the folk-jazz feel that underlays these delightful records. *So Far So Good* is a compilation that draws heavily on his best (but deleted) record, *Bless the Weather.* Jazz studio players and a subtle rhythm section on most cuts show Martyn cautiously and effectively extending Nick Drake's fluid manner. However, Martyn's "other" style, an overblown jazz rock, has yet to develop beyond the experimental instrumental "Glistening Glyndebourne." Several near misses are included on *So Far.* — B.T.

MARVELETTES
★ ★ ★ ★ **Anthology / Mo. (1975)**
The Marvelettes were a mysterious Motown "girl" group that lasted almost a decade and sported a number of lead singers and a raft of Motown production styles. *Anthology* is a splendid document of the evolution of Motown in the Sixties as well as a must for anyone who has ever felt the emotional pull of "Forever" or "When the Hunter Gets

Captured by the Game" or earlier hits like "Please Mr. Postman," "Beechwood 4-5789" and "Don't Mess with Bill." — J.MC.

MARVIN, WELCH AND FARRAR
★ ★ **Second Opinion / Sire (1971)** ¶
Hank Marvin and Bruce Welch were part of the British instrumental group the Shadows. The band was noted for Marvin's guitar style, exemplified by the 1960 hit "Apache," which influenced the generation of British guitarists led by Pete Townshend, Keith Richards and Eric Clapton. Unfortunately, this album with Australian John Farrar has nothing to do with that music, presenting instead an ersatz country-rock vocal harmony group. — J.S.

GROUCHO MARX
★ ★ **An Evening with Groucho / A&M (1972)**
He painted a mustache on his face and walked funny for a reason—see the movies. A genius maligned, this. — K.T.

CAROLYNE MAS
★ ★ ★ **Carolyne Mas / Mer. (1979)**
★ ★ **Hold On / Mer. (1980)**
★ ★ ★ **Modern Dreams / Mer. (1981)**
The diminutive Mas burst onto the New York music scene in 1979 with good songs, a powerful voice and a cocky guitar style, all of which resulted in a media blitz that hailed her as a female Bruce Springsteen before she'd even signed a record deal. This characterization proved to be a curse, and probably had something to do with the fact that Mas's musical partner, guitarist David Landau, was the younger brother of Bruce Springsteen's manager-producer Jon Landau. Though "Stillsane," the first song on her debut, is an obvious attempt to trade on the Springsteen reference, Mas was more at home on flat-out rockers like the great "Quote Goodbye Quote."

When *Hold On* once again failed to create a breakthrough, Landau was replaced by guitarist Rick DeSarno. British producers Jon Astley and Phil Chapman were brought in for *Modern Dreams,* which featured synthesizers prominently in the arrangements but still didn't quite do justice to Mas's promise. A beautiful rendition of Billy Nichols' stirring ballad "Under One Banner" saves the record. — J.S.

BARBARA MASON
★ ★ ★ **Give Me Your Love / Bud. (1973)** ¶
★ ★ **Lady Love / Bud. (1973)** ¶
★ ★ ★ **Transition / Bud. (1974)** ¶

★ ★ **Love's the Thing** / Bud. (1975) ¶
★ ★ **Sheba, Baby** / Bud. (1975) ¶
★ ★ **Locked in This Position** / Cur. (1977) ¶
★ ★ **I Am Your Woman, She Is Your Wife** / Prel. (1978)

Barbara Mason is Philadelphia's true first lady of soul. It also happens that she's been almost without competition for nearly a decade, but that's beside the point. Mason is no great shakes as a singer, but her offkey cooing and breathy phrasing give her an attractive vulnerability. Her early hits for Arctic ("Yes I'm Ready," "Oh How It Hurts") are long out of print, but her Buddah and Prelude albums are often quite appealing in small doses.

Give Me Your Love, Mason's best album, is mostly ballads (the title song is seductive, but uptempo), some with neat hook lines and titles ("Bed and Board," "You Can Be with the One You Don't Love"). *Transition,* the other exceptional disc here, finds Mason waxing philosophic about our times (she wrote all but one of the songs). — D.M.

DAVE MASON
★ ★ ★ **Alone Together** / Blue Th. (1970)
★ ★ **Headkeeper** / Blue Th. (1972)
★ ★ **Dave Mason Is Alive** / Blue Th. (1973)
★ ★ ★ **It's Like You Never Left** / Col. (1974)
★ ★ ★ **The Best of Dave Mason** / Blue Th. (1974)
★ ★ ★ **Dave Mason** / Col. (1974)
★ ★ **Split Coconut** / Col. (1975)
★ ★ ★ **Dave Mason at His Very Best** / ABC (1975)
★ ★ **Certified Live** / Col. (1976)
★ ★ **Let It Flow** / Col. (1977)
★ ★ **Mariposa de Orc** / Col. (1978)
★ ★ **Old Crest on a New Wave** / Col. (1980)

Mason was a key member of Traffic in its first and a couple of subsequent incarnations. *Alone Together* staked out the solo territory from which Mason has rarely strayed: a rather relaxed and reserved takeoff from hard rock, featuring somber, bittersweet melodies, basic guitar/keyboard arrangements, as well as Mason's restrained vocals and blues-derived though not bluesy electric guitar. His acoustic rhythm guitar accounted for the driving lightness of the songs, which moved but without breakneck tempos or flashy playing; some, however, were a trifle lengthy.

Side one of *Headkeeper* contained more alive but also unpolished continuations of his debut. The other side had fairly spirited live versions of earlier songs, plus a Traffic num-

ber, "Pearly Queen." *Dave Mason Is Alive* was almost entirely selections from his debut; adequate if unspectacular and somewhat rough, it benefited from Mark Jordan's tasteful piano and organ.

Best of and *At His Very Best* are almost identical compilations of the early studio material. *It's Like You Never Left* smoothed out some of the singer's few edges, while simultaneously picking up pace: it has more polished and full scoring but little bite. Still, the record had some of Mason's best writing. The backup band included Graham Nash singing and Stevie Wonder on harmonica. *Dave Mason* experimented with additional instrumentation: pedal steel, horns, strings, etc., which usually disguised and spoiled the continuing quality of Mason's material. But he erred with covers of Dylan and Sam Cooke, and his new band played without verve or flair, Mason no longer on lead guitar. *Split Coconut* shelved the orchestration and rocked out more with guitars. The band's plainness remained, although Mark Jordan made guest appearances, as did Crosby and Nash and, oddly, the Manhattan Transfer on a reggae-influenced Buddy Holly cover. Again, good material squandered, this time by overanxious arranging.

Certified Live unfortunately relied on the thin anonymity of the guitars/keys/bass/drums lineup. The surfeit of mediocre guitars from Mason and Jim Krueger detracted further, as did Mason's further attempts at husky soulful singing. Several weak covers were included; Mason's own songs spanned his whole career (including Traffic) but emphasized the earlier styles.

Let It Flow, Mariposa de Oro and *Old Crest* are Mason's softest efforts, padded with plenty of extra orchestration in an apparent pitch to MOR tastes. Nonetheless, the capable composer in Mason was evident though submerged. — C.W.

MASQUERADERS
★ ★ **Everybody Wanna Live On** / ABC (1975) ¶
★ ★ **Love Anonymous** / ABC (1977) ¶
★ ★ **The Masqueraders** / Bang (NA)

The Masqueraders are best known for two Sixties soul classics: "I'm Just an Average Guy" and "I Ain't Got to Love Nobody Else." Isaac Hayes' production on their comeback albums is labored and wooden, but "Traveling Man," a whimsical ballad from *Everybody,* stands out. — J.MC.

WAYNE MASSEY
■ **One Life to Live** / Poly. (1980)

Vapid crooner sings suburban cowboy ballads for the Moral Majority. The new Jim Nabors? — J.S.

MASTERPIECE
★ ★ **The Girl's Alright with Me / Whit. (1980)**
For most of its playing time, this album is absolutely nothing special, just Norman Whitfield whipping a pedestrian soul group through its paces. But on the title track, a remake of the Temptations' hit, they pull out a vocalist who is such a dead ringer for Eddie Kendricks it'll simply stop you in your tracks. Amazing. Pointless, but amazing. — D.M.

MASS PRODUCTION
★ **Three Miles High / Coti. (1977)** ¶
★ **Believe / Coti. (1977)** ¶
★ **Welcome to Our World / Coti. (1977)** ¶
★ **In the Purest Form / Coti (1979)**
★ **Massterpiece / Coti. (1980)**
★ **Turn Up the Music / Coti. (1981)**
Seventies disco funk with, as the name implies, more of a grind than a groove.
— D.M.

MATCHBOX
★ **Riders in the Sky / Rock. (1976), Br. imp.**
★ ★ **Settin' the Woods on Fire / Chis. (1978), Br. imp.**
★ ★ ★ **Rockabilly Rebel / Sire (1979)**
British rockabilly quintet does a nice job on *Rockabilly Rebel,* which avoids the freeze-dried impression most neo-rockabilly bands leave you with. — J.S.

MATERIAL
★ ★ ★ ★ **Memory Serves / Musician (1982)**
Genuinely hot guitar licks from Sonny Sharrock and Olu Dara's post-Miles cornet rescue this avant-funk concept group from the pretentiousness of Bill Lawell's sub–David Byrne lyrics and Michael Beinhorn's tape experiments. That is, what's supposed to render this pop is mostly sophomoric, but its roots in the contemporary jazz avant-garde are so firm that the best of the music is undeniable. Granted bonus star for featuring Henry Threadgill's alto sax on three cuts.
— D.M.

RONN MATLOCK
★ **Love City / Coti. (1979)**
Formula funk singer—the girth of Barry White, and a lot less imagination. — D.M.

MATRIX
★ **Tale of the Whale / War. (1979)**

★ **Wizard / War. (NA)**
Uninspired nine-piece fusion band. Nothing here Miles Davis can't do blindfolded and with one collapsed lung. — D.M.

IAN MATTHEWS
★ ★ ★ **Valley Hi / Elek. (1973)**
★ ★ ★ **Some Days You Eat the Bear . . . / Elek. (1974)**
★ ★ **Go for Broke / Col. (1976)**
★ ★ ★ **Stealin' Home / Mush. (1978)**
★ ★ **Siamese Friends / Rockb. (1979)**
★ ★ **Spot of Interference / RSO (1980)**
An original member of Fairport Convention (and one of the first to leave), Ian Matthews owns a winsome tenor voice that has rarely been sufficiently aggressive for the kind of folk-rock material ("Brown-Eyed Girl," for instance) that he likes to sing. His best effort, in fact, came on *Tigers Will Survive,* a now-deleted Vertigo LP that included his closest shot at a hit single, a splendid version of the Crystals' "Da Doo Ron Ron." *Tigers* is worth digging up; the Elektra sets are worth it for folk-rock fans and the more recent records are mostly notable because Matthews consistently chooses all the right songs, then sings and arranges them wrong.
— D.M.

MATUMBI
★ ★ **Point of View / EMI (1980)**
Noted British reggae-punk producer and dub wizard Dennis Bovell—who has worked with the Slits and Garland Jeffreys and has made a few mutant reggae solo LPs of his own—was a founding member and pivotal force of this band, a pioneer in the late-Seventies homegrown English reggae movement. Bovell's best instincts, however, were on vacation when the group recorded this pleasant but commercially diluted U.S. release. Lightweight pop-roots fare from people who should have known better. — D.F.

JOHN MAYALL
★ ★ ★ ★ ★ **Bluesbreakers—John Mayall with Eric Clapton / Lon. (1965)**
★ ★ ★ ★ ★ **Bluesbreakers / Lon. (1965)**
★ **Raw Blues / Lon. (1967)**
★ ★ ★ **Crusade / Lon. (1967)**
★ **The Blues Alone / Lon. (1967)**
★ ★ ★ **A Hard Road / Lon. (1967)**
★ **Bare Wires / Lon. (1968)**
★ **Diary of a Band, Vols. 1 and 2 / Lon. (1968)**
★ ★ ★ **Blues from Laurel Canyon / Lon. (1969)**
★ ★ **The Turning Point / Poly. (1970)**

★ Live in Europe / Lon. (1970)
★ ★ ★ Looking Back / Lon. (1970)
★ ★ Jazz-Blues Fusion / Poly. (1972)
★ ★ Thru the Years / Lon. (1972)
★ ★ Down the Line / Lon. (1973)
★ The Best of John Mayall / Poly. (1974)
★ New Year, New Band, New Company /
  ABC (1975)
★ ★ Notice to Appear / ABC (1975)
★ ★ A Banquet in Blues / Lon. (1976)
★ Lots of People / ABC (1977)
★ A Hard Core Package / ABC (1977)
★ ★ Primal Solos / Lon. (1977)
★ Last of the British Blues / ABC
  (1978)
★ The Bottom Line / DJM (1979)
★ No More Interviews / DJM (1979)

John Mayall became an important figure in the American rock scene because an extraordinary number of important musicians, especially guitarists, got their start playing in his bands, and because he was a British blues musician at a time when to be British, a musician and aware of the blues was to be hip by definition. Actually, however, Mayall was a pedestrian musical figure, more of the generation that spawned British blues revivalists such as Cyril Davies and Alexis Korner, and with the passion of a revivalist for false standards of purity. He gave Eric Clapton, Peter Green, Mick Taylor, Jack Bruce, Mick Fleetwood, John McVie, Aynsley Dunbar, Keef Hartley and a number of others important work when that was not easy to come by. But in the end, Mayall's own view of music was too narrow to keep any of his sidemen content and all of those with true skill went on to things both bigger and, though Mayall might deny it, substantially better.

His most significant records, then, are those which spotlight others. *Bluesbreakers* features a band effectively led by Eric Clapton, playing straight 12-bar Chicago blues. Clapton reaches so deep inside this music, though, that he elevates it above the usual pedestrian British blues style, and creates something quite authentic and genuinely moving from it. This is one of the outstanding examples of Clapton's playing anywhere. (There are two versions of the *Bluesbreakers* LP on the shelves; the one to buy is PS-492, with notes by Billy Altman.)

A Hard Road features guitarist Peter Green and bassist John McVie, just before they went off with another Mayall alumnus, Mick Fleetwood, to form Fleetwood Mac. The blues they play here is quite similar to early Fleetwood Mac (without Jeremy Spencer's loony slide playing, of course), and that

makes it burning, serious stuff, led by Green's sinuously beautiful lead lines.

Crusade features Mick Taylor, and while the record is not nearly as exceptional as *Bluesbreakers* and *A Hard Road*, it is at least interesting because Taylor left Mayall later for the Rolling Stones. *Crusade* also debuts Mayall's use of a horn section, which did surprisingly little to liberate him from the basic stodginess of his conceptions, primarily because the horns were used mostly to riff rather than to blow freely. Taylor, meanwhile, also appears on *Diary of a Band*, which is a set of live tapes from small British clubs, neither especially well recorded nor terribly well performed.

Basically, with the end of this cycle of albums, Mayall ceased to be very interesting. On *The Blues Alone*, he appears solo; Robert Johnson he ain't. And with *Bare Wires* he begins to move toward "progressive" rock and jazz ideas just as narrow-minded as his blues ones. Most of the group on that first album, led by drummer Jon Hiseman and hornman Dick Heckstall-Smith, left to form the more free-blowing Colosseum, and Mayall split for the States, where he lined up some L.A. players, made *Blues from Laurel Canyon* and has diddled around ever since.

Of his other albums on London, only *Looking Back*, a collection of singles from the 1964–69 period, and *Primal Solos*, which has some previously unheard Clapton, are worth much. His work for Polydor, ABC and DJM is just dismal, a veteran playing out the string, without much imagination. *Jazz Blues Fusion* features trumpeter Blue Mitchell, and *The Turning Point* kicked off Jon Mark and Johnny Almond's MOR-rock career. *Notice to Appear* was ineffectively produced by New Orleans hotshot Allen Toussaint, but a good deal of the rest is simply ground out, the one-time purist going through the motions. — D.M.

CURTIS MAYFIELD
★ ★ America Today / Cur. (1975)
★ ★ ★ Let's Do It Again / Cur. (1975)
★ ★ ★ Give, Get, Take and Have / Cur.
  (1976)
★ ★ ★ Never Say You Can't Survive / Cur.
  (1977)
★ ★ Short Eyes / Cur. (1977)
★ ★ ★ Do It All Night / Cur. (1978)
★ ★ Heartbeat / RSO (1979)
★ ★ Something to Believe In / RSO (1980)
★ ★ Love Is the Place / Bruns. (1981)

With the Impressions, Mayfield was one of the most inspired writers and singers of Sixties soul. His falsetto style was suitably modernized on his first few solo albums for Custom when it was distributed by Buddah. *Superfly,* the soundtrack to the blaxploitation film, was a simply great record, with marvelous singing and lyrics that undercut the film's lionization of dope dealing. "Freddie's Dead" and "Superfly" were major hits from that anti-decadent disco record, but it has somehow been deleted; find it if you're at all interested in Seventies black rock—it was one of the germinal albums, as important in its way as Marvin Gaye's, Stevie Wonder's and Sly Stone's stuff. The rest of these albums aren't nearly so good; *Let's Do It Again,* a soundtrack dominated vocally by the Staple Singers, is about the best. The rest is meandering funk that can usually be lived without, although occasionally Mayfield's chirping voice or his stinging guitar reappear for a few worthwhile moments. — D.M.

PERCY MAYFIELD
★ ★ ★ ★ **The Best of Percy Mayfield /
Spec. (NA)**
The influential West Coast blues singer of the Fifties. Set includes his best and best-known: "Please Send Me Someone to Love," "Cry Baby," "The Big Question," "Lost Love." — D.M.

MAZE
★ ★ **Maze / Cap. (1977)**
★ ★ **Golden Time of Day / Cap. (1978)**
★ ★ **Inspiration / Cap. (1979)**
★ ★ **The Hitter / Cap. (1979)** ¶
★ ★ **Joy and Pain / Cap. (1980)**
★ ★ **Live in New Orleans / Cap. (1981)**
This lazy jazz-funk ensemble, featuring vocalist/producer Frankie Beverly, managed several pop-R&B hits in 1977 and 1978—"Workin' Together," "While I'm Alone" and "Lady of Magic"—none of them terribly distinguished. The best parts of these albums are merely mediocre soul music. The worst would be laughed out of a cocktail lounge. — D.M.

MAC McANALLY
★ **Cuttin' Corners / RCA (1980)** ¶
★ **Mac McAnally / Ario. (NA)** ¶
★ **No Problem Here / Ario. (NA)** ¶
Typical self-pitying, country-inflected singer/songwriter wheeze. — D.M.

DAN McCAFFERTY
★ **Dan McCafferty / A&M (1971)**
Nazareth's vocalist makes a solo album. A Rod Stewart growler without the charm, McCafferty is for Nazareth fans only. — A.N.

C. W. McCALL
★ **Wolf Creek Pass / MGM (1975)**
★ **Black Bear Road / MGM (1975)** ¶
★ **Rubber Duck / Poly. (1976)** ¶
★ **Roses for Mama / Poly. (1977)** ¶
★ ★ **C. W. McCall's Greatest Hits / Poly.
(1978)**
★ **C. W. McCall and Co. / Poly. (NA)**
McCall cashed in on the mid-Seventies CB craze with "Convoy," written in 10-4-type lingo, then repeated it to death on this series of albums. "Convoy" was better as a movie; here it's just one long drawl, probably destined to be remembered only in the trivia contests of the Eighties. — D.M.

TOUSSAINT McCALL
★ ★ **Nothing Takes the Place of You / Ronn
(1957)**
Like "Boogaloo down Broadway" and "Why Can't We Live Together," McCall's "Nothing Takes the Place of You" is a homemade one-shot that transcends its own technical limitations. McCall is an organist, and this ballad-centered album is better than you might expect. — J.MC.

DENISE McCANN
★ **I Have a Destiny / Butter. (NA)**
★ **Tattoo Man / Butter. (NA)**
In no danger of being mistaken for Donna Summer (a fact some friendly soul might whisper into Denise's ear). — D.M.

PAUL McCARTNEY AND WINGS
★ ★ **McCartney / Cap. (1970)**
★ ★ ★ **Ram / Cap. (1971)**
★ ★ ★ **Wild Life / Cap. (1973)**
★ **Red Rose Speedway / Apple (1973)**
★ ★ ★ ★ **Band on the Run / Apple (1973)**
★ ★ ★ ★ **Venus and Mars / Cap. (1973)**
★ ★ ★ **Wings at the Speed of Sound / Cap.
(1976)**
★ ★ ★ ★ **Wings over America / Cap. (1977)**
★ ★ ★ **London Town / Cap. (1978)**
★ ★ **Back to the Egg / Col. (1979)**
★ ★ ★ **McCartney 2 / Col. (1980)**
★ ★ ★ ★ **Tug of War / Col. (1982)**
A home-produced solo excursion, *McCartney* was designed to publicize the official (1970) breakup of the Beatles, and Paul used it more as a megalomaniac's forum (the one-man band—McCartney is the album's sole musician) than as a vehicle for good material. His playing is rough and disingenuous, and there's only one good song on the record, "Maybe I'm Amazed."

Ram, on the other hand, is an all-out production effort that comes closer to reproducing the Beatles sound than any other solo album, and it includes a scattering of excellent material ("Smile Away," "Monkberry Moon Delight," "Uncle Albert/Admiral Halsey"). *Wild Life* has a crude but effective sound, since McCartney went right into the studio with wife Linda, Denny Laine and Denny Seiwell and laid down the tracks as quickly as possible. This boils down to a Wings audition.

Red Rose Speedway emphasizes the worst aspects of McCartney as solo artist and bandleader. The album is rife with weak and sentimental drivel and lacks any musical focus. But he turned around from that disaster and made a great album, *Band on the Run,* recorded in Nigeria. With only sparse help from Linda and a faithful Denny Laine, this turned out to be the real one-man show, and McCartney came up with aces, playing most of the instruments and writing his strongest collection of post-Beatles material—"Jet" and "Helen Wheels" especially.

Venus and Mars introduced a new Wings lineup, adding drummer Joe English and guitarist Jimmy McCullogh. Recorded in New Orleans, the album is a solid collection of good songs (particularly "Rock Show" and "Listen to What the Man Said") played well by the band and featuring some fine horn arrangements by Tony Dorsey. *Venus and Mars* pretty much served as a blueprint for the band's concert strategy, a successful plan judging by results of the Wings tour, documented by the three-record live set, *Wings over America.* McCartney's road show had a little something for everyone, but most of all the band proved it could rock and McCartney proved he hadn't forgotten his Little Richard imitation. The live set is also notable for the inclusion of Denny Laine's classic "Go Now" and the otherwise unreleased encore, a fiery rocker called "Soily."

Wings at the Speed of Sound, recorded in a hurry while the band was preparing for the tour, proves that they were sure enough of themselves to go on instinct and make a good album under extreme pressure. The McCartney wit is sharp on "Silly Love Songs," powered by one of his most melodic bass patterns. And chestnuts like "Beware My Love," Laine's pungent "Time to Hide" and the frolicking "Let 'Em In" give the record substance.

But *London Town,* released in 1978 after the group had been off the road for a while, finds McCartney and company succumbing to their vices: fake rock, pallid pop and unbelievable homilies make an unreal hodgepodge that's barely listenable next to Wings'

best work. *McCartney 2,* Paul's second homemade album, contains some nice instrumentals and the good single "Coming Up."

Tug of War is a tremendous effort that includes the sublime "Take It Away" with Ringo Starr on drums, as well as excellent collaborations with Stevie Wonder and Carl Perkins and a moving elegy to John Lennon, "Here Today." — J.S.

ALTON McCLAIN AND DESTINY
★ ★ ★ **Alton McClain and Destiny / Poly. (NA)**
★ ★ ★ **Gonna Tell the World / Poly. (1979)**
★ ★ ★ **More of You / Poly. (1980)**
Popular funk 'n' soul ensemble—journeyman fare. — D.M.

TOMMY McCLENNAN
★ ★ ★ **Cross Cut Saw / Roots (NA), Br. imp.**
Exciting, if raw, delta blues singer who recorded the basic version of "Bottle It Up and Go." These are from his 1939–42 Bluebird sessions, and while minor, are worth hearing. — D.M.

BILLY McCOMISKEY
★ ★ ★ **Makin' the Rounds / Green L. (NA)**
A fine instrumental presentation of Irish dance music. McComiskey, along with John Tabb, offers an American contribution to accordion playing on a par with contemporary native Irish musicians. — D.D.

DELBERT McCLINTON
★ ★ ★ ★ **Victim of Life's Circumstances / ABC (1975)**
★ ★ ★ ★ **Genuine Cowhide / ABC (1976)**
★ ★ ★ **Love Rustler / ABC (1977)**
★ ★ ★ **Second Wind / ABC (1978)**
★ ★ ★ **Keeper of the Flame / Capri. (1979)**
★ ★ ★ **Jealous Kind / Cap. (1980)**
★ ★ ★ **Plain from the Heart / Cap. (1981)**
McClinton makes consistently strong albums, though he isn't for everyone. A product of Texas and Louisiana roadhouses, he comes off a bit greasy, a bit compulsive, a bit dangerous but basically a vulnerable and bighearted guy just trying to stay one step ahead of whatever's chasing him, be that his shadow, a woman or some guy he just antagonized in a bar. *Victim,* containing brilliant originals, is in a "progressive country" mold, but a decidedly nonhackneyed one that thinks nothing of mixing Bobby Bland–type horns with pedal-steel guitar. *Genuine Cowhide* has but two originals; the others are rock & roll or rhythm & blues favorites. *Love Rustler* and *Second Wind* are mostly

oldies or contemporary songs by other writers, with only one original. Like their predecessors, the most recent McClinton albums are blue-eyed Southern soul that has little to do with country music, progressive or otherwise. — J.M.

CHARLIE McCOY

★ ★ **Charlie McCoy** / Monu. (1972)
★ ★ **Good Time Charlie** / Monu. (1973)
★ ★ **Fastest Harp in the South** / Monu. (1973)
★ ★ **Nashville Hit Man** / Monu. (1974)
★ ★ **Charlie McCoy Christmas** / Monu. (1974)
★ ★ **Charlie My Boy** / Monu. (1975)
★ ★ **Harpin' the Blues** / Monu. (1975)
★ ★ **The Real McCoy** / Monu. (1976)
★ ★ **Play It Again, Charlie** / Monu. (1976)
★ ★ **Country Cookin'** / Monu. (1977)
★ ★ **Charlie McCoy's Greatest Hits** / Monu. (1978)
★ ★ **Appalachian Fever** / Monu. (1979)
The fabled Nashville harmonica player, who made a rock reputation with his sometimes astonishing work on Bob Dylan's *Blonde on Blonde,* has never gone beyond tepid pop-country instrumentals with his own LPs, all of which are competent and dull. — D.M.

VAN McCOY

★ **Dancin'** / SSS (1975) ¶
★ ★ **From Disco to Love** / Bud. (1975)
★ ★ ★ **The Hustle** / H&L (1976) ¶
★ ★ **My Favorite Fantasy** / MCA (1978) ¶
★ ★ **Lonely Dancer** / MCA (1979)
Veteran soul producer cashed in early on Seventies dance crazes with "Disco Kid" and "The Hustle," both pop as well as R&B hits. McCoy is probably better known as a producer, and these records show why—they're all boogie-able party tracks, but they're also completely interchangeable. — D.M.

THE McCOYS

★ ★ **Hang On Sloopy** / Bang (1965)
★ ★ **You Make Me Feel So Good** / Bang (1966)
Led by Rick Derringer (then known as Rick Zehringer), the McCoys were a slightly above average mid-American garage band when "Hang On Sloopy" turned them into overnight stars in 1965. Their two Bang albums are populated mostly by energetic covers with a few tasty surprises (the Pretty Things' "SF Sorrow Is Born," "Stormy Monday") that gave clues to the band's possible growth. Their finest work came a bit later, though, on their two Mercury releases,

Infinite McCoys and *Human Ball* (both out of print). — B.A.

JIMMY McCRACKLIN

★ ★ ★ ★ **My Rockin' Soul** / United (NA)
★ ★ ★ **Jimmy McCracklin and His Blues Blasters** / Ace-Chis. (NA), Br. imp.
★ ★ ★ ★ **Rockin' Man** / Route 66 (NA), Br. imp.
★ ★ ★ **High On the Blues** / Stax (NA)
Fifties and Sixties pianist/vocalist best known for his 1958 hit, "The Walk" and "Just Got to Know." McCracklin's Modern material is very fine and reissued cheaply on the United set. The Chiswick LP is a ten-inch LP featuring some of his earliest sides, recorded from 1948 to 1950, while the Route 66 disc ranges from 1946 to 1955. The Stax set is a reissue of a 1971 LP produced by Al Jackson and Willie Mitchell, in the Memphis soul mood, on which McCracklin sounds surprisingly good. — D.M.

GEORGE McCRAE

★ ★ ★ ★ **Rock Your Baby** / TK (1974)
★ ★ ★ **George McCrae** / TK (1975)
★ ★ ★ **Diamond Touch** / TK (1976)
★ ★ ★ **We Did It** / TK (1979)
The record was "Rock Your Baby," the year was 1974, and it established Miami's TK Records as a force in black popular music—in fact it did a much better job establishing TK, and producers H. W. Casey (of KC and the Sunshine Band) and Rick Finch, than it did establishing McCrae, who has never quite lived up to it. "Rock Your Baby" remains, though, one of the great hit singles of the decade, a rolling soul groove with a marvelous falsetto trill. — D.M.

GEORGE AND GWEN McCRAE

★ ★ ★ **Together** / Cat (1976)
In which the leading husband-and-wife team (the only one) of Miami R&B do a Marvin Gaye and Tammi Terrell turn, not without some effect, but not with particularly terrific results, either. — D.M.

GWEN McCRAE

★ ★ ★ ★ **Rockin' Chair** / Cat (1975)
★ ★ **Something So Right** / Cat (1976)
★ ★ **Let's Straighten It Out** / Cat (1976)
Gwen McCrae is a tough, brassy singer who has been a mainstay of Miami's TK soul stable. *Rockin' Chair* is a collection of early TK singles, including her lone Top Forty hit, the title song. The record is hot, a little raunchy and mostly very good. Little Beaver is featured on guitar. But the other albums are de-energized. Beaver is absent, the tracks

are limp, and they're weighed down by dull horn and string charts. — J.MC.

THE McCRARYS

★ ★ **Just for You** / Cap. (NA)
★ ★ ★ **Loving Is Living** / Por. (1978) ¶
"You" was a substantial soul hit in 1978 for this family-style quartet, which echoes the Staple Singers in everything, but especially the voice of whichever sister (not identified) sings lead—she's a ringer for Mavis Staples, which is a kind of recommendation all by itself. Highlight of Portrait LP, beyond liner-note endorsement and harp riff by Stevie Wonder, is presence of such Motown session notables as the godlike bassist James Jamerson. — D.M.

ED McCURDY

★ **The Best of Ed McCurdy** / Trad. (NA)
McCurdy's best-known song, "Last Night I Had the Strangest Dream," is not included on this record. Nonetheless, there is a certain sense of the man: sentimental, humorous, boisterous and gentle—a Western version of Dave Van Ronk. He is assisted by Erik Darling and Billy Faier. — I.M.

COUNTRY JOE McDONALD

★ ★ ★ **Tonight I'm Singing Just for You** / Van. (1970)
★ ★ **Hold On It's Coming** / Van. (1971)
★ ★ **War War War** / Van. (1971)
★ **Incredible—Live** / Van. (1972)
★ **Paris Session** / Van. (1973)
★ ★ ★ **Country Joe** / Van. (1974)
★ **Paradise with an Ocean View** / Fan. (1975)
★ ★ ★ **The Essential Country Joe McDonald** / Van. (1976)
★ ★ ★ **Tribute to Woody** / War. (1976)
★ **Love Is a Fire** / Fan. (1976)
▫ **Rock and Roll Music from the Planet Earth** / Fan. (1978)
★ **Goodbye Blues** / Fan. (1979)
★ **Leisure Suite** / Fan. (1979)
Country Joe McDonald has retained the strengths he displayed when he debuted with the Fish in 1967—wit, a steady tone of populist outrage about war and things unecological, and a solid journeyman's musicianship. None of these virtues, unfortunately, has proved mightier than his flaws—a shortage of originality and raw talent.

His story is one of persistence: eight albums with the Fish from 1969 to 1971 and many solo LPs from 1971 till the present. Tellingly, the first two solo efforts, which are Joe's renditions of classics from Woody Guthrie (*Tribute to Woody*) and various country greats (*Tonight I'm Singing Just for You*), are the best. After that, beyond the wryly mesmerizing title track from *Hold On It's Coming*, there are very few stand-out tracks among these albums, which are full of complaints both personal ("Entertainment Is My Business") and political ("Tear Down the Walls"). An attempt to be a late-blooming rock & roller (*Rock and Roll from the Planet Earth*) was a most unnerving try from a man whose career was already out of joint with the times. — F.S.

McDONALD AND GILES

★ ★ ★ ★ **McDonald and Giles** / Coti. (1971) ¶
A very respectable album by two renegades from the original King Crimson. Ian McDonald, whose explosive reeds helped put Crimson on the map, absconded with that group's inventive drummer, Mike Giles, to produce this colorful album. The raucous, double-tracked tenor-sax maneuvers on the swinging finale to McDonald's "Suite in C" are guaranteed ear candy, and sort of McDonald's trademark. Giles' bassist brother, Peter, anchors down an effervescent rhythm section underpinning Stevie Winwood's heavenly piano. Where Winwood isn't playing keyboards, McDonald is—and he adds flute, guitar and a brilliant zither. Perhaps what is most important about this obscure get-together are the goofy, cryptic lyrics, which should be preserved in formaldehyde as the perfect example of at least one era's stony innocence. — B.M.

MISSISSIPPI FRED McDOWELL

★ ★ ★ ★ **Mississippi Delta Blues** / Arhoo. (1964)
★ ★ ★ ★ **Mississippi Fred McDowell** / Arhoo. (1967)
★ ★ **I Do Not Play No Rock and Roll** / Cap. (1969)
★ ★ **Mississippi Fred McDowell and His Blues Boys** / Arhoo. (1970)
★ ★ ★ ★ **Keep Your Lamp Trimmed and Burning** / Arhoo. (1973)
★ ★ ★ **Somebody Keeps Callin' Me** / Ant. (1976)
★ ★ **A Long Way from Home** / Mile. (NA)
★ ★ **Live in New York** / Oblivion (NA)
★ ★ ★ **Mississippi Fred McDowell** / Arc. Folk (NA)
★ ★ ★ ★ **Levee Camp Blues** / O.J.L. (NA)
★ ★ ★ **Mississippi Delta Blues** / Vogue (NA), Fr. imp.
Between the Rolling Stones' rewrite of McDowell's "You've Got to Move" on *Sticky Fingers* and Bonnie Raitt's general support

of his music (she asked him to tour with her at one point and frequently performs his songs), McDowell reached a far greater number of people than one would ordinarily expect of such a harsh-sounding rural bluesman. His own Capitol LP, *I Do Not Play No Rock and Roll,* was probably his best-selling album, but while it remains officially in print, it's difficult to track down in stores.

Keep Your Lamp, Somebody and *Live* were all issued posthumously, the live set recorded shortly before McDowell's death. *Keep Your Lamp,* however, was culled from various sessions (1965 to 1969) and features McDowell in a variety of settings—solo; with Johnny Woods on harmonica; with the Hunter's Chapel Singers; with Mike Russo and John Kahn on guitar and bass. It is his most representative album.

The Antilles material dates from the same sessions from which *I Do Not Play No Rock and Roll* emerged, while *Long Way from Home* was recorded by Pete Welding in 1966. The remaining Arhoolie sets are from the mid-Sixties; *Mississippi Fred McDowell and His Blues Boys* features Russo, Kahn and drummer Bob Jones. The repertoire throughout moves smoothly from blues to gospel and back.   — I.M.

RONNIE McDOWELL
★ ★ **Rockin' You Easy, Lovin' You Slow /** **Epic (1979)**
★ ★ **Going Going Gone / Epic (1980)**
★ ★ **Love So Many Ways / Epic (1980)**
★ ★ **Good Time Lovin' Man / Epic (1982)**
McDowell's most important music has a relationship to Elvis Presley: his "The King Is Gone" was the best of the posthumous Presley tribute discs, and McDowell supplied Elvis' voice for the 1979 TV movie on the King, starring Kurt Russell. These albums are unfortunately products of the new Nashville, which means they are just raw enough to escape being condemned for their utter slickness and emptiness. McDowell's voice is always fine, but he's never given more than mediocre material and arrangements.
— D.M.

McFADDEN AND WHITEHEAD
★ ★ ★ ★ **McFadden and Whitehead / Phil. (1979)**
★ ★ ★ **I Heard It in a Love Song / Phil. (1980)**
At their best, Gene McFadden and John Whitehead sound like a rejuvenated Harold Melvin and the Bluenotes—no surprise, considering that the duo wrote some of the Bluenotes' biggest hits, including "Bad Luck" and "Wake Up, Everybody." Unfortunately, McFadden and Whitehead are at their best less than the post-Pendergrass Bluenotes, and only "Ain't No Stoppin' Us Now" from *McFadden and Whitehead* can equal the Bluenotes' best.   — J.D.C.

KATE AND ANNA McGARRIGLE
★ ★ ★ ★ **Kate and Anna McGarrigle / War. (1975)**
★ ★ ★ ★ **Dancer with Bruised Knees / War. (1977)**
★ ★ ★ **Pronto Monto / War. (1978)**
★ ★ ★ ★ **Love Over and Over / Poly. (1982)**
Two sisters from Montreal make music that's crisp, nonelectric and utterly magical. Singing now in English, now in French, they suffuse their records with brightness and wit, proving that the inspired amateurism of the mid-Seventies could be dazzling.   — F.R.

BROWNIE McGHEE AND SONNY TERRY
★ ★ **Sonny Terry: Harmonica and Vocal Solos / Folk. (1952)**
★ ★ **Sonny Terry's Washboard Band / Folk. (1954)**
★ ★ **Brownie McGhee and Sonny Terry Sing / Folk. (1958)**
★ ★ **Brownie McGhee Sings the Blues / Folk. (1959)**
★ ★ **Preachin' the Blues / Folk. (1960)**
★ ★ **The Best of Brownie McGhee and Sonny Terry / Prest. (1960)**
★ ★ ★ ★ **Midnight Special / Fan. (1977)**
★ ★ ★ ★ **Back to New Orleans / Fan. (1972)**
★ ★ ★ **Live at the Second Fret / Prest. (NA)**
"Theirs is a unique form of song based strongly on the traditional country blues, modeled by the changing social climate and polished for a more universal appeal. Fortunately the tradition has not been subordinated to the shaping and polishing."

So wrote Gene Shay in his notes to *Live at the Second Fret,* in 1962. Harmonica player Terry and guitarist McGhee have been playing and singing together since 1939, with occasional timeouts for solo endeavors; for Terry to portray Lost John, the harp player in Broadway's *Finian's Rainbow;* and for them to spend two years acting together in *Cat on a Hot Tin Roof,* also on Broadway.

As close friends of Leadbelly (with whom they lived for a while), Woody Guthrie (with whom they appeared as the Woody Guthrie Singers) and Pete Seeger (with whom Sonny toured—a live album of their Carnegie Hall concert is on Folkways), they were never at a loss for material or engagements. And a great deal of their work is documented on record. The above sampling, however, dates approximately from 1952 through the mid-Sixties. There have been subsequent albums, including one in the early Seventies for A&M, but these represent Terry and McGhee, solo and together, in their prime.

A drummer is used on some of the sessions (*Sing* and the second of the two discs of *Back to New Orleans*), but is so distant in the mix that he remains unobtrusive. Indeed, part of the problem with some of the Sixties dates was that too many other musicians were thrown in to "compensate" for McGhee's and Terry's age. Yet, onstage even today, the pair remains as exuberant and forceful as ever.

The original mono version of *Sing* is preferable to its artificial stereo reissue, as *Preachin' the Blues* and the various solo albums (*Washboard Band* and *Harmonica and Vocal Solos* are ten-inch records) are suggested primarily as reference points to the breadth of Terry's and McGhee's endeavors and as an indication of where the duo sound came from.

The two Fantasy sets are excellent remasterings and repackagings of early Prestige/Bluesville material and beautifully illustrate the "modeling, shaping and polishing" process that has made Brownie's and Sonny's appeal extend well beyond the cult of blues fanatics. Theirs is a timeless music. — I.M.

BOB McGILPIN
■ **Get Up** / Butter. (NA)
■ **Bob McGilpin** / Casa. (NA)
■ **Superstar** / Butter. (NA)
Folkie disco, with the emptiest production and lightest-weight vocal delivery. McGilpin thanks God prominently on the back cover—with his talent he needs all the help he can get. — J.S.

MAUREEN McGOVERN
★ **Nice to Be Around** / 20th Cent. (1974) ¶
★ **Maureen McGovern** / War. (1979)
Uninteresting woman singer noted for the late-Seventies hit "Morning After." — J.S.

BAT McGRATH
★ ★ **From the Blue Eagle** / Amh. (1976)
★ ★ **The Spy** / Amh. (1978)
The present-day folksinger refuses to die. The difference between McGrath and his equally average predecessors (Eric Andersen, David Blue et al.) is the influence of the

Southern California rock of Jackson Browne in addition to Bob Dylan and Woody Guthrie. No big deal, just a spruced-up time warp. — D.M.

McGUFFEY LANE
■ **McGuffey Lane** / Atco (1980)
Superwimp MOR ersatz country schlock. Disgusting and unlistenable. Yech. — J.S.

ROGER McGUINN
★ ★ ★ **Roger McGuinn** / Col. (1973) ¶
★ ★ ★ **Peace on You** / Col. (1974) ¶
★ ★ ★ **Roger McGuinn and Band** / Col. (1975) ¶
★ ★ ★ ★ **Cardiff Rose** / Col. (1976) ¶
★ ★ ★ **Thunderbyrd** / Col. (1977) ¶
Roger McGuinn's solo career is a stylistic extension of the final versions of the Byrds, which he put together. McGuinn's distinctive, twangy voice and trademark rhythm-guitar harmonics give an overall evenness to his work that makes all but his least-inspired material sound pretty good. At his best, as on most of *Cardiff Rose* and bits and pieces from all the rest of his solo outings, McGuinn is a true original, one of the finest examples of a mature folk-rock stylist who isn't a sap. — J.S.

McGUINN AND HILLMAN
★ ★ **McGuinn and Hillman** / Cap. (1980)
Usual result from another L.A. game of musical chairs. — W.K.

McGUINN, CLARK AND HILLMAN
★ ★ **McGuinn, Clark and Hillman** / Cap. (1979)
★ ★ **City** / Cap. (1980)
Predictable vinyl versions of the Sixties equivalent to Richard Nader's rock & roll revival shows (that is, once-vital artists forced to trade endlessly on their past accomplishments in order to pay the rent). — W.K.

BARRY McGUIRE
★ ★ ★ **Eve of Destruction** / Dun. (1965)
★ **Seeds** / Myrrh (1973)
★ **Lighten Up** / Myrrh (1975)
★ **To the Bride** / Myrrh (1975)
★ **Jubilation** / Myrrh (1975)
★ **Jubilation, Too** / Myrrh (1976)
In the mid-Sixties, McGuire scored with the strident protest-song epic "Eve of Destruction." He went on to become a Jesus freak and write his sermons more directly. — J.S.

PETER McIAN
■ **Playing near the Edge** / Col. (1980)
Not nearly closely enough. — D.M.

LONETTE McKEE

★ ★ **Words and Music / War. (1978)**
Mainstream late-Seventies female soul singer/songwriter comes on like Hollywood's answer to Roberta Flack: that is, she is apparently humorless, she sings in overripe tones, and her lyrics are the height of pomposity. McKee gets even more jive when she tries to go uptempo. — D.M.

McKENDREE SPRING

★ **McKendree Spring / MCA (1969)**
★ **3 / MCA (1972)**
A truly rotten Seventies art/gimmick rock band led by the flatulent violin histrionics of Michael Dreyfuss, McKendree Spring is notable for recording the most obnoxious cover of Neil Young's oft-mangled wimp anthem, "Down by the River." This band's version was even worse than Buddy Miles'. — J.S.

BOB AND DOUG McKENZIE

★ ★ ★ **Great White North / Mer. (1981)**
Unaccountably funny comedy album by two SCTV comedians whose shtick is playing dumb, drunk Canadians. The Cheech and Chong of beer. — J.S.

SCOTT McKENZIE

★ **Stained Glass Morning / Ode (1970)** ¶
Folksy singer/songwriter scored with the late-Sixties hippie paean "San Francisco" (in which he advised visitors to the city to wear flowers in their hair), then quickly disappeared. This record does not include the hit. — J.S.

IAN McLAGEN

★ ★ ★ **Troublemaker / Mer. (1979)**
★ ★ ★ **Bump in the Night / Mer. (1981)**
As might be expected, these records provide a boozy good time as the ex-Faces keyboardist leads a crew of assorted friends (including Faces sidekick Ronnie Wood) through spirited sets of blues rocking jams. — J.S.

MURRAY McLAUCHLAN

★ ★ ★ **Boulevard / True (NA)**
★ ★ ★ **Hard Rock Town / True (NA)**
★ ★ ★ **Storm Warning / Asy. (NA)**
McLauchlan started out as a plucky Canadian folkie capable of great penny-novel-prose songwriting. These two albums represent his very late graduation into rock & roll, which lends his crudely drawn songs much needed power. *Hard Rock Town* actually finds McLauchlan leading a band, and with that album, the harsh realism of *Boulevard* achieves a poetic elegance and McLauchlan finally liberates

himself from a certain regional primitivism. — B.T.

DON McLEAN

★ **Tapestry / U.A. (1970)**
★ ★ ★ **American Pie / U.A. (1971)**
★ ★ ★ **Don McLean / U.A. (1972)**
★ **Playin' Favorites / U.A. (1973)**
■ **Homeless Brother / U.A. (1974)**
★ ★ **Solo / U.A. (1976)**
★ **Prime Time / Ari. (1977)**
★ **Chain Lightning / Millen. (1979)**
★ **Believers / Millen. (1981)**
"American Pie" is a tightly coded, symbolically charged "critical history" of rock & roll that serves as McLean's justification for saying goodbye to rock in favor of folk music. But McLean delivers it with such conviction that it becomes an anthem in spite of itself; in 1971 it seemed to sum up what a strange journey rock had taken us upon and how far adrift it had left us. "Vincent," McLean's follow-up ode to Vincent Van Gogh, shows his tendency to inflate insight into dogma, which is a lot more typical of his post-*Pie* work. McLean's chief concerns, the City as Babylon and Nature as Eden, are stifled by his New York liberal moralism. Although he found his most important lyrical sources in Phil Ochs and Bob Dylan, his tone is pure Pete Seeger, and emotionally he conveys a collegiate anger that might better be described as sophomoric petulance. His love songs sound like notes from the garret, and his odes to nature are mere catechism. Sanctimonious as he may be, however, McLean's not a purist: he's used folk in combination with rock, Dixieland and even ragtime, always to suit didactic ends. — B.T./D.M.

JIMMY AND KRISTY McNICHOL

■ **Jimmy and Kristy McNichol / RCA (1978)** ¶
TV tots just fooling around. Unbearable and insipid. — D.M.

CLYDE McPHATTER

★ ★ ★ ★ **Treasure of Love / Atl. (1980), Jap. imp.**
Includes the venerable R&B singer's fine post-Drifters hits, notably the title track, "Money Honey" and "Such a Night." Splendid Fifties singing, with tough bands and arrangements. — D.M.

BLIND WILLIE McTELL

★ **Last Session / Prest. (1956)**
★ ★ ★ ★ **The Early Years: 1927–1933 / Yazoo (1968)**

★ ★ ★ **Trying to Get Home** / Bio. (1970)
★ ★ ★ ★ **Atlanta Twelve String** / Atl. (1972)
★ ★ ★ ★ **1927–1935** / Yazoo (1973)
★ ★ ★ **King of the Georgia Blues Singers** / Roots (NA)
★ ★ ★ ★ **The Library of Congress Session** / Mel. (NA)

A blind street singer and twelve-string guitarist, McTell played blues, religious and country songs, ballads and pop tunes. He recorded under a variety of names for many labels, and although little is known of his life, much of the music remains readily available. And almost every young blues singer and interpreter has been influenced by McTell's guitar techniques and songwriting. His "Statesboro Blues," "Dying Crapshooter Blues" and "Trying to Get Home" are classics.

The Yazoo records are in amazingly good condition—the sound is crisp and clear throughout. *Trying to Get Home* and *Atlanta Twelve String* were recorded in 1949; the latter includes two cuts that had originally been released under the pseudonym Barrelhouse Sammy. Both LPs capture McTell pretty much at his peak. The Melodeon album is also beautiful; it dates from 1940. Recorded in a record shop in Atlanta, the 1956 *Last Session* is a rather sad footnote. McTell is caught at a point when the frustration of his lack of commercial success, liquor and age had overcome his physical and vocal dexterity. — I.M.

CHRISTINE McVIE
★ ★ ★ **The Legendary Christine Perfect Album** / Sire (1976) ¶

Rereleased after Fleetwood Mac's pop ascendance, this is the blues album that Christine Perfect (soon to be McVie) made after leaving Chicken Shack for a brief solo career before joining Mac. It's a solid and enjoyable set that features standard British blues playing and McVie's sublimely controlled blues voice. — J.B.M.

MEAT LOAF
★ ★ **Bat out of Hell** / Epic (1977)
★ **Dead Ringer** / Epic (1981)

Whatever elements made his bombastic rock opera mix of Spector, Springsteen and the kitchen sink into a multi-platinum success the first time around somehow got left out of the follow-up. Despite the attempt at duplication implied by its title, *Dead Ringer* is a critical and (surprisingly) commercial failure. Undoubtedly the heftiest footnote in rock history, and as important to it as Screaming Lord Sutch. — W.K.

MECO
★ ★ ★ **Star Wars and Other Galactic Funk** / Millen. (1977)
★ **Encounters of Every Kind** / Millen. (1977)
★ **The Wizard of Oz** / Millen. (1978)
★ **Moondancer** / Casa. (NA)
■ **Star Trek and the Black Hole** / Casa. (NA)
■ **Superman** / Casa. (NA)
■ **Meco Plays Music from** *The Empire Strikes Back* / RSO (1980)

Disco producer/auteur Tony Bongiovi's stable of session players clicked with this semi-solo strategy of covering the immensely popular themes from *Star Wars, The Wizard of Oz* and *Close Encounters of the Third Kind.* Rather than do the usual mindless ripoffs, however, the Meco versions are so cleverly arranged that the themes, when they do appear, work as surprise elements that are quite effective. The band's best moment is the side-long "Other Galactic Funk" from the first album, an interesting disco vamp based on a New Orleans second-line marching drum pattern. As Meco wore on, the formula became repulsive. — J.S.

THE MEDITATIONS
★ ★ ★ ★ **Message from the Meditations** / U.A. (1979)
★ ★ ★ ★ **Wake Up** / Double D (1980)
★ ★ ★ **Guidance** / Tad's (1980)

The best young reggae harmony group around but still little-known, the Meditations have a knack for catchy melody and clever lyrics. Their falsetto harmonies are often almost impossibly sweet and sometimes are employed for comic effect ("Woman Piabba"). Weak production values are their only liability. — R.F.G.

THE MEDITATION SINGERS
★ ★ ★ **Change Is Gonna Come** / Jewel (1971)

Though neither is apparent here, this gospel group spawned Laura Lee (whose mother is still its director) and Della Reese. An enjoyably modern group, they use arrangements that are decidedly nontraditional but still quite original and strangely compelling. — J.MO.

BILL MEDLEY
★ **Wings** / A & M (1971)
★ **Lay a Little Lovin' on Me** / U.A. (1978) ¶
★ ★ **Sweet Thunder** / Lib. (NA)
★ ★ **Right There and Now** / RCA (1982)

Talking about half of the Righteous Brothers is like talking about one Siamese twin, and listening to one is little improvement. — D.M.

RANDY MEISNER

★ **Randy Meisner / Asy. (1978)**
★ **One More Song / Epic (1980)**
Laid-back drivel from the former Eagle.
Makes John David Souther sound like Led
Zeppelin. — D.M.

MEKONS

★ ★ ★ **The Quality of Mercy Is Not Strnen**
/ Virgin (1979), Br. imp.
★ ★ ★ **The Mekons / Red Rhino (1980), Br.**
imp.
A bargain-basement Gang of Four, the
Mekons still have something to offer fans of
abrasive rock music. *The Quality of Mercy*
features jerky rhythms, defiantly lower-class
vocals and songs of boredom and romantic
frustration—all hallmarks of the British
punk scene. An occasional traditional chord
progression makes the rest bearable, while
some of the lyrics are almost cute in their
coyness about affairs of the (broken) heart.
Spare production and instrumentation pay
obeisance to the minimal funk rock then
starting to crowd punk out of the British
rock audience's limited attention
span.

The Mekons, with its near-anonymous
packaging, comes awfully close to pretentiousness; only the band's musical progression between albums makes it worthwhile.
Now fully into dance-oriented rock, they
spice things up with polyrhythmic instruments and vocals over steady drums. Lyrical
concerns have broadened to include empty
culture as well as empty lives. Challenging if
nonessential listening. — S.I.

MELANIE

★ **Photograph / Atl. (1976)** ¶
★ ★ **Phonogenic—Not Just Another Pretty**
Face / Mid. Int. (1978)
★ ★ **Best of Melanie / Bud. (1978)**
★ ★ ★ **Ballroom Streets /**
Tom. (1979)
Melanie epitomized the flower-child folksinger of the late Sixties. Her vocal range is
in fact quite exceptional, and her phrasing
often more sophisticated than she is given
credit for, but the determined innocence and
ingenuousness of her songs, their firm faith
in good vibes conquering all, was obnoxious
when she began recording and is now rather
hilariously dated in its naiveté.

Her first commercial success came when
she recorded "Candles in the Rain," a 1970
hit that called forth the spirit of Woodstock
itself. (As those who saw the movie will recall, the emcee asked everyone in the crowd
to light matches as a sign of solidarity—or

something.) Her only other substantial hit
came with "Brand New Key," in 1972.
"Candles" is on the Buddah *Best of* package,
"Key" on the deleted ABC *From the Beginning* set. *Phonogenic, Photograph,* and her
most recent album, *Ballroom Streets,* are
much more mature, and include several good
interpretations of contemporary songs. The
earlier material, however, is recommended
only for freshman mentalities, and only those
which are terribly romantic, at that.
— D.M.

THE MELODIANS

★ ★ ★ **Sweet Sensation / Mango (1981)**
When rocksteady was turning to reggae in
the late Sixties, the Melodians made a credible challenge to reigning harmony groups
such as the Paragons, Wailers and Uniques.
"Rivers of Babylon" alone assures them a
prominent niche in reggae history. Their
sweet, soulful singing will make you smile
and weep at the same time, and Leslie
Kong's chugging rhythms are the perfect
counterpoint. Only the skimpy playing time
and the omission of their Treasure Isle recordings keeps this from the essential category. — R.F.G.

HAROLD MELVIN AND THE BLUE NOTES

★ ★ ★ **Harold Melvin and the Blue Notes /**
Phil. (1972) ¶
★ ★ ★ ★ **Black and Blue / Phil. (1973)** ¶
★ ★ ★ ★ ★ **To Be True / Phil.**
(1975) ¶
★ ★ ★ ★ **Wake Up Everybody / Phil.**
(1975)
★ ★ ★ ★ **Collector's Item / Phil. (1976)**
★ ★ **Reaching for the World / ABC**
(1977) ¶
★ ★ **Now Is the Time / ABC (1977)** ¶
★ ★ **Blue Album / Source (1980)**
★ ★ **All Things Happen in Time / MCA**
(1981)
The lead singer's name was Theodore
Pendergrass, and he turned out some of the
strongest records produced by Kenny Gam-
ble and Leon Huff since their work with
Jerry Butler. The brilliant "Bad Luck," "If
You Don't Know Me by Now" and "Wake
Up Everybody" were among the greatest
disco-soul records of the middle Seventies,
with hot tracks and really ferocious vocal at-
tack. After the group broke up in 1976,
Melvin's regrouped forces churned out
inferior imitations for ABC and other
labels, while Pendergrass kept on with
the real thing for Gamble and Huff.
— D.M.

MEMBERS
★ ★ ★ **At the Chelsea Nightclub / Virgin (1979), Br. imp.**
★ ★ ★ **1980: The Choice Is Yours / Virgin (1980), Br. imp.**
Hard-hitting R&B-based British club band.
— J.S.

THE MEMPHIS JUG BAND
★ ★ ★ **The Memphis Jug Band, Vol. 1 / Roots (NA), Br. imp.**
★ ★ ★ **The Memphis Jug Band, Vol. 2 / Roots (NA), Br. imp.**
★ ★ ★ ★ **The Memphis Jug Band / Yazoo (NA)**
The seminal jug band of the late Twenties and early Thirties, led by vocalist/guitarist/harp player Will Shade, whose membership also included Walter Horton, Ben Ramey, Charlie Polk and a host of others over the years. The Yazoo set, as usual, duplicates the competition but with superior sound and packaging. — D.M.

MEMPHIS MINNIE
★ ★ ★ **Memphis Minnie, Vol. 1 / Blues C. (NA)**
★ ★ ★ ★ **Memphis Minnie, Vol. 2 / Blues C. (NA)**
★ ★ ★ ★ **The Early Recordings of Memphis Minnie and Kansas Joe / Pal. (NA)**
★ ★ ★ **Memphis Minnie, 1941–49 / Flyr. (NA)**
★ ★ ★ **Hot Stuff / Mag. (NA)**
Brilliant, big-voiced singer and blues guitarist was known as the female Big Bill Broonzy and once defeated Broonzy in a blues battle. Her husband, Kansas Joe McCoy, also played country blues, and her best work is the stuff they did together, which is on the Blues Classics Volume 2 and Paltram sides.
— J.S.

ANDY MENDELSON
★ **Maybe the Good Guy's Gonna Win / Ari. (1980) ¶**
Not this time. — J.S.

MENTAL AS ANYTHING
★ ★ ★ ★ **Get Wet / Virgin (1980), Br. imp.; Reg. (1979), Aust. imp.**
★ ★ ★ **Espresso Bongo / Reg. (1980), Aust. imp.**
★ ★ ★ ★ **Cats and Dogs / Reg. (1981), Aust. imp.**
From the lunatic fringe of Australian rock & roll, Mental As Anything sing songs with titles like "Troop Movements in the Ukraine" and "Theme from a Future TV Drama Se-

ries." By their third album, *Cats and Dogs* (a Top Ten album in Australia), they seem to have learned to play their instruments properly and think up words that do fit into the tunes, but thankfully this has in no way detracted from their amiably inspired amateurism. They still take cheerful delight in the ordinariness of things, and their images of love and romance all have a wonderfully domestic charm—Martin Plaza's "If You Leave Me Can I Come Too?" from *Cats and Dogs,* for instance, or Greedy Smith's description of the anguish of finding "Another Man's Sitting in My Kitchen" on *Get Wet.* All the members of the band write songs: not only Smith and Plaza but brothers Peter O'Dougherty and Reg Mombassa have contributed some fine numbers.

The 1979 Australian success of the single "The Nips Are Getting Bigger" led Virgin records to release Mental As Anything's first album in England, but neither of the subsequent records have been released outside Australia. It's a shame: their peculiar blend of suburban banality with a self-deprecating hilarity and true fan's affection for Sixties Top Forty music makes the Mentals one of Australia's most original and appealing acts.
— S.M.

NEIL MERRYWEATHER
■ **Neil Merryweather . . . John Richardson and Bores / Kent (NA)**
One of the most useless relics of Sixties West Coast psychedelic blues. Merryweather actually made a fairly listenable record once: *Word of Mouth "A Two Record Super-Jam,"* circa 1970, was bearable, but only because of the contributions of Steve Miller, Dave Mason, Barry Goldberg and a couple of others. Melt this one down. — D.M.

THE METERS
★ ★ ★ ★ **Cabbage Alley / Rep. (1972) ¶**
★ ★ ★ ★ ★ **Rejuvenation / Rep. (1974) ¶**
★ ★ ★ **Fire on the Bayou / Rep. (1975) ¶**
★ ★ ★ **The Best of the Meters / Virgo (1975)**
★ ★ ★ ★ **Cissy Strut / Is. (1975) ¶**
★ ★ **Trick Bag / Rep. (1976) ¶**
★ ★ ★ **New Directions / War. (1977) ¶**
The Meters' early style (represented on *Cissy Strut*) was revolutionary. As a quartet, the New Orleans-based group developed a bareboned, quirky brand of funk that leaned heavily on clipped rhythms and syncopated accents. The languid, off-center groove of songs like "Sophisticated Cissy" proved to be the forerunner of Seventies funk.

The group's Reprise albums sport an ex-

panded approach, with congas, acoustic piano and horns often incorporated. *Cabbage Alley* features mild reggae, second-line funk, ballads, rolling Professor Longhair piano chords (played by Art Neville) and some tasty horn charts by Allen Toussaint. *Rejuvenation* maintains their heavy commitment to New Orleans music, while at the same time taking dead aim at early-Seventies Sly Stone funk innovations. The album is a masterpiece. But not one of the albums since then has been able to expand on the possibilities suggested on *Rejuvenation*. *Trick Bag* is particularly disappointing because it shows a band stalled for lack of direction.
— J.MC.

MFSB
★ ★ **MFSB** / **Phil.** (1973)
★ ★ **Love Is the Message** / **Phil.** (1973)
★ ★ **Universal Love** / **Phil.** (1975) ¶
★ ★ ★ **Philadelphia Freedom!** / **Phil.** (1975) ¶
★ ★ **Summertime** / **Phil.** (1976)
★ ★ **The End of Phase 1** / **Phil.** (1977)
★ ★ **MFSB, The Gamble-Huff Orchestra** / **Phil.** (1978)
MFSB is the driving instrumental force—horns and rhythm section—behind the remarkable Philadelphia soul sound of producer Kenny Gamble and Leon Huff. But aside from "TSOP (The Sound of Philadelphia)," a major 1973 pop and R&B hit, and a decent version of "Philadelphia Freedom," this is a long way from the heyday of Booker T. and the MGs. For the most part, it's just competent dance funk. — D.M.

MIAMI
★ ★ ★ **The Party Freaks** / **Drive** (1974)
★ ★ ★ **Notorious Miami** / **Drive** (1976)
★ ★ ★ **Miami** / **Drive** (1979)
Surprisingly witty and funky Florida disco act. Led by producer Willie Clarke, abetted (on *The Party Freaks*) by the irrepressible Clarence Reid (a.k.a. Blow Fly). — D.M.

RAS MICHAEL AND THE SONS OF NEGUS
★ ★ ★ ★ **Nyabinghi** / **Troj.** (1974)
★ ★ ★ ★ ★ **Rastafari** / **Tuff Gong** (1975)
★ ★ ★ **Tribute to the Emperor** / **Troj.** (1976)
★ ★ ★ **Love Thy Neighbor** / **Jah Life** (1980)
★ ★ **Live** / **Lion.** (1981)
Synonymous with "roots," Ras Michael's roving band of singers, drummers, and dancers has been the most visible caretaker of Count Ossie's African cultural restoration project. Yet the Sons of Negus have not been afraid to use electric guitars to commu-

nicate their message, which is often couched in the stately cadences and melodies of Anglican hymns. On record, their loose communal playing sometimes seems unfocused, but the heartbeat funde drum (reggae's central pulse) is *always* there. *Rastafari* has purposeful, focused energy, while *Tribute* has the rock guitar. The later LPs get so spacy that they seem suitable only for the late-night dregs of heavy toking and meditation sessions. — R.F.G.

GORDON MICHAELS
★ **Stargazer** / **A&M** (1979)
Soulless light jazz entertainment without any function or sense of fun: typical studio pro pop. Not slick enough for background noise and too annoyingly proud of its own tastefulness and craftsmanship to be tolerated in the foreground. — D.M.

HILLY MICHAELS
★ **Calling All Girls** / **War.** (1980)
★ **Lumia** / **War.** (1981)
Jive new waver, a finger-popper in post-punk clothing. — D.M.

MICHELE
★ **Magic Love** / **West End** (1977)
Untransforming. — D.M.

BETTE MIDLER
★ ★ ★ ★ **The Divine Miss M** / **Atl.** (1972)
★ ★ **Bette Midler** / **Atl.** (1973)
★ **Songs for the New Depression** / **Atl.** (1975)
★ ★ ★ **Live at Last** / **Atl.** (1977)
★ ★ **Broken Blossom** / **Atl.** (1977) ¶
■ **Thighs and Whispers** / **Atl.** (1979)
★ ★ **The Rose** / **Atl.** (1979)
★ ★ **Divine Madness** / **Atl.** (1980)
When Bette Midler first began appearing in New York nightclubs, she was revelatory: a cabaret performer who was truly funny and had a firm grasp of rock and its offshoots. As a Seventies answer to Barbra Streisand, she was perfect. The flawed but historic first album captures her in all her gum-snapping, wisecracking naiveté—everything from the pathos of John Prine's "Hello in There" to the Andrews Sisters' "Boogie Woogie Bugle Boy" is here. This is the album that created nostalgia as we currently know it.

But Bette wilted in the spotlight, and little that she has come up with since is sufficient to explain her rabid cult. The readings grow more camp and turgid with each new album, and Midler seems less committed as well. There are bright spots: the spontaneous, screamingly funny dialogue on the *Live* album, which is also enhanced by her studio recording of "You're Moving Out Today." A few more songs like that and her hysterical, mismanaged career might finally amount to something. — D.M.

MIDNIGHT FLYER
★ ★ **Midnight Flyer** / Swan (1981)
A smooth outfit that serves as a showcase for the raucous vocals of former Stone the Crows singer Maggie Bell, Britain's answer to Janis Joplin. Bad Company's Mick Ralphs produced, and the whole affair sounds terribly professional. This also means that the grit in Bell's voice is so buried that the album sounds uncannily similar to Bette Midler in *The Rose*—that is, Joplin without the balls. — R.P.

MIDNIGHT OIL
★ ★ ★ **Midnight Oil** / Powd. (1978), Aust. imp.
★ ★ ★ ★ **Head Injuries** / Powd. (1979), Aust. imp.
★ ★ ★ **Place without a Postcard** / Powd. (1981), Aust. imp.
At their best, the Australian band Midnight Oil reminds you of an express train roaring past at a distance of about four feet. Loud and fierce in the finest rock & roll tradition, they manage to escape too close a connection with heavy metal largely through Rob Hirst's fiery and inventive drumming. The muscular melodies save the power chording from predictability, as do the dynamics of the interplay between guitarists Martin Rotsey and Jim Moginie. Most of Midnight Oil's songs belong to the social comment genre, raging at suburban passivity and political corruption with the energy and anger of the impassioned outsider. This commitment has been carried through in the band's consistent refusal to participate in the charades of rock & roll publicity, maintaining independence from the compromises dictated by major record labels. That integrity need not be a commercial liability is indicated by the fact that *Head Injuries* went gold without the benefit of mainstream AM radio play or appearances on the mindless TV shows that are the PR man's sine qua non of rock success in Australia. While singer Peter Garrett's furious onstage performance is legendary in Australia, the three albums on their appropriately named Powderworks label provide a good crystallization of Midnight Oil's fire and fervor. — S.M.

MIDNIGHT STAR
★ ★ **The Beginning** / Solar (1980)

★ ★ **Standing Together** / Solar (1981)
Upbeat eight-piece funk/disco unit sounds as if it has never recovered from John Travolta's *Saturday Night Fever* boogie numbers. Talk about clichés! — D.M.

THE MIGHTY CLOUDS OF JOY
★ ★ **Live at the Music Hall** / Pea. (NA)
★ ★ ★ **The Best of the Mighty Clouds of Joy** / Pea. (NA)
★ ★ **Presenting: The Untouchables** / Pea. (NA)
★ ★ **Mighty Clouds of Joy Sing Songs of Rev. Julius Cheeks and the Nightingales** / Pea. (NA)
★ ★ ★ **Live! At the Apollo** / Pea. (NA)
★ ★ ★ **Best of the Mighty Clouds of Joy** / Pea. (NA)
★ ★ **A Bright Side** / Pea. (NA)
The Mighty Clouds of Joy are one of the outstanding young modern-gospel quartets; they feature the lead voice of Joe Ligons rising out of a chorus of falsetto voices. Ligons also likes to preach à la the Reverend C. L. Franklin (Aretha's father), and if he sometimes sounds remarkably like Wilson Pickett, perhaps it's because he and Pickett both patterned themselves after Julius Cheeks of the Sensational Nightingales.

Yet the Clouds aren't always as sharp as they might seem from that description. Mainly, Ligons is an undisciplined singer who often screams for the sake of screaming. There are wonderful performances spread out over their albums—things like "We Think God Don't Care," from *Bright Side*, which sounds almost like a Sam and Dave ballad; "I Came to Jesus," from *Music Hall*; or Ligons' reading of "Burying Ground" on the Cheeks tribute album. But because of their inconsistencies, it's most advisable to stick with the two *Best of* LPs. There's little overlap in material between them, oddly enough; the earlier (Peabody 136) might contain slightly better songs, but on the later (Peabody 183), Ligons proves that as he grew, he did develop some subtlety and restraint. *Apollo* is the better of the two live albums because it offers more variety and a more exciting pace. Thanks in part to those high harmonies, the Mighty Clouds started sounding very much like the Impressions of the Curtis Mayfield era toward the end of the gospel phase of their career; and judging from the changes taking place in their arrangements, that's exactly what they were aiming for.
★ ★ ★ **It's Time** / Dun. (1974)
★ ★ **Kickin'** / ABC (1975)

★ **Truth Is the Power** / ABC (1977)
On paper, the Mighty Clouds' soul collaborations with Gamble and Huff look good.
They could possibly have been another Harold Melvin and the Blue Notes featuring
Theodore Pendergrass, given the similarities between Pendergrass and Ligons. But they
came along with too little too late. They hooked up with the production team just as
the Philly Sound was becoming mechanized and predictable. *It's Time* has a few flashy
surprises, but by *Kickin'* the group is grunting through poorly chosen material like an
"I've Got the Music in Me"/"Superstition" medley. On *Truth* they don't even have the
benefit of the Philly producers, and they sound like just about any anonymous soul
group.   — J.MO.

THE MIGHTY DIAMONDS
★ ★ ★ **Planet Earth** / V.F.L. (1978)
★ ★ ★ ★ **Deeper Roots** / V.F.L. (1979)
★ ★ ★ **Vital Selection** / Virgin (1981)
★ ★ ★ **Reggae Street** / Shan. (1981)
The Mighty Diamonds remain one of the most consistent harmony groups in reggae,
although since their 1977 classic *Right Time* they have not enjoyed the international rec-
ognition they deserve. *Planet Earth*'s tunefulness suffers from bland production, but
Deeper Roots restores the cutting edge needed to balance the sweet harmonies. *Vital
Selection* is an excellent compilation from their four Virgin LPs and *Reggae Street* is
an irresistibly melodic self-production.   — R.F.G.

MIGHTY FIRE
★ ★ ★ **No Time for Masquerading** / Elek. (1980)
Surprisingly enjoyable vocal quintet in Spinners/Whispers mold. Nothing new, but they
do the standard contemporary soul routine really well.   — D.M.

MIGHTY HIGH
■ **Mighty High** / MCA (1979)
Chicago meets Yes meets the Allman Brothers meets Uriah Heep.   — L.F.

AMOS MILBURN
★ ★ **Great R&B Oldies** / Blues Sp. (NA)
★ ★ ★ ★ **Amos Milburn and His Chicken Shackers** / Route 66 (NA), Br. imp.
The great Forties and Fifties blues shouter, exciting and influential. A good piano player
with a solid band, the Texas-bred Milburn is simply one of the finest vocalists of early
rhythm & blues. The evidence is on the vin-

tage sides on the Route 66 album, which unfortunately doesn't have his epochal
"Chicken Shack Boogie." The Blues Spectrum LP is quite recent, and Milburn
was ill when he made it—to be avoided.   — D.M.

BUDDY MILES
★ ★ ★ **Them Changes** / Mer. (1970)
★ ★ ★ **Carlos Santana and Buddy Miles Live** / Col. (1972)
The solo career of this clownish, heavy-handed ex–Electric Flag drummer is a series
of incredible gaffes, the likes of which have seldom been witnessed in the annals of popular music. His taste is awful, his playing is almost always overbearing, and he manages
to make more errors in judgment than seem possible. "Them Changes" is his anthem,
and a decent funk song, which in this context is miraculous.   — J.S.

JOHN MILES
★ **Rebel** / Lon. (1976) ¶
★ **Stranger in the City** / Lon. (1977) ¶
★ **Zaragon** / Ari. (1978)
★ **Sympathy** / Ari. (NA)
Eclectic English pop star borrows from everyone from Elton John to Yes. Slick, flashy,
often pretentious.   — S.H.

FRANKIE MILLER
★ ★ ★ **Once in a Blue Moon** / Chrys. (1973)
★ ★ ★ ★ **The Rock** / Chrys. (1973)
★ ★ ★ ★ **High Life** / Chrys. (1974)
★ ★ ★ **Full House** / Chrys. (1977)
★ ★ **Double Trouble** / Chrys. (1978)
★ ★ **Easy Money** / Chrys. (1980)
A raspy rhythm & blues belter, Miller resembles other singers (Otis Redding, Bob
Seger, Joe Cocker, Paul Rodgers) but sings mainly his own R&B-based material. *Once in
a Blue Moon* enlists the pub-rock of Brinsley Schwarz—tight and subtle, and very deriva-
tive of the Band. For *High Life,* Miller went to Georgia to team up with producer/
arranger/writer Allen Toussaint and a good studio team, including the Atlanta Rhythm
Section's fine guitarist, Barry Bailey. Miller's own more rock-directed quartet made the
meatier though less distinguished *The Rock.* *Full House* contains much the same band,
but also used studio aces like Chris Spedding and John "Rabbit" Bundrick. Here, with
mixed results, Miller resorts more than usual to nonoriginal material that goes
beyond the limits of straight R&B. *Double Trouble* and *Easy Money* returned him to
his own material, but he'd lost the spark.   — C.W.

JACOB MILLER
★ ★ ★ **Tenement Yard** / Top R. (1978)
★ ★ ★ **Dread, Dread** / U.A. (1979)
★ ★ ★ **Killer** / Top R. (1979)
★ ★ ★ **Wanted** / Top R. (1979)
★ ★ ★ **Mixed-Up Moods** / Top R. (1980)
★ ★ ★ **Lives On** / J. Gibbs (1980)
★ ★ ★ ★ **Greatest Hits** / Top R. (1980)

Some say Jacob Miller could sing anything, even opera, but his untimely death at age twenty-four magnified his legend and the genuine affection he had inspired in Jamaica. His work with Inner Circle has come under fire for its disco and R&B production values, but on his solo records, his strong vocals and excellent instrumental backing are unassailable. Only a shortage of truly outstanding tunes keeps his best records from the essential category. *Tenement Yard,* his debut (*Dread, Dread* is identical), contains his legacy, the title track. *Lives On* and *Mixed-Up Moods* are posthumous releases scraping the bottom of the barrel, but both contain great moments.   — R.F.G.

THE LEGENDARY JAY MILLER SESSIONS
★ ★ ★ ★ ★ **Tag Along** / Flyr. (1976), Br. imp.
★ ★ ★ ★ **Gonna Head for Home** / Flyr. (1976), Br. imp.
★ ★ ★ ★ **Rooster Crowed for Day** / Flyr. (1976), Br. imp.
★ ★ ★ ★ **Slim Harpo—Blues Hangover** / Flyr. (1976), Br. imp.
★ ★ ★ ★ **Lightning Slim—The Early Years** / Flyr. (1976), Br. imp.
★ ★ ★ ★ ★ **Al Ferrier and Warren Storm— Boppin' Tonight** / Flyr. (1976, Br. imp.
★ ★ ★ ★ ★ **Lazy Lester—They Call Me Lazy** / Flyr. (1976), Br. imp.
★ ★ ★ **Lonesome Sundown—Bought Me a Ticket** / Flyr. (NA), Br. imp.
★ ★ ★ **Katie Webster—Whooee Sweet Daddy** / Flyr. (1977), Br. imp.
★ ★ ★ ★ **Johnny Jano—King of Louisiana Rockabilly** / Flyr. (1977), Br. imp.
★ ★ ★ ★ **Louisiana Swamp Pop** / Flyr. (1977), Br. imp.
★ ★ ★ **Lightning Slim—Trip to Chicago** / Flyr. (1977), Br. imp.
★ ★ ★ ★ **Nathan Abshire and the Pine Grove Boys** / Flyr. (1977), Br. imp.
★ ★ ★ ★ ★ **Zydeco Blues** / Flyr. (1978), Br. imp.
★ ★ ★ ★ ★ **Rockin' Fever** / Flyr. (1978), Br. imp.
★ ★ ★ ★ **Lazy Lester—Poor Boy Blues** / Flyr. (1978), Br. imp.

★ ★ ★ ★ **Boppin' It!** / Flyr. (1980), Br. imp.
★ ★ ★ ★ ★ **Girl in the Tight Blue Jeans** / Flyr. (1980), Br. imp.
★ ★ ★ ★ **Bayou Boogie** / Flyr. (1980), Br. imp.
★ ★ ★ ★ **Slim Harpo—Got Love If You Want It** / Flyr. (1980), Br. imp.
★ ★ ★ ★ ★ **Too Hot to Handle** / Flyr. (1981), Br. imp.
★ ★ ★ ★ **Leroy Washington—Wild Cherry** / Flyr. (1981), Br. imp.
★ ★ ★ ★ ★ **Tribute to Harry Choates** / Flyr. (1981), Br. imp.
★ ★ ★ ★ ★ **Rusty and Doug Kershaw with Wiley Barkdull** / Flyr. (1981), Br. imp.
★ ★ ★ ★ ★ **Jimmy Newman and Al Terry** / Flyr. (1981), Br. imp.

Jay Miller, a shrewd producer and club owner in the small town of Crowley on the coastal crescent of South Louisiana, recorded an amazingly wide range of music between the late Forties and the early Sixties. During that time he cut country, Cajun, western, blues, R&B, rockabilly and early rock records of a consistently high standard, recording every talented artist in the South Louisiana area who wasn't already tied to a New Orleans studio.

Miller was a tireless supporter of good musicians who recorded hundreds of tapes, some of which were released on small regional labels of his own like Rocko, Zynn and Ringo. Often he would record artists, then take the tapes to larger labels and try to get contracts. As a result, most of the material he recorded was never released. Incredible as it may seem, this Comstock lode of essential music—recorded at a time when cross-fertilization of country, rock and blues styles was at its creative peak—was never commercially released until the mid-Seventies, when a British company, Flyright Records, embarked on a massive project of assembling Miller's legacy. Of the twenty-five LPs from Miller's vaults so far, there's not a single turkey, no boring exercises in nostalgia or nit-picking academicism, just beautifully evocative music in the widest imaginable range of American musical styles.

The records were made with a professionalism and musician's savvy that compares very favorably to that of other small label productions of the time. Astonishing instrumental performances are delivered offhandedly, and ingenious devices like the use of slapped newspapers, cardboard boxes and wire brushes for percussion effects give the project a loose, exciting style.

Tag Along, the first anthology, starts off at

a blistering pace with Rocket Morgan's title track backed up by his other fine performances of "What You Gonna Do," and "Gonna Walk You Home." Miller's session drummer Warren Storm kicks on "Troubles Troubles," "No No," "Kansas City," "Oh Nell" and "So Long, So Long." Miller's crack session guitarist, Pee Wee Trahen, contributes "Baby Hurry Home," Honey Boy Allen can be heard on "She's Gone, She's Gone," Wonder Boy Travis is represented by "You Know Yeah" and Joe Mayfield's "Look Out Baby" rounds out the set.

Gonna Head for Home and *Rooster Crowed for Day* are anthologies of Miller's blues records, including performances from Leroy Washington and the legendary harmonica player Lazy Lester. Miller leased a number of sides to Excello records, particularly songs by his best-known artist, Slim Harpo, who has two albums in the series, *Blues Hangover* and *Got Love If You Want It.* James Moore had been touring under the name of Harmonica Slim and playing harp behind another Miller artist, Lightning Slim, before he began his recording career with Miller, who changed the stage name to Slim Harpo. Most of the tracks on these two albums are either alternate takes of Excello releases or previously unissued songs. (See separate Slim Harpo review.)

The Early Years beautifully showcases country bluesman Lightning Slim ("Lightnin' Blues" is tremendous). Slim's expressive voice and excellent guitar playing are offset wonderfully by Wild Bill Philips' harmonica.

Boppin' Tonight is a hot rockabilly album, one side led by Al Ferrier's soulful country singing, with Brian Ferrier's tremendous guitar playing featured, and the other under the name of Miller's session drummer Warren Storm.

Lazy Lester was Miller's best session harmonica player and was also a valuable and innovative percussionist. *They Call Me Lazy* is a raucous, fantastic LP—the high-intensity delivery on the instrumental "Lester's Stomp" and "Lover Not a Fighter," with its great bass vocal track, shows off Lester as one of Miller's hottest acts. Katie Webster was Miller's great session piano player, and *Whooee Sweet Daddy* shows she could whoop it up as a leader, too, especially on the terrific version of "Mama Don't Allow."

King of Louisiana Rockabilly showcases the early rocking of Cajun Johnny Jano, who's backed here by Guitar Gable's band augmented by Miller's session bassist Rufus Thibodeaux. *Louisiana Swamp Pop* collects more early rock and R&B sides, notably

King Karl's "Walkin' in the Park" and "Goodbye Whiskey" and the Big Bopper's first record, the kicking "Boogie Woogie."

The predominant music in the area Miller worked was the alternately wild and somber Cajun music, and accordionist Nathan Abshire was one of its greatest practitioners. *Nathan Abshire and the Pine Grove Boys* is an essential Cajun record. The flip side of Cajun is the Zydeco of the French Louisiana blacks, and *Zydeco Blues,* which presents a side of Clifton Chenier and another side split between Fernest and the Thunders, Rockin' Dupsee, and Marcel Douglas and the Entertainers, is another indispensable collection.

Rockin' Fever, *Boppin' It*, *Girl in the Tight Blue Jeans*, *Bayou Boogie* and *Too Hot to Handle* are more superb anthologies of early rock & roll, rockabilly and R&B tunes. The work of blues guitarist Leroy Washington, another homegrown Louisiana product, is collected on *Wild Cherry.*

Tribute to Harry Choates (the well-known Cajun fiddler) is a loving project spearheaded by Abe Manuel's vocals and Rufus Thibodeaux on fiddle and, of course, includes a great version of the classic "Joli Blon." Another fiddler, the young Doug Kershaw, stars on the *Rusty and Doug Kershaw* set. *Jimmy Newman and Al Terry,* the most recent record in the series, demonstrates the depth of the material: it's an amazing record. Jimmy Newman's side presents his great heartthrob country-ballad style ("Wondering" and "I'll Have to Burn the Letters" are stand-outs), while Al Terry comes on like a Cajun Hank Williams with "I Wonder If I Can Lose the Blues This Way," a medley of "Diggy Liggy Lo/Big Texas" and an amazing version of "What Can I Do."   — J.S.

ROGER MILLER
★ ★ ★ ★ **Golden Hits of Roger Miller** / **Smash (NA)**
★ ★ **Off the Wall** / **Wind. (NA)**
★ ★ ★ ★ **The Best of Roger Miller** / **Mer. (NA)**

These days Roger Miller is perhaps best known for being the proprietor of Nashville's largest and most garish hotel, the King of the Road Inn—a little slice of Vegas right in the heart of Music City, whose cocktail lounge symbolizes country-as-banal-pop music. But from 1964, when he scored with "Dang Me," to 1966, when his success more or less faded out with "You Can't Roller Skate in a Buffalo Herd," Miller was a genuine pop-country eccentric whose recordings both epitomized the warm folksiness of country's good side and quickly capitulated to the homogeneous hominess of its dark, pre-outlaw days.

"King of the Road" and "Kansas City Star"—both released in 1964—were the height of Miller's writing and performing. The former, sung in a choking twang, was the story of a hobo; the irony was deliberate and endearing, much more humane than the kind of thing Randy Newman would get away with ten years later. "Kansas City Star," which was a pun on that city's most famous newspaper, was a sign that his creativity was fading fast and that he at least suspected it. The song is a marvelous description of a television personality who's content to be a hero in a small environment and doesn't really want the pressure of the big time. As Miller sang it, there was no doubt that the metaphor was personal.

But thereafter, Miller's knack for the vernacular evaporated into the usual pop-country unctuousness and sanctimony. Sojourns at Columbia and John Denver's Windsong Records didn't help much. But for a couple of years Roger Miller was a working-class hero. — D.M.

THE STEVE MILLER BAND
★ ★ ★ **Children of the Future** / **Cap.** (1968)
★ ★ ★ ★ **Sailor** / **Cap.** (1968)
★ ★ ★ ★ **Brave New World** / **Cap.** (1969)
Diehards contend that this was the Steve Miller Band's prime, and it's awfully hard to dispute the point. Produced by Glyn Johns, with Boz Scaggs contributing songs and vocals, these albums are unusually "British," particularly for a late-Sixties San Francisco-based band. From the beginning, Miller knew his formula—well-produced bunches of songs that ran together like rock & roll suites—and it's the same method that has made him a multi-platinum artist in the early Eighties.

The blues orientation of the first album, *Children of the Future,* softened by Scaggs' wistful "Baby's Calling Me Home," contrasts effectively with the rocking *Sailor,* which was highlighted by Miller's satiric raver, "Living in the U.S.A.," and Scaggs' all-stops-out "Dime-a-Dance Romance." *Living in the U.S.A.* is a twofer compilation of *Sailor* and the initial *Children* set.

Brave New World, without Scaggs but with an often puzzling Boz-like presence, continues in the seamless blues-rock style of the first two albums, with "Space Cowboy" and the title tune aptly capturing Miller's cogent, if occasionally banal, world view.
★ ★ **Number Five** / **Cap.** (1970)
★ ★ ★ ★ **Living in the U.S.A.** / **Cap.** (1971)

★ ★ **Rock Love** / **Cap.** (1971)
★ ★ ★ **Recall the Beginning** / **Cap.** (1972)
★ ★ ★ ★ **Anthology** / **Cap.** (1972)
This is a long and sleepy middle period in which the formula became tired and passé. Enlivened by an occasional stand-out tune, like "Your Saving Grace," this is generally a boring string of records in which Miller dabs bits of the blues and country into his rock formula, but fails to bring it to a full pop shine.
★ ★ ★ **The Joker** / **Cap.** (1973)
★ ★ ★ ★ **Fly Like an Eagle** / **Cap.** (1976)
★ ★ ★ ★ **Book of Dreams** / **Cap.** (1977)
★ ★ ★ **Steve Miller Band's Greatest Hits** / **Cap.** (1978)
★ ★ **Circle of Love** / **Cap.** (1981)
★ ★ ★ **Abracadabra** / **Cap.** (1982)
The simple blues figure that defined "The Joker" was to become the pattern for the albums that would secure Miller's mass success. The album, though, lacks the immediacy of the single—something that can't be said of the two LPs that followed.

Eagle and *Dreams,* recorded at the same time, are perfectly constructed albums, regurgitating old riffs with an undeniably professional polish that makes their derivation almost meaningless. Such singles as "Rock 'n' Me" (recycled Free, from *Eagle*) and "Jet Airliner" (based on Cream's "Crossroads" riff, from *Dreams*) were obviously retreads, but that didn't diminish the assured grace with which they monopolized AM radio in 1977 and 1978. Like Fleetwood Mac, Jefferson Starship and Bob Seger, Miller was a prototype late-Seventies rock phenomenon: a rocker who honed his craft in the Sixties and bided his time until the market was right for his well-produced encyclopedia of riffs. Seamless and smooth in style and presentation, Miller has ascended with the confidence that comes from thinking that you've always belonged there. But as *Circle of Love* demonstrated, confidence isn't always enough to excuse you from repeating yourself beyond endurance.

Abracadabra suggests, on the other hand, that Miller's command of beat and music basics will sustain him for a long time to come. — J.B.M./D.M.

MILLINGTON
★ **Ladies on the Stage** / **U.A.** (1978)
The Millington sisters' first group, Fanny, seemed to be a prospective great feminist hope in the early Seventies. This album, recorded half a dozen years and half a dozen albums down the line, makes apparent their

real desire: to be pop stars at any cost. The tragedy is that their original ideas were so far superior to this formula Hollywood trash. — D.M.

FRANK MILLS
■ **Music Box Dancer** / Poly. (1979)
■ **The Frank Mills Album** / Poly. (1980)
■ **Sunday Morning Suite** / Poly. (1981)
Easy-listening piffle. — J.D.C.

STEPHANIE MILLS
★ ★ **For the First Time** / Mo. (1975) ¶
★ ★ ★ **Whatcha Gonna Do?** / 20th Cent. (1979)
★ ★ **Sweet Sensation** / 20th Cent. (1980)
★ ★ ★ **Stephanie** / 20th Cent. (1980)
The teenage Mills was a sensation as Dorothy in *The Wiz*, the 1975 Broadway play that revived *The Wizard of Oz*. Unfortunately, her big voice was a bit too stagy and immature to carry off a pop record. But her Twentieth Century LPs aren't pop: they're disco. And since bombast is at the heart of modern dance recordings, Mills now fares very well indeed. — D.M.

ROY MILTON
★ ★ ★ ★ ★ **Roy Milton and His Solid Senders** / Sonet (NA), Br. imp.
★ ★ ★ ★ **R.M. Blues** / Vivid (NA), Jap. imp.
★ ★ ★ **The Great Roy Milton** / United (NA)
★ ★ **Great R&B Oldies** / Blues Sp. (NA)
★ ★ **Instant Groove** / Black and Blue (NA), Br. imp.
Seminal late Forties/early Fifties rhythm & blues shouter, best known for the marvelous "R.M. Blues." Of all the West Coast R&B singer/bandleaders, only Amos Milburn comes close to Milton's perfection of the jump-band form. The Sonet album collects his most important sides—including "R.M. Blues"—while the Vivid, a very expensive Japanese import, has much of the same material, with a few differences that make the investment worthwhile for genuine devotees of the genre. The others are remakes and not nearly as good, though Johnny and Shuggie Otis appear on the Blues Spectrum and Billy Butler plays guitar on the Black and Blue. — D.M.

MINK DeVILLE
★ ★ ★ ★ **Mink DeVille** / Cap. (1977)
★ ★ ★ ★ **Return to Magenta** / Cap. (1978) ¶
Singer Willy DeVille is cleverly derivative—he sounds like everyone from Lou Reed to the Isley Brothers. The caliber of his material made the Mink DeVille albums an immediate punk/new wave stand-out, though DeVille's roots are more clearly in New York's seamy R&B past. The highlights are the first album's "Mixed Up Shook Up Girl," a streetwise romance, and *Magenta*'s wild dance item, "Soul Twist." — J.B.M.

THE MIRACLES
★ ★ ★ **Renaissance** / Tam. (1973)
★ ★ **Do It Baby** / Tam. (1974)
★ ★ ★ **Don't Cha Love It** / Tam. (1975)
★ ★ **City of Angels** / Tam. (1975)
★ ★ **Power of Music** / Tam. (1976)
★ ★ ★ **Miracles Greatest Hits** / Tam. (1977)
★ ★ ★ **Love Crazy** / Col. (1977)
★ ★ **Miracles** / Col. (1977)
Without Smokey Robinson, the Miracles have had difficulty achieving a comfortable identity. *Renaissance* finds Robinson's replacement, William Griffin, attempting to imitate his predecessor's vocal style. Yet with a variety of producers (Marvin Gaye, Willie Hutch, Freddie Perren) and some good songs, *Renaissance* is a commendable soft-soul effort. *Do It Baby* again features a host of producers and some not-too-distinctive material, with one exception: the title song, produced by Perren, became the group's first post-Robinson hit single.

Perren produced all of *Don't Cha Love It*, mostly in the vein of *Do It Baby*—fluffy ballads and midtempo songs with snappy hooks. Perren also produced *City of Angels*, a concept album with songs written exclusively by the group. The lyrics are often embarrassingly trite, but Perren's arrangements are among his best, including the Griffin-led "Love Machine," the Miracles' biggest hit. The last Motown album, *Power of Music*, is also their first in-group production since the Robinson days. It sports neither distinctive songs nor arrangements. The Columbia albums reflect this independence, but without scoring heavily either artistically or commercially. — J.MC.

MI-SEX
★ ★ **Computer Games** / Epic (1980)
★ ★ **Space Race** / Epic (1980)
Dreary Australian techno-pop. Not as listenable as Icehouse, which doesn't say much. — J.D.C.

MISSISSIPPI SHEIKS
★ ★ **Stop and Listen Blues** / Maml. (NA) ¶
Made up of Lonnie Chatmon (fiddle) and Walter Vinson (guitar), the Sheiks were a black Thirties string band that catered to white audiences. "Sitting on Top of the World" was the Sheiks' "hit," and Vinson,

who claimed to have written it, is also said to have taught Charlie McCoy mandolin.
— I.M.

MISSOURI
★ ★ **Welcome Two Missouri** / Poly. (1979)
Uninventive manipulation of Allmans/ Skynyrd Southern rock ready-mades.
— D.M.

ADAM MITCHELL
★ **Redhead in Trouble** / War. (1979)
Who's this mellow-voiced wimp of a singer/ songwriter think he is? An album so lax and laconic that the only trouble Mitchell could conceivably cause is mass narcosis. — R.P.

GUY MITCHELL
★ ★ **American Legend** / Emba. (NA)
Mitchell was for the most part a fairly conventional pop singer of the early Fifties. In 1956, however, he cut a version of "Singing the Blues" that deserved its No. 1 status, Mitchell's throbbing voice cutting past Mitch Miller's lollipop arrangement. That record was especially influential in England (where Tommy Steele immediately covered it), and though Mitchell never repeated his success (at least not artistically) he is fondly remembered for his one shining moment, anyhow.
— D.M.

JONI MITCHELL
★ ★ ★ **Joni Mitchell** / Rep. (1968)
★ ★ ★ ★ **Clouds** / Rep. (1969)
★ ★ ★ **Ladies of the Canyon** / Rep. (1970)
At first encounter, Joni Mitchell came on like an enlightened but somewhat precious folkie, writing striking vignettes of romance but presenting them in an uncomfortably sterile manner. The first album, *Joni Mitchell,* did show effectively the varied hues that her later work would reflect: an alluring boisterousness ("Night in the City"), a sure hand at storytelling ("Marcie") and an almost mythic concept of romantic love ("Michael from Mountain"). Her second album, *Clouds,* found her singing with more confidence, and the songs reveal a developing maturity. Such tunes as "I Don't Know Where I Stand" and "That Song about the Midway" capture the emotional confusions of weakening romanticism.

Ladies of the Canyon, while it can't boast the extraordinary consistency of the songwriting on *Clouds,* nonetheless find Mitchell expanding musically, with added instrumentation pushing her toward her most fruitful period.
★ ★ ★ ★ ★ **Blue** / Rep. (1971)

★ ★ ★ ★ **For the Roses** / Asy. (1972)
★ ★ ★ ★ ★ **Court and Spark** / Asy. (1974)
With *Blue,* Mitchell's lyrical outlook became much more entwined with her own emotions, quickly establishing her as the most significant of the confessional singer/ songwriters. Her delicate but ever-adventurous vocals, bolstered by the album's quiet but assured instrumentation, left the songs to speak for themselves. The giddy hopefulness of "All I Want," the bittersweet regret of "Last Time I Saw Richard" and the sheer romantic wisdom of the title tune spoke eloquently.

For the Roses, a musically artier set than *Blue,* dealt with the romantic dilemma from an overtly feminine standpoint, even for Mitchell. Though occasionally ponderous— "Judgment of the Moon and Stars," in particular, suffers from this—the sweeping lyricism of "Cold Blue Steel and Sweet Fire" and the quiet intimacy of "Lesson in Survival," as well as the independence of will in *Roses'* every groove, make it one of her best.

Court and Spark remains Mitchell's most musical album: here the lyrics were pared to the essential bone, and the music accentuated the words as never before. We not only felt the romance in her voice on "Help Me," but the well-paced music of Tom Scott and crew sent a shiver of recognition up our spines. The emotional rushes that such a union created, such as the breathless bridge of "The Same Situation," gave Mitchell's songs a power far beyond mere words.
★ ★ ★ **Miles of Aisles** / Asy. (1974)
★ ★ **The Hissing of Summer Lawns** / Asy. (1975)
★ ★ ★ ★ **Hejira** / Asy. (1976)
★ ★ ★ **Don Juan's Reckless Daughter** / Asy. (1977)
★ ★ ★ **Mingus** / Asy. (1979)
★ ★ ★ **Shadows and Light** / Asy. (1980)
★ ★ ★ **Wild Things Run Fast** / Gef. (1982)
Recorded with Tom Scott and the L.A. Express, *Miles of Aisles* placed Mitchell in a cushy concert situation, where she could prove her newfound vocal chops. And on the early tunes, like "Cactus Tree" and "Rainy Night House," the updating is welcome. "Jericho," a song that later appears on *Don Juan,* is also a highlight, with the sturdy pop feel of the best of *Court and Spark.* A secondary, if entertaining, package.

Summer Lawns finds Mitchell spreading her introspective wings with sadly mixed results. Some of the songs are embarrassingly overdrawn, as if Mitchell reasoned that her stories could be better explained by too many details rather than a few well-chosen gems. The jazz feel she was developing was much better applied on *Hejira,* an album obsessed with lonesome revelry on a mythic and romantic highway. Here, Mitchell's increasingly airy voice blended with Jaco Pastorius' bass to create some sweeping moments of revelation. Despite an occasional lyrical gaffe, such songs as "Refuge of the Road" and "The Hissing of Summer Lawns" effectively embodied the mean contradictions with which an aging romantic must deal.

Don Juan's Reckless Daughter, a double album that should have been a single disc, seems to be another transitional LP, choking as it is with overblown ideas and an obsessively loose musical framework. *Mingus* is Joni's tribute to the dying jazz star; *Shadows and Light* was a good live set. Neither is among her more revelatory work. *Wild Things Run Fast* is a dignified set of songs about the problems of aging; in her diarist mode Mitchell is most eloquent on "Chinese Cafe" and "You Dream Flat Tires." But though Mitchell might be regretfully inconsistent of late, the spirit of romance and artistic wanderlust that percolates through her work makes her an important standard-bearer in the confessional singer/songwriter genre. — J.B.M.

PRINCE PHILLIP MITCHELL
★ ★ **Make It Good** / Atl. (1978)
★ **Top of the Line** / Atl. (NA)
Disco's pretensions to royalism meet Isaac Hayes–style confessional fantasies. This is sort of like Curtis Mayfield without the sincerity, especially on Mitchell's one genuine Good Idea: "Star in the Ghetto" from *Make It Good.* But the musical history of the Seventies proves nothing if not that the distance between good ideas and good music isn't a gap so much as a chasm. — D.M.

WILLIE MITCHELL
★ ★ ★ **Hold It** / Hi (NA)
★ ★ ★ **Best of Willie Mitchell** / Hi (NA)
★ ★ ★ **Willie Mitchell Live** / Hi (NA)
Mitchell has never had any hits of his own, and these albums contain only pedestrian funk. He is of interest chiefly as the producer of Al Green, Ann Peebles and many of the other Hi soul artists, as a first-rate mainstream-soul songwriter/producer and as the leader of the Hi Rhythm Section. — D.M.

MIZZ
★ **Mizz** / Casa. (NA)
You don't suppose they mean Ms., do you? Talk about blows against the empire . . . — D.M.

MOBERLYS
★ ★ ★ **The Moberlys / Safety First Records (1980)**
High-spirited homemade rock and soft pop from defunct Seattle band (named for school board president) which did much to spark revival of area's local scene in 1978–79. Probably no more inspired or timeless than scores of similar regional discs released, and barely distributed, at the end of the Seventies. Compositions show unusual fluidity, instrumental sound demonstrates band has done homework and tunes by band's Jim Basnight are illuminating examples of what pop rock sounds like to someone who came of adolescence during decade. Every city's rock scene deserved a band like the Moberlys, and it's likely that most had one. Side two is a live recording of unusual clarity.
— G.A.

MOBY GRAPE
★ ★ ★ ★ ★ **Moby Grape** / Col. (1967)
★ **Wow** / Col. (1968) ¶
★ ★ ★ **Great Grape** / Col. (1971) ¶
Moby Grape made only one good album, but what an album it is. That its debut LP is as fresh and exhilarating today as it was when it exploded out of San Francisco during 1967's summer of love is testament to the band's visionary concept of eclectic American music. Swirling within *Moby Grape* are elements of jazz, country, blues and plain old raveup rock & roll. Yet all of it is so well integrated into the group's execution (five members who all sing, write and play brilliantly) that it's impossible to pigeonhole any of the album's thirteen songs. Lead guitarist Jerry Miller and bassist Bob Mosley propelled the band instrumentally, but the two rhythm guitarists, Skip Spence and Peter Lewis, and drummer Don Stevenson also contributed heavily.

The Grape's rapid downhill slide remains one of the mysterious tragedies of the late Sixties. *Wow* was a complete failure, a double album that included a "bonus" jam LP that made absolutely no sense in terms of the group's strongest point: tight song construction. A half-dozen other albums are no longer available; they vary from solid country- and blues-influenced rock to sheer musical confusion. *Great Grape* is a moderately well-chosen anthology, but that first LP is really the one that matters. — B.A.

MODEL T SLIM
★ ★ ★ **Somebody Done Voodoo the Hoodoo Man** / Flyr. (1980)
Harp player influenced by both Sonny Boy

Williamsons, recorded in 1966–67. His version of the Junior Wells title classic is closer to delta blues than urban R&B. — D.M.

THE MODELS
■ **Yes with My Body / Wind. (1980)**
No, from my heart. — D.M.

THE MODELS
★ ★ ★ **AlphaBravoCharlieDeltaEcho . . . / Mush. (1980), Aust. imp.**
★ ★ ★ **Local and/or General / Mush. (1981), Aust. imp.**
Pop nouveau from Melbourne, Australia. Quirky rhythms, synthesizers and effects that are not overused, and glimpses of a sense of humor that is all too rare among those who graduate from art school into rock & roll. — S.M.

MODERN LOVERS
★ ★ ★ ★ **Modern Lovers / Beserk. (1976)**
★ ★ ★ **Modern Lovers Live / Beserk. (1977)**
Lead singer Jonathan Richman, a precursor of the late-Seventies new wave, is a perfectly innocent rock visionary whose best work is represented here on sides originally recorded in 1971 for Warner Bros. John Cale's production on *Modern Lovers* lends an ominous undercurrent to such songs as "Road Runner," a charmingly gauche tribute to AM radio, and "Pablo Picasso," a wryly corny lament about the rock artist and his attempt to attain respect. Richman went on to a solo career so ingenuous it became simply silly, while keyboard player Jerry Harrison joined up with Talking Heads. The live album is of similar vintage, though, and quite listenable. — D.M.

MO-DETTES
★ . . . **The Story So Far . . . / Deram (1980), Br. imp.**
Fashionable girl group, better live than on this thinly produced outing. Perhaps they'd be better off as models, where the material is already tailored. — ML.H.

ESSRA MOHAWK
★ ★ ★ **Essra Mohawk / Elek. (1974)**
★ ★ **Essra / Priv. (1977) ¶**
Better-than-average female singer/songwriter whose most distinctive characteristic is a bizarre streak she picked up from a brief Sixties stint with the Mothers of Invention. *Essra Mohawk* is her best work. — J.S.

MOLLY HATCHET
★ ★ ★ ★ **Molly Hatchet / Epic (1978)**
★ ★ ★ ★ **Flirtin' with Disaster / Epic (1979)**
★ ★ ★ **Beatin' the Odds / Epic (1980)**
★ ★ **Take No Prisoners / Epic (1981)**
★ ★ ★ **No Guts . . . No Glory / Epic (1983)**
No sooner did they emerge from the Jacksonville, Florida, club circuit than Molly Hatchet stepped into the boogie shoes of Lynyrd Skynyrd. Not because they had as much to say, mind you, but because Molly Hatchet came right to the point, matching gutsy guitar work with a hard-core boogie beat. It wasn't exactly a triumph of brawn over brain, but it came close. Unfortunately, singer Danny Joe Brown left the band after *Flirtin' with Disaster,* and his replacement, Jimmy Farrar, only partially filled the gap. In the post-Brown albums, the songs seem more like an excuse for jamming; too bad it was so sodden and cliché-ridden. By *Take No Prisoners,* the band had become pompous and product-oriented, a sort of boogie version of Angel. The sound improved considerably, however, when Brown returned for *No Guts.* — J.D.C.

THE MOMENTS
★ ★ ★ **Look at Me / Stang (1975)**
★ ★ **Moments with You / Stang (1977)**
★ ★ ★ **Patty / Stang (NA)**
★ ★ ★ **Sharp / Stang (NA)**
★ ★ ★ ★ **The Moments' Greatest Hits / Stang (NA)**
The Moments deserve better. For many years they've kept a steady string of hits on the charts in a genre (sweet soul) where groups come and go in the flicker of one hit 45. While the memory of faded groups like the Delfonics and Stylistics lingers, the Moments remain almost unknown outside of their primary audience: urban teens. Their clout is narrow, but intense. Not only is their list of soul hits enviable, but the group also writes and produces much of its own material, often with quite interesting results.

Though their 45s are impressive and lots of fun, the albums tend to be spotty, with a couple of exceptions: the most outstanding is *Greatest Hits,* which only recently was restored to the Stang catalogue. The other superior LP, *My Thing,* is unavailable. Of what's left, *Look at Me* features the frothy but delightful "Girls," as well as the creamy smooth title song. The other LPs are expendable. Anyway, if you've read this far, you probably already have them all, including *The Moments Live at the New York State Women's Prison.* — J.MC.

EDDIE MONEY

★ ★ ★ **Eddie Money / Col. (1977)**
★ ★ **Life for the Taking / Col. (1978)**
★ ★ **Playing for Keeps / Col. (1980)**
★ ★ **No Control / Col. (1982)**
Money sings in the hard-rock mold of Bob
Seger and Bruce Springsteen, although with
a lighter, more pop feel. His self-titled debut
album earned him two of 1978's best rock
hits, "Baby Hold On" and "Two Tickets to
Paradise." But subsequent albums fail to fol-
low up the success of the debut, and "I
Think I'm in Love," while a Top Thirty hit,
felt like a desperation move. — D.M.

T. S. MONK

★ ★ **House of Music / Mirage/Atl. (1980)**
The few remaining pop-culture democrats
among us will be gratified to note that,
though T.S. is the son of Thelonius, *House
of Music* is effectively an argument against
aristocracy. At least, that is, to the extent
that it demonstrates the old saw that while
rhythm may be natural as hell, imagination
isn't necessarily hereditary. In his abandonment of be-bop for boogie, the new Monk
may have earned a few contemporary kudos,
but he hasn't created anything that will last
nearly so long as the least of his old man's
creations . . . or the best of his disco-
oriented brethren's, for that matter. — D.M.

THE MONKEES

★ ★ ★ ★ **The Monkees' Greatest Hits / Ari.
(1969)**
★ ★ **More Greatest Hits of the Monkees /
Ari. (1982)**
Okay, the Monkees were TV's synthetic response to the Beatles, a mass-produced imitation of something relatively natural and
important. That doesn't mean they weren't
good—in fact, the group sometimes got excellent material and production from a variety of sources, notably Neil Diamond,
Tommy Boyce and Bobby Hart, and group
member Michael Nesmith. As drippy as
Davy Jones' ballads could be, "Another
Pleasant Valley Sunday," "I'm a Believer,"
"(I'm Not Your) Steppin' Stone" and several
of the other upbeat singles rank with the
best pop rock of the mid-Sixties era, which
is saying something. With the exception of
"Valleri," however, *More* goes too far.
— D.M.

MONOCHROME SET

★ ★ ★ **Strange Boutique / Dindisc (1980)**
★ ★ ★ **Love Zombies / Dindisc (1980), Br.
imp.**
Debonair art-school rock from suave British

bunch. Clever lyrics, smooth arrangements
employing Latin dance rhythms, and relaxed
vocalizing, but still more interesting than
stimulating. *Love Zombies* offers more enthusiasm than the reserved *Strange Boutique;*
both are for special tastes. — I.R.

BILL MONROE

★ ★ ★ ★ **Mr. Bluegrass / MCA (NA)**
★ ★ ★ **Bluegrass Ramble / MCA (1962)**
★ ★ ★ **Bluegrass Special / MCA (1963)**
★ ★ ★ ★ **I'll Meet You in Church Sunday
Morning / MCA (1964)**
★ ★ ★ **Bluegrass Instrumentals / MCA
(1965)**
★ ★ ★ ★ **The High, Lonesome Sound of Bill
Monroe / MCA (1966)**
★ ★ ★ **Bluegrass Time / MCA (1967)**
★ ★ ★ ★ **Bill Monroe's Greatest Hits /
MCA (1968)**
★ ★ ★ ★ **Bill and Charlie Monroe / MCA
(1969)**
★ ★ ★ **Voice from on High / MCA (1969)**
★ ★ ★ **Kentucky Bluegrass / MCA (1970)**
★ ★ ★ **Bluegrass Style / Cor. (1970)**
★ ★ ★ **Bill Monroe's Country Music Hall of
Fame / MCA (1971)**
★ ★ ★ **Road of Life / MCA (NA)**
★ ★ ★ ★ **Uncle Pen / MCA (1972)**
★ ★ ★ ★ ★ **Bean Blossom / MCA (1973)**
★ ★ ★ **Bill Monroe Sings Bluegrass Body
and Soul / MCA (NA)**
★ ★ ★ **Bill Monroe and His Bluegrass Boys
/ Cor. (NA)**
★ ★ ★ **Bill Monroe Sings Country Songs /
Cor. (NA)**
★ ★ ★ **Weary Traveller / MCA (NA)**
They call Monroe the father of bluegrass not
because he invented that variant of country
& western, but because he was its most ad-
venturous pioneer. The Kentucky native
began performing in the mid-Twenties with
his brother Charlie as the Monroe Brothers.
The album *Bill and Charlie Monroe* represents their early work, and some of Monroe's best. Bill played what he called "potato
bug mandolin"; Charlie played "houn' dog
guitar." Their first hit, written by Bill, was
"Kentucky Waltz" (1934), which gained
them and their backing group, the Bluegrass
Boys, a wide country audience. Monroe's instrumental style was characterized by peculiar tuning and intricate timing; among his
best-known instrumentals are "Get Up
John," "Blue Grass Ramble" and "Memories
of You."

Bill went solo in 1938 (Charlie retired
after World War II) and joined the Grand
Ole Opry a year later. He and the Bluegrass
Boys were among the troupe's featured art-

ists through the Sixties. The Bluegrass Boys were one of country's seminal groups, serving as a training ground for Lester Flatt, Earl Scruggs, Clyde Moody, Don Reno and many others. Monroe's best-known tune, "Blue Moon of Kentucky," was one of Elvis Presley's first great Sun records. Other memorable Monroe compositions include "Uncle Pen," "Gotta Travel On" and "Cheyenne."

Of the albums still available, the most exceptional are *Bean Blossom,* which is live, the best format for bluegrass; *I'll Meet You in Church,* a fine gospel recording; and several compilation albums of classic material (all rated four stars). Monroe's other material is spotty and sentimental, but at his best he is the invigorating spirit of bluegrass itself. — D.M.

CHRIS MONTAN
★ **Any Minute Now / 20th Cent. (1980)**
Writer/singer so slick and tasteful you'll want to strangle him before you've heard a full side. — D.M.

THE MONTCLAIRS
★ ★ ★ **Dreaming out of Season / Paula (1972)**
A soft-soul group from East St. Louis, the Montclairs made only one album, which is given over almost exclusively to creamy, falsetto ballads—all written by group member Phil Perry. Pre-disco teenage love music. — J.MC.

THE JAMES MONTGOMERY BAND
★ ★ **The James Montgomery Band / Is. (1976)**
★ ★ **Duck Fever / Waterh. (1978)** ¶
Long, repetitious, riff-dominated rhythm & blues by this Boston-based bar band squander Allen Toussaint's carefully tailored production on *James Montgomery Band.* Montgomery's smoothly nonchalant vocals work, but his capable harmonica playing is strangely scarce. There's a bit more harp on *Duck Fever,* but not enough to relieve the monotony entirely. — C.W.

LITTLE BROTHER MONTGOMERY
★ ★ **Farro Street Jive / Folk. (NA)**
★ ★ ★ **Home Again / Match. (NA)**
★ ★ **Tasty Blues / Prest. (NA)**
★ ★ ★ **Deep South Piano / Story. (1975)**
★ ★ **Blues / Folk. (NA)**
★ ★ **Church Songs / Folk. (NA)**
★ ★ ★ **Bajes Copper Station / Blues Bea. (NA)**
Blues and gospel singer/pianist started out in New Orleans and the Louisiana delta before moving to Chicago, where he established himself on his own and as an accompanist. — J.S.

MONTROSE
★ **Montrose / War. (1974)**
★ ★ **Paper Money / War. (1974)**
★ ★ **Warner Brothers Presents . . . Montrose / War. (1975)**
★ ★ ★ **Jump on It / War. (1976)**
★ ★ ★ **Open Fire / War. (1978)**
Considering Ronnie Montrose's rather impressive credentials as a guitarist (he's worked with Herbie Hancock, Van Morrison and Edgar Winter), the music he's made with his namesake band is disappointing. The group has had two incarnations, the first (represented on *Montrose* and *Paper Money*) featuring Sammy Hagar on lead vocals. *Montrose* is rehashed Mountain without even an update, although Ronnie is no Leslie West, and neither is Hagar. *Paper Money* tries to sound more progressively English and winds up equally redundant in a different field.

Stage two followed Hagar's departure, the 1975 breakup of the original unit and the reformation later that year. The new singer, Bob James, was obviously chosen for his resemblance to Hagar. Like its predecessors, *Presents* is faceless, unimaginative and plodding—ordinary in the extreme. *Jump on It* and *Open Fire* are improvements. The former is uptempo hard rock; the latter benefits from Edgar Winter's production, which adds funk and an ethereal touch. Nothing blindingly original, but competence has been achieved at last. — A.N.

MONTY PYTHON
★ ★ ★ **Matching Tie and Handkerchief / Ari. (1973)**
★ ★ **The Album of the Soundtrack of the Trailer of the Film of Monty Python and the Holy Grail / Ari. (1975)**
★ ★ ★ **The Worst of Monty Python / Bud. (1976)** ¶
★ ★ **Live at City Center / Ari. (1976)**
★ ★ **Life of Brian / War. (1979)**
★ ★ **Contractual Obligation Album / Ari. (1980)**
Puns, transvestites, double talk, studio effects and a smattering of obscenity from a clutch of English university grads. The live album's sound is very muddled and *Holy Grail* is dumb (though that's not true of the film), but *Matching Tie* contains a couple of bits of timeless genius: a cheese shop that contains no cheese and a marital squabble over rat-flavored pie. *Life of Brian* is the

soundtrack from the group's hit movie; *Contractual Obligation* describes itself. The early work on the Buddah set is Monty Python's best, although it may be too English (in approach and content) to be intelligible to non-Anglophilic Americans. — K.T.

THE MOODY BLUES
★ ★ **Go Now: The Moody Blues #1 / Lon. (1965)**
This album is now interesting mainly for the wonderful hit single "Go Now" and its near-hit followup. "From the Bottom of My Heart." The other ten songs are as thin and inept as anything by the Dave Clark Five. But as a souvenir of young adolescence, this timeworn LP is irreplaceable magic.
★ ★ ★ **Days of Future Passed / Deram (1967)** ¶
★ ★ **In Search of the Lost Chord / Deram (1968)** ¶
★ ★ **On the Threshold of a Dream / Deram (1969)** ¶
★ ★ **To Our Children's Children's Children / Thresh. (1970)** ¶
★ ★ **A Question of Balance / Thresh. (1970)** ¶
★ ★ **Every Good Boy Deserves Favour / Thresh. (1971)** ¶
★ ★ **Seventh Sojourn / Thresh. (1972)** ¶
★ ★ **This Is the Moody Blues / Thresh. (1974)** ¶
★ **Moody Blues Caught Live Plus Five / Lon. (1977)** ¶
★ ★ **Octave / Lon. (1978)** ¶
★ **Long Distance Voyager / Thresh. (1981)**
Slightly reorganized, the Moodys reappeared in 1967 with the landmark *Days of Future Passed,* the first of many attempts to unite the pop group with the symphony orchestra. Pretentious as it was (especially the spoken "poetic" introductions), it also has moments of real splendor in "Nights in White Satin" and "Tuesday Afternoon," both hits. Like all the group's material, the songs sound better with age.

The other albums follow a similar pattern. By mixing puerile philosophies (best/worst example: "Om" from *Lost Chord*) with easy, memorable melodies, and pleasant English vocal harmonies with the lessons learned from the London Festival Orchestra (expressed on Mellotron), the Moody Blues became gurus for a whole generation of illicit undergraduate pot smokers. Most of these sold millions, but contain little real imagination. "Ride My See-Saw," from *Chord,* is one exception, but the ideas came to a virtual dead end with *Seventh Sojourn,* and what's followed since the group's recent re-

grouping is dispensable, even on these pretentious terms. *This Is* is a good compilation for the uninitiated. — A.N.

EVE MOON
★ ★ ★ **Eve Moon / Cap. (1981)**
New York street singer/songwriter garnered her recording contract on the basis of her folk-oriented sidewalk sets (recorded on *Stars of the Streets,* a French-issued anthology of Manhattan's pavement-pounding artists). Her Capitol album is quite different—basic, rattling rock & roll. Moon's quirky but memorable songs make a nice peg for the change in style, so natural it almost seems planned that way. — R.P.

MOONDOG
★ ★ ★ ★ **Moondog 1 / Col. (NA)**
Louis Hardin, a.k.a. Moondog, is a blind musician/composer who built up a reputation for standing on streetcorners in midtown Manhattan dressed in archaic European garb. The marvelously eclectic symphonic work on this album is an obscure but worthwhile find. His melodic structures are classically inspired, while his use of percussion suggests a relationship with the more outside elements of rock and jazz rhythms. Moondog successfully sued Alan Freed in the late Fifties, forcing Freed to change the name of his radio show, originally called *Moondog's Rock and Roll Party.*
— J.S.

THE MOONGLOWS
★ ★ ★ ★ **Moonglows / Chess (1977)** ¶
One of the greatest R&B vocal groups of the Fifties, led by Bobby Lester and Harvey Fuqua. (Fuqua went on to become an important Motown producer/arranger/writer.) This doesn't contain "Sincerely," their huge 1955 hit, but it does have "Ten Commandments of Love," the 1959 smash, and a gaggle of other smooth, soulful croonings, including a previously unreleased gem, "Sweeter than Words." Fun and fundamental. — D.M.

DOROTHY MOORE
★ ★ ★ **Misty Blue / Mal. (1976)**
★ ★ **Dorothy Moore / Mal. (1977)**
★ ★ **Once Moore with Feeling / Mal. (1979)**
"Misty Blue" is one of those records—like Barbara Mason's "Yes I'm Ready"—that overpowers with its starkness, directness and simplicity. The album that followed up the single showed that Moore has the potential to do more with ballads, though mediocre material is a definite problem. The other two

LPs are a bit more pop-oriented, and also rather aimless. — R.G.

JACKIE MOORE

★ ★ ★ ★ **Make Me Feel Like a Woman / Kayv. (NA)**
★ ★ ★ **I'm on My Way / Col. (1979)**
★ ★ ★ **With Your Love / Col. (1979)**
Though Moore's best work was done for Atlantic ("Precious Precious") and is currently out of print, *Make Me Feel* serves her well. She is a blustery vocalist, and producer Brad Shapiro combines hardy lyrics with some tasteful, if not completely imaginative, arrangements. The Columbia albums are more polished but still soulful. — J.MC./D.M.

MELBA MOORE

★ **I Got Love / Mer. (1970)**
★ ★ **Peach Melba / Bud. (1975)** ¶
★ **This Is It / Bud. (1976)**
★ **Melba / Bud. (1976)**
★ **A Portrait of Melba / Bud. (1977)**
★ **Melba / Epic (1978)**
★ **Burn / Epic (1979)**
★ **Closer / Epic (NA)**
★ **Dancin' with Melba / Bud. (NA)**
★ **What a Woman Needs / EMI (1980)**
Melba Moore screeches, even more than Minnie Riperton did. One's tolerance for her albums depends on one's tolerance for the shrill. Nightclub cognoscenti seem to love it. *Peach Melba* does have a couple of reasonably modulated ballads, and the title tune of the Van McCoy disco album. *This Is It,* is reasonably pleasant. But her version of "Lean on Me" (the McCoy version) and "The Long and Winding Road" are nightmares. — R.G.

R. STEVIE MOORE

★ ★ ★ ★ **Phonography / HP Music (1976)**
★ ★ ★ **Stance / HP Music (1978)**
★ ★ ★ **Delicate Tension / HP Music (1979)**
Moore epitomizes the do-it-yourself philosophy, recording these remarkable records single-handedly at home on four-track machines and releasing them himself. He also works in a peculiar corner of pop music space where the alien progressive rock strains of Eno and Fripp, the prankish gags of the Residents, and wholesome American Sixties rock & roll intersect. What's even more peculiar is that for the most part it works.

Phonography is the most intriguing of the three records here. Moore originally recorded it as a demo disc, pressed up a hundred copies and sent it to record companies in 1976 (he has since reissued it in quantity). What those record companies thought of an album that featured everything from proto-new-wave rockers, stark guitar-and-voice ballads, *The Andy Griffith Show* TV theme, and snippets of Moore reciting biographical information has never been known. *Stance*—a sixteen-minute mini-LP—and *Delicate Tension* sound a little more polished but are no less fascinating. Moore's records are a refreshing experience—if you can find them. — D.F.

SCOTTY MOORE

★ ★ **Scotty Moore Plays the Big Elvis Presley Hits / Epic (NA), Br. imp.**
No one has a right to these songs more than Moore, who played on all of them ("That's All Right," "Hound Dog," "Heartbreak Hotel"). But if there's much doubt left in anyone's mind who really created the Elvis sound, one lesson should convince you that Moore wasn't the leader: these renditions are anything but outrageous. What brings them down, in the end, is their conservatism, as though Moore can't imagine where to go except to follow (softly) behind Elvis. Not a bad route to travel, though it's a road best taken noisily. — D.M.

TIM MOORE

★ ★ **Tim Moore / Asy. (1974)**
★ ★ **Behind the Eyes / Asy. (1975)**
★ **White Shadows / Asy. (1977)**
★ **High Contrast / Asy. (NA)**
This pop singer/songwriter won at the 1974 American Song Festival with "Charmer," from his first album, *Tim Moore,* a fine blend of MOR and rock with a Philly soul slant. The third and fourth LPs, *White Shadows* and *High Contrast,* show a marked decrease in song quality. — S.H.

JOHNNY MOPED

★ ★ **Cycledelic / Chis. (1978), Br. imp.**
Filthy bunch of spotty British punks with great names (Slimey Toad, the Berk Brothers, J. Moped) and no musical talent. A good deal of spirit and scatological humor don't adequately compensate for their basic badness; even the genealogy on the inner sleeve which draws connections to Chrissy Hyde (sic) fails to excuse them from songs like "Wee Wee" and "Darling Let's Have Another Baby." The only good laugh here is a painful version of Chuck Berry's "Little Queenie." Maybe drunks with no sense of pitch would find this good stupid fun; then again, maybe not. — I.R.

GAYLE MORAN

■ **I Loved You Then, I Love You Now** / War. (1979)

Bloated art-pop pomposities. Schmaltzy romantic pop posing as insightful sensitivity. The worst sort of est-ian cretinism. — D.M.

ANTHONY MORE

★ ★ ★ ★ **Flying Doesn't Help** / Quango (1979), Br. imp.

★ ★ ★ ★ **World Service** / Do-It (1981), Br. imp.

In the first half of the Seventies, More was one-third of the unique Slapp Happy; when that band folded into Henry Cow after several collaborative projects, More headed off on his own. These two recent solo albums are stunning, idiosyncratic works that are roughly describable as rock music, although More is not constrained by the conventions of the form. Sharing some common ground with John Cale, and Brian Eno's early solo work, More uses found sounds and complex structures to weave intense and moody songs that he sings in a variety of voices.

Flying Doesn't Help employs insidiously catchy melodies to clothe some fairly dark lyrical messages and adds audio vérité noises for flavoring. *World Service* offers more challenging music and lyrics and less prettiness to make it palatable, but succeeds as strongly as *Flying*. More is an experimental and convincing talent who has a lot to say on these records. — I.R.

MORNINGSTAR

■ **Morningstar** / Col. (1978) ¶

■ **Venus** / Col. (NA)

Purely wretched hard rock, the sort that's too mindless even to be pretentious. — D.M.

GARRETT MORRIS

■ **Saturday Night Sweet** / MCA (1980) ¶

At last *Saturday Night Live*'s original Token Negro achieves full equality with Chevy Chase—Garrett insists on singing with complete ineptitude, too. And he isn't funny, either! — D.M.

VAN MORRISON

★ ★ ★ ★ **Blowin' Your Mind** / Bang (1967)

★ ★ ★ ★ ★ **Astral Weeks** / War. (1968)

★ ★ ★ ★ ★ **Moondance** / War. (1970)

★ ★ ★ ★ **Van Morrison, His Band and Streetchoir** / War. (1970)

★ ★ ★ ★ **Best of Van Morrison** / Bang (1970)

★ ★ ★ ★ **Tupelo Honey** / War. (1971)

★ ★ ★ ★ **St. Dominic's Preview** / War. (1972)

★ **Hard Nose the Highway** / War. (1973)

★ ★ ★ **T.B. Sheets** / Bang (1972)

★ ★ ★ **It's Too Late to Stop Now** / War. (1974)

★ ★ ★ ★ **Veedon Fleece** / War. (1974)

★ ★ ★ **A Period of Transition** / War. (1977)

★ ★ ★ **Wavelength** / War. (1978)

★ ★ ★ ★ **Into the Music** / War. (1979)

★ ★ ★ ★ **Common One** / War. (1981)

★ ★ ★ ★ **Beautiful Vision** / War. (1982)

★ ★ ★ ★ **Inarticulate Speech of the Heart** / War. (1983)

Van Morrison has never been a terribly successful public artist, although he has occasionally sold a great many records, and some of his songs are well known. But his influence on musicians and critics has been enormous ever since he emerged from Belfast in 1966 with his band. Them, and its rock & roll masterpiece, "Gloria." (Even then, Van was upstaged; the Shadows of Knight's near-identical version made the American Top Ten.)

With Them, Morrison was a rough and tumble R&B singer—he sports a black eye on the cover of their second LP—who was capable of bringing Irish soul to Bob Dylan's "It's All Over Now Baby Blue" and demonic frenzy to the great harmonica-driven instrumental "Mystic Eyes." Since he's been on his own, Morrison's soul sources have deepened and expanded, so that he now seems less a great white R&B singer than like one of the very few rock artists who has invented a personal emotional equivalent of the blues.

The Bang sides were his post-Them solo debut, which produced one terrifically catchy single, "Brown-Eyed Girl" (1967), and several dreamy, Latin-rhythm personal songs, most notably "T.B. Sheets," "Ro Ro Rosey" and "He Ain't Give You None," all remarkably erotic in the best blues tradition. (The other Bang LPs are merely reworkings of the debut.)

Following the death of Morrison's producer, Bert Berns, the owner of Bang but best known as a soul writer/producer, Van moved to Warner Bros. Already living in America (*Blowin'* was made while Van lived in Cambridge, Massachusetts; he's since spent time in Woodstock, New York; Marin County, California; and L.A.). Morrison began to see himself as an immigrant everyman with a heavily mystical streak: he calls the result "Caledonia soul." *Astral Weeks,* a gorgeous song-cycle that appeared in 1968, was the first manifestation of this style. The record is nearly perfect, deeply emotive, elusively lyrical, musically both powerful and gentle.

Moondance was closer to straight soul, but the compact construction of songs like "Stoned Me," "Moondance," "Crazy Love" and the rest couldn't hide their searching spiritual concerns. *His Band and Streetchoir,* which contains his only Warners Top Ten hit, "Domino," and a pair of minor successes, "Blue Money" and "Call Me Up in Dreamland," is musically based in the sweet romantic soul of Curtis Mayfield and Smokey Robinson, though there is a devilish undercurrent of Fats Domino's New Orleans music as well.

Tupelo Honey was his last album of brief songs and contains some of his finest moments, particularly the hard-rocking "Wild Night." By now, however, Morrison was on the track of a truly personal voice, extremely singular, with roots in jazz as well as R&B. Always a part of his sound, these elements came to an exhilarating head in *St. Dominic's Preview.* That album's best songs—particularly the growling "Listen to the Lion" and the heart-wrenching "St. Dominic's Preview" and "Almost Independence Day"—are as soul-searching and soulful as any modern music.

Hard Nose the Highway was a failed sidestep, a compromise between the visionary demands of Morrison's work and his desire for a broad-based audience, a compromise more nearly perfected by *It's Too Late to Stop Now,* which weaves together his entire career, beginning with "Gloria," into a seamless act of will and devotion. *Veedon Fleece,* released in 1974, was more idiosyncratic—half a sendup of the superstardom that had eluded him, half a metaphysical voyage into his ancestry as a man and an artist. Its lack of public acceptance apparently pushed Morrison into a three-year retreat, broken by *A Period of Transition,* which more than lived up to its name. There are hints (notably "It Fills You Up" and "Heavy Connection") of a final, successful rapprochement between accessibility and vision, but the record finally falls short of its goal.

Into the Music completely realized the implications of his previous two albums, *A Period of Transition* and the more successful but still spotty *Wavelength.* It is an erotic/religious cycle of songs that culminates in the greatest side of music Morrison has created since *Astral Weeks.* Side two begins with a lurching yet somehow majestic Morrison original "Angelou," and concludes with

a version of "It's All in the Game," an Irish ballad written in 1914 (which had already been given an R&B interpretation in the Fifties by Tommy Edwards). In between, Morrison simply cuts loose all the vocal skyrockets at his command and lets the music surge and flow and ooze around him. This is shockingly transcendent stuff, absolutely intoxicating in its use of dynamics from a whisper to thunder, not forgetting silence itself.

Common One can become tedious because it never quite gains that height of soulfulness. Still, it's not easily dismissed: any record that features Morrison singing about "William Blake and the Eternals," a knowing equation with James Brown and the Famous Flames, contains mysteries whose depths are worth plumbing, even if the cost is sometimes an encounter with sententiousness.

Beautiful Vision is more focused than *Common One;* while it is still spiritually centered, it makes the most use of jazz rhythms since *Astral Weeks.* Not quite so radiant as *Into the Music, Vision* nevertheless represents the continuing vitality of Van Morrison.

Inarticulate Speech of the Heart is a largely instrumental album steeped in Irish folk and jazz allusions. At its best, this music has a soaring transcendence. At worst, it descends toward the banalities of fusion.

But all of this is of little consequence for those who know Morrison's songs and his singing. The bass playing of Richard Davis on *Astral Weeks,* which predates jazz-rock fusion by four years; Jack Schroer's beautiful sax work on several of the early Warner Bros. records; the constant drive of Morrison's songs, which often belies their tender sentiments—all mark him as an artist to be reckoned with. His influence has held considerable sway over such contemporaries as the Band, and he has in fact spawned a whole school of rock singers, which includes such notables as Bruce Springsteen, Bob Seger, Graham Parker, Frankie Miller and Thin Lizzy's Phil Lynott. Yet none of these has yet taken the spiritual basis of rock and R&B and the blues so far into an almost religious concept. Van Morrison remains unique, a great artist crying to be heard.
— D.M.

THE MORWELLS
★ ★ ★ **Best Of / Nighth. (1981)**
Such early Morwells singles as "Crab Race" and "Crazy Baldhead" were idiosyncratic diamonds in the rough. Their newer work

seems smooth, even tame by comparison, but it's still roots reggae, with a couple of moments of that off-the-wall greatness on every LP. *Best of* collects singles and LP cuts.
— R.F.G.

PABLO MOSES
★ ★ ★ ★ **A Song / Mango (1970)**
★ ★ ★ ★ **I Man I Bring / U.A. (1980)**
★ ★ ★ ★ **Pave the Way / Mango (1981)**
At times Pablo Moses seems like a laid-back, more cheerful Burning Spear, especially on the diamond-in-the-rough, countryish *I Man I Bring* (released as *Revolutionary Dream* in Jamaica). *A Song* seems deceptively smooth at first, but it's a polished diamond: hard rhythms, seamless musicianship, dynamic melodies. *Pave the Way* is a happy medium.
— R.F.G.

ELTON MOTELLO
★ ★ ★ ★ **Pop Art / Pass. (1980)**
A perceptive, tense little Englishman who didn't deserve to get lost in the mob of late-Seventies and early-Eighties electro-rockers. The songs are inventively structured and the balance between hot and cold in the sound is pretty near perfect. His despair is de rigueur modernist, but distinctive anyway. — L.F.

THE MOTELS
★ ★ ★ **The Motels / Cap. (1979)**
★ ★ ★ **Careful / Cap. (1980)**
West Coast new-wave quintet led by tough, smart vocalist Martha Davis plays a stripped-down combination of rock, R&B and reggae. — J.S.

MOTHER'S FINEST
★ **Mother's Finest / Epic (1976)**
★ ★ **Another Mother Further / Epic (1977)**
★ ★ **Mother Factor / Epic (1978)**
★ **Live / Epic (1979)**
★ **Iron Age / Atl. (1981)**
Like many musical crossbreeds in their early stages, Mother's Finest is a sound in search of an audience. Neither rock, soul nor disco, Mother's Finest bridges the gaps between Earth, Wind and Fire, Labelle and any number of white boogie bands. Of the group's five albums, the debut, *Mother's Finest,* is a lesser effort, with a sound far less integrated than the group itself (which has four black members, two white ones). Familiar rock riffs are coated with glossy, superfunk harmonies. *Another Mother Further,* the follow-up, is smoother and less frantic, with producer Tom Werman (who also works with Ted Nugent) rounding out the sound with strings and extensive use of synthesizer. Not

coincidentally, the best two tracks are the shortest ones: "Piece of the Rock" and "Hard Rock Lover," both pure stud rockers.
— G.K.

MOTORHEAD
★ **Motorhead / Chis. (1977), Br. imp.**
★ ★ **Bomber / Bronze (1979), Br. imp.**
★ **On Parole / Lib. (1980), Br. imp.**
★ ★ **Ace of Spades / Bronze (1980), Br. imp.**
★ ★ **No Sleep til Hammersmith / Bronze (1981), Br. imp.**
Led by bassist Lemmy, a longtime fixture of the British music scene, Motorhead is a three-piece heavy-metal band that delights the kids with its loud headbanger grind. Sufferable with smoke bombs. That this band has never caught on in America's wheat-belt heavy-metal heartland represents a mysterious lapse of bad judgment. — ML.H.

THE MOTORS
★ ★ ★ ★ **Motors / Virgin (1977)** ¶
★ ★ ★ ★ **Approved by the Motors / Virgin (1978)** ¶
★ ★ ★ ★ **Tenement Steps / Virgin (1980)**
Blazing hard-rock band led by ex–Ducks Deluxe pub rockers. The Motors' debut was one of the best straight rock records out of England during a year when new-wave bands, Elvis Costello and Graham Parker dominated the headlines. — J.S.

MOTT THE HOOPLE
★ ★ ★ ★ **Mott the Hoople / Atl. (1969)**
★ ★ ★ ★ **Brain Capers / Atl. (1972)**
★ ★ ★ ★ **All the Young Dudes / Col. (1972)**
★ ★ ★ ★ ★ **Mott / Col. (1973)**
★ ★ ★ **The Hoople / Col. (1974)**
★ **Mott the Hoople Live / Col. (1974)**
★ **Drive On / Col. (1975)**
★ **Shouting and Pointing / Col. (1976)**
★ ★ ★ **Greatest Hits / Col. (1976)**
Mott the Hoople, the group's debut, is an amazing record, one of the most perfect emulations of Dylan's *Blonde on Blonde* period; dense roller-rink organ blues and vocalist Ian Hunter's droning voice create a perfect atmosphere. The band did not have much to say ("Rock and Roll Queen" is the sole good original song), but the outside material included Sonny Bono's "Laugh at Me," which finally made sense without self-pity in this context; Doug Sahm's dramatic ballad, "At the Crossroads"; and the Kinks' "You Really Got Me," done as an overpowering instrumental. *Wildlife,* the group's disastrous second album for Atlantic, is now thankfully deleted. But on *Brain Capers,* the third, the band made one of the best heavy-metal re-

cords of the early Seventies: pounding and intelligent (if you can handle a song called "Death May Be Your Santa Claus"). All this time, Hunter's domination of the group was subtle but obvious; drummer Dale "Buffin" Griffin, bassist Overend Watts and particularly guitarist Mick Ralphs also played key roles.

When the band moved to Columbia in 1972 for *All the Young Dudes* (after almost breaking up in the wake of its remarkable lack of success in both England and America), it was accompanied by producer David Bowie, who cleaned up the sound, moved it to a point midway between heavy metal and *Blonde on Blonde* (an interesting and innovative niche) and gave the group two great songs: "All the Young Dudes," an explicitly gay anthem written by Bowie that almost became a U.S. hit, and Lou Reed's wonderful "Sweet Jane," a hymn of praise to the rock & roll muse.

Mott was even better, full of meditations on the group's artistic and commercial failures ("The Ballad of Mott the Hoople"), rock legends ("All the Way from Memphis," which Martin Scorsese used over the opening credits of *Alice Doesn't Live Here Anymore*) and English folk-rock psychological whimsy ("I Wish I Was Your Mother"). This is one of the great lost masterpieces of modern rock, ranking with Love's *Forever Changes* as a perfect mood piece.

Unfortunately, the group was never able to follow it up: *The Hoople, Mott*'s immediate successor, was spotty, largely because of Ralph's departure. And the rest was worse, leading up to *Drive On* and *Shouting and Pointing,* made after Hunter left for a solo career; both are shrill and pointless. The Columbia *Greatest Hits* anthology can't really bring all this together in a way that makes emotional sense; Atlantic's deleted collection of early Hoople material, *Rock and Roll Queen,* does a little better for the pre-*Dudes* stuff. But contemporary fans of mainstream rock could do worse than to pick up the four- and five-star records above while they remain in print; they're a profound influence on much of what has gone on with the new wave of the late Seventies and early Eighties.
— D.M.

MOUNTAIN
★ ★ ★ **The Best of Mountain / Col. (1973)**
★ ★ **Twin Peaks / Col. (1974)**
★ ★ **Avalanche / Col. (1974)**
The cream of American heavy metal in the early Seventies, Mountain had the formula down cold, building a plodding bass/drums/

keyboards rhythmic foundation for ex-Vagrant guitarist Leslie West's equally plodding leads. The late Felix Pappalardi (who helped launch heavy metal as Cream's producer) did his best Jack Bruce imitation on bass and wrote one of the band's best songs, "Theme from an Imaginary Western." That and the band's best-known song, "Mississippi Queen," are on the *Best of* collection.
— J.S.

THE MOVE
★ ★ ★ ★ **Fire Brigade / MFP (1971), Br. imp.** ¶
★ ★ ★ ★ ★ **The Best of the Move / A&M (1974)** ¶
★ ★ ★ ★ **California Man / Elect. (1974), Br. imp.** ¶
★ ★ ★ **The Move / MFP (1974), Br. imp.** ¶
The Move was formed in 1965 in Birmingham, England, and opened at the Marquee Club in London the next year. They created immediate excitement with a pop-art stage show heavily influenced by the Who, as was their sound. The group had a number of hit singles in Britain, beginning with "Night of Fear" in 1967, but never achieved more than a small cult following in the United States. As a result, most of the band's recorded history is to be found on imports.

The Best of the Move repackages the group's 1967 debut; it's an intriguing blend of pop melodies with loud but controlled drumming and Roy Wood's understated yet accomplished guitar, along with a dozen brilliant B sides, outtakes and failed singles. The import albums are also collections: *California Man* is the group's final material, including the excellent title single and "Do Ya," the band's best song and closest approximation of an American hit. *Fire Brigade* and *The Move* are more scattershot collections that include songs from several phases of the band's career.

Although they never achieved respectability at home—despite such autodestruct antics as smashing a TV set to smithereens as part of the act—the Move was highly influential on American art-rock bands. By 1970 the group was falling apart. Vocalist Jeff Lynne took the place of Jeff Wayne, with Wood and drummer Bev Bevan then forming Electric Light Orchestra, from which Wood soon departed for his own group, Wizzard. The band's later songs include most of the concepts ELO would make famous, the combination of classical motifs and Beatles melodies. — c.w.

THE MOVIES

★ **The Movies / Ari. (1976)** ¶
★ **India / RCA (1980)**
★ **Motor, Motor, Motor / RCA (1981)**
For everyone who fondly remembers the new
suit of clothes that good little boys once got
to wear for the holidays. *Clean* pop music,
but without the drama or the humor of soap
opera. Compared to this, Barbie dolls are
radical chic.   — D.M.

JUDY MOWATT

★ ★ ★ ★ **Black Woman / Ashandan/
Gener. (1979)**
I-Three Judy Mowatt's *Black Woman,* the
finest reggae LP by a woman, succeeds on
several levels. Her soulful singing stirs the
heart (she challenges the best R&B singers),
and the backing tracks are meaty chunks of
rhythm spiced with tasteful embellishments.
(Mowatt produced, arranged, and composed
much of the LP.) As a statement of black
womanhood, it is proud and assertive without being strident (on "Black Woman,"
"Slave Queen"). Fundamentally, though, it is
a religious work, informed by powerful faith
on "Sister's Chant," "Zion Chant" and "Joseph" (dedicated to Bob Marley).   — R.F.G.

MOXY

★ **Moxy / Mer. (1976)**
★ **Moxy II / Mer. (1976)**
★ **Ridin' High / Mer. (1977)**
★ **Under the Lights / Mer. (1978)**
The (very) poor man's Aerosmith.   — J.S.

THE MUFFINS

★ ★ ★ **Manna/Mirage / Ran. Rad. (1978)**
★ ★ ★ **Air Fiction / Muffins (1979)**
★ ★ ★ **185 / Ran. Rad. (1981)**
Artful if somewhat cerebral avant-rock tangents from the spiritual American cousins of
Henry Cow and Soft Machine. Their chops
are impressive, the compositions ambitious,
and while they often seem to embrace complexity for its own sake, there are times
when the Muffins can cook like the rock &
roll band they try not to be. Note: *Air Fiction,* half studio half live, was a limited edition of one thousand copies. Not to be confused with Martha and the Muffins.   — D.F.

GEOFF MULDAUR

★ **Motion / Rep. (1976)**
★ **Geoff Muldaur and Amos Garrett / Fly.
Fish (1978)**
★ **Blues Boy / Fly. Fish (1979)**
Muldaur, the former Jim Kweskin Jug Band
vocalist/instrumentalist, has never enjoyed
much popular success, either alone or with

his wife, Maria, who's done better by herself.
Eclectic and witty though he is, Muldaur
has never achieved sufficient direction to give
his music focus.   — I.M.

MARIA MULDAUR

★ ★ ★ **Maria Muldaur / Rep. (1973)**
★ ★ **Waitress in a Donut Shop / Rep. (1974)**
★ ★ ★ **Sweet Harmony / Rep. (1976)**
★ **Southern Winds / War. (1977)**
★ **Open Your Eyes / War. (1979)**
Formerly teamed with husband Geoff, this
veteran of the Boston folk scene (Kweskin
Jug Band) emerged in 1974 as a mature, sen-
sual stylist of great depth and versatility.
Her solo debut, *Maria Muldaur,* boasted de-
finitive versions of excellent songs by Dolly
Parton, Kate McGarrigle and Wendy Wald-
man among others, though it was David
Nichtern's "Midnight at the Oasis" that
earned her an enormous pop hit.
Waitress followed a similar format, but
the material and production were weaker.
Sweet Harmony ranged farther afield than
the debut for its material—the title song is a
Smokey Robinson ballad—and it was more
sophisticated, highlighted by a brilliant remake of Mildred Bailey's theme song,
"Rockin' Chair." But *Southern Winds,* an
attempt at contemporary funk produced by
Chris Bond (Hall and Oates), was a cata-
strophically wrong-headed disc, with weak
material and inept arrangements that
strained where Muldaur had formerly projected with ease. *Open Your Eyes* was more
of the same.   — S.H.

MARTIN MULL

★ **In the Soop / Van. (1971)**
★ **Martin Mull / Capri. (1972)**
★ **Martin Mull and His Fabulous Furniture
in Your Living Room / Capri. (1973)**
★ **Normal / Capri. (1974)**
★ **Days of Wine and Neuroses / Capri.
(1975)**
★ **No Hits, Four Errors / Capri. (1976)**
★ **I'm Everyone I've Ever Loved / ABC
(1977)**
★ **Sex and Violins / ABC (1978)**
★ **Near Perfect / Perfect / Elek. (1979)**
The best way to torpedo this artist-turned-
TV-star (he's had conceptual art exhibits at
major galleries and starred in the syndicated
Fernwood 2Night) is to give some samples of
his wit as it appears in his song titles:
"Noses Run in My Family," "Jesus Christ
Football Star," "Ego Boogie." Another tune
is said to be recorded by the Below Average
White Band. Mull does *not* have to be seen
to be dismissed unless you're just leaving

your sophomore year. Smug and obvious.
— K.T.

MOON MULLICAN
★ ★ ★ Seven Nights to Rock / Roun.
(1981)
"King of the Hillbilly Piano Players," Mullican often seems to have more in common
with jump blues à la Roy Brown and Wynonie Harris than with anything "country."
These are his finest sides, cut from 1946 to
1956 and originally released on King. They
include "Seven Nights to Rock," "Cherokee
Boogie" and "I'll Sail My Ship Alone." Mullican was a seminal influence on Jerry Lee
Lewis, and consequently on most rock & roll
pianists. As these sides show conclusively, he
was also a good singer and an excellent interpreter. — D.M.

HUGH MUNDELL
★ ★ ★ ★ Africa Must Be Free, by 1983 /
Mess. (1979)
★ ★ Jah Fire / Arawak (1981)
★ ★ Time and Place / MMLP (1981)
Another precocious reggae teenager. Mun-
dell's reedy tenor has a cutting edge and he's
written some good tunes. Africa finds Mun-
dell swimming in the sea of Augustus
Pablo's inspiration. Result? A unified master-
piece that takes stock of African diaspora.
The other LPs lack Pablo's consistent guid-
ance and thus offer only intermittent inspira-
tion. — R.F.G.

MUNICH MACHINE
★ ★ A Whiter Shade of Pale / Casa. (1978)
★ ★ Music Machine / Casa. (NA)
★ ★ Body Shine / Casa. (NA)
These Eurodisco session-group albums suffer
from some of the same problems that plague
all of producer Giorgio Moroder and Pete
Bellotte's projects. The concept of faceless
synthesizers combining with disembodied vocalists may be the underpinning of the form
that dominated mid-Seventies pop. Unfortunately, a voice with corporeal presence confronting all that mechanization is one hell of
a lot more invigorating, which is why the
only enduring Moroder/Bellotte records are
the ones they made with Donna Summer
(give or take the one they made with Debbie
Harry). — D.M.

MICHAEL MURPHEY
★ ★ ★ Geronimo's Cadillac / A&M (1972)
★ ★ ★ Cosmic Cowboy Souvenir / A&M
(1973)
★ ★ Michael Murphey / Epic (1974)
★ Blue Sky Night Thunder / Epic (1975)

★ Swans against the Sun / Epic (1975)
★ Flowing Free Forever / Epic (1976)
★ Lonewolf / Epic (1978)
★ Peaks, Valleys, Honkey-Tonks and Alleys
/ Epic (1979)
A "Cosmic Cowboy" country rocker with a
strong satirical thrust in his early songs,
Murphey moved relentlessly into banal John
Denver territory. "Geronimo's Cadillac" is
his best and best-known song, but it's been
done better by others (notably Hoyt Axton).
— S.H.

ELLIOTT MURPHY
★ ★ ★ Just a Story from America / Col.
(1977) ¶
★ ★ ★ Affairs / Courtesan
(1981)
★ ★ ★ Murph the Surf / Courtesan (1982)
Murphy made his first and best album for
Polydor in 1973 (Aquashow, deleted). Since
then, he's developed a remarkable lyrical
style—F. Scott Fitzgerald out of Lou Reed—
but hasn't added a discernible musical approach. His most recent albums are excellent
investigations of the mythical basis of twentieth-century American culture without sufficient musical interest to make the songs as
interesting as they'd need to be to enter that
mythology themselves. Murph the Surf is by
far the better of these. — D.M.

ANNE MURRAY
★ ★ Snowbird / Cap. (1970)
★ ★ Talk It Over in the Morning / Cap.
(1971)
★ Danny's Song / Cap. (1973)
★ ★ ★ Love Song / Cap. (1974)
★ ★ Country / Cap. (1974)
★ ★ ★ Highly Prized Possession / Cap.
(1974)
★ Together / Cap. (1975)
★ Keeping in Touch / Cap. (1976)
★ ★ Let's Keep It That Way / Cap.
(1978)
★ ★ New Kind of Feeling / Cap. (1979)
★ ★ I'll Always Love You / Cap. (1979)
★ ★ A Country Collection / Cap. (1980)
★ ★ Somebody's Waiting / Cap. (1980)
★ ★ Greatest Hits / Cap. (1980)
★ ★ Where Do You Go When You Dream?
/ Cap. (1980)
★ ★ Christmas Wishes / Cap. (1981)
Murray is a Canadian with a deep, throaty
voice that delivers an intense emotionalism
belied by her calm, polite performing demea-
nor. A former high school phys ed teacher,
her record company has always tagged her
with a girl-next-door image, and this has
been reinforced by the bulk of her material,

which is average MOR. But Murray also has an exciting, even dark, side to her: she has a strong cult among gay women, who have astutely perceived her firm independence of men even as she sings gloppy hetero-hymns to them—again, it is her voice that always rings out honestly.

Murray has also done a number of terrific Beatles covers, culminating in her gloriously tough and cheerful version of "You Won't See Me," on *Love Song,* her best album, though *Highly Prized Possession* is a close second (she makes "Day Tripper" her own on that one). The rest of these drown in the oily slickness of their production. This is nearly tragic, because Murray could be a great pop singer in a feminist era. Currently she is a moderately unpopular MOR tool.
— K.T.

JUNIOR MURVIN
★ ★ ★ **Police and Thieves / Mango (NA)**
Murvin isn't that great, but "Police and Thieves," the politicized reggae song that became his 1976 British hit and was later covered by the Clash, is a masterpiece. The album rates this highly on the strength of that song alone. — D.M.

SUSAN MUSCARELLA
■ **Rawflower / Pac. A. (NA)**
Next edition we're banishing hippies altogether. — D.M.

MUSCLE SHOALS HORNS
★ ★ ★ **Doin' It to the Bone / Ario.-Amer. (1971)**
★ ★ ★ **Born to Get Down / Bang (1976)**
Muscle Shoals is better known for its rhythm sections than its horns, but this is surprisingly hot-blooded funk without much embellishment, something like a Seventies version of the Mar-Keys. Highlights are the Bang album's torrid title track and a cover of the J. Geils Band's reggae hit, "Give It to Me."
— J.MC.

MUSIQUE
★ ★ **Keep On Jumpin' / Prel. (1978)**
The ones who perpetrated "(Push Push) In the Bush." No Nuremberg trial yet—the bonus star is for those (like me) who can't resist genuine mindlessness. — D.M.

CHARLIE MUSSELWHITE
★ ★ ★ ★ ★ **Stand Back / Van. (1967)**
★ ★ ★ ★ **Stone Blues / Van. (1968)**
★ ★ ★ **Tennessee Woman / Van. (1969)**
★ ★ ★ **Louisiana Fog / Cherry Red (NA)**
★ ★ ★ ★ ★ **Takin' My Time / Arhoo. (1971)**

★ ★ ★ ★ ★ **Goin' Back Down South / Arhoo. (1974)**
★ ★ ★ **Leave the Blues to Us / Cap. (NA)**
Musselwhite grew up in Memphis, where he learned to play blues guitar from Son Brimmer of the Memphis Jug Band, Furry Lewis and Gus Cannon. It was only after moving to Chicago and hearing Little Walter Jacobs that he switched to harmonica. Along with Paul Butterfield, Musselwhite became Little Walter's best white protégé. There isn't a lot of difference between Butterfield and Musselwhite stylistically except that Butterfield is a more elegant player and a better bandleader. Musselwhite sticks to basics and has never tried too strenuously to cross over to rock as Butterfield did.

Musselwhite's debut, *Stand Back,* is a great album that was overlooked simply because it didn't have the scope of Butter's *East West,* which is a shame, especially when you consider how many English blues bands were being accepted at the same time. Produced by Sam Charters, the record features an amazing band anchored by the incomparable Chicago drummer Fred Below and featuring guitarist Harvey Mandel and keyboardist Barry Goldberg. Goldberg produced the second album, which begins to show the strain of Musselwhite's lack of commercial exposure—Vanguard was putting the pressure on for some Butterfield-style sales. By the time of *Tennessee Woman,* it was apparent that Musselwhite was destined to suffer the traditional blues player's fate of constant obscurity. It wasn't until a few years later when he recorded for Arhoolie and was treated as a forgotten prize that Musselwhite found his proper niche, and his records for that label are excellent. On *Down South* he even plays some fairly good guitar.
— J.S.

MUTINY
★ ★ ★ **Mutiny on the Mamaship / Col. (1979)**
★ ★ ★ ★ **Funk Plus the One / Col. (1980)**
Jerome Bailey, a former drummer with the George Clinton, walked out of the Parliafunkadeliment Thang in a snit, and spends the better part of *Mamaship* singing about how unfunky the P-Funkers are, *especially* compared to Jerome Bailey. Not that it's just talk, either. *Mutiny* is on-the-one and then some, stomping a bottom-heavy groove that sounds like Hamilton Bohannon meets Bootsy. *Funk Plus the One* goes *Mamaship* one better by adding melody to the get-down. — J.D.C.

MX-80 SOUND
★ Hard Attack / Is. (NA) ¶
★ Out of the Tunnel / Ralph (1980)
New-wave/heavy-metal band plays stark, dissonant and ultimately boring rock that might best serve as soundtrack music for an extremely bad monster movie.   — J.S.

MYCHAEL
■ Neon Dreams / RCA (1979) ¶
Numbingly dull hard rock.   — D.M.

GARY MYRICK AND THE FIGURES
★ ★ ★ Gary Myrick and the Figures / Epic (1980)
★ ★ Living in a Movie / Epic (1981)
Gary Myrick is a good writer but not a particularly convincing one. His words and music convey a controlled hysteria that's exciting at first, but sounds increasingly contrived with each play. Not that the germ of originality is completely absent—parts of *And the Figures* are sheer eccentric genius— just buried under a lot of chaff.   — J.D.C.

MYSTIC MERLIN
★ Mystic Merlin / Cap. (1979)

★ Sixty Thrills a Minute / Cap. (1981)
I'm sure he was locked up years ago.
— D.M.

CEDRIC MYTON
★ ★ Congo Shanty / CBS (1979), Br. imp.
★ ★ ★ Image of Africa / CBS (1980), Br. imp.
★ ★ ★ ★ ★ Heart of the Congos / Go Feet (1980), Br. imp.
★ ★ ★ ★ Face the Music / Go Feet (1981), Br. imp.
A combination of Myton's exquisite harmonies, Lee "Scratch" Perry's demented production techniques and a heartfelt sincerity of belief in Jah Rastafari make *Heart of the Congos,* his very first LP rereleased on Go Feet, possibly the most soulful and inspirational reggae album outside of Bob Marley's earliest works. Although the singing remains beautiful, the middle two albums suffer from a certain underproduction, but *Face the Music,* on which Myton collaborates with that charming trombonist Rico, is a welcome return to fullness, despite its overall commerciality.
— ML.H.

NORMAN NARDINI AND THE TIGERS
★ ★ ★ **Eat'n Alive / Kam. S. (1981)**
In this era of prefix rock, a band that plays
unfettered, straight-ahead rock & roll is almost implausible. Near legends in their
hometown, Pittsburgh, the Tigers play somewhere on the East Coast every weekend of
the year, usually in bars, and usually to
rabid, partisan fans, mainly because Nardini
is a charismatic and endlessly energetic performer. This live album, which contains their
standard set of all original material, shows
the band to good advantage, playing good-
humored, cocky rock & roll as we have
come not to know it lately. — D.G.

WAZMO NARIZ
★ ★ ★ **Things Aren't Right / Illegal/IRS
(1979)**
★ ★ ★ **Tell Me How to Live / Big (1981)**
Nariz, an oddball who might be Jonathan
Richman's adult incarnation, is a suave, hy-
pertensive singer, a writer of endearing but
neurotic songs, and is probably a damn sight
too clever for his own good. Both albums
are smart and engaging, but promise humor
that isn't really apparent. Quirky but melodic music supports numbers like "Checking
Out the Checkout Girl," "Iron-on Courage"
and "The Refrigerator Saga." Fun for smart
alecks. — I.R.

GRAHAM NASH
★ ★ **Songs for Beginners / Atl. (1971)**
★ **Wild Tales / Atl. (1973)**
★ **Earth and Sky / EMI (1980)**
This former Hollie and Crosby, Stills and
Nash staple confuses simplicity with trite-
ness. *Beginners* contains the prototypical
"Simple Man." — S.H.

JOHNNY NASH
★ ★ ★ **I Can See Clearly Now / Epic
(1972)**

★ ★ **My Merry-Go-Round / Epic (1973) ¶**
★ **Let's Go Dancing / Epic (1979)**
Possessed of a strikingly affecting high tenor
and a rich gift for soulful phrasing, Johnny
Nash has nonetheless been the victim of his
own arrangements, which push him toward
the corny and commercial. Nash, who would
eventually settle in London, moved from the
United States to Jamaica to make his 1972
hit, "I Can See Clearly Now." The album of
the same name—that contains three Bob
Marley songs, two by John "Rabbit" Bundrick and one cowritten by Marley with
Nash—uses reggae rhythms to effectively
capture Nash's oddly innocent eroticism.
  Despite Bundrick's percolating keyboard
work, an intrusive and almost bubblegum-
style production job by Nash mars the other
two LPs, which reel between Philly soul, reggae and Stax-Volt attacks that never cohere.
— F.S.

THE NATIONAL LAMPOON
★ ★ ★ **Radio Dinner / Blue Th. (1972)**
★ ★ ★ ★ **Lemmings / Blue Th. (1973)**
★ ★ **Gold Turkey / Epic (1975)**
★ ★ **Goodbye Pop / Epic (1975)**
★ ★ **That's Not Funny, That's Sick / Label
21 (1978)**
★ **Animal House / MCA (1978)**
★ ★ ★ **Greatest Hits / Visa (1978)**
Like the magazine that spawned them, this
series of comedy albums begins brilliantly
and then peters out into material so pathetic
it gives new meaning to the term "sophomoric." *Lemmings,* based on the touring
revue that launched the careers of many of
Saturday Night Live's Not Ready for Prime
Time Players, is an inspired takeoff on rock
pomposity. The John Lennon, Bob Dylan
and Joan Baez parodies on *Radio Dinner* are
sheer genius. But the Epic albums disinte-
grate into cheap shots at the counterculture,
pop culture and just culture in general;

they're more exploitative of collegiate sensibility than reflective of it. *Animal House,* the soundtrack to the sometimes brilliant first *Lampoon* movie, falters for several reasons, not least of which is because the version of "Louie Louie" included here has been censored; John Belushi's marvelously filthy lyrics in the film deserve permanent enshrinement on disc. *Greatest Hits* and *That's Not Funny* are self-descriptive. — D.M.

NATIVE
★ Native / RCA (NA)
Bad disco. — J.S.

NATIVE SON
★ ★ Native Son / Inf. (1979)
★ ★ Savana Hot Line / MCA (1981)
Competent Japanese fusion group. — W.K.

NAZARETH
★ Razamanaz / A&M (1973)
★ Loud 'n' Proud / A&M (1974)
★ Rampant / A&M (1974)
★ ★ Hair of the Dog / A&M (1975)
★ Close Enough for Rock and Roll / A&M (1976)
★ Play'n' the Game / A&M (1976)
★ Hot Tracks / A&M (1977)
★ Expect No Mercy / A&M (1977)
★ No Mean City / A&M (1979)
★ Malice in Wonderland / A&M (1980)
★ Fool Circle / A&M (1981)
Dog food. Among the most mediocre of successful mid-Seventies British hard-rock groups, Nazareth's biggest claim to fame is a 1975 hit, "Love Hurts," which bears not a smattering of resemblance to the great Everly Brothers song of the same name. Dreadful stuff. — D.M.

HOLLY NEAR
★ ★ Hang in There / Red'd. (1973)
★ ★ A Live Album / Red'd. (1974)
★ You Can Know All I Am (with Jeff Langley) / Red'd. (1976)
★ ★ ★ Imagine My Surprise / Red'd. (1978)
★ ★ ★ Fire in the Rain / Red'd. (1981)
Pacifist/humanist/feminist/ex-folkie Holly Near is a force field more than an artist per se, and for like minds who prize putting one's ass on the line even in this noncommittal age, she's one hell of a motivator. Not that she wants to connect only with ideological kindred spirits; that's quite obvious on each LP. But until she addresses some major musical problems, her audience will stay small. *You Can Know* delineates these difficulties perfectly: undisciplined, eclectic song structures and embarrassing lyrical overstate-

ment. *Fire in the Rain* takes some brave new steps into jazz, pushing Near's glorious soprano voice to new expressiveness. — C.F.

FRED NEIL
★ ★ ★ ★ Everybody's Talkin' / Cap. (1969)
★ ★ ★ ★ The Other Side of This Life / Cap. (1970) ¶
★ ★ ★ Little Bit of Rain / Elek. (1970)
Reclusive Sixties folk-jazz singer/composer who played an avuncular role in relationship to folk rock—both Eric Burdon and Jefferson Airplane recorded Neil's "The Other Side of This Life"—but is perhaps better known for "Everybody's Talkin'," which Harry Nilsson made a hit on the soundtrack to *Midnight Cowboy. Everybody's Talkin',* on which Stephen Stills plays a pre–Buffalo Springfield guest role, also contains two marvelous little-known songs, "The Dolphins" and Neil's version of "Cocaine." Neil never had much commercial success and retreated by the mid-Sixties to Coconut Grove, Florida, where he has been peripherally engaged in dolphin research but has played little music ever since. — D.M.

BILL NELSON AND RED NOISE
★ ★ ★ Sound-on-Sound / Harv. (1979)
This initial outing from guitarist Nelson's post–Be Bop Deluxe band features the same blend of avant-garde art-rock ideas and hot licks done by the earlier group, but it doesn't surpass them. A cautious first step. — D.M.

RICKY NELSON
★ ★ ★ ★ ★ Legendary Master Series / U.A. (1971)
★ ★ Intakes / Epic (1977)
★ ★ Playing to Win / Cap. (1981)
★ ★ Four You / Epic (1981)
★ ★ Ricky / U.A. (NA), imp.
Because he first appeared on television's *Ozzie and Harriet* (which starred his parents) and began his rock & roll career in the same place, Nelson has been unjustly underrated. In fact he was a first-rate rock singer—if not a great one, he was at least leagues superior to the Bobby Vee/Fabian/Paul Anka finger-pop axis. Hits like "Travelin' Man," "Hello Mary Lou," "Teenage Idol" and "Poor Little Fool" were among the best in post-Elvis rock of the late Fifties. Nelson was supported by a terrific band, led by guitarist James Burton, who a decade later joined up with the King himself. If Nelson was a little closer to a crooner than a shouter, his work still holds up well. Had Pat Boone been this good, he wouldn't have had to go Christian.

The *Legendary Master Series* is a model of a reissue: excellent graphics and liner notes by Ed Ward say it all. It's not easy to find, though, and unfortunately, all of Nelson's Decca albums, including a pair of pretty good ones—the 1972 *Garden Party,* which contains the title cut, his last hit; and the 1970 *In Concert,* which features some terrific Dylan material—are out of print altogether. *Intakes* is not up to that level, but Nelson is definitely an artist worth hearing, one of rock's lost resources. *Ricky* reissues a Fifties record (minus two tracks); *Four You* and *Playing to Win* are marginally listenable pop country. — D.M.

SANDY NELSON

★ ★ ★ **Big Bad Boss Beat / Orig. Sound (NA)**
★ ★ ★ **Let There Be Drums / Imper. (1961)**
★ ★ ★ **The Very Best of Sandy Nelson / U.A. (NA), imp.**

In the post-Elvis, pre-Beatles rock world, Sandy Nelson held top rank with the Ventures as an instrumental influence. His axe was drums, and "Teen Beat," his 1959 hit for Original Sound, and "Let There Be Drums," a Top Ten smash for Imperial in 1961, were typically silly instrumentals of the period, which helped prepare an entire generation for such later episodes of ridiculous infatuation with instrumentals as Ginger Baker's Cream solo, "Toad," and the Surfaris' immortal "Wipe Out." Not an entirely benign historical force, but good for a laugh. — D.M.

TRACY NELSON

★ ★ **Deep Are the Roots / Prest. (1965)**
★ ★ ★ **Poor Man's Paradise / Col. (1975)**
★ ★ ★ **Sweet Soul Music / MCA (1975)** ¶
★ ★ **Time Is on My Side / MCA (1976)** ¶
★ ★ **Homemade Songs / Fly. Fish (1978)**
★ ★ **Doin' It My Way / Adel. (1980)**

As lead vocalist of Mother Earth, Tracy Nelson established herself as an acoustic blues and C&W singer with a large cult following. Members of Mother Earth were mostly from Texas, and steeped in rural tradition; Nelson grew up in Madison, Wisconsin, a college town where she became a folksinger. Together, she and the group made two superb (and long deleted) Mercury albums, *Living with the Animals* (1968) and *Make a Joyful Noise* (1969). But Nelson's solo albums often only suggest, rather than deliver, the full-throated power that has made her so popular.

Deep Are the Roots is a 1965 tribute to Ma Rainey and Bessie Smith. Nelson's strong, stately singing and Charley Musselwhite's fine harp work make it more than a period curio. *Poor Man's Paradise* encapsulates the country-rocking melancholy Nelson's roving sensibility also embraced in *Sweet Soul Music,* and *Time Is on My Side* shows her convincing way with bluesier tunes.

From 1967 to 1971, Nelson enjoyed a tenuous commercial viability, culminating in the fine religious-pastoral suite, *Bring Me Home,* and the deleted albums from that period include some real showstoppers: "Down So Low," "Soul of the Man," "I Need Your Love So Bad" and "You Win Again" are specimens of her strength and versatility. The available albums are products of a rich but quirky output. But it remains to be seen if Tracy Nelson's sometimes petulant intelligence will overshadow her strengths indefinitely. — F.S.

WILLIE NELSON

★ ★ ★ **Columbus Stockade Blues / Cam. (1970)**
★ ★ ★ **Shotgun Willie / Atl. (1973)**
★ ★ ★ **The Best of Willie Nelson / U.A. (1973)**
★ ★ ★ ★ ★ **Red Headed Stranger / Col. (1975)**
★ ★ **Yesterday's Wine / RCA (1975)**
★ ★ **What Can You Do to Me Now / RCA (1975)**
★ ★ ★ **Spotlight on Willie Nelson / Cam. (1975)**
★ ★ ★ **Country Willie / U.A. (1975)**
★ ★ ★ **The Sound in Your Mind / Col. (1976)**
★ ★ ★ **Willie Nelson Live / RCA (1976)**
★ ★ ★ ★ **Phases and Stages / Atl. (1976)**
★ ★ ★ ★ **The Troublemaker / Col. (1976)**
★ ★ ★ **Willie Nelson and His Friends / Plant. (1976)**
★ ★ **Wishing You a Merry Christmas / RCA (1976)**
★ ★ **Willie/Before His Time / RCA (1977)**
★ ★ ★ ★ **To Lefty from Willie / Col. (1977)**
★ ★ ★ **Stardust / Col. (1978)**
★ ★ ★ **There'll Be No More Teardrops Tonight / U.A. (1978)**
★ ★ ★ **One for the Road / Col. (1979)**
★ ★ ★ **Pretty Paper / Col. (1979)**
★ ★ ★ **San Antonio Rose / Col. (1980)**
★ ★ ★ **Sweet Memories / RCA (1979)**
★ ★ ★ **Minstrel Man / RCA (1981)**
★ ★ ★ **Greatest Hits and Some That Will Be / Col. (1981)**
★ ★ ★ **Somewhere over the Rainbow / RCA (1981)**

Like many of his peers, Willie Nelson began

his career singing in Texas honky-tonks in the late Fifties, before moving on to Nashville in the early part of the next decade, where he quickly acquired a reputation as a versatile country songwriter ("Night Life") and wrote at least one soul standard, "Funny (How Time Slips Away)," as well. Nelson also wrote "Crazy" for Patsy Cline and Faron Young's "Hello Walls." His early recordings—represented on the United Artists packages, they were originally done for Liberty—were also country hits, although they were a bit too raw for pop tastes. By 1964 Nelson was a fixture in the country establishment, a regular on the Grand Ole Opry and an RCA recording artist. But his talents didn't adapt well to the formula productions then the vogue, and by the early Seventies his dissatisfaction led him back to Texas, where he and Waylon Jennings, among others, spawned the so-called outlaw movement that returned country closer to its roots.

In 1972 Nelson became the first country artist signed to Atlantic Records. *Phases and Stages,* his first release for the label, gave him more latitude artistically than he'd been used to, and he used it well. But the soul- and rock-oriented company didn't really know what to do with him. After a disheartening second LP, *Shotgun Willie,* he moved to Columbia, with enough artistic autonomy to ensure his escape from the clutches of the CBS production pulverizer, Bill Sherrill.

His first Columbia release, *Red Headed Stranger,* was a genuine triumph that immediately brought country up to date with the trends in other forms of popular music. A concept album that owed as much to rock opera as to C&W, *Red Headed Stranger* was moving on several levels: as an allegorical autobiography, a religious parable and a fine country album that featured the hit single, "Blue Eyes Crying in the Rain." Yet while that album had won him a rock following as rabid as his country cult, Nelson hasn't quite been able to match *Red Headed Stranger.* The Columbia albums all have some worthwhile music, and they're far more adventurous than almost any other country records of recent years. But in the end, they seem to prove that even outlaw notions can be regulated and turned into formula.   — D.M.

NERVOUS REX
★ Nervous Rex / Dream. (1980)
New York new-wave outfit led by former rock critic Lauren Agnelli (a.k.a. Trixie A. Balm) caught producer Michael Chapman on the downslide, lacks enough performing

or songwriting talent of its own to compensate. Result is an attempt to be ingratiating that lives up to its own name in all the wrong ways.   — D.M.

MICHAEL NESMITH
★ ★ ★ And the Hits Just Keep On Comin' / Pacif. (1972)
★ ★ ★ Pretty Much Your Standard Ranch Stash / Pacif. (1973)
★ ★ ★ The Prison / Pacif. (1975)
★ ★ ★ Compilation / Pacif. (1977)
★ ★ ★ From a Radio Engine to the Photon Wing / Pacif. (1977)
★ ★ ★ Wichita Train Whistle Songs / Pacif. (1978)
★ ★ ★ Live at the Palais / Pacif. (1978)
★ ★ ★ Infinite Rider on the Big Dogma / Pacif. (1979)
Nesmith earned his name as a member of the Monkees, but his list of credits is more than enough to dispel the idea that he's as faceless as that band. Besides many of the Monkees' best songs, he also wrote "Different Drum" for the Stone Poneys (Linda Ronstadt's first hit); released a series of critically acclaimed country-rock albums for RCA (all out of print) after leaving the Monkees; and produced albums by Bert Jansch, Linda Hargrove and Ian Matthews. These albums give a good account of Nesmith's performance talents, although his most pompous tendencies coalesce on the concept album, *The Prison,* which is accompanied by a book and was later turned into a stage production.   — J.S.

MARK NESS
★ Mark Ness / Mid. Int. (NA)
More touchable than Eliot—but not much.   — D.M.

NETWORK
★ ★ Network / Epic (1977)
★ ★ ★ Nightwork / Epic (1978)
A seven-piece hard-rock band with middleweight credentials (Mike Ricciardella, the drummer and chief writer, came from Barnaby Bye; guitarist Mike Coxton played with the Illusion). Network's first album is screeching keyboard-oriented hard rock. But the second, *Nightwork,* settles down, thanks to better writing, George Bitzner's impressive keyboard work and a nice cover of "Halfway to Paradise."   — D.M.

THE NEVILLE BROTHERS
★ ★ ★ The Neville Brothers / Cap. (1978) ¶
★ ★ ★ ★ Fiyo on the Bayou / A&M (1981)
The Nevilles have been among New Orleans'

hottest rhythm sections for years, forming the backbone of the Wild Tchoupitoulas, among others. But their Capitol album, produced by Allen Toussaint, doesn't quite live up to their potential for drive and fire. The self-produced *Fiyo,* on the other hand, is as fine a set of New Orleans R&B workouts as anyone has put together in the past decade. — D.M.

NEW ADVENTURES
★ ★ **New Adventures / Poly. (NA)**
Same old crap. — D.M.

NEW BIRTH
★ ★ **Birth Day / RCA (1973)**
★ ★ **Best of the New Birth / RCA (1975)**
★ ★ ★ **Blind Baby / Bud. (1975)**
★ ★ **Reincarnation / RCA (1976)**
★ **Love Potion / War. (1976)**
★ ★ **Behold (The Mightly Army) / War. (1977)**
A self-contained vocal and instrumental group, New Birth has never enjoyed much pop success, and it has scored only sporadically on the R&B charts: "Dream Merchant," on the Buddah album, made it to No. 1 in 1975, and the group enjoyed a few other Top Twenty singles during that period, but never established a real identity. With good reason: the sound wavers from pure MOR (like the Main Ingredient or Fifth Dimension) to a version of soul harmony and straight funk groove. Lacking a really distinctive vocalist, this stuff just never jells. — D.M.

MICKEY NEWBURY
★ ★ ★ **Frisco Mabel Joy / Elek. (1971) ¶**
★ ★ **Rusty Tracks / ABC (1972)**
★ ★ ★ **Heaven Help the Child / Elek. (1973) ¶**
★ ★ ★ ★ **Live at Montezuma Hall / Looks Like Rain / Elek. (1973) ¶**
★ ★ ★ **I Came to Hear the Music / Elek. (1974) ¶**
★ ★ **Lovers / Elek. (1975) ¶**
★ **His Eye Is on the Sparrow / ABC (1978)**
★ ★ **The Sailor / MCA (1979)**
Newbury is one of the best of the new breed of Nashville singer/songwriters who came into prominence in the Seventies. Like his peers, Newbury specialized at first in writing material for other people—the Kenny Rogers and the First Edition hit, "Just Dropped In (To See What Condition My Condition Was In)," was his first big break, and since then his material has been covered by people as diverse as Jerry Lee Lewis, Roger Miller, Tom Jones, Pat Boone and Andy Williams.

Perhaps Newbury's best-known song since then is "Heaven Help the Child," but his best album is the double LP of a live set recorded at Montezuma Hall coupled with a reissue of his first album, the Jerry Kennedy–produced *Looks Like Rain.* — J.S.

NEW ENGLAND
★ ★ **New England / Inf. (1979)**
★ ★ **Explorer Suite / Elek. (1980)**
★ ★ **Walking Wild / Elek. (1981)**
Arena rock without the popularity; played with all the technical competence in the world and all the imagination the band's geographic name implies. — W.K.

NEW LOST CITY RAMBLERS
★ ★ ★ **New Lost City Ramblers, Vol. 1 / Folk. (1958)**
★ ★ ★ **Depression Songs / Folk. (1959)**
★ ★ ★ **New Lost City Ramblers, Vol. 2 / Folk. (1960)**
★ ★ ★ **New Lost City Ramblers, Vol. 3 / Folk. (1961) ¶**
★ ★ ★ **New Lost City Ramblers, Vol. 4 / Folk. (1962) ¶**
★ ★ ★ **American Moonshine and Prohibition / Folk. (1962)**
★ ★ ★ **New Lost City Ramblers, Vol. 5 / Folk. (1963) ¶**
★ ★ ★ **New Lost City Ramblers / Folk. (1964)**
★ ★ ★ **Modern Times / Folk. (1968)**
★ ★ ★ **"New" New Lost City Ramblers / Folk. (1972)**
★ ★ ★ **Remembrance of Things to Come / Folk. (1973)**
★ ★ ★ **On the Great Divide / Folk. (1975)**
One of the most important groups of the early-Sixties folk revival, the New Lost City Ramblers specialized in old-timey music, the sound of the Appalachian hills, the root stock from which commercial country & western music was developed in the late Twenties. Rather than the standard material developed by the Carter Family and Jimmie Rodgers, however, the Ramblers concentrated on older, less well-known songs that are the Carters' and Rodgers' source points or which were spun off from their reworkings of the tradition. The group was formed in the late Fifties by folklorist Mike Seeger (Pete's brother), who had done field recordings of some of the material; photographer John Cohen; and mathematician Tom Paley, who left the group in the early Sixties to pursue a teaching career and was replaced by Tracy Schwartz. All of the Ramblers' records are competent, and some of them are very high-spirited; the series, called simply

New Lost City Ramblers, is the earliest and probably the best of their catalogue.
— D.M.

RANDY NEWMAN
★ ★ ★ **Randy Newman** / Rep. (1968)
★ ★ ★ ★ **Twelve Songs** / Rep. (1970)
★ ★ ★ **Randy Newman Live** / Rep. (1971)
★ ★ ★ ★ **Sail Away** / Rep. (1972)
★ ★ ★ **Good Old Boys** / Rep. (1974)
★ ★ ★ **Little Criminals** / War. (1977)
★ ★ **Born Again** / War. (1979)
★ ★ ★ **Trouble in Paradise** / War. (1983)

Randy Newman is one of the most eccentric and talented of the late-Sixties pop performer/composers, possessed of an unusual melodic sense (derived not only from rock and blues but movie scores of the Thirties and Forties) and a pungently sardonic sense of humor. His first album, *Randy Newman,* was such an oddity when it was released that Reprise attempted to give it away though a series of tongue-in-cheek advertisements. That didn't help much commercially. *Twelve Songs,* which followed in 1970, was even more striking; Newman's sense of humor (in songs like "Suzanne," about an obscene telephone call; "Lucinda," about a girl swept up by a bleach cleaner; and "Mama Told Me Not to Come," later a hit for Three Dog Night, which concerned an improbable orgy attended by a naif) was more fully developed. The pathos he would bring to his best later work also began to emerge ("Let's Burn Down the Cornfield," "If You Need Oil") as his fascination with the South made its first appearance in "My Old Kentucky Home," a sort of backhanded tribute to Stephen Foster, among other things. But the most engaging aspect of the album is the playing of guitarist Ry Cooder and Newman's ragged-edged singing, which make everything from blues to pop songs fit together perfectly.

Newman has never been prolific, and *Live* was released in 1971 to fill the gap between *Twelve Songs* and *Sail Away.* It's a pleasant exposition of the songs on the first two albums, with a couple of minor additions. *Sail Away* was much more than that, a tour de force of social satire and some of Newman's best music. The title cut was an imaginary voyage on a slave ship, with the ship's captain promising Africans streets paved with gold; "Burn On," a tribute to the polluted Cuyahoga River, Cleveland's famous burning stream; "Dayton, Ohio—1903" an elliptical romance taking place in that town at the time of the Wright brothers' discovery of flight; and a couple of more puerile numbers,

"Political Science" ("Let's drop the big one") and "God's Song," in which the Lord appears as a monster who delights in holocaust. Despite slight flaws—those last two songs are a bit obvious, closer to Tom Lehrer than Bob Dylan in their targets and commentary—*Sail Away* is Newman's triumph.

Good Old Boys was Newman's first attempt at a cycle of thematically linked songs, and although it was much more popular than his earlier albums, its success was problematic. It is a series of sketches of the South, including "Rednecks," an imaginary defense of Lester Maddox against "smartass New York Jews," the offensiveness of which is not redeemed by Newman's Jewishness. The humor is exploitative of a region and people Newman comprehends less than well, although a couple of songs are both striking in their imagery and emotionally moving: "Louisiana 1927," about a famous flood; "A Wedding in Cherokee County," about a backwoods marriage to a freak; and the plaintive love song "Marie."

Little Criminals contained the hit single, "Short People," which offended plenty of people for the wrong reasons; it typified, however, a strain of smugness and cruelty that had developed in Newman's work. Accompanied by the Eagles and some really gorgeous string arrangements, he whipped his way through a batch of songs that lacked his usual bite, with only a couple of examples of the kind of nonformula pop his fans had come to expect. "Sigmund Freud's Impersonation of Albert Einstein in America" was about the best; it was originally written for the film of E. L. Doctorow's novel *Ragtime.* Nonetheless, *Little Criminals* won Newman a much larger audience than he had previously enjoyed. But *Born Again* was sub-Lehrer slapstick, its best song an encomium to ELO. *Trouble in Paradise* is a considerable musical rebound, if you consider Toto a great group. (Randy does.) Its attacks on New York, Los Angeles, and rock hangers-on are focused more precisely on their targets, even if his unrelieved misanthropy is getting to be a drag.   — D.M.

THUNDERCLAP NEWMAN
★ ★ ★ ★ **Hollywood Dream** / MCA (1973)

This remarkable one-shot assembled some of the strangest rock & roll minds of the past decade. Produced and recorded by Peter Townshend (who also played bass), the record combines Townshend protégés Andy Newman on piano and horns, Jimmy McCulloch (later of Stone the Crows and

Wings) on guitars, and Speedy Keen on drums and vocals. Keen also wrote the songs, some of which are enduring ("The Reason," "Look Around," "Accidents," "Something in the Air"). The band also does a neat cover of an obscure Dylan tune, "Open the Door, Homer." — J.S.

NEW MISSISSIPPI SHEIKS
★ ★ ★ **The New Mississippi Sheiks** / Roun. **(1980)**
The old Mississippi Sheiks, who launched themselves with the great "Sitting on Top of the World" in 1930, were one of the most popular string bands in history. Sam Chatmon, who was a marginal member of that group (which was led by his brother Bo), revived the concept along with fellow stringband vets Carl Martin and Ted Bogan in 1972. — J.S.

NEW MUSIK
★ ★ ★ **Sanctuary** / Epic **(1981)**
Catchy British electronic pop LP features popular rock-disco hit "Straight Lines." Leader Tony Mansfield's synthesizer work dominates the backing group's rhythm here as much as the sound overrides any substance. — W.K.

THE NEW RIDERS OF THE PURPLE SAGE
★ ★ ★ **New Riders of the Purple Sage** / Col. **(1971)**
★ ★ ★ **Powerglide** / Col. **(1972)**
★ ★ **Gypsy Cowboy** / Col. **(1973)**
★ ★ ★ **Adventures of Panama Red** / Col. **(1973)**
★ **Home, Home on the Road** / Col. **(1974)**
★ ★ **Brujo** / Col. **(1974)** ¶
★ ★ **Oh What a Mighty Time** / Col. **(1975)**
★ **New Riders** / MCA **(1976)**
★ ★ ★ **Best of** / Col. **(1976)**
★ **Who Are Those Guys?** / MCA **(1977)** ¶
★ **Marin County Line** / MCA **(1977)**
■ **Feelin' All Right** / A & M **(1981)**
This band got its start as the Grateful Dead's official warmup group during the Dead's performing heyday in the early Seventies. The Dead fans loved the Riders if only because Jerry Garcia would often sit in on steel guitar. So even though the Riders were a disorganized, second-rate country-rock outfit without a decent lead singer, the band gained instant recognition and a widespread following. The Riders traded off their hippie outlaw image deftly, drawing out their version of the cowboy caricature fairly successfully before running completely out of gas. If you want appropriate background

music for rustic keg parties in the wilderness, *New Riders of the Purple Sage, Powerglide* or *Panama Red* will do the trick. Otherwise, the New Riders are guaranteed to put you to sleep. — J.S.

JUICE NEWTON AND THE SILVER SPUR
★ **Juice Newton and the Silver Spur** / Cap. **(1975)**
★ **Come to Me** / Cap. **(1977)**
★ **After the Dust Settles** / RCA **(1977)**
★ **Well Kept Secret** / Cap. **(1978)**
★ **Juice** / Cap. **(1981)**
★ **Take Heart** / Cap. **(1981)**
Boring rock band fronted by an emotionally empty female singer who leads them where even fools would fear to tread, most nobably into a rotten version of Bob Seger's "Fire Down Below," on *Come to Me*. — D.M.

OLIVIA NEWTON-JOHN
■ **Let Me Be There** / MCA **(1973)**
■ **If You Love Me, Let Me Know** / MCA **(1974)**
■ **Have You Never Been Mellow** / MCA **(1975)**
■ **Clearly Love** / MCA **(1975)**
■ **Come On Over** / MCA **(1976)**
■ **Don't Stop Believin'** / MCA **(1976)**
■ **Making a Good Thing Better** / MCA **(1977)**
■ **Olivia Newton-John's Greatest Hits** / MCA **(1977)**
★ **Totally Hot** / MCA **(1978)**
★ **Physical** / MCA **(1981)**
Not only does this Australian country-pop singer possess the blank, open face of a Barbie doll, she also has what the French call *une voix chuchotante mannequinée,* which means (roughly) "a whispering fashion model voice" and denotes the kind of model turned pop singer—of which Twiggy is another example—who is a proliferous species in Europe. Each of Newton-John's hit singles—"If You Love Me, Let Me Know," "Have You Never Been Mellow," "Let Me Be There," "Let's Get Physical" and a blasé reading of Dylan's "If Not for You" are the most notorious—has made her place on the throne of the dude ranch/ski lodge subgenre of Seventies and Eighties mass-market pap more secure. These albums are almost indistinguishable from one another: you have only to buy one to know if you need music to go with your marshmallow sundaes. — B.T.

NEW YORK CITY BAND
★ **New York City Band** / Amer. Int. **(1979)**
This is actually the soundtrack to A.I.P.'s

flick *Sunnyside,* starring John Travolta's younger brother, Joey. The only other distinction this disco hackwork possesses is an audacious version of "Bo Diddley," set to drum machine and synthesizer. Chuck Berry wept. — D.M.

THE NEW YORK DOLLS
★ ★ ★ **New York Dolls / Mer. (1973)**
★ ★ ★ ★ **Too Much Too Soon / Mer. (1974)**
If there was ever a band before its time, it was the New York Dolls, the early-Seventies precursors of the punk scene. Caught between the glitter and punk eras, the Dolls squawked out hard rock that most often recalled the Stones and MC5, though they also had clear, if sonically obscure, R&B roots. Their debut, while featuring such stand-outs as "Looking for a Kiss" and "Personality Crisis," was marred by Todd Rundgren's heavy production hand. Shadow Morton had a tighter grasp on *Too Much Too Soon,* and the result was a frenetic attack. The unlikely highlight was a cover of Archie Bell and the Drells' "There's Gonna Be a Showdown." With singer David Johansen pouting out the song like an adolescent Mick Jagger, the title of the album told it all. — J.B.M.

NEW YORK MARY
★ ★ ★ **New York Mary / Ari. / Free (1976)**
★ **A Piece of the Apple / Ari. / Free (1977)**
A tight jazz-funk horn band in the style of the Brecker Brothers, but not as strong conceptually or improvisationally (which is not necessarily something to be ashamed of). The debut album, *New York Mary,* avoids clichés, but *Piece* wallows in 'em. — M.R.

THE NEW YORK ROCK ENSEMBLE
★ ★ ★ ★ **Roll Over / Col. (1970)** ¶
This is the group that made its name by wearing tuxedos, playing society gigs and trying to adapt Bach to rock. They failed miserably at all that overblown stuff, then went out and made this tremendous rock & roll album. "Running down the Highway," "Anaconda" and "Field of Joy" are all top-notch songs, and the band plays with good taste and fire. — J.S.

THE NICE
★ ★ **Elegy / Mer. (1971)** ¶
The Nice began life as a backup quartet for British singer P. P. Arnold, whom they often upstaged with their showmanship. Two of the members, keyboardist Keith Emerson and drummer Brian Davison, had been part of Gary Farr and the T-Bones, an early British R&B act. Guitarist David O'List was in the original Roxy Music, although he left before they made their first LP, while bassist Lee Jackson and Davison later appeared in Jackson Heights and Refugee, respectively. Emerson, of course, went on to Emerson, Lake and Palmer.

Nice's approach was more similar to ELP than any of the rest: they revamped jazz and classical themes with a heavy rock bias. The group's most famous numbers were evergreens like "Rondo" and "America" (from *West Side Story*), which gave Emerson all the room he needed for his flamboyant antics. Unfortunately, the group's most representative recordings were made for Andrew Loog Oldham's now-defunct Immediate label, and this Mercury set hardly does Nice justice. *Elegy* features awkward covers of Bob Dylan and Tim Hardin songs and a peculiarly weak rendition of the once spirited "America." The key to the future—Emerson's anyway—is a horribly simplistic and colorless Tchaikovsky adaptation. — D.M.

STEVIE NICKS
★ ★ ★ **Bella Donna / Mod. (1981)**
Bella Donna, or belladonna, is the second most hallucinogenic drug in the world, capable of inducing bizarre visual and mental distortions. The *most* hallucinogenic drug in the world is fame and success in rock & roll at the level of, say, Fleetwood Mac, the group of which Stevie Nicks is a member. *Bella Donna,* like all hallucinations, is odd, complex and rife with the sort of profundity that appears foolish once the drug wears off. Super-producer Jimmy Iovine assembled a super-crew to back Nicks, including Tom Petty and the Heartbreakers on the hit single, "Stop Dragging My Heart Around." This isn't a bad record, but a whole album's worth of Nicks' pseudo-mystical raspings is enough to make one start seeing things. — R.P.

NIGHT
★ ★ **Night / Planet (1979)**
★ ★ **Long Distance / Planet (1980)**
Journeyman rock endorsed by auteur producer Richard Perry is hardly less numbing than the run-of-the-mill variety, despite Nicky Hopkins' keyboards. — D.M.

ROBERT NIGHTHAWK
★ ★ ★ ★ **Bricks in My Pillow / Pearl (NA)**
★ ★ ★ **Robert Nighthawk and His Flames Live on Maxwell Street, 1964 / Roun. (NA)**
One of the definitive slide guitarists of the

Chicago blues scene. Nighthawk's single-string bottlenecking is both beautiful and influential. His earliest recordings under his own name (he recorded before World War II as Robert Lee McCoy) were for Chess and Aristocrat; these are no longer available. The Pearl LP features his marvelous 1952 sides for States and United, including some previously unissued. The Rounder release, the title of which is self-explanatory, is also pretty good. — D.M.

THE NIGHTHAWKS
★ ★ ★ ★ **Jacks and Kings** / Adel. (1977)
★ ★ ★ **The Nighthawks** / Mer. (1980)
Veteran D.C.-area blues band shows off barroom muscle on both sets. The Adelphi's a little less polished (an advantage) and features support from Pinetop Perkins and Guitar Junior, among others. The Mercury set isn't quite as fine. Either album is worth checking out, though, as a sample of how young white groups are helping to perpetuate genuine blues style and emotion.
— D.M.

MAXINE NIGHTINGALE
★ ★ ★ **Right Back Where We Started From** / U.A. (1976) ¶
★ ★ **Night Life** / U.A. (1977) ¶
★ ★ **Lead Me On** / Wind. (1979) ¶
★ ★ **Bittersweet** / Wind. (1981)
"Right Back Where We Started From" was one of the most infectious hits of 1976, the best sort of pop R&B. Recorded in England, it is Nightingale's sole first-rate song. The rest of the album named for it, as well as the other followups, are conventional and unexplosive. — D.M.

NIGHTLIFE UNLIMITED
★ **Nightlife Unlimited** / Casa. (NA)
Part of Casablanca's seemingly endless store of banal and tedious disco background music. — D.M.

WILLIE NILE
★ ★ ★ ★ **Willie Nile** / Ari. (1980)
★ ★ ★ **Golden Down** / Ari. (1981)
After Steve Forbert turned out not to be the new Dylan, there was a brief effort to pin that label on Willie Nile. Big mistake. Nile is to Forbert as Elvis Costello is to Joe Jackson; a gifted original, not a talented stylist. His self-titled debut does a wonderful job of capturing the interplay between Nile's folkie roots and rock and roll instincts; *Golden Down* gets dragged down by its overambitious production, some of which comes dangerously close to Springsteenism. — J.D.C.

JOHN JACOB NILES
★ ★ ★ ★ **John Jacob Niles Sings Folk Songs** / Folk. (1964)
★ ★ **The Best of John Jacob Niles** / Trad. (NA)
Crossing Kentucky mountain tradition with a vocal style that is reminiscent of Elizabethan balladeers, Niles was a concert artist performing folk songs some fifty years before the genre came into vogue. As a composer he is responsible for "I Wonder as I Wander," "Go 'Way from My Window" and the popular melody for "Black Is the Color of My True Love's Hair." His high tenor is magnificently captured on "I'm So Glad Trouble Don't Last Always," from the Folkways set (mostly reissues of 78 material). Joan Baez is probably the most prominent recorded practitioner of this style of folk interpretation. — I.M.

HARRY NILSSON
★ ★ ★ ★ **The Pandemonium Shadow Show** / RCA (1967) ¶
★ ★ **Aerial Ballet** / RCA (1968) ¶
★ ★ **Harry** / RCA (1969) ¶
★ ★ ★ **The Point** / RCA (1970)
★ ★ ★ ★ **Nilsson Sings Newman** / RCA (1970) ¶
★ ★ ★ **Aerial Pandemonium Ballet** / RCA (1971) ¶
★ ★ ★ ★ **Nilsson Schmilsson** / RCA (1971)
★ ★ **Son of Schmilsson** / RCA (1972)
★ ★ **A Little Touch of Schmilsson in the Night** / RCA (1973)
★ ★ ★ ★ **Pussy Cats** / RCA (1974) ¶
★ ★ **. . . That's the Way It Is** / RCA (1976) ¶
★ ★ **Knnillssonn** / RCA (1977) ¶
★ ★ ★ ★ **Nilsson/Greatest Hits** / RCA (1978) ¶
★ ★ **The World's Greatest Lover** / RCA (1978) ¶
★ **Early Tymes** / Sp. (NA) ¶
Aerial Ballet and *Harry,* art-pop songwriter Harry Nilsson's second and third albums, display him as a whimsical moralist who made music so wry it forced either smiles or grimaces; the principal instrument was his soft, high, perfectly pitched voice, while the imagery in his lyrics was cleverly domestic. Lots of aging urban folkies enjoyed these late-sixties recordings, because they seemed sensibly progressive: traditional songwriting tastefully orchestrated. On his second album, Nilsson covered Randy Newman's "Simon Smith and the Amazing Dancing Bear," to this day the most chirpily soup-headed song Newman's written. When *Nilsson Sings Newman* (now incomprehensibly out of print)

followed, it seemed clear what Nilsson was aiming for: mass success achieved by deleting the bitterness from Newman's odd melodies and impeccable wordplay.

The Point, the soundtrack of a television cartoon, further embedded Nilsson's cuteness. *Nilsson Schmilsson,* however, was his artistic breakthrough: where once his songs had been shy and chiding when they wanted to criticize ("Don't Leave Me," "Together," "I Guess the Lord Must Be in New York City"), here he decided to rock out, with all the energy and passion without prettiness that phrase implies. He hadn't totally abandoned the lovely lilting, but in a dreamy confection like "The Moonbeam Song," he inserted one word—"crap"—that made the whole thing work, both as a good song and a good MOR parody.

Son of Schmilsson is a clutch of unbearably clever and/or willfully cheesy outtake manqués, while *A Little Touch* is the opposite: a numbingly careful rendering of smooth crooning in styles and songs of the Twenties, Thirties and Forties. To make it authentic, Nilsson used orchestrator/ arranger Gordon Jenkins, who has performed the same tasks for Sinatra, Garland, Nat Cole and others. Given what had just preceded it, *A Little Touch* was bizarre: Was Nilsson serious? Was it camp? Was it a monumental sneer? Or a repentance? But the album was too cool and slick to make such questions interesting.

There ensued a two-year silence, during which Nilsson lived out the slob Schmilsson persona—according to the headlines, perpetually drunk and always ready to carouse with new pals John Lennon and Ringo Starr. (He had first received attention because the debut album had some Paul McCartney soundalikes that were shocking in their verisimilitude.) He thrashed back with the Lennon-produced *Pussy Cats,* which, in its limning of rock agony and absurdity, finds equals only in Lennon's own *Plastic Ono Band* and Neil Young's *Tonight's the Night.* An assemblage of offbeat covers ("Loop de Loop," "Subterranean Homesick Blues," "Rock around the Clock"), *Pussy Cats* is inspiring in its rage and heartbreaking in its cheerfulness. For someone who's never fully achieved stardom, Harry Nilsson knows and articulates more about it than almost anyone in rock.

That's the Way It is is another burp from the dyspepsia that resulted in *Pussy Cats,* but it lacks the discipline that made *Cats* so scarily anarchic, the firmness that's essential to portraying a person out of control. Nils-

son has become a whimsical amoralist, an artist who cannot find salvation or even much comfort in his art unless he is savaging it. All that prevents him from becoming an L.A. Artaud is his small protests: he likes to sleep late, he doesn't like to shave and he's almost proudly lazy. — K.T.

999
★ ★ **999 / U.A. (1978)** ¶
★ ★ **High Energy Plan / PVC (1979)**
★ ★ ★ **The Biggest Prize in Sport / Poly. (1980)**
★ ★ ★ **Concrete / Poly. (1981)**

999 started out as a dyed-hair, pseudo-punk outfit and has since become a modestly entertaining guitar group. No social relevance, please (we're British), but truly snappy six-string sound. For slow-motion head-banging. — W.K.

NITEFLYTE
★ ★ **Niteflyte / Ario.-Amer. (1981)**

Eurodisco act actually cracked Top Forty (barely) with "If You Want It." — D.M.

NINTH CREATION
★ ★ **Reaching for the Top / Prel. (1977)**

Semi-successful hard-core dance music. — D.M.

1994
★ **1994 / A&M (1978)**
★ **Please Stand By / A&M (1979)**

Heartland rock with an arty bent, presumably to excuse the lack of an interesting singer or much melody. — D.M.

NITTY GRITTY DIRT BAND
★ ★ **Uncle Charlie and His Dog Teddy / Lib. (1970)**
★ ★ **All the Good Times / U.A. (1972)**
★ ★ ★ ★ **Will the Circle Be Unbroken / U.A. (1972)**
★ ★ **Stars and Stripes Forever / U.A. (1974)**
★ ★ **Dream / U.A. (1975)**
★ ★ ★ **Dirt, Silver and Gold / U.A. (1976)**
★ ★ **The Dirt Band / U.A. (1978)**
★ ★ **American Dream / U.A. (1979)**

Unlike other country-rock groups (Poco or even the Eagles) who merely added country trappings to their light rock & roll, the Nitty Gritty Dirt Band began with a firmer commitment to bluegrass and rural C&W, blending in the electrified accouterments of rock. Formed in Long Beach, California, in 1965, the group has an underlying musical focus that's helped keep the Dirt Band (as it is now called) together through myriad personnel changes (Jackson Browne is one of many one-time group members) and ever-changing musical climates.

The Dirt Band's first album, *The Nitty Gritty Dirt Band,* yielded a hit single, "Buy for Me the Rain," by far their most middle-of-the-road 45. But that album, as well as their next three, are no longer available, leaving *Uncle Charlie and His Dog Teddy* to begin the story. *Uncle Charlie* demonstrated the band's savvy for picking material by up-and-coming songwriters. No less than three hit singles were culled from it: Michael Nesmith's "Some of Shelley's Blues," Kenny Loggins' "House at Pooh Corner" and the million-selling version of Jerry Jeff Walker's "Mr. Bojangles."

But it was not until the band moved from Los Angeles to Aspen, Colorado, that its identity became fixed and its albums began to gain a consistency of forethought and execution. *All the Good Times* (parts of which were recorded live) reflected not only the Dirt Band's new rural roots but also its affinity for modernized cornpone humor. That album also produced the last thing even approaching a hit single for the band, a swinging version of Hank Williams' "Jambalaya." The Dirt Band's acknowledged masterstroke, however, came in 1972. *Will the Circle Be Unbroken,* a three-record set, brought together three generations of musical Americana in a well-conceived, ornately packaged supersession. Traditional classics such as "Keep on the Sunny Side," "Orange Blossom Special" and "I Saw the Light" are performed with relish by country institutions like Mother Maybelle Carter, Earl Scruggs, Doc Watson, Roy Acuff, Merle Travis and Vassar Clements.

By their next album, *Stars and Stripes Forever,* the group was whittled down to a quartet (Jeff Hanna, John McEuen, Jim Ibbotson and Jimmie Fadden), and managed to represent its live show on two records. But this was a less successful attempt to sum up the band's career than the subsequent hits LP, *Dirt, Silver and Gold,* another three-record set, this one including early hits, unreleased masters and some new material. Between those two compilations was a single album, *Dream,* which stands as the band's last attempt to remain faithful to its bluegrass and country roots, including the obligatory Hank Williams song ("Hey Good Lookin'," with Linda Ronstadt on vocals) and an almost-hit version of the Everly Brothers' "(All I Have to Do Is) Dream."

On the surface, it would seem that the Dirt Band finally gave in to commercial pressures on *The Dirt Band.* It was a six-man band by this point, with Jim Ibbotson exiting and Merle Bregante, Al Garth (both of Loggins and Messina's band) and Richard Hathaway entering the fold. The LP is more song-oriented than its predecessors, and bluegrass influences give way to supplemental horns and strings. But *American Dream,* their only album since, was a disappointment. — G.K.

DON NIX

★ ★ **In God We Trust / Shel. (1971)** ¶
★ **Gone Too Long / Cream (1976)**
★ **Sky Rider / Shel. (NA)**
Jive white Memphis bluesman. *Gone Too Long* has worst possible version of the Byrds' "I'll Feel a Whole Lot Better." *In God* gets an extra star for the dignified participation of venerable real thing Furry Lewis, and the support of the Muscle Shoals Rhythm Section. — D.M.

RAB NOAKES

★ ★ **Red Pump Special / War. (1974)** ¶
★ ★ **Rab Noakes / MCA (1980)**
Competent singer, tedious songwriter, half a decade behind the times half a decade ago . . . hopelessly lost in space and time these days. — D.M.

KENNY NOLAN

★ ★ **Night Miracles/Casa. (NA)**
Singer/songwriter who penned "Lady Marmalade," "Get Dancin' " and "My Eyes Adored You" peddles his drip-dry sentiment on this solo debut. — J.S.

THE NOLAN SISTERS

★ ★ **Twenty Greatest Hits / Target (1978), Br. imp.**
★ ★ **The Nolan Sisters Collection / Pick. (1980), Br. imp.**
★ ★ ★ **Don't Make Waves / Epic (1980), Br. imp.**
★ ★ ★ **Nolan Sisters / Epic (1981), Br. imp.**
An Irish family of four sisters who practiced their MOR songs in London cabarets. Since joining Epic, they've left their Osmonds-like image behind them with tracks like "Who's Gonna Rock You" and "Chemistry." The Nolans were the first group to smash Japan's domestic charts in addition to the U.K.'s— they're not as straight as they look. — ML.H.

IAN NORTH

★ ★ ★ ★ **Neo / Aura (1979), Br. imp.**
★ ★ **My Girlfriend's Dead / Cach. (1981), Br. imp.**
New Yorker Ian North led Milk 'n' Cookies,

a band of would-be expatriate pop stars, to England in the mid-Seventies; since their breakup he has pursued a number of musical projects on his own. *Neo* is culled from recordings with several lineups of British musicians; the songs are clever but neurotic Anglo-American rock 'n' pop. *My Girlfriend's Dead* was done completely solo in New York, and tries to ape the cold synthesizer noises of Gary Numan with only marginal success. — I.R.

NOVA

★ ★ ★ **Vimania / Ari. (1976)** ¶
★ ★ ★ **Wings of Love / Ari. (1978)**
★ ★ ★ **Sun City / Ari. (1978)**
An Italian band influenced by the Mahavishnu Orchestra's acoustic stylings, Wayne Shorter's soprano sax attack, and British art-rock vocalizing. The resultant fusion is airy and pleasant, and on *Vimania,* guest drummer Narada Michael Walden pushes things incisively and contributes a catchy chart.
— M.R.

NRBQ

★ ★ ★ **NRBQ at Yankee Stadium / Mer. (1978)**
The initials originally stood for New Rhythm and Blues Quartet, but in fact these funky New York street guys play a mix of jazz and rock that swings and bops pretty hard, with a quirky sense of humor of the Michael Hurley variety. NRBQ made a series of Columbia albums, all now out of print, that are worth investigating, but this set is fine as well, in a modest way.
— D.M.

TED NUGENT

★ ★ ★ **Ted Nugent and the Amboy Dukes / Main. (1968)** ¶
★ ★ ★ **Ted Nugent / Epic (1975)**
★ ★ ★ **Free-for-All / Epic (1976)**
★ ★ **Marriage on the Rocks/Rock Bottom / Poly. (1976)**
★ ★ ★ ★ **Cat Scratch Fever / Epic (1977)**
★ ★ ★ ★ **Double Live Gonzo! / Epic (1978)**
★ ★ ★ **Weekend Warriors / Epic (1978)**
★ ★ ★ **State of Shock / Epic (1979)**
★ ★ ★ ★ **Scream Dream / Epic (1980)**
★ ★ ★ **Intensities in Ten Cities / Epic (1981)**
★ ★ ★ **Great Gonzos: The Best of Ted Nugent / Epic (1981)**
Ted Nugent has been recording since the mid-Sixties, when his Detroit-based band, the Amboy Dukes, had hits with a version of "Baby Please Don't Go" and their own quasi-psychedelic "Journey to the Center of the Mind." The original Dukes were a well-balanced rock band, typical of the time, with a decent singer, sloppy drummer and a half-inspired guitarist in Nugent. Subsequent editions of the group (the first recorded for Mainstream; later they made discs for Polydor and Warner Bros.) leaned more and more heavily on Nugent, a real wild man who viewed everything as a background for his undisciplined excursions into Jimi Hendrix fantasyland.

It wasn't until Nugent reached Epic Records and producers Tom Werman and Lou Futterman that he achieved some focus for his sheets of notes and piles of chords. Nugent is a formidable stylist in the heavy metal/psychedelic styles of the late Sixties and early Seventies. But if it weren't for his carnivorous and hysterical showmanship— and his unrestrained boastfulness about his alleged talents—he'd probably seem more old-fashioned than celebrated. As it is, he has become a star by making albums that capture all the frenzy of a convention of armed lunatics.

Nugent's demeanor is not inspired by drugs, but by sex and, he says, hunting—his blood lust and skills with rifle and bow and arrow are legendary. Oddly enough, this out-of-control image matches his playing so perfectly that his best records are his most recent, particularly *Scream Dream* and *Double Live Gonzo!,* the latter of which also serves as an excellent historical retrospective of his career. His other recent albums merely use and abuse the formula he established earlier.
— D.M.

GARY NUMAN

★ ★ ★ **Replicas / Atco (1979)**
★ ★ ★ **The Pleasure Principle / Atco (1979)**
★ ★ **Telekon / Atco (1980)**
★ **Tubeway Army/First Album / Atco (1981)**
★ ★ **Dance / Atco (1981)**
Gary Numan is essentially a trivialist, but a trivialist of great ability. Starting out in the sci-fi-obsessed Tubeway Army, Numan put out one album of lean but uninteresting punk (*Tubeway Army/First Album,* released in Britain in 1978) before discovering synthesizers. Numan used the synthesizer for burbling background as well as to support his simple, catchy hooks, and in so doing managed to turn the alienated-technician ethos of his idols Ultravox into a commercially successful sound. His first big hit was "Are 'Friends' Electric," from *Replicas,* followed by *Pleasure Principle*'s "Cars," which broke him in the United States. His well ran dry shortly after that; *Telekon* was tuneful but rather drab, while *Dance* makes an interest-

ing stab at imitating Eno's *Another Green World.* — J.D.C.

LAURA NYRO

★ ★ ★ ★ **Eli and the Thirteenth Confession /
Col. (1968)**
★ ★ ★ **New York Tendaberry / Col. (1969)**
★ ★ ★ **Christmas and the Beads of Sweat /
Col. (1970)**
★ ★ ★ ★ **Gonna Take a Miracle / Col.
(1971)**
★ ★ ★ **The First Songs / Col. (1973)**
★ ★ **Smile / Col. (1975)**
★ ★ **Season of Lights / Col. (1977)** ¶
★ ★ **Nested / Col. (1978)**

Laura Nyro was the hottest American songwriter in the pop and pop-R&B fields for a
period in the late Sixties and early Seventies.
She wrote "Stoney End" for Barbra Streisand; "Stoned Soul Picnic," "Sweet Blindness" and "Wedding Bell Blues" for the
Fifth Dimension; and Blood, Sweat and
Tears' "And When I Die." But her own performances were not as well received: booed
off the stage at the Monterey Pop Festival in
1967, she has never recovered, and remains
one of the current music scene's most shel-
tered and enigmatic figures.

Nyro has certain problems—a tendency to
be both obtuse and precious, platitudinous
and opaque—but of all the American singer/
songwriters of her era, she is certainly the
most soulful. Her best records—*Eli, The
First Songs* and the collaboration with
Labelle, *Gonna Take a Miracle*—fuse rock
and poetry with far more conviction and
emotional honesty than, say, Patti Smith.

After *Miracle* was released in late 1971,
Nyro did not record or make public appearances again until late 1975, when *Smile* appeared. Nyro still sounded about the same,
but in many ways that simply meant that
she was outdated, and she has not regained
her large cult or expanded it into anything
like mass success with the relatively mediocre LPs that have followed. — D.M.

GARY O
★ Gary O' / Cap. (NA)
Boring pop rock. — D.M.

BILLY OCEAN
★ Nights / Epic (NA)
Lightweight pop singer scored in 1976 with
"Love Really Hurts without You," trite
radio fodder. — D.M.

PHIL OCHS
★ ★ **All the News That's Fit to Sing** / Elek.
(1964)
★ ★ ★ **I Ain't a'Marchin' Anymore** / Elek.
(1965)
★ ★ ★ ★ **Phil Ochs in Concert** / Elek.
(1966)
As a former journalism student, Phil Ochs'
decision to become a "topical" songwriter
was appropriate. He started off in the Sixties
as an imitator of Bob Gibson, more out of
convenience than any sense of tradition. By
the time he recorded his first album, he was
already staking out his special territory, a
kind of romantic new left patriotism.

Despite the fast-fingered playing of Danny
Kalb (later lead guitarist for the Blues Project), *All the News That's Fit to Sing* is rather
drab, aside from Ochs' emulation of Woody
Guthrie, "The Power and the Glory" and an
inspired adaptation of Edgar Allan Poe's
"The Bells." On *I Ain't a'Marchin'*, Ochs'
second album and solo this time, he hits his
stride; the John Kennedy assassination and
the escalation of the Vietnam War created
an ethos of patriotic concern and protest in
which Ochs worked best. "Draft Dodger
Rag" and "I Ain't a'Marchin' Anymore" became antiwar theme songs, while "Here's to
the State of Mississippi" and "In the Heat of
the Summer" show just how much passion
Ochs could bring to the topical song.

On *Phil Ochs in Concert,* Ochs delivers his
strongest collection of protest songs, but his

voice—freed of the restraints of folk-music
vocals—soars away from the melodies into
dramatic phrasing. The influence of Bob
Dylan, moreover, prompted Ochs to pen several slightly "abstract" political songs like
"There But for Fortune" (a hit single for
Joan Baez), "Canons of Christianity" and his
first major narrative works, "The Ringing of
Revolution" and "Santo Domingo," both of
which are still amazingly moving. Although
In Concert offers his most advanced collection of protest songs, and the most droll be-
tween-song remarks ever recorded by anyone, it was the lone love song, "Changes,"
which caught the most attention.
★ ★ ★ **Pleasures of the Harbor** / A&M
(1967)
★ ★ ★ **Tape from California** / A&M (1968)
★ ★ ★ ★ **Rehearsals for Retirement** / A&M
(1969) ¶
★ ★ ★ **Chords of Fame** / A&M (1976)
Ochs' *Pleasures of the Harbor* was an all-
too-grand attempt to create his own *Blonde
on Blonde* and become a major songwriter/
poet. If Dylan could create a successful song
cycle by drawing on the poetics of Verlaine
and Rimbaud, then Ochs could pursue Keats
and Byron and the music of the nineteenth-
century art song. While they may work well
enough as baroque meditations on idealism
(in concert they did), "Cross My Heart,"
"I've Had Her," "Pleasures of the Harbor"
and "Flower Lady" sink into a slow melodrama with their Mozart-like piano awash in
dense strings. The most intriguing song on
the album is "Crucifixion," which is a
mythic narrative about the politics of assassination from Christ to Kennedy.

However much Ochs wanted to be the
songwriter/poet, *Pleasures* attains its special
charm through three comedy songs, "The
Party," "Miranda" and the celebrated
"Small Circle of Friends," with which his
public reputation is forever linked. The ar-

rangements here, unlike the "exalted" serious songs, played Dixieland and cocktail-piano stylings off Ochs' splendidly deadpan vocals.

The opening title track of *Tape from California* is Ochs' first, and quite successful, foray into rock & roll, helped by producer Van Dyke Parks. Then there is the straight folkie "Joe Hill," an autobiographical ballad and two beautifully martial antiwar songs, the last of which, "The War Is Over," was Ochs' most eccentric contribution to the mounting antiwar movement. The second side opens and closes with two very bad songs, "The Harder They Fall," based on elaborate puns, and a shy return to the themes of *Pleasures,* "The Floods of Florence." The centerpiece, however, is Ochs' explosive answer to Dylan's "Desolation Row"—"When in Rome." The song does nothing less than symbolically rewrite the entire history of the United States as a chaotic and apocalyptic epic, with Ochs playing all the lead parts in the first person. Performed solo, it marks the early stages of Ochs' personal disintegration, and it's brilliant.

The madness really breaks out on *Rehearsals for Retirement,* Ochs' bitter and extraordinary self-examination as a Sixties American hero. The Chicago Democratic Convention was a trauma from which Ochs, ever the sentimental patriot, never quite recovered. "My Life" closes the album like a door slamming on a cell, and not even the wit of "Where Were You in Chicago" defuses the scorched depression of the rest. *Rehearsals* has all the marks of an epitaph, but it is here that Ochs' wit, politics and poetic intentions ultimately meet and their vehicle is rock & roll, scruffily produced by Larry Parks. On this album, Ochs actually succeeds in becoming an American romantic, a scarred veteran of the Sixties with his soul still intact.

However, his psyche was shot, and his next project, an exploration of Americana, floundered on *Greatest Hits* (deleted). Van Dyke Parks' arrangements are too heavy, and the rapid decay of Ochs' writing, now that his political demons had departed to leave only anomie, brought the album down to numb sentimentality.

Released only in Canada, *Shoot Out at Carnegie Hall* (A&M, 1971) was Ochs' last gesture. Dressed in gold lamé and backed by a band (made up of the *Rehearsals* crew), he sang his best songs, "Okie from Muskogee" and medleys of Elvis Presley and Buddy Holly hits. Much of this material, but not the medleys, can be found on *Chords of Fame,* an anthology released after Ochs' suicide and distinguished by the alternate versions of sensual songs, including a march-band single of "Power and Glory," the live solo version of "Crucifixion" and the madcap singles (with Paul Rothchild producing) of songs from his first two albums.   — B.T.

OCONNOR
★ ★ **Come Alive / Bears. (1981)**
Funk 'n' fusioneer does little or nothing with the staples, despite Willie Mitchell's guidance.   — D.M.

HAZEL O'CONNOR
★ ★ **Breaking Glass / A&M (1980)**
★ ★ **Sons and Lovers / A&M (1980)**
This would-be new-wave English singer/ songwriter would be happier (if she had the pipes) singing arias in Wagnerian operas. At least that's what she seems to be attempting on these two unintentionally comic efforts.

Breaking Glass is the soundtrack album to the film that was an old-fashioned star vehicle for O'Connor. The film chronicles (what else?) the rise and fall of a "new-wave" singer and has as much to do with the spirit of contemporary British music as Barbra Streisand's *A Star Is Born* did with rock & roll.

On *Sons and Lovers,* O'Connor massacres "Danny Boy," transforming it into an apocalyptic battle march. And that's not the worst of it. Misguided, overblown nonsense.   — D.G.

MARK O'CONNOR
★ ★ ★ **Mark O'Connor / Roun. (1974)**
★ ★ ★ ★ **Markology / Roun. (1978)**
★ ★ ★ ★ **On the Rampage / Roun. (1979)**
Fiddle player O'Connor debuted as a leader at age fifteen in a stellar instrumental trio with Norman Blake on mandolin and Charlie Collins on guitar. O'Connor subsequently became a pioneer of new-wave bluegrass, dubbed "dawg music" by mandolinist David Grisman, whose group O'Connor joined. Grisman and guitarist Tony Rice, who was also part of the same Grisman ensemble, are all over *Markology,* which, astonishingly, reveals O'Connor as a master guitarist as well. *On the Rampage* features O'Connor on both guitar and fiddle. His only flaw is a tendency to play with such dazzlingly perfect technique that feeling can become a secondary consideration.   — J.S.

KENNY O'DELL
★ **Kenny O'Dell / Capri. (1974)**
★ **Let's Shake Hands and Come Out Lovin' / Capri. (NA)**

O'Dell has written some respectable country hits, like Charlie Rich's smash "Behind Closed Doors." Too bad he sings with an adenoidal whine that makes you wanna smack that noisy kid and tell him to shut up. — R.P.

ODETTA
★ **Odetta at the Gate of Horn / Trad. (NA)**
★ ★ ★ **The Essential Odetta / Van. (1973)**
Odetta is one of the most powerful folk-song stylists this country has produced. That her numerous recordings—some solo, some with rhythm section and some attempting folk rock, most out of print—have never aired the emotional intensity she reaches in live performance is sad. Perhaps a video disc would show her to better effect.
Odetta at the Gate of Horn is not the live album for which one would have hoped, and her voice matured considerably after the LP was made. *The Essential* was compiled from Carnegie Hall and Town Hall concerts, and because it's two discs long, it is more representative of her repertoire. — I.M.

ANDREW "VOICE" ODOM
★ ★ ★ ★ **Farther on down the Road / Blues. (1973)**
One of the many performers known as "B. B. King, Jr.": Odom was the St. Louis version. On this set, his excellent singing is pitched masterfully against the stinging guitar accompaniment of Earl Hooker. — J.S.

ODYSSEY
★ ★ ★ **Odyssey / RCA (1977)** ¶
★ **Hollywood Party Tonight / RCA (1978)** ¶
★ **Hang Together / RCA (1980)**
★ **I've Got the Melody / RCA (1981)**
"Native New Yorker" and "Weekend Lover," Top Forty hits for this two-man, three-woman black singing group in 1978, were both very much in the spirit of early Motown—cheery, soulful pop. Unfortunately, the followups are simply inept. — D.M.

OHIO PLAYERS
★ ★ **Ohio Players / Cap. (1974)** ¶
★ ★ ★ ★ **Fire / Mer. (1974)**
★ ★ ★ **Skin Tight / Mer. (1974)**
★ ★ ★ **Contradiction / Mer. (1976)**
★ ★ ★ ★ **Ohio Players Gold / Mer. (1976)**
★ **Angel / Mer. (1977)**
★ ★ **Mr. Mean / Mer. (1977)**
★ ★ **Best of the Ohio Players Early Years, Vol. 1 / Westb. (1977)**
★ ★ **Honey / Mer. (1978)**
★ ★ **Jass-Ay-Lay-Dee / Mer. (1978)**
★ **Everybody Up / Ari. (1979)**

★ ★ **Tenderness / Bdwalk (1981)**
★ ★ **Young and Ready / Acc. (1981)**
★ ★ **Ohio Players / Trip (NA)** ¶
★ ★ **Ohio Players / Up Fr. (NA)** ¶
★ ★ ★ **Sixteen Greatest Hits / Trip (NA)**
Dayton, Ohio's answer to the bizarre, post–Sly Stone funk sadomasochism of Parliament/Funkadelic. Formed in the early Seventies by reedman Clarence "Satch" Satchell, the band recorded a couple of inconsequential albums for Westbound Records, *Pain* and *Pleasure* (now out of print), known as much for the bondage cover art as for the music inside. The band's first hit single, a monotonous vamp called "Funky Worm," remains in print on the *Best of the Early Years* collection. When the Players switched to Mercury Records and adopted a more overtly Sly Stone–influenced style, immediate mass success followed. "Skin Tight" and "Fire" kicked off a series of monster R&B hits. Eventually the band ran out of hooks and degenerated into just another grinding wheel. *Fire* and the Mercury *Gold* collection present the group at its best. — J.S.

OINGO BOINGO
★ ★ **Oingo Boingo / IRS (1980)**
★ ★ ★ **Only a Lad / A&M (1981)**
Glib, somewhat slick and occasionally humorous new-wave group, whose sound is onomatopoeic. The title track of *Only a Lad* is the best moment. — J.S.

THE O'JAYS
★ ★ ★ ★ ★ **Back Stabbers / Phil. (1972)**
★ ★ ★ **The O'Jays in Philadelphia / Phil. (1973)**
★ ★ ★ ★ **Ship Ahoy / Phil. (1973)**
★ ★ **Live in London / Phil. (1974)**
★ ★ ★ **Survival / Phil. (1975)**
★ ★ ★ ★ **Family Reunion / Phil. (1975)**
★ ★ ★ **Message in the Music / Phil. (1976)**
★ ★ ★ **Travelin' at the Speed of Thought / Phil. (1977)**
★ ★ ★ **O'Jays Collector's Items / Phil. (1977)**
★ ★ ★ **So Full of Love / Phil. (1978)**
★ ★ ★ **Identify Yourself / Phil. (1979)**
★ ★ ★ **The Year 2000 / Phil. (1980)**
★ ★ ★ **The O'Jays / Up Fr. (NA)**
The O'Jays were probably the most faceless of all the groups who were the tools of Philadelphia soul producers Kenny Gamble and Leon Huff, but they have also been the most consistently successful, beginning with a string of R&B hits including "Lipstick Traces" (1965) and "I'll Be Sweeter Tomorrow" (1967), which are repackaged on the

Up Front collection along with similar R&B hits of the period.

Their early-Seventies recordings for Gamble and Huff's Neptune label (collected on *In Philadelphia*) reached much the same audience, but it was their 1972 hits "Back Stabbers" and "992 Arguments" (from *Back Stabbers*) that set the tone for the Philly International success story. Growling vocals rode on top of huge, complex productions that antedate disco but pick up on many of the seminal components of that sound, particularly the drums, which are mixed ever louder on succeeding releases. The group's string of singles successes has continued virtually unabated—"Love Train" and "Put Your Hands Together" in 1973, "For the Love of Money" in 1974, "I Love Music" in 1975 and so on.

The group's albums have been consistently danceable and the singing is always powerful, although recent LPs have succumbed somewhat to the specious quasi-mystical preaching of Gamble and Huff, who seem to have decided that disco is also the ideal medium for a kind of elusive spiritualism that smacks of the hippie rhetoric prevalent among Sixties white rock bands. None of this mars, however, the really awesome power of the best O'Jays music; *Back Stabbers* ranks with the best albums released in any genre in the past decade. — D.M.

DANNY O'KEEFE
★ ★ ★ **Danny O'Keefe / Coti. (1970)** ¶
★ ★ **Breezy Stories / Atco (1973)**
★ **So Long Harry Truman / Atco (1975)**
★ **American Roulette / War. (1977)**
★ **Seattle Tapes / First Amer. (1977)**
★ **Global Blues / War. (1978)**
Erratic singer/songwriter whose moment of glory, "Good Time Charlie's Got the Blues" (from *Danny O'Keefe*), was more than enough to base a career on. — J.S.

OLD AND IN THE WAY
★ ★ ★ ★ **Old and in the Way / Round (1975)** ¶
This live string band recording (from the Boarding House in San Francisco in 1973) is a treat. Old and in the Way was best known for presenting Grateful Dead guitarist Jerry Garcia in a nonelectric context. Though this was a convenient promotional hook, Garcia didn't really lead the band. Instead he played banjo and sang harmony vocals along with David Grisman, who added his excellent mandolin playing to the ensemble as well. Guitarist/vocalist Peter Rowan fronted

the band and contributed its two liveliest songs, "Midnight Moonlight" and "Panama Red." John Kahn played string bass, and bluegrass violin virtuoso Vassar Clements put on the finishing touches as featured soloist (his break on "Midnight Moonlight" is terrific). — J.S.

MIKE OLDFIELD
★ ★ **Tubular Bells / Virgin (1973)**
★ ★ **Ommadawn / Virgin (1975)** ¶
★ **Airborn / Virgin (1980)**
★ **QE2 / Virgin (1982)**
Oldfield, who had played bass and lead guitar in Kevin Ayers' band, was Virgin's first artist in 1973, and *Tubular Bells,* an ambitious fifty-minute composition, was an immediate success in Britain. The album consists of short, uncompelling melodies—based on rock, classical and British folk themes—repeated over and over at sluggish tempos, with various instruments (mostly fretted or keyboard) playing the same part. It's simplistic, monotonous and far too long, but fragmented into a 45 and released as the theme song from the film *The Exorcist,* it also became a pop smash in America.

The followup, *Hergest Ridge* (now deleted), was similar, although it emphasized the folk derivation and offered more colorful and pastoral textures and phrases. But *Ommadawn* capitalized on its predecessor's improvements, and added livelier, more forceful playing, as well as more catchy phrases. Still, it lacks sufficient imagination to sustain the composition over an entire LP. The same goes for the others. — D.M.

SALLY OLDFIELD
★ ★ ★ **Water Bearer / Chrys. (1978)**
This mysteriously beautiful album combines the British folk music and art-rock traditions in a tour de force by Oldfield, who plays a variety of keyboards, guitars and percussion instruments on the set. — J.S.

DAVID OLIVER
★ ★ **Jamerican Man / Mer. (1977)** ¶
★ ★ **David Oliver / Mer. (1978)**
★ ★ **Here's to You / Mer. (NA)**
★ ★ **Mind Magic / Mer. (NA)**
Destitute late soul mannerisms without enough grace to pass as even poor man's Chic. — D.M.

OLYMPIC RUNNERS
★ ★ **Don't Let Up / Lon. (1975)**
★ ★ **Hot to Trot / Lon. (1977)**
★ **Puttin' It On You / Poly. (1978)**
Mitch Mitchell and Ric Grech once planned

a supergroup that would have featured themselves and a guitarist they'd discovered, Joe Jammer. That plan fizzled, but Jammer went on to form the Olympic Runners, with Pete Wingfield (former Keef Hartley, Van Morrison, Colin Blunstone and Maggie Bell keyboardist). The format was transcendent disco, but it was sustained only for the group's first two albums, *Put the Music Where Your Mouth Is* and *Out-in-Front,* both of which London has deleted. What's left doesn't have the hot playing, although it does contain samples of Jammer's artfully Spartan guitar jabbing. Wingfield left to go solo, and made the 1976 hit, "Eighteen with a Bullet," in a vein similar to the Runners' early work. — B.M.

LENORE O'MALLEY
■ Lenore / Poly. (NA)
■ First Be a Woman / Poly. (NA) ¶
Tarty Eurodisco more notable for the chanteuse's gargantuan bosom than for the Phyllis-Schlafly-on-spanish-fly lyrical sentiments or the drum-machine rhythm track.
— D.M.

OMEGA
★ ★ Omega / Pass. (1975)
For everyone who'd like to grow up to be a synthesizer. — D.M.

ONE WAY WITH AL HUDSON
★ ★ ★ Love Is . . . One Way / MCA (NA)
★ ★ ★ One Way / MCA (NA)
★ ★ ★ Fancy Dancer / MCA (NA)
Successor to Al Hudson and the Soul Partners. Not as good as Hudson's 1977 album, *Cherish,* but it's solid contemporary soul, worth aficionado interest. — D.M.

THE ONLY ONES
★ ★ ★ Special View / Epic (1979)
★ ★ Baby's Got a Gun / Epic (1980)
Average British Beat, modern style. Best song is the first on *Special View,* "Another Girl, Another Planet"; it's downhill from there. — W.K.

ROY ORBISON
★ ★ ★ Greatest Hits / Monu. (1963)
★ ★ ★ ★ In Dreams / Monu. (1963)
★ ★ ★ More of Roy Orbison's Greatest Hits / Monu. (1964)
★ ★ ★ ★ Very Best of Roy Orbison / Monu. (1966)
★ ★ ★ The Original Sound of Roy Orbison / Sun (1969)
★ ★ ★ ★ ★ All-Time Greatest Hits / Monu. (1972)

★ ★ ★ Focus on Roy Orbison / Lon. (1976), Br. imp.
★ ★ ★ Regeneration / Monu. (1977)
★ ★ Laminar Flow / Asy. (1979)
★ ★ ★ Golden Hits / Buck. (NA) ¶
★ ★ ★ The Big O / Charly (NA), Br. imp.
★ ★ ★ Roy O / Charly (NA), Br. imp.
★ ★ ★ The Classic Roy Orbison / Lon. (NA), Br. imp.
★ ★ ★ Roy Orbison Sings / Lon. (NA), Br. imp.
Roy Orbison was one of the most singular rock stylists of the Fifties and Sixties; his string of hits is full of maundering, literally paranoiac self-pity, redeemed time and again by the extraordinary power of his quavering voice and the eccentric dynamism of the musical arrangements, which range from hard-edged rock & roll to the plushest ballads.

At Sun in the Fifties, Orbison was a journeyman rockabilly, heavily influenced by Elvis Presley both as a writer and as a singer. His hits were minor—"Rock House" and "Ooby Dooby" have lasted—but he occasionally came up with a track of gripping proportions: "Domino" features surf-style guitar five years too soon, while "Devil Doll" sets the stage for his truly major accomplishments of the next decade.

When he moved to Monument, where he was produced by Frank Foster, Orbison's style quickly divided into two parts. On the one hand, there was the nearly snarling blues/country shouter, whose quintessential movement comes with the seductive snarl on "Oh Pretty Woman." That song, and others like it, including "Mean Woman Blues" and "Candy Man," had a fair share of influence on the Beatles (who toured with him) and the rest of British rock & roll.

But Orbison's most fascinating records are chronicles of deep lust and even deeper fear: "Running Scared," "Love Hurts," "Only the Lonely"—these titles tell the story. In "Running Scared," the music builds from a whisper to a scream as Orbison recites an ultimate paranoid fantasy, imagining what might happen if his girl *possibly* saw someone who *might* attract her more than him, an anxiety rendered completely ironic because at the end he imagines that she doesn't. In general, these records were accompanied by the same surging Nashville rhythm section used for the other songs, but often abetted by female choruses and usually using strings to accentuate the rhythm. Only Phil Spector came close to this orchestral style of music, and only Spector matched Orbison's paranoia.

The Charly, Buckboard and Sun compila-

tions are of the material Orbison did for Sun in the Fifties, including the hits "Ooby Dooby" and "Rock House." The London records are from sessions after Roy's hit period (at Monument); they're generally a notch below his best, though there are sometimes minor delights hidden amongst them. The Monument *All-Time* is one of rock's more indispensable anthologies—its two records contain all the hits and a fair share of other oddities ("Leah" and "Shadaroba" reveal an unlikely bent for Orientalism). *Very Best* is a good one-disc sampling of the hits, while the other Monuments have been rendered redundant. The exception is *Regeneration,* the album that reunited Orbison and producer Frank Foster; it's less inspired than competent, but it is also always listenable.
— D.M.

ORCHESTRAL MANOEUVRES IN THE DARK
★ ★ ★ **Orchestral Manoeuvres in the Dark /**
Dindisc (1981)
★ ★ ★ **Architecture and Morality / Virgin/**
Epic (1981)
Tuneful, innovative two-man group led by the synthesizer work of Paul Humphreys and Andrew McCluskey. The group's approach is impressive (and unusual), since they are experimental yet keenly desirous of a mass audience. "Souvenir" (from *Architecture*), No. 3 hit single in England, proves their accessibility. — J.S.

THE ORCHIDS
★ ★ **The Orchids / MCA (1980)**
After his world-conquest plans for the Runaways fell through, impresario Kim Fowley decided he needed tarty innocence rather than sleazy insouciance. The results were actually more listenable than most such Fowley projects because he relied on girl-group fetishism rather than heavy-metal thunder. On the other hand, the Orchids gave little sign that there was anyone as talented as Joan Jett hidden among them. — D.M.

ORIGINAL MIRRORS
★ ★ ★ ★ **Original Mirrors / Ari. (1980)**
This hard-rocking, post-new-wave quintet led by ex–Deaf School vocalist Steve Allen plays toe-tapping R&B with a tough-edged bite that reflects its roots. "Could This Be Heaven" is the high point. — J.S.

THE ORIGINALS
★ ★ **Down to Love Town / Soul (1977)** ¶
★ ★ **Another Time, Another Place / Fan.**
(1978) ¶

★ ★ **Come Away with Me / Fan.**
(1978) ¶
★ ★ ★ ★ **Super Star Series, Vol. 9 / Mo.**
(1981)
The Originals have recorded two classic records, "The Bells," and "Baby I'm for Real," both produced by Marvin Gaye. Some of their best work is salvaged on the Motown anthology, but the other albums don't do the group justice. Without Gaye's guidance, the Originals lack distinctive personality and direction.
— J.MC.

ORION
■ **Orion Reborn / Sun (1979)**
■ **Sunrise / Sun (1980)**
■ **Country / Sun (1980)**
■ **Rockabilly / Sun (1981)**
■ **Fresh / Sun (NA)**
■ **Glory / Sun (NA)**
The idea here is that this is Elvis reborn, or that Elvis never died, just changed his name and went to work for Sun entrepreneur Shelby Singleton, or something equally likely. Actually, the concept is to confuse people with a mask and a glittery style, but the bottom line is second-rate Elvis impersonations (a third-rate idea to start with). There are people who claim to know Orion's "real" identity, but I'm not sure he deserves one.
— D.M.

TONY ORLANDO AND DAWN
★ **He Don't Love You / Asy. (1975)**
★ ★ **Greatest Hits / Ari. (1975)**
■ **Before Dawn / Epic (1975)**
■ **To Be with You / Elek. (1976)**
★ **The World of Tony Orlando and Dawn /**
Ari. (1976)
■ **I Got Rhythm / Casa. (NA)**
■ **Livin' for the Music / Casa. (NA)**
■ **Tony Orlando / Casa. (NA)**
Until he met up with producers Hank Medress and Dave Appel, Tony Orlando worked for CBS Records as a publishing executive. With the enormous success of "Tie a Yellow Ribbon 'round the Old Oak Tree" in 1973, he became a national celebrity, but one utterly without substance. The singles weren't the worst of it—imagine what the filler sounded like—but they were bad enough: one hoarse-throated throwback to the days of Frankie Laine after another. Garbage redeemed only slightly by success.
— D.M.

ORLEANS
★ ★ **Let There Be Music / Asy. (1975)**
★ **Waking and Dreaming / Asy. (1976)** ¶

★ **Before the Dance** / ABC (1978)
■ **Forever** / Inf. (1979)
■ **Orleans** / MCA (NA)
Supposedly the intelligent person's alternative to Eagles-Ronstadt-L.A.-session-rock, Orleans is masterminded by John and Joanna Hall, and is, if anything, more hollow and slick than that to which it is supposed to be an alternative. — K.T.

OZZY OSBOURNE
★ ★ **Blizzard of Oz** / Jet (1981)
★ ★ ★ **Diary of a Madman** / Jet (1981)
Helium-voiced Black Sabbath former frontman follows spiritual path of Alice Cooper. Dispensing bone-headed metaphysics over codified Brit hard-rock guitar, his Ozness ranks with the Addams Family and Creepy Crawlers as product for teen horror/laughs market. Featured role in big-screen buckets-of-blood production would seem a career imperative. Vocal novelty collectors; file with David Surkamp. — G.A.

OSIBISA
★ ★ ★ ★ **Osibisa** / MCA (1971)
★ ★ ★ ★ **Woyaya** / MCA (1972)
★ ★ **Welcome Home** / Ant. (1976)
★ **Ojah Awake** / Ant. (1977)
A quartet of Ghanaians transplanted to London, Osibisa makes music about happiness. At the core of the group's synthesis of intense, complex and primitive African rhythm and modern electric instrumentation (plus a wizard horn section) lies infectious joy. You can't tell it from the lyrics—most of which are in Swahili—but it's in the nature of their high-stepping Afro-Anglo blues jazz.
   The group put out three Warner albums, all of which are deleted, but MCA has kept their first and best two albums in print. These albums represent a fine introduction to the rites of hypnotic rhythm that define Osibisa. The stuff for Antilles is an embarrassment; to hear such brilliant players head for the disco formula is more than disappointing. Though they've never made a discernible commercial impact in America—despite having done the soundtrack for the second *Superfly* flick—Osibisa did make an important contribution by inventing a Western form of Patanga (Swahili for improvisation) atop a bed of Nigerian-style high-life music that isn't easily forgotten. — B.M.

OSIRIS
★ ★ ★ **Since before Our Time** / War. (NA)
It's hard to say why Osiris never hit while many other slinky funk outfits did—a roll of the dice, one supposes. Your better-than-average futurist fatback. — R.P.

LEE OSKAR
★ ★ **Lee Oskar** / U.A. (1976)
★ ★ **Before the Rain** / Elek. (1978)
War's only white member, this Dutch harp player recorded these LPs in 1976 and 1978, well after the band had peaked. Passing interest for diehard fans of War only. — D.M.

DONNY OSMOND
■ **Donny Osmond Album** / MGM (1971) ¶
■ **Portrait of Donny** / MGM (1972) ¶
■ **My Best to You** / MGM (1972)
■ **Alone Together** / MGM (1973) ¶
■ **Disco Train** / Poly. (1976) ¶
■ **Donald Clark Osmond** / Poly. (1977)
This is not the reincarnation of Shaun Cassidy. Well-crafted garbage—trash is too elevated a description. — D.M.

DONNY AND MARIE OSMOND
■ **I'm Leaving It All Up to You** / MGM (1974)
■ **Make the World Go Away** / MGM (1975)
■ **Donny and Marie** / Poly. (1976)
■ **New Season** / Poly. (1976) ¶
■ **Winning Combination** / Poly. (1978) ¶
■ **Goin' Coconuts** / Poly (1978)
The only people I've ever heard who deserved Andy Williams. Sometimes I wish they'd learn to ski and meet his ex-wife. — D.M.

MARIE OSMOND
■ **Paper Roses** / MGM (1973)
■ **Who's Sorry Now** / MGM (1975) ¶
■ **This Is the Way That I Feel** / Poly. (1977) ¶
Wretched excess, accent on wretched. — D.M.

THE OSMONDS
■ **Phase Three** / MGM (1972) ¶
■ **The Proud One** / MGM (1975) ¶
■ **Around the World Live in Concert** / MGM (1975)
■ **Brainstorm** / Poly. (1976) ¶
■ **Osmonds' Christmas Album** / Poly. (1976) ¶
■ **Osmonds' Greatest Hits** / Poly. (1977) ¶
■ **Steppin' Out** / Mer. (1978)
For Mormon Tabernacle Choir fans only. Some of these were hits; all of them deserve to be melted, except maybe the occasional Jackson 5 imitations. The heavy rock on *Phase Three* epitomizes stupidity. — D.M.

THE OTHER SIDE
■ **Rock-x-ing** / De-Lite (NA)
Features world's worst version of The Knickerbockers' pseudo-Beatles hit,

"Lies," and other lounge-rock ineptitudes.
— D.M.

JOHNNY OTIS

★ ★ ★ ★ Cold Shot / Kent (1969)
★ ★ ★ Live at Monterey / Epic (1971) ¶
★ ★ ★ ★ The Original Johnny Otis Show / Savoy (NA)
★ ★ ★ Guitar Slim Green's Stone Down
■ Blues / Kent (NA)

One of the most important figures in R&B history, Otis' list of accomplishments is impressive. The drummer/pianist/vibraphonist played with the Count Basie Orchestra before becoming a bandleader himself and scoring with the 1946 hit "Harlem Nocturne." This early work is represented on the Savoy collection. He later opened the first R&B club in Los Angeles, and his ribald jam sessions discovered and included such talents as Little Esther Phillips, Big Mama Thornton, Etta James, Hank Ballard and the Midnighters, and Jackie Wilson. The available material dates from Otis' comeback in the late Sixties. *Cold Shot* is the best Otis available, featuring Don "Sugar Cane" Harris and Otis' guitar-prodigy son Shuggie. The Monterey album (from the jazz, not pop, festival) features many of same associates, including Little Esther from the old days.
— J.S.

SHUGGIE OTIS

★ ★ ★ Here Comes Shuggie Otis / Epic (1970) ¶
★ ★ ★ Freedom Flight / Epic (1971)
★ ★ ★ Inspiration Information / Epic (1975) ¶
★ ★ ★ Preston Love's Omaha Bar-B-Q / Kent (NA)

This blues-based guitarist was well tutored by his father, legendary R&B bandleader Johnny Otis. *Here Comes,* Shuggie's debut, with white gospel singer Al Kooper, is of particular interest. On his own albums, Shuggie's performance suffers somewhat from his rather poor vocal ability.
— J.S.

JOHN OTWAY

★ ★ John Otway and Wild Billy Barrett / Poly. (1977), Br. imp.
★ ★ Deep and Meaningless / Poly. (1978), Br. imp.
★ ★ Where Did I Go Right / Poly. (1979) ¶
★ ★ Deep Thoughts / Stiff (1980), Br. imp.

Chaplin-esque ex-busker plies his British folk rock earnestly but without much success.
— J.S.

OUR DAUGHTER'S WEDDING

★ ★ ★ Digital Cowboy / EMI (1981)

New York-based sythesizer trio that at least has the wherewithal to play its instruments instead of vice versa. Our Daughter's Wedding hit big on the rock and disco dance club circuit with the independently released "Lawnchairs" in 1980. This five-song LP (which includes "Lawnchairs") reinforces the notion that synthesizer rock may be the bubblegum music of post-industrial America.
— G.A.

THE OUTLAWS

★ ★ Outlaws / Ari. (1975)
★ ★ Lady in Waiting / Ari. (1976)
★ ★ Hurry Sundown / Ari. (1977)
★ ★ Bring It Back Alive / Ari. (1978)
★ ★ Playin' to Win / Ari. (1978)
★ ★ In the Eye of the Storm / Ari. (1979)
★ ★ Ghost Riders / Ari. (1981)

A totally synthetic band who sound like every country boogie outfit from the Byrds to Poco and the Eagles, the Allmans to Marshall Tucker. Their chief songwriter, Henry Thomasson, is a master of the cut-and-paste method (a snippet of Richie Furay here, a soupçon of Bernie Leadon there). With excellent production by Paul Rothchild, and adequate musicianship, all Outlaws albums are full of Good Things from the Recording Industry. Or the Sara Lee banana cake of rock & roll. — A.N.

THE OUTSIDERS

★ ★ ★ Time Won't Let Me / Cap. (1966)
★ ★ Album # 2 / Cap. (1966)
★ ★ In / Cap. (1967)

Cleveland-based frat-rock group had two big hits in 1966: "Time Won't Let Me" and "Girl in Love." Thanks to Sonny Geraci's urgent vocals, the Outsiders' music straddled the line between rock and pop. Although *Time Won't Let Me* indicated the band might have some staying power on the strength of Tom King's well-crafted songs, inspiration quickly took a powder. *Album # 2* and *In* are notable not for the original numbers but for some energetic cover versions of some of the era's top pop hits— "(Just Like) Romeo and Juliet," "I Wanna Be Free," "Hanky Panky." This does not a career make, however, and the Outsiders called it quits in the late Sixties. Geraci later resurfaced singing lead for the group Climax ("Precious and Few"). — D.MC.

BUCK OWENS

★ ★ The Best of Buck Owens / Cap. (1964)
★ ★ Buck 'Em / War. (1976) ¶

★ ★ **Best of Buck Owens, Vol. 3** / **Cap.**
(1977)
★ ★ **Sweethearts in Heaven** / **Star.**
(1979)
★ ★ **Love Don't Make the Bars** / **War.**
(1981)
Owens came out of the Bakersfield, California, country music scene that also produced Wynn Stewart and Merle Haggard; he had an enormously popular series of country hits in the mid-Sixties, most of which were as much pop as country but only one of which—"I've Got a Tiger by the Tail"—made the pop Top Forty. Later he went on to star with Roy Clark on TV's *Hee Haw!* Capitol deleted most of his albums when he left the label for Warner Bros. in 1977—why not?—and leased the best early hits (including "Tiger") to Trip, which is the "essential" Owens album. The rest are pretty dull.
— D.M.

THE OZARK MOUNTAIN DAREDEVILS

★ ★ **The Ozark Mountain Daredevils** /
A&M (1973)
★ ★ ★ **It'll Shine When It Shines** / **A&M**
(1974)
★ ★ ★ **The Car over the Lake Album** /
A&M (1975)
★ ★ **Men from Earth** / **A&M (1976)**
★ ★ **Don't Look Down** / **A&M (1977)**
★ ★ **It's Alive** / **A&M (1978)**
★ ★ **Ozark Mountain Daredevils** / **Col.**
(1980)
A tribe of good ole boys who came out of the Missouri hills and Arkansas playing a mixture of traditional mountain music and bona fide American pop, the Ozark Mountain Daredevils sound like what might have happened if Jed Clampett had bought himself the Eagles to make records with. They've had several sizable pop hits, notably "If You Wanna Get to Heaven" from the eponymous first album. The Daredevils really hit their stride, though, on *Shine* and *Car over the Lake*. Since then they've been repeating a formula that has grown progressively more slick and less interesting.
— A.N.

OZO
★ **Listen to the Buddah** / **DJM (1976)** ¶
Post-psychedelic garbage. — J.S.

OZONE
★ ★ ★ **Walk On** / **Mo. (1980)**
★ ★ ★ **Send It** / **Mo. (1981) on It** / **Mo.**
(1981)
Commodores-style funk 'n' harmony group is more effective on ballads than uptempo material, but remains listenable throughout.
— D.M.

OZZ
■ **No Prisoners** / **Epic (1980)**
Guitarist Greg Parker was good enough to session for the likes of the Chi-Lites, Tyrone Davis and Buddy Miles, but when he decided to team up with heavy-metal vocalist Alexis T. Angel, he made a big mistake. Here's hoping you never have to listen to this album.
— J.S.

AUGUSTUS PABLO
★ ★ ★ **This Is Augustus Pablo / Kaya**
(1974)
★ ★ ★ **Ital Dub / Troj. (1976)**
★ ★ ★ ★ ★ **King Tubby Meets Rockers**
Uptown / Clock. (1976)
★ ★ ★ ★ ★ **Original Rockers / Greens.**
(1979)
★ ★ ★ ★ **King Tubby Meets Rockers in a**
Fire House / Shan. (1980)
★ ★ ★ **Dubbing Ina Africa / Abra. (1980)**
★ ★ ★ ★ **East of the River Nile / Mess.**
(1981)
Dub music is reggae stripped down to the
basics—bass and drums cranked up to the
limit and the entire arsenal of studio effects
used to remix a recording into a rhythmic
tour de force. Augustus Pablo, along with
Lee Perry, explored the limits of recording
studios to perfect dub. *King Tubby Meets
Rockers Uptown* was a mid-Seventies landmark that established dub as an art form.
All Pablo is interesting; *Ital Dub* and *This*
are nascent, mainly instrumental dub workouts. *Original Rockers* is a compilation of
impressive variety, while *East of the River
Nile* takes dub melodicism to new heights.
— R.F.G.

PABLO CRUISE
★ ★ **Pablo Cruise / A&M (1975)**
★ ★ **Nadia's Theme / A&M (1976)**
★ ★ ★ **Lifeline / A&M (1976)**
★ ★ ★ **Worlds Away / A&M (1976)**
★ ★ **Place in the Sun / A&M (1977)**
★ **Part of the Game / A&M (1980)**
★ **Reflector / A&M (1980)**
Mellow West Coast white R&B from a quar-
tet of vets from failed groups. Bassist Bud
Cockrell was in It's a Beautiful Day at that
band's low point, and the other three (key-
boardist Cory Lerios, guitarist David Jenkins
and drummer Steve Price) were in Stone-
ground. Jenkins is the best player of the lot

and the third album, *Lifeline,* includes a
couple of songs written by Ron Nagle, a little-known but interesting songwriter. But
Worlds Away scored big with a 1978 single,
"Love Will Find a Way," sort of a blander
version of Boz Scaggs' later work. — J.S.

PACIFIC GAS AND ELECTRIC
★ ★ **Get It On / Kent (1969)**
A soul-based band from the heyday of San
Francisco rock. Strident funk without pur-
pose. A couple of earlier albums for Colum-
bia are deleted. — D.M.

PAGES
★ **Pages / Epic (1978)**
★ **Future Street / Epic (1979) ¶**
★ **Pages / Cap. (1980)**
Vapid fusion-oriented pop. By the Capitol
album, the band had improved to the
level of very bad Steely Dan, to no
avail. — J.D.C.

ROBERT PALMER
★ ★ ★ **Sneakin' Sally through the Alley / Is.**
(1975)
★ ★ **Pressure Drop / Is. (1975)**
★ ★ **Some People Can Do What They Like**
/ Is. (1976)
★ ★ **Double Fun / Is. (1978)**
★ ★ **Secrets / Is. (1979)**
★ ★ **Clues / Is. (1980)**
★ ★ **Maybe It's Live / Is. (1982)**
White soul for snobs. Palmer's first album,
Sneakin' Sally, was more than promising, in-
fluenced equally by reggae, Allen Toussaint's
New Orleans rhythms and Little Feat's bi-
zarre attitudes. But each succeeding album
has been more narcissistic, as Palmer—
generally decked out in duds so ornately ex-
pensive they'd make Al Green blush—began
a treatise on high culture and soul slumming
that made Bryan Ferry's odyssey seem tame.
Revered by the sort of rock critics who

think that the sophomoric jokes of Sparks are the epitome of art rock, Palmer is in fact virtually soulless, the Fraud of Funk.
— D.M.

PARADISE EXPRESS
★ ★ **Paradise Express / Fan. (1979)**
Formula disco slightly redeemed by interestingly gritty lead singer, Vi Ann.   — D.M.

THE PARAGONS
★ ★ ★ **Return Of / Top R. (1981)**
★ ★ ★ **Riding High / Mango (1981)**
As one of the top three vocal groups during the mid-Sixties rocksteady era in Jamaica, the Paragons, with lead singer John Holt, had an enviable string of hits including "The Tide Is High" (recently trashed by Blondie), "Wear You to the Ball" and "On the Beach." These two reunion LPs show that their vocal blend is as warm and creamy as ever, but *Riding High* updates their hits with rather strained cleverness, while *Return Of* offers fresher-sounding new material.   — R.F.G.

PARIS CONNECTION
★ **Paris Connection / Casa. (1978)**
Eurodisco act fails to pull off its only interesting idea, a Righteous Brothers medley ("You've Lost That Loving Feeling/ Unchained Melody").   — D.M.

GRAHAM PARKER
★ ★ ★ ★ ★ **Howlin' Wind / Mer. (1976)**
★ ★ ★ ★ ★ **Heat Treatment / Mer. (1976)**
★ ★ ★ ★ **Stick to Me / Mer. (1977)**
★ ★ ★ **The Parkerilla / Mer. (1978)**
★ ★ ★ ★ ★ **Squeezing Out Sparks / Ari. (1979)**
★ ★ ★ **The Up Escalator / Ari. (1980)**
★ ★ **Another Gray Area / Ari. (1982)**
Howlin' Wind and *Heat Treatment,* both released in 1976, are extraordinary works of neoclassic rock & roll that draw their anger and emotional intensity from Bob Dylan, Van Morrison and the Rolling Stones, and at the same time anticipate the unsullied, scabrous explosion of punk. These are tough, passionate and hungry albums in which Parker refuses to accept anybody's vision of himself except his own. What his first two albums share with punk is the frightening implication that the culture around him is collapsing, that there is nothing to hold on to. If Parker's abnegation isn't as extreme as the punks', his best songs ("Pourin' It All Out," "Fool's Gold," "Don't Ask Me Questions") bray with danger and defeat, and even his most romantic songs ("Heat Treat-

ment" and "Hold Back the Night") have a fierce edge.

Where Parker differs from the punks and what he shares with Bruce Springsteen, Southside Johnny and Mink DeVille—the new guardians of rock & roll past—is his relation to rock history. This is more than a matter of choosing heroes (Van Morrison versus Iggy, say) or forms (R&B versus minimalism or primitivism, or whatever you want to call it). Parker sees rock & roll as a way out—in his case, as a way out of being a gas-station attendant—and rock tradition as a way of establishing order in a culture that has lost much of its meaning. The Rumour, Parker's five-piece band, turn almost every song into an epic stand of R&B belligerence and operatic intensity. By placing so much emphasis on traditional rock values, Parker avoids the pessimism of punk and the passivity of pop. The sound is steely-eyed and gritted-teeth.

On *Stick to Me* Parker's compromise comes close to collapsing. Bitterness reverts to impudence ("Problem Child"); sentiment turns maudlin ("Watch the Moon Come Down"); and for the first time, he has written throwaways ("The Raid," "New York Shuffle"). The situation is exacerbated by Nick Lowe's pollution of a mix, which buries the album's best cuts ("Soul on Ice," "Clear Head"). There are moments when Parker's vocals are barely audible. But for all its problems—most of which came about because the album was cut in a week—the record does live up to its title. It takes a while, but like the best method actors, Parker works by the accumulation of gesture and detail, and in the end *Stick to Me* has a power that can't be dismissed.

Parker followed *Stick to Me,* however, with a set that was undeniably disappointing. *The Parkerilla,* a two-disc live LP, merely rehashed the first two albums (only two songs are from *Stick*), added a sort of disco-single version of "Don't Ask Me Questions," which opened the set and had already appeared on the second album, and failed completely to convey the power of his public appearances. No oldies, nothing special—it was a remarkably shoddy set from a man of so much principle, and it undercut his credibility, even if the ostensible reasoning behind it was to escape the Mercury contract. That's no excuse for stealing money from fans with an inferior LP. Parker has a switchblade voice, but *Parkerilla's* a mugging.

Liberated from Mercury, Parker immediately produced (with Jack Nietsche at the board) the best record of his career,

Squeezing Out Sparks, which delivered on all the promise of his earliest LPs. *The Up Escalator* has some good songs ("Stupefaction," "Devil's Sidewalk"), but Parker's collaboration with the Rumour had run its course: the music is stiff and cold, the opposite of their best work together. But not as stiff and cold as *Gray Area,* which was made with a group of New York sessionmen from whom Parker is never able to evoke any empathy. — K.R./D.M.

JUNIOR PARKER

★ ★ ★ ★ **Junior Parker and Billy Love /**
  Charly (1977), Br. imp.
★ ★ ★ ★ **I Wanna Ramble / Ace (1982), Br.**
  imp.
★ ★ ★ ★ **Driving Wheel / Duke (NA)**
★ ★ ★ ★ **The Best of Little Junior Parker /**
  Duke (NA)

One of the finest of Sam Phillips' discoveries at Sun Records, Junior Parker was both an outstanding R&B vocalist and an exciting harp player, one of the key transitional figures in the transition between delta blues and R&B and R&B and rock & roll. Probably best known for having recorded the magnificent original version of "Mystery Train," Parker was a consistently interesting performer throughout the Fifties and much of the Sixties.

All of the material above is worthwhile. The half-album on Charly collects eight of the tracks Parker cut at Sun, including "Mystery Train." It would rate even higher if Billy Love's material were anywhere near as good. *I Wanna Ramble* collects tracks recorded between 1954 and 1956 for Duke Records. Where the Sun sides present Parker in a small ensemble setting, these often feature him with larger groups including horns. So do the albums on Duke itself. "Driving Wheel" is the title of his most imposing hit for that label, where he remained for a decade; the *Best of* is the better of these.

After leaving Duke, Parker recorded for Capitol, Bluesway, Mercury, Minit, United Artists and Groove Merchant. Little of what he cut there was up to his old standard, but if you're a blues and hard-core R&B fan, it's worth picking up when the bargain racks are in stock. Or if someone is considerate enough to reissue it.
  — D.M.

RAY PARKER, JR.

★ ★ ★ **Rock On / Ari. (1979)**
★ ★ ★ **The Other Woman / Ari. (1982)**
★ ★ ★ ★ **Greatest Hits / Ari. (1982)**

Parker is the best thing to happen to Motor City soul since Smokey Robinson left town. Best known for his hits with Raydio (the most important of which are included on *Greatest Hits*), Parker established his own identity with "The

Other Woman," which uses rock riffs, disco beats, soul choruses and every other trick in the book to create a slick pop gem. The rest isn't up to that standard—not quite—but doubters are advised to check out *Greatest Hits,* to hear what one of Sly Stone's more imaginative heirs is up to. — D.M.

PARLET

★ ★ **Play Me or Trade Me / Casa. (1978)**
★ ★ **Pleasure Principle / Casa. (1978)**
★ ★ **Invasion of the Booty Snatchers / Casa.**
  (1979)

His partisans talk less about Parlet than about George Clinton's other girl group, the Brides of Funkenstein, probably because (despite lead singer Jeannette Washington) Parlet is unsuccessful both artistically and commercially. In the end, these records go a long way toward suggesting that Clinton is as much hustler as genius, and that he's hustling more than just record companies. Listeners (not to mention critics) are liable to be bitten too. — D.M.

PARLIAMENT

★ ★ ★ **Chocolate City / Casa. (1975)**
★ ★ ★ ★ **The Clones of Dr. Funkenstein /**
  Casa. (1976)
★ ★ ★ **Mothership Connection / Casa. (1976)**
★ ★ ★ **Parliament Live / Casa. (1977)**
★ ★ ★ **Get Down and Boogie / Casa. (1977)**
★ ★ ★ ★ **Funkentelechy vs. the Placebo**
  Syndrome / Casa. (1977)
★ ★ ★ **Up for the Down Stroke / Casa. (1977)**
★ ★ ★ ★ **Motor Booty Affair / Casa. (1978)**
★ ★ ★ **Gloyhallastoopid / Casa. (1979)**
★ ★ ★ **Trombipulation / Casa. (1980)**

Parliament was the seedling from which the Parliafunkadelicment empire of maestro George Clinton grew. Originally a late-Sixties Detroit soul group ("[I Just Wanna] Testify" was their hit), Clinton has since taken the band (and its various offshoots, including Funkadelic, Bootsy's Rubber Band and the Horny Horns) into a nether world of black rock & roll. Funkadelic and Bootsy are more outrageously entertaining—a good deal of their music is simply power rock with a dance beat—but Parliament has been used for Clinton's major statements: *The Clones of Dr. Funkenstein* suggests a rather unpleasant vision of the future, while *Funkentelechy vs. the Placebo Syndrome* is actually a prescriptive manifesto concerning the sad state of the Seventies music world. Fascinatingly vulgar, like all of Clinton's projects, but also engaging in a rather diffuse way. — D.M.

ALAN PARSONS PROJECT

★ ★ **Tales of Mystery and Imagination /**
  20th Cent. (1976)

★ ★ ★ **I, Robot** / Ari. (1977)
★ ★ **Pyramid** / Ari. (1978)
■ **Eve** / Ari. (1979)
■ **Turn of a Friendly Card** / Ari.
(1980)
A dubious pretext for music, *Tales* (based on Poe's short stories) nonetheless has inspired moments from Pilot's infectious Beatles-derived rock, Andrew Powell's ornate arranging and Parsons' marvelously precise engineering. But melodramatic lyrics hurt. The followups are more rocking, less orchestrated versions of the same approach.
— C.W.

GRAM PARSONS
★ ★ ★ **G.P.** / Rep. (1973)
★ ★ ★ **Grievous Angel** / Rep. (1974)
★ ★ ★ **Sleepless Nights** / A&M
(1976)
★ ★ ★ ★ **Early Years** / Sierra (1979)
There are many who would agree that Gram Parsons' name should be appended not just to these four records but to the entire body of country rock. *Safe at Home,* now repackaged as *The Early Years,* Parsons' 1967 record with the International Submarine Band, is a treasure that shows the start of his Dynaflow mix of Merle Haggard and Arthur Crudup.

In 1968, Parsons joined with a Byrds incarnation that included Roger McGuinn, Chris Hillman and Clarence White to make the landmark *Sweetheart of the Rodeo;* "Hickory Wind," a song about his South Carolina boyhood that is perhaps his finest creation, is on that album. His 1970 collaboration with the Flying Burrito Brothers lent nine tracks to *Sleepless Nights;* the remaining three songs, bolstered by Emmylou Harris' loving attentions, are from the 1973 sessions for *Grievous Angel.*

G.P. is a sometimes lovely, sometimes wavering collection, with backups by Elvis Presley's band and Emmylou Harris; the same team made *Grievous Angel,* and the latter record shares the same mix of glories and thin spots. Parsons did a solo tour in support of that album in the winter and spring of 1973. His self-destructive ways stopped his heart and fixed him as a legend in October of that year. "His exit was perfect," says Elvis Costello with a certain sad truth. Parsons' influence is wide, deep and likely to last.
— F.S.

PARTNERS
★ **Last Disco in Paris** / Mar. (NA)
If it was all like this, the same would be true at my house. — D.M.

DOLLY PARTON
★ ★ ★ ★ ★ **The Best of Dolly Parton** / RCA
(1970)
★ ★ ★ ★ **Coat of Many Colors** / RCA
(1971)
★ ★ ★ ★ **My Tennessee Mountain Home** /
RCA (1973)
★ ★ ★ ★ **Love Is Like a Butterfly** / RCA
(1974)
★ ★ ★ ★ **Bargain Store** / RCA (1975)
★ ★ ★ **Dolly Parton in Concert** / RCA
(1975)
★ ★ ★ ★ ★ **The Best of Dolly Parton** / RCA
(1975)
★ ★ ★ **Dolly** / RCA (1975)
★ ★ **Mine** / Camd. (1975)
★ ★ **Just the Way I Am** / Camd. (1975)
★ ★ **I Wish I Felt This Way at Home** /
Camd. (1975)
★ ★ ★ **All I Can Do** / RCA (1976)
★ ★ ★ ★ **New Harvest . . . First Gathering** /
RCA (1977)
★ ★ **Here You Come Again** / RCA (1977)
★ ★ **Release Me** / Power. (1977)
★ ★ **Heartbreaker** / RCA (1978)
★ ★ ★ **In the Beginning** / Monu. (1978)
★ **Great Balls of Fire** / RCA (1979)
★ **Dolly, Dolly, Dolly** / RCA (1980)
★ **9 to 5 and Other Odd Jobs** / RCA (1980)
★ ★ ★ **Jolene** / RCA (NA)
In many ways Dolly Parton is the perfect country singer because she has all the right qualifications: she came from a poor family in the Tennessee mountains, and her stunted childhood has resulted in prolific songwriting about same. She's also the possessor of a stunning soprano voice and of a remarkable resemblance to the Big Rock Candy Mountain that all Southern kids were convinced actually existed. Dolly Parton *is* the South to many people; her lyrics are the embodiment of the proper Southern virtues of fundamentalist religion, respect for the family, worship of one's parents, praise for the right husband/lover and weepy, heartfelt laments over the wrongs suffered at the hands of a callous/drinking/running-around husband. Many country songwriters take all that and make it corny; Dolly makes it real and believable.

For many years she led a twin recording and performing career, solo and as half of a successful duo with Porter Wagoner. In 1973 she left the Porter Wagoner show, although he continued to produce her albums. Then in 1976 she left Wagoner completely and began to gear her career toward pop audiences. By 1978 she had succeeded, and *Here You Come Again* was her first gold album. It was also her least pleasing in years, with its slick California arrangements and production. That was a point she cheerfully conceded but argued convincingly that it gave her the pop audience she wanted and, simultaneously, that success afforded her the freedom to do whatever she wanted in the future.

The best representation of her work is contained in the two *Best of Dolly Parton* albums. So prolific is she that the albums are equally good, even though no one song appears on both. — C.F.

STELLA PARTON
★ **Country Sweet / Elek. (1977)**
★ **Stella Parton / Elek. (1978)**
★ **Love Ya / Elek. (1979)**
★ **Best of Stella Parton / Elek. (1980)**
Yeah, she's Dolly's sister. No, they don't have anything in common, musically or (ahem) physically. — D.M.

PASSAGE
★ **Passage / A&M (1981)**
Blandest soul trio left alive. — D.M.

PASSPORT
★ ★ **Looking Thru / Atco (1974)**
★ ★ **Cross-Collateral / Atco (1975)**
★ ★ **Infinity Machine / Atco (1976)**
★ ★ **Iguacu / Atco (1977)**
★ ★ **Sky Blue / Atl. (1978)**
★ ★ **Oceanliner / Atl. (1980)**
★ ★ **Blue Tattoo / Atl. (1981)**
On each of its albums, this German group plays similar-sounding fusion music. Built around leader Klaus Doldinger's tenor and soprano sax playing, and favoring somber yet steadily pulsing tunes, Passport is a poor man's Weather Report, but with much less percussive and compositional nuance. Competent but dull. — M.R.

BOBBY PATTERSON
★ ★ ★ **It's Just a Matter of Time / Paula (1972)**
For a couple of years in the early Seventies, Patterson was Jewel/Paula's man for all seasons. His lone album is stylistically varied, though centered in old-fashioned Southern soul. — J.MC.

CHARLEY PATTON
★ ★ ★ ★ ★ **The Founder of the Delta Blues / Yazoo (NA)**
★ ★ **The Immortal Charley Patton / O.J.L. (NA)**
★ ★ **The Immortal Charley Patton, Vol. 2 / O.J.L. (NA)**
Charley Patton wasn't nearly the first delta bluesman to record—he never made it to shellac until 1929—but he deserves the founder title anyway, not only because he was an enormous musical influence on all the men who came after him, from contemporaries like Willie Brown and Son House to Howlin' Wolf and Roebuck Staples, but also because his story is the very shape and outline of the romantic/mythic legend of the delta bluesman. Patton was born and raised the son of a plantation preacher, who beat him for his musical devilment. An uncommonly handsome man, Patton was a notorious womanizer and wife beater, an illiterate, an idler, what the notes to the Yazoo album call "the very stereotype of the 'bad plantation nigger.' " Of course he wound up becoming a preacher and a (fairly) young corpse, according to the yarns dead of poisoning or stabbing, but according to the state, dead of heart disease. Just where he was buried has never been determined.

And there is the music. Patton was not especially articulate—House and Brown and Wolf and a dozen others have created more striking and personal imagery in their blues. His technique was all rhythm, but it is a rhythm carried away with itself, thrust to such intimate extremes that Patton is eventually utterly identified with this singular sense of time, toying with it, tossing it back and forth between his guitar and his voice, working each of these instruments to contrast and complement the other. He exercises this technique on blues staples, nothing truly original: "Pony Blues," "Stone Pony Blues," "A Spoonful Blues," "Frankie and Albert," "Mississippi Boll Weevil Blues," "34 Blues" are all themes that have kicked around a while and will be developed better or more clearly or more poetically by Robert Johnson and his successors. But somehow there is nothing more powerful in all of American music—to say nothing of the blues—than Patton, the ultimate individualist, singing his songs in a cracked, parched voice that seems to leak out of his soul, picking his guitar in patterns only he can gauge in advance—torn, bitter, raging and exuberant, but on his own, outguessing the world and making it acknowledge some fragment of his genius. This is great music. Every bit of it is represented on the Yazoo compilation; the others simply repeat the same material, recorded between 1929 and his death in 1934, with inferior sound quality and less astute notes. Not that anyone is going to pin this particular performer down in print.
— D.M.

BILLY PAUL

★ ★ Ebony Woman / Phil. (1970) ¶
★ ★ ★ Going East / Phil. (1971) ¶
★ ★ ★ 360 Degrees of Billy Paul / Phil.
   (1972) ¶
★ ★ ★ Feelin' Good at the Cadillac Club /
   Phil. (1973) ¶
★ ★ ★ War of the Gods / Phil. (1973)
★ ★ Live in Europe / Phil. (1974)
★ ★ ★ Got My Head on Straight / Phil.
   (1975)
★ ★ ★ When Love Is New / Phil. (1975) ¶
★ ★ Let 'Em In / Phil. (1976)
★ ★ Only the Strong Survive / Phil. (1977)
★ ★ ★ The Best of Billy Paul / Phil. (NA)
★ ★ First Class / Phil. (NA)

When Billy Paul recorded *Feelin' Good*
(originally for Gamble Records), he was a
nimble-voiced cabaret-jazz singer. Despite
the title, it is not a live album; instead, Paul
scats his way through standards ("Blue-
sette," "Billy Boy") backed by an adept
acoustic rhythm section. Since then, Paul's
baritone has frayed around the edges and his
singing often finds him parodying his own
affectations.

Ebony Woman and *Going East* continue
loosely in the cabaret vein. The former is
filled with lightweight pop and jazz standards, while *Going East* is a successfully ambitious attempt to flesh out Paul's persona.
With the possible exception of "Magic Carpet Ride," the choice of songs on *Going East*
is judicious, while the arrangements combine
sophisticated horn and string charts with a
crisp but not cumbersome rhythm section.

Since then, Paul's music has been recorded
with MFSB's backup. "Me and Mrs. Jones,"
a pop smash, found him treading the line between MOR, cabaret and soul. It's a formula
that Gamble and Huff have turned to time
and again for his albums. As a result, there's
little to choose among them. The songs are
either lushly romantic or filled with pop social statements; both varieties have equally
erratic lyrics. Vocally, Paul tends to fall
back on familiar mannerisms. The only
album to avoid completely, however, is *Live
in Europe,* which is bogged down by a lumbering orchestra.   — J.MC.

LES PAUL

★ ★ New Sound, Vol. 2 (with Mary Ford) /
   Cap. (1951)
★ Les Paul Now / Lon. (1968)
★ ★ The World Is Still Waiting for the
   Sunrise / Cap. (1974)
★ Guitar Tapestry / Proj. (1976)
★ London Collectors—The Genius of Les
   Paul / Lon. (NA)

Les Paul is one of the most influential figures in rock—he perfected guitar amplification and built one of the great blues guitars,
the Gibson Les Paul—but his records aren't
much. The Capitol sets, with former wife
Mary Ford, are interesting period pieces
from the pre-Presley Fifties, but the rest are
sheer mood music, for Mantovani fans more
than rockers.   — D.M.

PAVLOV'S DOG

★ ★ Pampered Menial / Col. (1975) ¶
★ ★ At the Sound of the Bell / Col.
   (1976) ¶

Blue Oyster Cult on laughing gas. David
Surkamp's extraordinary, if hard-to-take,
voice (Marty Balin crossbred with a vacuum
cleaner) never quite jelled with the band's
technologically informed heavy-metal attack.
A few songs survive—"Late November"
from *Pampered Menial* and the wonderful
Mersey-like ballad, "Mersey," from *At the
Sound of the Bell*—but this will be remembered mainly for its eccentric qualities.
— J.B.M.

TOM PAXTON

★ Ramblin' Boy / Elek. (1964)
★ Outward Bound / Elek. (1966)
★ Morning Again / Elek. (1968)
★ The Things I Notice Now / Elek. (1969)
★ ★ The Compleat Tom Paxton / Elek.
   (1971)
★ New Songs from the Briarpatch / Van.
   (1977)
★ Heroes / Van. (1978)

A smugly sanctimonious product of the
early-Sixties folk movement, Paxton's performance abilities are extremely meager. His
best-known song, "The Last Thing on My
Mind," was written in 1963; after that, he
quickly declined into sentiment and a kind
of ham-handed political sermonizing about
obvious subjects. Somehow this has earned
him a cult following in England, although
America still can't be bothered. The Elektra
anthology *(Compleat)* is an overview for historians of the milieu in which Dylan was
nurtured. The rest are up for grabs to anyone who cares.   — D.M.

DEVIN PAYNE

★ Excuse Me / Casa. (NA)

Only if you swear you'll never do it again.
— D.M.

GORDON PAYNE

★ ★ Gordon Payne / A&M (1978)

Pleasant but unoriginal Croce-isms.   — D.M.

JOHN PAYNE BAND
★ ★ **Bedtime Stories / Ari. (1976)**
★ ★ **Razor's Edge / Ari. (1977)**
Payne's chief claim to fame is that he has frequently been a Van Morrison horn player. On his own he plays a blend of folk and funk that's peculiar though rarely exciting. — D.M.

PEACHES AND HERB
★ ★ **Greatest Hits / Epic (1968)**
★ ★ ★ **2 Hot! / Poly. (1978)**
★ ★ **Twice the Fire / Poly. (1979)**
★ ★ **Worth the Wait / Poly. (1980)**
★ ★ **Love Is Strange / Epic (NA)**
★ ★ **Saying Something / Poly. (1981)**
Despite a couple of Top Twenty hits ("Close Your Eyes," "Love Is Strange," "For Your Love"), the original Peaches and Herb (Francine Barker and Herb Fame) were the most supper club of Sixties soul duos. The Epic records are of that vintage. Compare them to anything by Sam and Dave, Mickey and Sylvia or Marvin Gaye and Tammi/Kim/Mary, if you need proof.

In 1978, Fame teamed up with Linda Greene, as the new Peaches, and scored a couple of more hits, the discofied "Shake Your Groove Thing" and the scintillating "Reunited," a beautiful revival of the soul sound he'd never quite mastered ten years before. Both of those are on *2 Hot!*, which contains little else that's appealing. The other Polydor records are seeking a formula that's never quite found, or at least isn't mastered when it is stumbled across. — D.M.

PEARL HARBOUR
★ **Pearl Harbour and the Explosions / War. (1980) ¶**
★ ★ ★ **Don't Follow Me, I'm Lost Too / War. (1980) ¶**
As lead vocalist with the Explosions, Pearl Harbour epitomized what was wrong with Bay Area new wave: she was jive, about as lively and radical as Grace Slick on codeine, and the band was even more listless. *Don't Follow Me*, recorded in England with production by Ian Dury/Clash sidekick Mickey Gallagher, is another story. It's juiced up with some rockabilly moves that Pearl actually pulls off with heart and heat. — D.M.

PEARLS BEFORE SWINE
★ ★ **One Nation Underground / ESP (1967)**
■ **Balaklava / ESP (1968)**
★ ★ **The Best of Pearls Before Swine / Adel. (1980)**
Between arty New York folk rock and the San Francisco eruption of 1967 there lay in wait a half-dozen bands like this. *One Nation Underground,* graced with a detail cover from Hieronymus Bosch's *Garden of Delights* that made the poster a big hit, is a classic example of wimp aggression. Between Tom Rapp's lisp, his rubber-band box guitars, windy eight-minute poetry lessons and kiss-off songs in Morse code, Pearls Before Swine's debut was, and remains, a disaster. On *Balaklava,* Rapp drops even the pretense of constituting a rock band and starts his long groan of pretentious Muzak. All his other attempts save *Balaklava* were mercifully deleted some time ago. This one is distinctive, any way, in its insane compulsion to garnish liberally with sound effects. — B.T.

ANN PEEBLES
★ ★ ★ **Part Time Love / Hi (1971)**
★ ★ ★ **Straight from the Heart / Hi (1972)**
★ ★ ★ **The Handwriting Is on the Wall / Hi (1975)**
★ ★ ★ **Tellin' It / Hi (1976) ¶**
★ ★ ★ **If This Is Heaven / Hi (1978)**
Born in East St. Louis in 1947, Ann Peebles grew up singing in her father's Baptist choir, a group estimable enough to back Mahalia Jackson (Peebles' idol) when she toured the Midwest. Peebles was discovered by Willie Mitchell, Al Green's producer, when she sat in with a club act while visiting Memphis. In 1971 she made *Part Time Love* with Mitchell, whose economical string and horn accompaniments were the ideal complement to a bottom-heavy rhythm section and Peebles' gritty, direct vocal style. Her debut, more straightforwardly bluesy than later sessions, bore little resemblance to Green's work with the same band—rather than recalling his keening melismata, she spoke out like the young Aretha Franklin.

Straight from the Heart, instrumentally a bit slicker than the 1971 record, cut even deeper vocally: "I Feel Like Breaking Up Somebody's Home Tonight" states a theme—loneliness—that is nicely underpinned by the concupiscent spunk of "99 Pounds" (a number written by her husband, Don Bryant).

Although Peebles' 1972 "I'm Gonna Tear Your Playhouse Down" had sold half a million copies in R&B markets, and several other singles had done well, 1974's brooding "I Can't Stand the Rain" (the excellent album of the same name is out of print) sold a surprising million copies as a crossover hit. Peebles has never cut any weak numbers, so anything available is recommended. *Tellin' It,* while it helps Peebles stake a claim as a songwriter, shows her as a somewhat domesticated stylist. *The Handwriting Is on the Wall,* is said by Willie Mitchell to be her best piece of work (it uses Mitchell's new production team). If so, Peebles' peak is still to come. — F.S.

DAVID PEEL AND THE LOWER EAST SIDE
★ **Have a Marijuana** / Elek. (1969)
The Sixties relic to end all Sixties relics: drug-crazed New York street freak arouses anthropological instincts of hip record company, which sends team of specialists to capture him in native environment. Status as the record that demolished the ban on drug references gives this one high marks in the blow-for-artistic-freedom department.
— F.R.

GEORGE PEGRAM
★ ★ ★ ★ **George Pegram** / Roun. (1970)
This landmark record signaled the beginning of Rounder Records' ambitious project to document American acoustic music. Produced by two of the company's cofounders, Ken Irwin and Bill Nowlin, this disc features breathtaking string quartet performances led by Pegram's sturdy banjo playing and singing and highlighted by Fred Cockerham's fiddle playing. — J.S.

TEDDY PENDERGRASS
★ ★ ★ ★ **Teddy Pendergrass** / Phil. (1977)
★ ★ ★ ★ **Life Is a Song Worth Singing** / Phil. (1978)
★ ★ ★ **Teddy** / Phil. (1979)
★ **Teddy Live** / Phil. (1979)
★ ★ ★ **T.P.** / Phil. (1980)
★ ★ **It's Time for Love** / Phil. (1981)
Pendergrass was the original lead singer of Harold Melvin and the Bluenotes; his solo albums have kept up the consistently high quality he showed there. Pendergrass is perhaps more confident as an uptempo stylist than as a ballad singer, but he acquits himself well on all sorts of material. One of the best products of the Gamble and Huff soul stable, he's lately lapsed into a formula so firm, he's virtually doing self-parody.
— D.M.

HOLLY PENFIELD
★ ★ **Full-Grown Child** / Dreaml. (1980)
Suburbia's idea of new wave. Singer/songwriter/pianist Penfield would be a passable rock chanteuse if the strength of her mind matched the strength of her vocal chords. "Tight Fit" is a great moment in vulgar rock sexism. — L.F.

PENGUINS
★ ★ ★ **Cool Cool Penguins** / Dooto (1955)
Their hit was "Earth Angel," a model of R&B harmony group slickness; the rest is similar but less inspired. — D.M.

THE PENTANGLE
★ ★ ★ ★ **The Pentangle** / Rep. (1968)
★ ★ ★ **Sweet Child** / Rep. (1969)
The original Pentangle idea was to bring together John Renbourne and Bert Jansch, two stellar British folk guitarists, Jacqui McShee, a crystal-voiced traditional ballad singer, and the jazz-oriented rhythm team of bassist Danny Thompson and drummer Terry Cox in order to breathe some life back into English folk music, a genre that was quite played out by the late Sixties.

The Pentangle, the band's first album, went further than could be hoped. The active jazz bottom, the Renaissance-music harmonies and the spirited exchanges between Renbourne and Jansch made Pentangle a virtuoso unit creating a terse, instrumentally based new folk style. Sparing use of McShee's voice brings out the mysteriously laconic circularity of the ballads, while the acoustic guitar duets converge with Cox and Thompson into occasionally powerful kinesics.

Sweet Child successfully experiments with minor variations on the group's basic formula. A double, half-live/half-studio album, *Child* features Renbourne on solo guitar doing short pieces that anticipate his extraordinary *Lady and the Unicorn* album, and Jansch, too, presents some of his nongroup songs (see *Bert Jansch Sampler,* on import). Cox and Thompson, after their own solo curios, lead the band through several excellent instrumentals which clearly show that their presence in Pentangle is the crucial ingredient. However, *Child*'s high points are still the full ensemble readings of traditional ballads.
★ ★ ★ **Basket of Light** / Rep. (1970) ¶
★ ★ **Cruel Sister** / Rep. (1971) ¶
★ **Reflection** / Rep. (1971) ¶
★ ★ **Solomon's Seal** / Rep. (1972) ¶
While *Basket of Light* marks the perfection of what had over the first two albums become Pentangle's characteristic ensemble sound, totally accommodating the traditional ballad to its flying instrumentals (and even incorporating "Sally Go Round the Roses" into the style), the album also marks the first step in the gradual withdrawal of Thompson and Cox into mere backup. Period-style percussion begins to predominate on *Basket* and Pentangle begins

progressively to lose its jazz feeling, and with it, its early conciseness and daring.

Nevertheless, *Cruel Sister* is the true dividing line. Side one serves as a retrospective of past achievements in style, completed with Renbourne's tender and very moving reading of "Lord Franklin" (the source of "Bob Dylan's Dream"). But the other side drags a side-long treatment of "Jack Orion" into the mistake of a grand "folk suite," an idea that has brought down several other English folk groups, including Fairport Convention. At some point Pentangle had started taking itself too seriously as an institution.

Reflection and *Solomon's Seal* have their bright spots, but these belong to individual members. With these records, Pentangle ceases to operate as a unit. The unusual amount of original material on *Reflection* suggests that they grew tired of the ballads. But the new material is ill-suited to the chemistry of the group. Cox and Thompson seem to have lost all interest, Renbourne and Jansch seem only less distracted and the album is overproduced. But the most telling mark is that Jacqui McShee, who was the haunted voice of the group, has reverted to mere folksinging. *Seal* suggested some sort of rebirth, particularly in the vocals, but that hope proved short-lived. — B.T.

PEOPLE'S CHOICE
★ ★ ★ **Boogie Down U.S.A.** / Phil. (1975) ¶
★ ★ ★ **We Got the Rhythm** / Phil. (1976) ¶
★ ★ ★ **Turn Me Loose** / Phil. (1978)
★ ★ ★ **People's Choice** / Casa. (NA)
People's Choice is a black rock band with limited scope, which just shows that limited doesn't always mean wretched. *Boogie Down*'s "Do It Any Way You Wanna," an unlikely pop hit in 1975, is typical of the group's songs: tough, clean, Philadelphia mix and some simple chanting. Lead singer Frankie Brunson often sounds like Screamin' Jay Hawkins, and combined with the band's updated, Philadelphia version of Booker T. and the MGs, usually does well. There's little to choose between these albums, all of which are mindless but fun. — J.MC.

PERE UBU
★ ★ ★ ★ **The Modern Dance** / Blank/Poly. (1978)
★ ★ ★ ★ **Dub Housing** / Chrys. (1979)
★ ★ ★ ★ ★ **Datapanik in the Year Zero** / Atl. (1979)
★ ★ ★ **New Picnic Time** / Chrys. (1979)
★ ★ ★ **The Art of Walking** / Rough T. (1980)

★ ★ ★ ★ **390 Degrees of Simulated Stereo, Ubu Live, Vol. 1** / Rough T. (1981)
Cleveland's Pere Ubu is one of the most important American avant-garde/new-wave rock bands of the late Seventies and early Eighties. Their early recordings (*Datapanik*, *Modern Dance*, *Dub Housing*) are the sounds of the American Urban Underground. Pere Ubu plays straight ahead rock & roll, twisted and contorted by singer/lyricist David Thomas, who sometimes sings, sometimes rambles, and rarely makes sense, and synthesist Allen Ravenstine, who is possibly the only true synthesizer artist in rock today. Ravenstine never plays musical notes with his synthesizer; instead he creates static backdrops, the kind of sounds you'd expect to come out of Three Mile Island during a meltdown. Bassist Tony Maimone and drummer Scott Krauss (recently replaced by Lounge Lizards/Feelies drummer Anton Fier) provide a steady and powerful rock backbeat. Guitarist Tom Herman, who left the band after *New Picnic Time,* provides what can only be called unusual guitar sounds. Herman's guitar doesn't screech or distort, it just doesn't do what you'd expect it to do, and at all the right (wrong?) times (the same goes for Thomas).

Datapanik, Modern Dance and *Dub Housing* are all basically rock albums. *New Picnic Time* and *The Art of Walking* are more avant-garde and perhaps a little unfocused. Ravenstine's synthesizer seems to be a little lower in the mix, and it's missed, but there are still moments of excellence. *390 Degrees* is a live album recorded wherever a tape machine was handy, whether it was a cassette machine or a four-track. The liner notes are good, and this is what you'd expect from a live Ubu gig. But what's missing in the live album are the visuals. David Thomas may be the funniest man in rock, but you have to see him live to really understand what Pere Ubu is all about. — K.L.

CARL PERKINS
★ ★ ★ ★ **Original Golden Hits** / Sun (1969)
★ ★ ★ ★ ★ **Blue Suede Shoes** / Sun (1969)
★ ★ ★ ★ **Rocking Guitarman** / Charly (1975), Br. imp.
★ ★ ★ ★ **Original Carl Perkins** / Charly (1976), Br. imp.
★ ★ **Long Tall Sally** / CBS (1977), Br. imp.
★ ★ ★ **Sun Sounds Special** / Charly (1978), Br. imp.
★ ★ ★ **Ol' Blue Suede's Back** / Jet (1978)
★ ★ ★ **Greatest Hits of Carl Perkins** / CBS (NA), Br. imp.

Perkins was one of the original great stars of Sam Phillips' Sun Records. Along with Jerry Lee Lewis, Elvis Presley and Johnny Cash, he put the stamp on rockabilly, a wild man's music. His best-known song is "Blue Suede Shoes" (although even that is often claimed as Presley's), but the stand-out track that reveals Perkins' rather astonishing guitar-playing ability is the more obscure "Dixie Fried." *Ol' Blue Suede's Back* is a 1978 comeback attempt (Perkins has more recently appeared in Cash's combo) that isn't bad, though the old stuff far surpasses it. The Charly albums are reissues of the Sun classics; the CBS material is later and blander. — D.M.

JOE PERRY PROJECT
★ ★ ★ **Let the Music Do the Talking / Col. (1980)**
★ ★ **I've Got the Rock 'n' Rolls Again / Col. (1981)**
With his smoldering solo debut, the guitarist who played Keith Richards to Steven Tyler's Mick Jagger in Aerosmith left his old band eating his heavy-metal dust. The combination of Perry's snappy gonzo riffing, a hellish rhythm section and Jack Douglas' meltdown production was unbeatable, especially when Perry and Project started gassing up the James Brown–style funk and customized Yardbirds ravers. Limited songwriting, however, got the better of them on album two. — D.F.

PERRY AND SANDLIN
★ ★ **For Those Who Love / Cap. (NA)**
★ ★ **We're the Winners / Cap. (NA)**
Supper-club soul, updated for the late Seventies. — D.M.

PERSIA
★ **Persia / Casa. (NA)**
I say it's Iran, and I say the hell with it. — D.M.

THE PERSUASIONS
★ ★ ★ ★ **We Came to Play / Cap. (1971)**
★ ★ ★ ★ **Street Corner Symphony / Cap. (1972)**
★ ★ ★ ★ ★ **Chirpin' / Elek. (1977)**
★ ★ ★ **Comin' at Ya / Fly. Fish (1979)**
The last (only?) great a cappella R&B group. Frank Zappa rescued the Persuasions from a life of total obscurity in Brooklyn about 1970, and recorded a pair of albums for his Bizarre label, which are now deleted. But the group was interesting enough to latch on to a Capitol contract almost immediately. Both of those albums (while they sold only

barely enough to remain in the catalogue) contain some fine singing—perhaps the best track is "Buffalo Soldier" from *Street Corner Symphony.* But the deleted A&M and MCA albums that followed the Capitol don't really do the Persuasions justice.

Chirpin', released in 1977 and one of the best albums in any genre put out in that year, is a complete triumph, as moving and evocative of street life as the best soul music, as energetic as early rock & roll. In "Looking for an Echo," the group found a song that told its story perfectly; in "To Be Loved," Joseph Russell came up with a great solo vehicle, nearly cutting Jackie Wilson's masterful original; "Sixty Minute Man" and "It's Gonna Rain Again" were simply great reflections of what such streetcorner harmonies were always all about. There isn't a bad track on *Chirpin',* and everyone vaguely interest in the amateur roots of rock ought to own it. — D.M.

PETER AND GORDON
★ ★ ★ **The Best of Peter and Gordon / Cap. (1966)**
Peter Asher was the brother of actress/model Jane Asher, Paul McCartney's first famous girlfriend, which encouraged McCartney to write "A World without Love" and give it to Asher's group, Peter and Gordon. It was a smash hit in 1964. But most of what Peter and Gordon did could be described as pre-folk-rock—their first album included "Freight Train" and "500 Miles" for instance. Their hits—"A World without Love," "I Don't Want to See You Again," "I Go to Pieces"—all had a folkish feel. But the group's best-known hit is probably "Lady Godiva," which is about the famous nude horsewoman, a puerile novelty.

Peter and Gordon are of current interest mostly because Asher went on to become the producer/manager of James Taylor and Linda Ronstadt. — D.M.

PETER, PAUL AND MARY
★ ★ **Peter, Paul and Mary / War. (1962)**
★ **Peter, Paul and Mary Moving / War. (1963)**
★ ★ ★ **Peter, Paul and Mary in the Wind / War. (1963)**
★ ★ **Peter, Paul and Mary in Concert / War. (1964)**
★ ★ ★ **A Song Will Rise / War. (1965)**
★ **See What Tomorrow Brings / War. (1965)**
★ **The Peter, Paul and Mary Album / War. (1966)**
★ ★ ★ **Album 1700 / War. (1967)**

★ **Late Again / War. (1968)**
★ **Peter, Paul and Mommy / War.
(1969)**
★ ★ **Best (Ten Years Together) / War.
(1970)**
■ **Reunion / War. (1978)**

Listening to Peter, Paul and Mary today,
one finds it difficult to fathom the profound
effect that their highly staged, impeccably arranged music had on the early Sixties. Having emerged from the Greenwich Village folk
scene at about the time Bob Dylan, Tom
Paxton, Eric Andersen and a host of others
were developing their songwriting and performing abilities, they had an enormous
fountain of new as well as traditional material at their disposal. And in combination
with manager Albert Grossman and musical
director Milt Okun, they hit upon the right
songs at the right time.

Given the late-Fifties success of people
such as the Kingston Trio and Harry Bela-
fonte, and the definition of folk music that
derived from that success, it was a natural
progression to the slickly stylized work of
Peter Yarrow, Paul Stookey and Mary
Travers, even if they were introducing the
songs of people who were shortly to become
known as "protest singers." Bob Dylan's version of "Blowing in the Wind" wouldn't
have sold the way it did without being
dressed up in Peter, Paul and Mary's three-
part harmonies, with crisp dual-guitar accompaniment.

The civil rights movement made social
consciousness acceptable at the mass level,
and gave focus to the general dissatisfactions
of the new breed of white, middle-class
socio-musical commentators. Peter, Paul and
Mary were among the first to put their popularity at the service of the cause. (And vice
versa.)

In the Wind, for example, pictures them
at the 1963 March on Washington, performing before the hundreds of thousands of people who lined the mall between the Lincoln
Memorial and the Washington Monument.
In Concert, the group's next set (and first
live album), exposed their political concerns
a little more directly, though not as pro-
nouncedly or as exploitatively as say, the
Chad Mitchell Trio.

A Song Will Rise was not one of their bet-
ter-selling albums, though it did much for
revitalizing a number of traditional and blues
tunes, adding "Motherless Child," "San
Francisco Bay Blues" (sparking interest in
Jesse Fuller) and "Cuckoo" to the standard
pop-folk repertoire.

It was *1700,* however, that finally brought

the political overtones into the foreground.
The civil rights movement had been overshadowed by the Vietnam War, and once
again Peter, Paul and Mary were among the
leading singing protesters. In addition, although they sneered in fear at the growing
importance of rock with "I Dig Rock and
Roll Music" (as they had done earlier with
"Blue" on *In Concert*), their sound matured
considerably.

It was at this point too, though, that the
group began to move in individual directions, Peter Yarrow in particular wanting to
assume a more political stance. The two albums that followed *1700* were, for all intents
and purposes, throwaways. *Ten Years Together* marked the formal end, the trio regrouping on rare occasions for benefit performances, more as a symbol of political
unity than of group allegiance.   — I.M.

TOM PETTY AND THE
HEARTBREAKERS

★ ★ ★ ★ **Tom Petty and the Heartbreakers
/ Shel. (1976)**
★ ★ ★ **You're Gonna Get It / Shel. (1978)**
★ ★ ★ ★ ★ **Damn the Torpedoes / Backs.
(1979)**
★ ★ ★ **Hard Promises / Backs. (1981)**
★ ★ ★ ★ **Long after Dark / Backs. (1982)**

Because his first albums appeared during the
first flush of new wave, and because Petty
and his Florida-bred band played mainstream rock with vigor and vitality, the first
two albums here were associated with punk
and its ilk. Petty instead works within the
narrower, perhaps more difficult tradition of
American rock & roll from the Byrds and
the Band to Bruce Springsteen and Bob
Seger: music informed by blues and country
and the British Invasion, but more than anything, a personal statement of emotional intensity.

Petty's clearly the leader of this group, not
only because he's the singer and songwriter
but also because he functions as a kind of
fulcrum for the talents of the others, most
notably organist Benmont Tench, whose
style is the ultimate extension of Al
Kooper's playing with Bob Dylan in the
mid-Sixties. Petty himself sounds remarkably
like Roger McGuinn, particularly on the
debut album's "American Girl," while some
of the band's other music is part of that long
strange search for a U.S. equivalent to the
Rolling Stones. With "Breakdown," from
You're Gonna Get It, the Heartbreakers
nearly found that sound. Unfortunately,
except for "Breakdown" and the scathing
"Listen to Her Heart," the second album

lacks the highlights of the first—it is less consistent, less fresh and poorly produced.

With *Damn the Torpedoes,* Petty made a breakthrough—this is one of the three great albums of late-Seventies American mainstream rock, along with Springsteen's *Born to Run* and Bob Seger's *Night Moves.* Like those records, *Torpedoes* is born from personal turmoil at the edge of despair, but it is ultimately an affirmation of idealism, a statement of faith in the transforming possibility of music. "Refugee," "Even the Losers," "Don't Do Me Like That" and even the seemingly slight "Century City" pack a wallop that's both sonic and emotional. Jimmy Iovine's production gave the band the density of sound and the sheer strength to convey Petty's best ideas perfectly.

Hard Promises is not quite so successful, but that is mostly a relative judgment. Petty's lyrics are more explicit and narrative-oriented than ever before, and the band's playing is on a par with *Torpedoes,* though a few of the songs ("Something Big," "The Criminal Kind") are not quite up to the earlier mark. On the other hand, "The Waiting," "Kings Road," Petty's duet with Stevie Nicks on "The Insider" and the toughest, most Stones-like rocker the band has ever done, "A Thing about You," made *Hard Promises* one of the more satisfying albums of its year, one of the few mainstream rock successes of the early Eighties. Encouragingly, Petty's commitment to his basic approach shows no signs of softening. — D.M.

PEZBAND
★ ★ **Pezband** / Pass. (1977) ¶
★ ★ **Laughing in the Dark** / Pass. (1978)
★ **Cover to Cover** / Pass. (1979)
Powerful, if not terribly distinctive pop from a Chicago-based rock band; its roots are more in British pop rock like Sweet and Amen Corner than in America, however, despite an appearance by Bruce Springsteen's saxman Clarence Clemons on *Laughing in the Dark.* — D.M.

P.F.M.
★ ★ ★ **Chocolate Kings** / Asy. (1976)
★ ★ ★ **Jet Lag** / Asy. (1977)
These are supposed to be Italy's top progressive musicians, and in fact the P.F.M. sound is comparable to the best of a topflight English progressive group like Genesis. The vocals are studied Peter Gabriel copies, too. The group has a great deal of other material available on earlier, deleted U.S. albums for Manticore (Emerson, Lake and Palmer's label) or on import. — A.N.

GREG PHILLINGANES
★ ★ **Significant Gains** / Planet (1981)
Phillinganes is a session player who has contributed hot licks to the Jacksons and others. None show up here, though; just soppy sentiment and a lot of unnecessary production. — J.D.C.

ANTHONY PHILLIPS
★ ★ ★ **Private Parts and Places** / Pass. (1978) ¶
★ ★ **Sides** / Pass. (1979)
★ ★ **1984** / Pass. (1981)
The original lead guitarist of Genesis returned in the mid-Seventies with a pleasant fusion of that group's art-rock pastoralism, and his own avant-garde notions. Not rock & roll, but not everything needs to be . . . I suppose. — D.M.

BRUCE (U. UTAH) PHILLIPS
★ ★ **Good Though** / Philo (1973) ¶
★ ★ **El Capitan** / Philo (1975) ¶
Phillips is a better entertainer and performer than either of these LPs indicates. Though his vocal and guitar abilities are severely limited, he is both an aficionado and a raconteur as regards railroads, hobos and the West. Rosalie Sorrels, Joan Baez and a number of progressive bluegrass and country bands have recorded his material. "The Telling Takes Me Home" and "Daddy, What's a Train?" are favorites along the summer folk festival route. — I.M.

ESTHER PHILLIPS (LITTLE ESTHER)
★ ★ ★ **And I Love Him** / Atl. (1965) ¶
★ ★ ★ ★ **Burnin'** / Atl. (1971) ¶
★ ★ ★ **From a Whisper to a Scream** / Kudu (1972)
★ ★ ★ **Alone Again (Naturally)** / Kudu (1972)
★ ★ ★ **Black-Eyed Blues** / Kudu (1973)
★ ★ ★ **Confessin' the Blues** / Atl. (1975)
★ ★ ★ **Little Esther Phillips** / Power (1975) ¶
★ ★ **Capricorn Princess** / Kudu (1976)
★ ★ ★ **You've Come a Long Way Baby** / Mer. (1977)
★ ★ ★ **All About Esther Phillips** / Mer. (1978)
★ ★ ★ **Here's Esther . . . Are You Ready?** / Mer. (1979)
★ ★ ★ **A Good Black Is Hard to Crack** / Mer. (1981)
Esther Phillips, a Texas-born blues and jazz singer, first emerged into the national spotlight as Little Esther in 1950, with "Cupid's Boogie" on Savoy. (That material is included on the Power Pak LP.) Extremely talented,

with a sensual streak derived from Dinah Washington, she has rarely repeated even R&B chart success: "Ring a Ding Doo" for Federal in 1952 and "Release Me," an R&B reworking of a country standard that made R&B Top Ten in 1962 for Lenox, are her only other R&B Top Ten hits. Phillips worked steadily with Johnny Otis' soul revue, however, and in 1964 came close to a hit with the Beatles' "And I Love Him" for Atlantic. She did a series of smoldering sides for that label (most notably the live LP, *Burnin'*) before moving into a more modern pop-jazz groove with her Seventies and Eighties LPs on Kudu and Mercury, all of which are pleasant examples of contemporary pop and jazz vocalizing. — D.M.

SHAWN PHILLIPS
★ ★ Contribution / A&M (1970)
★ ★ Second Contribution / A&M (1971)
■ Collaboration / A&M (1973)
★ Faces / A&M (1973)
★ ★ Furthermore / A&M (1974)
★ Bright White / A&M (1974)
★ ★ Do You Wonder / A&M (1975)
★ ★ Rumplestiltskin's Resolve / A&M (1976)
★ Spaced / A&M (1977)
★ Transcendence / RCA (1978)
Phillips was signed to A&M in 1969, when he delivered a trip of homemade albums to the company; the label boiled them down to form *Contribution*. Mostly he has mined a similar vein since then: folk and folk rock of the sort pioneered by Buffalo Springfield and Crosby, Stills and Nash. At his worst Phillips is a quavering wimp; his philosophy is the usual muck of romanticism and ecology. But at his best he deals comfortably with producer Paul Buckmaster's relatively lush arrangements, and on *Furthermore,* he collaborates capably with the British rock band Quartermass for some folk-classical mood music. — A.N.

PHILLIPS/MacLEOD
★ ★ Le Partie du Cocktail / Poly. (1979)
★ Phillips/MacLeod / Poly. (1980)
California rock notable chiefly for its blandness. — J.D.C.

PHILLY CREAM
★ ★ Philly Cream / WMOT (1979)
★ ★ No Time Like Now / WMOT (1981)
What this is, is your basic bar-band funk placed in a recording studio, where it loses its charm. Here we have plodding, unnecessary remakes of Sly Stone and Motown hits, James Brown's "Doin' It to Death" and Sam

and Dave's "Soul Man," concluding with a rousing "Join the Army," which is presumably what these guys have done since. — D.M.

PHOENIX
★ ★ Phoenix / Col. (1976) ¶
★ ★ In Full View / Char. (1980)
The logo suggests Aerosmith, but the sententious sentiment, purposeless hot-dog virtuosity and ASPCA vocals render this English trio's sound much closer to Emerson, Lake and Palmer pomp and piffle. — D.M.

PHOTOGLO
■ Photoglo / 20th Cent. (1980)
■ Fool in Love with You / 20th Cent. (1981)
Soft-rock balladeer pretentious enough to think he can get by with only one name. Even Little Richard used two. — D.M.

THE PHOTOS
★ ★ The Photos / Epic (NA)
Led by the Photo-genic Wendy Wu, this pop foursome have style but little panache. Outside of a nice reading of "I Just Don't Know What to Do with Myself," this band's image fades like a faulty Polaroid print. — R.P.

PHYREWORK
★ Phyrework / Mer. (NA)
Pheh. — D.M.

PIANO RED
★ ★ ★ Dr. Feelgood Alone / Arhoo. (1972)
★ ★ ★ Percussive Piano / Euphonic (NA)
★ ★ ★ Boogie Honky-Tonk / Oldie Bl. (NA)
Alias Doctor Feelgood, Red was a Georgia keyboardist with a rousing barrelhouse-to-honky-tonk style. — J.S.

WILSON PICKETT
★ ★ ★ ★ ★ The Best of Wilson Pickett / Atl. (1967) ¶
★ ★ ★ ★ ★ Wilson Pickett's Greatest Hits / Atl. (1973)
★ ★ Join Me and Let's Be Free / RCA (1977)
★ ★ ★ A Funky Situation / Big (1978)
★ ★ ★ I Want You / EMI (1979)
★ ★ ★ The Right Track / EMI (1981)
★ ★ ★ ★ The Sound of Wilson Pickett / Atl. (NA), Jap. imp.
★ ★ ★ Wickedness / Trip (NA) ¶
Wilson Pickett's work on Atlantic in the Sixties defined a style of soul music. Bold and cocky, Pickett—like James Brown—seemed to symbolize soul music at its most kinetic. His hits are among the period's most memorable and include "In the Midnight Hour,"

"Mustang Sally" and "I'm in Love." The songs on *Greatest Hits* span almost a decade and range from the unleashed fury of "I Found a True Love" (sung with the Falcons) to slicker but still powerful, Gamble-and-Huff-produced performances like "Don't Let the Green Grass Fool You."

Wickedness is a collection of songs from Pickett's pre-Atlantic tenure on the Double L label. Undisciplined and raw, the ballads remain forceful and moving. Included are his first two solo hits, "If You Need Me" and "It's Too Late." The RCA album—like its deleted brethren and the album Pickett made for his own Wicked label—lacks direction and distinctive material. It's representative of the musical identity crisis experienced not only by Pickett but by other soul stars of the Sixties struggling to find a niche in the mid-Seventies. Pickett came as close to a complete rapprochement with current styles as anyone with *A Funky Situation,* produced by Rick Hall in Pickett's Sixties stomping ground, Muscle Shoals. The record manages to update the tracks—including the inspired "Lay Me Like You Hate Me," a summation of Pickett's philosophy of romance—without losing the singer's distinctive style, as most recent veteran soul recordings have done. His EMI America records continue in this spirit. — J.MC.

PIECES
★ Pieces / U.A. (1979) ¶
Chicago-esque pop with disco flourishes. Eau de banality (i.e., stinks). — D.M.

THE PILGRIM TRAVELERS
★ ★ ★ Best of the Pilgrim Travelers / Spec. (NA)
★ ★ Best of the Pilgrim Travelers, Vol. 2 / Spec. (NA)
★ ★ ★ Shake My Mother's Hand / Spec. (NA)
Lou Rawls sang briefly with the Pilgrim Travelers, and though he's not featured on these albums, it's easy to see how he fit into this gospel group. They could sound like a group of hollerin' field hands (listen to "Standing on the Highway" on the first album), but the Travelers favored cooler, urbane vocals; some of their harmonies even sound detached. They were one of the most popular quartets, though their featured singers (Kylo Turner and Keith Barber) didn't have styles as distinctively personal as the best leads. Besides "Standing on the Highway," *Best of* contains Turner's magnificent "Mother Bowed" and a novelty called "Jesus Hits Like the Atom Bomb." The *Mother* album features "Peace of Mind" and "How Jesus Died" (rewritten by Ray Charles as "Lonely Avenue"). — J.MO.

JOHN PILLA
★ ★ Southbound / Van. (1966)
Only a middling folksinger, Pilla is justifiably much better known for his production work with Arlo Guthrie. — D.M.

RICK PINETTE AND OAK
★ Oak / Mer. (NA)
★ Set the Night on Fire / Mer. (NA)
Wooden heartland rock. — D.M.

PINK FAIRIES
★ ★ Kings of Oblivion / Poly. (1975) ¶
Proto-punk heavy metal from a trio that was an offshoot of the notorious British hippie-politico band the Deviants. Their first two albums, *Never Never Land* and *What a Bunch of Sweeties,* were never released in America, but this third LP adequately captured their neo-psychedelic bashing in spite of flat production and a slim songbook. Guitarist Larry Wallis went on to join the Stiff Records family of eccentrics. — D.F.

PINK FLOYD
★ ★ The Piper at the Gates of Dawn / Tower (1967)
★ ★ ★ A Saucer Full of Secrets / Cap. (1968)
★ ★ ★ Ummagumma / Harv. (1969)
★ More / Cap. (1969)
★ ★ Atom Heart Mother / Harv. (1970)
★ Relics / Harv. (1971)
★ ★ ★ ★ Meddle / Harv. (1971)
★ ★ Obscured by Clouds / Harv. (1972)
★ ★ ★ A Nice Pair / Harv. (1973)
Because they're a cult band with a mass audience, Pink Floyd has enjoyed a career of soaring ups and plummeting downs. The sound originated in late-Sixties British psychedelia, and Floyd's first two albums tortured song forms in the post–Sgt. Pepper manner. But those records also offered several instrumental space-rock seedlings that sprouted on *Ummagumma.*

At first, under Syd Barrett's leadership on *Piper,* the emphasis was on crazed songwriting. But with the harder rock sound of *Saucer,* the band developed a fruitful relationship between mannered experimentalism and aching lyricism, which it has never abandoned. However, these twin strains are not successfully synthesized until *Meddle.*

Ummagumma, a two-disc set, is a failed but fascinating experiment in the construction of avant-garde rock. On the studio sides, noise (electronic and documentary sounds), drone effects, mixed tempos and weirdly twisted song forms are mixed into sequences of fragmented pieces. It's something of a Pink Floyd notebook. The concert sides portray a very much advanced editing of the band that made *Saucer* the peak of its powers. It's here, incidentally, that Floyd creates the sounds of space-rock later developed into a major European genre by Hawkwind, Can, Tangerine Dream and others.

The lyrical soundtracks, *More* and *Obscured by Clouds,* are collections of light, often quasi-folkie ballads suggestive of impressionist sketches. Both were made to accompany European art films. The band retreats into polite but awkward poeticism and turns out music far more sentimental than the films.

Side one of *Atom Heart Mother* is an orchestral rethinking of the studio sides of *Ummagumma.* Not unlike something by the middle-period Deep Purple, Floyd breaks up into its component soloists and sets them in the context of a large orchestra playing a score of light classical fanfares. Even the several avant-garde sections late on the side fail to redeem the music's middle-brow pretensions. Side two is a rehash of ballad ideas left over from the movie scores.

The organization of *Meddle* is similar, but here the band has at last achieved a stylistic union of its aimless experimentalism and bland ballads. *Meddle*'s title track, which covers a whole side, flows out of a primal beep to create a play of stasis/hypnosis and pulse/pathos. Strangely, after several failed soundtracks, this music achieves its own cinematic mood, in a decidedly sci-fi genre. Unfortunately, side two is filler, mostly ballads, although this time they don't suffer from *Atom Heart Mother*'s indifferent performances.

A Nice Pair repackages *Piper* and *Saucer.* *Relics* collects singles from *Piper* through *More* and is of little interest.

★ ★ ★ ★ ★ **Dark Side of the Moon** / **Harv. (1973)**
★ ★ ★ **Wish You Were Here** / **Col. (1975)**
★ ★ ★ ★ **Animals** / **Col. (1977)**
★ ★ ★ ★ ★ **The Wall** / **Col. (1979)**
★ ★ ★ **A Collection of Great Dance Songs** / **Col. (1981)**

Dark Side of the Moon is Pink Floyd's masterpiece. The band improved its sound immeasurably (helped by engineer Alan Parsons) and took the leisure to develop its songs into perfect vehicles for its instrumental procedures. While the main interest on *Dark Side* is to maintain a rich lyricism

(aided by Dick Parry's saxophone and Clare Torry's vocals), the album also reintroduces *Ummagumma*'s experiments with noise and speech. These, together with bassist Roger Waters' lyrics, break *Dark Side*'s smooth surface with the flaky-epic urgency typical of the band's late albums.

Wish and *Animals* continue to work inside the style of *Dark Side,* but on those albums older Floyd ideas, like faster songs and harsh aural violence, are introduced into the majestic sweep. In these albums, Waters' lyrics become progressively bitter in their rather smug pessimism: *Animals* is little more than one long execution by Orwellian allegory. With a great deal of spotlighted solo space, all three albums document guitarist David Gilmore's emergence as Floyd's major instrumentalist, while keyboardist Rick Wright moves into the increasingly deep recesses of the band's music as the prime mover of Floyd's aural stagecraft.

The Wall is a two-disc conceptual work that produced the band's biggest (and best) hit, "Another Brick in the Wall, Part 2." The record is ultimately the culmination of the tendencies originally developed on *Wish* and *Animals;* it is arguably the band's best album, though the story is certainly one of its more pompous.

Pink Floyd is a band that's never thrown away a single idea. While this may have resulted in a dearth of imagination and a kind of standardization, as cited by its many critics, this narrowness has also kept Floyd from the dilettantism of its art-rock colleagues (Moody Blues; Emerson, Lake and Palmer) who lapse inexorably into glossy sentiment. — B.T./D.M.

PINK LADY
■ **Pink Lady** / **Elek. (1979)**
Japanese female duo had brief blush of pop success through short-lived TV series and marginal Top Forty single, "Kiss in the Dark," thanks to their Svengali, Paul Drew, former big-time radio programer. Something must have been lost in the translation, however: this is shtick so cloying and dumb that it might embarrass Cher . . . or even Sonny. — D.M.

THE PIONEERS
★ ★ ★ ★ **Longshot Kick de Bucket** / **Troj. (1970)**
★ ★ ★ **Greatest Hits** / **Troj. (1979)**
During the late Sixties, no group embodied early reggae as jauntily as the Pioneers, whose patois lyrics and close harmonies were immensely popular. *Long Shot* captures that

era beautifully, but *Greatest Hits* is dominated by the pop-oriented hits of their English heyday. — R.F.G.

PIPEDREAM
★ **Pipedream / MCA (1979)**
Not in your wildest fantasies. — D.M.

WARDELL PIPER
★ ★ **Wardell Piper / Mid. Int. (1980)**
Middleweight popper came close with "Gimme Something Real." — D.M.

THE PIPS
★ ★ **At Last . . . The Pips / Casa. (1978)**
★ ★ **Callin' / Casa. (1978)**
Without Gladys—that's kinda like glycerin without nitro. — D.M.

PIRATES
★ ★ **Out of Their Skulls / War. (1978)** ¶
★ ★ **Skull Wars / War. (1978)** ¶
★ ★ **Hard Ride / Pac. F.A. (1980)**
With the late Johnny Kidd as vocalist, the Pirates cut a seminal British rock single, "Shakin' All Over," and helped spawn the guitar styles of Townshend, Page, Beck et al. *Out of Their Skulls,* much of it live, includes a decent version of "Shakin' " (though not nearly as good as those by the Who and Guess Who) and a lot of rockabilly filler. Historians only. — D.M.

GENE PITNEY
★ **Just for You / Musi. (1961)** ¶
★ ★ ★ **Only Love Can Break a Heart / Musi. (1962)** ¶
★ ★ ★ **World Wide Winners / Musi. (1963)** ¶
★ ★ ★ **Big Sixteen / Musi. (1963)** ¶
★ ★ ★ **Big Sixteen, Vol. 2 / Musi. (1964)** ¶
★ ★ ★ **It Hurts to Be in Love / Musi. (1964)** ¶
★ **Looking through the Eyes of Love / Musi. (1965)** ¶
★ ★ **The Country Side of Gene Pitney / Musi. (1966)** ¶
★ ★ ★ **The Golden Hits of Gene Pitney / Musi. (1966)** ¶
★ **Young and Warm and Wonderful / Musi. (1966)** ¶
★ ★ **Sings Bacharach / Musi. (1967)** ¶
★ ★ **The Gene Pitney Story / Musi. (1967)** ¶
★ **She's a Heartbreaker / Musi. (1968)** ¶
★ ★ ★ **This Is Gene Pitney (Singing the Platters' Golden Platters) / Musi. (1969)** ¶
★ ★ ★ **A Golden Hour of Gene Pitney / Musi. (1972)** ¶

★ ★ **Pitney '75 / Bronze (1975), imp.**
★ ★ ★ **Sixteen Greatest Hits / Trip (NA)**
★ ★ ★ **Gene Pitney / Sp. (NA)**
★ ★ ★ ★ **Double Gold: The Best of Gene Pitney / Musi. (NA)**
★ ★ ★ **Town without Pity / Hallmark (NA)**
★ ★ ★ **Greatest Hits, Vol. 1 / Hallmark (NA)**
Gene Pitney is a very strange case. At times he seemed to be one of the classic minor rock singers—listen to "(I Wanna) Love My Life Away," on which he played every instrument, overdubbed his own voice a dozen times, and added a devastating cymbal clash to the final bar of every chorus, a remarkable feat for 1961. Others of his hits present him as a fine ballad singer, almost a male counterpart of Dionne Warwick—"Only Love Can Break a Heart," "Town without Pity," "Half Heaven, Half Heartache" and even "Mecca" all fit here. But he also recorded country songs, operated as a falsetto in duets with George Jones, and sang Italian love songs and the schlockiest Tin Pan Alley ballads. It's confusing, but "Love My Life Away," "Last Chance to Turn Around," "The Man Who Shot Liberty Valance," "Mecca" and a few others make Pitney's importance unmistakable, if rather ineffable.

Pitney also had some importance as a writer—notably "Hello Mary Lou" for Ricky Nelson—and as a discoverer of songwriters. He recorded as many Burt Bacharach and Hal David tunes as Warwick, although she was better known for it; had Carole King and Gerry Goffin songs in his repertoire; and was first to record Al Kooper's finest composition, "Just One Smile," later done by Blood, Sweat and Tears. Even Mick Jagger and Keith Richards wrote a song for him, the odd "That Girl Belongs to Yesterday"—and Pitney recorded with the Rolling Stones on their second album, along with crony Phil Spector. He is a significant figure for those reasons, as well.

Of these albums, the two-disc *Best of* is clearly the most worthy, although all of the *Greatest Hits* and other anthologies have much to recommend them. *Best of,* however, leans a little more heavily toward his hard-edged material, including "Love My Life Away," the rockingest number he ever did, and stays away from the country-Italian junk. *Golden Hour* is almost as good, but is dragged down by a few Italian songs.

The *Country Side of* is interesting but inferior to the George Jones duets. *It Hurts* contains the Jagger-Richards "That Girl Belongs to Yesterday," and is of value to collectors. (The song was an English hit for Pitney.) Avoid *Looking Through, Just for You,* and particularly *Young and Warm and Wonderful,* all of which emphasize his Anka-esque roots. Most of the rest are relics of the early Sixties era and consist of hits sandwiched with junk. *World Wide Winners* almost constitutes a greatest-hits LP, and has one of the classic schlock covers of the period. *This Is* is a curious experiment—Pitney as R&B vocalist—that almost works. *Pitney '75* was recorded after a long layoff, and gets an extra star just because his voice is in shape, which is more than can be said for either the material or arrangements. He is rumored to be recording again, but nothing has resulted since 1975. — D.M.

THE PLANETS
★ ★ The Planets / Mo. (1980)
Funk fundamentals—you'll be happier with a version a good deal less stripped down to basic banalities. — D.M.

PLANXTY
★ ★ ★ Planxty Collection / Shan. (1976)
★ ★ ★ ★ Cold Blow and the Rainy Night / Shan. (1979)
★ ★ ★ ★ ★ The Well below the Valley / Shan. (1979)
★ ★ ★ Planxty / Shan. (1979)
★ ★ ★ Prosperous / Tara (NA)
The key Irish group of the early Seventies, Planxty was formed by Donal Lunny out of the success of the *Prosperous* sessions. Though now defunct, Planxty was the most ambitious band of its type and displayed an awareness of other ethnic musics from Bulgarian to blues. *The Well below the Valley* is the best realization of the group's ideas and is a must for anyone interested in contemporary Celtic music. — D.D.

PLASTIC BERTRAND
★ ★ ★ Ca Plane pour Moi / Sire (1978)
Punk novelty from Belgian Euro-showbizzer who may not have been in on the joke. Surprisingly, the fey charm that made the title cut (translated: "This Life's for Me") a continental hit extends to the other tunes, but it seems unlikely that even Europeans could have swallowed this music—Edith Piaf meets the Beach Boys at a roller rink—whole. — G.A.

PLATINUM HOOK
★ Ecstasy Paradise / Mo. (NA)
★ It's Time / Mo. (1979)
Lead sinker, more likely. — D.M.

THE PLATTERS
★ ★ ★ The Platters / Sp. (1956)
★ ★ ★ ★ Encore of Golden Hits / Mer. (1960)
★ ★ ★ Double Gold Platters / Musi. (NA) ¶
★ ★ ★ ★ Sixteen Greatest Hits / Trip (NA) ¶
★ ★ ★ ★ More Encore of Golden Hits / Mer. (NA)
★ ★ ★ ★ Nineteen Hits / King (NA)
One of the slickest R&B groups of the Fifties, the Platters were probably the most palatable to straight pop (or antirock) tastes, the logical successors to the Mills Brothers and the Ink Spots. But at their best, with "Smoke Gets in Your Eyes," "Harbor Lights," "Only You" and "The Great Pretender," the group perfected the kind of funky smooch music that Curtis Mayfield's Impressions and Smokey Robinson's Miracles would later make an art form. — D.M.

PLATYPUS
★ Cherry / Casa. (NA)
★ Street Babies / Casa. (NA)
Lays eggs. — D.M.

PLAYER
★ ★ ★ Player / RSO (1977)
★ Danger Zone / RSO (1978)
★ Room with a View / Casa. (NA)
One of the several great singles from the hit disco movie *Saturday Night Fever,* "Baby Come Back" was probably a one-shot from this perfectly faceless Hall and Oates clone. For sure, as palatable as the self-titled debut album may be, it's also instantly forgettable: pop music as Chinese food. *Danger Zone* and *Room with a View* are less of the same. — D.M.

PLAYERS ASSOCIATION
★ ★ Players Association / Van. (1977)
★ ★ Turn the Music Up / Van. (1978)
★ ★ Born to Dance / Van. (1979)
★ ★ We Got the Groove / Van. (1980)
Occasionally vigorous funk 'n' fusion; more often, however, merely tepid. Led by Chris Hills, notorious in hippie days for leading Everything Is Everything, proprietors of the underground chant "Witchi Tai To." — D.M.

PLEASURE
★ ★ Dust Yourself Off / Fan. (1975)
★ ★ Accept No Substitutes / Fan. (1976)
★ ★ Joyous / Fan. (1977)
★ ★ Get to the Feeling / Fan. (1978)
★ ★ Future Now / Fan. (1979)

★ ★ **Special Things / Fan. (1980)**
Another dance-yourself-to-death concoction.
Nowadays, of course, it is often hard to tell
whether compulsive joggers or obsessive
dancers are more obnoxious. Pleasure's
mindless funk, however, seems to swing the
issue strongly toward the latter. — D.M.

POCKETS
★ **Come Go with Us / Col. (1977)**
★ **Take It On Up / Col. (1978)**
Utterly obnoxious black pop from 1977–78.
The bottom of the Philadelphia funk barrel.
Only for diehard dancers who've worn out
everything else—including their shoes.
— D.M.

POCO
★ ★ ★ ★ **Pickin' Up the Pieces / Epic
(1969)**
★ ★ **Poco / Epic (1970)**
★ ★ **Deliverin' / Epic (1971)**
★ ★ ★ **From the Inside / Epic (1971)**
★ ★ ★ **A Good Feelin' to Know / Epic
(1972)**
★ ★ **Crazy Eyes / Epic (1973)**
★ ★ **Seven / Epic (1974)**
★ ★ ★ **Cantamos / Epic (1974)**
★ ★ ★ **The Very Best of Poco / Epic
(1975)**
★ ★ ★ **Head over Heels / ABC (1975)**
★ ★ **Live / Epic (1976)**
★ ★ **Rose of Cimarron / ABC (1976)**
★ ★ **Indian Summer / ABC (1977)**
★ ★ **Legend / ABC (1978)**
★ ★ **Ride the Country / Epic (1979)**
★ ★ **Under the Gun / MCA (1980)**
Poco was founded in 1968 by two former
members of Buffalo Springfield, Richie Furay
and Jim Messina, along with three Colora-
dans, Rusty Young, Randy Meisner and
George Grantham. Their first album, *Pickin'
Up,* was an excellent combination of Beatles-
inspired harmony, melody and beat with
country & western's then-untapped rock possibilities. Furay's gorgeous tenor, Young's
rockified pedal steel and an imaginatively
tasteful mix of acoustic and electric guitars
trademark the debut. Meisner then left to
join first Ricky Nelson's Stone Canyon Band
and later the Eagles, and Tim Schmit replaced him as bassist on *Poco,* which streamlined but somewhat reduced the sound with
more electricity. But that album also wasted
almost a whole side with an unthrilling instrumental. *Deliverin'* was a faithful but routine live album, and after it, Messina left to
form Loggins and Messina. He was replaced
by Paul Cotton, who had been in Illinois
Speed Press. The Steve Cropper–produced

From the Inside lacks some of the early exuberance, but the care and sheer professionalism with which it was made echoes the
debut.

Cotton pushed the group in a somewhat
harder, simpler direction and *A Good Feelin'
to Know* took this several steps further. Recorded with a ragged toughness usually reserved for hard rock, the country influence
seemed nearly abandoned—disorienting but
good, if a bit drawn out. *Crazy Eyes,*
though, had no apparent course: tepid covers
of Gram Parsons and J. J. Cale songs and a
lengthy, orchestrated, cryptic title cut bogged
it down in correctness that left little room
for excitement.

Seven suffers severely from the departure
of Furay. Schmit was now the most important member—Furay wasn't replaced—and
while the songs were good enough, the playing was too long and wimpy. But *Cantamos*
brought back much of the old excitement; it
marked Young's emergence as a writer and
the more generous solo passages rocked hard
and fresh. *Very Best* is an excellent sampler
of this period; the subsequently released *Live*
has adequately performed material from several of the earlier discs.

Head over Heels had densely arranged and
recorded short songs—a modest excellence
rarely reached—but *Rose of Cimarron* lacks
raunch and drive. *Indian Summer* perks up
a bit but lacks the subtleties and imagination
of the group's best work. When Schmit became an Eagle (once more replacing Meisner), the Poco saga was pretty well finished,
although *Legend* eked out a hit in "Crazy
Love." Subsequent records are worthless.
— C.W.

BONNIE POINTER
★ ★ **Bonnie Pointer / Mo. (1978)**
★ ★ **Pointer / Mo. (1980)**
Those who try to tell you that this cast-off
Pointer Sister is a late-Seventies model of the
great Motown singers of the Sixties either do
not own *Mary Wells' Greatest Hits* or have
not listened to it lately. Not bad, sort of
tuneful, spritely melodies, but a long way
from the genius of yesteryear. Says the purist. — D.M.

THE POINTER SISTERS
★ ★ ★ **Pointer Sisters / Blue Th. (1973) ¶**
★ ★ **Live at the Opera House / Blue Th.
(1974) ¶**
★ ★ **That's a Plenty / Blue Th. (1974) ¶**
★ **Steppin' / Blue Th. (1975) ¶**
★ ★ ★ **Best of the Pointer Sisters / Blue Th.
(1976) ¶**

★ ★ **Having a Party** / Blue Th. (1977) ¶
★ ★ **Energy** / Planet (1978)
★ ★ **Priority** / Planet (1979)
★ ★ **Special Things** / Planet (1980)
★ ★ **Black and White** / Planet (1981)
Black woman vocal group whose gimmick was singing updated Andrews Sisters–type material from the Forties. The idea worked well enough in the early Seventies to net them a hit single, "Yes We Can Can." It was all downhill from there, except for their Top Ten 1978–79 hit, the Richard Perry production of Bruce Springsteen's "Fire," from *Energy*.   — J.S.

THE POLICE

★ ★ ★ **Outlandos d'Amour** / A&M (1978)
★ ★ ★ ★ **Regatta de Blanc** / A&M (1979)
★ ★ ★ ★ **Zenyatta Mondatta** / A&M (1980)
★ ★ **Ghost in the Machine** / A&M (1981)
An unlikely aggregation from the beginning—chief singer and bassist Sting was an actor who had never been in a band before, drummer Stewart Copeland had been playing with stodgy art rockers Curved Air—the Police were one of the more pleasurable spin-offs from the British new-wave revolution. Their first album was mere reggae-inflected power pop, helped along by an original and outstanding single, "Roxanne," which garnered them an audience.

With *Regatta de Blanc* and *Zenyatta Mondatta,* the group perfected its synthesis of light pop harmony and tight reggae rhythm, guitarist Andy Summers providing most of the instrumental coloration. "De Do Do Do, De Da Da Da," much less mindless than its title suggests, finally broke them into the U.S. Top Fifteen in 1980. *Zenyatta* suggested an approach that could be extended and used creatively throughout a long career.

But perhaps hampered by worries over its European image—where Sting had become almost a teenage idol—the group followed up with an overambitious conceptual LP, *Ghost in the Machine,* whose chief drawback was not its murky social theorizing (the title is extracted from Arthur Koestler) but its abandonment of the rudiments of the Police sound. Sting branched out as a horn player, and the distinctive rhythm and harmony blend that had earned the group its identity was buried under a self-indulgent and not especially intriguing experimentalism. Whether the Police can now go on with what the group is good at or whether future gaffes are necessary in order to justify the pretensions of this one is one of the more fascinating questions posed by contemporary rock.
— D.M.

POLYROCK

★ ★ ★ ★ **Polyrock** / RCA (1980)
★ ★ ★ ★ **Changing Hearts** / RCA (1981)
Polyrock is a minimalist rock band that understands the difference between simple music and simplistic music—their lack of ornamentation is not the product of a lack of imagination or skill. Quite the contrary. Polyrock's music is simple and effective because no motion is ever wasted. The band's major device is its arrangements, where instead of using instrumental texture to back the melody, the textural input actually *conveys* the melodic ideas, thus avoiding the usual dichotomy between theme and harmony. If that sounds academic, it's no accident; Polyrock's producer is composer Philip Glass, whose influence is particularly felt on the band's self-titled debut.   — J.D.C.

DAVID POMERANZ

■ **It's in Everyone of Us** / Ari. (1973) ¶
■ **Truth of Us** / Pac. F. A. (NA)
Jazz-pop singer/songwriter (who made earlier albums for MCA) comes a cropper with these shriekingly pretentious pop albums.
— S.H.

RUDY POMPILLI AND THE COMETS

★ ★ **Rudy's Rock** / Sonet (1976), Br. imp.
Bill Haley's saxophone player made his only solo album, with producer Sam Charters, as he was dying of cancer. Though he was once one of the best young saxophonists on the scene, his power had waned terribly by this point. Sadly, he didn't live to see the album released.   — J.S.

CHARLIE POOLE

★ ★ ★ **Old Time Songs, I** / Coun. (NA) ¶
★ ★ **Old Time Songs, II** / Coun. (NA) ¶
★ ★ **Legend of Charlie Poole** / Coun. (NA) ¶
Banjoist Poole and his North Carolina Ramblers were exponents of pre-bluegrass, country string-band music. Poole played his instrument using thumb and three fingers—as compared to the thumb and two-finger style later developed by Earl Scruggs. Known today as old-timey music, an idiom revitalized by the New Lost City Ramblers, these recordings (1925–1930) have been carefully remastered. The variations on traditional or "composed" pieces from the era ("Take a Whiff on Me" is heard as "Take a Drink on Me" on *Old Time Songs, I*) are of interest to both the scholar and the musician.
— I.M.

THE POP
★ ★ ★ **The Pop / Automatic (1977)** ¶
★ ★ ★ ★ **Go! / Ari. (1979)** ¶
★ ★ ★ **Hearts and Knives / Rhino (1981)**
This now-defunct San Francisco power-pop band had one truly distinguishing feature: an authentic, anomalous darkness pushing against the music's clean veneer. The Automatic release shows a lot of promise in spite of mushy production; the Rhino EP swan song has a couple of their most menacing, fully realized efforts. For overall consistency, *Go!* (with future Motel Tim McGovern sharpening the edge) is the one to grab. They coulda been contenders. — L.F.

IGGY POP
★ **The Idiot / RCA (1977)** ¶
★ ★ ★ **Lust for Life / RCA (1977)** ¶
★ **TV Eye—1977 Live / RCA (1978)** ¶
★ ★ **New Values / Ari. (1979)** ¶
★ ★ **Soldier / Ari. (1980)**
★ **Party / Ari. (NA)**
Iggy Pop was once the leader of the Stooges, the seminal punk-rock prototype. Here he's produced by David Bowie, who dominates on *The Idiot,* retreats on *Lust for Life* and nearly disappears on *TV Eye,* then plays out the string by making a series of albums in which he becomes the avant-garde Alice Cooper pushing out predictable shtick, some of it listenable, some of it not. By the time Iggy got this far, his maniacal inspiration was gone. Better to search for the now-deleted and sometimes brilliant Stooges albums—*Fun House* and *The Stooges* on Elektra, *Raw Power* on Columbia, all available as imports—but only if you thought the Sex Pistols were mellow. Some did. — D.M.

THE PORK DUKES
★ **Pork Dukes / Butt (NA)**
Punk as witty and interesting as its name. — D.M.

JOHNNY PORRAZZO
★ **Porrazzo / Poly. (1980)**
★ **Country Side of Johnny Porrazzo / Demand (NA)**
★ **Lighthouse / Demand (NA)**
Johnny Porrazzo is as obnoxious a pop singer as Billy Joel, but without a similarly redeeming gift for melody. — J.D.C.

POSITIVE FORCE
★ ★ **Positive Force / Sugar. (1981)**
Jive rap gab. — D.M.

JIM POST
★ **Colorado Exile / Fan. (1971)**
★ **Slow to 20 / Fan. (1972)**
★ **Rattlesnake / Fan. (1973)**
★ **Looks Good to Me / Fan. (1974)**
★ **Magic: In Concert / Fly. Fish (NA)**
★ **Shipshape / Fly. Fish (1981)**
The definition of the mediocre singer/songwriter. — D.M.

POTLIQUOR
★ ★ **Potliquor / Cap. (1979)** ¶
One of the first Southern rock bands, Potliquor hailed from Baton Rouge, Louisiana, and delivered a crude but powerful version of the by-now-traditional dueling guitars cliché. By 1979, years of failure had marked the band—the out-of-print records they cut for Janus in the early Seventies are much better. — J.S.

POUSETTE-DART BAND
★ ★ **Pousette-Dart Band / Cap. (1976)**
★ **Amnesia / Cap. (1977)**
★ **Never Enough / Cap. (1978)**
★ **Pousette-Dart Band 3 / Cap. (1980)**
Not quite folk, not quite rock. Jon Pousette-Dart's haunting melodies and raw yet tasteful electric slide guitar distinguish much of the debut, *Pousette-Dart Band,* as does Norbert Putnam's clear, spacious production. Yet at the same time a blandness lurks in other songs and Pousette-Dart's voice. But John Curtis' acoustic guitar is a neat complement.
Amnesia, Never Enough and *Pousette-Dart Band 3* follow the earlier record's worst tendencies and the slide is mostly missing. These are more rock oriented, with a slightly (and unconvincingly) heavier beat in parts. The sax and flute parts suggest interesting possibilities, which remain unexploited. — C.W.

POWDER BLUES BAND
★ ★ ★ **Uncut / Lib. (NA)**
★ ★ ★ **Thirsty Ears / Lib. (NA)**
Young, adept and powerful latter-day blues band. This ain't the real delta stuff by a long shot, but it's certainly enjoyable white-boy blues. — R.P.

ROGER POWELL
★ **Air Pocket / Bears. (1980)**
Why is it that the love of a boy for his automobile, his dog, even his guitar seems so warm and pleasant, while the love of a boy for his synthesizer seems so heartless and calculating? Probably because a lot less pretentious twaddle results from the former infatuations. — D.M.

ANDY PRATT
★ ★ **Andy Pratt / Col. (1973)**
★ ★ ★ **Resolution / Nemp. (1976) ¶**
★ ★ **Shiver in the Night / Nemp. (1977) ¶**
Andy Pratt is a promising prodigy in the pop school headmastered by the Beatles and the Beach Boys; he plays pop rock that is defined by its simple but catchy melodies, thick harmonies and finely glossed production. The Columbia album boasted some of Pratt's melodic talents—"Avenging Annie," unquestionably the album's highlight, ebbs and flows with the assurance of only the best pop—but his frail voice and occasionally cloying lyrics were emphasized by the tentative production. Done with producer Arif Mardin, though, *Resolution* is everything a pop album should be—simultaneously pretty and melodically compelling, sincere and yet self-aware, and clearly an effort of both pleasurable and professional expertise. *Shiver* is too baroque. Neither Mardin nor Pratt can really rock out, and they shouldn't have tried. — J.B.M.

PREACHER JACK
★ ★ **Rock 'n' Roll Preacher / Round. (1980)**
Semipro Boston area boogie-woogie pianist and blues shouter is backed here by George Thorogood's Destroyers and Sleepy LaBeef.
— J.S.

ELVIS PRESLEY/Early Years
★ ★ ★ ★ ★ **Elvis Presley / RCA (1956)**
★ ★ ★ ★ ★ **Elvis / RCA (1956)**
★ ★ ★ ★ **Lovin' You / RCA (1957)**
★ ★ ★ ★ **King Creole / RCA (1958)**
★ ★ ★ ★ ★ **For LP Fans Only / RCA (1959)**
★ ★ ★ ★ ★ **A Date with Elvis / RCA (1959)**
★ ★ ★ ★ ★ **The Sun Sessions / RCA (1976)**
Elvis Presley is by far the most important single figure in the history of rock & roll, and possibly the most important in American popular music, a giant of the modern era. We lean perilously close to toppling into blathering fandom, and thus dispense with historical detail, at least for this stage of his career. Presumably, every reader knows the outline of his initial success from "That's All Right" through "Heartbreak Hotel" and the great early RCA and Sun singles that accompanied them.

Suffice it to say that these records, more than any others, contain the seeds of everything rock & roll was, has been and most likely what it may foreseeably become. The most important of them by far are *The Sun Sessions,* the ten songs released by Sam Phillips' Memphis label before the Presley contract was sold to RCA, and *Elvis* and *Elvis*

Presley, the first two RCA LPs. *A Date* and *For LP Fans* contain a mixture of Sun and early RCA material; they were released during his incarceration in the armed forces. *King Creole* and *Loving You* are the soundtracks to his early movies. Each has some brilliant moments, thanks to the excellence of Jerry Leiber and Mike Stoller's songs, but they are nonetheless soundtrack LPs, with hints of the limitations discussed more thoroughly below.

ELVIS PRESLEY/The Soundtracks
★ ★ ★ **G.I. Blues / RCA (1960)**
★ ★ ★ **Blue Hawaii / RCA (1961)**
★ ★ ★ ★ **Girls! Girls! Girls! / RCA (1962)**
★ ★ **It Happened at the World's Fair / RCA (1963)**
★ ★ **Fun in Acapulco / RCA (1963)**
★ ★ **Kissin' Cousins / RCA (1963)**
★ ★ **Roustabout / RCA (1964)**
★ ★ **Girl Happy / RCA (1965)**
★ ★ **Harum Scarum / RCA (1965)**
★ ★ **Frankie and Johnny / RCA (1966)**
★ ★ **Paradise, Hawaiian Style / RCA (1966)**
★ ★ ★ ★ **Spinout / RCA (1966)**
★ ★ **Double Trouble / RCA (1967)**
★ ★ **Clambake / RCA (1967)**
★ ★ ★ **Speedway / RCA (1968)**
★ ★ ★ **Elvis Sings "Flaming Star" and Other Hits from His Movies / Camd. (1969)**
★ ★ ★ **Elvis Sings Hits from His Movies / Camd. (1972)**
★ ★ ★ **Double Dynamite / Camd. (1975)**
Elvis made nearly forty movies, not counting concert films and TV shows; almost all of them were completely dismal, and the LPs named after them, despite the occasional inclusions of studio "bonus" tracks, aren't much better. However, and this is crucial, there are exceptions: *G.I. Blues* has Presley fresh from the Army, before he got worn down by mediocre scripts and banal songs; *Girls! Girls! Girls!* has "Return to Sender," a great single; *Spinout* has some tough blues and a fine interpretation of a Dylan song, "Tomorrow Is a Long Time." Most of the rest of these are incompetent on all levels; Presley isn't trying, probably the wisest course in the face of material like "No Room to Rumba in a Sports Car" and "Rock-a-Hula Baby." When he does try, though, which is mostly when he's given something to try *with,* he's still one of the greats.

ELVIS PRESLEY/Post-Army Studio Albums: The Sixties
★ ★ ★ ★ **Elvis Is Back / RCA (1960)**

★ ★ ★ **Somethin' for Everybody** / RCA (1961)

★ ★ ★ **Pot Luck** / RCA (1962)

★ ★ ★ **Elvis for Everyone** / RCA (1965)

★ ★ ★ **Almost in Love** / Camd. (1970)

★ ★ ★ **I Got Lucky** / Camd. (1971)

★ ★ ★ ★ **Elvis Sings the Wonderful World of Christmas** / RCA (1976)

It's hard to admit it, but Presley did manage to sandwich a few indications of his vast natural talent on almost all of the studio albums released during the doldrums of the Sixties. This is most apparent on *Elvis Is Back,* recorded immediately following his release from the Army, when something (his future) was at stake. Although the power of his first recordings is diluted, it's still a fine record. Unlikely as it may seem, so is the Christmas LP, which contains a couple of strong blues and some convincing renditions of traditional songs. The rest is average, with an occasional surprise; worth looking into for the obsessed.

ELVIS PRESLEY/Gospel and Inspirational Albums

★ ★ ★ ★ ★ **His Hand in Mine** / RCA (1961)

★ ★ ★ ★ ★ **How Great Thou Art** / RCA (1967)

★ ★ ★ ★ **You'll Never Walk Alone** / Camd. (1971)

★ ★ ★ ★ ★ **He Touched Me** / RCA (1972)

★ ★ ★ **He Walks Beside Me** / RCA (1978)

Those who doubt that Presley was an intensely religious man have not heard these albums, almost all of which are among the most heartfelt he recorded. Except for the Camden, which lends toward secular inspirational songs, all are white gospel music and Presley's singing is nothing less than sublime; *How Great* even garnered a hit single, "Crying in the Chapel." *He Walks Beside Me* is a reissue of assorted gospel material with a couple of poor live songs added. It's noteworthy as one of RCA's first posthumous Presley releases but is otherwise dismissible.

ELVIS PRESLEY/The Great Comeback

★ ★ ★ ★ ★ **Elvis** / RCA (1968)

★ ★ ★ ★ ★ **From Elvis in Memphis** / RCA (1969)

★ ★ ★ ★ **From Memphis to Vegas** / RCA (1969)

★ ★ ★ ★ **Elvis Back in Memphis** / RCA (1970)

In 1968, Elvis withdrew from Hollywood, although he'd still make a couple more films there, to recenter his activities around live performances. This was first marked by a return to Memphis for recording sessions, and the initial album of the return, *From Elvis in Memphis,* is a masterpiece in which Presley immediately catches up with pop music trends that had seemed to pass him by during the movie years. He sings country songs, soul songs and rockers with real conviction, a stunning achievement. His Christmas 1968 TV special was even more remarkable, the first time in ten years Presley fans had been able to see him outside of a movie theater. He rose to the occasion magnificently, and rather than the banal show-business extravaganza that would have been so typical of his recent work, he came through with a set of hard-rocking blues and rock, represented on the show's soundtrack *(Elvis).* The other two albums attempt to continue such successes, with spottier results. The two-record *From Memphis to Vegas,* one disc of which was recorded live from his initial main-room casino shows, gave a hint of the uneven quality of what was to follow. Still, Presley had reestablished himself as the king of rock & roll, and he quickly became a major draw on both the concert circuit and in Vegas.

ELVIS PRESLEY/Live Albums

★ ★ ★ ★ **On Stage—February 1970** / RCA (1970)

★ ★ ★ **Elvis in Person** / RCA (1970)

★ ★ ★ ★ ★ **That's the Way It Is** / RCA (1970)

★ ★ ★ **As Recorded at Madison Square Garden** / RCA (1972)

★ ★ ★ **Elvis Aloha from Hawaii (Via Satellite)** / RCA (1973)

★ ★ ★ **Elvis Recorded Live on Stage at Memphis** / RCA (1974)

■ **Elvis Having Fun on Stage** / RCA (1974) ¶

★ ★ ★ **Elvis in Concert** / RCA (1977)

Live concerts gave Presley an ideal method to make equally speedy and shoddy recordings, a perfect substitute for soundtrack albums. Although only eight are represented here, there are far more than any other rock performer has ever released, and RCA probably has a few more shows in the can. Most of them are spotty, based on pseudo-events: a satellite broadcast to fifty countries *(Aloha),* his first-ever concert in New York *(Madison Square),* another return to *Memphis.* The best is *That's the Way It Is,* which is both a concert recording and a soundtrack, being the music from his final feature, a documentary of one of his shows, with a tremendous closing number, "Bridge over Troubled Water," the best version ever done of that war-horse. Being earlier than the others, *On Stage—February 1970* also isn't bad. The worst by far is *Having Fun on Stage,* two sides of tape-recorded byplay— bad jokes and about 10,000 requests for a glass of water.

ELVIS PRESLEY/Studio Albums of the Seventies

★ ★ ★ ★ I'm 10,000 Years Old / RCA (1971)
★ ★ ★ Love Letters from Elvis / RCA (1971)
★ ★ ★ Elvis Now / RCA (1972)
★ ★ Elvis Raised on Rock/For Ol' Times Sake / RCA (1973)
★ ★ ★ Elvis Good Times / RCA (1974)
★ ★ ★ ★ Promised Land / RCA (1975)
★ ★ ★ ★ Elvis Today / RCA (1975)
★ ★ ★ From Elvis Presley Boulevard, Memphis, Tennessee / RCA (1976)
★ ★ ★ Welcome to My World / RCA (1977)
★ ★ ★ Moody Blue / RCA (1977)

Although the live albums replaced the soundtracks as Presley's Seventies method of shrugging off his ability, his studio albums were of better quality than the ones he made in the previous era. Partly this was a matter of the variety of superior material available to him—a song like Billy Swan's "I Can Help" is tailor-made for the rollicking interpretation Elvis gives it on *Today,* which is sort of an updated rockabilly album. But Presley also did better with country sources *(10,000)* and the usual thrown-together assortments. Even something as ostensibly wrongheaded as *From Elvis Presley Boulevard* contains a magnificent performance of Timi Yuro's early-Sixties hit, "Hurt." Although rarely discussed, each of the albums in this group has more than a little to recommend it, and very few things to be said against it. Presley doesn't sound inspired very often, but he does sound committed, which is generally enough.

ELVIS PRESLEY/Compilations

★ ★ ★ ★ ★ Elvis' Golden Records, Vol. 1 / RCA (1958)
★ ★ ★ ★ ★ Elvis' Golden Records, Vol. 2 / RCA (1960)
★ ★ ★ ★ ★ Elvis' Golden Records, Vol. 3 / RCA (1963)
★ ★ ★ ★ ★ Elvis' Golden Records, Vol. 4 / RCA (1968)
★ ★ ★ ★ ★ World Wide Fifty Gold Award Hits, Vol. 1 / RCA (1970)
★ ★ ★ ★ World Wide Fifty Gold Award Hits, Vol. 2 / RCA (1971)
★ ★ ★ ★ ★ C'mon Everybody / Camd. (1971)
★ ★ Burning Love / Camd. (1972)
★ ★ Elvis Separate Ways / Camd. (1973)
★ ★ ★ ★ Elvis: A Legendary Performer, Vol. 1 / RCA (1974)
★ ★ Let's Be Friends / Camd. (1975)
★ ★ ★ Pure Gold / RCA (1975)
★ ★ ★ ★ Elvis: A Legendary Performer, Vol. 2 / RCA (1976)

Presley's songs have been frequently reassembled into a variety of packages, most of them tossed together without much consideration or respect. The leading offenders are the Camden packages, a hit or two (at most) surrounding pure trash; *Burning Love,* for instance, cashes in on Presley's last big pop hit (1972) by putting it on an album with lame songs from the movies. But at least the Camden packages have budget prices. *Pure Gold* tosses together some good hits, some bad, without annotation or reason; there's some decent music here, but the range is neither focused enough to be insightful nor broad enough to give a complete outline of Presley's skills.

The four-volume *Golden Records* series is far better. It isn't annotated either, but the covers are great—Volume 2, subtitled *Fifty Million Elvis Fans Can't Be Wrong,* features the King in his gold lamé suit, allegedly worth $10,000—and together the four discs provide all the hits, major and minor, through the mid-Sixties. The *World Wide Fifty Gold Award Hits* packages, which are four discs each, take the Presley story (or its highlights) through 1969, the final side of the great Volume 1 containing "In the Ghetto," "Kentucky Rain," "Suspicious Minds" and the other brilliant sides Presley made in his early return to Memphis recording studios. Volume 2 is weaker, since it is mostly B sides, but does contain the songs from his three early EPs, all of them worth having. But neither of these are annotated either; perhaps RCA feels commentary would be superfluous, gilding an obvious lily.

The real gems of this genre, however, are the two *Legendary Performer* albums, which are not only annotated (not particularly well) but also include things like photographs of the early days, pictures of Presley memorabilia, RCA contractual documents and the like. They also contain enough variety to give a true picture of Presley's career— famous mediocrities like "Blue Hawaii," alongside outtakes from the fabled Sun sessions.

ELVIS PRESLEY/Posthumous Releases

★ ★ ★ A Canadian Tribute / RCA (1977)

★ **Elvis on Stage / RCA (1977)**
★ **Sings for Children (And Grownups Too) /
RCA (1978)**
★ **Our Memories of Elvis / RCA
(1979)**
★ **Our Memories of Elvis, Vol. 2 / RCA
(1979)**
■ **Elvis Aron Presley / RCA (1980)**
★ **Guitar Man / RCA (1980)**
★ ★ ★ **This Is Elvis / RCA (1981)**
★ ★ **Elvis Presley's Greatest Hits, Vol. 1 /
RCA (1981)**
■ **I was the One / RCA (1983)**
Elvis's first posthumous release was actually
Elvis in Concert, the soundtrack to his
CBS-TV documentary special, shot during
the tour just preceding his death. But RCA
rammed that record out so quickly that it
was virtually simultaneous with his demise—
and anyway, he had at least his usual say
(however minimal) in its production.

RCA's next release revealed its strategy,
or complete lack of one. *Elvis Sings for Children (And Grownups Too)* amounts to a gesture of contempt, the complete trivialization
of a man who has just been heralded, in
obituaries and memorials around the world,
as a great American artist. The situation
seemed a setup for the kind of remakes RCA
has specialized in doing to Jim Reeves—
adding strings and voice arrangements that
"contemporize" music whose importance is
largely historical. At least this time the musical butchery was novel. Rather than adding
musicians, producer Felton Jarvis, with the
overt approval of Colonel Tom Parker and
Vernon Presley, subtracted them. Theoretically, these versions of Elvis with minimal
accompaniment highlighted his voice and allowed us to hear him in his "natural" state.
But Elvis was always a singer who was intimately involved with his musicians—even on
his worst material, he is leading the band,
not simply singing around it. Volumes 1 and
2 of *Our Memories of Elvis* and *Guitar Man*
are not entirely worthless, but only because
Elvis did have such a remarkable voice.
They are for completists only.

Elvis Aron Presley is an eight-record set
that supposedly contained important treasures from the RCA vaults. Needless to say,
it is dross, with almost nothing to recommend it, save perhaps the alternate take of
"Follow That Dream," an important hit not
found on any other U.S. LP.

This Is Elvis is the soundtrack to Malcolm
Leo and Andrew Solt's theatrical docudrama
about the King, and it does indeed contain
some treasures, including a revealing Fifties
interview (with a TV personality called Hy

Gardner), three live tracks from the Dorsey
Brothers TV appearances and one each from
the Milton Berle show and *The Ed Sullivan
Show.* The record also offers some of Pres-
ley's best, least-known songs—"I Got a
Thing about You, Baby," "Viva Las Vegas,"
"(Marie's the Name) His Latest Flame,"
"Merry Christmas, Baby"—in an intelligent
context.

But by Christmas of 1981, RCA was back
to its old tricks—this despite multi-million-
dollar lawsuits creeping up in Memphis.
Elvis Presley's Greatest Hits, Volume 1 was
anything but—yet another pointless rehash
of predictable old hits and pointless, perfunctory live material. Only a smoldering run-
through of "Steamroller Blues," also done
live, saves it from being utter rubbish. *I Was
the One* is worse: Presley classics "updated"
with new backing tracks, a genuine abomination. The question of when America's greatest musical figure will be presented with the
respect and consideration his artistry deserves remains unanswered. — D.M.

BILLY PRESTON
★ ★ ★ **The Wildest Organ in Town / Cap.
(1966)** ¶
★ ★ **I Wrote a Simple Song / A&M
(1972)** ¶
★ ★ **Music In My Life / A&M (1972)** ¶
★ ★ **Everybody Likes Some Kind of Music /
A&M (1973)** ¶
★ ★ ★ **Original Billy Preston—Soul'd Out /
GNP (1973)**
★ ★ **Kids and Me / A&M (1974)** ¶
★ ★ ★ **The Genius of Billy Preston / Sp.
(1975)**
★ ★ **It's My Pleasure / A&M (1975)** ¶
★ ★ **Billy / A&M (1976)** ¶
★ ★ **A Whole New Thing / A&M (1977)** ¶
★ **Late at Night / Mo. (1979)**
★ **Billy Preston and Syreeta / Mo. (NA)**
Billy Preston was a gospel-music prodi-
gy—he played the young W. C. Handy in
the film *St. Louis Blues*—and in his teens he
toured with Little Richard and Sam Cooke;
he recorded his first album for the latter's
Sar Records in 1964, then won a regular
spot on ABC-TV's *Shindig.* Ray Charles
then became his patron, and he made an
album with Charles' aid, which resulted in
the British hit single, "Billy's Bag." Later in
the Sixties, George Harrison took Preston
under his wing (an odd example of Krishna/
Christian ecumenicalism), and Preston par-
ticipated in the Beatles' *Get Back* and *Let It
Be* sessions. For Apple, he made his first
record to receive much white American
attention, "That's the Way God Planned

It," a pleasant gospel-rock attempt.

But it was after leaving Apple for A&M that Preston became a star. His initial A&M LP, *Simple Song,* earned him a No. 1 hit with "Outa Space," and his next two records *(Music Is My Life, Everybody Likes Some)* also produced hits, "Will It Go Round in Circles" and "Space Race." The records weren't much—tepid funk riffs with bellowed vocals and vaguely spiritual lyrics—but they kept him chic enough to earn a bid to appear as the Rolling Stones' keyboardist on the band's 1975 American tour. But his music since then has merely reworked the pallid formula established on the earlier records. Perhaps his most interesting work is the pre-Apple material available on the Springboard and GNP sets. — D.M.

THE PRETENDERS
★ ★ ★ ★ ★ **The Pretenders / Sire (1979)**
★ ★ ★ **The Pretenders II / Sire (1981)**
Chrissie Hynde, the lead singer and songwriter for the Pretenders, is the only woman to make distinctions of sex nonexistent in rock & roll. From her sheer authenticity as a three-dimensional woman whose sexuality is completely in sync with a superb rock sensibility, she has single-handedly reduced all other contemporary women in rock to any one of the number of clichés that abound about them.

The Pretenders is one of the most brilliant debut records in rock. From the Motown pleading of "Brass in Pocket" to the unrestrained joyousness of "Mystery Achievement" to the lovely "Stop Your Sobbing," the album holds endless delights. All the ambivalences of love, lust and hate are on display. There is no woman who loves rock who can't be thrilled by "Precious," when Chrissie wonders about getting pregnant against a backdrop of killer rock & roll—it just hasn't happened before. The rest of the Pretenders are neither subservient to Hynde nor condescending to her; the Pretenders are a group, and unlike certain other bands that make that claim, there is never any doubt about it.

Given that, *The Pretenders II* is a disappointment. The obvious pressure that Hynde was under to produce an achievement equal to the debut finds her reduced to occasional self-parody, especially on such embarrassing songs as "Pack It Up" and "The Adultress," where the subtle toughness on the first album becomes almost adolescent posturing. But the record has its moments; "Talk of the Town," "I Go to Sleep" and "English Rose" are as lovely and effective as anything on

The Pretenders. Given some freedom from intense public scrutiny, Chrissie Hynde is sure to make a contribution to rock & roll that will extend long through the Eighties. As it is, she's done more than her share.
— D.G.

THE PRETTY THINGS
★ ★ ★ **Silk Torpedo / Swan (1975)** ¶
★ ★ ★ **Real Pretty / Rare (1976)**
★ **Cross Talk / War. (1980)**
The Pretty Things were originally a spinoff from the Rolling Stones when bassist Dick Taylor (who'd been an original Stone) and guitarist Phil May formed the band in 1963. Their early sides, unavailable here but represented on the import collection *Attention! The Pretty Things!* (Fontana Special 6438 059, German), are raw-edged white R&B, drawing heavily on Bo Diddley, Chuck Berry and similar black urban R&B shouters. Today that style is dated but enormously attractive for its visceral energy and the streak of wildness that made the Prettys seem ribald even as the Stones edged ever nearer to the socially acceptable.

The group later expanded its base into psychedelia for a rock opera, *S.F. Sorrow,* released a year before *Tommy* but without much apparent influence on it. Taylor left shortly thereafter, and while some of the group's material since is well regarded in Anglophile rock circles, it's really only competent and conventional hard rock. One suspects the recordings for Led Zeppelin's Swan Song label were made more out of Jimmy Page's sense of historical obligation than because the band rates such attention these days.

Cross Talk is simply inexplicable, unless some corporate type out there in Burbank decided that it was hip and potentially profitable to release anything with a Sixties background. In the current environment, we can only be thankful that he misjudged our gullibility. — D.M.

DORY PREVIN
★ ★ **Mythical Kings and Iguanas / Media (1972)** ¶
★ ★ ★ **Mary C. Brown and the Hollywood Sign / U.A. (1972)** ¶
★ ★ **Dory Previn Live at Carnegie Hall / U.A. (1973)**
★ ★ **On My Way to Where / Media (1973)** ¶
★ ★ ★ **Dory Previn / U.A. (1974)** ¶
★ ★ **We're Children of Coincidence and Harpo Marx / War. (1976)** ¶
A talented if somewhat overbearing and ver-

bose songwriter with a horrible voice, Dory Previn's cult status never evolved into anything larger scale. She has more to offer devotees of Tin Pan Alley and soap operas than rock & roll fans. — J.S.

ALAN PRICE

★ ★ ★ This Price Is Right / Par. (1968) ¶
★ ★ ★ ★ O Lucky Man / War. (1973) ¶
★ ★ ★ Alan Price / Jet (1977) ¶
★ Lucky Day / Jet (1979)
★ Rising Sun / Jet (1980)

Former organist for Animals was one of the first to record Randy Newman *(This Price)*. His song cycle for *O Lucky Man* soundtrack uses rock as nastily witty Greek chorus commentary on the film's scenario. But its worthy Warner followup, *Between Today and Yesterday,* is a cutout. Price's later albums were never released in the U.S. and are available only via import, except for the mediocre sets on Jet. — S.H.

LLOYD PRICE

★ ★ ★ ★ Sixteen Greatest Hits / ABC (1972) ¶
★ ★ ★ Sixteen Greatest Hits / Trip (NA) ¶
★ ★ ★ ★ The ABC Collection / ABC (NA) ¶
★ ★ ★ ★ ★ Original Hits / Sonet (NA), imp.

His two big rock-era hits, "Personality" and "Stagger Lee," were characteristic of the sophisticated R&B Price was doing with rhythm & blues throughout the Fifties. (The best hit was probably "Lawdy Miss Clawdy" for Specialty in 1952, which is on the Sonet import.) Either of the ABC albums will fill you in on his later, slicker singing; Price was more than occasionally terrific at Jackie Wilson–era soul music. The Trip is unnecessary unless the ABCs are unavailable. The Sonet is vintage material and genuinely great. — D.M.

RAY PRICE

★ ★ ★ More Ray Price's Greatest Hits / Col. (1967)
★ ★ Danny Boy / Col. (1967)
★ ★ Christmas Album / Col. (1969)
★ ★ ★ ★ The World of Ray Price / Col. (1970) ¶
★ ★ ★ ★ Ray Price's Greatest Hits / Col. (1971)
★ ★ Welcome to My World / Col. (1971) ¶
★ ★ ★ ★ Ray Price's Greatest Hits / Col. (1971)
★ ★ ★ She's Got to Be a Saint / Col. (1973)
★ ★ You're the Best Thing That Ever Happened to Me / Col. (1974)
★ ★ ★ If You Ever Change Your Mind / Col. (1975) ¶

★ ★ Say I Do / Dot (1975) ¶
★ ★ ★ ★ The Best of Ray Price / Col. (1976)
★ ★ Rainbows and Tears / Dot (1976) ¶
★ ★ ★ Hank 'n' Me / Dot (1976) ¶
★ ★ ★ Reunited / Dot (1977)
★ ★ Like Old Times Again / ABC (NA)
★ ★ ★ Help Me / Col. (NA) ¶
★ ★ Ray Price / Col. (NA)
★ ★ San Antonio Rose / Col. (NA)
★ ★ Town and Country / Dimen. (NA)

Ray Price was known as the Cherokee Cowboy, not because he was part American Indian, but because he came from Cherokee County in East Texas, the same territory that produced Jim Reeves, whose songs his early honky-tonk weepers sometimes resemble. Price began recording in the late Forties, but it wasn't until he signed on with Columbia and with the Grand Ole Opry, in 1952, that he won a wide audience. In 1956, "Crazy Arms" became his first No. 1 national hit; it remains a country standard, as do "Same Old Me" and "Heartaches by the Number," among his grab bag of other hits in the Fifties. "Make the World Go Away" was his best Sixties recording, but while Price was continually commercially successful in that decade, he was one of the first honky-tonkers to resort to using strings and other pop arrangements on his records, with results that were at first energizing and later bathetic. The later sessions for ABC are exercises in mild competence. — D.M.

SAM PRICE AND THE "ROCK" BAND WITH KING CURTIS AND MICKEY BAKER

★ ★ ★ ★ Rib Joint / Savoy (1979)

Price was a journeyman pianist and vocalist blessed on these twenty-five sides with one of the hottest bands in rock history. Saxman Curtis and guitarist Baker were the definitive New York session stalwarts of the Fifties, when these tracks were cut (from 1956 to 1959). Their playing, alongside that of Price, drummers Panama Francis and Bobby Donaldson, bassists Leonard Gaskin, Jimmy Lewis and Al Lucas and additional guitarists Kenny Burrell and Al Casey, is hot, propulsive, like the missing link between the Timpani Five and Chuck Berry. — D.M.

CHARLEY PRIDE

★ ★ ★ ★ Country Charley Pride / RCA (1966)
★ ★ ★ Pride of Country Music / RCA (1967)
★ ★ The Country Way / RCA (1967)

★ ★ ★ **Make Mine Country** / RCA
(1968)
★ ★ **Songs of Pride . . . Charley, That Is** /
RCA (1968)
★ ★ ★ **Charley Pride in Person** / RCA
(1969)
★ ★ **The Sensational Charley Pride** / RCA
(1969)
★ ★ ★ **The Best of Charley Pride** / RCA
(1969)
★ ★ **Just Plain Charley** / RCA (1970)
★ ★ ★ **Charley Pride's Tenth Album** / RCA
(1970)
★ ★ ★ **Christmas in My Home Town** / RCA
(1970)
★ ★ ★ **From Me to You** / RCA (1971)
★ ★ ★ **Did You Think to Pray** / RCA
(1971)
★ ★ ★ **I'm Just Me** / RCA (1971)
★ ★ **Sings Heart Songs** / RCA (1971)
★ ★ ★ **Best of Charley Pride, Vol. 2** / RCA
(1972)
★ ★ **A Sunshiny Day with Charley Pride** /
RCA (1972)
★ ★ **The Incomparable Charley Pride** / RCA
(1972)
★ ★ **Songs of Love by Charley Pride** / RCA
(1973)
★ ★ **Sweet Country** / RCA (1973)
★ ★ **Amazing Love** / RCA (1973)
★ ★ **Country Feelin'** / RCA (1974)
★ **Pride of America** / RCA (1974)
★ ★ **Charley Pride—In Person** / RCA
(1975)
★ ★ **Charley** / RCA (1975)
★ ★ **The Happiness of Having You** / RCA
(1975)
★ ★ **Sunday Morning with Charley Pride** /
RCA (1976)
★ ★ **The Best of Charley Pride, Vol. 3** /
RCA (1976)
★ ★ **She's Just an Old Love Turned
Memory** / RCA (1977)
★ ★ **Someone Loves You, Honey** / RCA
(1978)
★ ★ **Burgers and Fries/When I Stop Leaving
(I'll Be Gone)** / RCA (1978)
★ ★ **You're My Jamaica** / RCA
(1979)
★ ★ ★ **There's a Little Bit of Hank in Me** /
RCA (1980)
Pride was the first black singer to break the
color line in the country music industry,
where racism is a matter of quiet but
determined policy. What's even more
impressive is that he did it at the height
of the civil rights era, when country
music and the Ku Klux Klan were all too
often synonymous (on the part of the
audience more than the performers for

the most part, but certainly not in all cases).
Pride became popular through the use of a
particularly ironic inversion—at a time when
white rock & rollers were building careers
on an ability to sound black, Pride made it
because he was a black who could sing white
so perfectly most rednecks never knew the
difference. The formula worked well because
he chose to do songs written especially for
him, rather than his own material, and he
could sing Hank Williams tunes as well as
anyone.

In order to be accepted by the country establishment Pride had to be exceptionally
good. He was: his deep, mellow voice was
an aural trademark absolutely made for
country music. But there was very little
room for expansion in the limited format set
for him, and as he continued to crank out
LP after LP, the voice became a familiar,
and banal, country music cliché. Pride's
later albums sound like the work of a well-
meaning and talented, but essentially directionless, industry hack, which is unfortunately what he's become. But the voice continues to sound great, and your chances of
finding a good love song on any Charley
Pride album are reasonably good.   — J.S.

PRINCE
★ ★ **For You** / War. (1978)
★ ★ ★ **Prince** / War. (1979)
★ ★ ★ ★ **Dirty Mind** / War. (1980)
★ ★ ★ ★ **Controversy** / War. (1981)
★ ★ ★ ★ ★ **1999** / War. (1982)
Minneapolis-based pop wunderkind (writer/
singer/keyboardist/guitarist) launched a successful career based on his own flaming androgyny and sexual licentiousness. While his
first album (released when he was only nineteen) was relatively unexplicit and suggested
Todd Rundgren imitating Smokey Robinson,
the second, with its racy dance-pop hit, "I
Wanna Be Your Lover," and its Jimi Hendrix guitar licks, revealed Prince to be a
funk-pop renegade. On *Dirty Mind,* Prince
exalted brother-sister incest, oral sex and les-
bianism, among other carnal delights. *Controversy* moved beyond sex to religion and
politics. Though the rhetoric was naive, the
music was hotter than ever—a heavily synthesized pop-funk lava through which
Prince's gasps and whines cut a sharp swath.
1999, a two-disc set, is a complete and convincing portrait of Prince as one of the great
contemporary naturals. On the title track
and "Little Red Corvette" especially,
he's brilliant, and his genius extends
through pop, rock, funk and sensual
soul.   — S.H.

PRINCE BUSTER

★ ★ ★ ★ ★ **Fab Greatest Hits / Melo. (1967)**

★ ★ ★ **Oldies but Goodies, Vol. 1 / Prince B. (1980)**

One of the original rappers when he ran a sound system in Jamaica during the early Sixties, Prince Buster's manic ska excursions directly inspired such ska revivalists as the Specials and Madness (whose name refer to a Buster tune). *Fab Greatest Hits* collects all the essential stuff (including a comically sexist diatribe, "The Ten Commandments," a minor hit in Texas!), while *Oldies* is a rawer sampling of his early Jamaican hits. Avoid most other Melodisc offerings. — R.F.G.

PRINCE FAR-I

★ ★ ★ **Under Heavy Manners / J. Gibbs (1978)**

★ ★ **Long Life / V.F.L. (1978)**

★ ★ ★ ★ **Message from the King / Virgin (1978)**

★ ★ ★ ★ **Cry Tuff Dub Encounter / Daddy Kool (1978)**

★ ★ ★ ★ **Free from Sin / Troj. (1979)**

★ ★ ★ ★ **Jamaican Heroes / Troj. (1981)**

★ ★ ★ **Rockers ina Suitcase / PRE (1981)**

One of the strangest reggae artists, Prince Far-I on record often sounds like a bullfrog trapped in an echo chamber located adjacent to a battlefield. In stentorian tones, he chants messages of inspiration and faith (he once recorded an entire LP of Bible verses) while the bass and drums thunder. What makes his records worthwhile rather than mere curiosities? The quality of the musicianship and the power of the rhythms. — R.F.G.

PRINCE JAZZBO

★ ★ ★ **Ital Corner / Clock. (1979)**

One of the earlier rapping DJs on the reggae scene, Prince Jazzbo's early efforts were often simple exercises in braggadocio. *Ital Corner,* his triumph, is aided in no small measure by the production genius of Lee Perry and the instrumental wizardry of the Upsetters. — R.F.G.

JOHN PRINE

★ ★ ★ **John Prine / Atl. (1972)**

★ ★ ★ **Diamonds in the Rough / Atl. (1972)**

★ ★ ★ ★ **Sweet Revenge / Atl. (1973)**

★ ★ ★ **Common Sense / Atl. (1975)**

★ ★ **Prime Prine / Atl. (1976)**

★ ★ ★ ★ **Bruised Orange / Asy. (1978)**

★ ★ ★ **Pink Cadillac / Asy. (1979)**

★ ★ ★ **Storm Windows / Asy. (1980)**

After over six albums of original songs, John Prine has evolved from a sentimental but witty folkie to a nihilistic but thoughtful soft rocker. Prine comes from working-class Chicago, and he's not only worked for the post office but served in the Army; all of that experience is reflected in his songs. His first album was his most popular, containing both "Sam Stone" and "Hello in There," which remain his best-known songs. The abuse of Vietnam vets and the neglect of old people, respectively, were just the sort of subjects a socially conscious folk-based singer/songwriter should have strummed about in the early Seventies, but because of Prine's corrosive cynicism and withering imagery, the songs soon seemed too pat. The far better things about the album were its shiveringly accurate feeling for white working-class life, as depicted in "Far from Me" and "Six O'Clock News," and an inclination toward lean, gutbucket country music that no young performer until Gary Stewart could equal.

The soupy melodrama of "Hello in There" increased on *Diamonds in the Rough,* which nonetheless included "Yes I Guess They Oughta Name a Drink after You," a glorious Hank Williams throwback.

Prine's disappointment at not becoming a star was palpable. On the cover of *Sweet Revenge,* he sprawled unshaven in the front seat of a convertible, pointy-toed cowboy boots thrust out and a hungover fuck-you expression beneath his shades. The music here is harder with country melodies, more smoothly complex lyrically, and more bitter and unforgiving in content. The softhearted songs, "Grandpa Was a Carpenter" and "Christmas in Prison," were redeemed by a modicum of sentimentality and a maximum of terse description.

Common Sense is Prine's greatest commercial failure but it is also his most daring and intermittently triumphant album. To those who loved "Sam Stone," *Common Sense* made no sense—Prine's sidewalk yowl and rock rhythms were unpalatable to old fans, and no new rock fans paid attention. In fact Prine was thrashing around for a new stance, a deceptively cheerful equivalent to Neil Young's *Tonight's the Night. Common Sense* concludes with a driving, hoarse version of Chuck Berry's "You Never Can Tell." *Prime Prine,* the best of album released during the two-year silence that followed, clarified nothing, being predictably chosen and folkie-minded.

Bruised Orange, released in mid-1978, was quiet, almost somber, a grouping of eccentric vignettes of urban working life, love songs and one hilarious blast at record-business promotional ploys, "Sabu Visits the Twin

Cities Alone." The best of the love songs, "If You Don't Want My Love," was written with Phil Spector, but Prine's best work was done on his own, abetted by Steve Goodman's perfect production touch. "Fish and Whistle," "That's the Way That the World Goes 'Round" and "Crooked Piece of Time" mask the toughness of their locales and stories with whimsical, gentle singing. *Bruised Orange* is an oddity, almost completely ignored by the public and radio alike, but it is nearly John Prine's masterpiece, a complete statement of one of the most interesting visions the Seventies has produced. — K.T./ D.M.

MADDY PRIOR
★ ★ **Woman in the Wings / Tak. (1978)**
★ ★ **Changing Winds / Tak. (1978)** ¶
Original folk music from Steeleye Span's once and former chanteuse. Over-earnest, over-orchestrated, but beautifully sung.
— B.C.

MADDY PRIOR AND JUNE TABOR
★ ★ ★ **Silly Sisters / Chrys. (1976)**
Terrific one-shot in which Steeleye Span's Prior teams up with the similarly inclined Tabor for a set of medieval to modern English folk music, but with far more bounce and joy than any of the Steeleye records. Much ironic commentary on male-female relationships, marital and otherwise. Splendid Sunday morning music for apostates.
— D.M.

PRISM
★ **Prism / Ario. (1977)**
★ **See Forever Eyes / Ario. (1978)**
★ **Armageddon / Cap. (1979)**
★ **Young and Restless / Cap. (1980)**
★ **Small Change (1981)**
Portentous progressive rock: a dab of Genesis, a smidgen of Yes. For synthesizer clones only. — D.M.

PRIVATE LINES
★ **Trouble in School / Pass. (NA)**
Flunked art. — D.M.

PROCOL HARUM
★ ★ ★ ★ ★ **A Whiter Shade of Pale / A&M (1967)** ¶
★ ★ ★ ★ **Shine On Brightly / A&M (1968)**
★ ★ ★ ★ ★ **A Salty Dog / A&M (1969)**
★ ★ ★ ★ **Home / A&M (1970)**
★ ★ **Broken Barricades / A&M (1971)**
★ ★ **Live with the Edmonton Symphony Orchestra / A&M (1972)**
★ ★ ★ **Grand Hotel / Chrys. (1973)**
★ ★ ★ ★ **The Best of Procol Harum / A&M (1973)**
★ ★ ★ ★ **Exotic Birds and Fruit / Chrys. (1974)**
★ ★ ★ **Procol's Ninth / Chrys. (1975)**
★ ★ ★ **Something Magic / Chrys. (1977)**
A Whiter Shade of Pale (originally released on Deram as *Procol Harum*) presented an imaginative, realized, and (for 1967) wholly unlikely combination of styles: Gary Brooker's excellent vocals echoed blues wailers like Ray Charles; Robin Trower's thickly distorted guitar recalled Eric Clapton's blues-based work with Cream; Matthew Fisher's cathedral organ borrowed from the seriousness, precision and majesty of classical composers; B. J. Wilson was a nimble and individual drummer; Keith Reid's lyrics owed much to Dylan's surrealistic *Blonde on Blonde* phase. The constant combination of piano (Brooker) and organ was largely unknown in rock at the time. *Shine On Brightly* continued this approach and included a long, shifting, multi-segmented magnum opus, one of rock's first.

Less a one-man show for Brooker (who had been writing almost all the music), *A Salty Dog* took many chances and succeeded brilliantly: grand orchestrations, subtle sound effects, quaint and somewhat rustic instruments, Fisher's gentle vocals, and ruder and more pared-down blues variations.

Fisher then quit and was replaced by Chris Copping (who doubled on bass), an adequate player but one without his predecessor's imagination. *Home* thus lacked the maturity, sweep and variety of earlier Procol, but did press further into harder rocking territory.

Broken Barricades erratically extended the heavier direction, failing twice with ragged, simplistic and poorly sung cuts from Trower. Elsewhere, the group was stale or longwinded, despite the prettiness of the title track, at the finish of which Wilson turns in some of his finest signatures.

Trower then left, and his successors have offered competent but not excellent similarity. The live LP had no new songs, and only smoothed out and drained the old arrangements with tasteful but sterilizing orchestration—too polite an approach for what was finally a rock group, whatever its obvious classical inspirations.

The Best assembed superior tracks from the first six albums, as well as some fine B sides and never-released tracks.

Grand Hotel had Brooker back in control, but except for Wilson, it's a faceless cast, and the record was only a pale reflection of the band's past. But *Exotic Birds and Fruit* nearly matched the best of the Fisher/ Trower days with its energetic paces, gentle melodies, gritty engineering and unabashed confidence. Given inspiring material, Procol showed it could still rise to the occasion.

Procol's Ninth (actually their tenth, including *The Best*) tried new tacks with some success: production from Jerry Leiber and Mike Stoller all but ignored the classical influence yet kept the group's basic sound intact. A horn-enlivened rock & roll song worked, as did an organ simulating bagpipes, but the Beatles' "Eight Days a Week" didn't.

Something Magic offered unconvincing and disjointed dollops of previous stylings; side two was a lengthy, boringly narrated indulgence. — C.W.

PROCTOR AND BERGMAN
★ ★ ★ ★ **TV or Not TV** / Col. (NA)
★ ★ **What This Country Needs** / Col. (NA)
★ ★ ★ **Give Us a Break** / Mer. (NA)
The performing half of the Firesign Theatre melds its characteristic Joycean wit with some hilarious slapstick routines. Their first album *(TV)* is the most successful of all the Firesign Theatre's side projects. — J.S.

THE PRODUCERS
★ ★ **The Producers** / Por. (1981)
Preppie pop rock—the kind of thing that makes you wish you'd devoted your life to baseball after all. — D.M.

PROFESSOR LONGHAIR
★ ★ ★ ★ **New Orleans Piano** / Atco (1953)
★ ★ ★ ★ **Live on the Queen Mary** / Harv. (1975)
★ ★ ★ ★ **Crawfish Fiesta** / Alli. (1980)
Roy Byrd, a.k.a. Professor Longhair, is widely acknowledged as the greatest New Orleans dance-hall pianist in the post–World War II era. His raucous, bawdy, half-chanted vocals over the wildest barrelhouse keyboard pounding you're ever likely to hear has strongly influenced New Orleans pianists, from Fats Domino to Mac Rebennack (a.k.a. Dr. John) and Allen Toussaint. Byrd's influence can be gauged, in fact, by comparing the 1953 version of "Tipitina" on *New Orleans Piano* to Dr. John's early-Seventies tribute on *Gumbo*.

New Orleans Piano collects Longhair's Atlantic sides from 1949 and 1953, including some previously unissued goodies like "Ball the Wall" and "Longhair's Blues Rumba."

Many characteristic sides for various obscure Southern labels are unfortunately unavailable (import pressings turn up from time to time), but this is a more-than-adequate representation of Byrd at the height of his powers. *Queen Mary,* recorded in 1975 at a party for Paul McCartney, shows how little those talents have diminished in twenty years. The material here is more traditional than on the Atco set, but it's still exciting, as is Byrd's relentless performance. *Crawfish,* released posthumously after Longhair's death in 1979, is also recent material. — J.S.

FRANK PROFFITT
★ ★ ★ **Reese, North Carolina** / Folk-Leg. (1962) ¶
★ ★ **Frank Proffitt Sings Folk Songs** / Folk. (1962) ¶
It was Proffitt's version of the traditional ballad "Tom Dooley," made world-famous by the Kingston Trio, that is credited with formally launching the late-Fifties folk revival. Proffitt himself, however, was a wellspring of ballads, first tapped by Frank Warner and later recorded by Sandy Paton, who went to Proffitt's home to make the tapes that resulted in both these albums. A tobacco farmer, carpenter and instrument maker, Proffitt was also known in folk circles for the fretless banjos he built and played. His own rendition of "Tom Dooley" is on the Folk-Legacy LP. — I.M.

THE PROOF
★ ★ **It's Safe** / Nemp. (1980)
Jersey bar-band competence. — D.M.

BRIAN PROTHEROE
★ ★ ★ **I/You** / Chrys. (1976)
An eclectic stylist, Protheroe suggests, though doesn't copy, other artists (Beatles, Donovan, Jethro Tull et al.) but has yet to forge his own musical identity. This LP, like his earlier deleted pair, skips from hints of jazz to rock to music hall to various permutations thereof. His keen and fresh melodies and bright tenor voice determine the music, and the spare arrangements (usually with his keyboards, and acoustic guitar in front), as well as Del Newman's sleek production, are nicely complementary. — C.W.

RICHARD PRYOR
★ ★ ★ ★ **Craps** / Laff (NA)
★ ★ ★ **Richard Pryor Meets Richard and Willie and the S.L.A.** / Laff (NA)
★ ★ ★ **Are You Serious** / Laff (NA)
★ ★ ★ **Black Ben** / Laff (NA)
★ ★ ★ **Wizard of Comedy** / Laff (NA)

★ ★ ★ **Who, Me? I'm Not Him** / Laff (NA)
★ ★ ★ **Richard Pryor** / Rep. (NA)
★ ★ ★ ★ **That Nigger's Crazy** / War. (1974)
★ ★ ★ **Was It Something I Said?** / Rep.
(1975)
★ ★ ★ ★ ★ **Bicentennial Nigger** / War.
(1976)
★ ★ ★ **Richard Pryor's Greatest Hits** / War.
(1977)
★ ★ ★ ★ ★ **Wanted** / War. (1978)
Richard Pryor is by far the most inspired
and hilarious comedian alive today. He is
also the most frightening, and his continual
scrapes with his wives, the law, drugs and
hospitals are a saga in themselves. In a good
many of his movie roles, Pryor stands just
this side of genius; in *Richard Pryor in Concert* (the soundtrack of which is *Wanted*), he
achieves it.

His album catalogue is nonetheless erratic,
with a tendency to fall back on the under-
the-counter stereotypes, sexual and racial, of
which the Laff party records are typical. But
even as the black Rusty Warren, Pryor is
never less than amusing. He changed his approach very little when he went to Warner
Bros., yet he has extended himself on occasion: *Wanted* is by far the most wide-ranging
work he has done, moving through all manner of characters and material that runs the
gamut from sweet Cosby-like tales of his
children's upbringing to angry political commentary. *Bicentennial Nigger* is his other
masterwork, a series of brutally revealing set
pieces whose last lines echo in the memory
for years. When Pryor achieves such a sublime transcendence of bitterness and rage, he
is perhaps funny only to the truly mindless
or the truly paranoid. But he also has managed at such moments to elevate stand-up
comedy to the level of genuine tragic art.
— D.M.

SNOOKY PRYOR
★ ★ ★ **Snooky Pryor** / Magpie (1978), imp.
★ ★ ★ **Real Fine Boogie** / Flyr. (NA), imp.
★ ★ **Shake Your Boogie** / Big Bear (NA),
imp.
★ ★ ★ **Pitch a Boogie** / P-Vine (NA)
Quite competent, but unexciting, Chicago
harmonica player and singer. Pryor's best
stuff is on Flyright, some J.O.B. sides from
the Fifties, and the material on Magpie and
P-Vine, which includes material dating back
to the Forties, is also real listenable. The Big
Bear is more contemporary. — D.M.

SNOOKY PRYOR AND JAMES MOODY
★ ★ **Snooky and Moody** / Flyr. (1980)

Uninspired early-Fifties Chicago blues performances. Better to check the Magpie LP of
Pryor on his own. — D.M.

ARTHUR PRYSOCK
★ ★ **Arthur Prysock '74** / Old T. (1973)
★ ★ **Love Makes It Right** / Old T. (1974)
★ ★ ★ **All My Life** / Old T. (1976)
★ ★ ★ **Silk and Satin** / Poly. (1977) ¶
★ ★ **Here's to Good Friends** / MCA (1978)
★ ★ ★ **Best of Arthur Prysock** / Verve (NA)
★ ★ ★ **This Is My Beloved** / Verve (NA)
★ ★ **Unforgettable** / King (NA)
Prysock was only sort of a blues singer in
the Delta to uptown sense; he was really a
part of the jazz scene. His biggest hit, "I
Didn't Sleep a Wink Last Night," came in
1952, although he was on the fringes of the
R&B scene, as a sort of minor-league Jimmy
Rushing, for many years thereafter. — D.M.

THE PSYCHEDELIC FURS
★ ★ ★ ★ **The Psychedelic Furs** / Col. (1980)
★ ★ ★ ★ **Talk Talk Talk** / Col. (1981)
On their audacious debut album, the Psychedelic Furs seemed to have the musical mak-
ings of a post-punk fave rave. Its relentless,
throbbing beat, crush of droning guitars and
wry saxophone asides quickly made the band
dance-club favorites; but what made the
group stand out from the pack was singer
Richard Butler, whose gritty voice and semi-
melodic delivery had a distinct Johnny Rotten charm to them. Adding to that charm
was Butler's distinctive word sense. Although he littered the songs with diffuse, almost disconnected images, it wasn't the
meaning so much as the words themselves
that counted. Butler's rhythmic delivery reduced his lyrics to so much verbal flotsam,
giving the words a percussive element that
fed the beat while simultaneously feeding off
its momentum.

Talk Talk Talk took a completely different
approach. Where *Psychedelic Furs* was vigor-
ously monolithic, *Talk* built off the charged interplay of the band members. On a rhythmic
level, the effect utilized the same circularity as
Butler's singing on the first album; where it dif-
fered was that the focus had become more melodic. The instrumental tracks were almost like
a wall of interlocking melody, held together by
resolute drumming and a more reflective, traditionally melodic Butler. At its best, like "Dumb
Waiters" or "Pretty in Pink," this is riveting
rock; at its worst, merely absorbing. A tremendous record.

P.S.: The "Psychedelic" is largely ironic,
nouveau psychedelia to the contrary.
— J.D.C.

PUBLIC IMAGE LIMITED
★ ★ ★ **Public Image Ltd.** / Virgin (1978), **Br. imp.**
★ ★ ★ ★ ★ **Metal Box** / Virgin (1979), **Br. imp**
★ ★ ★ ★ **Second Edition** / Is. (1979)
★ ★ ★ **Paris au Printemps** / Virgin (1980), **Br. imp.**
★ ★ ★ **Flowers of Romance** / War. (1981)
Answers the question: Whatever happened to Johnny Rotten?

But more importantly, Public Image Ltd. has helped to redefine the rock avant-garde. Depite muddled and meretricious rhetoric—rock is dead; they're not a rock band; the world is coming to an end; etc.—Rotten (now John Lydon), early Clash-mate Keith Levene and collaborators Jah Wobble, Jeanette Lee and Dave Crowe have on occasion pointed a genuinely new direction for rock that isn't simply a dead-end reprise of elitist ideas derived from other media.

They did this most effectively with their second album, *Metal Box,* released in the U.S. as *Second Edition.* The difference is much more than the title, however. *Metal Box* is a flat metal box, sort of like a film can, which holds three 12-inch 45 rpm discs that have an incredible sonic impact—this may be the hottest mastered record in history. It is certainly one of the most exciting, hypnotic and danceable, building wave after wave of post-disco synthesizer, percussion and guitar washes, over which Lydon's chanting, taunting, blistering, pestering, pleading and cowering voice hovers like a muse, a demon and a whimpering child.

Second Edition proves that it's not only the hot mixes that make this music so compulsively listenable: reduced to a pair of 12-inch LP sides, there's still lots here to enjoy. And the format of the U.S. release is considerably more convenient (plus you get the lyrics inked in on the back of the sleeve). Considering that *Metal Box* is one of the most expensive records ever issued—it goes for anywhere from $25 to $50 depending on the rapacity of your local shopkeeper—*Second Edition* is perhaps even the better buy.

Since then, unfortunately, Public Image Ltd. has disintegrated (Jah Wobble, longtime bassist, was expelled for using leftover band tapes for his solo record), restructured itself and floundered artistically. *Paris au Printemps* is a concert recording during which Lydon baits a hostile French crowd and the group runs through perfectly dull material

from the first, largely anti-papist LP. *Flowers of Romance* is more ambitious, but its Middle Eastern exotica and pretensions to seriousness give it far too much of the flavor of the stuffy art rock that Lydon professes to hate. — D.M.

PUNISHMENT OF LUXURY
■ **Laughing Academy** / U.A. (1979), **Br. imp.**
Awful Scottish new-wave quartet mixes leftfield S&M themes with neofascist imagery. Bend over. — J.S.

PURE PRAIRIE LEAGUE
★ ★ **Pure Prairie League** / RCA (1972)
★ ★ **Bustin' Out** / RCA (1975)
★ ★ ★ **Two Lane Highway** / RCA (1975)
★ ★ **If the Shoe Fits** / RCA (1976)
★ **Dance** / RCA (1976)
★ ★ **Takin' the Stage** / RCA (1977)
★ ★ **Just Fly** / RCA (1978)
★ **Can't Hold Back** / RCA (1979) ¶
★ **Firin' Up** / Casa. (1980)
★ **Something in the Night** / Casa. (1981)
Pure Prairie League's leaders, Craig Fuller and George Powell, come from Kentucky. Their debut (the self-titled LP) and *Bustin' Out* were agreeably quiet and modest blends of pop-rock songs with C&W arrangements; Fuller's writing and singing added a special gentleness. Fuller left before *Two Lane Highway,* where the group honed its earlier approaches, beefed up the guitars and investigated related stylings for greater variety. The other albums are slight variations on this approach. *Takin' the Stage* is a live LP. — C.W.

PUZZLE
★ **Puzzle** / ABC (1969)
Third-rate pop-rock from the progressive Seventies, which proves that neither Elvis Presley nor Alan Freed made a damn bit of difference: there's still one born every minute, and most of them become record-company executives. — D.M.

PYRAMID
■ **Pyramid** / Bang (1974)
Hippie utopianism at its most bland and platitudinous. Sanctimoniously dull enough to justify the punk revolt all by itself. — D.M.

PYRYMYD
★ **Pyrymyd** / Cap. (NA)
Y's guys. — D.M.

SIDNEY JOE QUALLS
★ ★ **I Enjoy Loving You / Dakar (1975)**
How about an entire album by somebody who sounds a lot like Al Green? The title song was a minor soul hit. — J.MC.

EDDIE QUANSAH
★ ★ **Awo Awo / Mango (1979)**
Abland synthesis of Afro, funk, pop and reggae that is less than the sum of its parts.
— R.F.G.

QUARTERFLASH
★ ★ **Quarterflash / Gef. (1981)**
FM-tailored audio wallpaper from an amalgam of Portland, Oregon, bar-circuit bands Pilot and Seafood Mama. Basic recipe: rock elements—Pretenders' guitar fills, Heart vocal mannerisms, Gerry Rafferty saxophone hooks—embedded in shimmering production surface. The LP's success via the single "Harden My Heart" is a monument to the crashing banality of contemporary U.S. radio. — G.A.

QUARTZ
★ ★ **Quartz / Mar. (NA)**
★ ★ **Camel in the City / Poly. (NA)**
Your dance-music basics. — D.M.

SUZI QUATRO
★ ★ **If You Knew Suzi / RSO (1978)**
★ ★ **Rock Hard / Dreaml. (1980)**
★ ★ **Suzi . . . and Other Four Letter Words / RSO (1979)**
Anglo-American pop tart whose migration from Motown to London in early Seventies, in association with Svengali/producer Mickey Most, resulted in some latter-day glitter-rock singles, notably "Can the Can" and "48 Crash," mindless variations on a formula perfected later by their writers, Nicky Chinn and Michael Chapman, with Sweet and Blondie. Quatro was semi-influential on all manner of Anglo-oriented American female singers, from the Runaways to Chrissie Hynde of Pretenders, but mostly as proof that women's rock could be done at all. Her posturing eventually became sufficiently ludicrous (and harmless) to be included as a regular part of the TV series *Happy Days*. Fester in peace. — D.M.

QUAZAR
★ ★ ★ ★ **Quazar / Ari. (1978) ¶**
The late Parliament-Funkadelic alumnus Glen Goins, whose bass playing defined George Clinton's style, scored a premature rock-disco hit with "Funk 'n' Roll (Dancing in the Funkshine)," which is the highlight of this posthumously released album. His chief cohort, drummer Jerome Brailey, went on to lead Mutiny, but Quazar is the truest heir of P-Funk, since it shows off P-Funk's rhythmic mainspring without suffering from George's cutesy-pie theorizing. This is conceptual funk that works as a matter of practice as well. — D.M.

QUEEN
★ **Queen / Elek. (1973)**
★ **Queen II / Elek. (1974)**
★ ★ **Sheer Heart Attack / Elek. (1974)**
★ ★ **A Night at the Opera / Elek. (1975)**
★ ★ **A Day at the Races / Elek. (1977)**
★ **News of the World / Elek. (1977)**
★ **Jazz / Elek. (1978)**
■ **Queen Live Killer / Elek. (1979)**
★ **The Game / Elek. (1980)**
★ ★ **Greatest Hits / Elek. (1981)**
This quartet of British college boys was assembled in 1972, and between the androgynous rich-kid posturings of vocalist Freddie Mercury and the metallic extravagances of Brian May's guitar, it bridged the gap between Led Zeppelin and David Bowie quite effectively, becoming one of the highest-grossing bands of the current era.

The debut albums are mostly fast, loud, guitar-dominated heavy rock, but taken considerably further than the genre's traditional blues base. *Queen II* has richer arrangements and a slightly less frenzied approach, which isn't always a blessing. The group's flamboyance couldn't always compensate for the weakness of its songwriting.

Sheer Heart Attack is streamlined: shorter songs, which are more hard than heavy, with an often simplified framework, although the ornate flourishes still obtrude. Mercury's piano playing also comes to the fore here. *A Night at the Opera,* which contains the classical hodgepodge "Bohemian Rhapsody," and *A Day at the Races* sharpened the now-varied attack. Queen effectively mimicked all the big-time British bands, moving through Zeppelin-like heaviness, Mercury's breathy vocals and piano, and May's more mainstream rock singing and guitar work. But *News of the World* took the band back closer to its heavy-metal base; the arrangements lack variety and the songs aren't just simple, they are redundant. *Jazz* was another bombastic farce, with no relation to the genre, while *The Game* dragged the group toward disco flamboyance, which was advantageous in gaining them hits but of no more artistic avail than any of its other strategies. *Live* is pointless. *Greatest Hits* is redundant to the single "Crazy Little Thing Called Love," the only listenable rock song in a dismal career.

? AND THE MYSTERIANS
★ ★ ★ ★ **96 Tears / London (1978), Jap. imp.**

The perfect Tex-Mex garage punk album of the Sixties. Makes Joe "King" Carrasco look like a fraud, and Iggy Pop like a tuneless wimp. Not for the faint of heart. — D.M.

QUICKSILVER MESSENGER SERVICE
★ ★ ★ **Quicksilver Messenger Service / Cap. (1968)**
★ ★ ★ ★ **Happy Trails / Cap. (1969)**
★ ★ ★ **Shady Grove / Cap. (1970)**
★ ★ **Just for Love / Cap. (1970)**
★ ★ **What about Me / Cap. (1971)**
★ ★ **Quicksilver / Cap. (1971)**
★ ★ **Comin' Thru / Cap. (1972)** ¶
★ ★ ★ **Anthology / Cap. (1973)**
★ ★ **Solid Silver / Cap. (1975)**

Quicksilver was probably the most overrated of the original batch of San Francisco groups. Its personnel was somewhat stellar— Dino Valenti wrote "Hey Joe" (under a pseudonym) and Jefferson Airplane's "Let's Get Together"; David Freiberg is now a member of Jefferson Starship; and English session veteran Nicky Hopkins appeared with the band during the *Shady Grove* period. But the group made only one noteworthy record, *Happy Trails,* which catches them live, at their peak, on versions of "Who Do You Love" and "Mona." Both tracks feature guitar extravaganzas by John Cipollina that are among the best instrumental work any San Francisco band did. They are the only hint available about where Quicksilver earned its reputation. — D.M.

QUINCY
★ **Quincy / Col. (NA)**

Heavy-handed pop group tries to sound new wave but only manages to come off as another broken-down glitter band with a rebuilt engine. — J.S.

LUTHER RABB
★ **Street Angel / MCA (1979)**
War bassist in funky but bleak solo effort.
— J.S.

RABBITT
★ ★ **Boys Will Be Boys / Capri. (NA)**
★ ★ **Croak and a Grunt in the Night /
Capri. (NA)**
Yet another mindless rock band signed by
Capricorn takes on Southern funk with un-
exciting results. Do not open until Easter.
— J.S.

EDDIE RABBITT
★ **Eddie Rabbitt / Elek. (1975)**
★ **Rocky Mountain Music / Elek. (1976)**
★ **Rabbitt / Elek. (1977)**
★ **Variations / Elek. (1978)**
★ **Loveline / Elek. (1979)**
★ ★ **Best Of / Elek. (1979)**
★ **Horizon / Elek. (1980)**
★ **Step by Step / Elek. (1981)**
Bland pop-country singer/ songwriter wrote
"Working My Way up to the Bottom" for
Roy Drusky, "Kentucky Rain" for Elvis
Presley and "Pure Love" for Ronnie Milsap
before beginning his own recording career.
He became one of the top country perform-
ers of the late Seventies, releasing a string of
hit singles: "Hearts on Fire," "You Don't
Love Me Anymore," "I Just Want to Love
You," "Suspicion," "Step by Step" and the
title track from the Clint Eastwood film
Every Which Way but Loose. Succeed-
ing LPs are less country, more MOR.
— J.S.

TREVOR RABIN
★ ★ **Trevor Rabin / Chrys. (1978)**
★ ★ **Face to Face / Chrys. (1979)**
The 1978 vogue term for Rabin's brand of
pop rock was power pop, which meant that
he had a cheery voice and a heavily chorded

electric guitar to back up his numbing songs
about romance and dance. — D.M.

YANK RACHELL
★ ★ **Mandolin Blues / Del. (NA)**
★ ★ **Yank Rachell / Blue G. (NA)**
As accompanist to Sleepy John Estes (who
returns the favor on *Mandolin Blues*), Rachell, a guitarist and mandolinist, is more
than competent. On his own, however, he's a
lot less rewarding, and from time to time
downright dull. Both of these are recent,
which doesn't help; his Twenties and Thirties music, on various anthologies, is a good
deal better. — D.M.

THE RACING CARS
★ ★ **Downtown Tonight / Chrys. (1977)**
★ ★ **Weekend Rendezvous / Chrys. (1977)**
★ ★ ★ **Bring on the Night / Chrys. (1978)**
English pop-rock band has never risen above
the level of nice humdrum melodies, tasteful
playing; it's the group's blandness—its aggra-
vating and unrelenting good taste—that does
it in. — D.M.

RADIATORS FROM SPACE
★ ★ ★ **TV Tube Heart / Chis. (1977), Br.
imp.**
The Radiators were in fact from Dublin, and
were one of the first punk groups to release
a record (in 1977). Their album shows some
real skill and talent, adding melodic invention, competent playing and a real pop sense
to what might have been routine genre fare.
The subject matter is predictable but not
bad, and the Radiators showed a lot more
promise than most of their contemporaries.
This remains, after several years, an enjoyable and significant record of the times.
— I.R.

GILDA RADNER
★ ★ ★ **Live from New York / War. (NA)**

The secret star of *Saturday Night Live* released the best solo comedy LP of any of the Not Ready for Prime Time Players. Features all the important Gilda TV characters. — J.S.

THE RAES
★ ★ **Dancing Up a Storm / A&M (NA)**
How to detect a disco album by a nonexistent group? They don't credit the singers. But then I wouldn't want a credit if I sang on this, either. — R.P.

R.A.F.
★ **R.A.F. / A&M (1980)**
★ **The Heat's On / A&M (1981)**
Lukewarm pop. — D.M.

GERRY RAFFERTY
★ ★ ★ **Can I Have My Money Back? / Blue Th. (1968)**
★ ★ ★ ★ **City to City / U.A. (1978)**
★ ★ **Night Owl / U.A. (1979)**
★ ★ **Snakes and Ladders / U.A. (1980)**
As a member of Stealers Wheel, Rafferty turned in an engaging British variation of Dylan's folk rock. On his own, he's done a more placid version of the same, highlighted by *City to City*'s "Baker Street," one of the most pleasant hit singles of 1978. The sax solo there is worth the price of admission, and the rest of the record follows suit. Subsequent LPs are only placid. — D.M.

THE RAIDERS
★ ★ **Greatest Hits, Vol. 2 / Col. (1970)**
★ ★ **Indian Reservation / Col. (1974)** ¶
After their hard-rocking beginnings as Paul Revere and the Raiders, this Seattle-bred, L.A.-based group settled into a more conventional mold, turning most of the proceedings over to vocalist Mark Lindsay, whose greatest aspiration, apparently, was to beat B. J. Thomas at his own game. "Indian Reservation" was the best they did, and it wasn't bad—but far inferior to the early stuff. — D.M.

THE RAINCOATS
★ ★ **The Raincoats / Rough T. (1980)**
Sure this is interesting for the new spaces these inspired amateurs discover, and because this band helps break gender barriers. It's also interesting to hear a cat howl for the first time, but *only* for the first time. One of those British new-wave acts that make better magazine copy than records. — R.P.

MA RAINEY
★ ★ ★ **Blues the World Forgot / Bio. (1968)**

★ ★ ★ ★ **Oh My Babe Blues / Bio. (1970)**
★ ★ ★ ★ **Queen of the Blues / Bio. (1972)**
★ ★ ★ ★ **Immortal / Mile. (1975)**
★ ★ ★ **Blame It on the Blues / Mile. (NA)**
★ ★ ★ **Down in the Basement / Mile. (NA)**
★ ★ ★ ★ **Ma Rainey / Bio. (NA)**
The so-called Mother of the Blues, Rainey was one of the finest classic blues singers of the early part of the century, and influenced greats such as Bessie Smith. Her most famous song, "C. C. Rider," probably adapted from an obscure folk source, has become one of the most-covered blues songs, making the transition to a rock hit in Chuck Willis' and Mitch Ryder's versions much later. She recorded a number of sides in the Twenties with barrelhouse pianist Georgia Tom Dorsey and guitarist Tampa Red. — J.S.

BONNIE RAITT
★ ★ ★ ★ **Bonnie Raitt / War. (1971)**
★ ★ ★ ★ **Give It Up / War. (1972)**
★ ★ ★ ★ **Takin' My Time / War. (1973)**
★ ★ **Streetlights / War. (1974)**
★ ★ ★ **Home Plate / War. (1975)**
★ ★ **Sweet Forgiveness / War. (1977)**
★ ★ **The Glow / War. (1979)**
Bonnie Raitt, the daughter of Broadway singer John Raitt, was playing on the Cambridge, Massachusetts, folk scene as early as 1967. Because she was managed by Dick Waterman, who also represented a number of country-blues figures (among them, Fred McDowell, John Hurt, Sippie Wallace and Son House), she frequently appeared with them in concert, which only fueled her ambition to become an authentic white blues performer.

Raitt began recording in 1971; her debut album, *Bonnie Raitt*, which was recorded at Dave Ray's studio in Minnesota and features Chicago bluesmen A. C. Reed and Junior Wells, is a straight blues affair, both engaging and sensitive. But it was with *Give It Up* that she came closest to perfecting her approach: she mingled her blues resources with a variety of contemporary and folk-oriented songs, coming up with classics in "Been Too Long at the Fair" and Eric Kaz's "Love Has No Pride." Her version of the latter remains definitive, despite the many subsequent covers. *Takin' My Time* is along the same lines, with a touch more electricity, highlighted by Jackson Browne's "I Thought I Was a Child" and Randy Newman's "Guilty."

But since then Raitt's recordings have generally been frustratingly inadequate. All of these records represent strategies designed to make her a star, and while Raitt's emotional sincerity is never called into question, the process has had less than salutary effects on the tone of her work.

Streetlights is the product of a collaboration with veteran soul producer Jerry Ragavoy and his philistine imagination. He came up with promising R&B-oriented material, but the arrangements are far too slick to accommodate Raitt's native funkiness. The record's most interesting moment is Joni Mitchell's "That Song about the Midway," a song whose involuted ambiguity couldn't be further from Raitt's bright-eyed irony.

Both *Home Plate* and *Sweet Forgiveness* were produced by Paul Rothchild, a man who should be consigned to making airline commercials; they are inexcusably banal attempts to turn Raitt into a Linda Ronstadt *manquée*. The fact that Raitt nearly overcomes on *Home Plate* doesn't excuse the concept. Rather than allowing herself to be melodramatic, Raitt is steamrollered, flattened out to accommodate a song selection that would enervate anyone. *Sweet Forgiveness* contained a remake of Del Shannon's "Runaway," which while quite awful was nearly a hit single; the streamlining homogenization continued after that "success" with *The Glow.* — B.T.

PHILIP RAMBOW
★ ★ ★ **Shooting Gallery / EMI (1979)**
★ ★ ★ **Jungle Law / Parlo./EMI (1981), Br. imp.**
Canadian Rambow has been a solo artist since the breakup of the Winkies in 1975. Yet due to contractual problems and a number of false starts (and despite several one-off appearances), he's released only two albums in six years. Rambow is a singer/songwriter/guitarist of above-average ability who bears comparison to John Hiatt; this pair of albums offer glimpses of real talent as well as a fair amount of dross. *Jungle Law* has great production and better-crafted songs; it covers a lot of ground from jazzy swing to soft ballads and driving rock & roll. *Shooting Gallery* has more raw emotion and topical lyricism. — I.R.

RAM JAM
★ **Ram Jam / Epic (1977)**
★ **Portrait of the Artist / Epic (1978)** ¶
Ram Jam is a godawful version of studio heavy metal, courtesy of former bubblegum producers Kastenatz-Katz. How this synthetic group got to make a second album is anybody's guess, but it probably has something to do with the fact that Ram Jam scored a minor hit single in 1977 with a re-

working of Leadbelly's "Black Betty." — D.M.

THE RAMONES
★ ★ ★ ★ **The Ramones / Sire (1976)**
★ ★ ★ ★ **Leave Home / Sire (1977)**
★ ★ ★ ★ **Rocket to Russia / Sire (1977)**
★ ★ ★ ★ **Road to Ruin / Sire (1978)**
Is this America's greatest rock band? Certainly it's the most amusing. Of all the Seventies punk rock bands, the Ramones were also the first latter-day punks to record. The Ramones know only one tempo—accelerated; their lyrical subject matter is puerile and inane, and the singer ain't real tuneful. As a result they are great, the embodiment of the amateur passion of rock & roll at a moment when it has nearly died out.
★ ★ ★ **End of the Century / Sire (1980)**
★ ★ **Pleasant Dreams / Sire (1981)**
Or are they? The Ramones present a classic critical conundrum, since their amateurishness and dumbness are attractive only if to some degree willful. With these records, those qualities began to seem as much the product of limitations and lack of talent as intention. And even if not, *Pleasant Dreams* represents the group's utter failure to become sufficiently professional to justify a multialbum career.

End of the Century is appealing primarily because of Phil Spector's production. But the joy has gone out of the Ramones' approach, and "Do You Remember Rock & Roll Radio" and "Danny Says," the best songs, represent the souring of their innocence. Spector turns in his best work in years—*Century* has the clarity such muddled jobs as Lennon's *Rock 'n' Roll* and Cohen's *Death of a Ladies Man* lack—but he only serves to emphasize the Ramones' shortcomings.

Pleasant Dreams is a dead end, a fainthearted reiteration of what made the Ramones initially intriguing. The problem with amateurism, it seems, is that you can't make a career of it. — D.M.

KENNY RANKIN
★ ★ **Like a Seed / Lit. Dav. (1972)**
★ ★ **Silver Morning / Lit. Dav. (1974)**
★ ★ **Inside / Lit. Dav. (1975)**
★ ★ **The Kenny Rankin Album / Lit. Dav. (1977)**
★ **After the Roses / Atl. (1980)**
MOR jazz-pop crooner is as bland as he is skillful at interpreting his and others' songs in a mellow, light scat style. Good mood music. Early Mercury albums, including minor classic, *Mindclusters,* out of print. — S.H.

RANKING JOE
★ ★ ★ **Saturday Night Jamdown Style /**
 Greens. (1980)
★ ★ ★ **Tribute to John Lennon / Tad's**
 (1981)
Ranking Joe cranks out countless DJ records, most of which are workmanlike, entertaining sets. He has little of significance to
say, but he'd be a good one to have at your
next yard-style sound-system jamdown.
— R.F.G.

RARE EARTH
★ ★ **Get Ready / Rare (1969)**
★ **Ecology / Rare (1970)**
■ **Rare Earth in Concert / Rare (1972)**
★ **Rare Earth / Prod. (1977)** ¶
★ **Band Together / Prod. (1978)** ¶
★ ★ **Super Star Series, Vol. 16 / Mo. (1981)**
Although they had some hits in the early
Seventies (the most notable was a cover of
the Temptations' "Get Ready," on the
album of the same name), Rare Earth re-
main remarkable because they were perhaps
the worst white-soul bar band ever formed,
and prospered on a Motown subsidiary.
Where was Berry Gordy—out to lunch?
— D.M.

THE RASCALS
★ ★ ★ ★ ★ **The Rascals' Greatest Hits /**
 Time-Peace / Atl. (1968)
The (Young) Rascals grew up in New Jersey, but were discovered on Long Island,
playing white R&B to socialites in the summer of 1965. Their gimmick was supposed to
be that they dressed in Edwardian costume,
but what gave them a string of great white
soul hits was the vocal prowess of Eddie Brigati and Felix Cavaliere.
  Brigati, Cavaliere (who played keyboards
as well as sang) and guitarist Gene Cornish
had originally played with Joey Dee and the
Starlighters ("Peppermint Twist") at the
Peppermint Lounge, the home of the twist;
drummer Dino Danelli was added when the
trio split from Dee. Signed to Atlantic Records in 1965 and coupled with the production team of Arif Mardin and Tom Dowd—
which would later assist Jerry Wexler so
ably in making Aretha Franklin's masterful
records—the group's first single, "Ain't
Gonna Eat Out My Heart Anymore," came
close to breaking out. But it was the second,
the rousing "Good Lovin'," which went to
No. 1 in early 1966, that really brought
them to fame. This spawned a string of hits,
the best known of which are the reflective
and sinuous "Groovin'" (1967) and "People
Got to Be Free" (1968), by which time the

name had been changed, from the Young
Rascals to the Rascals.
  "People Got to Be Free" was included in
an album that sowed the seeds of the group's
demise, *Freedom Suite,* which reflected an
attempt to join the psychedelic craze and
particularly Cavaliere's growing infatuation
with Eastern mysticism. In a pattern typical
of so many of the group's contemporaries,
the Rascals' musical worth declined as its
ambition soared, and by the early Seventies,
the band faded out, after switching to Columbia for one ill-fated LP. All that now remains in print is this glorious chronicle of a
group that ranks with Mitch Ryder and the
Detroit Wheels, and the Righteous Brothers
among white American soul singers. — D.M.

THE RASPBERRIES
★ ★ ★ ★ **The Raspberries' Best (Featuring**
 Eric Carmen) / Cap. (1976)
An exquisite anthology of Seventies pop rock
that's a throwback to the heyday of the
Beatles and Beach Boys. The Raspberries
came out of Cleveland in 1972 with a sound
that was already brilliantly homogeneous—
"Go All the Way" and "Tonight" (their first
two singles hits) were ringers for Paul
McCartney, thanks to Eric Carmen's vocals,
and the songs that followed lived up to a
similar standard. Such romanticism and nostalgia had no great depth, but it was great
entertainment. But in 1974, when Carmen
despaired of ever breaking through to more
substantial recognition, he came up with a
last-ditch effort called "Overnight Sensation
(Hit Record)" that painted his aspirations
with perfect bluntness. "Overnight Sensation" *is* the radio that leads to Carmen's
street of dreams, and in it, his vision of himself as the true inheritor of the innocence of
early-Sixties rock is justified completely.
  Unfortunately, "Overnight Sensation" and
the inspired album from which it came
(*Starting Over,* now deleted) were both relative commercial failures, and Carmen soon
left the band (which has since contributed
members to Fotomaker and Tattoo) for a
solo career in which he has, despite occasional hit singles, seemed more and more
like Barry Manilow for the prematurely senile. — D.M.

THE RASTAFARIANS
★ ★ **Orthodox / Rastafarians (1981)**
Rastas from Santa Cruz? On record they
sound like a slicker, less credible version of
Ras Michael and the Sons of Negus. A nice
try, but they lack both musical and spiritual
chops. — R.F.G.

THE RAVENS
★ ★ ★ ★ **The Greatest Group of All / Savoy (1978)**
Seminal doo-wop group. One of the first bird groups of the pre–rock & roll era, the Ravens, along with Sonny Til and the Orioles, bridged the gap between the age of the Ink Spots and Mills Brothers, and the rhythm & blues era, when secular black harmony merged with gospel.

This reissue spotlights the group's best material, recorded from 1945 through about 1948 (the liner notes, by Jack Sbarbori, very good in every other respect, are maddeningly vague about dates). Bass singer Jimmy Ricks is perhaps the outstanding member, but original first tenor Maithe Marshall is also remarkable. This album unfortunately does not contain two of the Ravens' best and most important recordings, "Ol' Man River" and the doo-wop precursor, "Count Every Star." But it does have "Write Me a Letter," and a remarkable version of "White Christmas," which predates Clyde McPhatter's with the Drifters by several years, as well as a side of previously unissued material. A must for collectors, or those at all interested in harmony singing. — D.M.

LOU RAWLS
★ ★ ★ **Stormy Monday / Cap. (1962)**
★ ★ ★ **Lou Rawls Live / Cap. (1966)**
★ ★ ★ **Soulin' / Cap. (1966)**
★ **Merry Xmas, Ho Ho Ho / Cap. (1967)**
★ ★ ★ **The Best of Lou Rawls / Cap. (1968)**
★ ★ ★ ★ **All Things in Time / Phil. (1976)**
★ ★ ★ **Naturally / Poly. (1976)** ¶
★ ★ ★ ★ **The Best from Lou Rawls / Cap. (1976)**
★ ★ ★ ★ **Unmistakably Lou / Phil. (1977)**
★ ★ ★ ★ **When You Hear Lou, You've Heard It All / Phil. (1977)**
★ ★ **Let Me Be Good to You / Phil. (1979)**
★ ★ **Sit Down and Talk to Me / Phil. (1979)**
★ ★ **Shades of Lou / Phil. (1980)**
Rawls is one of the many R&B singers trained in gospel groups. He got his start with the Pilgrim Travelers, then was signed as a pop singer by Capitol. In the Sixties, Rawls had several hits: "Dead End Street" and "Tobacco Road" pointed him out as one of the best new vocalists of his time. Capitol tried to mold Rawls in the same style as Nat King Cole, but ended up overproducing him and negating his talent, although the hits have a certain vitality.

It took Rawls a few label switches and some years to regain his composure after being slotted as a Las Vegas lounge act, but in the mid-Seventies he hooked up with Philadelphia International producers Gamble and Huff. They wrote and produced his next record, and suddenly Rawls had found himself once more. The high point of the collaboration so far is the 1977 smash hit, "You'll Never Find Another Love Like Mine," a magnificent performance that shows Rawls in top form and indicates that he still may not have tapped his full potential as a vocalist. He has also been seen and heard as the voice of Budweiser beer on commercials, from which *When You Hear* stems. — J.S.

DON RAY
★ ★ **The Garden of Love / Poly. (1978)**
Quasi-cosmic (shilling for carnal) disco clichés, rendered hot enough for occasional listenability by coproducer Cerrone. — D.M.

RAY, GOODMAN AND BROWN
★ ★ ★ **Ray, Goodman and Brown / Poly. (1979)**
★ ★ ★ **Ray, Goodman and Brown II / Poly. (1980)**
★ ★ ★ **Stay / Poly. (1981)**
Ray, Goodman and Brown are former Moments who have taken that group's sound, added some studio slickness and cashed in early on the R&B harmony revival. Although the singing is first-rate, the material is not; "Special Lady" from *Ray, Goodman and Brown* is well worth hearing, but the rest is well-harmonized fluff. — J.D.C.

THE RAYBEATS
★ ★ ★ ★ ★ **Guitar Beat / Jem (1981)**
One of the best rock & roll instrumental groups in recent years, the Raybeats built a solid reputation in new-wave clubs playing brilliantly tight sets featuring the often astonishing lead guitar playing of Jody Harris. Punk fashionmongers like to call them a surf band, but depending on your context you could swear they were a throwback to the free-for-all experimentation of the late Sixties, a sort of Quicksilver Messenger Service without the flab and hippie posturing. Proves there's still hope for the future of rock & roll. — J.S.

RAYDIO
★ ★ ★ **Raydio / Ari. (1978)**
★ ★ ★ **Rock On / Ari. (1979)**
★ ★ ★ **Two Places at the Same Time / Ari. (1980)**
★ ★ ★ **Woman Needs Love / Ari. (1981)**
Tight, funky horn band from Detroit scored pleasurable 1978 pop hit with reworking of "Jack and Jill" nursery rhyme. — D.M.

THE REAL KIDS
★ ★ **The Real Kids** / **Red S. (1977)**
Tough American rock falls into the chasm
between the ironic inspiration of the New
York Dolls and the ironic idiocy of the Ramones. Chuck Berry riffs punked up, humor-
lessly. — D.M.

EUGENE RECORD
★ ★ ★ **Eugene Record** / **War. (1977)**
★ ★ **Trying to Get to You** / **War. (1977)**
★ ★ **Welcome to My Fantasy** / **War. (1978)**
Record was the guiding light (songwriter
and lead vocalist) of the Chi-Lites, last of
the sweetly classic soul vocal groups. On his
own, he's still a fine songwriter, and on his
first solo album, he nearly matches the Chi-
Lites' romantic enthusiasm. Subsequent albums, however, show a tendency to dawdle
off into instrumental irrelevancies. — D.M.

THE RECORDS
★ ★ ★ **The Records** / **Virgin (1979)**
★ ★ ★ **Crashes** / **Virgin (1980)**
The Records were in the forefront of the
British power-pop explosionette of the late
Seventies; their debut album even includes a
hit record, "Starry Eyes." Beatles harmonies
and Byrds-like guitar work dominate these
consistently pleasant and tuneful albums.
— D.G.

LOUISIANA RED
★ ★ **Louisiana Red** / **Esceha (NA)**
Strong-voiced blues singer from Mississippi
went under the name Elmore James, Jr.,
down South, where he first acquired a reputation for playing good bottleneck acoustic
guitar and mouth harp. He later recorded
under the name Rocky Fuller with Muddy
Waters and Little Walter, and stayed with
Waters for a time. — J.S.

REDBONE
★ ★ **Redbone** / **Epic (1970)** ¶
★ ★ **Wovoka** / **Epic (1974)**
★ ★ ★ **Come and Get Your Redbone (The**
   Best of Redbone) / **Epic (1975)** ¶
★ ★ **Cycles** / **RCA (1977)** ¶
The only rock band led by full-blooded
North American Indians, Redbone was,
however, less influenced by Native American
culture than soul music. Pat and Lolly Vegas
were good songwriters (P. J. Proby had a hit
with "Niki Hoeky" in the Sixties) but more
limited performers. Despite such fine material as "The Witch Queen of New Orleans"
and "Niki Hoeky," the strained vocals make
a good deal of this unbearable. In "Come
and Get Your Love," though, the singing

was perfect, in a Marvin Gaye mold, and the
song became a Top Ten hit in 1974. The
RCA record is a misguided comeback; the
one to have, if you're interested in the
boundaries of rock and soul, is *Come and
Get Your Redbone.* — D.M.

LEON REDBONE
★ ★ ★ ★ **On the Track** / **War. (1976)**
★ ★ ★ **Double Time** / **War. (1976)**
★ ★ **Champagne Charlie** / **War. (1978)**
★ **Mystery Man** / **Acc. (1981)**
Redbone, a mysterious late-Sixties/early-
Seventies folk scene fixture who numbers
Bob Dylan among his admirers, coupled
with producer Joel Dorn and came up with
On the Track, a lovely album of pre–World
War II American music, with the ambiance
of an old 78. But *Double Time,* the follow-
up, made the approach seem more like a
pose than a commitment, and a smugly self-
conscious pose at that. And *Champagne
Charlie* made the debacle complete. — D.M.

THE RED CLAY RAMBLERS
★ ★ **The Red Clay Ramblers** / **Folk. (1974)**
★ ★ ★ **Stolen Love** / **Fly. Fish (1975)**
★ ★ ★ **Twisted Laurel** / **Fly. Fish (1976)**
★ ★ **Merchant's Lunch** / **Fly. Fish (1978)**
★ ★ **Chuckin' the Frizz** / **Fly. Fish (1979)**
This North Carolina group of college-
educated traditional music buffs earned its
recognition by providing the music for a
Broadway play, *Diamond Studs.* On vinyl,
the Ramblers have moved from an almost
musicological sense of tradition to a greater
awareness of taping technology and modern
nuance. Their facility with the two-step
string-band idiom is perhaps the most accessible form of old-timey music being performed in modern America. Comfortably accomplished instrumentalists and singers, the
Ramblers both pay tribute to, and infuse
with new life, neglected segments of our musical heritage. — R.P.

THE RED CRAYOLA
★ ★ **The Parable of Arable Land** / **Radar/**
   Int. Art. (1967; 1978)
★ **God Bless the Red Crayola and All Who**
   Sail with It / **International Artists (1968;**
   1978)
■ **Soldier Talk** / **Radar (1979)**
As a psychedelic novelty (from Texas yet),
the Crayola was a late-Sixties amusement—
the only band in the world ever to record a
motorcycle live in the studio. That was on
the inaugural disc, *Parable.* With *God Bless,*
the joke had already worn thin, but after
Radar reissued the first two albums in En-

gland, a band of arty post-punk minimalists attempted to carry the tradition onward, with particularly insipid results. — D.M.

OTIS REDDING
★ ★ ★ **Pain in My Heart** / **Atl.** (1965; rereleased 1981, Jap. imp.)
★ ★ ★ ★ **Otis Redding Live in Europe** / **Atco** (1966)
★ ★ ★ ★ **Otis Blue** / **Atl.** (1966; rereleased 1981, Jap. imp.)
★ ★ ★ ★ **History of Otis Redding** / **Atco** (1967)
★ ★ ★ ★ **The Immortal Otis Redding** / **Atco** (1968)
★ ★ ★ **The Dock of the Bay** / **Atl.** (1968; rereleased 1981, Jap. imp.)
★ ★ ★ **In Person at the Whisky Au Go Go** / **Atl.** (1968; rereleased 1981, Jap. imp.)
★ ★ ★ ★ **The Best of Otis Redding** / **Atco** (1972)
★ ★ ★ **The Otis Redding Story** / **Atco** (NA), imp.
★ ★ ★ **Otis** / **Atl.** (NA), imp.
★ ★ ★ ★ **Dictionary of Soul** / **Volt** (NA), imp.
★ ★ ★ ★ **The Great Otis Redding Sings Soul Ballads** / **Atl.** (NA), imp.
★ ★ ★ ★ **Otis Redding Sings Soul** / **Atl.** (NA), imp.
★ ★ ★ **The Soul Album** / **Volt** (NA), imp.
★ ★ ★ **Otis Redding Recorded Live** / **Atl.** (1982), imp.

Otis Redding was probably the most influential soul singer of the late Sixties, and on talent alone, he ranks with Marvin Gaye, Smokey Robinson, James Brown and Curtis Mayfield as one of the greatest. Redding's style was grittier and more maturely emotional than any of these, without Brown's hysteria or Mayfield's reserve; his hoarse shouting left a deep imprint on the music, which it has not yet fully discarded.

Despite this, Redding never achieved a major pop hit until after his untimely death in a plane crash in December 1967. Until the release of "Dock of the Bay," in early 1968, he was best known for having written Aretha Franklin's first No. 1 hit, "Respect," and for having wowed the hipsters at the Monterey Pop Festival the summer before. Yet Redding had recorded since 1962, and his songs include several now regarded as classics: "I've Been Loving You Too Long," "Mr. Pitiful" and "Try a Little Tenderness," the latter actually a reworked Forties ballad. But despite frequent cover versions of his songs, by Franklin, the Rolling Stones and

many others, Redding never reaped the benefits of his genius. His version of "Satisfaction," in which he repaid the Stones' several cops from him, came close. But "Dock of the Bay," a moody, introspective piece that set him solo against Steve Cropper's guitar and a very spare arrangement, was the song that put him over. It was almost as though radio and the public were atoning for ignoring Redding when he was alive.

Yet, as demonstrated by these albums, and the many Atlantic and Volt recordings from which they are derived (available as Japanese imports), Redding was a marvel: one of the great live showmen (*Live in Europe* is better than any other live rock or soul album I can think of), a masterful ballad singer and a true rocker in the spirit of his boyhood hero, Little Richard. Everything the man recorded—not only these albums but the cutouts as well—demands to be heard. — D.M.

THE REDDINGS
★ ★ ★ **The Awakening** / **Believe in a Dream** (1980)
★ ★ ★ **Class** / **Believe in a Dream** (1981)

Expecting the Reddings to sound like the Otis Redding Revue simply because Dexter and Otis III are Redding's sons and Mark Lockett his nephew is like expecting Caroline Kennedy to keep Soviet missiles out of Cuba—pointless and unfair. What the Reddings do is smooth, sophisticated funk, and the only reason to fault them is that their proficiency exceeds their originality or inventiveness. Still, considering their youth, it's reasonable enough to expect them to improve with time. — J.D.C.

HELEN REDDY
■ **I Don't Know How to Love Him** / **Cap.** (1971)
■ **Helen Reddy** / **Cap.** (1971)
★ ★ **I Am Woman** / **Cap.** (1972)
■ **Long Hard Climb** / **Cap.** (1973)
■ **Love Song for Jeffrey** / **Cap.** (1974)
■ **Free and Easy** / **Cap.** (1974) ¶
■ **No Way to Treat a Lady** / **Cap.** (1975)
★ ★ **Helen Reddy's Greatest Hits** / **Cap.** (1975)
■ **Music, Music** / **Cap.** (1976)
★ ★ **Ear Candy** / **Cap.** (1977)
■ **We'll Sing in the Sunshine** / **Cap.** (1978)
■ **Live in London** / **Cap.** (1978)
■ **Take What You Find** / **Cap.** (1979)
■ **Reddy** / **Cap.** (1980)

Helen Reddy could have been a feminist hero. Her 1972 No. 1 hit, "I Am Woman," was an anthem that signified the increasing political awareness of women, and Reddy might have commanded the loyalty of such people if she'd wanted to. Instead, she drifted off into the worst kind of romantic pop, even allowing her image to be reduced to a simple double entendre with *Free and Easy.* Since she was never any great shakes as a song stylist or interpreter anyway, the loss is her own. — D.M.

JEAN REDPATH
★ ★ **Frae My Ain Countrie / Folk-Leg. (1973)** ¶
Shortly after Redpath moved to the U.S. from Scotland in 1961, she found herself amidst the folksingers and songwriters in Greenwich Village, and performing at Gerde's Folk City: Jack Elliott, Bob Dylan, the Greenbriar Boys and others. Her own Scottish roots and songs were an entrée into the "folk revival," and she recorded for Prestige and Elektra at that time. *Frae My Ain Countrie* has the sort of ballads and other material she did on those now-deleted LPs. — I.M.

RED ROCKERS
★ **Condition Red / 415 (1981)**
★ ★ ★ **Good as Gold / Col. (1983)**
New Orleans Red Rockers attempt to capture and Americanize the sound and fury of the early Clash, but like most of the new wave of hard-core punkers they produce music so redundant and messages so garbled that it's hard to tell what they're advocating, if anything. The saving grace is a wonderful hyped-up cover of "Folsom Prison Blues," probably because it's the only tune that stands out from the rest.

However, *Good as Gold* reverses their form, presenting a solid, well-crafted set of songs highlighted by the inscrutable "China." — D.S.

THE REDS
★ **The Reds / A&M (1979)**
Lurching, graceless power pop—more annoying than invigorating. — D.M.

TAMPA RED
★ ★ ★ **Bottleneck Guitar 1928–1937 / Yazoo (1973)**
★ ★ ★ **The Guitar Wizard 1935–1953 / Blues C. (1974)**
★ ★ ★ ★ **The Guitar Wizard / RCA (1975)**
★ ★ ★ ★ **Bluebird No. 11 / Blueb. (NA)**
★ ★ ★ ★ **You Can't Get That Stuff No More / Oldie B. (NA)**
One of the most popular and frequently recorded urban blues performers of the late Twenties, Thirties and Forties, Tampa Red

has been credited by Big Bill Broonzy with inventing the slide-guitar blues technique, and his adaptation of the Hawaiian guitar sound to blues playing was very effective. He earned his living playing for nickels and dimes on the streets of Chicago, where he picked up his nickname (he was raised in Tampa).

His second record, "It's Tight Like That" (1928), became one of the most popular "race" records of all time. He was accompanied on his early material by pianist Georgia Tom Dorsey, and this period is well documented on the Yazoo album. The two *Guitar Wizard* releases, which don't duplicate each other despite having the same title, feature Red's later work (mid-Thirties to Fifties). These spirited records include a wide range of styles, from simple blues to hokum jumpers. His records with the Chicago Five were very popular with white audiences and included a lot of kazoo playing. Red's importance as a scene-maker in Chicago blues circles over the years is shown in the selection of sidemen on these dates, ranging from pianists Black Bob and Big Maceo to blues harpists Willie "Sonny Boy" Williamson and Walter "Shakey" Horton. — J.S.

BLIND ALFRED REED
★ ★ ★ **How Can a Poor Man Stand Such Times and Live? . . . The Songs of Blind Alfred Reed / Roun. (1972)**
Reed recorded these simple but lovely songs of religious conviction and social protest between 1927 and 1929. He had an excellent voice, more polished than was typical among West Virginia singers of the period, and while crude, his fiddle playing is effective. Ry Cooder fans will know the title tracks, but much of Reed's music deserves exploration. — D.M.

JERRY REED
★ ★ **Me and Jerry / RCA (1970)**
★ ★ ★ **The Best of Jerry Reed / RCA (1971)**
★ ★ **Tupelo Mississippi Flash / Camd. (1975)**
★ **Paper Roses / Camd. (1975)**
★ **Jerry Reed in Concert / RCA (1975)**
★ ★ **Red Hot Picker / RCA (1975)** ¶
★ ★ **Jerry Reed Rides Again / RCA (1975)**
★ ★ **Alabama Wild Man / Camd. (1976)**
★ ★ ★ **When You're Hot, You're Hot / RCA (1976)**
★ ★ **Both Barrels / RCA (1976)**
★ ★ **Me and Chet / RCA (1977)**
★ ★ **East Bound and Down / RCA (1977)**

★ ★ **Jerry Reed Sings Jim Croce / RCA (NA)**
★ ★ **Texas Bound and Flying / RCA (NA)**
★ ★ **Jerry Reed Live! / RCA (NA)**
★ ★ **Half Singin' and Half Pickin' / RCA (NA)**
★ ★ **Dixie Dreams / RCA (1981)**
Reed is a Nashville session guitarist who had two big hits—"When You're Hot, You're Hot" in 1971, "Amos Moses" in 1970—that he has never followed up, despite more than a decade of trying. Mostly because his picking and singing are strictly by formula—except on those singles, where he really sounds like the Alabama man of Burt Reynolds' dreams. — D.M.

JIMMY REED
★ ★ ★ ★ ★ **Jimmy Reed at Carnegie Hall / VJ (1962)**
★ ★ ★ **Just Jimmy Reed / VJ (1964)**
★ ★ ★ **The Best of Jimmy Reed / Cres. (1974)**
★ ★ ★ **Cold Chills / Ant. (1975) (NA)**
★ ★ ★ ★ **Upside Your Head / Charly (1980), Br. imp.**
★ ★ ★ ★ **High and Lonesome / Charly (1980), Br. imp.**
★ ★ ★ ★ **History of Jimmy Reed / Trip (NA)**
★ ★ ★ **Jimmy Reed / Archive of Folk (NA)**
★ ★ ★ **Wailin' the Blues / Trad. (NA)**
★ ★ ★ ★ **I'm Jimmy Reed / VJ (NA)**
★ ★ ★ ★ **Found Love / VJ (NA)**
★ ★ ★ **Blues Is My Business / VJ (NA)**
★ ★ ★ ★ **The Best of Jimmy Reed / VJ (NA)**
★ ★ ★ **Jimmy Reed Sings the Best of the Blues / VJ (NA)**
★ ★ ★ **Jimmy Reed at Soul City / VJ (NA)**
★ ★ ★ **The Legend, the Man / VJ (NA)**
★ ★ ★ **The Best of the Blues / Exodus (NA)**
★ ★ ★ ★ **The History of Jimmy Reed, Vol. 2 / Trip (NA)**
★ ★ **Jimmy Reed / AZ International (NA), Fr. imp.**
One of the most influential urban bluesmen of the Fifties, particularly on white rock musicians, Jimmy Reed developed his style as a youth in Mississippi and perfected it after moving north and becoming a foundry worker in Gary, Indiana, just outside Chicago. His style is typified by a steady four-bar beat, a walking bass line and his own distinctive vocals, halfway between a moan and a shout. This approach was later adapted and presented under various guises; it pops up in the early records of the Who, the Animals and even the Rolling Stones.

Reed's best-known songs, "Ain't That Loving You Baby," "Baby What You Want Me to Do," "Bright Lights Big City" and "Big Boss Man," were all recorded for Vee Jay in the Fifties and early Sixties, and are included on a dizzying array of labels—including the erratically available original, as a series of very fine reissues. Duplication is just about unavoidable. But his style was so homogeneous that it rarely faltered, and almost any of the records here will give a decent glimpse of his accomplishments.
— D.M.

LOU REED
★ ★ ★ **Lou Reed / RCA (1972) ¶**
★ ★ ★ **Transformer / RCA (1972)**
★ ★ ★ ★ **Rock 'n' Roll Animal / RCA (1974)**
★ ★ **Lou Reed Live / RCA (1975)**
★ ★ ★ **Coney Island Baby / RCA (1976)**
★ **Rock and Roll Heart / Ari. (1976)**
★ ★ **Walk on the Wild Side / RCA (1977)**
★ ★ ★ **Street Hassle / Ari. (1978)**
★ ★ **Take No Prisoners—Lou Reed Live / Ari. (1978)**
★ ★ **The Bells / Ari. (1979)**
★ ★ ★ **Growing Up in Public / Ari. (1980)**
★ ★ ★ ★ **Rock 'n' Roll Diary / Ari. (1980)**
★ ★ **Blue Mask / RCA (1982)**
★ **Legendary Hearts / RCA (1983)**
Lou Reed is the perfect rock critic's darling: limited, abrasive, a bad case of stunted musical development meeting profoundly pitiful lyrical confessions of self-loathing and nihilism. On occasion Reed has shown some real ability, primarily as a manipulator of rock traditions of singing and lyric writing, but his songs are repetitious, his addled production concepts make some of his best music virtually unlistenable, and his attempts to work in extended forms have all been disastrous. This includes the oft-heralded (now deleted) song cycle *Berlin,* which achieves a certain decadent splendor more because Bob Ezrin provided Reed with his first competence at the controls than because the songs actually hang together well. It goes trebly for *Metal Machine Music,* an album of abrasive electronic noise that is both an artistic and commercial hustle: Reed's experimentalism is definitely sub-Cage in that the intended effect is nothing more than cheap shock and perhaps critical credibility for being willing to indulge in such a monumentally nihilistic work. It hardly matters whether Reed intended *Metal Machine Music* as an elaborate joke on the public and his record company, or

whether he actually thought that he was making an important electronic work. The joke isn't particularly witty or original, and neither is the electronic music.

In the end, the only essential albums of Reed's solo career are *Rock 'n' Roll Diary,* which, by juxtaposing his later work with his early days in the Velvet Underground, makes it clear what a case of arrested development Reed really is; *Rock 'n' Roll Animal,* a live set featuring a remarkably skillful band led by guitarists Steve Hunter and Dick Wagner, the bulk of which went on to better things with Alice Cooper; and *Street Hassle,* Reed's most successful attempt to create a conceptual work, probably because he stays within the boundaries of conventional song form for the most part. *Street Hassle* is also a gesture of warmth from the nihilist, a bit of noblesse oblige upon discovering that he is mistaken for a grand old man by the punk insurrectionists of that period.

Of the rest, the debut, *Lou Reed,* is a muddle whose virtues are obliterated by an awful mix. *Transformer* is a dalliance with Bowie-esque sexual ambivalence—while it may be true that Bowie in fact took many of his tricks in this area from Reed, it must also be noted that Bowie uses them much more effectively.

The other Reed live albums (*Lou Reed Live* and *Take No Prisoners,* which is mostly a mordant standup-comic-with-guitar show) are a waste of breath. Reed's best live work, aside from that with the *Rock 'n' Roll Animal* band, was with the Velvet Underground, and it is also available on a couple of records, both of which are better than these.

Coney Island Baby returns Reed to his love of doo-wop harmony; it also manages some confessional songs that turn on more than self-loathing. The title song is one of the half-dozen best that he has written. *Rock and Roll Heart,* on the other hand, is ersatz and spongy, making no attempt to conceal its emotional fakery.

The Bells is another attempt to make electronic music, and though it is much more interesting than *Metal Machine Music,* there's nothing here that hasn't been done better by a number of others (Brian Eno, David Bowie again, Roxy Music). *Growing Up in Public* and his most recent RCA albums show Reed backing off a bit from his stance of decadent outrageousness, but without presenting sufficient musical development to earn him distinction as more than a minor artist, however great his influence on the punk era has been. — D.M.

THE REELS
★ ★ ★ **The Reels / Polyg. (1980)**
Agreeable, quirky Australian pop. Singer David Mason writes smart lyrics in a boppy, poppy setting for songs that verge on caricature but stay just the right side of cuteness. Unusually cheery synthesizer sounds dominate the lineup as they skip through jerky late-Seventies rhythms. The debut album, *The Reels,* includes several of the songs that were successful in Australia, such as "Prefab Heart." — S.M.

MARTHA REEVES
★ **We Meet Again / Fan. (1978)**
★ **Gotta Keep Moving / Fan. (1980)**
Martha Reeves' career since departing from the Vandellas has been a sad series of now-deleted conceptual mishaps shaped up by smartass auteurist producers: Richard Perry did a notable boondoggle for MCA in the mid-Seventies and no less than four producers turned executioner for her 1977 Arista set, *The Rest of My Life.* Reeves called that LP's gimmicky clutter "disco-designed," which is probably what she would say about these LPs, too. No excuse. — B.T.

CLARENCE REID
★ ★ ★ **On the Job / Als. (1976)**
Reid is a mainstay of the TK Records soul complex as Betty Wright's producer, and under his pseudonym, Blow Fly, he has also recorded a hilariously obscene series of R&B party albums in which he converts soul and disco charttoppers into risque expressions that verge on comedic pornography. His work on this album isn't that imaginative, but the songs are written with wit and Reid's performances have a kind of gravelly intensity that makes them memorable. — D.M.

CARL REINER AND MEL BROOKS
★ ★ ★ **2000 Years with Carl Reiner and Mel Brooks / War. (1973)**
★ ★ ★ **2000 and Thirteen / War. (1973)**
The premise in anyone else's hands would be trivial, lending itself to but a few quick yuks. But Mel Brooks portraying a 2,000-plus-year-old man inspires a blitz of dialect and absurdist humor that is surpassed only by Richard Pryor. Unlike Pryor, though, Brooks is apolitical, and the ancient Jew he impersonates bounces off things banal (food, historical celebrities) and abstract (the evolution of language, the family and religion). They say it was unrehearsed, but genial Reiner's questions sound carefully phrased and ordered; this does not spoil anything, however. — K.T.

THE REMAINS
★ ★ ★ ★ The Remains / Spoonfed (1978)
★ ★ ★ ★ Diddy Wah Diddy / Eva (1982),
   Fr. imp.
Led by guitarist/vocalist Barry Tashian, the
Remains were one of the finest American
bands during the British Invasion. Unfortunately, only one poorly recorded album was
issued at that time. These two sets both expand upon that basic set of material. The
Eva set includes nineteen songs, all of which
are also included on the Spoonfed set. Anyone who liked "Don't Look Back" on the
Nuggets collection, or simply has a fondness
for stripped-down mainstream American
rock of the period, will enjoy these.   — D.M.

RENAISSANCE
★ ★ ★ In the Beginning / Cap. (NA)
★ ★ ★ Prologue / Cap. (1972)
★ ★ ★ Ashes Are Burning / Cap. (1973) ¶
★ ★ ★ Turn of the Cards / Sire (1974)
★ ★ ★ Scheherazade and Other Stories /
   Sire (1975)
★ Live at Carnegie Hall / Sire (1976)
★ ★ Novella / Sire (1977)
★ ★ A Song for All Seasons / Sire (1978)
★ Azure d'Or / Sire (1979)
★ Camera, Camera / IRS (1981)
A classical rock group that, unlike its more
overbearing brethren, concentrated on a
lighter, almost folkier sound. The focus was
piano and acoustic guitar (as opposed to the
synthesizer/electric guitar lineup of Yes,
Emerson, Lake and Palmer and their ilk)
and the soaring voice of Annie Haslam. Unfortunately, their approach worked only sporadically, because for all the progressiveness
that the music was assumed to have had
(more by the group, probably, than anyone
else), the band's limitations prevented anything but the most redundant reiteration of
its style.
   Prologue and *Ashes Are Burning* (the first
two records of the post-Keith Relf/Jim
McCarty period; those two ex-Yardbirds had
formed the original outfit) displayed some
promise, but *Turn of the Cards* and *Scheherazade* seemed like carbon copies. The live
album was the beginning of the end. Their
inability to compose songs that would allow
for any fluidity or improvisation was fully
revealed by the note-for-note duplication,
supplemented by an orchestra, of their
"greatest hits." Renaissance's appeal, nonexistent in their native England and cultish at
best in America, declined afterwards, and
the remainder of the Sire material matches
this commercial decline with an artistic one.
The comeback attempt on IRS (whose head

honcho Miles Copeland had once managed
and produced them) was a ludicrous failure.
   — W.K.

RENALDO AND THE LOAF
★ ★ ★ Songs for Swinging Larvae / Ralph
   (1981)
Recorded in a living room by a pair of Englishmen known only as Renaldo M. and Ted
the Loaf, *Songs for Swinging Larvae* is a disturbing blend of tape loops, high-pitched vocals, Gregorian chants, metal combs, glockenspiels, bouzoukis, floodrums, hacksaw
blades, horse whinnies, otherworldly declamation and, apparently, an all-mouse chorus
on speed. Abstruse sounds understood as
music only by minds functioning in a coma
state from which death follows.   — D.MC.

JOHN RENBOURN
★ ★ ★ Sir John—Alot of Merrie Englandes
   / Rep. (1969) ¶
★ ★ ★ The Lady and the Unicorn / Rep.
   (1970)
★ ★ ★ John Renbourn / Rep. (1972) ¶
★ ★ ★ ★ Faro Annie / Rep. (1972) ¶
Renbourn and fellow folk guitarist Bert
Jansch were moving forces in the British
folk-rock group Pentangle, which was sort of
a mellow man's Fairport Convention in the
late Sixties and early Seventies. These LPs
feature a lot of flashy guitar work, but it's
ultimately somnolent: all of it good, and
Faro Annie especially so, but nothing really
breathtaking as this kind of folk music can
be at its best.   — D.M.

RENE AND ANGELA
★ Rene and Angela / Cap. (NA)
★ Wall to Wall / Cap. (NA)
Not the Patience and Prudence of today.
   — D.M.

R.E.O. SPEEDWAGON
★ ★ ★ R.E.O. Speedwagon / Epic (1971)
★ ★ ★ ★ R.E.O./T.W.O. / Epic (1972)
★ ★ ★ Ridin' the Storm Out / Epic (1973)
★ ★ Lost in a Dream / Epic (1974)
★ ★ This Time We Mean It / Epic (1975)
★ ★ R.E.O. / Epic (1976)
★ ★ R.E.O. Speedwagon—Live: You Get
   What You Play For / Epic (1977)
★ ★ You Can Tune a Piano But You Can't
   Tuna Fish / Epic (1978)
★ ★ Nine Lives / Epic (1979)
★ ★ High Infidelity / Epic (1980)
★ ★ A Decade of Rock 'n' Roll / Epic
   (1980)
★ ★ Good Trouble / Epic (1982)
It took R.E.O. Speedwagon seven albums to

earn a gold record, which makes it one of America's least successful but longest-lived bands commercially as well as aesthetically. Without a distinctive vocalist or material that's more than humdrum, R.E.O. Speedwagon has steadfastly maintained its status as a poor man's Jo Jo Gunne, a perennial opening act that's never quite qualified as a headliner.

The debut, *R.E.O. Speedwagon,* is interesting primarily for its "bar band makes good" atmosphere, complete with Jerry Lee Lewis piano riffs. *T.W.O.* showed added maturity and power; the version of "Little Queenie" is marred only by weak singing. But the three albums that followed *(Ridin' the Storm Out, Lost in a Dream,* and *This Time We Mean It)* are slicker and less energetic, a rejection of heavy-metal beginnings for a stab at Doobie Brothers–style pop rock. In 1976, with *R.E.O.,* the group returned to the *T.W.O.* approach, modified by some of the California influences of the three previous LPs. And while the 1977 *Live* seemed risky at the time—a two-record set for a band that had never been able to come across effectively on one?—it brought them gold, perhaps because of its predictability, which includes every bread-basket heavy-metal cliché down to the Chuck Berry encore. It was followed by *You Can Tune,* which is about as fresh as its title. The fish did not better with age, as subsequent R.E.O. material proved. However, it did dredge up a whole string of Top Forty hits in a bouncy, cute style. — A.N.

REPLACEMENTS
★ ★ ★ **Sorry Ma, Forgot to Take out the Trash / Twin T. (1981)**
Good-humored Minneapolis hard-core punk band that comes on like the early Ramones, but with a high-speed lead guitar on top of the frantic rhythm playing. Because they totally refuse to take themselves or what they do too seriously, they retain an air of fun and avoid the posturing that has affected so many groups like them for the worse. Who knows if we'll ever hear from them again? Who really cares? — D.S.

THE RESIDENTS
★ ★ ★ **Meet the Residents / Ralph (1974)**
★ ★ ★ **Third Reich 'n' Roll / Ralph (1975)**
★ ★ ★ **Fingerprince / Ralph (1976)**
★ ★ ★ ★ **Not Available / Ralph (1978)**
★ ★ ★ **Buster and Glen/Duck Stab! / Ralph (1978)**
★ ★ ★ ★ **Eskimo / Ralph (1979)**

★ ★ ★ **The Residents Commercial Album / Ralph (1980)**
★ ★ ★ **Mark of the Mole / Ralph (1981)**
These anonymous San Francisco-based comic avant-pop terrorists live on rock's lunatic fringe, conducting fascinating (if occasionally dense) experiments in sound texture and song structure with traces of inspiration as various as serious composers like Edgard Varèse and Luciano Berio, early Zappa/ Mothers circa *Freak Out* and *Lumpy Gravy,* and garage-punk. Their wicked sense of parody (the cover sendup of *Meet the Beatles* on their 1974 debut) and prankish promotional ways (limited edition records, playing one of their only two live shows wrapped in bandages) is refreshing compared to the humorless Madison Avenue approach of most record companies.

But it's not always easy to hear the music through the mischief. What at first may seem like arrhythmic banging, hokey voices and nonmelodies on *Meet the Residents* and *Fingerprince* is really traditional Western ideas of music turned over, under, sideways and down in novel, often dramatic combinations. The most accessible examples of this are *Third Reich 'n' Roll*—a collection of bizarre interpretations of Sixties rock classics like "In-a-Gadda-Da-Vida"—and the short songlike framework of *Buster and Glen/ Duck Stab!* (actually a compilation of two EPs). *Not Available* is probably their most successful record compositionally, a remarkably fluid work that combines Mike Oldfield's romantic gestures, the liquid electro-drift of German rock, and Zappa's Varèsian orchestral variations. On the other hand, their most conceptually ambitious record, *Eskimo*—a musique concrète opera of primitive Arctic life—is also the hardest to listen to. And the only problem with the *Commercial* album is that because of its forty 60-second songs (commercials, get it?) the best ideas are over before they can even get started.

The Residents, in summation, are a lot of things. Dull isn't one of them. — D.F.

MARTIN REV
★ ★ **Infidelity / Lust/Unlust (1980)**
Martin Rev is the musician half of the duo Suicide. This album is filled with synthesizers, sequencers and just about anything synthetic they could find. The music is usually very interesting, but on the better cuts (the first side in general), once you've really gotten into a piece, it's already faded out. — K.L.

PAUL REVERE AND THE RAIDERS
★ ★ ★ ★ **All-Time Greatest Hits / Col.**
(1972)
Although they're best remembered as a sort
of American answer to the British Invasion,
the Raiders were actually around for several
years before the Beatles struck; they even
had a local hit, "Like Longhair," in the Pacific Northwest in 1961. In 1965, Dick Clark
tapped them for his L.A. rock show, *Where
the Action Is,* and there the group's Revolutionary War costumes and lead singer Mark
Lindsay's ponytail made them seem a sort of
British Invasion band satire: not unlike a
pre-packaged Monkees. But the Raiders
began grinding out a series of hits in 1965,
with "Steppin' Out" and "Just like Me,"
that continued through 1967. The group's
best-known song is "Kicks," an antidrug
song written by Barry Mann and Cynthia
Weil, which manages to convey its message
without losing its cool.

The Raiders continued as a band of sorts
until the nether end of the Sixties, when
Mark Lindsay assumed command and the
name was shortened. Thereafter they pursued a pop-rock direction that was much less
satisfying. — D.M.

REVILLOS
★ ★ ★ **Rev Up / UK Snatzo/Dindisc (1980)**
The Rezillos apparently weren't crazy
enough, so singers Eugene Reynolds and Fay
Fife left that band to set up the Revillos. A
truly awesome creation, the Revillos are a
melting pot of mod glitter and camp/sf
threads visually, Sixties mock-commercial
sensibility and neo-punk pulse beat musically. *Rev Up* is packed with thirteen loving
pop parodies, including a Ventures-style instrumental ("Secret of the Shadow") and reworkings of "Cool Jerk" and "Hippy Hippy
Sheik" (sic). Thanks to Fay and the "Rev-
ettes," the Revillos often feature a girl-group
sound ("Bobby Come Back to Me," "Scuba
Boy Bop"). The album is largely an adrena-
line-pumper, but on the rare occasion when
the Revillos pause for breath ("Hungry for
Love," "On the Beach"), they prove to be
winsome as well as humorous. Hilarious
liner notes too. — S.I.

THE REVOLUTIONARIES
★ ★ **Black Ash Dub / Troj. (1978)**
★ ★ ★ **Reaction In Dub / Cha Cha (1979)**
★ ★ ★ **Gold Mine Dub / Greens. (1979)**
★ ★ ★ **Rockers Almighty Dub / Clock.
(NA)**
★ ★ **Negrea Love Dub / Troj. (1979)**
★ ★ ★ **Outlaw Dub / Troj. (1977)**

The Revolutionaries are Sly and Robbie's
band, the premier instrumental group in reggae. They've made countless dub LPs; none
are bad and several are outstanding. Only a
dub fanatic would need more than a couple.
— R.F.G.

THE RHEAD BROTHERS
★ **Dedicate / Harv. (NA)**
Sappy Seventies easy-listening rock. Others
preferred. — J.S.

RICE AND BEANS ORCHESTRA
■ **Rice and Beans Orchestra / Dash (1976)**
■ **Crossover / Dash (NA)**
Despite rootsy New Orleans title, the sine
qua non of this Miami disco formula act's
repertoire is "The Blue Danube Hustle, Part
One," and believe me, there's no need to
wait around for part two. — D.M.

TONY RICE
★ ★ ★ ★ **Tony Rice / Roun. (1976)**
★ ★ ★ ★ **Manzanita / Roun. (1978)**
★ ★ ★ ★ ★ **Mar West / Roun. (1980)**
★ ★ ★ ★ **The Bluegrass Album / Roun.
(1980)**
Rice is one of the best acoustic guitarists in
the world, a player of superb technical skill
and unparalleled feel who is primarily responsible, along with mandolinist David
Grisman, for the new wave of bluegrass performers who have expanded the traditional
medium into active modern form. Grisman
calls it dawg music; Rice calls it spacegrass.
Tony Rice and *Manzanita* are excellent collections of interpretative material featuring
Grisman and a number of other good players, including Richard Greene *(Tony Rice)*
and Sam Bush *(Manzanita)* on violin. *Mar
West* is a superb album of Rice originals and
a Miles Davis tune, "Nardis," which showcases an instrumental section that ranges
from bluegrass to jazz in a blaze of virtuosity. *The Bluegrass Album* is a pretty collection of solid performances of traditional material. — J.S.

CHARLIE RICH
★ ★ ★ ★ **Set Me Free / Epic (1968)**
★ ★ ★ ★ ★ **The Fabulous Charlie Rich /
Epic (1969)**
★ ★ ★ ★ **A Time for Tears / Sun (1970)**
★ ★ ★ ★ **Boss Man / Epic (1970)** ¶
★ ★ ★ ★ **The Best of Charlie Rich / Epic
(1972)** ¶
★ ★ ★ **Behind Closed Doors / Epic (1973)**
★ ★ ★ **Greatest Hits, Vol. 1 / Power (1974)**
★ ★ ★ **Greatest Hits, Vol. 2 / Power (1974)**
★ ★ ★ ★ **The Early Years / Sun (1974)**

★ Very Special Love Songs / Epic (1974)
★ ★ ★ Arkansas Traveller / Power (1974)
★ ★ The Silver Fox / Epic (1975)
★ ★ Every Time You Touch Me / Epic (1975)
★ ★ ★ She Loved Everybody but Me / Camd. (1975)
★ ★ ★ Too Many Teardrops / Camd. (1975)
★ Silver Lining / Epic (1976) ¶
★ ★ ★ Greatest Hits / Epic (1976)
★ ★ ★ Tomorrow Night / RCA (1976) ¶
★ ★ ★ ★ Lonely Weekends / Sun. (1969)
★ ★ Rollin' with the Flow / Epic (1977)
★ Take Me / Epic (1977) ¶
★ ★ ★ Big Boss Man/My Mountain Dew / RCA (1977) ¶
★ ★ Classic Rich / Epic (1978)
★ ★ Classic Rich, Vol. 2 / Epic (1978)
★ ★ I Still Believe in Love / U.A. (NA)
★ ★ ★ So Lonesome I Could Cry / Hi (NA)
★ Fool Strikes Again / U.A. (1979)
★ Nobody but You / U.A. (1979)
★ Once a Drifter / Elek. (1980)
★ I Do My Swingin' at Home / Epic (1981)
★ ★ ★ Sun's Best of Charlie Rich / Sun (NA)

Charlie Rich was perhaps the most inspired of all the singers who followed Elvis Presley and Jerry Lee Lewis out of Sam Phillips' Sun Studios, the birthplace of rockabilly. He is not only a first-rate rock singer—"Lonely Weekends" is his masterpiece in the genre—but also an adept country vocalist, a superb jazz-influenced pianist and a moving blues crooner. His early career was checkered, and many of that period's recordings are now released on a variety of repackages (Sun, Power Pak, Camden, RCA, Hi). Its peaks were "Lonely Weekends" (Sun, 1958) and "Mohair Sam" (Smash, 1963). The best sides he cut were done for Sun, but his best country singing was done at Smash, with producer Jerry Kennedy. Later he recorded for RCA's Groove subsidiary, and did a single album for Hi that is one of the fundamental country-meets-the-blues LPs.

In the late Sixties, Rich moved to Epic Records in Nashville and hooked up with producer Billy Sherrill. Their early collaborations were superb: culminating in *The Fabulous Charlie Rich,* which contains perhaps the greatest song ever written about a working-class loser—"Life Has Its Little Ups and Downs," written by Charlie's wife, Margaret Ann. But it was not until 1973's "Behind Closed Doors" that Rich became a big star. That song and a couple of the followups were excellent pop music, though not nearly

as country as their high ranking on that genre's charts would indicate. But after hitting the big time, Rich succumbed—to his drinking problem and to the blandishments of Vegas big bucks, which meant equally bathetic arrangements, to which Sherrill was already prone in any case. The last few years have been sad ones.
— D.M.

CLIFF RICHARD
★ ★ It's All in the Game / Epic (1964) ¶
★ ★ ★ I'm Nearly Famous / EMI (1976)
★ ★ ★ Every Face Tells a Story / EMI (1978)
★ ★ Green Light / EMI (1978)
★ ★ We Don't Talk Anymore / EMI (1979)
★ ★ I'm No Hero / EMI (1980)

Before the Beatles, Cliff Richard was England's answer to American rock. He began as a sort of mini-Elvis, with a backup group called the Shadows, who included a guitarist, Hank Marvin, an important influence on many British guitarists of the Sixties. But Richard converted to England's variety of fundamentalist Christianity, and whatever spark of spunk had been in his music was snuffed, though he continued to make the British charts throughout the Sixties. In the mid-Seventies, Rocket, Elton John's label, signed him up, and "I'm Nearly Famous" became his most successful American single. Unfortunately, nothing he's done since then amounts to much, just a more or less uninspired version of Elton's own style of pop-rock vision. — D.M.

LIONEL RICHIE
★ ★ ★ ★ Lionel Richie / Mo. (1982)

Because Richie is a crooner rather than a bopping funkster, he doesn't always get the critical respect he deserves. But "Truly," for all its romanticism, is as sweetly sung as any ballad in recent memory, and the rest of his album sustains that standard of quality. It would be nice to have him add some of the Commodores' style funk occasionally, but Richie is an exceptionally gifted pop stylist even without it. — D.M.

THE RICH KIDS
★ ★ ★ Ghosts of Princes in Towers / EMI (1978), Br. imp.

After leaving the Sex Pistols, bassist Glen Matlock put together a band with former Slik and future Ultravox member Midge Ure. The result, hard-rocking pop, loses most of its promise in Mick Ronson's dense production. — W.K.

JONATHAN RICHMAN
★ ★ **Jonathan Richman and the Modern Lovers / Beserk. (1976)** ¶
★ ★ **Rock and Roll with the Modern Lovers / Beserk. (1977)** ¶
★ ★ **Modern Lovers "Live" / Beserk. (1978)** ¶

In his original incarnation as the hyperthyroid lead singer of the Modern Lovers, Richman gave new hope to the socially inept. He looked like the kid who stumbled over his own feet in the high school lunchroom and got the shit kicked out of him by the football team on general principles: short hair, sloppy clothes, no cool. But a real genius for apt metaphor was expressed in songs like "Road Runner," "Pablo Picasso" and "Government Center."

On *Rock and Roll* and *"Live"* Richman lost his vision and became once more a teenage twerp, warbling about Veg-a-Matics and other garbage, replacing the Lover's flat punk rock with even flatter folkie music. Now you know *why* everybody picked on that kid in high school. — D.M.

RIDERS IN THE SKY
★ ★ ★ **Cowboy Jubilee / Roun. (NA)**
★ ★ ★ **Three on the Trail / Roun. (NA)**

This Western swing vocal group is precise and state of the art, but its approach is a little too academic. Of course, they cover "Ghost Riders in the Sky" (on *Three on the Trail*). — J.S.

TOMMY RIDGLEY
★ ★ ★ ★ **The New King of the Stroll / Flyr. (1976)**

Ridgley is one of the more interesting minor names in New Orleans R&B, and this album shows why. For the most part, these tracks were recorded in the early Sixties (several years after the Stroll was in vogue) for Ric, a local label. Ridgley began recording in the late Forties, and his best-known sides were done for Atlantic. He remains influenced by Fats Domino (not surprisingly, since both worked with writer/arranger Dave Bartholomew), though Ridgley's voice is more raspy and higher-pitched, closer to the other King of the Stroll, Chuck Willis. He's accompanied here by Huey Smith's Clowns (as Johnny Williams and the Tic Tocs) on "Should I Ever Love Again." Worthwhile listening for R&B fans. — D.M.

SHARON RIDLEY
★ ★ ★ **Stay a While with Me / Phil.-L.A. (1975)**

Better-than-average vocalist on a set of tradi-tional R&B ballads produced and written by Van McCoy and Joe Cobb. "You Sold Me a One-Way Ticket" is a high point, right out of Holland-Dozier-Holland. — J.S.

RIFF RAFF
★ ★ **Vinyl Futures / Atco (NA)**

Raucous noise—can be bettered elsewhere in genre, though. — D.M.

THE RIGHTEOUS BROTHERS
★ ★ ★ ★ ★ **The Righteous Brothers' Greatest Hits, Vol. 1 / Verve (1967)** ¶

Blue-eyed soul was all the rage from 1963 to 1966, thanks to the Rascals, Mitch Ryder and this duo. The Righteous Brothers were only Bill Medley and Bobby Hatfield, but they often sounded like a choir, adapting the approach of the Isley Brothers and Ike and Tina Turner to a male team sound. Their first hit, "Little Latin Lupe Lu," which also scored for Ryder, came on Moonglow Records in 1963. But in 1964 they joined Phil Spector's Philles label and immediately recorded one of the giants of the blue-eyed soul genre, "You've Lost That Lovin' Feelin'," which remains one of the best-produced rock records ever made, and one of the most wildly emotive. "Lovin' Feelin' " set a pattern for the group's other hits—Spector's Wall of Sound and tremulously paranoid lyrics in a call-and-response pattern were also the format of such hits as "Ebb Tide," "Just Once in My Life," "Soul and Inspiration" and "Go Ahead and Cry." All of these are here, and none of them miss a trick. Anyone who likes Hall and Oates, for instance, should faint when they hear *this* stuff. — D.M.

BILLY LEE RILEY
★ **Billy Lee Riley in Action / Cres. (1966)**

Riley was once a hot session guitarist for Sam Phillips at Sun, accompanying Jerry Lee Lewis, Roy Orbison and others in the heyday of rockabilly, and recording a few masterful sides himself. (The most well-known of them is the delightful "Flying Saucers Rock 'n' Roll," in which little green men come to this planet to boogie.) Such gems of nonsense and power are available on many of the Sun rockabilly compilation albums. The album above, recorded ten or more years later, is not so much mistitled as misspelled: *Billy Lee Riley Inaction* is more like it. — D.M.

JEANNIE C. RILEY
★ ★ ★ **Harper Valley P.T.A. / Plant. (1968)**
★ **Yearbooks and Yesterdays / Plant. (1969)**

★ Things Go Better with Love / Plant. (1969)
★ ★ Country Girl / Plant. (1970)
★ Generation Gap / Plant. (1970)
★ ★ Jeannie C. Riley's Greatest Hits / Plant. (1971)
★ ★ Jeannie / Plant. (1971)
★ Girls Girls Girls / Plant. (1977)
★ ★ Jeannie C. Riley and Fancy Friends / Plant. (NA)
★ ★ Twenty Great Hits / Plant. (NA)
★ ★ Wings to Fly / Heartw. (NA)
Jeannie C. Riley is famous for her cover of Tom T. Hall's anti-hypocrisy classic, "Harper Valley P.T.A." The song was hot enough to launch her career and prompt her manager, Shelby Singleton, to start a new record label (Plantation) behind it. But Riley never came up with another vehicle as good, and she slowly faded into country music history. — J.S.

RIMSHOTS
★ ★ ★ Party / Stang (1976)
★ ★ ★ Down to Earth / Stang (1976)
Competent funk, for all those who think that the primary musical sound at the core of the universe is probably "shooogity-boogity-shoop." And who knows, it might be true. — D.M.

JERRY RIOPELLE
★ ★ ★ Jerry Riopelle / Cap. (1971) ¶
★ ★ Second Album / Cap. (NA)
★ Take a Chance / ABC (NA)
Average and occasionally pleasant Seventies singer/songwriter with a penchant for understated funk arrangements. — J.S.

MINNIE RIPERTON
★ ★ ★ Perfect Angel / Epic (1974)
★ Come to My Garden / Janus (1974) ¶
★ ★ Adventures in Paradise / Epic (1975)
★ ★ Stay in Love / Epic (1977)
★ ★ Minnie / Cap. (1979)
★ ★ Love Lives Forever / Cap. (1980)
★ ★ Best of Minnie Riperton / Cap. (1981)
Riperton had a multi-octave voice, which made her the Yma Sumac of progressive soul. "Lovin' You" from *Perfect Angel* was a hit in 1975, but everything from then until her death from cancer in 1979 was downhill. — D.M.

THE RITCHIE FAMILY
★ ★ Arabian Nights / Mar. (1976)
★ ★ Life Is Music / Mar. (1976)
★ ★ African Queens / Mar. (1977)
★ ★ American Generation / Mar. (1978)

★ ★ Bad Reputation / Casa. (1980)
★ ★ Give Me a Break / Casa. (1980)
Miami soul's all-female answer to the Jackson Five lacks either the distinctive vocal personality of Michael Jackson or the group's excellent material. The tracks are hard, funky and tight, in the characteristic TK-combine fashion, but there's not enough coloration to make them worthwhile. — D.M.

JEAN RITCHIE
★ ★ ★ A Folk Concert / Folk. (1959) ¶
★ ★ ★ Concert at Town Hall / Folk. (1962)
★ ★ ★ Jean Ritchie and Doc Watson at Folk City / Folk. (1963)
★ ★ ★ None But One / Sire (1977) ¶
Ritchie hails from the Cumberland Mountains of Kentucky and was largely responsible for the popularization of the mountain dulcimer during the Sixties. *None But One* attempts, with intermittent success, to bridge the traditional/contemporary gap—a rock rhythm section just doesn't always adapt to her original or traditional songs. *Folk Concert* is shared with Oscar Brand and David Sear, and is more representative of her vocal and instrumental style (listen to "Shady Grove") than the Sire LP, although the recording quality of *Folk Concert* is exceptionally poor. The other Folkways recordings are technically, if not artistically, superior. — I.M.

TEX RITTER
★ ★ ★ Blood on the Saddle / Cap. (1960)
★ ★ ★ Hillbilly Heaven / Cap. (1961)
★ ★ ★ The Best of Tex Ritter / Cap. (1965)
★ ★ ★ An American Legend / Cap. (1973)
The John Wayne of country music—although Ritter wasn't as formidable a singer as Wayne was an actor. But like Wayne, Ritter has a reputation as both a cowboy and a reactionary of the old school. Ritter's best-known song, aside from a large repertoire of cowboy classics, was "Hillbilly Heaven," a maudlin epic that describes a dream in which Tex sees all the deceased heroes of country music. It has spawned innumerable parodies since, though it would be going too far to describe the song as influential—weird and gushingly sentimental are closer to the truth. — D.M.

SCARLET RIVERA
★ Scarlet Rivera / War. (1977)
★ Scarlet Fever / War. (1978)
Bob Dylan's Rolling Thunder Revue violinist makes discofied gypsy music, more notable

for its pretentiousness than its charm.
— D.M.

JOHNNY RIVERS

★ ★ Changes / Imper. (1966)
★ ★ ★ A Touch of Gold / Imper. (1969)
★ ★ ★ ★ Johnny Rivers / U.A. (1972)
★ ★ L.A. Reggae / U.A. (1972) ¶
★ ★ ★ Blue Suede Shoes / U.A. (1973)
★ ★ New Lovers and Old Friends / Epic (1975) ¶
★ ★ Wild Night / U.A. (1976) ¶
★ ★ Outside Help / Soul C. (1978) ¶
★ ★ ★ ★ Johnny Rivers' Golden Hits / Imper. (NA)
★ ★ Borrowed Time / RSO (NA)
★ ★ ★ Johnny Rivers' Greatest Hits / Imper. (NA)
★ ★ Romance / RSO (NA)
In the early Sixties, Rivers played the Los Angeles club circuit and eventually caught on at the Whiskey A Go Go, where the celebrity-studded crowds ate up his Baton Rouge-cum-New York white funk vocals and heavily rhythmic John Lee Hooker–derived boogie guitar playing. A live recording of Chuck Berry's "Memphis," from one of his Whiskey shows, became a hit, and Rivers was able to follow it with a couple more dance records (now all out of print) and singles ("Mountain of Love," "Maybellene," "Secret Agent Man," "I Washed My Hands in Muddy Water"), available on *Golden Hits.*

Rivers went on to become an MOR crooner, having some success with "Poor Side of Town" and "Tracks of My Tears"; a record executive (responsible for discovering the Fifth Dimension); and later a socially conscious Seventies singer/songwriter, covering James Taylor and recording "Come Home America," George McGovern's campaign song.   — J.S.

THE RIVINGTONS

★ ★ Papa-Oom-Mow-Mow / Lib. (1982)
One of the more marginal examples of recent major label reissue policy. "Papa-Oom-Mow-Mow" and "The Bird's the Word" are genuine R&B raunch classics, but whether you really need to hear "Mama-Oom-Mow-Mow" as well will tell you more about your own rock fanaticism than your taste. Of course I dug it.   — D.M.

ROADMASTER

★ Sweet Music / Mer. (1978)
★ Fortress / Mer. (1979)
★ Hey World / Mer. (1979)
American rock band of no discernible style, let alone genre. Unless poorly executed rock

cliché constitutes a genre. Two more LPs and it might.   — D.M.

HARGUS "PIG" ROBBINS

★ ★ Country Instrumentalist of the Year / Elek. (1977)
★ ★ Pig in a Poke / Elek. (1978)
★ ★ Unbreakable Hearts / Elek. (NA)
Robbins is a blind pianist who is one of Nashville's foremost sessionmen; he made his mark on rock by playing many of the piano parts on *Blonde on Blonde,* although his blindness apparently so intimidated Dylan that he was afraid to call Robbins by his studio nickname, "Pig." But these three LPs of C&W MOR don't do his talents justice; they're faceless Muzak for hayseeds.
— D.M.

MARTY ROBBINS

★ ★ ★ Gunfighter Ballads / Col. (1959)
★ ★ ★ More Gunfighter Ballads / Col. (1960)
★ ★ The Alamo / Col. (1960)
★ ★ More Greatest Hits / Col. (1971)
★ ★ Marty's Greatest Hits, Vol. 3 / Col. (1961)
★ ★ ★ Marty's Greatest Hits / Col. (1962)
★ ★ Return of the Gunfighter / Col. (1963)
★ ★ ★ What God Has Done / Col. (1966) ¶
★ ★ ★ The Drifter / Col. (1966)
★ ★ I Walk Alone / Col. (1968)
★ ★ My Woman, My Woman, My Wife / Col. (1970)
★ Christmas Album / Col. (1971)
★ ★ ★ The World of Marty Robbins / Col. (1971)
★ ★ ★ ★ All-Time Greatest Hits / Col. (1972)
★ ★ No Signs of Loneliness / Col. (1975) ¶
★ ★ ★ El Paso City / Col. (1976)
★ ★ Adios Amigo / Col. (1976)
★ ★ Don't Let Me Touch You / Col. (1977)
★ ★ Greatest Hits, Vol. 4 / Col. (1978)
★ ★ All-Around Cowboy / Col. (1979)
★ ★ The Performer / Col. (1979)
★ ★ With Love, Marty Robbins / Col. (1980)
★ ★ The Legend / Col. (1981)
★ ★ ★ El Paso / Col. (NA)
★ ★ Marty's Country / Col. (NA)
Best known today as a conventional country singer, Marty Robbins was a successful ballad singer in the mid-Fifties who helped bridge the gaps between country and rockabilly country and straight pop. His 1954 version of Arthur Crudup's "That's All Right" outsold Elvis Presley's superior Sun recording. But Robbins reached his pop peak in 1957, with "White Sport Coat," a Top Three

hit, and enjoyed a string of weepers that had considerable chart success and earned him the sobriquet "Mr. Teardrop."

Always more western-oriented than most country or rock singers, Robbins earned a No. 1 in 1959 with "El Paso," a gunfighter ballad of his own composition that led to the interesting series of *Gunfighter Ballads* and other cowboy-anthem albums. More recently he has recorded formula country songs, earning some occasional big country hits but not much pop success. — D.M.

ROCKIE ROBBINS
★ ★ **Rockie Robbins / A&M (1979)**
★ ★ **You and Me / A&M (1980)**
★ ★ **I Believe in Love / A&M (1981)**
Arghhh. MOR make-out soul, too well groomed—one's ears feel like they're wearing a three-piece suit that better not get wrinkled. Robbins has a pretty voice and each album has some pleasant listening, but hey, necking is not a nonwrinkle activity. He goes for a little much-needed roughness on *I Believe in Love,* which would be enjoyable if only his voice had been more predominant in the mix. And a pretty voice is all he's got. — L.F.

BRUCE ROBERTS
★ ★ **Bruce Roberts / Elek. (1977)**
★ **Cool Fool / Elek. (1979)**
This New York dandy is best known as one of lyricist Carole Bayer Sager's collaborators, but his solo work is distinguished more by perfect MOR production than by anything Roberts contributes. — D.M.

RICK ROBERTS
★ ★ **Windmills / A&M (1972)**
★ ★ **She Is a Song / A&M (1973)** ¶
★ ★ **The Best of Rick Roberts / A&M (1979)**
Roberts replaced Gram Parsons in the Flying Burrito Brothers, though not in the hearts of the group's fans. He cut these solo LPs between his stint with that group and the formation of Firefall, his current band. These feature plain pop melodies with country and bluegrass overtones, delivered with neither flair nor conviction and at usually lazy tempos. The few rocking moments lack strength. Roberts sports a sweet but unmoving tenor, and as an instrumentalist, he favors dull acoustic guitar strumming. Only the sometimes stellar backup musicians— David Crosby, Jackson Browne, Byron Berline and various Eagles—help raise this above the level of the really awful. — C.W.

PAUL ROBESON
★ ★ ★ **Ballad for Americans, Carnegie Hall Concert, Vol. 2 / Van. (1965)**
★ ★ ★ ★ **The Essential Paul Robeson / Van. (1974)**
A former All-American football player at Rutgers, a lawyer, concert artist, actor, humanitarian and leftist political activist, Paul Robeson was probably the most influential black performer of the late Forties and early Fifties for white audiences. His style, however, owes more to conventional operatic and popular singing than to any of the blues or gospel traditions of black culture. His rich baritone is best remembered for the searing interpretation of Jerome Kern's "Old Man River" and for the Earl Robinson cantata "Ballad for Americans." *The Essential* is a repackage of Volume 1 of his farewell Carnegie Hall concert (1958), coupled with another previously available LP of folk and classical concert pieces, in addition to "Ballad for Americans." *Ballad for Americans* includes more from the concert and some other material recorded about the same time. — I.M.

THE ROBINS
★ ★ ★ ★ **Best of the Robins / Cres. (1974)**
Excellent mid-Fifties R&B harmony group, whose reputation is enhanced by the fact that the same quartet later became the Coasters. "Smokey Joe's Cafe" is the big hit from this one. — D.M.

EARL ROBINSON
★ ★ **A Walk in the Sun / Folk. (1957)**
★ ★ **Earl Robinson Sings / Folk. (1960)**
Although rock will best remember Robinson as the composer of Three Dog Night's "Black and White," he was, more importantly, responsible for such cantatas as "Ballad for Americans" and "The Lonesome Train," and numerous TV and film scores. "Joe Hill," the labor anthem, and "The House I Live In" are also his compositions. His LPs are monotonous, but the songs are models of the craft. — I.M.

FENTON ROBINSON
★ ★ ★ ★ ★ **Somebody Loan Me a Dime / Alli. (1976)**
★ ★ ★ ★ ★ **I Hear Some Blues Downstairs / Alli. (1977)**
★ ★ ★ ★ **Mellow Blues Genius / P-Vine (NA), Jap. imp.**
Robinson is an exceptionally talented singer/ guitarist working in the urban blues tradition out of Chicago. He has been intelligently recorded by Alligator, one of the best labels

for contemporary blues, and his surefire, challenging solo style continues to push the boundaries of blues improvisation past previously recognized limits. Robinson is also a marvelous singer, who is equally adept at writing his own material as he is at covering standards. But it's his sometimes-incredible guitar playing that marks him as an original in a medium that prides itself on influence and imitation. — J.S.

L. C. "GOOD ROCKING" ROBINSON
★ ★ ★ **Ups and Downs / Arhoo. (1972)**
Blues-oriented multi-instrumentalist plays steel guitar, six-string and fiddle, all competently, but without inspiration.
— D.M.

SMOKEY ROBINSON
★ ★ ★ **Pure Smokey / Tam. (1974)**
★ ★ ★ ★ **A Quiet Storm / Tam. (1974)**
★ ★ ★ **Smokey's Family Robinson / Tam. (1975)**
★ ★ ★ **Deep in My Soul / Tam. (1977)**
★ ★ ★ **Big Time / Tam. (1977)**
★ ★ ★ **Love Breeze / Tam. (1978)**
★ ★ ★ **Smokin' / Tam. (1978)**
★ ★ ★ **Where There's Smoke / Tam. (1979)**
★ ★ ★ ★ ★ **Warm Thoughts / Tam. (1980)**
★ ★ ★ ★ **Being with You / Tam. (1981)**
★ ★ ★ **Motown Superstar, Vol. 18 / Mo. (NA)**
As the leader of the Miracles, Smokey Robinson had as much as anyone, even Berry Gordy, to do with formulating the Motown sound. When Smokey stepped away from the Miracles in the early Seventies (to become a Motown corporate vice-president), he swore he didn't want to make solo records, but his first, the now-deleted *Smokey* (Tamla 328), wasn't long in arriving. Interesting but erratic, it set the pattern for what followed. All of these albums have something to recommend them—most often Robinson's smooth tenor voice. But the best of all are those on which he wrote the material, generally much more reflective and personal than anything he tried with the Miracles. *Pure Smokey,* for instance, contains "Virgin Man," a fascinating attempt to explore male sexual inexperience and insecurity; *A Quiet Storm* is as romantic as songs he wrote for the Miracles, but more personally involved, and features one terrific groove, "Baby, That's Backatcha," for his voice; *Family Robinson* manages to make Robinson's sweetness come to terms with the contemporary black rock idiom, an explosive combination. *Motown Superstar* is an anthology of Robinson's

early solo work that adeptly excerpts all of the above albums.

Where There's Smoke represented Robinson's creative rebirth; at the advice of his son, he returned to a style closer to his Sixties one, and the result was his first major solo hit, "Cruisin'," a ballad as sinuous and sexy as any of his early best. This album also contains "Get Ready," a remake of the song he'd written for the Temptations in 1966, and one of the most danceable numbers of Smokey's solo career.

However, it was with *Warm Thoughts* that Robinson reestablished his complete mastery as a record maker. This album is his most wide-ranging solo work, but also his most completely realized. Stevie Wonder's "Melody Man," which is a tribute to one of his primary mentors; "Let Me Be the Clock" and "Into Each Rain Some Life Must Fall," extended-metaphor numbers akin to his best Miracles' songs; the disco-inflected "Heavy on Pride (Light on Love)"; and the touching duet with his wife, Claudette, on "Wine, Women and Song" make this one of the most sublime expressions of why they call it soul music in recording history. As Jean Renoir has written of Charles Chaplin, Smokey Robinson "takes note of the egotism and absurdity of the world, and like the early Christians, he meekly accepts it. It is an acceptance that softens the public heart and turns it away from violent solutions." This is the essence of Robinson's romantic convictions.

Being with You is not quite so transcendent, but it contains one masterpiece, the title track, the best ballad of Robinson's solo career, and an indication that as he enters his fifth decade as a man, his third as a performer, Smokey Robinson still has much important work ahead of him. — D.M.

SMOKEY ROBINSON AND THE MIRACLES
★ ★ ★ ★ **Greatest Hits from the Beginning / Tam. (1965)**
★ ★ ★ ★ ★ **Greatest Hits, Vol. 2 / Tam. (1968)**
★ ★ ★ **Tears of a Clown / Pick. (1970)**
★ ★ ★ ★ ★ **Anthology / Mo. (1974)**
★ ★ ★ ★ **Away We A-Go-Go / Mo. (1981)**
★ ★ ★ **Hi, We're the Miracles / Mo. (1981)**
★ ★ ★ **Doing Mickey's Monkey / Mo. (1981)**
★ **Live On Stage / Mo. (1981)**
Motown has deleted almost its entire catalogue of Sixties albums, except greatest-hits packages. The Miracles' *Hits from the Beginning* is the oldest Motown album still in

print. It contains twenty-two songs, all from the Miracles' earliest days. The material is ballad-oriented, and Smokey Robinson's falsetto sounds wildly erotic on songs like "You Can Depend On Me" and "I've Been Good to You." *Volume 2* is centered on the group's "classic" period, at the height of Robinson's powers as a songwriter, and includes mid-Sixties favorites like "The Tracks of My Tears," "I Second That Emotion" and "Going to A Go-Go." The *Anthology,* a three-record set, covers the Miracles from selected early hits through Robinson's departure. Naturally, there is a great deal of duplication among the first two greatest-hits sets and the *Anthology.* While the Sixties albums are no longer in the Motown catalogue, several have been reissued on Pickwick—but with modifications, including sleazier covers and fewer cuts per LP—nine songs from the original eleven to twelve. It seems a shoddy way to present some of soul's greatest music.

The four albums released in 1981 are reissues of mid-Sixties material and, with the exception of the poorly recorded *Live,* all are excellent. — J.MC.

TOM ROBINSON BAND
★ ★ ★ ★ **Power in the Darkness / Harv. (1978)**
★ ★ ★ **Tom Robinson Band TRB II / Cap. (1979)**
★ ★ **Sector 27 / IRS (1981)**
Overtly gay new-wave rock from England. Robinson is a bitter leftist polemicist, and songs like "Right on Sisters" are too full of rhetoric to be satisfying to any but the most doctrinaire ears. But the title song has a real majesty, and the group's English hit singles, "Grey Cortina" and "2-4-6-8 Motorway," have a raw hard-rock vitality that makes them work—and enhances the band's politics at the same time. — D.M.

VICKI SUE ROBINSON
★ ★ ★ **Never Gonna Let You Go / RCA (1976)**
★ ★ **Vicki Sue Robinson / RCA (1976)** ¶
★ ★ **Half and Half / RCA (1978)** ¶
★ ★ **Movin' On / RCA (1979)**
She started as an aspiring Broadway singer/actress, which may account for the uptown energy of "Turn the Beat Around," a truer "Boogie Down Broadway." The rest of *Never Gonna Let You Go* alternates ballads and Gloria Gaynor–type romps. *Vicki Sue Robinson* and *Half and Half* have Vicki moving downtown to the cabaret. It's "strictly for lovers," but she earns a shot on

the *Johnny Carson Show* before retiring to Atlantic City. — B.T.

ROCCO
★ ★ **Rocco / 20th Cent. (1976)** ¶
Undistinguished disco-funk from 1976. — D.M.

MAGGIE AND TERRE ROCHE
★ ★ ★ ★ **Seductive Reasoning / Col. (1975)**
This pair of New Jersey sisters operates in the Seventies post-folk idiom in much the same manner as Loudon Wainwright, joking their way through life's turmoil. Although they're a steady draw on the folk circuit and have recorded with third sister, Suzze, this LP is their only disc. But it's a winner. The Roches have a special interest in sexual neurosis that adds to their wit, and Maggie has a knack for getting away with outrageous rhymes: "clear to ya" and "cafeteria," for instance. The backup, by the Muscle Shoals Rhythm Section mostly, is superb, and the production—including a few tracks done by Paul Samwell-Smith and one by Paul Simon—is first-rate. Interesting for aficionados of the strange. — D.M.

THE ROCKATS
★ ★ **Live at the Ritz / Is. (1981)**
A recording of a show at Manhattan rock venue, LP's main claim to fame was speed with which it was pressed and distributed, primary note in publicity surrounding album release. Frantic and often clumsy renditions of songs older than band's members suggest the Rockats' grasp of rockabilly is tenuous at best. — G.A.

ROCKET 88
★ ★ ★ **Rocket 88 / Atl. (1981)**
Unknown Stone Ian Stewart and various celebrated sidekicks cook up some kind of storm in what passes in those circles for a wild, swinging set of blues. Ultimately pretty pedestrian, but vigorous and definitely less liable to cause brain damage than most other Stones' spinoffs and inheritors. — D.M.

THE ROCKETS
★ ★ ★ **The Rockets / Turn Up the Radio/ RSO (1979)**
★ ★ **No Ballads / RSO (1979)**
★ ★ ★ **Back Talk / Elek. (1981)**
Still another journeyman Detroit hard-rock band, heavy on the swagger and volume. Drummer John Badanjek and guitarist Jim McCarty both members of Mitch Ryder's Detroit Wheels in mid-Sixties. Badanjek (who calls himself Johnny Bee) went on to

work with Edgar Winter, Alice Cooper and Dr. John, while McCarty played with Siegel-Schwall Blues Band and the Buddy Miles Express and was third member of Cactus. Rockets' vocalist Dave Gilbert sang for Ted Nugent a decade ago. Despite richness of experience and connections, these three albums showcase a band hobbled by pedestrian ideas. *Back Talk* was produced by Jack Douglas, instrumental in the rise of Aerosmith. Rockets' first LP, 1977's *Love Transfusion,* was distributed by RCA and is no longer available. — G.A.

ROCKIN' SYDNEY AND HIS DUKES
★ ★ ★ **They Call Me Rockin' / Flyr. (1974)**
Swamp blues, wild, crude and rockin'. If you're looking for something to make Slim Harpo seem as cosmopolitan as Duke Ellington, you've hit the spot. Recorded in Louisiana between the late Fifties and 1965, *They Call Me Rockin'* includes all of Sydney's collector's classics; reference points for the uninitiated include Harpo, Cookie and the Cupcakes, Jimmy Reed and Freddy Fender at his least coherent. — D.M.

ROCKPILE
★ ★ ★ **Seconds of Pleasure / Col. (1980)**
Although the quartet of Nick Lowe, Dave Edmunds, Bill Bremner and Terry Williams had played on previous Lowe and Edmunds solo albums, contractual difficulties prevented any product from being released under the group name. It's a shame, then, that this is the only record that carries the Rockpile logo; while this LP is more than competent in the Chuck Berry/rockabilly/rock & roll style the band had played since its inception, the inspiration isn't there. Nick Lowe's penchant for off-the-wall songwriting (displayed fully on his own eclectic *Pure Pop for Now People*) is probably the missing ingredient. Surprisingly, it was the dominant Edmunds who left after the album's release, halting the acclaim that Rockpile's live reputation had secured. — W.K.

JESS RODEN
★ **Keep Your Hat On / Is. (1976)**
★ ★ **Blowin' / Is. (1977)**
★ ★ **Player Not the Game / Is. (1977)** ¶
★ ★ **Stonechaser / Is. (1980)**
Roden's a better-than-average blue-eyed soul singer from England whose recorded work is spotty. *Player Not the Game* is a decent studio effort, but the live set, *Blowin',* shows him and band in excellent form, a funk complement to Robert Palmer. — J.S.

JIMMIE RODGERS
★ ★ ★ **Jimmie the Kid / RCA (1961)** ¶
★ ★ ★ ★ **Country Music Hall of Fame: Jimmie Rodgers / RCA (1962)** ¶
★ ★ ★ ★ **Short but Brilliant Life of Jimmie Rodgers / RCA (1963)** ¶
★ ★ ★ ★ **My Time Ain't Long / RCA (1964)** ¶
★ ★ ★ ★ **Best of the Legendary Jimmie Rodgers / RCA (1965)**
★ ★ ★ ★ **Never No Mo' Blues / RCA (1969)** ¶
★ ★ ★ ★ **Train Whistle Blues / RCA (1969)** ¶
★ ★ ★ ★ **My Rough and Rowdy Ways / RCA (1975)**
★ ★ ★ ★ **A Legendary Performer / RCA (1978)** ¶
With the exception of Hank Williams, Jimmie Rodgers is undoubtedly the most important figure in country & western music; he was discovered in 1927, in the same Cumberland Mountains area where the Carter Family was also beginning its career. As the Singing Brakeman, it was Rodgers—far more than Woody Guthrie—who was the true voice of the Depression. Among his greatest records were "Blue Yodel," "Mule Skinner Blues," "Yodeling Cowboy Blues" and "Somewhere Down Below the Dixon Line," although dozens of his songs have entered the standard country and folk music repertoire.

Rodgers had been suffering from TB for several years before his first recordings, and he died in 1933 of that disease. This helped enhance his legend, and set the pattern for a great many other white recording stars (Hank Williams, Elvis, etc.) who burned out young. But his records remained best-sellers through the Fifties and into the Sixties. Each of them is of more than moderate value, although the *Legendary Performer* set is perhaps the best annotated. — D.M.

JIMMIE RODGERS
★ **Yours Truly / Roul. (1968)**
Not the country singer but a pop-folk stylist with the same name who had a few hits in the late Fifties; "Honeycomb" and "Kisses Sweeter than Wine" are the best known. His career ended after an alleged police beating. — D.M.

JOHNNY RODRIGUEZ
★ ★ ★ **Introducing Johnny Rodriguez / Mer. (1973)**
★ ★ **Reflecting / Mer. (1976)** ¶
★ ★ **Practice Makes Perfect / Mer. (1977)** ¶

★ ★ **Just for You** / Mer. (1977)
★ ★ ★ **Great Hits of Johnny Rodriguez** /
Mer. (NA)
★ ★ **Love Me with All Your Heart** / Mer.
(1978)
★ ★ **Rodriguez** / Epic (1979)
Chicano country singer got his start as guitarist in Tom T. Hall's band and eventually became Hall's protégé. Producer Jerry Kennedy went to work on him and Rodriguez soon had a string of Seventies country pop hits: "Pass Me By," "Ridin' My Thumb to Mexico," "That's the Way Loves Goes," "Just Get Up and Close the Door," "Hillbilly Heart" and "If Practice Makes Perfect." Like Freddy Fender, Rodriguez alternates singing Spanish and English verses.
— J.S.

THE RODS
★ **The Rods** / Ari. (1981)
Deep Purple meets Van Halen in central New York State. In the opening cut ("Power Lover"), the trio is already asking, "if you know what I mean," which at this point most everyone assuredly does. The Rods have a logo, a rap (David Feinstein wants to be known as "the meanest, loudest, fastest man ever to pick up a guitar") and a song entitled "Get Ready to Rock 'n' Roll." Uriah Heep also features in the formula someplace. Enough said? — G.A.

TOMMY ROE
★ ★ **Energy** / Monu. (1976)
★ ★ **Full Bloom** / Monu. (1977)
★ ★ **Sheila** / Acc. (NA)
Dull attempts at a Seventies comeback by the kid who did "Dizzy" and "Sweet Pea," which were obnoxiously catchy pop-rock hits of the middle Sixties. — D.M.

D. J. ROGERS
★ ★ ★ **D. J. Rogers** / Shel.
(1973)
★ ★ ★ **Love, Music and Life** / RCA
(1977) ¶
★ ★ ★ **Love Brought Me Back** / Col.
(1978) ¶
★ ★ **The Message Is Still the Same** /
Col. (NA)
★ ★ **Trust Me** / Col. (NA)
D. J. Rogers is a former member of gospel singer James Cleveland's choir, and Cleveland's influence still holds sway over Rogers' vocal delivery and phrasing. Also like Cleveland, Rogers possesses an unremittingly harsh singing voice. His albums are rhythmically stiff and tend to fall back on funk clichés, but midtempo songs and ballads reveal

a rude power that transcends much of the studio junk. Rogers is also a capable songwriter. — J.MC.

JIMMIE ROGERS
★ ★ **That's Alright** / Black and Blue (1974),
Br. imp.
★ ★ **Chicago Blues** / J.S.P. (NA), Br. imp.
★ ★ ★ **Jimmie Rogers** / Chess, (NA), Br.
imp.
Magnificent guitarist with the Muddy Waters Band for many years, Rogers' recordings on his own aren't as good as those with Muddy, but he played with many of the same fine musicians (Little Walter, Willie Dixon, Otis Spann, Walter Horton, Waters himself) and came up with some hot tracks that are definitely worth a listen, or three. They're collected—twenty-five of 'em—on the Chess import. The others are more recent, and not nearly as hot. — D.M.

KENNY ROGERS
★ **Kenny Rogers and the First Edition's**
Greatest Hits / Rep. (1971)
★ **Love Lifted Me** / U.A. (1974)
★ **Kenny Rogers** / U.A. (1975)
★ **Daytime Friends** / U.A. (1976)
★ ★ **Ten Years of Gold** / U.A. (1978)
★ **Love or Something Like It** / U.A. (1978)
★ ★ **The Gambler** / U.A. (1978)
★ **Every Time Two Fools Collide** / U.A.
(1980)
★ **Gideon** / U.A. (1980)
★ **Kenny** / U.A. (1980)
★ ★ **Share Your Love** / Lib. (1981)
★ **Kenny Rogers' Christmas** / Lib. (1981)
★ **Classics** / U.A. (1979)
★ ★ **Greatest Hits** / U.A. (1980)
Who would have thought, when Kenny Rogers and the First Edition scored a 1968 hit with "Just Dropped In to See What Condition My Condition Was In," that this prime-time psychedelia would later evolve into pop-country superstardom via "Ruby Don't Go to Town"? Who would have cared? But beginning with "Lucille" in 1977, and continuing with "The Gambler," from his conceptual MOR LP of the same name, Rogers has become the biggest name in slick country pop, a balladeer more sensual and sensible than Eddie Rabbitt, though not a bit less jive. The proliferation of his recordings is not especially meaningful—at his most ambitious, Rogers approaches occasional competence—and if you're a fan of such hits as "Lady" and "Don't Fall in Love with a Dreamer," you ought to be buying 45s anyhow. *The Greatest Hits* isn't a bad selection, but it isn't up-to-date. — D.M.

ROLLING STONES/The Early Years
★ ★ ★ ★ **The Rolling Stones / Lon. (1964)**
★ ★ ★ ★ **12 × 5 / Lon. (1965)**
★ ★ ★ ★ ★ **The Rolling Stones, Now! / Lon. (1965)**
★ ★ ★ ★ **Out of Our Heads / Lon. (1965)**
★ ★ ★ **December's Children (And Everybody's) / Lon. (1965)**
★ ★ ★ ★ ★ **Big Hits (High Tide and Green Grass) / Lon. (1966)**
★ **Got Live If You Want It / Lon. (1966)**
★ ★ ★ ★ ★ **Around and Around / Decca (NA), Br. imp.**

As everyone past infancy should know, the Rolling Stones in their initial incarnation were the greatest white blues and R&B band that ever was. This is not legend; it is fact. Unfortunately, the magnitude of their talent did not prevent them from making frequently spotty albums. Even in 1964, when the group first recorded, Keith Richards was the world's greatest Chuck Berry–style guitarist, Charlie Watts and Bill Wyman the most existentially funky rhythm section in music, and Brian Jones served as blues freak extraordinaire and musical director. But the early Mick Jagger's charisma could not make up for a lack of confidence and stylistic range. Although modeled after Muddy Waters, Slim Harpo, Solomon Burke and Otis Redding, too many of his vocals simply miss the mark. Worse, some of the early songs written by Jagger/Richards miss by more.

Around and Around, the import, is a fabulous look at the early days; it includes "Poison Ivy," the Stones' astounding version of Chuck Berry's "Bye Bye Johnny," and Jagger/Richards' best early song, "Empty Heart." It contains much of what's on *12 × 5* but is more coherently organized, and the liner photo of Jagger and the cop is a scream. On the other hand, the first LP (subtitled *England's Newest Hitmakers*) is the hardest R&B the Stones (or anyone) ever recorded. Besides "Not Fade Away," their first U.S. hit, it has another Berry marvel, "Carol"; "Tell Me," another strong original; and some first-rate Chicago blues. But it is also padded (with an instrumental version of "Can I Get a Witness," for one). *Now* is not—it is spare but powerful, and includes some benchmark Stones material: the obligatory Berry tune is "You Can't Catch Me," but the finest songs here are "Mona" and "Everybody Needs Somebody to Love," expropriated from Bo Diddley and Solomon Burke, respectively. *12 × 5* ranges from the wonderful "Time Is on My Side"—a true portent—to the

simply silly "Under the Boardwalk."

Out of Our Heads and *December's Children* let the focus slide slightly from blues/R&B to rock & roll. *Heads* includes some archetypal Jagger poses—"Satisfaction," "Play with Fire," "The Last Time," "The Under Assistant West Coast Promotion Man," as well as Burke's "That's How Strong My Love Is," Jagger's best pure soul vocal. It's padded, though, with a couple of jams. *Children,* despite "Get Off My Cloud" and "I'm Free," takes a distinct dip; "Route 66" and "As Tears Go By" haven't aged well, and the original writing is weak while the cover material scrapes the barrel bottom.

High Tide and Green Grass is both brutal and beautiful, one of the finest rock & roll collections ever assembled, not to mention its photography, which captures the essence of the early Rolling Stones completely. Besides being the cream of the six early American LPs, it also featured the first LP appearance of "19th Nervous Breakdown," which set the stage for the psychotic rock that would dominate the group's passions through *Aftermath* and much of the rest of its career. (Regrettably, it does not include the group's two other similar 1966 hits, "Mother's Little Helper" and "Have You Seen Your Mother Baby Standing in the Shadow.")

ROLLING STONES/The Middle Years
★ ★ ★ ★ ★ **Aftermath / Lon. (1966)**
★ ★ ★ ★ **Between the Buttons / Lon. (1967)**
★ ★ ★ **Flowers / Lon. (1967)**
★ ★ ★ **Their Satanic Majesties Request / Lon. (1967)**
★ ★ ★ ★ ★ **Beggar's Banquet / Lon. (1968)**
★ ★ ★ **Through the Past, Darkly (Big Hits, Vol. 2) / Lon. (1969)**
★ ★ ★ ★ **Let It Bleed / Lon. (1969)**
★ ★ ★ ★ **Hot Rocks 1964–1971 / Lon. (1972)**
★ ★ ★ ★ **More Hot Rocks (Big Hits and Fazed Cookies) / Lon. (1972)**
■ **Metamorphosis / Abkco (1975)**

With *Aftermath,* the change begun with *Out of Our Heads* was complete. No longer were the Stones simply recycling the blues and R&B of the masters; now they had evolved a rock & roll form of their own. It was still rooted in black music (in some ways, Richards' giant, fuzzy guitar tones were a compensation for the band's lack of horns), but now the style was distinctly their own.

Aftermath has everything: "Paint It Black," a tormented and demented hit; the misogyny of "Stupid Girl" and "Under My Thumb," which made Jagger infamous; dark brooding stuff like "Flight 505" and "Goin'

Home." The instrumentation is remarkably diverse—Brian Jones chips in with dulcimer and sitar, and there are a variety of keyboards—while Jagger's singing begins to reach maturity. The album's one flaw is its tendency to pander to the Stones' audience's flagellant tendencies, but I'm not sure that's the Stones' fault.

Between the Buttons is almost lighthearted in contrast, a kind of demonic folk-rock record. There are a number of obscure treasures here—"My Obsession," "Connection," "All Sold Out," "Complicated"—as well as the hits "Ruby Tuesday" and "Let's Spend the Night Together." *Flowers* includes those songs, plus "Have You Seen Your Mother," "Mother's Little Helper" and *Aftermath*'s "Lady Jane," not to mention one of the most embarrassing white-soul fiascoes on disc, "My Girl." It does have "Ride On Baby," "Sittin' on a Fence" and "Backstreet Girl." So does the English version of *Buttons* (Decca SKL 4852), which is a recommended alternative.

Satanic Majesties is a bad idea gone wrong. The idea of making a truly druggy answer to the cherubic joyousness of the Beatles' *Sgt. Pepper* was silly enough. Doing so by fuzzing up some pretty good songs with tape loops and early synthesizer experiments is thoroughly unforgivable. Only "2000 Man," "In Another Land" and "She's a Rainbow" redeem this one.

Beggar's Banquet is closer to what *Satanic* aimed for anyway. Its theme is dissolution, and from the opening song—the infamous "Sympathy for the Devil"—to the final number—the bathetically charming "Salt of the Earth"—it is terrifying. "Street Fighting Man" is the keynote, with its teasing admonition to do something and its refusal to admit that doing it will make any difference; as usual, the Stones were more correct, if also more faithless, philosophers than any of their peers.

Through the Past, Darkly has been rendered redundant by the *Hot Rocks* sets. The first of those collections is a hodgepodge of the obvious, but *More* contains some gems and rarities: the B side, "Child of the Moon" is available nowhere else; side four—which features blues numbers, some Chuck Berry and R&B remakes like "Fortune Teller" and "Poison Ivy"—has been available only on foreign LPs. *Metamorphosis* was assembled by the group's former manager, and consists of useless demos, outtakes from the 1968 to 1970 era, and a lot of sheer garbage. An early version of "Memo from Turner" is interesting, and "Don't Lie to Me" is

decently done, but a wise person would pass this up, if only out of respect for the group.

Let It Bleed is a transitional LP. It could as easily fall into the Seventies grouping, although one or two of its key tracks— "Midnight Rambler" and the title track, particularly—are leftovers of *Aftermath*-style demonism. Some of the most frightening and beautiful music the Stones have made is here—"Gimme Shelter" encapsulates the former, "You Can't Always Get What You Want" the latter, until you listen closely, at which point the categories revise themselves still more. But, perhaps because Brian Jones had died and Mick Taylor was not fully integrated as his replacement, the record is erratic. Richards' vocal on "You Got the Silver" is evocative, but "Monkey Man" is silly, "Country Honk" an abomination in the face of the original "Honky Tonk Women" single. Some of the rest is just okay. A good one, though—you wouldn't want to be without "You Can't Always Get What You Want" and "Gimme Shelter," which are about as terminal as the Sixties got.

ROLLING STONES/The Seventies and Eighties

★ ★ ★ ★ 'Get Yer Ya-Ya's Out!' The Rolling Stones in Concert / Lon. (1970)
★ ★ ★ ★ Sticky Fingers / Rol. (1971)
★ ★ ★ ★ Exile on Main Street / Rol. (1972)
★ Goat's Head Soup / Rol. (1973)
★ ★ ★ It's Only Rock 'n' Roll / Rol. (1974)
★ ★ Made in the Shade / Rol. (1975)
★ ★ ★ Black and Blue / Rol. (1976)
★ ★ ★ Love You Live / Rol. (1977)
★ ★ ★ Some Girls / Rol. (1978)
★ ★ Emotional Rescue / Rol. (1980)
★ ★ Sucking in the Seventies / Rol. (1981)
★ ★ ★ Tattoo You / Rol. (1981)
★ ★ Still Life / Rol. (1982)

This is a muddled era, framed by concert albums that contain some of the greatest music the Stones have made, and some of the most dreadfully disconcerting. If such a long-lived and volatile rock & roll band can be said to be in transition, then that's the explanation; others say it was over the moment Mick Taylor joined the group, replacing Brian Jones. (Jones died several weeks later.)

Taylor appeared on one track of *Let It Bleed*, but he made his presence felt with the Stones' 1969 tour of America, and with *Ya-Ya's* (one result of it). Partly as a result of Jones' absence, partly because of Taylor's stinging slide guitar and blues background, the group became much less pop-oriented, concocting instead a salacious and brutal rock sound. "Stray Cat Blues" was nasty on *Beggar's Banquet,* but on *Ya-Ya's* it is malicious. So is a good deal of Jagger's posing, which is an embarrassment thirteen years later. Still, there were moments in that show (including "Carol," "Love in Vain," "Little Queenie" and the twin classics that frame this album, "Jumpin' Jack Flash" and "Street Fighting Man") when one could believe, love and fear every aspect of the Stones' myth.

Sticky Fingers, then, came as something of a shock. Aside from "Brown Sugar" and "Bitch," which open the respective sides, it is the most subdued Rolling Stones record ever made. But its gentler side hides real fury: "Moonlight Mile" is beautiful, but listen closely and you'll hear a ravaged tale. "Wild Horses" is not so much wistful as bitter, and the rest is a restless rush in search of a self-assurance that never comes. Richards and Taylor work together well, while Paul Buckmaster's strings and Watts' drumming on "Moonlight Mile" are rock & roll landmarks.

Exile on Main Street made the mood of rebelliousness grown stale that dominated *Sticky Fingers* more explicit. It was an attempt to break past the limits maturity imposed, and about half the time it succeeded: "Rocks Off," "Rip This Joint" and Keith's sardonic "Happy" are truly fearsome—just plain mean. But even the Stones couldn't sustain that much spite for four sides; too much of *Exile* is simply forgettable, though the best of what's there is as essential as any Stones' music—which is to say, as any music at all. "Tumbling Dice," incidentally, may be the best thing they've ever recorded.

Goat's Head Soup is a mistake, a jumble or the beginning of the end, depending on whom you ask. Jagger's poses are encapsulated—or should I say, embalmed—forever here, with claptrap like "Dancing with Mr. D.," which wouldn't scare a four-year-old. Only "Heartbreaker" and "Angie" are up to the usual level.

Only Rock 'n' Roll managed to avoid the questions of decline by tossing together the usual recycled Chuck Berry with a terrific reggae song, "Luxury," and a knife-in-the-back ballad, "If You Really Want to Be My Friend." It's full of filler, but it is also the Rolling Stones as we know them, no small thing.

Black and Blue is the Rolling Stones as we may have to learn to like them. The hard rock they drew from Chuck Berry is dissipated here—only "Crazy Mama" and "Hand

of Fate" show a hint of it. There are some interesting, if eventually tedious, rhythm numbers, like "Hot Stuff," a reggae not half so good as "Luxury," and not much else. Except that Jagger sings better than ever—in fact, it could even be said that he sings, in the traditional sense, for the first time, on songs like "Memory Motel" (a half-mocking sequel to "Moonlight Mile"), "Melody" and "Fool to Cry." He's also stepping away from his devilish image, as befits someone nearing middle age. The combination may prove fascinating. *Love You Live* is a live album, has no new material (unless some old Fifties blues numbers count) and reveals nothing, though the playing is far superior to the group's dreadful 1975 U.S. tour. What will be interesting, though, will be whether rock's most famous (did someone say best?) group can survive to middle age.

Some Girls was the group's biggest seller ever, thanks to market expansion and a hit single in "Miss You," which took the discofied accents of *Black and Blue's* "Hot Stuff" and tightened them up. But the old energy of the Stones is gone for good—tracks like "Shattered" and "When the Whip Comes Down" are hollow echoes of the Stones' best moments. Only Keith Richards' scabrous "Before They Make Me Run" has any sort of emotional power, and then only because of Richards' then-current heroin bust. (He seems to have gotten off almost scot-free, hardly an outlaw's comeuppance.)

If *Some Girls* is disappointing, *Emotional Rescue* is downright depressing: a blatant and shameless retread. *Sucking* is an anthology of the Stones' most recent work, not especially intelligently selected. *Tattoo You* returned the band to hard rock and gave it a couple more hits, but the thrill is gone: these were rock & roll veterans playing out the string, doing it with pure competence and without a hint of inspiration. Only those utterly enamored of Jagger's every gesture (or terminally addicted to Charlie Watts' backbeat) need to chose this, among all the other Stones' product around. — D.M.

THE ROMANTICS
★ ★ ★ **The Romantics** / Nemp. (1979)
★ ★ **National Breakout** / Nemp. (1980)
★ ★ **Strictly Personal** / Nemp. (1981)

"What I Like about You," from *The Romantics,* is a perfect re-creation of the best of British Invasion pop—the kind of song that keeps you believing in the magic of rock & roll. Unfortunately, a few great songs and well-chosen covers do not make great albums, and the first two LPs from this De-

troit quartet suffer from a sameness that
eventually becomes dullness. The Romantics
have the form down, but they don't transcend it, expand on it or make it their own.
Strictly Personal shows the band turning to
light heavy metal with no real success. This
group may have greatness in them if they
can locate it. — D.G.

MAX ROMEO
★ ★ ★ **War Ina Babylon** / **Is.** (1976)
★ ★ **Open the Iron Gate** / **U.A.** (1978) ¶
★ ★ **Reconstruction** / **Mango** (1978)
★ ★ ★ **Holding out My Love to You** / **Shan.**
  (1981)

Romeo was known early on for making the
most risqué kind of reggae; it's got a tough
rhythmic bite but isn't useful except as a
dance mechanism, as the U.A. LP demonstrates. By the time of the Island set, he'd
switched his concerns to include Rastafarian
politics (Babylon is everywhere except Jamaica and mythic Ethiopia) with a considerable improvement in interest value. Recently
Max has been reaching for a widely accessible reggae-soul-pop fusion. *Reconstruction* is
a well-intentioned but unconsummated experiment, while *Holding* uses rhythm masters Sly and Robbie and Rolling Stone Keith
Richard to create unified pop. Inconsistent
material keeps it from the heights of *War
Ina Babylon.* — D.M./R.F.G.

ROMEO VOID
★ **It's a Condition** / **415** (1981)

Romeo Void made a splash with critics and
on the new-wave circuit in 1981, but its
debut album makes one wonder what anyone
sees in them. Silly, solipsistic rantings by a
singer who sounds as if she's perpetually
aping Mae West and competent but hardly
inspiring playing and material offer nary a
clue as to the attraction of this Bay Area
combo. — D.S.

RONIN
★ ★ ★ **Ronin** / **Mer.** (1980)

New York session heavies again form a band
of their own. The result might be labeled
Ichabod Crane rock, though in comparison
to other such efforts (from the Section to
Toto), Ronin has so much energy that it
seems like a triumph. Such comparisons can
only be labeled deceptive. — D.M.

LINDA RONSTADT
★ **Hand Sown . . . Home Grown** / **Cap.**
  (1969)
★ ★ **Silk Purse** / **Cap.** (1970)
★ ★ **Linda Ronstadt** / **Cap.** (1972)

★ ★ ★ **Don't Cry Now** / **Asy.** (1973)
★ ★ ★ ★ ★ **Heart Like a Wheel** / **Cap.**
  (1974)
★ ★ **Different Drum** / **Cap.** (1975)
★ ★ ★ **Prisoner in Disguise** / **Asy.** (1975)
★ ★ ★ **Hasten Down the Wind** / **Asy.**
  (1976)
★ ★ ★ **Greatest Hits** / **Asy.** (1976)
★ ★ **Simple Dreams** / **Asy.** (1977)
★ ★ ★ **A Retrospective** / **Cap.** (1977)
★ ★ **Living in the U.S.A.** / **Asy.** (1978)
★ ★ ★ **Greatest Hits, Vol. 2** / **Asy.** (1980)
★ **Mad Love** / **Asy.** (1980)
★ **Get Closer** / **Asy.** (1982)

As the most important interpretative singer
of the singer/songwriter age, Linda Ronstadt
is an anomaly. The irony of her success is
compounded by the fact that, while she has
a remarkable voice, Ronstadt is an utterly
horrid interpreter of contemporary rock and
soul material, frequently missing the essence
of a song and almost never cutting below the
surface. If the measure of an interpreter's
skill is the ability to enhance the nuances of
a song, to give listeners a fresh perspective
on some grand old chestnut or insight into
the work of a budding composer, Ronstadt
must be judged at best a competent craftsman, and at worst an empty-headed, soulless
dispenser of music as sheer commodity.

Ronstadt's soprano voice is so rare in its
purity of pitch and tone that she can actually override and obscure such issues. However, her technical ability has not always
been able to save her: her early recordings
(after she left the folk-rock group, the Stone
Ponys, which brought her from Arizona to
Los Angeles) founder for lack of a creative
direction. Neither Ronstadt nor any of her
early producers had any idea what to do
with that gorgeous voice.

Manager/producer Peter Asher, who
stepped in for *Heart Like a Wheel* (her final
Capitol album of new material, but released
after *Don't Cry Now*) was able to organize
Ronstadt's talent efficiently. With hard-edged
arrangements by supersession player Andrew
Gold, Ronstadt's voice was finally pitted
against fine material and pushed to convey
some of the spirit as well as the outline of
the songs. "You're No Good" and "When
Will I Be Loved" actually are better than
the Betty Everett and Everly Brothers' originals, and the title song, written by Anna
McGarrigle, represents Ronstadt's first important discovery of a new writer.

Ronstadt fulfilled the same role for Cali-
fornia singer/songwriters in the mid-
Seventies that Judy Collins did for East
Coast writer/performers in the late Sixties.

Indeed, it can be argued that Ronstadt's most important artistic contribution has been giving exposure of such new songwriting talents as McGarrigle, Karla Bonoff and Warren Zevon to a wider public. In all three cases, while these writers do not possess anything close to Ronstadt's instrument, their original versions of the songs Ronstadt has recorded are as good as hers.

Exacerbating this problem has been Asher's attempt to create a formula for Ronstadt's production. In part this strategy is brilliant: Asher's sound is state of the art, and until Ronstadt sequestered herself on Broadway with *The Pirates of Penzance,* it produced a steady steam of hits. But a fundamental part of Asher's approach was to have Ronstadt record "oldies"—material by writers such as Buddy Holly and Smokey Robinson. For anyone who loves the original versions of "That'll Be the Day," "Ooh Baby Baby" or Roy Orbison's "Blue Bayou," "Back in the U.S.A." by Chuck Berry and Little Anthony and the Imperials' "Hurt So Bad," Ronstadt's heartless renditions are a travesty verging on sacrilege. She has robbed the soul from some of the greatest songs in the rock pantheon, rendered them as arch and leaden as the embalmed show tunes of the previous generation.

Nor have Ronstadt's attempts to record the work of composers outside the Hollywood singer/songwriter axis fared much better. Although her version of Elvis Costello's "Alison" is much admired in certain quarters, her "reinterpretation" strikes me as opaque and impersonal—its most important innovation is a gender switch, for which Ronstadt hardly deserves credit. One might imagine a dozen female singers doing as good or better with this number. And her awkward, strident remake of the Rolling Stones' "Tumbling Dice" is worse, despite Mick Jagger's background involvement; this is not the return of "You're So Vain."

In the end, Ronstadt belongs to an era past, when technical precision and sheer talent was considered more significant than emotional interpretative ability. Her Broadway debut in a Gilbert and Sullivan operetta amounts to typecasting. As her single attempt to make an all-out rock & roll record, the hapless *Mad Love,* demonstrates, Linda Ronstadt has nothing to contribute to a genre steeped in transcendence and passion. — D.M.

ROOMFUL OF BLUES
★ ★ **Roomful of Blues / Is. (1977)**
Boston-based big band defines blues as a medium with horns, a rare thing in rock. They swing it a bit, but the material is too conventional and the singing too uninspired to make this the imaginative success it deserves to be. — D.M.

ROOT BOY SLIM AND THE SEX CHANGE BAND
★ **Root Boy Slim and the Sex Change Band / War. (1978)**
★ **Zoom / IRA (1979)**
The first album is a truly wretched 1978 version of the kind of college prank that would have been mildly funny in 1961. Slim growls, but not so handsomely as Howlin' Wolf, and the band plays with absolute lack of feel. Another gem for the second-year men. *Zoom* is more of the same. — D.M.

ROSE
★ ★ **Behind the Line / Millen. (NA)**
★ ★ **Worlds Apart / Millen. (NA)**
Mediocre soft rock. — D.M.

THE ROSEHIP STRING BAND
★ ★ **The Rosehip String Band / Fly. Fish (1976)**
Autoharp-led old-timey style band; sonic pleasantries done in by the impoverished cuteness of the original material. — D.M.

ROSE ROYCE
★ ★ **In Full Bloom / Whit. (1977)**
★ ★ ★ **Rose Royce Strikes Again / Whit. (1978)**
★ ★ **Rainbow Connection IV / Whit. (1979)**
★ ★ **Greatest Hits / Whit. (1980)**
★ ★ **Jump Street / Whit. (1981)**
This nine-man progressive soul band was formed by Norman Whitfield to back up his latter-day Temptations productions. Whitfield named the group, added female vocalist Gwen "Rose" Dickey, then used them as the soundtrack artists for *Car Wash,* which gave them their first hit singles, "Car Wash" and "I Wanna Get Next to You." The subsequent releases haven't been as successful as the *Car Wash* theme, which went to No. 1. But the group's popularity has endured for several years, and that's something these days. — D.M.

ROSE TATTOO
★ ★ ★ **Rock 'n' Roll Outlaw / Mirage (1980)**
★ ★ ★ **Assault and Battery / Mirage (1981)**
Rose Tattoo are Australian hard rockers whose gritty attack makes AC/DC sound wimpoid. It isn't just that Rose Tattoo bludgeon the beat and boast a lead singer

who makes Bon Scott seem like a crooner. The band's blues chops are entirely credible, and its use of slide guitar adds bite that mere bluster could never equal. Too bad the songs aren't similarly inspired. — J.D.C.

DIANA ROSS

★ ★ ★ ★ **Lady Sings the Blues / Mo. (1972)**
★ ★ ★ **Mahogany / Mo. (1975)** ¶
★ ★ ★ ★ **Diana Ross / Mo. (1976)** ¶
★ ★ ★ ★ **Diana Ross' Greatest Hits / Mo. (1976)**
★ ★ **An Evening with Diana Ross / Mo. (1977)** ¶
★ ★ ★ **Baby It's Me / Mo. (1977)** ¶
★ ★ ★ **Ross / Mo. (1978)**
★ ★ ★ **The Boss / Mo. (1979)**
★ ★ ★ **Diana / Mo. (1980)**
★ ★ ★ **To Love Again / Mo. (1981)**
★ ★ ★ **All the Great Hits / Mo. (1981)**
★ ★ ★ **Why Do Fools Fall in Love ? / RCA (1981)**
★ ★ ★ **Touch Me in the Morning / Mo. (1981)**
★ **Live at Caesar's Palace / Mo. (1981)**
★ ★ ★ **Silk Electric / RCA (1982)**
Ross's career since she left the Supremes in 1970 has been checkered, but not as spotty as her solo LPs. *Baby It's Me* is a 1977 super-production job by the always bombastic Richard Perry, which works half the time, more or less. *An Evening with Diana Ross,* a live set, is predictably dull. The soundtracks are also middling: *Mahogany* has that film's hit single plus lots of filler, *Lady Sings the Blues* some remarkable (although probably unpalatable to fans of the originals) versions of Billie Holiday songs crowded together with Michel Legrand's pop-jazz bathos, which fills out the score. *Diana Ross,* from 1976, is one of her best solo LPs, including "Mahogany" and "Love Hangover"; "Good Morning Heartache," the best song from *Lady;* and her great early hits, "Ain't No Mountain High Enough" and "Reach Out and Touch Somebody's Hand," as well as her two worst hits, "Touch Me in the Morning" and "Last Time I Saw Him." Her more recent material is slicker, but not better, "Endless Love" not excepted. — D.M.

DIANA ROSS AND MARVIN GAYE

★ ★ ★ ★ **Diana and Marvin / Mo. (1973)**
Essentially a reworking of the old Marvin Gaye and girl singer cliché, which he'd made work before with such lesser lights as Mary Wells, Kim Weston and the scintillating Tammi Terrell. This one has some moments, especially the singles, "Don't Knock My Love" and "My Mistake"—more moments, in fact, than most of the LPs either Ross or Gaye has recorded separately since 1973, when this one was released. — D.M.

DR. ROSS

★ ★ ★ **His First Recordings / Arhoo. (NA)**
★ ★ ★ **One-Man Band / Tak. (NA)**
★ ★ **The Harmonica Boss / For. (NA)**
★ ★ **The Harmonica Boss / Big Bear (NA), Br. imp.**
★ ★ **Blues and Boogie from Detroit / Escha (NA), imp.**
Ross's one-man band act is even more eclectic than Jesse Fuller's, a pure minstrel/ medicine show extravaganza of black folk tradition (not just blues). His best work is on Arhoolie, which features tracks cut in the Fifties for Sam Phillips at Sun. The Takoma set, recorded live in 1965, is also good. Ross's guitar style is modeled on fellow Detroiter John Lee Hooker's, his harp playing on Sonny Boy No. 1, his repertoire familiar, but he's basically a true individualist. Not exactly your heavyweight stuff, but fine listening, and an important part of American musical heritage. — D.M.

ROSSINGTON COLLINS BAND

★ ★ ★ **Anytime, Anyplace, Anywhere / MCA (1980)**
★ ★ ★ ★ **This Is the Way / MCA (1981)**
Even though Gary Rossington, Allen Collins and two other members of this group are alumni of Lynyrd Skynyrd, the Rossington Collins band is hardly a Skynyrd Mk. II. *Anytime, Anyplace, Anywhere* makes a few tentative steps in that direction; any comparisons would have to be tempered by the obvious differences between RCB singer Dale Krantz and the late Ronnie Van Zant. Krantz's voice, lighter and more flexible than Van Zant's, opens up territory for RCB that was inaccessible to Skynyrd, although at the cost of hard-core boogie credibility. No matter, because the Rossington Collins Band sounds more at home when stretching out through *This Is the Way* than when pumping up the beat on *Anytime, Anyplace, Anywhere.* More significantly, by breaking free of the hell-raising clichés the band could have easily fallen into, RCB comes closer to achieving the Southern rock transcendence promised (but not achieved) by the Allmans than any band since. — J.D.C.

ROUGH DIAMOND

★ **Rough Diamond / Is. (1977)**
A 1977 minor-league all-star band featuring vocalist David Byron, a man so talented that

he was thrown out of Uriah Heep, unquestionably the worst rock band ever to earn a gold album. Rough Diamond isn't any improvement. — D.M.

DEMIS ROUSSOS
★ **Happy to Be / Mer. (1976) ¶**
★ **Magic / Mer. (1976) ¶**
★ **Demis Roussos / Mer. (1978)**
Big-time European pop singer fails to cash in on U.S. market. In some countries, this Greek-born pop singer is outsold only by Abba. Here he looks like a hairier Kojak, and though his singing is passable, it's nothing that Johnny Carson and Ed McMahon (even) could get shook up about. — D.M.

THE ROWANS
★ **The Rowans / Asy. (1975)**
★ **Sibling Rivalry / Asy. (1976)**
★ **Jubilation / Asy. (1977)**
Jerry Garcia called this group of Marin County wimps the California Beatles when the boys' first album was released in the early Seventies. One presumes he was tripping at the time. The most godawful hippie mindlessness since It's a Beautiful Day. — D.M.

ROX
★ ★ **Rox / Bdwalk (1981)**
Purveyors of "D-d-d-d-d-d-dance," dumbest stutter record since you know what. — D.M.

ROXY MUSIC
★ ★ **Roxy Music / Atco (1972)**
★ ★ ★ **For Your Pleasure . . . / Atco (1973)**
★ ★ ★ ★ **Stranded / Atco (1973)**
★ ★ ★ ★ **Country Life / Atco (1974)**
★ ★ ★ ★ ★ **Siren / Atco (1975)**
★ ★ ★ ★ **Viva! Roxy Music / Atco (1976)**
★ ★ ★ ★ **Greatest Hits / Atco (1977)**
★ ★ ★ **Manifesto / Atco (1979)**
★ ★ ★ **Flesh and Blood / Atco (1980)**
Roxy Music was one of the most intelligent and musically compelling rock groups to come out of Britain in the Seventies, and given the fact that the original band housed singer Bryan Ferry and experimental wizard Brian Eno, it was also one of the most influential. Yet Roxy was, superficially, primarily Ferry's vehicle—with his mannered singing and lyrics drenched in self-aware ennui, his songs and visual style made him Chairman of the Board.

Roxy's first two albums are groping for a style. While Ferry's songs were generally strong, there was a disparity between Eno's attraction to eccentric instrumentation and Ferry's relatively straightforward tunes. *For Your Pleasure* found Ferry's songs and the band's treatment of them coming closer to fruition, but following its release, Eno left to pursue a solo career while Eddie Jobson was added on keyboards and electric violin. Roxy proceeded to make its best music.

At its high point Roxy came on like the Concorde, sleek and metallic. *Stranded* fairly exploded with rockers like "Street Life" and "Serenade," while more unusual uptempo tunes like "Amazona" crackled with sustain-drenched electricity. What set Roxy apart from other progressive and art-rock bands, though, was its incredible drive, sustained by saxophonist Andrew MacKay and guitarist Phil Manzanera, but founded in the drumming of Paul Thomas, and the band's various bassists, most often John Wetton, a King Crimson veteran. The slower, more tortured tunes further developed Ferry's lonely Everyman persona, an image that burst with fury from *Country Life*'s opening track, "The Thrill of It All." The slickest and most accomplished Roxy music yet, *Country Life* found the group at the peak of its maturity.

Siren's title is appropriate; it has that sort of effect on the listener. It is Roxy's masterpiece, calling the listener back by virtue of its finely honed instrumental attack and compelling lyrical attitude. "Love Is the Drug," Roxy's nearest approximation to an American hit single, set the scene of transitory love in a plastic world, while "She Sells" and "Sentimental Fool" pictured the participants in the charade as simultaneously pathetic and heroic. It is the album's music, though—steely sleek and fiery to the core—that makes it a touchstone album of Seventies art rock. While *Viva!* captured the group at its onstage best, and the *Greatest Hits* set is a fine sampler, *Siren* remains the album by which their best work will be remembered, at least for now. *Manifesto* and *Flesh and Blood,* released after the band split up between 1976 and 1978, were good of their kind, but they lacked the spark that made some of the earlier albums so grand. — J.B.M./D.M.

BILLY JOE ROYAL
★ **Billy Joe Royal / Mer. (NA)**
Royal hit in 1965 with "Down in the Boondocks," a piece of half-successful white soul that isn't included on this comeback attempt. Since Royal isn't nearly as adept as Tony Joe White at putting swamp rock across, you don't need this. — D.M.

THE ROYAL GUARDSMEN

■ Snoopy vs. the Red Baron / Laur. (1967)
★ Return of the Red Baron / Laur. (1967)
■ Snoopy and His Friends / Laur. (1967)
■ Snoopy for President / Laur. (1968)

One tepidly interesting comic-strip spinoff hit ("Snoopy vs. the Red Baron," 1966) does not excuse four albums of the same variety of insipid drivel. — D.M.

ROY C.

★ ★ Sex and Soul / Mer. (1973)
★ ★ More Sex and More Soul / Mer. (1977)

Anyone daft enough to make reggae on Long Island, in a Hempstead garage, deserves points for bravado. If Roy C. weren't so patently exploitative of women, he might get a lot more for his music, which is propulsive but formulaic. — D.M.

RUBBER CITY REBELS

■ Rubber City Rebels / Clone (1977)

Initiators of Akron, Ohio's post-punk art-rock scene. This band's responsibility for Devo and Pere Ubu reaching an international audience with their Kent State grad school glop is reason enough for the rating. The Rubber City Rebels' own brand of radar blips and Pac-Man noises is merely a side effect, like a splitting headache accompanying the announcement that you have a terminal illness. — D.M.

RUBEN AND THE JETS

★ ★ ★ Ruben and the Jets / Verve (1973) ¶

This album of brilliantly rendered Fifties R&B vocal tunes indicates Frank Zappa's love for the form and his consummate stylistic chops despite the fact that many people took the whole thing as a joke. Of course Zappa's sardonic wit does play a role here, but that's in the fictional casting of the Mothers of Invention as a pre-*American Graffiti* Fifties cultural parody, not in the music itself. — J.S.

RUBY AND THE ROMANTICS

★ ★ Greatest Hits Album / MCA (1977)

"Our Day Will Come" was their only claim to fame, and one is probably well advised to pick up that girl-group staple on the multitudinous oldies collections. — R.G.

RUDY

■ Just Take My Body / Poly. (NA)

Only if it's better than your music. — D.M.

DAVID RUFFIN

★ Who I Am / Mo. (1975) ¶

★ ★ Everything's Coming Up Love / Mo. (1976) ¶
★ In My Stride / Mo. (1977) ¶
★ ★ ★ David Ruffin at His Best / Mo. (1978)
★ ★ So Soon We Change / War. (1979)
★ ★ Gentleman Ruffin / War. (1980)
★ ★ ★ ★ My Whole World Ended / Mo. (1981)

When David Ruffin left the Temptations in 1969 and scored an immediate success with "My Whole World Ended (The Moment You Left Me)," his future seemed as bright as any singer in soul. His raspy leads on many Temptations songs had earned him a wide following—Rod Stewart draws heavily on Ruffin's singing in his interpretations of soul songs—that needed only nurture (adequate production, good material) to flower. Unfortunately, he began to suffer from a program of benign neglect from the Motown production corps, which tossed him around like a hot potato, and he's never lived up to a fraction of that promise. There are a few good moments on *At His Best,* but nothing any ordinary singer couldn't do on the rest.

My Whole World Ended is a reissue of Ruffin's first post-Temptations album, and by far the best thing here. — D.M.

RUFUS

★ ★ Rufus / MCA (1973) ¶
★ ★ ★ Rags to Rufus / MCA (1974) ¶
★ ★ ★ ★ ★ Rufusized / MCA (1974) ¶
★ ★ ★ Rufus . . . Featuring Chaka Khan / MCA (1975) ¶
★ ★ ★ ★ Ask Rufus / MCA (1977) ¶
★ ★ ★ Street Player / MCA (1978) ¶
★ Numbers / MCA (1979) ¶
★ Masterjam / MCA (1979) ¶
★ Camouflage / MCA (1981)
★ Party Till You're Broke / MCA (1981)

In reality Rufus *is* Chaka Khan. No one else in the group has anywhere near her distinctive talent. But the fact that she has always had a group behind her, to write with, tour with and work out arrangements with seems to have saved her from some of the hysterical, narcissistic excesses of a Natalie Cole or Melba Moore. From album to album, she's grown as a singer. At the time of "Tell Me Something Good" and "You Got the Love," she was a powerful, somewhat freakish AM singer, with an incredible range. By the time of "Sweet Thing" (on *Rufus . . . Featuring Chaka Khan*) and *Ask Rufus,* she's become a rhythmical sophisticated stylist. Her theme is always unrequited love, or at least uncertain love, and in all her best songs—"You Got the Love," "Stop On By," "Sweet

Thing," "Better Days," "Ain't Nothing but a Maybe"—she's addressed herself to uninterested or indifferent men.

Her lucky break came during the afternoon when Stevie Wonder sat in on their recording session, and cooked up "Tell Me Something Good," a ditty that outsold his own current singles. *Rags to Rufus* was something more than a showcase for its two hit singles—including "Smoking Room"—but not that much more. The next album, *Rufusized*, was a fully realized piece of work in what was to become a new genre—the middle ground between rock and soul. Khan had obviously been doing some thinking about Janis Joplin, but her sensibility was as different from Joplin's as from Aretha Franklin's or Gladys Knight's. There's a spacy, moody air about the woman that doesn't easily fit into any established genre. On *Numbers,* without Chaka, the band is lost.   — R.G.

THE RUMOUR
★ ★ ★ **Max / Mer. (1977)** ¶
★ ★ **Frogs, Sprouts, Clogs and Krauts / Ari. (1979)** ¶
★ ★ **Purity of Essence / Stiff (1980)** ¶
Graham Parker's backing group has never been able to establish any identity of its own. *Max* is the most comfortable of the Rumour's three records, its Band-like stylization closest to the soul-derived playing with which they supported Parker. *Frogs, Sprouts* is a failed attempt at modern synthesized pop; *Purity,* without lead singer and songwriter Bob Andrews, is a rather lifeless power-pop collection.   — W.K.

THE RUNAWAYS
★ ★ **The Runaways / Mer. (1976)**
★ ★ **Queens of Noise / Mer. (1977)**
★ ★ **Waitin' for the Night / Mer. (1977)**
Put together by Kim Fowley, the Runaways were meant to be a female punk rock band. They have yet to achieve either a musical style or the visual arrogance to make one unnecessary, so they remain a subcultural cartoon show. Their first album has all the marks of an Alice Cooper ripoff, including sequences from an imaginary girls' prison movie. On *Queens of Noise* the band manages a lumpen Mott the Hoople instrumental manner, while Joan Jett sings most of the lead vocals.   — B.T.

TODD RUNDGREN
★ ★ ★ ★ ★ **Something/Anything / Bears. (1972)**
★ ★ ★ **A Wizard, a True Star / Bears. (1973)**

★ ★ ★ **Todd / Bears. (1974)**
★ ★ **Todd Rundgren's Utopia / Bears. (1974)**
★ ★ **Initiation / Bears. (1975)**
★ ★ ★ **Another Live / Bears. (1975)**
★ ★ ★ **Faithful / Bears. (1976)**
★ ★ ★ **RA / Bears. (1977)**
★ ★ **Oops, Wrong Planet / Bears. (1977)**
★ ★ **Hermit of Mink Hollow / Bears. (1978)**
★ ★ ★ **Back to the Bars / Bears. (1978)**

Todd Rundgren is an artist caught between two worlds: he is a student of modern technology, capable of turning out densely experimental music that relies more on form and process than content, but he is also an incurable romantic with a penchant for writing light, soulful ballads. As a result, his recorded work has been remarkably inconsistent. A whiz in the studio (Rundgren learned his engineering and production crafts while fronting Philadelphia's Nazz in the late Sixties), the early part of his studio career found him more often than not making albums almost totally on his own, playing all (or almost all) the instrumental parts and singing both lead and background vocals. *Something/Anything,* his third album (*Runt* and the beautiful *The Ballad of Todd Rundgren* are both Ampex cutouts), featured only him on three of its four sides. It remains the definitive Rundgren opus, an ambitious, challenging and completely successful venture into everything from Motown parodies ("Wolfman Jack") to pop ("Saw the Light," a hit single) to hard rock ("Black Maria"). *A Wizard* crammed almost an hour's worth of music onto its two sides, with mixed results. The ethereal "Sometimes I Don't Know What to Feel" demonstrated Rundgren's keen understanding of Philly soul, and "International Feel" and "Just One Victory" rose to anthemic proportions as progressive rock classics. Yet such mindless electronic noodlings as "Dogfight Giggle" and "Rock and Roll Pussy" demolished the album's flow. *Todd,* another two-disc set, sought to place both sides of the Rundgren persona into a more cohesive and less manic format. But the songwriting was weak, for the first time in Rundgren's prolific career, and since that record, he has shunted back and forth from group leader (Utopia) to solo performer. For the last few years, Rundgren has seemed adrift, without focus. *RA* is Utopia's clearest work, reminiscent in spots of the Nazz; *Faithful,* which sported one side of cover versions of such Sixties standards as "Good Vibrations" and the Beatles' "Rain," is the best of his more current solo efforts.
— B.A.

RUSH

★ Rush / Mer. (1974)
★ Fly by Night / Mer. (1975)
★ Caress of Steel / Mer. (1975)
★ ★ All the World's a Stage / Mer. (1976)
★ ★ ★ 2112 / Mer. (1976)
★ ★ ★ A Farewell to Kings / Mer. (1977)
★ ★ ★ Hemispheres / Mer. (1978)
★ ★ ★ Permanent Waves / Mer. (1980)
★ ★ ★ Moving Pictures / Mer. (1981)
★ ★ ★ Exit . . . Stage Left / Mer. (1981)

Canadian heavy metal trio Rush began as a poor man's Led Zeppelin with a bone-crunching live sound that built up a modest following on the arena circuit, a period encapsulated by the early albums and climaxing with the earnest live set *All the World's a Stage.* The band's dogged determination to improve finally paid off when their sound and conception suddenly gelled on *2112,* a science fiction concept album that stands up favorably against similar efforts by British counterparts. At this point drummer Neil Peart, bassist/keyboardist Geddy Lee and guitarist Alex Lifeson had proven their instrumental chops and proceeded to improve their songwriting. That goal was finally achieved on the breakthrough *Permanent Waves,* with its excellent hit single "Spirit of the Radio" and the beautiful "Jacob's Ladder." Though Lee's banshee vocals continued to be a source of irritation for some, his tremendous synthesizer programing helped expand the band's range. By the time of the second live set, *Exit . . . Stage Left,* Rush had become one of the top arena attractions around. — J.S.

BOBBY RUSH

★ ★ ★ Rush Hour / Phil. (1979)

Veteran blues-soul performer turns in modernized version of American roots, featuring echoes of everyone from Howlin' Wolf to Stevie Wonder. "Evil Is," "I Can't Find My Keys" and a surreal version of producers Gamble and Huff's old Jerry Butler hit, "Hey Western Union Man," highlight a rare treasure. — D.M.

OTIS RUSH

★ ★ ★ ★ Right Place, Wrong Time / Bull. (1976)
★ ★ ★ ★ Groaning the Blues / Flyr. (1980)

If you think the horror stories so common to blues legend are a thing of the past, a quick account of the troubles that plagued Otis Rush will set you straight. Widely recognized as one of the finest contemporary blues guitarists/singers/bandleaders, Rush was

bounced around from label to label and almost always treated with the utmost shabbiness until Albert Grossman landed him a long-term recording contract with Capitol in 1971. Under the direction of ex–Electric Flag vocalist Nick Gravenites, Rush went into the studio and recorded a blockbuster album with a tremendous band that spotlighted his bright, economical guitar playing. Capitol never released the master, and Rush finally had to bargain with the company to buy the tapes so he could release the record elsewhere. Bullfrog finally put the set out in 1976, and the record stands as a modern blues classic.

Groaning the Blues is the fundamental stuff—the original sides that Rush recorded for Cobra. — J.S.

TOM RUSH

★ ★ Mind Rambling / Prest. (1963)
★ ★ ★ Blues, Songs, Ballads / Prest. (1965)
★ ★ ★ Tom Rush / Elek. (1965)
★ ★ ★ ★ Tom Rush—Take a Little Walk with Me / Elek. (1966)
★ ★ ★ ★ ★ The Circle Game / Elek. (1968)
★ ★ ★ Tom Rush / Col. (1970)
★ ★ Wrong End of the Rainbow / Col. (1970)
★ ★ ★ ★ Classic Rush / Elek. (1971)
★ ★ ★ Merrimack County / Col. (1972)
★ ★ Tom Rush / Fan. (1972)
★ ★ Ladies Love Outlaws / Col. (1974)
★ ★ ★ The Best of Tom Rush / Col. (1976)

Primarily known as an interpreter of other songwriters' material, Tom Rush is one of a handful of singers who helped alter the definition of folksinger in the Sixties. His early work on Prestige/Fantasy placed him squarely in the folk-blues vein of contemporaries John Hammond and Koerner, Ray and Glover. But when he moved to Elektra in the mid-Sixties, Rush began experimenting both with different types of songs and stylistic approaches. *Take a Little Walk with Me* featured one side of rockers arranged by Al Kooper, with fine versions of Bo Diddley's "Who Do You Love" and Buddy Holly's "Love's Made a Fool of You." *The Circle Game* is Rush's high-water mark, with songs by then-unknown Joni Mitchell, Jackson Browne and James Taylor, as well as a stand-out original composition, "No Regrets." The atmosphere is exemplified by Rush's version of Mitchell's "Urge for Going." Its low-key, sparse arrangement characterizes the educated, wistful and warm style Rush had evolved. Moving to Columbia at the end of the decade, Rush found immediate success with *Tom Rush,* which included one of his best-known pieces, "Lost My Drivin' Wheel." Unfortunately, he was becoming progressively more mellow and laid-back each time out, and his last few releases were pleasant but innocuous. — B.A.

JIMMY RUSHING

★ ★ ★ If This Ain't the Blues / Van. (1974)
★ ★ ★ ★ ★ Every Day I Have the Blues / Blues. (1973)
★ ★ ★ ★ ★ The Essential Jimmy Rushing / Van. (1978)
★ ★ ★ ★ ★ Mister Five by Five / Col. (1980)
★ ★ ★ Going to Chicago / Van. (NA)
★ ★ ★ Listen to the Blues / Van. (NA)

Rushing is perhaps the greatest of the Kansas City blues shouters (who included Big Joe Turner and Walter Brown). Born in Oklahoma City, Rushing recalls hearing Bessie Smith as an early turning point in influencing his musical direction; in 1929 he made his first recording with Walter Page's Blue Devils (Count Basie playing piano). Rushing then fronted Benny Moten's band before joining Basie for his greatest years. For fifteen years Rushing was the mainstay of Basie's greatest organization, bellowing and crooning against that band's powerful horn section, until economic pressures in the Forties forced Basie to disband in favor of a smaller group.

The Vanguard sides were recorded by John Hammond with a small group of Basie sidemen. *Essential* collects the best moments of that era. Rushing recorded several good records for Bluesway, and *Every Day I Have the Blues* is a fine representation of that period. There's no question that Rushing is best served working with a full band rather than the small combos he recorded with on the Vanguard sides, and here the Oliver Nelson Orchestra is a great foil. *Mister Five by Five* collects Basie's late-Fifties work for Columbia, again some with a full orchestra, some with interesting small combos like the Brubeck/Desmond group. These sides feature incredible performances: Rushing fronting a band with Buck Clayton, Coleman Hawkins and Jo Jones; Rushing fronting Benny Goodman's band; Rushing in a vocal duet with Helen Humes. — J.S.

RICHARD RUSKIN

★ ★ ★ Richard Ruskin / Tak. (1974)
★ ★ ★ Microphone Fever / Tak. (1976)
★ ★ ★ Six String Conspiracy / Tak. (1977)

West Coast acoustic guitarist records for John Fahey's Takoma label but doesn't play like Fahey, using shorter melodic fragments and covering standards with droll but effective humor. *Richard Ruskin* includes a version of "Teddy Bear's Picnic." — J.S.

BRENDA RUSSELL

★ Love Life / A&M (NA)
★ Brenda Russell / A&M (NA)

Hapless Hollywood session singer, once part of duo (Brian and Brenda). Ain't Tammi Terrell here, either. — D.M.

LEON RUSSELL

★ ★ ★ Leon Russell / Shel. (1970)
★ ★ Asylum Choir 2 / Shel. (1970)
★ ★ ★ ★ Leon Russell and the Shelter People / Shel. (1971)
★ ★ ★ Carney / Shel. (1972)
★ ★ ★ Hank Wilson's Back / Shel. (1973)
★ ★ Will o' the Wisp / Shel. (1975)
★ ★ ★ Best of Leon Russell / Shel. (1976)
★ ★ Americana / Parad. (1978)
★ ★ Life and Love / Parad. (1979)
★ ★ Looking Back / Olym. (1979)
★ ★ Live Album / Parad. (1981)

Russell was a session piano player in Los Angeles in the mid-Sixties. In his spare time, he recorded his own material at his home studio, including the two Asylum Choir albums that were released years later. After touring and recording with Delaney and Bonnie, he met Joe Cocker's producer, Denny Cordell. Russell was signed to work on Cocker's second album. Russell went on to lead Cocker's touring band, Mad Dogs and Englishmen, and to record a couple of fine solo albums, *Leon Russell* and *Leon Russell and the Shelter People*. The latter is his best record, combining three different bands on a variety of material including two of his best originals ("Stranger in a Strange Land," "Home Sweet Oklahoma") and interesting covers of Bob Dylan's "It's a Hard Rain Gonna Fall" and "It Takes a Lot to Laugh, It Takes a Train to Cry."

Russell's material thinned out and his abrasive singing could not save average songs, so his later albums suffer. His only worthwhile record in recent years was the tribute to Hank Williams, *Hank Wilson's Back*. — J.S.

MARY AND LEON RUSSELL

★ Wedding Album / Parad. (1976)
★ Make Love to the Music / Parad. (1977)

The Steve and Edie of Seventies rock. Yawn. — J.S.

MIKE RUTHERFORD

★ ★ Smallcreep's Day / Char. (1980)

The guitarist/bassist for Genesis makes an

enjoyable but hardly essential solo debut, heavy on the epic grandeur and cathedral keyboards but light on memorable tunes. The side-long title piece sounds like "Supper's Ready" warmed over.

    — D.F.

THE RUTLES
★ ★ ★ **The Rutles / War. (1978)**
A marvelously precise Beatles parody, done by ex–Bonzo Dog Band member Neil Innes, former Monty Python collaborator Eric Idle and, among others, lonesome George Harrison. — D.M.

MITCH RYDER
★ ★ ★ **How I Spent My Vacation / Seeds and Stems (1978) ¶**
★ ★ **Naked but Not Dead / Seeds and Stems (1979) ¶**
★ ★ ★ **Live Talkies / Line (1981), Ger. imp.**
Compilations of Ryder's great blue-eyed R&B hits with the Detroit Wheels ("Devil with a Blue Dress On / Good Golly Miss Molly," "Jenny Take a Ride," "Sock It to Me!") come and go with such rapidity that it's almost impossible to keep up with them. Anyone who spots one, now matter how tawdry the packaging, would be well advised to pick up on it. In addition to Ryder, one of the all-time honky blues singers, the Wheels featured John Badanjek, a great drummer, and guitarist Jim McCarty, an estimable guitarist. (The latter pair now lead the Rockets.)

    On his own in recent years, Ryder has recorded three albums of confessional-oriented hard rock. Despite the sometimes dated arrangements, *How I Spent My Vacation* is a searing documentary look at the real price of pop stardom in the Sixties: buggery, ripoffs and a complete abandonment of self-esteem, isolation and eventual loss of any hold on reality. *Naked but Not Dead* is still stuck in those hackneyed arrangements (as if Ryder had to go through his personal psychedelic period to make up for not keeping current back when). But the emergence of some radical political stances led directly to the success of *Live Talkies,* which mixes Ryder originals (notably his attack on Reagan and Bush), covers of R&B standards in the fashion of his hits ("Long Tall Sally / I'm Gonna Be a Wheel Someday," "Take Me to the River") and a pair of excellent Dylan covers, "Subterranean Homesick Blues" and "Wicked Messenger." This is by far the best of Ryder's comeback albums, and it lent real hope for the potential of his 1983 collaboration with John Cougar. Twenty years on, Ryder may possibly make himself a voice to be reckoned with once more. — D.M.

SUE SAAD AND THE NEXT
★ **Sue Saad and the Next / Planet (1980)**
Another entry in the Spandex-rock sweepstakes. Richard Perry produced this abysmal
album filled with songs that are about nasty
men or tough rock & roll chicks. The band
can't play; Saad can't sing and lacks even
Pat Benatar's shopping-mall arrogance.
— D.G.

SABU
★ **Sabu / MCA (NA)** ¶
Bad L.A. rock & roll from a reconverted
disco producer, Paul Sabu, who was respon-
sible for Ann-Margret's hit disco LP.
— J.S.

SAD CAFÉ
★ ★ ★ **Misplaced Ideals / A&M (1978)**
★ ★ **Facades / A&M (1979)**
★ ★ **Sad Café / Swan (1981)**
Studied and occasionally exciting British sextet trades on R&B and jazz influences. The
formula is solid, the playing is superb, but
they never break through the structure. *Misplaced Ideals,* a compilation from the
group's first two British releases, gives the
clearest picture of what they were trying to
do. — J.S.

SAGA
★ **Saga / Poly. (1978)**
★ **Images at Twilight / Poly. (1980)**
Aimless Canadian band essays Anglo art
rock. — D.M.

CAROLE BAYER SAGER
★ ★ **Carole Bayer Sager / Elek. (1977)**
★ **Too / Elek. (1978)**
★ **Sometimes Late at Night / Elek. (1982)**
Viewed as a singer/songwriter, Sager seems
schizoid—she has written a few great songs
("You're Moving Out," say) and some utter
rubbish, working with a variety of collabora-

tors (notably Marvin Hamlisch) and with a
wide range of performers, from Barbra Streisand and Bette Midler to Wayne Fontana
and the Mindbenders. Viewed as a song-mill
hack, working within the limitations of people like Carole King, but without King's inspiration, Sager is seen more accurately as
an uncaring professional, to whom songs
carry no more emotional weight than shoes.
That is, rather than a minor artist, Sager is
ultimately only the least interesting sort of
craftsperson. — D.M.

DOUG SAHM
★ ★ ★ ★ **Best of the Sir Douglas Quintet /
Tribe (1965)** ¶
★ ★ ★ **Honkey Blues / Smash (1968)** ¶
★ ★ ★ **Mendocino / Smash (1969)** ¶
★ ★ ★ ★ **Together after Five / Smash
(1970)** ¶
★ ★ ★ ★ **1 + 1 + 1 =4 / Phi. (1970)** ¶
★ ★ ★ **The Return of Doug Saldana / Phi.
(1971)** ¶
★ ★ **Doug Sahm and Band / Atl. (1973)** ¶
★ ★ ★ **Rough Edges / Mer. (1973)** ¶
★ ★ ★ **Texas Tornado / Atl. (1973)** ¶
★ ★ **Texas Rock for Country Rollers / Dot
(1976)** ¶
★ ★ ★ **Hell of a Spell / Tak. (1979)**
★ ★ ★ ★ **Best Of / Tak. (1980)**
★ ★ ★ ★ **Border Wave / Tak. (1981)**
Doug Sahm is a walking encyclopedia of
Texas music—blues, country, Western swing,
vintage rock & roll, Cajun, R&B, even Mexi-
can border music—all of which is melted
into a bright, pulsating sound nobody else
has ever matched. The LPs listed rank with
some of the most interesting and influential
recordings of the late Sixties and early Seventies, and are fairly easy to scare up in bargain bins. The Tribe album contains mid-
Sixties British-influenced rock (the hit was
"She's About a Mover") anchored by Augie
Meyer's simple, rhythmic Farfisa organ.

With its classic bar-band sound, this can legitimately be considered the only example of Texas punk rock. *Together,* with its relaxed and easygoing groove, its unlikely combination of cover versions and spacy originals and its irrepressible spirit, is perhaps Sahm's most coherent and consistent album. In this case, the sloppiness only adds to the atmosphere; *1+1+1=4* is more bluesy, more country and more precise, as well as better produced, but the Texas soul still carries it. In this period (1969 to 1970), Sahm's voice was at its richest and most commanding. His lyrics are also a perfectly natural mingling of the cosmic and the earthy; they often make a moral point but are seldom moralistic.

Honkey Blues, on which horns augment the Quintet, is what happens when the white blues move from San Antonio to Big Sur and live on a steady diet of sunshine acid. It revels in all that was good with the psychedelic experience, but because this expression is rooted in blues, it never gets too far gone. *Mendocino* is a denser version of the original Tribe sound, with its Cajun two-step and Tex-Mex rhythms. The album is largely composed of demos not intended for release, and is thus another slapdash affair, but it hardly suffers for that.

The same is true of *Rough Edges,* a compilation of outtakes that doesn't sound appreciably worse than Sahm's finished products. The *Saldana* LP is a much-celebrated return to his roots, on the west side of San Antonio, via "Wasted Days and Wasted Nights" and the like. The greasy barroom songs are among his best records, but the album's strength is diminished by a couple of ill-conceived and aimless acoustic ditties.

The first Atlantic album *(Doug Sahm and Band)* is a supersession, produced by Jerry Wexler with help from Bob Dylan, but as sterile and bloodless as Sahm's early work was sloppy and full of life. Though some rock and blues are included, it's also his first overtly country album. Side two of *Texas Tornado* is prime Sir Doug in style and substance, heavy on Chicano influence, but the first side is pretty dull.

Hell of a Spell is a blatant attempt at AOR radio commerciality, while *Border Wave* marks a return to the original Sir Doug style. The Takoma *Best Of* collects some of the Quintet's best Mercury material.
— J.M.O.

SAILOR
★ ★ **Sailor** / Epic (1974) ¶
★ ★ **Trouble** / Epic (1975) ¶

★ **Dressed for Drowning** / Cari. (1980)
Sailor's first two LPs were ersatz Roxy Music; their chief innovation was a calliope, rock's first and only use of that instrument as a regular part of anyone's sound. It didn't help much, but it was far superior to the Queen clones of *Dressed for Drowning.*
— D.M.

BUFFY SAINTE-MARIE
★ ★ ★ **It's My Way** / Van. (1964) ¶
★ ★ ★ **Many a Mile** / Van. (1965)
★ ★ ★ **Little Wheel Spin and Spin** / Van. (1966)
★ ★ **Fire and Fleet and Candlelight** / Van. (1967)
★ ★ **I'm Gonna Be a Country Girl Again** / Van. (1968)
★ ★ **Illuminations** / Van. (1969)
★ ★ ★ **The Best of Buffy Sainte-Marie** / Van. (1970)
★ ★ **The Best of Buffy Sainte-Marie, Vol. 2** / Van. (1971)
★ ★ **She Used to Wanna Be a Ballerina** / Van. (1971)
★ **Moonshot** / Van. (1972)
★ **Quiet Places** / Van. (1973)
★ ★ ★ **Native North American Child (An Odyssey)** / Van. (1974)
★ **Sweet America** / ABC (1976) ¶
Buffy Sainte-Marie is best known as a Native American (Indian) folksinger and a frequent member of the cast of *Sesame Street.* But the best of her songs—"Universal Soldier," "Many a Mile" and especially "Until It's Time for You to Go"—have a convincing universality. As a participant in the folk-music revival of the early Sixties, Sainte-Marie was respected as much for the "authenticity" of her Cree background as for her rather underestimated talents as a writer. Her voice, a soprano with heavy vibrato, is perhaps too eccentric to gain her mass popular acceptance. And as she attempted to bridge the gap between the narrow world of folk and the broader horizons outside it, she has been subject to some egregious gaffes: *Moonshot,* in which she plays a sex-kittenish role, is downright embarrassing. The best of her work remains her early Vanguard albums, particularly *Many a Mile* and *It's My Way.* — D.M.

ST. PARADISE
★ **St. Paradise** / War. (1979)
Power trio has fine heavy-metal lineage— Ted Nugent, Montrose, Sammy Hagar— which only goes to show the difference between rock & roll and horse racing.
— D.M.

THE SAINTS

★ ★ **I'm Stranded / Sire (1977)** ¶
★ ★ ★ **Eternally Yours / Sire (1978)** ¶
★ ★ ★ **Prehistoric Sounds / Harv. (1978),**
  Br. imp.

In 1976, just as punk was emerging in England, the Saints in Brisbane, Australia, released "I'm Stranded" on their own independent label. A minor classic of the genre, the single got better reviews in England than at home, and the band immediately packed its bags. They achieved a modicum of success with the *I'm Stranded* album, which verges on the indecipherable but includes an unlikely cover of "Kissing Cousins" alongside more typically punkoid anger and angst.

Eternally Yours makes more accessible the literate, often vitriolic lyrics of guitarist Ed Kuepper and singer Chris Bailey. The addition of brass shifts the music from pure punk to a sort of warped soul, and Bailey's offhand snarl has become more self-consciously mannered. *Prehistoric Sounds* develops Kuepper and Bailey's wonderfully morbid perspective, in songs like "Swing for the Crime," "Everything's Fine" and "Church of Indifference." More horns contribute to an original sound that is best described as a melodic drone. The Saints disintegrated in 1978, but Kuepper has continued in the same vein with Laughing Clowns, who have achieved some recognition in Australia. Chris Bailey put together a new Saints lineup in 1980 with a rather more straightforward rock & roll sound and a great independent EP titled "Paralytic Tonight, Dublin Tomorrow." — S.M.

ST. TROPEZ

★ ★ **Belle de Jour / Butter. (NA)**
★ ★ **Je t'Aime / Butter. (NA)**

Disco internationalism—dance music's last resort. — D.M.

SALSOUL ORCHESTRA

★ ★ ★ **Salsoul Orchestra / Sals. (1975)**
★ ★ ★ **Nice 'n' Naasty / Sals. (1976)**
★ ★ ★ **Magic Journey / Sals. (1977)**
■ **Charo and the Salsoul Orchestra / Sals.**
  (1977)
★ **Up the Yellow Brick Road / Sals.**
  (1978) ¶
★ ★ **How High / Sals. (NA)**
★ ★ **Street Sense / Sals. (NA)**

A hot disco band, not really an orchestra. Most of the time, this group's very facelessness is an advantage; nothing gets in the way of the steaming tempos. But when they make attempts to expand their horizons—on the godawful *Charo* set and *The Wizard of Oz*

fiasco—the results have been pretty dire. Covers are often fascinating for their blatant sexism; chief case in point is *Nice 'n' Naasty*. — D.M.

SALSOUL STRINGS

■ **How Deep Is Your Love / Sals. (NA)**

Shameless elevator Muzak, discofied. — D.M.

SAM AND DAVE

★ ★ ★ ★ **The Best of Sam and Dave / Atl.**
  (1969)
★ ★ **Sweet and Funky Gold / Gusto (1978)**
★ ★ ★ **Sam and Dave / Rou. (NA), Ger.**
  imp.
★ ★ ★ ★ **Double Dynamite / Atl. (1980),**
  Jap. imp.
★ ★ ★ ★ **Soul Men / Atl. (1980), Jap.**
  imp.
★ ★ ★ ★ ★ **Hold On I'm Comin' / Atl.**
  (1980), Jap. imp.

Once Sam and Dave stood side by side with Otis Redding as the most formidable purveyors of Memphis soul. But Redding's death marked the beginning of a sharp decline for the two-fisted, double-punch brand of soul that Sam Moore and Dave Prater proffered, and in the Seventies the pair all but disappeared. Though their peak was brief (1965–1969), the hits ("Soul Man" and "Hold On I'm Comin'" were the biggest) gathered on the *Best of* are landmark Sixties pop music. The Atlantic imports are the original Sam and Dave releases of the late Sixties—every track is fine. Gusto offers remakes of the hits. Roulette's material is pre-Atlantic and not bad. — J.M.C. / D.M.

SAM THE BAND

★ **Play It Again, Sam / Casa. (NA)**

This could be the beginning of a terrible headache. — J.S.

DAVID SANCIOUS AND TONE

★ **David Sancious / Chel. (NA)** ¶
★ ★ ★ **Forest of Feelings / Epic (1975)**
★ ★ **Transformation / Epic (1976)**
★ ★ **Dance of the Age of Enlightenment /**
  Ari. (1978) ¶
★ ★ **True Stories / Ari. (1978)**

Sancious has served as an extremely able sideman for an unlikely combination of Seventies stars: Bruce Springsteen and Stanley Clarke (he recorded only with the former). The *David Sancious* LP was made during his tenure with Springsteen and is less directly jazz rock than the others. *Forest* is the most appealing of the rest, incorporating the variety of jazz, classical, rock & roll and African modes that made Sancious a special favorite with Springsteen cultists. — D.M.

CARL SANDBURG

★ **Carl Sandburg Sings Americana / Ev. (NA)**
★ ★ **The Great Carl Sandburg / Lyr. (NA)**
The poet/historian/folklorist periodically recorded some of the songs he compiled in his book *American Songbag,* and an out-of-print album of that name (Caedmon TC-2025) is really preferable to the two currently available LPs. There is a gentleness in his voice that communicates enormous warmth, and *Songbag* (book and record) served as a source of traditional songs for many a latter-day folkie. The Lyrichord set features more tracks than the Everest, with six cuts duplicated on each. — I.M.

SANFORD-TOWNSEND BAND

★ ★ ★ **Smoke from a Distant Fire / War. (1976)**
★ ★ **Duo Glide / War. (1978)**
★ ★ **Nail Me to the Wall / War. (1979)**
This white-soul songwriting team's funk-rocking debut was produced by Jerry Wexler and Barry Beckett at Muscle Shoals Sound Studios in Alabama and lives up to that studio's reputation for fine R&B sessions. The band is tight and inspired; several of the songs (particularly "Smoke from a Distant Fire," a 1977 hit single) are good, and the Wexler-Beckett production glosses it all beautifully without stifling the players. The others are less inspired, as the two seem unsure of themselves without the direction of Wexler and Beckett. — J.S.

SAMANTHA SANG

★ ★ **Emotion / Priv. (1978) ¶**
★ **From Dance to Love / U.A. (NA)**
Sang was a virtual unknown until Bee Gee Barry Gibb took her to Criteria Studios in Miami and produced *Emotion*'s title song, which became a Top Ten hit in early 1978, during that year's Bee Gees explosion. The sound is pure Bee Gees, and one wonders just what the singer contributed beyond her disembodied vocal. The rest of the album, produced by Miami vets Albhy Galuten and Karl Richardson, and the followup lack even this much interest. — D.M.

SANTA ESMERALDA

★ ★ ★ ★ **Don't Let Me Be Misunderstood / Casa. (1977)**
★ ★ ★ **House of the Rising Sun / Casa. (1978)**
★ ★ **Beauty / Casa. (1978)**
★ ★ **Another Cha Cha / Casa. (NA)**
★ ★ **Don't Be Shy Tonight / Casa. (NA)**
This Spanish disco group reworked white rhythm & blues hits of the British Invasion for the late-Seventies disco market—and with good effect. "Don't Let Me Be Misunderstood," an eight-minute suite of the Animals' 1965 hit, is the best of the group's work, thanks to a ferocious lead singer, Leroy Gomez. The *Don't Let Me* album also contains a remarkable version of Van Morrison's "Gloria." *House of the Rising Sun,* released in 1978, is less skillful, mostly because of Gomez' departure. Nonetheless, it probably is more attractive to most rock fans' ears than other disco products. Santa Esmeralda should have quit at that point. — D.M.

SANTANA

★ ★ ★ ★ **Santana / Col. (1969)**
★ ★ ★ ★ **Santana: Abraxas / Col. (1970)**
★ ★ ★ ★ **Santana 3 / Col. (1971)**
★ ★ ★ ★ **Caravanserai / Col. (1972)**
★ ★ ★ **Welcome / Col. (1973)**
★ ★ ★ ★ **Santana's Greatest Hits / Col. (1974)**
★ ★ ★ **Borboletta / Col. (1974)**
★ ★ ★ ★ **Amigos / Col. (1976)**
★ ★ ★ **Festival / Col. (1977)**
★ ★ ★ **Moonflower / Col. (1977)**
★ ★ **Inner Secrets / Col. (1979)**
★ ★ **Marathon / Col. (1979)**
★ ★ **Zebop / Col. (1981)**
Carlos Santana, a Mexican guitarist from the Tijuana region, went to San Francisco during the hippie daze and first earned recognition playing on the second Al Kooper–Mike Bloomfield super session. With a variety of other Latin musicians from the area, most notably the poll-winning Central American percussionist José "Cepito" Areas and drummer Mike Shrieve, he formed his own band and recorded an eponymous debut LP in 1969.

An appearance at Woodstock set the stage for great commercial prosperity. *Abraxas,* the second album, featured a reworking of Latin master Tito Puente's "Oye Como Va," which garnered them a hit single. *Santana 3* added Coke Escovedo and guitar protégé Neal Schon to the lineup; it was the culmination of the band's early style. Since then, Santana albums have alternated between Carlos Santana's solo LPs and his occasional collaborations, including one with Mahavishnu John McLaughlin, with whom he shares a guru, Sri Chinmoy.

With *Caravanserai,* Santana became a

jazz-rock fusion band, with emphasis on Latin percussion devices. The lineup included Schon, Areas, Shrieve and several additions, most prominently conga players James Mingo Lewis and Armando Peraza. *Borboletta* was a disappointing followup. But *Amigos* is more interesting, as Santana attempted to recapture his Latin roots. Since *Festival,* the group has drifted from occasionally fiery improvisation to increasingly desperate AOR radio banalities, with an unfortunate emphasis on commercial pandering. Still, Santana remains one of the pioneers of both Latin-jazz electric fusion and jazz rock. — D.M.

CARLOS SANTANA
★ Carlos Santana and Buddy Miles Live / Col. (1972)
★ ★ ★ Love, Devotion, Surrender / Col. (1973)
★ ★ Illuminations / Col. (1974)
These are the Mexican-American guitarist's solo LPs, which are more conceptually adventurous but generally less listenable than his work with the Santana group. The album with Miles is essentially a casual jam; *Illuminations* (with Alice Coltrane) and *Love, Devotion, Surrender* (with John McLaughlin) attempt to do for guitar what John Coltrane did for saxophone, with only middling success at best. — D.M.

SASSY
★ ★ Sassy / Drive (NA)
Doncha gimme no lip. — D.M.

MERL SAUNDERS
★ ★ Heavy Turbulence / Fan. (1972)
★ ★ Fire Up / Fan. (1974)
Saunders, a Northern California keyboardist, doesn't have much to say on these extra-mellow albums. — J.C.C.

MERL SAUNDERS AND JERRY GARCIA
★ ★ ★ Live at the Keystone / Fan. (1973)
The association between Jerry Garcia, guitarist, vocalist and composer for the Grateful Dead, and Merl Saunders, a Northern California keyboardist of some renown, does not really deliver much on this extra-mellow album recorded live at San Francisco's Keystone. Combining old and new standards like "Positively 4th Street," "That's All Right, Mama" and "My Funny Valentine" with indolent funk-rock instrumental treatments, this band often threatens to succumb to blissful torpor. Saunders plays a lot of swirling chords, but Garcia never really rises to

the level of inspiration he's often shown with the Dead. — J.C.C.

SAVOY BROWN
★ ★ Getting to the Point / Par. (1968) ¶
★ ★ ★ Blue Matter / Par. (1969) ¶
★ ★ ★ A Step Further / Par. (1969) ¶
★ ★ ★ Raw Sienna / Par. (1970) ¶
★ ★ Looking In / Par. (1970) ¶
★ ★ ★ Street Corner Talking / Par. (1971) ¶
★ ★ ★ Hellbound Train / Par. (1972) ¶
★ ★ Lion's Share / Par. (1972) ¶
★ Jack the Toad / Par. (1973) ¶
★ ★ Boogie Brothers / Lon. (1974) ¶
★ Wire Fire / Lon. (1975) ¶
★ Skin 'n' Bone / Lon. (1976) ¶
★ ★ ★ London Collector—The Best of Savoy Brown / Lon. (NA)
★ ★ Savage Return / Lon. (1978)
Despite countless personnel changes, Savoy Brown's one constant, guitarist Kim Simmonds, endures with his fluid boogie-blues style. The first four albums *(Point, Matter, Further* and *Sienna)* feature a strange, croaking blues vocalist, Chris Youlden; both *A Step Further* and *Blue Matter* also contain some live recordings, and "Savoy Brown Boogie" from the former is the band's definitive statement, although the basic premise is better presented through Youlden's vocal on "Train to Nowhere" on *Blue Matter.*

Dave Peverett, later of Foghat, replaced Youlden on *Looking In,* and he was fully integrated over the next three albums. But with *Jack the Toad* a decline set in, partially because another capable vocalist, Dave Walker, had left. The rest is simply a matter of playing out the string of tired, recycled blues riffs. — A.N.

SKY SAXON BLUES BAND
★ A Full Spoon of Seedy Blues / GNP (1967)
The Sonny Bono of the psychedelic age. — B.A.

LEO SAYER
★ ★ ★ Silverbird / War. (1973) ¶
★ ★ ★ Just a Boy / War. (1975)
★ Another Year / War. (1975) ¶
★ ★ ★ Endless Flight / War. (1976)
★ ★ Thunder in My Heart / War. (1977) ¶
★ ★ Leo Sayer / War. (1978) ¶
★ ★ Here / War. (1979)
★ ★ Living in a Fantasy / War. (1980)
An excellent English pop-rock singer, Sayer is only a fair writer. His first two albums, *Silverbird* and *Just a Boy,* were done during a period when Sayer appeared onstage in

mime makeup, exploiting a lonely Pierrot persona. With *Endless Flight* Sayer went Hollywood, thanks to Richard Perry's lush production, and scored two No. 1 hits, "You Make Me Feel Like Dancing" and "When I Need You." Since then he's learned to grin on talk shows and generally act so cute it's revolting, and not even Perry's studio expertise has been able to save him from banality. — S.H.

BOZ SCAGGS

★ ★ ★ ★ **Boz Scaggs / Atl. (1971)**
★ ★ ★ **Moments / Col. (1971)**
★ ★ ★ **Boz Scaggs and Band / Col. (1971)**
★ ★ ★ ★ **My Time / Col. (1972)**
★ ★ ★ **Slow Dancer / Col. (1974)**
★ ★ ★ ★ **Silk Degrees / Col. (1976)**
★ ★ ★ **Down Two, Then Left / Col. (1977)**
★ ★ **Middle Man / Col. (1980)**
★ ★ ★ **Hits / Col. (1980)**

After leaving the Steve Miller Band in the late Sixties, Boz Scaggs recorded a solo album in Muscle Shoals, Alabama, that earned him instant notoriety. *Boz Scaggs* (produced by *Rolling Stone*'s Jann Wenner) featured that town's crack rhythm section, led by guitarist Duane Allman, whose extended solo on "Loan Me a Dime" is one of the high points of both men's careers. Scaggs has an easy, lilting voice and a knack for writing terrific rock & roll hooks into his songs. His subsequent recordings switched back and forth between hard rock and ballad R&B (*My Time* has two burning rockers, "Dinah Flo" and "Full-Lock Power Slide") before settling into softer material. His reputation as a crooner grew slowly until he scored big in 1976 with the hit single "Lowdown," from *Silk Degrees. Down Two, Then Left* attempted to continue that cool R&B success a little too cautiously, leaving Scaggs a bit too cold for comfort. — J.S.

ARMAND SCHAUBROECK STEALS

★ ★ ★ **A Lot of People Would Like to See Armand Schaubroeck Dead / Mirror (1974)**
★ ★ **I Came to Visit, But Decided to Stay / Mirror (1975)**
★ ★ **Live at the Holiday Inn / Mirror (1975)**
★ ★ ★ **Ratfucker / Mirror (1977)**
★ ★ **Shakin' Shakin' / Mirror (1978)**

A legend at least in his own city—Rochester, New York—Armand Schaubroeck is a music-store proprietor who ran for public office, put up billboards protesting the draft and records decidedly bent albums of a punky Lou Reed-ian quality. He only gets two stars for most of the albums listed here, but not because of any serious artistic defects—Schaubroeck is simply an acquired taste.

His obsessions are all found on life's underbelly—the criminal element, disenfranchised kids, psychological horror (his "Sister Ray"-like adaptation of Edgar Allan Poe's "Bells" on *I Came to Visit*)—and his most successful albums are those where the intensity of those obsessions is matched by the fury of his performance. *A Lot of People* is a harrowing three-record musico-documentary based on Schaubroeck's stay in jail, and *Ratfucker* is a graphic tour of street-gang evil: both are marked by dark bluesy structures and Schaubroeck's ominous dry monotone. A little more accessible are the pop twists of *Shakin' Shakin',* but the two-record *Live at the Holiday Inn* is marred by overloud overdubbed audience static. — D.F.

HELEN SCHNEIDER

■ **So Close / Wind. (1977)** ¶
■ **Let It Be Now / Wind. (1978)** ¶

The kind of pop we'd hoped rock had eliminated. Pop this adult and sophisticated reaches mindless vulgarity via the back door. — D.M.

SCIENTIST

★ ★ ★ **Scientist vs. Prince Jammy / Troj. (1978)**
★ ★ ★ **Heavyweight Dub Champion / Greens. (1980)**
★ ★ ★ **Scientist vs. Space Invaders / Greens. (1980)**
★ ★ ★ ★ **Scientific Dub / Clock. (1981)**
★ ★ ★ **Rids the World of Vampires / Greens. (1981)**

Scientist is one of the best mixers of reggae—clear, precise and polished. His dub LPs (and there are a ton of them) usually sound wonderful, but lately he's relied too much on gimmicky concepts and electronic ephemera. *Scientific Dub* combines strong rhythms with understated mixing, and this stands out. — R.F.G.

TONY SCIUTO

★ ★ ★ **Island Nights / Epic (1980)**

Amiable adult-contemporary fare, but a little too slick for its own good. Sciuto is a strong writer but doesn't seem totally convinced by the stylization he's adopted. Still, it's more listenable than Kenny Loggins. — J.D.C.

THE SCOOTERS

★ ★ **Young Girls / EMI (1980)** ¶
★ ★ **Blue Eyes / EMI (1982)**

Faceless post-Knack power pop. — W.K.

SCORPIONS

★ ★ Fly to the Rainbow / RCA (1976)
★ ★ In Trance / RCA (1976)
■ Virgin Killer / RCA (1977)
★ Taken by Force / RCA (1978) ¶
★ Tokyo Tapes / RCA (1978)
★ ★ Love Drive / Mer. (1979)
★ ★ Animal Magnetism / Mer. (1980)
German hard-rock band influenced by Deep Purple and Uriah Heep. Guitarist Michael Schenker later joined UFO. — J.S.

JACK SCOTT

★ ★ ★ Jack Scott Rocks / Rock & Roll (NA)
★ ★ ★ Jack Scott on Groove / RCA (NA), Br. imp.
★ ★ Jack Scott Rocks On / Leroy (NA)
Minor but influential late-Fifties rock & roll balladeer, best known for "What in the World's Come over You," "Burning Bridges" and "My True Love," as well as the latter-day rockabilly classic "The Way I Walk" (recently covered by the Cramps). Scott was a limited performer at best, and none of these shows him at his absolute best, but the Rock & Roll set comes close, and the *Groove* material, though straying closer to country, isn't bad. The Leroy album is of more recent vintage, and should be avoided. — D.M.

TOM SCOTT

★ ★ ★ Great Scott! / A&M (1972)
★ ★ ★ Tom Scott and the L.A. Express / Ode (1974)
★ ★ ★ Tom Cat / Ode (1975)
★ ★ New York Connection / Ode (1975)
★ ★ Tom Scott in L.A. / RCA (1977)
★ ★ Blow It Out / Epic (1977)
★ ★ Intimate Strangers / Col. (1978)
★ ★ Street Beat / Col. (1979)
★ ★ ★ Best of Tom Scott / Col. (1980)
★ ★ Apple Juice / Col. (1981)
★ Rural Still Life / MCA (1982)
Reedman Scott, perhaps the best known L.A. studio horn player, brought functionally tasty licks and arrangements to a host of albums. But only one of his own—*Great Scott!*—features him as a soloist and conceptualizer of any note. *Great Scott!* isn't just one thing; at times it features a little late-Sixties space sensibility, but it also includes modal jazz and a bit of rock. Still, it's elegantly musical, and Scott does better than his usual antiseptic copping of original styles.

The two L.A. Express albums (*Tom Cat's* the second) are heavily arranged (not strings, but with a certain density), small-group fusion, featuring nice, if brief, solos by the Ex-

press members (who include guitarists Larry Carlton and Robben Ford, bassist Joe Sample and drummer John Guerin). There's plenty of guitar-horn dueling and ample funky backbeat.

Since then Scott has made a series of lukewarm, quasi-funk, mood music discs for easy listening fanatics only. — M.R.

GIL SCOTT-HERON

★ ★ ★ Pieces of Man / Fly. (1973)
★ ★ ★ The Revolution Will Not Be Televised / Fly. (1975)
★ ★ ★ ★ First Minute of a New Day / Ari. (1975)
★ ★ ★ From South Africa to South Carolina / Ari. (1975) ¶
★ ★ ★ It's Your World / Ari. (1976) ¶
★ ★ ★ ★ Bridges / Ari. (1977) ¶
★ ★ ★ Secrets / Ari. (1978) ¶
★ ★ ★ 1980 / Ari. (1980)
★ ★ ★ Real Eyes / Ari. (1980)
★ ★ ★ Reflections / Ari. (1981)
★ ★ ★ The Mind of Gil Scott-Heron / Ari. (NA)
Scott-Heron began recording in the early Seventies as one of those black jazz poets who bop along every few years; he was more politically astute than most, though hardly more musical. But in 1974 Scott-Heron and his partner, Brian Jackson, composed "The Bottle," a savage attack on drugs and alcohol in minority communities. It was a pop hit, and deservedly so: the *First Minute* album shows why, particularly given Scott-Heron's newfound ability (willingness?) to actually sing. *Bridges* contains his best song since "The Bottle," the utterly chilling antinuclear ode, "We Almost Lost Detroit." — D.M.

THE SCRUFFS

★ ★ Wanna Meet the Scruffs? / Powerplay (1977)
The Scruffs played middlin' to almost bad power pop as if their lives depended on it on this record—which makes this a perfect memento of new wave's banner year in America. Smart, vulnerable lyrics and a few tasty tracks suggest that talent became misplaced in the mannerisms of a movement. — L.F.

EARL SCRUGGS

★ ★ Earl Scruggs—His Family and Friends / Col. (1971)
★ ★ ★ I Saw the Light / Col. (1972)
★ ★ Live at Kansas State / Col. (1972)
★ ★ ★ Dueling Banjos / Col. (1973)
★ ★ ★ Earl Scruggs Revue / Col. (1973)
★ ★ Where the Lilies Bloom / Col. (1974) ¶

★ ★ ★ **Rockin' 'Cross the Country** / Col. (1974) ¶
★ ★ ★ **Anniversary Special, Vol. 1** / Col. (1975) ¶
★ ★ ★ **Earl Scruggs Revue, Vol. 2** / Col. (1976) ¶
★ ★ ★ **Earl Scruggs Revue Live from Austin City Limits** / Col. (1976)
★ ★ **Strike Anywhere** / Col. (1977) ¶
★ ★ ★ **Banjoman** / Sire (1977)
★ ★ **Today and Forever** / Col. (1979)

As half of Flatt and Scruggs, Earl Scruggs was one of the most important popularizers of bluegrass and a significant banjo stylist. On his own, the influence continues, but the output hasn't been as good. — D.M.

GARY AND RANDY SCRUGGS
★ ★ **The Scruggs Brothers** / Van. (NA)

The sons of Earl Scruggs attempt to adapt their father's bluegrass style to a rock format, with dismal results. Not lively enough to be one or the other, the album is too condescending to effect a workable merger.
— D.M.

SEA LEVEL
★ ★ ★ **Sea Level** / Capri. (1977)
★ ★ ★ **Cats on the Coast** / Capri. (1978)
★ ★ ★ **On the Edge** / Capri. (1978)
★ ★ ★ **Long Walk on a Short Pier** / Capri. (1979)
★ ★ ★ **Ball Room** / Ari. (1980)

When Chuck Leavell, the former Allman Brothers keyboard player, put together his own band following the group's demise, he came up with a terrific pun for its title (C. Leavell, get it?) and an interesting approach: adapting the Allman's modal blues rock to the jazz from which it was derived. The debut album seemed like a new, bluesier direction for fusion, but having seen the light, Sea Level was apparently unable to follow it. *Cats on the Coast* and *On the Edge* simply meander in search of focus. On recent LPs, Leavell's front-man role has been taken over by Randall Bramblett, with no discernible change in the group's sound. — D.M.

SEALS AND CROFTS
★ **Year of Sunday** / War. (1971) ¶
★ **Summer Breeze** / War. (1972) ¶
★ **Diamond Girl** / War. (1973) ¶
★ **Seals and Crofts 1 and 2** / War. (1974) ¶
■ **Unborn Child** / War. (1974) ¶
★ ★ **Seals and Crofts Greatest Hits** / War. (1975)
■ **I'll Play for You** / War. (1975) ¶
★ **Get Closer** / War. (1976) ¶

■ **Sudan Village** / War. (1976) ¶
■ **Takin' It Easy** / War. (1978)
■ **Longest Road** / War. (1980)

Folk-rock duo spins contemporary MOR of above-average intensity, relying on pretty tunes with exotic flourishes ("Summer Breeze" and "Diamond Girl" were their biggest mid-Seventies hits) and a spiritual angle: both are members of the Bahai faith, which got them into considerable trouble with their viciously antifeminist "Unborn Child," which derided abortion. *Get Closer* tried to bring them nearer to MOR soul, an attempt that clicked for the title song, and not much else. Since then, they've returned to their previous style. — D.M.

TROY SEALS
★ ★ **Troy Seals** / Col. (1976) ¶

Seals is best known as a writer of country cowboy songs, and on the basis of this solo LP, it's likely to remain that way. — D.M.

SON SEALS
★ ★ ★ ★ **Son Seals Blues Band** / Alli. (1974)
★ ★ ★ ★ **Midnight Son** / Alli. (NA)
★ ★ ★ ★ **Live and Burning** / Alli. (NA)

One of the best of the new generation of Chicago blues guitarists. He started off as a drummer, backing Robert Nighthawk, before switching to guitar and eventually joining Earl Hooker's band. Albert King later hired him as a drummer, and Seals' drumming in King's band is on the *Live Wire/Blues Power* album. In the Seventies, Seals took over Hound Dog Taylor's gig at Chicago's Expressway Lounge and began whipping his band into shape. Records show Seals to be a good blues singer in the Junior Parker tradition and an excellent, sure-toned guitarist. His lightning-fast runs will undoubtedly delight fans of better-known white blues guitarists who aren't as good. — J.S.

THE SEARCHERS
★ ★ ★ ★ **The Searchers** / Sire (1979)
★ ★ ★ ★ **Love Melodies** / Sire (1981)

With people like Tom Petty and the Records making liberal use of the Byrdsy folk-rock sound they pioneered during the first British Invasion, the Searchers got a chance to come off the cabaret circuit they've been touring on since the late Sixties. The results are splendid; the singing is inspired and the legendary jangling guitar work is sharp and bright. Granted one extra star each for sticking it out so long and making two examples of rock's rarest achievement: the comeback record that matches the original stuff. — W.K.

SEATRAIN

★ ★ **Seatrain / A&M (1969)** ¶
★ ★ **Seatrain / Cap. (1971)**
★ ★ ★ **Marblehead Messenger / Cap. (1971)**
Seatrain was formed in California by bassist/
flutist Andy Kulberg and drummer Roy Blu-
menfeld after the Blues Project broke up.
But their Capitol debut album, which earned
considerable critical acclaim in 1969, placed
heaviest emphasis on violinist Richard
Greene, who had experience with Bill Mon-
roe's bluegrass group and the Jim Kweskin
Jug Band. Greene was missing on *Marble-
head Messenger,* recorded in London with
George Martin producing, and on the A&M
LP, so these albums are considerably less attractive. — D.M.

JOHN SEBASTIAN

★ ★ ★ **John Sebastian / Rep. (1970)**
★ **Welcome Back / Rep. (1976)** ¶
After the Lovin' Spoonful broke up, Sebastian recorded a self-titled solo album for Reprise that, while pleasant listening, was the
epitome of strained, tie-dyed soulfulness.
This approach continued for a series of now-
deleted efforts, each of which reduced the
memories of "Do You Believe in Magic?"
and "Summer in the City" a bit further. The
last straw, however, was "Welcome Back,"
the theme song for Gabe Kaplan and John
Travolta's TV show. The song was a hit, but
both it and the album are nearly worthless
artistically. — D.M.

THE SECRET

★ **The Secret / A&M (1979)** ¶
Overarranged pop with jittery singing that's
hard to take for a whole record, delivered at
the same rushed tempo that the Kinks fall
into with their worst material. — W.K.

SECRET AFFAIR

★ ★ **"Glory Boys" / I-Spy (1979), Br. imp.**
★ **Behind Closed Doors / I-Spy (1980), Br.
imp.**
Born out of the British Mod revival and led
by vocalist/trumpet player Ian Page, Secret
Affair shares the original Mods' flair for
flashy suits and patchy anthems. Sometimes
powerful, as on "Time for Action" from the
first LP, more often pompous and arrogant,
especially when augmented by strings on *Behind Closed Doors.* — ML.H.

SECTOR 27

★ ★ ★ **Sector 27 / IRS (1980)**
Answer to trivia question: Whatever happened to Tom Robinson, rock's first overtly
gay rock hitmaker? After two albums of po-

lemicized new wave, he formed this artier,
more oblique band, which had some U.K.
success with heartfelt single "Martin's
Gone" but generally lacked the emotional
vigor of the original Tom Robinson Band,
and certainly had no intentions of lightening
up sufficiently for another "2-4-6-8 Motorway." Not bad, but you've heard lots like it
before. — D.M.

NEIL SEDAKA

★ ★ ★ **Sedaka's Back / R. (1974)** ¶
★ ★ **Breaking Up Is Hard to Do / Camd.
(1975)**
★ ★ **Oh Carol / RCA (1975)**
★ ★ **Neil Sedaka Sings His Greatest Hits /
RCA (1975)**
★ ★ **The Hungry Years / R. (1975)** ¶
★ ★ **Pure Gold / RCA (1976)**
★ **Steppin' Out / R. (1976)** ¶
★ **Song / Elek. (1977)**
★ ★ **Neil Sedaka's Greatest Hits / R.
(1977)** ¶
★ ★ **Sedaka: The Fifties and Sixties / RCA
(1977)** ¶
★ **The Many Sides of Neil Sedaka / RCA
(1977)** ¶
★ **All You Need Is the Music / Elek. (1978)**
★ **In the Pocket / Elek. (1980)**
★ **Neil Sedaka / Elek. (1981)**
After a promising beginning as a classical pi-
anist (Arthur Rubinstein selected him as the
best New York classical player in 1956), the
Brooklyn-born Sedaka conceived an interest
in writing pop songs. He teamed up with a
high-school crony, Howard Greenfield (Sedaka was the melodist; Greenfield added lyrics), and began selling songs to LaVern
Baker, the Tokens and Dinah Washington.
He scored biggest, however, with "Stupid
Cupid" by Connie Francis in 1958.
   Like Carole King and Jerry Goffin, Ellie
Greenwich and Jeff Barry and others, Se-
daka/Greenfield soon became a familiar New
York composing team of the pop hits of the
era. But in 1959 Sedaka turned to recording
his own material; "The Diary" was his first
hit, but it was minor compared to the international best-seller that followed—"Oh
Carol," written for King. Sedaka followed
this with a succession of nasal teen-dream
items, including "Happy Birthday Sweet Sixteen," "Calendar Girl" and the best of them,
"Breaking Up Is Hard to Do." These and
the other, lesser songs Sedaka made during
the post-Presley, pre-Beatles years are collected on the various RCA and Camden anthologies.
   In 1973, after a ten-year layoff, Sedaka
began performing again. He recorded three

albums in the U.K.—*Solitaire, The Tra La Days Are Over* and *Laughter in the Rain*—before getting a compilation of them released on MCA (now *Sedaka's Back*) through the auspices of Elton John. "Laughter in the Rain" became a major hit for him, and the Captain and Tennille scored even bigger with his "Love Will Keep Us Together." The first album Sedaka made for Elton John's Rocket Records, the mistitled *The Hungry Years,* seemed to reestablish him as a major pop writer/performer. Sedaka had also been a more attractive singer than his teen-idol competitors, and his early Rocket work seemed to indicate that he had matured into an Elton-like pianist/vocalist. But subsequent releases have shown him to be much more like a second-rate Barry Manilow, without much of John's hard-rocking sensibility. — D.M.

THE SEEDS

★ ★ ★ **The Seeds / GNP (1966)**
★ ★ ★ **A Web of Sound / GNP (1966)**
★ **Future / GNP (1967)**
★ ★ **Merlin's Music Box / GNP (1967)**
★ ★ **Fallin' Off the Edge / GNP (1977)**
"Two great chords—five great albums!" reads the epitaph at the beloved Seeds' mythical grave site, a spot in Southern California where marijuana plants and magic mushrooms grow wild, and toward which most God-fearing punk bands of the Seventies bowed at sunset each day.

That the Seeds were able to parlay their distinctly limited talents as writers, singers and musicians into a rather long and sucessful career is one of the more miraculous stories in rock fabledom. Lead singer Sky Saxon's world view was limited to two subjects—sex and drugs—and his snarling vocals were accompanied by some of the most amateurishly oddball music ever recorded by modern recording equipment—in particular, the organ and piano of Daryl Hooper, whose idea of a creative solo was to play the same riff over and over at varying octaves. It is highly doubtful that their music could have been any worse than it was. Their singular charm lay in the fact that, due to their lack of skills, their music could not have been any better, either.

The Seeds sports their biggest hit, "Pushin' Too Hard," and Saxon's best composition, "Can't Seem to Make You Mine," but true believers usually rally around their second LP, *A Web of Sound.* This LP includes plenty of psychedelic numbers, like "Rollin' Machine," "Tripmaker" and "Mr. Farmer," and the band's magnum opus, "Up in Her Room," a fourteen-and-a-half-minute

account of lovemaking that features two breaks for cigarettes (Saxon obviously worked fast).

Future is the group's flower-power concept album, and its best track, "Two Fingers Pointing on You," was performed by the band in *Psych Out,* their lone film appearance (the movie starred Jack Nicholson as the ponytailed leader of an acid-rock band in Haight-Ashbury during the summer of love; of such stuff, friends, are legends made). *Merlin's Music Box* is supposed to be a "live" album, but sounds curiously like outtakes from previous LPs with prerecorded audience screams. Still, the record does include the classic "900 Million People Daily All Making Love," and Saxon's Arab getup on the back cover does pre-date Dylan by a good eight years.

Fallin' Off the Edge consists of more outtakes and previously unreleased songs, taking the place of *A Full Spoon of Seedy Blues,* a blues LP with liner notes by Muddy Waters ("I sincerely believe that at last America has produced a group to be another Rolling Stones"). That all records but *Full Spoon* are still available is proof positive that there is, at times, justice in the universe. Pass the hookah. — B.A.

MIKE SEEGER

★ ★ ★ **American Folk Songs / Folk. (1957)**
★ ★ ★ **Old Time Country Music / Folk. (1962)**
★ ★ ★ **Tipple, Loom and Rail / Folk. (1966)**
Since the mid-Fifties, Mike Seeger—son of ethnomusicologist Charles Seeger, brother of Peggy and half-brother of Pete—has carried on his family's folk-music tradition, with a special interest in the Appalachian Mountain music that forms the basis of C&W.

In the early Fifties, he traveled through the rural South, collecting folk songs and discovering a number of important performers, including Dock Boggs. Beginning around 1955, he began performing such material at a variety of coffeehouses and festivals; by 1958 he had helped form the most important old-timey group of the folk revival, the New Lost City Ramblers. His solo albums include the same kind of material, which is performed with musicological expertise, but also with a great deal of authentic emotion, lacking the sanctimonious politicking of Pete's similar recordings of international folk music. — D.M.

PEGGY SEEGER

★ ★ **Penelope Isn't Waiting Any More / Roun. (1973)**

A folk album of feminist consciousness-raising songs. — J.S.

PEGGY SEEGER AND EWAN MacCOLL
★ ★ ★ ★ **At the Present Moment / Roun. (1973)**
★ ★ ★ **Folkways Record of Contemporary Songs / Folk. (1973)**
It was ironic for MacColl to win a Grammy in 1972 as a writer of "The First Time Ever I Saw Your Face." For more than a decade the song had been a standard of the contemporary folk repertoire. It was symbolic, however, of the scant attention the songwriter/singer/interpreter has received here. Similarly, Seeger's work is better known and respected in Britain, where the two reside. (She is, of course, the sister of Mike and half-sister of Pete Seeger.) They have recorded dozens of albums of radical protest songs composed in the folk idiom, traditional ballads and other works. Both MacColl and Seeger inspired many of the protest singers of the Sixties folk revival, and they themselves remain vital commentators to this day. — I.M.

PETE SEEGER
★ ★ **Original Talking Union / Folk. (1955)**
★ ★ **Pete Seeger Sings American Ballads / Folk. (1957)**
★ **Pete Seeger with Sonny Terry at Carnegie Hall / Folk. (1958)**
★ ★ **American Favorite Ballads III / Folk. (1959)**
★ **Pete Seeger with Memphis Slim and Willie Dixon at the Village Gate / Folk. (1960)**
★ ★ **American Favorite Ballads IV / Folk. (1961)**
★ ★ **American Favorite Ballads V / Folk. (1962)**
★ **Pete Seeger at the Village Gate, Vol. 2 / Folk. (1962)**
★ ★ ★ ★ **We Shall Overcome / Col. (1963)**
★ **Songs of Struggle and Protest: 1930–1950 / Folk. (1964)**
★ ★ **Dangerous Songs / Col. (1966)**
★ ★ **Pete Seeger Sings Woody Guthrie / Folk. (1967)**
★ **Pete Seeger's Greatest Hits / Col. (1967)**
★ ★ ★ **Waist-Deep in the Big Muddy and Other Love Songs / Col. (1967)**
★ ★ **Young vs. Old / Col. (1969)**
★ ★ **The World of Pete Seeger / Col. (1972)**
★ ★ **Broadside / Folk. (NA)**
★ ★ **Pete Seeger Sings Leadbelly / Folk. (NA)**
★ **Sing with Seeger / Disc (NA)**
★ ★ ★ **Three Saints, Four Sinners and Six Other People / Odys. (NA)**

Carl Sandburg called Seeger "America's tuning fork." Although he would no doubt deny it, Seeger more than anyone was responsible for the sparks that ignited the folk revival of the Fifties and Sixties. During the earlier decade, Seeger's radical belief in humanitarian socialism found him at odds with both Senator Joseph McCarthy and the House Un-American Activities Committee. Seeger's refusal—on Fifth Amendment grounds—to testify before the committee resulted in his being blacklisted by television and radio, although Columbia continued to record him.

Despite his lack of media exposure, Seeger was at the forefront of the civil rights and anti–Vietnam War movements. Throughout the Sixties, he reached audiences by touring constantly in this country and abroad; through his travels and concerts, he taught more people the choruses of such songs as "We Shall Overcome," "Little Boxes," "A Hard Rain's A-Gonna Fall," "Where Have All the Flowers Gone" and "Guantanamera"—among dozens of others—than could reasonably have been expected of a single human being.

Seeger has neither an exceptional voice nor an outstanding banjo or guitar style. What he does possess is the unique ability to make friends of total strangers, using his music and gestures as common denominators. In fact, Americans may have more trouble than anyone else with Seeger, for his entertainment, while educational, can also be preachy and sanctimonious on political issues.

Seeger has recorded extensively. The list here represents perhaps half of what he has put on disc as a soloist. There are also recordings by him and the Almanac Singers (which included Lee Hays, Woody Guthrie and Millard Lampell) and the Weavers. This list is only a sampling, but it is impressive on several levels. Each LP, whether recorded live or in a studio, is a concert unto itself. Seeger is a master of programing and of the singalong, and his concerts always strike a balance between traditional ballads, international folk songs, freedom songs, political commentaries and satires, instrumentals, new songs in the folk idiom and others. With the exception of the *American Favorite Ballads* series, on which Seeger becomes a human songbook, that kind of balance is struck throughout his catalogue. The emphasis may shift slightly, but the effect is always of a broad overview of life. Even when the same songs overlap from LP to LP, the performances change sufficiently to keep them fresh.

The Folkways titles are generally self-explanatory, although when other performers share the billing, their roles are generally minor. Memphis Slim and Willie Dixon are barely audible, for instance. The sound quality of the Folkways LPs, most of which have been recorded with a single microphone, is also poor. And on the reprocessed stereo of the Leadbelly and Guthrie collections, the electronic effect robs the albums of naturalness. However, all of these records are historically most valuable. *Broadside* is particularly recommended as an example of Seeger's excellent ear for material from the "topical" songwriters of the early Sixties.

The Columbia recordings, dating through the mid-Sixties, are generally well recorded. *We Shall Overcome,* loaded heavily with the freedom songs of the civil rights movement, is perhaps Seeger's best concert recording. It was obviously a highly emotional night and Seeger was at his peak vocally.

"Waist-Deep in the Big Muddy" was the song that brought Seeger back to national television after seventeen years, with two appearances on *The Smothers Brothers Comedy Hour.* The first time, censors nixed the anti–Vietnam War song; the ensuing uproar gained him a return invitation and he sang the song.

Three Saints is a set of story songs, excellent for children or adults. *World* and *Greatest Hits* are collections of material associated with Seeger, although many were popularized by other artists. They're both satisfactory introductory sets. — I.M.

THE SEEKERS
★ ★ Best of the Seekers / Cap. (1967)
Australian pop-folk group hit in the middle Sixties with the theme from *Georgy Girl* and "I'll Never Find Another You." They produced fluffy Peter, Paul and Mary–style vocals, then faded out to reappear a couple of years later as the New Seekers, equally banal. — D.M.

BOB SEGER
★ ★ ★ Ramblin' Gamblin' Man / Cap. (1969) ¶
★ ★ ★ Mongrel / Cap. (1970) ¶
★ ★ ★ ★ Smokin' O.P.'s / Cap. (1972, 1977)
★ ★ ★ ★ Seven / Cap. (1974, 1977)
★ ★ ★ Beautiful Loser / Cap. (1975)
★ ★ ★ ★ Live Bullet / Cap. (1976)
★ ★ ★ ★ ★ Night Moves / Cap. (1977)
★ ★ ★ ★ Stranger in Town / Cap. (1978)
★ ★ Against the Wind / Cap. (1980)
★ ★ ★ Nine Tonight / Cap. (1981)
★ ★ ★ ★ ★ The Distance / Cap. (1983)

From 1965, when he made his first single for Cameo-Parkway, through 1977, Bob Seger was rock's foremost case of talent in the wilderness. In those years, Seger made a series of great rock singles in a style influenced by Dylan, the Stones, John Fogerty and Wilson Pickett. An adept writer and a brilliant vocalist, Seger still could not get a hit—outside of his native Detroit, where most went Top Ten. And along the way, a fine series of LPs for Warner Bros., particularly *Back in '72,* has been allowed to disappear. But *Night Moves* turned the corner for Seger in 1977, and he is now highly regarded almost everywhere.

Of the earlier albums, *Ramblin' Gamblin' Man* and *Mongrel* sound relatively dated, although Seger's "Ramblin' Gamblin' Man," a white R&B song, is a gem, and *Mongrel's* Creedence-like "Lucifer" is nearly as good. *Smokin' O.P.'s* contains only one Seger original, "Heavy Music," which had been a Detroit hit in 1967. The rest of this eccentric LP is diverse—Chuck Berry's "Let It Rock," Stephen Stills' "Love the One You're With," plus staples like "Bo Diddley" and "Turn on Your Lovelight"—but it's notable mostly for Seger's voice and some guitar work by Bobby Bland veteran Mike Bruce.

Seven and *Beautiful Loser* are the albums that paved the way for Seger's breakthrough; on the former, he assembled the Silver Bullet Band, and on the latter, he attempted some ballad material that, although too crude to work perfectly, at least allowed him some additional range. Each, of course, contains a hard-rock hit (in Detroit only): *Beautiful* has "Katmandu," *Seven* has "Get Out of Denver."

Live Bullet is one of the best live albums ever made, and a fitting documentary history of Seger's career. In spots, particularly during the medley of "Travelin' Man"/"Beautiful Loser" on side one, Seger sounds like a man with one last shot at the top. The desperation, oddly enough, was what pushed the record far past a concert LP's ordinary boundaries, paving the way for *Night Moves,* that wonderful chronicle of the moments when age becomes irrelevant and innocence gains experience. *Stranger in Town* picked up where *Night Moves* left off, perfectly balancing Springsteen-affected ballads with brutally hard rock.

Against the Wind, unfortunately, saw Seger needlessly retrenching into a conservative musical formula: alternating soft (AM radio) ballads with pumped-up (FM radio) rockers. His singing remained impeccable and remarkable, but his arrangements lost their bite and his lyrics their focus. Even the most basic rock songs on *Wind* seem churned out, rather than built up from an internal intensity, as his best earlier ones had. In the title song, Seger described his dilemma perfectly by admitting he wasn't sure what to leave in and what to leave out. Perhaps *Against the Wind,* then, suffers simply from Seger having made the wrong decisions.

Commercially, *Against the Wind* eclipsed every other Seger record; artistically, it represented an unignorable and undeniable decline. *Nine Tonight* is a live album, released as a holding action while Seger prepared his next studio set. It is sharp and confident but doesn't have the sense of breakthrough of *Live Bullet,* and the arrangements are predictable rehashes of the album tracks. As a reprise of the first period of Seger's success, it functions well enough, but that period has been so brief, it's hardly begging for a summary.

Seger reclaimed his place in the contemporary American rock pantheon with *The Distance,* his finest musical achievement and a distinct return to his lyrical roots as well. *The Distance* has the clearest and most powerful sound of any Seger record (thanks largely to producer Jimmy Iovine and engineer Shelly Yakus), and it avoids the banal balladry of *Against the Wind.* It's also intimately involved with creating the kind of characters Seger offered on *Night Moves, Beautiful Loser* and *Stranger in Town:* working- and middle-class Middle Americans struggling against their emotional and economic circumstances, not always winning but never ceasing to fight. In songs like "Even Now," "Makin' Thunderbirds," "Little Victories" and a version of Rodney Crowell's "Shame on the Moon," Seger reestablishes his claim to top stature among American rockers. Only Bruce Springsteen and Jackson Browne can write as well as he can, and Seger sings rings around both.

It is hard to think of any performer in rock history who has flirted with commercialized mediocrity as fully as Seger did in the late Seventies and rebounded with such striking artistic power. In the Eighties he will be a name to reckon with.
— D.M.

SELDOM SCENE
★ ★ ★ **Act 1** / Rebel (NA)
★ ★ ★ **Act 2** / Rebel (NA)
★ ★ ★ **Act 3** / Rebel (NA)
★ ★ ★ **Old Train** / Rebel (NA)
★ ★ ★ **Recorded Live** / Rebel (NA)

★ ★ ★ **The New Seldom Scene Album** / Rebel (NA)
★ ★ ★ **Act 4** / Sugar. (NA)
This is bluegrass' most promising light, as evidenced by the group's topping the polls of *Muleskinner News* as best group during the late Seventies. Dobro player Mike Auldridge is an accomplished sessionman and solo artist; Ben Eldridge is a facile and intelligent banjo stylist; and singers John Duffey and John Starling are notable for their warm, rich vocals. Given to mixing traditional tunes with contemporary material by such writers as Tom Paxton, Rodney Crowell, Herb Pederson and Steve Goodman, the Seldom Scene cross the bluegrass generation gap: the group is adored by both young and old fans.

Of special interest are the resonant *Live* set, recorded at Washington's Cellar Door club, and *The New Seldom Scene* LP, which includes vocal harmonies by Linda Ronstadt, who also featured Starling on her own albums. The epitome of low-key, friendly, down-home hip, Seldom Scene is fast becoming a bluegrass institution. — R.P.

SELECTER
★ ★ ★ ★ **Too Much Pressure** / Chrys. (1980)
★ ★ ★ **Celebrate the Bullet** / Chrys. (1981)
One of the best of Britain's "two-tone" bands, Selecter play reggaefied dub with a hard rocking edge. Their interracial lineup gave rise to the generic description, and the resultant interplay made *Too Much Pressure* a strong debut, particularly for Pauline Black's distinctive lead vocals. The record is studded with good songs: "On My Radio," "Missing Words," "Street Feeling," "My Collie (Not a Dog)," the title track and "James Bond." On *Celebrate the Bullet,* the material isn't quite as strong; the record is principally a showcase for the group's instrumental chops. — J.S.

THE SENSATIONAL NIGHTINGALES
★ **Almighty Hand** / Pea. (1976)
★ ★ ★ **Songs of Praise** / Pea. (NA)
★ ★ ★ **Glory Glory** / Pea. (NA)
★ ★ **Travel On** / Pea. (NA)
★ ★ **Prayed Too Late** / Pea. (NA)
★ ★ ★ **Best of the Sensational Nightingales** / Pea. (NA)
★ ★ ★ **Heart and Soul** / Pea. (NA)
★ ★ **It's Gonna Rain Again** / Pea. (NA)
★ ★ **You and I and Everyone** / Pea. (NA)
The Reverend Julius Cheeks, for years the mainstay of the Nightingales, was one of the

wild men of gospel music, a tireless shouter and a flamboyant showman. He has had an ineradicable influence on soul music. Wilson Pickett modeled his singing after Cheeks in almost every respect, as the most cursory listening reveals. James Brown also picked up quite a few tips from Cheeks, particularly in his phrasing.

Unfortunately, Cheeks appears on none of these albums except on some of the *Best of* affair, which is chock full of such unvarnished gospel as "Burying Ground," "Standing at the Judgment" and "Prayed Too Late." Singing lead on the other albums are Herbert Robertson and Charles Johnson. But Cheeks' influence remained long after he himself left, especially on Robertson. (Johnson is a bit sweeter.) So the Nightingales continued to rate as one of the leading contemporary quartets through the Sixties. Perhaps they favored less feverishly paced material than before, but they could still cut loose when they wanted to.

They also remained very much the purists, which ultimately worked against them. While soul music absorbed their influence and then other gospel groups absorbed soul's influence, the Nightingales modernized only slightly, and in largely insignificant ways. Also, while they did later start to use some new instruments and arranging ideas, they continued to sing only religious material. If anything, they got slightly more country-sounding as the years passed. Aside from that, they lost Robertson and got less interesting. — J.MO.

RONNIE SESSIONS
★ **Ronnie Sessions / MCA (1977)**
Jive pop-country novelty junk. — D.M.

707
★ **707 / Casa. (1980)**
★ **The Second Album / Casa. (1981)**
Second-rate Toto. — J.D.C.

SEVENTH WONDER
★ **Climbing Higher / Parach. (NA)**
★ **Seventh Wonder / Parach. (NA)**
★ **Thunder / Choc. (NA)**
Parapsychological disco band later turned into an R&B vocal group with steel guitars behind lead vocalist Marvin Patton. — J.S.

THE SEX PISTOLS
★ ★ ★ ★ **Never Mind the Bollocks, Here's the Sex Pistols / War. (1977)**
★ ★ ★ **The Very Best of the Sex Pistols / Col. (1978), Br. imp.**

★ ★ ★ **The Great Rock 'n' Roll Swindle / Virgin (1980), Br. imp.**
The Sex Pistols were unquestionably the most radical new rock band of the Seventies. Their initial single, "Anarchy in the U.K.," was widely banned in England, got them thrown off their first record label (EMI) and still made the Top Ten. The group's nihilistic politics, coupled with their basic punk-rock musical approach, was startling, the best example of deliberate vulgarity rock has ever produced. Stretched over an album, the relentless power of Johnny Rotten's scabrous vocals, Steve Jones' stinging guitar and the blitzkrieg of sound can become a bit wearing, but the best tracks, including "Anarchy," "God Save the Queen" and "Pretty Vacant," are as challenging as anything recorded since the advent of Elvis Presley himself. Not for the faint of heart, but if that's your problem, you may have wandered into *Bollocks* by mistake. The group broke up, appropriately enough, after making only this record, and bassist Sid Vicious died an ugly death in early 1979, but Rotten continues with Public Image Limited. Further releases are a tribute to the Pistols' inventiveness in a very short span and Malcolm McLaren's marketing shrewdness—not necessarily in that order. — D.M.

PHIL SEYMOUR
★ ★ ★ **Phil Seymour / Bdwalk (1981)**
Debut from Dwight Twilley's bandmate which raises question of how much of that act's style and character stemmed from its namesake and how much from Seymour, who loses little of duo's pop ingenuousness in transition to solo work. However, the presence of Twilley's other member Bill Pitcock and two Twilley-written tunes ("Love You So Much," "Then We Go Up") indicates Seymour's separation isn't total. Also along for these sessions are 20/20's Ron Flynt and Steve Allen and Rodney Crowell associate Emory Gordy. The results are graceful and affecting and pay tribute to most of the right stuff—Byrds, Del Shannon, Bobby Fuller ("Let Her Dance"), rockabilly (in fine version of "Trying to Get to You") —without moving beyond the "promising" category. Seymour's vocals are competent, if not inspired. Seymour and Pitcock's compositions err on the side of slightness. — G.A.

SHADOW
★ ★ **Love Lite / Elek. (1979)**
★ ★ **Shadow / Elek. (NA)**
★ ★ **Shadow in the Streets / Elek. (NA)**

Mediocre soul group has shown just enough mid-chart action to keep its career going.
— D.M.

THE SHAGGS
■ **Philosophy of the World / Roun. (1980)**
This all-woman power trio from New England plays music so stilted and unappealing that lovers-of-the-bizarre like NRBQ, who were instrumental in getting them recorded, find them brilliant primitives. That is what's known as perverse. — J.S.

SHAKERS
★ **Yankee Reggae / Asy. (1976)**
Berkeley's only contribution to reggae was a batch of white boys who couldn't quite get the beat right, sang miserably and, in short, lived up to the generally impoverished Bay Area rock tradition. — D.M.

THE SHAKIN' PYRAMIDS
★ ★ ★ ★ ★ **Skin 'Em Up / Virgin (1981)**
With a vocalist and a mere two acoustic guitars, the Shakin' Pyramids do something to rockabilly that all the latest, fully electrified bands haven't been able to—you can dance to it again. Their recent work with skiffle king Lonnie Donegan is something to look out for. — ML.H.

SHAKIN' STREET
★ ★ **Shakin' Street / Col. (1980)**
Former Dictators guitarist Ross the Boss fronts post-punk heavy-metal group whose highlight is the cracked voice of lead singer Fabienne Shine, one woman who's not afraid to wallow in rock at its most turgid and tumescent. Nothing to brag about, but any band with the audacity to name itself after the MC5's best song can't be all bad, either.
— D.M.

SHALAMAR
★ ★ ★ **Big Fun / Solar (1979)**
★ ★ ★ **Three for Love / Solar (1981)**
★ **Go for It / Solar (1981)**
Pop-soul trio from Los Angeles proved the ideal vehicle for Solar's ace producer/writer Leon Sylvers III to show off his whipped-cream style. "The Second Time Around," the gold single from *Big Fun* (their third album, and the first with Donny Hathaway soundalike Howard Hewett replacing Gerald Brown) established them as a hitmaking act. On *Three for Love,* Sylvers refined his surf-side pop-soul bubblegum style to a peak of polish. *Go for It* was neither as careful nor as catchy. — S.H.

SHAM 69
★ ★ ★ **Tell Us the Truth / Sire (1978) ¶**
★ ★ **Hersham Boys / Poly. (1979)**
Punk group with an admirably brittle sound, but given to lyrics of the most ideologically pure political stripe. For safety-pin leftists, or anyone who thinks the Clash are too pop.
— D.M.

SHA NA NA
■ **Best of Sha Na Na / Bud. (1976)**
★ **Sha Na Na Is Here to Stay / Bud. (1977)**
In 1969, when Sha Na Na was formed by a group of students at Columbia University, the notion of nostalgia for Fifties rock was still reasonably novel. Onstage, the group's slick choreography and its impersonations of the look of such greaser archetypes as Gene Vincent and Eddie Cochran was at least amusing. But in the studio, the group had nothing new to add; the harmonies were purified and lost all soul. Despite a successful appearance at Woodstock (oh, irony!), the group never developed sufficient original material or personality to become more than cartoons of real rock. This junk-food aroma was only enhanced when the group somehow managed to acquire a network TV show in 1976. Only one member of the group, original guitarist Henry Gross, has gone on to anything like authentic success. — D.M.

DEL SHANNON
★ ★ ★ ★ **Tenth Anniversary Album / Suns. (1971), Br. imp.**
★ ★ ★ **Del Shannon Live in England / U.A. (1973) ¶**
★ ★ ★ ★ **The Vintage Years / Sire (1975) ¶**
★ ★ ★ **Drop Down and Get Me / Elek. (1981)**
★ ★ ★ ★ **The Best of Del Shannon / Pick. (NA)**
Shannon was one of the genuinely great rockers of the interregnum between Elvis and the Beatles: The evidence is in his hatful of hit singles, from the saucy "Little Town Flirt" and "Hats Off to Larry" to the brilliantly paranoiac "Keep Searchin'," "Stranger in Town" and "Runaway." He was also a first-rate songwriter, contributing "I Go to Pieces" to Peter and Gordon among others. In a way Del Shannon stands as the missing link between the raw, unself-conscious rock of the Fifties and the more consciously craftsmanlike rock of the Sixties.

The Sire set is definitive, collecting all the important hits (which are also on the Sunset and Pickwick sets) but including, in addition, many of Shannon's more obscure works. The live album also features the hits but in versions too hurried and nostalgic for comfort.

Tom Petty produced *Drop Down and Get Me,* which sounds something like Shannon's early work but is more country-flavored. Shannon sings well, and organist Benmont Tench is inspired, but the material lacks the narrative sweep of his best hits of the Sixties. — D.M.

DEE DEE SHARP
★ ★ ★ **Happy 'bout the Whole Thing / Phil. (1975)** ¶
★ ★ ★ **What Color Is Love / Phil. (1977)** ¶
★ ★ ★ **Dee Dee / Phil. (NA)**

Famed for her tinny (and mostly forgettable) Cameo-Parkway novelty songs of the early Sixties ("Ride," "Mashed Potatoes"), Sharp teamed up with husband Kenneth Gamble's Philadelphia soul production team for these pleasant, if unexceptional, offerings. — J. MC.

BILLY JOE SHAVER
★ ★ ★ ★ **Old Five and Dimers Like Me / Monu. (1973)**
★ ★ ★ **When I Get My Wings / Capri. (1976)** ¶
★ ★ ★ **Gypsy Boy / Capri. (1977)** ¶
★ ★ ★ **I'm Just an Old Chunk of Coal (But I'm Gonna Be a Diamond Someday) / Col. (1982)**

Shaver is one of the most celebrated of the new breed of Nashville singer/songwriters led by Kris Kristofferson and Waylon Jennings. He wrote most of the material for Jennings' *Honky Tonk Heroes* album and has had his songs covered by Kristofferson, Tom T. Hall, Willie Nelson, Bobby Bare and Tex Ritter. *Old Five and Dimers* is his classic set, which his Capricorn and Columbia albums cannot match, despite the presence of better-than-average material and production assistance from Bob Johnston. — J.S.

MARLENA SHAW
★ **Marlena / Blue N. (NA)** ¶
★ ★ **From the Depths of My Soul / Blue N. (1973)** ¶
★ ★ ★ **Who Is This Bitch Anyway / Blue N. (1975)**
★ **Just a Matter of Time / Blue N. (1976)**
★ ★ ★ **Sweet Beginnings / Col. (1977)**
★ ★ ★ **Acting Up / Col. (1978)** ¶

Marlena Shaw sounds like the soft side of Esther Phillips; she's capable of the same sardonic phrasing, the same sexuality, but she also has a yearning and coyness reminiscent of the young Nancy Wilson. It's been hard for Shaw to find a proper studio setting for her talent, and as a result her career has more misses than successes.

Marlena is an abomination; her salty vocals are constantly warring with Wade Marcus' sugary strings, and her attempts to sing behind the beat clash with the rigid orchestrations. *Depths* is a slight improvement, because the material is more contemporary, a tentative compromise between Shaw and her arranger.

It wasn't until *Bitch,* an album she largely cowrote with Bernard Ighner, that Shaw was allowed to show off her stuff, especially her improvisational raps. Here one gets the sense of an intelligent woman doing the singing, with a nasty but nice sense of humor. But lackluster sales sent her back to a factorylike disco approach with producer Bert deCoteaux. DeCoteaux supplied her with a variety of current and slightly out-of-date soul songs and a conventional female backup trio. It just didn't work: singing the Spinners, Shaw sounds silly. But the Columbia albums modulated that approach. *Beginnings* featured an improvised monologue on "Go Away Little Girl," which became her first hit single. Shaw and deCoteaux now seem to have established some type of sensible working relationship. — R.G.

SHEILA AND B. DEVOTION
★ ★ ★ **Sheila and B. Devotion / Carr. (NA)**
★ ★ ★ **Singing in the Rain / Casa. (NA)**

Ambitious, not always successful attempts to create dance-rock synthesis. Produced by Nile Rodgers and Bernard Edwards of Chic. — D.M.

PETE SHELLEY
★ ★ ★ ★ **Homosapien / Is. (1981)**

After the Buzzcocks and a year-long absence, Pete Shelley is back in the land of flesh and blood. Maybe Shelley is not as searing on his own as he was with the original Buzzcocks (of "Spiral Scratch" fame), but his voice is more versatile and his songs are undercut with urgency, which might have something to do with the Roland microprocessor computer he uses or with producer Martin Rushent, who resuscitated Human League. — ML.H.

ALLEN SHELTON
★ ★ ★ **Shelton Special / Roun. (1977)**

Good instrumental record led by Shelton's deft banjo playing. — J.S.

T. G. SHEPPARD
★ ★ **T.G. / War. (1978)**
★ ★ **Daylight / War. (1978)**

★ ★ **Three-quarters Lonely / War. (1979)**
★ ★ **Smooth Sailin' / War. (1980)**
★ ★ **I Love 'Em All / War. (1981)**
Straightforward country-pop singer, whose reputation is at least partly based on being a marginal member of Elvis' Memphis Mafia, under his real name, Bill Browder. Sheppard's hits ("Do You Wanna Go to Heaven," "Devil in the Bottle," "Don't Touch Me," "Tryin' to Beat the Morning Home") are not quite as smarmy slick as Eddie Rabbitt's—which is probably why they don't cross over—but that's the general genre.
— D.M.

THE SHEPPARDS
★ ★ ★ ★ ★ **The Sheppards / Solid S. (1980)**
This Chicago quintet plus guitarist, a veritable missing link between doo-wop and soul, was virtually unknown until Solid Smoke released these eighteen scintillating sides, some of the most shimmering harmony known to mankind. Lead vocalists Millard Edwards and Murrie Eskridge are both outstanding, and teenaged guitarist Kermit Chandler is a revelation. The highlights are "Island of Love," the closest they came to a hit, and "Tragic," with wonderful echo and venomous revenge lyrics, plus a guitar part that shreds everything it touches. But everything here is outstanding—one of the finds of the past decade. — D.M.

THE SHERBS
★ ★ ★ **The Skill / Atco (1981)**
An Australian group that began life as a wimp-rock outfit called Sherbert toughens up its sound, shortens its name and releases an interesting, if derivative, album of minimalist power pop. Dire Straits without the mystery.
— D.MC.

JOHNNY SHINES
★ ★ ★ **Sittin' on Top of the World / Bio. (1972)**
★ ★ ★ **Johnny Shines and Company / Bio. (1972)**
★ ★ ★ ★ **Johnny Shines / Advent (1974)**
★ ★ ★ **Hey Ba-Ba-Re-Bop / Roun. (1978)**
One of the finest Mississippi *and* Chicago bluesmen, Shines began his career traipsing after Robert Johnson and later moved to the city. He is very fine on his own, only slightly less adept with a small Chicago band. His best recordings are on Flyright's *Dust My Broom* (listed under Robert Jr. Lockwood and Johnny Shines), but Shines is one of the few bluesmen retaining his creativity today. The Advent album, which features him both

solo and electric, was cut in the Seventies and it's superb, and the Rounder set, also very recent, is just about as good. Shines' forte is interpreting the songs of Robert Johnson; he does some of them on all of the albums above. — D.M.

ELLEN SHIPLEY
★ ★ ★ **Ellen Shipley / RCA (1979)** ¶
★ ★ ★ **Breaking through the Ice Age / RCA (1980)**
New York-based singer who's been lumped together with Ellen Foley, Carolyne Mas and other turn-of-the-decade female rockers, Shipley has shown a greater ability than the others to write convincingly. The problem with these records is her inexperience with fronting a full-bore rock band; when they turn it up, she can sound shrill. Still, when the mood is properly set, as on *Ice Age*'s "Lost without Your Love," Shipley's singing comes through and carries both albums.
— W.K.

THE SHIRELLES
★ ★ ★ **The Shirelles / Ev. (1981)**
★ ★ ★ **The Very Best of the Shirelles / U.A. (NA), Br. imp.**
★ ★ ★ ★ ★ **The Shirelles Sing Their Very Best / Sp. (NA)** ¶
In the late Fifties and early Sixties, the Shirelles spearheaded the "girl group" movement, which also included the Crystals, Ronettes, Chiffons, Orlons and scads of others. The Shirelles were the first of these and one of the best, numbering among their hits such legitimate classics of the era as "Soldier Boy," "I Met Him on a Sunday," "Will You Love Me Tomorrow," "Baby It's You" and a half-dozen other statements of romantic adolescent innocence. The Springboard set contains almost all of them, though some of the group's original, but now deleted, collections on Scepter are more attractively presented. — D.M.

SHIRLEY AND LEE
★ ★ ★ ★ **The Best of Shirley and Lee / Ace (1973), Br. imp**
Very fine New Orleans rhythm & blues duets, including the hits "Let the Good Times Roll" and "Feel So Good." Most of these were recorded between 1952 and 1956, and along with Mickey and Sylvia's somewhat slinkier sides, represent the beginning of one of rock & roll's grand traditions: the sultry boy-girl duet, in which as little as possible is left to the imagination.
— D.M.

THE SHIRTS

★ ★ The Shirts / Cap. (1978) ¶
★ Street Light Shine / Cap. (1979) ¶
★ Inner Sleeve / Cap. (1980)
Like Mink DeVille, the Shirts wound up at
CBGB's not because the group was terribly
new wave in its approach but because the
joint happened to be in the neighborhood.
But unlike DeVille, the Shirts aren't motivated by a soul crusade, just a desire to
make pop music. Pleasant but formulaic pop
rock. — D.M.

THE SHOES

★ Present Tense / Elek. (1979)
★ Tongue Twister / Elek. (1980)
AOR bore. There's nothing here that Bread
didn't do better. — D.G.

SHOOTING STAR

★ ★ Shooting Star / Virgin/Atl. (1979)
★ ★ Hang On for Your Life / Virgin/Epic
(1981)
English label signs young Midwestern rockers playing sophisticated heavy metal, hoping
to gain a foothold in the American market;
band makes two well-aimed records and still
no go. *Shooting Star* showed some intelligence and promise; *Hang On for Your Life*
shows only desperation. — I.R.

SHOTGUN

■ Shotgun / MCA (1977)
■ Good, Bad and Funky / MCA (1978)
■ Shotgun 3 / MCA (1978) ¶
■ Shotgun 4 / MCA (1980) ¶
■ Kingdom Come / MCA (1981)
These guys play like somebody took a .12
gauge to their instruments. Rock at its
dumbest. — J.S.

SIDE EFFECT

★ ★ Side Effect / Fan. (1974)
★ ★ What You Need / Fan. (1977)
★ ★ Goin' Bananas / Fan. (1978)
★ ★ Rainbow Visions / Fan. (1978)
★ ★ After the Rain / Elek. (1980)
★ ★ Portraits / Elek. (1981)
★ ★ ★ Greatest Hits / Fan. (NA)
The poor man's Dr. Buzzard's Original "Sa-
vannah" Band. Since the concept of Broad-
way soul only carried Buzzard through one
album successfully, this is for addicts only.
— D.M.

BEN SIDRAN

★ ★ ★ Puttin' In Time on Planet Earth /
MCA (1974)
★ ★ ★ Free in America / Ari. (1976) ¶
★ ★ ★ ★ The Doctor Is In / Ari. (1977) ¶

★ ★ ★ A Little Kiss in the Night / Ari.
(1978) ¶
★ ★ ★ Cat and the Hat / A&M (1979)
Benjamin Sidran, a Ph.D. in philosophy/
musicology, grew up in Racine, Wisconsin,
joined up with Steve Miller and Boz Scaggs
at the University of Wisconsin (they taught
him that rock & roll wasn't dirty), then traveled to England to write his doctoral thesis
on the growth of black music in the U.S. (it
was published in 1971 as *Black Talk*). But
along with his studies, Sidran has found time
to play session piano (and vibes) with Miller,
Scaggs, Eric Clapton, Peter Frampton, the
Rolling Stones and Tony Williams. He has
also produced albums by Miller, Williams
and Jon Hendricks, and while producing
Miller's *Brave New World* he helped corral
Paul McCartney to play drums on "Kow
Kow" and sing on "My Dark Hour."
  When Sidran decided to take the solo
plunge, it was sort of casual and nonprofit
funk-filled jazz and goofiness that he came
up with. These albums are exemplary "easy
swinging," laid-back professionalism. His
piano turns a nasty trick and his vocals and
lyrics owe a great deal to the wit and slow-
burn contortions of his mentor, Mose Allison. — B.M.

PAUL SIEBEL

★ ★ ★ Woodsmoke and Oranges / Elek.
(1970)
★ ★ ★ Jack-Knife Gypsy / Elek.
(1971) ¶
Good Woodstock-area folksinger and songwriter. — J.S.

SIEGEL-SCHWALL BAND

★ ★ The Siegel-Schwall Band / Van.
(1966)
★ ★ Say Siegel-Schwall / Van. (1967)
★ ★ Shake / Van. (1968)
★ Siegel-Schwall '70 / Van. (1970)
★ Three Pieces for a Blues Band / Deutsche
Grammophon (1973) ¶
★ ★ The Best of Siegel-Schwall / Van.
(1974)
This was Chicago's "other" white blues
group of the Sixties, but unlike their neighbors the Butterfield Blues Band, Siegel-
Schwall was not steeped in blues tradition,
but emphasized a kind of neo-psychedelic
improvisation on blues themes that has
weathered the years with little grace. Still,
the early Vanguard sets are far superior to
the later one ('70) and the windy, pretentious symphonic fraud for Deutsche Grammophon. — D.M.

BUNNY SIGLER
★ ★ ★ **That's How Long I'll Be Loving You / Phil. (1974)** ¶
★ ★ ★ ★ **Keep Smilin' / Phil. (1974)** ¶
★ ★ ★ **My Music / Phil. (1976)** ¶
★ ★ ★ **Let Me Party with You / Gold (1978)** ¶
★ ★ ★ **I've Always Wanted to Sing . . . / Gold (1979)** ¶
★ ★ ★ **Let It Snow / Sals. (NA)** ¶

Bunny Sigler's first two Philadelphia International albums were released only months apart. Despite the fact that *Keep Smilin'* has only three songs not found on *That's How Long,* the additions do wonders, making the "rerelease" a smart, iconoclastic gumbo of modern Philly soul. *Keep Smilin'* not only reflects such sources of inspiration as Marvin Gaye, the early Impressions and streetcorner doo-wop, but it also is imbued with infectious good humor—quite apart from the increasingly ponderous paeans of mentors Gamble and Huff. Though *My Music* has several outstanding songs, including one bit of zaniness about a trip to Ghana, the LP is disappointing. Many of Sigler's more eccentric impulses have been curtailed in favor of stock Philly disco charts. Still, *Keep Smilin'* and a handful of earlier singles remain as a testament to Bunny Sigler's talents.   — J. MC.

THE SILENCERS
★ ★ **Rock 'n' Roll Enforcers / Prec. (NA)**
★ ★ **Romantic / Epic (NA)**
Spirited, melodic white R&B in a late Geils mode. Guitarist Warren King and vocalist Frank Czuri are the mainstays.   — J.S.

SILICON TEENS
■ **Music for Parties / Sire (1980)**
Synthesizer versions of Fifties classics and dreary originals. Pray that your parties are never this dull.   — J.D.C.

SILK
★ ★ **Silk / Prel. (NA)**
★ ★ **Smooth as Silk / Prel. (NA)**
★ ★ **Midnight Dancer / Phil. (NA)**
More disco cosmopolitanism. Back to the land is beginning to look more attractive.   — D.M.

SHEL SILVERSTEIN
★ **Freakin' at the Freakers Ball / Col. (1973)**
Silverstein is a *Playboy* cartoonist who has contributed many novelty songs (most notably Loretta Lynn's "One's on the Way" and Dr. Hook's "Cover of Rolling Stone") to the country and pop charts. As a singer, however, he's mostly a pretty good draftsman.
    — D.M.

SILVETTI
★ **Concert from the Stars / Sire (1978)**
★ **Spring Rain / Sire (NA)** ¶
One of those Eurodisco concept groups, in which anonymous voices soar over anonymous synthesized strings and formula rhythms. In the right hands, this can be great stuff, but impresario Bebu Silvetti's no Giorgio Moroder—he's not even any Jacques Morali, when you get right down to it.
    — D.M.

DAVID SIMMONS
★ ★ ★ **Hear Me Out / WMOT (1978)**
★ ★ ★ **The World Belongs to Me / WMOT (NA)**
Soul crooner in the Teddy Pendergrass/Isaac Hayes league. His voice is as good as Teddy's, his tempos as turgid as Isaac's, and like both his mentors, he suffers from a lack of first-rate material and a pretentiously macho view of sex. Given a song as good as any of Pendergrass' best, though, Simmons could actually make a horse race out of the Seventies' soul-stud sweepstakes.
    — D.M.

JOHN AND ARTHUR SIMMS
★ ★ **John and Arthur Simms / Casa. (1980)**
Unexceptional funk and ballads.   — J.D.C.

CARLY SIMON
★ **Carly Simon / Elek. (1970)**
★ **Anticipation / Elek. (1971)**
After several false starts (including an album with sister Lucy as the Simon Sisters on Columbia), Carly Simons' recording career began with these inflated, clumsily revisionist folkie albums in 1970 and 1971. Successive left-field summertimes hits, "That's the Way I Always Heard It Should Be" and "Anticipation," later a ketchup commercial, probably saved both albums from the remainder bins, and the frequently flat-voiced Simon from immediate obscurity. Despite lifeless performances, both singles proved to be pop masterpieces expressive of the postfeminist woman—sexually independent but still expecting the find the easy permanence of romantic marriage someday soon.

Although prophetic of Simon's career, these singles were not typical of the first two albums. The rest of the songs have no such thematic redemptions, except for the pop-star snapshot "Legend in Your Own Time." The Paul Simon–style "Reunions" and

"Dan, My Fling," not to mention the apocalyptic "Share the End," are way outside Carly's reach both as performer and songwriter (even with poet/collaborator Jacob Brackman).

★ ★ ★ **No Secrets / Elek. (1972)**
★ ★ **Hot Cakes / Elek. (1974)**
★ **Playing Possum / Elek. (1975)**

Richard Perry was the perfect producer to give shape to Carly Simon's vast confusions. His slick cut-and-paste production gives both her writing and her studio performances a semblance of form; his massed but subtly deployed studio firepower covered Simon's anemic vocals with pleasant salvos of sound. However, that marvel of female sarcasm and Simon's real claim to pop genius, "You're So Vain" (from *No Secrets*), is untypical. Most of Simon's songs continue the themes of her early singles, but in a postmarital mode: proud family chronicles—from both childhood and her marriage to James Taylor—some vague pop feminism and some ambivalent love songs.

Perry's work with Simon starts strongly with *No Secrets,* almost an autobiographical concept album, slips into hit-and-miss with *Hot Cakes,* practically a James Taylor/Carly Simon duet LP, and falls apart with *Playing Possum,* in which Perry presses a variety of unsuitable stylized settings, from disco to lounge jazz, on Simon, who winds up panting for breath.

★ ★ ★ **The Best of Carly Simon / Elek. (1975)**
★ ★ ★ **Another Passenger / Elek. (1976)**
★ ★ ★ **Boys in the Trees / Elek. (1978)**
★ ★ **Come Upstairs / War. (1980)**
★ ★ **Torch / War. (1981)**

On *Another Passenger,* produced by Ted Templeman, Simon achieves a narrow but solid new start. Cowriter Jacob Brackman returns after a long absence, and she has picked up some needed lessons in phrasing, mostly from James Taylor. On the best songs, including the title cut, Simon uncovers herself and reflects her age and her class. (She is the daughter of one of the founders of Simon and Schuster.) She has abandoned the inane persona of a college-educated housewife about to enter transactional analysis that had progressively taken over her songs. The lessons learned from Perry aren't forgotten, but Simon at least seems really comfortable. At times she is even conversant with the arrangements. *Boys in the Trees* is something of a compromise between Perry's lushness and Templeman's relatively sparse approach, thanks to the guiding hand of Arif Mardin. If Simon is never quite as soulful as

she'd like to be, she's given consistently appropriate support.

The *Best of* collection is Simon's best album, since she is primarily a singles artist. Here her early singles can be heard without suffering through the slbums. Some fans, however, have probably found alternative favorites. Few need bother following Simon's dreadful descent into *Come Upstairs* and *Torch.* — B.T.

JOE SIMON

★ ★ ★ ★ **The World of Joe Simon / Sound. (1973)**
★ ★ ★ **Get Down / Spring (1975)** ¶
★ ★ **Love Vibrations / Spring (1978)**
★ ★ ★ **A Bad Case of Love / Spring (NA)** ¶
★ ★ ★ **Easy to Love / Spring (NA)** ¶
★ ★ ★ **Joe Simon Today / Spring (NA)**

Joe Simon is a smooth-voiced soul singer whose immense popularity has diminished only slightly since he began recording for Sound Stage Seven in 1966. With producer John Richbourg (best known as disc jockey John R.), Simon scored a series of brilliantly mellow soul hits, including "Teenager's Prayer," "Nine Pound Steel" and "The Chokin' Kind," the latter a 1969 million-seller. Since he's moved to his own label, Spring, Simon's career has been more erratic in terms of quality. "Drowning in the Sea of Love," produced by Gamble and Huff, was a smash in 1972 on both pop and soul stations, but since then he's been more confined to black audiences. Unfortunately, a great deal of his early and superior work for Spring has been deleted, and the Sound Stage Seven LP remains the only collection of his early work. — D.M.

LUCY SIMON

★ **Stolen Time / RCA (1977)** ¶

Carly's opera-trained sister. Only for those who enjoy subsistence on a steady diet of white bread. — D.M.

PAUL SIMON

★ ★ ★ ★ ★ **Paul Simon / Col. (1972)**
★ ★ ★ ★ ★ **There Goes Rhymin' Simon / Col. (1973)**
★ ★ ★ **Live Rhymin' / Col. (1974)**
★ ★ ★ ★ ★ **Still Crazy after All These Years / Col. (1975)**
★ ★ ★ ★ **Greatest Hits, Etc. / Col. (1977)**
★ ★ ★ **One Trick Pony / War. (1980)**

Paul Simon was half of Simon and Garfunkel, which understates the matter considerably: he was the duo's writer, and it is for their songs, more than anything, that Simon and Garfunkel are remembered. Since he struck out on his own, in 1971, he has recorded a series of albums that are among the greatest popular music anyone in the current era has attempted.

Paul Simon, the first LP, set the stage for his growth: it is rougher and more expansive than any of the Simon and Garfunkel recordings, with several quirky reggae numbers made in Jamaica and a sense of lost innocence that says much about the necessity for the group's demise. *There Goes Rhymin' Simon* is based on blues and gospel music; the record's biggest hit, "Loves Me Like a Rock," was recorded with the Dixie Hummingbirds, which makes it as close to real gospel as a Jewish kid from Queens is ever likely to come. *Still Crazy* is a chronicle of experience, frequently using broken marriage as a metaphor; it is Simon's most mature work, and his most musically sophisticated, relying, for instance, on interrelationships of notes from song to song for part of its cohesion and emphasizing piano rhythms over guitar figures. In "Fifty Ways to Leave Your Lover," "My Little Town" (the Simon and Garfunkel reunion), the title cut and several other songs, Simon's writing reached a new level of sophistication.

Unfortunately, he has produced very little since then. *Live Rhymin'* was released to fill the temporal gap between the second and third solo albums, and *Greatest Hits, Etc.,* which contained a pair of good new songs, "Stranded in a Limousine" and "Slip Slidin' Away," served the same function. *One Trick Pony* is the soundtrack of Simon's movie, which he wrote and starred in. It has one superb song, "Ace in the Hole," and much listenable music, but generally seems dated. Simon then returned to duetting with Art Garfunkel. — D.M.

SIMON AND GARFUNKEL
★ ★ **Wednesday Morning, 3 A.M. / Col. (1965)**
★ ★ **Sounds of Silence / Col. (1966)**
★ ★ ★ **Parsley, Sage, Rosemary and Thyme / Col. (1966)**
★ ★ ★ ★ ★ **Bookends / Col. (1968)**
★ ★ **The Graduate / Col. (1968)**
★ ★ ★ **Bridge over Troubled Water / Col. (1970)**
★ ★ ★ ★ **Simon and Garfunkel's Greatest Hits / Col. (1972)**
★ ★ ★ **The Concert in Central Park / War. (1982)**

With their socially relevant but gentle folk rock, Simon and Garfunkel quietly bridged the Sixties generation gap. *Wednesday Morning,* their debut, made no waves until pro-

ducer Tom Wilson grafted an electric guitar to a song called "Sounds of Silence," which proceeded to become one of the biggest and best folk-rock hits. Paul Simon's elliptical, imagistic writing soon became very big on the rock-lyrics-are-poetry circuit, but he was really an expert popular-song craftsman, influenced by both folk and rock but owing allegiance to neither. A string of hits followed, many featuring Art Garfunkel's beautiful tenor voice. *Parsley,* an early if vague concept album, contained more than its share of successes: the beautiful "Homeward Bound," the Eleanor Rigby–like "For Emily Whenever I May Find Her," and "59th Street Bridge Song (Feelin' Groovy)," a big hit for Harper's Bizarre.

Ironically, "Scarborough Fair/Canticle," an adaptation of a pair of traditional songs, made Simon and Garfunkel superstars when it and an additional number written by Simon, "Mrs. Robinson," were used as themes for Mike Nichols' 1967 film, *The Graduate.*

It was on *Bookends* and *Bridge,* however, that the pair really hit their stride. *Bookends* was more directly conceptual than even *Parsley,* a kind of snapshot album of American life in the late Sixties: "Mrs. Robinson," "America," "Fakin' It" and "At the Zoo" were hits (all were written by Simon, of course). "Bridge over Troubled Water" was perhaps the most influential and certainly the most recorded number of the latter half of the Sixties; it is an almost breathtakingly perfect song, and its roots in black gospel enable it to escape the sometimes cloying sweetness of the rest of the album. *Bridge* became an unheard-of success, selling four million copies in the U.S. and many millions more abroad.

Unfortunately, that saccharine tendency makes many of these records seem extremely dated today. *Greatest Hits* remains the best example of Simon and Garfunkel's work together. Simon's solo recordings are far superior to all except two or three of the duo's best songs. Yet their 1981 reunion in Central Park is a brilliant updating of their sound—perhaps because it omits the duo's more precious tendencies. — D.M.

NINA SIMONE
★ ★ ★ **The Best of Nina Simone / Phi. (1969)**
★ ★ ★ **The Best of Nina Simone / RCA (1970)**
★ ★ ★ **Here Comes the Sun / RCA (1971)**
★ ★ ★ **Baltimore / CTI (1978)**
★ ★ ★ **It Is Finished / RCA (NA)**

★ ★ ★ ★ **The Finest of Nina Simone / Beth. (NA)**
Dusky-voiced singer/keyboardist earned her nickname, "The High Priestess of Soul," through deeply personal interpretations of everything from Gershwin to Dylan to African folk songs. One of the most intellectual soul singers of her generation, Simone metamorphosed from a moody jazz-pop stylist into a political voice whose expressions of black rage and pride remain unmatched in their emotional intensity.

Simone debuted in the late Fifties on Bethlehem, for whom she had her first and biggest hit, "I Loves You Porgy," The Philips *Best of* collects highlights from six albums recorded between 1964 and 1967 and includes "I Put a Spell on You" and Simone's searing black-consciousness manifesto, "Four Women." RCA's *Best of* seems a somewhat arbitrary selection from her next half-dozen albums (from 1967 to 1970).
— S.H.

SIMPLE MINDS
★ ★ **Life in a Day / Zoom (1979), Br. imp.**
★ ★ ★ **Real to Real Cacophony / Zoom (1979), Br. imp.**
★ ★ ★ **Empires and Dance / Zoom (1980), Br. imp.**
★ ★ ★ **Sons and Fascination/Sister Feeling Call / Virgin (1981), Br. imp.**
★ ★ ★ **Themes for Great Cities / Stiff (1981)**
This Glasgow-based band has been heavily inspired by the sounds of Roxy Music. There are layers of synthesizers and treated guitars on these records, and lead singer Jim Kerr sounds just like Bryan Ferry. Simple Minds' records to date have suffered from a certain sameness, using the same beat and musical ideas a little too often. *Sons and Fascination/ Sister Feeling Call* was released as a limited edition double album, has since been released separately and is their best work to date.
— K.L.

FRANKIE LEE SIMS
★ ★ ★ **Lucy Mae Blues / Spec. (NA)**
Texas country bluesman rocks out on these Fifties sides. — D.M.

VALERIE SIMPSON
★ ★ ★ ★ **Keep It Comin' / Mo. (1977)**
This includes a fair share of material from Simpson's 1972 solo album, *Exposed,* including the scarifying half-a-cappella "Sinner Man," which is Joni Mitchell meets Aretha Franklin in its confessional intensity. For the most part, Simpson is better off here than as part of a duo with Nicklas Ashford, simply because there's more chance for an articulate personality to emerge. But Ashford's production presence is a key to the way the record works, and it's impossible to imagine either she or he writing songs without the other. Since they've cowritten "Let's Go Get Stoned," "Ain't Nothing Like the Real Thing" and what sometimes seems like the other third of Motown's greatest hits (the ones Holland-Dozier and Smokey Robinson didn't pen), that's high praise, indeed.
— D.M.

FRANK SINATRA
★ ★ ★ ★ ★ **The Frank Sinatra Story in Music / Col. (1958)**
★ ★ ★ ★ **In the Beginning (1943–1951) / Col. (1972)**
★ ★ ★ ★ **Songs for Young Lovers / Cap. (1954)**
★ ★ ★ ★ ★ **In the Wee Small Hours / Cap. (1955)**
★ ★ ★ ★ ★ **Songs for Swingin' Lovers / Cap. (1956)**
★ ★ ★ ★ ★ **A Swingin' Affair / Cap. (1957)**
★ ★ ★ ★ ★ **Where Are You / Cap. (1957)**
★ ★ ★ ★ ★ **Come Fly with Me / Cap. (1958)**
★ ★ ★ ★ ★ **Only the Lonely / Cap. (1958)**
★ ★ ★ ★ **Come Dance with Me / Cap. (1959)**
★ ★ ★ **No One Cares / Cap. (1959)**
★ ★ ★ ★ **Nice 'n' Easy / Cap. (1960)**
★ ★ ★ ★ **Sinatra's Swingin' Session / Cap. (1961)**
★ ★ ★ **All the Way / Cap. (1961)**
★ ★ ★ **Come Swing with Me / Cap. (1961)**
★ ★ ★ **Ring-a-Ding Ding / Rep. (1961)**
★ ★ ★ **Sinatra Swings / Rep. (1961)**
★ ★ ★ **I Remember Tommy / Rep. (1961)**
★ ★ ★ **Point of No Return / Cap. (1962)**
★ ★ **Sinatra and Strings / Rep. (1962)**
★ ★ **Sinatra and Swingin' Brass / Rep. (1962)**
★ **All Alone / Rep. (1962)**
★ ★ ★ **Sinatra and Basie / Rep. (1963)**
★ ★ **The Concert Sinatra / Rep. (1963)**
★ ★ **Sinatra's Sinatra / Rep. (1963)**
★ **Days of Wine and Roses, Moon River and Other Academy Award Winners / Rep. (1964)**
★ ★ **It Might as Well Be Swing / Rep. (1964)**
★ **Softly as I Leave You / Rep. (1964)**
★ **Sinatra '65 / Rep. (1965)**
★ ★ ★ ★ **September of My Years / Rep. (1965)**
★ ★ ★ **A Man and His Music / Rep. (1965)**
★ ★ **My Kind of Broadway / Rep. (1965)**
★ **Moonlight Sinatra / Rep. (1966)**

★ ★ **Strangers in the Night** / Rep. (1966)
★ **Sinatra at the Sands** / Rep. (1966)
★ **That's Life** / Rep. (1966)
★ ★ ★ **Francis Albert Sinatra and Antonio Carlos Jobim** / Rep. (1967)
★ ★ ★ **Francis A. Sinatra and Edward K. Ellington** / Rep. (1967)
★ ★ **Frank Sinatra's Greatest Hits** / Rep. (1968)
★ **Cycles** / Rep. (1968)
★ **My Way** / Rep. (1969)
★ **A Man Alone** / Rep. (1969)
★ **Watertown** / Rep. (1970)
★ **Sinatra and Company** / Rep. (1971)
★ ★ **Frank Sinatra's Greatest Hits, Vol. 2** / Rep. (1972)
★ ★ ★ **Ol' Blue Eyes Is Back** / Rep. (1973)
★ **Some Nice Things I've Missed** / Rep. (1974)
★ **The Main Event** / Rep. (1974)
★ ★ ★ **Trilogy: Past, Present and Future** / Rep. (1980)
★ ★ ★ **She Shot Me Down** / Rep. (1981)

Frank Sinatra's voice *is* pop music history. From a crooner, who injected a softened version of Billie Holiday's jazz phrasing into Bing Crosby's creamy ballad style, Sinatra evolved into the definitive saloon stylist of the Fifties and from there into a punchy swinger whose occasionally surly roughness was echoed by pop rockers such as Billy Joel and Neil Diamond.

Sinatra's big-time career began in 1939 when he was hired as a vocalist by bandleader Harry James, with whom he worked for six months before joining Tommy Dorsey. The sides he cut with Dorsey and the Pied Pipers (including the classic standards "I'll Never Smile Again," "Oh, Look at Me Now" and "This Love of Mine") are available on RCA Victor and RCA Camden. The mellow "note-bending" style of Ziggy Elman, Dorsey's trombonist, is said to have been a big influence on Sinatra's shaping of vowels.

In 1942, Sinatra decided to become a soloist, reaching his peak of popularity as a bobby-sox idol two years later in an historic performance at New York's Paramount Theater. Though most of the nearly two hundred and fifty sides he cut with Columbia are out of print, *The Frank Sinatra Story in Music*, a two-disc Columbia Special Products package, is the definitive anthology of "The Voice" at its most seductive, and it traces his career from the earliest Harry James sides (reissued after Sinatra became a star) through such bold early-Fifties swing hits as "Castle Rock" and "The Birth of the Blues." *In the Beginning*, which contains twenty

cuts, sticks to Sinatra's more successful Columbia singles, which were seldom his best records, and its sound is crudely rechanneled into stereo. *Story* is far preferable, with its matchless performances of "Laura," "I'm Glad There Is You," and "I Concentrate on You," etc. Here is Sinatra's bel canto baritone at its purest—a distillation of the homefront American dream in wartime. No male pop singer before or since has offered eroticism so tenderly, even though many have tried, including Tony Bennett, Vic Damone, Al Martino, Jerry Vale, Jack Jones, Barry Manilow . . . the list is endless.

When Sinatra moved to Capitol in 1953, his personality changed from a questing romantic to a worldly sophisticate, alternately pleasure-loving and rueful. At Columbia, Sinatra had worked almost exclusively with one arranger/conductor (Axel Stordahl), who supplied him with a hearts-and-flowers chamber orchestra sound. At Capitol, Sinatra rotated primarily among three— Nelson Riddle, Gordon Jenkins and Billy May—with whom he made seven masterpieces in five years. Capitol has reissued them in various formats, including twofers, with new titles, and deletions in repertoire.

With Nelson Riddle *(Songs for Young Lovers, Songs for Swingin' Lovers, A Swingin' Affair, Nice 'n' Easy)*, Sinatra reached the summit of his recording career. Riddle's tasty jazz orchestra arrangements of songs like "You Make Me Feel So Young," "It Happened in Monterey" and "I've Got You under My Skin" buoyed Sinatra to an all-time peak of mellow exuberance on *Swingin' Lovers*. And on the more reflective *Only the Lonely*, Riddle's delicately moody arrangements blended jazz solos into a colorful orchestral palette.

Gordon Jenkins, who has always favored heavy Mahlerian string arrangements, Sinatra used for his dark-night-of-the-soul albums like *Where Are You* and *No One Cares*. On *Where Are You*, their one perfect collaboration, Sinatra's singing exuded a towering angst that bordered on the sepulchral; the album contains great remakes of "I'm a Fool to Want You" and "Laura."

With Billy May, Sinatra moved into the harder swing that dominated his Sixties output after putting out a brilliant medium-tempo album, *Come Fly with Me*, in the Nelson Riddle mold. The move from pop-jazz orchestration into harder, brassier swing coincided with the deterioration of Sinatra's velvety tone, for which he compensated with snappier, more aggressive phrasing.

Many of the albums Sinatra made for his

own record company, Reprise, beginning in 1961 were simultaneous exercises in nostalgia and attempts to improve on past performances. But even as Sinatra continued to refine his style, the voice became ever more frayed, and his choices of new songs and new writers to boost (Rod McKuen? Bob Gaudio? Jake Holmes?) were less than inspired. On turning fifty, Sinatra reteamed up with Gordon Jenkins to make *September of My Years*, which summed up the punchy sentimentality of a whole generation of American men. The centerpiece, "It Was a Very Good Year," is an exceptionally eloquent expression of middle-aged erotic nostalgia.

Sinatra's biggest hits in the Sixties, "Strangers in the Night" (1966), "That's Life" (1966), "Cycles" (1968) and "My Way" (1969), became the centerpieces of uneven albums. *Ol' Blue Eyes Is Back* (1973) was the first of several carefully planned comebacks. It was superseded several years later by the three-record *Trilogy*, in which Sinatra considered the past, present and future, respectively, with arrangers Billy May, Don Costa and Gordon Jenkins. While Jenkins' conception of Sinatra's future consisted of a fatuous self-penned oratorio, May's swing side was up to Sinatra's late-Fifties standards, and Costa's contemporary side yielded Sinatra's biggest Seventies hit, "Theme from New York, New York." *She Shot Me Down*, made mostly with Jenkins, is memorable for Sinatra's thoughtful versions of Alec Wilder's last two songs, "South to a Warmer Place" and "A Long Night." Released on the eve of Sinatra's sixty-sixth birthday, it showed him still going strong.

Like Presley and Dylan—the only other white male American singers since 1940 whose popularity, influence and mythic force have been comparable—Sinatra will last indefinitely. He virtually invented modern pop song phrasing. — S.H.

THE SINCEROS
★ ★ ★ ★ **Sound of Sunbathing / Col. (1979)**
★ ★ ★ **Pet Rock / Col. (1981)**
Wonderful British pop-rock quartet led by guitarist/songwriter Mark Kjeldsen parlayed singalong choruses and slick playing into a delightfully tuneful debut. "Take Me to Your Leader" compares favorably to the Cars at the height of that band's popularity; "Little White Lie," "Worlds Apart" and "Quick, Quick Slow" are also stand-outs. On *Pet Rock*, the sound is the same but the ideas aren't as good. — J.S.

SINGERS AND PLAYERS
★ ★ ★ **War of Words / 99LP (1981)**
And now for something completely different: new-age reggae. This U.K. collaboration between Jamaican-based musicians (Style Scott, Bim Sherman, Prince Far-I), U.K.-based West Indians, and U.K. new-wavers yields an entrancing mix of roots rhythms and electronics—cool, hard and substantial. More insightful material could have produced a classic. — R.F.G.

SHANDI SINNAMON
★ **Shandi Sinnamon / Asy. (1976)**
An artist who undoubtedly admires Helen Reddy for her singing rather than her politics. And she's just about as awful, too. — D.M.

SINS OF SATAN
■ **Thou Shalt Boogie Forever / Bud. (NA)**
Lunch break's over, back on your heads! — J.S.

SIOUXSIE AND THE BANSHEES
★ ★ **The Scream / Poly. (1978), Br. imp.**
★ ★ **Join Hands / Poly. (1979), Br. imp.**
★ ★ **Kaleidoscope / Poly. (1980), Br. imp.**
★ ★ **Ju Ju / Poly. (1981), Br. imp.**
★ ★ ★ **Greatest Hits / Poly. (1981), Br. imp.**
Siouxsie wears great clothes and knows how to use makeup well. Her musical ability, at least as evidenced by her recorded work, is minimal. Neither danceable nor lyrically interesting, these albums are uniformly ghoulish, self-indulgent and monotonous, and Siouxsie's flirtations with anti-Semitism make them even less appealing, if only as documents of London scene-making. The tedium is relieved only by a few songs such as "Hong Kong Garden" and "Spellbound," which are available on the greatest-hits compilation. — D.G.

SISTER SLEDGE
★ ★ **Circle of Love / Atco (1975) ¶**
★ ★ **Together / Coti. (1977) ¶**
★ ★ ★ **We Are Family / Coti. (1979)**
★ ★ **Love Somebody Today / Coti. (1980)**
★ ★ **All American Girls / Coti. (1981)**
This talented teenage family group has been unable to come up with a hit record, partly because of material that usually lacks distinction. The disco-based *We Are Family* was their commercial breakthrough. — J.MC.

SKAFISH
■ **Skafish / Illegal (1980)**
New-wave frog prince rides his enormous

proboscis and a songwriting style that celebrates the joys of insanity into a truly forgettable record. This is one fish with a short shelf life. Get the old newspapers! — J.S.

RICKY SKAGGS
★ ★ ★ ★ **Waitin' for the Sun to Shine /**
Epic (1981)
★ ★ ★ ★ **"Family and Friends" / Roun.**
(1982)
★ ★ ★ **Highways and Heartaches / Epic**
(1982)
Despite the high ratings, it's fair to say that Skaggs has not quite lived up to his potential—which only means that he is capable of making nearly perfect bluegrass and country music. A veteran of several backing groups (notably the Stanley Brothers, the Clinch Mountain Boys and Emmylou Harris' group), Skaggs combines a brilliant bluegrass singing style with modern country material, and he keeps his arrangements fairly traditional. Given really outstanding material, he could be amazing.

Each of the albums here has something to recommend it. *Waitin' for the Sun to Shine* is Skaggs' commercial breakthrough set, thanks largely to the high lonesome title track. Also worth hearing are "Don't Get above Your Raising," "Your Old Love Letters" and "So Round, So Firm, So Fully Packed." *Highways and Heartaches* isn't quite as strong, but "Heartbroke" and "Don't Let Your Sweet Love Die," plus Rodney Crowell's "One Way Rider" and Bill Monroe's "Can't You Hear Me Callin' " suggest Skaggs' aptitude for not only all country styles but all country eras, from ancient to postmodern. The Rounder set was in fact recorded (and originally released) before either of the Epic sets, and it hews closer to traditional styles, particularly bluegrass. Skaggs' parents appear on the beautiful "River of Memory" and "Won't It Be Wonderful There," and his wife, Sharon, and her family offer "Hallelujah I'm Ready." This is earthier, less contemporary than the Epic albums, and just as worthwhile. It would have been a shame for Skaggs to remain so totally a rustic—he deserves the broader audience his slicker new material brings him—but it would be a shame if he lost contact with such powerful roots. That he has kept himself this close to home so far is cause for rejoicing. — D.M.

THE SKATALITES
★ ★ ★ **African Roots / U. A. (1978)** ¶
The Skatalites were the foremost band playing ska, the predecessor of reggae. This is a little rugged on Yankee ears, but the fundamentals for what the Wailers and Maytals would later make popular are firmly embedded here. Since *African Roots* is a relatively recent recording, try to find the band's seminal early-Sixties material on Studio One, especially *Best of* and *Ska Authentic.* — D.M. /R.F.G.

SKATT BROTHERS
★ **Strange Spirits / Casa. (NA)**
Ex-Kiss road manager and musical buddy Sean Delaney create a more rockified model of the Village People. But this supposedly cruiser-bruiser stuff is just limp-wristed posing. Strange spirits indeed, the Skatt Brothers certainly aren't of any note for their music. — R.P.

SKY
★ **Sky 3 / Ari. (NA)**
Classical-pop guitarist John Williams leads this meandering outfit through its semi-pastoral moods as if he were sleepwalking. Come to think of it, maybe he is. — J.S.

PATRICK SKY
★ ★ ★ **Patrick Sky / Van. (1965)**
■ **Songs That Made America Famous / Adel.**
(1973)
★ ★ **Two Steps Forward—One Step Back /**
Lev. (1975) ¶
As a singer/songwriter during the Sixties (as represented on the Vanguard LP), Sky combined an offbeat sense of humor with a serious love of traditional music. But after two albums for Vanguard (the second is deleted) and two for MGM (also out of print), Sky did *Songs That Made America Famous* on his own. He claimed that the language and subject matter were too offensive and vulgar for any major label to release it, but with the exception of Mike Hunt's "The Pope," the record just isn't really funny. Sky is currently concentrating on traditional music and building Irish uilleann pipes, and that's the side of his career chronicled on the Leviathan LP. — I.M.

SKYBOYS
★ ★ **Skyboys / First Amer. (1979)**
Sunny country pop in L.A. cowboy vein, from Pacific Northwest unit with roots in both country and rock. Skyboy Ken Parypa is brother of two members of seminal Sixties rockers the Sonics. — G.A.

SKYHOOKS
★ ★ ★ **Living in the Seventies / Mush.**
(NA), Aust. imp. ¶

★ ★ ★ **Ego Is Not a Dirty Word** / **Mush. (1975), Aust. imp.** ¶
★ ★ **Straight in a Gay Gay World** / **Mush. (1976), Aust. imp.**
★ ★ **Guilty until Proven Insane** / **Mush. (1977), Aust. imp.**
★ ★ **Live! Be in It** / **Mush. (1978), Aust. imp.**
★ ★ ★ **Best of Skyhooks** / **Mush. (1979), Aust. imp.**
★ **Hot for the Orient** / **Mush. (1980), Aust. imp.**

When Skyhooks made it to No. 1 on the Australian charts in 1975, it v as a signal that things had changed in Oz's rock & roll. The music had an eclectic, urgent, witty quality. The clear, trebly sounds of the two guitars, the clever rhythmic and melodic interplay and the constructions of the songs themselves—all knew about the last twenty years of American and British rock and pop, but did more than simply echo them.

Skyhooks' songs are about Carlton and Toorak, not Pasadena and Kansas City. When they sang about cars, they sang about Falcons and Holdens, not Chevvies and Mustangs. Bass player Greg Macintosh wrote songs that crystallized the experience of growing up in urban Australia.

"Love on the Radio" is a song about the transmutation of emotion into commodity, on which magic the huge profits of popular culture are founded. It's a song that makes sense to anyone who's grown up with radio anywhere. "Living in the Seventies," Skyhooks' first No. 1 hit, is a brilliantly edgy, nervous, funny evocation of urban neurosis. "Horror Movie" refers to the luridly numbing effects of TV news shows. And the ambivalent selfishness of modern romance is summed up in "Love's Not Good Enough."

Skyhooks first gained popularity with audiences from the university suburb of Carlton, in Melbourne. But after curly-haired surfer larrikin Graeme "Shirley" Strachan joined as singer, they became one of the top bands in the country. Their stage act was theatrical to the point of burlesque, but always with an edge of self-parody that rescued it from tastelessness. The somewhat bizarre spectacle of ten thousand fourteen-year-old girls singing along with songs like "You Just Like Me 'Cos I'm Good in Bed" and "All My Friends Are Getting Married" was commonplace in 1975–76.

Confusingly, the first U.S. album, *Ego Is Not a Dirty Word* (on Mercury, now deleted), has the same name and cover as the second Australian album but is in fact a compilation of their first two records; while the second U.S. album, *Living in the Seventies,* has the same title and cover as the first Australian release but, apart from the title track, is really the third, less successful Australian record.

The best of Skyhooks can be heard on the first U.S. record. By the next some of the freshness has gone. The nervy, uptempo pace is unrelieved and quickly becomes wearing, and the lyrics begin to seem forced, merely reflecting rather than illuminating the world they evoke. The first two Australian releases are worth seeking out, as they include some gems of local reference—"Balwyn Calling" and "Carlton" among them—that have been filtered out of the U.S. releases. It's a pity: if Australians can take their rock & roll filled with references to Memphis or Amarillo, surely an American audience could have absorbed a bit of Australiana.

Early in 1977 guitarist Red Symons departed and was replaced by Bob Spencer; in 1978 Shirley Strachan left. But the band had already begun to lose its originality, humor and lightness of touch, and the later albums tend to a more conventional harder rock style, the lyrics only intermittently recalling the inspiration, wit and irony of the early days. — S.M.

SKYLINERS
★ ★ ★ **Since I Don't Have You** / **Orig. Sound (NA)**
The title track was one of the best moody pop ballads of 1959; it sounded so funky, in a manner derived from the Platters, that it was hard to believe the quintet was white. Subsequent singles, collected here from the originals released on Calico, still featured the resonant lead singing of Jimmy Beaumont but lacked the great spark of the first hit. — D.M.

SLADE
★ **Sladest** / **Rep. (1973)** ¶
★ **Nobody's Fools** / **War. (1976)** ¶
A number of people were briefly convinced in the early Seventies that Slade, a group of working-class louts from the English Midlands, were about to be the Next Big Thing. They were, at least in England, thanks to such trebly, metallic shouters as "Mama Weer All Crazee Now" and "Gudbuy T'Jane" (the spelling is theirs, not ours). Those moments came a few years before the over-the-hill-and-soon-to-be-far-away *Sladest* and *Nobody's Fools.* The high-water marks for this quartet of ferocious hard-core rockers were a pair of deleted LPs, *Slade Alive* and *Slayed?,* whose straight-for-the-gut ap-

proach has influenced a number of later bands, most notably Kiss. Produced and managed by former Animals bassist and Jimi Hendrix manager Chas Chandler.
— B.A.

SLAPP HAPPY
★ ★ **Sort Of** / Rec. (1972/1981), imp.
★ ★ ★ ★ **Acnalbasac Noom** / Rec. (1972/1981), imp.
★ ★ ★ **Slapp Happy** / Virgin (1974), imp.
★ ★ ★ ★ **Desperate Straights** / Virgin (1974), imp.

Slapp Happy was one of the first and certainly one of the most deviant groups on the Virgin label. Employing a variety of musical idioms from waltzes to bossa novas and tangos, and combining them with staggeringly literate lyrics, Slapp Happy managed to sound alternately sinister and cheerful, and always intriguing.

Guitarist and vocalist Peter Blegvad, pianist Anthony More and vocalist Dagmar Krause, whose eerie high-pitched voice was the group's most arresting feature, later joined the group Henry Cow, and Slapp Happy broke up in 1975. — D.G.

SLAUGHTER
★ **Bite Back** / DJM (1980)
Hard-core British punkaboogie recorded three years too late to be an interesting historical artifact and about one hundred years too early for the band's abilities. — W.K.

SLAVE
★ ★ ★ **Slave** / Coti. (1977) ¶
★ ★ **The Hardness of the World** / Coti. (1977) ¶
★ ★ ★ **The Concept** / Coti. (1978) ¶
★ ★ ★ **Just a Touch of Love** / Coti. (1979)
★ ★ ★ **Stone Jam** / Coti. (1980)
★ ★ ★ **Show Time** / Coti. (1981)

This ten-piece disco band's first album, *Slave,* got some exposure in dance palaces, where its all-out thump made up for the utter inanity of the rest of it. *The Hardness of the World* lacked panache, but *The Concept* and followups snapped with Parliafunkadelic-styled wit and imagination. Time for a *Greatest Hits* set here. — D.M.

H.Y. SLEDGE
★ **Bootleg Music** / SSS (NA)
Pounded out. — D.M.

PERCY SLEDGE
★ ★ ★ ★ **The Best of Percy Sledge** / Atl. (1969)

★ ★ ★ **Percy Sledge: Star Collection** / Midi (1972), Fr. imp.
★ ★ ★ **Percy Sledge: Star Collection, Vol. 2** / Midi (1973), Fr. imp.
★ ★ ★ **The Golden Voice of Soul** / Midi (1974), Fr. imp.
★ ★ ★ **I'll Be Your Everything** / Capri. (1974) ¶
★ ★ ★ ★ **Two Originals of Percy Sledge** / Atl. (1975), Ger. imp.
★ ★ ★ **Greatest Hits** / Gusto (1981)
★ ★ ★ ★ **Percy!** / Monu. (1983)

Through the middle Sixties, Percy Sledge, along with producers Quin Ivy and Marlin Greene, made a series of melodramatically heartrending soul ballads—"Warm and Tender Love," "When a Man Loves a Woman," "Out of Left Field," "Take Time to Know Her"—that remain emotional classics for romantics of all ages. Sledge's tenor voice was fitted to gospel-like backgrounds, which gave the often maudlin lyrics a properly portentous cast. This is a bit dated, in terms of approach and message, but truly wonderful stuff; the *Best of* has the great majority of Sledge's worthwhile sides. The Capricorn album reunites Sledge with Quin Ivy, and although there aren't any masterpieces, it's a smoothly listenable update of the approach.

Gusto's *Greatest Hits* are remakes. The imports are vintage Atlantic material, with some interesting and audacious song choices, particularly on *The Golden Voice of Soul. Percy!* is a solid contemporary LP of Sledge singing in his old style—very satisfying when it works. — D.M.

SLICK
★ ★ **Slick** / WMOT (1979)
★ ★ **Go for It** / WMOT (NA)
More like oil than Grace, this self-defining disco group is characteristically (for WMOT's stable) faceless. — D.M.

GRACE SLICK
★ ★ ★ **Conspicuous Only in Its Absence** / Col. (1968)
★ ★ ★ **Collectors Item** / Col. (1971)
★ ★ **Baron Von Tollbooth and the Chrome Nun** / Grunt (1973)
★ ★ **Manhole** / Grunt (1974)
■ **Dreams** / RCA (1980)
★ **Welcome to the Wrecking Ball** / RCA (1981)

The two Columbia albums are essentially the same: material from Slick's pre-Jefferson Airplane band the Great Society, including elongated versions of "White Rabbit" and "Somebody to Love." *Manhole* was recorded during the days of the Jefferson Airplane's disintegration and bears the appropriate scars of the time. — J.S.

THE SLICK BAND
★ ★ **The Earl Slick Band** / Cap. (1976)
★ ★ ★ **Razor Sharp** / Cap. (1976)
Before forming this band, Earl Slick was best known as David Bowie's guitarist, circa the *Young Americans* LP. Although singer Jimmie Mack wrote most of the material, the group's apparent purpose is to create a setting for Slick's firestorm guitar playing. In that capacity, it serves well, grinding out solid, simple bottom. Mack works inside the Anglo-screamer rock tradition and writes passable lyrics about barroom sex and violence.

On *Earl Slick,* the band is apparently still figuring out its basic strategy, and Mack's songs overuse the Bad Company midtempo strategy; Slick botches the multi-tracked guitar technique developed in his Bowie stint. *Razor Sharp* is much improved, reducing Mack's role to something more functional, and the band pushes steadily to showcase Slick's searing solos and flash fills. — B.T.

THE SLITS
★ **Cut** / Ant. (1979), Br. imp.
After being together three years, this English all-female group finally made a record; it reveals no singing ability, a rudimentary handling of musical instruments and rather poor reggae-influenced songwriting. Yet this do-it-yourself incompetence is precisely the point, claim the group's admirers. Obviously, then, for hard-core Anglophilic ass kissers only.
— W.K.

SLY AND THE FAMILY STONE
★ ★ ★ **A Whole New Thing** / Epic (1967) ¶
★ ★ ★ ★ **Life** / Epic (1968)
★ ★ ★ **Dance to the Music** / Epic (1968)
★ ★ ★ **High Energy** / Epic (1975) ¶
A Whole New Thing was an apt title; with one album, Sly Stone and his sexually and racially integrated band assaulted black music conventions and irreparably changed its direction and focus. Sly built songs like "Dance to the Music" and "Life" on James Brown's rhythmic innovation while adding fresh elements: disembodied group vocals, scattershot horn charts and lyrics with a point of view. The early Sly Stone records are undisciplined, but they contain a ferocious spirit and energy that borders on the anarchic.
★ ★ ★ ★ ★ **Stand!** / Epic (1969)
★ ★ ★ ★ ★ **Greatest Hits** / Epic (1970)

Both *Stand!* and *Greatest Hits* exuded an optimism that was fitting for the time. "Stand," "Everybody Is a Star" and "Hot Fun in the Summertime" were as representative of the Woodstock sensibility (and mood) as any twenty-minute Grateful Dead guitar jam. The optimism wasn't confined to the lyrics or stance, either. The brashness of early singles like "Dance to the Music" was replaced by a gentler tone that one might guess meant peace of mind.
★ ★ ★ ★ ★ **There's a Riot Goin' On** / Epic (1971) ¶
There are few pop albums this powerful. Though the record yielded two hit singles, white listeners were alienated by it, perhaps purposely. Sly made fun of his old songs; the remake of "Thank You Falettinme Be Mice Elf Again" as "Thank You for Talkin' to Me Africa" is chilling. The title cut was timed at 0:00, and through most of the record, Sly sounded stoned. Not a pleasant buzz either, but something a whole lot more vicious. Greil Marcus said it best: "The record was no fun." Woodstock was over.
★ ★ ★ ★ **Fresh** / Epic (1973) ¶
★ ★ ★ **Small Talk** / Epic (1974) ¶
★ ★ ★ **High on You** / Epic (1975) ¶
★ ★ ★ **Heard Ya Missed Me, Well I'm Back** / Epic (1976) ¶
★ ★ ★ **Back on the Right Track** / War. (1979)
★ ★ **Ten Years Too Soon** / Epic (1979)
★ ★ ★ ★ **Anthology** / Epic (1981)
Sly hasn't been quite the same since *Riot. Fresh* featured a glossy Richard Avedon cover and "If You Want Me to Stay," a hit single that beat a hasty retreat from the wormy truths of "Family Affair." Black funk, rock and disco groups borrowed heavily from *Riot*'s rhythms but ignored the message for the trappings. By *Small Talk,* Sly was competing with a host of imitators who could do Sly Stone better than Sly. And with the Ohio Players, an audience didn't have to worry about hearing what it didn't want to hear, confronting what was most painful to confront. A 1976 issue of *Jet* magazine provided the final irony: Sly Stone, on whose back the Seventies black music explosion was built, was broke.
— J.MC.

SLY AND ROBBIE
★ ★ **Sixties, Seventies and Eighties** / Mango/Taxi (1982)
Who'd a thunk it? Reggae's hardest, rootsiest rhythm section doing an LP of standards (would you believe "Only Sixteen," "Watermelon Man" and a Beatles tune?) and, gasp,

singing. A worthy effort, but the whole affair sounds forced. — R.F.G.

THE SMALL FACES
★ ★ ★ **Ogden's Nut Gone Flake / Abkco (1968)**
★ ★ ★ **First Step / War. (1970)** ¶
★ **Playmates / Atl. (1977)** ¶
★ ★ **78 in the Shade / Atl. (1978)** ¶
This hardly looks like the catalogue of an important British rock band, but the Small Faces (later, simply the Faces) never had much luck in the States. All of their early mod R&B records are out of print in the U.S. (a deleted Sire anthology is well worth picking up), as is the group's first Immediate album, *There Are but Four Small Faces,* which contained their pop-psychedelic hit, "Itchykoo Park."

The equally psychedelic concept album, *Ogden's Nut Gone Flake,* a strange combination of program music, fairy tale and soul-based rock, remains, and it's fairly wonderful, one of the least pretentious and most artistically successful spinoffs of the *Sgt. Pepper* era. Lead singer Steve Marriott never sounded more leprechaunish. *First Step* is the group's first album with Rod Stewart and Ron Wood replacing Marriott (who left to form Humble Pie). It's back to rock and soul, quite admirably done but nowhere near as much fun as the band's stage show.

Playmates presents the original group (Marriott, Ian McLagan, Kenny Jones) minus bassist Ronnie Lane, who's virtually dropped out of sight. *Playmates* is a disaster, mostly because of the shoddy material, though the fact that Marriott blew out his voice in the latter stages of Humble Pie's boogying days doesn't help. *78* is a minor rebound, but with the departure of drummer Kenny Jones to join the Who, probably a last gasp. — D.M.

SMALL TALK
★ **Small Talk / MCA (1981)**
Boring rock band. — D.M.

SMASH
■ **Smash / Source (NA)**
Flop. — D.M.

BESSIE SMITH
★ ★ ★ ★ ★ **Any Woman's Blues / Col. (1970)**
★ ★ ★ ★ ★ **The World's Greatest Blues Singer / Col. (1971)**
★ ★ ★ ★ ★ **Empty Bed Blues / Col. (1971)**
★ ★ ★ ★ ★ **The Empress / Col. (1971)**
★ ★ ★ ★ ★ **Nobody's Blues but Mine / Col. (1972)**
These records are the crown jewels of Columbia's ambitious jazz repackaging program, the John Hammond collection. Five double sets cover virtually the entire recorded history of one of the greatest, most influential musicians of the twentieth century. Bessie Smith's impact is so widespread it's almost impossible to gauge. She turned the blues into a modern jazz form, outdistancing most of her accompanists with her uncanny sense of phrasing and clear, powerful tone. The young Louis Armstrong played with Smith and was undoubtedly affected. Billie Holiday brought Smith's style into a jazz vocal context and passed it on to all those who in turn followed her, while Smith's impact on straight blues comes down through Mahalia Jackson and Big Mama Thornton.

World's Greatest covers Smith's first and last sessions, in 1923 and 1933. The first recordings were extremely crude, but the 1933 set, produced by Hammond, combines Smith with a fine band composed of trumpeter Frankie Newton, trombonist Jack Teagarden, Benny Goodman on clarinet, tenor saxophonist Chu Berry, Buck Washington on piano, Bobby Johnson on guitar and Billy Taylor on bass.

The other records present Smith in a variety of contexts, often accompanied by the solo piano of James P. Johnson. Some of the collections' best moments, however, are the exchanges between Smith and Louis Armstrong, the only musician at the time who could nearly match Smith's uncanny ability to bend notes and completely personalize even the most trite material. The version of W. C. Handy's "St. Louis Blues," done in 1925, is an amazing recording. — J.S.

CLAY SMITH
★ **Decoupage / Monu. (NA)**
Overdue to live up to its title. — D.M.

ERNIE SMITH
★ ★ ★ **To Behold Jah / Gener. (1977)**
★ **Ska Reggae / Gener. (1981)**
Ernie Smith has had hits in Jamaica since the late Sixties, but since moving to Canada, he has attempted to fuse the reggae pulse with Latin and Afro rhythms, topped by soul-inflected vocals and rock guitar. On *To Behold Jah,* this fusion yields results ranging from pleasant to inspired (on the title cut). *Ska Reggae* is an egregious rehash of ska, rocksteady and reggae hits. — R.F.G.

HUEY "PIANO" SMITH AND THE CLOWNS

★ ★ ★ ★ ★ **Huey "Piano" Smith and the Clowns** / Vivid/Ace (1979), Jap. imp.
★ ★ ★ ★ ★ **Rockin' Pneumonia and the Boogie Woogie Flu** / Sue (NA), Br. imp.

The finest New Orleans R&B this side of Professor Longhair. Smith is basically known today only for "Rockin' Pneumonia," but the thirteen other tracks on the Sue album, and the dozen more, without duplication, on the Ace set, argue forcefully that he was one of the best bandleaders in rock & roll history. The most notable graduates of his group were Bobby Marchan and Frankie Ford, but all of the players were ace, and with the addition of Marchan, Smith was blessed with a pair of fine vocalists. The Ace LP is also available as a Japanese import, with liner notes, but since the notes are in Japanese, this may not justify the price, which is considerably higher, even for an import.
— D.M.

MARGO SMITH

★ **Don't Break the Heart That Loves You** / War. (1978)
★ **Just Margo** / War. (1979)
★ **A Woman** / War. (1979)
★ **Diamonds and Chills** / War. (1980)

Boring country-pop singer in the Patsy Cline mold, but hasn't a shred of Patsy's soul.
— D.M.

PATTI SMITH

★ ★ ★ ★ **Horses** / Ari. (1975)
★ **Radio Ethiopia** / Ari. (1976)
★ ★ ★ ★ **Easter** / Ari. (1978)
★ ★ **Wave** / Ari. (1979)

Patti Smith began her career as a poet and critic, published in a variety of periodicals, but mostly *Creem* and *Rolling Stone*. At her best, those vocations have an expansive effect on her approach to music; at her worst she's an arrogant amateur, with more pretenses than anyone in the history of rock & roll. Which is to say that even at her worst she's one of the most interesting figures in contemporary rock & roll and potentially the first really compelling female rocker since Janis Joplin.

Horses, her debut LP, is Smith at her most overtly poetic, perhaps because several key songs were developed in the context of poetry readings, in which Smith would be backed only by Lenny Kaye's electric guitar. Her version of "Gloria" is one of the most remarkable ever done, and "Land," a takeoff on Wilson Pickett's "Land of 1,000 Dances," is a psychic horror story unmatched by any-

one since Jim Morrison. Smith's voice is never more than winsomely evocative, but on this album she uses it to good effect. Not so on *Radio Ethiopia*: the Kaye-led group, inferior to her in imagination if not technique, simply overwhelms her and drowns her out.

Easter returns Smith to the forefront with amazing success. "Because the Night," a composing "collaboration" with Bruce Springsteen, became a Top Twenty hit single, hardly what the ordinarily scatological Smith could have been expected to turn out; the rest of the album is hard-driving rock, as eerie as anything she'd done before, and more sensual. Her flaws aren't completely tamed, naturally, but *Easter* at least pointed the way to a sound that is both palatable and uncompromising. *Wave* was a decent followup, but fans were left dangling when Smith threw over her career for domesticity. Chrissie Hynde may fill the market gap, but artistically, Patti's absence is regrettable and she is irreplaceable. With luck, she'll return.
— D.M.

REX SMITH

■ **Rex** / Col. (NA)
■ **Where Do We Go from Here?** / Col. (1978)
■ **Sooner or Later** / Col. (1979)
■ **Forever** / Col. (1980)
■ **Everlasting Love** / Col. (1981)

A pirate's penance? No reason you've gotta pay, too. Anyone who fashions a career from wooing Linda Ronstadt on Broadway *deserves* Gilbert and Sullivan justice. — D.M.

SLIM SMITH

★ ★ ★ ★ **Late and Great** / Micron (NA)
★ ★ ★ **Memorial** / Troj. (1981)

The late Slim Smith, lead singer of top Sixties vocal group the Uniques, was venerated in Jamaica for his high sweet singing. While his R&B doo-wop-style crooning and Sixties soul-style emoting may seem dated now, the quality of both his vocals and his classic rocksteady rhythms is undeniable. Both LPs compile some of his best material. — R.F.G.

SMOKIE (SMOKEY)

★ ★ **Smokey** / MCA (1975) ¶
★ ★ **Smokie—Midnight Cafe** / RSO (1976)
★ ★ **Bright Lights and Back Alleys** / RSO (1977)

One of those concept groups that go so far toward demolishing the hopes of an aspiring auteurist producer. With this, Mike Chapman (Suzi Quatro, Blondie, the Knack) falls flat on his face—and not only for lack of sufficient talent to mold. It kind of tells you something about who the real engine of creation in rock & roll might be, don't it? Hooks galore, and pretty faces. All that's missing is brains. — D.M.

SNAKEFINGER
★ ★ ★ ★ **Chewing Hides the Sound / Ralph (1979)**
★ ★ ★ **Greener Postures / Ralph (1981)**
Both of these records were for the most part co-composed and produced by the Residents. On *Chewing Hides the Sound* the music is comparable to Beefheart or Zappa. Philip "Snakefinger" Lithman is a very interesting guitarist who plays straight-ahead lead guitar (with a few detours) as well as slide and toy guitar. The material here (especially on *Chewing*) is humorous, and the music varies from warped rock to a cover version of "I Love Mary." — K.L.

SNEAKER
★ ★ **Sneaker / Hands. (NA)**
Pop rock adequate as radio filler, not much else. — D.M.

SNIPS
★ ★ ★ **Snips and the Video Kings / Jet (1978), Br. imp.**
★ ★ ★ ★ **La Rocca / EMI (1981), Br. imp.**
Ex–Sharks and Baker-Gurvitz Army singer Snips (real name: Steve Parsons) made an enjoyable but unspectacular debut as a bandleader fronting an aggregation called the Video Kings. The album was surprising only inasmuch as it showed Snips as a songwriter with a flair for hooky pop tunes—unexpected considering his past credits. *La Rocca*, produced by guitarist Chris Spedding, his former bandmate in Sharks, is a more ambitious and ultimately more satisfying effort, marred only by occasional lyrical excesses. "Nine O'Clock," a collaboration with Ultravox's Midge Ure that appears on *La Rocca,* is Snips at his best: hard, tuneful pop rock that doesn't insult the intelligence. — D.S.

PHOEBE SNOW
★ ★ ★ ★ **Phoebe Snow / Shel. (1974)**
★ ★ ★ **Second Childhood / Col. (1976)**
★ ★ ★ **It Looks Like Snow / Col. (1976)**
★ ★ ★ **Never Letting Go / Col. (1977)**
★ ★ **Against the Grain / Col. (1978)**
★ ★ ★ **Best of Phoebe Snow / Col. (1981)**
★ ★ ★ **Rock Away / Mirage (1981)**
One of the most gifted voices of her generation, Phoebe Snow can do just about anything stylistically as well as technically. Her rich, throbbing alto, with its stratospheric outer limits, is a genuine phenomenon, and

she backs up her technique with tough, gutsy emotionality. The question that's still unanswered is how best to channel such talent. Snow's debut, a left-field hit in 1974, was propelled by the hit single "Poetry Man," and it presented her as a moody folk-jazz chanteuse with rock leanings. After ugly legal hassles with her original label, Shelter, Snow signed with Columbia and made *Second Childhood* with producer Phil Ramone. Jazzier in style, more introspective in mood, it juxtaposed a swinging "No Regrets" alongside eccentric original ballads with parapsychological themes. The disappointing sales of *Second Childhood* prompted Snow to move toward harder R&B-rock with producer David Rubinson. Highlights of *It Looks Like Snow* include vibrant, punchy renditions of "Teach Me Tonight" and "Don't Let Me Down."

Reteamed with Phil Ramone on *Never Letting Go,* Snow turned in a stunning remake of "Love Makes a Woman," among other savvy revivals. On *Against the Grain,* Snow's lilting version of Paul McCartney's "Every Night" outdistanced Barry Beckett's pedestrian R&B-rock production. Finally, Snow left Columbia, which released a *Best of. Rock Away,* her Mirage debut, is a straight-ahead pop-rock album made with members of Billy Joel's band. Though it wasn't the answer, it contained some strong, focused performances and Snow's most down-to-earth original songs since her first album. — S.H.

GINO SOCCIO
★ ★ ★ **Outline / War./RFC (1979)**
★ ★ ★ **Closer / Atl. (NA)**
★ ★ ★ **S-Beat / War. (NA)**
An early and effective exponent of dance rock, Soccio attacks the fusion from the disco side, but his groove is embedded in rock, without becoming leaden. — D.M.

SOFT MACHINE
★ ★ ★ ★ ★ **Third / Col. (1970)**
★ ★ ★ **Fourth / Col. (1971)**
★ ★ ★ **Six / Col. (1973) ¶**
★ ★ ☆ **Seven / Col. (1974)**
Soft Machine was the most prestigious and musically accomplished of the experimental groups to come out of England in the Sixties, melding rock, jazz and classical styles into a kind of noncommercial, prefusion music. Led by the brilliant percussionist Robert Wyatt, this band's first three albums are landmarks in experimental rock. Unfortunately the first two are now out of print, but the breakthrough record, *Third,* remains.

On that one, the band expanded from a trio to eight pieces and fomented an instrumental interlace seldom heard in a rock context. At one time, four different horn lines race each other while the twisted rhythm section chugs it all along like crazy clockworks. Wyatt's "Moon in June" is a masterpiece.

Wyatt departed after *Third,* leaving the conceptual reins to organist Mike Ratledge. Under his direction, the band was less inspired, playing the sort of aimless noodling that eventually gave this kind of music a bad name.   — J.S.

SONNY AND CHER
★ ★ ★ ★ **The Best of Sonny and Cher** / Atco (1972) ¶
★ ★ **The Two of Us** / Atco (NA) ¶
★ ★ **Sonny and Cher "Live"** / MCA (1974) ¶
★ ★ ★ **The Beat Goes On** / Atco (1975) ¶
Having learned the ropes of the music business as a percussionist with Phil Spector's studio orchestra, Sonny Bono was able to successfully re-create Spector's Wall of Sound on many of his early hits, written by him and performed with his wife, Cher. Their pre-Seventies material holds up rather well. The *Best of* collection features the duo's string of Top Ten smashes in the mid and late Sixties ("Bang Bang," "Baby Don't Go"); *The Beat Goes On*'s title track is a classic period piece of pop culture, and "Laugh at Me," Sonny's lone solo hit, is a disarming let-me-do-my-thing anthem; the *Live* double LP is from their Vegas act and is a souvenir of prime-time Sonny and Cher, replete with Cher's constant rank-outs of Sonny. In light of subsequent events, it's hard to say just what was acting and what was real. Recommended mostly for those with a taste for the perverse.   — B.A.

SONS OF CHAMPLIN
★ ★ ★ **Loosen Up Naturally** / Cap. (1969) ¶
★ **Sons** / Cap. (1969) ¶
★ ★ ★ ★ **Follow Your Heart** / Cap. (1971) ¶
★ ★ ★ **Sons of Champlin** / Ario. (1976) ¶
★ ★ ★ **Circle Filled with Love** / Ario. (1976) ¶
★ ★ ★ **Loving Is Why** / Ario. (1977) ¶
The Sons of Champlin bill themselves as the longest-living Marin County rock band. They've consistently eschewed the spotlight since their inception in 1965, and they became one of the first rock groups to use horns for soloing in a jazz-influenced context. The double set, *Loosen Up Naturally,* includes some pretty hot playing and sounded very good when released in the late Sixties, though it dated fast. The band indulges in some inane cosmic lyrics and falls prey to the noodling tendencies that often plague such efforts. *Follow Your Heart* is the most focused record, and it has aged well. The Ariola albums date from the band's mid-Seventies comeback, but by that time the group wasn't offering anything novel and had to rest on its status as a hippie legend.   — J.S.

ROSALIE SORRELS
★ ★ ★ **If I Could Be the Rain** / Folk-Leg. (1967) ¶
★ ★ **Always a Lady** / Philo (1976) ¶
★ ★ **Monuments of Happiness** / Philo (1977) ¶
Sorrels drifts in and out of view, her infrequent albums appearing on various labels. A singer, songwriter, raconteuse and poet, she adds great sensitivity to her music, whether she is singing any of the title tracks here or one of Bruce "Utah" Phillips' union or train songs. Phillips' songs are well represented on the Folk-Legacy set, on which Sorrels is accompanied by Mitch Greenhill. Some of the stories ("Mehitabel's Theme" on *Always a Lady*) work better in concert than on record, but when Sorrels is singing, she can swing on a jazz beat or rock with a country flavor along with the best.   — I.M.

THE SORROWS
★ ★ **Love Too Late** / Pav. (NA)
★ ★ **Teenage Heartbreak** / Pav. (NA)
Typical power pop: ersatz adolescence.   — D.M.

THE SOS BAND
★ ★ ★ **SOS** / Tabu (1980)
★ ★ **Too** / Tabu (1981)
Energetic if unimaginative funk band. Turned moralistic on the second album, and went so far as to cover Seals and Croft's anti-abortion number, "Unborn Child." A definite bad sign.   — J.D.C.

THE SOUL CHILDREN
★ ★ ★ **Where Is Your Woman Tonight?** / Epic (1977) ¶
★ ★ ★ **Open Door Policy** / Stax (NA)
The Soul Children are a durable Southern trio with a twist: each member (two male, one female) is a qualified lead vocalist. The group specializes in an intense, rugged brand of gospel soul, a style long out of fashion in black music. Still, they've managed to keep an audience, like many others in the genre, through a series of other-man, other-woman love songs. But *Where Is Your Woman To-*

night? suffers from the occasionally intrusive and sloppy production of David Porter. The Don Davis–produced *Finders Keepers* is concise and truer to the verities of the genre, but it's an Epic cutout. Since then, the group has made a variety of uptempo dance singles for Fantasy's revived Stax label collected in *Open Door Policy.* — J.MC.

THE SOUL STIRRERS

★ ★ ★ ★ ★ **The Soul Stirrers Featuring Sam Cooke / Spec. (NA)**
★ ★ ★ ★ **The Gospel Soul of Sam Cooke with the Soul Stirrers, Vol. 1 / Spec. (NA)**
★ ★ ★ **The Gospel Soul of Sam Cooke with the Soul Stirrers, Vol. 2 / Spec. (NA)**
★ ★ ★ ★ **The Original Soul Stirrers / Spec. (NA)**

The Soul Stirrers rose to gospel prominence with Rebert Harris as lead singer, but his successors included Sam Cooke and Johnnie Taylor. Under Harris, the group was the first to add a fifth member to the quartet lineup, so the lead singer could step out front and take solo lines while still keeping the four-part harmonies intact.

Cooke was gospel's first real sex symbol, and his work also pushed the group sound far enough toward pop that it wasn't exactly a shock when he left gospel for pop. *The Soul Stirrers Featuring Sam Cooke* is the best of their albums because it demonstrates this process by including one of Cooke's gospel showcases ("Wonderful") and one of his leaning-toward-pop masterpieces (the desolate "Touch the Hem of His Garment"). But the album also contains a key Harris-Paul Foster lead ("By and By") and one of the best efforts ("The Love of God") by Taylor, who started out very much a Cooke imitator, just as Cooke began as a Harris imitator.

There's much overlap among the Specialty albums. Those interested solely in Cooke should check out both volumes of *Gospel Soul.* The first is slightly superior, due to the spectacular moaning of "Jesus Wash Away My Troubles" and the way Cooke builds and builds on "Peace in the Valley." His voice is already as sweet as it ever got on his pop sides, but the addition of a rough edge, and arrangements that really let him stretch out, lead some to argue that his gospel sides are his greatest achievements.

★ ★ **Best of the Soul Stirrers / Check. (1966)** ¶
★ ★ **The Gospel Truth / Check. (1967)**
★ ★ **Going Back to the Lord Again / Spec. (NA)**

Willie Rogers and Martin Jacox share leads on the Checker albums; while Rogers in particular shows great potential, both pale next to the earlier Specialty work. Richard Miles replaces Rogers on the later Specialty LP, and both the instrumentation and singing are a bit more modern (as is the material, such as a version of "Let It Be"). Finally, search for a copy of the out-of-print *Gospel Music, Volume 1/Soul Stirrers* (Imperial LM-94007). This is mostly a cappella sides from the late Forties by the Harris-led group, and is a marvelous showcase for the relaxed but insistent style that first won the Soul Stirrers fame. — J.MO.

SOUL SYNDICATE

★ ★ **Uptown Harvest / Epip. (1980)**
★ ★ **Was, Is and Always / Epip. (1980)**

Led by master reggae guitarist Earl "Chinna" Smith, the Soul Syndicate has been one of the few reggae bands to exist outside of the studio. Varied gigs have given them fluency in a variety of styles—Santa on drums, Fullwood on bass and Smith are stand-outs. Unfortunately, these records suffer from a lack of identity. — R.F.G.

JOE SOUTH

★ ★ ★ **Joe South's Greatest Hits / Cap. (1970)**

In the early Sixties, South made his reputation in Atlanta and Nashville as a top-notch session guitarist and songwriter. Among his hits are "Games People Play," "Walk a Mile in My Shoes," "Hush," "Down in the Boondocks" and "I Never Promised You a Rose Garden." Unfortunately, most of his catalogue is out of print, but well worth looking for in the cutout bins, especially his groundbreaking 1968 classic, *Introspect.* — J.S.

JOHN DAVID SOUTHER

★ **John David Souther / Asy. (1972)** ¶
★ **Black Rose / Asy. (1976)**
★ ★ **You're Only Lonely / Col. (1979)**

Talented Texas singer/songwriter (he co-wrote "The Best of My Love" for the Eagles and wrote "Faithless Love" for Linda Ronstadt) followed a promising solo debut with the whiny *Rose* LP. The title track of the Columbia LP, a neat Roy Orbison clone, is the best thing he's ever done—or probably ever will. — S.H./D.M.

THE SOUTHER-HILLMAN-FURAY BAND

★ ★ **The Souther-Hillman-Furay-Band / Asy. (1974)**
★ **Trouble in Paradise / Asy. (1975)** ¶

This was supposed to be a supergroup: Chris Hillman made his reputation as a Byrd, Richie Furay as a member of the Buffalo Springfield and Poco, John David Souther as a kind of Jackson Browne manqué who also wrote songs for sometime girlfriend Linda Ronstadt. But it never jelled, and what seemed promising in 1975 was all through by 1976. The three subsequently pursued solo careers. — S.H.

SOUTHSIDE JOHNNY AND THE ASBURY JUKES
★ ★ ★ ★ **I Don't Want to Go Home** / Epic (1976)
★ ★ ★ ★ **This Time It's for Real** / Epic (1977)
★ ★ ★ ★ **Hearts of Stone** / Epic (1978)
★ ★ ★ ★ **Havin' a Party with Southside Johnny and the Asbury Jukes** / Epic (1979)

Because they're from Asbury Park, New Jersey, are produced by Miami Steve Van Zandt of the E Street Band, and have recorded several of Bruce Springsteen's songs, Southside Johnny and the Asbury Jukes have been identified with Springsteen's musical style. This is far from an apt comparison: Springsteen's antecedents are much broader than this combination of doo-wop and Stax/New Orleans rhythm & blues.

But all of these records are charming, and with *Hearts of Stone,* Southside and Van Zandt have begun to exert a vision of their own. The first album, *Go Home,* which features Springsteen's monumental "The Fever" and guest appearances by Lee Dorsey and Ronnie Spector, is perhaps slightly superior to the second for its energy and enthusiasm, although *This Time* has better Van Zandt material. But the group's best LP is *Hearts:* the horns have the punch of rock & roll guitars; Southside sings with great assurance; the material is superlative (the Springsteen title track and Van Zandt's "This Time Baby" are pop songs Leiber and Stoller could envy); and the rhythm and guitar sections have all the drive great rock requires. *Havin' a Party* is a fine sampler of the first three, Van Zandt–produced albums, concluding with a rousing live version of the Sam Cooke oldie that gives the album its title.
★ ★ ★ **The Jukes** / Mer. (1979)
★ ★ **Love Is a Sacrifice** / Mer. (1980)
★ ★ ★ ★ **Reach Up and Touch the Sky— Southside Johnny and the Asbury Jukes Live!** / Mer. (1981)

In 1979 the Jukes left Epic and Van Zandt behind them. *The Jukes* is a valiant but vain attempt to redefine an identity away from the Asbury Park/Springsteen crowd, but the weakness of the material (mostly written by guitarist Billy Rush) can't be overcome, despite good production by Barry Beckett in Muscle Shoals. *Love Is a Sacrifice* has somewhat stronger material—mostly that which Johnny cowrote—but it's undone by the band's self-production, which is simply amateurish.

The live album is another story, since it gets to use all the great songs from the band's Epic period, and exhibits the Jukes' growth into a tight-knit stage ensemble. Southside himself is simply a terror onstage, and the side four medley of Sam Cooke songs is one of the best things in the Jukes' repertoire.

But this still leaves open the question of what the Jukes can hope to achieve without the aid of Miami Steve, Springsteen or someone like them. Southside Johnny has proven himself one of the era's most soulful rock vocalists, but whether he will ever again have material and direction worthy of his talent is another question. — D.M.

SPACE
★ **Deliverance** / Casa. (1978)
★ **Just Blue** / Casa. (1979)

The group name no doubt refers to its sound, a fusion between space rock and disco, but it's tempting to pretend the name really means what's between their ears. — J.D.C.

SPANDAU BALLET
★ ★ **Journeys to Glory** / Reform. (1981), Br. imp.

How did the new romantics become the new funk-salsa explosion in England? Don't ask. Highly derivative in one quick jump from synthesizer to funk bop, Spandau Ballet is seemingly enthralled not with any musical style so much as with themselves. Not even a thousand changes of clothing can boost this fashion. — ML.H.

THE SPANIELS
★ ★ ★ **The Spaniels** / Lost Nite (NA)
★ ★ ★ ★ **Great Googley Moo!** / Charly (1981), Br. imp.

Exceptional doo-wop quintet best known for "Goodnight Sweetheart Goodnight" (1954) sounds just fine on both of these collections. The Charly set has superior annotation and a somewhat better song selection ("Great Googley Moo!" itself is fantastic), but the Lost Nite also has "Goodnight Sweetheart Goodnight" and includes some material not on the Charly compilation. — D.M.

LUCILLE SPANN
★ ★ ★ **Cry Before I Go / Blues. (1974)**
Otis Spann's wife Lucille dedicated this LP to her late husband. She sings emotionally with the help of pianist Detroit Junior and guitarists Mighty Joe Young and Eddie Taylor, who also rise to the occasion. — J.S.

OTIS SPANN
★ ★ ★ ★ **Blues Never Die / Prest. (1964)**
★ ★ ★ **Cryin' Time / Van. (1970)**
★ ★ ★ ★ **Otis Spann with Luther Johnson, Muddy Waters Blues Band / Muse (1973) ¶**
★ ★ ★ ★ **Chicago Blues / Test. (NA)**
★ ★ ★ **Otis Spann / Arc. Folk (NA)**
★ ★ ★ **Otis Spann vs. the Everlasting Blues / Spivey (NA)**
A tremendous piano player and fine singer, Spann nailed down the keyboard spot in Muddy Waters' highly influential Fifties and Sixties outfit, and he played on many of the Waters classics. His high-powered, technically dazzling style created the standard for postwar hard blues piano, and thus for the rock keyboardists (especially the English ones), who picked up cues from the blues revival of the Sixties. Spann backed such notable white blues players as Paul Butterfield and Mike Bloomfield (on the landmark *Fathers and Sons* album, with Waters) and Fleetwood Mac.

Spann's own records are high-energy sets, recorded with a wide range of sidemen, including Robert Lockwood Jr. and, often, members of the Waters band. Waters gave him plenty of space, but naturally, Spann's separate efforts offer even greater opportunity to show off his fast-fingers roll. Vocally he was no slouch either, singing in a smooth but edgy voice influenced in no small amount by Waters. Spann died in 1971 at age forty, but left a recorded legacy that testifies to his powers. — J.S.

DANNY SPANOS
★ ★ ★ **Danny Spanos / Wind. (NA)**
Ex–Sly and the Family Stone drummer in an earnest but unspectacular debut featuring session guitarist Earl Slick. — J.S.

THE SPARK GAP WONDER BOYS
★ ★ ★ **Cluck Old Hen / Roun. (1970)**
Good New England-based bluegrass group of young players keeping alive an old tradition. Dave Doubilet and Neil Rossi switch off on a number of instruments, while George Nelson sticks to the guitar. Their adaptations of standards like "The Black Mountain Rag" and "Colored Aristocracy" mesh well with remakes of numbers associated with particular old-timers like Charlie Poole's "Take a Drink on Me" and "The Milwaukee Blues." — J.S.

SPARKS
★ **Sparks / Bears. (1972) ¶**
★ **Woofer in Tweeter's Clothing / Bears. (1973) ¶**
★ ★ **Kimono My House / Is. (1974)**
★ ★ **Big Beat / Col. (1976) ¶**
★ **Introducing Sparks / Col. (1977) ¶**
★ **No. 1 in Heaven / Elek. (1979)**
★ **Whomp That Sucker / RCA (1981)**
All-American weirdos Ron and Russ Mael *(Sparks)* go to England to get rich and famous *(Woofer in Tweeter's Clothing)*. The objective is to hit it big in a foreign land and then return home to conquer the masses who ignored them before they went to England to get rich and famous. The plan goes awry when they bomb in the U.S. after scoring hits in the U.K. *(Kimono My House)*. They decide to move back home to California, assuming that the failure was caused by losing touch with their roots. They abandon the speeded-up music-hall approach and opt for somewhat less outré rock *(Big Beat)*. No one seems to care. They then decide to start from scratch again *(Introducing Sparks)*, but old fans have disappeared and new ones are few and far between.

Sustained smarm is the best description of their more recent work. Docked one star per album for being somewhat responsible for Queen. — B.A.

SPECIALS
★ ★ ★ ★ **Specials / Two-Tone (1979)**
★ ★ ★ ★ **More Specials / Two-Tone (1980)**
Dominated by the loony Man Ray-esque presence of Jerry Dammers, the Specials premiered so-called new ska on their euphonious first album. Their blend of irresistible dance rhythms and humanist politics on "A Message to You Rudy" and "Too Much Too Young" brought them both critical and commercial acclaim in England. *More Specials,* a broadening of their initial attack with more fluid and less aggressive melodies, is enriched by veteran Jamaican trombonist Rico Rodrigues. Theirs has been a progression rather than a cashing in on their original hit formula. "Ghost Town," the powerfully haunting song written about the 1981 riots in England, is easily one of the best songs of the decade and is available on an import EP. At the end of 1981, however, the group announced its breakup. — ML.H.

PHIL SPECTOR
★ ★ ★ ★ ★ **Phil Spector's Christmas LP /
Spector (NA)** ¶
★ ★ ★ ★ ★ **Phil Spector's Greatest Hits /
Spector (NA)** ¶

Both of these albums contain performances by a variety of artists, but they are really the result of only one man's work and vision. Phil Spector, rock's first boy genius, made the producer a cult hero with his Sixties Wall of Sound singles on his own Philles Records. (Earlier he had been the protégé of Leiber and Stoller and had worked with the Drifters and Ben E. King.) The *Christmas* album is a masterpiece of sentimentality that achieves a trio of unbelievable peaks: Darlene Love's keening "Christmas (Baby Please Come Home)"; the Crystals' atomic reworking of "Santa Claus Is Comin' to Town"; Spector's maudlin voiceover "thank you" and benediction on the final track, "Silent Night," which presages Simon and Garfunkel's *Parsley, Sage, Rosemary and Thyme* move by several years.

The cream, though, is really on *Greatest Hits.* Spector's good-bad-but-not-evil genius was perfectly suited to singles, so the compilation album is his grandest idiom. This package includes the best songs he did with the Ronettes ("Be My Baby," "Walking in the Rain" and "Baby, I Love You"), the Crystals ("Da Doo Ron Ron," "Then He Kissed Me," "He's a Rebel," "Uptown"), and Darlene Love ("[Today I Met] The Boy I'm Gonna Marry," "Wait 'Til My Bobby Gets Home"), who were his major performers at Philles. Also on the LP are majestically paranoid Righteous Brothers hits ("You've Lost That Lovin' Feelin'," "Unchained Melody," "Just Once in My Life," "Ebb Tide") and a host of one-shots: a bizarre version of "Zip-a-Dee-Doo-Dah" by Bobb B. Soxx and the Blue Jeans; Curtis Lee's swinging "Pretty Little Angel Eyes"; the Teddy Bears' "To Know Him Is to Love Him," Spector's initial hit and the one for which he took the title from his father's tombstone; Ike and Tina Turner's classic flop, "River Deep—Mountain High," the most overrated rock single ever made; and a final blast of bombast, Sonny Charles and the Checkmates' "Black Pearl." Genius in every groove, and only one sin: Spector must be the only man in the world who thinks he produced Ben E. King's "Spanish Harlem," as well as cowriting it with Jerry Leiber.
— D.M.

CHRIS SPEDDING
★ ★ ★ **Chris Spedding / EMI (1976)** ¶

★ ★ ★ **Friday the Thirteenth / Pass. (1981)**
Superlative English session guitarist hoisted by his own petard: should he go for the Anglo-flash technique he helped pioneer or the raw rock & roll he obviously admires? The answer is to the left of Dave Edmunds and the right of Brian Eno, which ain't nowhere, but also isn't terribly satisfying.
— D.M.

JEREMY SPENCER
★ ★ **Flee / Atl. (1979)**
Former Fleetwood Mac guitarist, recovered from a spell in a religious cult, but not enough so as to regain his sense of humor. Everything Spencer played in the original Mac was high energy and hilarious; this stuff is simply tired and turgid. — D.M.

JIMMIE SPHEERIS
★ **Isle of View / Col. (1972)**
★ **Jimmie Spheeris / Col. (1973)** ¶
★ **The Dragon Is Dancing / Epic (1975)** ¶
★ **Ports of the Heart / Epic (1976)** ¶
The hippie ethic refuses to die, as demonstrated by this character, so laid-back that he gives new meaning to the word limpid.
— D.M.

SPIDER
★ ★ **Spider / Dreaml. (1980)**
★ ★ **Between the Lines / Dreaml. (1981)**
New York–based rock group, produced by Dreamland proprietor Mike Chapman, almost managed a hit with "New Romance." Like the rest, it's typical Chapman post-punk power pop, more slick than exciting.
— D.M.

SPINETTA
★ **Only Love Can Sustain / Col. (1980)** ¶
Dan Fogelberg in Gino Vanelli's clothing.
— J.D.C.

SPINNERS
★ ★ ★ ★ ★ **Spinners / Atl. (1973)** ¶
★ ★ ★ ★ **Mighty Love / Atl. (1974)**
★ ★ ★ **New and Improved Spinners / Atl. (1974)** ¶
★ ★ ★ ★ ★ **Pick of the Litter / Atl. (1975)** ¶
★ ★ ★ ★ **Spinners Live / Atl. (1975)** ¶
★ **Happiness Is Being with the Spinners / Atl. (1976)** ¶
★ ★ **Yesterday, Today and Tomorrow / Atl. (1977)** ¶
★ ★ **Spinners/8 / Atl. (1977)** ¶
★ ★ ★ ★ **The Best of the Spinners / Atl. (1978)**
★ ★ **Dancin' and Lovin' / Atl. (1979)**

★ ★ **Love Trippin'** / Atl. (1980)
★ ★ **Superstar Series, Vol. 9** / Mo. (1981)
★ ★ ★ **Can't Shake This Feelin'** / Atl. (1981)
★ ★ **The Original Spinners** / Mo. (1981)
★ ★ **The Best of the Spinners** / Mo. (1981)
More than a decade ago, trying to analyze his feelings about the two most fashionable New Wave film directors, critic Andrew Sarris concluded that while Jean-Luc Godard was decidedly more brilliant, more innovative and more profound, as time went by, the gentle, leisurely insights of François Truffaut became more valued. I don't think the metaphor has to be stretched very far to apply to the Spinners. They've never received the praise addressed to the O'Jays, the Blue Notes or Al Green; the very smoothness and gentleness in their music has often been used against them. Yet few soul albums of the Seventies are as genuinely pleasurable as *Pick of the Litter, Mighty Love* and *Spinners*. The critic inside us tends to condemn them for being so instantly likable, so easy to listen to. But the Spinners have a definite, strong resonance and an intelligence that goes deeper than their supposedly bubblegum surface.

The key to their success has always been writer/producer/arranger Thom Bell. He saw in the Spinners a chance to expand beyond the overly ornate falsetto groups he had previously worked with (the Delfonics, for example). *Spinners*, their first album, contains four classic singles—"I'll Be Around," "Could It Be I'm Falling in Love," "One of a Kind (Love Affair)" and the meditative "How Could I Let You Get Away." It still sounds more like a collection of singles than a genuinely conceptual album, but the singles are so great that it hardly matters.

On *Mighty Love,* Bell created his first listenable and coherent LP, allowing Philippe Wynne to stretch out and explore his gospel roots. *New and Improved* sounds a bit old and tired and is salvaged mainly by Dionne Warwick's guest shot on "Then Came You." On that number, the Bell/Spinners style— with its call-and-response structure imposed upon cascading strings and vocal backups— reaches its pinnacle. *Pick of the Litter* was the collaboration's last great success; there are no monumental songs on it, but the group sang with utter professionalism. And many of the songs are very good: "Just as Long as We Have Love" with Warwick, and "Honest I Do," for example. There's something so tight about the record, including its deep understanding of counterpoint, the

grace with which the singers switch leads and, most of all, its ability to express joy simply and directly.

Despite awkward orchestrations and a lame rhythm section, the *Live* album allowed Wynne to show off on the ballads. *Happiness* was the beginning of the end, although *Yesterday, Today and Tomorrow* is in many respects worse, save for Wynne's swan song, "Throwing a Good Love Away," a number that owes as much to Gene Kelly as Otis Redding, but nevertheless works.

Spinners/8 and subsequent releases feature Jonathan Edwards replacing Wynne. Edwards is monstrously talented—he plays Willie Mays to Wynne's cool Joe DiMaggio— and onstage he can really spark the group, but Bell never quite figured out what to do with all his talent, and neither have the group's other producers. So, these days, the group's sound never jells; if it did, the Spinners could still deliver a plenitude of pleasure. The 1978 anthology of hits certainly does, though not so much as *Spinners, Mighty Love* and *Litter,* which have a force all their own.

The Motown albums reissue rather uninspired Sixties material, the exception being the hit, "It's a Shame," which helped Bell contrive the group's formula. — R.G./D.M.

DAVID SPINOZZA
★ ★ ★ **Spinozza** / A&M (1978)
Hot young New York session guitarist turns in a surprisingly effective set of jazz rock. Powerful and concise like Spinozza's best backup work. — D.M.

SPIRIT
★ ★ ★ ★ **Twelve Dreams of Dr. Sardonicus** / Epic (1967)
★ ★ ★ ★ **Spirit** / Epic (1968)
★ ★ ★ **The Family That Plays Together** / Epic (1969)
★ **Feedback** / Epic (1972)
★ ★ ★ ★ **Best of Spirit** / Epic (1973)
★ ★ **Potatoland** / Rhino (1981)
Spirit was one of the strangest and best bands to come out of the anything-goes attitude that surrounded California rock in the late Sixties. Drummer Ed Cassidy was a jazz journeyman who'd played with Gerry Mulligan, Thelonious Monk and Cannonball Adderley and was old enough to be the father of all the other players in the band. In fact, he later became the stepfather of Spirit's guitarist, Randy California, who studied with Jimi Hendrix just as that guitarist was codifying his amazing style. Keyboardist John Locke, bassist Mark Andes and vocalist Jay

Ferguson rounded out a strange lineup that played jazz-rock hybrid long before anyone thought of matching those styles.

Best of, which duplicates the first album but adds the otherwise unavailable *Clear Spirit,* is recommended. *The Family That Plays Together* includes the group's most accessible single, "I Got a Line on You." *Twelve Dreams* is the band's most adventurous and probably best record, notable for advanced production technique and a few excellent songs: "Nothin' to Hide," "Nature's Way," "Animal Zoo" and "Mr. Skin." The band splintered, Ferguson and Andes forming Jo Jo Gunne, California going solo, while Cassidy recruited new players and kept on. *Feedback* is all that remains from that period.

Cassidy and California later re-formed Spirit to record for Mercury, but the records were parodies of the band's former greatness, laying out every psychedelic cliché imaginable. All of them are now deleted. *Potatoland* was a similarly unsuccessful reunion attempt. — J.S.

THE SPIRIT OF MEMPHIS QUARTET
★ ★ ★ ★ **The Spirit of Memphis Quartet /
King (1978)**
Little-known but exceptionally fine jubilee gospel singing, recommended not only to those with an affection for gospel harmony (who will love lead vocalist Jet Bledsoe and tenor Willie Broadnax) but also to aficionados of doo-wop and R&B harmony. — D.M.

VICTORIA SPIVEY
★ **Victoria Spivey with the Easy Riders Jazz
Band / GHB (1965)** ¶
★ **Blues Is Life / Folk. (1976)**
★ ★ **Victoria Spivey and Her Blues / Spivey
(NA)**
★ ★ **Queen and Her Nights / Spivey (NA)**
★ ★ **Recorded Legacy of the Blues / Spivey
(NA)**
Spivey was a blues sex symbol of the Twenties, but her records, even with the remarkable guitarist Lonnie Johnson, were inconsistent and mostly forgettable. The available material is little more than historical notation. — J.S.

THE SPIZZLES
★ ★ ★ **Spikey Dream Flowers / A&M
(1980)**
The further adventures of Spizz Energy/ Athletico Spizz 1980. Spizz' sf lunacy is as endearing as ever, but the tension between the modestly accomplished backup and his wildly erratic singing suggests that maybe punks are better off when they really *don't* know what they're doing. — J.D.C.

SPLIT ENZ
★ ★ **Mental Notes / Mush. (1975), Aust.
imp.**
★ ★ ★ **Second Thoughts / Mush. (1976),
Aust. imp.**
★ ★ ★ **Dizrhythmia / Mush. (1977), Aust.
imp.**
★ ★ ★ **Frenzy / Mush. (1979), Aust. imp.**
★ ★ **Beginning of the Enz / Mush. (1980),
Aust. imp.**
★ ★ ★ ★ **True Colours / A&M (1980), Aust.
imp.**
★ ★ ★ **Waiata / A&M (1981), Aust. imp.**
New Zealand's major contribution to pop music, Split Enz wandered five years in the cult-status wilderness before history caught up with their peculiarities.

A genuinely odd band, the early Enz were noted for their bizarre appearance and music, which most nearly approximated British art rock in its self-conscious weirdness, which veered between the operatic and the burlesque. In 1976 Roxy Music's Phil Manzanera took them temporarily under his wing, and re-recorded most of the 1975 album *Mental Notes,* the results being released as *Second Thoughts.*

By the late Seventies the new-wave aesthetic made Split Enz's taste for geometric extremes in music, hair and dress seem far less eccentric. Lineup changes following the departure of Phil Judd, who with singer Tim Finn had founded the band, moved them toward an an increasingly accessible sound. Producer David Tickle added focus, and a cleaner, tighter, sharper sound, and the Australian success of "I See Red" was quickly followed by 1980's *True Colours* and the brilliant single "I Got You" with its compelling, neurotic chorus. *True Colours* brought Eddie Rayner's electronic keyboards to the fore, and a taut Eighties urgency replaced a penchant for touches of the British music hall. The Enz's now somewhat muted strangeness perfectly tempered their newly acquired pop sensibility. The success of *True Colours* was also partly due to the emergence of guitarist Neil Finn (Tim's little brother) as a songwriter and vocalist. (As a further concession to the Eighties the album was elaborately packaged with cover art in a variety of color combinations and a laser-etched graphic on the vinyl.)

The successful formula—without the fancy graphics—was repeated with *Waiata* in 1981, though none of the songs quite

matched the pop triumph of "I Got You."
— S.M.

SPLODGE

★ ★ ★ **Splodgenessabounds / Deram
(1980), Br. imp.**

A pioneer and front runner of the "punk-
pathetique" genre, Max Splodge chronicles
the everyday problems of runny noses and
buying beers in overcrowded clubs, as on his
chart smash "Two Pints of Lager and a
Packet of Crisps," which appears on this
album in dub form.   — ML.H.

MARK SPOELSTRA

★ **Mark Spoelstra / Folk. (NA)**

In the Sixties folk movement, Spoelstra was
known for having done alternative service
time as a conscientious objector long before
Vietnam became a hot issue. This gave his
first records for Elektra special interest, but
by the time he made this early-Seventies
Folkways album, Spoelstra seemed just another dated folkie, locked permanently out of
time with too much integrity and not enough
music to get him to the next stop.   — D.M.

SPOOKY TOOTH

★ ★ ★ ★ **Spooky Two / A&M (1969) ¶**
★ **Ceremony / A&M (1970) ¶**
★ ★ ★ ★ **The Last Puff / A&M (1970)**
★ ★ ★ **Tobacco Road / A&M (1971)**
★ ★ ★ **You Broke My Heart So I Busted
Your Jaw / A&M (1973)**
★ ★ **The Mirror / Is. (1974)**

If there was ever a *heavy* band, Spooky
Tooth had to be it. Featuring two vocalists
prone to blues-wrenching extremes (Gary
Wright and Mike Harrison) and an instrumental attack composed of awesomely loud
keyboards and guitars, Spooky Tooth came
on like an overwhelming vat of premedicated
goo. *Tobacco Road,* which put the title tune
and Janis Ian's "Society's Child" into this
bluesy heavy-metal context, contained the
germ of the style. But with *Spooky Two,* the
band applied the bombastic combination
with more dramatic panache; the result is an
album that's still heavy after all these years.
Spooky Two's blockbuster was "Evil
Woman," with growling stretches of lead
guitar roaring out of the song's belly, which
itself was framed by a cathedral-loud blues
organ. Totally overdone, and perhaps because of that, a total knockout. Whether it
was a ballad ("Hangman Hang My Shell on
a Tree") or riff-rocker ("Better by You, Better by Me"), *Spooky Two* played it at full
throttle. Similarly, *Ceremony,* a concept LP
done with the French electronic musician

Pierre Henry, went full tilt; the cumbersome
musical and lyrical concept made this last
album sound like it was done by a bunch of
gentle-hearted folkies. *Ceremony* was a
dreadful musical and commercial tailspin;
Gary Wright left to go solo.

Harrison re-formed Spooky Tooth to include guitarist Henry McCulloch and keyboardist Chris Stainton from the Grease
Band; the album that resulted, *The Last
Puff,* was a smashing comeback, though it
failed to revive the commercial fires. A
sprightly cover of Elton John's "Son of Your
Father" and a doomsday interpretation of
the Beatles' "I Am the Walrus" brandished
all the chutzpah of the best Spooky Tooth.
Though subsequent moments would sometimes hit these peaks (Harrison rejoined for
You Broke My Heart and left the memorable
"Wildfire"; Mick Jones was a part of this
band), Spooky Tooth would remain the right
band at the wrong time.   — J.B.M.

THE SPORTS

★ ★ ★ **Reckless / Mush. (1978), Aust. imp.**
★ ★ ★ ★ **Don't Throw Stones / Mush.
(1978), Aust. imp.**
★ ★ ★ ★ **Suddenly / Mush. (1980), Aust.
imp.**
★ ★ ★ **Sondra / Mush. (1981), Aust. imp.**

The Sports belong to that generation of musicians who grew up immersed in the great
pop and soul music of the Sixties, and their
songs reflect those traditions while avoiding
direct imitation. Some of the best of those
tracks can be found on the 1979 U.S. Arista
release *Don't Throw Stones*—the ballad
"Reckless," for instance, or "Mailed It to
Your Sister," which has an R&B tinge recalling the band's origins in Melbourne as a
good-timey, funny, rockabilly-flavored dance
band (a phase that's best reflected in the
1978 Australian album *Don't Throw Stones*).
Also included is "Who Listens to the
Radio," the Sports' one successful U.S. single.

Steve Cummings is an excellent singer and
his distinctive phrasing and delivery make
him arguably the finest vocalist Australian
rock & roll has produced. Cummings' is the
essential sensibility behind the Sports, and
his songs on the early records idiosyncrati-
cally evoke suburban pop culture, peopled by
characters reading *True Confessions* or detective novels, or doing homework with the
radio on. You get the impression that Cummings' songs would find their spiritual home
in suburban kitchens with formica-top tables
and in teenage bedrooms with posters on the
wall of the kids who made Sixties hits of

songs like Jackie de Shannon's "When You Walk in the Room" and the Easybeats' "Wedding Ring," the two nonoriginal songs covered on the Sports' albums.

Several of the songs originally released on *Reckless* were re-recorded for U.S. release on *Don't Throw Stones.* In the intervening period guitarist Martin Armiger had replaced the rockabilly-influenced Ed Bates, and his sharp and lucid playing gave a harder edge to the band's sound, complementing Andrew Pendlebury's sweeter, more lyrical guitar work. Armiger also brought a more contemporary approach to the Sports' songwriting, though a number of his songs, such as the disturbing "Hit Single" and "Terror Hits," were omitted from the U.S. releases.

The concerns of the later albums tend to be rather darker, and the music becomes increasingly complex—the good humor seems to have been exchanged for greater sophistication, with varying results. At its best this trade-off produced great pop like *Suddenly*'s "Strangers on a Train" and "Blue Hearts" or the somber and affecting "Go" from the same record, and "Softly Softly" and "Face the Tiger" from *Sondra.* But at times on these albums the Sports seem to be pursuing more mainstream pop forms, and can be accused at some times of blandness and at others of forced cheerfulness.

The band's best records, *Don't Throw Stones* and *Suddenly,* produced by Englishman Pete Solley, were remixed for release in the U.S. Unfortunately they've been deleted from Arista's catalogue, but they can still be found in the bargain bins of many American record stores. — S.M.

DUSTY SPRINGFIELD
★ ★ ★ ★ **Dusty Springfield's Golden Hits** / Phi. (1966)
★ ★ ★ **It Begins Again** / U.A. (1978)
★ ★ **Never Trust a Man in a Rented Tuxedo** / U.A. (1978) ¶

Dusty Springfield was one of the most ingratiating of the Sixties "girl" singers—the breathy romanticism of her hits ("I Only Want to Be with You," "Stay Awhile," "You Don't Have to Say You Love Me," "Wishin' and Hopin' ") demands she be thought of as a girl, rather than a woman, too. Those hits are on the Philips LP.

Since then, Springfield has been recorded several times in a more mature style, as a sort of rock & roll Peggy Lee. Only one of the United Artists attempts remains in the catalogue, and it's rather bland. But her (deleted) 1969 Atlantic LP, *Dusty in Memphis,* was a genuine pop classic, including a version of "Son of a Preacher Man" that comes close to cutting Aretha Franklin's. — D.M.

RICK SPRINGFIELD
★ **Beginnings** / Cap. (1972)
★ **Wait for the Night** / Chel. (1974) ¶
★ ★ **Working Class Dog** / RCA (1981)
★ **Comic Book Heroes** / Col. (1982)
★ **Success Hasn't Spoiled Me Yet** / RCA (1982)
★ **Living in Oz** / RCA (1983)

Former preppie heartthrob as star of TV soap *General Hospital* had early career as teen idol, although his Capitol, Chelsea and Columbia sides never got him off the ground. Breakthrough came with "Jessie's Girl," fervid confession of lust from *Working Class Dog.* Since then Springfield has churned out slick, sort of listenable pop fodder: just for you, if you think Bruce Springsteen and Tom Petty would be perfect if only they wore *designer* jeans. — D.M.

BRUCE SPRINGSTEEN
★ ★ ★ **Greetings from Asbury Park, New Jersey** / Col. (1973)
★ ★ ★ ★ **The Wild, the Innocent, and the E Street Shuffle** / Col. (1973)
★ ★ ★ ★ ★ **Born to Run** / Col. (1975)
★ ★ ★ ★ **Darkness on the Edge of Town** / Col. (1978)
★ ★ ★ ★ ★ **The River** / Col. (1980)
★ ★ ★ ★ ★ **Nebraska** / Col. (1982)

Record companies often like to tout verbally imaginative young songwriters as "the new Bob Dylan," which is a phrase now widely regarded as the kiss of death. Among many other things, Bruce Springsteen is the exception that proves the rule. He is the most brilliant American rock & roll performer to emerge in the last decade, with a truly remarkable verbal facility. But Springsteen's lyrical talent is only the equal of his strengths as a composer, as a live performer and as a guitarist. Although Columbia pushed his *Greetings* debut as a "Dylan"-styled album because of its astonishing verbosity, Springsteen was a rocker from the beginning, in a league with English writer/ performers like Keith Richards, Pete Townshend and Van Morrison. He was much more than any postfolkie word wizard.

Greetings is a collection of excellent songs whose public rejection has more to do with overhype and underproduction than with the music that's on it. Springsteen immediately established his feel for both street scenes and human relationships in such songs as "Growin' Up," "For You" and "Blinded by the Light." The latter became a hit (in a

bowdlerized version) for Manfred Mann's
Earth Band in 1976. Springsteen's producer
wanted a singer/songwriter-oriented album,
and the conflict between this approach and
the performer's R&B and English rock roots
finally drags the record down, but not without
some remarkable moments.

*The Wild, the Innocent, and the E Street
Shuffle* resolved the musical conflict, leaving
Springsteen with a fine soul-based band to
complement a set of songs intimately linked
conceptually. Side two of this album is practically
a suite, beginning and ending with
scenes of urban poverty and romance ("Incident
on 57th Street," "New York City Serenade");
the rock anthem "Rosalita," a hilarious
statement of purpose, is sandwiched
between them. Springsteen continued his interest
in both character and narrative in the
lyrics, and his song structures, which used
multiple bridges, varying choruses and meter
stretched until it almost snapped, were easily
the most influential and inventive since Van
Morrison's.

Still, *Wild* had little or no commercial impact,
despite the fact that Springsteen's stage
show had attracted a particularly rabid cult
in the Northeast and among critics. *Born to
Run,* released in September 1975, was so
widely anticipated that it landed Springsteen
on the covers of both *Time* and *Newsweek*
during the same week in October. The
album popped him loose commercially, and
with good reason: it is a production masterpiece,
a celebration of the joys of the street,
rock & roll and the ecstasy of life lived on
its sweet edge.

Born to Run was a concept album in
every important sense—its Phil Spector–
influenced production gave it a continuity of
sound, and the progression from the opening
"Thunder Road" to the final "Jungleland"
was not only diurnal but (despite the many
characters involved) really one long story.
But in achieving this homogeneity of purpose,
Springsteen sacrificed nothing, made no
concessions to nonrock: "Born to Run," the
record's hit single, is the crust of classic rock
& roll, and numbers like "Backstreets,"
"She's the One" and "Tenth Avenue Freezeout"
dig even deeper. *Born to Run* was
Springsteen's assertion that he could do it
all, that he was not just another rocker but a
truly great one; clarity of purpose and mammoth
ambition drip from the grooves.

Springsteen didn't release his next album,
Darkness on the Edge of Town, until more
than two years later. *Darkness* rejected the
Spectorian embellishments and much of the
joy of *Born to Run* in favor of more bitter

truths and more biting music. Springsteen finally
cut loose as a guitarist, and his singing
changed from simple rock & roll to a bellow
of rage and pain. *Darkness* is a stark and
brutal record, and while its best songs
("Badlands," "The Promised Land," "Racing
in the Streets," "Adam Raised a Cain"
and "Darkness on the Edge of Town") have
a great deal of compassion and a kind of
hope against hope, for the most part Springsteen
is asserting the pain of lost innocence
and betrayals both personal and public.

The River, released after another two-year
hiatus, is by far Springsteen's most mature
work, and arguably his most consistent. It is
a sprawling record, and its ambition outstrips
anything else that Springsteen has attempted,
if only because he attempts to have
it both ways, retain the innocent freshness of
Born to Run while not backing off from the
hard-won realities of *Darkness.* So *The River*
contrasts "I Wanna Marry You," a Drifters-like
ensemble vocal, with the stark, almost
folk purity of the title track, as close to a
great protest song as anyone wrote in the
early Eighties; the songs themselves often intermingle
these qualities, so that even seemingly
exuberant rockers like "Hungry
Heart," "Out in the Streets" and "Cadillac
Ranch" possess an underlayer of desperate,
frustrated foreboding.

The River takes the tales of *Born to Run*
and *Darkness on the Edge of Town* to their
logical conclusion; both lyrically and musically,
its final numbers ("Ramrod," "The
Price You Pay," "Drive All Night" and
"Wreck on the Highway") summarize and
complete a version of the single tale Springsteen
began to tell with *Born to Run.* Their
encapsulation of these themes suggests that a
period of his work has been completed, but
in their more explicit politics and their more
balanced portrayal of the world he sees,
these songs also suggest a future direction
for his work.

"Hungry Heart," from *The River,* finally
gave Springsteen a genuine mass audience,
and he then was forced to confront the inertia
and dilution of spirit and energy that accompanies
such notoriety. *Nebraska* was a
startling response, a set of ghostly, semi-acoustic
songs fixated on death and defeat,
without much (if any) acknowledgment of
the overriding exhilaration and joy that dominate
all Springsteen's other albums. *Nebraska*
is a great statement of rock & roll
pessimism, which also serves as a challenge
to Springsteen's audience (in the fashion of
Bob Dylan in the Sixties) and a cogent response
to the deadening effect of the spirit of

Reaganism presently abroad in America. If there had been any doubt, this album firmly and finally placed Bruce Springsteen among the greatest, most ambitious artists rock has produced. — D.M.

SPUNK
★ ★ **Tighten It Up / Gold Coast Records (NA)**
Tired funk. — D.M.

SPY
★ **Spy / Kir. (1980)**
More vapid pomp rock from the folks who brought you Kansas. — J.D.C.

SPYRO GYRA
★ ★ **Spyro Gyra / Amh./MCA (1978)**
★ ★ **Morning Dance / Inf. (1979)**
★ ★ **Carnaval / MCA (1980)**
★ ★ **Catching the Sun / MCA (1980)**
★ ★ **Freetime / MCA (1981)**
The music made by this late-Seventies fusion band is deceptively perfect fare for the novice jazz listener afraid to make the leap from pop music to more authentic and demanding terrain. Electric rock instrumentation, catchy melodies and squeaky clean production that firmly place the music in a pop context are combined with a facile ability to handle all fashionable time signatures and to solo with competent, if anonymous, skill. A propulsive Latin flavor runs through most of these records, but the slickness of the arrangements and the sterility of the production would level any exotic element into MOR numbness. Would-be dabblers are hereby warned that any relation between this and a notion of serious jazz is purely accidental. — S.F.

SQUEEZE
★ ★ **U.K. Squeeze / A&M (1978)**
★ ★ ★ **Cool for Cats / A&M (1979)**
★ ★ ★ ★ **Argybargy / A&M (1980)**
★ ★ ★ ★ **Eastside Story / A&M (1981)**
English rock quintet formed by the brilliant songwriting team of Chris Difford and Glenn Tilbrook has expanded from punchy, post-punk irreverence to rival Lennon and McCartney in the fecundity of its pop ideas and the polish of its execution. Produced by John Cale, *U.K. Squeeze* yielded their first Top Ten English hit, "Take Me I'm Yours." Highlights of the more sophisticated *Cool for Cats* included the title track, "Up the Junction" and "Slap and Tickle." The pure pop tunefulness of "Pulling Mussels (from the Shell)" and "If I Didn't Love You," from *Argybargy,* propelled by Tilbrook's McCartney-esque vocals became Squeeze's character-

istic sound, though Difford's occasional raffish interjections muss things up a bit.

Squeeze has suffered some unsettling personnel shake-ups. After *Cool,* John Bentley replaced Harry Kakoulli on bass, and the talented keyboard clown, Jools Holland, departed after *Argybargy,* to be replaced temporarily by ex-Ace member, Paul Carrack. Carrack sang Squeeze's most soulful hit, "Tempted," from *Eastside Story,* but left the group in the fall of 1981. *Eastside Story,* whose styles run from fake country ("Labeled with Love") to art pop ("F-Hole"), is a near-perfect pop-rock album of pithy vignettes that fuse Beatle-esque lyricism with new-wave wit. — S.H.

CHRIS SQUIRE
★ ★ ★ ★ **Fish Out of Water / Atl. (1975)**
★ ★ ★ **Don't Say No / Cap. (1981)**
The Yes bassist presents a fine approximation of the whole group, even down to his Jon Anderson–inspired singing. Squire prefers long cuts that excellently and subtly vary the same passage. His loud, thick bass is both an anchor and a lead instrument; few guitars, lots of majestic orchestrations. — C.W.

JIM STAFFORD
★ **Jim Stafford / Poly. (1974)**
Stafford enjoyed a brief mid-Seventies vogue, which earned him a summer replacement TV show and a hit record, "Spiders and Snakes," a wretched pop interpretation of the Garden of Eden story. If you must, the hit's here—along with gallons of other garbage. — D.M.

STAINLESS STEAL
★ **Can-Can / War. (1978)**
That's Offenbach's can-can. Stainless, maybe; painless, definitely NOT. Producer/ songwriter Pete Bellote should stick to working with Donna Summer and Giorgio Moroder. Clichés abound. — D.M.

MICHAEL STANLEY BAND
★ **Friends and Legends / MCA (1973)**
★ ★ **You Break It . . . You Bought It / Epic (1975)**
★ ★ ★ **Ladies' Choice / Epic (1976)** ¶
★ ★ ★ **Stagepass / Epic (1977)**
★ ★ **Cabin Fever / Ari. (1978)**
★ ★ **Greatest Hits / Ari. (1979)**
★ ★ **Heartland / EMI (1980)**
★ ★ **North Coast / EMI (1981)**
Although it has yet to make a dent outside its native Ohio, the Michael Stanley Band is competent, though it's hampered by the lack

of a unique sound. *Friends and Legends* was actually a Stanley solo album, released in 1973, before he put the group together. *You Break It* is pleasant but restrained; *Ladies' Choice* is more adventurous, with solid riffs, some added and well-done synthesizer work and even a dash of reeds. Like most live albums, *Stagepass* is a good souvenir for staunch fans but offers little for the uninitiated. Subsequent releases fail to provide a breakthrough, but Stanley's long-lived Midwestern following suggests he'll eventually find a broader audience. — A.N.

THE STANLEY BROTHERS
★ ★ ★ ★ ★ **The Best of the Stanley Brothers / Star.-Gusto (1975)**
★ ★ ★ ★ **The Stanley Brothers and the Clinch Mountain Boys Sing the Songs They Like Best / Star.-Gusto (1975)**
★ ★ ★ ★ **For the Good People / Star.-Gusto (1975)**
★ ★ ★ **Folk Song Festival / Star.-Gusto (1975)**
★ ★ **The Stanleys in Person / Power (1975)**
★ ★ ★ **Hymns of the Cross / King-Gusto (1976)**
★ ★ **Banjo in the Hills / Star.-Gusto (1976)**
★ ★ ★ **Good Old Camp Meeting Songs / King-Gusto (1976)**
★ ★ ★ **Folk Concert / Star.-Gusto (1976)**
★ ★ ★ **Sixteen Greatest Hits / Star.-Gusto (1977)**
★ ★ ★ ★ **The Stanley Brothers and the Clinch Mountain Boys / King-Gusto (1977)**
★ ★ ★ ★ **Twenty Bluegrass Originals / Gusto Deluxe (1978)**
★ ★ ★ ★ ★ **Sixteen Greatest Gospel Hits / Gusto (1978)**
★ ★ ★ ★ **"I Saw the Light" / Gusto (1980)**
★ ★ ★ ★ **The Columbia Sessions, 1949–1950 / Roun. (1980)**
★ ★ ★ **Old Country Church / Gusto (1981)**
★ ★ ★ **Their Original Recordings / Mel. (NA)**
★ ★ ★ **Uncloudy Day / County (NA)**
Those young folkies who took up banjo strumming in the early Sixties had the right idiom—bluegrass—but the wrong focus. The beauty of bluegrass lies in its great singers and in the way their high lonesome voices blend with one another and with the banjos, fiddles, mandolins and guitars of the string band.

Ralph Stanley is a great banjoist, as good as anybody this side of Earl Scruggs, but it was the intertwining of his voice with brother Carter's that gave the Stanleys their

stature as the finest exponents of bluegrass in the late Fifties and Sixties. Bill Monroe was more of an originator, Flatt and Scruggs more virtuosic, but the Stanleys had something more important: soulfulness. Whether singing folk songs, traditional hymns, country songs or bluegrass standards, the Stanleys created music that had a consistent intensity and purposefulness.

As a result, they remain the only bluegrass group that can truly be said to possess vision. In their best music, songs such as "Mountain Dew," "How Mountain Girls Can Love," "I'm a Man of Constant Sorrow," "It's Raining Here This Morning," "Little Maggie," "Wildwood Flower," "Gathering Flowers for the Master's Bouquet" and "Little Birdie," the Stanleys offer a completely self-expressive world view. This vision is conveyed even when they sing songs made famous by others (compare their version of "Mollie and Tenbrooks" to Bill Monroe's original, for instance).

The ultimate proof of their greatness rests with "Rank Stranger," which is a frightening glimpse of the biblical hell on earth. The sense of loneliness and abandonment here is bone-chilling in its completeness, and the yearning for salvation is utterly glorious.

Starday, King, Gusto and Power Pak are all spinoffs of the same company, and these albums reissue the Stanleys' brilliant recordings made for Starday/King which were originally released from the late Forties right through the Sixties. (Carter Stanley, who usually took the lead vocals, died in 1966.) The only one of these albums to avoid is *Banjo in the Hills,* which is all-instrumental. Even the live sets *(The Stanleys in Person, Folk Song Festival, Folk Concert)* are interesting. Melodeon's album, pressed from old 78s, sounds surprisingly good. The Rounder collection, which features early material, has some beautiful tracks, particularly "Have You Someone (in Heaven Awaitin')" and "The White Dove." The County album, recorded in a single evening's session in 1963 at a Baltimore studio above a used car lot, has some wonderful moments, especially Ralph Stanley's singing on "Precious Memories" and the ensemble work on the title track. — D.M.

MAVIS STAPLES
★ ★ ★ **A Piece of the Action / Cur. (1977) ¶**
★ ★ ★ **Mavis Staples / Stax (1978)**
★ ★ ★ **Oh, What a Feeling / War. (1979)**
As the lead singer with the Staple Singers, Mavis Staples is one of the most remarkable voices in soul and gospel. On *Piece of the*

Action, a soundtrack album produced by Curtis Mayfield, unfortunately, she is rather underutilized. These albums have some high points, but they pop up infrequently and unexpectedly from the tepid vocal and instrumental riffing that fills them out. — D.M.

THE STAPLE SINGERS
★ ★ ★ **Pray On / Epic (1967)** ¶
★ ★ ★ **Great Day / Mile. (1975)** ¶
★ ★ **Use What You Got / Fan. (NA)**
★ ★ **Twenty-fifth Day of December / Fan. (NA)**

The Staple Singers allegedly sold out gospel music, but the truth is they were mostly outside the gospel mainstream from their inception. Their style had little to do with close-harmony jubilee or shouting quartet; instead, they harkened back to the days of the lone singer with untutored piano or guitar. Pops Staple's guitar playing was redolent of both black and white country influences; Mavis' sexy contralto may have been an ideal gospel vehicle, but her phrasing and diction always showed considerable outside influence.

This batch of albums is from the early Sixties, their "folk-gospel" phase. They sang traditional hymns and spirituals—generally, but not strictly, Pops on the uptempo songs, Mavis on the slow ones—that were as well known to white people as to black. They also sang Bob Dylan and Woody Guthrie songs, as well as songs with religious themes that don't fit any particular definition. *Pray On* is the closest thing here to a traditional gospel album, but even it's not *that* close. *Great Day* offers both the most variety and the largest number of familiar songs. — J. MO.

STARGARD
★ ★ ★ **What You Waitin' For / MCA (1977)**
★ ★ ★ **The Changing of the Guard / War. (1979)**

Moderately successful disco funk group in Earth, Wind and Fire spirit (which figures, since *Changing* was produced by Verdine White of EWF). The female trio dedicates the Warners LP to Minnie Riperton, another obvious influence, but since this is one of those situations in which the band members are more prominently credited than the group itself, it's hard to say whose show this is. — D.M.

STARPOINT
★ ★ **Starpoint / Casa. (1980)**
★ ★ **Keep On It / Casa. (1981)**

Fairly creative disco production. Nice multivocal style and a Sly-style tune "Stand"

called "I Just Wanna Dance with You." — J.S.

EDWIN STARR
★ ★ **Edwin Starr / 20th Cent. (1977)** ¶
★ ★ **Clean / 20th Cent. (1978)** ¶
★ ★ **H.A.P.P.Y. Radio / 20th Cent. (1979)** ¶
★ ★ **War and Peace / Mo. (1980)**
★ ★ ★ **Superstar Series, Vol. 3 / Mo. (1981)**
★ ★ **Best of Edwin Starr / 20th Cent. (NA)**

As a minor-league Motown singer, Starr had a couple of fine moments in the late Sixties: "25 Miles" was a good Wilson Pickett derivative, and "War" helped introduce social commentary into soul. But the Twentieth Century-Fox records reduce Starr's once-powerful voice to a mannerism, and the arrangements don't give him the space to belt. Check out the Motown reissues. — D.M.

RINGO STARR
★ ★ ★ **Sentimental Journey / Cap. (1970)**
★ ★ ★ **Beaucoups of Blues / Cap. (1970)** ¶
★ ★ ★ ★ ★ **Ringo / Cap. (1973)**
★ ★ ★ **Goodnight Vienna / Cap. (1974)**
★ ★ ★ **Blast from Your Past / Cap. (1975)**
★ ★ **Ringo's Rotogravure / Atco (1976)** ¶
★ ★ **Ringo the 4th / Atco (1977)** ¶
★ ★ **Bad Boy / Por. (1977)** ¶
★ ★ **Stop and Smell the Roses / Bdwalk (1981)**

Of all the Beatles, Ringo Starr seemed the least likely to pursue a successful solo career after the group broke up. His first solo records were accordingly strange—*Sentimental Journey,* a catalogue of pop standards done with lush string arrangements, and *Beaucoups of Blues,* a straight country album produced by Pete Drake.

Then producer Richard Perry assembled a spectacle of an album around the goofy Beatles drummer, and when the dust settled, *Ringo* yielded two blockbuster singles, "Photograph" and "You're Sixteen." Ringo's solo career was made. *Goodnight Vienna,* the followup, included a cameo by John Lennon on the title track, which he wrote, and another hit with "Nono Song." Despite ambitious production and able studio backing, Ringo's albums for Atco, Portrait and Boardwalk are lifeless, much inferior to the Capitol solos. *Blast* is a nice greatest-hits set that includes the previously unavailable single written about the Beatles breakup, "Early 1970." — J.S.

STARS ON
★ ★ ★ **Stars on Long Play / Radio (1981)**
★ ★ ★ **Stars on Long Play 2 / Radio (1982)**

For those who just landed, the first side of

the first *Stars* LP consists of a fifteen-minute medley of twenty-nine Beatle songs set to a standardized handclap-thud disco beat, and tricked up to sound *just like* John, Paul, etc. There's something else on the second side, but you won't play it. (Doesn't sound like the Beatles.) Five thousand years of civilization for this? — S.I.

STARZ
■ Starz / Cap. (1976)
■ Violation / Cap. (1977)
■ Attention Shoppers / Cap. (1978)
■ Coliseum Rock / Cap. (1978)
Miniaturized Kiss, in comparatively worse taste. — J.S.

THE STATES
★ The States / Chrys. (1979)
★ Picture Me with You / Bdwalk (1981)
Tedious, uninspired radio fodder. The only sign of cleverness is the cover artwork on the debut album. — I.R.

CANDI STATON
★ ★ Young Hearts Run Free / War. (1976)
★ ★ Music Speaks Louder Than Words / War. (NA)
★ ★ House of Love / War. (NA)
★ ★ Chance / War. (1979)
★ ★ Candi Staton / War. (1980)
Candi Staton's early, Rick Hall–produced recordings (for Fame) remain her best work, though all are out of print. These albums feature different producers, none wholly sympathetic to Staton's special gifts, although "Young Hearts Run Free" was a 1976 pop hit. Bob Monaco, producer of *Music,* sabotages the singer with watery charts, while Dave Crawford, who did the other LPs, found himself so bankrupt for rhythm ideas that he used the same melodic hook on three *Young Hearts* songs. The most impressive item here is a beautiful gospel song, "Take My Hand, Precious Lord" on *House of Love.* — J.MC.

STATUS QUO
★ ★ Piledriver / A&M (1973) ¶
★ ★ Hello / A&M (1974) ¶
★ ★ Quo / A&M (1974) ¶
★ ★ On the Level / Cap. (1975) ¶
★ ★ Status Quo / Cap. (1976) ¶
★ ★ Live / Cap. (1977) ¶
★ ★ Status Quo Live / Cap. (1977)
★ ★ Rockin' All Over the World / Cap. (1978) ¶
In 1968, Status Quo had a worldwide hit with "Pictures of Matchstick Men," a phased-guitar rocker. They did not resurface

until 1972, having changed in the meantime from arty pop to full-tilt boogie band. *Piledriver,* with riff-riddled boogie grunge like "Don't Waste My Time" and "Oh Baby," inspired massive boot-thumping in England and a somewhat smaller following in the U.S. The rest of the records repeat the formula: strongly accented beat with noxiously simple guitar chords and a few shouted catch phrases. — A.N.

STEALER'S WHEEL
★ ★ ★ ★ Stuck in the Middle with You / A&M (1978)
Great Beatle-esque group led by songwriters Joe Egan and Gerry Rafferty scored big with the title track, which they cowrote and which, like the rest of the album, was produced by Jerry Lieber and Mike Stoller. Rafferty went on to an even more successful solo career. — J.S.

STEELEYE SPAN
★ ★ ★ ★ Hark! The Village Wait / Chrys. (1970)
★ ★ ★ ★ Please to See the King / Chrys. (1971)
★ ★ ★ ★ Ten Man Mop or Mr. Reservoir Butler Rides Again / Chrys. (1971)
★ ★ ★ Below the Salt / Chrys. (1972)
★ ★ ★ Parcel of Rogues / Chrys. (1973)
★ ★ ★ ★ Now We Are Six / Chrys. (1974)
★ ★ ★ ★ Commoner's Crown / Chrys. (1975)
★ ★ ★ ★ All around My Hat / Chrys. (1975)
★ ★ Rocket Cottage / Chrys. (1976)
★ ★ ★ Storm Force Ten / Chrys. (1977)
★ ★ ★ ★ The Steeleye Span Story—Original Masters / Chrys. (1977)
★ ★ ★ Live at Last / Chrys. (1978)
Steeleye Span was one of the earliest and most prolific groups to combine rock with traditional British Isles folk music. *Hark! The Village Wait* featured acoustic fretted instruments with lots of vocal harmonies; occasional electricity, as well as a session drummer, gave the rock setting. Two duos— Gay and Terry Woods, Tim Hart and Maddy Prior—provided depth and variety; ex–Fairport Conventioneer Ashley Hutchings played bass.

The Woodses then left. Martin Carthy, a mainstay in acoustic folk until then, and fiddler Peter Knight joined. *Please to See the King* and *Ten Man Mop* gave the quintet a sharper, more electric timbre, with Prior's vocals in the forefront. No drummer appeared, but the group often utilized miscellaneous percussion instruments for strong rhythm.

Hutchings then left, as did Carthy, and

the group took a decidedly more muscular, rockish turn. But newcomer Bob Johnson's electric guitar was too loud and raw. The previous subtlety and distinction were gone, and thus *Below the Salt* and *Parcel of Rogues* suffered: these have the same spirit, but a somewhat different and inferior presentation.

Now We Are Six added Nigel Pegrum on drums, as well as wind instruments and even synthesizer, and Steeleye Span had never sounded better or cleverer. But three throwaways—two cuts from a primary-school choir and an inexplicable remake of "To Know Him Is to Love Him," with David Bowie on saxophone—marred the album. Technically, however, the record benefited from its production consultant: Ian Anderson of Jethro Tull.

Commoner's Crown topped them all: thoughtful, imaginative and varied arranging—a masterful synthesis of folk and rock, neither overshadowing the other. Peter Sellers, of all people, added a slice of whimsy to one cut.

All around My Hat plunged more deeply into rock, largely through Mike Batt's production and louder guitars. For the first time, Steeleye Span sounded like rock turning to folk, rather than the reverse—a less adventurous approach perhaps, yet handled well. But *Rocket Cottage* continued the trend to a poor end. The six were heavy-handed, almost clumsy—a pale reduction of their past triumphs.

Story is an excellent two-record set spanning all previous albums. — C.W.

STEELY DAN
★ ★ ★ ★ **Can't Buy a Thrill / MCA (1972)**
★ ★ ★ ★ **Countdown to Ecstasy / MCA (1973)**
★ ★ ★ **Pretzel Logic / MCA (1974)**
★ ★ ★ **Katy Lied / MCA (1975)**
★ ★ ★ **The Royal Scam / MCA (1976)**
★ ★ ★ ★ **Aja / MCA (1977)**
★ ★ ★ **Greatest Hits / MCA (1978)**
★ **Gaucho / MCA (1980)**
Steely Dan's first two albums (*Can't* and *Countdown*) presented the group as a polished studio rock band, which scored a couple of hit singles, including "Do It Again" and "Reeling in the Years," despite a penchant for obscure lyrics and dissonant guitar patterns. With *Pretzel Logic,* the dissonance and beatnik poesy began to take over, and while the band was still capable of something as fine as "Rikki Don't Lose That Number," it was also growing much more pompous.

After *Pretzel,* Steely Dan became the exclusive province of songwriters Walter Becker and Donald Fagen; the results, *Katy Lied* and *Royal Scam,* have been defended as innovation and as ideology, but not necessarily as listenable. Steely Dan's art rock was by now edging ever closer to jazz, the vocals had deteriorated, the lyrics were often obscure for their own sake and the group's stature seemed to infect the records with an unparalleled pretentiousness. *Aja* reflects some musical lightening up: it is more frankly into musical merger, with less pretense about being a rock band and with liner notes just sophomoric enough to undercut the grad-school inflations of the lyrics. *Gaucho,* apparently their last LP, demonstrates why they broke up; it's the kind of music that passes for jazz in Holiday Inn lounges, with the kind of lyrics that pass for poetry in freshman English classes. Donald Fagen's solo LP is a far better bet. — D.M.

JIM STEINMAN
■ **Bad for Good / Epic (1981)**
Good for nothing, more like it. — W.K./ D.G.

STEPPENWOLF
★ ★ ★ ★ **Steppenwolf / Dun. (1968)**
★ ★ ★ **Steppenwolf the Second / Dun. (1968)**
★ **At Your Birthday Party / Dun. (1969)** ¶
★ **Early Steppenwolf / Dun. (1969)** ¶
★ ★ **Steppenwolf Live / Dun. (1970)**
★ **Steppenwolf Seven / Dun. (1970)**
★ ★ ★ **Steppenwolf Gold / Dun. (1971)**
★ ★ **For Ladies Only / Dun. (1971)** ¶
★ ★ ★ **16 Greatest Hits / Dun. (1973)**
★ **Hour of the Wolf / Epic (1975)**
★ ★ ★ **16 Great Performances / ABC (NA)**
★ ★ ★ **ABC Collection / ABC (NA)** ¶
★ **Reborn to Be Wild / Epic (NA)** ¶
Steppenwolf evolved from a Canadian group of legendary freneticism, Sparrow. Their first two albums made them mid-Sixties biker favorites, thanks to such items as "Born to Be Wild" and "Magic Carpet Ride." Leader John Kay then tried his hand at a political-commentary concept album (the awful and deleted *Monster*) and trailed off into anachronism, moving from Dunhill to Epic along the way. The self-titled first LP remains the best, and should be picked up in lieu of one of the virtually identical greatest-hits repackages. — J.S.

STERLING
★ **City Kids / A&M (1980)**
This occasionally flashy, often grunting ram-

rod rock tries for a sleek contemporary sound, but it's as retrograde as an act can get. — R.P.

CAT STEVENS

★ ★ Mona Bone Jakon / A&M (1970)
★ ★ ★ Tea for the Tillerman / A&M (1971)
★ ★ Teaser and the Firecat / A&M (1971)
★ ★ Catch Bull at Four / A&M (1972)
★ Foreigner / A&M (1973)
★ Buddah and the Chocolate Box / A&M (1974)
★ ★ ★ Cat Stevens' Greatest Hits / A&M (1975)
■ Numbers / A&M (1975)
■ Izitso / A&M (1977)
★ Back to Earth / A&M (1978)
★ ★ Cat's Cradle / Lon. (NA)

Stevens began recording for Deram (now released on London) in 1966; his second single, "Matthew and Son," was a Top Ten hit in his native England in 1967. But in 1968, Stevens contracted tuberculosis and spent a year recuperating in a clinic. He recovered in time to release *Mona Bone Jakon* in 1970, perfectly timed for the beginning of the singer/songwriter era.

Stevens was recording with a basic rock band (guitar, bass and drums), and together with producer Paul Samwell-Smith they made his next album, *Tea for the Tillerman,* a classic of British pop. Stevens had a knack for writing sensitive but straightforward songs like "Father and Son" and his first American hit, "Wild World." The album established him in America. *Tea* was followed by another strong set, *Teaser and the Firecat.* But since then he's become infatuated with Eastern mysticism, numerology and a pretentious, light classical music approach. He has not handled much of this complexity well, and the simple warmth of his early songs is now buried in a mass of needless ostentation. — D.M.

RAY STEVENS

★ ★ ★ Ray Stevens' Greatest Hits / Barn. (NA) ¶
★ ★ Nashville / Barn. (NA) ¶
★ ★ ★ Very Best of Ray Stevens / Barn. (1975) ¶
★ ★ Just for the Record / War. (1976) ¶
★ ★ Feel the Music / War. (1977) ¶
★ The Feeling's Not Right Again / War. (1979)
★ Shriner's Convention / RCA (1980)
★ One More Last Chance / RCA (1981)

Stevens began his career as a rock novelty singer whose biggest hit was a semibrilliant comic turn, "Ahab the Arab," recorded back about 1962; phase two (the Barnaby LPs) found him a pop-country singer with several hits on the C&W chart; phase three finds him floundering at Warner Bros. and then RCA, not turning out anything distinctive. The "Ahab" era novelties are on Barnaby's hits anthologies, but in re-recorded versions; search for Mercury's cutouts, which have the originals and a spark of imagination.
— D.M.

SHAKIN' STEVENS

★ ★ Legend / Parlo. (1970), Br. imp.
★ ★ I'm No D.J. / CBS (1971), Br. imp.
★ ★ Rockin' and Shakin' / Contour (1972), Br. imp.
★ ★ Shakin' Stevens and the Sunsets / Phi. (1974), Br. imp.
★ ★ Shakin' Stevens / Track (1978), Br. imp.
★ ★ The Legend / EMI (1979), Br. imp.
★ ★ ★ This Ole House / Epic (1980), Br. imp.
★ ★ ★ At the Rockhouse / Magnum Force (1980), Br. imp.
★ ★ ★ Shakin' Stevens / Epic/NuDisk (1980)
★ ★ ★ Get Shakin / Epic (1980)

British rockabilly revivalist whose biggest claim to fame until 1980 was appearing on-stage as Elvis Presley in Jack Goode's posthumous tribute to the King, which ran in London's West End, quite successfully, just after Elvis' death. (*Legend* was produced by Dave Edmunds, who also contributed rockabilly fanatic sleeve notes.) In 1980, Stevens began working with steel guitarist B. J. Cole and lead guitarist Albert Lee (Head Hands and Feet), at which point his revivalism took root and resulted in "This Ole House," "Marie Marie" and "You Drive Me Crazy," probably the best and certainly the most authentic hits of the U.K.'s renewed rockabilly craze. All you need to hear are on the U.S. LP *(Get Shakin');* the rest are luxuries.
— D.M.

B. W. STEVENSON

★ ★ B. W. Stevenson / RCA (1972) ¶
★ ★ The Best of B. W. Stevenson / RCA (1977) ¶
★ Lost Feeling / War. (1977) ¶
★ On the Christmas Night / MCA (1979)
★ Lifeline / MCA (1980)

Stevenson clicked in 1973 with "My Maria" and "Shambala," both on the RCA albums. These were the very best sort of folkish Seventies rock: tough vocals, driving backings. They deserved their chart status. Unfortunately, since then he has not come up with anything half so interesting. — D.M.

AL STEWART

★ ★ **Past, Present and Future / Janus (1974)** ¶
★ ★ **Modern Times / Janus (1975)** ¶
★ ★ ★ **The Year of the Cat / Janus (1976)**
★ ★ **The Early Years / Janus (1978)** ¶
★ ★ **Time Passages / Ari. (1978)**
★ ★ **24 Carrots / Ari. (1980)**
★ ★ **Indian Summer / Ari. (1981)**

Scottish singer/songwriter who has been recording for over a decade but enjoyed his biggest success with the title song from *The Year of the Cat,* in 1976. *Past, Present and Future* is a concept album about European history, though Stewart seems without the insight to make such an outrageous proposition more than amusing. — D.M.

AMII STEWART

★ ★ **Knock on Wood / Ari. (1979)**
★ **Paradise Bird / Ari. (1980)**
★ **I'm Gonna Get You Love / Hands. (1981)**

Stewart's disco remake of Eddie Floyd's soul hit, "Knock on Wood" made No. 1 in 1979. But Stewart's followups (even the attempt to redo "Light My Fire") weren't nearly as danceable or pleasurable. "Knock on Wood" was probably the best disco remake of a soul song, but you'll want to prove it with the twelve-inch single, not with any of these LPs. — D.M.

BILLY STEWART

★ ★ ★ **I Do Love You / Chess (1965)** ¶
★ ★ ★ **Summertime / Chess (1966)** ¶
★ ★ ★ **Billy Stewart Teaches Old Standards New Tricks / Chess (1967)** ¶
★ ★ ★ ★ **Billy Stewart Remembered / Chess (1970)** ¶
★ ★ ★ **Cross My Heart / Cadet (NA)** ¶
★ ★ ★ ★ **The Greatest Sides / Chess (1982)**

Stewart had perhaps the most eccentric vocal style in the history of soul. He weighed 300 pounds, but his range was extremely high and he was capable of amazing trills at the upper end of it. Such glossolalia brought an extremely weird dimension to "Summertime," the *Porgy and Bess* standard he made a hit in 1966. That, and "I Do Love You," a hit in both 1965 and 1969, were the highlights of his career. Stewart died in 1970. *The Greatest Sides* is a wonderful collection of his best and most important material, including both the above hits, "Fat Boy," "Sitting in the Park" and more. — D.M.

GARY STEWART

★ ★ ★ **You're Not the Woman You Used to Be / MCA (1975)** ¶
★ ★ ★ ★ **Out of Hand / RCA (1975)**
★ ★ ★ **Steppin' Out / RCA (1975)**
★ ★ ★ ★ **Your Place or Mine / RCA (1977)**
★ ★ ★ **Little Junior / RCA (1978)**
★ ★ ★ **Gary / RCA (1979)**
★ ★ ★ **Cactus and Rose / RCA (1980)**
★ ★ ★ ★ **Greatest Hits / RCA (1981)**

For anyone who likes both honky-tonkin' country music and basic rock & roll, Gary Stewart is a dream come true. He combines both genres seamlessly into something more elusive than ordinary country rock. His ferocious mountain tenor, heavy on the vibrato, attacks songs like a rocker's voice, but his records are clearly a product of Nashville (although they've progressed away from the Music City mainstream). Stewart sings drinking, fighting and cheating songs, but he keeps his distance: he's paying tribute to the country forms he loves, not singing about himself.

The MCA album is old demos released after he became a star; the singing is vibrant but not fully developed. But the songs represent his most fanciful storytelling on record. Of the RCA albums, *Out of Hand* is an unbeatable collection of honky-tonk songs on which his singing overcomes a slightly muddled production. *Steppin' Out* is a more self-conscious country primer: a bluegrass song, a standard, some stinging Southern rock, some "progressive" songs. *Your Place* is Stewart's most subtly distinctive yet—bigbeat country that's harmonically reminiscent of *Blonde on Blonde* (of all things); on the uptempo numbers, Stewart's singing even evokes the mid-Sixties Dylan. *Little Junior* isn't quite that fine, but it does reflect Stewart's growing comfort with his unique formal merger.

Since then, he's been treading water all too comfortably. The *Greatest Hits* collection is intelligently compiled and the first side is genuinely intense. — J.MO.

JOHN STEWART

★ ★ ★ **California Bloodlines / Cap. (1969)**
★ **Willard / Cap. (1970)** ¶
★ ★ **Cannons in the Rain / RCA (1973)**
★ ★ ★ **Phoenix Concerts Live / RCA (1974)** ¶
★ **Wingless Angels / RCA (1975)** ¶
★ ★ **Fire in the Wind / RSO (1977)**
★ ★ ★ **Bombs Away Dream Babies / RSO (1979)**
★ ★ ★ **Dream Babies Go to Hollywood / RSO (1980)**

One man's Americana, deeper than John Denver's, but still laced with corn, appropriately enough for a former member of the Kingston Trio. — S.H.

ROD STEWART

★ ★ ★ ★ **The Rod Stewart Album** / Mer. (1969)
★ ★ ★ ★ **Gasoline Alley** / Mer. (1970)
★ ★ ★ ★ ★ **Every Picture Tells a Story** / Mer. (1971)
★ ★ ★ ★ **Never a Dull Moment** / Mer. (1972)
★ ★ ★ **Sing It Again, Rod** / Mer. (1973)
★ ★ ★ ★ **Atlantic Crossing** / War. (1975)
★ ★ ★ ★ **A Night on the Town** / War. (1976)
★ ★ ★ **Best of Rod Stewart** / Mer. (1976)
★ ★ ★ **Best of Rod Stewart, Vol. 2** / Mer. (1976)
★ ★ ★ **Foot Loose and Fancy Free** / War. (1977)
★ ★ **Blondes Have More Fun** / War. (1978)
★ ★ ★ **Rod Stewart's Greatest Hits** / War. (1979)
★ ★ **Foolish Behaviour** / War. (1980)
★ ★ ★ **Tonight I'm Yours** / War. (1981)
★ ★ **Rod Stewart and Steampacket** / Sp. (NA) ¶
★ ★ **Rod Stewart and the Faces** / Sp. (NA) ¶

Rod Stewart is one of the great rock singers of the Seventies. He began his career in England, performing with a variety of small-time bands (some of his early material is represented on the Springboard packages) before joining the Jeff Beck Group in 1969, where he established himself. By 1970 he had joined the Faces and begun recording a memorable series of solo albums; the Faces broke up in 1975 and Stewart has continued on his own since then.

The Rod Stewart Album, his debut, and *Gasoline Alley,* which followed, reveal more of Stewart's folk roots than he would ever show again. But it was with *Every Picture Tells a Story* that he finally realized his full promise, turning in a diverse collection of vocals, including folk-rock numbers like Tim Hardin's "Reason to Believe"; flat-out rock like the title cut, which is as imaginatively lyrical as the best of Jerry Lee Lewis and (thanks to Mickey Waller's drumming) just as powerful; and the poignant ballad "Maggie May," his first hit single. Stewart also toyed with soul music, recording the Temptations' "Losing You" in a style that reflected the influence of both the Tempts' David Ruffin and soul master Sam Cooke. *Never a Dull Moment* repeated this mix with

slightly less successful results. The Mercury repackages (the two *Best ofs* and *Sing It Again, Rod*) also include material from his fourth and weakest solo LP, *Smiler,* now deleted.

In 1975, Stewart moved to Warner Bros., where he began working with veteran producer Tom Dowd, who teamed him with a variety of American sessionmen. *Atlantic Crossing,* the first of their collaborations, was spotty, but *A Night on the Town* was terrific, revealing Stewart's skills as both writer and interpreter, and at the same time gaining him a second and even bigger hit single, "Tonight's the Night." But he then decided to become a sex symbol rather than a rock & roller, and *Foot Loose and Fancy Free,* while not truly awful, came as a real disappointment to those who knew the vitality of his early work. Since then he has straddled the line between prancing fool and competent entertainer as if he'd never owned any dreams of artistry. *Tonight I'm Yours,* one of the classics of pure recorded vanity, ends the discussion with a thud. — D.M.

STIFF LITTLE FINGERS

★ ★ ★ ★ **Inflammable Material** / Rough T. (1979)
★ ★ ★ ★ **Nobody's Heroes** / Chrys. (1980)
★ ★ ★ **Hanx!** / Chrys. (1980)
★ ★ ★ **Go for It** / Chrys. (1981)

Punk rockers from Northern Ireland come on with enough energy to solve the home crisis single-handedly. The relentless backbeat and mean, dramatic power chords are even more reminiscent of the spirit of early Who than the Clash (a band Stiff Little Fingers is often favorably compared to), and there's nary a weak niche in the band's aggressively streetwise songwriting stance. The British debut contained several instant classics, particularly "Alternative Ulster," "Suspect Device," "State of Emergency" and "White Noise." *Nobody's Heroes* introduced the group to the U.S. via such chestnuts as "Fly the Flag," "Nobody's Hero," "Bloody Dub," "I Don't Like You" and "Tin Soldiers." *Hanx!* is a live album. *Go for It* shows the band improving musically and in recording quality, especially on the great title track, but not writing as much inspired material as before, although "Roots, Radicals, Rockers and Reggae" does the trick. — J.S.

STEPHEN STILLS

★ ★ ★ **Stephen Stills** / Atl. (1970)
★ ★ ★ **Stephen Stills 2** / Atl. (1971)
★ ★ ★ **Manassas** / Atl. (1972)
★ **Down the Road** / Atl. (1973)

■ **Steven Stills Live / Atl. (1975)**
★ **Stephen Stills / Col. (1975)**
★ ★ ★ **Still Stills / Atl. (1976)** ¶
★ **Illegal Stills / Col. (1976)**
★ ★ **Thoroughfare Gap / Col. (1978)**
As a member of the Buffalo Springfield and Crosby, Stills, Nash (and Young), Stephen Stills was always a more notable guitarist than writer, and his singing ranged from moving to limpid. It remained in the latter category, and his writing was only occasionally worthwhile, on his solo discs. The best of them are the first Atlantic LP, which includes "Love the One You're With," the second, which has "Change Partners," and *Still Stills,* an anthology that has both plus his "Go Back Home" collaboration with Eric Clapton. *Manassas* isn't really a solo LP at all—it's a rock band, featuring ex–Byrd and Flying Burrito Brother Chris Hillman, and it has its moments. The Columbia stuff is garbage, the relic of a burnt-out career.
— D.M.

STILLS-YOUNG BAND
★ ★ **Long May You Run / Rep. (1976)**
Stephen Stills and Neil Young in a collaboration that's a long way from their days in the Buffalo Springfield. The album is redeemed only by Young's biting title track, a mock tribute to a car and a girl—in that order. — D.M.

STILLWATER
★ **Stillwater / Capri. (1977)**
★ **I Reserve the Right / Capri. (1978)**
Anonymous Southern folk rock. — J.S.

STINGRAY
★ **Stingray / Carr. (1981)**
Competent and well arranged but plodding and basically uninteresting heavy-metal band from South Africa. This could be any number of other faceless late-Seventies heavy-metal outfits, all equally talented and equally undistinguished. — J.S.

ALAN STIVELL
★ ★ ★ **Renaissance of the Celtic Harp / Roun. (1972)**
★ ★ ★ ★ ★ **Live at the Olympia / Fon. (1972)**
★ ★ ★ ★ **From Celtic Roots / Fon. (1974)**
★ ★ ★ ★ **Journee à la Maison / Roun. (NA)**
★ ★ ★ **Disco de Oro / Phi. (NA)**
★ ★ ★ **Alan Stivell, Vol. 1 / Impact (NA)**
★ ★ ★ **Alan Stivell, Vol. 2 / Impact (NA)**
Stivell is to Celtic music what Ravi Shankar is to Indian music. He is synonymous with Breton music and culture. A multi-instrumentalist (pipes, harp, flute and bombarde), he is considered the virtuoso of Celtic harp. His large ensemble arrangements, particularly well revealed on the live album, transcend the limitations of folk, rock and classical forms. All of the albums are recommended, but those featuring electric guitarist Dan ar Bras *(Celtic Roots, Live)* should appeal to even the casual listener.
— D.D.

FRANK STOKES
★ ★ ★ ★ **Creator of the Memphis Blues / Yazoo (NA)**
★ ★ ★ **Frank Stokes / Roots (NA), Br. imp.**
Very early, very fine Memphis bluesman who was half of the Beale Street Sheiks. Stokes had some elements of minstrelsy in his approach, and also worked with fiddler Will Batts. The Yazoo set is exceptionally fine; the Roots is also good, though it duplicates some tracks with inferior sound. Stokes can also be heard on an album he shares with the Mississippi Sheiks, *Sittin' on Top of the World,* on Biograph. — D.M.

STONEBOLT
★ ★ **Stonebolt / Parach. (1978)**
★ ★ **Keep It Alive / RCA (1980)** ¶
★ ★ **New Set of Changes / RCA (NA)**
Typical AOR cannon fodder: a little Eagles-ish harmony, some recycled George Harrison guitar, nice bland wash of synthesized strings in the background. Very listenable unless you make the mistake of paying attention, in which case you'll wish you could light the fuse on that cannon. — D.M.

THE STONE PONEYS
★ ★ ★ **The Stone Poneys Featuring Linda Ronstadt / Cap. (1975)**
Linda Ronstadt as a green but strong-voiced lead singer in a folk-rock band noted primarily for the hit "Different Drum," written by Monkee Mike Nesmith. — J.S.

ROB STONER
★ ★ ★ ★ **Patriotic Duty / MCA (1980)**
Stoner is an accomplished session musician (his credits range from backing Don McLean's "American Pie" to serving as musical director for Bob Dylan's Rolling Thunder Revue) who was one of the earliest proponents of the rockabilly revival via his legendary early-Seventies outfit Rockin' Rob and the Rebels. This set presents Stoner's rockabilly blasting into the Eighties with such cruisers as "Hotel 1-2-3," "Seven Days," "What Round Is This" and "I Came I Saw I Left." — J.S.

STONE'S THROW
★ **Suppressed Desire** / Sire (NA)
My sentiments exactly. — D.M.

STRANGELOVES
★ ★ **I Want Candy** / Bang (1965)
Billing itself as Australian to cash in on the 1965 British invasion, this New York City trio crossed "Hand Jive" with a typical high-school football cheer to produce the pulsat-ingly delightful "I Want Candy." Today, the song is wonderfully dated, invoking blissful, nostalgic tingles—the highlight of an other-wise laughably weak collection of the same song rewritten a dozen times. — A.N.

STRANGLERS
★ ★ **IV Rattus Norvegicus** / A&M (1977)
★ ★ **No More Heroes** / A&M (1977)
★ ★ **Black and White** / A&M (1978)
★ ★ **Stranglers IV** / IRS (1979)
★ ★ **The Raven** / U.A. (NA)
★ ★ ★ ★ **X Certs** / U.A. (1979)
New-wave band strongly reminiscent of one of the original Sixties punk-rock groups, the Music Machine, but with additional Jim Morrison pretensions. The live *X Certs* shows them at their best. — J.S.

THE STRAWBS
★ ★ ★ ★ **Just a Collection of Antiques and Curios** / A&M (1970)
★ ★ ★ **From the Witchwood** / A&M (1971)
★ ★ ★ ★ **Grave New World** / A&M (1972)
★ ★ ★ **Bursting at the Seams** / A&M (1973)
★ ★ ★ **Hero and Heroine** / A&M (1974)
★ ★ ★ **Ghost** / A&M (1975)
★ ★ ★ **Nomadness** / A&M (1975) ¶
★ ★ ★ ★ **Deep Cuts** / Oy. (1976)
★ ★ ★ **Burning for You** / Oy. (1977)
★ ★ ★ **The Best of the Strawbs** / A&M (1978)
★ ★ ★ **Deadlines** / Ari. (1978) ¶
The Strawbs came out of the same English folk-rock scene that produced Steeleye Span and Fairport Convention, with whom they shared singer Sandy Denny. The group also gave Rick Wakeman his start. But the real leader of the band was vocalist/guitarist Dave Cousins, and it is Cousins' range of in-terests, from classical to folk to art rock, that made the Strawbs one of the more inter-esting—if least commercially viable—folk-rock groups of the Seventies. — D.M.

STRAY CATS
★ **Stray Cats** / Ari. (1981)
★ ★ **Gonna Ball** / Ari. (1981), Br. imp.
With petrified quiffs trembling from street excitement, this New York three-piece swept Britain with twelve songs that could have been written in 1956 but, unfortunately for us, have been saved until now. Rockabilly with a new-romantic flair. — ML.H.

STREEK
★ ★ **Streek** / Col. (NA)
Next edition, all the mediocre funk 'n' fusion acts who can't spell their own names prop-erly get docked one notch for ruining our hopes for literacy in these times. — D.M.

STREET CORNER SYMPHONY
★ ★ **Harmony Grits** / Bang (1975)
★ ★ ★ **Little Funk Machine** / ABC (1977) ¶
Harmony, the first album by this five-piece soul-singing group, isn't much, but the sec-ond is a pleasant surprise, mostly because of production by Willie Hutch and a rhythm section that includes drummer James Gad-son and bassist James Jamerson, studio stal-warts of Motown's heyday. — D.M.

STREETHEART
★ ★ ★ **Under Heaven over Hell** / Atl. (1979)
Surprisingly listenable Canadian hard rock, in a toned-down Humble Pie (i.e., subdued Steve Marriott) mold. The versions of "Under My Thumb" and "Here Comes the Night" aren't a patch on the Stones or Them, though. — D.M.

STREET PLAYER
★ ★ **Street Player** / Ario.-Amer. (NA)
★ ★ **Dancin' Fever** / Ario.-Amer. (NA)
The endless boogie refuses to die. — D.M.

BARBRA STREISAND
★ ★ ★ ★ **The Barbra Streisand Album** / Col. (1963)
★ ★ ★ **The Second Barbra Streisand Album** / Col. (1963)
★ ★ ★ ★ **The Third Album** / Col. (1964)
★ ★ ★ **Funny Girl (original cast)** / Cap. (1964)
★ ★ ★ **People** / Col. (1965)
★ ★ **My Name Is Barbra** / Col. (1965)
★ ★ **My Name Is Barbra, Two** / Col. (1966)
★ ★ **Color Me Barbra** / Col. (1966)
★ ★ **Je M'Appelle Barbra** / Col. (1966)
★ ★ ★ **Simply Streisand** / Col. (1967)
★ ★ **A Christmas Album** / Col. (NA)
★ ★ **A Happening in Central Park** / Col. (1967)
★ **What About Today** / Col. (1967)
★ ★ **Funny Girl (original soundtrack)** / Col. (1968)
★ ★ ★ ★ **Barbra Streisand's Greatest Hits** / Col. (1970)
★ ★ ★ ★ **Stoney End** / Col. (1971)

★ ★ ★ **Barbra Joan Streisand** / Col. (1972)
★ ★ **Live Concert at the Forum** / Col. (1972)
★ ★ **Barbra Streisand . . . And Other Musical Instruments** / Col. (1973)
★ ★ ★ ★ **The Way We Were** / Col. (1974)
★ **Butterfly** / Col. (1974)
★ **Classical Barbra** / Col. (1976) ¶
★ ★ ★ **Lazy Afternoon** / Col. (1975)
★ **A Star Is Born (original soundtrack)** / Col. (1976)
★ ★ ★ **Streisand Superman** / Col. (1977)
★ ★ **Songbird** / Col. (1978)
★ ★ ★ ★ ★ **Barbra Streisand's Greatest Hits, Vol. 2** / Col. (1978)
★ ★ **Wet** / Col. (1979)
★ ★ ★ ★ **Guilty** / Col. (1980)
★ ★ ★ ★ **Memories** / Col. (1981)

The most influential mainstream American pop singer since Frank Sinatra, Barbra Streisand has remained an intimidating force on the pop scene for twenty years. In the early Sixties she succeeded Judy Garland as queen of the vaudeville-cum-torch tradition of Fanny Brice and Helen Morgan. In the Seventies she was the inspiration for cabaret-rock performers like Bette Midler, Barry Manilow, Melissa Manchester, and Peter Allen.

A minor role in the Broadway musical *I Can Get It for You Wholesale* catapulted Streisand to stardom in 1962, when she was still a teenager. Her first solo album, the following year, instantly established her as a major recording star. With their mixture of quality theatrical standards and nightclub songs arranged with lavish good taste by Peter Matz and others, her first three albums still stand as genre classics. The quintessential early Streisand cut was her "ironic" version of "Happy Days Are Here Again," from the first album, which she delivered as an operatically hysterical lament.

In 1964, Streisand was cast by Ray Stark to play his late mother-in-law, Fanny Brice, in the Broadway production of *Funny Girl.* It became her most famous role, both on Broadway and in the movies. Through the Sixties, Streisand ignored rock in favor of standards and special material. *My Name Is Barbra, My Name Is Barbra, Two* and *Color Me Barbra* were spinoffs of TV specials and featured elaborate medleys. The studio albums *Je M'Appelle* and *Simply Streisand* were, respectively, an uneven collaboration with arranger/composer Michel Legrand, and Streisand's best album of standards since the *Third.*

Streisand didn't seriously take on the songwriters of her own generation until *What About Today,* which contained three Beatles songs produced and performed in an unwieldy theatrical style. But with *Stoney End,* recorded with rock producer Richard Perry, Streisand finally found a wailing pop-rock vocal style that was suitable for Carole King and Laura Nyro ballads. A second collaboration with Perry, *Barbra Joan,* featured a beautiful medley of Burt Bacharach-Hal David ballads. But Streisand was never able to sing hard rock convincingly, and on the eccentric *Butterfly,* produced by her boyfriend Jon Peters, she sounded way out of her depth. *The Way We Were,* however, was more on the mark—an opulent pop-rock album that mixed rock ballads with Hollywood schmaltz; the title cut, from the movie, became her first No. 1 hit.

By the early Seventies, Streisand's singing had gained in depth and assurance what it had lost in histrionic enthusiasm. All her interpretations were marked by an imperious sense of command. *Lazy Afternoon* (produced by Rupert Holmes) was a winning throwback to prerock days, while *Superman* was a thoroughly modern pop-rock album in which she communicated an almost voracious glee over the commercial success of *A Star Is Born,* the musically insipid "home movie" she made with Jon Peters. On *Songbird* (highlighted by a powerful version of "Tomorrow" from the musical *Annie*), and *Wet* (all of whose songs had images of water), Streisand's imperiousness, combined with uneven material and formulaic arrangements, made for a disturbing remoteness. *Wet* introduced Streisand's disco duet with Donna Summer, "No More Tears (Enough Is Enough)."

Streisand hit her musical career peak with *Guilty,* an audacious collaboration with the Bee Gees' Barry Gibb, who produced and wrote all the tunes and sang on two cuts. Here Streisand's pop-operatic aspirations found a perfect aural launching pad in Gibb's celestial arrangements with their light pop-funk underpinnings. The consistency of *Guilty* is matched by Streisand's two greatest-hits collections. The first volume, released in 1970, is highlighted by "People," "Free Again" and the novelty "Second Hand Rose," and presents a definitive portrait of Streisand the theatrical diva. *Volume 2* showcases the Seventies pop-rock belter and includes "The Way We Were" and "You Don't Bring Me Flowers" (her No. 1 duet with Neil Diamond), along with movie themes and album highlights. *Memories,* which duplicates much of *Volume 2,* also contains two previously unrecorded songs, plus a remake of "Lost inside of You," from *A Star Is Born.* — S.H.

STRIKER

★ Striker / Ari. (1978) ¶
Failed aspirants to Foreigner's muscle-rock crown. — D.M.

STUFF

★ ★ ★ Stuff / War. (1976)
★ ★ ★ More Stuff / War. (1977)
★ ★ ★ Stuff It / War. (1978)
★ ★ Live in New York / War. (1980)
A group of top pop and soul studio musicians (bassist Gordon Edwards, keyboardist Richard Tee, guitarists Cornell Dupree and Eric Gale, drummer Christopher Parker). The playing is predictably slick and fiery. — J.S.

THE STYLISTICS

★ ★ ★ ★ The Stylistics / H&L (1971) ¶
★ ★ ★ ★ Round 2 / H&L (1972) ¶
★ ★ ★ ★ Rockin' Roll Baby / H&L (1973) ¶
★ ★ ★ ★ Let's Put It All Together / H&L (1974) ¶
★ ★ Heavy / H&L (1974) ¶
★ ★ ★ ★ Best of the Stylistics / H&L (1975) ¶
★ ★ ★ Thank You Baby / H&L (1975) ¶
★ ★ ★ You Are Beautiful / H&L (1975) ¶
★ ★ ★ In Fashion / Mer. (1978) ¶
★ ★ ★ Love Spell / Mer. (1979) ¶
★ ★ ★ Hurry Up This Way Again / Phil. (1980) ¶
★ ★ ★ Closer Than Close / Phil. (1981) ¶
★ ★ ★ Wonder Woman / H&L (NA) ¶
★ ★ Once upon a Juke Box / H&L (NA) ¶
★ ★ ★ ★ The Fabulous Stylistics / H&L (NA) ¶

For three years in the early Seventies, Russell Thompkins really was what Robert Christgau called him—nothing less than a Wimp God, the last grand exponent of classic falsetto R&B harmony. "You Make Me Feel Brand New," "Betcha by Golly, Wow," "Break Up to Make Up," "You Are Everything" and "People Make the World Go 'Round," all written and produced by Thom Bell and Linda Creed, are as good a run of hits as anybody had in the decade. And "Rockin' Roll Baby" took the formula uptempo, with results nearly as mythic as vintage Chuck Berry.

Unfortunately, the group eventually split with Bell and Creed, and though Thompkins remains a great singer, neither material nor production nor the general direction of the group's career has amounted to much since then. Hugo and Luigi and Marty Bryant and Bill Perry's post-Bell productions were wimp-pop without the genius (although Van McCoy's arrangements kept the group pretty hip), Teddy Randazzo guided them competently but without much distinction at Mercury, and since transferring to Philly International, the group hasn't been able to do anything with the tired TSOP soul machine.

It is tempting to see the Stylistics solely as a producers' vehicle, but that isn't really fair. Simply sustaining the notion of a straight harmony group after the Sly Stone revolution in black pop required a fair amount of conceptual dedication, and a specific identity, and Thompkins remains the perfect soul neoclassicist, the last true representative of the tradition of Clyde McPhatter to Eddie Kendricks; he's far more dedicated to this ideal than, say, Michael Jackson, or even Eugene Record. And the boundaries suggested by those reference points perfectly define the limitations and strengths of the Stylistics. — D.M.

STYX

★ Styx / Wood. (1972)
★ ★ Styx II / Wood. (1973) ¶
★ ★ Serpent / RCA (1974)
★ ★ Miracles / Wood. (1974)
★ ★ ★ Equinox / A&M (1974)
★ ★ ★ Crystal Ball / A&M (1976)
★ ★ Best of Styx / Wood. (1977)
★ ★ ★ Grand Illusion / A&M (1977)
★ ★ Pieces of Eight / A&M (1978)
★ ★ Cornerstone / A&M (1979)
★ ★ Paradise Theater / A&M (1980)
★ ★ Lady / RCA (NA)
Styx is a superbly teenage American response to the flashy British art rock (Yes, etc.) that blended unusual melodies, spirited vocals and just enough technical gymnastics to score heavily in the teen market. The RCA records, originally released on Wooden Nickel, came before the rise, and aren't worth much. *Equinox* and *Crystal Ball* gave the group its first successes, although the latter repeats most of the former. *Grand Illusion,* the third in the series, also exposed the band's limitations as writers—further progress seems unlikely. — A.N.

SUBURBAN LAWNS

★ ★ ★ Suburban Lawns / IRS (1981)
New-wave quintet with a Velvet Underground fixation tries hard to sound like Talking Heads. "Gossip" and "Flying Saucer Safari" feature some good guitar playing by John McBurney. — J.S.

THE SUBURBS
★ ★ ★ **In Combo** / Twin T. (1979)
★ ★ ★ **Credit in Heaven** / Twin T. (1981)
In an era of bands pretending to be cryptic, remote and strange, Minneapolis' Suburbs are apparently the genuine item. They pirate devices from British Invasion, Bowie, funk, Talking Heads, "new music" and twist it all into aural art that must be processed almost as visual information to be enjoyed. Both records are a Rorschach test worth taking, although the group's deliberate obtuseness can be wearing over the four sides of *Credit.*
— L.F.

BRUCE SUDANO
★ ★ ★ **Fugitive Kind** / Millen. (1981)
Former member of Brooklyn Dreams (and Donna Summer's husband) comes closer to the rock & roll Dreams never quite reached, but remains a bit on the slick, pop side of the ledger. Quite strongly sung and adeptly arranged, though. — D.M.

SUE ANN
★ ★ ★ **Sue Ann** / War. (1981)
With a little more power and personality, Sue Ann could have turned her Pete Bellotte-produced debut into the rock/funk fusion Donna Summer aimed for with *The Wanderer.* That she came as close as she did bodes well, especially considering the lameness of the material. — J.D.C.

SUGARLOAF
★ ★ ★ **Don't Call Us, We'll Call You** / Clar. (1975)
This Colorado band had an early-Seventies pop hit, "Green-Eyed Lady," then faded from sight. Trying to regain a recording deal, it was spurned rather imperiously by CBS. This resulted in Jerry Corbetta's amusing song, "Don't Call Us, We'll Call You," in which the CBS phone number is spelled out—touch-tone style—for the world. That was another hit, but the band quickly dropped from sight anyway. CBS has since changed its number. — D.M.

SUICIDE
★ ★ ★ **Suicide** / Red S. (1977) ¶
★ ★ ★ ★ **Alan Vega/Martin Rev/Suicide** / Ze/Ant. (1980)
★ ★ ★ **Suicide** / Red S. (1980)
Consisting of singer Alan Vega and Martin Rev on minimal keyboards and rhythm box, this primal New York electronic duo specializes in confrontation. Suicide first surfaced from Manhattan's art scene in the early Seventies, often sharing the stage with the New York Dolls at the legendary Mercer Arts Center, ducking bottles and battling hecklers antagonized by their transistorized apocalyptic blues.

Vega's Presley-cum-Iggy psychobilly attack and Rev's primitive heartbeat accompaniment rival the best horror-show Stooges and the Velvets' "Sister Ray" for sheer rock & roll terror. The pair's debut *Suicide* is a tough album to swallow. It is also a pioneering punk work, an essential link between the guitar-driven blitz of punk rock and the electronic pulse of later groups like Joy Division. One of the group's biggest fans, Ric Ocasek of the Cars, produced *Alan Vega/Martin Rev/Suicide,* adding almost orchestral grace to Rev's keyboards without compromising their savage urban drive. For the uninitiated this is the best place to start.

The second *Suicide* LP is basically a reissue of the first, with extra tracks and a flexi-disc of a typical live Suicide gig, complete with the sound of breaking glass—against the stage. — D.F.

YMA SUMAC
★ ★ ★ **Voice of the Xtabay** / Cap. (1950)
★ ★ **Legend of the Sun Virgin** / Cap. (1952)
★ ★ **Inca Taqui** / Cap. (1963)
★ ★ **Mambo** / Cap. (NA)
Sumac arrived in the mid-Fifties from the Peruvian mountains, and immediately became an unpronounceable household name because of her eight-octave range. (*Xtabay*—now re-released as side A of a disc that also includes *Inca Taqui*—was her hit, or milestone, or whatever.) Patti Smith for xenophiles. — D.M.

HUBERT SUMLIN
★ ★ ★ **Groove** / Black and Blue (NA), Br. imp.
★ ★ ★ **Hubert Sumlin and Carey Bell** / L+R (NA), Br. imp.
★ ★ ★ **Funky Roots** / Vogue (NA), Br. imp.
Howlin' Wolf's guitarist in solo sets, some electric, some acoustic, which are pretty passable. — D.M.

DONNA SUMMER
★ ★ **Love to Love You Baby** / Oasis (1975)
★ **A Love Trilogy** / Oasis (1976)
★ **The Four Seasons of Love** / Oasis (1977)
★ ★ ★ **I Remember Yesterday** / Casa. (1977)
★ ★ ★ **Once upon a Time** / Casa. (1977)
★ **Live and More** / Casa. (1978)
★ ★ ★ ★ **Bad Girls** / Casa. (1979)
★ ★ ★ ★ **On the Radio: Greatest Hits, Vols. 1 and 2** / Casa. (1979)
★ ★ ★ ★ ★ **The Wanderer** / Gef. (1980)

Working with producers Pete Bellotte and Giorgio Moroder in Munich and L.A., Donna Summer perfected a version of disco that was the height of the genre's aspirations to artistry. In five years, Summer managed to move from the ultimate sex queen—"Love to Love You Baby," her first hit, was nothing less than sixteen minutes of simulated orgasm, a genius novelty—to committed, introspective, even religious artist.

She didn't really hit her stride on LP until the initial concept sets, *I Remember Yesterday* and *Once upon a Time.* Both of these expanded on her basic danceable premise not only with hints of a story line—nostalgia for her pop past on the former, a kind of Cinderella fairy tale on the latter—but with echoes of Motown and rock & roll. The live album is dismal—Summer is a perfect recording studio artist in that she has little or no idea of what to do when confronted with situations calling for spontaneous interaction with a crowd. This stiffness results in her least listenable disc.

Bad Girls, however, presented Summer's boldest declaration of independence from disco stereotyping. "Hot Stuff" and the title track both moved along with typical late-Seventies dance rhythm bounce and also incorporated powerful, surging Rolling Stones-style guitar chords. This trend was extended—not to say perfected—on *The Wanderer,* in which Summer's songwriting also took a turn toward the personal, expressing not only her keen feeling for urban paranoia but also her commitment to Christianity. On this album, Summer, Bellotte and Moroder actually function as a sort of high-tech rock band; with the possible exception of Michael Jackson's *Off the Wall,* no one has made a contemporary pop dance record with so much stylistic depth, grace and power.

On the Radio is a marvelous collection of Summer's hits through "Bad Girls" and "Hot Stuff," including "No More Tears (Enough Is Enough)," her duet with Barbra Streisand. Together with *Bad Girls* and *The Wanderer,* it establishes Summer's credentials as one of the most important new artists of the Seventies. — D.M.

SUN
★ ★ ★ **Live On, Dream On** / Cap. (1976) ¶
★ ★ **Wanna' Make Love** / Cap. (1976)
★ ★ **Sun-Power** / Cap. (1977)
★ ★ **Sunburn** / Cap. (1978)
★ ★ **Destination: Sun** / Cap. (1979)
★ ★ **Sun over the Universe** / Cap. (1980)
★ ★ **Force of Nature** / Cap. (1981)
This post–Sly Stone hard-disco group from Dayton, Ohio, came from a parent group called the Overnight Low Show Band, which contributed three members to the Ohio Players. The band's sound is hard-edged funk and features tightly arranged ensemble riffing in the manner of the Commodores. "Wanna Make Love (Come Flick My Bic)" from *Live On* became a substantial hit in 1976. — J.S.

ROY SUNDHOLM
★ ★ **The Chinese Method** / Poly. (1979)
He's no Scandinavian Springsteen, but this Norwegian-born singer/songwriter (and former Graham Parker roadie, no less) at least has a breezy rock & roll-spirited, R&B-spiced writing style going for him. Unfortunately, his debut album is deep-sixed by drab arrangements and soulless production. — D.F.

SUNNYLAND SLIM
★ ★ ★ ★ **Slim's Shout** / Prest. (NA)
★ ★ ★ ★ **Sad and Lonesome** / Jewel (NA)
★ ★ ★ ★ **She Got That Jive** / Airw. (NA)
Chicago-based vocalist/pianist with a reputation as an excellent accompanist as well as leader of his own fine sessions. Here he is presented with several good groups of musicians. *Slim's Shout* features King Curtis on sax; *Sad and Lonesome* uses Walter Horton's harp; *She Got That Jive* showcases guitarists Eddie Taylor and Hubert Sumlin. — J.S.

SUNSHINE BAND
★ ★ **Sound of Sunshine** / TK (NA)
Same old story, without KC. — D.M.

SUPERTRAMP
★ ★ **Supertramp** / A&M (1970)
★ ★ **Indelibly Stamped** / A&M (1971)
★ ★ ★ **Crime of the Century** / A&M (1974)
★ ★ ★ **Crisis? What Crisis?** / A&M (1975)
★ ★ ★ ★ **Even in the Quietest Moments . . .** / A&M (1977)
★ ★ ★ **Breakfast in America** / A&M (1979)
★ ★ ★ **Paris** / A&M (1980)
After its classic period *(The Yes Album* through *Close to the Edge),* Yes left a mid-Seventies void in art rock that has been filled by Genesis and Supertramp. Both bands have the capacity to turn out well-honed avant-garde technotronics with a minimum of murky subterfuge. They also stretch out (but not too far), and on occasion get fairly outside (but they know how and when to reel it back in). The most substantial difference between the two is that Supertramp can write a hook, the missing element in the genre since the early days of Yes. Another

important distinction is that while Genesis has grown less creative over the years, Supertramp has grown exponentially, improving as players while perfecting the hit formula epitomized by "Ain't Nobody but Me."
— B.M.

THE SUPREME ANGELS
★ ★ ★ ★ ★ Supreme / Nashb. (1972)
★ ★ ★ Shame on You / Nashb. (1974)
★ ★ In Love with God / Nashb. (1976)
★ ★ ★ ★ If I'm Too High / Nashb. (NA)
This is probably the hippest and flashiest of the young, Seventies-style gospel groups. Lead singer Howard Hunt is very heavily influenced by Wilson Pickett (a blatant example of soul pointing the way for gospel, rather than vice versa); many of the group's arrangements rely on a relaxed, loping Jimmy Reed-type beat; the organ is jazzy; and guitarist Alfonso Dent sounds like he just stepped out of a South Side Chicago blues bar.

It's a virtual tossup between *Supreme* and *If I'm Too High*, with the nod going to *Supreme* because it offers a more interesting batch of songs, ranging from a truly inspired gospel version of "Lucky Old Sun" to a funereal "Precious Lord," a fine, slow vehicle for Hunt's improvisatory preaching and shouting style. The problem with the last album is that the Angels went too far with their soul leanings, so that the title song, which spotlights the high sweet lead of Gregory Kelly, is nothing but a soul ballad with religious lyrics. With its horns, strings and flute, it could be the Chi-Lites. But the arrangement, as with many cuts here, is soul at its most pedestrian. However, "You Can't Get to Heaven (by Living Like Hell)," with its crazed piano, is well worth hearing.
— J.MO.

THE SUPREMES
★ ★ ★ ★ Meet the Supremes / Mo. (1966)
★ ★ ★ I Hear a Symphony / Mo. (1966)
★ ★ ★ ★ Supremes A Go-Go / Mo. (1966)
★ ★ ★ ★ Supremes A Sing Holland-Dozier-Holland / Mo. (1967)
★ ★ ★ ★ ★ Anthology: Diana Ross and the Supremes / Mo. (1974)
★ Supremes / Mo. (1976)
★ ★ The Supremes at Their Best / Mo. (1978) ¶
★ ★ ★ ★ Superstar Series, Vol. 1 / Mo. (1981)
★ The Supremes at the Copa / Mo. (1968)
When Holland-Dozier-Holland stopped writing and producing the Supremes in the late Sixties, many looked at it as the end of an

era. Together, that trio plus Diana Ross had created a remarkable string of hit singles in the mid to late Sixties that were the epitome of the Motown sound; they are included on the *Anthology* package and are virtually all great. The other Seventies albums, however, feature little by Holland-Dozier-Holland, and nothing at all by Ross. As a result, there's little here of more than cursory interest. *Superstar Series* is a hits package. The Sixties albums are recent reissues, and with the exception of *At the Copa,* worth hearing.
— R.G./D.M.

SURF PUNKS
■ My Beach / Epic (1980)
The idea of combining Ventures-style surf songs with Ramones-style punk is a great one—too bad the Surf Punks didn't come up with it. Instead, we get a whole album devoted to deriding "valleys" (folks who aren't surfers) and crowing about how good the surfing life is. Which is probably closer to the current surfer culture than a Ventures/Ramones marriage, but since when is that an excuse? Suggested sequel: *My Record Player.*
— J.D.C.

ALFONZO SURRETT
★ ★ ★ Comin' Out / MCA (1980)
With his smooth voice, strong melodic sense and resolutely danceable rhythm arrangements, Surrett comes off like Peabo Bryson with weaker songs but more on-the-one. And weak songs are easily remedied.   — J.D.C.

SURVIVOR
★ ★ ★ Survivor / Scotti (1979)
★ ★ ★ Premonition / Scotti (1981)
Survivor is like Bachman-Turner Overdrive without the hits—not bad until you realize that without the hits, BTO was pretty boring.   — J.D.C.

SUTHERLAND BROTHERS AND QUIVER
★ ★ ★ Reach for the Sky / Col. (1975) ¶
★ ★ ★ Slipstream / Col. (1976) ¶
★ ★ ★ Down to Earth / Col. (1978) ¶
★ ★ When the Night Comes Down / Col. (1979)
Prior to their amalgamation, the Sutherland Brothers (Gavin and Iain) had made two folk-rock albums, while Quiver had made a pair of undistinguished hard-rock LPs. In 1973, the collaboration sparked a Top Twenty hit (on Island) called "You Got Me Anyway," which felt like the best kind of Dylan-esque rock. Although the Sutherlands received some British acclaim as authors of

Rod Stewart's "Sailing," the group itself never again made much U.S. impact. *Reach* has a fantastic song, "Arms of Mary," surrounded by lots of passable ones; *Slipstream* is just the passable stuff, while *Down to Earth* and *When the Night* find the remnants of Quiver altogether absent, leaving the field entirely to the Sutherlands, who lack punch. — D.M.

SUZY Q

★ **Get On Up and Do It Again** / Atl. (NA)
Disco hackwork. — D.M.

SWAMP DOGG

★ ★ ★ **Finally Caught Up with Myself** / MCA (NA)
★ ★ ★ **Swamp Dogg** / Wiz. (NA)
★ ★ ★ **I'm Not Selling Out, I'm Buying In** / Tak. (1981)
★ ★ ★ ★ **The Best of Swamp Dogg** / War Bride (1982)
Jerry Williams, a.k.a. Swamp Dogg, has for some years been soul music's chief eccentric, parlaying a gravelly voice and trenchant wit into a cohesive, if bizarre and somewhat dated, style. Williams writes the most explicit and hilarious tales of philandering this side of Clarence Reid's Blowfly persona, although he also has a certain sentimental streak (not to mention a penchant for arcane political commentary).

The essential Swamp Dogg—given that his early masterpiece *Total Destruction to Your Mind* is long out of print—is the War Bride *Best of*. In addition to *Total Destruction*'s title track, it also contains the somewhat psychedelic protest number "Synthetic World," the brutal Wilson Pickett/Joe Tex parody "Wife Sitter," and the bulk of the other really memorable tunes Dogg has cut for a number of labels over the past fifteen years. Not for the faint of heart, but for those with a sufficiently eclectic and unembarrassable view of the world, fine stuff. The others are for hard-core soul deviants only. — D.M.

BILLY SWAN

★ ★ ★ ★ **I Can Help** / Col. (1975) ¶
★ ★ ★ **Rock and Roll Moon** / Col. (1975) ¶
★ ★ ★ ★ ★ **Billy Swan** / Col. (1976) ¶
★ ★ ★ **Four** / Col. (1976) ¶
★ ★ ★ **Billy Swan at His Best** / Monu. (1978)
★ ★ ★ **You're OK, I'm OK** / A&M (1978) ¶
★ ★ ★ **I'm Into Lovin' You** / Epic (1981)
Swan is labeled "progressive rockabilly"—definitely for lack of a better term. He owes a lot to the Beatles for ideas about harmony singing and to Motown or Forties jump-blues bands for ideas about using horns. It's a modern Southern roadhouse sound, greatly influenced by the music of the original rockabilly artists (Presley, Jerry Lee Lewis et al.), but in Swan's hands it sounds something like the Beatles singing Buddy Holly. Though he has a fondness for novelty tunes, Swan's specialty is the adult love song; his urgent, nervous singing style somehow makes him sound guarded and outreaching at the same time, a truly Seventies attitude.

"I Can Help" is his best-known song, and the album marks an impressive debut. Though perhaps his most country-sounding, it owed obvious debts to Memphis rockabilly, and the material is outstanding. The second, *Moon*, is clearly a descendant of the first, but rocks a little harder. The third, *Billy Swan*, on which his sound finally jells, is one of the great lost Seventies albums—passionate songs and singing with white-hot musicianship. *Four* was cut in Muscle Shoals, Alabama, and has more of a soul feel, with increased use of strings and horns. *You're OK, I'm OK* and *I'm Into Lovin' You* find Swan shifting his recording base to L.A. and nearly becoming swamped in psychobabble. The result was that he found himself back where he started, playing keyboards for Kris Kristofferson. — J.B.M.

THE SWAN SILVERTONES

★ ★ ★ ★ **Love Lifted Me** / Spec. (NA)
★ ★ ★ **My Rock** / Spec. (NA)
★ ★ ★ ★ **The Swan Silvertones** / Exo. (NA)
Lead singer Claude Jeter's falsetto shriek is the touchstone for countless soul stylists, and when Al Green's voice runs up or down the scale or slides all around the beat, it is in blatant imitation of Jeter. The Swans also boasted the more modern "hard" singing of Solomon Womack; a classic screamer in Robert Crenshaw; and later, one of gospel's tightest arrangers in Paul Owens. *Rock* is only barely the lesser of the two Specialty albums; the title song is a Swans calling card, but so is "How I Got Over" from the *Love* LP, and the latter also contains "Glory to His Name" and a powerfully understated "I'm A-Rollin'." The Exodus sides are considered inferior, but are likely to be of more interest to rock fans, as they're in a modern "hard" style more similar to soul: especially "Mary Don't You Weep," with Louis Johnson building the lead and Jeter's falsetto filling in the spaces. — J.MO.

SWEAT BAND

★ ★ ★ ★ **Sweat Band** / Uncle Jam (1980)

Sweat Band is yet another of George Clinton's Parliafunkadelicment Thang spinoffs, spun out by Bootsy Collins and featuring such P-Funk stalwarts as Mike Hampton, Gary Shider, Bernie Worrell, Maceo Parker and Fred Wesley. Although a good part of it is amiable fluff, enough of it combines a loopy sense of humor with solid funk to make it Collins' best album since *Stretching Out in a Rubber Band.* — J.D.C.

SWEET
★ ★ ★ **Desolation Boulevard / Cap. (1975)**
★ ★ **Give Us a Wink / Cap. (1976)**
★ ★ **Off the Record / Cap. (1977)**
★ ★ **Level Headed / Cap. (1978)**
★ ★ **Cut above the Rest / Cap. (1979)**
★ ★ **Sweet VI / Cap. (1980)**
Sweet made Who-like pop-rock singles that were massive hits in England from 1973 through 1975, the pre-punk heyday of bands like Slade. Sweet was slicker and flashier than those, but also less inspired; the real story was the songs of Nicky Chinn and Mike Chapman, who also wrote for Suzi Quatro. In America, Sweet scored mildly with "Action" (from *Wink*), "Blockbuster" (their best song), "Little Willy" and *Desolation*'s "Fox on the Run." — D.M.

SWEETBOTTOM
★ ★ ★ **Angels of the Deep / Elek. (1978)**
★ ★ **Turn Me Loose / Elek. (1979)**
With a name like that, this fusion group should be left for dead, but they play too well to dismiss them. Guitarist Martin Appel is particularly good. — J.S.

SWEET PEOPLE
★ **Sweet People / Poly. (NA)**
Nice guys finish last. — D.M.

SWEET TALKS
★ ★ **Sweet Talks / Mer. (NA)**
You'll have to speak a bit sweeter than that to get me to invest. — D.M.

SWEET THUNDER
★ **Sweet Thunder / Fan./WMOT (1978)**
★ **Horizon / Fan./WMOT (NA)**
Absolutely listless late Philly group. Like the Delfonics meet MFSB on Quaaludes. — D.M.

STEVE SWINDELLS
★ ★ ★ **Fresh Blood / Atco (1980)**
Swindells, a keyboard player and songwriter whose odd credits include a stint with the Hawklords and a tune on the *McVicar* soundtrack album, is teamed here with

Simon King and Huw Lloyd-Langton from the Hawkwind family and Nic Potter, who was of Van der Graaf Generator and the Tigers. On this album, however, Swindells' grand but downcast songs are sung in a strong, dramatic voice; the music is powerful and wide-screen. An impressive first effort. — I.R.

SWITCH
★ ★ ★ **Switch / Gor. (1978)**
★ ★ ★ **Switch 2 / Gor. (1979)**
★ ★ ★ **This Is My Dream / Gor. (1980)**
★ ★ ★ **Reaching for Tomorrow / Gor. (1980)**
★ ★ ★ **Switch 5 / Gor. (1981)**
Funk group's lack of crossover success in these tepid times just might be proof of its quality. For the most part, even the hits ("There'll Never Be," "I Call Your Name," "Love Over and Over Again" all made the soul Top Ten) are run-of-the-mill post-disco funk and ballads, but their groove has a certain integrity. Nothing as brilliantly melodic as the Commodores' best, but far superior to the likes of Air Supply, if you catch my drift. — D.M.

KEITH SYKES
★ ★ ★ **I'm Not Strange, I'm Just Like You / Backs. (1980)**
★ ★ ★ **It Don't Hurt to Flirt / Backs. (1981)**
California writer/rocker varies his approach from Marty Balin-esque white soul to vaguely new-wave offerings; arrangements and melodies are first-rate, the lyrics lack much depth, the singing wavers between strained and ingratiating. Sexism rears its ugly head a bit too often to take Sykes with full seriousness—especially on the second album. — D.M.

ROOSEVELT SYKES
★ ★ ★ **Honeydripper / Prest. (1960)** ¶
★ ★ ★ **Blues / Folk. (1961)** ¶
★ ★ ★ ★ **Country Blues Piano Ace 1929–1932 / Yazoo (1971)** ¶
★ ★ ★ **Feel Like Blowing My Horn / Del. (1973)** ¶
Sykes is regarded as one of the key developers of the modern blues piano style—a combination of barrelhouse boogie, prominent right-handed rhythm patterns and 12-bar blues structure. He is also a formidable blues singer and a prolific songwriter.

The albums listed above represent various phases of his career. The Yazoo set traces his early accomplishments, solo as well as with a number of vocal accompanists. The Prestige and Folkways LPs were made in the early Sixties; the former draws on the jazz aspect of his talents (and features King Curtis on tenor sax), while the latter concentrates on Sykes' bluesier side (solo and with his protégé, Memphis Slim). The Delmark album, recorded in 1973, places him in a modified Chicago blues context.

Oddly, Sykes' lifelong theme song, the self-composed "Honeydripper," a hit for him in the Thirties, isn't on any of these albums, though another of his popular numbers, "The Night Time Is the Right Time," can be found on a set he shares with Little Brother Montgomery (*Urban Blues,* Fantasy). — I.M.

SYLVAIN SYLVAIN
★ ★ ★ ★ Sylvain Sylvain / RCA (1979) ¶
★ ★ ★ ★ Syl Sylvain and the Teardrops / RCA (1981)
After contributing to fellow ex–New York Doll David Johansen's first two solo albums, Syl Sylvain got a chance to step out on his own. And he delivered the goods with two solid records that show off an ear for classic rock & roll sounds in a form lighter than the old Dolls' stuff. Timeless pop by a man who takes the tradition of rock and its positive effect on people seriously. — W.K.

EDMUND SYLVERS
★ ★ ★ Have You Heard / Casa. (NA)
Thanks to brother Foster, Edmund can lay claim to being part of the first family of post-disco dance music. And he doesn't do such a bad job himself. — D.M.

THE SYLVERS
★ ★ Showcase / Cap. (1976) ¶
★ ★ ★ Something Special / Cap. (1976) ¶
★ ★ ★ New Horizons / Cap. (1977) ¶
★ ★ ★ Best of the Sylvers / Cap. (1978) ¶
★ ★ Forever Yours / Casa. (1978)
★ ★ Concept / Solar (1981)
After a career largely kept alive by one Foster Sylvers hit ("Misdemeanor") and innumerable appearances on the cover of the black teen magazine *Right On!*, the Sylvers found consistent commercial success in the mid-Seventies with former Jackson Five producer Freddie Perren. Perren's production style harks back to the classic Motown sound, and his hot, concise tracks, coupled with some appropriately frothy Keni St. Lewis lyrics, have given this family group a string of sometimes annoying ("Boogie Fever") and sometimes fun ("Hot Line") pop hits. — J.MC.

SYLVESTER
★ ★ Sylvester / Fan. (1977)
★ ★ Step Two / Fan. (1978)
★ ★ ★ Stars / Fan. (1979)
★ ★ Living Proof / Fan. (1979)
★ ★ ★ Sell My Soul / Fan. (1980)
★ ★ ★ Too Hot to Sleep / Fan. (1981)
When he first began recording in 1973, for Blue Thumb, Sylvester was disco's only screaming black drag queen, like Little Richard out of the closet. But in recent years, he's modified his sexual thrust and come up with these hot dance albums, lightly likable except for his more mannered exhortations. — D.M.

SYLVIA
★ Sylvia / Vibr. (1977)
★ Lay It on Me / Vibr. (1977)
★ Brand New Funk / Vibr. (1977)
The original heavy-breathing disco, from the former distaff member of Mickey and Sylvia ("Love Is Strange"). She also owns All-Platinum Records, of which Vibration is a subsidiary. The hit was "Pillow Talk" from *Sylvia.* — J.S.

SYNERGY
★ Electronic Realizations for Rock Orchestra / Pass. (1975)
★ Sequencer / Pass. (1976)
★ Cords / Pass. (1978)
★ Games / Pass. (NA)
★ Audion / Pass. (NA)
Not really a group at all, just New Jersey synthesizer whiz Larry Fast and his multiple machines. Truly pompous antirock b.s. — D.M.

SYREETA
★ ★ ★ Syreeta / Mo. (1972) ¶
★ ★ ★ One to One / Tam. (1977) ¶
★ ★ ★ Rich Love, Poor Love / Mo. (1977) ¶
★ ★ ★ Syreeta / Tam. (1980)
★ ★ ★ Set My Love in Motion / Tam. (1981)
Stevie Wonder's former wife was produced by him on the Motown label, and she turned in her best work. The Tamla LPs are not as successful, mostly because she's only an average vocalist who lacks inspiration. A latter duet with G.C. Cameron was slightly more successful. — D.M.

HERMAN SZOBEL
★ ★ Szobel / Ari. (1976)
Classically trained, Zappa-influenced pianist; nephew of impresario Bill Graham. — J.S.

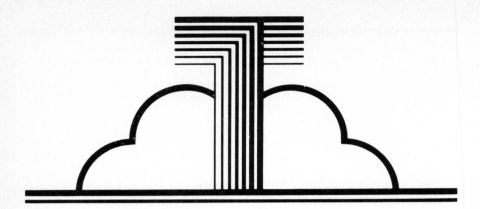

TALKING HEADS
★ ★ ★ ★ **Talking Heads 77 / Sire (1977)**
★ ★ ★ **More Songs about Buildings and Food / Sire (1978)**
★ ★ ★ **Fear of Music / Sire (1979)**
★ ★ ★ ★ **Remain in Light / Sire (1980)**

Talking Heads came out of New York's seminal punk scene at about the same time as Blondie, the Patti Smith Group, Television and Richard Hell's Voidoids, yet never really had much in common musically with those bands. Lighter and with distinct R&B overtones, the sound of *Talking Heads 77* was as distinct and idiosyncratic as that of, say, Smith's *Horses* or Television's *Marquee Moon,* but more obviously detached from rock & roll tradition. *More Songs* is essentially an extension of the ideas proposed by *77,* from the self-conscious modernism burlesqued by the title to the cooled-down R&B stylizations that earned the group its first hit, a cover of Al Green's "Take Me to the River." That album also began a period of collaboration with producer Brian Eno, a relationship that provided the band with some of its most challenging and problematic music. Although *Fear of Music* had some brilliant moments, including the apocalyptic urgency of "Life during Wartime" and the remarkably ethereal "Air," much of the album was weighted down by Eno's obtrusive production devices. Some ground was regained by *Remain in Light,* where the vitality of African performance techniques and funk-based rhythms employed by the band considerably offset the manipulative production process used in editing the album; but even then the music on disc was not nearly as exciting as the concert performances of the same material using an expanded version of Talking Heads. — J.D.C.

IAN TAMBLYN
★ ★ ★ **Closer to Home / GRT (1977)** ¶

Organic Canadian folk pop, with songs and arrangements recalling Bruce Cockburn's romantic grace. Tamblyn's singing is as fresh and clear as a cool mountain breeze. You've heard it all before, but not always done so tastefully. — D.F.

TAMS
★ ★ **Tams / ABC (1964)** ¶
★ ★ **At the Top / MCA (NA)**

Group that scored in 1963 with "What Kind of Fool?" is ineffectively revived for a mid-Seventies dance record. Boo-wop. — D.M.

TANGERINE DREAM
★ ★ **Stratosfear / Virgin (1977)** ¶
★ ★ **Encore—Tangerine Dream Live / Virgin (1977)** ¶
★ ★ **Thief / Elek. (1981)**
★ ★ **Exit / Elek. (1981)**

Kings of the synthesizer, German-style, or the machine takes over. These are neither much better, nor much worse, than the group's import albums, but they *are* cheaper. For technocrats and energy brats. — D.M.

MARC TANNER BAND
★ ★ **No Escape / Elek. (1979)**
★ ★ **Temptation / Elek. (1980)**

Tanner's a talented guitarist with a workmanlike approach to his rock & roll, but nothing on either of these albums is inspired or inflammatory enough to make you understand why they were cut. — R.P.

TANTRUM
★ **Rather Be Rockin' / Ova. (1979)**
★ **Tantrum / Ova. (NA)**

The band plays a bearable AOR background mush, but even though the concept of three female lead singers is innovative, it'd be a lot more successful if one of them wasn't thoroughly annoying, or if any were discernably gifted. — D.M.

THE TAPES
★ ★ ★ **Party / Pass. (1980)**
The Dutch apply the lessons of *Talking Heads 77* to tales of alienated Europa—with a little Brecht, Stravinsky and Roxy Music thrown in for good measure. The results are interesting. And the Tapes are apparently only the visible tip-off to an active new music underground in Holland. — D.F.

TARNEY AND SPENCER
★ ★ ★ **Three's a Crowd / A&M (1978)**
★ ★ ★ **Run for Your Life / A&M (1979)**
Australian pop-rock duo spins a sound reminiscent of the later Fleetwood Mac. *Three's a Crowd* features the Climax Blues Band in a session role. — J.S.

A TASTE OF HONEY
★ ★ **A Taste of Honey / Cap. (1978)**
★ ★ **The Hitter / Cap. (1979)** ¶
★ ★ **Another Taste / Cap. (1979)**
★ ★ **Twice as Sweet / Cap. (1980)**
Disco group notable principally for having a pair of women instrumentalists and scoring a major 1978 hit with "Boogie Oogie Oogie," almost but not quite the "Surfin' Bird" of the new beat. — D.M.

RICHARD TATE
★ ★ **Richard Tate / ABC (1977)** ¶
Reasonably engaging McCartney-esque pop rock. Complex surfaces but no depth. — D.M.

BERNIE TAUPIN
★ **He Who Rides the Tiger / Asy. (1980)**
Elton John's lyricist in what should be an embarrassingly bad solo LP. — J.S.

TAVARES
★ ★ ★ ★ **Check It Out / Cap. (1974)** ¶
★ ★ ★ **Hard Core Poetry / Cap. (1974)** ¶
★ ★ ★ **In the City / Cap. (1975)** ¶
★ ★ ★ **Sky High! / Cap. (1976)** ¶
★ ★ ★ ★ **Love Storm / Cap. (1977)**
★ ★ ★ ★ **The Best of Tavares / Cap. (1977)**
★ ★ ★ **Future Band / Cap. (1978)**
★ ★ ★ **Madame Butterfly / Cap. (1979)** ¶
★ ★ ★ **Supercharged / Cap. (1980)**
★ ★ ★ **Love Uprising / Cap. (1980)**
★ ★ ★ **Loveline / Cap. (1981)**
Tavares is a family soul quintet without a particularly distinctive vocal personality. Nevertheless, as a vehicle for two sets of producers, the group has made several first-rate contributions to the pop-soul arena in the middle and late Seventies.

Tavares' first three albums *(Check It Out, Hard Core Poetry* and *In the City)* were pro-duced by Brian Potter and Dennis Lambert, who downplayed traditional two- and three-part soul harmonies in favor of a more homogenized unison approach. With intelligent song selection and tasteful (if sometimes bland) production, Lambert and Potter gave Tavares a string of mildly soulful ballad hits ("Check It Out," "She's Gone").

Ex-Motown producer Freddie Perren took over after *In the City,* and while he too works a pop-soul bag, the difference is noticeable. Perren's tracks are hotter (in the classic Motown mold), and his arrangements tend to feature more old-fashioned soul group devices. The lyrics are often lightweight ("Whodunit"), but the songs have a spirit and energy missing from Lambert and Potter's work.

Since 1980, Tavares has worked with several different producers without achieving any clear stylistic direction. — J.MC.

TAXXI
★ ★ **Day for Night / Fan. (1981)**
Limp blues-rock trio. — J.S.

CARMOL TAYLOR
★ ★ ★ ★ **Song Writer / Elek. (1976)**
A nice little slice of Nashville from a singer who doesn't deserve her obscurity. The country cookers bubble with verve, the ballads shed the proper tear, and Taylor and some all-star Nashville pickers even turn out a fine cover of Chuck Berry's "Back in the U.S.A." — R.P.

CHIP TAYLOR
★ ★ **Some of Us / War. (1974)** ¶
★ ★ **Somebody Shoot Out the Jukebox / Col. (1976)** ¶
★ ★ **Chip Taylor's Saint Sebastian / Cap. (1979)**
Taylor is best known as a songwriter: in the Sixties, two of his songs, "Wild Thing" and "Angel of the Morning," became big one-shot pop hits for the Troggs and Merilee Rush, respectively. On his own, the sound's closer to C&W, laconic but not terribly effective because he isn't a particularly impressive singer. — D.M.

EDDIE TAYLOR
★ ★ ★ **I Feel So Bad / DJM (1976)**
★ ★ ★ **Bad Boy a Long Way from Home / P-Vine (1978), imp.**
★ ★ ★ **My Heart Is Bleeding / L&R (1980), Br. imp.**
★ ★ ★ ★ ★ **Big Town Playboy / Charly (1981), Br. imp.**
The great Chicago singer, guitarist and writ-

er. His Vee Jay recordings (the bulk of them on *Big Town Playboy*, the rest on *Street Talkin'*, a Muse album he shares with Elmore James) are some of the finest urban blues ever made. Of the later material above—all of it from the Seventies—the DJM set, which includes backing from Philip Walker and George Smith, is about the best. — D.M.

HOUND DOG TAYLOR
★ ★ ★ **Hound Dog Taylor and the Houserockers / Alli. (1971)**
★ ★ ★ ★ **Natural Boogie / Alli. (1974)**
★ ★ ★ ★ **Beware of Dog / Alli. (1976)**
Excellent Chicago slide guitarist plays no-holds-barred barroom boogie, and plays it as well as it comes. The posthumously released live album, *Beware of Dog*, captures Taylor at his hottest, in front of a club full of dancing, howling fans. — J.S.

JAMES TAYLOR
★ ★ ★ ★ ★ **Sweet Baby James / War. (1970)**
★ ★ ★ **Mud Slide Slim and the Blue Horizon / War. (1971)**
★ ★ **One Man Dog / War. (1972)**
★ ★ **Walking Man / War. (1974)**
★ ★ ★ ★ **Gorilla / War. (1975)**
★ ★ **In the Pocket / War. (1976)**
★ ★ ★ ★ **James Taylor's Greatest Hits / War. (1976)**
★ ★ ★ ★ **JT / Col. (1977)**
★ ★ **Flag / Col. (1979)**
★ ★ **Dad Loves His Work / Col. (1981)**
The prototypical Seventies singer/songwriter, Taylor blends folk, traditional, R&B and jazz influences into an acoustically based pop song style, as expressive as it is understated. Taylor's auspicious 1969 Apple debut is out of print. *Sweet Baby James*, which made him a star, introduced the famous "Fire and Rain"; it holds up as a spare, compelling musical statement. *Mud Slide Slim* reflects, often eloquently, the confusion that followed success.

On *Gorilla*, Taylor broke out of a downward drift with some pure R&B ("How Sweet It Is") and a steamy masterpiece, "You Make It Easy." *JT* contains a great interpretation of the Jimmy Jones R&B hit, "Handy Man," and a sly gem, "Secret o' Life." Taylor's singing has gained in strength over the years, as evidenced by the stunning remakes of "Carolina on My Mind" and "Something in the Way She Moves," on the *Greatest Hits* collection. A fine writer who has produced at least a handful of modern standards, Taylor is perhaps an even finer singer; his assimilation of American-roots styles evokes classic male American types. — S.H.

JOHNNIE TAYLOR
★ ★ ★ **Eargasm / Col. (1976)**
★ ★ **Rated Extraordinaire / Col. (1977) ¶**
★ ★ **Disco 9000 / Col. (1977)**
★ ★ **Reflections / RCA (1977) ¶**
★ ★ ★ ★ **The Johnnie Taylor Chronicle / Stax (1977)**
★ ★ **Ever Ready / Col. (1978) ¶**
★ ★ **She's Killing Me / Col. (1979)**
★ ★ **New Day / Col. (1980)**
★ ★ **Best of Johnnie Taylor / Col. (1981)**
Taylor's early Stax hits (collected on *Chronicle*) are riveting Southern funk, highlighted by "Who's Making Love." But he is also a warm balladeer with a relaxed, easygoing delivery derived from his biggest vocal influence, Sam Cooke. *Eargasm* is largely in one mold—heavily produced blues ballads—though "Disco Lady," a catchy novelty hit (1976) crammed full of sexual innuendo, pointed the unfortunate direction for the rest of what's here, summed up by *Rated Extraordinaire*'s air-brushed sleaze ("Your Love Is Rated X"). — J.MC.

LITTLE JOHNNIE TAYLOR
★ ★ ★ **Open House at My House / Ronn (1973)**
★ ★ ★ **Little Johnnie Taylor / Ronn (1978)**
★ ★ ★ ★ **Part Time Love / Charly (1980), Br. imp.**
★ ★ ★ ★ **I Shoulda Been a Preacher / Red L. (1981), Br. imp.**
★ ★ ★ **Raw Blues / Stax (NA)**
Though often confused with his better-known namesake, the Johnnie Taylor who did "Disco Lady," Little Johnnie Taylor has carved his own distinct identity. The title song on *Open House* was a novelty blues hit (perhaps the last of its kind), and the Ronn albums feature a cross section of ballads, Southern R&B and blues. Taylor has a grainy, dry voice that's most effective on his half-spoken, half-sung blues songs. The Red Lightnin' and Charly sides are from the mid-Sixties, the Stax material a bit later. "Part Time Love" is Taylor's best-known hit, and well worth hearing, as are the others. — J.MC./D.M.

KATE TAYLOR
★ **Kate Taylor / Col. (1978) ¶**
★ **It's in There / Col. (1979)**
Kate Taylor once seemed the most promising member of her musical family, which includes brothers James, Livingston and Alex. But that was with her early-Seventies album

on Atlantic. On these albums she attempts to go the Linda Ronstadt oldies route and it just doesn't work; she hasn't the feeling for old rock that Ronstadt and producer Peter Asher contrive, and seems more at home with the kind of singer/songwriter material brother James writes. — D.M.

KOKO TAYLOR
★ ★ ★ I Got What It Takes / Alli. (1975)
★ ★ ★ The Earthshaker / Alli. (1978)
★ ★ ★ From the Heart of a Woman / Alli. (NA)

Taylor is that rarity, a contemporary *female* Chicago blues performer. She's been around town for twenty years as a sort of gravel-voiced distaff answer to Howlin' Wolf—her early Chess singles, collected on a single deleted Chess LP, include a definitive version of Willie Dixon's "Wang Dang Doodle," which is principally associated with Wolf. The Alligator albums date from the Seventies, and all present her in fine form. *Earthshaker* features a remake of "Wang Dang Doodle," and somewhat stronger material overall than the rest. — D.M.

LIVINGSTON TAYLOR
★ ★ Three Way Mirror / Epic (1979)
★ ★ Man's Best Friend / Epic (1980)
★ ★ Echoes / Capri. (1981)

Livingston made a pair of earlier albums produced by critic Jon Landau in the early Seventies, when recording James' siblings was all the rage. These LPs are just as laid-back, featuring the same minimal attempts at going funky as his brothers' and sister's records. But Liv's singing is a bit less apathetic. — D.M.

MONTANA TAYLOR
★ ★ ★ ★ Montana's Blues / Oldie B. (1977)

This extremely obscure solo barrelhouse piano player/singer would be a forgettable footnote if his delivery wasn't so sharp and spirited. This collection sums up the Chicago-based Taylor's work, ranging from the only official recordings he did in 1929 to a radio broadcast from 1946. — J.S.

ROGER TAYLOR
★ ★ ★ Fun in Space / Elek. (1981)

Roger Taylor is the drummer from Queen. He plays almost all the instruments on this album, but the material isn't that much different from what Queen does (i.e., heavy metal). It doesn't have Freddie Mercury on it, there are no hokey operatic vocals on it (à la Mercury), and it sounds as good as anything Queen has done in the last few years. — K.L.

TED TAYLOR
★ ★ Shades of Blue / Ronn (1969)
★ ★ You Can Dig It / Ronn (1970)
★ ★ Taylor Made / Ronn (1973)
★ ★ Keepin' My Head Above Water / MCA (1978) ¶
★ ★ ★ Keep Walkin' On / Charly (NA), Br. imp.

Taylor is a Southern R&B singer with an affecting nasal falsetto. These albums collect vintage Taylor recordings from the late Sixties and early Seventies; the production is sometimes cheesy, but a strolling blues on *Shades of Blue* ("Days Are Dark") and some pop-R&B ballads are of interest. — J.MC.

TUT TAYLOR
★ ★ Friar Tut / Roun. (1972)
★ ★ ★ The Old Post Office / Fly. Fish (1975)
★ ★ Dobrolic Plectoral Society / Tak. (1976)

Taylor is Nashville's premier dobro player who, together with guitarist Norman Blake, is responsible for much of the backup work on any number of country and country-rock albums recorded in that city. Among others, John Hartford has featured them on his solo outings. Although the dobro is essentially an accompanying instrument, it holds up surprisingly well in its featured role here. The Takoma set has the most varied instrumentation (the bass is unduly prominent), but the Flying Fish album is the one most closely linked to the latter-day "progressive/hot licks" school of bluegrass—flashy but always tastefully executed. — I.M.

TAZMANIAN DEVILS
★ ★ ★ Tazmanian Devils / War. (1980)
★ ★ Broadway Hi-Life / War. (1981)

San Francisco quintet combined reggae rhythms with Fifties rockabilly and surf music rhythms for an interesting debut, but by the second album they ran out of gas. — J.S.

BRAM TCHAIKOVSKY
★ ★ ★ Strange Man, Changed Man / Poly. (1979)
★ ★ Pressure / Poly. (1980)
★ ★ Funland / Ari. (1981)

Former member of the Motors seemed to be in the vanguard of Britain's post-punk reaction, power pop. The hit (from *Strange Man*) was "Girl of My Dreams"; too bad that, like everyone else in that short-lived movement, one was all he had in him. — W.K.

THE TEARDROP EXPLODES
★ ★ ★ **Kilimanjaro / Mer. (1980)**
★ ★ **Wilder / Mer. (1982)**
The main problem with Liverpudlian songwriter and vocalist Julian Cope is that his music is too obviously Doors-like. Still, "Is Vic There," "Treason" and "Reward" from the first LP are catchy tunes. *Wilder,* though, doesn't live up to its name. — ML.H.

TEAZE
★ **One Night Stands / Cap. (1979)**
Bad Canadian heavy-metal quartet produced by April Wine's Myles Goodwyn. — J.S.

TEENAGE HEAD
★ ★ **Frantic City / Attic (1980), imp.**
Canadian group takes its name from an old Flamin' Groovies song and tries to duplicate the Groovies' mix of Fifties rock, British Invasion harmony and punk (in this case, Seventies English as opposed to Sixties American) energy. The combination rarely works, mainly because of inadequate songwriting. — W.K.

TEENA MARIE
★ ★ ★ **Wild and Peaceful / Mo. (1979)**
★ ★ ★ ★ **Lady T / Mo. (1980)**
★ ★ ★ ★ **Irons in the Fire / Mo. (1980)**
★ ★ ★ ★ ★ **It Must Be Magic / Mo. (1981)**
First cliché: Teena Marie could sing the phone book and make it work. Second one: Mobs of songwriters have tried to make jazz complexity affable and pop affability musically and emotionally complex. This pint-sized young white girl is doing it.

Mentor Rick James produced and wrote most of *Wild and Peaceful.* His signature has stayed on her handling of internal rhythms and horns, which is just fine; that juicy foundation ballasts her precocious plunders of jazz, sweet soul and rock. By *Irons in the Fire,* it's her ballgame; she's writing most of the songs, arranging lots of the rhythm and vocal tracks, and coproducing. Ah, youth.

It Must Be Magic is superb thinking man's dance music. Ordinary lyrical concerns are made extraordinary by Teena's idiosyncratic imagery and wordplay. Your booty and your brain are equally motivated. — L.F.

TELEVISION
★ ★ **Marquee Moon / Elek. (1977)**
★ ★ **Adventure / Elek. (1978)**
Somewhat mysteriously, Television was the most widely touted band to emerge from the New York new wave. But *Marquee Moon* showed the group as the exclusive project of guitarist Tom Verlaine, an interesting Jerry Garcia–influenced guitarist who lacked melodic ideas or any emotional sensibility. After releasing a similar LP *(Adventure)* in 1978, the group broke up, with Verlaine recording two records on his own. — D.M.

TELEX
★ **Neurovision / Sire (1980)**
It ought to go without saying that this Eurodisco synthesizer pop is mechanistic and chilling. The only possible interest here is the vocals, which are emotionally distanced in the manner of Bryan Ferry, without displaying any inkling of the occasional warmth and wit on which Ferry's success is founded. — D.M.

TEMPTATIONS
★ ★ ★ ★ **Meet the Temptations / Gor. (1964)**
★ ★ ★ ★ **Temptations' Greatest Hits, Vol. 1 / Gor. (1966)**
★ ★ ★ ★ **In a Mellow Mood / Gor. (1967)**
★ ★ ★ ★ ★ **Anthology with Diana Ross and the Supremes / Mo. (1968)**
★ ★ ★ **Cloud Nine / Gor. (1969)**
★ ★ ★ ★ **Temptations' Greatest Hits, Vol. 2 / Gor. (1970)**
★ ★ ★ **Psychedelic Shack / Gor. (1970)**
★ ★ ★ **Puzzle People / Gor. (1970)**
★ ★ ★ ★ **Masterpiece / Gor. (1973)**
★ **A Song for You / Gor. (1975)** ¶
★ ★ **Do the Temptations / Gor. (1976)** ¶
★ **Hear to Tempt You / Atl. (1977)** ¶
★ ★ ★ ★ **Anthology / Mo. (1977)**
★ **Bare Back / Atl. (1978)** ¶
★ ★ ★ ★ ★ **The Temptations Sing Smokey / Gor. (1979)**
★ ★ **Power / Gor. (1980)**
★ ★ **Temptations / Gor. (1981)**
The best-known and commercially most successful of all the male Motown groups of the Sixties, the Temptations have had an erratic career that runs the full range from post-doo-wop harmony to Sly Stone–influenced modern funk and includes more than its share of hits.

The Temptations released their first records in 1961 and had their first hit, "Dream Come True," the next year, but it wasn't until 1964, with Smokey Robinson's "The Way You Do the Things You Do" (contained on the remarkable *The Temptations Sing Smokey*), that the group began to achieve consistent success, largely through the brilliance of lead vocalists Eddie Kendricks (tenor) and David Ruffin (baritone). Through 1968, the group had a streak of major hits, most notably 1965's "My Girl" and "Since I Lost My Baby"; 1966's "Ain't Too Proud to Beg," "Beauty Is Only Skin Deep" and "I Know I'm Losing You"; the next year's "You're My Everything" and 1968's "I Wish It Would Rain." But with "Cloud Nine," which began to venture farther from basic group harmony, Ruffin left the group and was replaced by Dennis Edwards from the Contours. The Temptations were now teamed with Norman Whitfield, a producer heavily influenced by Sly and the Family Stone's innovations, who earned them another series of hits in a looser, funkier style including "Get Ready," "I Can't Get Next to You," "Psychedelic Shack" and "Ball of Confusion." But after "Just My Imagination," a 1971 return to the ballad style, Kendricks also left to go solo. Kendricks was never satisfactorily replaced, and although the Temptations' 1972 hit "Papa Was a Rollin' Stone" is a landmark Seventies recording that helped usher in an age of increased sophistication both lyrically and musically for black pop music, the group has really never been the same. Kendricks and Ruffin record solo with sporadic success. — D.M.

10 C.C.
★ ★ Original Soundtrack / Mer. (1975) ¶
★ ★ How Dare You / Mer. (1976)
★ ★ Deceptive Bends / Mer. (1977)
★ ★ Live and Let Live / Mer. (1977)
★ ★ Bloody Tourists / Poly. (1978)
★ ★ The Things We Do for Love / Poly. (1979) ¶
★ ★ Greatest Hits / Poly. (1979)
★ ★ Look Hear / War. (1980)
A melange of art-rock smarminess and pop-song parodies that have occasionally clicked as hits ("I'm Not in Love" was the most notable). Critically overrated, mostly because the group's fascination with pop formulas and studio technology is sufficiently pretentious to seem imposing to a bunch of college boys. — D.M.

TEN YEARS AFTER
★ ★ ★ Ten Years After / Deram (1967)
★ ★ ★ Undead / Deram (1968)
★ ★ ★ A Space in Time / Col. (1971)
★ ★ ★ Rock and Roll Music to the World / Col. (1972)

★ Alvin Lee and Company / Deram (1972)
★ ★ Recorded Live / Col. (1973)
★ Positive Vibrations / Col. (1974)
★ ★ Goin' Home: Their Greatest Hits / Deram (1975) ¶
★ The Classic Performances of Ten Years After / Col. (1976)
★ ★ ★ London Collector: Ten Years After / Lon. (NA)
Ten Years After began performing in 1967 (a decade after Elvis became a star), with a blues/jazz fusion led by Chick Churchill's Brian Auger–inspired organ and Alvin Lee's Jim Hall–like guitar. Early on, Lee established himself as the focus of the group, with a hyperkinetic, staccato guitar solo style. (See "Spoonful," from *Ten Years After.*) *Undead* contained the first of the group's classic numbers, however: "I'm Going Home." Thereafter, the group began to move away from blues and jazz stompers (on *Undead,* they'd actually recorded Woody Herman's "Woodchopper's Ball") toward writing their own rock-blues-based material.

With *Sssh, Cricklewood* and *Watt,* Ten Years After hit its popular peak. (Those albums are now replaced with a selection on *London Collector: Ten Years After.*) Lee had made a big impression on the guitar-struck masses with his performance at Woodstock (and later, in the movie). His reputation as a blazingly fast guitarist came to dominate the group's image, much to Lee's own displeasure. The music grows repetitious, though the group has become more technically adept. *Alvin Lee and Company* and *Goin' Home* are both scrapings from the bottom of the barrel, released after the group left to join Columbia in 1972.

The Columbia records feature some change of direction: on the first two, Lee tones down, attempting to accommodate his fiery style to the band, even toying with strings and electronic effects. *Recorded Live* regressed: this 1973 set included virtually nothing that wasn't being done in 1969. By the time of *Positive Vibrations,* Lee was already out touring under his own name and Columbia simply used *Classic Performances* as a mop-up reissue from the band's waning days. — A.N.

TERRY
★ Confessions of a Sinner / Mer. (NA) ¶
Please do your penance elsewhere. — D.M.

JOE TEX
★ ★ ★ Another Woman's Man / Power (1977)

★ ★ ★ **Bumps and Bruises** / Epic (1977) ¶
★ ★ ★ **Rub Down** / Epic (1978) ¶
★ ★ ★ **London Collector—Super Soul** / Lon.
(NA) ¶

Joe Tex, who died in 1982, was a journey-man Southern soul singer with a flair for down-home storytelling. While during the Seventies, his voice lost the falsetto edge that marked his classic hits ("Hold What You've Got," "The Love You Save," available on his deleted Atlantic albums), the Epic al-bums are charmingly anachronistic LPs spurred by a hot Nashville session band. The Power Pak album features sides recorded for Mercury, between the Atlantic and Epic pe-riods. The London album features obscure Sixties singles.   — J.MC.

TEXAS PLAYBOYS

★ ★ ★ **Texas Playboys Today** / Cap.
(1977) ¶
★ ★ ★ **Original Texas Playboys** / Cap.
(1977) ¶
★ ★ ★ **Live and Kickin'** / Cap. (1978)

Bob Wills' old band has carried on the Western swing tradition since his death. That's what these discs are about, and for what they are, they're good, although one is not as likely to be surprised by the band without Wills.   — D.M.

SISTER ROSETTA THARPE

★ ★ ★ **What Are They Doin' in Heaven?** /
ALA (1961)
★ ★ ★ ★ ★ **The Best of Sister Rosetta**
Tharpe / Savoy (1979)
★ ★ ★ **Gospel Train** / MCA (1980)

It's said that Elvis Presley used to run home from school each day to hear Sister Rosetta Tharpe evangelize over the radio. The tradi-tional hymns on the Savoy set—"Precious Memories," "Last Mile of the Way," "Peace in the Valley," "99½ Won't Do," "Precious Lord," "Walking up the King's Highway" and others—will convince you Elvis was right again. Tharpe was a grand singer and a better guitarist, and her ear for material was uncanny: "This Train" is unforgettable, as are several of her others. The MCA set con-tains tracks recorded between 1946 and 1948 with a variety of groups, and isn't as suc-cessful as the more sparely accompanied Savoy sides. The ALA material, from the early Sixties, was recorded well after she'd passed her prime.   — D.M.

THEM

★ ★ ★ ★ **Them** / Par. (1965) ¶
★ ★ ★ **Them Again** / Par. (1966) ¶

★ ★ ★ ★ **Them Featuring Van Morrison** /
Par. (1972)
★ ★ ★ **The Story of Them** / Lon. (1976)
★ ★ ★ **Backtrackin'** / Lon. (NA) ¶

This hard-nosed Irish R&B band made minor inroads in the British Invasion with several hits—"Gloria," "Here Comes the Night" and "Mystic Eyes." Their recording career spanned only three years, and the group might well be forgotten if it weren't for lead singer Van Morrison. Thanks to Morrison, Them's sound was as tough and sinewy as the Animals and Stones, and Mor-rison himself was particularly fierce at this stage.

Van was an original even then, and his raspy, vaguely threatening vocals fit Them's punch-it-out approach perfectly. *Them* is the album that spawned all three hits and the band is never better than on "Mystic Eyes"—pounding, relentless drums and bass anchoring a rhythm section stretched by organ washes and incessant staccato guitar. Morrison carries the load: shaking maracas, bleating drunkenly through his talking har-monica, singing in an unrestrained growl that twists to a climactic, inarticulate scream. The true source of raw power, this is some of the most visionary music ever made. *Them Again* includes more of the same, with horns added for James Brown's "Out of Sight" and Morrison at his interpre-tive best on Bob Dylan's "It's All Over Now Baby Blue."

Them Featuring Van Morrison reissues the first two records (minus two tracks each) in a single package. *Backtrackin'* and *The Story of Them* collect previously unavailable mate-rial from British singles and albums. The title track from *Story of Them* is a minor classic in the autobiographical talking-blues vein also used by the Animals ("The Story of Bo Diddley") and Rolling Stones ("Stoned"). A must for fans of Van Morri-son's brooding defiance, as are all of these.
— J.S.

THIN LIZZY

★ **Fighting** / Mer. (1975)
★ ★ ★ **Jailbreak** / Mer. (1976)
★ ★ **Johnny the Fox** / Mer. (1976) ¶
★ ★ **Live and Dangerous** / War. (1978)
★ **London Collector: Rocker** / Lon. (NA)
★ **Night Life** / Mer. (1974)
★ ★ **Bad Reputation** / Mer. (1977)
★ **Black Rose—A Rock Legend** / War.
(1979)
★ **Chinatown** / War. (1980)
★ ★ **Renegade** / War. (1982)

This Irish quartet has been kicking around the British Isles since the early Seventies, led by Phil Lynott's throaty, Van Morrison-like vocals and songwriting. Most of the time it's been nothing much more than a good bash, but the group reached a commercial-artistic peak in 1976 with *Jailbreak,* which included a hit single, "The Boys Are Back in Town," which remains the best absorption of Bruce Springsteen's Morrison influence to date. Since then it's been back to the hammer and tongs approach (*Johnny the Fox,* a concept LP, notwithstanding). The *London Collector* set represents the group's first recording, which has a tendency to stray in the direction of art rock; the Warner Bros.' live set is a 1978 compendium of the band's best material over the years, including "The Boys . . ." and a nice version of Bob Seger's "Rosalie." — D.M.

THIRD WORLD
★ ★ Third World / Is. (1976)
★ 96 Degrees in the Shade / Is. (1977)
★ Journey to Addis / Is. (1978)
★ ★ Live / Prisoner in the Street / Is. (1980)
★ ★ Rock the World / Col. (1981)

Perfectly mediocre reggae, emblematic of the music's decline in recent years. When this half-white, half-rasta band plays "Slavery Days," the Burning Spear classic, all the ominous elements are discarded, leaving nothing but sinewy dance music, slick but not devoid of deep emotion. By 1980, Third World's once-promising synthesis of reggae, Afrofunk and pop had degenerated into a recycling of clichés with soft-focus production. *Live* has a few flashes of electricity, which the band can still generate on occasion. — D.M./R.F.G.

.38 SPECIAL
★ ★ .38 Special / A&M (1977)
★ ★ ★ Special Delivery / A&M (1978)
★ ★ ★ ★ Rockin' into the Night / A&M (1979)
★ ★ ★ ★ Wild-Eyed Southern Boys / A&M (1981)

At first this group seemed like a soft-focus Lynyrd Skynyrd, which was not surprising considering that the band's frontman is Ronnie Van Zant's younger brother Donnie, that bassist Larry Junstrom was once in Lynyrd Skynyrd and that the band learned primarily from being in close proximity to Skynyrd and often jamming with them. By the time of *Rockin',* though, the band had matured into one of Southern rock's finest products. The twin guitars of Jeff Carlisi and Don

Barnes are the focal point of the band's sound, and the two mesh in a unique style that is well presented on "Robin Hood." *.38 Special* came into its own commercially on the hard-rocking *Wild-Eyed Southern Boys.* On the title track of that album you can hear them at their best. — J.S.

B. J. THOMAS
★ ★ Reunion / ABC (1975) ¶
★ ★ B. J. Thomas / MCA (1977) ¶
★ ★ Everybody Loves a Rain Song / MCA (1978)
★ ★ ★ Best of B. J. Thomas / Exact (1980)
★ ★ Some Love Songs Never Die / MCA (1981)
★ ★ ★ B. J. Thomas Sings His Very Best / Sp. (NA) ¶
★ ★ Help Me Make It / ABC (NA) ¶
★ ★ ★ Sixteen Greatest Hits / Trip (NA) ¶
★ ★ ★ The ABC Collection / ABC (NA) ¶
★ ★ ★ Best of B. J. Thomas / Star. (NA)
★ ★ For the Best / MCA (NA)

This Oklahoma-based country-rock singer had a series of pop ballad hits from 1966 through 1972, many of them of surprisingly high quality. The first was a version of Hank Williams' "I'm So Lonesome I Could Cry" in 1966. This was followed by "Hooked On a Feeling" in 1968, the No. 1 "Raindrops Keep Falling on My Head" in 1969 and "I Just Can't Help Believing" in 1970. But the best of all was the final one, "Rock and Roll Lullabye," which appropriated some Beach Boys falsetto for its final chorus.

The ABC Collection is far more interesting than the other hits collections, and the other albums are mere country pop, not worth bothering with. — D.M.

CARLA THOMAS
★ ★ ★ ★ The Best of Carla Thomas / Atl. (NA) ¶

The queen of Memphis soul during its mid-Sixties heyday has hardly been visible in the Seventies. Never a major talent on a level with Sam and Dave or Otis Redding (with whom she cut "Tramp"), Thomas did develop a soft, vulnerable persona (best expressed in "B-A-B-Y") that was a refreshing contrast to the raw, gritty music of her Stax-Volt stablemates. Her father is pioneer Memphis singer/DJ Rufus Thomas. — J.MC.

DAVID THOMAS
★ ★ ★ ★ The Sound of the Sand and Other Songs of the Pedestrian: David Thomas and the Pedestrians / Rough T. (1981)

David Thomas is the lead singer of Pere Ubu. The music here is similar to that of

Pere Ubu, but since Thomas has used other musicians, there's a slightly different sound. The album was cut at 45 rpm, so the sound is excellent (it really does make a difference) and there are over 37 minutes of music. Richard Thompson has been brought in to play guitar, Philip Moxham (of Young Marble Giants) is on bass, Anton Fier (of the Raincoats, Feelings, Lounge Lizards and now Ubu) is on drums and Allen Ravenstine (Ubu) is on EML synthesizers. The music ranges from slow rock ("The New Atom Mine") to heavy percussion ("The Cricket in the Flats"). There's also a cover version of "Sloop John B." Overall, the compositions and sound are better than that heard on the last few Ubu albums. David Thomas is in high form on this album, so if you're a fan of Pere Ubu, you won't be disappointed.
— K.L.

EVELYN THOMAS
★ ★ ★ **I Wanna Make It on My Own / Casa. (1978)**
★ ★ **Have a Little Faith in Me / AVI. (NA)**
Thomas is a more-than-passable dance-beat chanteuse undone by the fact that her only up-to-snuff material is the title track of her Casablanca LP. Singers require more support than this. — D.M.

HENRY THOMAS
★ ★ ★ ★ **Ragtime Texas / Her. (1974)**
Fantastic Texas country bluesman of the Twenties sings, plays guitar, whistles and throws in panpipes for good measure, all in a deeply spirited delivery. This great collection includes his entire recorded output with incisive and amazingly detailed annotation. A fine record. — J.S.

IAN THOMAS BAND
★ ★ **Goodnight Mrs. Calabash / Chrys. (1976)**
Canadian singer/songwriter leads nondescript five-piece group. — J.S.

IRMA THOMAS
★ ★ ★ **Irma Thomas / Bandy (NA)**
★ ★ ★ **Safe with Me / RCS (1979)**
★ ★ ★ ★ **In Between Tears / Charly (1980), Br. imp.**
The very fine New Orleans vocalist. Her vintage sides for Canyon, Rocker and Fungus labels (produced by Swamp Dogg Williams) are collected on the Charly LP, while the others are more recent, and surprisingly successful, issues. — D.M.

JAH THOMAS
★ ★ ★ **Dance Pon de Corner / Jah Life (1979)**
★ ★ ★ **Hear It in the News / Tad's (1980)**
Jah Thomas would be just another yard-style reggae DJ—impossible to appreciate away from the sound-system dance—but for two factors: his heavy, smoky baritone and his lyrics, which offer interesting, if limited, social commentary. — R.F.G.

RAMBLIN' THOMAS
★ ★ ★ ★ **Chicago Blues / Bio. (NA)**
Wonderful examples of country blues by a major practitioner. Thomas, a Texan, recorded for Paramount in the Twenties; these are his vintage sides. — D.M.

RUFUS THOMAS
★ ★ **If There Were No Music / Avid (1977)**
★ ★ **I Ain't Gettin' Older, I'm Gettin' Better / Avid (1977)**
★ ★ ★ **Rufus Thomas / Gusto (1980)**
Former Memphis disc jockey who made a name for himself as a recording artist with a string of salaciously comedic soul numbers for Stax: "Do the Funky Penguin" and "Walking the Dog" are probably the best known. The Avid discs contain none of these, and the Stax items are out of print. The Gusto disc contains remakes of the Stax material—not bad, but seek the real thing. Thomas is the father of soul singer Carla Thomas. — D.M.

TIMMY THOMAS
★ ★ ★ **You're the Song I've Always Wanted to Sing / Glades (1974)**
★ ★ ★ **The Magician / Glades (1976)**
★ ★ ★ **Touch to Touch / Glades (1978)**
★ ★ ★ **Timmy Thomas Live / Glades (1979)**
Minor Florida soul singer, from the same stable that produced Betty Wright and K.C. and the Sunshine Band, but inferior to most of the rest. Interesting groove, but not enough distinction. — D.M.

LINVAL THOMPSON
★ ★ **I Love Marijuana / Troj. (1978)**
★ ★ ★ ★ **Six Babylon / Clock. (1979)**
Reportedly, Linval Thompson gave up a career in engineering to sing reggae and embrace Rastafarianism. He's a capable singer, writer and producer, but not strong enough to transcend routine material. *Six Babylon* features outstanding material and production. — R.F.G.

RICHARD AND LINDA THOMPSON
★ ★ ★ **Richard Thompson starring as Henry the Human Fly / Is. (1972), Br. imp.**

★ ★ ★ **Live (More or Less)** / **Is.**
(1977)
★ ★ ★ **First Light** / **Chrys. (1978)**
★ ★ ★ **Richard Thompson (guitar, vocal)** /
Is. (1976), Br. imp.
★ ★ ★ **Strict Tempo!** / **Elixir (1981), Br.**
imp.
★ ★ ★ ★ **Shoot Out the Lights** / **Hann.**
(1982)
The Thompsons (Richard was lead guitarist
of Fairport Convention) have released several other albums, but of them, only *Pour
Down like Silver* (1975), the most plainspo-
ken of Richard's adventures in Sufi songwriting, is a major loss. *Live* contains a fine live
disc alongside his first solo disc; *Richard
Thompson (guitar, vocal)* has the live stuff
and a more interesting selection of studio
tracks. *Strict Tempo!* is all instrumental, a
showcase but no more. *Henry the Human
Fly* is early, not very exceptional folk rock,
in which Thompson begins to explore some
of the ideas that reach fruition on *Shoot Out
the Lights,* a legitimate Eighties masterpiece,
on which the songwriting, singing (especially
by Linda) and Richard's extraordinary guitar
playing combine to make majestic, epic
music. "Wall of Death" is the greatest
amusement-park song ever written, and one
of the scariest pieces of music anyone in the
rock era has composed.
Naturally, when they had released *Shoot
Out the Lights* and begun to get some overdue recognition, the Thompsons dissolved
their musical partnership. — D.M.

THE THOMPSON TWINS
★ ★ **A Product of . . .** / **Ari. (1981), Br.**
imp.
Atypical British pop: a conglomeration of
pop, reggae, funk and African rhythms. The
music is engaging but lacks real substance.
— ML.H.

ALI THOMSON
★ **Take a Little Rhythm** / **A&M (1980)**
★ **Deception Is an Art** / **A&M (1981)**
A Paul McCartney clone on the title track
of *Rhythm* (a minor hit), Thomson comes
up with nothing so imaginative on the other
LP. — D.M.

BIG MAMA THORNTON
★ ★ ★ **Big Mama Thornton with the**
Chicago Blues Band / **Arhoo. (1967)**
★ ★ **Sassy Mama** / **Van. (1975)**
★ ★ ★ **Jail** / **Van. (1975)**
★ ★ **She's Back** / **Back. (NA)**
★ ★ ★ **Big Mama Thornton in Europe** /
Arhoo. (NA)

It was Willie Mae "Big Mama" Thornton's
recording of the Jerry Leiber and Mike Stoller song "Hound Dog" that first rocked the
charts, although it was Elvis Presley's later
version that topped them. Fronting Johnny
Otis' band at the time, and appearing on
package shows with Little Esther (Phillips),
Thornton also wrote "Ball and Chain," later
popularized by Janis Joplin.
The Chicago Blues Band of the Arhoolie
LP features Muddy Waters, James Cotton
and Otis Spann, and the excitement of the
moment is readily sensed, even though the
staple songs of Thornton's career aren't included. Thornton has a big voice, in the traditions of Bessie Smith and Ma Rainey, and
in 1966, when the Arhoolie sessions were
done, she was still in relatively full command of it.
The subsequent albums lack the urgency
of her earlier work—the Backbeat set was
done in the early Seventies, the Vanguards in
1975—and the backup groups (unidentified
on Backbeat, various top session musicians
on the Vanguard LPs) lack the cohesiveness
that comes from years of playing together or
at least from playing in the same idiom. *Jail,*
however, does have her singing "Hound
Dog," "Ball and Chain" and "Little Red
Rooster." — I.M.

GEORGE THOROGOOD AND THE
DESTROYERS
★ ★ **George Thorogood and the Destroyers** /
Roun. (1977)
★ ★ **Move It On Over** / **Roun. (1978)**
★ **Better Than the Rest** / **MCA (1979)**
★ ★ **More George Thorogood and the**
Destroyers / **Roun. (1980)** ¶
Hard-working white bluesman with the pro-
verbial heart of gold, Thorogood is nonethe-
less a fairly dull recording artist. Possessed
of a limited voice, he does straightforward
versions of rocking blues classics (only a
couple of originals here), unburdened by either drawn-out arrangements or, sadly, the
spark of his influences. — W.K.

3-D
★ **See It Loud** / **Poly. (1980)**
★ **3-D** / **Poly. (1980)**
Westchester bar band switches from heavy
metal to Cars soundalikes, cutting its fashion
to fit the times, not too well or too wisely.
Pathetic. — D.M.

THE THREE DEGREES
★ ★ **New Dimensions** / **Ari. (NA)** ¶
★ ★ **So Much Love** / **Rou. (NA)**
Venerable girl group that had its first chart

luck in 1970 with a remake of the Chantels' "Maybe," which doesn't come close to the original, then moved on to Philadelphia International, where the trio was the voice humming along on the MFSB smash "TSOP (The Sound of Philadelphia)." On their own, the girls managed another Top Ten hit, "When Will I See You Again," later in 1974. But with the Philly International albums long deleted, there's nothing here to get excited about.   — D.M.

THREE DOG NIGHT
★ ★ ★ **Three Dog Night / Dun. (1969)** ¶
★ **Captured Live / Dun. (1969)** ¶
★ ★ ★ ★ **Joy to the World—Greatest Hits / Dun. (1974)**
★ ★ **American Pastime / ABC (1976)** ¶
From about 1969 through the mid-Seventies, Three Dog Night was the slickest Top Forty singles band in America. Fronted by three lead singers (the best known of whom was Cory Wells), the group presented a modified soul revue as polished as a Vegas lounge band's, for white audiences who had often never seen anything like it.

At their best (on singles, rarely on LPs), Three Dog Night were skillful reductionists, giving mass appeal to songwriters as eccentric as Randy Newman ("Mama Told Me Not to Come"), Laura Nyro ("Eli's Coming") and Harry Nilsson ("One") long before most of the hard-rock in crowd picked up on them. The group was also capable of a certain kind of R&B stylization; in their hands, Otis Redding's "Try a Little Tenderness" might have lost most of its specific gravity, but it was Three Dog Night's version that introduced the song to most Americans.

But on LP, the group was never able to produce anything substantial. Production extravaganzas, farcical concepts and other attempts at artistic outreach all went wanting; the result is that only the *Joy to the World—Greatest Hits* collection of their singles remains in print.
— D.M.

THREE OUNCES OF LOVE
★ ★ **Three Ounces of Love / Mo. 1978** ¶
Despite their Commodores and Holland-Dozier-Holland connections, Berry Gordy's answer to the Three Degrees and Love Unlimited could use a whole lot less romance and a whole lot more imagination—not to mention some decent material.   — D.M.

THUMBS
★ ★ ★ **The Thumbs / Ramona (1981)**
Wichita group released this album on its own label. It's pretty undistinguished and horribly amateurish, with the exception of "I Wasn't

Born on the Fourth of July," in which these Kansas boys simply pour out their heartland souls onto the vinyl. Since there's no single, this makes the album worth having, at least for those who love sub-Springsteen passion.
— D.M.

THUNDER
★ ★ **Thunder / Atco (NA)**
★ ★ **Headphones for Cows / Atco (1981)**
Poor man's ZZ Top.   — J.S.

BOBBY THURSTON
★ ★ ★ **Main Attraction / Prel. (NA)**
★ ★ ★ **You Got What It Takes / Prel. (NA)**
More attractive than most latter-day disco. Thurston makes the most of a good set of pipes, as well as danceable rhythm.   — D.M.

STEVE TIBBETS
★ ★ ★ **Steve Tibbets / Frammis (1979)**
★ ★ ★ ★ **Yr / Frammis (1981)**
Both these albums were recorded, produced, engineered, performed and released by Steve Tibbets himself. The first album is a synthesizer-guitar album, and although Tibbets uses a few too many clichés, he proves that he has the talent to make those clichés work. On *Yr,* Tibbets goes wild: the album is a startling combination of electric guitar, tabla, acoustic guitar, kalimba and a little synthesizer. Tibbets weaves from heavy rock to several kalimbas playing a duet and it never falters. The guitar work is never short of excellent and Tibbets uses sitars, dulcimers, mandolins and any other stringed instrument he can get his hands on.   — K.L.

TIERRA
★ ★ ★ **Tierra / Sals. (NA)**
★ ★ ★ **City Nights / Bdwalk (NA)**
★ ★ ★ **Together Again / Bdwalk (1981)**
Solid low-rider rock—not up to the level of War's best, but one of the better efforts in the Chicano rock & roll genre since Ritchie Valens went down.   — D.M.

TIGERS
★ **Savage Music / A&M (1980)**
Rock & roll hackwork.   — D.M.

SONNY TIL AND THE ORIOLES
★ ★ ★ ★ **Greatest Hits / Collectables (NA)**
A fine collection of Til's cool tenor leads and the Orioles brilliant harmonies. "Crying in the Chapel," their great 1953 hit that kicked off the craze for bird-named doo-wop vocal groups at the dawn of the rock era, is included, as are their other early recordings, including the very first, "It's Too Soon to Know," from 1947. Nicely annotated, too.   — D.M.

TILT
★ Music / Parach. (1978)
Retch. Heavy-metal machismo with the
added disadvantage of intelligible lyrics.
— D.M.

THE TIME
★ ★ ★ The Time / War. (1981)
Promising debut from Minneapolis sextet
that departs from disco and new-wave conventions to present ebullient witty jams on
time-honored themes of lust, egotism and romance. If "The Stick" isn't as clever a car-
as-sexual-metaphor tune as Grace Jones'
"Pull Up to the Bumper," it's at least more
convincingly raunchy, an element the Time
couples with elegance to give album its
major motif. Band's chance to record came
through sponsorship of another Minneapolis
eroticist, Prince. — G.A.

TIN HUEY
★ ★ Contents Dislodged during Shipment /
War. (1979)
New-wave band with too much of a debt to
standard-issue heavy metal to make it stick.
— J.S.

TKO
★ ★ Let It Roll / Inf. (1979) ¶
Musically a combination of mid-period
Stones, glam rock and vocal bombast à la
Heart (whose management company backed
the group), TKO was on the ropes before
the opening bell when its label, Infinity,
folded after issuing debut. LP's main asset
was Brad Sinsel's tunes, its main defect his
overwrought vocals. — G.A.

TOBY BEAU
★ Toby Beau / RCA (1978) ¶
★ More Than a Love Song / RCA (1979) ¶
★ If You Believe / RCA (1980)
★ My Angel Baby / RCA (1981)
Awful Midwestern rock band that found a
following (God knows how) in the late Sev-
enties with their ridiculously hammer-headed
and dull brand of rock. — D.M.

LILY TOMLIN
★ ★ ★ This Is a Recording / Poly. (1971)
★ ★ ★ And That's the Truth / Poly. (1972)
★ ★ ★ ★ Modern Scream / Poly. (1975)
★ ★ ★ ★ Lily Tomlin on Stage / Ari.
(1977) ¶
Tomlin is the greatest comic monologuist
since Ruth Draper. Her first two albums,
Recording and *Truth,* feature the most pop-
ular characters she created on TV's *Laugh-
In,* Ernestine and Edith Ann. *Modern*

Scream is a more ambitious aural collage
(Tomlin interviews herself playing a variety
of characters), which includes some of the
material that went into her 1977 Broadway
triumph, captured with *On Stage.* Tomlin's
stand-up comedy dissolves in and out of social criticism and tour-de-force acting—
hilarious, astute, occasionally chilling.
— S.H.

TOMMY TUTONE
★ ★ Tommy Tutone / Col. (1980)
★ ★ Tommy Tutone 2 / Col. (1981)
Or is that Ned Nuwave? One of far too
many L.A. acts who substitute a supposedly
smart and sharp approach for rock & roll innovation. Tommy Tutone's style is a lot like
a Hollywood film set—it looks right, but if
you peek behind the facade, you discover it's
all a matter of creative fakery. — R.P.

GARY TOMS EMPIRE
★ Blow Your Whistle / Pip (1975) ¶
★ Turn It Out / MCA (1977) ¶
★ Let's Do It Again / Mer. (1978)
One of hundreds of one-shot disco acts, the
Empire had its moment with "Blow Your
Whistle," a raucous Kool and the Gang de-
rivative. — J.MC.

TOM TOM CLUB
★ ★ Tom Tom Club / Sire (1981)
Led by Talking Heads' rhythm section (Tina
Weymouth and Chris Frantz), the Tom Tom
Club offer music that's more obviously
danceable but much less interesting than the
mother group's rhythmic workouts on *Remain in Light.* Most of the music is also less
catchy than the Heads' work, and the supposedly mysterious female chanting vocals
come off as self-consciously arty. The one
saving grace is the beat-crazy dance single
"Wordy Rappinghood"—a smart look at the
joys and sins of the band's own hyper-verbal
milieu. — J.F.

TONIO K.
★ ★ Life in the Food Chain / Epic (1979) ¶
★ ★ Amerika / Ari. (1980)
If Warren Zevon is Jackson Browne as were-
wolf, what's this guy? How about Warren
Zevon as simple smartass? These LPs rock
pretty hard considering their L.A. origins,
but a bit too glibly for their own good.
— D.M.

TOOTS AND THE MAYTALS
★ ★ ★ ★ ★ Funky Kingston / Is. (1965)
★ ★ ★ ★ From the Roots / Troj. (1973)
★ ★ ★ ★ Reggae Got Soul / Is. (1976)

★ ★ **Pass the Pipe** / Mango (1979)
★ ★ ★ ★ **Best of Toots** / Troj. (1979)
★ ★ ★ **Just Like That** / Mango (1980)
★ ★ ★ **Toots Live** / Mango (1980)

Toots Hibbert is unquestionably one of the greatest vocalists to appear in popular music in the past decade. Together with the Maytals, he helped found reggae (and gave it its name) in the Sixties, and the group's series of singles is one of the most pleasurable things to be found in the Jamaican idiom. As a singer, Toots is sort of a sweet Antilles version of Otis Redding—he occasionally sings Redding's material in concert and the effect is startling.

Funky Kingston is virtually a greatest-hits album, released years after most of the material became popular in Jamaica. It includes three of the finest reggae vocals ever made ("Time Tough," "Pressure Drop," "Pomp and Pride") plus a couple of amazing American pop covers, "Louie Louie" and "Country Road." *Reggae Got Soul* is an awkward but moving compromise between reggae and North American soul music. *From the Roots* is peak Leslie Kong-produced nascent reggae, while *Best of* collects the best of three eras: rocksteady, reggae and funk. By *Pass the Pipe,* Toots' soul-reggae fusion half became lugubrious, but *Just Like That* is a spry return to roots, and *Live* captures all the sweat and peerless energy of Toots live.
— D.M./R.F.G.

TORONTO
★ ★ **Lookin' for Trouble** / A&M (1980)
★ ★ **Head On** / A&M (1981)

Heart with new-wave costuming. They're pretty good players, though, and "5035," from *Head On,* is a fine song. — J.S.

PETER TOSH
★ ★ ★ ★ **Legalize It** / Col. (1976)
★ ★ ★ ★ **Equal Rights** / Col. (1977)
★ ★ ★ ★ **Bush Doctor** / Rol. (1978)
★ ★ **Mystic Man** / Rol. (1979)
★ ★ ★ ★ **Wanted Dread or Alive** / EMI (1981)

One of the original Wailers (along with Bob Marley and Bunny [Livingston] Wailer), Tosh's solo albums, although they've never had much non-Jamaican airing, are excellent, pure reggae, truer to the spirit and form of the music than Marley's more celebrated work. *Equal Rights* is the best of these, if only because it has a version of the Wailers' "Get Up, Stand Up." *Bush Doctor* features a duet with Mick Jagger on the Temptations' "Don't Look Back" but also a softening of

Tosh's raw musical and abrasive political posture. Not a sellout but enough to sow seeds of doubt. Tosh's continuing efforts to find an appropriate medium to communicate with a global audience (rock reggae? disco reggae? funky reggae?) reached a low point with *Mystic Man*'s bland production and uneven material. *Wanted,* however, integrates rock guitar with roots rhythms (some of the best Sly and Robbie playing ever) to produce a successful synthesis and a couple of masterpieces in "Rastafari Is" and "Wanted."
— D.M./R.F.G.

TOTO
★ **Toto** / Col. (1978)
★ **Hydra** / Col. (1979)
★ **Turn Back** / Col. (1980)

This conglomeration of L.A. session musicians made a hit out of a debut album that is all chops and no brains. Formula pop songs, singing that wouldn't go over in a Holiday Inn cocktail lounge. Since then they've gotten slicker, remained vacuous and seem to grow more popular every day. Cockroaches are expected to outlast the human race, too. — D.M.

ALLEN TOUSSAINT
★ ★ ★ **Life, Love and Faith** / Rep. (1972) ¶
★ ★ ★ ★ **Southern Nights** / Rep. (1975) ¶
★ ★ ★ **Motion** / War. (1978) ¶

Legendary New Orleans R&B producer's recent solo albums (he recorded now unavailable material for a number of small labels) are exemplary versions of mellow Southern soul. The only problem is that Toussaint sometimes gets too mellow, but his songwriting and arrangement genius overcomes any conceptual problems. The title track from *Southern Nights,* his best record, was covered by Glen Campbell with remarkable success. — J.S.

TOWER OF POWER
★ ★ ★ **Bump City** / War. (1972)
★ ★ ★ ★ **Tower of Power** / War. (1973)
★ ★ ★ ★ **Back to Oakland** / War. (1974)
★ ★ ★ ★ **Urban Renewal** / War. (1975) ¶
★ ★ ★ **In the Slot** / War. (1975) ¶
★ ★ ★ ★ **Tower of Power Live and in Living Color** / War. (1976)
★ ★ ★ **Ain't Nothin' Stoppin' Us Now** / Col. (1976)
★ ★ ★ **We Came to Play** / Col. (1978) ¶
★ ★ **Back on the Streets** / Col. (1979)

This Oakland-based big band is noted for its super-funky live performances and has managed to translate a good deal of that energy onto vinyl. Though the band was always tight and the trademark five-piece horn section could blow up a storm from the start, it wasn't until the third album, *Tower of Power,* that the sound jelled. Vocalist Lenny Williams provided the focal point for the band's energy, and the three albums that feature him fronting the band, *Tower of Power, Back to Oakland* and *Urban Renewal,* are as fine a set of R&B records as have been released in the Seventies. Williams gave the band tremendous breadth on ballad material, but his uptempo vocals (as on the hit "What Is Hip") really took off. A couple of different vocalists have tried to fill Williams' shoes since then without much success, so the band has relied on its instrumental firepower and arrangement sense to make up the difference. The live set shows just how hot they can get in concert.   — J.S.

HENRY TOWNSEND
★ ★ ★ Music Man / Adel. (1973)
★ ★ ★ ★ Mule / Nighth. (1980)
Townsend is a tremendous country-blues guitar and piano player from St. Louis. His clever improvisations make even his later work (which is represented by these two albums) interesting, although he's been active since the Twenties. *Mule* features several tracks with Yank Rachell.   — J.S.

TOWNSEND, TOWNSEND, TOWNSEND AND ROGERS
★ Townsend, Townsend, Townsend and
   Rogers / Choc. (NA)
The disco equivalent of Arthur Hurley and Gottlieb. Corporate boogie. Yecch.   — D.M.

PETER TOWNSHEND
★ ★ ★ ★ Who Came First / MCA (1972) ¶
★ ★ ★ ★ ★ Rough Mix / MCA (1977)
★ ★ ★ ★ ★ Empty Glass / Atco (1980)
The Who's guitarist and principal songwriter is one of the most important figures in the past fifteen years of rock & roll. His first two solo albums (*Rough Mix,* the second, is actually a collaboration with a former Face, Ronnie Lane) are more overtly involved with his spiritual master, Meher Baba, than his group efforts can afford to be. On the first, this is not necessarily an advantage: Townshend's version of Jim Reeves' "There's a Heartache Following Me" is fine and moving, but his version of Baba's prayer, "Parvadigar," is a bit wearing to heathen ears. But the album is saved by the rock numbers. "Pure and Easy," contained on the Who's *Odds and Sods* in a group version, is one of the best songs Townshend's ever written, and "Nothing Is Everything" is far superior to

the Who's version of the same song, "Let's See Action."
   Rough Mix is a triumph: "Street in the City" ranks with Townshend's most adventurous productions, and "My Baby Gives It Away" is a classically styled rocker, while Lane's eccentric fusion of British folk and hard rock is consistently moving, particularly on such songs as "Annie."
   Townshend's third solo album, *Empty Glass,* was by far his best; it is also the one that's most like a Who record, with stinging guitar and forceful, angry vocals. If there had been any doubt that Townshend himself was Roger Daltrey's singing role model, *Empty Glass* dispelled it. And the record's obsessions—aging, spirituality, sex, children, desperate passion, the falling apart of tradition and the general loss of humanity in modern times—are consistent with the thrust of his Who material. "Let My Love Open the Door," one of Townshend's perfectly ambiguous paeans to romance and Baba, was a Top Ten hit, making *Empty Glass* his most successful personal venture on every level.
   — D.M.

TRAFFIC
★ ★ ★ ★ Mr. Fantasy / U.A. (1968)
★ ★ ★ ★ ★ Traffic / U.A. (1968) ¶
★ ★ ★ Last Exit / U.A. (1969) ¶
★ ★ ★ ★ The Best of Traffic / U.A. (1970) ¶
★ ★ ★ ★ John Barleycorn Must Die / U.A.
   (1970) ¶
★ ★ ★ Welcome to the Canteen / U.A.
   (1971) ¶
★ ★ The Low Spark of High Heeled Boys /
   Is. (1971)
★ ★ ★ Shoot Out at the Fantasy Factory /
   Is. (1973)
★ ★ Traffic on the Road / Is. (1974)
★ ★ ★ When the Eagle Flies / Asy. (1974) ¶
★ ★ ★ Heavy Traffic / U.A. (1975) ¶
★ ★ More Heavy Traffic / U.A. (1975) ¶
Traffic was a band with talent to burn. Its nominal figurehead, Stevie Winwood, powered the group with his searing blues singing and intelligent keyboard and guitar playing. Dave Mason, whose singing, songwriting and guitar playing would have made him the focal point of most other bands, was overshadowed here by Winwood, and the lineup was completed by the angular funk drumming of Jim Capaldi and hipster fills from saxophone-flautist Chris Wood.
   At its best, Traffic was a band to be reckoned with. The first two Traffic albums are late-Sixties classics, an eclectic combination of blues, folk, jazz and rock that was polyglot without ever becoming overextended.

Mr. Fantasy, released shortly after *Sgt. Pepper* and masterfully produced in similar fashion by Jimmy Miller, is one of the most durable products of that very dated era. *Traffic* was more fully mature. "Feelin' Alright," "Who Knows What Tomorrow May Bring" and "You Can All Join In" are timeless songs, some of the best moments of their era.

After Mason's departure for a solo career, Traffic was never really the same. *John Barleycorn* was Winwood's swan song as a major talent; the album concentrated more on the folk and jamming elements of the band, and it was particularly effective as a trio record. It includes three stand-out songs: the title track, "Empty Pages" and "Freedom Rider." *Canteen* added a new rhythm section and Latin percussion and reunited Dave Mason with the band for a one-shot tour. The record's fairly good, especially in comparison to the lethargic *On the Road.* Traffic's later work is desultory, with Winwood apparently just going through the motions after his disastrous flirt with superstardom in Blind Faith. He even wrote a song called "Sometimes I Feel So Uninspired," an accurate account of his creative powers. Some of the old spark seemed to return for *When the Eagle Flies*, but nothing has appeared since then.

Since all of Traffic's important work is on the first two albums, the compilation packages are redundant. — J.S.

TRAMMPS
★ ★ ★ The Legendary Zing Album / Bud. (1975) ¶
★ ★ ★ Where the Happy People Go / Atl. (1976) ¶
★ ★ Disco Inferno / Atl. (1976) ¶
★ ★ Trammps III / Atl. (1977) ¶
★ ★ ★ The Best of the Trammps / Atl. (1978) ¶
★ ★ Mixin' It Up / Atl. (1980)
★ ★ Slipping Out / Atl. (1980)

The Trammps have been one of disco's most idiosyncratic groups. The band's early singles on Buddah updated ancient R&B classics and featured Jimmy Ellis' straining, gritty tenor against the basso profundo of Earl Young, a style continued on the group's best (though unfortunately deleted) LP, *Trammps* (Golden Fleece). But when the dictates of disco began to demand longer songs, the group foundered on bloated workouts. The Buddah singles are stretched to six-minute-plus lengths on the *Zing* album and the Atlantic LPs feature similarly inflated material. Despite some hot tracks ("Where the Happy

People Go," "Disco Inferno") and the appeal of Ellis' voice, the excess baggage becomes wearing. — J.MC.

TRAPEZE
★ Trapeze / Thresh. (1970)
★ ★ Medusa / Thresh. (1970)
★ ★ You Are the Music . . . We're Just the Band / Thresh. (1972)
★ Final Swing / Thresh. (1974)
★ Hot Wire / War. (1974) ¶
Break a leg. — W.K.

HAPPY AND ARTIE TRAUM
★ ★ ★ Mud Acres, Music among Friends / Roun. (1972)
★ ★ Life on Earth / Roun. (1974)
★ ★ Hard Times in the Country / Roun. (1975)
★ ★ Woodstock Mountain / Roun. (1977) ¶
★ ★ Silly Songs and Modern Lullabies / Briar (NA)

Together or as soloists, backup musicians and songwriters, the Traums were all-around participants in the folk revival. Although two fine Capitol albums are out of print, these LPs represent the traditional foundations and contemporary folk influences that contribute to their sound. Though *Mud Acres* also features Maria Muldaur, Eric Kaz and John Herald, it is the Traums who shape the tone and whose folk-blues-country mesh is one of the building blocks of a Northeastern sound further developed by Dylan, the Band, the Muldaurs and others. — I.M.

PAT TRAVERS
★ ★ ★ Pat Travers / Poly. (1976)
★ ★ ★ Makin' Magic / Poly. (1977)
★ ★ ★ Putting It Straight / Poly. (1977)
★ ★ ★ Heat in the Streets / Poly. (1978)
★ ★ ★ Go for What You Know / Poly. (1979)
★ ★ ★ Crash and Burn / Poly. (1980)
★ ★ ★ Radio Active / Poly. (1981)

Technically adept Canadian blues-rock guitarist has the standard Eric Clapton fixation but seems to be able to take it somewhere. — J.S.

MERLE TRAVIS
★ ★ ★ ★ Merle Travis' Guitar / Cap. (1956) ¶
★ ★ ★ ★ ★ The Best of Merle Travis / Cap. (1967)
★ ★ ★ Merle Travis and Joe Maphis / Cap. (1978) ¶

Merle Travis is influential both as a writer—responsible for "Sixteen Tons" and "Dark as

a Dungeon" among others—and as a guitarist. He adapted five-string banjo picking to guitar playing, a style now called "Travis picking." The Capitol *Best of* contains his finest work, including the originals of "Sixteen Tons" and "Dark as a Dungeon."
— D.M.

JOHN TRAVOLTA
★ ★ **John Travolta** / Mid. Int. **(1976)** ¶
★ ★ **Can't Let You Go** / Mid. Int. **(1977)** ¶
★ ★ **Travolta Fever** / Mid. Int. **(1978)**
The pop face of 1978 actually began recording a couple of years previously, though no one noticed much until *Saturday Night Fever* and *Grease.* Frankly, though, Travolta's a lot more interesting dancing to the Trammps and the Bee Gees than he is slogging his way through modernized Frankie Avalon concoctions. — D.M.

TREFETHEN
■ **Am I Stupid or Am I Great** / Pac. A. **(NA)**
You can't be serious. Was the guy who suggested this title into sabotage or what? Honesty maybe. — D.M.

T. REX
★ ★ ★ **Electric Warrior** / Rep. **(1971)**
★ ★ ★ **The Slider** / Rep. **(1972)**
Marc Bolan formed Tyrannosaurus Rex during the English hippie craze, and made a couple of delightful pop-mystical LPs in a psychedelic folkie vein. But in the early Seventies, Bolan aimed for bigger game—the teen idol market—which required more punch. He built "Bang a Gong," the highlight of *Electric Warrior,* around a Pete Townshend-style fuzz chord riff, and the abbreviated T. Rex had an international hit in 1971. But despite a succession of followups in the same innocently slinky mold, Bolan was never able to follow up his one chart success, and *The Slider* is the only other LP still in print. Bolan died in 1977. — D.M.

TRIGGER
■ **Trigger** / Casa. **(1978)**
"Melodic" hard rock performed with no discernible wit, imagination, or for that matter, ability. Occasional ineptly recycled Raspberries riffs are what pass for highlights.
— D.M.

TRILLION
★ **Trillion** / Epic **(1979)**
★ **Clear Approach** / Epic **(1980)**
Did the name stand for how many records these turkeys expected to sell, or how much their record label wasted on them? — R.P.

TRIPLE S CONNECTION
★ ★ ★ **20th Century-Fox Presents Triple S Connection** / 20th Cent. **(1979)**
Delfonics-style light soul harmony over a well-blended disco groove. More smoochable than danceable, but what's the problem with that? Produced by Chicago's answer to Thom Bell, Bunky Sheppard. — D.M.

TRIUMPH
■ **Rock 'n' Roll Machine** / RCA **(1979)**
■ **Just a Game** / RCA **(1979)**
■ **Progression of Power** / RCA **(1980)**
■ **Allied Forces** / RCA **(1981)**
Brain-busting, bone-crushing, synapse-snapping, death-dealing, etc., etc. . . . ROCK & ROLL. At least that's the way record companies usually try to sell this sort of proto-fascist junk. (Docked one star each for plotting world domination from Canada; I mean, at least if these guys were German, they might even be a little frightening instead of quite a bit laughable.) — W.K.

TRIUMVIRAT
★ **Mediterranean Tales** / Elect. **(1972)** ¶
★ **Illusions on a Double Dimple** / Harv. **(1974)**
★ **Spartacus** / Cap. **(1975)**
★ **Old Love Dies Hard** / Cap. **(1976)**
★ **Pompeii** / Cap. **(1977)**
★ **A La Carte** / Cap. **(1979)**
Finland's contribution to Seventies progressive rock. For Focus fans or complete xenophiles only. — J.S.

TROOPER
■ **Trooper** / MCA **(1975)**
★ **Two for the Show** / MCA **(1976)** ¶
★ **Knock 'Em Dead** / MCA **(1977)** ¶
★ **Thick as Thieves** / MCA **(1978)**
■ **Flying Colors** / MCA **(1979)**
■ **Hot Shots** / MCA **(1980)**
Randy Bachman's mid-Seventies heavy-metal discovery. Senescent Bachman-Turner Overdrive. — J.S.

ROBIN TROWER
★ ★ **Twice Removed from Yesterday** / Chrys. **(1973)**
★ ★ ★ **Bridge of Sighs** / Chrys. **(1974)**
★ ★ ★ **For Earth Below** / Chrys. **(1975)**
★ ★ ★ **Long Misty Days** / Chrys. **(1976)** ¶
★ ★ ★ **In City Dreams** / Chrys. **(1977)**
★ ★ ★ **Robin Trower—Live!** / Chrys. **(1977)**
★ ★ **Caravan to Midnight** / Chrys. **(1978)**
★ **Victims of the Fury** / Chrys. **(1980)**
Procol Harum's original guitarist, Robin Trower earned a respectable following on both sides of the Atlantic for his powerful

and incisive style. He had a knack for shaping a thick, rich sustain from his vintage Les Paul guitar with total control, building towering lead-guitar passages that perfectly complemented the big, keyboard-dominated sound of Procol Harum.

By the time of Procol's *Broken Barricades* LP, Trower had switched to a Fender Stratocaster and a totally different style. This would take him away from the group and on to a solo career. It was definitely fashioned from the Jimi Hendrix school, although Trower cleaned things up and refined certain nuances in terms of bent notes and finger vibrato. *Twice Removed from Yesterday*'s material and execution was still at a nascent stage, and the aura of Hendrix hung too thick for most to penetrate.

But the audience obviously appreciated Trower's aesthetic of continuity and he continued to refine his sound on subsequent albums. *Bridge of Sighs* and *For Earth Below* had better songs, and the addition of drummer Bill Lordan on the latter album helped tighten things up. *Live!* recorded in Sweden, gave Trower more space to stretch out his improvisations. Concentrating on subtle vibrato and long, shaped notes, he does his best work on slower tunes like "Daydream," where his lyricism prevails. Faster and more popular numbers like "Rock Me Baby" and "Little Bit of Sympathy" have a certain energy, but they suffer from comparison with the originals.

The last few albums exhibit a softer, more understated approach that lacks the fire of Trower's earlier work. For hard-core rock guitar fans. — J.C.C.

TRUSSEL
★ ★ **Love Injection** / Elek. (1980)
Title track was a middleweight soul hit. — D.M.

ERNEST TUBB
★ ★ ★ ★ **The Ernest Tubb Story** / MCA (1959)
★ ★ ★ **Ernest Tubb's Golden Favorites** / MCA (1961)
★ ★ ★ **Ernest Tubb's Greatest Hits** / MCA (1968)
★ ★ ★ ★ **Ernest Tubb and His Texas Troubadors** / Voc. (1975)
★ ★ **Legend and the Legacy** / Cachet (1979)
★ ★ ★ **Ernest Tubb, Vol. 2** / MCA (NA)
★ ★ ★ **I've Got All the Heartaches I Can Handle** / MCA (NA)
Tubb is the link between Jimmie Rodgers and Hank Williams in the honky-tonk country tradition. Tubb and Rodgers never met,

but Tubb's family became friendly with Rodgers' widow in San Antonio, and she gave him Rodgers' old guitar and arranged for Tubb to record for RCA's Bluebird subsidiary in 1936. In 1940, Tubb signed with Decca Records, for whom he has recorded for nearly forty years, although these are his only remaining catalogue LPs. Tubb became a regular member of the Grand Ole Opry in 1943, after a couple of appearances in Westerns. Later in the Forties, he became one of the first country stars to sing at Carnegie Hall.

Tubb has never been a giant record seller; rather, he is a key influence on many rockabilly and country performers of the present (Asleep at the Wheel in particular). His best-known songs include "Walking the Floor over You," "Our Baby's Book," "My Tennessee Baby," "Have You Ever Been Lonely," "Take Me Back and Try Me One More Time," "Tomorrow Never Comes" and a couple of duets: "Goodnight Irene," the Leadbelly song, sung with Red Foley in 1950, and "Mr. and Mrs. Used to Be" with Loretta Lynn in 1964. — D.M.

THE TUBES
■ **The Tubes** / A&M (1975)
■ **Young and Rich** / A&M (1976)
★ **Now** / A&M (1977)
★ **What Do You Want from Live** / A&M (1978)
★ **Remote Control** / A&M (1979)
★ ★ **T.R.A.S.H.** / A&M (1981)
★ ★ **Completion Backward Principle** / Cap. (1981)
The Tubes are a San Francisco troupe that *earns* the title shock-rock. They specialize in a kind of satirical cabaret that emphasizes ambisexuality, outré social and political humor, and hard rock twisted into comedic shape. Their best-known song, "White Punks on Dope," is an unlikely freaks' anthem, but most of the time this material doesn't deserve preservation on wax. What's funny when spontaneous and visual becomes turgid and shrill on repeated listenings, and vocalist Fee Waybill has the most unique range in rock: two notes, both flat. — D.M.

TANYA TUCKER
★ ★ ★ **Delta Dawn** / Col. (1972)
★ ★ ★ **What's Your Mama's Name** / Col. (1973) ¶
★ ★ ★ **Would You Lay with Me** / Col. (1974)
★ ★ **Tanya Tucker** / MCA (1975)
★ ★ ★ ★ **Tanya Tucker's Greatest Hits** / Col. (1975)

★ ★ **Lovin' and Learnin'** / MCA
(1976) ¶
★ ★ **Here's Some Love** / MCA (1976) ¶
★ ★ ★ **You Are So Beautiful** / Col.
(1977) ¶
★ ★ **Ridin' Rainbows** / MCA (1977) ¶
★ ★ ★ **Tanya Tucker's Greatest Hits** /
MCA (1978)
★ ★ ★ **TNT** / MCA (1978)
★ ★ **Tear Me Apart** / MCA (1979)
★ ★ **Dream Lovers** / MCA (1980)
★ ★ **Should I Do It** / MCA (1981)
Tanya Tucker began recording in 1972 when
she was only thirteen, in a pop-country style
developed with producer Bill Sherrill. She
immediately scored two minor pop crossover
hits, "Would You Lay with Me in a Field of
Stone" and "Blood Red and Going Down."
But when she left Columbia and Sherrill,
and as she aged, she lost much of her popu-
lar attraction. Whether she will ever regain a
substantial audience is still open to question.
— D.M.

TOMMY TUCKER
★ ★ ★ **Mother Tucker** / Red L. (1980), Br.
imp.
★ ★ **Live and Well** / Orna. (1981)
The late creator of "Hi Heel Sneakers," the
original of which is not on either of these
Seventies sessions. *Mother Tucker,* however,
offers an alternate take of "Hi Heel Sneakers," and though it's not as good, the rest of
the album is pretty solid. The Ornament is
not. — D.M.

IKE TURNER
★ ★ ★ ★ ★ **I'm Tore Up** / Red L. (1978),
Br. imp.
★ ★ ★ ★ **Ike Turner and His Kings of
Rhythm** / Ace (NA), Br. imp.
★ ★ ★ ★ **Kings of Rhythm** / Flyr. (1981),
Br. imp.
Though a generation of rock & rollers know
him only as Tina's foil, Ike Turner is in fact
a major figure in postwar rhythm & blues.
Turner was a great talent scout, who located
a good many of Sam Phillips' and Chess Rec-
ords' blues stars, and he was a fine band-
leader long before he ever hooked up with
Annie Mae Bullens (a.k.a. Tina). *I'm Tore
Up,* with sides by Ike Turner and His
Rhythm Rockers featuring vocalist Billy
Gayles, is as searing as early-Fifties R&B
ever got, a masterpiece of funky heat, driven
by Turner's biting guitar. The Ace is of
lesser quality, though not much, and the
Flyright consists of previously unissued
songs recorded for Cobra, the Chicago blues
label, in 1958, with vocals by Jackie Brens-

ton ("Rocket 88") among others. All are
worth hearing. — D.M.

IKE AND TINA TURNER
★ ★ ★ ★ ★ **River Deep—Mountain High** /
A&M (1969) ¶
★ ★ ★ **What You Hear Is What You Get** /
U.A. (1971) ¶
★ ★ ★ ★ **The World of Ike and Tina Turner**
/ U.A. (1973) ¶
★ ★ ★ ★ **The Soul of Ike and Tina Turner** /
Kent (1973)
★ ★ **Sixteen Great Performances** / ABC
(1975) ¶
★ ★ ★ ★ **Ike and Tina Turner's Greatest
Hits** / U.A. (1976) ¶
★ ★ **The Edge** / Fan. (1980)
★ ★ ★ ★ **Ike and Tina Turner's Festival of
Live Performances** / Kent (NA)
★ ★ ★ ★ **Please, Please, Please** / Kent (NA)
★ ★ ★ ★ **Too Hot to Hold** / Sp. (NA) ¶
★ ★ **Airwaves** / U.A. (NA)
Ike Turner began his career as an A&R man
for a variety of labels, turning over talent to
Modern and Sun among others. (Howlin'
Wolf was among his discoveries.) He joined
forces with his wife, Tina, in the mid-Fifties,
and they had several hits through the early
Seventies in a variety of R&B styles. The
early records for Sue are perhaps their best,
but the remakes of such classics of that period as "A Fool in Love" (on *River Deep*)
and the United Artists' *World of* aren't bad.
   A 1969 tour with the Rolling Stones won
the duo a white rock following, which was
both deserved (they had one of soul's most
dynamic shows) and finally ruinous (it encouraged Tina's tendency to screech rather
than sing and incited the Turners' dual capacity for silly salacious byplay). Nonetheless, the recordings for United Artists from
the early Seventies are solid, although the
Blue Thumb, United Artists and Fantasy
material recorded later is far weaker.
   The Kent records are solid Sixties R&B,
featuring Tina's voice above Ike's always
tight rhythm arrangements, with a band led
by his fine guitar playing. *River Deep* is a
Phil Spector production and one of the true
anomalies of rock & roll; the title song's failure to become a hit single drove Spector into
retirement for several years. Yet when the
album was finally rereleased in the early Seventies, it was a hodgepodge in which Turner's bluesy productions clash with Spector's
silken Wall of Sound. It never lives up to
what Spector claimed for it, although it occasionally comes close enough to be a must
for fans of either performer or producer.
— D.M.

BIG JOE TURNER

★ ★ ★ **Have No Fear, Big Joe Turner Is Here** / Savoy (1977)
★ ★ ★ ★ ★ **The Boss of the Blues** / Atl. (1981)
★ ★ ★ ★ **Joe Turner** / Atl. (NA), Jap. imp.
★ ★ ★ ★ **Jumpin' the Blues** / Arhoo. (NA)
★ ★ ★ ★ ★ **The Best of Big Joe** / Atl. (NA), Jap. imp.
★ ★ ★ **Texas Style** / Black & Blue (NA), Fr. imp.
★ ★ ★ **Turn on the Blues** / United (NA)
★ ★ ★ **Still Boss of the Blues** / United (NA)
★ ★ ★ **The Soul of Big Joe** / United (NA)
★ ★ ★ ★ ★ **Early Big Joe** / MCA (NA)
★ ★ ★ **Big Joe Turner** / Spivey (NA)
★ ★ ★ **Really the Blues** / Big Town (NA), imp.
★ ★ ★ **Joe Turner and Count Basie** / Pablo (NA)
★ ★ ★ **The Things I Used to Do** / Pablo (NA)
★ ★ ★ **Everyday I Have the Blues** / Pablo (NA)
Big Joe Turner has been recording for almost half a century, in every style from boogie-woogie and Kansas City jazz to rhythm & blues and rock & roll, and he is still making fine music today. An adept pianist in his younger years, he (along with Pete Johnson) pioneered boogie-woogie in the late Thirties, and this was one of the more magnificent developments of American music, as expressed on the vintage sides collected on *Early Big Joe*. The Savoy and Arhoolie recordings from the Forties are also inspired and passionate.

In the Fifties, Turner moved to Atlantic and became a pop star, recording first R&B-based jazz (see *Boss of the Blues*) and then outright rock & roll, including the epochal "Shake Rattle and Roll" (heard on *The Best of Big Joe*, a must). All the Atlantic material is terrific.

Since then he has traipsed all over the musical map. The United LPs collect R&B sides, while most of the rest focus on his jazz credentials. His most recent work is for Pablo, which is the label of impresario Norman Granz. Though the settings are pretty stuffy, Turner makes them rock. — D.M.

SPYDER TURNER

★ **Music Web** / Whit. (1977) ¶
★ **Only Love** / Whit. (1979)
Turner earned his legend with a late-Sixties one-shot, a version of Ben E. King's "Stand by Me" into which he interpolated the styles of King, Sam Cooke, Otis Redding, Smokey Robinson, James Brown and other soul heroes of the day. (And inspired a monumentally silly but famous rock essay by Sandy Pearlman—later Blue Oyster Cult's producer—called "The Raunch Epistomology of Spyder Turner.") These are comeback LPs, but Turner didn't really have anywhere to go back *to*. — D.M.

TINA TURNER

★ ★ **Acid Queen** / U.A. (1975) ¶
★ ★ **Rough** / U.A. (1979)
★ ★ **The Queen** / Sp. (NA) ¶
Without Ike Turner's grand sense of groove and melody, Tina is left on her own to shout and screech without much purpose. Stick with the Ike and Tina sides. — D.M.

THE TURTLES

★ ★ ★ ★ **Greatest Hits** / Sire (1974) ¶
★ ★ ★ **Turtles 1968** / Rhino (1982)
★ ★ ★ **It Ain't Me Babe** / Rhino (1982)
Complete with liner notes from former Turtles Flo and Eddie, *Greatest Hits* runs the gamut from the seminal folk-rock "It Ain't Me Babe" to the memorable pop schlock "Elenore" and "Happy Together" to a look at where they are now (a 1966 Warren Zevon song called "Outside Chance," performed like a cross between the Rolling Stones and ? and the Mysterians). Period music to be sure, but what a fine period!

You don't need the others unless you're a folk-rock fanatic. — J.B.M.

TUXEDOMOON

★ ★ ★ ★ **Half-Mute** / Ralph (1980)
★ ★ ★ ★ **Desire** / Ralph (1981)
Tuxedomoon are masters of sound texture. They blend synthesizers, violins, saxophones, guitars, tapes and vocals into the oddest shapes. Their first album, *Half-Mute*, is an album of experimental music. *Half-Mute*'s "59 to 1" is quite catchy, while "Nazce" is a quiet and moody avant-garde tune. On *Desire*, they began to stretch out and use textures more to their advantage. On *Half-Mute* they use a sax, a violin and a bass for texture, while on *Desire* a string section appears on several songs (especially "Holiday for Plywood") and many more overdubs, without ever cluttering up (or muddying) the final product. — K.L.

20/20

★ ★ ★ **20/20** / Por. (1979)
★ ★ ★ **Look Out!** / Por. (1981)
Underrated Los Angeles band signed in record-label power-pop panic of 1978–79. First album is masterful distillation of nostalgia for Sixties music scene, contemporary L.A.

youth culture and eternal rock obsessions—
love, sex, drugs, cars and guitars. None of
the other L.A. power-pop bands even came
close to 20/20's satisfyingly multilayered,
densely textured lyrical and instrumental
sound. First album's surprising approach and
signatures ("Out of This Time" is a completely unexpected Hendrix tribute) made it
one of year's best debuts. *Look Out!* displays
darker concerns. Motif, as carried by "Nuclear Boy," "American Dream" and "Life in
the U.S.A.," seems to be threat of social
breakdown, nuclear war, impossibility of relationships, etc. If their optimism flagged on
second disc, 20/20's intelligence didn't, but
youthful freshness of debut gives it slight
edge. — G.A.

DWIGHT TWILLEY
★ ★ ★ Sincerely / MCA (1976)
★ ★ ★ Twilley Don't Mind / Ari. (1977) ¶
★ ★ ★ Twilley / Ari. (1979)
★ ★ ★ Scuba Divers / EMI (1982)
Beatles and Byrds influences abound in this
Tulsa boy's albums. The best moment is on
the first album (originally released on home-
town Shelter): his 1975 hit single, "I'm on
Fire," rockabilly for moderns. — J.S.

THE TWINKLE BROTHERS
★ ★ ★ Love / V.F.L. (1979)
★ ★ ★ ★ Country Men / Virgin (1980)
★ ★ ★ Me No You / Twinkle (1981)
One of the most exquisite harmony groups
in reggae, the Twinkle Brothers have yet to
achieve the recognition merited by their ten-
plus years of quality performances. *Love*
lacks the high points of earlier Virgins, but
Country Men may be their best ever. *Me No
You* features the masterful "Rasta Pon
Top." — R.F.G.

CONWAY TWITTY
★ ★ ★ To See My Angel Cry / MCA
(1970) ¶
★ ★ ★ Hello Darlin' / MCA (1970)
★ ★ ★ ★ Greatest Hits, Vol. 1 / MCA
(1972)
★ ★ You've Never Been This Far Before /
MCA (1973)
★ ★ Conway Twitty's Honky Tonk Angel /
MCA (1974)
★ ★ I'm Not Through Loving You Yet /
MCA (1974)
★ ★ Linda on My Mind / MCA (1975)
★ ★ ★ High Priest of Country Music /
MCA (1975)
★ ★ Twitty / MCA (1975)

★ ★ Now and Then / MCA (1976)
★ ★ ★ Greatest Hits, Vol. 2 / MCA
(1976)
★ ★ ★ Play Guitar Play / MCA (1977) ¶
★ ★ I've Already Loved You in My Mind /
MCA (1977) ¶
★ ★ Georgia Keeps Pulling On My Ring /
MCA (1978)
★ ★ Conway / MCA (1978)
★ ★ Very Best of Conway Twitty / MCA
(1978)
★ ★ Cross Winds / MCA (1979)
★ ★ Heart and Soul / MCA (1980)
★ ★ Rest Your Love on Me / MCA
(1981)
★ ★ I'm Not Used to Loving You / Cor.
(NA)
Twitty originally scored with "It's Only
Make Believe," a 1958 No. 1 hit. He fol-
lowed it the next year with "Mona Lisa,"
before tripping over from rockabilly into
straight country, where he has become a
major force, albeit a conservative one. His
records continually top the country charts,
and occasionally when he combines his big
baritone voice, his still-acute guitar playing
and his top-notch group, The Twitty Birds,
he makes a record that breaks through the
stifling conventions of current country pop.
— D.M.

TYCOON
■ Tycoon / Ari. (1978) ¶
■ Turn Out the Lights / Ari. (1981)
Dynamics left over from flop film scores; vocals wrenched from hoarse throats; rhythms
recycled from large machinery; lyrics dedicated to the propagation of sexism and other
idiotic stereotypes. A name that says it all—
this is the music industry's idea of progressive. Which is to say that compared to Tycoon, Journey is the Rolling Stones, and
Rush has transcended Jimi Hendrix.
— D.M.

THE TYMES
★ ★ ★ Best of the Tymes / Abkco (1974)
★ ★ Turning Point / RCA (1976) ¶
★ ★ Diggin' Their Roots / RCA (1977) ¶
A very late, somewhat minor doo-wop group
from Philadelphia, the Tymes first scored in
1963 with "So Much in Love" and followed
it up with "Wonderful Wonderful." But by
the end of 1964, they were on their way
back to obscurity. The Abkco collection is
the one to get—the RCA discs were attempts to revive the group with a more modern style. — D.M.

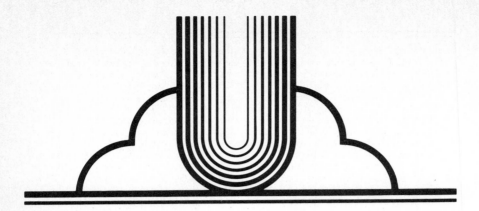

UB40

★ ★ ★ ★ **Signing Off** / Grad. (1980), Br. imp.
★ ★ ★ ★ **Present Arms** / Dept. (1981), Br. imp.
★ ★ ★ **Present Arms in Dub** / Dept. (1981), Br. imp.
★ ★ ★ ★ **UB44** / Dept. (1982), Br. imp.
★ ★ ★ ★ **The Singles Album** / Dept. (1983), Br. imp.

UB40's thundering sax-and-guitar music was one of the two best things to emerge from Britain's brief ska revival. The other was the English Beat, and if UB40 has never quite acquired the musical diversity and pop sheen of that band, they certainly make up for it by recording songs that not only speak in terms of political outrage ("Madame Medusa," the most vicious imaginable attack on Maggie Thatcher, "The Earth Dies Screaming," a scarifying blast against nuclear war, "One in Ten," a bitter rant against unemployment) but also completely reflect their passion and frustration. One of the most underrated bands of the decade; absolutely shameful that they've never had a single U.S. record released, especially as these were all British hits. *The Singles Album* reissues material from the period of the first album. — D.M.

UFO

★ ★ **Force It** / Chrys. (1975)
★ ★ **Phenomenon** / Chrys. (1976)
★ ★ **No Heavy Petting** / Chrys. (1976)
★ ★ **Lights Out** / Chrys. (1977)
★ ★ **Obsession** / Chrys. (1978)
★ ★ **Strangers in the Night** / Chrys. (1978)
★ ★ **No Place to Run** / Chrys. (1979)
★ ★ **The Wild, the Willing and the Innocent** / Chrys. (1981)

UFO began as a power trio with lead vocalist; its chief distinction was the thick chording and agile (if unrevolutionary) lead guitar playing of Michael Schenker. *Force It, Phenomenon* and *No Heavy Petting* were produced by Leo Lyon, of Ten Years After. Ten Years After keyboard player Chick Churchill also turns up on *Force It.* With *Petting,* a permanent keyboardist was added to flesh out the sound; subsequent releases used more artillery—horns and strings even—in an attempt at greater substance. Not much of it worked. — C.W.

U.K.

★ ★ ★ **U.K.** / Poly. (1978)
★ ★ ★ **Danger Money** / Poly. (1979)
★ ★ **Night after Night** / Poly. (1979)

Progressive rock supergroup led by former Yes/King Crimson percussionist Bill Buford and ex–Roxy Music synthesizer whiz Eddie Jobson turned in competent job with first three LPs, all the rage among technophiles in 1979. — D.M.

UK SUBS

★ ★ **Another Kind of Blues** / RCA (1979)
★ ★ **Kicks** / Stiff (1982)

Heavy on the baloney. Hold the mayo. — J.S.

ULTIMATE

★ **Ultimate** / Casa. (1979)

Charmless disco Muzak. — D.M.

ULTRAVOX

★ ★ ★ **Ultravox!** / Is. (1977) ¶
★ ★ **Ha! Ha! Ha!** / Is. (1977), Br. imp.
★ ★ ★ **Systems of Romance** / Ant. (1978), Br. imp.
★ ★ ★ **Three into One** / Ant. (1980), Br. imp.
★ ★ ★ ★ **Vienna** / Chrys. (1980)
★ ★ ★ **Rage in Eden** / Chrys. (1981)

Originally a quintet fronted by punky Bowie-cum-Ferry poseur John Foxx, Ultravox epitomized the British late-Seventies transition from glam-rock flash to stark holocaust electro-dance music on their Brian Eno–produced debut. The bittersweet whine of Billy Currie's violin and Foxx's melodramatic airs (particularly on the dark monologue "My Sex," a not-so-distant relative of Bowie's "My Death") gave them an effective Berlin cabaret menace later exploited to a greater degree on the synthesizer-heavy *Systems of Romance,* the first of their three albums produced by German techno-rock chief Conny Plank. (Just for the record, *Ha! Ha! Ha!* is no laughing matter, a collection of mostly robotic Roxy Music cops like "Hiroshima Mon Amour." The compilation *Three in One* summarizes the band's Island/Antilles years.)

John Foxx's departure to make solo records nearly finished the band. But a major rethink—a super-synthesizer sound with a propulsive rock-disco beat and Euro-romantic trappings—and the introduction of dapper vocalist Midge Ure made all the difference on *Vienna,* a 1980 U.K. smash. Then-hot Gary Numan publicly acknowledged Ultravox (by then a four-piece) as a major influence, and the support of the burgeoning new romantic underground didn't hurt. Still, it is the snappy melodic kick and graceful keyboard orchestrations of songs like "Sleepwalk" and "Passing Strangers" that distinguish Ultravox from the rest of the post-punk electro-pop pack. They still wear their pretensions on a sleeve (for which *Rage in Eden* gets docked a star), but at least they do it with style. — D.F.

UNCLE LOUIE
★ ★ **Uncle Louie's Here / Mar. (NA)**
More Florida-bred dance-funk product. — D.M.

THE UNDERTONES
★ ★ ★ ★ **The Undertones / Sire (1979)**
★ ★ ★ **Hypnotized / Sire (1980)**
★ ★ ★ ★ **Positive Touch / Harv. (1981)**
Teenage group that came roaring out of Ireland with a hard and fast debut reminiscent of punk's masterpiece of pop form, the Ramones' *Rocket to Russia.* Although *Hypnotized*'s opening number promised "More Songs about Chocolate and Girls," the adolescent, sledgehammer approach gave way a bit to some ballads and acoustic guitars. With *Positive Touch,* the emphasis was firmly on diversity; producer Roger Bechirian (engineer on several Elvis Costello albums) helped the band achieve a stunning variety of sounds, textures and tempos, all delivered with the usual charming Under-

tones brevity. Whether this maturing of their craft can be fully reconciled with the punk energy that initially drove them remains to be seen. — W.K.

UNION GAP
★ **Lady Willpower / Col. (1969)**
★ ★ ★ **Union Gap's Greatest Hits / Col. (1970)**
Powered by Gary Puckett's searing lead vocals, the Union Gap racked up a series of hits from 1967 to 1968—"Woman, Woman," "Young Girl," "Lady Willpower" and "Over You." The group was strictly a singles band, so the *Greatest Hits* set is the only one that makes sense. — J.S.

UNIQUES
★ ★ ★ **Uniquely Yours / All Pl. (1966)**
★ ★ ★ **Uniques / All Pl. (1969)**
★ ★ ★ **Golden Hits / All Pl. (1972)**
More post-doo-wop Jersey rhythm & blues, à la the Montclairs and Sylvia. — D.M.

PHIL UPCHURCH
★ ★ **Phil Upchurch / Cadet (1969)** ¶
★ ★ **The Way I Feel / Cadet (1969)** ¶
★ ★ **Phil Upchurch / Mar. (1978)**
★ ★ ★ **Feeling Blue / Mile. (NA)**
Upchurch is from Chicago, and his guitar playing is basically derived from blues and funk, with an undercurrent of Charlie Christian in his phrasing. His early albums show off a tough guitar sound with spurts of inventiveness bouncing off occasionally inappropriate choral and orchestral backgrounds.

Unfortunately, most of Upchurch's career has been marked by formula playing and funk anonymity. Upchurch's style is fluid and clean but colorless. A tendency to become a guitar chameleon (too many sessions) is best expressed on the Marlin *Phil Upchurch,* his most commercial effort. The first side is produced by John Tropea, and Upchurch unconsciously assumes a Tropean style. On side two, George Benson produces, and guess who Phil turns into as of the first few notes? *Feeling Blue* is the only recommendation here. — J.C.C.

UPSETTERS
★ ★ **Super Ape / Is. (1977)**
★ ★ ★ ★ **Scratch and Co. / Clock. (1980)**
★ ★ ★ **The Upsetter Collection / Troj. (1981)**
★ ★ ★ **Blackboard Jungle Dub / Clock. (1981)**
The Upsetters were the house band for the ever-creative Lee Perry during the late Sixties and early Seventies when he was creat-

ing some of reggae's most imaginative records. Members of the Upsetters went on to become the Wailers. *The Upsetter Collection* compiles late-Sixties/early-Seventies singles, some of which are classics. The Clocktower LPs compile dubs of Perry productions of the Upsetters and other artists during the early Seventies. Always interesting.
— R.F.G.

URBAN HEROES
★ Who Said / Hands. (NA)
Not me. — D.M.

URBAN VERBS
★ ★ Urban Verbs / War. (1980)
★ ★ Early Damage / War. (1981)
Progressive synthesizer-dominated music; for Eighties hippies. — W.K.

URIAH HEEP
■ Uriah Heep / Mer. (1970)
■ Salisbury / Mer. (1971)
★ Look at Yourself / Mer. (1971)
★ Demons and Wizards / Mer. (1972)
■ Magician's Birthday / Mer. (1972)
■ Uriah Heep Live / Mer. (1973)
■ Sweet Freedom / War. (1973)
■ Wonderworld / War. (1974) ¶
■ Return to Fantasy / War. (1975) ¶
★ Best of Uriah Heep / Mer. (1976)
■ High and Mighty / War. (1976) ¶
■ Firefly / War. (1977) ¶
■ Innocent Victim / War. (1978) ¶
■ Fallen Angel / Chrys. (1978)
A mutant version of Deep Purple, Uriah Heep has to be considered one of the worst commercially successful bands of the Seventies. Good points: sincerity and an organist (Ken Hensley) far more intelligent and capable than the group. Bad points: one of the most strident and annoying singers (David Byron) in rock history. The problem is that Byron gets the material he deserves. — J.S.

U ROY
★ ★ ★ ★ U Roy / Attack (1974)
★ ★ ★ ★ Dread in-a Babylon / Virgin (1976) ¶
★ ★ ★ Rasta Ambassador / State L. (1977)
★ ★ ★ Natty Rebel / State L. (1978)
★ ★ ★ ★ Jah Son of Africa / State L. (1979)
★ ★ ★ Greatest Hits / State L. (1979)
★ ★ ★ Love Gamble / State L. (1980)
★ ★ ★ ★ ★ Version Galore / Treasure Isle (NA)

One of the original masters of the reggae-derived "dee jay" style, U Roy's a scabrous conversationalist with a more-than-funky beat, but definitely not the thing for the faint of heart or those with any antipathy to marijuana, which he treats as a true sacrament. Around 1969–70, U Roy inaugurated a whole new era of reggae talk-over. Where earlier efforts had consisted of extravagent boasting or comic storytelling (with the exception of a few Prince Buster social commentaries), U Roy put a message in his rap, invented a singsong style that played off the rhythms of the music *and* integrated both rhythm and content into the prerecorded hits he used as takeoff points. *Version Galore,* if you can find it, has his seminal early hits (*U Roy* has a few others), while later records show his continued vitality. *Greatest Hits* compiles late-Seventies high points but not, as implied, his greatest hits.
— D.M./R.F.G.

URUBAMBA
★ ★ ★ ★ Urubamba / War. (1974) ¶
This album of Peruvian folk music was recorded by Paul Simon, who has used this group on some of his recordings, both solo and with Simon and Garfunkel. It is surprisingly charming, the South American flute and drums carrying a series of high-pitched but soothing melodies that are calm without becoming Muzak. — D.M.

USA-EUROPEAN CONNECTION
★ ★ USA-European Connection / Mar. (NA)
★ ★ Come into My Heart / Mar. (1978)
Passable internationalized dance music.
— D.M.

U2
★ ★ ★ ★ ★ Boy / Is. (1980)
★ ★ ★ ★ October / Is. (1981)
★ ★ ★ ★ War / Is. (1982)
Young Irish group whose echoed vocals and strong, jagged playing (supplied mainly by aptly named guitarist The Edge) is one of the Eighties' most promising sounds. Although the mystical atmosphere these two records conjure up could lead the group into numbing Led Zeppelin territory, their youth and innate pop sense will probably keep the music simple and direct. *Boy* and *War* confirm this judgment.
— W.K.

VALDY
★ **See How the Years Have Gone By /
A&M (1975)**
★ **Valdy and the Hometown Band / A&M
(1976)**
Valdy is a minor Canadian pop music institution who has successfully played out the semi-amateur folksinger role for more than a decade. Despite the slickness of his records, Valdy's songs are moral rather than mellow, full of message rather than mellifluence. His performances are notorious for their arrogant displays of "country man" sermonizing.

After recording two studio LPs and one live one in Canada, Valdy went to L.A. to record a U.S. greatest-hits package, *See How the Years*. Producer Paul Rothchild offers a tastefully dressed-up L.A. session band and Valdy sounds quite at ease, if a bit comatose.

Valdy and the Hometown Band, produced by Claire Lawrence, marks a slight change in Valdy's writing. Instead of posing as Legendary Canadian Mountain Man, Valdy becomes a trans-Canada tourist and produces full-color, National Film Board songs. The Hometown Band, a very flexible Vancouver-based group that also records on its own, provides an intelligently eclectic backup without the pretensions of ponderous rootsi-ness that are Valdy's usual stock in trade.
— B.T.

RITCHIE VALENS
★ ★ ★ **The History of Ritchie Valens / Delfi
(1981)**
★ ★ ★ ★ **The Best of Ritchie Valens / Delfi
(1981)**
Ritchie Valens is unfortunately best known as the youngest rocker to die in the plane crash with Buddy Holly and the Big Bopper. But Valens was much more: still a teenager when he died, he was a star before he gradu-ated from *junior* high school, and had he lived, he would almost certainly have been the first Hispanic-American rock star. He was an exciting guitarist, his singing had a joyous innocence and his songs were reflec-tive of his heritage and experience: "La Bamba," perhaps his biggest hit, is a tradi-tional Mexican tune rocked to death, and "Donna," a beautiful ballad, is about his Anglo girlfriend, whose family tried to pre-vent her from dating Valens because he was a Chicano.

History is a three-record boxed set, with the usual packaging paraphernalia. It's more than anyone but scholars and fanatics needs to hear. But the *Best of* boils it down to just the good stuff, and that's well worth a listen, even for those who don't share the memory.
— D.M.

JOHN VALENTI
★ **I Won't Change / RCA (NA)**
Pop singer who'd be better off if he did.
— D.M.

FRANKIE VALLI
■ **Frankie Valli Is the Word / War. (1978)**
■ **Very Best of Frankie Valli / MCA (1979)**
■ **Heaven above Me / MCA (1981)**
In plain English, the word is garbage. De-spite his association with the Four Seasons, Valli's career is really notable because he has managed to extend the nasal whining of the Fabian/Frankie Avalon style well into the Seventies and Eighties. Pure pop for poor fools. — D.M.

LON AND DERREK VAN EATON
★ **Who Do You Out Do / A&M (1975)** ¶
Passable melodic pop, unambitious and un-individual. Economic arranging, medium tempos, lots of vocal harmonies. Suitably modest production from Richard Perry and Bill Schnee. — C.W.

LUTHER VANDROSS

★ ★ ★ ★ **Never Too Much** / Epic (1981)
★ ★ ★ ★ **Forever, for Always, for Love** /
Epic (1982)

Vandross has for years been one of New York's most successful session singers, and with these two albums, his rich, resonant tenor has made him a star out front. Vandross is also an accomplished writer and arranger who knows how to balance slickness and passion, making his craftsmanship seem effortless. *Never Too Much* is a bit too much the one-man show, but *Forever* is a breakthrough, especially the opening medley of Luther's "Bad Boy" with Sam Cooke's "Having a Party," a hit, and the cover of the Temptations' "Since I Lost My Baby," in which Luther proves why he deserves to be considered one of the most promising vocal groups around, as well as a solo artist. — J.D.C./D.M.

THE VAN DYKES

★ ★ ★ ★ **"No Man Is an Island"** / Solid S.
(1982)

The subtitle is "Lone Star Soul from Fort Worth's Finest," and that's the essential information about this vocal trio. Well, that and the fact that this album contains fourteen scintillating sides, some previously unissued, highlighted by the wonderful title track, the closest the Van Dykes ever came to a national R&B hit. — D.M.

VANGELIS

★ **Heaven and Hell** / RCA (1975)
★ **Albedo 0.39** / RCA (1976)
★ **Spiral** / RCA (1977)
★ **Beaubourg** / RCA (1978)
★ **China** / Poly. (1979)
★ ★ **Chariots of Fire** / RCA (1982)

Greek piano prodigy makes his records in England. Allegedly this is rock, but if that's true, then the guy who wrote the soundtrack for *2001* is Buddy Holly. Classical mediocrity became world famous with mawkish *Chariots* soundtrack music. A frequent collaborator with Jon Anderson, formerly of Yes, which is indictment enough in these parts. — D.M.

VAN HALEN

★ ★ ★ **Van Halen** / War. (1978)
★ ★ ★ **Van Halen 2** / War. (1979)
★ ★ ★ **Women and Children First** / War.
(1980)
★ ★ **Fair Warning** / War. (1981)

1978's heavy-metal surprise was a Southern California band that grinds out a variety of variations on the basic "Louie Louie" thump theme, most notably a version of the Kinks' earlier variation, "All Day and All of the Night." The second album is as imaginative as its title. Subsequent LPs revealed guitarist Eddie Van Halen to be the premier heavy-metal technician of the Eighties, and vocalist David Lee Roth to be the most obnoxious singer in human history, an achievement notable in the face of long tradition and heavy competition. Eddie's wizardry makes it sorta worthwhile in the end, though *Fair Warning* hints that they're running dry. — D.M.

VANILLA FUDGE

★ ★ ★ **Vanilla Fudge** / Atco (1967)

One of the most absurd albums ever made— soul music, "In-A-Gadda-Da-Vida" style. When this album was released, the notion of a psychedelic version of the Supremes' "You Keep Me Hangin' On" was so perfect that the Fudge actually found itself with a hit single. Grand organ playing, lugubrious drumming, vocals that define wretched excess, pure period fun. Ages better than some "serious" art rock of the era. — D.M.

GINO VANNELLI

■ **Crazy Life** / A&M (1973)
★ **Powerful People** / A&M (1974)
★ **Storm at Sunup** / A&M (1975)
■ **The Gist of the Gemini** / A&M (1976)
■ **A Pauper in Paradise** / A&M (1977)
★ **Brother to Brother** / A&M (1978)
■ **Nightwalker** / Ari. (1981)
■ **Best of Gino Vannelli** / A&M (1981)

Teamed with his keyboardist brother, John, and under the tutelage of Herb Alpert, Gino Vannelli has progressed from mere schlock to monumental vulgarity, creating a mammoth new "My Way" out of MOR melodies and his brother's post–Pink Floyd Muzak.

Vannelli is primarily a crooner, but capable of twisting loudly in the sonic wind whooshing from the synthesizers. He is a parody of romantic agony, a pop Prometheus unbound by taste or prodded by imagination. Studio technology, the budget to use it, and Gino's temperamental self-image are the sole sources of development from the suburban wedding music of *Crazy Life* to the errant disco of *Powerful People* to the unavoidable crystallization of style begun with *Storm at Sunup*. Perhaps a few of Vannelli's epic arrogations might work, were it not for his lyrics that extend bottomless narcissism and chilling stupidity beyond sodden sentimentality straight into complete hilarity. — B.T.

DAVE VAN RONK

★ **Black Mountain Blues** / Folk. (1959)
★ **Dave Van Ronk Sings Earthy Ballads and Blues** / Folk. (1961) ¶
★ ★ ★ **Dave Van Ronk** / Fan. (1972)
★ ★ **In the Tradition** / Prest. (NA)
★ ★ ★ **Sunday Street** / Philo (1976)
★ ★ **Dave Van Ronk, Folksinger** / Prest. (NA)
★ ★ **Inside Dave Van Ronk** / Rep. (NA)

This is just a bare sampling of Van Ronk's recorded work. One of the majors behind the folk revival, both as a performer and as host to many would-be folkies newly arrived in New York, Van Ronk's initial loves were blues and jazz. Eventually he integrated the songs of contemporary writers—Bob Dylan, Joni Mitchell, even Jacques Brel—into his gruffly tender style.

The Folkways sets are more interesting for material than sound quality, which is poor, and Van Ronk's often instructive blues guitar work is largely inaudible. The Fantasy two-disc set is a repackaging of his first two Prestige LPs, *Folksinger* and *Inside,* both recorded in 1962. They feature some of his best-known interpretations—most notably "Cocaine Blues," "He Was a Friend of Mine" (perhaps the first cover of a Dylan song), "Motherless Child" and "Fair and Tender Ladies." *In the Tradition* finds Van Ronk singing as part of the Red Onion Jazz Band (Dixieland, of course) on six songs and performing solo blues on the remainder.

Sunday Street is representative of Van Ronk's periodic forays into a sound that links his traditional efforts to the pop idiom—which is not to say that it's a pop record. But together with a now out-of-print Polydor LP, it covers his performing repertoire (he has often re-recorded songs over the years as his approach to them changes) in a faithful yet accessible fashion. — I.M.

RANDY VANWARMER

★ ★ **Warmer** / Bears. (1979)
★ **Terraform** / Bears. (1980)

One-hit wonder: "Just When I Needed You Most" (from *Warmer*) got sappy singer/songwriter to No. 4 in 1979. Subsequent efforts are entirely lackluster. — D.M.

TOWNES VAN ZANDT

★ ★ ★ **High, Low and In-Between** / Toma. (1971)
★ ★ ★ **The Late, Great Townes Van Zandt** / Toma. (1972)
★ ★ ★ **Delta Momma Blues** / Toma. (1978)
★ ★ ★ **Townes Van Zandt** / Toma. (1978)
★ ★ ★ **Our Mother, the Mountain** / Toma. (1978)
★ ★ ★ **Townes Van Zandt Live** / Toma. (1978)
★ ★ ★ **Flyin' Shoes** / Toma. (1979)

The Jackson Browne of Texas. Which means that Van Zandt's country inflection is a bit more authentic, his mysticism is firmly grounded in pop psychology, his melodies have a hummable sameness, and he isn't much of a vocalist. On the other hand, Townes is a hell of a lot better alternative than, say, John David Souther. — D.M.

JOHNNY VAN ZANT

★ ★ ★ **No More Dirty Deals** / Poly. (1980)
★ ★ ★ **Round Two** / Poly. (1981)

The third son of Jacksonville rock patriarch Lacy Van Zant, Johnny sings better than Ronnie did with Lynyrd Skynyrd and rocks as hard as his brother Donnie does in .38 Special. His debut features a stirring tribute to the late Ronnie, "Standing in the Darkness," which is loosely based on the Skynyrd classic "Free Bird." — J.S.

THE VAPORS

★ ★ ★ ★ **New Clear Days** / Lib. (1980)
★ ★ ★ **Magnets** / Lib. (1981)

The Vapors turned out one of 1980's most engaging singles with "Turning Japanese," possibly a pop ode to masturbation. Surprisingly, it's not the only good thing on their debut album, *New Clear Days.* David Fenton, the band's writer and auteur, composed a series of stories (it's hard to tell just what the unifying concept is, something about war, Japan and madness) that are full of sweet adolescent psychotics seemingly left over from Pete Townshend's and Ray Davies' early songs. "Sixty Second Interval" and "Waiting for the Weekend," in particular, are as satisfying and memorable as any music released in the past few years. Unfortunately, *Magnets* lacks the imagination of the debut, and in late 1981 the Vapors broke up. — D.G.

VAPOUR TRAILS

★ **Vapour Trails** / War. (1979)

All the predictable claptrap of L.A. rock, made less excusable because the group traveled all the way from London to indulge itself. — D.M.

SYLVIE VARTAN

■ **I Don't Want the Night to End** / RCA (1979) ¶

In the mid-Sixties, Vartan showed a lot of flair. All white go-go boots, fishnet stockings and miniskirts, she was France's answer to

Sandie Shaw—Le Pop Star who sang mournful ballads in a voice reeking with sincerity and emotion. There is nothing to recommend on this album, however. The kind of music that passes for rock on made-for-TV movies, it's the worst kind of slick pop-disco.
— D.G.

BOBBY VEE
★ ★ ★ **Bobby Vee's Golden Greats / U.A. (NA)**
★ ★ **Tribute to Buddy Holly / Sunset (1978), Br. imp.**
Minnesota rocker whose career allegedly began when he filled in for Buddy Holly the night after the plane crash; later actually recorded an album with the Crickets, and some of Buddy's material. The vocal resemblance is slender, but Vee did do a good job on some of his own slight pop-rock hits of the early Sixties, notably "Red Rubber Ball," "Take Good Care of My Baby" and "The Night Has a Thousand Eyes." These, and his other hit material, are collected on the United Artists set above. But the Vee record to seek is the British-only *Legendary Master Series* set, with annotation by Greil Marcus. Incidentally, Bob Dylan plays piano on none of the above. — D.M.

TÁTA VEGA
★ ★ **Full Speed Ahead / Tam. (1976)** ¶
★ ★ ★ **Totally Táta / Tam. (1977)** ¶
★ ★ **Try My Love / Tam. (1979)**
★ ★ **Givin' All My Love / Tam. (NA)**
Táta Vega is an exception to the glut of current, anonymous Motown acts. Though her debut LP, *Full Speed Ahead,* is perfunctory disco, *Totally Táta* shows intelligence and some varied ideas. The influences on *Totally Táta* include Stevie Wonder, Marvin Gaye and Jackson Five, but the album's unfortunate commercial failure may preclude any further musical ambitiousness. — J.MC.

THE VELVET UNDERGROUND
★ ★ ★ ★ ☆ **The Velvet Underground and Nico / Verve (1967)** ¶
★ ★ ★ **White Light, White Heat / Verve (1967)** ¶
★ ★ ★ **The Velvet Underground / MGM (1969)** ¶
★ ★ ★ ★ **Loaded / Coti. (1970)**
★ ★ ★ **The Velvet Underground Live at Max's Kansas City / Coti. (1972)**
★ ★ ★ ★ ★ **1969 Velvet Underground Live / Mer. (1974)**
Few groups in the history of popular music have broken down as many barricades as the Velvet Underground did in its all-too-brief

existence. The Velvets' foresight into the directions that electric music was taking (dissonance, feedback, extended improvisation) and their forays into taboo lyrical subject matter (the decadence of the idle rich, the horrors and joys of drugs, the realities of life on the street) were so out of step with what was going on in the music world around them in the late Sixties and early Seventies that they never gathered more than a very small cult following. Yet the Velvets' influence hovers over all present music seeking to do more than merely entertain. Leader Lou Reed's almost cinéma vérité songwriting style rang with an honesty and compassion that few songwriters ever reach, and the band's uncompromising, committed playing is arguably *the* source of most post-punk/new-wave music.

The group's first album, *The Velvet Underground and Nico,* with its famous Andy Warhol banana cover, features such classics as "Waiting for the Man," "Heroin," "Venus in Furs" and "I'll Be Your Mirror," with the ever-mysterious Nico on lead vocals on several tracks, and John Cale's viola and piano helping to shape the various moods and images evoked by the band's music. The second and third LPs, *White Light White Heat* and *The Velvet Underground,* are also masterpieces, though on completely different levels. *White Light* is a turbulent, almost chaotic assault of electric music. *The Velvet Underground* is the most low-key of the group's records, with several beautiful ballads ("Candy Says," "I'm Set Free," "Pale Blue Eyes") and some extraordinary rhythm guitar by Reed on "What Goes On."

Loaded is the original band's final testament. It's the most accessible of the Velvets' records, featuring such charged rockers as "Rock and Roll" and "Head Held High" and some passionate ballads ("New Age," "Oh! Sweet Nuthin' ").

Of the two live albums released after the band's demise, the Mercury double-LP set is recommended slightly above the Max's record because it features a few previously unrecorded songs and captures neatly the often-overlooked ability of the group to rock out gracefully without compromising its music or attitudes. Reed's heartfelt singing, Sterling Morrison's sympathetic lead work, Doug Yule's innocent, supportive vocals and fine bass work (he replaced Cale after the second album), and Maureen Tucker's primitive, solid drumming are displayed here to the fullest and make the set a glorious document of the music. — B.A.

THE VENTURES
★ ★ ★ ★ **Walk Don't Run** / Lib. (1960)
★ ★ ★ **The Ventures Play Telstar and Lonely Bull** / Lib. (1963)
★ ★ ★ **Golden Greats by the Ventures** / Lib. (1967)
★ ★ ★ **Tenth Anniversary Album** / Lib. (1970)
★ ★ ★ **TV Themes** / U.A. (NA) ¶
★ ★ ★ **Very Best of the Ventures** / Lib. (1975)
★ ★ ★ **The Ventures Play the Country Classics** / Lib. (NA)

Textbook instrumental rock & roll, West Coast school, brought to us through the Sixties courtesy of Bob Bogle (guitar/bass), Nokie Edwards (guitar), Don Wilson (guitar) and Mel Taylor (drums). These four journeyman musicians helped blaze a path for many aspiring rockers through their tough, nononsense treatment of rock & roll classics and popular movie and TV themes of the day.

The Ventures' big hit, "Walk Don't Run," is a marvel of rock & roll balance, with the dark and echoey lead guitar part that put the Mostite Company on the map; it survives as the era's signature sound. The current discography is confused to say the least, and you're more likely to find out-of-print Ventures albums in the cutout bins than anything on this list. But rejoice in the fact that they all sound the same, so it really doesn't matter anyway. Stiff snare and cymbal sound, pulsing bass and metallic guitars spitting out popular melodies through a wash of echo and vibrato. What more could the young musician ask for? — J.C.C.

TOM VERLAINE
★ ★ ★ ★ **Tom Verlaine** / Elek. (1979)
★ ★ ★ ★ **Dreamtime** / War. (1981)

The former leader of Television combines a sense of imminent personal disaster with a sense of devotion, plays desperate, searing guitar combining the best aspects of Neil Young and Jerry Garcia, and seems to haunt his own records like a premature ghost. — B.C.

THE VIBRATORS
★ ★ ★ ★ **Pure Mania** / Col. (1977) ¶
★ ★ ★ **V2** / Col. (1978) ¶
★ ★ ★ **Batteries Included** / CBS (1980), Br. imp.

Too professional to be termed hard-core punk, too raw to qualify as power pop, the Vibrators' *Pure Mania* might have been the record that the term "new wave" was coined to quantify. Or maybe not—certainly, to the extent that new wave is a marketing slot, the Vibrators never really qualified. How *do* you sell a band whose most pungent rhymes revolve around S&M and whose blitzkrieg attack is relentlessly thunderous? Not at all, at least not in America.

V2 is a letdown, the energy dissipated with nothing but the cheap thrills of secondhand kinkiness to compensate. *Batteries Included* is a thoroughly unnecessary anthology, since everything you need is on the first album. Waverers about punk, though, should beware: *Pure Mania* can be enough to push you over the edge into true belief. — D.M.

SID VICIOUS
★ ★ **Sid Sings** / Virgin (1979)

At his best, he sings some Eddie Cochran tunes and "My Way," (the one written by Paul Anka, not Eddie's), all of which are genuine highlights of the Sex Pistols movie, *The Great Rock and Roll Swindle*, on whose soundtrack album they are heard in their proper context. This record is not only redundant but deliberately ghoulish, a necrophilic exploitation of the most rancid and destructive side of punk. — D.M.

THE VILLAGE PEOPLE
★ ★ **Village People** / Casa. (1977)
★ ★ ★ **Macho Man** / Casa. (1978)
★ ★ ★ **Cruisin'** / Casa. (1978)
★ ★ ★ **Go West** / Casa. (1979)
■ **Live and Sleazy** / Casa. (1980)
■ **Renaissance** / RCA (1981)

Late-Seventies disco group (all male) raised the gay visual stereotype to an art form: an Indian, a leather freak, etc. Everything but a sissy, which would not have worked, because their big hit was "Macho Man," a dumb but inspired dance chant. It was followed by "YMCA," which was more frank and just as stupid, if equally danceable. Kiss for grownups. — D.M.

GENE VINCENT
★ ★ ★ **Bluejean Bop** / Cap. (1956/1976), Fr. imp.
★ ★ ★ **Gene Vincent Rocks and the Bluecaps Roll** / Cap. (1958/1976), Fr. imp.
★ ★ ★ **A Gene Vincent Record Date** / Cap. (1959/1978), Fr. imp.
★ ★ ★ **Sounds Like Gene Vincent** / Cap. (1959/1978), Fr. imp.
★ ★ ★ **Twist Crazy Times** / Cap. (1960), Fr. imp.
★ ★ ★ **Gene Vincent** / Lon. (1967), Belg. imp.

★ ★ ★ **The Day the World Turned Blue** /
Bud. (1970), Ger. imp.
★ ★ ★ **The Gene Vincent Story, Vol. 5** /
Cap. (1973), Fr. imp. (Also issued as:
Pioneers of Rock / Starline (1972), imp.)
★ ★ ★ **Les Pionniers du Rock** / Cap. (1972),
Fr. imp.
★ ★ ★ ★ **The Gene Vincent Story, Vol. 1** /
Cap. (1973), Fr. imp.
★ ★ ★ ★ **The Gene Vincent Story, Vol. 2** /
Cap. (1973), Fr. imp.
★ ★ ★ ★ **The Gene Vincent Story, Vol. 3** /
Cap. (1973), Fr. imp.
★ ★ ★ **The Gene Vincent Story, Vol. 4** /
Cap. (1973), Fr. imp.
★ ★ ★ **The Gene Vincent Story, Vol. 6** /
Cap. (1973), Fr. imp.
★ ★ ★ **The Gene Vincent Story, Vols. 7–8** /
Cap. (1973), Fr. imp.
★ ★ ★ ★ **The Bop That Just Won't Stop** /
Cap. (1974)
★ ★ ★ **Gene Vincent and the Bluecaps** /
Cap. (1976), Fr. imp.
★ ★ ★ ★ **Rock 'n' Roll Legend** / Cap.
(1977), Fr. imp.
★ ★ ★ **Gene Vincent's Greatest** / Cap.
(1977)
★ ★ ★ **Gene Vincent's Greatest, Vol. 2** /
Cap. (1979), Br. imp.
★ ★ ★ **Forever Gene Vincent** / Roll. R.
(1980)
★ ★ ★ **Crazy Beat** / Cap. (NA), Fr. imp.
★ ★ ★ **Gene Vincent Memorial Album** /
Cap. (NA), Fr. imp.
★ ★ ★ ★ **Greatest Hits** / Cap. (NA), Br.
imp.
★ ★ **Rhythm in Blue** / Blue Cap (NA), Can.
imp.

Gene Vincent's genius is maddeningly elusive. Superficially his career seems extremely
minor: His only really important U.S. hit
was "Be-Bop-A-Lula," which seems to mark
him as a minor artist, if one of the best of
the early wave of Presley-influenced singers.
And though Vincent was much more popular in Europe, particularly in England, even
that nation's record charts don't tell the full
story of the quantity and quality of music—
almost all of it rock & roll—that he recorded.

The basic problem is the lack of a well-
packaged, competently annotated anthology.
French Capitol has an exhaustive series of
Vincent issues, but asking someone to sort
through twelve to fifteen discs of material
(not all of it excellent) is too much. (Seven
albums—*Gene Vincent and the Bluecaps,
Roll, Record Date, Sounds Like, Twist Crazy
Times,* and *Crazy Beat,* plus the four-record
boxed set, *Rock 'n' Roll Legend*—do incorporate Vincent's entire Capitol output, but
that's still far too vast a repertoire for casual
listening.)

However, a mere glance at a representative sampling of Vincent material demonstrates that he recorded an incredible
amount of fine material, maintained a basic
stylistic identity from 1956 through his death
in 1971 (from complications due to injuries
suffered in his 1960 car crash with Eddie
Cochran, plus damage due to alcoholism)
and simply possessed one of the finest voices
in the history of the music.

Vincent is probably at his best when simply rocking out on his early Capitol sides,
but he never abandoned rock for country, as
most fellow rockabilly-oriented performers
did. The result is that even the Belgian import, *Gene Vincent,* which is a reissue of a
1966 set originally on Challenge, and the
German import, *The Day the World Turned
Blue,* which was cut in 1970, only a few
months before Vincent's death, have a great
deal of rock & roll spirit and a sound that
has its share of continuity with Vincent's
early work. Even more startling is the gorgeous version of "Bring It On Home to
Me," on the otherwise highly marginal Rollin' Rock album, which is cluttered with imitations and tributes.

The best of Vincent's early rock & roll
tracks—"Be-Bop-a-Lula," "Woman Love,"
"Who Slapped John," "Race with the
Devil," "Git It"—establish him as an important pioneer, and the bulk of them can even
be found on the ridiculously tossed together,
ten-tracks-per-disc American collections. But
Vincent is one performer still due his perfect
tribute album. — D.M.

EDDIE "CLEANHEAD" VINSON
★ ★ ★ ★ **Jammin' the Blues** / Black L.
(1975)
★ ★ ★ **Eddie Cleanhead Vinson** / Trip
(NA)
★ ★ ★ ★ ★ **Cherry Red Blues** / King
(NA)
★ ★ ★ ★ **Wee Baby Blues** / Black and Blue
(NA)
★ ★ ★ ★ **The Original Cleanhead** /
Bluestime (NA)

One of the best Southwest blues singers, Vinson hails from Houston, Texas, and made a
name for himself singing and playing alto
saxophone in Cootie Williams' band. He
scored a hit in 1945 with "Kidney Stew
Blues" and a cover of Joe Turner's "Cherry
Red." Vinson's strong voice and falsetto
tricks carried him easily into the Sixties and
Seventies blues contexts. — J.S.

THE VIOLINAIRES

★ ★ **Stand by Me / Check (1965)**
★ ★ **The Fantastic Violinaires in Concert /
Check. (1969)**
★ ★ ★ **Please Answer This Prayer / Check.
(1971)**

Wilson Pickett is said to have sung briefly
with the Violinaires, though if he recorded
with them, it's undocumented. He's not on
these albums, but the group is from Detroit,
and shares stylistic similarities with Detroit
soul singers. The background vocals on the
live album's "My Mother Used to Hold
Me," for example, instantly recall Pickett's
"I Found a Love." This is one of the most
modern-sounding gospel groups, all high-
squealing voices and vocal arrangements full
of background *ooh*s and *ee*s. Through the
Sixties, their progress paralleled soul as
much as gospel. *Please* features modern instrumentation and vocals, and even songs
that deal with such subjects as dope and
Vietnam. It's fair to say that soul was at
least as big an influence on them as they
were on it. — J.MO.

VIOLINSKI

★ ★ ★ **No Cause for Alarm / Jet (1979)** ¶
Mik Kaminski played violin in the Electric
Light Orchestra until a few albums ago;
Mike De Albuquerque was ELO's first bassist. Created as a vehicle for Kaminski (who
is billed on the front cover), Violinski almost
became a real group, featuring not only violin but also the songs and keyboards of John
Marcangelo and De Albuquerque's guitar
work. The results vaguely resemble ELO in
spots, but *No Cause for Alarm* lacks Jeff
Lynne's lethal pop hooks, the bottom provided by cellos, though Violinski is more adventurous and less clichéd than ELO. Pleasant, well-crafted and harmless. — I.R.

VISAGE

★ ★ ★ **Visage / Poly. (1981)**
Only genuinely interesting exponents of new-
romantic honky funk, thanks to guitarist
Midge Ure (ex-Magazine). — D.M.

THE VOGUES

★ ★ **The Vogues' Greatest Hits / Rep.
(1970)**

Sappy mid-Sixties vocal group had one great
hit, "Five O'Clock World," and then closed
down shop. — D.G.

ERIC VON SCHMIDT

★ ★ **Eric Von Schmidt with Rolf Cahn /
Folk. (1961)**
★ ★ **The Folk Blues of Eric Von Schmidt /
Prest. (NA)**

A composer, blues interpreter and artist/
illustrator, Von Schmidt sang intermittently
throughout the Fifties and early Sixties, although music took second place to his artistic pursuits. He was immortalized by an
aside about him that Bob Dylan offered on
his debut album. Both of these sets date
from the early Sixties, the Folkways LP
offering a more interesting song selection,
the Prestige recording featuring blues and
jug-band style support from Geoff
Muldaur, Robert Jones and Fritz
Richmond. — I.M.

ROGER VOUDOURIS

★ **Roger Voudouris / War. (1978)**
★ **Radio Dream / War. (1979)**
★ **A Guy Like Me / War. (NA)**

Strained pop cliché with overmodulated bass
for "rock" flavor. — D.M.

VOYAGE

★ **Voyage / Mar. (1977)**
★ **Fly Away / Mar. (1978)**

It's hard to imagine a sterner test of pop
acumen than being asked to discern the le-
gitimizing function of these albums. Certainly, dancing isn't all there is to it—although a
dance beat is about all that distinguishes the
music from random elevator noises. Perhaps
Voyage proposes some more epistemological
lesson. After all, it can't be that any record
executive thought this amalgamation of disco
clichés made it as dance-floor fodder. Can it?
— D.M.

VOYAGER

★ **Halfway Hotel / Elek. (1979)**
★ **Act of Love / RCA (1980)**

Strained versions of pop's most banal ideas:
Elton John-isms meet Doobie Brothers
ready-mades in a web of Billy Joel ballad bathos. — D.M.

RICHARD WAGNER

★ ★ **Richard Wagner** / Atl. (1978) ¶

As Dick Wagner, he's an ace session guitarist (notably with Alice Cooper and Lou Reed), often ably paired with this album's producer, Bob Ezrin. But here he and Ezrin have created music as murkily intended and nearly as pretentious as the inexplicable name change. To see what Wagner really can do, check out whatever remains of the Frost catalogue on Vanguard, or Reed's *Rock 'n' Roll Animal.*
— D.M.

BUNNY WAILER

★ ★ ★ ★ **Blackheart Man** / Is. (1976)
★ ★ ★ **Protest** / Is. (1977)
★ ★ ★ ★ ★ **Bunny Wailer Sings the Wailers** / Mango (1980)
★ ★ ★ ★ **Rock 'n' Groove** / King Solomonic (1981)

Bunny Wailer (né Livingston) was an original member of the Wailers, and thus a crucial figure in reggae's development. After Bob Marley converted the group to mere backup in the mid-Seventies, Bunny recorded *Blackheart Man,* darker and yet more listenable than much of Marley's latter-day guitar noodling. Like subsequent LPs, it contains a healthy dose of Rastafarianism, including the always murky Rasta political pronouncements, a tendency that gets altogether out of hand on *Protest.*

Bunny Wailer Sings the Wailers is his masterpiece, coolly rootsy versions of early songs by the group, including "I Stand Predominate," "Rule This Land," "Hypocrite" and "Walk the Proud Land." *Rock 'n' Groove* lacks such exquisite material, but with this record Wailer becomes a kind of reggae patriarch, creating a sound both sinuous and tough—the very best of reggae's undiluted pleasures, rendered utterly contemporary. — D.M.

THE WAILING SOULS

★ ★ ★ **Wild Suspense** / Mango (1979)
★ ★ ★ ★ **Fire House Rock** / Greens. (1981)
★ ★ ★ ★ **Wailing** / Jah Guidance (1981)

Back in the early Sixties, the Wailing Souls used to hang around Studio One with the Wailers and learn singing techniques from Wailer mentor Joe Higgs. The Wailers went on to international stardom while the Souls languished in obscurity (only one release up to 1979, an excellent Studio One LP). Unsurprisingly, their international debut on Mango showed a vocal similarity to early Wailers. *Fire House Rock* upgraded the production, introduced killer material and gave the Souls a few 1980–81 hits. — R.F.G.

LOUDON WAINWRIGHT III

★ ★ ★ **Loudon Wainwright III** / Atl. (1970) ¶
★ ★ ★ **Album II** / Atl. (1971) ¶
★ ★ ★ **Album III** / Col. (1973)
★ ★ ★ **Attempted Mustache** / Col. (1973)
★ ★ **Unrequited** / Col. (1975)
★ ★ **T-Shirt** / Ari. (1976) ¶
★ ★ **Final Exam** / Ari. (1978) ¶
★ ★ ★ **Live One** / Roun. (1979)

Acoustic singer/songwriter and brilliant middle-class satirist. Onstage, Wainwright is Chaplin through the eyes of Artaud, filtered through Dylan. *Album III* has his only hit, the bizarre one-shot, "Dead Skunk." The Atlantic albums contain his least comic, most mordant material; the Arista LPs have his most bitter and freakish. — S.H.

THE WAITRESSES

★ ★ ★ **Wasn't Tomorrow Wonderful?** / Poly. (1982)

A collection of chirpy wiseass songs—some truly witty, others mere novelty fluff. The lead singer sounds like Deborah Harry with her IQ doubled, and even though her talky delivery and the music's relentless bouncy

beat make the album overly samey, several choice cuts like the sarcastic "No Guilt" are both screamingly funny and relatable.
— J.F.

TOM WAITS

★ ★ ★ ★ Closing Time / Asy. (1973)
★ ★ ★ Heart of Saturday Night / Asy. (1974)
★ ★ ★ Nighthawks at the Diner / Asy. (1975)
★ ★ ★ Small Change / Asy. (1976)
★ ★ ★ ★ Foreign Affairs / Asy. (1977)
★ ★ ★ ★ Blue Valentine / Asy. (1978)
★ ★ ★ Heart Attack and Vine / Asy. (1980)

Tom Waits is probably the most beatnik-influenced figure in rock & roll—his best work is a cross between one of Jack Kerouac's amphetamine verbal rambles and a psychotic short-order chef's midnight diatribe. This obscures, unfortunately, his talents as a composer (*Small Change* and *Closing Time* each contain several winning songs), and his gravel-voiced poetic renditions can become tedious for all but cultists. Waits is a punk of the old school, hard-bitten and determinedly scrounging, worth watching, if not always able to transcend his own excessive wordiness. *Blue Valentine,* an album containing a remarkable version of *West Side Story*'s "Somewhere" and a lot of actual music instead of polysyllabic monotone mumble, is his best effort since the debut. — D.M.

RICK WAKEMAN

★ ★ ★ Six Wives of Henry VIII / A&M (1973)
★ ★ ★ Journey to the Center of the Earth / A&M (1974)
★ ★ Myths and Legends of King Arthur / A&M (1975)
★ ★ No Earthly Connection / A&M (1976)
★ ★ White Rock / A&M (1977) ¶
★ ★ Rick Wakeman's Criminal Record / A&M (1977)
★ ★ Rhapsodies / A&M (1979)

Classically trained ex-Strawbs and Yes keyboardist lets his imagination run wild on these bloated solo efforts full of wholesale clips from his favorite composers. Wakeman's attempt at making program music for the various themes the albums are supposed to represent is ludicrous, but enough decent playing surfaces through the smoke screen to save this stuff from the recycling vat. His first solo outing, *Six Wives,* remains Wakeman's best. — J.S.

WENDY WALDMAN

★ ★ ★ ★ Love Has Got Me / War. (1973) ¶
★ ★ Gypsy Symphony / War. (1974) ¶
★ ★ Wendy Waldman / War. (1975) ¶
★ ★ Main Refrain / War. (1976)
★ ★ ★ ★ Strange Company / War. (1978) ¶

Los Angeles–based singer/songwriter made a formidable debut at age twenty-two with *Love Has Got Me,* a gorgeous collection of songs filled with romantic wanderlust. Working in styles that ranged from acoustic folk to Gershwin-esque torch, Waldman exhibited the writing potential of a young Laura Nyro or Joni Mitchell. But the record bombed, and subsequent albums were relatively spotty. Finally, on *Strange Company,* Waldman moved into the L.A. pop-rock mainstream without sacrificing her unusually sophisticated harmonic style. Few contemporary writers have evoked the will to love with such an intense mixture of spirituality and earthiness. — S.H.

BOBBI WALKER

★ ★ ★ Diamond in the Rough / Casa. (NA)
Better-than-average disco chanteuse.
— D.M.

JERRY JEFF WALKER

★ ★ ★ Viva Terlingua / MCA (1973)
★ ★ ★ Jerry Jeff Walker / MCA (1973) ¶
★ ★ ★ ★ Walker's Collectibles / MCA (1974)
★ ★ ★ Ridin' High / MCA (1975)
★ ★ ★ ★ It's a Good Night for Singin' / MCA (1976)
★ ★ ★ A Man Must Carry On / MCA (1977)
★ ★ ★ Contrary to Ordinary / MCA (1978)
★ ★ ★ Jerry Jeff / Elek. (1978)
★ ★ ★ Too Old to Change / Elek. (1979)
★ ★ ★ ★ Best of Jerry Jeff Walker / MCA (1980)
★ ★ ★ Reunion / South Coast (1981)

Walker's best-known song is "Mr. Bojangles," a 1970 hit for the Nitty Gritty Dirt Band. Associated with the Austin, Texas, outlaw country scene, his band—The Lost Gonzos—is perhaps the best in the genre. His records tend to sound too similar, and they have a tendency toward hippie sentimentalism and sanctimoniousness. But at his best he is a wryly humorous and moving performer, worth hearing by country-rock buffs. — D.M.

JIMMIE (J.J) WALKER

★ Dyn-O-Mite / Bud. (1975) ¶
A young black comic whose stage persona is quite different from the sunny, sassy charac-

ter portrayed on TV's *Good Times,* the role
that made his club career commercially viable. He spins out already dated one-liners
about black style. — K.T.

JUNIOR WALKER AND THE ALL STARS

★ ★ ★ ★ Shotgun / Pick. (1965) ¶
★ ★ ★ ★ Greatest Hits / Soul (1969)
★ ★ ★ ★ ★ Anthology / Mo. (1974)
★ Whopper Bopper Show Stopper / Soul
 (1976) ¶
★ Smooth / Soul (1978)
★ Back Street Boogie / Whit. (1979)
★ ★ ★ ★ Superstar Series, Vol. 5 / Mo.
 (1981)

Even in his salad days, Junior Walker was a
soul-music anomaly. As a member of the
mid-Sixties Motown stable, Walker managed
a steady stream of hot party hits ("Shotgun," "I'm a Roadrunner") using a honking
saxophone style that had its roots in late-
Forties and early-Fifties R&B. Walker's
voice and saxophone shared a similar tone:
both gruff and ragged with an appealing affability. Though his early Motown hits resembled the records of his label counterparts
only in the velocity of the band tracks, by
the late Sixties, Walker was funneled into
more muted and produced settings. With increased emphasis on vocals and more lyrical
saxophone solos, Walker maintained his popularity with ballad and midtempo hits like
"What Does It Take (To Win Your Love for
Me)."

After a commercial decline and a recording absence of several years, Walker was resurrected by Motown in the mid-Seventies,
when party hits (as a part of disco) became
a black pop staple again. *Whopper Bopper,
Smooth,* and *Back Street Boogie* are results
of that era, but the best of the comeback
LPs, *Hot Shot* (produced by Brian Holland
and emphasizing Walker's gruffer side), is
out of print. — J.MC.

SAMMY WALKER

★ Song for Patty / Folk. (1975)
★ Blue Ridge Mountain Skyline / War.
 (1978) ¶

Walker was originally presented to the world
under the aegis of the late Phil Ochs as yet
another "new Bob Dylan." But in Walker's
hand, Dylan's influence became a matter of
studied mannerism, too crude for belief.
Rather than extending the styles Dylan originated, Walker simply mimics Dylan's style,
with all its many limitations. The result is
something worse than mediocre—it's as insulting as unintentional parody gets. — D.M.

T-BONE WALKER

★ ★ ★ ★ The Truth / Bruns. (1968)
★ ★ ★ I Want a Little Girl / Delmark
 (1973)
★ ★ ★ ★ T.B. Blues / Atl. (1975), Fr. imp.
★ ★ ★ ★ ★ T-Bone Walker / Blue N. (1975)
★ ★ ★ Stormy Monday Blues / Charly
 (1978), Br. imp.
★ ★ ★ ★ T. Bone Jumps Again / Charly
 (1980), imp.
★ ★ ★ Feeling the Blues / Black and Blue
 (NA)
★ ★ ★ Well Done / Home C. (NA)

T-Bone Walker was the most influential of
the Texas blues guitarists, and his style can
be heard in B. B. King, Eric Clapton, Albert
King, Buddy Guy, Albert Collins, Freddie
King and dozens of others. When he began
recording in the Thirties, the blues was a
rural and acoustic genre, but by the time he
died in 1975, he'd helped turn it into something electric, faster, jazzier and much more
modern.

Walker played with both large jazz orchestras and on his own, his voice and electric
guitar (which he helped pioneer) accompanied by a brass section. In the end, he ranks
with Muddy Waters and B. B. King, Robert
Johnson and Blind Lemon Jefferson, and
Charlie Patton as one of the kings of blues;
today, his influence is evident everywhere.
The Blue Note collection is truly his best
music, with excellent liner notes and discographical information compiled by Pete
Welding. The Atlantic and Charly sets aren't
far behind, though. — D.M.

WALL OF VOODOO

★ Wall of Voodoo / IRS (1980)
★ Dark Continent / IRS (1981)

L.A. electronic music quintet makes self-
proclaimed "aural nightmare" music. Take it
from them and pass on this stuff. — J.S.

JAMES WALSH GYPSY BAND

★ ★ James Walsh Gypsy Band / RCA
 (1978)

Minnesota-based eight-piece group presents
an eclectic group of songs ranging from folk
ballads to acid-rock throwbacks to smooth,
Chicago-style big band rock. Guitarist Jim
Behringer flashes a few good moments.
— J.S.

JOE WALSH

★ ★ ★ The Smoker You Drink, the Player
 You Get / MCA (1973)
★ ★ ★ So What? / MCA (1974)
★ You Can't Argue with a Sick Mind /
 MCA (1976)

★ ★ ★ **But Seriously Folks . . . / Asy.**
(1978)
★ ★ ★ **The Best of Joe Walsh / MCA**
(1978)
★ ★ **There Goes the Neighborhood / Asy.**
(1981)
The former James Gang lead guitarist takes
his band, Barnstorm, through a collection of
fiery rockers and cool, sweaty neofunk instrumentals on the MCA albums, originally
put out on ABC. The classic is "Rocky
Mountain Way" from *The Smoker. Sick
Mind* is a live album made while Barnstorm
was on the wane. *But Seriously Folks* is a riotous disc, made after Walsh joined the Eagles; it contains his 1978 hit single, "Life's
Been Good," which may be the most important statement on rock stardom anyone has
made in the late Seventies. — J.S.

DEXTER WANSEL
★ ★ **Life on Mars / Phil. (1976)**
★ ★ **What the World Is Coming To / Phil.**
(1977)
★ ★ **Voyager / Phil. (1978)**
★ ★ **Time Is Slipping Away / Phil. (1979)**
★ ★ **Individuals / Col. (NA)**
Gamble-Huff arranger/keyboardist Wansel's
solo albums with the house band for that
team's Philadelphia International label are
somewhat better-than-average instrumental
sets, highlighted by Wansel's accomplished
synthesizer work and the usual funk wallpaper that characterizes such projects. — J.S.

WAR
★ ★ ★ **All Day Music / U.A. (1971)**
★ ★ ★ ★ **The World Is a Ghetto / U.A.**
(1972)
★ ★ ★ **Deliver the Word / U.A. (1973)**
★ ★ **War Live / U.A. (1974)**
★ ★ ★ ★ **Why Can't We Be Friends / U.A.**
(1975)
★ ★ ★ ★ **War's Greatest Hits / U.A.**
(1976)
★ ★ **Love Is All Around / ABC (1976)**
★ ★ ★ **Platinum Jazz / Blue N. (1977)**
★ ★ **Galaxy / MCA (1977)**
★ ★ ★ **Youngblood / U.A. (1978)**
★ ★ ★ **Music Band / MCA (1979)**
★ ★ ★ **Music Band 2 / MCA (1980)**
War is perhaps the most underrated black
band of the Seventies; its best songs outstrip
even the Commodores and the Isley Brothers
for sheer funk power.
  The septet began recording with Eric Bur-
don (of the Animals) in 1970 and immedi-
ately scored with "Spill the Wine." By 1971,
Burdon was exhausted but the band carried
on. "All Day Music," the title song of their

second album, was a 1971 hit and established their lean style: creaking electric
backup underneath powerful vocal shouts.
But it was the second hit, "Slippin' into
Darkness," that signified War's ability to
capture the mood of its time. That song, like
"The World Is a Ghetto," its brilliant followup, is nothing less than haunting.
  The ABC album is recycled Burdon tracks
and mediocre, as is the first MCA album.
But the United Artists albums are of uniformly high quality, stinging and angry at
their peaks, with a throbbing beat that qualifies them as a variety of disco but without
any of the mechanistic menace normally associated with that genre. — D.M.

ANITA WARD
★ ★ **Songs of Love / Juana (1979)**
★ **Sweet Surrender / Juana (1980)**
"Ring My Bell" was as sweet as any pop-
dance hit of its year, harkening back to the
TK organization's beginnings with George
McRae's "Rock Your Baby." But Ward was
never able to sustain that much interest over
a full album side—seek out the twelve-inch
single instead. — D.M.

THE WARD SINGERS
★ ★ **I Feel the Holy Spirit / Savoy (NA)**
★ ★ ★ ★ **Lord, Touch Me / Savoy (NA)**
★ ★ ★ **Meeting Tonight / Savoy (NA)**
★ ★ ★ **Packing Up / Savoy (NA)**
★ ★ ★ **Surely God Is Able / Savoy (NA)**
★ ★ ★ **That Old Landmark / Savoy (NA)**
★ ★ ★ ★ ★ **The Best of the Famous Ward**
  Singers of Philadelphia, Pennsylvania /
  Savoy (1978)
Founded by mother Gertrude Ward and perpetuated by daughter Clara, the Ward Singers are best known for the pop-gospel songs
they've performed for white nightclub audiences from L.A. and Vegas to New York
and Miami. Recordings of that era, primarily
under the tutelage of Clara, aren't even considered here, for they are shameless self-
exploitation, giving the white folks what they
want to hear, whereas the earlier Ward
groups were among the best and most moving gospel ever had to offer.
  Clara's influence is everywhere in soul
music; Aretha Franklin's first recordings
were unabashed exact copies of Clara's piano
and singing. The group also had other lead
singers that were easily Clara's equal, most
notably the incandescent Marion Williams.
The Wards were the first gospel group to
utilize multiple lead singers, and one assumes that's because they simply had too
many good voices to waste all but one on

backgrounds and harmonies. (Others were Kitty Parham, Frances Steadman, Martha Bass, Willa Ward.) Mother Gertrude, Clara and Marion, in particular, all boasted range and pitch better heard than described, and their phrasing was dramatic even by gospel standards.

Touch Me is the album that best captures the group's overall scope and sense of dynamics, yet brilliant performances are scattered throughout the other albums. Williams' two best-loved songs ("Surely God Is Able" and "Packing Up") each head an LP, for example. And the *Meeting* album is a fascinating and well-thought-out document, with one side simulating an old campground meeting, the songs linked together by a theme chorus that weaves through the whole side.

Since the first edition, Savoy has issued *The Best of* compilation, which features most of the group's finest material, especially that with the incandescent Williams. — J.MO.

LEON WARE
★ **Inside Is Love / Fab. (1979)**
★ **Musical Massage / Gor. (1980)**
★ **Rockin' You Eternally / Elek. (1981)**
Session bassist Ware's solo repertoire is unusual only because he proves himself a mediocre singer as well as an unimaginative band leader and composer. Occasional "fusion" touches do little to alleviate the basic banality of his pop-soul love songs; if there's anything to admire here, it's Ware's continuing ability to convince record companies that he deserves a shot. — D.M.

JENNIFER WARNES
★ ★ ★ **Jennifer Warnes / Ari. (1977)**
★ ★ ★ **Shot through the Heart / Ari. (1979)** ¶
An excellent Los Angeles-based singer in the Linda Ronstadt mold, Warnes has released two very careful and tasteful albums marked by a rare discrimination in choice of intelligent country-pop songs. "Right Time of the Night," and "Up Where We Belong," her 1982 duet with Joe Cocker from the first album, were sizable hits. — S.H.

PAUL WARREN AND EXPLORER
★ ★ **One of the Kids / RSO (1980)**
Paul Warren played guitar for Ray Manzarek's Nite City; as a reward he got his own band and this album. The cover art's great, the album ain't. Back to the minors. — I.R.

DIONNE WARWICK
★ ★ ★ **Dionne / War. (1972)** ¶
★ ★ ★ **Just Being Myself / War. (1973)** ¶
★ ★ ★ **Then Came You / War. (1975)** ¶
★ ★ ★ **Track of the Cat / War. (1975)** ¶
★ ★ ★ **Only Love Can Break a Heart / Musi. (1977)** ¶
★ ★ ★ **Love at First Sight / War. (1977)** ¶
★ ★ **Dionne / Ari. (1979)**
★ ★ **No Night So Long / Ari. (1980)**
★ ★ **Hot Live and Otherwise / Ari. (1981)**
★ ★ **Friends in Love / Ari. (1982)**
★ ★ ★ ★ ★ **Dionne Warwick: More Greatest Hits / Sp. (NA)** ¶
★ ★ ★ ★ **Dionne Warwick Sings Her Very Best / Sp. (NA)** ¶
★ ★ ★ ★ **Dionne Warwick Sings One Hit After Another / Sp. (NA)** ¶
★ ★ ★ ★ **The Golden Voice of Dionne Warwick / Sp. (NA)** ¶
Dionne Warwick was something of an anomaly in Sixties pop music. She was black, yet not an R&B singer, though she wasn't a straight pop interpreter like Nancy Wilson, either. Instead, Warwick walked a thin line between the genres, and the result, thanks to her long collaboration with producer/writers Burt Bacharach and Hal David, was an impressive stream of hit records. The string began in 1962 with "Don't Make Me Over," continuing with "Anyone Who Had a Heart," "Walk On By," "You'll Never Get to Heaven," "Who Can I Turn To," "Message to Michael," "Trains and Boats and Planes," "I Just Don't Know What to Do with Myself" and "Alfie," among many others, before it petered out in 1971 with "Make It Easy on Yourself." This is among the best romantic music ever made, and Warwick's best singles as collected on the various Springboard repackages (the originals were on Scepter) still make fine listening. But when she began recording for Warner Bros. in 1972, she lost her touch, and except for "Then Came You," a single recorded with the Spinners in 1976, she's never quite regained it, despite a succession of labels, approaches and producers. — D.M.

WAS (NOT WAS)
★ ★ **Was (Not Was) / Ze/Is. (1981)**
"Out Come the Freaks" was genuinely worthwhile bizarro soul from the Hollywood/Motown beatnik duo. But that's not on the album, which is pretentious honky funk in the early-Eighties art-rock mold. — D.M.

WASHBOARD SAM
★ ★ ★ ★ **Washboard Sam / RCA (1971)**
★ ★ ★ ★ **Washboard Sam / Blues C. (NA)**
Vintage Thirties and Forties sides from charming, very popular prewar Chicago

bluesman, who was often accompanied by Big Bill Broonzy among others. — D.M.

LALOMIE WASHBURN
★ ★ **My Music Is Hot** / Parach. (1977)
Pleasant disco singer works well within disco conventions without ever suggesting the ability or inclination to transcend or transmute them. — D.M.

GENO WASHINGTON
★ **That's Why Hollywood Loves Me** / DJM (1979)
This isn't the Geno who had a minor U.S. hit with "Gino Is a Coward," back before the Beatles; this is the one who was the dance darling of the original London Mods, England's version of a swinging soul man. Isolated in the U.K., that's how Geno must have seemed twenty years ago. Unfortunately, he's asked here to compete as a recording artist with the real item—and he falls far short. Anglophiles are advised to steer clear, for fear of having basic illusions smashed to smithereens. — D.M.

WATER AND POWER
★ ★ ★ **Water and Power** / Fan. (NA) ¶
Better-than-average vocal trio's offering is slickly produced and well written and performed R&B. Nothing really stands out, which is the only thing keeping this from being a spectacular debut. — J.S.

MUDDY WATERS
★ ★ ★ ★ **Muddy Waters at Newport** / Chess (1960), Fr. imp.
★ ★ ★ **Muddy Waters at Newport, 1960** / Chess (1960)
★ ★ ★ **Fathers and Son** / Chess (1962), Fr. imp.
★ ★ ★ ★ **Folk Singer** / Chess (1964)
★ **Muddy, Brass and the Blues** / Chess (1966)
★ ★ ★ ★ **The Real Folk Blues** / Chess (1966), Fr. imp.
★ ★ ★ ★ ★ **Sail On** / Chess (1969)
★ ★ ★ ★ **They Call Me Muddy Waters** / Chess (1970)
★ ★ ★ **Muddy Waters Live** / Chess (1971)
★ ★ ★ ★ **Good News** / Syndicate Chapter (1971), Br. imp.
★ ★ ★ ★ ★ **McKinley Morganfield** / Chess (1971)
★ ★ ★ ★ ★ **Back in the Early Days** / Syndicate Chapter (1971), Br. imp.
★ ★ ★ ★ **The London Muddy Waters Sessions** / Chess (1972)
★ ★ ★ ★ **Can't Get No Grindin'** / Chess (1973)

★ ★ **Mud in Your Ear** / Musi. (1973)
★ ★ ★ **Unk in Funk** / Chess (1974)
★ ★ ★ **Muddy Waters at Woodstock** / Chess (1975)
★ ★ ★ **After the Rain** / Chess (1977)
■ **Electric Mud** / Chess (1977), Fr. imp.
★ ★ ★ ★ **Hard Again** / Blue S. (1977)
★ ★ ★ ★ **Muddy Waters** / Chess (1977), Fr. imp.
★ ★ ★ **I'm Ready** / Blue S. (1978)
★ ★ ★ **Muddy "Mississippi" Waters, Live** / Blue S. (1977)
★ ★ ★ ★ **Blues Roots, Vol. 2** / Chess (1982), Ger. imp.
★ ★ ★ ★ **Rolling Stone** / Chess (1982)
★ ★ ★ ★ ★ **Chess Masters** / Chess (1982), Br. imp.
★ ★ ★ ★ ★ **Chess Masters, Vol. 2** / Chess (1982), Br. imp.
★ ★ ★ ★ **More Real Folk Blues** / Chess (NA), Fr. imp.

The first of the great Chicago bluesmen. Waters grew up on a Mississippi plantation (as McKinley Morganfield), where he made some field recordings during World War II. In the mid-Forties he arrived in Chicago, and in 1948 he burst on the city's blues scene.

Through the years, he became widely hailed as one of America's great musical resources. Among Chicago bluesmen, only Howlin' Wolf could match Waters for vision, authority and dignity. Because he was also a formidable bandleader, Waters would appear to have a slight edge as the more influential of the two, but their rivalry was legendary.

From Waters' bands came a host of blues stars: Otis Spann, Little Walter, Junior Wells, Fred Below, Walter Horton, Jimmy Rogers, James Cotton, Leroy Foster and Buddy Guy, among many others. And from his guitar, voice and harp came a flow of classic blues songs: "Hoochie Coochie Man," "Mannish Boy," "Got My Mojo Workin'," "Rollin' Stone" and "You Shook Me" are only some of the more famous numbers Waters either wrote or popularized. Waters was beloved and venerated not just in Chicago's blues community, but also by the folk revivalists of the late Fifties and early Sixties, and by the white rock musicians, particularly English ones, of the Sixties: the Rolling Stones, of course, named themselves after his great song.

Waters made his greatest music for Chess; the cream of it is collected on the two-disc *McKinley Morganfield*. More recently, Waters recorded a series of LPs for the Blue Sky label, produced by Johnny Winter, that feature a number of his former sideman (no-

tably Cotton and Rogers) and both old songs and new ones. Through his sixties, Muddy Waters remained as vital as men twenty years younger. He died in May 1983.
— D.M.

DOC WATSON
★ ★ ★ ★ **Doc Watson and Son** / Van. (1965)
★ ★ **Doc Watson** / Van. (1966)
★ ★ **Home Again!** / Van. (1967)
★ ★ ★ ★ **Southbound** / Van. (1967)
★ **Good Deal! (In Nashville)** / Van. (1968)
★ ★ **Doc Watson on Stage** / Van. (1970)
★ ★ **The Essential Doc Watson** / Van. (1973)
★ ★ ★ **Memories** / U.A. (1975)
★ **Doc and the Boys** / U.A. (1976)
★ ★ ★ **Watson Family** / Folk. (NA)
Doc Watson is frequently heralded as the best flat-picking guitarist in the country. It is not simply the breakneck speed at which he is capable of playing, but rather that every tune comes from deep within him, growing out of the Carter Family/Clarence Ashley/Jimmie Rodgers traditions on which he was raised.

Watson came to national prominence during the early Sixties, playing the Newport Folk Festival as well as clubs and concerts in Los Angeles, New York and all points between. Although his repertoire—in number of songs—seems endless, Doc has generally limited himself to items within the country traditions mentioned above. His occasional forays into more contemporary songs (other than original compositions) have rarely been successful. Rhythm sections and other extraneous instruments take too much away from Doc's own playing.

Similarly, his best recorded work has featured himself solo or with his son Merle or guitarist John Pilla and perhaps a string bass. Thus *Doc Watson and Son* and *Southbound,* though among his earliest sets for Vanguard (1966 and 1967, respectively), remain the most representative of his playing. Doc's vocals have become surer over the years, and the flash of his flat-picking has somehow mellowed without losing its cutting edge. But the repertoire on each is a good cross section of the types of songs Doc performs best—from "Deep River Blues" to "Tennessee Stud" to "Little Darling Pal of Mine."

On Stage and *Essential* are both live sets—no date on the former, the latter emanating from Doc's Newport appearances in 1963 and 1964. Other than the applause, however, they have nothing on *Southbound* or *Doc Watson and Son.*

Memories is an interesting concept album put together by Merle, reflecting the traditional roots of Doc's music and, in the case of "You Don't Know My Mind Blues," accounting for a certain boomerang effect: "Our arrangement of this old Bar-B-Q Bob tune," writes Merle on the inner sleeve, "shows the Allman Brothers' influence in our blues." Merle was most assuredly smiling when he wrote those words. Once again, though, the rhythm section (as on *Good Deal!*) is intrusive rather than supportive.

As for the remaining albums in the catalogue, Doc couldn't make a *bad* album if he tried. It's more a matter of the similarity in the kinds of tunes and the occasional re-recordings of favorites making them somewhat redundant. His impact on people ranging from John Herald (who played on *Doc Watson*) to the Allmans, however, is undisputed. And his ability to make tradition breathe is unequaled. — I.M.

JOHNNY GUITAR WATSON
★ ★ ★ **Listen** / Fan. (1973)
★ ★ ★ **I Don't Want to Be a Lone Ranger** / Fan. (1975)
★ ★ ★ **Ain't That a Bitch** / DJM (1976)
★ ★ ★ **A Real Mother for Ya** / DJM (1977)
★ ★ ★ **Funk beyond the Call of Duty** / DJM (1977)
★ ★ ★ **Gangster of Love** / Power (1977) ¶
★ ★ ★ **Giant** / DJM (1978)
★ ★ ★ **What the Hell Is This?** / DJM (1979)
★ ★ ★ **Love Jones** / DJM (1980)
★ ★ ★ **Johnny Guitar Watson and the Family Clone** / DJM (1981)
★ ★ ★ **That's What Time It Is** / Atl. (1981)
★ ★ ★ **Very Best of Johnny Guitar Watson** / MCA (NA)
★ ★ **I Cried for You** / Cadet (NA) ¶
After a recording career that included frantic B. B. King–styled guitar blues, soul duets with Larry Williams and cocktail blues piano *(I Cried),* Johnny Guitar Watson emerged on Fantasy in the mid-Seventies with a unique concoction of blues, funk and middle-class soul. Like Junior Walker, Watson has a matching vocal and instrumental tone: lean and sandpaper grainy. To his credit, Watson uses a deft, small band on his records, avoiding studio overkill. His best songs ("I Don't Want to Be a Lone Ranger," "Real Mother") are either tongue-in-cheek or just plain silly, and all the recent albums are infused with a humor that, while neither profound nor transcendent, makes them just plain fun.
— J.MC.

WAX
★ ★ Wax Attack / RCA (1980) ¶
★ ★ Do You Believe in Magic / RCA (1981)
Disco-harmony competence. — D.M.

THE WEAVERS
★ ★ ★ ★ ★ The Weavers at Carnegie Hall /
Van. (1961)
★ ★ Reunion at Carnegie Hall, 1963 / Van.
(1963) ¶
★ The Weavers' Reunion, Part Two / Van.
(1965) ¶
★ The Weavers' Songbook / Van. (1967)
★ ★ The Weavers' Greatest Hits / Van.
(1971)
★ ★ ★ Best of the Weavers / MCA (NA)
For anyone interested in the roots of the folk
revival of the Fifties and Sixties, the Weavers
are the group to hear. The original incarnation—Pete Seeger, Ronnie Gilbert, Lee Hays
and Fred Hellerman—was an outgrowth of
the Almanac Singers of the Forties. The
songs were carefully arranged for multipart
harmony and the performances were sparked
by spiritual energy. Though Erik Darling,
the first replacement for Seeger when the latter set out on his own, was an able banjoist
and singer, it is clear today that Seeger provided the intangible element that made the
Weavers hitmakers ("Goodnight Irene," "On
Top of Old Smokey," both for Decca in 1950).
  The original Carnegie Hall concert LP
stands as testimony to the sharp image cut
by the quartet. It is one of the few recordings from that era that still holds tremendous emotional power. Recorded Christmas
Eve, 1955, the renditions of "Kisses Sweeter
Than Wine," "Rock Island Line" and
"Goodnight Irene" (there are twenty songs
altogether) are definitive in the context of a
commercial folk idiom that didn't betray its
origins.
  The reunion LPs feature the original quartet plus Darling, Bernie Krause and Frank
Hamilton (also members at various times).
They were recorded in 1963. Seeger leads a
singalong on Tom Paxton's "Ramblin' Boy,"
and "San Francisco Bay Blues" and
"Guantanamera" are also added to the repertoire. But the enlarged ensemble doesn't always adapt to the highly structured arrangements.
  Greatest Hits consists of live takes with
the original members. Poor in sound quality,
the two studio LPs lack the enthusiasm of
the live ones. — I.M.

JIMMY WEBB
★ ★ ★ Land's End / Asy. (1974)
★ ★ ★ El Mirage / Atl. (1977) ¶

Major Sixties songwriter ("By the Time I
Get to Phoenix," "Wichita Lineman," "Mac-
Arthur Park," "Up, Up and Away," "Didn't
We," etc.) is a quirky but expressive inter-
preter of his own ultra-romantic material.
His three out-of-print Reprise albums, espe-
cially Letters, are also worth scouting out.
  — S.H.

WE FIVE
★ ★ You Were on My Mind / A&M (1965)
★ Take Each Day as It Comes / A.V.I.
(1977)
Australian folk-rock singers who had a hit
with the title cut for the A&M LP in the
mid-Sixties, an Ian and Sylvia song that was
arranged in a way that gave early indication
of how Tin Pan Alley would co-opt the supposedly pristine American folk-rock movement. This is We Five's sole interest almost
two decades later, and it is more sociopolitical than musical. — D.M.

BOB WEIR
★ ★ ★ Ace / War. (1972) ¶
★ ★ ★ Heaven Help the Fool / Ari. (1978)
Grateful Dead lead singer and rhythm guitarist Weir was the first member of that
band to release a solo album. Ace was more
of a Grateful Dead album than any of the
band's other solo offshoots, featuring the
Dead as players and including a number of
songs (particularly "Playing in the Band"
and "One More Saturday Night") that became concert standards for the group.
  Heaven Help the Fool was Weir's attempt
to break away from the Grateful Dead
image. The album was recorded with a
harder-edged band and presents Weir as a
Boz Scaggs–style crooner. The title track,
"Bombs Away" and "Salt Lake City" are
the album's stand-outs. — J.S.

TIM WEISBERG
★ ★ ★ Tim Weisberg / A&M (1971)
★ Hurtwood Edge / A&M (1972)
★ ★ Dreamspeaker / A&M (1973)
★ ★ Tim Weisberg 4 / A&M (1974)
★ ★ Listen to the City / A&M (1975)
★ ★ Live at Last / A&M (1976)
★ ★ Tim Weisberg Band / U.A. (1977)
★ ★ Rotations / U.A. (1978)
★ Party of One / MCA (1980)
★ Travelin' Light / MCA (NA)
★ Nadia's Theme / A&M (NA)
This talented but mellow flutist insists on
turning jazz chops and a rock background
into undifferentiated Muzak mush. He
should play his concerts in supermarkets.
  — J.S.

TIM WEISBERG AND DAN FOGELBURG
★ ★ **Twin Sons of Different Mothers / Epic (1978)**

Smooth, post-rock cocktail-lounge Muzak made a big hit in 1978. Whatever blandness Fogelburg lacks, Weisberg makes up for in spades. The combination ought to be marketed as an insomnia cure. — D.M.

BOB WELCH
★ ★ ★ **French Kiss / Cap. (1977)**
★ ★ **Three Hearts / Cap. (1979)**
★ **Other One / Cap. (1979)**
★ **Man Overboard / Cap. (1980)**
★ **Bob Welch / RCA (1981)**

Welch was a key member of Fleetwood Mac in the years immediately preceding that band's sudden rise to fame. His presence in the group yielded mixed results—Welch is a good guitarist and has written some very good songs, but he never seemed to be able to put it all together. When he left Fleetwood Mac and formed Paris, a boring power trio, it seemed he'd succumbed to his own worst instincts.

French Kiss, however, has its moments. Half the songs are pretty good, Welch handled most of the difficult production and arrangement tasks himself with good results, and some of the Fleetwood Mac crew joined up to remake Welch's best song with that band, "Sentimental Lady" (originally on Mac's *Bare Trees*). Fittingly enough, Welch's version became a substantial hit single this time around. Followup releases have been ineffectual. — J.S.

CORY WELLS
★ **Touch Me / A&M (1978)** ¶
★ **Ahead of the Storm / A&M (NA)**

Former Three Dog Night lead singer sounds forlorn without the rest of the pack. Strained and soulless. — D.M.

JUNIOR WELLS
★ ★ ★ ★ ★ **Hoodoo Man Blues / Del. (1965)**
★ ★ ★ ★ **It's My Life, Baby / Van. (1966)**
★ ★ ★ **Comin' at You / Van. (1968)**
★ ★ ★ **Southside Blues Jam / Del. (1970)**
★ ★ ★ **In My Younger Days / Red L. (1971), Br. imp.**
★ ★ ★ **On Tap / Del. (1974)**
★ ★ ★ ★ **Blues Hit Big Town / Del. (1977)**
★ ★ ★ **Pleading the Blues / Isabel (1980), imp.**
★ ★ ★ ★ **Messing with the Blues / P-Vine (NA), Jap. imp.**

Junior Wells replaced Little Walter on harmonica in Muddy Waters' influential Chicago blues band during 1954, then did a stint in the Army. He really hit his stride as a recording artist with *Hoodoo Man Blues* in 1965, one of the best Chicago blues recordings. Wells is a master showman, and his performances with guitarist Buddy Guy have been among the best received by the rock audience. But his style is sometimes a deterrent here: he is too flashy for some of the blues' more stately traditions. When held in check, as on the *Hoodoo Man* session and the four-star performances above, he is an excellent harmonica stylist and a better-than-average vocalist as well. — D.M.

KITTY WELLS
★ ★ ★ **Dust on the Bible / MCA (1959)**
★ ★ ★ ★ **Kitty Wells Story / MCA (1963)**
★ ★ ★ **Kitty Wells' Greatest Hits / MCA (1968)**
★ ★ ★ **Country Heart / Voc. (1969)**
★ ★ ★ **Best of Kitty Wells / Exact (1980)**
★ ★ **Kitty Wells / RCA (NA)**

From 1952 straight through the Sixties, Kitty Wells was the almost undisputed queen of country music. She earned her stature with "It Wasn't God Who Made Honky Tonk Angels," continued it with a series of hits including "Making Believe," "One by One" and "I Can't Stop Loving You" in the Fifties, and sustained it in the Sixties with "Day into Night," "Unloved Unwanted" and "Will Your Lawyer Talk to God." The best of her music is collected on *Story.* — D.M.

MARY WELLS
★ ★ **Bye Bye Baby / Mo. (1961)**
★ ★ ★ **Two Lovers / Mo. (1962)**
★ ★ ★ ★ **Mary Wells' Greatest Hits / Mo. (1963)**
★ ★ ★ **My Guy / Mo. (1964)**
★ ★ **In and Out of Love / Epic (NA)**

One of Motown's early teen queens, Wells had a first-rate series of early-Sixties hit singles: "My Guy," "The One Who Really Loves You," "Two Lovers" and "You Beat Me to the Punch." All of them would have been sultry if her breathlessness hadn't rendered them adolescently harmless. They're still fun to listen to, though, and the *Greatest Hits* is one of Motown's better collections. — D.M.

DAVID WERNER
★ **Imagination Quota / RCA (1975)** ¶
■ **David Werner / Epic (1979)**

Midwestern glitter rock. — S.H.

HOWARD WERTH AND THE MOONBEAMS
★ ★ **King Brilliant / R. (1975)** ¶

When Elton John formed his own record

label in the mid-Seventies, he decided he needed a hard-rock band for its roster. This amalgam of Rolling Stones clichés was his solution. Which says more about Elton than Werth. — D.M.

FRED WESLEY
★ ★ ★ **A Blow for Me, A Toot to You /**
  Atco (1977) ¶
★ ★ ★ **Say Blow by Blow Backwards / Atl.**
  (NA)
Ex–James Brown trombonist and horn-section captain turns in a neat but direction-less solo work with a lot of funk riffing and some (but not enough) hot playing. — J.S.

WEST, BRUCE AND LAING
★ ★ **Why Dontcha / Col. (1972)**
★ ★ **Whatever Turns You On / Col.**
  (1973) ¶
★ ★ ★ **Live 'n' Kickin' / Col. (1974)** ¶
A grotesque attempt to revive Cream using the basest of retreads, Mountain, as a foun-dation. Leslie West's guitar playing is laugh-ably inept in comparison with Eric Clap-ton's, but as power trios go, the presence of Jack Bruce on bass helps this one approach respectability (only on the live record).
— J.S.

HEDY WEST
★ ★ ★ **Old Times and Hard Times / Folk-**
  Leg. (1967) ¶
Best known as the author of "500 Miles," West's repertoire here is descended from her Georgia family, including lyrics composed by her father, the poet-activist Don West. West was looked to by folk-revival singers and topical songwriters as a firsthand source of lore and information concerning the Appala-chian coal miners and their union struggles.
— I.M.

WET WILLIE
★ ★ **Wet Willie / Capri. (1971)** ¶
★ ★ ★ **Wet Willie II / Capri. (1972)** ¶
★ ★ ★ **Drippin' Wet / Capri. (1973)**
★ ★ ★ **Keep On Smilin' / Capri. (1974)** ¶
★ ★ ★ **Dixie Rock / Capri. (1975)** ¶
★ ★ ★ ★ **The Wetter the Better / Capri.**
  (1976) ¶
★ ★ ★ **Left Coast Live / Capri. (1977)** ¶
★ ★ ★ ★ **Manorisms / Epic (1978)**
★ ★ ★ **Wet Willie's Greatest Hits / Capri.**
  (1978) ¶
★ ★ **Which One's Willie? / Epic (1979)**
Rock & roll is chronically derivative, but no-where was this as obvious as during the South's rise to rock prominence after the All-man Brothers Band's breakthrough—nearly everybody seemed to be flogging the same

whipping post with a blues-rock style applied to the jamming sensibilities of hard, heavy-metal rockers like Cream. Soon enough, the wheat was separated from the chaff, and though a long career with Capricorn resulted in only minimal commercial success, Wet Willie proved itself one of the region's most vibrant and consistent bands.

Most other Southern bands seasoned their blues rock with country influences, but Wet Willie fired its music with hard-biting R&B. Though the band's debut album, *Wet Willie,* jelled into little more than a studied blue-print of the approach, with *II,* Willie could deliver credible covers of tunes like Otis Redding's "Shout Bamalama" alongside its own cookers like "Red Hot Chicken." The highly charged live album, *Drippin' Wet,* showed that the band's barroom approach effectively complemented the beer-swilling nature of its music. With his combination of a rocker's dynamics and a soul man's re-straint, Jimmy Hall became the best vocalist of the Southern school.

Mass acceptance almost came with the single success of "Keep On Smilin'," which added a thicker slice of gospel styling to Willie's synthesis. "Dixie Rock," the title tune of the LP that followed, pushed Wet Willie to another level—this was the most rocking tune they'd done, owing as much to British hard rock as to the Stax sound. Though this element never dominated, the stylistic addition pushed the band toward its best Capricorn work.

The Wetter the Better cooked everything up right—Ricky Hirsch's guitar was sharper than ever and new singer/keyboardist Mi-chael Duke contributed two stand-out rock-ers, "No, No, No" and "Teaser." The high-light, though, was "Everything That Cha Do (Will Come Back to You)," which found Hall's voice and Hirsch's guitar effortlessly binding the circular rhythms of this song about karma. *Left Coast Live,* the last album on which Hirsch appears (he left to join Gregg Allman), again effectively captured the band's dynamism and particularly shows Hirsch's growth during his tenure with the band.

Regrouping with a new contract at Epic (Jimmy Hall and Michael Duke remain prin-cipals), Wet Willie returned with *Manorisms.* It's the band's most heavily produced album (thanks to Gary Lyons), but the high gloss did nothing to diminish the rhythmic soul of "Make You Feel Love Again," the Spector-cum-Springsteen Wall of Sound of "Rain-man" and the homespun joy of "Streetcorner Serenade." But after some further personnel changes, the group ran out of steam with

Which One's Willie and soon sundered.
— J.B.M.

THE WHISPERS
★ ★ ★ **One for the Money** / Solar (1976) ¶
★ ★ ★ **Open Up Your Love** / Soul T. (1977)
★ ★ ★ **Headlights** / Solar (1978) ¶
★ ★ ★ **Whisper in Your Ear** / Solar (1979)
★ ★ ★ **Happy Holidays to You** / Solar (1979)
★ ★ ★ **This Kind of Lovin'** / Solar (1981)
★ ★ ★ **Imagination** / Solar (1980)
★ ★ ★ ★ **Best Of** / Solar (1982)

The initials of Solar Records, the label the Whispers record for, stand for Sound of Los Angeles, so it is not without coincidence that the group embodies the sound of Los Angeles soul. L.A. music as a rule reflects a normalization of the prevailing national style, and the Whispers are no exception. Their sound, an equal blend of vocal and production values (characteristic of R&B vocal group music) extends the lush, pop-soul sounds of the Gamble-Huff Philly school, without matching any of the latter's distinctive lyrics, melodies or vocal stylings. From the first album to the last, there is little difference here save for a bit more of a nod to funk. Pick any one of the above with which to mellow out at night. — A.F.

IAN WHITCOMB
★ **You Turn Me On!** / Tower (1965) ¶
★ ★ **Ian Whitcomb's Mod Mod Music Hall** / Tower (1966) ¶
★ **Yellow Underground** / Tower (1967) ¶
★ **Sock Me Some Rock** / Tower (1968) ¶
★ ★ **Under the Ragtime Moon** / U.A. (1972) ¶
★ ★ **Crooner Tunes** / Great N. (1976)
★ ★ **Ian Whitcomb's Red Hot Blue Heaven** / First Amer. (1977)
★ ★ **Ian Whitcomb: The Rock & Roll Years** / First Amer. (1979)
★ **Instrumentals** / First Amer. (1980)

A student of history at Trinity College in Dublin, young Ian Whitcomb became an overnight pop star completely by accident in 1965 when a novelty bopper called "You Turn Me On" (recorded as a joke) suddenly leapt into the Top Ten. The followup, a version of the blues "This Sporting Life," reportedly inspired Bob Dylan's producer Tom Wilson to try a similar piano-organ arrangement on "Like a Rolling Stone." There was, however, nothing inspirational about the corny Carnaby Street–pop filler of his debut album.

But Whitcomb was not really teen heartthrob material. His first musical love has always been Tin Pan Alley and its relations—British music hall, ragtime, the songs they don't seem to write anymore. And his records since have been faithful tributes to the music of the good old days, performed not with academic admiration but with the good humor of a true fan. *Red Hot Blue Heaven, Crooner Tunes* and *Under the Ragtime Moon* (produced by Neil Innes and regrettably out of print) are the best of the lot, although *The Rock & Roll Years* (which includes the single "You Turn Me On") is an engaging overview of Whitcomb's sideline rock efforts. The Tower stuff is long-deleted and *Instrumentals* is an ill-conceived album of ragtime piano covers of "Wooly Bully" and "Louie Louie." But worth seeking out is Whitcomb's English two-record compilation *After the Ball,* a collection of original pop songs from the turn of the century designed as a companion to his historical study of the music of the same name.
— D.F.

BARRY WHITE
★ ★ **I've Got So Much to Give** / 20th Cent. (1973)
★ ★ **Stone Gon'** / 20th Cent. (1973)
★ ★ **Rhapsody in White** / 20th Cent. (1974)
★ ★ **Can't Get Enough** / 20th Cent. (1974)
★ ★ **Barry White's Greatest Hits** / 20th Cent. (1975)
★ ★ **Is This Whatcha Want** / 20th Cent. (1976) ¶
★ ★ **Barry White Sings for Someone You Love** / 20th Cent. (1977)
★ ★ **The Man** / 20th Cent. (1978) ¶
★ ★ **The Message Is Love** / Unli. (1979)
★ **I Love to Sing the Songs I Sing** / 20th Cent. (1979)
★ **Sheet Music** / Unli. (1980)
★ **Best of Our Love** / Unli. (1981)
★ **Beware** / Unli. (1981)
★ ★ **Greatest Hits, Vol. 2** / 20th Cent. (1981)

White enjoyed a brief vogue in the mid-Seventies with a series of steamy seduction records in which he promised his baby virtually everything, in a way still acceptable to the FCC. He might have reigned forever as a black matinee idol, and held the title as king of smooch disco, had he not revealed himself to be the possessor of one of music's most corpulent frames. Somehow, the modern Rudolph Valentino shouldn't be overweight and wear a cluster of huge rings.

You pick from these records. They literally all sound the same: pleasant pop-funk riffs over which White can growl, the aural equivalent of static on your baby's telephone wire. — D.M.

BUKKA WHITE
★ ★ ★ **Sky Songs, Vol. 1** / Arhoo. (1965)
★ ★ ★ **Sky Songs, Vol. 2** / Arhoo. (1965)
★ ★ ★ **Big Daddy** / Bio. (1974)
★ ★ ★ **Mississippi Blues** / Tak. (NA)
White was one of the earliest delta country-blues musicians, roughly contemporaneous with the great Charlie Patton and even greater Robert Johnson. White lived longer, but his output wasn't quite as magnificent. Still, these recordings are an important source of delta styles, and White did have a powerful bottleneck style.
— D.M.

MICHAEL WHITE
★ ★ **X Factor** / Elek. (1978)
White is a talented, sometimes even inspiring electric jazz violinist. Producer George Duke is a far too commercial and lavish arranger. Guess who wins. — R.P.

WHITEFACE
★ **Whiteface** / Mer. (NA)
A truly loud and irritating heavy rock band. Not just loud and irritating like most, but *truly* loud and irritating. Need I say it again? — R.P.

WHITESNAKE
★ ★ ★ **Ready an' Willing** / Mirage (1980)
★ ★ ★ **Live . . . in the Heart of the City** / Mirage (1980)
★ ★ **Come an' Get It** / Mirage (1981)
Because three out of six Whitesnakers are Deep Purple alums—singer David Coverdale, drummer Ian Paice and keyboardist Jon Lord—you'd be right in assuming that Whitesnake carries a certain amount of the Deep Purple punch. Where the bands differ is in the use of that punch; Purple, particularly in the Richie Blackmore days, went straight for the gut in a show of bluster, while Whitesnake, thanks to Mickey Moody, uses more finesse to flatten the listener. By *Come an' Get It*, however, the winds of change had caught up with Whitesnake, rendering the band a breezy imitation of Foreigner. — J.D.C.

WHITE WITCH
★ **White Witch** / Capri. (1978)
★ ★ **Spiritual Greeting** / Capri. (1978)
Mid-Seventies Southern answer to Black Sabbath led by guitarist Buddy Richardson. The only thing this group had going for it was the fine production of Ron and Howard Albert at Miami's Criterion Recording Studios, on *Spiritual Greeting.* — J.S.

THE WHO
★ ★ ★ ★ ★ **The Who Sing My Generation** / MCA (1966)
★ ★ ★ ★ **Happy Jack** / MCA (1967)
★ ★ ★ **The Who Sell Out** / MCA (1967)
★ ★ **Magic Bus—The Who on Tour** / MCA (1968)
★ ★ ★ **Tommy** / MCA (1969)
★ ★ ★ ★ **The Who Live at Leeds** / MCA (1970)
★ ★ ★ ★ ★ **Who's Next** / MCA (1971)
★ ★ ★ ★ ★ **Meaty, Beaty, Big and Bouncy** / MCA (1971)
★ ★ ★ ★ **Quadrophenia** / MCA (1973)
★ ★ ★ ★ **Odds and Sods** / MCA (1974)
★ ★ ★ ★ **The Who by Numbers** / MCA (1975)
★ ★ ★ ★ **Who Are You** / MCA (1978)
The early Who albums present one of the most interesting problems posed in rock & roll history. The band was considered at the time to be much better in live performance than on record, yet these records transcend their flaws. *The Who Sing My Generation* (now available only in tandem with *Magic Bus*) is one of the most influential rock albums ever released. The generation of punk rockers takes its cue from this record. Roger Daltrey's singing is crude and the recording quality leaves a lot to be desired, but the energy of the record is unbelievable. Two songs, "My Generation" and "The Kids Are Alright," became anthems for the Mods in England yet went almost unnoticed in the U.S. Guitarist (and songwriter) Pete Townshend's feedback technique made "My Generation" and the instrumental "The Ox" sonic marvels of the time. Bassist John Entwistle, for whom the latter track was named, added subtly to the mayhem as drummer Keith Moon cascaded his rolls through it all at breakneck speed.

Happy Jack (now available only in tandem with *Sell Out*) presents better-conceptualized material, but it's less energetic than the first record. The title track became the Who's first American hit. Entwistle unveiled his exceptional songwriting ability and multi-instrumental prowess with "Boris the Spider" and "Whiskey Man." More importantly, the album includes a suite of songs, "A Quick One While He's Away," that Townshend referred to as a "mini-opera." In "A Quick One," Townshend worked out organizational ideas and musical themes he would later use in *Tommy.*

The Who Sell Out is a failed concept

album, but it's a brilliant failure. The idea was to re-create the ambiance of AM radio programming, fusing new Who songs with fake commercials written by Townshend. Side one pulls this off, climaxing with what may be the Who's most powerful single, "I Can See for Miles." The concept breaks down, however, on the second side. "Real," the last song on the album, is another mini-opera that anticipated *Tommy* directly, with a long instrumental break that was reproduced in *Tommy* as "Underture."

Magic Bus—The Who on Tour was a quickie package thrown together by MCA because *Tommy* was overdue. There are several good songs on the record, particularly "Magic Bus," "Pictures of Lily" and "Call Me Lightning," but this is really for collectors only. *Meaty, Beaty, Big and Bouncy* shows what the Who could really do with the singles anthology idea.

Tommy is Townshend's acknowledged masterpiece, the record that put the Who on the map. Using a few standard Who chord progressions as motifs, Townshend constructed a virtual theory of essential rock forms, running each progression through its possibilities. But the record was only a blueprint for what *Tommy* would become when the Who performed it live. The story line is a bit fractured, and it's further confused by the inclusion of two John Entwistle songs, but the band's instrumental work is exemplary, especially Moon's relentless drumming. "Pinball Wizard" became a huge hit single.

Live at Leeds gives an indication of what the Who was capable of in concert. It's a remarkably powerful, if diffuse, record, a good example of the kind of energy that the Who generates live. Side one lines up the killer combination of "Young Man Blues," "Substitute," "Summertime Blues" and "Shakin' All Over." The album was packaged as a mock bootleg and includes a lot of interesting scrapbook material, including Townshend's notes for "My Generation," the contract for the band's engagement at the Woodstock festival, a receipt for a case of smoke bombs and a poster advertising the band's early gigs at the Marquee Club in London.

Townshend's big problem at this point was trying to come up with a sequel to *Tommy.* He finally settled on a science fiction film project called *Life House,* which would include a live Who performance and expand the band's stage concept to include prerecorded tapes for backing rhythm. The project broke down in production, and the Who went into the studio to salvage what it could

of the wealth of material Townshend had written for it. When they finished, they had what may well be the finest rock record ever made.

Who's Next is so different from what the band had put out on record before that it sounds like it was recorded by a different group. For the first time the Who was able to capture the live energy of a concert in the studio, and the result was devastating. Glyn Johns engineered and deserves a lot of credit, but *Who's Next* is an individual triumph for each member of the band as well as a solid group effort. Some of Townshend's most beautiful songs are here—"Bargain," "Song Is Over," "Goin' Mobile" and "Won't Get Fooled Again." Entwistle's "My Wife" is his best song and a lot of people's favorite track on the record. Moon faced the difficult task of maintaining his abandoned drumming style while matching the rigid rhythmic structure of the backing tapes on "Baba O'Riley" and "Won't Get Fooled Again." The tapes added the promised technological edge to the band's sound, and Townshend's use of a guitar distortion device called an envelope follower on "Goin' Mobile" is amazing. But the final and most convincing triumph is Daltrey's. His singing had improved on *Tommy,* the first album on which he really came to life, and of course all his screaming blood and thunder was dutifully caught on *Live at Leeds.* Daltrey's singing on *Who's Next,* however, is stunning, and definitely one of the strongest rock vocal performances on record. His scream at the climax of "Won't Get Fooled Again" is a moment of pure rock transcendence.

Meaty, Beaty, Big and Bouncy is the album that proves what a great singles band the Who is. The British and American hits—"I Can't Explain," "The Kids Are Alright," "Happy Jack," "I Can See for Miles," "Pinball Wizard," "The Magic Bus" and "Substitute"—are all here, as well as gems like "I'm a Boy," "Anyway, Anyhow, Anywhere," "Boris the Spider," "Pictures of Lily" and "The Seeker."

Quadrophenia was Townshend's recapitulation of the Mod years in the form of a concept album. Here he took the use of electronic tapes to extend the limits of the Who's sound as far as he could, programing dense, symphonic textures throughout the record. As he did in *Tommy,* Townshend used motifs throughout the record, but this time in a much more complex formula. He also had Entwistle overdub entire horn sections. The project was so ambitious that it swamped the Who in its scope and ended up more like a Townshend solo project, with the Who as session musicians, than a full-fledged Who album. Daltrey's vocals are strained and often buried in the mix. Despite this flaw, *Quadrophenia* remains a rich and rewarding listening experience, especially on headphones. "The Real Me," "The Punk Meets the Godfather" and all of side three are classic Who performances.

Odds and Sods assembles a number of semi-legendary Who songs that never made it to albums. It's not what you'd call the band's most timeless work, but all of it is interesting and some of it is great. Entwistle's sardonic account of life on the road, "Postcard," leads off. Townshend's antismoking commercial written for the American Cancer Society, "Little Billy," is also here, as well as "Glow Girl," a part of the original idea for *Tommy,* and a trio of songs from the *Life House* project which were left off *Who's Next*: "Pure and Easy," "Naked Eye" and "Long Live Rock." Also included is the first single recorded by the band when they were called the High Numbers, "I'm the Face."

The Who by Numbers is the strangest and one of the most moving Who albums. Townshend's songs were written at a point when he was feeling depressed and frustrated, and deal directly with the problems faced by an aging rocker who wonders if he can still keep it together. "However Much I Booze," "How Many Friends" and "In a Hand or a Face" reflect Townshend's angst. "Dreaming from the Waist," a powerful rock song with Daltrey's best vocal on the record, seems to lament the characteristic impulsiveness of rock & roll stardom, while "Blue Red and Grey" openly denounces the crazy lifestyle in favor of a measured life in which every moment is savored. "Slip Kid" and "Squeeze Box" are neat little songs written as potential singles ("Squeeze Box" was released as a single and did well, though not spectacularly). Entwistle's one contribution, "Success Story," is almost an answer piece to Townshend's soul-searching. The autobiographical track pounds away furiously as Entwistle makes wry observations about various aspects of his band's career, then gives a heartfelt defense of rock & roll at the end.

Who Are You picks up where the song leaves off. Released in 1978, after a three-year hiatus, it shows the Who drastically changed but seemingly revitalized. Moon's drumming lacks power, but Daltrey has never sung better than on "Guitar and Pen," "Trick of the Light," a brilliant Entwistle heavy-metal pastiche, and the winding title track, which became a midsummer hit. The album's topic was sustaining rock & roll past thirty, and while this angered many Who fans, who felt that eternal youth is the rock & roll promise, it fit with the band members' situation. And Townshend left the record open-ended: if "Music Must Change," on which Moon doesn't even play, seemed the end of the band's basic approach, "Love Is Coming Down" promised at least that there would be more of the relentless honesty the Who had always delivered. "Who Are You" itself lived up to that promise, a pounding statement of identity lost and found.

Unfortunately, Keith Moon died of a drug overdose only weeks after the record's release.

★ ★ ★ ★ **The Kids Are Alright** / MCA (1979)
★ ★ ★ **Quadrophenia** / Poly. (1979)
★ ★ ★ ★ **Face Dances** / War. (1981)
★ ★ ★ **Hooligans** / MCA (1981)
★ ★ ★ **It's Hard** / War. (1982)

Moon's live swan song with the band was tracks recorded for *The Kids Are Alright* film—"My Wife," "Won't Get Fooled Again" and "Baba O'Riley." The rest of this two-disc soundtrack LP collects amazingly rare and valuable live performances from different concerts and television shows over a period of almost fifteen years. Moments like the versions of "My Generation" from the Smothers Brothers show, "A Quick One While He's Away" from the Rolling Stones Rock & Roll Circus and the "Sparks"/"Pinball Wizard"/"See Me, Feel Me" sequence from Woodstock are worth the price of the record alone.

Quadrophenia is another, less successful soundtrack, although the film itself is a major element in the group's history. Though the songs culled from the original recording are remixed to better effect, the concept was stronger in its complete presentation.

Face Dances debuted the new lineup, with Moon's replacement Kenney Jones and keyboardist John "Rabbit" Bundrick added to flesh out the group's sound. Theoretically, Moon's death had freed Townshend to create a "new" Who sound, and the band had already toured with both new members, but the addition of Rabbit's keyboards didn't drastically alter the studio sound because the Who had always made good use of keyboard session players on previous albums.

Too many expectations were built up for *Face Dances,* and when the record failed to be a breakthrough along the lines of *Who's Next,* it was almost universally and in some cases incredibly unfairly condemned. Lost in

the controversy were such gems as Townshend's beautiful hymn to his work, "Daily Records," one of his best Meher Baba tributes, "Don't Let Go the Coat," the hot-rocking "You Better You Bet" and the live showstopper "Another Tricky Day," as well as two fine Entwistle songs, "The Quiet One" and "You." Producer Bill Szymczyk recorded the best vocal sound the Who has ever gotten, but ended up taking a lot of the blame for the commercial failure of *Face Dances,* which was more likely due to the band's failure to support the record with a U.S. tour. *Face Dances* is a very good record that suffers from not being the great one people wanted it to be. *Hooligans* is little more than a closet-cleaning effort by MCA after the band left for Warner Bros. Of course it's an interesting closet. *It's Hard,* the record that accompanied the final tour in 1982, was a major disappointment despite several good songs—"Cry If You Want" "Eminence Front" and "Athena."
— J.S.

RUSTY WIER
★ ★ ★ **Don't It Make You Wanna Dance / 20th Cent. (1975)**
Wier is a pretty good Texas singer/songwriter, a kind of minor-league Jerry Jeff Walker, with an excellent voice and a penchant for picking excellent sidemen to flesh out his material.   — J.S.

WILD BILL'S BLUE WASHBOARD BOYS
★ ★ ★ **Baby Yum Yum / Flyr. (1978)**
Boisterous if not inspired zydeco-based blues from 1969, leased from Goldband Records in Lake Charles, Louisiana. The emphasis on washboard (rubboard) in the rhythm section makes this version of zydeco seem more primitive than the better-known style popularized by Clifton Chenier.   — D.M.

WILD CHERRY
★ **Wild Cherry / Epic (1976)**
★ **Electrified Funk / Epic (1977)**
★ **I Love My Music / Epic (1978)**
■ **Only the Wild Survive / Epic (NA)**
White boys playing quintessentially unfunky music. The hit (1976) was "Play That Funky Music (White Boy)."   — K.T.

THE WILD TCHOUPITOULAS
★ ★ ★ ★ **The Wild Tchoupitoulas / Is. (1976)** ¶
The Wild Tchoupitoulas make American roots music—an ebullient brand of hard-core, second-line New Orleans funk. The

Tchoupitoulas are a street gang who long ago put down their weapons for songs and Mardi Gras parade costumes. The Meters provide instrumental backup and production assistance. A remake of the Meters' "Hey Pocky-A-Way" is the high point.
— J.MC.

WILDWEEDS
★ **Wildweeds / Van. (1970)**
Terrific argument for defoliating hippies, redeemed (slightly) by a fairly creditable version of Big Boy Crudup's "My Baby Left Me," easily the best Elvis imitation ever done by a singer wearing patchouli oil.
— D.M.

REV. ROBERT WILKINS
★ ★ ★ ★ **The Original Rolling Stone / Her. (1980)**
★ ★ ★ **Before the Reverence / Mag. (NA)**
Fine gospel-blues performer from the Twenties and Thirties; Wilkins is best known for his song "Prodigal Son," which the Rolling Stones recorded on *Beggars' Banquet.* Despite its obnoxious "father of rock 'n' roll" liner notes, the Herwin has most of the same material as the Magpie and better sound.
— D.M.

DENIECE WILLIAMS
★ ★ ★ ★ **This Is Niecy / Col. (1976)**
★ ★ ★ **Songbird / Col. (1977)** ¶
★ ★ ★ ★ **That's What Friends Are For / Col. (1978)**
★ ★ ★ **When Love Comes Calling / Col. (1979)**
★ ★ ★ **My Melody / Col. (1981)**
Best known for her 1978 duet with Johnny Mathis, Williams benefits from Maurice White's sparse and restrained production on all of these albums. Williams has a billowy soprano perfect for the pleasant love songs she favors, although the aim is sometimes prettiness rather than substance.
— J.MC.

DON WILLIAMS
★ ★ ★ **Don Williams, Vol. 1 / MCA (1974)**
★ ★ ★ **Don Williams, Vol. 2 / MCA (1974)**
★ ★ ★ **Don Williams, Vol. 3 / MCA (1974)**
★ ★ ★ **You're My Best Friend / MCA (1975)**
★ ★ ★ ★ **Greatest Hits / MCA (1975)**
★ ★ ★ **Harmony / MCA (1976)**
★ ★ ★ **Country Boy / MCA (1977)**
★ ★ ★ **Expressions / MCA (1978)**
★ ★ ★ **Best of Don Williams, Vol. 2 / MCA (1979)**
★ ★ ★ **Portrait / MCA (1979)**

★ ★ ★ **I Believe in You / MCA (1980)**
★ ★ ★ **Especially for You / MCA (1981)**
★ ★ ★ **Visions / MCA (1982)**
Williams' deep bass voice and soulful songwriting made him one of the most successful country-pop performers of the mid to late Seventies, during which time he recorded a string of hits that were as good as they were popular—"Amanda," "I Wouldn't Want to Live if You Didn't Love Me," "Say It Again," "She Never Knew Me," "Ties That Bind," "Till the Rivers All Run Dry" and "We Should Be Together." Williams' songs have come to the attention of rock musicians and have been recorded by Eric Clapton and Peter Townshend. — J.S.

HANK WILLIAMS JR.
★ ★ ★ **Fourteen Greatest Hits / MGM (1976)**
★ ★ ★ **One Night Stands / Elek. (1977) ¶**
★ ★ ★ **New South / Elek. (1977)**
★ ★ ★ **Family Tradition / Elek. (1979)**
★ ★ ★ **Whiskey Bent and Hell Bound / Elek. (1980)**
★ ★ ★ **Habits Old and New / Elek. (1980)**
★ ★ ★ **Rowdy / Elek. (1981)**
Hank Williams Jr. faced an impossible task: as the son of the greatest figure in country music history he was expected to live up to (and perhaps live out) the grandeur and tragedy of his father's career. Although his father died when he was only four, Williams has been performing his father's music in concert, from his preadolescent years.

More recently, after a stint recording conventional country for MGM, Williams has begun to break into the outlaw country mold. The process began with his final MGM album, the deleted *Hank Williams Jr. and Friends,* one of the landmarks of recent country. It is both personal and potent, with more of a rock tinge than anything since. After a mountain-climbing accident in 1976, in which he nearly lost his life, Williams came back to record the Elektra records, all of which have strong moments but lack the consistent sense of breakthrough which characterizes *Friends.* — D.M.

HANK WILLIAMS SR.
★ ★ ★ ★ **I Saw the Light / MGM (1972)**
★ ★ ★ ★ ★ **Twenty-four of Hank Williams' Greatest Hits / MGM (1974)**
★ ★ ★ **Hank Williams Live at the Grand Ole Opry / MGM (1976)**
★ ★ ★ **Home in Heaven / MGM (1976) ¶**
★ ★ ★ ★ ★ **Twenty-four Greatest Hits, Vol. 2 / MGM (1977)**
★ ★ ★ ★ **Hank Williams Sr.'s Greatest Hits / MGM (NA)**
★ ★ ★ ★ **Very Best of Hank Williams / MGM (NA)**
★ ★ ★ ★ ★ **The Immortal Hank Williams / MGM (NA), Jap. imp.**
Only Jimmie Rodgers can compare with Hank Williams as a country music figure, and even Rodgers is outstripped by Williams' influence on later developments in rock & roll; Elvis Presley, Buddy Holly and Bob Dylan, to name just three, owe a great deal to his writing and singing style, to his lyrical vision and to his itinerant-minstrel way of life. Williams recorded for only six years—from 1947 to 1953—yet even today, twenty-five years after his death, he is regarded with semi-religious awe in Nashville.

Williams has been called a folksinger, which is not altogether inaccurate. His sound was very basic, his voice and guitar backed by a band without drums. But the yodeling and the perspective of his singing could only have come from the tradition founded by Jimmie Rodgers and the Carter Family.

But unlike most country musicians, Williams did not sing songs of resignation and despair but of exhilaration, resilience, and occasionally, nearly mystical illumination. The greatest of them include: "I'm So Lonesome I Could Cry," "Cold Cold Heart," "Moaning the Blues," "Long Gone Lonesome Blues," "Kawliga," "I'll Never Get Out of This World Alive," "Jambalaya," "Honky Tonk Blues" and "Settin' the Woods on Fire." Williams never found a way out of the social dead end of country, but in his songs are the seeds of rock & roll, which in the hands of Elvis Presley, Holly and others became the exit for thousands.

The ultimate Williams set is *The Immortal,* a ten-disc boxed set that's enormously expensive ($100–$125) but worth every cent because it contains virtually every recorded note he sang. — D.M.

JERRY WILLIAMS
★ **Gone / War. (1979)**
Journeyman white funk. If soul music is about emotional ease, Williams flunks out immediately. He's strident even on his cover of Otis Redding's "I've Got Dreams to Remember." The star is for at least having enough good taste to record such a gem; he doesn't get more because his execution fails his ideas. — D.M.

LARRY WILLIAMS
★ *That* **Larry Williams / Fan. (1978)** ¶
★ ★ ★ **Original Hits / Sonet (NA), imp.**
★ ★ ★ **Slow Down / Spec. (NA), imp.**
Williams was a Fifties novelty R&B singer who had hits with "Bony Moronie" and "Dizzy Miss Lizzy," the latter covered by the Beatles. The Fantasy comeback LP contains nothing but mediocre funk, but the imports are the real thing. — D.M.

LENNY WILLIAMS
★ ★ ★ **Choosing You / MCA (1977)**
★ ★ **Spark of Love / MCA (1978)** ¶
★ ★ **Love Current / MCA (1979)** ¶
★ **Let's Do It Tonight / MCA (1980)**
Ex–Tower of Power vocalist goes solo in a much mellower context with fair results. — J.S.

MARION WILLIAMS
★ ★ ★ ★ **Lord, You've Been Mighty Good to Me / John Hammond Records (1982)**
Shamefully, this is the only available solo recording by the greatest living gospel singer—some would argue the greatest living American singer in any genre. Fortunately, Williams' Savoy recordings with the Ward Singers are still in print on *The Best of the Famous Ward Singers of Philadelphia, Pennsylvania,* which is highly recommended. Anyone who comes across any of Williams' Vee Jay (reissued on Trip) albums with the Stars of God would be well advised to pick them up.
Lord You've Been Mighty Good to Me is an only partially successful attempt to accommodate contemporary gospel trends, but producer Tony Heilbut and Williams stay as close to possible to the spare, traditional approach that so well enhances her beautiful, vibrant voice. Those interested in blues singing stylists, as well as gospel, will find Williams fascinating, if not as overpowering here as in some other contexts. Her influence on such performers as Little Richard and the Isley Brothers is still striking and important. — D.M.

MASON WILLIAMS
★ ★ **Mason Williams Phonograph Record / War. (1968)**
★ **Hand Made / War. (1970)** ¶
★ **Mason Williams Listening Matter / Ev. (NA)** ¶
★ **Feudin' Banjos / Olym. (NA)**
★ **Fresh Fish / Fly. Fish (1978)**
Williams earned a reputation as a writer/performer on the Smothers Brothers' late-Sixties television show. He wrote some fairly

interesting pop songs—"Classical Gas" from *Phonograph Record* was a hit—but never quite broke through. *Phonograph Record* was an early attempt to record a pop-folk song cycle, something like Van Dyke Parks' first album, but much less interesting. The rest is mere silliness. — D.M.

MAURICE WILLIAMS AND THE ZODIACS
★ ★ ★ ★ **The Best of Maurice Williams and the Zodiacs / Relic (NA)**
They're best (probably only, in some quarters) known for the exhilarating "Stay," but the twenty-one tracks collected here will convince you that this South Carolina quartet was one of the greatest of all doo-wop groups. The Zodiacs (known as the Gladiolas when they recorded the original "Little Darling" for Excello in 1955) hit No. 1 with "Stay" in late 1960, and these sides, initially issued as Herald 45s, include that song and the ones that followed, most notably "Come Along," "Come and Get It," "Running Around" and "We're Lovers." — D.M.

OTIS WILLIAMS AND HIS CHARMS
★ ★ ★ ★ **Otis Williams and His Charms Sing Their All-Time Hits / King (NA)**
★ ★ ★ ★ **Sixteen Hits / King (1978)**
Reissues of fine R&B sides by this doo-wop quintet. "Hearts of Stone" is a rock classic by any standard, "Ling Ting Tong" was one of the first great rock nonsense syllables, and "Ko Ko Mo (I Love You So)" isn't far behind. *Sixteen Hits* has all the essentials and four more tracks, but both albums have worthwhile nuggets. — D.M.

PAUL WILLIAMS
■ **Wings / A&M (1971)**
★ **Just an Old Fashioned Love Song / A&M (1971)**
■ **Life Goes On / A&M (1972)**
■ **Here Comes Inspiration / A&M (1974)**
★ **Phantom of the Paradise / A&M (1974)**
■ **Little Bit of Love / A&M (1974)**
■ **Ordinary Fool / A&M (1975)** ¶
★ **Classics / A&M (1977)**
■ **Little on the Windy Side / Por. (NA)**
Williams is the most facile and bubble-headed of Seventies pop writers; his melodies are straight from advertising, and his lyrics are unctuous statements of things he may know about but has never felt. If one must suffer his banalities, it is far better to do so in the versions recorded by artists like the Carpenters and Three Dog Night. At least they can vocalize a bit; the composer cannot. — D.M.

ROBERT PETE WILLIAMS

★ ★ ★ Sugar Farm Blues / Blues Bea.
(1972), Br. imp.
★ ★ ★ ★ Louisiana Blues / Tak. (1980)
★ ★ ★ ★ Angola Prisoner's Blues / Arhoo.
(NA)
★ ★ ★ ★ Those Prison Blues / Arhoo.
(NA)
★ ★ ★ ★ Free Again / Prestige (also
contained in the two-LP set *Robert Pete
Williams and Snooks Eaglin,* on Fantasy)
★ ★ ★ When I Lay My Burden Down /
So. (NA)

One of the greatest guitarists in blues history, Robert Pete Williams is a singular character. Discovered in Louisiana State Prison (at Angola) in 1959, he immediately stunned listeners with his eccentric rhythms and original attack. His style is so bold and raw it requires some close attention at first, but anyone willing to listen intently will be amply rewarded. Aside from the *Sugar Farm* set, recorded in Europe when Williams was well up in age, all of these records are exceptionally fine, both for guitarists and anyone who cares about the blues, not as a rigid form but as a means of deep expression. — D.M.

ROBIN WILLIAMS

★ ★ ★ Reality . . . What a Concept / Casa.
(1979)

This is a relative disappointment, because (on TV as Mork, anyhow), Williams is the fastest, most associatively brilliant verbal wit since Jonathan Winters. Here the jokes are verbal, altogether too hip and druggy, and recorded live in concert—what you might call the most slipshod way of making a concert LP, and far from the best. If Williams ever decides to take album-making seriously, he could be the first comic to eclipse or extend the work of the Firesign Theatre. But you won't be able to tell it by listening to this. — D.M.

ROBIN WILLIAMSON

★ ★ Journey's Edge / Fly. Fish (1977)
★ ★ American Stonehenge / Fly. Fish
(1978)
★ ★ Songs of Love and Parting / Fly. Fish
(NA)

Pleasant, quiet post-folk-rock music from a former member of the Incredible String Band. — D.M.

SONNY BOY WILLIAMSON (JOHN LEE WILLIAMSON)

★ ★ ★ Sonny Boy Williamson / Blues C.
(NA)

★ ★ ★ ★ Sonny Boy Williamson, Vol. 2 /
Blues C. (NA)
★ ★ ★ ★ Sonny Boy Williamson, Vol. 3 /
Blues C. (NA)
★ ★ ★ ★ Sonny Boy Williamson / RCA
(NA)
★ ★ ★ ★ Sonny Boy Williamson, Vol. 2 /
RCA (NA)

The irony of Rice Miller (Sonny Boy No. 2) taking the original Sonny Boy's name is that the imitator/pretender turned out to be the superior artist. There is nothing as shattering here as the second Sonny Boy's best tracks. The difference is that while both Sonny Boys were great harp players, only No. 2 could sing.

All of these records, reissues of sides from the Thirties and Forties, are good, but none is essential. — D.M.

SONNY BOY WILLIAMSON (RICE MILLER)

★ ★ ★ ★ Bummer Road / Chess (1969)
★ ★ ★ ★ ★ This Is My Story / Chess
(1972)
★ ★ ★ ★ One Way Out / Chess (1974), Fr.
imp.
★ ★ ★ ★ King Biscuit Time / Arhoo. (1976)
★ ★ ★ ★ Sonny Boy Williamson / Chess
(1977), Fr. imp.
★ ★ ★ ★ The Real Folk Blues / Chess (NA),
Fr. imp.
★ ★ ★ ★ More Real Folk Blues / Chess
(NA), Fr. imp.
★ ★ ★ Sonny Boy Williamson and Memphis
Slim in Paris / Cres. (NA)
★ ★ Final Sessions, 1963–64 / Blue Night
(NA), imp.
★ ★ A Portrait in Blues / Story. (NA)

This is the second Sonny Boy (real name, Rice Miller). The second Sonny Boy, like the first, was one of the best harmonica players the blues has produced. Williamson was a convincing lyricist as well, and a formidable vocalist. Several of his songs—"Don't Start Me to Talkin' " most prominently, but also "One Way Out," "Nine Below Zero" and "Fattening Frogs for Snakes"—have become rock-bar and blues-band staples.

Williamson was born in rural Mississippi, and like so many others, followed a seemingly inevitable route to Chicago in the late Forties. He was supported by many of the genre's best players (Muddy Waters, Willie Dixon, Robert Jr. Lockwood, Otis Spann, Fred Below, Buddy Guy and Jimmy Rogers, among others), all of whom seemed to have learned a great deal from his novel approach to blues. In Williamson, the medium is at its most lyrical without ever sacrificing any of its raw power. The best of the Chess LPs, *This Is My Story,* is a classic of the blues, and a fundamental source point of rock. — D.M.

WILLIE JOHN
★ ★ ★ **Fifteen Original Hits / King (NA)**
One of soul music's greatest voices, although his best shot at a hit single, "Fever," was stolen by Peggy Lee. Willie John's gospel-like falsetto was a major influence on James Brown (who recorded a tribute LP in the late Sixties after John died in a West Coast prison), and because of Brown, on a whole generation of singers. "Talk to Me," "All Around the World" and the other songs here stake Willie's claim as one of rock's least-remembered fathers. — D.M.

CHUCK WILLIS
★ ★ ★ ★ ★ **I Remember Chuck Willis /**
 Warner-Pioneer (1963, 1980), Jap. imp.
★ ★ ★ ★ ★ **Chuck Willis—My Story / Col.**
 (1980)
Willis was already a seasoned rhythm & blues performer, a veteran of Red McAllister's band, when he hooked up with Atlanta's influential disc jockey Zenas Sears in 1951. Sears became Willis' manager and got him signed to Okeh, where he recorded the fourteen cuts included on *My Story,* quickly exhibiting a real gift for blues songwriting and producing the classics "I Feel So Bad," "My Story" and "Don't Deceive Me," all in the finest style of pre–rock & roll jump blues. Altogether, Willis recorded forty sides for Okeh, finally leaving in 1954 for Atlantic. *My Story* collects the best of them.

At Atlantic, Willis turned his attention more and more to rock & roll, and by the time of his untimely death in 1958 (from a stomach ulcer), he was known as "The King of the Stroll" (because it was his hit, "Betty and Dupree," which Dick Clark's *American Bandstand* regulars preferred to do that step to). *I Remember Chuck Willis* collects the bulk of Willis' plaintive and boisterous Atlantic R&B numbers, notably "What Am I Living For" and "Hang Up My Rock & Roll Shoes," the bizarre posthumous single; "From the Bottom of My Heart" and "Just One Kiss," a pair of great original ballads; and "C.C. Rider" and "Betty and Dupree," two blues standards that Willis rearranged sufficiently to make them important early rock & roll hits.

Willis' abilities were multiple. He had a fine sweet voice, his songwriting was superb, his instinct for arrangement was outstanding, and his lyrics were both witty and insightful.

While not a flamboyant performer, he added to rock & roll lore of the period by wearing a turban in all of his performances. These two releases represent his work well, though if Warner-Pioneer ever reissues *King of the Stroll* (you can bet domestic Atlantic never will) jump on that, too. It contains such other breathtakingly incisive ballads as "Ease the Pain," "It's Too Late" (recorded by Eric Clapton on *Layla*) and "My Crying Eyes." Although his career was short (he was only thirty when he died), Willis stands as one of the most remarkable and important Fifties performers. — D.M.

BOB WILLS AND HIS TEXAS PLAYBOYS
★ ★ ★ **Bob Wills and His Texas Playboys /**
 MCA (1958)
★ ★ ★ **Bob Wills Sings and Plays / Lib.**
 (1963) ¶
★ ★ ★ **King of the Western Swing / MCA**
 (1968)
★ ★ ★ **Time Changes Everything / MCA**
 (1969)
★ ★ ★ ★ **Bob Wills Plays the Greatest**
 String Band Hits / MCA (1969)
★ ★ ★ **The Best of Bob Wills and His Texas**
 Playboys / MCA (1969)
★ ★ ★ **Living Legend / MCA (1969)**
★ ★ ★ **Bob Wills in Person / MCA (1971)**
★ ★ ★ ★ **Bob Wills Anthology / Col.**
 (1973)
★ ★ ★ **For the Last Time / U.A. (1974)**
★ ★ ★ **The Best of Bob Wills and His Texas**
 Playboys / MCA (1975)
★ ★ ★ **Fathers and Sons / Epic (1975)**
★ ★ ★ **Remembering . . . / Col. (1976) ¶**
★ ★ ★ **Bob Wills in Concert / Cap. (1976)**
★ ★ ★ **Twenty-four Great Hits / MGM**
 (NA)
★ ★ ★ **Western Swing Along / RCA (NA)**
Born in 1905, by 1933 Bob Wills had become a major bandleader in Texas and Oklahoma, leading the twenty-five-piece Texas Playboys on radio stations throughout the region, and recording for Columbia in a fashion of his own device. Essentially, Wills merged country & western music with swing jazz; the resultant combination was far from hick and numbered Charlie Parker, among others, among its aficionados.

Wills' band emphasized both stringed instruments (guitars and his own fiddle) and a horn section, which makes it unique in C&W styles. Among his great hits, the best of them recorded for Columbia in the Thirties, were "Rose of San Antone," "Texas Playboy Rag," "Mexicali Rose," "Take Me Back to Tulsa" and "The Yellow Rose of

Texas." The familiarity of those titles speaks as well as anything for the remarkable power of his music. Along with Hank Williams Sr. and Jimmie Rodgers, Wills is one of the grandfathers, on the country side, of rock. — D.M.

AL WILSON
★ ★ I've Got a Feeling / Play. (1976)
Al Wilson is a contemporary singer with a voice and style that treads a watery line between Las Vegas gloss and urban soul. Without a distinctive vocal personality, Wilson has nevertheless managed to score several hits with unassuming midtempo material. Listening to an Al Wilson record is like eating at Howard Johnson's. — J.MC.

JACKIE WILSON
★ ★ ★ ★ Jackie Wilson Sings the Blues / Bruns. (1960)
★ ★ ★ ★ My Golden Favorites / Bruns. (1960)
★ ★ ★ ★ My Golden Favorites, Vol. 2 / Bruns. (1960)
★ ★ ★ Body and Soul / Bruns. (1962)
★ ★ Jackie Wilson Sings the World's Greatest Melodies / Bruns. (1963)
★ ★ Nobody but You / Bruns. (1963)
★ ★ Baby Workout / Bruns. (1963)
★ ★ ★ Spotlight on Jackie Wilson / Bruns. (1965)
★ ★ ★ Whispers / Bruns. (1967)
★ ★ Manufacturers of Soul (with Count Basie) / Bruns. (1968)
★ ★ I Get the Sweetest Feeling / Bruns. (1968)
★ ★ Do Your Thing / Bruns. (1969)
★ ★ It's All a Part of Love / Bruns. (1970)
★ ★ You Got Me Walking / Bruns. (1971)
★ ★ ★ ★ Jackie Wilson's Greatest Hits / Bruns. (1972)
★ ★ Beautiful Day / Bruns. (1972)
★ Nowstalgia / Bruns. (1974)
★ ★ ★ ★ ★ The Jackie Wilson Story / Epic (1983)
Despite his vocal and performing genius (he may have been the best pure vocalist of his generation), Jackie Wilson led an aimless and uneven recording career. With few exceptions, Wilson's output suffered from hack, over-orchestrated arrangements, heavy-handed choral accompaniment and dubious song selection. Still, the sheer power and virtuosity of Wilson's voice overcame many of the obstacles. Consider his biggest hit: "Night," backed with "Doggin' Around." "Night" is a supper-club ballad that borders on schmaltz, but Wilson turns it into a real showstopper, flaunting his operatic range (a

gimmick he used to even greater effect on his version of "Danny Boy"). The flip side, "Doggin' Around," is a quasi-blues song that he reworks into a wrenching emotional showpiece.

Wilson's early LP output mixes melodramatic ballads with brassy uptempo dance numbers ("Baby Workout" was his biggest hit in that mold) and the occasional blues (one of his best albums is the hard to find Sings the Blues). The titles—World's Greatest Melodies, Body and Soul—reflect the bent.

In the mid-Sixties, Wilson found a sympathetic producer, Chicago soul entrepreneur Carl Davis, to produce two of his more memorable hits: "Whispers" and the ageless "Higher and Higher." For a time, the association gave Wilson's career a needed shot in the arm, but by 1970 the Davis-produced records were mediocre at best. Wilson had some minor Seventies hits but scarcely anything of interest to anyone but devoted fans. It's somehow fitting that the album released just prior to his heart attack and subsequent complete incapacitation was a tribute to Al Jolson. A hodgepodge of previously unreleased, Davis-produced singles came out a year later. The Epic set, compiled and annotated by Joe McEwen, is a beautiful and thorough demonstration of Wilson's skills. It has all the hits and several rarities. — J.MC./D.M.

LARRY JON WILSON
★ ★ ★ New Beginnings / Monu. (1975)
★ ★ ★ Let Me Sing My Song to You / Monu. (1976)
★ ★ ★ Loose Change / Monu. (1977)
★ ★ ★ Sojourner / Monu. (1979)
Wilson has one of those smooth, big-voiced backwoods baritones that can crawl around a well-carved country song like a limber raccoon. His records are all solid, if not stellar, examples of good basic country & Southern music without all the floss found in the usual Nashville dross.

TONY WILSON
★ ★ ★ Catch One / Bears. (1979)
Unconventional only because this LP of singer/songwriter sensitivities is made by a black man—but then that's unconventional enough to make a song like "Africa" interesting for formal reasons alone. Wilson's choice of cover material is adventuresome enough to point up his limitations, which boil down to oversensitivity: thus Dylan's "Forever Young," Randy Van Warmer's "Just When I Needed You Most." But if there's doubt about roots here, check out

"New Orleans Music," whose funkiness even discoid producers Ron and Howard Albert cannot obscure. — D.M.

JESSE WINCHESTER
★ ★ ★ **Third Down 110 to Go / Bears. (1972) ¶**
★ ★ ★ **Learn to Love It / Bears. (1974) ¶**
★ ★ ★ **Let the Rough Side Drag / Bears. (1976)**
★ ★ ★ **Nothing but a Breeze / Bears. (1977)**
★ ★ ★ **A Touch on the Rainy Side / Bears. (1978) ¶**
Winchester grew up in Memphis, a serviceman's son, but when he became eligible for the draft in 1967, he split to Canada. In 1970, he met the Band's Robbie Robertson and Robertson induced his then-manager, Albert Grossman, to record Winchester. The resulting album, produced by Robertson and on the long-defunct Ampex label, was widely acclaimed, mostly for its fine collection of songs including "Yankee Lady," "Biloxi" and "The Brand New Tennessee Walt."

Winchester didn't return to vinyl until 1972, when he recorded a Todd Rundgren-produced LP, which was not so enthralling. But *Learn to Love It* fared better, and since then he's recorded fairly prolifically in a mildly interesting country-rock vein. Although he became a Canadian citizen in 1973, Winchester did not return to this country until the Carter amnesty of 1977. Since he'd never been around before, it wasn't much of a comeback, but he continues to work steadily in both countries today. — D.M.

PAM WINDO AND THE SHADES
★ ★ ★ **It / Bears. (1982)**
Pam Windo, wife of freethinking reed man Gary Windo, fronts this Woodstock cult band with a certain odd yet compelling glee. New wave for the smart and sassy country squire set. — R.P.

COLIN WINSKI
★ **Rock Therapy / Tak. (1980)**
Having distinguished himself as "Rollin' " Colin Winski, guitarist/vocalist with Ray Campi, he and other band members split from their mentor and secured opening spot on Western U.S. Clash tour—which looks to have been Winski's fifteen minutes of fame. This subsequent solo LP is vapid, mostly wrongheaded and not much fun. Performing rockabilly well is no guarantee of knowing how to record it. — G.A.

STEPHANIE WINSLOW
■ **Crying / War. (1980)**

Cloying, disgustingly banal record by pop chanteuse Winslow includes pointless covers of Fleetwood Mac's "Say You Love Me" and Roy Orbison's "Crying." — J.S.

EDGAR WINTER
★ ★ **Entrance / Epic (1970)**
★ ★ ★ ★ **Edgar Winter's White Trash / Epic (1971)**
★ ★ ★ ★ **Roadwork / Epic (1972)**
★ ★ ★ ★ **They Only Come Out at Night / Epic (1972)**
★ ★ ★ **Shock Treatment / Epic (1974) ¶**
★ ★ **Jasmine Nightdreams / Blue S. (1975) ¶**
★ ★ ★ **Edgar Winter Group with Rick Derringer / Blue S. (1975) ¶**
★ ★ ★ **Recycled / Blue S. (1977) ¶**
★ ★ **Edgar Winter Album / Blue S. (1979)**
★ ★ **Standing on Rock / Blue S. (NA)**
In the beginning (about 1970), Edgar Winter was just the older brother of Johnny Winter, who was then heralded as the greatest white blues guitarist of them all. *Entrance,* an eccentric Texas jazz-rock combination, made that distinction seem the only one Edgar was likely to earn. But a bit later he put together one of the most soulful white horn bands ever assembled, White Trash, and together they made a pair of fine records—*Edgar Winter's White Trash* (which includes "Keep Playin' That Rock and Roll") and the live *Roadwork.* This music had its roots in Southwestern roadhouses and kicked just that viciously. Edgar came up with a huge hit in 1973, with "Frankenstein," from *They Only Come Out at Night,* heavy rock recorded with the band that included Derringer. He's never repeated that success, however. — D.M.

JOHNNY WINTER
★ ★ ★ ★ **Johnny Winter / Col. (1969)**
★ ★ ★ ★ **Second Winter / Col. (1969)**
★ ★ ★ ★ **Johnny Winter And / Col. (1970)**
★ ★ ★ **Live / Col. (1971)**
★ ★ ★ ★ **About Blues / Janus (1971) ¶**
★ ★ ★ ★ **Still Alive and Well / Col. (1973)**
★ ★ ★ **John Dawson Winter III / Blue S. (1974) ¶**
★ ★ ★ **Saints and Sinners / Col. (1974)**
★ ★ ★ **Captured Live / Blue S. (1976)**
★ ★ ★ ★ **Nothin' but the Blues / Blue S. (1977)**
★ ★ ★ **White Hot and Blue / Blue S. (1978)**
★ ★ ★ **Raisin' Cain / Blue S. (1980)**
★ ★ ★ **Before the Storm / Janus (NA) ¶**
★ ★ ★ **Austin, Texas / U.A. (NA) ¶**
Johnny Winter came out of Texas in 1969 after woodshedding there for the better part of a decade, and was immediately heralded

as America's best young white blues guitarist—the acclaim was all the more powerful because he, like his brother Edgar, is an albino. He was almost immediately signed by Columbia to a lucrative long-term contract. But because he was more committed to blues than rock, and because of a nasty heroin problem, Winter never realized his commercial promise.

The Janus and United Artists packages are recordings made in Texas during the mid-Sixties; they are straight blues and not bad, although the two-record Janus package *(Before the Storm)* is pretty thin. Winter's best blues playing is on *Johnny Winter,* the first Columbia LP, and *Nothin' but the Blues,* cut with some of the same people who made Muddy Waters' *Hard Again* (produced by Johnny). His rock ventures peaked early, with *Second Winter,* which includes a wonderful version of Bob Dylan's "Highway 61 Revisited," and *Johnny Winter And,* recorded with the remnants of the McCoys, including Rick Derringer. *Still Alive and Well,* his first album after being cured of his addiction, is also an interesting pop collection, with more than the usual share of straight blues work. — D.M.

JONATHAN WINTERS
★ ★ **Laugh Live / Col. (1973)**
Winters' way with a sound effect is incomparable and unerring, but much more effective, naturally, if you can see him doing the impossible. His records unfortunately tend to emphasize Winters' least appealing character—a despised, lisping homosexual. For the rest, inspired mimicry with uninspired premises to showcase it. — K.T.

RUBY WINTERS
★ **"I Will" / Millen. (1978)**
Soul ballads sung as if Nancy Wilson, not Aretha Franklin, were the Queen of Soul, and funky included plastic covers on the couch. — D.M.

STEVE WINWOOD
★ ★ ★ ★ **Steve Winwood / Is. (1977)**
★ ★ ★ ★ ★ **Arc of a Diver / Is. (1980)**
Winwood, the driving force behind both the Spencer Davis Group and Traffic, went into seclusion in the mid-Seventies before releasing his long-awaited first solo album, *Steve Winwood.* His haunting vocal style and effortlessly brilliant keyboard playing is featured well on a number of understated R&B vamps like "Hold On" and "Time Is Running Out" and his classic ballad style is shown on the beautiful "Let Me Make Something in Your Life." One of the most

interesting aspects of the record is Winwood's collaboration with ex–Bonzo Dog Band leader Viv Stanshall on "Vacant Chair," which is an odd yet straightforward and heartfelt lyric from someone known only for his comedy material.

It was another Stanshall-Winwood composition, "Arc of a Diver," that keyed Winwood's triumphant album of the same name. Here Stanshall's surrealistic imagery is set off eerily by the stark moonlight colors of Winwood's keyboards. On this set Winwood played all the instruments himself and developed a stunning conceptual unity in the process. "While You See a Chance" became an enormous hit, and its simple melodicism makes it one of those songs you never grow tired of. In fact every song on the album has a melodic hook that remains an insistent memory. — J.S.

THE WIPERS
★ ★ ★ **Is This Real? / Park Avenue (1980)**
★ ★ ★ **Youth of America / Park Avenue (1981)**
Portland, Oregon, power trio in the forefront of American punk's end-of-the-decade retreat to the suburbs. *Is This Real?* achieved a grittiness of execution and attack which, like the area's rock of two decades ago, belies the Pacific Northwest's pastoral reputation. The Wipers survived critical accolades from East Coast critics to make a second LP, *Youth of America,* as pointed and energetic as their first, in the process deserting Portland for New York. — G.A.

WIRE
★ ★ ★ ★ **Pink Flag / Harv. (1977)**
★ ★ ★ **154 / War. (1979)**
There's a cleanness of line and lack of distortion to this music that belies its place in the punk-rock pantheon; its motives are too self-consciously arty for that. But the British quartet plays at the furious pace of a punk group, cramming more than twenty songs— almost all of them intelligent ones—on the debut LP. The followups, *Chairs Missing,* available only as an import, and *154,* slow the breakneck pace a fraction, but confirm the initial impression that this could have been one of the major groups of the Seventies' new wave. *154* showed its limits and that seems to have been the end of it. — D.M.

WISHBONE ASH
★ ★ **Wishbone Ash / MCA (1970)**
★ **Pilgrimage / MCA (1971)**
★ ★ ★ **Argus / MCA (1972)**
★ ★ **Wishbone Four / MCA (1973)**

★ ★ Live Dates / MCA (1973)
★ Locked In / Atl. (1976) ¶
★ New England / Atl. (1976) ¶
★ ★ Front Page News / MCA (1977) ¶
★ No Smoke Without Fire / MCA (1978)
★ Just Testing / MCA (1979)
★ Number the Brave / MCA (1981)

Wishbone Ash never quite fit into any rock genre. They were simply a British hard-rock act, with overtones of art rock (like Yes) and boogie music (like Ten Years After), without a central personality, but capable of slugging it out on one-night stands throughout the U.S. and U.K. They earned their share of fans that way, but without developing any distinct musical style. *Argus* came closest to giving them an identity. Of the rest, the Atlantics are mush; the live LP is probably the next best bet for the curious. — D.M.

JAH WOBBLE

★ ★ ★ The Legend Lives On: Jah Wobble in Betrayal / Virgin (1980) ¶

Hard to imagine that Wobble was really expelled from Public Image Ltd. for appropriating these particular tracks (which Messrs. Lydon and Levene still claim were corporate property). Maybe it's just that what Wobble uses to overlay the basic doom-rock of PIL's conception isn't very interesting. No reason for any but complete PIL fanatics to hear this. — D.M.

HOWLIN' WOLF

★ ★ ★ ★ ★ Evil / Chess (NA)
★ ★ ★ Howlin' Wolf: Chess Blues Masters / Chess (NA)
★ ★ ★ ★ Big City Blues / United (1966)
★ ★ ★ ★ The Legendary Sun Performers: Howlin' Wolf / Charly (NA), Br. imp.
★ ★ ★ ★ The London Howlin' Wolf Sessions / Chess (1971)
★ ★ ★ Change My Way / Chess (1977)
★ Live and Cookin' at Alice's Restaurant / Chess (NA)
★ Message to the Young / Chess (1971)
★ ★ ★ ★ The Back Door Wolf / Chess (1973)
★ This Is Howlin' Wolf's New Album / Cadet C. (NA), Br. imp.
★ ★ ★ ★ From Early Til Late / Blue Night (NA)
★ ★ ★ ★ ★ The Real Folk Blues / Chess (1966), Br. imp.
★ ★ ★ ★ ★ More Real Folk Blues / Chess (1967), Br. imp.
★ ★ ★ ★ ★ Going Back Home / Syndicate Chapter (NA), Br. imp.
★ ★ ★ ★ ★ Heart Like Railroad Steel: Rare and Unreleased Recordings, Vol. 1 / Blues Ball (NA)
★ ★ ★ ★ ★ Can't Put Me Out: Rare and Unreleased Recordings, Vol. 2 / Blues Ball (NA)

Howlin' Wolf was one of the most heroic and gigantic figures in American musical history, a sharecropper's son whose bitterness, anger, dignity and humor never failed him, a growling singer, buzzsaw guitarist, acid-etched writer and storehouse of pointed vulgarity and abandon unmatched in all the annals of the blues. Born Chester Burnett on a Mississippi plantation, and thus providing one of the most direct links to the delta blues tradition, Howlin' Wolf (along with Muddy Waters) revolutionized the urban blues in Chicago after World War II.

Wolf's connections to the blues were more than casual. He married Willie Brown's sister, and his half-sister married the second Sonny Boy Williamson, Rice Miller. If all that Wolf had done was synthesize the country blues he heard around him in his youth—the delta blues of Robert Johnson, Charley Patton, the original Sonny Boy, Tommy Johnson and the like—and transfer it to the electrified North, he would be a performer of major importance. What made him an artist was his vision and strength, his massive, lunging presence onstage and his eloquent, brooding, vivid songwriting. From beginning to end—from "I Ain't Superstitious" and "Smokestack Lightnin' " to "Coon on the Moon"—Wolf was a breed apart, and though he sometimes seemed gruff and blustering, every pose was a means to an end. No one who knows the pulse and poetry of Wolf's music can doubt his claim to artistry.

Wolf created his music out of the staple emotions of the blues—fear raised to a keen edge, lust as something to wallow in, introspection so withering it sneers at pity and laughs at scorn. And his ability to communicate ideas as subtle as these is already present in his first recordings, made in Memphis under the auspices of a talent scout named Sam Phillips, who leased his work to Chess and Modern (whence it has wound its way to what's left of Chess and such labels as United, Kent, Charly and Syndicate Chapter). The early material is savage, crude and unforgettable. The records to hear are the United, the Charly and especially *Going Back Home,* which traces Wolf from 1948 to 1958 with an especial emphasis on the earlier period.

"How Many More Years," Wolf's first hit, drew him to Chess and Chicago full-time, and it was there that he really made his mark. It seems especially appropriate somehow that Wolf moved to the city, for though a man so unbending is an odd sight in any society, he certainly has less place in a rural community than in an urban one, where his refusal of anonymity makes an incredibly potent statement. Wolf's music must be heard through a wall of echofied fake stereo on *Chess Blues Masters,* unfortunately; on the other Chess LPs, which are perhaps lesser selections—*Blues Masters* has just about everything in the way of material—the dense, seismic power of his music cuts across better, giving an inkling of how Wolf could have been the ground-zero inspiration for such latter-day blues bands as the Rolling Stones and the Yardbirds.

Wolf's greatest album, *Howlin' Wolf* (Chess 1469, deleted) with a picture of a rocking chair on the cover, is worth tracking down, too. In the first edition of this book, Greil Marcus called it "the finest of all Chicago blues albums," and maybe it is. Certainly, it was made by the finest of all Chicago blues singers: Muddy Waters may have led better bands, but it was Howlin' Wolf who left his signature on all that he touched.

The records to beware are obvious from the ratings, but worth noting is that the Cadet Concept LP is a complete travesty, an attempt from the late Sixties to psychedelicize Wolf's music; the cover notes boast of Wolf hating the record, and for this gesture alone, all remaining copies should be shot on sight. *Message to the Young* is a similar, though slightly less contemptuous, attempt to make Wolf "contemporary," this time through the use of soul-music conventions. Apparently Chess never got the picture: Wolf's music is enduring and timeless on its own, and after fad and fashion have gone their way, his best music continues to sound swell. *Live* deserves to be boycotted, on the other hand, because it was recorded late in Wolf's life (he died in 1976), when he was not up to his own standards, and because it is so poorly recorded.

Wolf's final album, *The Back Door Wolf,* is some kind of triumph, however. The songs range over Wolf's life span from ancient delta blues to Watergate and the Apollo moonshot program, and his easy mastery of such a broad set of songs, coupled with the spare, sympathetic backings he's given, make this album a minor Wolf masterpiece, and perhaps his finest memorial. To the end, a great one.   — D.M.

BILL WITHERS
★ ★ **Making Music** / Col. (1975) ¶
★ ★ **Naked and Warm** / Col. (1976) ¶
★ ★ **Menagerie** / Col. (1977) ¶
★ ★ **'Bout Love** / Col. (1978)
★ ★ ★ **Best of Bill Withers** / Col. (1980)
Withers began recording in 1972 for Clarence Avant's Sussex label, after serving in the Navy and as a computer operator. His early songs (recorded for Sussex Records), while funky enough, had an almost folkish feel, and he scored with several warm, pop-styled soul numbers, including "Ain't No Sunshine," the gospelly "Lean on Me" and "Use Me," both of which made the Top Ten. Since joining Columbia in 1975, however, he has lost his touch, caught between the macho of disco and his own artistic diffidence—he's too shy to be Barry White, and his natural demeanor is currently out of vogue. Some pleasant moments here, but the Sussex records are the ones worth tracking down.   — D.M.

JIMMY WITHERSPOON
★ ★ ★ **Mean Old Frisco** / Prest. (1963)
★ ★ ★ **Goin' to Chicago Blues** / Prest. (1963)
★ ★ ★ **Blue Spoon** / Prest. (1964)
★ ★ ★ ★ **Best of Jimmy Witherspoon** / Prest. (1964)
★ ★ ★ **Some of My Best Friends Are the Blues** / Prest. (1964)
★ ★ ★ **Blues for Easy Livers** / Prest. (1966)
★ ★ **The Spoon Concerts** / Fan. (1972)
★ ★ ★ **Spoonful** / Blue N. (1975)
★ ★ ★ **Goin' to Kansas City Blues** / RCA (1975)
★ ★ ★ **Groovin' and Spoonin'** / Orig. Jazz (NA)
★ ★ ★ **Spoon in London** / Prest. (NA)
★ ★ ★ **A Spoonful of Blues** / United (NA)
★ ★ ★ **Big Blues** / J.S.P. (NA), Br. imp.
Jimmy Witherspoon is perhaps the best-known survivor of the Kansas City blues scene that produced so much fine music in the Thirties. He is a more jazz-oriented bluesman than the Chicago and delta performers, using more sophisticated arrangements—often featuring horn charts.

Witherspoon, whose best-known song is "Ain't Nobody's Business," was probably most influential on such R&B singers as Bobby Bland, although he also made a (now-deleted) LP with Eric Burdon for MGM.   — D.M.

BOBBY WOMACK
★ ★ ★ **Communication** / U.A. (1971) ¶
★ ★ ★ **Understanding** / U.A. (1972)

Too often, Bobby Womack seems the musical equivalent of baseball star Dick Allen. Like Allen, whose statistics have never kept pace with his abilities, Womack has never been as consistent as his considerable talent might allow. After years of indifferent success as a solo singer, he recorded *Communication* and *Understanding* in sessions only a few days apart. Though erratic, those LPs show a matured singer/songwriter and sport some of Womack's best work, including "That's the Way I Feel About Cha" and "Woman's Gotta Have It."

★ ★ ★ ★ **Facts of Life** / U.A. (1973) ¶
★ ★ **Lookin' for a Love Again** / U.A. (1974) ¶
★ ★ ★ ★ **Greatest Hits** / U.A. (1974) ¶
★ ★ ★ **I Don't Know What the World Is Coming To** / U.A. (1975) ¶
★ ★ **Bobby Womack Goes C&W** / U.A. (1976) ¶

Though he's had success in an uptempo vein ("I Can Understand It," "Lookin' for a Love"), Womack works best in a narrative ballad approach. On one side of *Facts of Life,* he collects a string of such cuts, believable love songs that have the type of subdued passion that marked many Sam Cooke hits. A cover of "The Look of Love" is also included on *Facts,* and on other albums he takes awkward stabs at C&W and rock. As his own producer, Womack doesn't always temper such musical ambition with good taste.

★ ★ ★ **Home Is Where the Heart Is** / Col. (1976) ¶
★ ★ ★ ★ **Safety Zone** / U.A. (1976) ¶
★ ★ ★ **Pieces** / Col. (1977) ¶
★ ★ **Roads of Life** / Ari. (1979) ¶

In an attempt to curb his excesses, U.A. contracted David Rubinson to produce *Safety Zone.* Using an L.A. session band, Rubinson concocted some smart rhythm tracks and with the exception of one slip into plastic psychedelia, *Safety Zone* sticks close to the feel of Womack's earlier work. Womack's Columbia albums are returns to self-production, and the problems of the past creep up again: strong original tunes are mixed with misguided cover material.
— J.MC.

STEVIE WONDER

★ ★ ★ **A Tribute to Uncle Ray** / Mo. (1963)
★ ★ ★ **The Jazz Soul of Little Stevie Wonder** / Mo. (1963)
★ ★ ★ ★ **The Twelve-Year-Old Genius** / Mo. (1963)
★ ★ ★ ★ **Down to Earth** / Mo. (1966)
★ ★ ★ ★ **Uptight** / Mo. (1966)

★ ★ ★ ★ **Down to Earth** / Mo. (1967)
★ ★ ★ ★ **I Was Made to Love Her** / Mo. (1967)
★ ★ ★ ★ **For Once in My Life** / Mo. (1968)
★ ★ ★ ★ ★ **Stevie Wonder's Greatest Hits** / Tam. (1968)
★ ★ ★ **My Cherie Amour** / Mo. (1969)
★ ★ ★ ★ **Signed, Sealed and Delivered** / Mo. (1970)
★ ★ ★ **Where I'm Coming From** / Mo. (1971)
★ ★ ★ ★ **Stevie Wonder's Greatest Hits, Vol. 2** / Tam. (1971)
★ ★ ★ ★ ★ **Talking Book** / Tam. (1972)
★ ★ ★ ★ ★ **Music of My Mind** / Tam. (1972)
★ ★ ★ ★ ★ **Innervisions** / Tam. (1973)
★ ★ ★ ★ **Fulfillingness' First Finale** / Tam. (1974)
★ ★ ★ ★ **Songs in the Key of Life** / Tam. (1976)
★ ★ ★ ★ ★ **Looking Back** / Tam. (1977)
★ ★ ★ **Journey through the Secret Life of Plants** / Tam. (1979)
★ ★ ★ ★ ★ **Hotter Than July** / Tam. (1980)
★ ★ ★ **With a Song in My Heart** / Mo. (1981)
★ ★ ★ ★ ★ **Stevie Wonder's Original Musiquarium I** / Tam. (1982)

Stevie Wonder has the revered stature that anyone who has consistently created daring, imaginative, widely heard and exciting American popular music for more than two decades deserves. What's more remarkable is that he has achieved this status while still in his mid-thirties, and after making the incredibly difficult transition from teen star to mature musician. Only Michael Jackson, of contemporary performers, has even a chance of matching Stevie's remarkable track record.

Wonder has been a hitmaker since 1963, when "Fingertips Pt. 2," his third single, became a No. 1 hit. His early records generally fell within the boundaries of the Motown formula sound: "Fingertips," with its raucous harmonica and wild shouts, was at the raw edge of the Motown spectrum, but "Castles in the Sand" went all the way in the other direction. Meantime, the hits piled up, "I Was Made to Love Her," "For Once in My Life," "Uptight," "My Cherie Amour," "Yester-Me, Yester-You, Yesterday," "Shoo-Be-Doo-Be-Doo-Da-Day," "A Place in the Sun," and "Blowin' in the Wind" all making the Top Ten before the Sixties were out. (Wonder had seven other pop Top Forty hits in the decade, a remarkable record.) These hits are contained on the greatest-hits anthologies as well as on the later *Looking Back,* which features enough material from Wonder's next period to make the earlier albums less essential.

However, the various Sixties albums listed here, reissued over the past couple of years in Motown's ambitious program, serve at least to refute the idea that Motown issued only weak, padded albums of show tunes and the like. Wonder certainly recorded his share of standards and ballads (and he wrote his share too), but in his hands they're anything but flimsy or superfluous. These records, with hard-driving R&B set up against pure smooch music, are an early indication of the scope of Stevie's ambition: He wanted to sing everything from Bob Dylan to Frank Sinatra, to work in every format from gutter blues to elegant swing.

Beginning with *Where I'm Coming From,* Wonder shook loose of the Motown production format and began to explore a much more personal vision. That first step was a bit tentative, but within a year he had turned out a pair of extraordinary albums, *Talking Book* and *Music of My Mind.* These albums and their successors pioneered stylistic approaches that helped to determine the shape of pop music for the next decade. Wonder incorporated influences from Sly Stone, Curtis Mayfield, Jimi Hendrix and Gamble and Huff, but he was also the most intelligent user of synthesizers west of Pete Townshend; he wrote smoldering bluesy rockers like "Superstition" alongside finger-popping ballads such as "You Are the Sunshine of My Life"; he played many, if not all, of the instrumental parts himself; and his lyrics, while sometimes obtuse, could also be extraordinarily trenchant, as on "Living for the City," from *Innervisions*, arguably his finest album.

Of all Wonder's mid-Seventies work, only *Fulfillingness' First Finale,* released soon after a 1974 car crash, is less than central to the most significant developments of its period. This does not mean that it is all equally important or effective. *Songs in the Key of Life,* a two-disc set with a seven-inch EP, is so sprawling that it is virtually impossible to absorb all of it, and many of Wonder's lyrics drift off into some kind of psychobabble. However, even here the best of his music is a tour de force of modern recording possibilities.

Journey through the Secret Life of Plants, created as a film soundtrack, was widely dismissed as pure indulgence. But the composition is integrated in a fashion altogether remarkable among popular recordings, achieving a kind of classic ebb and flow

among the tracks, and although it is undeniably strange, there is a certain fascination in hearing Wonder's lyrics, which grant a gracious intellect even to plant life. *Hotter Than July* shows Wonder's latter-day immersion in Caribbean and African culture, and *Original Musiquarium I,* while primarily an anthology of previously released material, makes as strong a case for Wonder's talents as Neil Young's *Decade* does for his. On the strength of its new tracks—"Front Line," "Do I Do," "That Girl" and "Ribbon in the Sky"—what Wonder does next is almost certain to be fascinating. — D.M.

BRENTON WOOD
★ **Come Softly / Cream (NA)**
Does not contain "Oogum Boogum" or "Gimme Little Sign." — D.M.

LAUREN WOOD
★ **Cat Trick / War. (1981)**
★ **Lauren Wood / War. (1982)**
Wood has all of Joni Mitchell's jazzy pretensions without their justification: that is, she lacks the lyrical sophistication to convince you that her aspirations are a match for her insights. Probably because the latter are altogether lacking in depth. — D.M.

RON WOOD
★ ★ ★ **I've Got My Own Album to Do / War. (1974)** ¶
★ ★ ★ **Now Look / War. (1975)**
★ ★ ★ **Mahoney's Last Stand / Atco (1976)**
★ ★ **Gimme Some Neck / Col. (1979)**
★ ★ ★ **1234 / Col. (1981)**
Wood was the bassist in Jeff Beck's 1969 group. When the band split up, he and vocalist Rod Stewart joined the Faces, where Wood played guitar, and in 1975, after Stewart left the Faces, Wood became a Rolling Stone. The way to Stones-hood was paved by *I've Got My Own,* Wood's first solo album, which includes guest appearances by Keith Richards and Mick Jagger, among others. But his 1975 solo LP, *Now Look,* is better; his version of Gib Guilbeau's "Big Bayou" actually cuts Stewart's. Most of this is loose, energetic and more attractive for its feel than its precision—Wood is a cracked-voice singer, but his slide-guitar style is stinging and distinctive. *Mahoney's Last Stand* was a soundtrack collaboration between Wood and Face Ron Lane; the movie was released only in Canada, but the music has the same jaunty appeal as the solo records.

Gimme Some Neck, his first solo album as a full-fledged Stone, was a gross disappointment, Wood merely going through the super-star solo album motions. But *1234* is a different story. Although Wood never regains the joyous tempo of his Faces period, his vocals are the best neo-Dylan yowling anyone's come up with in years, a droll way to celebrate his usual superficial concerns. — D.M.

ROY WOOD
★ ★ **On the Road Again** / War. (1979)
Ex-Move leader Wood's only in-print solo LP is the least interesting of his records. Wood's eccentric wit and excellent musicianship are much more in evidence on the Fifties revival set *Eddie and the Falcons,* on the brilliant *Boulders,* which would rate five stars if it was in print, and on *Mustard* and *Wizzard's Brew.* — J.S.

WRECKLESS ERIC
★ ★ ★ ★ **Big Smash/ Stiff** / Epic (1980) ¶
Pop-trash masterpieces from hard-drinking sawed-off songmaster whose twisted talent was spawned in the British punk uproar. The songs superficially exalt the pop conventions to which they conform, only to trash them. Instrumentation and arrangements are harsh and hokey in turn, the teen dream an Eighties nightmare, a smoking ruin of affairs gone bad, betrayal, unrequited lust. Eric's from-the-pavement songs owe more to mid-Sixties Kinks than to the humorless, irony-hating punk scene with which he's associated in the U.S.; a bleak paranoia, here effectively satirized, is one of his few links with that sensibility. "Take the Cash" and "A Pop Song" join the top rank of tunes written about the record biz. This joint Stiff/Epic release incorporates an earlier Stiff American LP. — G.A.

BETTY WRIGHT
★ ★ ★ ★ **Danger: High Voltage** / Als. (1974)
★ ★ ★ **Explosion** / Als. (1976)
★ ★ **This Time for Real** / Als. (1977)
★ ★ ★ **Betty Wright Live** / Als. (1978)
★ ★ ★ **Travelin' in the Wright Circle** / Als. (1979)
★ ★ ★ **Betty Wright** / Epic (NA)
An energetic, spunky performer, Betty Wright hasn't been able to transfer her considerable talents into sustained commercial success. Her early hits ("Clean Up Woman," "The Babysitter") are gritty novelty records, but they're out of print and the albums are a mixed bag. *Danger: High Voltage* is the best; it's a cross section of exuberant, varied dance songs and poignant ballads, recorded during the peak of Miami soul. The subsequent albums show a distressing lack of direction

and often bog down with hack productions. — J.MC.

GARY WRIGHT
★ ★ **Dream Weaver** / War. (1975)
★ **Light of Smiles** / War. (1976) ¶
★ **Touch and Gone** / War. (1977) ¶
★ **Headin' Home** / War. (1979)
Keyboard veteran of Spooky Tooth, hit big in 1975 with a syrupy ballad, "Dream Weaver," from the album of the same name. Since then he's indulged himself with increasing flatulence in a spacy, mystical froth of synthesizers and remarkably poor vocalizing. — D.M.

O. V. WRIGHT
★ ★ ★ **O. V. Wright** / MCA (1965)
★ ★ ★ **Nucleus of Soul** / MCA (1966)
★ ★ ★ ★ **Eight Men and Four Women** / MCA (1967)
★ ★ ★ ★ **A Nickel and a Nail/Ace of Spades** / MCA (1970)
★ ★ ★ ★ **Memphis Unlimited** / MCA (1973)
★ ★ ★ **Into Something I Can't Shake Loose** / Hi (1975)
★ ★ ★ **The Bottom Line** / Hi (1978)
★ ★ ★ **We're Still Together** / Hi (NA)
O.V. Wright's best records are the Sixties soul sides he made for Backbeat (now put out by MCA), particularly the sometimes chilling "Ace of Spade." His voice is unique, a dark and moody instrument that's a holdover from the heyday of Southern soul. The Hi albums contain strong performances marred by Willie Mitchell's dreary string charts. — J.MC.

WRIGHT BROTHERS FLYING MACHINE
★ **Wright Brothers Flying Machine** / Casa. (1978)
Grounded by its own banalities. — D.M.

THE WRITERS
★ **All the Music That's Fit to Play** / Col. (1978) ¶
★ **All in Fun** / Col. (NA)
Sessionmen, the best known being percussionist Ralph McDonald and guitarist Hugh McCracken, indulge themselves in the usual turgid jazz rock. This is almost enough to make you appreciate Toto, especially since the meandering music here proves conclusively that writers are the one thing that these chops-*meisters* ain't. — D.M.

MICHAEL WYCOFF
★ ★ **Come to My World** / RCA (1980)
Everything Wycoff didn't learn from Stevie

Wonder, he picked up from George Benson (after Benson put down his guitar). The very definition of second-rate. — D.M.

TAMMY WYNETTE
★ ★ ★ **Your Good Girl's Gonna Go Bad /** Epic (1967) ¶
★ ★ ★ ★ **D-I-V-O-R-C-E / Epic (1968)**
★ ★ ★ ★ **Stand by Your Man / Epic (1969)**
★ ★ ★ **Inspiration / Epic (1969)** ¶
★ ★ ★ ★ ★ **Tammy's Greatest Hits / Epic (1969)**
★ ★ ★ **Christmas with Tammy / Epic (1970)** ¶
★ ★ ★ **Tammy's Greatest Hits, Vol. 2 / Epic (1971)**
★ ★ ★ **Bedtime Story / Epic (1972)**
★ ★ ★ **First Songs of the First Lady / Epic (1973)** ¶
★ ★ ★ **Kids Say the Darndest Things / Epic (1973)** ¶
★ ★ ★ **Woman to Woman / Epic (1974)** ¶
★ ★ ★ **Another Lonely Song / Epic (1974)** ¶
★ ★ ★ **Tammy's Greatest Hits, Vol. 3 / Epic (1975)**
★ ★ ★ **I Still Believe in Fairy Tales / Epic (1975)** ¶
★ ★ ★ **Till I Can Make It on My Own / Epic (1976)**
★ ★ ★ **You and Me / Epic (1976)** ¶
★ ★ ★ **Let's Get Together / Epic (1977)**
★ ★ ★ **One of a Kind / Epic (1977)**
★ ★ ★ **Womanhood / Epic (1978)**
★ ★ ★ **Tammy's Greatest Hits, Vol. 4 / Epic (1978)**
★ ★ ★ **Just Tammy / Epic (1979)**
★ ★ ★ **Only Lonely Sometimes / Epic (1980)**
★ ★ ★ **You Brought Me Back / Epic (1981)**

A former hairdresser from Tupelo, Mississippi, Tammy Wynette had become the most important female vocalist in country music by the end of the Sixties. She began recording in 1966 and quickly turned out a series of hits, including "Your Good Girl's Gonna Go Bad," "D-I-V-O-R-C-E," "Take Me to Your World" and "Stand by Your Man." Through the Seventies and Eighties, and despite her marriage to and subsequent divorce from champion honky-tonker George Jones, Wynette has settled into a formula country approach, abetted by producer Billy Sherrill's rather treacly taste in arrangements and material. But both *D-I-V-O-R-C-E* and *Stand by Your Man* are modern country LPs worth hearing, and the first *Greatest Hits* collection is a must. — C.F.

PHILLIPE WYNNE
★ ★ ★ **Starting All Over / Coti. (1977)**

As lead vocalist for the Spinners, Wynne did some wonderful things. But on his own, he can't match them, at least not in his initial solo outing. Disappointing. — D.M.

X
★ ★ **Los Angeles** / Slash (1980)
★ **Wild Gift** / Slash (1981)
★ **Under the Big Black Sun** / Slash
(1982)

Despite raves in every publication from *Time* to *The New York Rocker,* despite being hailed as the greatest Los Angeles rock band since the Doors (whose organist, Ray Manzarek, has produced the group), the songs of leaders John Doe and Exene Cervenka basically boil down to a rehash of the aesthetized decadence and musical desiccation typified by the Doors and the group's other obvious (and inevitable) influence. But Doe and Cervenka possess only a smidgen of Lou Reed's ability to delineate the demimonde, and Exene lacks even a hint of Jim Morrison's pop charm. (If anything, she sounds like a more hapless version of Grace Slick.) Lyrically, X prattles a great deal about soul, but it is hard to think of another band so well-reviewed whose music is so directionless and abrasively unemotional. And if X has compensating glories (as the Stooges, Dolls, Sex Pistols and early Clash did), they're well hidden on these discs.

Symptomatically, the group's only album with major-league distribution, *Under the Big Black Sun,* laid an egg commercially. Not terribly surprising in the end, since like all bohemian avant-gardists, X protects itself carefully from any claims of the larger marketplace. But like others of that stripe, their failure to find an audience is less the result of a cultural conspiracy than of the band's utter failure to meet any of the requirements of genuinely popular culture. Critics may be required to contort themselves into positions in which this kind of rubbish represents a major statement, but there's no reason for anyone whose hip credentials don't depend upon it to do likewise.
— D.M.

X RAY SPEX
★ ★ **Germ Free Adolescents** / EMI (1978),
Br. imp.

Original arty-pretentious British punk rockers, best known for "O Bondage Up Yours" and lead vocalist Poly Styrene. Presumably the abandonment of pop form, soulless vocals and arrhythmic beat make an important aesthetic/political comment about modern nihilism and dehumanization . . . or something. No one listens to this stuff for amusement. — D.M.

XTC
★ ★ ★ **White Music** / Virgin (1978), Br.
imp.
★ ★ ★ **Go Two** / Virgin (1978), Br. imp.
★ ★ ★ ★ **Drums and Wires** / Virgin (1979)
★ ★ ★ ★ **Black Sea** / Virgin (1980)

Anglo art-pop's 1978 debuts were less than impressive, perhaps because the punkish competition was a bit stiff that year. As Andy Partridge's sense of twisted pop began to dominate Colin Moulding's penchant for skewed art, however, XTC became more and more one of the highlights of the contemporary British scene. That is, this is one of the few arty avant-gardists of the post-punk moment that can really rock out, which means that it sweats enough to earn its pretensions (and maybe even its nihilism). — D.M.

YACHTS
★ ★ ★ SOS / Poly. (1979)
★ ★ ★ ★ Yachts without Radar / Poly.
(1980)
Cinematically conceived pop as appealing
and powerful as music of more well-known
Squeeze. Bouncing, kinetic arrangements, alternately powered and punctuated by Henry
Priestman's keyboards, carry lyrics that jive
punfully even as they make a point, although
too many of the songs are about screwings
in the record biz. First LP exhibits less verve
and command than second outing, the
title of which commemorates band's
separation from U.K.'s Radar Records.
— G.A.

STOMU YAMASHTA
★ ★ ★ Red Buddah / Van. (1974)
★ ★ ★ ★ Go / Is. (1976)
★ ★ ★ Go Too / Ari. (1977) ¶
★ ★ ★ Go—Live from Paris / Is. (1978)
Japanese composer/percussionist whose bizarre ideas and musical eclecticism have
made him well respected in varied musical
circles but keep him a mystery to the general
public. Yamashta's musical productions (all
his records are related to one of several multimedia presentations he has either put together or is still planning) combine elements
of jazz, rock, classical and electronic music
deftly, and sometimes arbitrarily—hence his
difficulty in reaching a mass audience. *Man
from the East,* a strange but fascinating stage
show featuring elements of Japanese Kabuki
theater, spawned the *Red Buddah* album,
which is the best demonstration of Yamashta's astounding technique as a percussionist. The other records are part of a project that Yamashta intends as a recapitulation
of all his influences. *Go,* which includes a
fine performance on keyboards from Steve
Winwood, is the most accessible record Yamashta has made. — J.S.

JIMMY YANCEY
★ ★ ★ ★ ★ Chicago Piano / Atl. (1972)
★ ★ ★ ★ ★ Jimmy Yancey / Oldie B. (NA)
★ ★ ★ ★ ★ The Immortal Jimmy Yancey /
Oldie B. (NA)
Possibly the best of all the barrelhouse piano
practitioners, Yancey brought a quiet eloquence and nuance to the style that the
rough-and-tumble barroom soundtrack genre
lacked elsewhere. Yancey played for himself
and did not actively pursue recording dates,
so his output is limited but precious. By day
he worked as a professional baseball player
and later as a groundskeeper for the Chicago
White Sox; at night he would play his piano.
The Oldie Blues sides collect his earliest
work, from 1939 on *Immortal* and from
1943 on the other, which also includes a rare
and beautiful private party recording. The
Atlantic sides are reissues of an eloquent session made just a few weeks before his death
in 1951 with Jimmy's wife, Mama Yancey,
singing on some tracks. — J.S.

GLENN YARBROUGH
■ The Best of Glenn Yarbrough / RCA (1970)
■ The Best of Glenn Yarbrough / Trad. (NA)
Less appropriate titles could not have been
found for either of these LPs. Although Yarbrough had a hit with "Baby the Rain Must
Fall" (around which the RCA collection is
built), his best work was unquestionably as a
member of the Limeliters. That group's
RCA catalogue is out of print, but it was a
typical example of early-Sixties pop folk. The
Tradition LP is slightly more in tune with
the Limeliters style than the obnoxiously orchestrated MOR RCA set. Better to check
the cutout bins for RCA's Limeliters releases. — I.M.

THE YARDBIRDS
★ ★ ★ ★ ★ The Yardbirds Great Hits / Epic
(1967) ¶

★ ★ ★ **Eric Clapton and the Yardbirds with Sonny Boy Williamson / Mer. (1970) ¶**
★ ★ ★ ★ **Yardbirds Favorites / Epic (1977) ¶**
★ ★ ★ **Eric Clapton and the Yardbirds / Sp. (NA)**
★ ★ ★ **Shapes of Things / Sp. (NA) ¶**

One of the great Sixties rock groups, the Yardbirds were influential on other musicians beyond the bounds of their own commercial impact, which in this country amounted mostly to a handful of hit singles: "Heart Full of Soul," "I'm a Man," "For Your Love" and "Shapes of Things." These were rock at a certain edge, beginning to prepare itself for the massive guitar frenzy and experimentation of the psychedelic age.

Keith Relf was probably the most limited singer in any of the significant British groups, but the Yardbirds' guitarists—Eric Clapton, Jeff Beck and Jimmy Page, in sequence—were all true originals: Clapton's fiery blues style dominates the Springboard LPs, while Beck and Page take over on the Epic repackages. The Yardbirds helped introduce almost every significant technical innovation in the rock of their period: feedback, modal playing, fuzztone, etc. Their influence can't be overestimated. Cream, Led Zeppelin and heavy metal in general would have been inconceivable without them. — D.M.

YELLOW MAGIC ORCHESTRA
★ ★ **Yellow Magic Orchestra / A&M (1979)**
★ ★ ★ **BGM / A&M (1981)**

Bland, trite synthesizer pop lacking the conceptual sophistication of Kraftwerk or the instrumental assurance of Tomita. *Yellow Magic Orchestra* features a nice imitation of a Space Invaders machine, though. — J.D.C.

YES
★ ★ ★ **Yes / Atl. (1969)**
★ ★ **Time and a Word / Atl. (1970)**
★ ★ **The Yes Album / Atl. (1971)**
★ ★ ★ **Fragile / Atl. (1971)**
★ ★ ★ **Close to the Edge / Atl. (1972)**
★ ★ **Yessongs / Atl. (1973)**
★ **Tales from Topographic Oceans / Atl. (1973)**
★ ★ **Relayer / Atl. (1974)**
★ ★ **Yesterdays / Atl. (1975)**
★ **Going for the One / Atl. (1977)**
★ **Tormato / Atl. (1978)**
★ **Drama / Atl. (1980)**
★ **Yesshows / Atl. (1980)**

Classical rockers with hearts of cold, Yes entered the Seventies as a creative example of post-*Pepper's* artistic aspirations, a musicianly alternative to the growing metal monster rock was becoming. It left the decade as perhaps the epitome of uninvolved, pretentious and decidedly nonprogressive music, so flaccid and conservative that it became the symbol of uncaring platinum success, spawning more stylistic opponents than adherents.

The heart of Yes's approach was never really the dazzling displays of technical perfection that each band member could conjure up in abundance. The center of attention, and therefore also the blame for their eventual artistic numbness, should be granted to Jon Anderson and his continual obsession with quasi-mystical themes and words. The early records, with Peter Banks and Tony Kaye, relied on outside material to some degree and avoided the problems that Anderson's progressively obscure vision would bring to later albums. With the addition of guitarist Steve Howe *(The Yes Album)* and keyboard flash Rick Wakeman *(Fragile),* Anderson began delving deeper into extended lyrical forays that had a certain fairy-tale charm, but ultimately served only as an extra texture in the complex sound tapestry. The peak of Yes's experimentation was reached on *Fragile* and *Close to the Edge,* the latter especially reaching highs that were not again attained. From that point, massive arena success and a growing split between the relaxed, meat-eating Wakeman and the uptight, health-conscious Anderson and Howe led to their demise.

Almost no platinum-level group in the Seventies had anything new to offer after the release of their live albums, and Yes was no exception. *Yessongs* serves as an estimable live greatest-hits package, although the sound isn't quite up to snuff. On *Tales from Topographic Oceans,* the bottom fell out. Featuring only one song on each of its four sides, the music veered from what was rapidly becoming the lush Yes version of Muzak to some of the most jarring and nauseating guitar noise heard since the psychedelic Sixties. Fans weren't the only ones puzzled; Rick Wakeman, with a potentially lucrative solo career awaiting, took off in utter confusion over the group's intents. By now, though, the band could shrug off the loss of its only charismatic member and simply mix a new element into their formula; in this case, keyboardsman Patrick Moraz, who lasted only one studio album.

The final evidence of growing institutional insufferableness was reached with the release of solo records by each band member, a move that traditionally demonstrates divisiveness and the unwillingness to channel personal effort and growth into the group. Wakeman's return, *Going for the One,* promised change—no Roger Dean cover, and the relatively straightforward, hard-rocking title track—but quickly became business as usual. The almost new-wave simplicity (for Yes) that *One* conveyed was less an effective reduction of valid ideas than an admission of total artistic bankruptcy. After *Tormato* (whose tomato-splattered cover looked like the critics heard what was inside before the shrink wrap was added), Wakeman and Anderson split for good, and the group rolled on by picking up two ex-Buggles (of pop novelty "Video Killed the Radio Star" fame), Geoff Downes and Trevor Horn. If the release of all those solo records hadn't already put them on the same level of crass corporate rapacity as Kiss, then surely this move did. Yes had become a machine whose reputation was larger and more important than any of its human components; as with all such companies, the bottom line was money, not art or the welfare of its employees. Who cared if the final product was now a bland assembly-line concoction? Apparently no one. — W.K.

YIPES!

★ Yipes! / Millen. (1979)
★ A Bit Irrational / Millen. (1980)
Hard-rock tedium. Nothing to get excited about. — D.M.

DENNIS YOST AND THE CLASSICS FOUR

★ ★ Stormy / Acc. (NA)
Hits by late-Sixties Southern group that contributed members to Atlanta Rhythm Section. Yost is a strained white soulman, in the manner of David Clayton-Thomas more than Mitch Ryder or Felix Cavaliere, but "Spooky," his best hit, is a gem nonetheless. "Stormy" and the rest are dispensable; this is definitely a group for singles collectors. — D.M.

JESSE COLIN YOUNG

★ ★ Together / War. (1972) ¶
★ ★ Song for Juli / War. (1973) ¶
★ ★ The Soul of a City Boy / Cap. (1974)
★ ★ Light Shine / War. (1974) ¶
★ ★ Songbird / War. (1975) ¶
★ ★ On the Road / War. (1976)
★ ★ Love on the Wing / War. (1977) ¶
★ ★ American Dreams / Elek. (1978)
Young was a quixotic force as leader of the Youngbloods, one of the more eccentric manifestations of late-Sixties folk rock. On his own, he was a lot more like a soap-opera caricature of northern California hippies— rusticated without relief or groove or much more than the usual pious combination of good times and happy vibes. This extensive catalogue is one long, numb muddle. — D.M.

JOHNNY YOUNG

★ ★ ★ Johnny Young and His Chicago Blues Band / Arhoo. (1966)
★ ★ ★ Chicago Blues / Arhoo. (1968)
Journeyman Chicago guitarist and singer doubles on mandolin, which makes him more interesting than most of the current competition. — D.M.

KAREN YOUNG

★ ★ ★ Hot Shot / West End (1979)
Listenable disco starlet—not Donna Summer, but not bad. Title track made some noise on both pop and soul charts. — D.M.

MIGHTY JOE YOUNG

★ ★ Legacy of the Blues, Vol. 4 / Sonet (1972), Br. imp.
★ ★ Chicken Heads / Ova. (1974)
★ ★ Love Gone / Ova. (1976)
★ ★ Mighty Joe Young / Ova. (1976)
★ ★ Bluesy Josephine / Black and Blue (1976), imp.
★ ★ Blues with a Touch of Soul / Del. (NA)
A rather pedestrian young Chicago blues guitarist. Young earned his nickname more for his size than for his guitar style, a rather bland synthesis of Freddie King and Luther Allison. — D.M.

NEIL YOUNG

★ ★ ★ Neil Young / Rep. (1969)
★ ★ ★ ★ Everybody Knows This Is Nowhere / Rep. (1969)
★ ★ ★ After the Gold Rush / Rep. (1970)
★ ★ ★ Harvest / Rep. (1972)
★ Journey through the Past / Rep. (1972)
These are the records that Young made between the time when he split with Buffalo Springfield, where he made his early reputation, and his initial burst of fame and abnegation. Young was already some kind of West Coast mysterioso hero, and the enigmatic *Neil Young,* a curious mixture of folkie piety and Spector-ian lushness, did nothing to dispel this aura. Its highlights are the alienation anthem, "The Loner," and the Dylan-esque dirge epic, "The Last Trip to Tulsa."

With *Everybody Knows This Is Nowhere,* Young hooked up with a California bar band, Crazy Horse. Crazy Horse's guitarist, Danny Whitten, seems to have been responsible for inducing Young to make more streamlined, though no less long-winded ("Down by the River" is one thing, "Cowgirl in the Sand" quite another) rock & roll. "Cinnamon Girl" is the finest rocker Young recorded in this period.

Harvest and *Gold Rush,* recorded after Whitten's death but with the remnants of Crazy Horse (Nils Lofgren picking up the slack), were Young's most popular records, producing the hit singles "Heart of Gold," "Old Man" and "Only Love Can Break Your Heart." They weren't nearly so raw as *Eveverybody Knows This Is Nowhere,* and not nearly as ambitious. They were, indeed, very good examples of the singer/songwriter style then dominating the pop charts—though Young joined Crosby, Stills and Nash at this time in order to toughen up their sound, only such a trio of wimps would have thought of him as a hard-rocker.

Journey through the Past is Young's first attempt at over-self-mythologizing. Ostensibly the soundtrack to the terrible movie of the same name, which he directed, *Journey* is actually an attempt to catalogue Young's creativity (and some of his influences), as if the artist were critically evaluating his own career to date. But at this point Young seemed little more than an erratic West Coast folk-rocker or an eccentric singer/songwriter.

★ ★ ★ **Time Fades Away / Rep. (1973)**
★ ★ **On the Beach / Rep. (1974)**
★ ★ ★ ★ ★ **Tonight's the Night / Rep. (1975)**
★ ★ ★ ★ **Zuma / Rep. (1975)**
This is Young's most hard-rocking and least murky period, a time when his music seemed to have a clear-cut direction, and his career a consciously creative shape. *Time Fades Away* was Young's response to the realization that his popular success as a singer/songwriter had boxed him in. It is a live album, sporting a group of previously unrecorded songs and featuring a band of Hollywood session players playing extraordinarily raw, nearly atonal rock & roll. Its best numbers—"Last Dance," "Time Fades Away," "Yonder Stands the Sinner"—have the aura of doom characteristic of all Young's work in this period. Its worst—"Don't Be Denied"—fall back into the hippie simplisms of Young's more overweening work with Buffalo Springfield. *On the Beach* takes this even further; this album's apocalyptic prophecy is rendered all but unlistenable by Young's grating, whining delivery.

With *Tonight's the Night,* however, Young came up with a record as beautifully nightmarish as his intentions. Conceived as an elegy to Whitten (and roadie Bruce Barry), the record chronicles the post-hippie, post-Vietnam demise of countercultural idealism, and a generation's long slow trickle down the drain through drugs, violence and twisted sexuality. The music, played with a revamped version of Crazy Horse, is nothing less than scathing, and Young's parched, wracked voice is perfectly in tune with the thrust of his lyrics. This is Young's only conceptually cohesive record, and it is a great one.

Zuma is in many ways the obverse of *Tonight's the Night:* most of it retains the hard-rock sound of the new Crazy Horse, but Crosby, Nash and Young harmonizing provides its conclusion. And while *Zuma* continues to portray all kinds of romance savagely, the perspective has moved from social comment to the purely personal (and often vindictive). When *Zuma* works, as on "Cortez the Killer," "Drive Back" and one or two others, it is brilliant. When it does not, however, it returns to the fuzzy platitudes of Young's worst early work: the final "Through My Sails" is as maudlin as Buffalo Springfield's "Broken Arrow," and with less excuse.

★ ★ ★ ★ ★ **Decade / Rep. (1978)**
Decade is the most purposeful recording of Young's career. A triple-disc anthology of all his work up to this period, beginning with Buffalo Springfield and concluding with excerpts from his reunion with Stephen Stills (as a duo, in 1977), *Decade's* overt purpose is to establish Young's credentials as a major rock artist, on a level with Dylan, Lennon and Presley.

Superficially, the evidence is convincing. At this stage, Young had created an extremely diverse body of work, and the best of it ("Ohio," "Cinnamon Girl," "Southern Man," "Helpless," *Tonight's the Night,* "Like a Hurricane," "Cortez the Killer") is as good as the best rock of any American artist of the Sixties and Seventies. But for all his virtues, Young embedded his good ideas in a trove of bad ones, and his realized concepts are forever juxtaposed (except on *Decade*) with his worst. With the exception of *Tonight's the Night,* he has never been able to make a fully realized concept album, not a terribly significant flaw except that he kept on making half-realized ones. By excerpting the most successful moments from these failures, Young almost managed to convince you they were triumphs.

Up to the point it covers, *Decade* qualified Young as one of the most important performers of the Seventies, if not all time, and certainly one of the few Americans who had a mainstream pop music career that showed signs of developing into a major artistic personality.

★ ★ ★ **American Stars 'n' Bars / Rep. (1977)**
★ ★ **Comes a Time / Rep. (1978)**
★ ★ **Hawks and Doves / Rep. (1979)**
★ ★ ★ ★ **Rust Never Sleeps / Rep. (1979)**
★ ★ ★ **Live Rust / Rep. (1980)**
★ ★ **Re-ac-tor / Rep. (1981)**
★ **Trans / Gef. (1982)**

These are the albums Young has made since *Decade* (except for *American Stars 'n' Bars,* issued slightly earlier but which belongs here because of its construction and sound). They demonstrate conclusively that whatever Young may have shown the world about his relative strengths with *Decade,* there were weaknesses in his work almost as significant. With one exception, each of these records in turn is more conceptually conceited and more scattershot in its effects.

American Stars 'n' Bars seemed a slight downturn from *Zuma* and *Tonight's the Night,* basically a return to the country and folk implications of Young's pre-*Time Fades Away* material, perhaps as an attempt to regain his footing on the radio. Although both the title and the cover fumble to convey some overriding truth about America, and Young's relationship to it (as a musician; as an immigrant—he's Canadian by birth; as a star—who knows?), the record never gets around to clarifying its purpose (if it has one). The best track, an eight-minute tour de force of electric guitar feedback and extended metaphor (Smokey Robinson meets Jimi Hendrix on Bob Dylan's old block) is "Hurricane." It is sandwiched between two of the worst songs of Young's career, "Will to Love," a paean to the lust of the salmon, and "Homegrown," a homily for grassgrowers that would have been embarrassing if recorded by David Peel. Most of the rest is Young harmonizing with the likes of Linda Ronstadt and the genuinely awful Nicolette Larson. Larson is the dominant supporting performer on *Comes a Time* as well, an even messier stylistic hodgepodge—its best song, Ian Tyson's "Four Strong Winds," wasn't even written by Young.

These records establish a pattern for Young's other releases to date, with their mixture of country folk songs and rock & roll "experiments." The former are too often desiccated, and the latter are almost invariably stillborn, resting on a guitar style that seemed brilliant as a schematic at the time of *Zuma* and now seems like nothing so much as a thunderingly unimaginative dead end. Though some of Young's rawness is deliberate, a good deal of the rest is simply sloppy.

Young has never learned the basic craftsmanship and sense of detail required to make the kind of ambitious conceptual statements to which these records aspire. Were he content to be judged as a songwriter, Young might be a genuine genius. But even his songs suffer from his lack of craft: far too many of them are windy exertions to no clear purpose, reiterations of a philosophy that hasn't been amplified or expanded since Buffalo Springfield's "Broken Arrow."

That is not to say that Young does not make remarkable music from time to time. *Rust Never Sleeps* comes very close to realizing everything he intends for it. In "Powderfinger," Young wrote as brilliant a statement of American nihilism and despair as any rock writer has created; in "Pocahontas," he found an amusing new way to tackle his romanticized fantasies of the Indians; and in "Thrasher," he came up with a unique extended metaphor to express his disgust with and distrust of technology. On the other hand, Young's attempt to extend the concept of this album with *Live Rust* results in a murky web of pretentious noise and comment, which adds little to the original versions of the songs, and if anything, may be the most lifeless, stilted work he has done. (Even more pretentious, though less murky, is his synthesizer farce, *Trans.* Unless it's a joke, which is fairly unlikely.)

(Worse yet are Young's occasional attempts at overt political commentary, which range from the addlepated—"T-Bone" on *Re-ac-tor,* "Welfare Mother" on *Rust Never Sleeps*—to the outright reactionary—"Union Man" on *Hawks and Doves.*)

Because he lacks the commitment or the focus to develop his ideas (or even select well among them), Young remains a minor artist—albeit one with major potential, if he should apply himself diligently enough to develop it. — D.M.

STEVE YOUNG
★ ★ ★ **Seven Bridges Road / Blue C. (1975)**
★ ★ ★ ★ **Renegade Picker / RCA (1976)** ¶
★ ★ ★ ★ **No Place to Fall / RCA (1977)** ¶

Young is some kind of country songwriter. His "Lonesome, On'ry and Mean," with its loping pace and grim evocation of the plight of a drifter pursued by inner demons, is the best thing Waylon Jennings ever recorded. Young's own version of it (on *Renegade Picker*) approaches Jennings' intensity; he possesses the same kind of husky baritone and remarkable ability to sustain notes. A fine, overlooked, underrated country performer. — C.F.

LONNIE YOUNGBLOOD
★ ★ **Lonnie Youngblood / Radio (1981)**
Overinflated funk featuring third-rate Junior Walker licks. — J.D.C.

THE YOUNGBLOODS
★ ★ ★ **Youngbloods / RCA (1967)**
★ ★ ★ ★ **Best of the Youngbloods / RCA (1970)**
★ ★ ★ ★ **This Is the Youngbloods / RCA (1972)**
One of the best of the late-Sixties bands to come under the psychedelic umbrella, the Youngbloods played music that was really much too conservative by the standards of the day to be called acid rock. Led by reconstructed folkie Jesse Colin Young, the band was more a white R&B outfit than anything else. After knocking around for a while, a version of "Get Together" became a hit and the band enjoyed moderate popularity. Young put together his own label, Raccoon Records, released a pair of great albums by Michael Hurley and some Youngbloods projects, then promptly went broke.

At various times the Youngbloods have had quite a few albums out, but now most of them, even the legendary *Elephant Mountain,* are deleted. The remaining records, especially the *This Is* compilation, do give a good, if fractured, account of the band. — J.S.

YOUNG MARBLE GIANTS
★ ★ ★ **Colossal Youth / Rough T. (1980), Br. imp.**
Future primitive, a melodic minimalist Fairport Convention. The band broke up in early 1981. — B.C.

ZAPP
★ ★ **Zapp / War. (1980)**
Studio group is concoction, primarily, of
Roger Troutman, who has poached Prince's
territory as rapper/rocker by reducing himself to one name and adding a little rock &
roll to the act. *Zapp* is overproduced with
the aid of Bootsy Collins. Although apparently part of George Clinton's Grand Funk
Army, it stumbles over its own grunting emphasis on bassistry. Dull and predictable,
this mess nonetheless made it to No. 1 on
the R&B charts at the turn of the decade.
— D.M.

FRANK ZAPPA/THE MOTHERS OF INVENTION
★ ★ ★ ★ **Freak Out / Verve (1966)** ¶
★ ★ ★ ★ **Absolutely Free / Verve (1967)** ¶
★ ★ ★ ★ ★ **We're Only in It for the Money
/ Verve (1968)** ¶
★ ★ ★ **Mothermania / Biz./Verve (1969)** ¶
★ **The Worst of the Mothers / Verve
(NA)** ¶
The Mothers of Invention, led by Frank
Zappa, shocked the Sixties "underground"
into early self-recognition with the intellec-
tual arrogance and wit of *Freak Out.* Here
at last was an album that interjected the
ironic modes of pop art (as practiced by
Rosenquist, Warhol and Dine) into rock &
roll and made it work. Dylan's lyrics had already put down love-song clichés, and others
had attempted arty experiments with rock,
but Zappa took the whole form through a
grand mutation.
One disc of the double record consists of
robust parodies of mid-Sixties suburbia.
Zappa knew his pop ready-mades well
enough to render them into effective songs
like "You Didn't Try to Call Me" and
"How Could I Be Such a Fool," but it was
Ray Collins' extraordinary pop-operatic vocals that best conveyed the not-so-mock rage.

The other disc is rock's first experimental
music masterpiece, influenced mainly by
such modern composers as Edgar Varèse,
but with an anarchist aggression that is far
more defiantly celebratory than arty. "Help,
I'm a Rock" and "The Return of the Son of
Monster Magnet" created an enduring aural
landscape over which Zappa's mythic heroes—from Suzy Creamcheese to his current
sadistic libertine of "The Torture Never
Stops"—have quested in various stages of
numbed distress ever since.
Stuck in among these avant-garde excursions is "Trouble Comin' Everyday."
Zappa's own brilliantly ugly vocal growls
over the Mothers' lunging ancestor, heavy-
metal rock. Along with "Help, I'm a Rock,"
"Trouble" darkly anticipates the political
themes of imprisonment and suffocation that
obsess Zappa on *Absolutely Free* and *We're
Only in It for the Money.*
Both of those albums should have dated
badly. While often hailed for Zappa's "montage" editing, which turned regular rock-
song forms inside out, the popularity of the
LPs rests on satire. Surprisingly, they have
dated very little. Aside from a few topical
references, the prison/insane asylum/
shopping mall algebra still stings and the essentially structural intelligence of Zappa's
montage remains awesome.
Absolutely Free takes on "straight" America with "Brown Shoes Don't Make It,"
"Plastic People" and "America Drinks and
Goes Home" to create a pop horror show
worthy of Hans Bellmer's dolls, whose violent overtones Zappa was deliberately evoking in his live shows.
We're Only in It for the Money was intended to serve as a Brechtian (as in "alienation effect") answer to *Sgt. Pepper's Lonely
Hearts Club Band,* and it is a relentless savaging of "hip" America, for which the
Beatles' album was providing an appropri-

ately naive soundtrack. Zappa's tone is never less than ominous. His montage techniques are now perfected, and he weaves chillingly munchkin pop-song sections into white noise, spoken sections and Varèsian segments mounting up to his horrific "The Chrome Plated Megaphone of Destiny." The suitable text, he tells us in his liner notes, is Kafka's "In the Penal Colony," while the music itself is a frightening indication that if Zappa expected anything of the Sixties, it was the antichrist, not the Aquarian Age. Still, "Mother People" posits a cautiously rationalist humanism as something to which his fans might aspire. As he would reveal with his next albums, Zappa wasn't really the Dada nihilist of his public reputation.

The compilation albums should be avoided. Zappa was working in a strict album format, although he himself put *Mothermania* together, which makes it preferable.

★ ★ ★ ★ **Uncle Meat / Biz. (1969)**
★ ★ ★ ★ **Weasels Ripped My Flesh / Biz. (1970)**
★ ★ ★ ★ **Burnt Weeny Sandwich / Biz. (1970)**

Uncle Meat, the last album recorded by the original Mothers, was part of Zappa's sustained effort to use *musical* means to create extended works. (*Lumpy Gravy,* Zappa's deleted first solo album, is also part of this process.) Although the montage techniques are still used to great advantage, they are now joining together longer and more discrete elements. The effect achieved is a blend rather than a collision. As the Mothers grew into a superb instrumental ensemble, Zappa also worked in extended, jazzlike solos, and his appropriations from modern composers also continued.

Here Zappa the moralist-satirist temporarily disappears, replaced by an incarnation as metaphysician. The vocal fragments, spoken parts and even the songs consist largely of autobiographical allusions, poetic texts, linguistic games and gnomic manifestos on aesthetics. The result is Zappa's most personal work. *Meat* and the later-released *Weeny* and *Weasels* (consisting of selections from the vast career retrospective Zappa once planned) are the best records by Zappa and the Mothers of Invention.

The missing artifact from this period is *Ruben and the Jets,* the set of doo-wop parodies that are autobiographical in another way. The set is deleted, which is unfortunate, although Zappa's sincere affection for doo-wop's aching sweetness was overwhelmed by sheer weariness and a dry sense

of something neither Zappa nor the Mothers could emotionally entertain.

★ ★ **Mothers Live at the Fillmore East— June 1971 / Biz. (1971)**
★ **Just Another Band from L.A. / Biz. (1972)**
★ ★ ★ **The Grand Wazoo / Rep. (1973)**

This is Zappa's most disorganized period, because so much of his work immediately following the dissolution of the Mothers is deleted. The best album, *Hot Rats* (Bizarre), was a long-awaited guitar showcase for Zappa, who had previously repressed his own playing on records. *Chunga's Revenge* featured Flo and Eddie, and was recorded just before the formation of a second Mothers lineup. Zappa's sarcastic intelligence is indefatigable here, but it's quite clear that both his icy anger and serious imagination were spent before *Chunga* was recorded.

The band that recorded *Live at the Fillmore* and *Just Another Band* had taken on the character of a cynical joke. These Mothers could play excitingly and entertainingly, but in the end the albums witness a woeful attenuation of Zappa's best ideas and instincts. *The Grand Wazoo* is a return to the full horn-section arranging he'd almost forsaken after *Uncle Meat.* In its modest way— Zappa has seldom been so understated— *Wazoo* is a fusion-music gem that almost manages to sound like art rock.

★ ★ ★ **Over-Nite Sensation / Discr. (1973)**
★ ★ **The Roxy and Elsewhere / Discr. (1974)**
★ ★ ★ **One Size Fits All / Discr. (1974)**
★ ★ **Bongo Fury / Discr. (1975)**

On these albums, Zappa achieves a nicely formulaic plateau. Having discarded, or stored away, most of his compositional experiments. Zappa now writes regular rock songs that in turn resemble Chicago, Santana and John McLaughlin in structure, though usually a quirky beat change or keyboard flourish acts as a signature. The lyrics are cozily scatological, casually pornographic or smugly satirical. As *Roxy* demonstrates, Zappa has found a congenial audience that considers him a showbiz eccentric in between the heated mathematical guitar solos that have become his main order of business. The studio albums are better, simply because they're more amply produced and cleverly arranged than *Roxy.*

Bongo Fury is a collaboration with Captain Beefheart and a depressing edition of more of the same, a very minor *Trout Mask Replica* lyrically, with the band restlessly twanging.

All these records are enjoyable, if only for

the pleasure of Zappa being very much his competent self. However, they do suggest that the cautiously rational humanist in him has overcome his imagination. — B.T.

FRANK ZAPPA

★ ★ ★ **Studio Tan** / War. (1978)
★ ★ ★ **Sleep Dirt** / War. (1979)
★ ★ ★ **Orchestral Favorites** / War. (1979)
★ ★ ★ ★ **Sheik Yerbouti** / Zappa (1979)
★ ★ ★ ★ **Joe's Garage Act I** / Zappa (1980)
★ ★ ★ ★ **Joe's Garage Acts II and III** / Zappa (1980)
★ ★ ★ ★ **Tinseltown Rebellion** / Bark. (1981)
★ ★ ★ ★ ★ **You Are What You Is** / Bark. (1981)
★ ★ ★ ★ **Shut Up 'n Play Yer Guitar** / Bark. (1981)
★ ★ ★ ★ **Shut Up 'n Play Yer Guitar Some More** / Bark. (1981)
★ ★ ★ ★ **Return of the Son of Shut Up 'n Play Yer Guitar** / Bark. (1981)

If Zappa had seemed in a cul-de-sac with his mid-Seventies work, which is arguable, his departure from Warner Bros. Records seemed to spur him on creatively. With virtually everything he had done up to that point tangled in litigation, Zappa was forced to start from scratch, and he came up with an ambitious program. His first move was the projected release of the long-anticipated multi-LP work, *Läther,* which was a collection of canned and live music that represented the cutting edge of Zappa's experiments through the Seventies. Warner Bros. cut that idea short by claiming that some of the proposed music for *Läther* was actually owed them and released part of the *Läther* concept on *Studio Tan, Sleep Dirt* and *Orchestral Favorites.*

Sheik Yerbouti saw Zappa returning to his most devastating satire and social criticism, zeroing in on pop sentimentality with "I Have Been in You" and "Broken Hearts Are for Assholes" and the late-Seventies disco set with "Dancing Fool" and "Jewish Princess."

Joe's Garage continued the sociopolitical commentary with Zappa's most fully realized conceptual LP since *We're Only in It for the Money.* This three-disc, two-package science fiction concept presents a future world in which music has been outlawed and musicians are punished severely for breaking the law. In the course of this sweeping collection Zappa manages to look back with fondness on a bygone era in the title track, satirically gibe sexual mores in "Catholic Girls," L. Ron Hubbard in "A Token of My Extreme," groupies in "Crew Slut" and wet T-shirt nights in "Wet T-Shirt Nite," then include a beautifully introspective, mostly instrumental song of alienation, "Outside Now." Above all, *Joe's Garage* is a masterful piece of production, which indicated the future direction of Zappa's technologically advanced approach to arranging and recording music.

Tinseltown Rebellion is a mostly live document of Zappa's crack touring outfit at the outset of the Eighties, featuring a lot of new material, including several songs that would become standards—the title track, "Fine Girl," "Easy Meat," "The Blue Light" and "Bamboozled by Love."

You Are What You Is ties together all the threads of Zappa's renaissance, combining his renewed satiric voice with his most advanced recording techniques. Guest vocal appearances by Motorhead and Jimmy Carl Black from the classic Mothers band and one of the best collections of songs Zappa's ever assembled make this one of his finest records ever. "Teenage Wind" is a hilarious parody of concert-going clichés over the years, "Harder Than Your Husband" is a great C&W spoof, and "Doreen," "Goblin Girl," "Conehead" and "Mudd Club" are Zappa's finest cameo songs.

You Are What You Is contains Zappa's most direct attack on hypocrisy in a suite of songs aimed at the religion-for-profit video evangelists who have proliferated in the Eighties—"The Meek Shall Inherit Nothing," "Dumb All Over" and "Heavenly Bank Account."

Fans of Zappa's instrumentals and arrangement strategies will find the *Shut Up* series particularly worthwhile. The records are made up of strictly instrumental tunes featuring Zappa guitar solos in a variety of contexts. One of the most interesting tracks, "Canard du Jour" from *Return of,* is a duet between Zappa on bouzouki and Jean-Luc Ponty on baritone violin. — J.S.

ZAP POW

★ ★ **Zap Pow** / Mango (NA)
★ ★ **Reggae Rules** / Rhino (NA)

Zap Pow can be enjoyable live (they've gigged the Jamaican tourist circuit) but their blend of funk, soul and reggae lacks identity or edge. — R.F.G.

WARREN ZEVON

★ ★ ★ ★ ★ **Warren Zevon** / Asy. (1976)
★ ★ ★ ★ **Excitable Boy** / Asy. (1978)
★ ★ **Bad Luck Streak in Dancing School** / Asy. (1980)
★ ★ ★ ★ ★ **Stand in the Fire** / Asy. (1980)
★ ★ ★ **The Envoy** / Asy. (1982)

Zevon is one of the best young writer/ performers to emerge in the past few years, and one of the toughest rockers ever to come out of Southern California. *Warren Zevon,* his debut LP, received a great deal of attention because of Jackson Browne's production, but Zevon has a tougher, more ribald style than Browne, both lyrically and musically. "Carmelita," one of his best songs, is about a lonesome L.A. drug addict, and both "Desperadoes under the Eaves" and "Mohammed's Radio" paint less than flattering portraits of Hollywood life. *Excitable Boy,* which contains Zevon's hit single, "Werewolves of London," was not quite as successful as the first LP, even though it was more popular. Producers Browne and Waddy Wachtel aided Zevon in firming up his sound, but the material on side two is terribly weak—among the most obvious filler any major rock artist has recorded. Still, "Roland the Head less Thompson Gunner," "Excitable Boy" and "Lawyers, Guns and Money" make even the second album substantial.

Bad Luck Streak in Dancing School is an erratic set of songs, the failed funk of "Jungle Work" and the pretentious poesy of "Empty Handed Heart" offset by the rock-hard intensity of "Wild Age" and "Play It All Night Long" and the exuberance of "Jeannie Needs a Shooter." (Two semiclassical pieces, "Interlude No. 1" and "Interlude No. 3," unfortunately tip the scales in the wrong direction.)

Stand in the Fire is a live album, and it's Zevon's best recording yet. The material ranges over all three of his previous albums, plus two good new songs and a raveup on "Bo Diddley" and "Bo Diddley's a Gunslinger." The pace is ferocious and the band (a group of unknowns led by guitarist David Landau) pushes Zevon to his limit, yet he remains sufficiently contained to focus everything he does. Wild and joyous, undercutting every hint of sentimentality with a kernel of toughness (and every tough-guy pose with an admission of hope), *Stand in the Fire* represents Zevon as the best kind of writer/ performer: smart enough to teach, quick enough to learn, dedicated enough to hold both ends together. *The Envoy,* despite some nice moments, is not close to that level. — D.M.

THE ZOMBIES

★ ★ Time of the Zombies / Epic (1973)
★ ★ ★ Early Days / Lon. (NA)

Early Days incorporates the band's original incarnation as one of the artier British Invasion groups, courtesy of the relatively spooky hit, "Tell Her No," which sparked the career of Rod Argent. *Time of the Zombies* sports an almost-all-new group (except for Argent) who hit in the States with "Time of the Season." This version of the group also launched Colin Blunstone. Both bands are better—if less typically—represented by their hit singles, available on any number of multi-artist anthologies superior to these collections. — D.M.

ZOOM

■ Zoom / A&M (1974)

Inconsequential Seventies pop. — J.S.

TAPPER ZUKIE

★ ★ ★ ★ Man Ah Warrior / Meroe (1977)
★ ★ ★ MPLA / V.F.L. (1978)
★ ★ ★ Tapper Roots / V.F.L. (1978)
★ ★ ★ Peace in the Ghetto / V.F.L. (1978)
★ ★ ★ ★ Black Man / Stars (1979)

Rocker Patti Smith championed reggae DJ Tapper Zukie in the late Seventies (she and Lenny Kaye released his debut on their own Meroe label), and he's justified their push with his energetic delivery and often acute messages. *Man Ah Warrior* remains a rough, punky stand-out. — R.F.G.

ZZ TOP

★ ★ First Album / War. (1970)
★ ★ Rio Grande Mud / War. (1972)
★ ★ Tres Hombres / War. (1973)
★ ★ Fandango / War. (1975)
★ ★ Tejas / War. (1976)
★ ★ ★ The Best of ZZ Top / War. (1977)
★ ★ ★ Deguello / War. (1979)
★ ★ ★ El Loco / War. (1981)

This Texas boogie band enjoyed a vogue during 1975 and 1976, when its concerts broke attendance records set by the Beatles, among others. But on record, ZZ Top was never more than a poor man's Lynyrd Skynyrd—some rural feeling but mostly just numbing guitar drive. Rock & roll can be mindless fun, but it never deserved to be this empty-headed. — D.M.

Anthologies, Soundtracks and Original Casts

★ ★ ★ ★ Ace Story, Vol. 1 / Ace (1981), Br. imp.
Artists include: Frankie Ford, Earl King, Frankie Lee Sims, Huey "Piano" Smith, Joe Tex, The Phaetons, Mac Rebennack, the Supremes, Joe and Ann, Jimmy Clanton, Alvin "Red" Tyler, Hershel Almond, Bobby Marchan, Morgus and the Ghouls.

Fine collection of New Orleans rhythm & blues, featuring the classics "Sea Cruise" (Ford), "Rockin' Pneumonia and the Boogie Woogie Flu" (Smith) and "Hey Little Girl" (Sims). A bit thinner than a collection from such a seminal label ought to be, though. (Incidentally, the Supremes here are a male quintet, no relationship to the Motown group.) — D.M.

★ ★ ★ Ace Story, Vol. 2 / Ace (1981), Br. imp.
Artists include: Junior Gordon, Lightnin' Hopkins, Mercy Baby, Frankie Ford, Eddie Bo, Bobby Marchan and the Clowns, the Blue Dots, Gene and Al's Spacemen, Little Shelton, Lloyd Price, Joe Dyson, Eddy Seacrest, Charles Brown and Amos Milburn, Jimmy Clanton.

Weak selection from the New Orleans R&B label. Some good blues tracks, but Ford, Price, Brown and Milburn are heard on trivialities, while Clanton's "Go Jimmy Go" is so nasal it's hard to believe it wasn't recorded in South Philly. Marchan's "Rockin' behind the Iron Curtain" is one of the wittier recordings of Huey Smith's old sidekicks, though. — D.M.

★ ★ ★ ★ Ace Story, Vol. 3 / Ace (1982), Br. imp.
Artists include: Sonny Boy Williamson, Huey Smith and His Rhythm Aces, Mercy Baby, Alvin "Red" Tyler, Albert Scott, Bobby Marchan, Huey Smith and His New Clowns, the
Blue Dots, the Supremes, Jerry McCain, Junior Gordon with the Huey Smith Orchestra, Mack Rebennack and His Orchestra, Joe Tex.

Probably the finest of the three packages, with fine sides from Smith and associates Marchan and Gordon and solid New Orleans R&B from the rest. No classics, but everything here is substantial. — D.M.

★ ★ ★ ★ ★ Ain't That Good News / Spec. (NA)
Artists include: Swan Silvertones, Original Gospel Harmonettes, Five Blind Boys of Alabama, Sam Cooke and the Soul Stirrers, Bessie Griffin, Chosen Gospel Singers, Meditation Singers, Pilgrim Travelers.

Black gospel masterpieces—a legitimate sacred *Best of* from vintage Fifties recordings, including Cooke's best religious number, "Touch the Hem of His Garment." — D.M.

★ ★ ★ Aladdin Magic / U.A. (1979), Br. imp.
Artists include: Big "T" Tyler, Shirley and Lee, Marvin and Johnny, Starlighters, Amos Milburn, Gene and Eunice, Louis Jordan, Fatso and Flaire, Thurston Harris, Sugar and Pee Wee, Jimmy Liggins, Clarence Garlow, Great Gates, Skinny Dynamo.

Nice selection of Fifties R&B from the Los Angeles–based label. The Shirley and Lee material (also available on a separate album) includes the hit "Feel So Fine" and three other tracks, and their rough/smooth dialectic sums up the basics of the Aladdin approach. This is relatively urbane black pop of its period, hailing back to the kind of jump blues represented here by Jordan and Liggins. — D.M.

★ ★ ★ ★ **All About Trains / RCA**
(NA)
Artists include: Hank Snow, Jimmie
Rodgers.

As anyone who's ever toyed with a harmonica knows, there is something particularly musical about railroads. Here two important country artists sing songs with rail themes—some of these are more or less folk numbers, but all of them qualify as excellent Americana and first-rate C&W. Rodgers, of course, is better, but what did you expect from the Singing Brakeman? Sea chanteys? — D.M.

★ ★ ★ ★ **Duane Allman Anthology / Capri.**
(1972)
Artists include: Aretha Franklin, King Curtis,
John Paul Hammond, Boz Scaggs, Delaney
and Bonnie, Cowboy, Eric Clapton and
Duane Allman, Derek and the Dominos,
Hourglass, Wilson Pickett, Clarence Carter,
Duane Allman, Allman Brothers Band.

Before he became a star with the Allman Brothers Band, Duane Allman was a heavyweight Muscle Shoals session guitarist. This posthumously released album gives a fair picture of his range—while the Franklin and Pickett sides have pop songs ("The Weight" and "Hey Jude" respectively) poorly suited to their styles, Derek and the Dominos' "Layla" and Boz Scaggs' "Loan Me a Dime" are not only the very best work of these artists but are among Allman's greatest hits. The Allman Brothers tracks are better heard in the context of the band. The only genuine rarity is the Johnny Jenkins side (he was the singer for whom Otis Redding was originally chauffeur), the Clapton/Allman duet and the Duane Allman solo spot on "Goin' Down Slow." — D.M.

★ ★ ★ **Duane Allman Anthology, Vol. 2 /**
Capri. (1974)
Artists include: Duane Allman, Aretha Frank-
lin, King Curtis, Otis Rush, Ronnie Hawkins,
Wilson Pickett, Arthur Conley, Hourglass,
Lulu, Herbie Mann, Johnny Jenkins, Boz
Scaggs, Sam Samudio, Delaney and Bonnie,
Allman Brothers Band, Duck and the Bear.

A spottier set than Volume 1. There isn't anything as grand as "Layla" here, though Johnny Jenkins' "Walk on Gilded Splinters" is fine funk and Aretha's "It Ain't Fair" is one of her best. — D.M.

★ ★ ★ ★ **All of My Appointed Time / Stash**
(1978)
Artists include: Golden Gate Jubilee Quartet,
Kings of Harmony, Blue Jay Singers, Soul

Stirrers, the Georgia Peach and the Harmonaires, Bessie Griffin, Golden Harps, Marion Williams.

A marvelous selection that spans forty years of a cappella gospel singing. Side one is male groups and vocalists, highlighted by the Golden Gate's scintillating "Standing by the Bedside of a Neighbor" and the R. H. Harris–led Soul Stirrers' classic "Well Well Well." Side two features female singers, concluding with a pair of tremendous 1976 recordings by Marion Williams, including the title track. Skillfully selected, intelligently annotated by Anthony Heilbut. — D.M.

★ ★ ★ **All Platinum Gold / All Pl.**
(NA)
Artists include: Donnie Elbert, Retta Young,
Sylvia George Kerr, Brother to Brother, Mo-
ments, Hank Ballard, Chuck Jackson, What-
nauts, Linda Jones, Shirley and Company,
Derek Martin, Rim Shots.

Spotty collection of Jersey soul and disco that spans this decade's black pop styles. Included are some inferior more recent items by Jackson and Ballard, which don't match their early stuff, and a couple of inspired one-shots: Elbert's bizarre falsetto parody of Diana Ross on "Where Did Our Love Go" and Shirley and Company's wildly kinky "Shame Shame Shame," in which Shirley and friends drive a Cadillac customized so completely it's got a diamond in the back. The rest ranges from perfunctory funk to ho-hum harmony. — D.M.

★ ★ **All This and World War II**
(Soundtrack) / 20th Cent.
(1976)
Artists include: Ambrosia, Elton John, Leo
Sayer, Bee Gees, Bryan Ferry, Roy Wood,
Keith Moon, Rod Stewart, Four Seasons,
David Essex, Jeff Lynne, Helen Reddy, Lyn-
sey de Paul, Richard Cocciante, Frankie
Laine, Johnson Brothers, Status Quo, Henry
Gross, Frankie Valli, Tina Turner, Peter Ga-
briel, Will Malone/Lou Reizner, London
Symphony Orchestra.

Soundtrack for a 1976 movie that coupled World War II battle footage with Beatle songs. If that doesn't make sense, you get the idea. Obviously there are some terrific singers here, but there are also some unaccountably silly ones, and the material isn't necessarily well chosen for even the best of them. There's little chance that anyone who was properly matched—say, Peter Gabriel to "Strawberry Fields Forever"—would be able to survive the glutinous London Symphony arrangements. Only Rod Stewart, who sticks in an electric guitar on "Get Back," prevails. — D.M.

★ ★ ★ **The American Dream: The Cameo-Parkway Story 1957–1962 / London (1975), Br. imp.**
Artists include: the Rays, Zacherle, Charlie Grace, Applejacks, Chubby Checker, Bobby Rydell, Orlons, Dovells, Dee Dee Sharp, Don Covay, Jo Ann Campbell.

Hits of the Philly dance/pop label, reissued by its U.K. licensee. Cameo-Parkway's cheesy dance hits could sometimes be tremendously exciting (Chubby Checker's "Let's Twist Again," the Dovells "Bristol Stomp" and "Hully Gully Baby," Dee Dee Sharp's "Ride!"), and they helped pioneer the girl-group sound with the Orlons' "The Wah-Watusi" and "Don't Hang Up." But too much here is on the level of "The Girl from Wolverton Mountain," "Limbo Rock," "Mexican Hat Rock" and "Dinner with Drack." And then there's Bobby Rydell, a smirking Neil Diamond before his time. — D.M.

★ ★ ★ ★ **The American Dream: The London-American Legend / London (1975), Br. imp.**
Artists include: Carole King, Little Eva, Raindrops, Ran-dells, Dale and Grace, Cookies, Castaways, Chartbusters, Strangeloves, Derek, Vogues, Knickerbockers, McCoys, Sam Cooke, Maxine Brown, Bobby Parker, Betty Harris, Barbara Mason, Dobie Gray, Erma Franklin, Exciters, Bobby "Boris" Pickett, Terry Stafford, Neil Diamond.

Sixties pop sides recorded by various American companies but issued in Britain on Decca's London-American label. The hits here include Cooke's "You Send Me," Little Eva's "Loco-motion," "Piece of My Heart" by Erma Franklin (whence came Janis Joplin's mangling), "Liar Liar" by the Castaways, "I Want Candy" by the Strangeloves, and several others worth having. Annotation is more than adequate, but there are two discs here, so expect to pay through the nose. For an eclectic view of the early Sixties it's hard to beat this set, though. — D.M.

★ ★ ★ ★ ★ **American Graffiti (Soundtrack) / MCA (1973)**
Artists include: Bobby Freeman, Bill Haley and the Comets, Flash Cadillac, Lee Dorsey, Crests, Buster Brown, Del Shannon, Platters, Fleetwoods, Tempos, Skyliners, Diamonds, Beach Boys, Monotones, Chuck Berry, Clovers, Johnny Burnette, Big Bopper, Five Satins, Regents, Silhouettes, Buddy Holly, Fats Domino, Mark Dinning, Cleftones, Buddy Knox, Heartbeats, Spaniels, Joey Dee and the Starlighters, Sonny Til and the Orioles, Dell-Vikings, Booker T. and the MGs, Flamingos, Frankie Lymon.

The music used in the 1974 hit film, which was mostly a series of fast-paced clichés about adolescence in the pre-Beatle Sixties. What made the movie work was the soundtrack, which had captured the beat and excitement of the era's radio. That means you have to sit through the Regents' "Barbara-Ann" and the Crests' "Sixteen Candles," which are almost insufferable, to get at gems like the Diamonds' "The Stroll" and "Little Darlin' " and the Dell-Vikings' "Come Go with Me." The big names (Berry, Holly, Domino, Beach Boys) are represented by the obligatory well-known hits. There isn't a true rarity in the bunch, but this is still one of the all-time party records and a fairly accurate picture of a 1963 golden oldies weekend. — D.M.

★ ★ ★ ★ **American Graffiti, Vol. 2 / MCA (NA)**
Artists include: Beach Boys, Dorados, Little Richard, Jerry Butler, Jody Reynolds, Everly Brothers, Ritchie Valens, Joe Jones, Jewel Akens, Chris Montez, Jimmy Reed, Toni Fisher, Bobby Helms, Harold Dorman, Ronnie Hawkins, Dorsey Burnette, Johnny Tillotson, Jimmie Rodgers, Lenny Welch, Teddy Bears, Wilbur Harrison, Kathy Young, Fendermen, Hollywood Argyles, Little Anthony and the Imperials, Olympics, Buddy Holly.

Not a soundtrack—at least none of this is in the movie—but an extension of the boss beat weekend concept of Volume 1. There are fewer obligatory nods to big names here—the only superstars are Holly, the Beach Boys and the Everlys—which leaves room for at least a few things more obscure and harder to obtain on LP: Jody Reynolds' death classic "Endless Sleep," Harold Dorman's original "Mountain of Love," the Teddy Bears singing Phil Spector's first production of "To Know Him Is to Love Him" and the great "Western Movies" by the Olympics. While this isn't everything you'll want to hear by Ritchie Valens or Jerry Butler, it's certainly all you need from Dorsey Burnette, Jimmie Rodgers (the pop singer) and Lenny Welch. And though they have the wrong version of "The Big Hurt"—Timi Yuro (not to mention Elvis Presley) cuts Toni Fisher to *shreds*—who could be without the Hollywood Argyles' "Alley Oop"? — D.M.

★ ★ ★ **American Hot Wax (Soundtrack) /
A&M (1978)**
*Artists include: Big Beat Band, Delights, Professor LaPlano and the Planotones, Clark
Otis, Chuck Berry, Chesterfields, Screamin'
Jay Hawkins, Timmy and the Tulips, Jerry
Lee Lewis, Jackie Wilson, Moonglows, Drifters, Mystics, Buddy Holly, Maurice Williams
and the Zodiacs, Little Richard, Cadillacs,
Elegants, Turbans, Bobby Darin, Frankie
Ford, Spaniels.*

Soundtrack from the 1978 biography of pioneer DJ Alan Freed is like the movie: half
of it is great. The problem is the first disc
that includes cinematic groups rather than
the real thing who fairly butcher the hits.
The tracks by Berry, Hawkins and Lewis are
acceptable live versions done for the film's
climactic concert sequence; they're of interest
mainly to collectors. But this does have
some great stuff, beginning with Jackie Wilson, the Moonglows and the Drifters, and
including the Mystics' "Hushabye," "Zoom"
by the Cadillacs, the great Maurice Williams
falsetto on "Stay," the rumbling "When You
Dance" by the Turbans, Frankie Ford's raucous "Sea Cruise" and two enduring smooch
classics—the sort Freed specialized in playing—"Goodnight It's Time to Go" by the
Spaniels and the achingly lovely "Little
Star" by the Elegants. — D.M.

★ ★ ★ **Animal House (Soundtrack) / MCA
(1978)**
*Artists include: John Belushi, Sam Cooke,
Bobby Lewis, Paul and Paula, Stephen Bishop, Chris Montez.*

This film about early-Sixties college life
contains some pretty good period pieces, including "Twistin' the Night Away" and
'Wonderful World" by Cooke, "Tossin' and
Turnin'" by Lewis and "Let's Dance" by
Montez. The soundtrack also features John
Belushi's high point as a vocalist, "Louie,
Louie." — J.S.

★ ★ ★ **Another Man Done Gone / Flyr.
(1978)**
*Artists include: Willie Moore, Guitar Shorty,
Willie Rockmore and Bruce Upshaw, Baby
Tate, Jack Harp, Buddy Boy Jenkins, Henry
Johnson, Elbert Freeman and Nathaniel
Ford, Bud Grant, Bill Bryant, Ed Green,
Baby Tate and Peg Leg Sam, Dave Dickerson.*

Nineteen tracks of pleasant if unexceptional country blues, recorded between 1962
and 1971, in locations ranging from Albany,
New York (Moore), to Crestview, Florida
(Harp). — D.M.

★ ★ ★ ★ ★ **Anthology of American Folk
Music, Vol. 1: Ballads / Folk. (NA)**
*Artists include: Dick Justice, Nelstone's Hawaiians, Clarence Ashley, Coley Jones, Bill
and Belle Reed, Buell Kazee, Chubby Parker
and His Old Time Banjo, Uncle Eck Dunford, Burnett and Rutherford, Buster Carter
and Preston Young, Carolina Tar Heels, G.B.
Grayson, Kelly Harrell, Edward L. Crain,
Furry Lewis, Carter Family, Williamson
Brothers and Curry, Frank Hutchison, Charlie Poole with the North Carolina Ramblers,
Mississippi John Hurt, William and Versey
Smith, Bently Boys, Masked Marvel.*

The first two-disc, boxed, lavishly annotated set of Moe Asch's monumental tribute
to the country's musical heritage. All of this
is pre–World War II; most of it is pre-
Depression. The remastering from old 78s
occasionally leaves something to be desired,
but this set, with its companion volumes, is
the fundamental source of folk music preservation. The Poole, Hurt, Masked Marvel,
Carolina Tar Heels and Clarence Ashley
tracks are all vintage masterpieces. — D.M.

★ ★ ★ ★ ★ **Anthology of American Folk
Music, Vol. 2: Social Music / Folk. (NA)**
*Artists include: "Uncle Bunt" Stephens, J.W.
Day (Jilson Setters), Prince Albert Hunt's
Texas Ramblers, Delma Lachney and Blind
Uncle Gaspard, Andrew and Jim Baxter, Eck
Robertson and Family, Floyd Ming and His
Pep-Steppers, Henry Thomas, Jim Jackson,
Columbus Fruge, Joseph Falcon, Breaux
Freres, Cincinnati Jug Band, Frank Cloutier
and Victoria Cafe Orchestra, Reverend J. M.
Gates, Alabama Sacred Harp Singers, Middle
Georgia Singing Convention No. 1, Reverend
Sister Mary Nelson, Memphis Sanctified Singers, Elders MacIntosh and Edwards Sanctified Singers, Reverend Moses Mason, Bascom
Lumar Lunsford, Blind Willie Johnson, Carter Family, Ernest Phipps and His Holiness
Singers, Reverend F. W. McGee, Reverend D.
C. Rice and His Sanctified Congregation.*

Volume 2 of the masterful collection is devoted to the music Americans have listened
to at parties, in churches and at dances. The
church dominates, not only in quantity but
in quality. Johnson's "John the Revelator"
is amazing, on the gospel-blues side, but
so is the Carters' country-gospel "Little
Moses." — D.M.

★ ★ ★ ★ ★ **Anthology of American
Folk Music, Vol. 3: Songs / Folk.
(NA)**
*Artists include: Clarence Ashley, Buell Kazee,
Cannon's Jug Stompers, Didier Herbert, Rab-*

bit Brown, "Dock" Boggs, Bascom Lumar Lunsford, Mr. and Mrs. Ernest V. Stoneman, Stoneman Family, Memphis Jug Band, Carter Family, Clemo Breaux and Joseph Falcon, Blind Lemon Jefferson, Sleepy John Estes, Ramblin' Thomas, Julius Daniels, Clemo Breaux with Joe Falcon and Ophy Breaux, Uncle Dave Macon, Mississippi John Hurt, J. P. Nestor, Ken Maynard, Henry Thomas.

The concluding volume of this exhaustive documentation of American folk styles may be the best listening of the three. Nearly every track here is winning, and some of it is absolutely essential to an understanding of the resources upon which rock & roll was built: listen to Rabbit Brown, for instance. — D.M.

★ ★ ★ ★ **Anthology of the Banjo / Trad. (NA)**
Artists include: Mason Williams, David Lindley, Joe Maphis, Erik Darling, Mike Seeger, Jim McGuinn, Billy Cheatwood.

Good anthology of folk and country banjo styles that dates from the early-Sixties folk revival. Rockers will be most curious about Jackson Browne sideman David Lindley, who shines on "Mad Mountain Medley," his only extant recording before his work with Kaleidoscope on the group's debut LP, and the track by McGuinn, made before he formed the Byrds or changed his name to Roger. Hilarious liner notes. — D.M.

ANTHOLOGY OF THE BLUES (Series)
★ ★ ★ **Arkansas Blues / Kent (NA)**
Artists include: Baby Face Turner, Drifting Slim, Sunny Blair, Robert Dudlow Taylor, James "Peck" Burtis, Junior Brooks.
★ ★ ★ **Blues from the Deep South / Kent (NA)**
Artists include: Pinetop Slim, Dixie Blues Boys, Leroy Simpson, Big Bill Dotson, Arkansas Johnny Todd, Mr. Harris and Arkansas Johnny Todd.
★ ★ ★ **California Blues / Kent (NA)**
Artists include: Johnny "Guitar" Watson, George Smith, James Reed, Walter Robertson, Johnny Fuller.
★ ★ ★ **Detroit Blues / Kent (NA)**
Artists include: John Lee Hooker, Eddie Kirkland, Eddie Burns, Sylvester Cotton.
★ ★ ★ ★ **Memphis Blues / Kent (NA)**
Artists include: Howlin' Wolf, Joe Hill Lewis, Walter Horton, Bobby Bland and Junior Parker, Bobby Bland, Willie Nix.
★ ★ ★ **Mississippi Blues / Kent (NA)**
Artists include: Boyd Gilmore, Houston Boines, Charley Booker.

★ ★ ★ ★ **Texas Blues / Kent (NA)**
Artists include: Little Son Jackson, Smokey Hogg, Jesse Thomas, Alexander Moore, Lowell Fulsom, Charlie Bradix.
★ ★ ★ **West Coast Blues / Kent (NA)**
Artists include: Mercy Dee, Jimmy Nelson, Pee Wee Crayton, James Reed, Saunders King, J.W. Walker, Roy Hawkins.

Excellently produced series, well annotated, gives a look at some of the second-level blues performers of each important region west of the Mississippi and up North. Probably of interest only to blues fanatics, however. — D.M.

★ ★ ★ **Anthology of Folk Music, Vol. 1 / Sine (NA)**
Artists include: Pete Seeger, Odetta, Alan Lomax, Etta Baker, Ed McCurdy, David Hammond, Italian Brass Band, Leadbelly, Woody Guthrie, Josh White, Lightnin' Hopkins, Clancy Brothers and Tommy Makem, Sonny Terry and Brownie McGhee, Glenn Yarbrough, Glen Campbell, John Lee Hooker, Mississippi State Penitentiary.

A much more erratic sampling of American traditional music. Some of the names are well known and important—Seeger, Guthrie, Leadbelly, Hopkins, Terry and McGhee, Hooker—but some of them are atrocious performers, particularly Yarbrough and Campbell. Not bad, but decidedly inferior to the Folkways' anthology of American folk-music sets. Five discs. — D.M.

★ ★ ★ **Anthology of Folk Music, Vol. 2 / Sine (NA)**
Artists include: Judy Collins, Theodore Bikel, Will Holt, Dillards, Oscar Brand, Ed McCurdy, Odetta, Mason Williams, Glen Campbell, A. L. Lloyd, John Jacob Niles, Clancy Brothers and Tommy Makem, Ewan MacColl, Mary O'Hara, Mississippi State Penitentiary, Woody Guthrie and Cisco Houston, Pete Seeger, Lightnin' Hopkins, Sonny Terry and Brownie McGhee, John Lee Hooker, Hoyt Axton, Leadbelly, Josh White, Limeliters, Eric Weisberg and Marshall Brickman, the Band.

The same flaws as Volume 1 in this set pertain to this four-disc followup. And some of the artistic inclusions are unaccountable: the Band's "Up on Cripple Creek" and "Rag Mama Rag" are *not* folk music. — D.M.

★ ★ **Anthology of the Twelve-String Guitar / Trad. (NA)**
Artists include: Glen Campbell, Mason Williams, Bob Gibson, James McGuinn, Howard Roberts, Joe Maphis, Billy Strange.

Passable country and folk guitar instrumentals. All that might be of interest to non-guitarists are the McGuinn (he's now Roger, late of the Byrds) and Maphis selections. — D.M.

★ ★ **Any Which Way You Can (Soundtrack) / Viva (1980)**
Artists include: Ray Charles and Clint Eastwood, Glen Campbell, David Frizzell and Shelly West, Fats Domino, Jim Stafford, Johnny Duncan, Gene Watson, Texas Opera Company, Cliff Crofford, John Durrill.

All that rescues this set from Clint and Sondra's tunelessness is Charles (who sounds good paired with *anybody*) and Fats, whose "Whiskey Heaven" is his best track in a decade (just about his only one, of course). The country performers are mostly just going through the motions. — D.M.

★ ★ **Apocalypse Now (Soundtrack) / Elek. (NA)**
Artists include: The Doors, Flash Cadillac.

Coppola's film may have had something to do with the Doors revival, as their classic "The End" was brought back as an even scarier nightmare vision than it used to be. The soundtrack is marred by the omission of the Diga Rhythm Band's *River Music* material, which was released as a separate LP. — J.S.

★ ★ ★ **Atlantic Blues Special / Atl. (NA), Jap. imp.**
Artists include: Tommy Ridgley, Guitar Slim, Ivory Joe Hunter, Stick McGhee and His Buddies, T-Bone Walker, Al King, Ray Agee.

Nice but (given the title) a long way shy of necessary. This disc collects fourteen late Forties/early Fifties blues sides, the most notable of which are Hunter's "Since I Met You, Baby" and McGhee's "Drinkin' Wine Spo-Dee-O-Dee." The rest is good and the four tracks by Slim and the equal number by Walker are hard to find these days, but unless you're a particular fan of one of the above, you can probably live without this one. — D.M.

★ ★ ★ **Atlantic Do Wap Special / Atl. (NA), Jap. imp.**
Artists include: Versatiles, Diamonds, Cookies, Regals, Crescendos, Bobbettes, Cardinals, Penguins, Sh-Booms, Diamonds, Romeos, Pearls.

Mostly minor vocal harmony groups of the early days of Atlantic (the title is an eccentric translation of doo-wop). These are all nice nuggets, but unless you're a complete collector, you won't mind passing this one up (particularly at the always outrageous price of Japanese imports). — D.M.

★ ★ ★ **Atomic Cafe (Soundtrack) / Roun. (1982)**
Artists include: Golden Gate Quartet, Karl and Harty, Sonny Boy Williamson, Buchanan Brothers, Lowell Blanchard with the Valley Trio, Jackie Doll and His Pickled Peppers, Billy Hughes and the Rhythm Buckaroos, Sons of the Pioneers, Commodores, Sonny Russell, Five Stars, Skip Stanley, Slim Gaillard Quartette, Little Caesar with the Red Calendar Sextette, Spirits of Memphis Quartet, Louisiana Red.

Seventeen songs on nuclear themes from the anti-bomb documentary. Highlights are the Golden Gate's "Atom and Evil" (a masterpiece) and the Spirits of Memphis' "Atomic Telephone" and Sonny Boy Williamson's "Win the War Blues." The rest centers on bluegrass and rockabilly and is mostly trivial. — D.M.

★ ★ ★ **At the Hop / MCA (NA)**
Artists include: Danny and the Juniors, Jimmy Rodgers, Pat Boone, Del Vikings, Lloyd Price, Barry Mann, Royal Teens, Del Shannon, Tommy Roe, Chantays, Surfaris, Barry McGuire, Impressions, the Mamas and the Papas, Grass Roots, Steppenwolf, Richard Harris, Three Dog Night.

This collection of classic oldies includes everything but the kitchen sink, which is its problem. The dross is mixed indiscriminately with great songs like the title track, "Who Put the Bomp," "Short Shorts," "Runaway," "Sheila," "Pipeline," "Wipeout" and "It's All Right." This could have made one great single disc, but as a double album it's a flabby mess. — J.S.

★ **Award Winners / RCA (NA)**
Artists include: Charley Pride, Chet Atkins, Ronnie Milsap, Dave and Sugar, Dolly Parton, Jim Ed Brown and Helen Cornelius, Atkins String Company, Nashville Brass and Danny Davis, Chet Atkins and Les Paul, Dickey Lee.

Impoverished collection of Seventies country-pop hits. All that saves this from the trash bin is Atkins' duet with Paul, and that one is available on an LP of similar duets. — D.M.

★ ★ ★ **Babylon (Soundtrack) / Tak. (1981)**
Artists include: Yabby You, Michael Prophet, Cassandra, I Roy, Aswad.

The British film *Babylon* follows in the footsteps of *Rockers* and *The Harder They Come*, as does its soundtrack. There's some evocative incidental music by Dennis Bovell as well as some excellent obscurities. — R.F.G.

★ ★ ★ ★ **Bachelor Blues / Neon (1982)**
Artists include: Hound Dog Taylor, James Cotton, Jimmy Rogers, Homesick James, Betty Everett, Little Mack, Carl Jones, Lee Jackson, Slim Willis, Rudy Robinson.
Semiclassic Chicago blues, from serious though second-rank names. "I Know You Don't Love Me" (James) and a pair by Jimmy Rogers are the highlights. Betty Everett, sounding more feisty than ever, is a pleasant surprise. — D.M.

★ ★ ★ **Bang and Shout Super Hits / Bang (NA)**
Artists include: Van Morrison, Neil Diamond, Strangeloves, Donald Height, Erma Franklin, McCoys, Derek, Freddie Scott, Jackie Moore, Jerry O.
Relics of pop-rock (and pop-soul) past. The Morrison track, "Brown Eyed Girl," is pure genius; the McCoys and Strangeloves are ancestral punk rock; Diamond was at his best on Bang and "Cherry Cherry" was his best there. But most importantly, this record has Erma Franklin (Aretha's sister) doing the original "Piece of My Heart," which will make you forget Janis Joplin's strident version PDQ. (Scott and Moore are interesting, but very minor, soul performers.) — D.M.

★ ★ ★ ★ **Barefoot Rock and You Got Me / Duke (NA)**
Artists include: Junior Parker, Bobby Bland.
Two of the best modern R&B singers split a disc, one side each, just as they once shared a band. Bland is a better singer, in a way, but Parker is tons more challenging, both to his band and his listeners. This will make anyone a fine introduction to either man (or both). — D.M.

★ ★ ★ ★ **Beach Beat Classics / Ripete (1980)**
Artists include: Catalinas, Tymes, Fantastic Shakers, Band of Oz, Bob Collins and the Fabulous Five, Cannonball, Tempests, Swinging Medallions, Showmen, Willie Tee, Billy Stewart, Garnett Mimms and the Enchanters, Lenny O'Henry, Prophets, Ernie K-Doe, Chairmen of the Board.
Marvelous collection (especially side two) features the sort of light, danceable soul

that's perfect for hot-weather hops at the shore. These records, probably unknown in the rest of the country for the most part, are regarded as classics by soul fans from Virginia through South Carolina, and the best of them deserve that stature. You won't find much better than the Showmen's "39-21-46," Lenny O'Henry's "Across the Street," "Ms. Grace" by the Tymes and Ernie K-Doe's "Te-Ta-Te-Ta-Ta." Some of the later, more self-referential material (e.g., "Shaggin' " by Band of Oz) isn't quite up to snuff, however. — D.M.

★ ★ ★ ★ ★ **Beach Beat Classics, Vol. 2 / Ripete (1980)**
Artists include: Drifters, Globetrotters, Futures, Jerry Butler, Jim Gilstrap, Trammps, Platters, Chairmen of the Board, Ravens, O'Jays, Maurice Williams and the Zodiacs, Tams, Intruders.
The best of Ripete's collections of soul singles regarded as dance classics on the Atlantic seaboard. This contains such legitimate gems as "Everything's Tuesday" (Chairmen), "(I'm Just Thinking About) Cooling Out" (Butler), "Kissing in the Back Row" (Drifters), "Hold Back the Night" (Trammps) and "May I" (Zodiacs), as well as some more minor but always lovely pleasures. — D.M.

★ ★ ★ **Beach Beat Classics, Vol. 3 / Ripete (1981)**
Artists include: Embers, Fantastic Shakers, Dale Van Horn, Poor Souls, Love Committee, Drifters, Clifford Curry, Chairmen of the Board, Roscoe Gordon, Wilbert Harrison, Jewell and the Rubies, Maurice Williams and the Zodiacs, Tams, Intrigues, Dallas Frazier, Louis Prima and Keely Smith.
By this time, Ripete was beginning to scrape the bottom of the beach-music barrel, symbolized by the inclusion of the awful "Elvira" (Frazier) and the ludicrous "Just a Gigolo" (Prima and Smith). Even the name groups here turn in minor efforts, though Williams' "Stay" is a major classic and the Curry tracks aren't bad. — D.M.

■ **Beatlemania (Original Broadway Cast) / Ari. (NA)**
There are twenty-two Beatle-composed songs here, performed by the puppets from the stage show that enjoyed a long run on Broadway. This horrible piece of garbage is the best evidence that the Beatles didn't make it on haircuts alone—and that some record companies are utterly shameless. Get the plague first. — D.M.

★ ★ ★ ★ **The Beat of the Beach / Ari.**
(1982)
Artists include: James and Bobby Purify,
Showmen, Clifford Curry, Lee Dorsey, Aaron
Neville, Garnet Mimms, Showmen, Box Tops,
Don Gardner and Dee Dee Ford, Wilbert
Harrison, Drifters, General Johnson, Patty
and the Emblems, Shirley and the Shirelles,
Nino Tempo and April Stevens, O'Jays,
Trammps, Van Dykes, Gladys Knight and the
Pips, Delfonics.

The highlights of this selection of soulful
sides, which were or ought to have been Atlantic Coast beach favorites, are the three
1968 numbers by the Showmen, along with a
pair by Clifford Curry, James and Bobby Purify's "I'm Your Puppet" (one of the gentlest
hits ever), and the Trammps' "Hold Back
the Night." But it's all solid. — D.M.

★ ★ ★ **Bebop Singers / Prest. (NA)**
Artists include: Annie Ross, Eddie Jefferson,
Joe Carroll.

Jefferson and Ross are two of the best jazz
singers of the past thirty years. For anyone
interested in vocal experiments and scat singing, this should prove of value. The highlight
is Ross' "Twisted." — D.M.

★ ★ ★ **Beserkely Chartbusters / Beserk.**
(NA)
Artists include: Earth Quake, Greg Kihn,
Jonathan Richman, Rubinoos.

Mostly this sampler from the original
American new-wave label is flaccid. Kihn,
Earth Quake and the Rubinoos have a very
tame idea of what rocking out means. But
Jonathan Richman reaches his peak with
this album's "New Teller," "Government
Center" and the grand "Road Runner." The
latter is so sick it has to be heard to be believed. — D.M.

★ ★ ★ ★ **The Best of Baton R&B / Flyr.**
(1980)
Artists include: Marie Knight, Ann Cole, Big
Mike Gordon, Chris Kenner, Frankie Tucker,
The Hearts, The Rivileers, The Fidelitys, The
Kings.

New York and New Orleans rhythm &
blues circa 1954–58. The major "name" here
is Kenner; these are his first sides, and while
they aren't as exceptional as those he later
did for Atlantic/Instant, they're good
enough. The other acts tend to be heavily influenced by the New Orleans stalwarts of the
period, most notably Little Richard and Fats
Domino; the New Yorkers add Clyde Mc-
Phatter and Frankie Lymon as sources. The
Rivileers' track is "A Thousand Stars," the

teenage-profound ballad Kathy Young and
the Innocents later made a smooch-rock
classic. — D.M.

★ ★ **Best of the Blues / Sine (NA)**
Artists include: Jimmy Witherspoon and
Groove Holmes, Jimmy Witherspoon, Light-
nin' Hopkins, Ray Charles, John Lee Hooker,
Sonny Terry and Brownie McGhee, Big Joe
Williams, Leadbelly, Josh White, Big Bill
Broonzy, Jimmy Reed, Memphis Slim, Otis
Spann.

An unfocused collection of blues styles.
Some good tracks—particularly the Leadbelly, Hooker and Spann numbers—but not
enough cohesion. Better overviews of the
genre are available. — D.M.

★ ★ **Best of the Blues, Vol. 2 / Sine (NA)**
Artists include: Sonny Terry and Brownie Mc-
Ghee, Bessie Smith, Louis Armstrong, King
Oliver, Leadbelly, Fats Waller, Big Joe Wil-
liams, Jimmy Witherspoon and Richard
"Groove" Holmes, Lightnin' Hopkins, Cisco
Houston, Johnny Hammond, John Lee Hook-
er, Gary Davis, Junior Wells, Otis Spann,
James Cotton, Otis Rush.

Again blues without definition: what links
King Oliver and Fats Waller with James
Cotton and John Lee Hooker, much less
what connects Otis Spann and Johnny Hammond, is mysterious except to collectors,
who already have this stuff in more reasonable formats. — D.M.

★ ★ ★ **Best of Burt Bacharach / Trip (NA)**
Artists include: Dionne Warwick, Dusty
Springfield, Timi Yuro, Jerry Butler, Bobby
Vinton, Jackie DeShannon, Shirelles, Chuck
Jackson, B. J. Thomas, Gene Pitney, Tommy
Hunt, Buddy Greco.

Bacharach, with partner Hal David, was
one of the most formidable pop songwriters
of the Sixties. This isn't quite his greatest
hits, because if it were, it would be a Dionne
Warwick LP with guest appearances by Presley, DeShannon and the Shirelles. But it
gives a good picture of the kind of romantic
material Bacharach and David wrote, and
the sort of artists for whom they wrote it.
Highlights: Shirelles' "Baby It's You," Jackson's "Any Day Now," Pitney's "The Man
Who Shot Liberty Valance," from the great
John Ford film, and Warwick's "Anyone
Who Had a Heart," "Walk On By," "Alfie"
and "Do You Know the Way to San Jose."
Bacharach not only cowrote but coproduced
all of the Warwick tracks with David.
— D.M.

★ ★ ★ ★ ★ **Best of the Chicago Blues / Van. (NA)**

Artists include: Junior Wells, J. B. Hutto, Otis Spann, Johnny Young, Big Walter Horton, Jimmy Cotton, Buddy Guy.

Indispensable collection of Sixties sides recorded by Sam Charters. This is a compilation of tracks from the three original single albums in the series. — J.S.

★ **Best of a Great Year, Vol. 3 / RCA (NA)**

Artists include: Eddy Arnold, Chet Atkins, Bobby Bare, Skeeter Davis, Jim Ed Brown, George Hamilton IV, Johnny Bush, Floyd Cramer, Nashville Brass and Danny Davis, Waylon Jennings, Dickey Lee, Dolly Parton, Kenny Price, Jerry Reed, Jim Reeves, Johnny Russell, Charlie Rich, Connie Smith, Hank Snow, Nat Stuckey, Porter Wagoner, Dottie West, Dolly Parton and Porter Wagoner, Norro Wilson.

Four sides of C&W banality and corn relieved intermittently by the simple competence of Rich, Jennings, Reeves and Parton, who keep better company elsewhere. — D.M.

★ ★ ★ **The Best of the Groups / Scepter (1972)**

Artists include: Guess Who; Vanilla Fudge; Animals; Rocky Fellers; Canned Heat.

The great revelation here is none of the well-known groups. Most of their material is early outtakes, and in the Fudge's case, particularly, would have been better left unresurrected, though there is a case to be made that "Shakin' All Over" is the quintessential Guess Who track (if not the quintessence of a certain stream of rock), while the Animals' "Bo Diddley" is fine and funny. Nevertheless, the Rocky Fellers, a Latino precursor of the Jackson Five, top 'em all with their now-forgotten hits, "Killer Joe" and "Like the Big Guys Do." If you like soulful, this is a good place to go—especially in contrast to the bombast that surrounds it. — D.M.

★ ★ ★ **The Best of Philadelphia International Records / Phil. (1981)**

Artists include: Lou Rawls, Three Degrees, O'Jays, Billy Paul, McFadden and Whitehead, Teddy Pendergrass, Jones Girls, People's Choice.

This is a long way from being what it claims. Any record that omits Pendergrass's best records (made with Harold Melvin and the Blue Notes), plus Philadelphia International's signature tune, MFSB's "TSOP," can hardly claim best-of status. But what's here is very fine, from McFadden and Whitehead's tough "Ain't No Stoppin' Us Now" to the Three Degrees' "When Will I See You Again." — D.M.

★ ★ ★ **Big Bad Boss Beat / Orig. Sound (NA)**

Artists include: Champs, Dee Dee Sharp, B. Bumble and the Stingers, Sandy Nelson, Preston Epps, Ernie Fields, Gary "U.S." Bonds, Bill Doggett, Revels.

Early-Sixties rock, mostly instrumental. Rolling Stone contributor Langdon Winner played piano on "Church Key" by the Revels, but in that kind of company what stands out is the classic outer-space recordings of Bonds: "Quarter to Three" and "New Orleans" will set your pacemaker aflutter. The Champs' "Tequila" isn't bad, and Preston Epps' "Bongo Bongo Bongo" and "Bongo Rock" make him the Perez Prado of rock & roll. This should get a bonus star for its title, unquestionably the product of inspiration. — D.M.

■ **Big Dance Records in the Big Apple / Ari. (NA)**

Artists include: Alexander's Disco Time Band, Polly Brown, Atlanta Disco Band, Jackie Robinson, Pretty Maid Company, Charlie Calello.

Wretched dance disc. — D.M.

★ ★ ★ ★ ★ **Birmingham Quartet Anthology / Clanka Lanka (1980), Swed. imp.**

Artists include: Golden Leaf Quartette, Birmingham Jubilee Singers, Four Great Wonders, Famous Blue Jay Singers, Dunham Jubilee Singers, Ravizee Singers, Bessemer Sunset Four, Heavenly Gospel Singers, Kings of Harmony, C.I.O. Singers.

Some of the most beautiful harmony singing ever recorded resides in these two discs, remastered from sides recorded on 78s in Jefferson County, Alabama, between 1926 ("He Took My Sins Away," Birmingham Jubilee Singers) and 1953 ("Shall I Meet You Over Yonder," Blue Jay Singers). The bulk of what's here is spiritual texts rendered in close four-part harmony. "Holy Is My Name" by the Dunham Jubilee Singers, "I Am Thinking of a City," by the Ravizee Singers, "He'll Understand" by the Four Great Wonders and "I Wouldn't Mind Dying" by the Golden Leaf Quartette are among the finest examples of this music ever collected. This is a must set for anyone interested in gospel music, doo-wop harmonies or the richest traditions of American song. — D.M.

★ ★ **The Bitter End Years / Rox. (NA)**
Artists include: Peter, Paul and Mary, Lime-liters, Tom Paxton, Pete Seeger, Judy Collins, Phil Ochs, Everly Brothers, Simon Sisters, Tom Rush, Josh White, Theodore Bikel, Jerry Jeff Walker, John Denver, Melanie, Arlo Guthrie, John Prine, James Taylor, Bette Midler, John Sebastian, Isley Brothers, Dion, Van Morrison, Curtis Mayfield, Lily Tomlin, Robert Klein, Joan Rivers, David Steinberg, Woody Allen, David Frye.

For a dozen years or more, the Bitter End was New York's chief new artist showcase. At first it specialized in folk, then folk rock, but in the end it was open to all. Apparently, a tape recorder was running full time but caught little that was exceptional. Van Morrison, Dion, Prine, and maybe Midler are worth hearing. So are some of the rest—but elsewhere. — D.M.

★ ★ **Black Slavery Days / Clappers (1980)**
Artists include: The Skulls, Mercenaries, Original Survivors, the Arrows.

Interesting concept—every cut is by a group from St. Ann's parish in Jamaica, birthplace of Bob Marley and Burning Spear. Well-performed militant rockers that let down only with the undistinguished composing. — R.F.G.

★ ★ ★ ★ ★ **Bless My Bones: Memphis Gospel Radio, The Fifties / P-Vine (1982), Jap. imp.**
Artists include: Songbirds of the South, Spirit of Memphis Quartet, Dixie Nightingales, Brewsteraires, Rev. W. H. Brewster and Brewsteraires, Queen C. Anderson & Brewster Singers, Southern Wonders, Sounset Travelers.

Marvelous collection of radio transcriptions of gospel singing groups heard in Memphis during the Fifties. The influence of the music runs deeply through rock and soul music: Reverend Brewster held gospel sings that the young Elvis Presley (and many other white and black youths) attended, while the Songbirds of the South manage to utter in one song—"99½ Won't Do"—the message of two of Wilson Pickett's Memphis hits (the title and "in the midnight hour"), references that will seem tangential only to those who have not experienced them firsthand. Recommended. — D.M.

★ ★ ★ **Blue Collar (Soundtrack) / MCA (NA)**
Jack Nitzsche's track for director/screenwriter Paul Schrader's film about Detroit auto workers. This makes it for two reasons: the inclusion of Howlin' Wolf's "Wang Dang Doodle," and Captain Beefheart's reworked "I'm a Man," here called "Hard Workin' Man." — D.M.

★ ★ ★ ★ **Bluegrass for Collectors / RCA (NA)**
Artists include: J. E. Mainer and the Mountaineers, Bill Monroe and the Bluegrass Boys, Charlie Monroe and the Kentucky Pardners, Riley Puckett, Gid Tanner and the Skillet Lickers.

Fine collection of classic pre–World War II bluegrass, highlighted by the Monroe Brothers and Gid Tanner. — D.M.

★ ★ ★ ★ **Blues at Newport—1963 / Van. (NA)**
Artists include: Brownie McGhee and Sonny Terry, Mississippi John Hurt, John Hammond, Reverend Gary Davis, John Lee Hooker, Dave Van Ronk.

Fine set from one of the early-Sixties festivals that helped so much in publicizing the rediscovered bluesmen like Hurt. Hurt, in fact, *owns* this set, with his wonderful "Candy Man," "Trouble I've Had It All My Days" and "Frankie." McGhee and Terry, Davis and white popularizers Hammond and Van Ronk rise admirably to the occasion, as does Hooker, although he is clearly at his best with an electric band, which the purism of the Newport committee would not allow. — D.M.

★ ★ **Blues Brothers (Soundtrack) / Atl. (1980)**
Artists include: James Brown, Aretha Franklin, Blues Brothers, Cab Calloway, Ray Charles.

You can hardly fault the cast, and Aretha, for one, turns in such a rousing performance (of "Think") that it makes the project almost worthwhile. But whether or not they knew it, Jake and Elwood (Dan Aykroyd and John Belushi, though not in that order) were perpetuating a batch of racist stereotypes: basically, that all bluesmen are either "blind ignorant niggers" (to paraphrase Elvis Costello) or plain weird. Aretha, Ray, James and Cab are here, in the end, because they needed the exposure; they're good because they're good. The listener must make his own compromise. — D.M.

★ ★ ★ **The Blues Came down from Memphis / Charly (NA)**
Artists include: Doctor Ross, James Cotton, Willie Nix, Rufus Thomas, Jimmy DeBerry, Sammy Lewis, Little Milton.

Mostly marginal postwar Chicago blues recorded by Sam Phillips for the Sun label before he became involved in rock & roll. To some extent these sides anticipate the Chicago blues styles Chess and others would record. Perhaps the most interesting moment is Rufus "Hound Dog" Thomas' "Bear Cat," which blueprints Presley's later recording of "Hound Dog." — J.S.

★ ★ **Blues from Big Bill's Copa Cabana / Chess (NA)**
Artists include: Muddy Waters, Buddy Guy, Sonny Boy Williamson, Howlin' Wolf, Muddy Waters, Willie Dixon and Buddy Guy.

A Sixties session from Chicago blues disc jockey Big Bill Hill's nightclub. Nothing really exceptional here, although the Dixon, Waters, Guy trio is a rarity. — D.M.

★ ★ ★ ★ **Blues Piano—Chicago, Plus / Atl.**
Artists include: Little Johnny Jones, Floyd Dixon, Little Brother Montgomery, Meade Lux Lewis.

Classic early-Fifties piano recordings are among Ahmet Ertegun and Jerry Wexler's earliest experiments. — J.S.

★ ★ ★ ★ **Blues Project / Elek. (NA)**
Artists include: Dave Van Ronk, John Koerner, Ian Buchanan, Geoff Muldaur, Mark Spoelstra, Danny Kalb, Dave Ray, Eric Von Schmidt.

Early-Sixties collection of young folk-blues guitarists. The outstanding performers here are Koerner, Van Ronk and Ray. Danny Kalb would later perform in a band called the Blues Project. And Ian Buchanan turns in a nice song called "Winding Boy," though he dropped from sight immediately afterward. This record is legendary because Bob Dylan plays under a pseudonym on one track—we'll let you figure out which song, and what name. It won't take long. — D.M.

★ ★ ★ ★ **The Border (Soundtrack) / MCA (1982)**
Artists include: Ry Cooder, Ry Cooder and Willie Greene, Jr., Freddy Fender, Sam Samudio, John Hiatt, Brenda Patterson, Jim Dickinson.

Cooder composed almost the entire score here, most of it in collaboration with others (Dickinson wrote a couple of tunes, Samudio two others). Together these men and women manage to capture the heartbreaking reality of life on the Mexican-American border, at least as effectively as Tony Richardson's fine film. And in the effortless way in which the Anglo and Hispanic performers work together, they suggest the ground for a cure. — D.M.

★ **Bound for Glory (Soundtrack) / U.A. (NA)**
Only Hollywood would make a Woody Guthrie biography starring the TV master of kung fu, David Carradine. Well, David's not as good as Bruce Lee was at martial arts, he can't act as well as his father, and while he may not be much worse at singing than his brother Keith, he isn't much better. Stick with Arlo Guthrie and his old man. — D.M.

★ ★ **Breakout: Top Forty Hits of Today / Col. (NA)**
Artists include: Mott the Hoople, Ten Years After, Andy Pratt, Hollies, Looking Glass, Loggins and Messina, Dr. Hook, Chi Coltrane.

Tepid collection of AOR fare offers testimony to the creative bankruptcy of Seventies rock. — J.S.

THE BRISTOL RECORDER
★ ★ ★ ★ **First Edition / Wavelength (NA), Br. imp.**
Artists include: Electric Guitars, Joe Public, Various Artists, Circus Circus.
★ ★ ★ ★ **The Recorder / Bristol Recorder (NA), Br. imp.**
Artists include: the X-Certs, Peter Gabriel, Fish Food, the Radicals, the Welders.
★ ★ ★ ★ **Recorder Three / Bristol Recorder (NA), Br. imp.**
Artists include: P. B. Davies, Essential Bop, Robert Fripp, Ekomé, the Thompson Twins.

A combination record and magazine, the *Bristol Recorder* captures the spontaneity of the local music scene in this southern British city. Inside the album's gatefold sleeve, political commentary—Bristol's St. Paul's ghetto was the scene of intense rioting in 1981—and band interviews accompany unusual tracks. Most of the album is quite uncommercial; its appeal really lies in the appearances of Peter Gabriel, Robert Fripp and the Thompson Twins. Ekomé, an expatriate dance and drum troupe from Ghana, gives a sparkling performance in the third issue. — ML.H.

★ ★ ★ ★ **Brunswick's Greatest Hits / Bruns. (NA)**
Artists include: Chi-Lites, Artistics, Barbara Acklin, Jackie Wilson, Young-Holt Unlimited, Lost Generation, Tyrone Davis, Little Richard.

Vintage soul from the label that did so much to bring you the second payola scandal of 1973–76. The Wilson and Chi-Lites sides are triumphal, the Davis is tougher than it first appears, and Little Richard is mediocre compared to his Specialty stuff, although "Baby Don't You Tear My Clothes" is a great reworking of a Beatles idea. Only Young-Holt and Lost Generation are lousy. — D.M.

■ **Bye Bye Birdie / RCA (1963)**
This 1963 LP featuring Dick Van Dyke, Ann-Margret and Bobby Rydell (Paul Lynde's absent, fortunately for him, unhappily for us) is offered as evidence that Robert Stigwood did not invent the insipid rock musical, but was only extrapolating from a long, ignoble tradition. — D.M.

★ ★ ★ **Cadence Classics, Vol. 1 / Barn. (NA)**
Artists include: Everly Brothers, Johnny Tillotson, Chordettes, Eddie Hodges, Link Wray.
This is mostly banal pop, although the Everly Brothers songs are strong—especially "Bye Bye Love"—and Link Wray's lone contribution is his best song, "The Rumble," an instrumental that still cooks. — D.M.

★ ★ **Cadence Classics, Vol. 2 / Barn. (NA)**
Artists include: Chordettes, Everly Brothers, Eddie Hodges, Johnny Tillotson, Charlie McCoy, Link Wray.
Buy an Everly Brothers anthology instead. This time not even Link Wray saves the set. — D.M.

★ ★ **Cadence Classics, Vol. 3 / Barn. (NA)**
Artists include: Everly Brothers, Chordettes, Marion Marlowe, Lenny Welch, Don Shirley Trio, Johnny Tillotson, Archie Bleyer, Julius La Rosa, Bill Hayes.
Whaddya want this for? Julius La Rosa? Buy the Everly Brothers alone and you'll feel better about it. — D.M.

★ ★ **California Jam 2 / Col. (1978)**
Artists include: Aerosmith, Heart, Santana, Ted Nugent, Dave Mason, Mahogany Rush.
Live heavy metal with a little Dave Mason and Santana for pacing. — J.S.

★ **California U.S.A. / Col. (NA)**
Artists include: Walter Egan, Jan and Dean, Rondells, Flo and Eddie, American Spring.
Rotten collection of L.A. wimp-rock saved only by Flo and Eddie's irony. — J.S.

★ ★ ★ **Calling Rastafari / Nighth. (1982)**
Artists include: Culture, the Ital, the Mighty Diamonds.
Most of these cuts are available (in one form or another) elsewhere, but it's unlikely that you'll find a more consistent set of recordings by some of reggae's greatest harmony groups. — R.F.G.

★ ★ ★ ★ **Car Wash (Soundtrack) / MCA (1976)**
1976 discofied soundtrack was one of the year's best-selling albums, thanks to Rose Royce's title track. The song made that group a hit, although nothing of the rest of Rose Royce's music, or the background score, or the Pointer Sisters' art-deco funk matches up to it. The movie, naturally, was mediocre. — D.M.

★ ★ ★ ★ **Catch This Beat / Is. (1980), Br. imp.**
Artists include: Ethiopians, Peter Tosh, the Melodians, Derrick Harriot, Ken Boothe, others.
Around 1966 in Jamaica, rocksteady superseded the hot, mainly instrumental ska with slower, tricker rhythms, more prominent guitars and more soulful singing. *Catch This Beat* collects gems from that era, though its range is limited, leaving out prime Treasure Isle and Studio One material. — R.F.G.

★ ★ ★ ★ ★ **Chicago Blues Anthology / Chess (NA)**
Artists include: Robert Nighthawk, Johnny Shines, Memphis Slim, Jimmy Rogers, Willie Mabon, Floyd Jones, Elmore James, Big Bill Broonzy and Washboard Sam, Big Boy Spires, John Brim, Otis Rush, J. B. Lenoir, Eddie Boyd, Buddy Guy.
First-rate compilation of Chicago blues tracks, most of some importance, recorded from 1949 to 1964 by the city's chief blues label. Broonzy and Washboard Sam are near the end of the line, but Lenoir, Elmore James and Shines are at the peak of their abilities. Superb notes by Pete Welding. An excellent source for anyone interested in Chicago blues beyond Waters/Wolf/Williamson/Walter. — D.M.

★ ★ ★ ★ **Chi-Town Show Down / Solid S. (1982)**
Artists include: Esquires, Marvelows.
Nicely packaged battle-of-the-bands concept LP, featuring seven solid soul sides by the Esquires ("Get on Up") on side one and a half-dozen more, including the ecstatic "I Do," by the Marvelows on side two. Minor but substantial. — D.M.

★ ★ ★ ★ **Chicago/The Blues/Today! Vol. 1 / Van. (NA)**
Artists include: Junior Wells, Chicago Blues Band, J. B. Hutto and His Hawks, Otis Spann.

Excellent Sixties recordings produced by Sam Charters. The Wells sides, with Buddy Guy on guitar and Fred Below on drums, are particularly fine. — J.S.

★ ★ ★ ★ **Chicago/The Blues/Today! Vol. 2 / Van. (NA)**
Artists include: Johnny Shines, James Cotton, Homesick James.

The second of these great Sixties blues recordings. — J.S.

★ ★ ★ ★ **Chicago/The Blues/Today! Vol. 3 / Van. (NA)**
Artists include: Johnny Young, Big Walter Horton, Homesick James.

More of the great Sixties blues sessions recorded by Sam Charters. Walter Horton plays harp on every track on the record, with Charlie Musselwhite adding a second harmonica on Horton's tracks. — J.S.

★ ★ ★ ★ **Chicago Slickers 1948 to 1953 / Nighth. (NA)**
Artists include: Little Walter, Floyd Jones, Johnny Shines, John Brim, Homesick James, Delta Joe, Robert Nighthawk, Big Boy Spires, Earl Hooker, Forest City Joe.

Good collection of early postwar amplified Chicago blues. Some of these tracks are pretty rare; all of them are worth listening to. Two of Little Walter's earliest tunes, "I Want My Baby" and "Just Keep Lovin' Her," are included, and benefit from top-flight accompaniment, including Muddy Waters. "Ramblin' " is considered to be Johnny Shines' masterpiece. — J.S.

★ ★ ★ ★ **Club Ska '67 / Mango (1980)**
Artists include: The Skatalites, Roland Alphonso, Desmond Dekker, the Gayladds, Rita Marley, Baba Brooks, Justin Hines.

Just as much quality as the *Intensified* volumes but fewer tracks (twelve instead of sixteen) and a preponderance of familiar material ("Songs of Navarone," "Shanty Town," "Phoenix City"). But it's the only place you can get Justin Hines' "Rub Up, Push Up" and Rita Marley's early hit "Pied Piper." — R.F.G.

★ ★ ★ ★ **Concert for Bangla Desh / Apple (NA)**
Artists include: Ravi Shankar and Ali Akbar Khan and Alla Rakah, George Harrison, *Billy Preston, Ringo Starr, George Harrison and Leon Russell, George Harrison and Eric Clapton, Leon Russell, Leon Russell and Don Preston, Bob Dylan.*

The Big Event of 1972, recorded live at Madison Square Garden, proceeds supposedly to UNICEF. But the only music that's really happening is Dylan's—he hadn't been onstage for a long time, and really puts out. "Just Like a Woman" is an utter revelation, the best version he's ever done of it, and his other numbers (which range from "Blowin' in the Wind" and "Mr. Tambourine Man" to the unlikely "It Takes a Lot to Laugh It Takes a Train to Cry") aren't far behind. Aside from Dylan, the highlight is George Harrison and Eric Clapton's reprise of their Beatles' duet on "While My Guitar Gently Weeps." — D.M.

★ ★ **Country Boy and Country Girl / RCA (NA)**
Artists include: Jim Reeves and Dottie West, Bobby Bare and Skeeter Davis, Hank Snow and Anita Carter, Bobby Bare, Norma Jean and Lynn Anderson, Jimmy Dean and Dottie West, Waylon Jennings and Anita Carter, Archie Campbell and Linda Mann, Connie Smith and Nat Stuckey, Dottie West and Don Gibson.

This volume of duets is far from the best of that odd C&W subgenre, probably because George Jones, the best duet singer in country, never recorded for RCA. — D.M.

★ **Country Chart Busters, Vol. 1 / Col. (NA)**
Artists include: Earl Scruggs, Tanya Tucker, Lynn Anderson, Freddy Weller, Barbara Fairchild, Johnny Cash, Sonny James, Bob Luman, Carl Smith, Jody Miller, Johnny Paycheck.

Mediocre assembly of Columbia's country artists. The best items are Cash's "Oney" and Tanya Tucker's splendidly weird "Bloody Red and Going Down." — D.M.

★ **Country Chart Busters, Vol. 2 / Col. (NA)**
Artists include: Tammy Wynette, Tanya Tucker, Jody Miller, Charlie McCoy, Ray Price, Sonny James, Freddy Weller, Lynn Anderson, Johnny Cash, Earl Scruggs, Johnny Duncan.

Another grab bag of CBS country performers. Anything here worth having—only Wynette's "D-I-V-O-R-C-E"—is available with more interesting companions elsewhere. — D.M.

★ **Country Chart Busters, Vol. 3 / Col. (NA)**
Artists include: Lynn Anderson, Barbara

Fairchild, Carl Smith, Tanya Tucker, Sonny James, Freddy Weller, Charlie Rich, Ray Price, David Houston, George Jones, Tammy Wynette.

Another lousy grab bag.   — D.M.

★ **Country Chart Busters, Vol. 4 / Col. (NA)**
Artists include: Charlie McCoy, George Jones, George Jones and Tammy Wynette, Tommy Cash, Bob Luman, Johnny Cash, Johnny Duncan, Barbara Fairchild, Stonewall Jackson, Mac Davis.

When they get to Mac Davis on one of these anthologies, you *know* they're scraping the bottom of the barrel.   — D.M.

★ **Country Chart Busters, Vol. 5 / Col. (NA)**
Artists include: Charlie Rich, Johnny Paycheck, Jody Miller, Tammy Wynette, Freddy Weller, Sonny James, David Houston, Lynn Anderson, Connie Smith, Barbara Mandrell.

The final installment in Columbia's exploration of the rube potential of the C&W audience is just as dismal as the first four.   — D.M.

★ ★ ★ ★ ★ **Country Cooking: Fourteen Bluegrass Instrumentals / Roun. (1971)**
Landmark album of new-wave bluegrass instrumentals. Guitarist Russ Barenberg, fiddler Kenny Koseyk, bassist John Miller and multi-instrumentalist Tony Trischka all became prominent players in the field.   — J.S.

★ ★ **Country 45s / Epic (NA)**
Artists include: George Jones, Johnny Paycheck, Charlie Rich, Tanya Tucker, Tammy Wynette, David Houston, David Houston and Barbara Mandrell, Barbara Mandrell, Freddy Weller, Jody Miller, Sandy Posey, Johnny Duncan.

Decent selection of Seventies C&W hits. Producer Billy Sherrill, with his fondness for big, bland arrangements, did too many of these for our taste, but Jones, Wynette, Rich and Tucker all perform respectably. Wynette's "Stand by Your Man" is a true masterpiece, but it's available in better company elsewhere. Freddy Weller ought to lay off the Chuck Berry songs. "Promised Land" is a message whose irony he seems unable to appreciate.   — D.M.

★ ★ ★ ★ **Country Gospel Song / RBF (1971)**
Artists include: Ernest Phipps and His Holiness Singers, Alfred G. Karnes, Blind Willie Johnson, Blind Mamie Forehand, Smith Brothers, Lonnie McIntosh, Rev. J. M. Gates, the Carter Family, Uncle Dave Macon, Freeman Quartet.

Splendid set of Southern religious music, recorded in the Twenties and Thirties, which features some of the most outstanding performers, black as well as white, in the entire sacred genre: Blind Willie Johnson's talents were as immense as the Carter Family's, of course, but Reverend Gates and Ernest Phipps were also outstanding. And the others are not far below this standard.   — D.M.

★ ★ ★ **Country Hits of the Fifties / Cap. (NA)**
Artists include: Tennessee Ernie Ford, Jean Shepard, Ferlin Husky, Hank Thompson, Freddie Hart, Sonny James, Faron Young, Jean Shepard and Ferlin Husky, Skeets McDonald, Tommy Collins.

Nice assemblage of Fifties C&W hits. Ford's "Sixteen Tons" is a kind of rockabilly, and Thompson's "The Wild Side of Life" might be. James' "Young Love" was the most familiar pop hit of this bunch.
   — D.M.

★ ★ ★ **Country Hits of the Forties / Cap. (NA)**
Artists include: Tex Williams, Tennessee Ernie Ford, Margaret Whiting and Jimmy Wakely, Merle Travis, Tex Ritter, Jimmie Davis, Al Dexter, Jimmy Wakely, Leon Payne, Jack Payne, Jack Guthrie.

Solid set of country hits from the post–World War II era. Ritter, Ford and Davis are all significant C&W grandfathers (though none of these songs, except perhaps Ford's "Mule Train," are among their best) and Jimmie Davis, who sings "You Are My Sunshine," went on to become governor of Alabama, a process George Wallace is unlikely to reverse.   — D.M.

★ ★ **Country Hits of the Sixties / Cap. (NA)**
Artists include: Glen Campbell, Wanda Jackson, Wynn Stewart, Faron Young, Buck Owens, Tex Ritter, Merle Haggard, Roy Clark, Sonny James, Ferlin Husky.

So-so collection, inferior to the Forties and Fifties volumes of the series. The highlights are Haggard's "Today I Started Loving You Again" and Faron Young's "Hello Walls." Tex Ritter's "I Dreamed of a Hillbilly Heaven" is a kitsch classic.   — D.M.

★ **Country Love, Vol. 2 / Col. (NA)**
Artists include: Patti Page, Ray Price, Tommy Cash, Statler Brothers, Judy Lynn, Tammy Wynette, Charlie Rich, Lynn Anderson, Sammi Smith, Stonewall Jackson, Carl Smith, Marty Robbins, Sonny James, Arlene Harden, Barbara Mandrell, Johnny Cash,

Jody Miller, David Houston, Nashville Strings, Carl Perkins.

Utterly undistinguished package of Columbia's country roster. — D.M.

★ **Country Love, Vol. 3 / Col. (NA)**
Artists include: Arlene Harden, Barbara Mandrell, Lynn Anderson, Marty Robbins, Charlie McCoy, Tammy Wynette and George Jones, Tammy Wynette, David Houston, George Jones, David Houston and Barbara Mandrell, Jody Miller, Charlie Rich, Johnny Paycheck, Ray Price, Connie Smith, Freddy Weller, Barbara Fairchild, Johnny Cash and June Carter, Sonny James, Tanya Tucker.

Columbia raids its catalogue without rhyme or reason. Symptom: Barbara Mandrell's "Treat Him Right" is included both here and on Volume 2 of the series. Wasn't *anybody* paying attention? — D.M.

★ ★ ★ **Countryman (Soundtrack) / Mango (1982)**
Artists include: Bob Marley and the Wailers, Wally Badarou, Rico, Steel Pulse, Aswad, Dennis Brown, Toots and the Maytals, Fabulous Five, Jah Lion, Human Cargo, Lee Perry, Wally Badarou and Rebop Kwaku Baah.

From the 1982 film that tried to redo *The Harder They Come* legend, not with much success. The material here that's by familiar names (Wailers, Maytals, Steel Pulse and Aswad, even) is solid, but too much is by the rather limited Wally Badarou and a batch of other reggae also-rans. — D.M.

★ ★ ★ **Country Music and Bluegrass at Newport—1963 / Van. (NA)**
Artists include: Jim and Jesse, Morris Brothers, Clint Howard and Doc Watson, Clarence Ashley, Clint Howard, Mac Wiseman, New Lost City Ramblers, Tom Logan, Doc Watson.

Good selection of genre favorites as performed at the influential folk festival in its peak year. Infectious and fun. — D.M.

★ ★ ★ **Country's Greatest Hits / Col. (NA)**
Artists include: Johnny Cash, George Morgan, Billy Walker, Jimmy Dean, Carl Smith, Marty Robbins, Little Jimmy Dickens, Roy Acuff, Johnny Horton, Carl Perkins, Ray Price, Lefty Firzzell, Claude King, Lonzo and Oscar, Charlie Walker, Tommy Collins, Stonewall Jackson, Statler Brothers, Flatt and Scruggs, Johnny Cash and June Carter.

A spotty set, but one with highlights:

Cash's "I Walk the Line," Price's "Release Me," Horton's "North to Alaska," Acuff's "Wabash Cannonball" and Robbins' "El Paso." Perkins, however, is represented by a remake of "Blue Suede Shoes" that pales next to his spectacular Sun original. — D.M.

★ ★ ★ ★ **Creation Rockers, Vol. 1 / Troj. (1979)**
Artists include: Baba Brooks, Niney, Big Youth, Sugar Minott, Augustus Pablo, Gregory Isaacs, Carlton and the Shoes.
★ ★ ★ ★ **Creation Rockers, Vol. 2 / Troj. (1979)**
Artists include: Alton Ellis, Slim Smith, the Wailers, Peter Tosh, Dennis Brown, Mikey Dread.
★ ★ ★ ★ **Creation Rockers, Vol. 3 / Troj. (1979)**
Artists include: Johnny Osbourne, the Upsetters, Linval Thompson, Sugar Minott, the Clarendonians, I Roy.
★ ★ ★ ★ **Creation Rockers, Vol. 4 / Troj. (1979)**
Artists include: Don Drummond, Wailing Souls, Junior Byles, Niney, Black Uhuru, Augustus Pablo.
★ ★ ★ ★ **Creation Rockers, Vol. 5 / Troj. (1979)**
Artists include: Alton Ellis, the Techniques, Wailing Souls, Big Youth, Horace Andy, Trinity.
★ ★ ★ ★ **Creation Rockers, Vol. 6 / Troj. (1979)**
Artists include: Jackie Mittoo, the Maytals, I Roy, Johnny Clark, the Morwells, Freddie McKay.

Another magnificent historical survey by Trojan (there have been some lousy ones). Each volume offers twelve cuts which move from late Ska-era to late-Seventies reggae rockers. There's not a bad cut in the series, and each volume contains priceless rarities, such as the Interns (the Wailers in disguise) on Volume 3, Niney's magnificent "Blood and Fire" on Volume 1 and Black Uhuru's otherwise unavailable "Born Free" on Volume 4. All equally essential. — R.F.G.

★ ★ **Dark Muddy Bottom Blues / Spec. (NA)**
Artists include: John Lee Hooker, Pinebluff Pete, Big Joe Williams, Lightnin' Hopkins, Clarence London, Country Jim.

Fifties blues from Texas and the West Coast, primarily. Highlights are Hooker, Hopkins and Williams; the others are extremely minor. — D.M.

★ ★ ★ ★ **Days of Heaven (Soundtrack) / Pac. A. (1979)**
Ennio Morricone's haunting soundtrack for Terence Malick's cryptic but beautifully photographed non-Western. Morricone's music is completely capable of standing on its own (it makes more sense than the picture much of the time), and he has rarely sounded any better than he does here. — D.M.

★ ★ ★ **Death Wish (Soundtrack) / Col. (1975)**
Herbie Hancock effectively scored this 1975 film about Central Park vigilantism. It's the usual jazz-rock fusion blend. — D.M.

★ ★ ★ **A Decade of Gold (1955–1965) / Era (NA)**
Artists include: Gogi Grant, Teddy Bears, Castells, Donnie Brooks, Dorsey Burnette, Art and Dotty Todd, Jewel Akens, Dave Dudley, Chris Montez, Castaways, Hollywood Argyles, Pastel Six, Larry Verne, Fendermen.
Lightweight rock with a few exceptions on the positive side: Teddy Bears' "To Know Him Is to Love Him" is Phil Spector's earliest production; the Castaways' "Liar Liar" is a terrific 1965 Minnesota one-shot; the Hollywood Argyles' "Alley Oop," the Fendermen's "Muleskinner Blues" and Dave Dudley's "Six Days on the Road" are all memorable novelties. — D.M.

★ ★ ★ **Dells vs. Dramatics / Cadet (NA)**
Artists include: Dells, Dramatics, Dells and Dramatics.
Two top-flight soul groups combine with surprising effectiveness. Each group is represented by four tracks separately, and they join forces on "Love Is Missing from Our Lives" and "I'm in Love." — D.M.

★ ★ ★ ★ **Delta Blues Heavy Hitters 1927–1931 / Her. (NA)**
Artists include: William Harris, Blind Joe Reynolds, Skip James.
Great collection of early delta blues recorded between 1927 and 1931. Marred only by the poor quality of the existing versions of these rare records, the set features some fierce playing, particularly Harris on "Kansas City Blues" and "Bull Frog Blues" and James on "Outside Woman Blues" and the electrifying "Devil Got My Woman." Note how closely James' 1931 recording of "Outside Woman Blues" was followed by Cream nearly fifty years later. — J.S.

★ ★ ★ ★ **Detroit Blues 1948–54 / Nighth. (NA)**
Artists include: Slim Pickens, Walter Mitch-

ell, L. C. Green, Sam Kelly, Playboy Fuller, Robert Henry, Baby Boy Warren, Henry Smith.
Because of poor distribution, Detroit-made postwar blues records never achieved the notoriety of their Chicago counterparts, but as this excellent set proves, it wasn't because Detroit blues was any less exciting or innovative. — J.S.

★ ★ **Disco Express / RCA (NA)**
Artists include: Tymes, Faith, Hope and Charity, Bill Harris, Charles Drain, Blood Hollins, Zulema, Brothers, Destiny, Choice Four.
Seventies dance-party album has some decent tracks—Faith, Hope and Charity's "To Each His Own," Charles Drain's "What You Don't Know"—but not enough. — D.M.

★ **Disco Funk / RCA (NA)**
Artists include: Brother Soul, Con-Funk-Shun, Lillian Hale, Hudson County, Madeira, People, T.C.B., Third Time Around.
Bottom-of-the-barrel Seventies dance music, each performance interchangeable with a dozen other rhythm machines. — D.M.

★ ★ ★ **Disco Party / Nat. (1979)**
Artists include: Thelma Houston, Marvin Gaye, Smokey Robinson, the Supremes, Diana Ross, Táta Vega.
Rather lackluster collection, not surprisingly, since Motown wasn't one of the greater disco labels. Best thing here is probably Vega's "Come In Heaven (Earth Is Calling), Pt. 2," although Diana's "Love Hangover" and Marvin's "Got to Give It Up" are also to be reckoned with. — D.M.

★ ★ ★ **Dr. Demento's Delights / War. (NA)**
Artists include: Allan Sherman, Possum, R. Crumb and His Cheap Suit Serenaders, Spike Jones and His City Slickers, Doodles Weaver, Napoleon XIV, Holy Modal Rounders, Ben Gay and the Silly Savages, Harry "The Hipster" Gibson, Jim Kweskin Jug Band, Jef Jaisun.
Pop and rock oddities compiled and annotated by well-known discophile Barrett Hansen. Too crazy for mass consumption, and definitely not approved by the Vinyl Conservation Society, but the Rounders' "Boobs a Lot," Napoleon XIV's widely banned "They're Coming to Take Me Away, Ha Ha" and Kweskin's "If You're a Viper" are worth it for those with a penchant for the truly silly. — D.M.

★ ★ ★ ★ **Doo Wop / Spec. (NA)**
Artists include: Chimes, Monitors, Larry Williams, Vernon Green and the Phantoms, Jesse and Marvin, Marvin and Johnny, Four Flames, Roddy Jackson, Roy Montrell, King Perry and the Pied Pipers, Bob "Froggy" Landers, Rene Hall Band, Joe Lutcher.

Oldies comedy from the Fifties. These really were hits—some of them—and John Lennon immortalized Larry Williams' "Bad Boy" on *Beatles VI.* Strictly for laughs but a good time, graphically well presented.
— D.M.

■ **Doonesbury's Jimmy Thudpucker (and the Walden West Rhythm Section Greatest Hits) / Wind. (NA)**
From the 1977 Christmas special. Thudpucker is supposed to be Garry Trudeau's fantasy of a union between John Denver and Bob Dylan, and unfortunately he lives up to the synthesis. B-o-r-i-n-g. — D.M.

★ ★ ★ **Down behind the Rise / Nighth. (NA)**
Artists include: Jesse Thomas, Frankie Lee Sims, Lightnin' Hopkins, Beverley Scott, Willie Lane, Wright Holmes, Johnny Beck.

Collection of Southwestern country-blues guitarists recorded between 1947 and 1953. The range of material is interesting: amplified country blues by Jesse Thomas ("D. Double Due Love You," "Same Old Stuff," "Another Friend Like Me," "I Wonder Why," "Gonna Write You a Letter," "Gonna Move to California"), a kind of Western swing approach with bass and lap steel guitar from Frankie Lee Sims ("Don't Forget Me Baby"), and some of Lightnin' Hopkins' rarest material ("Jazz Blues," "Henny Penny Blues"). — J.S.

★ ★ ★ **Dreamgirls (Original Cast) / Gef. (1982)**
Dreamgirls is a project whose significance has been overlooked. Consider that at the very moment when American radio and TV broadcasting of music had retreated into phony "separate but equal" rhetoric, the biggest musical property on Broadway was a retelling of the Motown story, in terms that made it clear how central to American folklore Berry Gordy's (and Diana Ross') rise to celebrity and wealth really was. Unfortunately, while it is effective on stage, Henry Krieger's score suffers rather predictably on record. The diction is stagy and thus seems forced and unnatural to ears accustomed to soul and pop phrasing. On the other hand, the music has more authenticity than most. It's hard to think of another musical this side of *The Wiz* that deserved a rating even

this high. And *Dreamgirls* is serious in a way that *The Wiz* never dreamed of being. But seeing, not hearing, is believing.
— D.M.

★ ★ ★ **Drop Down Mama / Chess (NA)**
Artists include: Johnny Shines, Robert Nighthawk, Big Boy Spires, Honey Boy Edwards, Floyd Jones, Claude Smith.

Second-echelon Chicago blues performers. Shines' "So Glad I Found You" and "Joliet Blues," Nighthawk's venerable "Sweet Black Angel" and Jones' "Dark Road" are standouts. A nice complement to the Chess *Chicago Blues Anthology.* — D.M.

★ **Dueling Banjos from *Deliverance* (Soundtrack) / War. (1972)**
From the 1972 John Boorman film that was supposed to take star Burt Reynolds and poet/author James Dickey into the artistic big time. Instead, the only hit this produced was Eric Weisberg's title track and some other banjo numbers that are much less exciting. — D.M.

★ ★ **Dynamite Instrumentals / Ext (NA)**
Artists include: Jools Holland and His Millionaires, Duane Eddy, the Surfaris.

Unfocused album of instrumentals does include a couple of great songs: "Wipe Out," "Pipeline," "Rebel Rouser" and "Raunchy."
— J.S.

★ ★ ★ ★ **East Side Revue / Ramp. (1969)**
Artists include: Cannibal and the Headhunters, Premiers, Mark and the Escorts, Ronnie and the Pomona Casuals, Sisters, Frankie Olivera, Blendells, Pagents, Atlantics, Mixtures, Enchantments, Jaguars, Heartbreakers, Ambertones, Alfred and Joe, Romancers, Salas Brothers, Li'l Ray, Slauson Brothers, Blue Satins, Village Callers, Royal Checkmates, Aldermen, the Epics, Back Seat, Sammy Lee and the Summits, the Flirtations, Sunday Funnies, East Side All Stars, David and Ruben, the Runabouts, the Impals, East Side Kids, the Midniters.

Fabulous collection of vintage rock & soul from the little-noted but highly influential East Los Angeles Chicano rock scene. The best-known tracks here are the original "Land of 1,000 Dances" (Cannibal and the Headhunters) and "Farmer John" (Premiers), but these two discs offer an excellent selection of surf music, hard rockers and ballads, plus some garage psychedelia. Especially worthy of note are "I Wanna Do the Jerk" by Ronnie and the Pomona Casuals, the Blendells' "Dance with Me," the two Salas Brothers tracks, "Karen" by Li'l Ray, and "House of Wax" by the Aldermen. Any exploration of Latin-influenced rock & soul ought to begin here. — D.M.

★ ★ ★ ★ ★ **Echoes of a Rock Era: The Early Years / Rou. (NA)**
Artists include: Sonny Til and the Orioles, Faye Adams, Bo Diddley, Penguins, Cadillacs, Moonglows, Chuck Berry, Nutmegs, Jesse Belvin, Heartbeats, Frankie Lymon, Crows, Chuck Willis, Fleetwoods, Jimmie Rodgers, Buddy Knox, Rays.

Excellent Fifties anthology, drawing from a variety of sources—Chess (Berry's "Roll Over Beethoven" and "Maybellene," Diddley's "Bo Diddley," "Sincerely" by the Moonglows), Atlantic ("Gee" by the Crows and Chuck Willis' "C. C. Rider"), West Coast harmony groups (Penguins' "Earth Angel"), gospel R&B (Til's "Crying in the Chapel") and Southwestern rockabilly (Knox' "Party Doll"). Only the Jimmie Rodgers tracks are truly weak, and while there's nothing really obscure, the presentation is very attractive. — D.M.

★ ★ ★ ★ **Echoes of a Rock Era: The Groups, Vol. 1 / Rou. (NA)**
Artists include: Crows, Harptones.

Two prime Fifties vocal groups from the East Coast, doo-wopping to their—and your—hearts' content. Lush and soulful, if a bit primitive. The Crows are best remembered for "Gee," the Harptones for "Sunday Kind of Love." Not as good for general interest as the survey LPs in the series, but fine for aficionados of streetcorner soul. — D.M.

★ ★ ★ ★ **Echoes of a Rock Era: The Groups, Vol. 2 / Rou. (NA)**
Artists include: Heartbeats, Shep and the Limelites.

Seminal New York group harmony from the Fifties. The general survey LPs in this series are great starter sets for rock fans; these are for collectors. The Heartbeats' best song was "A Thousand Miles Away," but the group's brooding wistfulness sustains its sides. Shep and the Limelites came up with the unsettling ballad "Daddy's Home," contributing a haunted quality that pervades the group's material here. — D.M.

★ ★ ★ ★ **Echoes of a Rock Era: The Later Years / Rou. (NA)**
Artists include: Maxine Brown, Carla Thomas, Shirelles, Chubby Checker, Cleftones, Silhouettes, Lee Dorsey, Bobby Lewis, King Curtis, Mary Wells, Ben E. King, Little Eva,

Dave "Baby" Cortez, Joey Dee and the Starliters, Essex, Joe Henderson, Lou Christie.

Final volume of this fine survey gives a nice look at rock just before the Beatles: Motown is represented with Mary Wells' "My Guy," Atlantic with Ben E. King's "Don't Play That Song" and King Curtis' great "Soul Twist," Stax with Carla Thomas' "Gee Whiz," girl groups by the Shirelles' "Baby It's You" and "Dedicated to the One I Love," New Orleans by Lee Dorsey's "Ya Ya," one-shot pop by Little Eva's immortal "The Locomotion," and so forth. Some froth (Cleftones, Lou Christie) but general excellence. — D.M.

★ ★ ★ ★ **Echoes of a Rock Era: The Middle Years / Rou. (NA)**
Artists include: Monotones, Silhouettes, Dee Clark, Chantels, Jimmie Rodgers, Little Anthony and the Imperials, Coasters, Flamingos, Wilbur Harrison, Johnny and the Hurricanes, Crests, Fiestas, Billy Bland, Maurice Williams and the Zodiacs, Joe Jones, Maxine Brown, Dovels, Joey Dee and the Starliters.

Rock and R&B from about 1958 to around 1962—the latter part of the harmony-group era (Monotones' "Book of Love," Coasters' "Poison Ivy" and "Charley Brown," the Chantels' "Maybe" and Maurice Williams' "Stay" are all masterpieces of that genre) to the beginning of the twist (Joey Dee and the Starliters' "Peppermint Twist" is perhaps the best of the dance-craze discs). The only clinkers are Jimmie Rodgers (the pop one, of course) and the Crests, whose "Sixteen Candles" is teen exploitation music, not rock. Attractively packaged. — D.M.

★ ★ ★ ★ ★ **Eighteen King Size Country Hits / Col. (NA)**
Artists include: Cowboy Copas, Moon Mullican, Grandpa Jones, Carlisle Brothers, Bonnie Lou, William Raney, Joe Osborne, Hawkshaw Hawkins, Delmore Brothers, D. Reno and R. Smiley, Clarence Moody, Stanley Brothers, J. Cardwell, Pop Eckler.

Excellent sampler of C&W sides made for King, the Cincinnati-based label that made most of its impact in the Forties and Fifties. Well annotated by Sire Records owner, Seymour Stein, and highlighted by the bluegrass of the Delmore and Stanley Brothers, and the honky-tonk singing of Cowboy Copas and Hawkshaw Hawkins.

Even better is the companion volume, *Eighteen King Size Rhythm and Blues Hits,* released at the same time but now deleted. It features profoundly important material by

James Brown, Little Willie John and Hank Ballard, among others, with ample commentary, again by Stein. Seek out both. — D.M.

★ ★ ★ **Endless Beach / Epic (1982)**
Artists include: Tyrone Davis, Robert John, Spellbinders, Wild Cherry, Otis Leavell, Tower of Power, Billy Butler and the Enchanters, Spiral Starecase, Major Lance, Tina Charles, Jimmy Hall, Essence, Tymes, Ron Moody and the Centaurs.

Collection of CBS's beach music-related material is a bit thin on the ostensible collection, but contains good sides by Davis, John, Butler, Hall, Tymes and Charles. Smarmily packaged. — D.M.

★ ★ **England's Greatest Hit Makers / Lon. (NA)**
Artists include: Rolling Stones, Kathy Kirby, Them, Tom Jones, Unit Four Plus Two, Bern Elliott, Mike Leander Orchestra, Bachelors, Lulu and the Lovers, Zombies, Johnny Howard Band, Billy Fury, Applejacks, Dave Berry.

Your Anglophilia has to run pretty deep to want this collection of dated English pop from the mid-Sixties. The Stones' track is the obscure but easily available "Surprise Surprise"; Them checks in with "Little Girl"; the Zombies with "Nothing's Changed." Aside from those, the most interesting item here is Unit Four Plus Two's "Woman from Liberia," which is hardly as good as their hit, "Concrete and Clay." In context this is rot, and instructive to anyone who believes the British Invasion was all gold—but it isn't worth more than a couple of bucks, for any purpose. — D.M.

★ ★ ★ ★ ★ *E.T.:* **Narrated by Michael Jackson; Produced by Quincy Jones; Music by John Williams / MCA (1982)**
MCA undoubtedly meant this to be just a simple Christmas exploitation package, designed to cash in on the holiday market and be forgotten. But in Michael Jackson they got more than the perfect narrator; they acquired such an icon of innocence that he takes the story into a whole other realm. Although he sings only one song (the rather bathetic "Someone in the Dark"), Jackson commands your full attention in his enthusiasm and total belief in the story. At key moments his voice seems to crack, as though he, too, were moved to tears by this simple story (which evokes Leslie Fielder's theories of white men and aliens in all sorts of different contexts). The result is beautiful, whimsical, exciting and totally charming, a kitsch masterpiece at the very least and an impor-

tant collaboration between significant artists (Spielberg and Jackson; forget Quincy Jones and John Williams, even if you *can* tell them apart). If rock & roll is sense and sensibility as much as form, then this is the real item. — D.M.

★ **Every Which Way but Loose (Soundtrack) / Elek. (1979)**
Artists include: Eddie Rabbitt, Mel Tillis, Sondra Locke, Cliff Crawfors, Charlie Rich.

Country-pop soundtrack to a bad Clint Eastwood film. — J.S.

■ **Evita (Original Cast) / MCA (NA)**
The best thing about this 1976 "rock" opera, based on the life of Evita Perón, the Argentine Rasputin, and written by the *Jesus Christ Superstar* team of Andrew Lloyd Webber and Timothy Rice, is the reappearance on record of former Manfred Mann lead singer Paul Jones. Unfortunately Jones has lost his touch, a problem exacerbated by the surroundings: wooden singing, horrid songwriting and a stupid concept. — D.M.

★ **Fabulous Sixties / Ext (NA)**
Artists include: Sam and Dave, Blood, Sweat and Tears, Classics IV.

Grab-bag approach with no good reason for existence. — J.S.

★ ★ ★ **John Fahey, Leo Kottke and Peter Lang (NA)**
Sampler of Takoma's three most prominent folk-blues-based guitarists. Fahey is a genius, but Kottke and Lang are only slightly his inferiors. All of this is pleasant, although every one of them is better when given more space to stretch out. — D.M.

★ ★ ★ **Fantasy Blues Two-Fer Giants / Fan. (NA)**
Artists include: Jimmy Witherspoon, Lightnin' Hopkins, Reverend Gary Davis, Furry Lewis, Memphis Slim, John Lee Hooker, Jesse Fuller, Sonny Terry and Brownie McGhee, Tom Rush, Dave Van Ronk, Holy Modal Rounders.

Interesting collection that's not really blues at all but a sampling of the best blues and folk from Prestige albums, which Fantasy now owns and reissues. The last three artists—Rush, Van Ronk and the Rounders—are all white folkies who depart in various ways from black blues tradition. The first nine are all for the real bluesman, though, and while this isn't anyone's best work, these Fifties and Sixties recordings have a certain vitality and make a nice introduction to mostly country (only Hooker and Witherspoon are electric or band artists) blues. — D.M.

★ ★ ★ ★ **Fifteen Original Big Hits, Vol. 1 / Stax (1981)**
Artists include: Dramatics, Shirley Brown, Booker T. and the MGs, William Bell, Emotions, Eddie Floyd, Bar-Kays, Johnnie Taylor.

Excellent collection of Stax hits including "Woman to Woman" by Brown, "Soul Limbo" by Booker T., "Who's Making Love" by Johnnie Taylor and "In the Rain" by the Dramatics. — J.S.

★ ★ ★ **Fifteen Original Big Hits, Vol. 2 / Stax (1981)**
Artists include: Booker T. and the MGs, Emotions, Albert King, Carla Thomas, Isaac Hayes, Dramatics, Staple Singers, Johnnie Taylor.

Good collection of Stax hits including "Time Is Tight" by Booker T., "Cheaper to Keep Her" by Taylor and "Theme from *Shaft*" by Hayes. — J.S.

★ ★ ★ **Fillin' In Blues / Her. (NA)**
Artists include: Jim Jackson, Furry Lewis, Cannon's Jug Stompers, Washboard Walter, Slim Barton and Eddie Mapp, Cow Cow Davenport, James "Boodle It" Wiggins, Piano Kid Edwards, Ishmaen Bracey, Charley Taylor.

Blues anthology whose only organizing principle is rarity—hence the name, as well as the suggestion that this is a collectors-only set. One side is country blues, one is barrelhouse piano; all of the material is from 1928–30 and a few gems are included, like Jim Jackson's great version of "Hesitation Blues" and the Gus Cannon's Jug Stompers sides "Last Chance Blues" and "The Rooster Crowing Blues." — J.S.

★ ★ ★ ★ **A Fistful of Dollars (Soundtrack) / RCA (NA)**
This outstanding score by Ennio Morricone is interesting to rock fans because the Italian composer uses electric guitar to create effects more deadly than most rock musicians. Morricone's influence has seeped into several young electric guitarists since this picture appeared in the late Sixties. (The film is Clint Eastwood's second cosmic Western with director Sergio Leone.) — D.M.

★ ★ ★ **FM (Soundtrack) / MCA (1978)**
Artists include: Jimmy Buffett, Doobie Brothers, Eagles, Dan Fogelberg, Foreigner, Billy Joel, Randy Meisner, Steve Miller, Tom Petty and the Heartbreakers, Queen, Linda Ronstadt, Boz Scaggs, Bob Seger, Steely Dan, James Taylor, Joe Walsh

Had it not been released in 1978—the year of *Saturday Night Fever*—this soundtrack from the flop movie about rock radio might have been regarded as a true phenomenon, since it spent a fair share of time in the Top Ten. Even so, this is a peculiarly flawed picture of what went on in rock in the late Seventies.

The bias toward California rock is extreme, symbolized by the inclusion of two Linda Ronstadt cover versions, "Tumbling Dice" and "Poor Poor Pitiful Me," both of them demonstrably inferior to the Rolling Stones and Warren Zevon originals. There is also a bent toward lightweight pop of all kinds (thus, Billy Joel's "Just the Way You Are"), and a complete underrating and underestimation of hard rock: why Foreigner's "Cold as Ice" formula crap and Queen's contemptible neofascist chant "We Will Rock You" rather than the Who and Lynyrd Skynyrd, two acts who actually record for MCA?

Producer Irving Azoff, who manages the Eagles, Steely Dan, Buffett, Meisner, Scaggs, Fogelberg and Walsh, seems to have let his taste dictate the contents. Especially given Steely Dan's otherwise unavailable title track, this could have been the new *Woodstock,* a comprehensive overview of a contemporary moment in rock. Instead, that place goes to *Saturday Night Fever,* which at least accurately reflects the energy and scope of disco. — D.M.

★ ★ ★ ★ **Fourteen Golden Recordings from the Vaults of Duke Records, Vol. 1 / ABC (NA)**
Artists include: Bobby "Blue" Bland, Johnny Ace, Casuals, Willie Mae Thornton, O.V. Wright, Junior Parker, Torros, Clarence "Gatemouth" Brown, Rob Roys, Roy Head, Joe Hinton.

Fine sampler of R&B from the Texas-based Duke label. Most of these are minor R&B hits from the Fifties and Sixties. Bland's "There Ain't Nothing You Can Do" and "Further up the Road" are among his best. Head's "Treat Her Right" and Hinton's "Funny" take the R&B-country fusion beyond rockabilly. Ace's "Pledging My Love" is a genre masterpiece. There's some surprisingly good group vocalizing—the Casuals' "So Tough," "Dance with Me" by the Torros—a peculiar black-consciousness item by Wright ("Ace of Spades") and, of course, Thornton's "Hound Dog," which is where

Elvis learned it. Annotation is only adequate, which is all that holds this back. — D.M.

★ ★ ★ ★ **Fourteen Golden Recordings from the Vaults of Vee Jay Records** / ABC (NA)
Artists include: Dells, Gene Chandler, Betty Everett and Jerry Butler, Dee Clark, Gladys Knight and the Pips, Jimmy Reed, Jerry Butler, John Lee Hooker, Betty Everett, Eddie Harris.

Interesting collection of hits from the formidable Chicago label, one of the few black-owned ones of the Fifties and Sixties. "Duke of Earl," by Chandler, is a classic rock mystery: who is the Duke and why? The Everett/Butler duet on "Let It Be Me," Butler's own "He Will Break Your Heart" and Gladys Knight's "Every Beat of My Heart" are transitional records between R&B and soul of some importance, while Reed and Hooker's blues are both well known because they were so easily adapted to rock & roll by the British bands, particularly the Animals. — D.M.

★ ★ ★ ★ ★ **Alan Freed's Memory Lane** / Rou. (1962)
Artists include: Dells, Jerry Butler, Flamingos, Crests, Sonny Til and the Orioles, Jacks, Five Satins, Moonglows, Teen Queens, Rays, Little Anthony and the Imperials, Robert and Johnny, Mello Kings, Jesse Belvin.

The fact that this is a fine collection of slow-dance R&B ballads is secondary to the fact that it's narrated by Freed, giving those who missed the first great rock disc jockey's radio shows a chance to hear him. Freed probably isn't at the peak of his form—this album and its nonnarrative companion, *Alan Freed's Top Fifteen,* were made for George Goldner's End label after Freed's career had been destroyed in the payola witch hunt. But it's still a thrill to hear the voice that started it all, and if none of these tracks are obscure—well, maybe the Jacks' "Why Don't You Write Me"—that's a tribute to the prescience of his (and Goldner's) taste. — D.M.

★ ★ ★ ★ **Alan Freed's Top Fifteen** / Rou. (1962)
Artists include: Wilbert Harrison, Buster Brown, Etta James, Santo and Johnny, Nutmegs, Spaniels, Dee Clark, Shirelles, Lee Dorsey, Silhouettes, Faye Adams, Charlie and Ray, Cadillacs, Rivileers, Edna McGriff.

Not as exceptional as *Alan Freed's Memory Lane*—he doesn't narrate it—but this LP has more diversity. And, presuming he really picked the cuts, the album confirms the excellence of the great DJ's taste. You can imagine, with awe, that this is what the music on his shows sounded like, and be overwhelmed by its scope: "Kansas City" by Harrison and "Fanny Mae" by Brown are hard rockers, while the beautiful "Shake a Hand" by Faye Adams is a barely secular gospel derivative. — D.M.

★ ★ ★ ★ **Friends of Old-Time Music** / Folk. (1964)
Artists include: Doc Watson and Gaither Carlton, Hobart Smith, Mississippi John Hurt, Almeda Riddle, Stanley Brothers, Clarence Ashley and Doc Watson, Jesse Fuller, Dock Boggs, Roscoe Holcomb, Howard Price and Watson.

Lovely set includes live performances by some of the most important bluegrass and mountain music performers, highlighted by the Stanleys and Watson and Ashley, alongside some of the great delta bluesmen, highlighted by the gentle genius of Hurt. Roscoe Holcomb's "Pretty Fair Miss All in a Garden" is not to be forgotten. — D.M.

★ **Fritz the Cat (Soundtrack)** / Fan. (NA)
Artists include: Bo Diddley, Billie Holiday, Alice Stuart, Jim Post, Merl Saunders, Cal Tjader, Bernard Purdie.

Very spotty record, from Ralph Bakshi's animated feature based on R. Crumb's horny cartoon feline. Diddley and Holiday are overwhelmed by the trio of West Coast mediocrities, who noodle aimlessly over the rest of the disc. — D.M.

★ ★ ★ **From the Historic Vaults of Duke** / Peacock / ABC (NA)
Artists include: Bobby Bland, Johnny Ace, Junior Parker, John Roberts, Lamp Sisters, Ernie K-Doe, Paulette Parker, Clarence and Calvin, O. V. Wright, Jeanette Williams, Roy Head, Willie Mae Thornton, Insights.

Much more spotty than its companion volume, *Fourteen Golden Recordings,* this set nonetheless gives a pretty good picture of the actual Duke release pattern. The Lamp Sisters' "Today Will Be Yesterday, Tomorrow" is a nice R&B oddity, but the Bland and Parker selections are poor, and the rest is simple middle-level R&B, without much distinction. — D.M.

★ ★ ★ ★ **From Jubilee to Gospel** / JEMF (1980)
Artists include: Wings over Jordan, Wiseman Sextette, Utice Institute Jubilee Singers, Virginia Female Singers, Birmingham Jubilee

Singers, Cornfed Four, Golden Gate Quartet, Norfolk Jazz Quartet, Famous Blue Jays of Alabama, Dunham Jubilee Singers, Bill Landford Four, Heavenly Gospel Singers, the Georgia Peach and Her Gospel Singers, Selah Jubilee Singers, Alphabetical Four, Fairfield Four.

Subtitled "A Selection of Commercially Recorded Black Religious Music, 1921–1953," this set is at its best documenting the middle of the period, when the pure doo-wop gospel harmony was developed and reached its most exquisite development. There is extensive annotation, thanks no doubt to a grant from the National Endowment for the Arts, a rare instance of the American government having a shred of cultural self-respect. — D.M.

★ ★ ★ ★ ★ From Spirituals to Swing / Van. (NA)
Artists include: Benny Goodman Sextet, Count Basie, Helen Humes, Hot Lips Page, Kansas City Six, James P. Johnson, New Orleans Feetwarmers, Golden Gate Quartet, Sonny Terry, Joe Turner and Pete Johnson, Pete Johnson, Meade Lux Lewis, Albert Ammons, Big Bill Broonzy, Sonny Terry and Bull City Red, Mitchell's Christian Singers, Ida Cox.

John Hammond's memorable 1936 Carnegie Hall concert delivers just what it promises: spirituals, swing and everything in between, including blues, ragtime, hot New Orleans jazz—the works. Probably of value only to historians and collectors—the recordings are not great—but a nice perspective on the development of black American music, nonetheless. — D.M.

★ ★ ★ From the Vaults / Nat. (1979)
Artists include: Temptations, Diana Ross and the Supremes, Marvelettes, Marvin Gaye, Monitors, Spinners, Smokey Robinson and the Miracles, Martha Reeves and the Vandellas, Gladys Knight and the Pips, Mary Wells.

Nice idea: take out some old (1962–1966), previously unreleased tracks by the most famous artists (give or take the Tops and Marvin Gaye) of Motown's halcyon days and package them together. The result isn't very revealing—there's nothing resembling a lost hit here, though it's nice to hear the Miracles' "It's Fantastic" and the Vandellas' "Undecided Lover"—but it remains a good idea. Who knows? Gaye and Stevie Wonder may actually have left some treasure in the archives. — D.M.

★ ★ ★ Georgia Sea Island Songs / New W. (1977)
Artists include: John Davis, Joe Armstrong, Bessie Jones, Willis Proctor, Henry Morrison, with various groups.

Like all of New World's packages of American folk music, this is splendidly annotated and at least decently recorded. It is in fact a compilation of recordings made for the Library of Congress by Alan Lomax in 1960 and 1961 among black singers on the islands just off the southern Atlantic coast. The tunes include ancient folk ballads and many hymns, performed in a primitive but fascinating style that has links both to African performances and to the kind of Pentecostalism expressed in Sacred Harp and similar white, mainland sacred music. — D.M.

★ ★ ★ Get Down and Boogie / Casa. (NA)
Artists include: Donna Summer, Giorgio, Parliament, Roberta Kelly, Smoke.

Mixed bag of funk and disco material. Summer is the siren of the dance floor, and "Love to Love Ya Baby" was the first indication of how and why: this is her best and most sultry moan and groan. Parliament's "Give Up the Funk" is probably the most accessible kind of music that leader George Clinton makes. But the rest of this is just the dance formula, done without much distinction, unless you like Giorgio's Muzak-inspired "Nights in White Satin." — D.M.

★ ★ ★ Get Your Ass in the Water and Swim Like Me! / Roun. (1976)
This is a collection of "narrative poetry from black oral tradition," according to the subtitle, but what it really is is a set of "toasts," long, rhyming scatological tales, reminiscent of the dozens, which include such classic stories as "Titanic," "Stackolee," "Signifying Monkey" and "Joe the Grinder and G.I. Joe." If you want to understand the roots of rap music—which are not in the toasting of Jamaican DJs—check this out. There's no music, and the performers are uncredited (though all are male), but the beat is on the one, anyhow. — D.M.

■ Godspell (Original Cast) / Ari. (1973)
■ Godspell (Soundtrack) / Ari. (1973)
One of Broadway's lamer attempts to go counterculture, with a musical based on Saint Matthew's gospel. In language the authors would pretend to understand, somebody's going to earn an awful lot of bad karma for these electrified recyclings of Rodgers and Hart. Don't mess with the Kid. — D.M.

★ ★ ★ ★ **Going down the Valley: Vocal and Instrumental Style in Folk Music from the South / New W. (1977)**
Artists include: Shortbuckle Roark and Family, Ben Jarrell, Shelor Family, Pope's Arkansas Mountaineers, Bela Lam and His Greene County Singers, the Carter Brothers and Son, Ernest V. Stoneman and His Dixie Mountaineers, the Perry County Music Makers, Uncle Dave Macon and His Fruit Jar Drinkers, Gid Tanner and His Skillet Lickers, Charlie Poole and the North Carolina Ramblers, Ashley and Abernathy, Callahan Brothers, Allen Brothers, Fort Worth Doughboys, Taylor-Griggs Louisiana Melody Makers, Coon Creek Girls, Wade Mainer, Zeke Morris and Steve Ledford.

Excellent assemblage of mostly mountain music, with both key performers (Poole, Macon, Stoneman, Tanner) and key songs ("Little Maggie," "Corrina, Corrina," "Cotton-Eyed Joe", "Old Joe Clark") well represented. — D.M.

★ ★ ★ ★ **Golden Age of Rhythm and Blues / Chess (NA)**
Artists include: Bluejays, Coronets, El-Rays, Moonglows, Moonlighters, Orchids, Flamingos, Five Notes, Ravens, Quintones, Tornadoes, Students, Sentimentals, Lee Andrews and the Hearts, Monotones, Pastels, Revels, Sonics, Miracles.

Chess Records is thought of as a blues label, but it also produced some of the dreamiest doo-wop of the Fifties. These harmony groups are mostly Chicago based (the big exception is the Miracles, whose "Bad Girl" was done before Berry Gordy dreamed up Motown). Unfortunately, given the inclusion of so many obscure groups, this collection is not annotated, but the best of it—"Bad Girl," the Moonglows' "Sincerely," Lee Andrews and the Hearts' "Teardrops," the Flamingos' "I'll Be Home" and "The Vow," and particularly "I'm So Young" by the Students—is downright essential. — D.M.

★ ★ ★ **Golden Hits from the Gang at Bang / Bang (NA)**
Artists include: Neil Diamond, McCoys, Strangeloves, Exciters.

Anthology of mid-Sixties hits that range from Diamond's formula pop rock ("Cherry Cherry" and "Solitary Man") to the Exciters' pop soul and primordial punk rock (Strangeloves with "I Want Candy" and "Cara-lin," and the McCoys with "Hang On Sloopy" and "Fever"). Worth having for the latter. — D.M.

★ ★ ★ **Golden Soul (in Aid of the World's Refugees) / Atl. (NA)**
Artists include: Otis Redding, Ray Charles, Roberta Flack, Wilson Pickett, King Curtis, Ben E. King, Drifters, Sam and Dave, Spinners, Percy Sledge, Joe Tex, Aretha Franklin.

This album's proceeds go to UNICEF, and it is an interesting, if limited, look at the development of Atlantic's version of soul from Charles' "What'd I Say" (1955) to Flack's "Feel Like Makin' Love" (1974). What happens in between is the story of R&B's development into soul and the ability of the music to surpass nomenclature barriers. Everything here represents the artist at the height of his/her powers. Unfortunately, there is no annotation. Ideally, one should look for the eight-volume *History of Rhythm and Blues* (now deleted), which tells Atlantic's story in much more detail. Failing that, however, this has to do. — D.M.

★ ★ **Golden Summer / U.A. (NA)**
Artists include: Beach Boys, Marketts, Fantastic Baggys, Jan and Dean, Surfaris, Frogmen; Frankie Avalon, Dick Dale and the Deltones, Trashmen, Tradewinds, Jack Nitzsche, Annette Funicello, Routers, Ventures.

A concept collection gone wrong. Inferior Beach Boys selections (where's "Surfin' USA"?), some poor covers ("Pipeline" by the Ventures, when the hit version by the Chantays is far, far superior), and some pure nonsense: Annette and Frankie carry the concept too far. In fact the best stuff here is *not* about surfing: Nitzsche's "Lonely Surfer," the Tradewinds' "New York's a Lonely Town" and the Trashmen's gibberish masterpiece, "Surfin' Bird," are among the truest ancestors of the punk rock of the Ramones and Sex Pistols. — D.M.

★ ★ ★ **The Good, the Bad and the Ugly (Soundtrack) / U.A. (1968)**
From the 1968 Sergio Leone film starring Clint Eastwood. Hugo Montenegro parlayed the theme song into a pop hit. But composer Ennio Morricone's arrangement is tougher, more electric; it could pass for a kind of post-Hendrix rock. Still, this is the least exciting of Morricone's Leone scores. — D.M.

★ ★ ★ **Good Old Country Gospel / RCA (NA)**
Artists include: Chet Atkins, Floyd Cramer, Jim Reeves, Skeeter Davis, Dolly Parton, Porter Wagoner and the Blackwood Brothers, Connie Smith, Dottie West.

A rather skimpy assortment, of which the Wagoner track with the Blackwood Brothers is most worthwhile. Hearing the other singers here do hymns is like watching the most outrageous Saturday-night reveler arrive for church next morning: his contrition may be suspect, but not his faith. It's a shame there isn't at least one selection here, though, from Elvis Presley's three wonderful gospel LPs. — D.M.

★ ★ ★ Gospel at Its Best / Pea. (NA)
Artists include: Dixie Hummingbirds, Inez Andrews, Sensational Nightingales, Pilgrim Travelers, Jackson Southernaires, Mighty Clouds of Joy, Loving Sisters, Biblical Gospel Singers, Five Blind Boys, Williams Brothers.

A fine collection of Fifties and Sixties gospel music, which might make a nice supplement to Columbia's *Gospel Sound* sets. The Hummingbirds, Nightingales, Pilgrim Travelers, Blind Boys and Mighty Clouds are all among the most important groups in the genre. — D.M.

★ ★ ★ The Gospel Ship: Baptist Hymns and White Spirituals from the Southern Mountains / New W. (1977)
Artists include: Ike Caudill, D. N. Asher, Howard Adams, Rev. I. D. Beck, George Spanger, Ruby Vass, Hobart Smith, Preston Smith, Texas Gladden, Almeda Riddle, Ollie Gilbert, Neill Hampton, Mountain Ramblers.

Nice collection for those desiring an overview, but without anything fundamental or sufficiently luminescent to make it indispensable. Riddle's "I Am a Poor Wayfaring Stranger" and Smith's "See That My Grave Is Kept Clean" are worth knowing, however. — D.M.

★ ★ ★ ★ ★ The Gospel Sound, Vol. 1 / Col. (NA)
Artists include: Blind Willie Johnson, Reverend J. M. Gates, Arizona Dranes, Golden Gate Jubilee Quartet, Mahalia Jackson, Mitchell's Christian Singers, Abyssinian Baptist Choir, Dixie Hummingbirds, Dorothy Love Coates, Staple Singers, Angelic Gospel Singers and the Dixie Hummingbirds, Marion Williams.

A splendid double-disc gospel compilation with material spanning the era from Johnson's 1927 "Motherless Children" and "If I Had My Way" to Coates' 1968 "Strange Man." The annotation is by Tony Heilbut, the best critic in the field. This is part of Columbia's John Hammond Collection, and is packaged and chosen with that venerable gentleman's usual perspicacity. These two volumes are perhaps *the* fundamental overview of black gospel styles. — D.M.

★ ★ ★ ★ ★ The Gospel Sound, Vol. 2 / Col. (NA)
Artists include: Blind Willie Johnson, Eddie Head and Family, Marion Williams, Arizona Dranes, Golden Gate Jubilee Quartet, Mahalia Jackson, Reverend J. M. Gates, Dorothy Love Coates and the Gospel Harmonettes, Pilgrim Travelers, Staple Singers, Bessie Griffin, Mitchell's Christian Singers, R. Harris and the Christian Singers.

The second lovely volume of black gospel music, presented as part of Columbia's John Hammond Collection and annotated by Tony Heilbut. Fundamental for anyone with an interest in America's black musical heritage. — D.M.

★ ★ The Graduate (Soundtrack) / Col. (NA)
This album made Simon and Garfunkel huge stars in 1968, but it's too skimpy on Paul Simon songs—"Mrs. Robinson" and "Sounds of Silence" as well as the inevitable "Scarborough Fair" and a couple of others—while the set is filled out with the usual background music. This album doesn't hold up much better than the Mike Nichols–directed period picture it is derived from. — D.M.

■ Grease (Original Cast) / MGM (NA)
★ Grease (Soundtrack) / RSO (1978)
The Broadway show is concrete evidence that that medium ought to be legally barred from any association with rock & roll, or the Fifties. Dumb, obvious and boring. The film version is a different matter: John Travolta might have been a great greaser if he'd been able to avoid the travesty of his surroundings. While any movie with an affection for Sandra Dee and Fabian is a movie we can do without, this is slightly redeemed by the presence of "You're the One That I Want," a 1978 hit in which Travolta and Newton-John capture a sliver of the sound and innocent spirit of the era. A smart guy would save himself a lot of dough by springing for the single and forgetting about this dud. — D.M.

★ ★ ★ ★ ★ Great Bluesmen / Van. (NA)
Artists include: Homesick James, John Lee Hooker, Sleepy John Estes, Muddy Waters, Jesse Fuller, Reverend Gary Davis, Mance Lipscomb, Mississippi John Hurt, Junior Wells, Johnny Shines, Son House, Sonny Terry, Joe Turner and Pete Johnson, Brownie McGhee and Sonny Terry, Otis Spann, Big

Bill Broonzy, Lightnin' Hopkins, Johnny
Young, James Cotton, Jimmy Rushing, Skip
James, J. B. Hutto, Fred McDowell, Ida Cox,
Robert Pete Williams, Otis Rush.

The full scope of blues: delta stylists like
Hurt and House, to relatively sophisticated
Kansas City performers (Rushing, Turner,
Johnson) and a good deal of Chicago material—Waters, Cotton, Spann, James, Rush,
Hutto, Young. Also some eccentrics and
transitional figures: Broonzy, Fuller, Hooker,
Lipscomb, Davis, Estes. Perfunctorily annotated, but nonetheless, this is a comprehensive blues perspective, although little of it
(perhaps only Hurt's "Moanin' the Blues") is
definitive. — D.M.

★ ★ ★ ★ Great Bluesmen at Newport / Van.
(NA)
Artists include: Robert Pete Williams, Sonny
Terry and Brownie McGhee, John Lee Hook-
er, Son House, Skip James, Sleepy John
Estes, Willie Doss, Mississippi Fred McDo-
well, Mississippi John Hurt, Reverend Gary
Davis, Lightnin' Hopkins, Dock Reese.

Fine selection of live, mostly delta-based
folk-blues artists, from the 1963 and 1964
Newport Folk Festivals, at which nearly all
the major rediscovered bluesmen appeared.
Those shows were occasions, and often the
performances reflect it. The annotation, unfortunately, is completely inadequate, and
Estes, for instance, is clearly well past his
prime. — D.M.

★ ★ ★ ★ ★ Great Golden Gospel Hits, Vol.
1 / Savoy (NA)
Artists include: James Cleveland, Gospel Har-
monettes, Roberta Martin Singers, Imperial
Gospel Singers, Ward Singers, Davis Sisters,
Five Blind Boys, Gospel Clefs, Caravans, Alex
Bradford, Staple Singers, Gay Sisters.

A fine representation of black religious
music from the label that has done the most
to preserve its treasures. These tracks range
from the late Forties through the Sixties,
and feature a great many of this music's biggest names. Dilettantes and beginners will
get more from Columbia's Gospel Sound as
an overview, but those interested in the continuing breadth and vitality of gospel as a
musical genre should investigate this, and its
companion volumes. — D.M.

★ ★ ★ ★ ★ Great Golden Gospel Hits, Vol.
2 / Savoy (NA)
Artists include: James Cleveland, Caravans,
Gospel Harmonettes, Rosie Wallace, Dorothy
Norwood, Gospel Clefs, Southwestern Michi-
gan Choir, Reverend Charles Watkins, Ro-

berta Martin Singers, Five Blind Boys, Robert
Anderson, Raspberry Singers.

The second excellent collection in Savoy's
series. — D.M.

★ ★ ★ ★ ★ Great Golden Gospel Hits, Vol.
3 / Savoy (NA)
Artists include: James Cleveland, Reverend
Cleophus Robinson, Dr. C. J. Johnson, Banks
Brothers, Jesse Dixon, Dorothy Norwood,
Southwestern Michigan Choir, Caravans, Gos-
pel Wonders, Vill Moss, D. Barrett, Angelic
Choir.

Collection sustains its quality through the
third set in Savoy's series. — D.M.

★ ★ ★ Great Golden Gospel Hits, Vol. 4 /
Savoy (NA)
Artists include: James Cleveland, Dorothy
Norwood, Jesse Dixon, Davis Sisters, Rosetta
Tharpe, Roberta Martin Singers, Angelic
Choir, James Herndon, Caravans, Voices of
Tabernacle, Hulah Gene and Carolyne, Bill
Moss.

The concluding volume of Savoy's gospel
collection has fewer big names than the others but is still a fine selection. — D.M.

★ ★ Great Moments at the Grand Ole Opry
/ RCA (NA)
Artists include: Minnie Pearl, Connie Smith,
Sonny James, Chet Atkins, Bobby Bare,
Hank Snow, Don Gibson, Dolly Parton, Jim
Reeves, Porter Wagoner, Johnny Russell and
Archie Campbell, Ronnie Milsap, Billy Walk-
er, Dottie West, Jim Ed Brown.

Doesn't deliver on the title's promise.
These are mostly average tracks from a
group of average singers, with a handful of
exceptions: Parton, Reeves, Wagoner and
Bare, who turn in interesting versions of predictable songs. — D.M.

★ ★ ★ ★ The Great Rap Hits / Sugar.
(1980)
Artists include: Sequence, Super Wolf, Sugar
Hill Gang, Spoonie Gee, Lady B., Funky
Four Plus One.

When released in 1980, this looked like an
excellent overview of a fad. Today its major
virtue is inclusion of the first big rap record,
"Rapper's Delight" by Sugar Hill Gang, and
an early track by Funky Four Plus One. But
it doesn't do an adequate job of surveying
what has become an important genre. — D.M.

★ ★ ★ Great Soul Hits / Bruns. (NA)
Artists include: Jackie Wilson, Young-Holt
Unlimited, Barbara Acklin, Artistics, Gene
Chandler, Big Maybelle.

A collection of Brunswick's R&B successes. Wilson's "Doggin' Around" and "Lonely Teardrops" are masterful, Acklin's "Love Makes a Woman" and the Artistics' "I'm Gonna Miss You" acceptable soul, Young-Holt and Chandler's sides undistinguished, while Big Maybelle's "Candy" and "The Trouble I've Seen" are tough blues, a bit out of place in such company. — D.M.

★ ★ ★ **Greatest Country Hits of the Seventies, Vols. 1–3 / Col. (NA)**
Artists include: Larry Gatlin, Willie Nelson, Johnny Cash, Mickey Gilley, Johnny Paycheck.

Mixed bag of country songs ranging from good to banal stuff. Volume 1, which includes Paycheck's "Take This Job and Shove It," gets a slight edge. — J.S.

★ ★ **Greatest Country and Western Hits / Col. (NA)**
Artists include: Jimmy Dean, Marion Worth, Marty Robbins, Ray Price, Flatt and Scruggs, Johnny Cash, Carl Smith, Claude King, Lefty Frizzell, Carl Butler, Stonewall Jackson, Little Jimmy Dickens.

Undistinguished selection of Columbia's big country hits is hardly anybody's greatest: Cash's "Ring of Fire" might be his, but how can anyone stand the insufferable *Beverly Hillbillies* TV theme, "Ballad of Jed Clampett," assigned to Flatt and Scruggs? Jimmy Dean's "Big Bad John" and Claude King's "Wolverton Mountain" are both country-pop novelties that haven't dated well. Forget about this. — D.M.

★ ★ ★ **Greatest Folksingers of the Sixties / Van. (NA)**
Artists include: Ian and Sylvia, Rooftop Singers, Buffy Sainte-Marie, Joan Baez, Cisco Houston, Country Joe and the Fish, Odetta, Richard and Mimi Fariña, Phil Ochs, Eric Andersen, Jim Kweskin and the Jug Band, Doc Watson, John Hammond, Jack Elliott, Mississippi John Hurt, Judy Collins and Theodore Bikel, Weavers, Bob Gibson and Hamilton Camp, Tom Paxton, José Feliciano, Staple Singers, Joan Baez and Bob Gibson, Flatt and Scruggs, Bob Dylan and friends, Peggy Seeger and Ewan MacColl, Paul Butterfield Blues Band, Chamber Brothers, New Lost City Ramblers, Tommy Makem, Oscar Brand and Jean Ritchie, Pete Seeger.

The definition of "folk music" here is so broad that it encompasses everything from a purist like Pete Seeger to a Puerto Rican pop singer like José Feliciano; renegades like Bob Dylan and Country Joe and the Fish

and traditionalists like Watson, Brand and Ritchie; ancient bluesmen like Hurt, bluegrass traditionalists like Flatt and Scruggs, modern white bluesmen like Hammond and Butterfield, and old-timey revivalists like the Ramblers.

Still, during the scattered decade that was the Sixties, the term "folk" had just about that many applications. The music here is representative of the various permutations of what folk fans found themselves exposed to in those years. The Dylan track, by the way, is a version of "Blowin' in the Wind" recorded at the 1963 Newport Folk Festival, the same place where Dylan would be attacked two years later for going electric. Nothing else here is terribly obscure, and the lack of notes hurts. — D.M.

★ ★ ★ **Greatest Gospel Gems, Vol. 1 / Spec. (NA)**
Artists include: Sam Cooke and the Soul Stirrers, Brother Joe May, Pilgrim Travelers, Five Blind Boys, Alex Bradford, Dorothy Love Coates and the Gospel Harmonettes, Swan Silvertones, Robert Anderson, Chosen Gospel Singers, Wynona Carr, Soul Stirrers.

The first of two excellent compilations of Specialty's Fifties gospel recordings. — D.M.

★ ★ ★ **Greatest Gospel Gems, Vol. 2 / Spec. (NA)**
Artists include: Alex Bradford, Johnnie Taylor and the Soul Stirrers, Sam Cooke and the Soul Stirrers, Meditation Singers, Pilgrim Travelers, Brother Joe May, Five Blind Boys, Brother Joe May and the Pilgrim Travelers, Swan Silvertones, Reverend James Cleveland, Dorothy Love Coates and the Gospel Harmonettes.

Second Specialty gospel compilation is especially interesting because it features gospel recordings by no less than three future soul singers: Cooke, of course; Johnny Taylor, who replaced Cooke in the Soul Stirrers and went on to record "Who's Makin' Love" and "Disco Lady"; and Laura Lee, famous now for "Women's Love Rights," but much earlier a member of the Motown-based Meditation Singers. — D.M.

★ ★ ★ **Greatest Hits from England / Par. (1967)**
Artists include: Fortunes, Tom Jones, Them, Moody Blues, Hedgehoppers Anonymous, Los Bravos, Unit Four Plus Two, Jonathan King, Zombies, Kathy Kirby, Noel Harrison, Nashville Teens.

Oddly enough, this collection is a pretty

good presentation of the second wave of the British Invasion, and far superior to London's *England's Hit Makers,* which is a kind of companion volume. There's nothing by the Stones here, but that's made up for by the gaggle of punk-prototype hits that are included: Them's "Gloria," "Go Now" by the Moody Blues, Los Bravos' odd "Black Is Black," the Zombies' "She's Not There" and especially the most raunchy of them all, "Tobacco Road" by the Nashville Teens. Although a good deal of the rest is sentimental pop, Jonathan King's "Everyone's Gone to the Moon" is at least futuristic sentimentality and Tom Jones' "It's Not Unusual" is the bluesiest item he has ever recorded. — D.M.

★ ★ **Greatest Songs of Woody Guthrie /**
   Van. (NA)
Artists include: Woody Guthrie, Cisco Houston, Weavers, Odetta; Country Joe McDonald, Jack Elliott, Woody Guthrie and Cisco Houston, Babysitters, Jim Kweskin, Joan Baez.
   This could have been a magnificent set. Guthrie ranks with Hank Williams, Jimmie Rodgers and the Carter Family as a pre-rock songwriter of enormous imagination, vitality and humanity. At times, in fact, this set can't help living up to its hero's legend: particularly on his own numbers ("This Land Is Your Land," "Hard Traveling," three others), but also on Elliott's "Talking Fish Blues" and "1913 Massacre," and Kweskin's "Buffalo Skinners." The others treat Guthrie too much as a national monument to get at the spirit of roughneck fun and the utter lack of pious sanctimoniousness that lies at the heart of his musical vision—a problem epitomized by Joan Baez' reading of the outlaw ballad "Pretty Boy Floyd." — D.M.

★ ★ **Guitar Album / Poly. (NA)**
Artists include: Eric Clapton, Roy Buchanan, Rory Gallagher, T. Bone Walker, Ellen McIlwaine, Stone the Crows, Link Wray, John McLaughlin, Area Code 615.
   Right players, but mostly the wrong songs. This scattershot collection features Buchanan and Gallagher at their best (Buchanan's "The Messiah Will Come Again" is the highlight of his solo career), Clapton with some good material ("Slunky," "Let It Rain," "Have You Ever Loved a Woman") from his Derek and the Dominos period. Wray and McLaughlin have done better elsewhere, Stone the Crows produced "Maggie Bell" but not much noteworthy guitar, and McIlwaine's eccentric approach doesn't make sufficient sense in this limited slot. — D.M.

★ ★ ★ **Guitar Boogie / RCA (NA)**
Artists include: Eric Clapton, Jimmy Page, Jeff Beck.
   Early blues recordings from these British guitarists are of interest mostly to collectors. — J.S.

★ **Guitar Greats / Ev. (NA)**
Artists include: Glen Campbell, Dick Rosmini, Joe Maphis, Billy Strange, Fred Gerlach, Jim Helms, Tommy Tedesco, Joe Maphis and James McGuinn, James McGuinn, Mason Williams.
   Only players will be interested in this set of tunes by Sixties folk and country sidemen, the best known of whom today are McGuinn, Campbell and Maphis. The others are forgotten, not necessarily regrettably. — D.M.

★ **Guitar Heroes / Epic (NA)**
Artists include: Boston, Cheap Trick, REO Speedwagon, Molly Hatchet, Johnny Winter.
   Bad collection of heavy-metal tracks. — J.S.

★ ★ ★ **Guitar Player / MCA (NA)**
Artists include: B. B. King, Lee Ritenour, Joe Pass, Larry Coryell.
   Good collection of mostly jazz guitar playing. — J.S.

★ **Guitar Players / Main. (NA)**
Artists include: Amboy Dukes, Jay Berliner, David T. Walker and Arthur Wright, Lightnin' Hopkins, Brownie McGhee, Jim Raney, David Spinoza, Jack Wilkins.
   All that saves this collection from the trash bin is the Amboy Dukes' "Baby Please Don't Go," which was Ted Nugent's pro debut and a punk-rock prototype, and the Hopkins and McGhee blues tracks. The rest, including well-known sessionman Spinoza's "Thank You," is the sort of tepid jazz funk Mainstream makes its speciality. — D.M.

★ ★ ★ **Guitar Star / Red L. (NA), Br. imp.**
Artists include: Mighty Joe Young, Fenton Robinson, Bobby Parker, Magic Sam, Wayne Bennet, Big Moose, Johnny Littlejohn, Letty Bates.
   Recordings from the Fifties and Sixties by a good cross section of Chicago guitarists, including Robinson's 1967 cut of "Somebody Loan Me a Dime." — J.S.

★ **Guitars That Destroyed the World / Col.**
   (NA)
Artists include: Sanatana/Buddy Miles,

Johnny Winter And, Ten Years After, West, Bruce and Laing, Mountain, Spirit.

Pointless collection of heavy metal distinguishes none of the participants. — J.S.

■ **Hair (Original Broadway Cast) / RCA (1969)**
■ **Hair (Original Cast) / RCA (1968)**
■ **Hair (Soundtrack) / RCA (1979)**
What the squares thought the Sixties were about. If you must hear "Aquarius," you'll be a lot better off with the Fifth Dimension's version, which was a hit. — D.M.

★ ★ **Happytimes—Rockin' and Rollin' / Ext (NA)**
Artists include: Dixie Cups, Drifters, John Fred and the Playboy Band, Lesley Gore, Jan and Dean.
Uninspired collection of oldies includes "Chapel of Love," "Under the Boardwalk," "Judy in Disguise" and "Surf City." — J.S.

★ ★ ★ **Happy Trails / U.A. (NA)**
Artists include: Roy Rogers, Billie Jo Spears, Slim Whitman, Dave Dudley, Willie Nelson, Crystal Gayle, Bob Wills and the Texas Playboys, Johnny Darrell, Jean Shepherd, Bobby Goldsboro, George Jones, Walter Brennan, Del Reeves, Warren Smith, Freddy Fender, Patsy Cline, Bob Wills and Tommy Duncan.
Solid country sampler. Nelson's "Funny How Time Slips Away" and "Night Life" are two of his first compositions, and two of his best; Wills' "San Antonio Rose" is immortal. Jones' "She Thinks I Still Care" ranks with his best, too, and Fender's "Wasted Days and Wasted Nights" is the only really remarkable thing his long career has produced. But perhaps this album's strongest inclusion is Dudley's one-shot hit, "Six Days on the Road." — D.M.

★ ★ **Hard Country (Soundtrack) / Epic (NA)**
Artists include: Michael Murphy, Tanya Tucker, Jerry Lee Lewis, Joe Ely.
Mostly bad soundtrack is helped by the inclusion of Jerry Lee's "I Love You So Much It Hurts" and Ely's "West Texas Waltz." — J.S.

★ ★ ★ ★ ★ **The Harder They Come (Soundtrack) / Is. (1975)**
Artists include: Jimmy Cliff, Scotty, Melodians, Toots and the Maytals, Slickers, Desmond Dekker.
The greatest reggae sampler, and the soundtrack to the Jamaican outlaw picture that had tremendous impact on college crowds in the Northeast and in San Francis-

co, where the reggae cult began to bloom. Cliff's title song, "You Can Get It If You Really Want," "Many Rivers to Cross" and "Sitting in Limbo" are the strongest, purest reggae he's ever done. The Maytals' "Pressure Drop" and "Sweet and Dandy" are treasures. The other songs, while done by obscure artists, are up to the standard of the above: the Melodians' "Rivers of Babylon" is particularly haunting. But the song that says it all—catches Jamaican politics and the culture that nurtures reggae and the sensibility of the film—is the Slickers' "Johnny Too Bad," a virtual anthem of Third World rebellion. This album isn't platinum, or even gold, but it is as influential as anything released in the Seventies: witness the Rolling Stones, Patti Smith and the Clash, among others. A must. — D.M.

★ ★ ★ **Havana Jam / Col. (NA)**
Artists include: Weather Report, Stephen Stills, CBS Jazz All-Stars, Kris Kristofferson.
Good live documentary recordings of the late-Seventies Cuban-American exchange concert. — J.S.

★ ★ ★ **Havana Jam 2 / Col. (NA)**
Artists include: Weather Report, CBS Jazz All-Stars, Cuban Percussion Ensemble, Irakere.
More live recordings from the same event. — J.S.

★ ★ ★ **Heaven's Gate (Soundtrack) / Lib. (1980)**
Artists include: David Mansfield, Doug Kershaw.
The soundtrack of the most overrated flop in movie history (it wasn't *that* bad, but then how could it have been?) is also not bad. David Mansfield operates on a sort of sub-Cooder level of American folk music sources for twelve of the tracks, and on the thirteenth Kershaw cuts loose with "Mamou Two Step" to lively up the place. You could do lots worse. — D.M.

★ ★ **Heavy Metal (Soundtrack) / Asy. (NA)**
Artists include: Sammy Hagar, Devo, Blue Oyster Cult, Cheap Trick, Don Felder, Black Sabbath, Journey, Grand Funk Railroad.
Pretty lightweight assortment of heavy-metal tracks make up the soundtrack to the animated film of the same name. — J.S.

★ **Heavy Traffic (Soundtrack) / Fan. (NA)**
Track to Ralph Bakshi's second animated feature (followup to *Fritz the Cat*) features silly versions of "Scarborough Fair," none of them by Simon and Garfunkel. — D.M.

★ ★ ★ ★ **Jimi Hendrix and Otis Redding Live at the Monterey International Pop Festival / Rep. (1970)**

Great performances by two now-deceased immortals, caught at the festival at which both made their national breakthroughs. Otis is at his raving best on one side, while on the other, Hendrix gives what may have been his greatest show ever: the versions of "Wild Thing" and "Like a Rolling Stone" are everything they should, and could, have been. A lot more than just a memory here. — D.M.

★ **Here Comes Some Soul from Otis Redding and Joe Curtis / Als. (NA)**

A cheat: on the cover, Redding's billing is about three times as large as Curtis'. And while Curtis is a fair journeyman soul man himself, this isn't his best work—much less Redding's. — D.M.

★ ★ **High Water Blues: Field Recordings of Mississippi and Louisiana Blues, 1965–1970 / Flyr. (NA)**

Artists include: Isaiah Chattman, L. V. Conerly, John Henry "Bubba" and Melvin Brown, Fiddlin' Joe Martin, Houston Stackhouse, Woodrow Adams, Cary Lee Simmons, Boogie Bill Webb, Charlie and Willis Taylor.

Thin collection of primarily acoustic material; well annotated, but only Martin and Stackhouse (especially on "Return Mail") are really exceptional, and Martin can be heard to better advantage elsewhere. — J.S.

★ ★ **History of Bell U.K. (1970–1975) / Ari. (NA)**

Artists include: Hello, Glitter Band, Gary Glitter, Showaddywaddy, Bay City Rollers, Linda Lewis, Pearls, Drifters, Barry Blue, Slik.

British hit singles from the kind of power pop labels over there. Unfortunately, aside from sweet-voiced Linda Lewis, whose "It's in His Kiss" is superior to any of her American releases, this is pretty tame stuff. These Drifters are a long way from the originals, and unless the ersatz excitement of the Rollers' "Keep on Dancing" is your idea of high energy, there's mighty thin pickings in this batch for anyone but a terminal Anglophile. — D.M.

★ ★ ★ **History of British Blues / Sire (1973)**

Artists include: Cyril Davies Rhythm and Blues All-Stars, Alexis Korner Blues Inc., Spencer Davis R&B Quartet, Yardbirds, Graham Bond Organization, Downliners Sect, *John Mayall's Bluesbreakers, Aynsley Dunbar Retaliation, Fleetwood Mac, Savoy Brown, Duster Bennett, Chicken Shack, T. S. McPhee, Jo Ann Kelly, John Lee's Groundhogs, Gordon Smith, Christine Perfect, Key Largo, Climax Blues Band, Jellybread, Mike Vernon.*

First-rate assembly of British interpretations of blues. In the Sixties, some of these were names to contend with, and some of them still are, though not necessarily the same ones. Current Fleetwood Mac fans won't recognize that group, which was playing straight-ahead Chicago-style blues on "Homework," or even Christine McVie, who works under her maiden name, Christine Perfect, on "Crazy 'bout You Baby" and with Chicken Shack on "It's Okay with Me Baby."

Davies and Korner are important because it was their bands from which the Rolling Stones, among others, sprang. The Yardbirds, represented by "Baby What's Wrong," were at their bluesiest with the original guitarist, Eric Clapton. So was John Mayall, when Clapton was in his Bluesbreakers. McPhee founded the Groundhogs, while Savoy and Climax went on to Seventies success in the States. Downliners Sect has undergone something of a revival in the punk era, while Mike Vernon, to move to the opposite pole of the album's concern, is more noteworthy for the bluesmen he recorded than for his own performances. — D.M.

★ ★ ★ **History of British Rock, Vol. 1 / Sire (1974)**

Artists include: Kinks, Dave Clark Five, Bee Gees, Manfred Mann, Donovan, Mungo Jerry, Rod Stewart, Troggs, Gerry and the Pacemakers, Peter and Gordon, Walker Brothers, Searchers, Wayne Fontana, Uriah Heep, Hollies, Small Faces, Billy J. Kramer, Mindbenders, Silkie, Vanity Fare, Dusty Springfield, Freddy and the Dreamers, Cliff Richard, Honeycombs, Swinging Blue Jeans, Merseys, Status Quo, Pretty Things.

While no anthology that omits the Rolling Stones and Beatles can claim to be a definitive look at British rock in the Sixties and early Seventies, this two-disc set does a commendable job of surveying both top-rank artists (Kinks, Manfred Mann, Rod Stewart, Small Faces, Hollies) and some significant minor ones. If Dave Clark Five and Mungo Jerry are remembered only by fanatics and trivia buffs, the Troggs' "Wild Thing" and "Needles and Pins" by the Searchers are worth remembering for their energy, excitement and influence (particularly on punk and new-wave rock, but also on heavy-metal

and California harmony groups). The best of Sire's trio of historical investigations.
— D.M.

★ ★ ★ ★ **History of British Rock, Vol. 2 / Sire (1974)**
Artists include: Beatles, Peter and Gordon, Billy J. Kramer and the Dakotas, Cilla Black, Dave Clark Five, Searchers, Gerry and the Pacemakers, Kinks, Sandie Shaw, Donovan, Rod Stewart, Hollies, Chad and Jeremy, Manfred Mann, Troggs, Dusty Springfield, Van Morrison, Tremeloes, Small Faces, Cream, Who, Badfinger, Bee Gees, Elton John, Deep Purple, Julie Driscoll/Brian Auger Trinity, Arthur Brown, Thunderclap Newman.

More Sixties period pieces. The Beatles' track is a bad one, the version of "Ain't She Sweet" from the Tony Sheridan period in Germany—while a great many of the Merseybeat artists who originally followed the Beatles out of Liverpool and London today sound very weak: Kramer and the Dakotas, Black, Gerry and the Pacemakers, Chad and Jeremy, and Peter and Gordon (who are even represented by their best songs) all suffer from this. And a bit of the selection is more pop than rock—that applies to the Bee Gees and Elton John, but more especially to the Tremeloes and the Donovan track.

Yet there are still some gems here: Manfred Mann's "Mighty Quinn," a great Dylan version; the Kinks' "All Day and All of the Night," Cream's "Sunshine of Your Love" and the Who's "Call Me Lightning," all magnificently powerful; and some lost obscurities, particularly "Fire" by Brown and Thunderclap Newman's exhilarating "Something in the Air." — D.M.

★ ★ ★ ★ **History of British Rock, Vol. 3 / Sire (NA)**
Artists include: Searchers, Beatles, Animals, featuring Eric Burdon, Gerry and the Pacemakers, Kinks, Troggs, Donovan, Them, Olivia Newton-John, Dusty Springfield, Manfred Mann, Peter and Gordon, Badfinger, Elton John, Derek and the Dominos, David Bowie, Billy J. Kramer and the Dakotas, Unit Four Plus Two, Zombies, Dave Clark Five, Matthew's Southern Comfort, Python Lee Jackson, Chris Farlowe, Cream, Deep Purple, Mary Hopkin, Bee Gees.

The final set in Sire's series ends disappointingly—still no Rolling Stones, and weak choices from the Beatles, John, the Animals and Deep Purple—but with some encouraging and interesting material nonetheless.

Newton-John doesn't belong here; neither does Hopkin. And while Kramer and the Dakotas as well as Gerry and the Pacemakers are certainly overrepresented, Cream's "Anyone for Tennis" is sufficiently obscure to be treasured, while Them's "Here Comes the Night," the Zombies' "She's Not There" and Farlowe's "Out of Time" are well worth having. Chances are this is for collectors more than casual fans, but the Sire series is still a fine adjunct to a collection with any pretensions to being comprehensive, even if no volume is strong enough to single out.
— D.M.

★ ★ ★ **The History of Northwest Rock, Vol. 1 / Great N. (1976)**
Artists include: Frantics, Dave Lewis, Sonics, Kingsmen, Don and the Goodtimes, Sir Raleigh and Coupons, Ian Whitcomb, Bards, Springfield Rifle.

★ ★ ★ **The History of Northwest Rock, Vol. 2 / Great N. (1978)**
Artists include: Paul Revere and the Raiders, Don and the Goodtimes, Sonics, Springfield Rifle, Bards, Kingsmen, Dave Lewis, Dimensions, New Yorkers, Ian Whitcomb.

★ ★ ★ **The History of Northwest Rock, Vol. 3 / Great N. (1980)**
Artists include: Springfield Rifle, London Taxi, Bumps, Breakers, Jack Horner and the Plums, Sonics, Bards, Live Five, Magic Fern, P. H. Phactor, Brave New World, Kingsmen.

It's actually amazing how many solid American rock bands emerged from the Pacific Northwest (Washington and Oregon) in the early through mid-Sixties. The Raiders, Kingsmen, Sonics and Wailers make this one of the most productive regions for a certain kind of garage/surf/protopunk rock— raunchy, male-oriented, beer-fed and utterly uneloquent, but passionate and amusing nevertheless. Unfortunately, these three discs spread the good stuff a bit thin and don't contain anything by the original Wailers ("Tall Cool One"), who may have been the best and were certainly the most accomplished band in the region. By Volume 3, we're edging into garage psychedelia that is corny and unimaginative. Still, the best tracks here (mostly by the groups listed above plus occasional winners from Don and the Goodtimes and Springfield Rifle) are well worth hearing, at least by aficionados of the period. — D.M.

★ ★ ★ ★ **The History of Surf Music, Vol. 1 / Rhino (1982)**
Artists include: Dick Dale, Chantays, Belairs, Blazers, Pyramids, Lively Ones, Original Sur-

faris, Crossfires, Eddie and the Showmen, Sentinals, Tom Starr and the Galaxies, Challengers, Surfaris.
★ ★ ★ **The History of Surf Music, Vol. 2 / Rhino (1982)**
Artists include: Beach Boys, Dan and Jean, Dee D. Hope, Trashmen, Turtles, Jan and Dean, Bruce Johnston, Tradewinds, Beach Girls, Surfaris.

If it's true, as many suspect, that surf music is the only genre in rock in which the instrumentals are superior to the vocal numbers, the contrast between these two LPs is instructive. Aside from the Beach Boys and Tradewinds, most of the vocal album (2) is puerile or hokey. And the great exception is "Surfin' Bird" by the Trashmen, which is virtually an instrumental (the vocal gibberish can hardly be described as singing) and may not even be surf music, since the group hailed from Minnesota and were actually ripping off an R&B group, the Rivingtons.

The instrumental album, on the other hand, is a virtually seamless joy, perfect for hot afternoons no matter how far from the beach you might be. The classics are here, of course—"Pipeline," "Miserlou," "Penetration," "Wipe Out"—but even the more minor numbers such as "K-39" (Challengers) have enough drive to make you kind of embarrassed for Jimi Hendrix's anti-surf bigotry.

Avoid the other two volumes in this series, however. One is a set of songs by "revivalist" surf groups, none of them illuminating, and the other is an entire set by the Challengers, which goes too far for anyone but total fanatics. — D.M.

★ **Hit 45s of the Seventies, Vols. 1 and 2 / Epic (NA)**
Artists include: Hollies, Dave Loggins, Michael Murphy, Looking Glass, Wild Cherry, Johnny Rivers.
Another worthless collection of garage-sale leftovers from the company vaults. — J.S.

★ **Hits of the Mersey Era / Cap./EMI (NA)**
Artists include: Gerry and the Pacemakers, Billy J. Kramer and the Dakotas, Swinging Blue Jeans, Cilla Black, Freddie and the Dreamers, Hollies.
Aside from the Hollies, this is fluff—and "Stay" isn't a particularly good Hollies track. All of these groups were influenced by the Beatles, but they were among the first to pull the rock side of that foursome into the background in favor of conventional show-business song values. The Blue Jeans'

"Hippy Hippy Shake" is almost worth the time, although more because amateurish enthusiasm dates better than pop warbling. Everything that's here and worthwhile is included, among more interesting company, on Sire's three-volume *History of British Rock,* anyhow. — D.M.

★ ★ ★ **Hollywood Knights (Soundtrack) / Casa. (1980)**
Artists include: Brooklyn Dreams, Bruce Channel, Martha and the Vandellas, Wilson Pickett, Ray Charles, Four Seasons, Chiffons, Surfari.
Uneven soundtrack has some great songs like "Hey Baby," "Quicksand," "Heat Wave" "In the Midnight Hour," "He's So Fine," "One Fine Day" and "Wipe Out." — J.S.

★ ★ ★ **Honky Tonkin' / RCA**
Artists include: Waylon Jennings, Gary Stewart, Willie Nelson, Bobby Bare, Guy Clark.
Excellent collection of country songs, including "Bloody Mary Morning," "Crazy Arms," "She's Actin' Single (I'm Drinkin' Double)." — J.S.

★ ★ **Hustle Hits / De-Lite (1976)**
Artists include: Gary Toms Empire, Crown Heights Affair, Kool and the Gang, Kay Gees, Zakariah, Yambu.
The hustle is the only new dance *step* introduced by the Seventies' disco movement; it's a kind of easy-to-learn tango, but more licentious. This is fine stuff for it, or more free-form movement, particularly Kool and the Gang's tracks ("Spirit of the Boogie," "Mother Earth"), although how easy it is to adapt conventional pop songs to the beat is indicated by Zakariah's "Girl from Ipanema" and Yambu's "Sunny," the latter a reworking of the great Bobby Hebb hit. — D.M.

★ **In Concert / RCA (NA)**
Artists include: Charley Pride, Dolly Parton, Ronnie Milsap, Dolly Parton and Ronnie Milsap, Jerry Reed, Chet Atkins, Jerry Reed and Chet Atkins.
Miserable collection of RCA's country artists in performance. The highlights are all Parton's. — D.M.

★ ★ ★ **Indianapolis Jump / Flyr. (1976)**
Artists include: Shirley Griffith and J.T. Adams, Yank Rachell and Shirley Griffith, Pete Franklin, Bertha Lee Jones, Scrapper Blackwell, James Easley.
Adequate late-Fifties through mid-Sixties

blues sampler of recordings made in Indianapolis (surprisingly, a minor center of prewar blues recording). Rachell is the best-known performer, Griffith (a male) has the best voice, but everyone is up to snuff, if you like country blues. — D.M.

★ **In Harmony / War. (NA)**
Artists include: Doobie Brothers, James Taylor, Carly Simon, Lucy Simon, Bette Midler.
Album of children's songs recorded for *Sesame Street.* — J.S.

★ ★ **In Harmony 2 / Col. (NA)**
Artists include: Billy Joel, James Taylor, Dr. John, Bruce Springsteen.
Some good moments, especially Springsteen's version of "Santa Claus Is Coming to Town." — J.S.

★ ★ **In the Heat of the Night (Soundtrack) / U.A. (1967)**
Quincy Jones' score is notable principally for Ray Charles' singing on the title song. The rest is unobtrusive background music, including the other vocals (a second by Charles, and one each from Gil Bernal and Glen Campbell). — D.M.

★ ★ ★ **Intensified! Original Ska 1962–1966 / Mango (1979)**
Artists include: Roland Alphonso, Eric Morris, Baba Brooks, Charms, Shenley Duffus, Don Drummond and Drumbago, Skatalites, Maytals, Tommy McCook, Stranger Cole, Derrick and Patsy, Justin Hines.
★ ★ ★ **Intensified! Original Ska 1963–1967 / Mango (1979)**
Artists include: the Maytals, Skatalites, Lord Brynner and the Sheiks, Marguerita, Don Drummond, Eric Morris, Roland Al and the Soul Brothers, Stranger Cole, Sir Lord Comic, Desmond Dekker and the Four Aces, Soul Brothers, Ethiopians.
Nicely compiled, sketchily annotated sets of pre-reggae Jamaican hits, the most interesting by the Skatalites, Maytals, Hines and Ethiopians. Necessary for reggae cultists, interesting for amateurs, slinky for dancing. — D.M.

★ ★ ★ **An Introduction to Gospel Song / RBF (1972)**
Artists include: Fisk University Jubilee Quartet, Tuskegee Institute Singers, Pace Jubilee Singers with Hattie Parker, Rev. J. M. Gates and Congregation, Rev. F. W. McGee and Congregation, Sister Ernestine Washington with Bunk Johnson's Jazz Band, Elder Lightfoot Solomon Michaux and His "Happy Am I" Choir and Orchestra, Rev. Utah Smith and Congregation, Morth McLease and her sons, the Spirit of Memphis Quartet.
Samuel Charters compiled this arresting survey of black spiritual singing, ranging from the earliest recorded examples (the Fisk University Jubilee Quartet's "Roll Jordan Roll," made in 1913) through the mid-Fifties with the Spirit of Memphis group. The early music can be too stiff and formal for any but historical tastes, but by side two you're into fairly exciting territory, though only Gates and the Spirit of Memphis Quartet are among gospel's top rank of performers. — D.M.

★ ★ ★ **Irie Reggae Rockers / J. Gibbs (1979)**
Artists include: Dennis Brown, the Mighty Diamonds, Ruddy Thomas, Marcia Aitken.
A bouncy, slick collection of faultlessly performed "lovers' rock" reggae, pop-oriented with emphasis on soulful remakes. Tuneful but too seamless. — R.F.G.

★ ★ **It Takes Two / Nat. (1978)**
Artists include: Marvin Gaye and Tammi Terrell, Thelma Houston and Jerry Butler, Syreeta and G. C. Cameron, Diana Ross and Marvin Gaye, the Supremes and the Four Tops, Art and Honey, Blinky and Edwin Starr, Diana Ross and the Supremes and the Temptations, Marvin Gaye and Kim Weston.
A nice idea—putting the best of Motown's boy/girl matchups on a single disc—but there's not nearly enough Marvin Gaye and company, nothing at all by Stevie and Syreeta and far too much by Art and Honey and Blinky and Edwin Starr, while the various supper-club numbers by the Supremes and friends are a genuine drag. — D.M.

★ ★ ★ **Jack Ruby Hi-Fi / Clappers (1980)**
Artists include: Ken Boothe, Earth's Last Messengers, Lenox Miller, the Revealers.
An off-the-wall collection produced by top sound-system impresario and producer (see Burning Spear) Jack Ruby. Four extended vocal tracks that metamorphose into spacy dub instrumentals. It's all good, and "Hypocrites" by Earth's Last Messengers is exceptional. — R.F.G.

★ ★ ★ **Jackson Blues 1928–1938 / Yazoo (NA)**
Artists include: Ishman Bracey, Charlie McCoy, Walter Vincent, Arthur Pettis, Bo Carter, Tommy Johnson, Willie Lofton, Mississippi Sheiks, Mississippi Mudder, Willie Harris.

Collection of sides from the overlooked but important area of Jackson, Mississippi, headed by "Lonesome Home Blues," "Black Mare Blues" and "Bye Bye Blues" from Tommy Johnson, the most influential musician from the area. — J.S.

★ ★ **Jamaica Ska / Rhino (1981)**
Artists include: The Maytals, the Blues Busters, Byron Lee and the Dragoneers.

Most of this LP was popular in Jamaica in the early Sixties, but these tracks tend to be slicker styles of ska or minor examples of these performers' work. Worthwhile for the historically curious or collectors. The Blues Busters (a duo heavily influenced by Sam Cooke) have the best stuff here. — R.F.G.

■ **Jesus Christ Superstar (Original Broadway Cast) / MCA (1972)**
★ **Jesus Christ Superstar (Original London Cast) / MCA (1972)**
★ ★ **Jesus Christ Superstar (Soundtrack) / MCA (1973)**
Broadway cast LP is only the highlights of the Andrew Webber–Timothy Rice score. The other two are complete, and the consistent element is Yvonne Elliman, who turns in a good performance (as Mary Magdalene) singing "I Don't Know How to Love Him." The soundtrack has the advantage of Murray Head's version of "Superstar," the Judas soliloquy. But mostly this is a sappy hippie's version of St. Matthew's Gospel, which ought to be equally odious to true believers of all faiths, if only for the musical pablum it offers as a substitute for conviction. — D.M.

★ ★ ★ **Jewels, Vol. 1 / SSS (NA)**
Artists include: Tommy James, Ad Libs, Peggy Scott and Jo Jo Benson, Jerry Lee Lewis, Rugbys, Shangri-Las, Bill Justis, Alive and Kickin', Dixie Cups, Jelly Beans, Three Degrees, Carl Perkins.

Good collection, but compiled without rhyme or reason. Perkins' "Blue Suede Shoes" and Lewis' "Whole Lotta Shakin' Goin' On" are the only masterpieces, but the girl-group hits—"Boy from New York City" (Ad Libs), "Leader of the Pack" (by the hallowed Shangri-Las, toughest broads in the universe), "Chapel of Love" (Dixie Cups) and "I Wanna Love Him So Bad" (Jelly Beans)—are all worth hearing again. Not so the Three Degrees' "Maybe," which pales next to the Chantels' original. — D.M.

★ **Jewels, Vol. 2 / SSS (NA)**
Artists include: Billy Hemmons and Clay's

Composite, Betty La Vette, Gloria Taylor, Johnny Adams, Wilbert Harrison, Big John Hamilton, George Perkins and the Silver Stars, Peggy Scott and Jo Jo Benson, Calvin Leavy, Hank Ballard, Mickey Murray.

Ringers all. There isn't a song here worth doing more than once that someone else hasn't done better. Hearing the immensely talented Ballard wasted on Kristofferson's "Sunday Mornin' Comin' Down" moves me to tears for all the wrong reasons. — D.M.

★ ★ **The Joe Gibbs Family Merry Rockers Xmas / J. Gibbs (1979)**
Artists include: Dennis Brown, the Mighty Diamonds, Ruddy Thomas, Trinity.

This really *is* Christmas standards done reggae style (a side-long medley on side one, four songs on side two) that is a surprisingly pleasing mix of tongue-in-cheek humor, absurd juxtapositions and genuinely beautiful singing on perennial favorites. — R.F.G.

★ ★ ★ **Johnny Otis Show Live at Monterey / Epic (NA)**
Artists include: Johnny Otis, Esther Phillips, Eddie Vinson, Big Joe Turner, Ivory Joe Hunter, Roy Milton, Gene Conners, Roy Brown, Shuggie Otis, Margie Evans, Pee Wee Crayton, Delmar Evans.

Otis was one of the Fifties' leading talent scouts and impresarios as well as an R&B bandleader of some repute, although "Willie and the Hand Jive," a reworking of the Bo Diddley riff, is his only well-remembered hit. This is a recording of a 1970 appearance that featured his revue of that period: Phillips, Brown, Milton, Hunter and Turner are all primordial soul shouters who retained a good deal of their performance acumen well past their prime. (Only Phillips and Turner have accomplished much since then, though.) This is also probably the best presentation on record of Shuggie Otis, a fine blues guitarist. Good set for parties attended by pop music historians. — D.M.

★ ★ **Frank Johnson's Favorites / Ralph (NA)**
Artists include: Tuxedomoon, Fred Frith, Ranaldo and the Loaf, MX-80 Sound, the Residents, Snakefinger, Yello, Art Bears.

This is basically a Ralph Records sampler—mainly non-LP B sides, or cuts that just didn't fit on the albums. There's really nothing special here except for a hysterical cover of the Beatles' "Flying" by the Residents. — K.L.

■ **Joseph and the Amazing Technicolor Dreamcoat (Original cast) / MCA (NA)**
A rock "cantata" by Andrew Lloyd Webber and Timothy Rice, the pair who brought you *Jesus Christ Superstar* and *Evita*. This one's from the Old Testament, which makes the wrath one feels at such an undisguised artistic ripoff in keeping with the period. More in keeping than the music or lyrics, anyway. — D.M.

★ ★ **Joyride (Soundtrack) / U.A. (NA)**
Half this record is dominated by old-time Hollywood arranger Jimmie Haskell, but it also includes six songs by Electric Light Orchestra, including the hit "Tightrope." But none of it is sufficiently outstanding to be of interest to anyone except a hard-core ELO follower. — D.M.

★ **Kent State (Soundtrack) / RCA (NA)**
Artists include: Richie Havens, Grace Slick, John Sebastian.
Ridiculous "nostalgia protest" album of songs from the TV movie soundtrack. — J.S.

★ ★ ★ **King Cobras: Chicago Kings of the Harmonica, 1956–58 / Flyr. (1980)**
Artists include: Little Willie Foster, Louis Myers, Sonny Boy Williamson, Charles Clark, Sunnyland Slim, Arbee Stidham, Shakey Horton.
Uneven and poor sound quality sampling of Chicago blues harpists recorded between 1956 and 1958. — J.S.

★ ★ ★ ★ ★ **King-Federal Rockabillys / King (1978)**
Artists include: Mac Curtis, Charlie Feathers, Joe Penny, Ronnie Molleen, Hank Mizell, Bill Beach, Bob and Lucille.
Rockabilly is probably the most overrepresented reissue music of all; it's a thin genre, and for the most part the cream was quickly skimmed off. This album is perhaps the best single compilation of the type, aside from those released by Sun. The Charlie Feathers tracks are exceptionally fine, particularly the justly famous "One Hand Loose," while Hank Mizell's "Jungle Rock" is a prophetically primitive masterpiece. Also excellent are the Mac Curtis tracks. — D.M.

★ ★ ★ ★ **The "King Kong" Compilation / Mango (1981)**
Artists include: Desmond Dekker and the Four Aces, Maytals, Melodians, Ken Boothe, Tyrone Evans, Pioneers, Delroy Wilson, Bruce Ruffin, Ansell Collins.

Excellent set of late Sixties/early Seventies tracks produced by legendary Jamaican producer Leslie Kong before his untimely demise. Classics include Dekker's "Israelites," the Maytals' "Monkey Man," "It Mek" (Dekker), "Rivers of Babylon" (Melodians) and "Long Shot Kick de Bucket" (Pioneers). Justifies Kong's stature as one of the truly revered figures of reggae music. — D.M.

★ ★ ★ ★ **King of Comedy (Soundtrack) / War. (1982)**
Artists include: Pretenders, B. B. King, Talking Heads, Bob James, Rickie Lee Jones, Robbie Robertson, Ric Ocasek, Ray Charles, David Sanborn, Van Morrison.
Producer Robertson has come up with a soundtrack better than its movie by wheedling from his performers some of the best performances of their recent careers: "Back on the Chain Gang" (Pretenders), " 'Tain't Nobody's Bizness (If I Do)" (King), "Wonderful Remark" (Morrison) and "Come Rain or Come Shine" (Charles) rank with their very best work. Unfortunately, the disc is also saddled with the jazzy Muzak of Bob James and David Sanborn, as if there was a rule against consistently interesting soundtrack recordings. — D.M.

★ ★ ★ ★ **Lake Michigan Blues, 1934–41 / Nighth. (NA)**
Artists include: Robert Nighthawk, Yank Rachell, Tampa Red, Sonny Boy Williamson, Robert Lockwood.
Great record of seminal Chicago blues from the late Thirties and early Forties featuring some excellent Tampa Red sides ("Worried Devil Blues," "She Don't Know My Mind, Part 2") as well as Red's protégé, Tampa Kid ("Baby Please Don't Go"). The historic recording debuts of Sonny Boy Williamson and Robert Nighthawk, which blueprinted the Chicago styles of the postwar era, are included here, and Robert Lockwood's "Little Boy Blue" features an amazing performance on bottleneck guitar. — J.S.

★ ★ ★ ★ **The Last Waltz (Soundtrack) / War. (NA)**
Artists include: Band, Ronnie Hawkins, Neil Young, Joni Mitchell, Neil Diamond, Dr. John, Paul Butterfield, Muddy Waters, Eric Clapton, Bobby Charles, Van Morrison, Bob Dylan.
The soundtrack from Martin Scorsese's troubling cinematic obituary filmed at the Band's final performance on Thanksgiving, 1976, at Winterland in San Francisco. This

was a sort of last gasp for rock's old guard, and it is the oldest players, with a couple of exceptions, who come off best. The Band runs through its old repertoire with less gusto than it has sometimes shown, but Muddy Waters comes up with as grand a version of his classic "Mannish Boy" as he has ever done. Dr. John's "Such a Night" and Ronnie Hawkins' "Who Do You Love" are also lively. No one is embarrassing— though this show was mostly about past glory, you'd never know it from the heart Van Morrison puts into "Tura Lura Lura" or Neil Young's soul-searching "Helpless." And for one moment the Band comes completely to life, when drummer Levon Helm duets on "Mystery Train" with Paul Butterfield. Eerie, sometimes nerve-racking as this is, it might work for anyone but old fogeys. In some weird way this is a small triumph, in keeping with the ostentatious understatement of the Band's career. — D.M.

★ ★ ★ **Laurie Golden Goodies / Laur. (NA)**
Artists include: Music Explosion, Chiffons, Gary "U.S." Bonds, Royal Guardsmen, Jarmels, Dion and the Belmonts, Mystics, Gerry and the Pacemakers.

Good selection of hits. The Chiffons' "He's So Fine" and Dion's "Runaround Sue" and "Teenager in Love" are well-known early-Sixties masterworks. The Mystics' lovely "Hushabye," and the Jarmels' "A Little Bit of Soap" aren't but ought to be. The best stuff of all is a kind of outer-space rock & soul music perfected by U.S. Bonds on "Quarter to Three" and "New Orleans," two of the most poorly recorded and most exciting of all post-Presley, pre-Beatles hits. The Royal Guardsmen's "Snoopy vs. the Red Baron" records ought to be buried, though. Unannotated. — D.M.

★ ★ ★ ★ **Leiber and Stoller: Only in America / Atl. (1980), Ger. imp.**
Artists include: Jay and Americans, Dino and Sembello, Coasters, Big Mama Thornton, Dion, Drifters, Ben E. King, LaVern Baker, Trini Lopez, Nancy Sinatra and Lee Hazelwood, Maria Muldaur, Wynonie Harris, Isley Brothers, Clovers, Cheers.

Erratic but interesting two-disc collection makes a case for Leiber and Stoller as Great American Artists or thereabouts. It pretty much works, too, thanks to an emphasis on their work with the Coasters, Drifters and Ben E. King. But when they stray from R&B, Leiber and Stoller get as corny as the next guy: the title track (Jay and the Americans), "Jackson" (Sinatra and Hazelwood),

"Neighborhood" (Dino and Sembello) and even "Black Denim Trousers and Motorcycle Boots" are self-conscious in a way that "Yakety Yak," "Hound Dog," "Kansas City" (even though whoever decided to include the Lopez version should get his or her head examined), "Stand by Me," "Ruby Baby," "There Goes My Baby," "On Broadway," "That Is Rock & Roll" and their other greatest hits (where's "What About Us"?) never are. Great artists, great Americans, too true to have to prove it, makes you wonder why they bother. Robert Palmer's notes are good but don't explain. — D.M.

★ ★ ★ **Let's Clean Up the Ghetto / Phil. (1977)**
Artists include: Lou Rawls, Philadelphia International All-Stars, Dee Dee Sharp Gamble, Teddy Pendergrass, Three Degrees, O'Jays, Billy Paul, Archie Bell and the Drells, Intruders, Harold Melvin and the Blue Notes.

Producers Kenneth Gamble and Leon Huff gathered together the leading lights of their record company to make this LP; the profits (if there have been any) to go to "Community Development Programs" (their capitals). The All-Stars are an assemblage of the artists listed, and they aren't bad on the title track. But unfortunately, with the exception of the Blue Notes' interpretation of Fred Neil's "Everybody's Talkin'," the material isn't adequate. Only Sharp, the Three Degrees and the Intruders fare well, probably because they get songs from their albums, rather than newly recorded social consciousness songs done especially for this project. — D.M.

★ ★ ★ **Let's Do It Again (Soundtrack) / Cur. (NA)**
One of Curtis Mayfield's better blaxploitation film tracks, principally because it features the Staple Singers, who got a hit from the title track. Not as superb as *Superfly* (one of the best soundtracks ever made in any genre), but a decent example of Seventies black genre music. — D.M.

★ ★ ★ **Let's Have a Ball: Brownie McGhee and His Buddies, 1945–1955 / Magpie**
Artists include: Jack Dupree, Stick McGhee, Big Chief Ellis, Sonny Terry, Ralph Willis, Alonzo Scales, Brother Blues, Bobby Harris, Brownie McGhee.

Guitarist/vocalist McGhee is a sideman on all tracks except two (where he is leader). Usually he appears in duos and trios, and not surprisingly, he's shown to best advantage with his latter-day partner, Sonny

Terry. Jazzy, rocking blues make up the bulk of this set, the individual highlight of which is brother Stick McGhee's "Drinkin' Wine Spo-Dee-O-Dee," which is seminal rock & roll, recorded in 1947. Although the cover notes this material was recorded in New York, and the dates, there are unfortunately no other notes. — D.M.

★ ★ ★ ★ **Life in the European Theatre / War. (1981)**
Artists include: The Clash, the Jam, the Beat, the Specials, XTC, Peter Gabriel, Ian Dury and the Blockheads, Madness, Bad Manners, the Stranglers, the Undertones, Echo and the Bunnymen, the Au Pairs.

After President Reagan's crass observations about a limited nuclear war in Europe, Survival Music put together a peacetime compilation. With songs like "London Calling" from the Clash, the Jam's "Little Boy Soldiers" and XTC's "Living through Another Cuba," this is pretty heady stuff. Only Ian Dury keeps his wits about him in "Reasons to be Cheerful—Part Three." Recording royalties from this album have been donated to Friends of the Earth, European Nuclear Disarmament and the Anti-Nuclear Campaign. Politics aside, an excellent cross section of the current British scene. — ML.H.

★ ★ ★ **Like 'Er Red Hot / Duke (NA)**
Artists include: Bobby "Blue" Bland, Clarence "Gatemouth" Brown, Little Jr. Parker, Paul Perryman, Johnny Ace, Casuals, Rob Roys, Ernie Harris, Torros, Willie Mae Thornton.

Good collection from the Texas soul and blues label, but not as solid as ABC's reissue compilations, *From the Historic Vaults of Duke/Peacock.* Only Perryman is unrepresented there. Still, if you can't find the others, this will more than do you: Bland's "Farther up the Road," Parker's "Next Time You See Me" and Ace's "Pledging My Time" are among the greatest R&B made in the Fifties and Sixties—tough, committed music. And Thornton (usually referred to as "Big Mama") contributes a version of "Hound Dog" from which, of course, Elvis Presley modeled his. — D.M.

■ **Lipstick (Soundtrack) / Atl. (NA)**
The movie was supposed to make Margaux Hemingway, the model, a star, but left her still a model. The soundtrack was supposed to make French synthesizer-rocker Michel Polnareff a household name in rock circles, but left him a laughingstock. Drivel. — D.M.

★ ★ **Live and Let Die (Soundtrack) / U.A. (1973)**
Wings got a hit single from Paul McCartney's title song to this James Bond film, which would put them right up there with Carly Simon and Shirley Bassey—except that "Live and Let Die" actually has exciting passages. The rest of the score is John Barry's usual decent pop jazz. — D.M.

★ **Live at Bill Graham's Fillmore West / Col. (1969)**
Artists include: Nick Gravenites, Mike Bloomfield, Bob Jones, Taj Mahal.

Beware the album that headlines the impresario, an old rock epigram ought to read. Unlike John Hammond Sr., Graham is no philanthropist. As well intentioned as this set may once have been, it is now grossly outdated (like *Live at CBGB's,* for that matter). Bloomfield's "Oh Mama" is an exercise in wretched excess, and the Gravenites and Mahal tracks are below their usual standards. Nobody we've met remembers Jones, which his "Love Got Me" deserves. — D.M.

★ ★ **Live at CBGB's / Atl. (NA)**
Artists include: Tuff Darts, Shirts, Mink DeVille, Laughing Dogs, Miamis, Sun, Stuart's Hammer, Manster.

An odd reflection of New York's so-called new wave, circa winter 1976–77. None of the scene's big stars are here—that means Patti Smith, Television, the Ramones and Talking Heads, in case you're wondering what big star means in this context. But Mink DeVille has made a pair of good rock and soul albums, and the Darts and Shirts both landed record deals, although the resulting albums weren't much. But by now the record is primarily a period piece. — D.M.

★ ★ ★ ★ **Living Chicago Blues Vols. 1–3 / Alli. (1978)**
Artists include: Jimmy Johnson, Eddie Shaw, Left Hand Frank.

Alligator is an outgrowth of the quest by *Living Blues* magazine to keep Chicago blues players alive and in demand, and these anthologies are the immediate results of that quest. Volume 1, which features a tremendous performance from Eddie Shaw leading Howling Wolf's band, with Hubert Sumlin on guitar, is a must. — J.S.

★ ★ ★ ★ **Living Chicago Blues, Vols. 4–6 / Alli. (1980)**
Artists include: A. C. Reed and the Spark

Plugs, Scotty and the Rib Tips, Lacy Gibson, Detroit Junior, Luther "Guitar Junior" Johnson.

The second group of contemporary Chicago blues recordings from Alligator. Volume 6, with Guitar Junior and Detroit Junior, is especially recommended. — J.S.

★ ★ ★ ★ **The Long Riders (Soundtrack) / War. (1980)**
Ry Cooder's soundtrack to Walter Hill's last-of-the-cowboy movies is a successful evocation of what we understand as the mood and spirit of the West. And to think John Ford was often stuck with Dmitri Tiomkin! — D.M.

★ ★ ★ **Looking for Mr. Goodbar (Soundtrack) / Col. (1977)**
Artists include: Thelma Houston, Commodores, O'Jays, Donna Summer, Diana Ross, Bill Withers, Boz Scaggs, Marlene Shaw.

A rather creepy film, this movie about a good Irish Catholic girl who screws around and doesn't fall in love in a discothèque setting, nevertheless offers a hell of a dance record as its soundtrack. The Commodores' "Machine Gun" and O'Jays' "Backstabbers" are their very best songs, and both Ross' "Love Hangover" and Scaggs' "Low Down" are top-notch. The rest is only so-so, but the groove is galvanizing. — D.M.

★ ★ ★ **Lost Soul, Vol. 1 / Epic (1982)**
Artists include: Brenda and the Tabulations, Bill Coday, Gwen McCrae, Jackie Moore, Essence, Soul Children, Z. Z. Hill, Betty LaVette, Mavis Staples with the Staple Singers, Vibrations.
★ ★ ★ **Lost Soul, Vol. 2 / Epic (1982)**
Artists include: Chairmen of the Board, Brenda and the Tabulations, Philly Devotions, Joe Tex, Roger Hatcher, Bobby Womack and Brotherhood, Howard Tate, Essence, Gwen McCrae, Don Covay and Goodtimers.
★ ★ ★ **Lost Soul, Vol. 3 / Epic (1982)**
Artists include: Tyrone Davis, Bobby Womack, Thelma Jones, Gwen McCrae, Z. Z. Hill, Lou Courtney, Fontella Bass, Obrey Wilson, Laura Lee, Mattie Moultrie.
Nice way for CBS to empty out its vault of minor soul masterworks. Actually, there's nothing astonishing in its obscurity on any of these sets, but each includes a few pieces that genuinely deserve preservation: Hill's "Love Is So Good When You're Stealing It," "Lead Me On" by McCrae, Mavis Staples' tour de force "Crying in the Chapel,"

"Finders Keepers" by Chairmen of the Board and "Ain't Got Nobody to Give It To" by Howard Tate are only the most arresting examples. Nice for fans, primarily. — D.M.

★ ★ ★ ★ **Lowdown Memphis Harmonica Jam 1950–1955 / Nighth. (NA)**
Artists include: Hot Shot Love, Joe Hill Louis, J. D. Horton, Mumbles, Willie Nix, Woodrow Adams, Chicago Sunny Boy.
Very interesting set of harmonica-based tracks provide a kind of conceptual bridge between pre- and postwar blues style in Memphis. The city's jug-band tradition is strongly in evidence, especially on the one-man-band performances by Joe Hill Louis, whose "Walkin' Talkin' Blues" and "Street Walkin' Woman" were Sam Philips' first productions. Mumbles is a pseudonym for the great harmonica player Walter Horton. On "Seems Like a Million Years" and "Bakershop Boogie," sessions led by drummer Willie Nix, the young James Cotton plays harmonica. — J.S.

★ ★ ★ **Mackintosh and T.J. (Soundtrack) / RCA (NA)**
Artists include: Waylon Jennings, Johnny Gimble, Willie Nelson, Ralph Mooney, Waylors.
Waylon Jennings provides most of the music for this late-Seventies modern cowboy-trucker flick. His "All Around Cowboy" and "Bob Wills Is Still the King," Mooney's "Crazy Arms" and Nelson's "Stay a Little Longer" are the right honky-tonk for the occasion, loose and easy. Still, the set is too unfocused to achieve much. — D.M.

★ ★ ★ **Mar-Vel Masters, Vols. 1–3 / Cowboy Carl Records (1978–79)**
Artists include: Chuck Dallis, Harold Allen, Slim O'Mary, Harry Carter, Bill Ferguson, Shorty Ashford, Bobby Sisco, the Beverly Sisters, Ramsey Kearney, Rem Wall, Paul Parker, Billy Nix, Lorenzo Smith, Jack Bradshaw, Herbie Duncan, Jack Bradshaw, Bob Burton, Ray Lynn, Troy Robinson, Mel Kimbrough, Jim Gatlin, Stony Calhoun, Bill Lillpop, Basil Smith, J. T. Watts, Bob Burton, Tex Justus, Ronnie Durbin.
Not every C&W/R&B fusion made it to Hitsville in the Fifties—or necessarily deserved to. These discs encapsulate the seventeen-year, 140-release history of Indiana-based Mar-Vel Records, intrepid entrepreneur Harry Glenn and his unlikely roster of hillbilly twisters, country queens, rock & roll Apaches, guitar boppers and redneck hip-

sters. Even in 1976, Glenn was roaming Indiana highways selling 45s like Chuck Dallis' "Moon Twist" and "Come On Let's Go" out of his car. There are great anonymous performances here and also extraordinary wretchedness—Billy Hall's "Ooga Booga Boo Boo." But all of it is the authentic tribal music of the people Albert Goldman despises. Volume 2, *Hillbilly Boogie*, concentrates only country jump and Western swing; volumes 1 and 3 are labeled "rock & roll, rockabilly, country rock," but anything goes. — G.A.

★ ★ ★ **Memphis Country / Sun (NA)**
Artists include: Johnny Cash, Jerry Lee Lewis, Charlie Rich, David Houston, Jack Clement, Carl Perkins, Barbara Pittman, Dale Wheeler, Conway Twitty, Warren Smith, Roy Orbison, Texas Bill.
Straight country from the great rockabilly home label. Lewis' "You Win Again," Cash's original "I Walk the Line" and Rich's "Sittin' and Thinkin' " are all among their best work, but Perkins, Orbison and Twitty are better on rockers. Clement's "Ten Years" is worth hearing, too, though. — D.M.

★ **Midnight Cowboy (Soundtrack) / U.A. (1969)**
John Barry scored most of this early-Seventies statement on New York lowlife. The exception is Nilsson's "Everybody's Talkin'," which made the Fred Neil song a Top Ten hit; Nilsson has a couple of other tracks, too, but that's all that anyone would want to hear. — D.M.

★ ★ ★ **Mighty Motown / Nat. (1978)**
Artists include: Rick James, Marvin Gaye, Mandre, Smokey Robinson, High Inergy, Thelma Houston, Táta Vega, Switch, Jermaine Jackson, Diana Ross.
Nothing major here, but if you're not a singles buyer, "Full Speed Ahead" (Vega), "I Want You" (Gaye), "Sexy Lady" (James) and "Love So Fine" (Robinson) are worth knowing. And High Inergy's "You Can't Turn Me Off (In the Middle of Turning Me On")" is one of the classic Motown numbers of the late Seventies. — D.M.

★ ★ ★ ★ **Mississippi Blues / Yazoo (NA)**
Artists include: William Harris, Skip James, Son House, Charlie Patton, John Byrd.
Excellent collection of delta blues recorded between 1927 and 1941, with superb sound reproduction and extensive notes. — J.S.

★ ★ ★ ★ ★ **The Mississippi Blues, Vols. 1–3 / O.J.L. (NA)**
Artists include: Bukka White, Willie Brown, Kid Bailey, Robert Wilkins, Skip James, Son House, Louise Johnson, Charlie Patton, Jaydee Short, Blind Willie Reynolds, Hambone Willie Newbern, Johnny Temple, Big Joe Williams, Rosie Mae Morre, Robert Johnson.
Indispensable collection of Mississippi blues recordings. — J.S.

★ ★ ★ **Mississippi Bottom Blues / Maml. (NA)**
Artists include: Otto Virgial, Charlie Patton, Freddie Spruell, Long Cleve Reed and Papa Harvey Tull, Tommy Bradley.
Collection of delta blues sides highlighted by the great Charlie Patton. — J.S.

★ ★ ★ **Mississippi River Blues / Flyr. (NA)**
Artists include: Luciouss Curtiss, Willie Ford and others.
1939 Library of Congress field recordings from Natchez. — J.S.

★ **Moment by Moment (Soundtrack) / RSO (NA)**
Artists include: Yvonne Elliman, Michael Franks, Charles Lloyd, Stephen Bishop.
Wimp soundtrack music. — J.S.

★ ★ ★ ★ **Monkey Business / Troj. (1980)**
Artists include: the Upsetters, Clancy Eccles, the Maytals, King Stitt, Desmond Dekker.
This LP succeeds in capturing the best of the early reggae era but offering nothing but tunes that hit big in the skinhead/blue-beat-era U.K. Most of these selections are well-known (and frequently compiled—for example, the Pioneers' "Long Shot," Desmond Dekker's "Hanty Town"), but every cut is worthwhile. King Stitt's offerings are great examples of early DJ rapping and Lee Perry's Upsetter cuts (the nucleus of the Wailers came from the Upsetters) are some of his best work. — R.F.G.

★ ★ ★ ★ **More American Graffiti / MCA (1975)**
Artists include: Chantels, Bill Haley and the Comets, Larry Williams, Coasters, Betty Everett, Dion and the Belmonts, Little Richard, Brenda Lee, Cadillacs, Gene Chandler, Buddy Holly and the Crickets, Danleers, Lloyd Price, Crows, Carl Dobkins, Tune Weavers, Carole King, Little Eva, Kingsmen, Jerry Butler, Dubs, Shirelles.
Third and final volume of MCA's double-disc oldies compilation again has little or

nothing to do with the George Lucas flick. But the collection's a good one, without anything terribly obscure but with a few hard-to-find gems (King's "It Might As Well Rain Until September," the Kingsmen's "Louie Louie," which misses most collections, and "Could This Be Magic" by the Dubs), plenty of Holly and Little Richard, and few, if any, ringers. — D.M.

★ ★ ★ **Motortown Revue Live / Mo. (1969)**
Artists include: Originals, Blinky, Bobby Taylor, Temptations, Gladys Knight and the Pips, Stevie Wonder.

★ ★ ★ **Motortown Revue, Vol. 2 / Mo. (1964)**
Artists include: Temptations, Kim Weston, Marvelettes, Mary Wells, Marvin Gaye, Martha and the Vandellas, Stevie Wonder.

★ ★ ★ **Recorded Live at the Apollo, Vol. 1 / Mo. (1963)**
Artists include: Contours, Supremes, Marvin Gaye, Marvelettes, Little Stevie Wonder, Mary Wells, Miracles.

Probably because the greatness of Motown is inherent in the preplanning and discipline associated with the recording studio, there's nothing especially scintillating on any of these sets. But they do recapture a smidgen of the excitement of the old Motown package shows, and a chance to hear the early Smokey Robinson, the young Stevie Wonder and such half-forgotten treasures as Weston, the Contours and Taylor are not to be missed. At least not if you really love the hits. — D.M.

★ ★ **Motown's Great Interpretations / Nat. (1977)**
Artists include: Smokey Robinson and the Miracles, Michael Jackson, Diana Ross, Dynamic Superiors, Supremes and Four Tops, Spinners, Temptations, Originals, Gladys Knight and the Pips, Junior Walker and the All Stars, David and Jimmy Ruffin, Thelma Houston.

Side one is sort of passable. True, Smokey's "I Heard It through the Grapevine" comes in fourth, behind not only Marvin and Gladys but also Creedence. True, hearing Diana Ross cover Aretha Franklin is not so much enlightening as weird. And heaven knows, the idea of the Supremes and Four Tops singing anything together, much less "Hello Stranger," is like mating a bunny and a bull. But there is a nice version of "Ain't Nothing Like the Real Thing" by the Dynamic Superiors which is weird because it

wants to be, and Michael Jackson singing "My Girl" feels like destiny.

On side two, performers on the level of Thelma Houston and the Originals cover material such as "Wichita Lineman" and "Me and Bobby McGee," a bad idea in the first place. Yuck. — D.M.

★ **Motown Show Tunes / Nat. (1977)**
Artists include: Diana Ross, G. C. Cameron, Marvin Gaye, Smokey Robinson, Willie Hutch, Diana Ross and the Supremes, Jackson Five, Edwin Starr, Thelma Houston, Four Tops.

The kind of album that gives Motown LPs their bad reputation (largely undeserved). But who *wants* to hear Smokey sing "An Old-Fashioned Man" or the Four Tops do "The Sound of Music"? Maybe Berry Gordy, but not us—or you either, most likely. On the other hand, this album does include music from *Trouble Man, Cooley High, Lady Sings the Blues, Foxy Brown, The Mack, Hell Up in Harlem* . . . the whole cycle of blaxploitation (so-called) pictures that helped to make the early Seventies such an exciting time for black pop culture. Long gone, of course, and much lamented by those who recall. — D.M.

★ ★ ★ ★ **Motown Story / Mo. (NA)**
Artists include: Barrett Strong, Marvellettes, Marvin Gaye, Smokey Robinson and the Miracles, Stevie Wonder, Martha and the Vandellas, Diana Ross and the Supremes, Mary Wells, Temptations, Four Tops, Junior Walker and the All-Stars, Gladys Knight and the Pips, Jimmy Ruffin, Marvin Gaye and Tammi Terrell, Supremes and Temptations, Jackson Five, Originals, Supremes.

Five-record documentary history of the great black pop label. Nearly every major hit the label has ever had is included, and all of its major artists—Gaye, Robinson and the Miracles, Ross and the Supremes, Jackson Five, Four Tops, Wonder, Knight and the Pips, Temptations, Martha and the Vandellas. But the narrative introductions to each song are intrusive for less than scholarly listening, even though some convey interesting information (Robinson on how he came to write "I Second That Emotion"; Levi Stubbs of the Four Tops on why he didn't understand the lyric of "Reach Out I'll Be There"). Still, there is so much essential music here that the package rates top ranking anyway. Insufficient liner notes, probably because the real annotation is in the grooves. — D.M.

★ ★ ★ **Muddy and the Wolf / Chess (1982)**
Artists include: Muddy Waters, Howlin' Wolf.
A repackaging of parts of their sessions
with Anglo-American rock heavyweights.
Wolf's session works, probably because he
can bend anything to his will, but Muddy
sounds consistently uncomfortable throughout his set. Funny, because one would have
thought that Mike Bloomfield and Paul Butterfield, Duck Dunn and Sam Lay (plus Otis
Spann himself) would have been at least as
simpatico a band as Eric Clapton, Stevie
Winwood, Ian Stewart, Bill Wyman and
Charlie Watts, plus Hubert Sumlin his own
bad self. Figure it's the rhythm section,
where the drummer rules the roost: Dunn
cuts Wyman, but Watts demolishes Lay.
And rock covers paper anyhow, because why
the hell did Chess reissue this stuff when so
many of both Waters' and Wolf's classics remain out of print? — D.M.

★ **Music from** *Outlaw Blues* / **Cap. (NA)**
*Artists include: Steve Fromholz, Peter Fonda,
Peter Fonda and Susan St. James, Charles
Bernstein, Hoyt Axton.*
Almost all wrong. Fromholz and Axton
deliver their usual journeyman country-rock
performances, but what business has Fonda
got singing, much less doing duets with St.
James? Bernstein's tracks are background
score. As big a mess as the picture.
— D.M.

MUSIC IN THE WORLD OF ISLAM
★ ★ ★ ★ ★ **Volume 1: The Human Voice /**
Tan. (1976), imp.
*Artists include: Ismail Ali Hasan and Abdel
Hamid Abdel Aziz, Habibola Halika, Amir
Mohammed of Aqcha and Baba Hakim,
Salim Alān and the pearl divers, Wa-
simxzama Khan Naseri and Nazir Ahmad,
Dunya Yunis, Mehein fin Baqid and Dahai
fin Baqid, Hateim Atiya Khalil Sayed, Aqi
Pishak of the Teka Turkoman family, Sufis
in the Khalif's mosque in Bagdad.*
★ ★ ★ **Volume 2: Lutes / Tan. (1976),**
imp.
*Artists include: Salman Shukur, Sultan
Hamid, Aboubekr Zerga, Hussein Ali Zodeh,
Baba Hakim, Erol Sayin, Jalal zur Fonun,
Khan Mohammad, Aqi Pishak, Mohammad
Omar.*
★ ★ ★ **Volume 3: Strings / Tan. (1976),**
imp.
*Artists include: Jalal Khan, Abdul Rahim
and Mishri Khan, Bahir Hashim Al-Rajab,
Juma īad Semahin, Abdou Badjé, Abdullah
Mohammad of the Beni Amer tribe, Pyara
Khan, Aydemir Cerdet, Parvis Meshkotian,*
Amari *Baharu Qenyé of Wollo, Hadja Ouled,
Hasan Ali Al-Naqib, Aladin, Shumar Khan,
Nur Mohammad.*
★ ★ ★ **Volume 4: Flutes and Trumpets /**
Tan. (1976), imp.
*Artists include: Kammo Khan, Niyazi Sayin,
Sian ditta Quadri, Nubarak Ali, Rehmat
Khan, Jalit Hussain, Samad Khan, Baluch
Khan, Hassan Naheed, Gopal, Manudin,
Ramjar, Aligar, Shabudin, Bumi.*
★ ★ ★ **Volume 5: Reeds and Bagpipes /**
Tan. (1976), imp.
*Artists include: Pempa, Shakar Khan, Ismail
Karaleniz, Rajab bin Khamis, Qashqai no-
mads, Taghan, Emilio and Dominico Ruffo,
Mustafa Pelibas, Karo Batak people, Mah-
mood Ali Ibrahim, Hassan Farhat.*
★ ★ ★ ★ **Volume 6: Drums and Rhythms /**
Tan. (1976), imp.
*Artists include: Malang, Mohammad Akram
Rohnawaz, Orchestra of the Sultan of Dosso,
Shahabudin, Ramishwar, Shankar, Sushilko-
mar, Mrs. Sultana Abdulla and the Awal* tar
*players, Misri Khan, Jamal Khan, Abdul
Rahim and Rahim Bux, Abdul Whab, Salim
Alān and the pearl divers, Ustad Tabib Hussain, Al Haq sect, Mohammad Ismaili, Faro-
marz Payyar.*
Recorded by Jean Jenkins and Poul Rov-
sing Olsen in the far-flung outposts of the
Moslem sphere, this six-record anthology
spans the music from Africa to Indonesia.
Although challenging to listen to continuous-
ly, it features many priceless gems, including
the beautiful Dunya Yunis, the Lebanese
mountain singer who stars in a much mutated form on Eno and Byrne's *My Life in
the Bush of Ghosts.* — ML.H.

★ ★ ★ ★ **The Music of Africa / BBC**
Hori. (1971), Br. imp.
Taken from the BBC archives, this compilation of traditional African music is all-
encompassing. From Ethiopia, an extract
from the Ethiopian Orthodox Church service
sung in the ecclesiastical Ge'ez language;
from Algeria, the dance music of the Ouled
Näil people—even a Mauritanian griot performing a Tukolor guitar solo. The description of unusual instruments in the liner notes
(notably King Tutankhamen's silver trumpet,
recorded for the first time in 1939) documents this record's call of the exotic.
— ML.H.

★ **Nashville (Soundtrack) / ABC (1975)**
Robert Altman's country music film suffered, among other things, from the lack of
an adequate score. Richard Baskin's C&W
pastiche can't fill out the movie—or the

disc—sufficiently to hold interest. Only Keith Carradine's stud posturing, "I'm Easy," has adequate melodic and lyrical interest to work away from the action. — D.M.

★ ★ **Ned Kelly (Soundtrack) / U.A. (NA)**
Artists include: Kris Kristofferson, Waylon Jennings, Mick Jagger, Tom Ghent.

Jagger starred in this film biography about an infamous Australian outlaw. His singing isn't much (one song, "Wild Colonial Boy"), nor is Ghent's, but Jennings offers the title track and a bit more, while Kristofferson comes up with three passable tunes. This is for hard-core Stones fans only, though why *Ned Kelly* is still in print and the far superior Jagger score of *Performance* is deleted is beyond the reckoning of any humans except Warner Bros. accountants. — D.M.

★ ★ ★ **New and Old Sounds / U.A. (NA)**
Artists include: Bob Marley, Meditation, Dillinger, Delroy Wilson, Ken Boothe, Dobby Dobson, Burning Spear, Heptones, Jackie Mittoo.

Selection of vintage reggae tracks. Marley's "One Love" is among his earliest recordings, as are the Heptones' "In the Groove" and "Pretty Looks Isn't All." Burning Spear's tracks don't compare with the group's later recordings, but Boothe's "This Is the Time" is one of his most solid. — D.M.

★ ★ ★ **Jimmy Newman and Al Terry: Their Earliest Recordings 1949–1952 / Flyr. (1981)**
One side each for these Southern Louisiana Cajun country singers from the early Fifties. Newman's more interesting, since he's more ethnic. Terry, in fact, is a fairly conventional country honky-tonk stylist who might have simply slipped over the border from Texas. — D.M.

★ ★ ★ **New Orleans Jazz and Heritage Festival / Fly. Fish (1979)**
Artists include: Clifton Chenier, Irving McLean, Roosevelt Sykes, Henry Butler, Ironing Board Sam, Onward Brass Band, Robert Pete Williams, Mamous Hour Cajun Band, Eubie Blake, New Orleans Ragtime Orchestra, Charles Mingus, Youth Inspirational Choir.

Not as good as the Island set, but an interesting array of talent from ragtime to blues to jazz to gospel to Cajun zydeco, omitting only rock and R&B. Which is the basic *reason* it's not as good, of course. — D.M.

★ ★ ★ ★ ★ **New Orleans Jazz and Heritage Festival / Is. (NA)**
Artists include: Allen Toussaint, Lee Dorsey, Ernie K-Doe, Robert Parker, Irma Thomas, Earl King, Lightnin' Hopkins, Professor Longhair.

This sure ain't jazz. In fact, it is the cream of the city's rhythm & blues tradition, which definitely falls into the Heritage category. Toussaint has never sounded better than he does in this live, open-air context, as he plays for his neighbors. His "Shoorah Shoorah" and "Play Something Sweet" are particularly free and effective here.

Dorsey, K-Doe, Thomas, King and Longhair have sounded better but not much. Each is represented by his or her most famous song—K-Doe's "Mother-in-Law," Dorsey's "Holy Cow" and "Workin' in a Coal Mine," Parker's "Barefootin'," Thomas' "I Done My Part" and King's "Trick Bag" lead up to Longhair's "Tipitina" and "Mardi Gras in New Orleans." There is still great pleasure and power to be found in these songs, although all of the originals were cut before the advent of the Beatles.

The only ringer is Hopkins, who is actually a Houston bluesman. But he contributes "Baby Please Don't Go" and "Mojo Hand" like a good country neighbor, so the historical inaccuracy is more than excusable. — D.M.

★ ★ ★ **Newport Broadside / Van. (NA)**
Artists include: Jim Garland, Ed McCurdy, Phil Ochs, Peter La Farge, Joan Baez and Bob Dylan, Pete Seeger and Bob Dylan, Tom Paxton, Sam Hinton, Bob Davenport, Freedom Singers.

Political folksinging (so-called topical songwriting) from the 1963 folk festival. Much of this has now dated, particularly the songs by doctrinaire writers like Paxton and Ochs. Dylan's duet on "With God on Our Side" is historically interesting, but his alliance with the sanctimonious Pete Seeger on the rare "Ye Playboys and Playgirls" is slightly embarrassing today. But it is mostly the Dylan performances that lend this set much interest now. — D.M.

★ ★ ★ **Newport Folk Festival '63 (Evening Concert) / Van. (NA)**
Artists include: Ian and Sylvia, Freedom Singers, Joan Baez, Bob Dylan, Sam Hinton, Mississippi John Hurt, Jack Elliott, Rooftop Singers.

Surprisingly, in two decades this set has not dated much. It helps that the political rhetoric and pious folklore mongering (that walked hand in hand) have been kept to a minimum here. Hurt's "C. C. Rider," "Stagolee," "Coffee Blues" and "Spikedriver Blues" give a sense of what magic his rediscovery and appearance here must have been, while Dylan's "Blowin' in the Wind" is so overwhelming to the crowd that the rejection of his rock & roll by a similar audience a couple of years later is unimaginable. The rest isn't up to par, although Elliott's "Diamond Joe" isn't bad. — D.M.

★ ★ ★ **Newport Folk Festival '64 (Evening Concerts) / Van. (NA)**
Artists include: Pete Seeger, Sleepy John Estes, Buffy Sainte-Marie, José Feliciano, Rodrigues Brothers, Phil Ochs, Frank Proffitt, Jim Kweskin and the Jug Band.

This isn't nearly as exciting as the 1963 set, not only because Dylan is missing but because there isn't any other performer who can match Hurt's brilliant appearance. Estes' "Corinna" is moving, Proffitt's "Tom Dooley" takes the song back from the Kingston Trio into the tradition where it belongs, and Kweskin's Maria Muldaur feature, "I'm a Woman," is good fun. But Seeger and Ochs are doctrinaire, and have not dated well, and the appearance of Feliciano is inexplicable at such a purist gathering. — D.M.

NEWPORT FOLK MUSIC FESTIVAL 1959–1960
★ ★ ★ **Volume 1 / Folk. (NA)**
Artists include: O.J. Abbott, Willie Thomas and Butch Cage, Pat Clancy, Mike Seeger, Pete Seeger, Alan Mills, Frank Hamilton.
★ ★ ★ **Volume 2 / Folk. (NA)**
Artists include: Brownie McGhee and Sonny Terry, New Lost City Ramblers, Frank Warner, Fleming Brown, Guy Carawan, John Greenway.

Before the big folk revival boom of the Sixties, Newport was much more traditionally oriented than its later topical politics would indicate. The outstanding performers here are not as well known as those on the other Newport sets released by Vanguard, but "I'm a Stranger Here" by Hamilton on Volume 1 and Volume 2's "Asheville Junction" by Warner as well as Guy Carawan's moving "We Shall Overcome" are all worth hearing. — D.M.

★ ★ **9-30-55 (Soundtrack) / MCA (NA)**
This film, based on a young man's James Dean fanaticism, is pre–rock & roll in its music orientation. It contains "In the Jailhouse Now" by Webb Pierce and Kitty

Wells' "Making Believe," both strong country standards, a Leonard Rosenman score that isn't much, plus narration by Richard Thomas that is good enough to belie his earlier role as John-Boy in TV's *The Waltons*. Interesting for trivia fans. — D.M.

★ ★ ★ ★ **NME Dancin' Master / New Musical Express (1981)**
Artists include: Tom Browne, Linx, Grace Jones, Talking Heads, Elvis Costello and the Attractions, Beggar and Company, Funky Four Plus One, Ian Dury and the Blockheads, Kid Creole and the Coconuts, the Lounge Lizards, the Polecats, Lloyd Coxone, Madness, the Beat, Grandmaster Flash and the Furious Five, Junior Giscombe, the B-52's, Susan, the Jam, Dennis Bovell, the Plastics, James White and the Blacks, the Teardrop Explodes, U2.

The perfect nightclubbing tape for parties at home, the *NME Dancin' Master*, compiled by England's leading music weekly, captures all the moods. For the exotic, Grace Jones' "Feel Up" and "Stomping at the Corona" by the Lounge Lizards, for the kitsch, the Plastics' "Last Train to Clarksville" and "Traison (C'est Juste Une Histoire)" by the Teardrop Explodes—there's even a swooning instrumental version of "Give Me Back My Man" from the B-52's. But the party tracks are definitely the joint: Grandmaster Flash's "Birthday Party," Talking Heads' "Cities," Costello's "Big Sister," Kid Creole's "There but for the Grace of God" and James Black's "Contort Yourself." Now that you've got the music, all you need are the drugs. — ML.H.

THE NONESUCH EXPLORER SERIES
★ ★ ★ **The Soul of Flamenco (1965)**
★ ★ ★ **Bouzoukee—the Music of Greece (1965)**
★ ★ ★ **The Koto Music of Japan (1965)**
★ ★ **Caledonia! The MacPherson Singers and Dancers of Scotland (1965)**
★ ★ ★ **The Pennywhistlers (1965)**
★ ★ ★ **Japanese Koto Classics (1965)**
★ ★ ★ **The Real Mexico in Music and Song (1965)**
★ ★ ★ ★ ★ **Music of Bulgaria (1965)**
★ ★ ★ **Geza Music of Japan (Music from the Kabuki Theatre) (1966)**
★ ★ ★ ★ ★ **The Real Bahamas in Music and Song (1966)**
★ ★ **The Sound of the Sun (Steel Band/ Trinidad) (1966)**
★ ★ ★ **Flower Dance (Japanese Folk Melodies) (1966)**
★ ★ ★ ★ **Los Chiriguanos of Paraguay (Guarani Songs and Dances) (1966)**

★ ★ ★ ★ The Pennywhistlers: A Cool Day and Crooked Corn (1966)
★ ★ ★ ★ ★ A Bell Ringing in the Empty Sky (Japanese Shakuhachi Music) (1967)
★ ★ ★ Kingdom of the Sun (Peru's Inca Heritage) (1967)
★ ★ ★ ★ Folk Fiddling from Sweden (1969)
★ ★ ★ ★ A Harvest, A Shepherd, A Bride (Village Music of Bulgaria) (1969)
★ ★ ★ ★ ★ In Praise of Oxala and Other Gods (Black Music of South America) (1970)
★ ★ ★ ★ In the Shadow of the Mountain (Bulgarian Folk Music) (1970)
★ ★ ★ ★ The Persian Santur (Music of Iran) (1971)
★ ★ ★ ★ Escalay: The Water Wheel (Oud Music of Nubia) (1971)
★ ★ ★ Village Music of Yugoslavia (1971)
★ ★ ★ Fiestas of Peru (Music of the High Andes) (1972)
★ ★ ★ Caribbean Island Music (1972)
★ ★ ★ ★ The Irish Pipes of Finbar Furey (1972)
★ ★ ★ ★ ★ P'ansori (Korea's Epic Vocal Art and Instrumental Music) (1972)
★ ★ ★ ★ Village Music of Turkey (1972)
★ ★ ★ ★ China (Shantung Folk Music and Traditional Instrumental Pieces) (1972)
★ ★ ★ ★ ★ Afghanistan (Music from the Crossroads of Asia) (1973)
★ ★ ★ Irish Pipe Music (Hornpipes, Airs and Reels) (1973)
★ ★ ★ ★ A Persian Heritage (Classical Music of Iran) (1973)
★ ★ ★ Music in the Karakorams of Central Asia (1974)
★ ★ ★ ★ Turkey/A Musical Journey (1975)
★ ★ ★ ★ Mexico (Fiestas of Chiapas and Oaxaca) (1976)
★ ★ ★ ★ Japan (Traditional Vocal and Instrumental Music: Shakuhachi) (1976)
★ ★ ★ ★ Shakuhachi: The Japanese Flute (1977)
★ ★ ★ The Real Bahamas, Vol. 2 (1978)
★ ★ ★ ★ ★ Qawwali (Sufi Music from Pakistan) (1978)
★ ★ ★ Japan (Kabuki and Other Traditional Musics) (1978)
★ ★ ★ China (Music of the Chinese Pipa) (1979)
★ ★ ★ ★ ★ The Nonesuch Explorer (Treasures of the Explorer Series) (1971)

The Nonesuch Explorer Series began life as the Nonesuch International Series in late 1964 as a vehicle for licensing foreign tapes and records and releasing them in America. When Tracey Sterne was brought in to head Nonesuch in late 1965 she changed the name

and changed everything else in the series, bringing a style and a grace that changed the way foreign/world music is now presented and listened to.

As recently as the mid-Sixties, Indian music (one of the oldest and most complex musics in the world) was still catalogued at Juilliard under "primitive musics," and the records of international music available to the general public were few and far between. They consisted of brightly packaged bits of exotica that turned musicians (not to mention their cultures) into travesties of themselves (titles like *Fiesta! The Chihuahua Music of Mexico* and *The Happy Hawaiians* abounded) or very dry-looking field recordings with indecipherable notes and with track titles designed to scare off all but the staunchest ethnomusicologist ("Child hitting small animal while singing," "Man playing odd-looking three-stringed instrument").

Ms. Sterne programmed her records of world musics as carefully as classical and pop albums (often more carefully), making sure the pieces all fit together into a unified whole), packaged the records with attractive line drawings and watercolors that gave them the distinction and sophistication of the best *New Yorker* covers, and began finding and commissioning recordings of music that, at least in America, had never been available to a general public: music of Bali, Java, Afghanistan, Burundi, Turkey, Bulgaria, Nubia, and on and on. In an unprecedented move, she often relied on producers who were involved with the pop world and who brought a freshness and vitality to the recordings: Joe Boyd (who produced Fairport Convention, Nick Drake, and the Incredible String Band), Peter Siegel (who produced Paul Siebel and Elliott Murphy) and Bill Leader (who produced Pentangle) all contributed productions (and often then brought a sense of world music and of new possibility to the pop records they were recording).

During the late Sixties and early Seventies, much of the cross-pollination that took place in pop music, the openness and receptivity, came in no small part from the sudden availability of so much previously unheard music. The Incredible String Band, the Grateful Dead, Ry Cooder, Kate and Anna McGarrigle, and Melanie all recorded songs from *The Real Bahamas* albums; Simon and Garfunkel used harmonies they'd learned from *Music of Bulgaria;* Tim Buckley developed his own version of the Balinese monkey chant on *Golden Rain,* guitarists like John Martyn, Richard Thompson and Robbie

Basho (as well as Grateful Dead percussionist Mickey Hart) learned from the oud playing of Hamza El Din on *Escalay: The Water Wheel;* John McLaughlin's post-Mahavishnu band, Shakti, featured Indian violinist L. Shankar, who was first heard on *Pallavi;* and the list goes on.

The records are well recorded, beautifully documented, and best of all, *cheap* (at a list price of $5.98, they generally sell for $4.00 to $4.49). *Music of Bulgaria, The Real Bahamas, Vol. 1, The Water Wheel, A Bell Ringing in the Empty Sky, Javanese Court Gamelan, Vol. 2, Burundi* and *Afghanistan* are all classic recordings and belong in every collection, but for the uninitiated the best place to start might be *The Nonesuch Explorer,* a two-record set featuring thirty of the best selections from various albums.
— B.C.

Indian/Tibetan
★ ★ ★ The Music of India (1965)
★ ★ ★ ★ Classical Music of India (1966)
★ ★ ★ Dhyanam/Meditation (South Indian Vocal Music) (1966)
★ ★ Bhavalu/Impressions (South Indian Instrumental Music) (1966)
★ ★ ★ ★ Kalpana (Instrumental and Dance Music of India) (1966)
★ ★ ★ Ramnad Krishnan: Vidwan (Songs of the Carnatic Tradition) (1966)
★ ★ ★ The Ten Graces Played on the Vina (Music of South India) (1966)
★ ★ ★ ★ Sarangi (Instrumental Music of North India) (1968)
★ ★ ★ Pulse of Tanam (Ragas of South India) (1969)
★ ★ ★ Indian Street Music (1969)
★ ★ ★ Ramnad Krishnan (South Indian Classical Music) (1971)
★ ★ ★ Pallavi (South Indian Flute Music) (1973)
★ ★ ★ ★ ★ Tibetan Buddhism (Tantras of Gyuto/Mahakala) (1973)
★ ★ ★ ★ Kashmir (Traditional Songs and Dances) (1974)
★ ★ ★ Master of the Sarangi (Classical Music of India) (1975)
★ ★ ★ ★ ★ Tibetan Buddhism (Tantras of Gyuto/Sangwa Dupa) (1975)
★ ★ ★ Festivals of the Himalayas (1975)
★ ★ ★ The Bengel Minstrel (Music of the Bauls) (1975)
★ ★ ★ ★ Kashmir (Traditional Songs and Dances, Vol. 2) (1976)
★ ★ ★ ★ ★ Tibetan Buddhism (The Ritual Orchestra and Chants) (1976)
★ ★ ★ ★ Ladakh (Songs and Dances from the Highlands of Western Tibet) (1977)
★ ★ ★ ★ Festivals of the Himalayas, Vol. 2 (1978) ·
★ ★ ★ ★ Tibetan Buddhism (Shedur: A Ghost Exorcism Ritual) (1978)
★ ★ ★ ★ Nectar of the Moon (Vichitra Vina Music of Northern India) (1981)

The breadth of these recordings (not to mention the breadth of India's music) is staggering. While some of the recordings of ragas seem overly polite and bloodless, best left to be played in the backs of Indian restaurants, the recordings made in Kashmir, Ladakh and the Himalayas are fierce and overpowering, featuring drumming usually associated with the trance musics of Morocco and vocals that are awe-inspiring. Most of these albums were produced by David Lewiston, a former pupil of composer Thomas DeHartmann and a fine ethnomusicologist who brings a particularly sensitive ear to these recordings and whose productions of Tibetan chant are overwhelming and highly recommended. — B.C.

African
★ ★ ★ Voices of Africa (High-Life and Other Popular Music) (1966)
★ ★ ★ ★ The African Mbira (Music of the Shona People of Rhodesia) (1971)
★ ★ ★ ★ The Soul of Mbira (Traditions of the Shona People of Rhodesia) (1973)
★ ★ ★ ★ ★ Animals of Africa (Sounds of the Jungle, Plain and Bush) (1973)
★ ★ ★ ★ ★ Music from the Heart of Africa/ Burundi (1974)
★ ★ ★ Africa: Ceremonial and Folk Music (1975)
★ ★ ★ ★ ★ Africa: Witchcraft and Ritual Music (1975)
★ ★ ★ Africa: Drum, Chant and Instrument Music (1976)
★ ★ ★ ★ Africa: Shona Mbira Music (1977)
★ ★ ★ Africa: Ancient Ceremonies, Dance Music and Songs of Ghana (1979)
★ ★ ★ ★ Music of the Upper Volta: Savannah Rhythms (1981)

The recent interest in (and exploitation of) African music make these recordings all the more important. The double drum ideas heard in Adam and the Ants, Bow Wow Wow, Liquid Liquid, Duran Duran and many other bands can be heard (to better advantage) on *Music from the Heart of Africa: Burundi,* and aficionados of Talking Heads, the Police and David Byrne and Brian Eno's experiments will find familiar rhythms and sounds on *Witchcraft and Ritual Music, Savannah Rhythms* and *Drum, Chant and Instrument Music. Animals of Af-*

rica is just that: an entire album devoted to the sounds of lions, hyenas, zebras and wildebeests out on the plains. — B.C.

Indonesian
★ ★ ★ **The Balinese Gamelan (1966)**
★ ★ ★ **Tahiti: The Gauguin Years (Songs and Dances of Tahiti) (1966)**
★ ★ ★ ★ **Golden Rain (The Ramayana Monkey Chant) (1967)**
★ ★ ★ **The Jasmine Isle (Music of the Javanese Gamelan) (1968)**
★ ★ ★ ★ **Music for the Balinese Shadow Play (1970)**
★ ★ ★ ★ **Javanese Court Gamelan (1971)**
★ ★ ★ ★ **Gamelan Semar Pegulingan (Gamelan of the Love God) (1972)**
★ ★ ★ ★ ★ **Javanese Court Gamelan, Vol. 2 (1977)**
★ ★ ★ ★ ★ **Javanese Court Gamelan, Vol. 3 (1979)**
★ ★ ★ **Island Music of the South Pacific (1981)**

Javanese music is the slowest in the world, seeming to exist in a dream-time of falling and rising tempos and recurrent interior rhythms. The gamelan, a series of tuned gongs and/or bowls that sound like a cross between vibes and careless evening bells, is supplemented with bamboo flute, rebab (a raspy violin) and occasionally a vocal chorus. Bali, only two miles from Java, produces the fastest music in the world, as bright and fierce as Java's is shadowy and playful. Their monkey chant (documented on *Golden Rain*) is one of the most stunning vocal exercises ever recorded (and sounds right at home next to records of Yoko Ono, Ornette Coleman and Don Cherry). Volumes 2 and 3 of *Javanese Court Gamelan* are among the most beautiful albums ever recorded and sound like they could be sisters of Van Morrison's *Astral Weeks.* — B.C.

★ ★ ★ **No Nukes (Soundtrack) / Asy. (NA)**
Artists include: Bruce Springsteen, Crosby, Stills and Nash, John Hall, Bonnie Raitt, Gil Scott-Heron.

Soundtrack from the film documentary of the antinuclear MUSE concerts features some great material, like Springsteen's, and some terrible material, like Crosby, Stills and Nash's. — J.S.

★ ★ ★ **Novo Rock / Arabella Eurodisc (1980), Fr. imp.**
Artists include: The Beat, the Pop, Secret Affair, Ian Gomm, the Outline, John Hiatt, An-
thony More, Iggy Pop, Herman Brood, the Opposition, Simple Minds, the A's, the Sports, Nina Hagen, Lene Lovich.

Not readily available in English-speaking countries, this French sampler of newer rock (circa 1979–80) is an odd-man-out collector's item, especially with Herman Brood's "Hot Shot" and the delightful trio of Brood, Lene Lovich and Nina Hagen doing "I Love You Like I Love Myself," from the *Cha Cha* soundtrack. — ML.H.

★ ★ ★ **No Wave / A&M (NA)**
Artists include: Squeeze, Police, Joe Jackson, Klark Kent, Stranglers, Dickies.

Good anthology of late Seventies/early Eighties new-wave bands in the IRS stable. — J.S.

★ ★ ★ ★ ★ **Nuggets / Sire-H (NA)**
Artists include: Standells, Electric Prunes, Strangeloves, Knickerbockers, Vagrants, Mouse, Shadows of Knight, Blues Project, Seeds, Remains, Barbarians, Castaways, Magicians, 13th Floor Elevators, Count Five, Leaves, Michael and the Messengers, Cryan Shames, Blues Magoos, Amboy Dukes, Chocolate Watch Band, Mojo Men, 3rd Rail, Sagittarius, Nazz, Premiers, Magic Mushrooms.

Probably the most delightfully unpretentious collection of mid-Sixties artifacts imaginable, thanks to the compilation and witty annotation by critic/historian Lenny Kaye, who went on to play guitar for Patti Smith's group. These are somewhat bluesy, somewhat psychedelic, always amateurish, and for the most part, utterly unself-conscious in their naiveté. Anyone who doesn't understand the nostalgia of certain old-timers for that golden age of rock blossoming into art needs to hear this, and anyone who does comprehend that feeling needs to own it.

There are stars here before their time (Ted Nugent in the Amboy Dukes; Leslie West in the Vagrants; Todd Rundgren in the Nazz). There are local legends: the Dukes in Detroit, the Shadows of Knight in Chicago, Nazz in Philly, Vagrants and Blues Project in New York, the Barbarians and Remains in Boston, Mouse (and the Traps) and the Elevators in Texas. But most of all, these are witty three-minute attempts at hit singles, often with a bizarre cast: "Moulty" is the story of how the Barbarians' hook-handed drummer got that way. "Lies" by the Knickerbockers is the most perfect copying of the Beatles ever done; you could say the same thing about Mouse's "Public Execution" and Bob Dylan. "Psychotic Reaction" by Count Five is a great jumbling of the Yardbirds'

"I'm a Man" extrapolation; the Leaves' "Hey Joe" and the Seeds' "Pushin' Too Hard" are folk rock that manages to get raunchy.

There is a great deal of distorted blues and high school stud posturing—"Dirty Water" by the Standells, the Vagrants' "Respect," "No Time Like the Right Time" by the Blues Project, and the Blues Magoos' "Tobacco Road," for instance. Anyone who remembers can't resist these songs; anyone who has forgotten will blush in disbelief; those who never knew don't know what they're missing. — D.M.

★ ★ ★ ★ Oi! / EMI (1981), imp.
★ ★ ★ ★ Strength thru Oi, Vol. 2 / Decca (1981), imp.
Artists include: Oi!Oi!Oi!, Cockney Rejects, Peter and the Test Tube Babies, 4-Skins, Postmen, Exploited, Terrible Twins, Max Splodge and Desert Island Joe, Slaughter and the Dogs, Garry Johnson, the Strike, Infra-Riot, the Last Resort, Criminal Class, the Toy Dolls, Barney Rubble, Cock Sparrer, Splodge and the Shaven Heads.

The famous albums that were blamed for the July 1981 riots in England. After the skinhead with clenched fists and bullet haircut on the cover of Volume 2 was identified as a recruiter for the neofascist British Movement organization, Decca deleted its LP. Both albums are a garage-band celebration of a no-hope future. Rock & roll and sports are the only two ways of escaping any ghetto, although it is unlikely that these raw screams of protest from skinhead bands will find a mass audience. Puts the Ramones to shame; exhilarating, yet at the same time terribly depressing. — ML.H.

★ ★ ★ Okeh Chicago Blues / Epic (1982)
Artists include: Big Boy Edwards, Victoria Spivey and Her Chicago Four, Curtis Jones, Roosevelt Scott, Peter Chatman and His Washboard Band, Brownie McGhee, Champion Jack Dupree, Roosevelt Sykes, Tony Hollins, Peter Cleighton, Memphis Minnie, Little Son Joe, Big Bill and His Rhythm Band, the Yas Yas Girl, Johnny Shines, Muddy Waters, Big Joe Williams.

This set is a conceptual mistake: it features blues recorded in Chicago, but very little that's in the style associated with that town. Instead we have a great deal of jumping, uptown piano blues, a bit of transported country blues and only a few tracks that reflect the synthesis of delta blues and electricity Waters and his cohorts began to achieve in the late Forties. (It's a shame that Epic couldn't put together a selection of Okeh's fine delta sides—or some of its gospel music, for that matter.)

The highlights are near the end, with four fine previously unissued performances by Shines, three otherwise unavailable sides from Waters and the excellent material by Williams. "Bad Whiskey Blues" (Yas Yas Girl), "I Am Sailin' " (Memphis Minnie) and "Confession' the Blues" (Cleighton with an ace band) are also worth knowing about. — D.M.

★ ★ ★ ★ ★ Okeh Rhythm and Blues / Epic (1982)
Artists include: Smiley Lewis, Chuck Willis, Big Maybelle, Screamin' Jay Hawkins, Titus Turner, Larry Darnell, Johnnie Ray, Billy Stewart, Schoolboys, Sheppards, Treniers, Paul Gayten, Little Joe and Thrillers, Doc Bagby, Red Saunders, Little Richard, Ravens, Sandmen, Marquees.

Exceptionally fine selection of R&B material originally issued in the Fifties and the early Sixties on Okeh. Highlights are everywhere, but especially not to be overlooked are "Please Say You Want Me" (Schoolboys), "Pretend You're Still Mine" (Sheppards), "Peanuts" (Little Joe), "Baby You're My Only Love" (Stewart) and "Hey Little Schoolgirl" (Marquees). Hits are abundant, from Ray's "Cry" and "I Put a Spell on You" by Hawkins to Big Mama Thornton's original version of "Whole Lotta Shakin' Goin' On." — D.M.

★ ★ ★ ★ Okeh Soul / Epic (1982)
Artists include: Major Lance, Billy Butler and the Enchanters, Walter Jackson, Opals, Artistics, Vibrations.

Nice but imperfect survey of Chicago soul of the early to middle Sixties. Lance's hits are all here: "Monkey Time," "Um, Um, Um, Um, Um, Um," "The Matador," along with several lesser numbers. But the bulk of the album is a tribute to the influence of Curtis Mayfield, who is as pervasive in his style as he is conspicuous in his absence as a performer, and to the production skills of Carl Davis, who did all but two of the tracks. Without Jerry Butler, the Impressions and Betty Everett, this can't be a really accurate survey of the region during this period, but it's a fine sampling nonetheless. — D.M.

★ ★ ★ ★ ★ Okeh Western Swing / Epic (1982)
Artists include: Al Bernard, Emmett Miller and His Georgia Crackers, Roy Newman and

His Boys, Blue Ridge Playboys, Range Riders, W. Lee O'Daniel and His Hillbilly Boys, Crystal Springs Ramblers, Bob Wills and His Texas Playboys, Saddle Tramps, Sons of the Pioneers, Light Crust Doughboys, Hi Neighbor Boys, Hank Penny and His Radio Cowboys, Swift Jewel Cowboys, Sweet Violet Boys, Ocie Stockard and His Wanderers, Hi-Flyers, Sons of the West, Adolf Hofner and His Orchestra, Slim Harbert and His Boys, Spade Cooley, Leon McAuliffe and His Western Swing Band.

A marvelous collection, the perfect introduction to "cowboy jazz" for novices, a nice complement to the collections of aficionados. Wills, who is to Western swing what Elvis is to rockabilly (i.e., a figure who explodes past the boundaries of the genre), gets a whole side of middle-Thirties classics, each one a winner. But such less well-known but also exciting performers as McAuliffe, the Pioneers, Miller, the Range Riders, the Light Crust Doughboys and Hank Penny are also worth a listen. Spade Cooley is worth his own album (and he's got one in another CBS series). — D.M.

★ ★ **The Oldies / Doo (NA)**
Artists include: Penguins, Souvenirs, Pearls, Calvanes, Pipes, Romancers, Silks, Medallions, Meadowlarks, Crescendos.

An assortment of *very* minor doo-wop artists. Even the Penguins, the best-known group here, are represented not by "Earth Angel," their greatest hit, but by the more obscure (but not bad) "Please Mr. Junkman." Cultists only. — D.M.

★ ★ ★ **Oldies but Goodies, Vol. 1 / Orig. Sound (1959)**
Artists include: Five Satins, Penguins, Teen Queens, Mello Tones, Don Julian, Medallions, Shirley and Lee, Cadets, Sonny Knight, Jaguars, Etta James, Oscar McLollie.

Leadoff volume of Original Sound's impressive oldies series (unannotated, of course) comes up with more than its share of winners: "In the Still of the Night" (Five Satins), "Earth Angel" (Penguins), "Let the Good Times Roll" (Shirley and Lee), "Stranded in the Jungle" (Cadets) and "Dance with Me Henry" (Etta James). More R&B than rock & roll oriented, though "Stranded" is so riotous that it qualifies in both directions. — D.M.

★ ★ ★ **Oldies but Goodies, Vol. 2 / Orig. Sound (1960)**
Artists include: Clovers, Heartbeats, Jesse

Belvin, Crows, Velvetones, Nutmegs, Charts, Joe Turner, Peppermint Harris, Tony Allen, Turbans, Faye Adams.

The best tracks here include Turner's "Shake Rattle and Roll," a cornerstone of R&B's evolution into a sound attractive to whites; Adams' gospel-like "Shake a Hand"; "Devil or Angel" by the Clovers and "Gee" by the Crows, two of Atlantic's best early group records; "Story Untold" by the Nutmegs, "1,000 Miles Away" by the Heartbeats, "When You Dance" by the Turbans and "Good Night My Love" by Belvin, all swell R&B hits. — D.M.

★ ★ ★ ★ **Oldies but Goodies, Vol. 3 / Orig. Sound (1961)**
Artists include: Dell-Vikings, Frankie Ford, Little Anthony and the Imperials, Flamingos, Little Richard, Dells, Preston Epps, El Dorados, Huey Smith, Shields, Jerry Butler, Gene and Eunice.

The quality here is unassailable; if there were adequate (or any) liner notes in this series, it would be a five-star disc. "Come Go with Me" by the Dell-Vikings, the Imperials' lush "Two People in the World," "Lovers Never Say Goodbye" by the Flamingos and the Dells' "Oh What a Night" are the best sort of group rhythm & blues. Butler's "For Your Precious Love" is a masterpiece of solo crooning. Smith's pounding "Don't You Just Know It," Ford's honking "Sea Cruise" and Little Richard's shouted "Long Tall Sally" are among the greatest hits of New Orleans rock and R&B. For weirder tastes, too, there is Preston Epps with the decidedly mortal "Bongo Rock." Put this set in a time capsule and you'll probably confuse people three hundred years from now. But you'll also exhilarate them. — D.M.

★ ★ ★ ★ **Oldies but Goodies, Vol. 4 / Orig. Sound (1962)**
Artists include: Gloria Mann, Rays, Five Satins, Six Teens, Mickey and Sylvia, Dubs, Chantels, Jerry Lee Lewis, Sandy Nelson, Norman Fox and the Rob Roys, Barrett Strong, Carl Perkins.

This album comes as close to the modern era as anything in Original Sound's series by including Strong's "Money," the first Motown hit. Alongside "Blue Suede Shoes" by Perkins and Lewis' "Whole Lotta Shakin' Goin' On," this is perhaps the hardest-driving set in the Original Sound series. Not that frontier material is neglected: the Satins' "To the Aisle" and "Could This Be Magic" by the Dubs are drippingly romantic. Nelson's "Teen Beat" drum tour de force has dated, but Mickey and Sylvia's salacious R&B novelty, "Love Is Strange," has not. — D.M.

★ ★ ★ ★ Oldies but Goodies, Vol. 5 / Orig. Sound (1963)

Artists include: Elegants, Rosie and the Originals, Skyliners, Paradons, Dominoes, Maurice Williams, Shep and the Limelites, Channels, Hollywood Argyles, Bobby Day, Preston Epps, Jewels.

Mostly obscure, mostly beautiful. The Elegants' "Little Star" is an achingly pure group vocal; "Angel Baby" by Rosie and the Originals is a profoundly silly one. The Skyliners' "Since I Don't Have You" is a teenager's dream, while the Dominoes' "Sixty Minute Man" is his fantasy. Some of these simply transcend themselves: "Stay" by Maurice Williams is a reckless lover's plea; "Daddy's Home" by Shep and the Limelites is a tortured step toward adulthood; "Hearts of Stone" by the Jewels adds that fitting touch of adolescent self-pity. Not that there is no silliness here: if the Argyles' "Alley Oop" doesn't satisfy you, check Preston Epps, who returns (he was last seen in Volume 3) with "Bongo Bongo Bongo." Huh? — D.M.

★ ★ ★ ★ Oldies but Goodies, Vol. 6 / Orig. Sound (1964)

Artists include: Gary "U.S." Bonds, Fireflies, Bill Doggett, Dion, Safaris, Skyliners, Gene Chandler, Dee Dee Sharp, Little Caesar and the Romans, Dee Clark, Gladys Knight and the Pips.

This album contains Little Caesar's ode to such things, "Those Oldies but Goodies (Remind Me of You)." As if to demonstrate why that's so, it also features Bonds' "Quarter to Three," a space sound from the past, Doggett's primitive instrumental "Honky Tonk," Chandler's mysterious "Duke of Earl" (who is this man and what does he want?), Sharp's dance hit "Mashed Potato Time," Dee Clark's "Raindrops" and the debut appearance of Knight and the Pips, on the ballad "With Every Beat of My Heart." — D.M.

★ ★ ★ Oldies but Goodies, Vol. 7 / Orig. Sound (1965)

Artists include: Tommy Edwards, Gary "U.S." Bonds, Mark Dinning, Paris Sisters, Ritchie Valens, Chimes, Jerry Butler, Jimmy Jones, Champs, Dion, Barbara George, B. Bumble and the Stingers.

This set contains more of the teen-exploitation music (Edwards, Dinning, Paris

Sisters, Jones, even B. Bumble) than is usual in the Original Sound series. But it also has some memorable moments: "New Orleans" by Bonds, "I Know" by George, "Tequila" by the Champs, Dion's "Run-around Sue" and Butler's "He Will Break Your Heart." Best of all, it has Valens' heartbreaking "Donna," which makes you wonder what he might have achieved if he hadn't decided to board a certain airplane back in 1959. — D.M.

★ ★ ★ ★ Oldies but Goodies, Vol. 8 / Orig. Sound (NA)

Artists include: Dixie Cups, Terry Stafford, Bobby Darin, Ritchie Valens, Inez Foxx, Troy Shondell, Dale and Grace, Carla Thomas, Blue Jays, Coasters, Ernie Fields, Ernie Freeman.

Nice blend of the obvious and the obscure. Dixie Cups' "Chapel of Love" is a good New Orleans girl-group hit, Darin's "Splish Splash" is one of Atlantic's first white rock records, Carla Thomas' "Gee Whiz" one of Stax' first hit productions, the Coasters' "Searchin'" an immortal. On the ballad side, there's Stafford's "Suspicion," which Elvis elevated to an anthem of paranoia; Shondell's "This Time" and the soaring "Lover's Island" by the Blue Jays. For pure fun, this has "La Bamba," Valens' reworking of a Mexican folk melody, and Foxx's "Mockingbird," a similar restructuring of a Yankee folk song. — D.M.

★ ★ ★ Oldies but Goodies, Vol. 9 / Orig. Sound (NA)

Artists include: Timi Yuro, Casinos, Esther Phillips, Don and Juan, Cathy Jean and the Roommates, J. Frank Wilson, Bobby Day, Del Shannon, Bobby Fuller, Castaways, Jewel Akens, Bobby Bland.

One of the series' weaker sets. Aside from Bland's "Turn on Your Lovelight," Shannon's "Runaway," Fuller's "I Fought the Law," the Castaways' "Liar Liar" and "What's Your Name" by Don and Juan, most of these are dispensable or worse: do you want to hear J. Frank Wilson's morbid "Last Kiss" ever again? — D.M.

★ ★ ★ ★ Oldies but Goodies, Vol. 10 / Orig. Sound (NA)

Artists include: Righteous Brothers, Frankie Avalon, Shirelles, Tune Weavers, Duprees, Johnny Ace, Chuck Berry, Isley Brothers, Fats Domino, Bo Diddley, Sam the Sham and the Pharaohs, Olympics.

Another solid set. Domino, Isleys, Berry, Diddley and Shirelles tracks are the more or less obvious sort. So is "You've Lost That Lovin' Feelin' " by the Righteous Brothers, but it's too good not to merit special mention. Less well known but still charming are "You Belong to Me" by the Duprees, Ace's "Pledging My Love" and two grandly silly novelties, "Hully Gully" by the Olympics and Sam the Sham's "Wooly Bully." Big drawback: Frankie Avalon's "Venus," which deserves to be napalmed. — D.M.

★ ★ ★ ★ **Oldies but Goodies, Vol. 11 / Orig. Sound (NA)**
Artists include: Righteous Brothers, Little Anthony and the Imperials, Bobby Hebb, Mary Wells, Classics IV, Harvey and the Moonglows, Little Richard, Kingsmen, Diamonds, Chuck Berry, Angels, Soul Survivors.

Perhaps the best set in the series: diverse, unusual, exciting. "Soul and Inspiration" is one of the Righteous Brothers' best, while "Goin' Out of My Head" *is* Little Anthony's best. Hebb's "Sunny" is a marvelous ballad, and Wells' "My Guy" one of the all-time Motown standards. Richard's "Tutti Frutti" and "Maybellene" by Berry are definitive examples of their music. The Moonglows' "Ten Commandments of Love" is a perfect doo-wop choice, while the Classics IV's "Traces" shows what happened to that sound in the Sixties. The Angels' "My Boyfriend's Back" is probably the most blustering of the girl-group hits. But the heart and soul of rock is captured exquisitely by such minor gems as the incoherent "Little Darlin' " (Diamonds), the raunchy "Louie Louie" (Kingsmen) and the unlikely but pungent "Expressway to Your Heart" (Soul Survivors), the latter being the oddest record Gamble and Huff ever made. — D.M.

★ ★ ★ ★ **Oldies but Goodies, Vol. 12 / Orig. Sound (NA)**
Artists include: Everly Brothers, Delfonics, Lenny Welch, Ruby and the Romantics, James and Bobby Purify, Impressions, Box Tops, Chuck Berry, Jerry Lee Lewis, Little Richard, Fontella Bass, Contours.

Continues the pattern of the best LPs in the series: some rock & roll (Berry, Lewis, Richard), a big ballad (Welch's "Since I Fell for You"), a lot of mainstream soul (Impressions, Purify Brothers, Bass, Contours, Delfonics). This works even better than most, maybe because the kind of Sixties soul it includes—Bass' "Rescue Me," the Contours' wild "Do You Love Me," Purify Brothers' "I'm Your Puppet"—is less often anthologized than the Fifties R&B earlier discs in the series rely upon. And the girl-group

number, Ruby and the Romantics' "Our Day Will Come," is one of the few in that genre that's truly erotic. — D.M.

★ ★ ★ ★ **Oldies but Goodies, Vol. 14 / Orig. Sound (NA)**
Artists include: Platters, Dionne Warwick, Crests, Brenda Lee, Lloyd Price, Dinah Washington, Bill Haley and the Comets, Martha and the Vandellas, Chiffons, Wilson Pickett, McCoys, Shirelles.

Hardly a miss in the bunch. This is, of course, really the thirteenth volume in the previously available series—maybe someone at Original Sound is superstitious. But whatever the number, there's barely a miss in a group including "Smoke Gets in Your Eyes" (Platters), "Don't Make Me Over" (Warwick), "I'm Sorry" (Lee), "Sixteen Candles" (Crests—a little wimpy, but it's the only one), "Just Because" (Price), "Unforgettable" (Washington), Haley's "Rock around the Clock," the Vandellas' "Dancing in the Street" (an anthem), the Chiffons' "He's So Fine" (possibly the best girl-group hit of all), "Funky Broadway" (Pickett), "Hang on Sloopy" (McCoys) and "Will You Still Love Me Tomorrow" (Shirelles). If this set had been pieced together with a shred more scholarship—if it had notes, I mean—this, like the other four-star LPs in the series, would rate a full five. — D.M.

★ ★ **Old N' Golden / Jamie (NA)**
Artists include: Fantastic Johnny C, Tommy McLain, Barbara Lynn, Barbara Mason, James Boys, Volcanoes, Sunny and the Sunglows, Crispian St. Peters, Cliff Nobles and Company, Brenda and the Tabulations, Showstoppers, Dale and Grace, Della Humphrey, Helene Smith, Duane Eddy, Kit Kats.

Random assortment of old rock and R&B hits has a few, but not quite enough, rarities to make it worthwhile: Johnny C's "Boogaloo Down Broadway," the Showstoppers' "Ain't Nothin' but a House Party," Eddy's "Rebel Rouser" and Dale and Grace's "I'm Leaving It Up to You" are about the best of this spotty lot. — D.M.

★ ★ ★ ★ **Old Time Music at Newport—1963 / Van. (NA)**
Artists include: Doc Watson, Clarence Ashley, Jenes Cottrell, Dock Boggs, Maybelle Carter, Dorsey Ashley, Clinton Howard, Fred Price and Doc Watson.

Nice selection of mountain music from early-Sixties folk festival marks the reblossoming of Appalachian music. Carter's "Storms Are on the Ocean" is a wonder,

and the final Ashley-Howard-Price-Watson quartet features versions of "The Intoxicated Rat," "Wreck on the Highway" and "Weaveroom Blues" that capture the essential community feeling of the genre.
— D.M.

★ ★ ★ ★ **Once Upon a Time in the West (Soundtrack) / RCA (NA)**
Sergio Leone's fourth and final Western is a kind of cosmic Marxist view of life and death. Supposedly country rocker Gary Stewart's favorite album, this is composer Ennio Morricone at the height of his powers. He uses electric guitars in a way that slashes and bleeds, his orchestra is percussive in a manner akin to recent rock, and the evocative power of his compositions is alternately chilling and exultant. Leone's best film; Morricone's best score. — D.M.

★ ★ ★ **One Big Happy Family / Mango (NA)**
Artists include: Toots and the Maytals, Bob Marley, Burning Spear, Steel Pulse, I Jah Man and others.
A good sampler from Mango's reggae roster. Most of the cuts are easily obtained elsewhere except for the indispensable Burning Spear masterpiece "Social Living." — R.F.G.

★ ★ **One Flew Over the Cuckoo's Nest (Soundtrack) / Fan. (1976)**
Passable score by Jack Nitszche has too few electronic elements to qualify as rock, although the presence of the legendary Lonely Surfer and Spector arranger lends it some interest. — D.M.

★ ★ ★ **Original Golden Hits of the Great Groups / SSS (NA)**
Artists include: Ad Libs, Jelly Beans, Dixie Cups, Shangri-Las, Butterflys, Tradewinds.
But for the inclusion of the Tradewinds' "New York's a Lonely Town," this would be a decent sampler of girl-group records. The final track throws the focus off, not that the producers care. In this incoherent context, the two Shangri-Las songs—"Leader of the Pack" and "Remember (Walking in the Sand)"—and the Dixie Cups' set—"People Say," "Chapel of Love"—stand out. — D.M.

★ ★ ★ ★ **Original Greatest Gospel Hits / Gusto (1978)**
Artists include: Nightingales, Trumpeteers, Harmonizing Four, Consolers, Little Abraham Swanson, Alfred Bolden.

Rather minor but always invigorating collection of gospel tracks, the best of them by the Sensational Nightingales, who feature Reverend Julius Cheeks. Good notes and budget price make this one of better offers on current shelves. Gusto should be commended for keeping so much valuable material widely available; larger companies could learn a lesson from this smaller label. — D.M.

★ ★ ★ ★ **Original Memphis Rock and Roll / Sun (NA)**
Artists include: Carl Perkins, Carl Mann, Bill Justice, Carl McVoy, Warren Smith, Jerry Lee Lewis, Roy Orbison, Charlie Rich, Billy Lee Riley.
The only American Sun collection (in England, there are a dozen or more). The obvious items are here—Orbison's "Ooby Dooby" and Rich's "Lonely Weekends" to go with Lewis' "Whole Lotta Shakin' Goin' On" and "Great Balls of Fire" as well as Perkins' "Honey Don't" and "Blue Suede Shoes." But with a couple of exceptions (Riley's raucous "Red Hot" and Mann's "Mona Lisa"), the rest is pretty poorly chosen. — D.M.

★ ★ **Original New York Rock and Roll / SSS (NA)**
Artists include: Tradewinds, Evie Sands, Dixie Cups, Alvin Robinson, Ad Libs, Jelly Beans, Shangri-Las.
Weak selection of tracks from the old Shadow Morton production company, Red Bird Records. Shangri-Las' "Leader of the Pack" and the odd, snowbound surfer song, "New York's a Lonely Town" by the Tradewinds, are the best things here. But they're available in better company elsewhere. (Charly Records, the British label, has a pair of Red Bird collections that are much much better chosen and presented.) — D.M.

★ ★ **Original Rock and Roll / Power (NA)**
Artists include: Carl Perkins, Jimmy Clanton, Ad Libs, Roy Orbison.
Poorly packaged sampler. Only Clanton's "Just a Dream" is mildly obscure. Everything else is easily available elsewhere. — D.M.

★ ★ **Original Rock and Roll, Vol. 2 / Power (NA)**
Artists include: Platters, Boyd Bennett, Coasters, Bobby Lewis, Bill Doggett.
Another poorly packaged compilation— nothing special here. — D.M.

★ ★ ★ ★ Original Rock Oldies—Golden Hits, Vol. 1 / Spec. (NA)

Artists include: Little Richard, Larry Williams, Lloyd Price, Monotones, Sam Cooke, Johnnie and Joe, Arthur Lee Maye and the Crowns, Chimes, Tony Allen and the Champs, Don and Dewey.

First-rate collection of the label's Fifties hits, beautifully packaged. Richard's "Rip It Up" and "Long Tall Sally," Price's "Lawdy Miss Clawdy" and the Monotones' "Book of Love" are the best-known selections, but the other tracks are fine and Sam Cooke's very early pop single, "I'll Come Running Back to You," is a must for his fans. — D.M.

★ ★ ★ ★ Original Rock Oldies—Golden Hits, Vol. 2 / Spec. (NA)

Artists include: Little Richard, Tommy Tucker, Larry Williams, Tony Allen and the Champs, Don and Dewey, Clifton Chenier, Johnny Fuller, Chimes, Lloyd Price, Sam Cooke.

Not as stellar as the first set, but still solid. Richard is represented by "Good Golly Miss Molly" and "Lucille," Price by the less well-known "Baby Please Come Home," Don and Dewey by "Justine," Cooke by another early pop ballad, "Forever." But the highlight is one of the most outrageous hits ever made, Tommy Tucker's "High-Heeled Sneakers," an invitation to transvestism (I guess). — D.M.

★ ★ Original Surfin' Hits / Cres. (NA)

Artists include: Sentinals, Rhythm Kings, Soul Kings, Jim Waller and the Deltas, Bob Vaught and the Renegaids, Dave Myers and the Surftones, Breakers.

Very minor surf music. You have to still love *Gidget* movies and lust in your heart after Annette Funicello to have any desire to hear these. — D.M.

★ ★ Patty (Soundtrack) / Stang (NA)

Blaxploitation flick about you-know-who and the SLA. A couple of nice songs from the Moments and Chuck Jackson can't make this more than passable, however. — D.M.

★ Permanent Wave / Epic (NA)

Artists include: After the Fire, Kursaal Flyers, Cortinas, New Hearts, Diodes, Only Ones, Vibrators.

Bad anthology of new-wave tracks mixed with unrelated material for filler. — J.S.

★ Phantom of the Paradise (Soundtrack) / A&M (1975)

Brian De Palma's rock version of *The Phan-*

tom of the Opera was cinematically brilliant, but burdened with a stupefying Paul Williams score that rendered everything around it false. Here all you get is Williams' stupefaction, a miserable prospect; there is a kind of hatred for hard rock here that emerges as soured contempt. A competent performance by Jeffrey Commanor on a couple of oldies pastiches is all that keeps this one from biting the dust. — D.M.

★ ★ ★ ★ Philadelphia Classics / Phil. (1977)

Artists include: MFSB, Three Degrees, O'Jays, Harold Melvin and the Blue Notes, Intruders.

A better set than the label's *Greatest Hits,* largely because it includes the three or four earliest smashes they had: "TSOP" (MFSB), "I Love Music" (O'Jays), "I'll Always Love My Mama" (Intruders), "Bad Luck" (Melvin). And with that as a basis, this two-disc anthology can hardly miss. — D.M.

★ ★ ★ Piano Blues: 1927–1937 Stomp 'Em Down / Oldie (NA)

Artists include: James "Boodle It" Wiggins, Bob Call, Raymond Barrow, "Spider" Carter, Ell-Zee-Floyd, John Oscar, Joe Pullum, Walter (Cowboy) Washington.

Good collection of barrelhouse-to-ragtime piano playing by some minor but worthwhile players recorded between the late Twenties and the late Thirties. James "Boodle It" Wiggins delivers a version of the traditional "Keep a Knockin' an You Can't Get In." — J.S.

★ ★ ★ Pick Hits of the Radio Good Guys, Vol. 1 / Laur. (1964)

Artists include: Chiffons, Dimensions, Gary "U.S." Bonds, Passions, Dion, Randy and the Rainbows, Jarmels, Tokens, Mystics.

A spotty mid-Sixties period piece, before the disc jockey became such a figure of calculated hipness that his (or her) personality evaporated altogether. This is AM music, and some of it (Bonds' two songs, the Mystics' "Hushabye," the Jarmels' "A Little Bit of Soap" and, of course, Dion and the Chiffons) is the best kind of Top Forty sound. Some of it isn't too good and all of it is available in better-produced packages, though the cover is quaint. — D.M.

★ ★ ★ ★ ★ Please Warm My Weiner / Yazoo (NA)

Artists include: Whistling Bob Howe and Frankie Griggs, Georgia Tom and Tampa Red, Hokum Boys, Butterbeans and Susie, Yazoo All Stars, Memphis Minnie, Bo Carter.

Hilarious sides of the bawdiest hokum blues sides ever recorded. R. Crumb artwork is most appropriate. — J.S.

★ ★ **Porgy and Bess / RCA (NA)**
A great idea: get Ray Charles to sing the male lead of Gershwin's great operetta. It went wrong when Cleo Laine, a white British jazz singer with a stilted demeanor, was picked to play Bess. With Sarah Vaughan, Ella Fitzgerald and, to pick randomly but more wisely, Aretha Franklin still living, that's like asking Helen Reddy to play Superfly's girlfriend. For Charles fanatics only. — D.M.

★ ★ ★ ★ ★ **Powerhouse for God: Sacred Speech Chant and Song in an Appalachian Baptist Church / University of North Carolina Press (1982)**
One of the greatest documentary recordings ever made. Scholar Jeff Todd Titon spent five years with the congregation of the Fellowship Independent Baptist Church in Stanley, Virginia. What he emerged with is recordings of worship services, including altar calls and hymns beautifully sung by the membership and featuring vocals led by Reverend John Sherfey, one of the finest spiritual singers since Skip James. Also here is testimony, much of it moving, by Edith Cubbage and by Reverend Sherfey (side four is his life story). Marvelously packaged. You'll probably need to get it from the University of North Carolina Press directly: P.O. Box 2288, Chapel Hill, N.C. 27514. It's worth the effort, both for the gorgeous music and for the splendid honesty and eloquence of the testimony. — D.M.

★ ★ ★ ★ **Precious Lord (Great Gospel Songs of Thomas A. Dorsey) / Col. (NA)**
Artists include: Marion Williams, Alex Bradford, Sallie Martin, Dixie Hummingbirds, R. H. Harris, Bessie Griffin, Delois B. Campbell.
Dorsey was the greatest of the black gospel composers and this is a grand testament to the fact. Williams shines on "Take My Hand Precious Lord," "What Could I Do?" and three others; other important songs include "Hide Me in Thy Bosom," "Peace in the Valley," "Never Turn Back," "If You See My Savior," "Old Ship of Zion" and "My Desire." A nice supplement to Columbia's *Gospel Sound* collections. — D.M.

★ **The Progressives / Col. (NA)**
Artists include: Weather Report, Soft Machine, Charles Mingus, Don Ellis, Paul Win-
ter, Maynard Ferguson, John McLaughlin Mahavishnu Orchestra, Walter Carlos, Bill Evans, Ornette Coleman, Albert Dailey, Keith Jarrett.
Beware the record-company assessment of the avant-garde. I'd like someone to explain just what Don Ellis and John McLaughlin ultimately have in common, much less Paul Winter and Charles Mingus. Some good progressive stuff here, but if you're aware enough to tell the difference, you don't need this sampler. If you're not, it will only mislead you. — D.M.

★ **Propaganda / A&M (NA)**
Artists include: Granati Brothers, Joe Jackson, Police, Reds, Squeeze.
Bad new-wave anthology. — J.S.

★ ★ ★ **Pure Soul / Kent (NA)**
Artists include: B. B. King, Lowell Fulsom, Elmore James, Little Richard, Vernon and Jewell, Z. Z. Hill.
Pure nothing but still a pretty decent compilation. King, Fulsom and James play pretty much straight blues: King's "Eyesight to the Blind," a Sonny Boy Williamson song, Fulsom's "Black Nights" and James' "Dust My Blues" are all worth hearing. Richard and Hill, Vernon and Jewell are R&B (the former more properly rock & roll) artists. Nothing exceptional from them, unfortunately. — D.M.

★ ★ ★ **Ramblin' on My Mind (Train and Travel Blues) / Mile. (NA)**
Artists include: Johnny Young, Carl Hodges, Leroy Dallas, Jimmy Brewer, Honeyboy Edwards, Big Joe Williams, Connie Williams, Dr. Isaiah Ross, John Lee Granderson, Bill Jackson, Elijah Brown, W. B. "Piano Bill" Bryson.
Thematically organized anthology of minor blues performers. Has its moments. — D.M.

★ ★ **Rancho Deluxe (Soundtrack) / U.A. (NA)**
Modern cowboy flick for which country hippie Jimmy Buffett provided six songs, none of them terribly memorable. Fodder for the Buffett clique and no one else. So laid-back it doesn't have to prove it. — D.M.

★ ★ **Raw Blues / Lon. (NA)**
A hodgepodge of the label's blues repertoire: British performers like John Mayall and Eric Clapton plus some minor work by Otis Spann and Champion Jack Dupree. Nothing

special here that isn't more accessible in a better format somewhere else. — D.M.

★ ★ ★ ★ ★ **Rebel Music / Troj. (1980)**
Artists include: Dennis Brown, Gregory Isaacs, Bob Andy, the Heptones, Big Youth, U Roy, Peter Tosh, Derrick Harriott.

Another historical retrospective from Trojan, "Rebel Music" focuses on classic reggae, from late rocksteady to mid-Seventies rockers. The quality is stunningly high throughout—most of this sounds entirely fresh today. A few especially valuable tracks: Tosh's "Maga Dog," Isaacs' "Rock Away," Junior Byles' "Beat Down Babylon," and Dennis Brown's original "Money in My Pocket". — R.F.G.

★ ★ ★ ★ ★ **The Red Bird Story, Vol. 1: The Hit Factory / Charly (NA), Br. imp.**
Artists include: Shangri-Las, Dixie Cups, Ad Libs, Jelly Beans, Tradewinds, Sid Barnes, Sam Hawkins, Robbins.
★ ★ ★ **The Red Bird Story, Vol. 2: The New York Sound and the New Orleans Connection / Charly (NA), Br. imp.**
Artists include: Butterflies, Jeff and Ellie, "Shadow" Morton, Ad Libs, Robbins, Evie Sands, Dixie Cups, Alvin Robinson.

A pair of hit collections from the fine New York City Sixties label. Side one is a dominated by some of the finest girl group tracks ever cut, Shadow Morton's productions of the Shangri-Las, and the New Orleans whimsy of the Dixie Cups, with interesting genre items by the Ad Libs and Jelly Beans to fill it out. (There's also the great East Coast surf disc, "New York's a Lonely Town," by the Tradewinds.) Volume 2 is thinner, with only the Dixie Cups tracks up to the level of the best on the earlier set. But this does have "Iko Iko," which is a necessity in any well-rounded collection. — D.M.

★ ★ **Redneck Mothers / RCA (NA)**
Artists include: Johnny Russell, Gary Stewart, Willie Nelson, Steve Young, Bobby Bare, Tennessee Pulleybone, Jerry Reed, Vernon Oxford.

Country music for anthropologists. RCA apparently couldn't make up its mind about whether to fill this set out with more outlaw performers like Stewart, Nelson and Young or attempt to force a few of its more mainstream C&W artists like Bare and Reed into the mix, in hope of country-rock crossover. Aside from "Renegade Picker" and "Tobacco Road" by Young, Stewart's "Honky Tonkin' " and Bare's "Up Against the Wall,

Redneck Mother" (an outrageous hillbilly exploitation tune), slim pickin's around here. — D.M.

★ ★ ★ **Reggae Spectacular / A&M (NA)**
Artists include: Jimmy Cliff, Blue Haze, Bob and Marcia, Glen and Dave, Harry J. and the Allstars.

Pretty minor reggae, except Cliff's. And most of his tracks are better presented on *The Harder They Come* soundtrack, or his own LPs. — D.M.

★ ★ ★ **Remember How Great, Vol. 1 / Rou. (NA)**
Artists include: Heartbeats, Frankie Lymon, Flamingos, Fiesta, Monotones, Chuck Berry, Little Anthony and the Imperials, Lee Dorsey, Lee Anderson and the Hearts, Robert and Johnny, Etta James, Chantels.

Predictable assortment of Fifties hits, from hard rock (Berry) to doo-wop (Heartbeats, Monotones). Always nice to hear Lymon and Dorsey, but you can do better than this. — D.M.

★ ★ ★ **Remember How Great, Vol. 2 / Rou. (NA)**
Artists include: Moonglows, Frankie Lymon, Maurice Williams and the Zodiacs, Five Satins, Shirley and Lee, Coasters, Sonny Til, Billy Bland, Penguins, Bobby Freeman, Cadillacs.

Decent but predictable Fifties assortment. — D.M.

★ ★ ★ **Remember How Great, Vol. 3 / Rou. (NA)**
Artists include: Joe Jones, Silhouettes, Edsels, Wilbur Harrison, Don and Dee Dee Ford, Chantels, Coasters, Harptones, Drifters, Crests, Jerry Butler, Bo Diddley.

Another decent selection, this one with a few fairly obscure items: Don and Dee Dee Ford's "I Need Your Lovin' " is as pounding as any rock ever made, and the Harptones' "Sunday Kind of Love" is as smooth as good R&B gets. — D.M.

★ ★ ★ **Remember How Great, Vol. 4 / Rou. (NA)**
Artists include: Spaniels, Nutmegs, Flamingos, Mello Kings, Chantels, Dreamlovers, Little Anthony and the Imperials, Willows, Ben E. King, Dave "Baby" Cortez, Moonglows.

A little more coherent than the other volumes in the series, because it focuses on groups, except for King's grand "Don't Play That Song" and Cortez' awful "Happy Organ." The rest is solid enough but unexceptional. Chantels' "He's Gone" is a good one that doesn't pop up often. — D.M.

★ ★ ★ **Remember How Great, Vol. 5 / Rou. (NA)**
Artists include: Cleftones, Bobbettes, Chuck Berry, Ben E. King, King Curtis, Tempos, Ray Barretto, Dubs, Rays, Buddy Knox, Essex, Gloria Mann.

A few more oddities than the other volumes in the series, but still nothing truly exceptional. Worth noting are Barretto's "Watusi," to this day the only substantial salsa hit of the rock era, and the Essex's "Easier Said Than Done." — D.M.

★ ★ ★ **Rhythm and Rock: The Best of Chess, Checker, Cadet / Chess (1981), Br. imp.**
Artists include: Little Tommy Tucker, Clarence Henry, Dale Hawkins, Bo Diddley, Jackie Brenston, Ko Ko Taylor, Dave Baby Cortez, Chuck Berry, Jimmy McCarklin, Eddie Fontaine, Rusty York, Little Walter.

Very fine selection of mostly R&B sides from the Chicago group of labels. Highlights include Tucker's hit version of "High-Heeled Sneakers," Henry's "Ain't Got No Home," "Suzie Q" (Hawkins), "Rocket 88" (Brenston), "Wang Dang Doodle" (Taylor) and "My Babe" (Walter), plus, of course, the Berry and Diddley numbers. Well worth digging up. — D.M.

★ ★ ★ ★ ★ **Rhythm of Resistance (Soundtrack) / Virgin (1978), imp.**
Artists include: Babsy Mlangeni, Malombo, Mparanyana and the Cannibals, Ladysmith Black Mambazo, Jonny and Sipho, Mahotella Queens, Abafana Baseqhudeni.

Movie soundtrack is a tribute to the black liberation struggle in apartheid South Africa. Among several gems, these are diamonds in the rough: "Inkunzi Ayi Hlabi Ngokusima" by Jonny and Sipho, "Igula Lamasi" by Mahotella Queens and "Ubu Gowele" by Abafana Baseqhudeni. Yet another album in David Byrne's touring collection of ethnic music. — ML.H.

★ ★ ★ ★ ★ **Risky Blues / King (NA)**
Artists include: Bull Moose Jackson, Wynonie Harris, the Dominoes, the Swallows, Eddie "Lockjaw" Davis.

Gems from the King vault, all with frankly sexual themes: Jackson's "Big Ten Inch Record"; Harris' "Keep On Churnin' "; the Swallows' "It Ain't the Meat"; the Dominoes' "Sixty Minute Man." — J.S.

★ ★ **Roadie (Soundtrack) / War. (1980)**
Artists include: Cheap Trick, Pat Benatar, Joe Ely, Alice Cooper, Teddy Pendergrass, Eddie Rabbitt, Styx, Blondie.

Music-biz movie soundtrack with very little to recommend it. — J.S.

★ ★ ★ ★ **Rockabilly Stars, Vol. 1 / Epic (1981)**
Artists include: Town Hall Party, Everly Brothers, Little Jimmy Dickens, Marty Robbins, Johnny Horton, Collins Kids, Billy Brown, Carl Perkins, Link Wray, Ersel Hickey, Carl Smith, Scotty Moore, Bob Luman, Mac Curtis, Johnny Cash, Allan Rich, Mickey Gilley, Charlie Rich.

★ ★ ★ **Rockabilly Stars, Vol. 2 / Epic (1981)**
Artists include: Collins Kids, Everly Brothers, Sid King and the Five Strings, Little Jimmy Dickens, Carl Perkins, Lorrie Collins, Larry Collins, Ronnie Self, Link Wray, Sleepy LaBeef, Rick Nelson, Billy Lee Riley, Bob Luman, Johnny Cash, Mickey Gilley.

★ ★ ★ **Rockabilly Stars, Vol. 3 / Epic (1982)**
Artists include: Little Jimmy Dickens, Everly Brothers, Collins Kids, Joe Maphis and Larry Collins, Ronnie Self, John D. Loudermilk, Johnny Cash, Jimmy Murphy, Cliff Johnson, Johnny Horton, Onie Wheeler, Rose Maddox, Jaycee Hill, Carl Perkins, Sid King and the Five Strings, Werly Fairburn, Bobby Lord, Lorrie Collins, Leon Smith.

The problem with these sets is that their definition of rockabilly is far too broad. The Carl Perkins and Charlie Rich tracks were made late in their careers, and have little musical resemblance to rockabilly. Marty Robbins was poaching on Elvis' turf from the beginning, smoothing all the nuances over. Mickey Gilley has never been closer to rockabilly than his genetic relationship to Jerry Lee Lewis.

That out of the way, there are some interesting pieces here. Volume 1 has a certified masterpiece, Charlie Rich's beautiful blues, "Feel Like Going Home," a solo Scotty Moore workout on "Milk Cow Blues," and Link Wray's "Raw Hide," as well as a couple of legitimate rockabilly efforts by the Collins Kids and the Everly Brothers' "The Sun Keeps Shining." There's also Ersel Hickey's original "Bluebirds over the Mountain," not as good as the Beach Boys version (or the picture of Hickey that's on the cover).

Volume 2 is notable mostly for an abundance of Collins Kids numbers (also available on a separate Collins Kids LP).

"Keep a Lovin' Me" (Everlys), "I Got a Thing about You Baby" (Billy Lee Riley, creating a model for Elvis Presley) and the pair of Wray numbers are also worth a listen.

Volume 3 features more good stuff from the Everlys and Collinses, John D. Loudermilk's original of "Tobacco Road," a nice Rose Maddox track and Leon Smith's "Little Forty Ford." It also contains the most previously unissued material of the series. — D.M.

■ **Rock and Roll: Evolution or Revolution? / Laur. (NA)**
Given this kind of documentary, is there anyone out there who can't answer the question? Positive proof that the Sixties weren't entirely golden. — D.M.

★ ★ ★ **Rock and Roll Festival, Vol. 1 / Kent (NA)**
Artists include: Little Richard, Joe Houston, Etta James, B. B. King, Ike and Tina Turner, Cadettes, Ikettes, Jacks, Elmore James, Shirley Gunter and the Queens, Teen Queens, Oscar McLollie, Marvin and Johnny, Jessie Belvin.

Most of the more familiar names here are represented by their most familiar tracks. James' and King's tracks, in fact, are their signature songs, "Dust My Blues" and "Rock Me Baby" respectively. Worth noting: "Cherry Pie" by Marvin and Johnny, "Convicted" by McLollie and "Oop Shoop" by Gunter. Good set with a smattering of the unusual. — D.M.

★ ★ ★ **Rock and Roll Is Here to Stay / Gusto (NA)**
Artists include: Danny and the Juniors, Bill Haley and the Comets, Gary U.S. Bonds, Dobie Gray, American Breed, Classics IV, Kingsmen.

Oldies anthology with few clinkers and some gems, like "Louie Louie," "See You Later Alligator," the title track, "Quarter to Three," "Traces" and "Drift Away." — J.S.

★ ★ ★ **Rock and Roll Show / Gusto (NA)**
Artists include: Bill Doggett, Chuck Berry, Sammy Turner, Jerry Lee Lewis, Moonglows, Billy Ward and the Dominoes, Screamin' Jay Hawkins, Coasters, Frankie Ford.

Nothing terribly rare here, but Berry and Lewis are well represented (two tracks each of their original hits), and the Moonglows, Ford, Coasters, Hawkins and Dominoes tracks are all their best. Only Doggett's "Honky Tonk" and "Lavender Blue" by Turner seem minor. — D.M.

★ ★ ★ ★ **Rock and Roll Show / Gusto (NA)**
Artists include: Bill Doggett, Chuck Berry, Jerry Lee Lewis, Moonglows, Coasters, Frankie Ford, Screamin' Jay Hawkins.

Great collection of Fifties classics includes "Honky Tonk," "Sweet Little Sixteen," "Great Balls of Fire," "Reelin' and Rockin'," "Whole Lotta Shakin' Goin' On," "Roll Over Beethoven," "I Put a Spell on You," "Charlie Brown," "Sea Cruise." — J.S.

★ ★ ★ ★ ★ **Rockers / Mango (1979)**
Artists include: Inner Circle, Mighty Maytones, Junior Murvin, Heptones, Peter Tosh, Jacob Miller, Junior Byles, Bunny Wailer, Gregory Isaacs, Rockers All Stars, Kiddus I, Burning Spear, Third World, Justin Hines and the Dominoes.

The film *Rockers* operated in the tragicomic realm of everyday ghetto life in contrast to the myth-making of the first reggae film *The Harder They Come*. The *Rockers* soundtrack one-ups its most worthy predecessor with more material (sixteen tracks), uniformly excellent selection (including stand-outs by Junior Byles, Kiddus I, Mighty Maytones, Bunny Wailer and the otherwise unavailable a capella version of Spear's "Jah No Dead") and programing (side two plays like a song cycle). An essential overview/introduction to contemporary reggae. — R.F.G.

★ **Rock Guitar Greats, Vol. 1 / Sp. (NA)**
Artists include: Jimi Hendrix, Eric Clapton, Jimmy Page, Sonny Boy Williamson, Jeff Beck.

It will come as news to Williamson's admirers that the master blues harpist is a guitar great as well. But this sleazy ripoff, which contains the most mediocre material done by each performer, is hardly the place to find out about it. Williamson is actually represented on some tracks cut with Clapton's Yardbirds in England. The rest are outtakes that should have stayed that way. — D.M.

★ **Rock Guitar Greats, Vol. 2 / Sp. (NA)**
Artists include: Eric Clapton, Jeff Beck, Rory Gallagher, Stevie Winwood, Jimi Hendrix, Jimmy Page and Sonny Boy Williamson, Ron Wood and the Faces.

More outtakes from diverse sources. Wood's "Collibosher" with the Faces may have been the worst thing they ever recorded; Beck's "New York City Blues" is the Yardbirds retitled and so forth. The Hendrix selection is a real atrocity. — D.M.

★ ★ ★ **Rock 'n' Roll High School (Soundtrack) / Sire (1979)**
Artists include: Ramones, Brian Eno, Nick Lowe, Devo, Eddie and the Hot Rods, Brownsville Station, Chuck Berry, Alice Cooper.

Once you get past the punk-rock hook, this is a great collection of songs with school-related themes, like Berry's "School Days," Cooper's "School's Out" and Brownsville Station's "Smoking in the Boys Room." — J.S.

★ ★ ★ **Rock-O-Rama, Vol. 1 / Abkco (NA)**
Artists include: Chubby Checker, Tymes, Orlons, Bobby Rydell, Dee Dee Sharp, Question Mark and the Mysterians, Charlie Gracie, Terry Knight and the Pack, Dovells, Rays.

Erratic collection from the Cameo-Parkway label, which Abkco owner Allen Klein now controls. This ranges from Rydell's dismal teen-idol schlock to Checker's twist hits, the minor girl-group dance hits of the Orlons and Sharp to such punk classics as Question Mark's "96 Tears," and Dovells' boisterous "You Can't Sit Down." Not bad, altogether. — D.M.

★ ★ **Rock-O-Rama, Vol. 2 / Abkco (NA)**
Artists include: Bobby Rydell, Dovells, Tymes, Orlons, Dee Dee Sharp, Chubby Checker, Zacherle, Candy and the Kisses, Charlie Gracie, Question Mark and the Mysterians, Don Covay, Jo Ann Campbell.

Much weaker than Volume 1 of this series and equally uneven. The good Dovells, Question Mark and Checker tracks appear on the other set; Rydell contributes even more limp work. Highlight: Zacherle's "Dinner with Drac," which is better than "Monster Mash." Lowlife: Campbell's "The Girl from Wolverton Mountain," a truly horrid novelty. — D.M.

★ ★ ★ **Rock's World Revolution: The Roots / Legr. (1979)**
Artists include: Gary "U.S." Bonds, Frank Guida and the Swedish All Star Orchestra, Jimmy Soul, Gregory Cafone, Church Street Five, Tommy Facenda, Lenis Guess.

Useful largely if you don't have any Bonds sides (this has "New Orleans," "School Is Out," "Dear Lady Twist" and the inevitable "Quarter to Three'), or if you want to hear "Nite with Daddy G," the Church Street

Five disc Bonds wails about (and sings over) in the inevitable one. — D.M.

★ **Rock Vocal Greats / Sp. (NA)**
Artists include: Jimi Hendrix, Jeff Beck and the Yardbirds, Animals, featuring Eric Burdon, Jack Bruce/Ginger Baker/Dick Heckstal, Gregg and Duane Allman, Rod Stewart, Stevie Winwood and the Spencer Davis Group, Rory Gallagher.

Some great names make some lousy music. Beck isn't even the vocalist on his track. Hendrix, Animals, Allmans and Stewart are all shown at their very worst. — D.M.

★ ★ **Rocky (Soundtrack) / U.A. (1977)**
Included mostly because soundtrack composer Bill Conti's theme song, "Gonna Fly Now," became a catchy 1977 hit. But nothing much but mush for the rest of it. The story is a good rock-star-type fable, though. Might have made an interesting Elvis vehicle—there was a guy who could take a punch. — D.M.

■ **Roller Boogie / Casa. (NA)**
Artists include: Cher, Johnnie Coolrock, Mavis Vegas Davis, Earth, Wind and Fire, Bob Esty.

Soundtrack for a bad roller-disco movie. — J.S.

★ **Roots of Rock / Ev. (NA)**
Artists include: Jimi Hendrix, Little Richard.

Mediocre assortment of rerecorded Richard tracks and Hendrix halfway humiliating himself doing "Lawdy Miss Clawdy." Forget it. — D.M.

★ ★ ★ ★ ★ **The Roots of Rock and Roll / Savoy (NA)**
Artists include: Wild Bill Moore, Paul Williams, Hal Singer, "Big Jay" McNeely, Sam Price, Johnny Otis, Nappy Brown, Huey "Piano" Smith, Varetta Dillard, Big Maybelle, Ravens, Clarence Palmer and the Jive Bombers, Luther Bond and the Emeralds.

Wonderful selection of late-Forties and early-Fifties R&B hits shows the development of R&B styles toward something identifiable as rock & roll. (Smith's "You Make Me Cry" and Maybelle's "Candy" are very close to rock, indeed.) There is an accent on sax performers here—McNeely, Moore and Price are some of the best honkers of the era. Williams' "The Hucklebuck" kicked off an early rock-style dance fad, the Ravens was one of the seminal vocal groups of the period (inspiring a variety of other groups to name themselves after birds), and Moore's "We're Gonna Rock, We're Gonna Roll" is one of rock's earlier anthems. Excellent annotation. (Since 1978, Savoy has released ten more titles in this series.) — D.M.

★ ★ ★ **Roxy London WC2 (January–April 1977) / EMI (NA)**
Artists include: Johnny Moped, Eater, X-Ray Spex, Buzzcocks, Slaughter and the Dogs, Unwanted, Wire, Adverts.
Selection of live tracks from the London punk club that only existed during the period indicated. Some of the genre's best groups—X-Ray Spex, Buzzcocks, Wire, Adverts—are represented, although everyone else is generally unworthy of vinyl. Check X-Ray's "Oh, Bondage, Up Yours" for a kick. — D.M.

★ **RSO Chartbusters / RSO (NA)**
Artists include: Andy Gibb, Player, John Stewart, Yvonne Elliman, Frankie Valli.
Bad Seventies AOR anthology. — J.S.

★ ★ ★ **Rural Blues / Fan. (NA)**
Artists include: Robert Pete Williams, Snooks Eaglin.
Selection of tracks, originally done for Prestige, by two minor country bluesmen. Interesting for blues fans. — D.M.

★ ★ ★ ★ **San Francisco Blues Festival, Vols. 1–3 / Solid S. (1981)**
Artists include: Roy Brown, Lowell Fulson, Jimmy Rogers, Phillip Walker, Isaac Scott, Big Mama Thornton, Little Joe Blue, Sugar Pie DeSanto.
Good collections of live recordings from the Bay Area's active blues festival. Volume 1, which features a side each of Fulson and Brown, is the best. — J.S.

★ ★ **Saturday Night Disco / De-Lite (NA)**
Artists include: Made in U.S.A., Crown Heights Affair, Kool and the Gang, Kay Gees.
Saturday Night Fever cash-in attempt. Kool's "Open Sesame" is a hot track, but the rest is nothing special. — D.M.

★ ★ ★ ★ ★ **Saturday Night Fever (Soundtrack) / RSO (1977)**
Artists include: Bee Gees, Yvonne Elliman, Walter Murphy, Tavares, David Shire, Kool and the Gang, Ralph McDonald, K.C. and the Sunshine Band, MFSB, Trammps.
This set sold about 15 million copies in 1977 and 1978, so chances are you've heard of it, at least. Truth to tell, it dispels a lot of foolish notions about disco: this is a fabulous pop album, with great warmth, and very little of it is mechanistic (with the exception of David Shire's background music, and even that's atmospheric enough to work). Most of the best moments belong to the Bee Gees— "Stayin' Alive" would be a classic in any idiom—but the Trammps' "Disco Inferno" is the single most propulsive track here. Does for the Seventies what *Woodstock* did for the Sixties: defines an era's taste, and celebrates it. — D.M.

★ ★ ★ **Saturday Night Pogo / Rhino (NA)**
Artists include: Winos, Berlin Brats, Droogs, Needles and Pins, Motels, Vom, Low Numbers, Dogs, Young Republicans, Daddy Maxfield.
Pretty funny anthology of L.A. punk bands. — J.S.

★ ★ ★ **Seattle Syndrome / Engram Records (1981)**
Artists include: X-15, the Pudz, Student Nurse, the Beakers, Jim Basnight, the Fastbacks, the Refuzors, the Fartz, the 88's, Blackouts, the Macs, Phillipo Scrooge, K7SS, Savant, Body Falling Downstairs.
Compilation of fifteen Seattle bands that at least indicates regional experiments in pop equal to much-fawned-over U.K. provincial output. Material stretches from inevitable Talking Headom to Eno ambient doodlings through the low-rent heavy-metal suburb of the Eighties, punk. Best cuts: X-15's "Vaporized," sf Bowie; Blackouts' "Young Man," alienation à la Medium, Medium; twerp power pop of "We'll Always Be in Love" and deranged rockabilly boogie "Party 88." Student Nurse (represented here by "Discover Your Feet") became something of a New York dance club cult item during the summer of 1981. — G.A.

★ ★ ★ **The Secret Policeman's Ball / Is. (1980)**
Artists include: John Cleese, Peter Cook, Billy Connolly, Michael Palin, Terry Jones, Eleanor Bron, John Fortune, Rowan Atkinson.
★ ★ ★ **The Secret Policeman's Ball: The Music / Is. (1980)**
Artists include: Pete Townshend, Tom Robinson, Neil Innes, John Williams, Pete Townshend and John Williams.
★ ★ ★ **The Secret Policeman's Other Ball / Is. (1982)**
Artists include: Sting, Jeff Beck and Eric Clapton, Bob Geldof and Johnny Fingers, Phil Collins, Donovan, the Secret Police.
Beware the first album listed—unless you're terminally addicted to British come-

dy. Connolly is gross enough to translate (except that his damn Scots accent is so thick), Palin, Cleese and Jones are familiar to Python bits, and all are better seen than heard. *The Music* is probably what you want, at least if you're a Townshend fan, since it includes not only his duet with Williams on "Won't Get Fooled Again" but also "Drowned" and "Pinball Wizard" as solo acoustic pieces. But in the end this is really just for fanatics of a different stripe.

The best music here may be on *Other Ball*, which features a clashing raveup between Beck and Clapton, Sting doing to "Roxanne" and "Message in a Bottle" roughly what Townshend does for his chestnuts, and Geldof trying to do the same for "I Don't Like Mondays." Even Collins isn't bad.   — D.M.

■ **Sgt. Pepper's Lonely Hearts Club Band (Soundtrack) / RSO (1978)**
Artists include: Peter Framptom, Aerosmith, Steve Martin, Bee Gees, George Burns, Earth Wind and Fire, Billy Preston, Alice Cooper, Sandy Fariña, Paul Nicholas, Frankie Howard, Dianne Steinberg, Stargard.

An utter travesty. The discovery, on screen, that there is no plot (except a kind of parboiled cross between *Magical Mystery Tour* and *Yellow Submarine*), that absolutely no one in the picture can act (*especially* not Frampton and the Bee Gees) and that the special-effects crew apparently worked with two tons of dry ice and a box of scotch tape pales next to the musical travesty perpetrated on the Beatles' most influential work. (Not all of the music comes from *Sgt. Pepper*, of course.) Aerosmith ("Come Together") and Earth, Wind and Fire ("Got to Get You into My Life") turn in passable performances, but that's no excuse for being involved with this holocaust. Two million people bought this album, which proves that P. T. Barnum was right and that euthanasia may have untapped possibilities. Easily the worst album of any notoriety in this book.   — D.M.

★ ★ ★ ★ ★ **Shagger's Delight / Ripete (1981)**
Artists include: Dominoes, Earl Bostic, Bill Doggett, Five Royales, Platters, Checkers, Sticks McGhee, Platters, Lamplighters, Kingpins.

Because it features hard-core R&B of the Fifties, most of it fairly unfamiliar, this is probably the best of Ripete's anthologies of "beach music," the gritty but lightly danceable soul preferred by drunken frat boys on the lower eastern seaboard. If you can dig the Royales' "Monkey Hips and Rice," the Dominoes' "Sixty Minute Man," McGhee's "Jungle Juice" or the likes of "Good Rockin' Tonight" in Harris' great version, you'll love this. And if not, are you sure you're in the right book?   — D.M.

★ **Sheba, Baby (Soundtrack) / Bud. (NA)**
Van McCoy score for mediocre blaxploitation flick features a few tracks by Barbara Mason and Monk Higgins, none of which rises to the level of listenability.   — D.M.

★ ★ ★ **Six Pak, Vol. 1 / Lone (NA)**
Artists include: Willie Nelson, Ray Wylie Hubbard, Cooder Browne, Don Bowman, Steve Fromholz, Geezinslaw Brothers.

Collection of so-called outlaw country artists fares better at the hands of Nelson's Lone Star label than through a big corporation: these guys now seem like friends rather than freaks. The highlights, in addition to Willie's two songs, are Hubbard's "Up Against the Wall, Redneck Mother" and Fromholz' "Heroes" and "Fool's Gold," although Don Bowman's "Willon and Waylee" will give country-outlaw initiates a smile.   — D.M.

★ ★ ★ ★ **Sixteen Greatest Original Bluegrass Hits / Star. (1977)**
Artists include: Flatt and Scruggs, Stanley Brothers, Buzz Busby, Jimmy Martin and Bob Osborne, Carly Story, Bill Clifton, Hylo Brown, New Grass Revival, Charlie Monroe, Jim and Jessie, Moore and Napier, Jim Eanes, Country Gentlemen, Mac Wiseman, Stonemans, Reno and Smiley.

Not quite what it claims—these songs cover sixteen artists, and none of them is named Bill Monroe, for one thing—but for the most part a solid collection nonetheless. Good set for beginners, though *Thirty Years of Bluegrass* is better.   — D.M.

★ ★ **Sixteen Rock Guitar Greats / Trip (NA)**
Artists include: Jimi Hendrix, Jeff Beck, Yardbirds, Rory Gallagher, Ron Wood and the Faces, Spencer Davis Group, Lonnie Mack, Big Bill Broonzy, Elmore James, Arthur "Big Boy" Crudup, Canned Heat, Jimmy Page and Sonny Boy Williamson.

Sometimes dire, sometimes excellent sampler of tracks from a variety of performers not all of whom—Crudup, James and Broonzy, for instance—are rockers. The Page and Williamson, Wood and Faces, and unfortunately, Hendrix tracks are poor. The Yardbirds—from the Eric Clapton era—are strong. Gallagher is his usual rollicking self, and the Spencer Davis version of "Dimples" is one of vocalist Stevie Winwood's finest moments, though it has nothing to do with guitar playing. — D.M.

★ ★ **Sixteen Rock Vocal Greats / Trip (NA)**
Artists include: Rod Stewart, Long John Baldry, Spencer Davis Group, Yardbirds, Rory Gallagher, Jimi Hendrix, Brian Auger, Cream, Liverpool Roadrunners, James Taylor, Animals.

A few gems, much dross. Stewart's tracks are wretched; Baldry may be the most overrated of all the obscure English singers; the Davis tracks pop up on almost every Trip and Springboard anthology, a distinction of which their mild virtues are hardly worthy; Taylor's work is from his pre-Apple career. The Animals, Yardbirds, Cream and Gallagher aren't bad, Auger is acceptable, and Hendrix gets a halfway decent treatment, thanks to the inclusion of his "Red House" blues. — D.M.

★ ★ ★ **Sixty Years of Country Music / RCA (1982)**
Artists include: Henry Gilliland and A. C. "Eck" Robertson, Vernon Dalhart, Jimmie Rodgers, Carter Family, Montana Slim, Milton Brown and His Musical Brownies, Bill Boyd and His Cowboy Ramblers, Blue Sky Boys, Hackberry Ramblers, Bill Monroe and His Blue Grass Boys, Elton Britt, Sons of the Pioneers, Hank Snow and His Rainbow Ranch Boys, Elvis Presley, Don Gibson, Jim Reeves, Chet Atkins, Eddy Arnold, Jerry Reed, Charley Pride, Waylon Jennings, Dolly Parton, Ronnie Milsap, Alabama.

A nice complement to the *Smithsonian Collection of Classic Country Music*, especially since it ranges so far back (to "Arkansas Traveler" by Robertson and Gilliland, "The Prisoner's Song" by Dalhart and the Rodgers and Carter tracks). Every genre is represented, bluegrass especially well, and the inclusion of Presley, Jennings and Parton gives a much clearer picture of the best contemporary country approaches than the Smithsonian set does. — D.M.

★ **Skateboard (Soundtrack) / RCA (NA)**
Exploitation film about the skateboard craze that infected late-Seventies' teenagers produces exploitation music aimed at same market, only less effectively. — D.M.

■ **Skatetown U.S.A. (Soundtrack) / Col. (NA)**
Artists include: Dave Mason, Heatwave, John Sebastian.
More music to roller-disco by. — J.S.

★ ★ ★ ★ **Sly and Robbie Present Taxi / Is. (1981)**
Artists include: Jimmy Riley, Tamlins, Junior Delgado, Dennis Brown, Sly Dunbar, Wailing Souls, Black Uhuru, General Echo, Gregory Isaacs, Viceroys.

A dozen hot reggae productions by top team of Sly Dunbar and Robbie Shakespeare. Highlights are "Sweet Sugar Plum" and "Old Broom" (Wailing Souls), "Heart Made of Stone" (Viceroys) and "Oh What a Feeling" (Isaacs). — D.M.

★ ★ ★ ★ ★ **The Smithsonian Collection of Classic Country Music / Smithsonian (1981)**
Artists include: A. C. "Eck" Robertson, Fiddlin' John Carson, Grayson and Whittier, Uncle Dave Macon and His Fruit Jar Drinkers, Vernon Dalhart, Charlie Poole with the North Carolina Ramblers, Gid Tanner and His Skillet-Lickers, Smith's Sacred Singers, East Texas Serenaders, Darby and Tarlton, Buell Kazee, Bradley Kincaid, Carl T. Sprague, Ernest V. Stoneman, Carter Family, Jimmie Rodgers, Arthur Smith, Riley Puckett, Cliff Carlisle and His Buckle Busters, Coon Creek Girls, Mac and Bob, Callahan Brothers, Blue Sky Boys, Delmore Brothers, Monroe Brothers, Rouse Brothers, Red Foley, Karl and Harty, Lulu Belle and Scotty, J. E. Mainer's Mountaineers, Rex Griffin, Roy Acuff, Gene Autry and Jimmy Long, Sons of the Pioneers, Patsy Montana and the Prairie Ramblers, Montana Slim, Stuart Hamblen and His Covered Wagon Jubilee, W. Lee O'Daniel and His Light Crust Doughboys with Leon Huff, Shelton Brothers, Jimmie Davis, Bill Boyd and His Cowboy Ramblers, Milton Brown and His Brownies, Bob Wills and His Texas Playboys, Leo Soileau and His Three Aces, Woody Guthrie, Chuck Wagon Gang, Cliff Bruner's Texas Wanderers, Ernest Tubb, Wiley Walker and Gene Sullivan, Ted Daffan's Texans, Elton Britt, Al Dexter and His Troopers, Tex Ritter, Molly O'Day and the Cumberland Mountain Folks, Jack Guthrie and His Oklahomans, Bailes Brothers, Gene Autry, Merle Travis, Eddy Arnold, Tex Williams and His Western Caravan, Johnny and Jack and Their Tennessee Mountain Boys, Jimmy Dickens, Maddox Brothers and Rose, Red Foley, Grandpa Jones, Cowboy Copas, Moon Mullican and the Showboys, Slim Whitman, Hank Snow and His Rainbow Ranch Boys, Leon Payne, Pee Wee King and His Golden West Cowboys, Martha Carson, Floyd Tillman, Lefty Frizzell, Carl Smith, Hank Thompson and His Brazos Valley Boys, Kitty Wells, Wilma Lee and Stoney Cooper with Their Clinch Mountain Clan,

Hank Williams, Chet Atkins, Webb Pierce, Johnny Cash, Tennessee Ernie Ford, Everly Brothers, Jim Reeves, Ray Price, Bobby Helms, Louvin Brothers, Johnny Horton, Marty Robbins, Rusty and Doug, Patsy Cline, Buck Owens, George Jones and Melba Montgomery, Bill Monroe and His Blue Grass Boys, Flatt and Scruggs, Stanley Brothers, Mac Wiseman, Jim and Jesse and the Virginia Boys, Osborne Brothers, Bill Clifton and His Dixie Mountain Boys, Reno and Smiley, Lilly Brothers, Hylo Brown, Jimmy Martin and the Sunny Mountain Boys, Kenny Baker, Doc Watson, Charlie Moore and the Dixie Partners, Cliff Waldron and the New Shades of Grass, Country Gentlemen, Seldom Scene, Dave Dudley, Bobby Bare, Porter Wagoner, Roger Miller, Charley Pride, Tom T. Hall, Dolly Parton, Merle Haggard, Loretta Lynn, Tammy Wynette, George Jones, Moe Bandy, Flying Burrito Brothers, Willie Nelson.

To call this eight-disc compilation ambitious is to understate the case considerably. It is the most far-ranging and thoroughly researched package of American vocal music ever issued, and by and large a complete success. One might quibble here and there: How Elvis Presley and Jerry Lee Lewis can be omitted when not only the Everly Brothers but even the Flying Burrito Brothers are included is a mystery, and especially since some countrypolitan performers (Pride, Horton, Reeves) seem no less marginal to the development of the pure genre. Maybe annotator Bill Malone is having some latter-day revenge against the rockabilly spearhead that almost fatally wounded country in the late Fifties? In any event, both annotation and sound quality are superb, and this is well worth whatever it takes or costs to get hold of it. — D.M.

★ **Smokey and the Bandit (Soundtrack) / MCA (NA)**
This Burt Reynolds film produced a score with some barely passable Jerry Reed and Bill Justis country songs and a lot of incidental CB dialogue. — D.M.

★ ★ ★ ★ **Solar Galaxy of Stars Live / Solar (NA)**
Artists include: Whispers, Shalimar, Lakeside, Dynasty.
Excellent anthology, especially worthwhile for the Whispers tracks. — J.S.

★ ★ ★ ★ **Solar's Greatest Hits / Solar (1982)**

Artists include: Whispers, Shalamar, Carrie Lucas, Lakeside, Dynasty.
Representative selection of Dick Griffey label's contemporary soul hits. The real maestro would seem to be producer Leon Sylvers III, however. Side one is seamless, but side two weakens on just those tracks where Sylvers didn't work. — D.M.

★ ★ ★ **Sorcerer (Soundtrack) / MCA (NA)**
Tangerine Dream's score for William Friedkin's film noir mistake is much more affecting on the screen, but serviceable on disc for fans of electronic improvisations. — D.M.

★ ★ ★ ★ **Soul Deep, Vol. 1 / Atl. (1981), Jap. imp.**
Artists include: James Carr, Rozetta Johnson, Peggy Scott and Jo Jo Benson, C. P. Love, Jackie Moore, Z. Z. Hill, Percy Sledge, Dee Dee Warwick, Judy Clay, Otis Clay, Mighty Sam, J. P. Robinson.
More Sixties vintage soul from the Japanese revival. The highlights are fairly numerous, though nothing will be of much interest to the uninitiated. Still, "Hold On" (Carr), "Cover Me" (Moore), "(Home Just Ain't Home At) Suppertime" (Hill), "Faithful and True" (Sledge) and two female responses to male classics, Warwick's "Suspicious Minds" and Judy Clay's "Sister Pitiful," are well worth a listen. — D.M.

★ ★ ★ **Soul Gold / SSS (NA)**
Artists include: Mickey Murray, Johnny Adams, Sil Austin, Johnny Soul, Betty Harris.
Interesting collection of R&B hits, highlighted by Murray's "Shout Bamalama." — J.S.

★ ★ ★ ★ **Soul to Soul / Tad's (1979)**
Artists include: Barry Brown, Rod Taylor, Ranking Barnabas, Carlton Livingston, Horace Andy.
A solid collection of hard, dub-style productions of vocalists, and DJs—strictly dance-hall-style reggae. Georgi McKay's "Money Money" and Ranking Barnabas' "Whip Them" are worth the price of the LP alone, but there are no weak cuts. — R.F.G.

★ ★ ★ ★ **Soul Years / Atl. (NA)**
Artists include: LaVern Baker, Booker T. and the MGs, Ray Charles, Drifters, Aretha Franklin, Clovers, Coasters, Otis Redding, Spinners, Brook Benton, Bobbettes, Ruth Brown, Solomon Burke, Clarence Carter, Chords, Wilson Pickett, King Floyd, Ivory Joe Hunter, Sam and Dave, "Stick" McGhee,

Percy Sledge, Joe Tex, Joe Turner, Chuck Willis, Betty Wright.

While this hardly makes up for the deletion of the great eight-volume *History of Rhythm and Blues,* which was superbly chosen and annotated, it's a nice two-disc overview of Atlantic's progress as this country's foremost (with Motown, anyway) black music label. It covers the Fifties in much detail—highlights include Willis' "C. C. Rider," Turner's groundbreaking "Shake, Rattle and Roll," Baker's "Tweedle Dee," "Money Honey" from the first Drifters, "Yakety Yak" by the Coasters. "One Mint Julep" by the Clovers, "Sh-Boom" by the Chords, and Hunter's "Since I Met You Baby," among others of that period, are also included. Its Sixties representatives are even more stellar: Franklin's "Respect" and "Natural Woman," Redding's "Dock of the Bay," the MGs' "Green Onions," Pickett's "In the Midnight Hour," "When a Man Loves a Woman" by Sledge, and Burke's "Just out of Reach," among others. The Seventies performances are more limited but still solid: King Floyd's "Groove Me," Wright's "Clean Up Woman" and the Spinners' "I'll Be Around."

Best of all, a chance to hear Ray Charles' "What'd I Say" and "I Got a Woman," which did more to popularize secular-gospel fusion than any other hits of the Fifties, and the Drifters' "There Goes My Baby," which introduced strings into R&B, paving the way for its development into soul music, and gave the wonderful Ben E. King his start.

A good set, lacking only organization (the sequence is scattered) and annotation to make it perfect. — D.M.

★ ★ **The Sounds of Asbury Park / Visa (NA)**
Artists include: Lord Gunner Group, Sonny Kenn and Friends, Ken Viola and Friends, Paul Whistler, Kog Nito and the Geeks, Lisa Lowell.

Collection of Asbury Park groups and musicians, some of whom predated Bruce Springsteen's identification with that town, but none of whom can overcome the temptation to sound too much like him, often with very embarrassing results. — J.S.

★ ★ ★ **Southbound / Van. (NA)**
Artists include: John Pilla, Merle Watson and Doc Watson, Doc Watson.

Good album of old-timey guitar playing. Doc Watson is the best there is at it, and Pilla is his protégé, Merle is his son. — D.M.

★ ★ ★ **South's Greatest Hits, Vol. 1 / Capri. (1977)**
Artists include: Allman Brothers Band, Charlie Daniels, Elvin Bishop, Outlaws, Marshall Tucker Band, Gregg Allman, Atlanta Rhythm Section, Lynyrd Skynyrd, Amazing Rhythm Aces, Dr. John, Wet Willie.

Showcases a variety of post–Allman Brothers Southern rock performers. There are some fine songs here—notably Dr. John's "Right Place Wrong Time," Wet Willie's "Keep on Smilin'," Skynyrd's "Sweet Home Alabama," "Ramblin' Man" by the Allmans and Bishop's "Fooled Around and Fell in Love," though the latter is a pop hit without much regional feeling. The groove is generally steady and easy, but somehow one can't help feeling that these performances are all shown to better advantage in the context of their original LPs. — D.M.

★ ★ ★ **South's Greatest Hits, Vol. 2 / Capri. (NA)**
Artists include: Marshall Tucker Band, Atlanta Rhythm Section, Charlie Daniels Band, Outlaws, Allman Brothers Band, Elvin Bishop Sea Level, Stillwater, Wet Willie.

Second set in series lacks anything as strong as Lynyrd Skynyrd's "Sweet Home Alabama" from the first, but does nicely with Tucker's "Heard It in a Love Song," Atlanta Rhythm Section's "So in to You," Allmans' "Jessica" and Willie's "Street Corner Serenade." But the Outlaws are dreadful and Daniels isn't much better—neither is Stillwater, for that matter. Of the additions and more recent groups here, only Sea Level indicates that there is much life left in the Southern hard-rock genre. — D.M.

★ ★ **Souvenirs of Music City, U.S.A. / Plant. (NA)**
Artists include: Jeannie C. Riley, Charlie Rich, Jimmy C. Newman, Hank Locklin, Leroy Van Dyke, Gordon Terry, James O'Gwynn, Rita Remington, Roy Orbison, David Allan Coe, Willie Nelson, Carl Perkins, Johnny Cash, Ray Pillow, Rex Allen Jr., Sleepy LaBeef, George Jones, Little David Wilkins, Carl Belew, David Houston.

A hodgepodge. The only sizable country hit here is Riley's "Harper Valley P.T.A." The Rich, Orbison, Perkins, Cash and LaBeef tracks are from Sun Records, but only LaBeef's "Black Land Farmer" is moderately rare, and the others are better heard on Sun anthologies. Nelson, Jones and Coe are at least interesting, but most of the rest is mediocre. — D.M.

★ ★ ★ ★ ★ **Phil Spector Wall of Sound /
Phil Spector International (1981),
Br. imp.**
*Artists include: Crystals, Ronettes, Darlene
Love, Righteous Brothers, Bob B. Soxx and
the Blue Jeans, Dion, Ike and Tina Turner,
the Phil Spector Wall of Sound Orchestra,
Bonnie and the Treasures, April Stevens,
Modern Folk Quartet, Alley Cats, Betty Wil-
lis, Treasures.*
Magnificent nine-disc boxed collection of
Spector's greatest work, including two vol-
umes by the Ronettes, one each by the Crys-
tals, Love, the Righteous Brothers, Bob B.
Soxx and Dion, plus scattered hits and
misses by others. Also features the legendary
Phil Spector's Christmas Album (a.k.a. *A
Christmas Gift for You*). Pricey but precious.
— D.M.

★ ★ ★ **Spirituals to Swing (John Hammond's
Thirtieth Anniversary Concert—1967) /
Col. (NA)**
*Artists include: George Benson, Marion Wil-
liams, Count Basie, Joe Turner, Cafe Society
Band, Joe Turner and Pete Johnson, John
Handy, Big Mama Thornton.*
Obviously, this thirtieth-anniversary show
can't hope to compete artistically with the
music produced at Hammond's groundbreaking 1937 concert, which brought black
American music to Carnegie Hall and highbrow America for what amounted to the
first time. But it has its fair share of good
moments—especially from Williams, Basie
and Turner. — D.M.

★ ★ ★ ★ **Spitballs / Beserk. (1978)**
*Artists include: Jonathan Richman, Greg
Kihn, Sean Tyla, the Rubinoos, and others.*
This fine collection of reworked oldies by
various artists on Beserkley's roster—
including Jonathan Richman, Greg Kihn,
Sean Tyla and the Rubinoos—works as a
well-programed Sixties party record. And although some of the vocals (especially Richman's on the Dixie Cups' "Chapel of Love")
almost knock one star off, the splendid
reworkings of the Bobby Fuller Four's
"Let Her Dance" and the Raiders'
"Just Like Me" put it right back on.
— W.K.

★ **Spy Who Loved Me (Soundtrack) / U.A.
(NA)**
This Marvin Hamlisch score is bone-dull except for Carly Simon's theme-song hit, "Nobody Does It Better," which is heard to better advantage on her album. — D.M.

★ ★ ★ **Stan's Soul Shop / Charly (1981), Br.
imp.**
*Artists include: Stanley Winston, George Per-
kins, Eddie Giles, Clarence Carter, Reuben
Bell, Clay Hammond, Roscoe Robinson,
Montclairs, Bob Camille, Bobby Powell,
Bobby Patterson, Soul Stirrers, Eddie Steele,
Casey Jones, Johnny Gilliam.*
Minor but nice soul sides from Jewel re-
cords; all were originally issued in the late
Sixties or early Seventies. Hammond, Win-
ston, Carter and Robinson are particularly
worth hearing. Very tough and Southern.
— D.M.

★ ★ ★ **Starday-Dixie Rockabillys / Gusto
(NA)**
*Artists include: Link Davis, Rudy "Tutti"
Grayzell, Benny Joy, Groovey Joe Poovey,
Cliff Blakeley.*
Interesting collection of novelty rockabilly
tunes. — J.S.

★ **Stardiscs / Lon. (NA)**
*Artists include: Larry Page Orch, André
Gagnon, John Miles, Hodges, James and
Smith, Al Green, Olympic Runners, Blood-
stone, Nature Zone, Steve Bender.*
With exception of Al Green's "Full of
Fire," this is all dross. Even Miles and
Bloodstone aren't up to their best tricks
here. — D.M.

★ **Star Wars (Soundtrack) / 20th Cent.
(1977)**
John Williams' score, discofied by a couple
of artists, made some commercial inroads in
1977, yet nothing like the ones made by the
movie. Title theme isn't bad, but the rest is
dispensable. — D.M.

★ ★ **The Story of Star Wars / 20th Cent.
(NA)**
Dialogue, music and sound effects from the
film. More interesting than the score alone,
but strictly for cultists, nonetheless. — D.M.

★ ★ **Steppin' Out (Disco's Greatest Hits) /
Poly. (NA)**
*Artists include: Chakachas, Isaac Hayes,
Bionic Boogie, Roy Ayers, Don Ray, Gloria
Gaynor, Fatback Band, Kongas, Joe Simon,
Trax, Crystal Grass.*
Doesn't live up to the subtitle. Gaynor's
"Never Can Say Goodbye," which is as pro-
pulsive as any disco music ever made, and
Simon's sweet-tempered "I Need You, You
Need Me" are the best of a pretty dull as-
sortment. — D.M.

★ ★ **Steppin' Out / Mid. Int. (NA)**
*Artists include: Silver Convention, Carol
Douglas, Touch of Class, Liquid Pleasure,
Andrea True Connection.*

Passable disco sampler. "Fly Robin Fly"
by Silver Convention is about the best of it,
although former porno starlet True's "More
More More" has its own fascination.

★ ★ ★ ★ ★ **Story of the Blues / Col. (NA)**
*Artists include: Fra-Fra Tribesmen, Missis-
sippi John Hurt, Blind Willie McTell, Lead-
belly, Blind Lemon Jefferson, Charley Patton,
Texas Alexander, Peg Leg Boy Fuller and
Sonny Terry, Brownie McGhee, Joe Williams
and Sonny Boy Williamson, Big Bill Broonzy,
Joe Turner and Pete Johnson, Otis Spann,
Elmore James, Johnny Shines, Barbecue Bob
and Laughing Charley, Henry Williams and
Eddie Anthony, Mississippi Jook Band, Mem-
phis Jug Band, Bessie Smith, Lillian Glinn,
Bertha Hill, Butterbeans and Susie, Leroy
Carr and Scrapper Blackwell, Faber Smith
and Jimmy Yancey, Peetie Wheatstraw, Casey
Bill and Black Bob, Bo Carter, Robert John-
son, Bukka White, Memphis Minnie.*

Fantastic assortment of pre–World War II
blues. Includes all the major figures: Johnson, Patton, Bessie Smith, James (who
stretches toward Chicago-style city blues of
the postwar era), Broonzy, McGhee and
Terry, Hurt, Leadbelly, Jefferson. Plus an assortment of band tracks, piano blues—nearly
every style of blues imagined so far is
represented here. Recommended; well annotated. — D.M.

★ ★ ★ **Sunday Down South / Sun (NA)**
*Artists include: Johnny Cash, Jerry Lee
Lewis.*

Two rockabillies remember their religious
roots. Hymns for be-bop backsliders, or
something like that. Don't step on my pa-
tent-leather Easter shoes? Good stuff anyhow. — D.M.

★ ★ ☆ ★ **Super Country Hits of the 1940s /
Gusto (1978)**
*Artists include: Delmore Brothers, Cowboy
Copas, Pop Eckler, Patsy Montana, York
Brothers, George Morgan, Jimmy Dickens,
Wayne Raney, Rose Maddox, Kenny Roberts.*

Good selection of old Starday label hits includes "Candy Kisses" (Morgan), "Filipino
Baby" (Copas), "Philadelphia Lawyer" (Maddox) and "Money Marbles and Chalk" (Eckler). Also a pair of nice bluegrass-style hits,
"Blues Stay Away from Me" (Delmores) and
"River of Tears" (Yorks). — D.M.

★ ★ ★ **Super Country Hits of the 1950s /
Gusto (1978)**
*Artists: Jimmy Dickens, Benny Banres,
George Jones, Skeeter Davis, Jack Cardwell,
Bobby Helms, Arlie Duff, Bonnie Lou, War-
ner Mack, Carlisles.*

Comparatively lackluster selection of pe-
riod hits. About the best is "Why Baby
Why" (Jones), though "The Death of Hank
Williams" (Cardwell) is a nice curio.
— D.M.

★ ★ **Super Groups / Pick. (NA)**
*Artists include: Mighty Clouds of Joy, Jack-
son Southernaires, Dixie Hummingbirds,
Highway Q.C.'s, Sensational Nightingales.*

Poorly packaged set nonetheless contains
some fine music from several male groups
that are among the biggest names in black
gospel. — D.M.

★ ★ ★ **Super Hits, Vol. 1 / Atl. (1967)**
*Artists include: Percy Sledge, Sam and Dave,
Wilson Pickett, Young Rascals, Joe Tex,
Booker T. and the MGs, Barbara Lewis, Ar-
etha Franklin, Eddie Floyd, Mar Keys.*

All that's left of Atlantic's old five-volume
series of its R&B pop crossover hits. Not a
bad song in the bunch; also nothing rare,
and silly notes. You can get this stuff—most
of it, anyhow—in better condition on this
label's *The Soul Years*. — D.M.

★ ★ ★ **Super Oldies of the Fifties, Vol. 1 /
Trip (NA)**
*Artists include: Little Anthony and the Impe-
rials, Crows, Five Satins, Danleers, Chantels,
Cadillacs, Dubs, El Dorados, Lloyd Price,
Mystics, Little Richard, Lee Andrews and the
Hearts, Bobby Freeman, Jimmy Clanton,
Jesters, Johnnie and Joe, Penguins, Sonny Til
and the Orioles, Ritchie Valens, Harptones.*

Decent oldies set, unannotated, with no
surprises except possibly Freeman's "Do
You Want a Dance," a Sixties record.
— D.M.

★ ★ ★ **Super Oldies of the Fifties, Vol. 2 /
Trip (NA)**
*Artists include: Flamingos, Frankie Lymon,
Sam Cooke, Teen Queens, Heartbeats, Mono-
tones, Wilbur Harrison, Shirelles, Lloyd
Price, Charts, Olympics, Dion, Little Richard,
Dave "Baby" Cortez, Dee Clark, Bobby Day,
Spaniels, Ritchie Valens, Frankie Ford, Dubs.*

No real surprises here, but some nice oddities: the Spaniels' "Stormy Weather," a
beautiful ballad; the somewhat hilarious
"Western Movies" by the Olympics; Price's

"Stagger Lee," rather than the usually anthologized "Lawdy Miss Clawdy."
— D.M.

★ ★ ★ ★ **Super Oldies of the Fifties, Vol. 3 / Trip (NA)** ¶
Artists include: Platters, Diamonds, Crests, Little Richard, Scarlets, Harptones, Jerry Lee Lewis, Five Satins, Channels, Willows, Crew Cuts, Lloyd Price, Spacemen, Eugene Church, Lee Andrews and the Hearts, Continentals.

Some relative rarities here, highlighted by Price's "I'm Gonna Get Married" and Lee Andrews and the Hearts' "Try the Impossible." But beware "Sh-Boom," by the Crew Cuts; it is a white cover version of the infinitely superior black original done by the Chords.   — D.M.

★ ★ ★ **Super Oldies of the Fifties, Vol. 4 Trip (NA)** ¶
Artists include: Moonglows, Platters, Tune Weavers, Crests, Jerry Lee Lewis, Little Richard, Kodaks, El Dorados, Spaniels, Paragons, Harptones, Jacks, Wailers, Channels, Marvin and Johnny, Eternals, Velvets, Donnie Owens.

Good one for doo-wop aficionados, with the tracks from the Moonglows, Spaniels, El Dorados, Harptones, Jacks and Paragons. Also for anarchists, with Little Richard performing not only his own hit, "Lucille," but also Larry Williams' "Short Fat Fanny." "Rockin' in the Jungle" by the Eternals is a cute spinoff from the Cadets' "Stranded in the Jungle."   — D.M.

★ ★ **Super Oldies of the Fifties, Vol. 5 / Trip (NA)** ¶
Artists include: Platters, Channels, Tommy Edwards, Shirley and Lee, Diamonds, Anita Bryant, Jack Scott, Cadillacs, Fire Flies, Shepherd Sisters, Phil Phillips, Champs, Jerry Wallace, Johnny Preston, Jerry Butler, Paul Evans, Thomas Wayne, Johnny and the Hurricanes, Tony Bellus, Della Reese.

Bad pop singers (Bryant) and silly novelties like Evans' "Seven Little Girls (Sittin' in the Back Seat)," Preston's "Running Bear." Little good stuff: Diamonds do the "Stroll," Platters have "Smoke Gets in Your Eyes," Butler "For Your Precious Love," which launched his career, and that of the Impressions. Plus two hot instrumentals, "Red River Rock" by Johnny and the Hurricanes and "Tequila" by the Champs. Still, too spotty for comfort.   — D.M.

★ ★ ★ **Super Oldies of the Fifties, Vol. 6 / Trip (NA)** ¶

Artists include: Crests, Platters, Three Friends, Moonglows, Dell-Vikings, Little Richard, Spaniels, Teen Chords, Faye Adams, Jerry Lee Lewis, Starlights, Cadillacs, Continentals, Jimmy Reed, Lloyd Price, Sam Cooke, Huey "Piano" Smith.

Odds and ends in this erratic collection. The better sides include: Price's "Where Were You on Our Wedding Day," Reed's "Honest I Do," "Only Sixteen" by Cooke, "Rockin' Pneumonia and the Boogie Woogie Flu" by Smith, Little Richard's three tracks, the Dell-Vikings' "Come Go with Me," Lewis' hilarious (but intense) "High School Confidential" and the Platters' "My Prayer." Not to mention "Secret Love" by the Moonglows. But some of this is bubblegum light— two songs by the Crests is enough to give you cavities, fluoride or no fluoride.
— D.M.

★ ★ ★ ★ **Super Oldies of the Fifties, Vol. 7 / Trip (NA)** ¶
Artists include: Big Bopper, Channels, Cadets, Platters, Crests, Diamonds, Jack Scott, Little Richard, Magnificents, Collegians, Paragons, Cadillacs, Moonglows, Jesters, Dells, Jesse Belvin, Etta James, Lloyd Price, Flamingos.

No set that includes "Chantilly Lace" (Bopper), "Stranded in the Jungle" (Cadets), two by Little Richard, "Oh What a Night" (Moonglows) and "Goodnight My Love" (Belvin) can be dismissed out of hand. Especially when it finishes with the Flamingos' "I'll Be Home."   — D.M.

★ ★ **Super Oldies of the Fifties, Vol. 8 / Trip (NA)** ¶
Artists include: Fleetwoods, Fats Domino, Santo and Johnny, Eddie Cochran, Clovers, Bill Haley and the Comets, Frankie Avalon, Penguins, Teen Queens, Bill Doggett, Falcons, Fabian, Five Satins, Jimmy Clanton, Dubs, Mickey and Sylvia.

Heavily padded: the Five Satins' "In the Still of the Night" and Clanton's "Just a Dream" appear on Volume 1 of the series, and there's just no excuse for remembering Fabian and Frankie Avalon, unless you like to torture yourself. Three tracks by Haley seems excessive, too. Highlight: "Love Is Strange" by Mickey and Sylvia, a grand track rarely anthologized.   — D.M.

★ ★ ★ **Super Oldies of the Sixties, Vol. 1 / Trip (NA)** ¶
Artists include: Shirelles, Kingsmen, Jive Five, Dion, Chantels, Kathy Young, Shells, Angels, Cascades, Gene Chandler, Dave "Baby" Cortez, Del Shannon, Ron Holden, Rosie and the

Originals, Troy Shondell, Frankie Avalon, Les Cooper, Little Caesar and the Romans.

Decent selection of pre-Beatles Sixties hits includes some girl groups (Shirelles, Angels, Chantels), some doo-wop and assorted New York-style harmony (Jive Five, Dion, Rosie and the Originals), some teen-exploitation music (Avalon, Shondell, Cortez) and some oddball gems: "Louie Louie," the raunch rock classic by the Kingsmen; "Duke of Earl," Gene Chandler's mysterious lament-tribute; Shannon's "Runaway"; and Little Caesar's anthemic (if nasal) "Those Oldies but Goodies." — D.M.

★ ★ ★ **Super Oldies of the Sixties, Vol. 2 / Trip (NA)** ¶
Artists include: Shep and the Limelites, Capris, Dale and Grace, Lee Dorsey, Chiffons, Dee Clark, Blue Jays, Dionne Warwick, Harold Dorman, Paul Evans, Joe Jones, Anita Bryant, Paul Peterson, Shirelles, James Darren, Fendermen, Sam Cooke, Freddie Scott, Dovells.

A good sampler, among other things, for those who think that rock between the time Presley entered the army and the Beatles entered the American charts was all wimps and no successes. In fact, as shown by Dorsey's "Ya Ya," the Chiffons' "He's So Fine," Harold Dorman's wild "Mountain of Love," Scott's "Hey Girl" and the Fendermen's "Muleskinner Blues," this was a fertile era, particularly for black performers: Cooke's "Wonderful World" has become a standard, for instance. But the impression that there was a great deal of bathetic pop (Anita Bryant) and purely exploitive teen-market music (Peterson, Darren) isn't altogether wrong. A bag as mixed as the era it draws upon. — D.M.

★ ★ ★ **Super Oldies of the Sixties, Vol. 3 / Trip (NA)** ¶
Artists include: Chuck Jackson, Barbara Lynn, Jerry Butler, Ike and Tina Turner, Shirelles, Wilson Pickett, Jimmy Hughes, Maxine Brown, Joe Henderson, Gladys Knight and the Pips, Dionne Warwick, Mongo Santamaria, Patti LaBelle and the Bluebelles, Betty Harris, King Curtis.

This amounts to a survey of black musical styles of the early (pre-Beatle) Sixties. Jackson (represented by "Any Day Now"), Butler ("He Will Break Your Heart," "Moon River"), Brown ("All in My Mind," "Funny") and Warwick ("Don't Make Me Over") were crooners—ballad singers who brought a world of emotion to pop ballads that no white singers had done, and yet con-

veyed the songs conventionally enough to enjoy substantial white pop appeal. Pickett ("If You Need Me"), Ike and Tina ("It's Gonna Work Out Fine," "Poor Fool"), Harris ("Cry to Me"), even Lynn ("You'll Lose a Good Thing") are tougher, more directly black in their approach. Curtis ("Soul Twist") and Santamaria ("Watermelon Man") contribute two of the era's funkiest instrumentals. Nice set. — D.M.

★ ★ ★ **Super Oldies of the Sixties, Vol. 4 / Trip (NA)** ¶
Artists include: Bobby Lewis, Randy and the Rainbows, Dion, Del Shannon, Terry Stafford, Jimmy Charles, Don and Juan, Barbara George, Trashmen, Volumes, Shirelles, Paragons, Beach Boys, Cathy Jean and the Roommates, Dixie Cups, Don Gardner and Dee Dee Ford, Dual, Inez Foxx, Angels, Chris Kenner.

In addition to the usual teen-exploitation music, R&B one-shots, girl groups and wild novelties, this set begins to get into the kind of heavily produced (Shannon) but somehow more authentic (Beach Boys) music that paved the way for the Beatles and the British Invasion. Still, the highlight of the set is a nonsense song, the Trashmen's "Surfin' Bird," which proves that all great art knows where the garbage dump lies. — D.M.

★ ★ ★ **Super Oldies of the Sixties, Vol. 5 / Trip (NA)** ¶
Artists include: Toys, Little Eva, B. J. Thomas, Happenings, Beach Boys, Turtles, Robert Parker, Chad and Jeremy, Shelley Fabares, Dionne Warwick, Mitch Ryder and the Detroit Wheels, Gerry and the Pacemakers, Betty Everett, Raindrops, Cookies, Classics, Shirelles, Shangri-Las, Dobie Gray.

A nice sampling of hits from the period immediately before and just after the emergence of the Beatles. The British selections (Pacemakers, Chad and Jeremy) are the weakest of the bunch; Fabares' "Johnny Angel" is pure pubescent exploitation. But there are a number of indications of the way in which Phil Spector's Wall of Sound approach was beginning to have an effect (Toys, Happenings, Thomas, even Little Eva); a different sort of resonance appears in the girl-group sides (Shangri-Las, Shirelles) that indicates that performers, writers and producers were beginning to see themselves as camp. The R&B selections are few but strong—Parker's "Barefootin' " is the best. Plus two tracks from the best blue-eyed soul group in the land—at least until the advent of the Righteous Brothers and the Young

Rascals—Mitch Ryder and the Detroit Wheels. The Beach Boys ("Surfer Girl") move into a ballad style, and the Turtles ("It Ain't Me Babe") signify the arrival of Bob Dylan, folk rock and bohemian California as factors in rock. — D.M.

★ ★ ★ ★ **Super Oldies of the Sixties, Vol. 6 / Trip (NA)** ¶
Artists include: Percy Sledge, Sam and Dave, Don Covay, Bobby Freeman, Otis Redding, Capitols, Slim Harpo, Dionne Warwick, Brenton Wood, Joe Jeffrey Group, James Brown, Jerry Butler and Betty Everett, Esquires, B. B. King, Packers, Alvin Cash, Tommy Tucker, Meters, Maxine Brown.

A diversity of mid-Sixties soul music. Atlantic and Stax are well represented by Redding, Sam and Dave, Sledge, Cash and Covay (whose "Mercy Mercy" might be an outline for Mick Jagger's vocal style). King's "Rock Me Baby" is a definitive version of his blues style. Butler and Everett continue a version of doo-wop tradition, while Warwick takes black balladry into mainstream pop. In a way, though, the most fascinating numbers here are the wildest: Freeman's "C'mon and Swim" was produced by Sly Stone and is unlike most dance discs of the period in its unleashed ferocity, Tucker's "High-Heeled Sneakers" is utterly bizarre, Harpo's "Scratch My Back" has sexual connotations that it's hard to believe were permissible fifteen years ago and the Meters' "Cissy Strut" is virtually a schematic diagram of the fundamental New Orleans rhythm pattern. — D.M.

★ ★ ★ **Super Oldies of the Sixties, Vol. 7 / Trip (NA)** ¶
Artists include: J. Frank Wilson, Soul Survivors, Shangri-Las, Gerry and the Pacemakers, Chad and Jeremy, Dionne Warwick, Happenings, Dixie Cups, B. J. Thomas, Turtles, Royal Guardsmen, Jackie Lee, Beach Boys, Ad Libs, Jelly Beans.

Despite some good last-gasp girl-group selections (Shangri-Las, Dixie Cups, Ad Libs, Jelly Beans), most of this is too wimpy to be listenable today. Gerry and the Pacemakers and Chad and Jeremy were among the least consequential British groups, the Beach Boys' "Surfin' " is the dullest of that group's teen-craze discs, and the Happenings, Wilson and the Royal Guardsmen explicit rock without contributing anything to it. But Lee's dance record, "The Duck," is nice, as are Warwick's two ballads, and the Soul Survivors' "Expressway to Your Heart" is a fine hunk of period soul music. — D.M.

★ ★ ★ **Super Oldies of the Sixties, Vol. 8 / Trip (NA)** ¶
Artists include: Turtles, B. J. Thomas, Tommy James, Dionne Warwick, Brenton Wood, Deon Jackson, John Fred and the Playboy Band, Mitch Ryder and the Detroit Wheels, Toussaint McCall, Happenings, Aaron Neville, Chiffons, Forum, Leaves, Bobby Fuller Four, Seeds, Count Five.

Mixed bag. There is some fine hard rock here: Fuller's "I Fought the Law," "Psychotic Reaction" by Count Five, "Hey Joe" by the Leaves and "Pushin' Too Hard" by the Seeds are all minor but strong. Ryder's tracks are powerful white R&B. Jackson and Wood contribute nice black pop hits, while Fred's "Judy in Disguise (with Glasses)" is a great *Sgt. Pepper* takeoff. Too much of the rest is too pop, insufficiently rocking not to have dated. — D.M.

★ ★ **Super Oldies of the Sixties, Vol. 9 / Trip (NA)** ¶
Artists include: Duprees, Crests, Dionne Warwick, Roommates, Beach Boys, Chimes, Janie Grant, Embers, Jan and Dean, Champs, Premiers, Tradewinds, B. J. Thomas, Raindrops, Johnny Crawford, Evie Sands, Jerry Wallace, Chad and Jeremy, Jack Scott.

This is mostly very minor, and often it's awful (Sands, Crests, Roommates, Crawford, Chad and Jeremy, Wallace). Scott's "What in the World's Come over You" is an odd rockabilly ballad, "Surfin' USA" is one of the Beach Boys' best (although "Heart and Soul" is probably Jan and Dean's worst) and aside from that, there's not a lot here. — D.M.

★ ★ **Super Oldies of the Sixties, Vol. 10 / Trip (NA)** ¶
Artists include: Lesley Gore, Dickey Lee, Duprees, Leroy Van Dyke, Vogues, Cowsills, Flares, Every Mother's Son, B. J. Thomas, Cannibal and the Headhunters, Jay and the Techniques, Dionne Warwick, Roger Miller, Sam the Sham and the Pharaohs, Gentrys, Shangri-Las.

Weak pop set, little rock or soul. Big exception is Cannibal and the Headhunters' "Land of 1,000 Dances." Jay and the Techniques have a continually listenable pop-soul item, "Apples Peaches Pumpkin Pie," and Warwick is her usual fine self. "Wooly Bully" (Sam the Sham) is a genuine weirdo, but like Gore's "It's My Party," it is more memorable than playable, today. Which is still an improvement over most of the rest of what is here. — D.M.

★ ★ ★ **Super Oldies of the Sixties, Vol. 11 / Trip (NA)** ¶
Artists include: Nat Kendricks and the Swans, Billy Preston, Patti LaBelle and the Blue-belles, John Lee Hooker, Wilson Pickett, Manhattans, Baby Washington, Ike and Tina Turner, Gene Chandler, Lloyd Price, Jimmy Reed, Jennell Hawkins, Joe Simon, Gladys Knight and the Pips, Jimi Hendrix, Chantels.

Decent soul collection from the period, with some blues (Reed, Hooker) additions. The songs by Preston and Hendrix are not the sort of thing that would be remembered but for the success those two enjoyed in later years. — D.M.

★ ★ ★ **Super Oldies cf the Sixties, Vol. 12 / Trip (NA)** ¶
Artists include: Angels, Lesley Gore, Platters, Bobby Hebb, B. J. Thomas, Mark Dinning, Standells, Left Banke, Cowsills, Knickerbock-ers, Stan Getz/Astrud Gilberto, Duprees, Crests, Dionne Warwick, David Rose, Friend and Lover, Jerry Butler, Johnny Crawford, Rochell and the Candles.

Mediocre. For every "Dirty Water" by the Standells, there's Getz and Gilberto; for every "Walk Away Renee" by the Left Banke, there's the rank pop instrumental of David Rose. Nice stuff by Butler, Gore (even), Hebb dragged down by silliness of much of the rest. — D.M.

★ ★ **Super Oldies of the Sixties, Vol. 13 / Trip (NA)** ¶
Artists include: Bobby Goldsboro, Exciters, Cher, Dennis Yost and Classics IV, Bob Lind, Animals, Jackie De Shannon, Johnny Bur-nette, Buddy Knox, Buckinghams, Rivingtons, Bobby Vee, Little Anthony and the Imperials, Dick and Dee Dee, Jay and the Americans, Turtles, Ventures, Capris.

Mixed bag: for every lushly romantic bal-lad like the Capris' "There's a Moon Out Tonight," there's a lushly stupid pop song like Goldsboro's "Honey." Despite the Ani-mals, De Shannon, and the inspired insipid-ity of "Bird's the Word" by the Rivingtons, there's not much here that you can't get in better company elsewhere. — D.M.

★ ★ ★ **Super Oldies of the Sixties, Vol. 14 / Trip (NA)** ¶
Artists include: Little Anthony and the Impe-rials, Gene McDaniels, Jay and the Ameri-cans, Johnny Burnette, Bobby Goldsboro, Jackie De Shannon, Rivieras, Timi Yuro, Cher, C.O.D.s, Bobby Vee, Dennis Yost and the Classics IV, Sugarloaf, Animals,

Rivingtons, Fabian, Frankie Avalon, Ernie K-Doe.

Final volume of the set epitomizes its vir-tues (good rock and R&B tracks by Bur-nette, Anthony and the Imperials, Animals, Rivingtons and K-Doe) and imperfections (the teen-idol muck of Fabian, Avalon and Cher, the sentimental pop of Goldsboro, the wretched "Michael" by the C.O.D.s). — D.M.

★ ★ ★ ★ **Super Super Blues Band / Check. (NA)**
Artists include: Muddy Waters, Howlin' Wolf, Bo Diddley.

Three of the Chess stable's best combine on their classics: Waters' "Long Distance Call," Wolf's "Spoonful" and "Red Roost-er," Diddley's "Diddley Daddy." — D.M.

★ ★ ★ ★ **Surfin' Roots / Fest. (1977)**
Artists: Beach Boys, Pyramids, Dick Dale and His Del-Tones, Frogmen, Marketts, Dave Myers and Surftones, Rumblers, Annette, Chantays, Sentinals, Kenny and the Cadets, Annette and the Beach Boys, Surfaris, Denels, Rendezvous.

Basically excellent set of surf songs, in-cludes "Pipeline" (Chantays), "Latinia" (Sentinals), "Let's Go Trippin' " and "Misir-lou" (Dale), "Penetration" (Pyramids), plus "Wipe Out," "Surfer Girl," and some fluff from Annette that pulls it back from five stars. — D.M.

★ ★ ★ **Swamp Blues / Ex. (NA)**
Artists include: Clarence Edwards, Whisper-ing Smith, Henry Gray, Silas Hogan, Arthur "Guitar" Kelly.

Excello was always the oddest, funkiest, most down-home of blues labels, and this collection shows why. It's not just the cru-dity of the music—which seems lost between plantation sounds of Mississippi and Muddy Waters' breakthrough up north—but also their themes: Arthur Kelly's "No. 10 at the Station and No. 12 Is on the Road," which must be the most long-winded restatement of the mystery-train theme, for instance. Con-sistently intriguing. — D.M.

★ ★ ★ ★ **Taxi Presents Sounds of the Eighties / Taxi (1980)**
Artists include: Jimmy Riley, Junior Delgado, Dennis Brown, Black Uhuru, the Tamlins.

Although many of these cuts are available on other LPs, this selection is all killer, no filler. The Black Uhuru cuts are particularly useful, since they are from the difficult-to-find *Showcase* LP. Together they form the first fruition of Sly and Robbie's production approach. — R.F.G.

★ ★ ★ TCB (Soundtrack) / Mo. (NA)
Artists include: Diana Ross, Supremes, Temptations.
Good collection of Motown classics includes nothing not widely available on anthologies of the individual artists' work. — J.S.

★ ★ Tell Me That You Love Me Junie Moon (Soundtrack) / Col. (NA)
Folk ideologue Seeger and Pacific Gas and Electric, a minor San Francisco group, provide the background music for Otto Preminger's improbable and sentimental story of three misfit losers, one facially disfigured, one an epileptic, one a wheelchair-bound homosexual. If you can figure out the cinematic combination, you can probably fathom the musical one. — D.M.

★ ★ ★ Texas Country / U.A. (NA)
Artists include: Willie Nelson, Freddy Fender, Asleep at the Wheel, Bob Wills and the Texas Playboys.
A fine set, without much depth, but a good representation of the artists included. Nelson and Wills made good music, though not their best, for United Artists—both are represented, however, by a selection of their best-known titles. Fender, by far the most minor figure here, has four sides, of which only the anthology-perennial, "Wasted Days and Wasted Nights," amounts to much. But Asleep at the Wheel's five songs are from the group's first album, and it may be the best music they have ever made, particularly the versions of "Take Me Back to Tulsa" and "Cherokee Boogie." Good set. — D.M.

★ ★ ★ Texas Guitar—From Dallas to L.A. / Atl. (NA)
Artists include: T-Bone Walker, Al King, Guitar Slim, R. S. Rankin, Lawyer Houston.
Good collection of Texas guitarists. In retrospect, the absence of Johnny Copeland seems a serious omission. — J.S.

★ ★ ★ That Summer! / Ari. (1979)
Artists include: Ian Dury and the Blockheads, Mink DeVille, Elvis Costello, the Boomtown Rats, Zones, the Only Ones, Wreckless Eric, Patti Smith Group, the Ramones, the Undertones, Eddie and the Hot Rods, Nick Lowe, Richard Hell and the Voidoids.
Elvis Costello meets the Voidoids. British soundtrack from *That Summer!* movie is a power-pop-cum-punk sampler. Curious but

good nonetheless, especially with Richard Hell's underground hit, "Blank Generation." — ML.H.

★ ★ ★ The Thing (Soundtrack) / MCA (1982)
Score of John Carpenter's ultrahorrific picture is by Ennio Morricone but doesn't rank with his best work. — D.M.

★ ★ ★ ★ Thirty Years of Bluegrass / Gusto (1977)
Artists include: Stanley Brothers, Flatt and Scruggs, Reno and Smiley, Country Gentlemen, Hylo Brown, Jimmy Martin and Bob Osborne, Scotty Stoneman, Benny Martin, Tommy Jackson, Jim and Jesse, Bill Clifton, Mac Wiseman, Bill Emerson, Allen Shelton, Red Allen, New Grass Revival, Kentucky Travelers, Grandpa Jones, Bill Harrell, Jim Eanes, Stringbean, Stoneman Family, Charlie Monroe, Moore and Napier, Buzz Busby, Carl Story.
Best one-volume survey of the genre. All the right names are present, plus such songs as the Stanleys' "How Mountain Girls Can Love" and "Rank Strangers," Flatt and Scruggs' "Salty Dog" and "Roll in My Sweet Baby's Arms," "Orange Blossom Special" by Benny Martin, "Cotton-Eyed Joe" by Tommy Jackson, "Beautiful Blue Eyes" by Red Allen and the Stoneman Family's "Wreck of Number Nine." — D.M.

★ ★ ★ ★ This Is How It All Began, Vol. 1 / Spec. (NA)
Artists include: Chosen Gospel Singers, Soul Stirrers, Mercy Dee, Alex Bradford, John Lee Hooker, Frankie Lee Sims, Roy Milton, Percy Mayfield, Joe Liggins, Four Flames, Jimmy Liggins, Camille Howard, Swan Silvertones.
Fine selection of gospel, blues and R&B sounds influential on the development of modern rock and soul. — D.M.

★ ★ ★ ★ This Is How It All Began, Vol. 2 / Spec. (NA)
Artists include: Lloyd Price, Guitar Slim, Jesse Belvin and Marvin Phillips, Tony Allen and the Champs, Little Richard, Larry Williams, Sam Cooke, Art Neville, Jerry Byrne, Don and Dewey.
Fine album of early rock and soul performances, includes early secular singing from Cooke, two Richard hits, a pair of Williams novelties, Price's "Lawdy Miss Clawdy," and other solid L.A. and New Orleans sides. — D.M.

★ ★ ★ ★ **This Is Reggae Music, Vol. 1 / Is. (NA)**
Artists include: Zap Pow, Wailers, Jimmy Cliff, Lorna Bennett, Joe Higgs, Heptones, Maytals, Owen Gray.
While it's hardly as fundamental as *The Harder They Come,* this sampler offers some fine reggae, including the Wailers' "I Shot the Sheriff" and "Concrete Jungle," the Heptones' "Book of Rules" and the Maytals' "Funky Kingston" and "Louie Louie."
— D.M.

★ ★ ★ **This Is Reggae Music, Vol. 2 / Is. (NA)**
Artists include: George Dekker, Peacemakers, Scotty and Lorna Bennett, Rudie Mowatt, Third World, Augustus Pablo, Heptones, Arthur Louis, Desi Young, Burning Spear.
Collection of minor reggae tracks nonetheless includes the outstanding "Marcus Garvey" by Burning Spear, Arthur Louis' odd cover of Dylan's "Knocking on Heaven's Door" and the Heptones' "Country Boy."
— D.M.

★ ★ ★ ★ **This Is Reggae Music, Vol. 3 / Is. (NA)**
Artists include: Junior Murvin, Lee Perry, Max Romeo, Justin Hines and the Dominoes, Aswad, Jah Lion, Burning Spear, Prince Jazzbo and the Upsetters, Peter Tosh, Bunny Wailer.
Fine collection of Jamaican hits includes Murvin's "Police and Thieves," Romeo's "War in a Babylon," Burning Spear's "Man in the Hills," "Rastaman" by Wailer and "No Sympathy" by Tosh—all important reggae artists and/or songs. — D.M.

★ ★ ★ **Times Square (Soundtrack) / RSO (NA)**
Artists include: Suzi Quatro, Pretenders, Roxy Music, Gary Numan, Talking Heads, Joe Jackson, XTC, Ramones, Lou Reed, Patti Smith.
Good collection of Seventies/Eighties material highlighted by Pretenders "Talk of the Town," Talking Heads' "Life during Wartime" and Patti Smith's "Pissing in a River."
— J.S.

★ ★ ★ **To Mother / Spec. (NA)**
Artists include: Pilgrim Travelers, Alex Bradford, Five Blind Boys, Detroiters, Soul Stirrers, Bessie Griffin, Swan Silvertones.
Tributes to Mom and her faith in God from a number of gospel's leading lights.
— D.M.

★ **Tommy (Soundtrack) / Poly. (1975)**
Before Robert Stigwood butchered *Sgt. Pepper,* he did the same for the Who's rock opera *Tommy,* although with considerably more justification: Roger Daltrey, the Who's vocalist, starred (albeit with Ann-Margret, the doyenne of Elvis flicks), and composer Pete Townshend added some new incidental music. But while Townshend's increased use of synthesizer on the soundtrack is interesting, most of the vocals are not: Ann-Margret, Jack Nicholson and Oliver Reed don't have an octave of range among them; Elton John's version of "Pinball Wizard" is feeble next to the original; and Tina Turner's "Acid Queen" is a screeching parody of the Who's, and of her own soul-slut persona. No excuse for this while you can still obtain the original. — D.M.

★ ★ ★ **A Touch of Soul, Vol. 1 / Atl. (1981), Jap. imp.**
Artists include: New Foundation, Enticers, Webs, Soul Brothers Six, Barbara Brown, Lorraine Johnson, Margie Alexander, Irma Thomas, Baby Washington, Laura Lee.

★ ★ ★ **A Touch of Soul, Vol. 2 / Atl. (Jap. imp.) 1981**
Artists include: Mike Williams, J. P. Robinson, Soul Brothers Six, Mighty Sam, Otis Clay, Ted Taylor, Walter Rhodes, Rudy Mockabee.
Minor but potent collections of soul singles from Atlantic's mid-Sixties archives. Volume 1 focuses on women, Volume 2 on men. Especially funky are the Soul Brothers Six, Irma Thomas, Otis Clay, and Enticers numbers. — D.M.

★ ★ ★ ★ ★ **The Trojan Story / Troj. (1980)**
Artists include: Derrick Morgan, Jimmy Cliff, the Ethiopians, Lee Perry, the Clarendonians, Stranger Cole.
The scope of this three-LP boxed set is staggering—fifty tracks spanning all of Jamaican pop music from late-Fifties pre-ska to early-Seventies proto-reggae. Essential for anyone who wants to understand the development of Jamaican music, this set includes priceless rarities by Lee Perry (one of his few solo vocal outings), Laurel Aitken's "Bartender," Derrick Morgan's Ja standard "Fat Girl," the stirring gospel sound of the Mellow Larks' "Time to Pray" and the original "A Message to You Rudie."
— R.F.G.

★ ★ ★ ★ **Twenty Bluegrass Originals: "Hymns" / Gusto (1978)**
Artists include: Stanley Brothers, Carl Story,

Lewis Family, Wade Mainer, Reno and Smiley, Acorn Sisters, Moore and Napier, Reno and Harrell, Jimmy Martin, Bailey Brothers, Jim and Jesse, Wilma Lee and Stony Cooper.

Excellent selection of bluegrass religious songs by some of the top names in the field. Highlights include "Rank Strangers" (Stanleys), "I'm Using My Bible for a Roadmap" (Reno and Smiley), "White Dove" (Martin), "Jacob's Vision" (Stanleys), "Unclouded Day" (Lewis Family") and "Purple Robe" (Stanleys). — D.M.

★ **Twenty Golden Souvenirs (Of Music City) / Plant. (NA)**
Artists include: Johnny Cash, Jerry Lee Lewis, Charlie Rich, Leroy Van Dyke, Jimmy C. Newman, Hank Locklin, Charlie Walker, John Wesley Ryles, Willie Nelson, Dave Dudley, David Allan Coe, Jeannie C. Riley, James O'Gwynn, Murry Kellum, Gordon Terry, Paul Martin, Rufus Thibodeaux, Rex Allen Jr., Jimmie Davis, Rita Remington.

Even the best-known performers here are represented by minor examples of their work. The others are minor, indeed. — D.M.

★ ★ **Twenty Great Country Hits / RCA (NA)**
Artists include: Chet Atkins, Bobby Bare, Jim Ed Brown, Jessi Colter, Floyd Cramer, Nashville Brass, Waylon Jennings, Ronnie Milsap, Dolly Parton, Jerry Reed, Charlie Rich, Jim Reeves, Johnny Russell, Hank Snow, Gary Stewart, Porter Wagoner, Porter Wagoner and Dolly Parton, Billy Walker, Dottie West.

Scattershot collection of RCA's acts. Bare, Jennings, Reed, Rich and Stewart are represented by excellent examples of their work. Others aren't. — D.M.

★ **Twenty Great Hits / Plant. (NA)**
Artists include: Jimmy C. Newman, David Allan Coe, Rex Allen Jr, Eddie Burns, James O'Gwynn, John Wesley Ryles, Linda Martell, Tennessee Guitars, Robbie Harden, Ruby Wright, Sleepy LaBeef, Ray Pillow, Debbie Lori Kaye, Harlow Wilcox, Little David Wilkins, Jeannie C. Riley, Dee Mullins, Maxine Brown, Tokyo Matsu, Leroy Van Dyke.

Very minor country collection. — D.M.

★ ★ ★ **Twenty Greatest Rhythm and Blues Hits / Kent (NA)**
Artists include: B. B. King, Jimmy Witherspoon, Roosevelt Sykes, Elmore James, Jimmy McCracklin, Pee Wee Crayton, Howlin' Wolf, S. King, Smokey Hogg, Lowell Fulsom, Lightnin' Hopkins, Roscoe Gordon,

John Lee Hooker, Jimmy Nelson, Junior Beasley.

Fine collection of mostly 12-bar blues artists. King is particularly well represented with three tracks, including his momentous "Sweet Sixteen," while Hooker chips in with "Boogie Chillen," and James with the inevitable "Dust My Blues" and "Standing at the Crossroads." — D.M.

★ ★ **Twenty Super Rhythm and Blues Hits / Kent (NA)**
Artists include: B. B. King, Etta James, Ikettes, Joe Houston, Lowell Fulsom, Pee Wee Crayton, Young Jessie, Jimmy Witherspoon, Cadets, John Lee Hooker, Ike and Tina Turner, Jacks, Johnny "Guitar" Watson.

Good selection includes everything from novelties like "Stranded in the Jungle" (Cadets) to doo-wop like "Why Don't You Write Me?" (Jacks) and straight 12-bar blues (King). — D.M.

★ ★ **Uncle Sam Goes Reggae / J. Gibbs (1980)**
Artists include: Tyrone Taylor, Ruddy Thomas, George Nooks, Marcia Aitken.

Nothing but reggae do-overs here, ranging from the inspired ("Can't Stop Rasta," a dynamic version of Michael Jackson's "Don't Stop Til You Get Enough") to the lame (Thomas' version of Billy Joel's "Just the Way You Are"). — R.F.G.

★ ★ ★ **Underground Blues / Kent (NA)**
Artists include: Elmore James, B. B. King, Howlin' Wolf, Jimmy Reed, Lightnin' Hopkins, John Lee Hooker.

By "underground" Kent presumably means artists who were influential upon the white rock-blues groups of the Sixties, and this is a representative sampling of names, if not always of repertoire. (James and King are not given their best songs; Wolf's and Hooker's are perhaps overfamiliar.) Good introduction to the originals that may be familiar in versions by the Animals, Stones, and so forth. — D.M.

★ ★ ★ **Urban Blues / Fan. (NA)**
Artists include: Roosevelt Sykes, Little Brother Montgomery.

Two blues pianists, not necessarily major ones, on a set of songs originally recorded for Prestige. Title is a bit misleading, since this hardly gives a sampling of the full range of urban blues styles. Nice music anyway. — D.M.

★ ★ **Urban Cowboy (Soundtrack) / Asy. (NA)**
Artists include: Jimmy Buffett, Joe Walsh, Dan Fogelberg, Mickey Gilley, Johnny Lee, Bonnie Raitt, Kenny Rogers, Boz Scaggs, Bob Seeger, the Eagles.
Uneven soundtrack collection of country-rock tunes for the John Travolta flop.
— J.S.

★ ★ **Volunteer Jam / Capri. (1976)**
Artists include: Charlie Daniels Band, Marshall Tucker Band.
Live set of minor Southern rockers is hardly the cream of the genre. — D.M.

★ ★ ★ **Wackies Selective Showcase / Wac. (1979)**
Artists include: Jezzreel, Leroy Sibbles, Wayne Jarret, Horace Andy.
This collection is unified by the trademark super-spacy Wackies' production style, which bathes everything in shimmering clouds of echo. The material here is strong enough to stand up—"This World" is one of former Heptone Leroy Sibbles' best solo outings.
— R.F.G.

★ ★ ★ ★ **Walking Blues / Flyr. (1979)**
Artists include: Son House, Fiddlin' Joe Martin, Willie Brown, Leroy Williams, Willie "61" Blackwell, David Edwards.
This is worthwhile for the four Son House tracks alone, but especially because it is so well annotated (including a separate booklet that comments on the tracks at great length). The selection is from Library of Congress recordings made in the Forties by Alan Lomax. The revelation is Blackwell, a bluesman so surreal he almost bridges the gap between Rabbit Brown and Bob Dylan virtually singlehandedly. Check his "Junior's a Jap Girl's Christmas," a nonlinear ode to World War II patriotism. — D.M.

★ ★ **Walnut Valley Spring Thing / Tak. (NA)**
Artists include: John Hartford, Tut Taylor and Don Humphreys, New Grass Revival, Merle Travis, Cathy Barton, Hutchison Brothers.
Live recordings from the bluegrass festival. Highlight is Travis, working out on some of his best songs—"Smoke That Cigarette," "Dark as a Dungeon," "White Heat."
— D.M.

★ ★ **The Wanderers (Soundtrack) / War. (NA)**
Artists include: Four Seasons, Shirelles, Lee Dorsey, Angels, Ben E. King, Isley Brothers, Contours.
Carefully selected Fifties period piece concentrates too much on the Four Seasons.
— J.S.

★ ★ ★ **The Warriors (Soundtrack) / A&M (1979)**
Artists include: Barry DeVorzon, Arnold McCuller, Kenny Vance, Mandrill, Joe Walsh, Genya Ravan, Eric Mercury, Desmond Child.
Barry DeVorzon's background junk gets too much space, and Vance's pseudo-Latin act is silly, Ravan's posturing pointless and Mandrill's funk overarranged. But that still leaves Arnold McCuller's powerful "Nowhere to Run," Joe Walsh's witty and potent "In the City" and Desmond Child's affecting "Last of an Ancient Breed," not bad in this day and age. In a just world we could just buy the singles, but this world lacks justice, among many other things. — D.M.

★ **Welcome to L.A. (Soundtrack) / U.A. (NA)**
Score from confused picture about Hollywood scene is less than worthy. Keith Carradine is a lot less comfortable with these Richard Baskin songs than with the ones in *Nashville*, and Baskin's own singing is expendable, to be charitable. — D.M.

★ ★ **West Side Story (Original Cast) / Col. (NA)**
★ ★ ★ **West Side Story (Soundtrack) / Col. (NA)**
This is a fairly successful attempt to exploit the rock ambiance of the Fifties. None of the tunes—written by Leonard Bernstein, after all—is a rocker, but the "Jet Song" has entered the rock consciousness (as a takeoff point for Alice Cooper parodies, if nothing else) and "Somewhere" is a great ballad, although it lacked an "inside" interpretation until Tom Waits did his. These songs were influential, in their way, in making juvenile delinquency (thus, rock) a subject matter fit for middlebrows. — D.M.

★ ★ ★ **Where the Buffalo Roam (Soundtrack) / MLA (NA)**
Artists include: Neil Young, Jimi Hendrix, Bob Dylan, Creedence Clearwater Revival, Temptations.
Good collection of some canned and some original material, highlighted by Neil Young singing "Home on the Range." — J.S.

★ **White Mansions / A&M (NA)**
Artists include: Jessi Colter, Waylon Jennings,

John Dillon, Steve Cash, Waylon Jennings and Jessi Colter, John Dillon and Jessi Colter, Steve Cash, John Dillon and Waylon Jennings, Voices of Deliverance.

Genuinely horrid attempt to tell the story of the Civil War from the South's perspective; written by an Englishman, this manages to misinterpret the politics of the era, and repeats every social cliché about the period. It gets one star because Jennings sings a few of the songs as though he means business. — D.M.

★ ★ ★ **White Spirituals from the Sacred Harp / New W. (1977)**
Field recordings of the Alabama Sacred Harp Convention, massed choirs of dozens, sometimes hundreds, of voices singing traditional hymns without instrumental accompaniment. Although these songs were collected by Alan Lomax in 1959, they represent a tradition closer to two hundred years old: the shape note hymn singing of Protestant fundamentalists. Haunting and beautiful, though strange to noninitiates at first. — D.M.

★ ★ ★ **Wild Wild Young Women / Roun. (NA)**
Artists include: Janis Martin, the Collins Kids, the Nettles Sisters, Jean Chapel, Sparkle Moore, Joan King, Rose Maddox.

Fantastic collection of women rockabilly artists from the Fifties. Many of these sides are extremely rare. Highlights are Janis Martin's "My Boy Elvis" and Rose Maddox's "Wild, Wild Young Men." — J.S.

★ ★ ★ **Windy City Blues: The Transition from 1935 to 1953 / Nighth. (NA)**
Artists include: Pinetop, State Street Boys, Washboard Sam, Robert Lee McCoy, Sonny Boy Williamson, Robert Lockwood, Guitar Pete Franklin, Tampa Red, Tony Hollins, Johnny Shines.

This anthology traces the growth of the blues scene in Chicago from the rural blues up from the South in the prewar era to the postwar electric style most people associate with Chicago blues. Pianist Aaron "Pinetop" Sparks duets with guitarist Henry Townsend on "Every Day I Have the Blues." The State Street Boys, led by Big Bill Broonzy, anticipate the Fifties style with the 1935 record "Sweet to Mama." Robert Lockwood flashes the tradition learned from his stepfather, Robert Johnson, on "Dust My Broom" from 1951, while in the same year old-timer Tampa Red stakes further claim to his leg-endary slide guitar style via "Green and Lucky Blues." — J.S.

★ ★ ★ ★ **Wiser Dread / Nighth. (1981)**
Artists include: Bunny Wailer, the Ital, the Morwells, Jackie Brown, Sang Hugh.

You say you never heard of the Ital, Jackie Brown or Sang Hugh? This magnificent collection of obscure Jamaican singles from the Seventies offers priceless examples of roots music—spare, infectious rhythms, soaring harmonies and heart-stopping vocalizing informed by a palpable spirituality. — R.F.G.

★ ★ ★ **Wizards from the Southside / Chess (1982)**
Artists include: Howlin' Wolf, Muddy Waters, John Lee Hooker, Little Walter, Bo Diddley, Sonny Boy Williamson.

Blues classics from the vaults. No surprises, but the Walter, Wolf and Waters sides are all genuinely major, and it's more than nice to have them back in print. Execrably annotated, however. — D.M.

★ ★ ★ **The Wiz (Original Cast) / Atl. (1975)**
★ **The Wiz (Soundtrack) / MCA (1978)**
In making the original-cast album of the black Broadway revival of *The Wizard of Oz,* producer Jerry Wexler circumvented many problems by adding a soul rhythm section. The result is that the intensity of the performances transcends the stagy phrasing. Stephanie Mills, who plays Dorothy, is the chief offender in the latter regard; Tasha Thomas and Dee Dee Bridgewater turn in convincing performances that show both as musicians as much as actresses.

The soundtrack had many advantages; recorded with top-flight studio musicians, its stars are musical ones first: Diana Ross, Michael Jackson, and the pair together. But it never jells because the arrangements are precisely as flatulent as the Broadway ones Wexler eschewed. As disastrous on the turntable as it was on the screen. — D.M.

★ ★ ★ **Woodstock (Soundtrack) / Coti. (1970)**
Artists include: John B. Sebastian, Canned Heat, Richie Havens, Country Joe and the Fish, Arlo Guthrie, Sha-Na-Na, Country Joe McDonald, Joan Baez, Crosby, Stills and Nash, Crosby, Stills, Nash and Young, the Who, Joe Cocker, Santana, Ten Years After, Jefferson Airplane, Sly and the Family Stone, Butterfield Blues Band, Jimi Hendrix.

Even if it's as embarrassingly dated as antihippie ideologues would argue (and the worst of it definitely is), even if too much space is given over to Baez, McDonald and Crosby, Stills and Nash and even though many important performers (Joplin, the Band, Creedence) are omitted, there are enough classic performances here to justify the rating: Ten Years After are blindingly bluesless, Sly is either revivalist in his frenzy or protofacist but either way fascinating, the Who were never more aggressive, and Joe Cocker grinds out his soul with vengeance. And there is Jimi's last long sad blast, a virtual definition of his galvanizing genius and charismatic presence. Plus the Airplane and Santana, for those whose tastes run that way. — D.M.

★ **World of Country Giants / Col. (NA)**
Artists include: Marty Robbins, Ray Price, Johnny Horton, Tommy Cash, Tammy Wynette, Johnny Cash, David Houston, Carl Smith, Stonewall Jackson, Bob Luman, Lynn Anderson, Freddy Weller, Jody Miller, Carl Perkins, Jerry Reed, David Rogers, Sammi Smith, Johnny Duncan.
Country names at their worst. Chief (almost only) exception is Johnny Cash's version of Dylan's "Don't Think Twice, It's All Right." — D.M.

★ ★ **Yes Nukes / Rhino (NA)**
Artists include: Pop, Twisters, Cliché, Nu Kats, Soul Dads, Weirdos, Runaways, Wedge.
Uneven new-wave collection. — J.S.

■ **You Light Up My Life (Soundtrack) / Ari. (NA)**
Spawned Debby Boone's career with the title song. But this doesn't even have the hit version. Symptomatic of how much rock has *not* changed pop music.
— D.M.

Index to Artists
in the First Edition

The following artists, all of whose material is now out of print, have entries in the first edition of the *Record Guide* only:

Aalon
Ace Spectrum
David Ackles
Arthur Adams
Jay Boy Adams
A Foot in Coldwater
Jan Akkerman and Kaz
  Lux
Allman and Woman
Alquin
Shirley Alston
Amazing Blondel
American Flyer
American Gypsy
American Tears
Bill Amesbury
Angelo
Aorta
Area Code 615
Jose "Chepito" Areas
Arizona
Arrogance
Arthur Hurley and
  Gottlieb
Atlanta Disco Band
Attitudes
Avalanche
Frankie Avalon
David Axelrod
Ayers Rock

Baby
Bachelors
Randy Bachman
Back Street Crawler
Ginger Baker
Baker-Gurvitz Army
Long John Baldry
Banco
Bandit
Rose Banks

Barclay James Harvest
Nickey Barclay
Barrabas
David Batteau
Bazuka
Beaver and Krause
Beaverteeth
The Beckies
Beers Family
William Bell
Jesse Belvin
Benny and the Jets
Mike Berry
Karen Beth
Biddu Orchestra
Bill and Taffy
Billion Dollar Babies
Black Blood
Bloodstone
Blue Swede
Colin Blunstone
Boa
Tommy Bolin
Angelo Bond
Boney M
Ken Boothe
Booty People
Bottom Line
Boxer
Bonnie Bramlett
Brave Belt
Brewer and Shipley
Brian and Brenda
Albert Brooks
Dianne Brooks
Arthur Brown
John Lee and Gerry Brown
Keisa Brown
Maxine Brown
Mel Brown
Brownsville Station

Lord Buckley
Bulldog
Eric Burdon and War
Tucky Buzzard
David Byron

Brian Cadd
Camel
G. C. Cameron
Carl Carlton
Carmen
Buzz Cason
David Cassidy
Caston and Majors
Cats
Steve Cauthen
Felix Cavaliere
Chairmen of the Board
Chakachas
Cathy Chamberlain
Champion
Chanter Sisters
Charlie and the Pep Boys
Chicken Shack
Chocolate Milk
Choice Four
Chordettes
Keith Christmas
Gavin Christopher
George Clinton
Clover
Odia Coates
Wayne Cochran
Phil Cody
Dennis Coffey
Stephen Cohn
Cold Blood
David Courtney
Lou Courtney
Cowboy
Crackin'